W9-DAB-773

TORTS

PERSONAL INJURY LITIGATION

FIFTH EDITION

TORTS

PERSONAL INJURY LITIGATION

FIFTH EDITION

WILLIAM P. STATSKY

Australia • Brazil • Japan • Korea • Mexico • Singapore • Spain • United Kingdom • United States

Torts: Personal Injury Litigation, Fifth Edition
William P. Statsky

Vice President, Career and Professional Editorial: Dave Garza

Director of Learning Solutions: Sandy Clark

Senior Acquisitions Editor: Shelley Esposito

Managing Editor: Larry Main

Senior Product Manager: Melissa Riveglia

Editorial Assistant: Danielle Klahr

Vice President, Career and Professional Marketing: Jennifer Baker

Marketing Director: Deborah Yarnell

Marketing Manager: Erin Brennan

Marketing Coordinator: Erin DeAngelo

Production Director: Wendy Troeger

Production Manager: Mark Bernard

Content Project Management: PreMediaGlobal

Senior Art Director: Joy Kocsis

Senior Technology Product Manager: Joe Pliss

Library of Congress Control Number: 2010932271

ISBN-13: 978-1-4018-7962-4

ISBN-10: 1-4018-7962-4

Delmar
5 Maxwell Drive
Clifton Park, NY 12065-2919
USA

Cengage Learning is a leading provider of customized learning solutions with office locations around the globe, including Singapore, the United Kingdom, Australia, Mexico, Brazil, and Japan. Locate your local office at: **international.cengage.com/region**

Cengage Learning products are represented in Canada by Nelson Education, Ltd.

To learn more about Delmar, visit **www.cengage.com/delmar**

Purchase any of our products at your local college store or at our preferred online store **www.cengagebrain.com**

Printed in the United States of America
2 3 4 5 6 7 14 13 12 11

DEDICATION

For Pat, Jessie, Gabe, Randy, Carlie, Ava, Hailey, Myles, Kaia, Moxie, Rainy, and Milosc

BY THE SAME AUTHOR

For all publications by William Statsky, see:
statsky.blogspot.com

The California Paralegal: Essential Rules, Documents, and Resources. Clifton Park, N.Y.: Delmar Cengage Learning, 2008 (with S. Sandberg)

Case Analysis and Fundamentals of Legal Writing, 4th ed. St. Paul: West Group, 1995 (with J. Wernet)

Essentials of Paralegalism, 5th ed. Clifton Park, N.Y.: Delmar Cengage Learning, 2010

Essentials of Torts, 3d ed. Clifton Park, N.Y.: Delmar Cengage Learning, 2011

Family Law: The Essentials, 2d ed. Clifton Park, N.Y.: Delmar Cengage learning, 2004

Family Law, 5th ed. Clifton Park, N.Y.: Delmar Cengage Learning, 2002

The Florida Paralegal: Essential Rules, Documents, and Resources. Clifton Park, N.Y.: Delmar Cengage Learning, 2009 (with B. Diotalevi & P. Linquist)

Inmate Involvement in Prison Legal Services: Roles and Training Options for the Inmate as Paralegal. Chicago: American Bar Association, Commission on Correctional Facilities and Services, 1974

Introduction to Paralegalism: Perspectives, Problems, and Skills, 7th ed. Clifton Park, N.Y.: Delmar Cengage Learning, 2009

Legal Desk Reference. St. Paul: West Group, 1990 (with B. Hussey, M. Diamond, & R. Nakamura)

The Legal Paraprofessional as Advocate and Assistant: Training Concepts and Materials. New York: Center on Social Welfare Policy and Law, 1971 (with P. Lang)

Legal Research and Writing: Some Starting Points, 5th ed. Clifton Park, N.Y.: Delmar Cengage Learning, 1999

Legal Thesaurus/Dictionary: A Resource for the Writer and Computer Researcher. St. Paul: West Group, 1985

Legislative Analysis and Drafting, 2d ed. St. Paul: West Group, 1984

The New York Paralegal: Essential Rules, Documents, and Resources. Clifton Park, N.Y.: Delmar Cengage Learning, 2009 (with R. Sarachan)

The Ohio Paralegal: Essential Rules, Documents, and Resources. Clifton Park, N.Y.: Delmar Cengage Learning, 2008 (with K. Reed & B. Moore)

Paralegal Employment: Facts and Strategies for the 1990s, 2d ed. St. Paul: West Group, 1993

Paralegal Ethics and Regulation, 2d ed. St. Paul: West Group, 1993

The Pennsylvania Paralegal: Essential Rules, Documents, and Resources. Clifton Park, N.Y.: Delmar Cengage Learning, 2009 (with J. DeLeo & J. Geis)

The Texas Paralegal: Essential Rules, Documents, and Resources. Clifton Park, N.Y.: Delmar Cengage Learning, 2009 (with L. Crossett)

Rights of the Imprisoned: Cases, Materials, and Directions. Indianapolis, Ind.: Bobbs-Merrill Company, 1974 (with R. Singer)

What Have Paralegals Done? A Dictionary of Functions. Washington, D.C.: National Paralegal Institute, 1973

CONTENTS IN BRIEF

CONTENTS

TABLE OF CASES

CHAPTER 14

CHAPTER 15

CHAPTER 16

CHAPTER 17

CHAPTER 18

CHAPTER 19

CHAPTER 20

CHAPTER 21

CHAPTER 22

CHAPTER 23

CHAPTER 24

CHAPTER 25

CHAPTER 26

CHAPTER 27

CHAPTER 28

TABLE OF EXHIBITS

PREFACE

Thousands of injuries occur every day on the road, at work, in department stores, on the playground, and at home. The incidence of property damage is equally extensive. Although most of these mishaps never find their way into the legal system, many are caused by wrongs that we call *torts*. In addition to providing compensation to victims, one of the major objectives of tort law is behavior modification. A premise of tort litigation is that one of the most effective ways to force people to avoid injuring others or damaging their property is to hang the threat of a lawsuit over their heads. These are some of the dynamics we will explore in this book.

It is an exciting time to study tort law. Throughout the country there is considerable controversy over whether our system of tort litigation is causing more societal ills than it is solving. Horror stories abound on talk shows and editorial pages. An example is the seventeen-year-old Michigan high school student who sued Nintendo and Toys "R" Us, where she bought a Nintendo video game console. Her suit claims that she has an inflamed thumb from playing too much Nintendo. Her doctor calls the condition "Nintendinitis" (a word that will send you to over 20,000 sites via Google). The suit alleged that the condition prevents the plaintiff from writing, from typing—and, of course, from playing Nintendo games! Such cases have prompted calls for tort reform. The chapters of this book will help place these calls into perspective.

The Internet has also stirred controversy. The legal system is having tremendous difficulty trying to figure out what role it should play in the still-burgeoning life of the World Wide Web. Should there be tort remedies to cover unsavory activity such as plagiarism, theft of media, personal attacks (e.g., cyberbullying), and privacy invasions (e.g., cyberstalking)? Communications technology in the twenty-first century continues to force the legal system to confront such questions.

Torts is one of the first courses taught to first-year students in law school. This is because the study of tort law can provide excellent insight into the common law, the practice of law, and legal skills, particularly legal analysis. Paralegal students can also tap into this insight. In a personal injury practice of law, the attorney–paralegal team makes an important contribution. In many offices, the team is inseparable. To achieve this work environment, one of the first steps is to understand the principles of tort law that the attorney applies in personal injury cases. This understanding is one of our major goals.

CHAPTER FORMAT

Each chapter includes features designed to assist the student in understanding the material:

- A chapter outline at the beginning of each chapter provides a preview of the major topics in the chapter.
- Chapter objectives, also at the beginning of each chapter, present a more detailed listing of the themes and skills covered in the chapter.
- Exhibits and tables are used extensively to clarify concepts and present detailed information in an organized chart form.
- Assignments that ask the student to apply concepts to particular fact situations are included within most chapters.

- At the end of each chapter, there is a Check the Cite exercise in which the student is sent to a specific case found on the Internet that is relevant to the material covered in the chapter.
- Also at the end of each chapter there is an Internet research project in which the student is asked to conduct state-specific Internet research on a topic covered in the chapter.
- Following each project assignment there is an exercise called Ethics in a Torts Practice, which asks the student to read a fact situation and identify ethical problems that may exist. These exercises may tangentially cover the topic of the chapters in which they are found. Their main purpose, however, is to review the major ethical issues that apply to any law office.
- A chapter summary at the end of each chapter provides a concise review of the main concepts discussed.
- Key terms are presented in boldface type the first time they appear in each chapter. Also a list of key terms is found at the end of each chapter to help review important terminology introduced in that chapter.
- Helpful Websites are added at the end of each chapter to provide additional materials on the topics of the chapter.
- Margin definitions are presented for each term in boldface type in the chapter.
- Examples are used extensively to highlight critical doctrines and practices.
- After the discussion of a major tort in a chapter, there is a comprehensive checklist called Definitions, Relationships, Paralegal Roles, and Research References. It is designed to provide the "big picture" by making connections between the particular tort examined in the chapter and related material on other torts discussed in other chapters. The checklist also serves as an on-the-job refresher for individual torts.

CHANGES IN THE FIFTH EDITION

- Many new and revised examples and exhibits are included.
- Each chapter begins with chapter objectives.
- Margin definitions have been added in each chapter.
- New assignments and exercises at the end of each chapter include Check the Cite, Project, and Ethics in a Tort Practice.
- Each chapter concludes with review questions.
- The comprehensive charts on each of the major torts (Definitions, Relationships, Paralegal Roles, and Research References) have been moved from the beginning of the discussion of the tort to the conclusion of the discussion.
- The Chapter 1 overview of case law as a source of tort law includes an excerpt from a case found online, which is the same case found in a traditional reporter.
- Chapter 1 contains a new chart comparing tort actions and criminal prosecution for the same conduct.
- Chapters 1–4 and 12 include new end assignments: Project and Ethics in a Tort Practice.
- Chapters 5–11 and 13–29 include new end assignments: Check the Cite, Project, and Ethics in a Tort Practice.
- Chapters 1–29 contain review questions at the end of the chapters.
- Material on civil procedure in Chapter 3 has been cut back.
- Chapters 5–26 contain separate exhibits on the elements of each tort covered in the chapters.
- Chapter 5 contains a new chart comparing civil and criminal battery and assault.
- Chapter 5 also contains additional material on damages in battery actions.

- Chapter 6 covers the relationship between assault and the Internet offenses of cyberstalking and cyberbullying.
- Chapter 7 contains a new chart comparing privilege and immunity.
- Chapter 9 covers emotional wrongs committed on the Internet and the tort of intentional infliction of emotional distress.
- Chapter 9 also examines whether the families of the victims of 9/11 can sue for intentional infliction of emotional distress.
- Chapter 10 asks whether spam can constitute trespass to chattels and whether electronic data can be converted.
- The overview of negligence in Chapter 12 adds coverage of gross negligence and ordinary negligence.
- Chapter 16 discusses the causation issues involved in the Columbine massacre and the settlement fund set up to compensate families of the 9/11 terrorist attack.
- Chapter 17 covers comparative negligence principles that applied to the 1993 World Trade Center bombing.
- Chapter 19 gives additional background on the Stella hot coffee case and raises the question of whether there can be strict liability for defective websites and movies.
- Chapter 20 adds the RICO litigation to the strategies leveled against the tobacco industry.
- Chapter 23 discusses the case against Craigslist for public nuisance and the statutory immunity given to the firearms industry.
- Chapter 26 adds additional material on wrongful discharge and deceptive trade practices.
- Appendix A extensively expands the state and federal resources available online on torts law and practice.

TEACHING AIDS AND SUPPLEMENTS

Student StudyWARE™ CD-ROM

The new accompanying CD-ROM includes interactive StudyWARE™, providing additional material to help students master the important concepts in the course. This CD-ROM includes

- study guide with extensive review questions
- multiple-choice and true/false quizzing
- case studies with multiple-choice follow-up questions
- flash cards

Instructor's Manual

An Instructor's Manual and Test Bank by the author of the text accompanies this edition and has been expanded to incorporate changes in the text and to provide comprehensive teaching support. It includes the following:

- teaching options, such as lecture ideas and suggestions for using selected assignments
- answers to Check the Cite, Ethics in a Torts Practice, and Review Questions
- a test bank of 450 questions, which include a variety of questions in true/false, multiple-choice, completion, matching, and essay formats

Instructor Resources

Delmar Cengage Learning's Instructor Resources to accompany *Torts: Personal Injury Litigation* can provide valuable assistance with course design and student evaluation.

This instructor CD-ROM allows you anywhere, anytime access to all of your resources:

- The **Instructor's Manual** contains various resources for each chapter of the book.
- The **Computerized Test Bank** in ExamView facilitates the generation of tests and quizzes. With many questions and different styles to choose from, you can easily create customized assessments for your students. You can also add your own unique questions.
- Customizable **PowerPoint® Presentations** focus on key points for each chapter.

(PowerPoint® is a registered trademark of the Microsoft Corporation.)

All of these instructor materials are also posted on our website in the Online Resources section.

WebTUTOR WebTutor™

The WebTutor™ supplement allows you, as the instructor, to take learning beyond the classroom. This online courseware is designed to complement the text and benefit students and instructors alike by helping manage time, prepare for exams, organize notes, and more. WebTutor™ allows you to extend your reach beyond the classroom.

Web Page

Visit our website at www.paralegal.delmar.cengage.com, where you will find valuable information such as hot links and sample materials to download, as well as other Delmar Cengage Learning products.

Please note that the Internet resources are of a time-sensitive nature and URL addresses may often change or be deleted.

SUPPLEMENTS AT-A-GLANCE

SUPPLEMENT:	WHAT IT IS:	WHAT'S IN IT:
Student CD-ROM	Software program (CD-ROM in the back of the book). StudyWARE™ is like the student's own private tutor, reinforcing text material in an interactive environment!	StudyWARE™ software with additional quizzing, case studies with multiple-choice follow-up questions, flash cards, and study guide.
Online Instructor's Manual	Resources for the instructor, posted online at www.paralegal.delmar.cengage.com in the Online Resources section	• Instructor manual with lecture ideas, suggested answers, and test bank with answer key • PowerPoint® presentations
Instructor Resources CD-ROM INSTRUCTOR RESOURCES	Resources for the instructor, available on CD-ROM	• Instructor manual with lecture ideas, suggested answers, and test bank with answer key • Computerized test bank in ExamView with many questions and styles to choose from to create customized student assessments • PowerPoint® presentations
WebTutor™ WebTUTOR™	WebTUTOR™ supplemental courseware complements Cengage Learning paralegal textbooks by providing interactive reinforcement that helps students grasp complex concepts. WebTUTOR™ allows you to know quickly what concepts your students are or aren't grasping.	• Automatic and immediate feedback from quizzes and exams • Online exercises that reinforce what they've learned • Flashcards that include audio support • Greater interaction and involvement through online discussion forums
Torts Online Course	Robust Online Course available on both Blackboard and WebCT. (Availability upon request for eCollege, Angel, Desire2Learn, and more.) The course can be used along with this textbook or any book for an introductory course. See a demo at http://cengagesites.com/academic/?site=4074.	Includes 16 lessons with introduction, objectives, lecture outline, video activities, journal activities, group activities, Internet activities, discussion questions, ethics questions, glossary terms, weblinks, study notes, and quizzing for the student. Instructor materials include PowerPoint slides and test banks.

ACKNOWLEDGMENTS

Many thanks to the reviewers who made valuable suggestions for improving this text:

Linda Anderson
Woodbury College
Burlington, VT

Beverly Broman
Duff's Business Institute
Pittsburgh, PA

Mimi Flaherty
RETS Technical Center
Charlestown, MA

Christie Highlander
Southwestern Illinois College
Belleville, IL

Elizabeth Mann
Greenville Technical College
Greenville, SC

Alvin McDonald
New Mexico State University at Alamagordo
Alamagordo, NM

Christine Thiltgen
American River College
Sacramento, CA

CHAPTER

1

INTRODUCTION TO TORT LAW AND PRACTICE

CHAPTER OUTLINE

- Scope
- Definitions and Purposes
- Elements of All the Torts
- Categories of Torts
- Introduction to Causation
- Relationship Between Tort Law and Other Areas of the Law
- Sources of Tort Law

CHAPTER OBJECTIVES

After completing this chapter, you should be able to:

- Understand the financial and human scope of unintended injuries in society.
- Define tort, damages, criminal law, civil law, and related concepts.
- Know the four purposes of tort law.
- Know what is meant by stating a tort cause of action.
- Distinguish among intentional torts, negligence, and strict liability.
- Know the meaning of proximate cause.
- State the two tests for actual cause (cause in fact).
- State the relationship between tort law and the following areas of the law: contract law, criminal law, civil procedure law, family law, constitutional law, estate law, state and local government law, real property law, insurance law, and environmental law.
- Define the primary authorities and state how they relate to a torts (personal injury) practice.
- Define the major secondary authorities and state how they can be helpful in a torts (personal injury) practice.

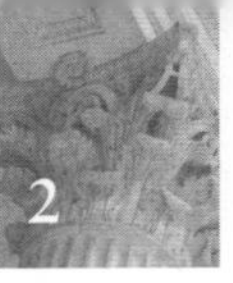

SCOPE

tort A civil wrong (other than a breach of contract) that causes injury or other loss for which our legal system deems it just to provide a remedy such as damages. Injury or loss can be to the person (a personal tort), to movable property (a personal property tort), or to land and anything attached to the land (a real property tort).

damages 1. Monetary payments awarded to compensate someone for a legally recognized wrong (noun). 2. Causes harm or other loss (verb). (The word *damage* means injury, impairment, or other loss to person or property.)

diversity of citizenship The disputing parties are citizens of different states. This fact gives jurisdiction (called diversity jurisdiction) to a United States district court when the amount in controversy exceeds $75,000.

Accidental or unintentional injuries take a staggering toll on society. Each year, the total economic cost of such injuries is $652 billion according to the National Safety Council. This includes medical expenses, property damage, wage losses, productivity losses, legal costs, police costs, and related administrative expenses. Each year, over 23 million people need medical attention and 120,000 die from unintended injuries.[1]

Some of these injuries are caused by **torts**, which brings us to the subject of this book. Broadly speaking, a tort is a civil wrong that can be redressed by awarding **damages.** A more precise definition is that a tort is a civil wrong (other than a breach of contract) that causes injury or other loss for which our legal system deems it just to provide a remedy such as damages. We'll have more to say about this definition shortly when we examine the categories of personal torts, personal property torts, and real property torts. See Exhibit 1–1 for statistics on tort cases in selected state courts in the country.

Federal courts also handle tort cases when the parties suing each other are citizens of different states **(diversity of citizenship)** or when the suit is against the federal government for a tort committed by a federal employee. Fourteen percent of all civil cases filed in U.S. district courts (the main federal trial court) are tort claims. Plaintiffs won about 51 percent of these cases. The median award for plaintiffs in *state* courts is $24,000. The median award in *federal* courts is considerably larger, $179,000.[2]

Our goal in this book is to help you understand the law behind these statistics and the roles played by paralegals in a legal system designed to determine when injured parties should be compensated for losses caused by torts.

DEFINITIONS AND PURPOSES

remedy 1. The means by which a right is enforced or the violation of a right is prevented, compensated for, or otherwise redressed. 2. To correct.

jurisdiction 1. The authority or power of a court to resolve a dispute. Its *personal jurisdiction* is its power to order a particular defendant to do or to refrain from doing something. Its *subject matter jurisdiction* is its power to hear certain kinds of cases. 2. The geographic area over which a particular court has authority.

criminal law The law that governs crimes alleged by the government. Criminal law defines crimes, punishments, and procedures for investigation and prosecution. Also called penal law.

civil law 1. The law that governs rights and duties between private persons or between private persons and the government concerning matters other than the commission of a crime. 2. Any law other than criminal law. 3. The statutory or code law applicable in Louisiana and in many Western European countries other than England.

When someone harms or damages the person or property of another, the primitive instinct of the victim is often to strike back. Our legal system functions as a check against this instinct so that the peace of the realm is not disturbed. If a conflict is not resolved informally among the parties, society asks that the parties seek a **remedy** in court. In the medical world, a remedy is something that cures or treats an ailment. In the law, a remedy is a means by which the enforcement of a right is sought or the violation of a right is prevented, compensated for, or otherwise redressed.

There are two kinds of disputes over which courts have **jurisdiction**: criminal disputes and civil disputes. (Jurisdiction is the authority or power of a court to resolve a dispute.) These disputes are based on the two major categories of law:

- **criminal law**: The law that governs crimes alleged by the government.
- **civil law**: The law that governs rights and duties between private persons or between private persons and the government concerning matters other than the commission of a crime. (A separate meaning of civil law is the law that applies in Louisiana and some European countries.)

Criminal law covers those wrongs that are serious enough to be classified as crimes, e.g., murder and burglary. Civil law covers civil wrongs, which essentially consist of everything other than criminal wrongs. Tort law is one of the branches of civil law. Another familiar branch is contract law.

The word tort comes from the Latin word "tortus," meaning twisted, and from the French word "tort," meaning injury or wrong. As we have seen, the complete definition of tort is a civil wrong (other than a breach of contract) that causes injury or other loss for which our legal system deems it just to provide a remedy such as damages.

The same conduct can constitute both a tort and a crime. The proceedings in which torts and crimes are litigated, however, are separate and substantially different. A dramatic example of the difference can be seen in the O. J. Simpson trials

Exhibit 1–1 Tort trials in state courts in the nation's 75 largest counties (For comparable data in the federal courts, see Exhibit 20–2 in Chapter 20.)

	Year of trial collection			Percent change	
Type of tort trial characteristic	**1996**	**2001**	**2005**	**1996–2005**	**2001–2005**
How many tort trials were disposed?					
All tort trials	**10,278**	**7,948**	**7,038**	**–31.5%**	**–11.5%**
Automobile accident	4,994	4,235	3,545	–29.0	–16.3
Medical malpractice	1,201	1,156	1,219	1.5	5.5
Premises liability	2,232	1,268	1,067	–52.2	–15.8
Intentional tort	491	375	352	–28.4	–6.1
Product liability	421	158	225	–46.7	42.2
What percentage of plaintiffs won?					
All tort trials	**48.2%**	**51.6%**	**48.0%**	**–0.3%**	**–6.8%**
Automobile accident	57.5	61.2	61.0	6.1	–0.4
Medical malpractice	23.3	26.8	19.4	–17.0	–27.7
Premises liability	39.6	42.0	38.9	–1.7	–7.3
Intentional tort	57.0	56.8	50.4	–11.5	–11.2
Product liability	44.9	44.2	37.9	–15.6	–14.2
How much did prevailing plaintiffs win?					
All tort trials	**$38,000**	**$30,000**	**$31,000**	**–18.4%**	**3.3%**
Automobile accident	22,000	18,000	16,000	–27.3	–11.1
Medical malpractice	354,000	464,000	679,000	91.8	46.3
Premises liability	71,000	65,000	90,000	26.8	38.5
Intentional tort	40,000	41,000	100,000	150.0	143.9
Product liability	241,000	495,000	748,000	210.4	51.1
What percentage of plaintiffs won punitive damages?					
All tort trials	**3.3%**	**5.3%**	**3.6%**	**8.5%**	**–33.3%**
Automobile accident	0.7	2.1	1.6	134.3	–22.0
Medical malpractice	1.1	4.9	2.6	144.7	–46.1
Premises liability	4.5	1.5	0.5	–89.5	–68.9
Intentional tort	24.0	36.4	24.3	1.2	–33.3
Product liability	7.7	4.2	1.3	–83.8	–70.4
How long did disposition of tort case take?					
All tort trials	**21.8 mo.**	**21.5 mo.**	**23.0 mo.**	**5.3%**	**6.7%**
Automobile accident	18.9	19.8	20.0	5.6	1.0
Medical malpractice	29.7	28.6	30.7	3.5	7.6
Premises liability	24.6	22.6	24.0	–2.5	6.0
Intentional tort	20.6	20.2	25.3	22.8	25.2
Product liability	32.4	25.5	30.0	–7.5	17.4

Source: Bureau of Justice Statistics, *Tort Bench and Jury Trials in State Courts, 2005*, Table 12, p. 12 (November 2009) (bjs.ojp.usdoj.gov/content/pub/pdf/tbjtsc05.pdf). Note: The table includes all jury trials, bench trials, trials with a directed verdict, trials that ended in a judgment notwithstanding the verdict, and jury trials for defaulted defendants concluded in a sample of the nation's 75 most populous counties. Product liability includes cases of asbestos exposure. Data from *Civil Justice Survey of State Courts* (1996, 2001, and 2005). Data can be obtained from the University of Michigan Inter-University Consortium for Political and Social Research.

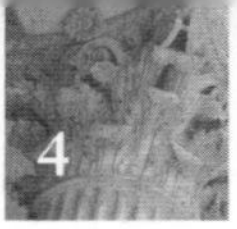

that gripped the attention of the nation in the 1990s. In a criminal trial, the former football star was acquitted of murdering two persons. In a subsequent civil trial, however, he was found liable for wrongfully causing the deaths of the same two people. These are not inconsistent results because the **standard of proof** is significantly different in criminal and civil cases. In a criminal case, the elements of the crime must be established against the defendant beyond a reasonable doubt, whereas in most civil cases, the elements of the tort or other cause of action must be established against the defendant by a **preponderance of the evidence**. One can conclude that the preponderance of evidence establishes that someone committed a certain act, and also conclude that there is some reasonable doubt about whether he or she committed it. See Exhibit 1–2 for more examples of the differences between civil and criminal cases.

standard of proof How believable or convincing a version of a fact must be before the trier of facts (usually a jury) can accept it as true.

preponderance of the evidence The standard of proof that is met when the evidence establishes that it is more likely than not that the facts are as alleged.

Exhibit 1–2 Tort action and criminal prosecution for the same misconduct: Two separate proceedings.

Example	**Facts: Jim pushes Mary against the wall, grabs her purse containing valuable jewelry, and flees.**	
	Tort Case	**Criminal Case**
The wrong committed	The tort of conversion (wrongfully taking another's personal property).	The crime of robbery (using force or violence to take personal property from the person of another).
Nature of the wrong	A private wrong. Jim took Mary's private property.	A public wrong. When robbery occurs, the public peace has been disturbed.
Court hearing the case	A suit for the tort of conversion is a civil action heard in a civil court.	A robbery prosecution is a criminal action heard in a criminal court.
Parties	Mary sues Jim. The moving party is Mary, who is the plaintiff; Jim is the defendant. Someone accused of committing a tort is an alleged tortfeasor.	The state prosecutes Jim. The moving party is the state. Jim is the defendant, also called the accused. (Mary is the complaining witness.)
Standard of proof	Mary must prove the elements of the tort of conversion by a preponderance of the evidence.	The state must prove the elements of robbery beyond a reasonable doubt.
Representation	Mary can represent herself or she can hire (and pay for) a private attorney to represent her. Jim can represent himself or he can hire (and pay for) a private attorney to represent him.	The state is represented by the prosecutor (sometimes called the district attorney). Jim may be able to represent himself or he can hire (and pay for) a private attorney to represent him.
Right to counsel	If Jim cannot afford a private attorney, in most cases he does not have the right to be represented by assigned counsel paid by the state.	If Jim cannot afford a private attorney, in most cases he has the right to be represented by assigned counsel paid by the state.
Procedural rules	Rules of civil procedure	Rules of criminal procedure
Testimony of defendant	The defendant (Jim) may be forced to testify.	The defendant (Jim) has a constitutional right to silence; he cannot be forced to incriminate himself.
Jury verdict	Many states allow jury verdicts by less than unanimous vote.	Most states require jury verdicts by unanimous vote.
Conclusion of proceeding	The defendant is found liable or not liable. The final judgment of the court includes a determination of liability.	The defendant is found guilty or not guilty. If guilty, the final judgment includes the punishment imposed during sentencing.
Monetary payments	A defendant who is found liable may be forced to pay money (damages) to the victim of the tort.	A defendant who is found guilty may be forced to pay restitution to the victim of the crime. The defendant might also be incarcerated and forced to pay a fine. The fine is paid to the state, not to the victim.

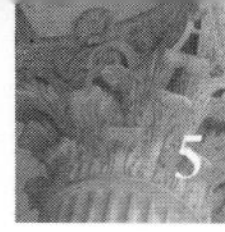

There are four major purposes of tort law: peace, deterrence, restoration, and justice.[3]

1. *Peace:* To provide a peaceful means for adjusting the rights of parties who might otherwise "take the law into their own hands." A courtroom is a neutral setting where allegations can be aired in order to reach a rational resolution that the parties and the community can accept.
2. *Deterrence:* To deter wrongful conduct. Tort litigation takes place in public. The media is free to report what occurs in court. News that certain conduct forced someone into court and led to the payment of a large money judgment can encourage the public to avoid that kind of conduct for fear of being subjected to a similar fate. This is sometimes called the "behavior modification" purpose of tort law. It has the effect of encouraging socially responsible behavior such as making safer automobiles and removing ice from sidewalks.
3. *Restoration:* To restore injured parties to their original position, insofar as this is possible, usually by compensating them for their injury. This is sometimes referred to as being **made whole**. Of course, it is often impossible to restore someone to the condition that existed before the injury occurred. If you negligently break my leg, I may never be restored to full health. Yet by providing compensation (damages), I am being made as whole as is humanly possible.
4. *Justice:* To identify those who should be held accountable for the harm that resulted. A tort case can involve one or more victims and one or more defendants alleged to have a role in causing a particular injury. The law of torts is designed to sort through the involvement of all of the participants in order to identify who is **culpable** or blameworthy and to determine who, in fairness, should be made to pay.

made whole Restored to the condition that existed before the wrong was committed against the victim insofar as this is possible. To be compensated for a loss.

culpable At fault; blameworthy.

Whenever someone suffers a serious loss caused by another, our tort system could become involved. If it does, the overriding question of tort law—and the theme of this book—is whether that loss should be shifted to someone else in light of the peace, deterrence, restoration, and justice objectives of tort law.

ELEMENTS OF ALL THE TORTS

Every tort is a **cause of action**, which is simply a legally acceptable reason for bringing a suit. When you state a tort cause of action, you list the facts that give you a right to judicial relief against the **tortfeasor**—the wrongdoer who has committed the tort. Causes of action are rules. Every rule can be broken down into the component parts that we call **elements.** (As we will see in Chapter 2, the complete definition of an element is as follows: a portion of a rule that is one of the preconditions of the applicability of the entire rule.) The elements of the torts and related causes of action that we will study in this book are listed in Exhibit 1–3. For each cause of action, you are told what elements must be supported by facts in order to "state" the cause of action. When a party has offered sufficient evidence covering every element of a cause of action, that party has presented what is called a **prima facie case** that will entitle the party to prevail unless the other side offers more convincing counterevidence.

cause of action 1. A legally acceptable reason for bringing a suit. A rule that constitutes a legal theory for bringing a suit. 2. The facts that give a person a right to judicial relief. When you state a cause of action, you list the facts that give you a right to judicial relief against the wrongdoer. When you state a tort cause of action, you list the facts that give you a right to judicial relief against the tortfeasor.

tortfeasor A person who has committed a tort.

element A portion of a rule that is one of the preconditions of the applicability of the entire rule. A cause of action is a rule. Hence, a cause of action has elements.

prima facie case A party's presentation of evidence that will prevail unless the other side offers more convincing counterevidence.

CATEGORIES OF TORTS

There are three main categories of torts:

- intentional torts
- negligence
- strict liability torts

These categories are not ironclad. There are some torts that overlap the categories, as we will see.

Exhibit 1–3 Torts and related causes of action: The elements.

1. Abuse of Process
(Chapter 8)
1. The use of criminal or civil process
2. For improper or ulterior motive

2. Alienation of Affections
(Chapter 22)
1. The defendant intended to diminish the marital relationship (love, companionship, and comfort) between the plaintiff and the latter's spouse
2. Affirmative conduct by the defendant
3. Affections between the plaintiff and spouse were in fact alienated
4. The defendant caused the alienation

3. Assault (Civil)
(Chapter 6)
1. Act
2. Intent to cause (a) an apprehension of an imminent harmful or offensive contact or (b) the imminent harmful or offensive contact itself
3. Apprehension of an imminent harmful or offensive contact with the plaintiff's person
4. Causation of the apprehension

4. Battery (Civil)
(Chapter 5)
1. Act
2. Intent to cause (a) an imminent contact with the plaintiff's person or (b) an apprehension of such contact
3. Contact that is harmful or offensive
4. Causation of the harmful or offensive contact

5. Civil Rights Violation
(Chapter 27)
1. A person acting under color of law
2. Deprives someone of a federal right

6. Conversion
(Chapter 10)
1. Personal property (chattel)
2. The plaintiff is in possession of the chattel or is entitled to immediate possession
3. Intent to exercise dominion over the chattel (a serious interference)
4. Dominion
5. Causation of the serious interference

7. Criminal Conversation
(Chapter 22)
The defendant had sexual relations with the plaintiff's spouse (adultery).

Defamation (two torts: libel and slander)

8. Libel
(Chapter 24)
1. Written defamatory statement by the defendant
2. Of and concerning the plaintiff
3. Publication of the statement
4. Damages:
   a. In some states, special damages never have to be proven in a libel case
   b. In other states, libel per se does not require special damages, but libel per quod does
5. Causation

9. Slander
(Chapter 24)
1. Oral defamatory statement by the defendant
2. Of and concerning the plaintiff
3. Publication of the statement
4. Damages:
   a. Special damages are not required for slander per se
   b. Special damages are required for slander per quod
5. Causation

10. Disparagement
(Chapter 26)
1. False statement of fact
2. Disparaging the plaintiff's business, products, or title to property
3. Publication
4. Intent
5. Special damages
6. Causation

11. Enticement of a Child or Abduction of a Child
(Chapter 22)
1. The defendant intended to interfere with the parent's custody of the child.
2. Affirmative conduct by the defendant:
   a. to abduct or force the child from the parent's custody,
   b. to entice or encourage the child to leave the parent, or
   c. to harbor the child and encourage the latter to stay away from the parent's custody.
3. The child left the custody of the parent.
4. The defendant caused the child to leave or to stay away.

Exhibit 1–3 (Continued)

12. Enticement of Spouse
(Chapter 22)
1. The defendant intended to diminish the marital relationship between the plaintiff and the latter's spouse.
2. The defendant engaged in affirmative conduct either:
   a. to entice or encourage the spouse to leave the plaintiff's home, or
   b. to harbor the spouse and encourage the latter to stay away from the plaintiff's home.
3. The plaintiff's spouse left home.
4. The defendant caused the plaintiff to leave home or to stay away.

13. False Imprisonment
(Chapter 7)
1. An act that completely confines the plaintiff within fixed boundaries set by the defendant
2. Intent to confine the plaintiff or a third party
3. Causation of the confinement
4. The plaintiff was either conscious of the confinement or suffered actual harm by it

14. Injurious Falsehood
(Chapter 26)
1. False statement of fact
2. Harmful to the pecuniary interest of the plaintiff
3. Publication
4. Intent
5. Special damages
6. Causation

15. Intentional Infliction of Emotional Distress
(Chapter 9)
1. An act of extreme or outrageous conduct
2. Intent to cause severe emotional distress
3. Severe emotional distress is suffered
4. Defendant is the cause of this distress

16. Interference with Contract Relations
(Chapter 26)
1. An existing contract
2. Interference with the contract by the defendant
3. Intent to interfere
4. Damages
5. Causation

17. Interference with Prospective Advantage
(Chapter 26)
1. Reasonable expectation of an economic advantage
2. Interference with this expectation
3. Intent to interfere
4. Damages
5. Causation

Invasion of Privacy (four torts)

18. Appropriation
(Chapter 25)
1. The use of the plaintiff's name, likeness, or personality
2. For the benefit of the defendant

19. False Light
(Chapter 25)
1. Publicity
2. Placing the plaintiff in a false light
3. Highly offensive to a reasonable person

20. Intrusion
(Chapter 25)
1. An act of intrusion into someone's private affairs or concerns
2. Highly offensive to a reasonable person

21. Public Disclosure of Private Fact
(Chapter 25)
1. Publicity
2. Concerning the private life of the plaintiff
3. Highly offensive to a reasonable person

22. Malicious Prosecution
(Chapter 8)
1. Instigation of criminal proceedings
2. Without probable cause
3. With malice
4. The criminal proceedings terminate in favor of the accused

23. Misrepresentation
(Chapter 26)
1. Statement of fact
2. Statement is false
3. Scienter (intent to deceive)
4. Justifiable reliance
5. Actual damages

24. Negligence
(Chapter 12)
1. Duty
2. Breach of duty
3. Proximate cause
4. Damages

Nuisance (two torts)

25. Private Nuisance
(Chapter 23)
1. An act
2. Unreasonable interference with the use and enjoyment
3. Of private land
4. Based on negligence, intent, strict liability, or violation of a statute, ordinance, or regulation
5. Causation

Exhibit 1–3 (Continued)

26. **Public Nuisance**
    (Chapter 23)
    1. An act
    2. Unreasonable interference with the use and enjoyment
    3. Of a right common to the general public
    4. Based on negligence, intent, strict liability, or violation of a statute, ordinance, or regulation
    5. Causation

27. **Prima Facie Tort**
    (Chapter 26)
    1. Infliction of harm
    2. Intent to do harm (malice)
    3. Special damages
    4. Causation

28. **Seduction**
    (Chapter 22)
    The defendant had sex with the plaintiff's minor daughter by force or with the consent of the daughter.

29. **Strict Liability for Abnormally Dangerous Conditions or Activities**
    (Chapter 11)
    1. Existence of an abnormally dangerous condition or activity
    2. Knowledge of the condition or activity
    3. Causation
    4. Damages

30. **Strict Liability for Harm Caused by Animals**
    (Chapter 11)
    Domestic Animals
    1. Keeping a domestic animal that the owner has reason to know has dangerous propensities
    2. Harm caused by the animal due to that specific propensity

    Wild Animals
    1. Keeping a wild animal
    2. Harm caused by the animal

31. **Strict Liability in Tort**
    (Chapter 19)
    1. Seller
    2. A defective product that is unreasonably dangerous to person or property
    3. User or consumer
    4. Physical harm (damages)
    5. Causation

32. **Trespass to Chattels**
    (Chapter 10)
    1. Personal property (chattel)
    2. The plaintiff is in possession of the chattel or is entitled to immediate possession
    3. Intent to dispossess or intermeddle
    4. Dispossession or intermeddling
    5. Causation of the dispossession or intermeddling

33. **Trespass to Land**
    (Chapter 23)
    1. An act
    2. Intrusion on land
    3. In possession of another
    4. Intent to intrude
    5. Causation of the intrusion

Warranty (three causes of action)

34. **Breach of Express Warranty**
    (Chapter 19)
    1. A statement of fact that is false
    2. Made with the intent or expectation that the statement will reach the plaintiff
    3. Reliance on the statement by the plaintiff
    4. Damage
    5. Causation

35. **Breach of Implied Warranty of Fitness for a Particular Purpose**
    (Chapter 19)
    1. Sale of goods
    2. By a merchant of goods of that kind
    3. The merchant has reason to know the buyer's particular purpose in buying the goods
    4. The merchant has reason to know that the buyer is relying on the merchant's skill or judgment in buying the goods
    5. The goods are not fit for the particular purpose
    6. Damage
    7. Causation

36. **Breach of Implied Warranty of Merchantability**
    (Chapter 19)
    1. Sale of goods
    2. By a merchant of goods of that kind
    3. The goods are not merchantable
    4. Damage
    5. Causation

37. **Wrongful Civil Proceedings**
    (Chapter 8)
    1. Initiation of civil proceedings
    2. Without probable cause
    3. With malice
    4. The proceedings terminate in favor of the person against whom the civil proceedings were brought
    5. Some states add an additional element of special injury or interference caused by the civil proceedings

38. **Wrongful Discharge**
    (Chapter 26)
    1. Termination of an employee by an employer
    2. Retaliation
    3. Violation of public policy

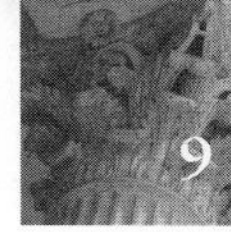

Intentional Torts

An **intentional tort** is a tort in which a person either desired to bring about the result or knew with substantial certainty that the result would follow from what the person did or failed to do. Some of the major intentional torts are battery, assault, trespass, and false imprisonment. Many of the cases asserting these torts are relatively straightforward. An easy battery case, for example, occurs when one person punches another in the nose. Other cases, however, are not so easy:

intentional tort A tort in which a person either desired to bring about the result or knew with substantial certainty that the result would follow from what the person did or failed to do.

EXAMPLE

Jim rides his bicycle through a large puddle of water directly in front of a bench where Mary is sitting. The water splashes on Mary who now sues Jim for battery. *Mary v. Jim* (battery)

When we study battery, we will see that a main issue in the battery case of *Mary v. Jim* will be whether Jim desired to hit Mary with the water or knew with substantial certainty that this would happen if he rode through the water.

It is often difficult to get into someone's head to prove desire. Hence, plaintiffs can use the alternative test of substantially certain knowledge. Compare the following two cases:

- I place a lighted match to the newspaper you are reading, which then catches fire. Assume that I was just joking around; I didn't want the newspaper to go up in flames.
- I light a cigarette in a room full of gasoline vapors, which then explode. Assume that I did not want this explosion to occur.

In the first case, a jury would probably conclude that I had substantially certain knowledge that your newspaper would catch fire when I placed a lighted match to it. To reach this result, the jury would rely on common sense and the everyday experience of all adults. The jury, however, might not conclude that I had substantially certain knowledge that the explosion would result in the second case. I may have been stupid to light a cigarette in that room, but stupidity or carelessness is not the same as substantially certain knowledge.

In the case of *Mary v. Jim,* suppose (a) that the jury believes Jim when he asserts that he never wanted (desired) to splash Mary (perhaps because he was riding the bike so fast when he turned a sharp corner that he never saw anyone on the bench) or (b) that the jury concludes he did not know with substantial certainty that he would splash her (perhaps because he was riding the bike so slowly). In short, the jury believes Jim when he says that he splashed Mary by accident. If the jury accepts this version of the facts, there is no intentional tort because the element of intent has not been proven. There is, however, another tort that Jim may have committed: negligence.

Negligence

Negligence is the failure to use reasonable care that an ordinary prudent person would have used in a similar situation, resulting in injury or other loss. An example might be colliding with someone while driving under the influence of medication that causes intense drowsiness. An ordinary prudent person taking such medication would not drive. Hence the driver was negligent.

negligence The failure to use reasonable care that an ordinary prudent person would have used in a similar situation, resulting in injury or other loss.

To understand the distinction between negligence and intentional torts, we need to compare an *unreasonable risk of harm* and a *substantial certainty of harm:*

- negligence: The heart of a plaintiff's negligence case is to show that the defendant created an *unreasonable risk of harm*, which is a risk that an ordinary prudent person would not take.
- intentional tort: The heart of a plaintiff's intentional tort case is to show that the defendant wanted (desired) the harm to result or knew that there was a *substantial certainty of harm* based on what the defendant did or failed to do.

In our bicycle example of *Mary v. Jim,* assume that Mary does not sue for battery because of the difficulty of proving intent. Instead, she sues Jim under a negligence cause of action. Now the question will be whether Jim was so careless in riding the bike near the bench that he created an unreasonable risk of splashing people with water. The answer may depend on a variety of facts (which a paralegal might be asked to help uncover through interviewing and investigation) such as:

- how fast Jim was riding,
- how deep was the puddle,
- whether Jim knew his riding through other puddles in the area was causing splashes,
- how visible to Jim was Mary on the bench, etc.

A jury might believe that Jim never wanted (desired) to splash Mary and that he did not have substantially certain knowledge that he would splash her, but still come to the conclusion that he created an unreasonable risk of splashing her and that an ordinary prudent person would not have taken this risk. Hence, he committed negligence. In later chapters, we will examine other examples of this important distinction between negligence and intentional torts.

Strict Liability

strict liability Responsibility for harm even if one did not intend the harm and used reasonable care to try to prevent it. Responsibility for harm whether or not the person causing the harm was at any fault or engaged in any moral impropriety. Also called absolute liability and liability without fault.

liable Obligated in law; legally responsible.

The general meaning of **strict liability** (also called *absolute liability* or *liability without fault*) is responsibility for harm whether or not the person causing the harm was at any fault or engaged in any moral impropriety. If the defendant engages in a certain kind of conduct that causes harm, liability will result irrespective of intent or negligence. An example would be performing an abnormally dangerous activity such as blasting. If the plaintiff is injured because of the explosion of the defendant's dynamite, the latter will be responsible (i.e., **liable**), regardless of whether the defendant desired to injure the plaintiff or knew with substantial certainty that the plaintiff or anyone else would be injured (intent), and regardless of whether the defendant acted unreasonably in setting off the explosive (negligence). As we will see, however, it is sometimes difficult to distinguish strict liability from negligence, especially in the area of products liability.

One final caution about definitions of legal terminology: use the definitions as points of departure only. The most dangerous definitions are the ones that give the appearance of universality. The meaning of a word or phrase may change when the context changes. In the practice of law, great care is needed to *localize* all definitions by determining what a particular court in your state meant by a word or phrase. Also, keep in mind that as courts struggle to do justice, they sometimes stretch the definitions to accommodate the result they want to reach on the facts before them. Again, consider all definitions as no more than starting points from which you need to make further inquiry.

INTRODUCTION TO CAUSATION

proximate cause A cause that is legally sufficient to impose liability for the results of one's wrongful act or omission. There are two components of proximate cause: actual cause (which answers the question of who was the cause in fact of the harm or other loss) and legal cause (which answers the question of whether the harm or other loss was the foreseeable consequence of the original risk).

In Chapter 15 we will study causation extensively. Since causation will be referred to throughout the book, a brief introduction is in order here. **Proximate cause** is a cause that is legally sufficient to impose liability for the results of one's wrongful act or omission. Unfortunately, courts use the phrase proximate cause in different ways. In this book, we will use it to mean both actual cause and legal cause:

- actual cause, which answers the question of who was the cause in fact of the harm or other loss
- legal cause, which answers the question of whether the harm or other loss was the foreseeable consequence of the original risk

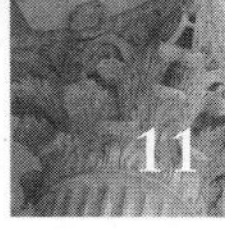

For now, let's focus on **actual cause**, which means cause in fact as established by one of the following two tests:

- **but-for test**: Would the event (e.g., the injury) have happened without the act or omission of the party? But for the act or omission, would the event have occurred?
- **substantial-factor test**: Did the party have a significant or important role in bringing about the event (e.g., the injury)?

Either test is sufficient to establish actual cause. The but-for test is used when there is only one alleged cause of an event in question. The substantial-factor test is used primarily when more than one causal entity is alleged.

actual cause Cause in fact. Causation established either by the but-for test or by the substantial-factor test. But-for test: can it be said that an event (e.g., the injury) would not have occurred without the act or omission of the party? Substantial-factor test: can it be said that the party's acts or omissions had a significant or important role in bringing about the event?

but-for test Would the event (e.g., the injury) have happened without the act or omission of the party? But for the act or omission, would the event have occurred? Also called the *sine qua non* test.

substantial-factor test Did the party's acts or omissions have a significant or important role in bringing about the event (e.g., the injury)?

EXAMPLES

- *But for.* George fires his gun at Bill. Bill's left arm is paralyzed by the bullet. But for the gunshot wound, Bill's arm would not have been paralyzed. Therefore, George's act of firing the gun was the actual cause of the paralysis.
- *Substantial factor.* Ajax Manufacturing Co. and Winthrop, Inc., pour chemicals into a stream. After they do so, the stream is so polluted that it is no longer suitable for fishing.
  — The dumping by Ajax had a significant role (i.e., was a substantial factor) in making the river unfishable. Therefore Ajax was an actual cause of this result.
  — The dumping by Winthrop had a significant role (i.e., was a substantial factor) in making the river unfishable. Therefore Winthrop was an actual cause of this result.

Again, in Chapter 15 we will have a lot more to say about these two tests for actual cause and we will also cover legal cause, the second component of proximate cause.

RELATIONSHIP BETWEEN TORT LAW AND OTHER AREAS OF THE LAW

The study of tort law will involve us in many other areas of the law:

Contract Law

When you buy a toaster, you have entered a **contract** of purchase. If the appliance explodes in your face when you try it for the first time, you may have an action for a breach of contract (you did not receive the functioning toaster you paid for) *and* an action for a tort (you were injured by the toaster). Most of the law of products liability grows out of such situations. Furthermore, it can be a tort to cause or induce someone to breach a contract.

contract A legally enforceable agreement. An agreement supported by consideration, which can be an act, a forbearance (not performing an act), a promise to perform an act, or a promise to refrain from performing an act.

Criminal Law

When Ted punches Bob in the face, two wrongs have probably been committed. Bob has been *personally* injured. He can bring a tort action against Ted for civil battery. In addition, as we have seen, the public has been injured. The public peace has been violated. The state prosecutor can bring a criminal action against Ted for a crime that might be called "battery" or "assault and battery." The tort action and the criminal action are separate proceedings (see Exhibit 1–2). We need to examine the relationship between torts and crimes. For example, is it a tort to encourage the prosecutor to bring a criminal action that turns out to be groundless? We will answer this question when we study the tort called malicious prosecution.

Civil Procedure Law

A tort may lead to a lawsuit where civil procedure law governs jurisdiction, pleadings, discovery, trial, and appeal. We will review some of these topics with an emphasis on paralegal roles during the different stages of tort litigation. We will also cover **alternative dispute resolution (ADR)** such as arbitration and mediation.

alternative dispute resolution (ADR) A method or procedure for resolving a legal dispute without litigating it in a court or administrative agency. Examples include arbitration and mediation.

Family Law

There are a number of tort doctrines that are designed to protect the family. Examples include damages for loss of consortium and suits for wrongful adoption. In addition, family members can commit torts against each other. Whether they are allowed to sue for such torts depends on the scope of the intrafamily tort immunity, which we will be examining.

Constitutional Law

To deprive someone of federal civil rights under color of law can be what is called a constitutional tort. Constitutional law is also significant in suits for defamation (libel and slander) brought against the media.

Estate Law

What happens when the wrongdoer dies before being sued by the injured party? Can the wrongdoer's estate be sued? Suppose the injured party dies before suing the wrongdoer. Can the estate of the injured party sue the wrongdoer? If so, who receives the award of damages in the suit? We will examine these questions under the topics of survival and wrongful death.

State and Local Government Law

Can a city or state be sued in tort? Can a tort action be brought against the United States (federal) government? Answers to such questions involve the doctrine of sovereign immunity.

Real Property Law

There are a number of torts that are committed by or against landowners and land occupiers. These real estate torts sometimes raise questions such as What is land? and What is the possession of land?

Insurance Law

Insurance law has a major impact on tort litigation, particularly on the question of whether the parties will settle their dispute. Also, in many states, insurance companies can be sued for "bad faith" in how they handle policy claims made against them.

Environmental Law

Environmental rules and regulations can have an important impact on certain negligence and nuisance cases as well as in the area of mass tort litigation and toxic torts.

SOURCES OF TORT LAW

Where does tort law come from? Who writes the rules for establishing tort liability through litigation? Where are these rules found? These are our concerns in this section. Although many of these themes may be covered in a legal research course, it is helpful to reinforce them in the context of tort litigation.

Primary Authority

Primary authority is any law that a court could rely on in reaching a decision. Examples include court opinions, statutes, constitutions, administrative regulations, administrative decisions, charters, ordinances, and rules of court. See Exhibit 1–4 for the definitions of these categories of primary authority and examples of how they could be involved in tort litigation.

primary authority Any law (e.g., case or statute) that a court could rely on in reaching a decision.

Exhibit 1–4 Categories of primary authority involved in a tort case.

Category	Definition	Example
(a) Opinion	A court's written explanation of how it applied the law to the facts before it to resolve a legal dispute. Also called *case* or *decision*. (Most tort law is created in opinions.) (The word *case* has two other meanings: a pending matter on a court calendar and a client matter handled by a law office.)	The case of *Smith v. Jones* rules that Jones negligently injured Smith in an automobile collision.
(b) Statute	A law passed by the federal or state legislature declaring, commanding, or prohibiting something. Also called *act* and *legislation*. (Statute, act, and legislation are sometimes used in a broader sense to include laws passed by any legislature, which would include ordinances passed by a city council.)	Davis is injured in one of the elevators at Macy's Department Store. In the suit, Davis alleges that Macy's violated § 236 of the state's statutory code, which requires a monthly safety inspection of all elevators.
(c) Constitution	The fundamental law that creates the branches of government, allocates power among them, and defines some basic rights of individuals.	A story in *Time* magazine links Harris with the illegal drug trade. Harris sues for libel. *Time* argues that the suit violates the First Amendment right to freedom of the press.
(d) Administrative Regulation	A law written by an administrative agency and designed to explain or carry out the statutes, executive orders, or other regulations that govern the agency. Also called *administrative rule*.	Simpson suffers food poisoning after eating a product of General Foods Inc. The suit alleges that General Foods failed to follow § 137.3, a regulation of the Food and Drug Administration on proper food labeling.
(e) Administrative Decision	An administrative agency's resolution of a controversy (often following a hearing) on the application of the regulations, statutes, or executive orders that govern the agency. Sometimes called administrative *ruling*.	In *Perry v. Commissioner,* the State Workers' Compensation Board rules that Perry is not entitled to benefits because his injury did not arise out of his employment.
(f) Charter	The fundamental law of a municipality or other local unit of government, authorizing it to perform designated governmental functions.	Adams can sue Portland for the injury caused by a city police officer; Adams is allowed to bring this suit because § 26 of the Portland charter waives sovereign immunity for injuries wrongfully caused by municipal employees within the scope of employment.
(g) Ordinance	A law passed by the local legislative branch of government (e.g., city council, county commission) that declares, commands, or prohibits something. (Same as a statute, but at the local level.)	Kelly sues Parker for trespass to land when Parker's cows damage Kelly's land. Parker argues that Kelly did not have the kind of fencing around his land required by § 22(g) of the County Ordinance on farm animal control.
(h) Rules of Court	The procedural laws that govern the mechanics of litigation (practice and procedure) before a particular court. Also called court rules.	Richardson sues his doctor for negligence. Under Superior Court Rule 38, all medical malpractice cases must be first heard by a magistrate, who must prepare a pretrial order before the case can commence in Superior Court.

Opinions Court opinions (referred to as case law) are the foundation of tort law. In fact, the major way in which tort law comes into existence is through what is called **common law**. This is judge-made law created in the absence of statutes or

common law Judge-made law in the absence of statutes or other controlling law.

other controlling law. In effect, the courts create tort law when there is a vacuum. If, for example, the court has a dispute before it that has never been litigated in the courts and is not governed by any statute or constitutional provision, the court can create law to govern that dispute. What it creates is called the common law. An example is invasion of privacy, which, as we will see in Chapter 25, consists of four separate torts. The courts created privacy tort law at a time when there were few or no statutes in this area. When a court creates common law, it relies primarily on the customs and values of the community from time immemorial. Very often these customs and values are described and enforced in old opinions, which are heavily referred to (i.e., cited) by modern courts in the continuing process of developing the common law.

reporter A volume (or set of volumes) of court opinions. Also called case reports. (See the glossary for an additional definition.)

Court opinions are printed in volumes called **reporters**. For example, in Exhibit 1–5 you will find the first page of the opinion called *Austria v. Bike Athletic Co.*, printed in volume 810 of the Pacific Reporter, 2d Series. (The same opinion can be found online. See Exhibit 1–6.) *Austria* is a products liability case in which a high

Exhibit 1–5
Excerpt from a torts court opinion found in a reporter: *Austria v. Bike Athletic Co.*, 107 Or. App. 57, 810 P.2d 1312 (Ct. App. 1991).

1312 Or. 810 Pacific Reporter, 2d Series

107 Or.App. 57

John Austria, as guardian ad litem for Richard Austria, a minor, and John Austria and Perla Austria, husband and wife, Respondents.

v.

BIKE ATHLETIC CO., a foreign corporation, Colgate-Palmolive Co., a foreign corporation, and Kendall Research Center, a foreign entity, Appellants,

and

Renato Pizarro, M.D., Defendant

A8707–044789; CA A63376.

Court of Appeals of Oregon.

Argued and Submitted Nov. 21, 1990.

Decided May 1, 1991.

Parents of football player severely injured by blow to head during football practice brought suit against designer and manufacturer of football helmet, alleging defective design. The Circuit Court, Multnomah County, Richard L. Unis, J., entered judgment for plaintiffs, and defendants appealed. The Court of Appeals, Deits, J., held that there was evidence from which jury could conclude that player's injuries were caused by defects in football helmet.

Affirmed.

1. **Products Liability 60**
In order to prove that football player's injuries were caused by defects in football helmet, it was not necessary to prove amount of force received by player as result of blow, amount of force that he would have received had he been wearing helmet of alternative design or amount of force required to cause type of head injury he suffered.

2. **Products Liability 83**
Evidence, when combined with inferences drawn therefrom, was sufficient to allow jury to conclude that defective helmet caused football player's head injury; there was evidence about how and why player was struck, what a football helmet is supposed to do to reduce consequences of collision, that hematoma resulted from precisely the kind of trauma that helmets are designed to prevent, that properly designed helmet would have greatly reduced likelihood of hematoma and that helmet was not adequately designed to reduce that likelihood.

3. **Products Liability 88**
There was sufficient proof to submit to jury allegation that football helmet was improperly designed or manufactured so that it would allow energy of blow to be transmitted to head of user without absorbing sufficient amounts of energy so as to prevent closed head injuries.

James N. Westwood, Portland, argued the cause for appellants.

W. Eugene Hallman, Pendleton, argued the cause for respondents.

Before RICHARDSON, P.J., and NEWMAN and DEITS, JJ.

DEITS, Judge.

Richard Austria was severely injured by a blow to the head during football practice. Through his guardian ad litem, he sued the designer and manufacturer of the football helmet that he was wearing, alleging that its defective design was the cause of his injury. The jury returned a verdict for plaintiffs and defendants appeal, arguing, primarily, that the trial court erred in denying their motions for directed verdict, because there was insufficient evidence of causation. We affirm.

In September, 1985, Richard Austria was a sixteen year old high school junior. He was injured during football practice when the knee of another player forcefully struck the front of his helmet. Although he was dazed by the collision, he walked off the field on his own and seemed to suffer few ill effects. Approximately two weeks later, however, he experienced severe headaches. On October 1, he collapsed during football practice. A CT scan indicated that Richard had a subdural hematoma....

Exhibit 1–6 Excerpt from a torts court opinion found online in Westlaw: *Austria v. Bike Athletic Co.*, 107 Or. App. 57, 810 P.2d 1312 (Ct. App. 1991). If this opinion had not yet been printed in a traditional reporter, its Westlaw citation might be *Austria v. Bike Athletic Co.*, 1991 WL 253716342 (Ct. App. 1991).

H

Austria v. Bike Athletic Co.
107 Or.App. 57, 810 P.2d 1312
Or.App.,1991.
May 01, 1991 (Approx. 4 pages)

West Reporter Image (PDF)

107 Or.App. 57, 810 P.2d 1312, 67 Ed. Law Rep. 1302, Prod.Liab.Rep. (CCH) P 12,906

Court of Appeals of Oregon.
John AUSTRIA, as guardian ad litem for Richard Austria, a minor, and John Austria and Perla Austria, husband and wife, Respondents,
v.
BIKE ATHLETIC CO., a foreign corporation, Colgate-Palmolive Co., a foreign corporation, and Kendall Research Center, a foreign entity, Appellants,
and
Renato Pizarro, M.D., Defendant.

A8707-04478; CA A63376.
Argued and Submitted Nov. 21, 1990.
Decided May 1, 1991.
Reconsideration Denied June 26, 1991.

Review Denied Aug. 20, 1991.

Parents of football player severely injured by blow to head during football practice brought suit against designer and manufacturer of football helmet, alleging defective design. The Circuit Court, Multnomah County, Richard L. Unis, J., entered judgment for plaintiffs, and defendants appealed. The Court of Appeals, Deits, J., held that there was evidence from which jury could conclude that player's injuries were caused by defects in football helmet.

Affirmed.

school student sued a helmet manufacturer after being severely injured in the head during football practice. Hundreds of thousands of tort opinions such as this can be found in the many sets of reporter volumes in a law library and in online databases.

Statutes The statutes passed by legislatures affect tort litigation in three significant ways:

Statutes can change the common law Generally, statutes are superior in authority to court opinions. If the legislature desires to change the common law that has been developed by the courts, it can pass a statute making this change. Such a law is called a statute in **derogation** of the common law.

derogation A partial repeal or abolition of a law. For example, a statute in derogation of common law changes the common law.

Statutes can define the standard of care When a defendant is sued for negligence, one of the claims often made by the plaintiff is that the defendant violated a statute, e.g., a traffic statute or a license statute. In such cases, the court must examine the relationship between the common law of negligence and the statute that has allegedly been violated. As we will see in Chapter 14, the specific question is whether the statute will be used by the court to define the standard of care to which the defendant will be held.

Statutes can create new torts Occasionally the legislature will create an entirely new tort cause of action. The state of Minnesota, for example, recently decided that the traditional torts did not sufficiently cover the harm caused when one person coerces another into prostitution. Consequently, the Minnesota legislature created the following new cause of action:

> Minnesota Statutes Annotated § 611A.81. Cause of action for coercion for use in prostitution

> Subdivision 1. Cause of action created.
> (a) An individual has a cause of action against a person who:
> (1) coerced the individual into prostitution;
> (2) coerced the individual to remain in prostitution; [or]
> (3) used coercion to collect or receive any of the individual's earnings derived from prostitution. . . .

This cause of action for coerced prostitution did not exist at common law. It is a creation of the legislature.

In the same manner, the legislature could pass a statute that creates a new defense to an existing cause of action or could set limits on the amount and kind of damages that can be awarded for certain torts that are successfully established. For example, some states have statutes that limit the amount of damages that can be awarded in a medical malpractice case.

statutory code A collection of statutes organized by subject matter rather than chronologically by date enacted.

Statutes are printed in volumes called **statutory codes**. For example, in Exhibit 1–7 you will find the beginning of § 2-621 in *Illinois Annotated Statutes*. (The same statute can be found online at www.ilga.gov.) This section of the statute provides some of the requirements for bringing products liability litigation against manufacturers and other defendants.

Exhibit 1–7
Excerpt from a page in a statutory code on a torts issue: *Illinois Annotated Statutes*, chapter 110, § 2-621 (West 1983).

110 ¶ 2–621 CODE OF CIVIL PROCEDURE
Code of Civ.Proc. § 2–621

2–621. Product liability actions
§ 2–621. Product liability actions. (a) In any product liability action based on any theory or doctrine commenced or maintained against a defendant or defendants other than the manufacturer, that party shall upon answering or otherwise pleading file an affidavit certifying the correct identity of the manufacturer of the product allegedly causing injury, death or damage. The commencement of a product liability action based on any theory or doctrine against such defendant or defendants shall toll the applicable statute of limitation and statute of repose relative to the defendant or defendants for purposes of asserting a strict liability in tort cause of action. . . .

Administrative Regulations In a number of areas, administrative agencies and their regulations have a large role in tort litigation. At the state level, the best example is the workers' compensation agency or board that covers occupational accidents. At the federal level, an example of an important agency is the United States Consumer Product Safety Commission, as we will see when we examine products liability.

administrative code A collection of administrative regulations organized by subject matter rather than chronologically by date enacted.

Administrative regulations are printed in volumes often called **administrative code** or code of regulations. For example, in Exhibit 1–8 you will find § 1118.1 in *Code of Federal Regulations*. (The same administrative regulation can be found online at www.gpoaccess.gov/cfr.) This section covers investigations conducted by the United States Consumer Product Safety Commission on products alleged to be unsafe, such as athletic equipment used in school sports.

Secondary Authority

secondary authority Any nonlaw (e.g., a legal treatise) that a court could rely on in reaching a decision.

Secondary authority is any nonlaw that a court could rely on to reach its decision. Examples include legal encyclopedias, legal treatises, legal periodical literature, and annotations. There are two main values of secondary authorities. First, they often contain extensive footnotes that will lead you to court opinions and other primary authorities on the tort (or other) topic you are examining. Second, they are usually written in a clear, basic writing style. Since they often cover the fundamentals, they are excellent starting points for the novice who needs a quick overview or summary of the law. This background can be valuable in understanding the sometimes more difficult-to-read primary authority.

Consumer Product Safety Commission

PART 1118—INVESTIGATIONS, INSPECTIONS AND INQUIRIES UNDER THE CONSUMER PRODUCT SAFETY ACT

Subpart A—Procedures for Investigations, Inspections, and Inquiries

Sec.
1118.1 Definitions, initiation of investigations, inspections, and inquiries and delegations.
1118.2 Conduct and scope of inspections.
1118.3 Compulsory processes and service.
1118.4 Subpoenas.
1118.5 Investigational hearings.
1118.6 Depositions.
1118.7 Rights of witnesses at investigational hearings and of deponents at depositions.
1118.8 General or special orders seeking information.
1118.9 Motions to limit or quash subpoenas and general or special orders and delegation to modify terms for compliance.
1118.10 Remedies for failure to permit authorized investigation.
1118.11 Nonexclusive delegation of power.

Subpart A—Procedures for Investigations, Inspections, and Inquiries

§1118.1 Definitions, initiation of investigations, inspections, and inquiries and delegations.

(a) *Definitions.* For the purpose of these rules, the following definitions apply:

(1) *Act* means Consumer Product Safety Act (15 U.S.C. 2051, et seq.).

(2) *Commission* means the Consumer Product Safety Commission.

(3) *Firm* means a manufacturer, private labeler, distributor, or retailer of a consumer product, except as otherwise provided by section 16(b) of the Act.

(4) *Investigation* is an undertaking by the Commission to obtain information for implementing, enforcing, or determining compliance with the Consumer Product Safety Act and the regulations, rules, and orders issued under the Act.

Exhibit 1–8
Excerpt from an administrative regulation on a torts issue: 16 Code of Federal Regulations § 1118.1 (2008).

Courts can rely on secondary authority, although they are not required to do so. Secondary authority can only be **persuasive authority**, which means that the court is free to accept or reject the authority in rendering its decision. When a dispute is in litigation, the main focus of the court is on primary authority. Secondary authority is of interest to the court when the legal issue before the court is a difficult one or when it is relatively novel. Otherwise, courts generally prefer that parties do not cite secondary authority in documents submitted to the court during litigation.

persuasive authority Any authority that a court could rely on in reaching its decision, even though it is not required to rely on it. (The opposite of persuasive authority is **mandatory authority**, which is any authority a court must rely on in reaching its decision.)

Assume that you are working on a products liability case and that you want to find relevant discussions of the law in secondary authority. Here are some examples of law books you might use:

Legal Encyclopedia A **legal encyclopedia** is a multivolume set of books that summarizes almost every important legal topic. Two of the major legal encyclopedias are *Corpus Juris Secundum* (see Exhibit 1–9 for a sample page) and *American Jurisprudence 2d* (see Exhibit 1–10 for a sample page), both published by West Group.

legal encyclopedia A multivolume set of books that summarizes almost every important legal topic.

Legal Treatise A **legal treatise** is a book written by a private individual (or by a public official writing as a private citizen) that provides an overview, summary, or commentary on a legal topic. Perhaps the most famous and widely used legal treatise is *Prosser and Keeton on the Law of Torts* (5th ed. 1984). See Exhibit 1–11 for a sample page. The *Prosser and Keeton* book has been extensively updated by *The Law of Torts* (2000) by Dan B. Dobbs.

legal treatise A book written by a private individual (or by a public official writing as a private citizen) that provides an overview, summary, or commentary on a legal topic.

Another extremely important legal treatise is *Restatement of Torts,* published by a private organization of scholars, the American Law Institute. Many courts are greatly influenced by the *Restatement,* particularly when these courts are dealing with questions or issues that are relatively new for their states. Products liability litigation is a major example of this; a large number of courts have agreed with and have adopted positions of the *Restatement* on strict liability in tort. These positions are found within the volumes of *Restatement (Second) of Torts* (see Exhibit 1–12). As we will see in Chapter 19, some controversial changes were made in the most recent addition to the field, *Restatement (Third) of Torts: Products Liability.*

Exhibit 1–9
Excerpt from a page in a volume of *Corpus Juris Secundum* on a torts issue: 72 *Corpus Juris Secundum* Supplement § 66 (2006).

72 C.J.S.Supp. PRODUCTS LIABILITY §§65–66

Assuming facts favorable to plaintiff suing a cigarette manufacturer for cancer or death resulting from cancer because of cigarette smoking, recovery might be grounded on negligence,[67] fraud for misrepresentation,[68] implied warranty,[69] or strict liability in tort.[70] While a manufacturer of cigarettes is strictly liable for foreseeable harm resulting from a defective condition in the product when the consumer uses the product for the purposes for which it was manufactured and marketed,[71] there is no absolute liability for the harmful effects of which no developed skill or foresight can avoid.[72] Thus the manufacturer of cigarettes cannot be held absolutely liable for cancer, or a consumer's death from cancer, allegedly caused by smoking cigarettes,[73] where plaintiff's claim negatives scientific foreseeability, peculiar defects in cigarettes, and cancer consequences to a substantial segment of the public.[74]

§66. Toys, Games, and Athletic or Recreational Equipment

The concept of products liability applies to a manufacturer of toys, games, and athletic or recreational equipment.

Library References

Products Liability 60.

The concept of products liability applies to a manufacturer of toys, games, and athletic or recreational equipment.[75] Thus, the manufacturer may be liable under the doctrine of strict liability in tort for injury caused by a defective condition unreasonably dangerous to the user or consumer of such products.[76] Liability may also be grounded on negligence.[77] The manufacturer is not an insurer of safety of the equipment[78] and does not guarantee that it will not wear out and will last forever.[79] The manufacturer should anticipate the reasonably foreseeable risks in the use of the product.[80]

The manufacturer of toys, games, and athletic or recreational equipment, is under a duty to test and inspect the products for safety before marketing them,[81] but a wholesaler or retailer has been held not to have a duty to inspect products packaged by, and received from, a reputable manufacturer.[82] While a manufacturer has a . . . .

67. U.S.—Lartigue v. R. J. Reynolds Tobacco Co., C.A.La., 317 F.2d 19, certiorari denied 84 S.Ct. 137, 375 U.S. 865, 11 L.Ed.2d 32.
68. U.S.—Lartigue v. R. J. Reynolds Tobacco CO., C.A.La., 317 F.2d 19, certiorari denied 84 S.Ct. 137, 375 U.S. 865, 11 L.Ed.2d 92.
69. U.S.—Lartigue v. R. J. Reynolds Tobacco Co., C.A.La., 317 F.2d 19, certiorari denied 84 S.Ct. 137, 375 U.S. 865, 11 L.Ed.2d 92.
70. U.S.—Lartigue v. R. J. Reynolds Tobacco Co., C.A.La., 317 F.2d 19, certiorari denied 84 S.Ct. 137, 375 U.S. 865, 11 L.Ed.2d 92.
71. U.S.—Lartigue v. R. J. Reynolds Tobacco Co., C.A.La., 317 F.2d 18, certiorari denied 84 S.Ct. 137, 375 U.S. 865, 11 L.Ed.2d 92.
72. U.S.—Lartigue v. R. J. Reynolds Tobacco Co., C.A.La., 317 F.2d 19, certiorari denied 84 S.Ct. 137, 375 U.S. 865, 11 L.Ed.2d 92.
73. U.S.—Hudson v. R. J. Reynolds Tobacco Co., C.A.La., 427 F.2d 541—Green v. American Tobacco Co., C.A.Fla., 409 F.2d 1166, certiorari denied 90 S.Ct. 912, 397 U.S. 911, 25 L.Ed.2d93—Lartigue v. R. J. Reynolds Tobacco Co., C.A.La., 317 F.2d 19, certiorari denied 84 S.Ct. 137, 375 U.S. 865, 11 L.Ed.2d 92.
74. U.S.—Hudson v. R. J. Reynolds Tobacco Co., C.A.La., 427 F.2d 541.
75. Ind.—Dudley Sports Co. v. Schmitt, 279 N.E.2d 266, 151 Ind.App.217.

Golf cart

Purchaser of allegedly defective golf carts could maintain action against manufacturer to recover for loss of his bargain and cost of making repairs, even though parts were purchased from a dealer and not directly from the manufacturer.

Mich.—Cova v. Harley Davidson Motor Co., 812 N.W.2d 800, 26 Mich.App.602.

76. Baseball sunglasses

U.S.—Filler v. Rayex Corp., C.A.Ind., 435 F.2d 336.

Exhibit 1–10
Excerpt from a page in a volume of *American Jurisprudence 2d* on a torts issue: 63 *American Jurisprudence 2d* § 1 (2008).

§ 1. GENERALLY; "PRODUCTS LIABILITY" DEFINED

The term "products liability," a phrase almost unknown to the legal profession in earlier years, is now almost universally applied to the liability of a manufacturer, processor, or nonmanufacturing seller for injury to the person or property of a buyer or third party caused by a product which has been sold. The subject matter of products liability was formerly dealt with under such legal classifications as "negligence," "torts," or "sales." Particularly in light of the development of the doctrine of strict liability in tort, however,[1] it is clear that "products liability" has become a legal heading or subject in its own right.

The paradigmatic products liability action is one where a product which is reasonably certain to place life and limb in peril, and is distributed without reinspection, causes bodily harm, and a manufacturer is liable regardless of whether it is negligent because public policy demands that responsibility be fixed wherever it will most effectively reduce the hazards to life and health inherent in defective products that reach the market.[2] Typically, the term "products liability" covers any liability of a manufacturer or other seller or a product, where personal injury or damage to some other property is caused by a defect in the product.[3] The manufacturer's duty of care includes protection against property damage, which traditionally means damages to other property caused by a defective product; such damage is so akin to personal injury that the two are treated alike.[4]

Products liability may also include any liability arising because some defect causes loss or destruction of the product itself.[5]. . .

[1]§§ 517 et seq.

[2]East River S.S. Corp. v Transamerica Delaval, 476 US 858, 90 L Ed 2d 865, 106 S Ct 2295, CCH Prod Liab Rep ¶ 11008, 1986 AMC 2027, 1 UCCRS2d 609 (not followed on other grounds by Washington Water Co. v Graybar Elec. Co., 112 Wash 2d 847, 774 P2d 1199, CCH Prod Liab Rep ¶ 12233).

[3]Greenman v Yuba Power Products, Inc., 59 Gal 2d 57, 27 Cal Rptr 697, 377 P2d 897, 13 ALR3d 1049 (which first judicially applied the doctrine of strict liability in tort).

[4]East River S.S. Corp. v Transamerica Delaval, 476 US 858, 90 L Ed 2d 865, 106 S Ct 2295, CCH Prod Liab Rep ¶ 11008, 1986 AMC 2027, 1 UCCRS2d 609 (not followed on other grounds by Washington Water Power Co. v Graybar Elec. Co., 112 Wash 2d 847, 774 P2d 1199, CCH Prod Liab Rep ¶ 12233).

[5]See, for example, Gherna v Ford Motor Co. (1st Dist) 246 Cal App 2d 639, 55 Cal Rptr 94 (an action for the sudden destruction of a car by fire because of an alleged defect therein).

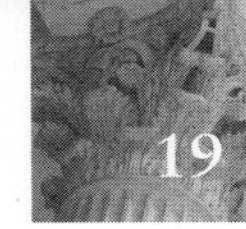

Exhibit 1–11
Excerpt from a page of a legal treatise on a torts issue: W. Page Keeton et al., *Prosser and Keeton on the Law of Torts* § 95 (5th ed. 1984).

Chapter 17

PRODUCTS LIABILITY

Table of Sections

§95. Theories of Recovery and Types of Losses

Products liability is the name currently given to the area of the law involving the liability of those who supply goods or products for the use of others to purchasers, users, and bystanders for losses of various kinds resulting from so-called defects in those products.

At the very outset, it is important to make a distinction between two types of product conditions that can result in some kind of loss either to the purchaser or a third person. One is a dangerous condition of the product or, if one prefers, a product hazard;[1] the other is the inferior condition or . . . .

1. A recent government estimate placed the number of consumer product injuries (both in and out of the home) at 36 million for 1977. See Prod.Saf. & Liab.Rep. (BNA), June 29, 1979, 511. The total cost of such injuries to the nation has been estimated at $20 billion or more per year. Owen, Punitive Damages in Products Liability Litigation, 1976, 74 Mich.L.Rev. 1258–59 n. 2.

677

Exhibit 1–12
Restatement (Second) of Torts (1979).

Legal Periodical Literature A legal periodical is an ongoing publication (e.g., one published six times a year) containing articles, case notes, and other information on legal topics. When published by law schools, legal periodicals are often called law reviews or law journals, e.g., *Harvard Law Review, Yale Law Journal.* Two of the main indexes to legal periodical literature are the *Current Law Index* and the *Index to Legal Periodicals and Books.* See Exhibit 1–13 for a sample page from the *Index to Legal Periodicals and Books.*

Exhibit 1–13
Excerpt from a page in the *Index to Legal Periodicals and Books* that includes citations to legal periodical literature on torts issues.

SUBJECT AND AUTHOR INDEX 199

Prodan, Pamela
The legal framework for Hydro-Quebec imports, 28 *Tulsa L.J.* 435–75 Spr '93

Products liability
See also
Strict liability
Tobacco industry

Apportionment of damages—Third Circuit predicts Pennsylvania courts would not allow jury to apportion liability in a cigarette smoking, asbestos exposure case—Borman v. Raymark Industries, Inc., 960 F.2d 327 (1992). R.K. Shuter, student author. 66 *Temp.L.Rev.* 223–38 Spr '93

Cipollone v. Liggett Group, Inc. [112 S.Ct. 2608 (1992)]: one step closer to exterminating the FIFRA presumption controversy. C. E. Boeh, student author. 81 *Ky.L.J.* 749–78 Spr '92/'93

Constitutional law—pre-emption—the Federal Cigarette Labeling and Advertising Act's express pre-emption provision defines the pre-emptive reach of the Act and must be construed narrowly. Cipollone v. Liggett Group, Inc., 112 S.Ct. 2608 (1992). M. A. Bakris, student author. 70 *U.Det.Mercy L.Rev.* 487–512 Wint '93.

Dangerous products and injured bystanders. R.F. Cochran, Jr. 81 *Ky.L.J.* 687–725 Spr '92/'93

Drugs
California
Kill or cure? Pogash. 13 *Cal.Law.* 48–51 + Je/'93

Motor vehicles
The tide has turned. L. E. Cohen. 29 *Trial* 75–9 Ja '93

Alaska
Products liability in Alaska—a practitioner's overview. T. A. Matthews. 10 *Alaska L.Rev.* 1–32 Je'93

California
Don't kill the messenger 'till you read the message: products liability verdicts in six California counties, 1970–1990. S. Daniels, J. Martin. 16 *Just.Sys.J.* 69–95 '93

European Community countries
The asbestos problem and the European Economic Community. E. R. Bothwell, student author. 31 *Column. J. Transnat'l L.* 205–30 '93

Michigan
Uniform Commercial Code—Article 2—the economic loss doctrine bars an action in tort and a buyer's sole remedy is found under Article 2, where a product purchased for commercial purposes causes economic loss. Neibarger v. Universal Cooperatives, Inc., 486 N.W.2d 612 (Mich.1992). C. W. Fabian, student author. 70 *U.Det.Mercy L.Rev.* 513–29 Wint '93

Annotations An annotation is a set of notes and commentary on issues in court opinions. The major annotations are published by West Group in books called *American Law Reports.* These books print the annotations as well as the court opinions that contain the issues treated in the annotations. The main units of *American Law Reports* are A.L.R., A.L.R.2d, A.L.R.3d, A.L.R.4th, A.L.R.5th, A.L.R.6th, A.L.R. Fed., and A.L.R. Fed. 2d. Annotations provide excellent leads to case law on thousands of issues such as torts and other areas of the law. For an example of a tort annotation, see Exhibit 1–14.

Tort Law Online

online 1. Connected to another computer or computer network, often through the Internet. 2. Residing on a computer and available for use; activated and ready for use on a computer.

It is now possible to obtain a great deal of **online** information that is relevant to a torts practice from free and fee-based sites on the Internet. In addition to research

Products Liability—Sports
76 ALR4th 201

76 ALR4th

ANNOTATION

PRODUCTS LIABILITY: COMPETITIVE SPORTS EQUIPMENT

by

Lee R. Russ, J.D.

§7. **Football helmets—liability of manufacturers and sellers**

[a] **Failure to protect against spinal injury—liability supportable**

In the following products liability cases involving claims that a football helmet was defective in failing to protect its wearer against injuries to the spine, the courts held that, under the particular circumstances presented, there was sufficient evidence of liability to support a judgment in favor of the plaintiff or to reverse a judgment in favor of the manufacturer of the helmet at issue.

Finding several evidentiary rulings to have been erroneous, the court in Galindo v. Riddell, Inc. (1982, 3d Dist) 107 Ill App 3d 139, 62 Ill Dec. 849, 437 NE2d 376, CCH Prod Liab Rep ¶ 9374, reversed a judgment for the maker of a "TK-2" football helmet who was sued by a high school football player for spinal injuries sustained while attempting to make a tackle in a varsity football game. The helmet consisted of a plastic shell on the outside, with a grey rubber pad and cloth strap suspension system on the inside. The plaintiff was paralyzed from the neck down as a result of a dislocation fracture at the fifth and sixth cervical vertebrae. The plaintiff sued on theories of strict liability. . . .

Exhibit 1–14
Excerpt from the first page of an annotation on a torts issue: Lee R. Russ, *Products Liability: Competitive Sports Equipment,* 76 American Law Reports, 4th 201 (1990).

into cases, statutes, and other authorities, a law firm often needs to do factual research. Examples include obtaining information about the manufacturer of a product, the weather conditions on the day of an accident, the assets of a defendant, or the location of a potential witness.

The two major fee-based online services are Westlaw and LexisNexis. They have extensive databases containing primary and secondary authority. One of the particularly useful databases that each provides is a *jury verdict service.* It allows you to search court records to find out what jury verdicts have been returned for specific bodily injuries caused by different categories of accidents. Such information can be invaluable in deciding whether to settle a case and in making a presentation to a liability insurance company.

Greater caution is needed when using free Internet sites than when using the fee-based ones like Westlaw and LexisNexis. In general, the free sites are not as accurate, current, comprehensive, or easy to use as the fee-based sites. Many government sites are free and reliable, although they are rarely as user-friendly as fee-based sites. For an example of a government site relevant to a torts practice, see Exhibit 1–15.

See also the Helpful Websites section at the end of the chapter for sites that a torts practice would find helpful.

PROJECT

Exhibit 1–3 lists a large number of torts. Go to websites of attorneys who practice law in your state. Find law firms that mention any ten of the torts in Exhibit 1–3. Limit yourself to one law firm per tort. For each site you find, give the name of the firm, quote the sentence from the site that mentions the tort, give the web address of the page of the quote, and give the date you visited the site to find the quote. Example: Law offices of Smith and Smith. "We handle malicious prosecution cases." www.smithlawoffice.com (visited December 10, 2011). To locate law firms in your state, run a search in Google, Bing, or other search engine that contains the name of your state, the word "attorney," and the tort you are checking. Example: Pennsylvania attorney negligence. See also the links to trial attorneys in Appendix A.

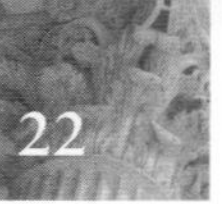

Exhibit 1–15 Example of an Internet site relevant to tort law: Consumer Product Safety Commission (www.cpsc.gov).

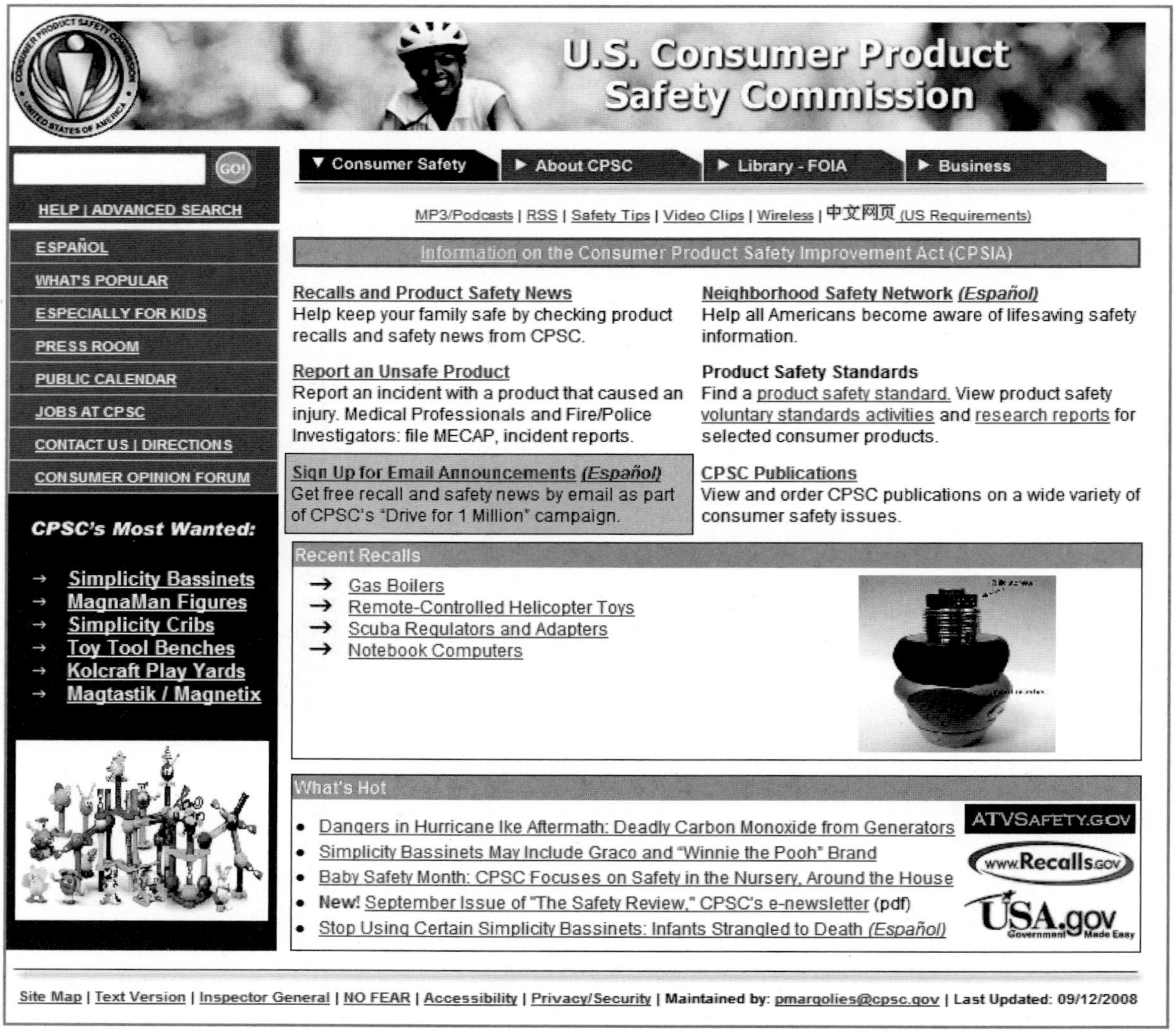

U.S. Consumer Product Safety Commission

GO!

HELP | ADVANCED SEARCH

▼ Consumer Safety ▶ About CPSC ▶ Library - FOIA ▶ Business

MP3/Podcasts | RSS | Safety Tips | Video Clips | Wireless | 中文网页 (US Requirements)

ESPAÑOL
WHAT'S POPULAR
ESPECIALLY FOR KIDS
PRESS ROOM
PUBLIC CALENDAR
JOBS AT CPSC
CONTACT US | DIRECTIONS
CONSUMER OPINION FORUM

Information on the Consumer Product Safety Improvement Act (CPSIA)

Recalls and Product Safety News
Help keep your family safe by checking product recalls and safety news from CPSC.

Neighborhood Safety Network *(Español)*
Help all Americans become aware of lifesaving safety information.

Report an Unsafe Product
Report an incident with a product that caused an injury. Medical Professionals and Fire/Police Investigators: file MECAP, incident reports.

Product Safety Standards
Find a product safety standard. View product safety voluntary standards activities and research reports for selected consumer products.

Sign Up for Email Announcements *(Español)*
Get free recall and safety news by email as part of CPSC's "Drive for 1 Million" campaign.

CPSC Publications
View and order CPSC publications on a wide variety of consumer safety issues.

CPSC's Most Wanted:

→ Simplicity Bassinets
→ MagnaMan Figures
→ Simplicity Cribs
→ Toy Tool Benches
→ Kolcraft Play Yards
→ Magtastik / Magnetix

Recent Recalls

→ Gas Boilers
→ Remote-Controlled Helicopter Toys
→ Scuba Regulators and Adapters
→ Notebook Computers

What's Hot

- Dangers in Hurricane Ike Aftermath: Deadly Carbon Monoxide from Generators
- Simplicity Bassinets May Include Graco and "Winnie the Pooh" Brand
- Baby Safety Month: CPSC Focuses on Safety in the Nursery, Around the House
- New! September Issue of "The Safety Review," CPSC's e-newsletter (pdf)
- Stop Using Certain Simplicity Bassinets: Infants Strangled to Death *(Español)*

ATVSAFETY.GOV
www.Recalls.GOV
USA.gov Government Made Easy

Site Map | Text Version | Inspector General | NO FEAR | Accessibility | Privacy/Security | Maintained by: pmargolies@cpsc.gov | Last Updated: 09/12/2008

ETHICS IN A TORTS PRACTICE

You are a paralegal working in the law office that represents Ed Harris, who is being sued for negligence by George Adams. The negligence case arose out of a car accident, which Adams claims was caused by Harris. Immediately after the accident, Adams called the police when Harris threatened to kill Adams because of Adams's "crazy driving." Another law firm is representing Harris in the criminal case in which Harris is being charged with criminal harassment. One day in the office, Harris asks you a legal question about his criminal case. You happen to know the correct answer. Because your firm is not representing Harris on the criminal case, you answer the question. Any ethical problems?

SUMMARY

A tort is a civil wrong (other than a breach of contract) that causes injury or other harm for which our legal system deems it just to provide a remedy such as damages. A remedy is the means by which a right is enforced or the violation of a right is prevented, compensated for, or otherwise redressed. Criminal law governs a suit brought by the government for the commission of a crime. Civil law governs a suit between private persons or between private persons and the government over a matter other than the commission of a crime. Tort law is one of the branches of civil law. The same conduct can constitute both a tort and a crime. Tort and criminal cases, however, involve separate proceedings. There are four major purposes of tort law: to provide a peaceful means for adjusting the rights of parties; to deter wrongful conduct; to try to restore injured parties to their original position; and to identify who, in fairness, should be responsible for the harm that resulted.

A cause of action is a legally acceptable reason for bringing a suit. Tort causes of action have elements. To state a tort cause of action is to assert facts that support each element of the tort committed by the tortfeasor. A prima facie case is a party's presentation of evidence that will prevail unless the other side offers more convincing counterevidence. There are three main categories of torts: intentional torts (the actor desires the result or knows with substantial certainty that it will occur), negligence (the actor creates an unreasonable risk of harm), and strict liability torts (the actor engages in conduct for which the law imposes liability regardless of intent or negligence). Proximate cause is a cause that is legally sufficient to impose liability for the results of one's wrongful act or omission. The two components of proximate cause are actual cause and legal cause. The two tests for actual cause are the but-for test and the substantial-factor test.

Primary authority is any law that a court can rely on in reaching a decision. The major primary authorities are court opinions, statutes, constitutions, administrative regulations, administrative decisions, charters, ordinances, and rules of court. Common law is judge-made law in the absence of statutes or other controlling law. A good deal of tort law is common law. Statutes can change the common law, define the standard of care in negligence cases, and create new torts and defenses. Secondary authority is any nonlaw that a court can rely on to reach a decision. Examples include legal encyclopedias, legal treatises, legal periodical literature, and annotations. Secondary authority is helpful in finding and explaining primary authority. There is a great deal of legal and factual information relevant to a torts litigation practice that is available online from both free and fee-based sites on the Internet.

KEY TERMS

tort *2*
damages *2*
diversity of citizenship *2*
remedy *2*
jurisdiction *2*
criminal law *2*
civil law *2*
standard of proof *4*
preponderance of the evidence *4*
made whole *5*
culpable *5*
cause of action *5*
tortfeasor *5*
element *5*
prima facie case *5*
intentional tort *9*
negligence *9*
strict liability *10*
liable *10*
proximate cause *10*
actual cause *11*
but-for test *11*
substantial-factor test *11*
contract *11*
alternative dispute resolution (ADR) *12*
primary authority *13*
opinion *13*
statute *13*
constitution *13*
administrative regulation *13*
administrative decision *13*
charter *13*
ordinance *13*
rules of court *13*
common law *13*
reporter *14*
derogation *15*
statutory code *16*
administrative code *16*
secondary authority *16*
persuasive authority *17*
mandatory authority *17*
legal encyclopedia *17*
legal treatise *17*
online *20*

REVIEW QUESTIONS

1. What is the financial scope of accidental or unintentional injuries every year?
2. What is a tort?
3. Distinguish between civil and criminal disputes.
4. What are the four purposes of tort law?
5. How do you state a cause of action?
6. What is the effect of stating a prima facie case?
7. What is an intentional tort?
8. How does an intentional tort differ from negligence?
9. Distinguish between unreasonable risk of harm and substantial certainty of harm.
10. How do intentional torts and negligence differ from strict liability?
11. What is proximate cause?
12. What are the two components of proximate cause?
13. What are the two tests for actual cause (cause in fact)?
14. Give examples of how tort law can relate to the following areas of law: contract law, criminal law, civil procedure law, family law, constitutional law, estate law, state and government law, real property law, insurance law, and environmental law.
15. What is primary authority?
16. Define the following primary authorities: opinion, statute, constitution, administrative regulation, administrative decision, charter, ordinance, and rules of court.
17. What is common law?
18. What are the three ways that the statutes of the legislature can affect tort law?
19. What is secondary authority?
20. What are the main categories of secondary authority?
21. How can a torts practice use secondary authority?
22. What is the *Restatement of Torts*?
23. What kinds of online research can be used in a torts practice?

HELPFUL WEBSITES

OVERVIEW OF TORT LAW ONLINE

- Findlaw
  www.findlaw.com
  (type "torts" in the search box; also click links to "Accidents & Injuries")
- Washlaw
  www.washlaw.edu/subject/torts.html
- Hieros Gamos, Guide to Tort Law
  www.hg.org
  (click "Law & Practice," then "Legal Malpractice," "Libel/Slander," "Malpractice," "Personal Injury," "Product Liability," "Torts," "Workers' Compensation," etc.)
- MegaLaw
  www.megalaw.com
  (click "Law Topic Pages" for links to damages, libel, personal injury, torts, etc.)
- **Legal Information Institute**
  topics.law.cornell.edu/wex/Tort
- **LexisNexis Torts Capsule Summary**
  www.lexisnexis.com/lawschool/study/outlines/html/torts/index.asp
- **Personal Injury Law**
  www.lawguru.com
  (click "Personal Injury Law")

GENERAL LAW (including Tort Law) ON THE INTERNET: FREE SITES

www.plol.org
scholar.google.com
scholar.google.com/advanced_scholar_search?hl=en&as_sdt=2000
www.justia.com
law.lexisnexis.com/webcenters/lexisone
findacase.com
www.infogrid.com/legal.htm
www.law.stanford.edu/library/research
www.lexisweb.com
openjurist.org

DATA ON INJURIES AND TORTS

www.cdc.gov/nchs/injury.htm
www.nsc.org
www.cdc.gov/mmwr
www.ojp.usdoj.gov/bjs/civil.htm

GOVERNMENT AGENCIES

- Consumer Product Safety Commission
  www.cpsc.gov
- National Highway Traffic Safety Administration (NHTSA)
  www.nhtsa.dot.gov

- National Transportation Safety Board
  www.ntsb.gov
- Occupational Safety and Health Administration
  www.osha.gov

TORT REFORM/ATTACKS ON THE TORT SYSTEM

- American Tort Reform Association
  www.atra.org
- Junk Science Review
  www.junkscience.com
- National Patient Safety Foundation
  www.npsf.org
- Overlawyered
  overlawyered.com
- Center for Justice and Democracy
  www.centerjd.org
- U.S. Tort Liability Index
  special.pacificresearch.org/pub/sab/2008/Tort_Index
- Faces of Lawsuit Abuse
  facesoflawsuitabuse.org/stories

MEDICAL RESEARCH

www.medscape.com
www.nlm.nih.gov

TORT ATTORNEYS FOR PLAINTIFFS

- American Association for Justice
  www.atlanet.org

TORT ATTORNEYS FOR DEFENDANTS

- Defense Research Institute
  www.dri.org

ENDNOTES

1. U.S. Census Bureau, *Statistical Abstract of the United States*, table 194, p. 127 (2009); National Safety Council (www.nsc.org).
2. Administrative Office of the U.S. Courts, *Civil Master File, fiscal year 2001* (www.uscourts.gov); United States Department of Justice, Bureau of Justice Statistics (www.ojp.usdoj.gov/bjs/abstract/fttv03.htm).
3. Adapted from John W. Wade et al., *Torts* 1 (9th ed. 1994).

Student StudyWARE™ CD-ROM
For additional materials, please go to the student CD in this book.

CHAPTER

2

LEGAL ANALYSIS IN TORT LAW

CHAPTER OUTLINE

- Structure of Legal Analysis
- Issue
- Rule
- Application
- Conclusion

CHAPTER OBJECTIVES

After completing this chapter, you should be able to:

- Understand the value of legal analysis in the performance of a paralegal's job.
- State the three objectives of legal analysis.
- Describe the role of legal analysis in fact gathering, advocacy, and outcome prediction.
- Know how to do a preliminary assessment of a torts problem.
- Identify and handle missing important facts in the legal analysis of a torts problem.
- Break a rule into its elements in order to identify legal issues.
- Know the importance of definitions of elements in rules and where to find such definitions.
- Line up facts with each of the elements as a checklist when writing a memorandum of law that applies rules to facts.
- Explain some of the major differences between legal analysis in an exam answer and in a memorandum of law.
- Know how to do a factor analysis.
- Present a counteranalysis and conclusion.

STRUCTURE OF LEGAL ANALYSIS

legal analysis The application of one or more rules to the facts of a client's case in order to answer a legal question that will help (1) prevent a legal dispute from arising, (2) resolve a legal dispute that has arisen, or (3) prevent a legal dispute from becoming worse.

primary authority Any law (e.g., case or statute) that a court could rely on in reaching a decision.

The foundation of all the other skills in the delivery of legal services is the skill of **legal analysis**, also referred to as legal reasoning. There is no better way to *mis*prepare oneself to work in a law office than by memorizing a lot of law or by learning to go through the steps of a task by rote. The skill of legal analysis will help you to avoid this approach to job assignments.

This chapter will present an introduction to the fundamentals of legal analysis, a skill that attorneys learn and perfect in three grueling years of law school and in a lifetime of diligent practice. Given the vast scope of the topic, our coverage in this chapter is limited to the basics. Paralegals can increase their effectiveness as part of the torts-litigation team by understanding the specific purpose and general framework of legal analysis. This understanding is our goal.

Legal analysis is the application of **primary authority** to facts in order to solve a legal problem. Primary authority is any law that a court could rely on in reaching a decision. As we saw in Exhibit 1–4 in Chapter 1, the major categories of primary authority are court opinions or case law (containing the common law), statutes, constitutions, administrative regulations, administrative decisions, charters, and ordinances. For now, we will refer to any primary authority as a rule. In tort law, these rules (particularly opinions and statutes) define the tort causes of action (see the list in Exhibit 1–3 of Chapter 1) and their defenses.

Here is a more comprehensive definition of legal analysis:

> *Legal analysis* is the application of one or more rules to the facts presented by a client in order to answer a legal question that will help:
> (1) avoid a legal dispute from arising,
> (2) resolve a legal dispute that has arisen, or
> (3) prevent a legal dispute from becoming worse.

The central legal dispute in tort law centers on the determination of who, if anyone, is liable (i.e., legally responsible) for an injury or harm that has occurred. Legal analysis helps us make this determination.

One of the benefits of effective legal analysis is that it will enable you to perform other critical skills such as those listed in Legal Analysis Guideline #1:

Legal Analysis Guideline #1

- *Additional Fact Gathering.* Legal analysis will help you identify further facts you need to try to obtain through client interviewing and field investigation.
- *Advocacy.* Legal analysis will help you:
  (a) make the most reasonable argument on how a rule applies to the facts in a manner most helpful to the client of the law office where you work, and
  (b) make the most reasonable argument on how a rule applies to the facts in a manner most helpful to the *opponent* of the client of your office (the best way to prepare a case against opponents is to anticipate what their arguments are likely to be).
- *Prediction.* Legal analysis will help you make an educated guess of what a particular court (or other tribunal such as an administrative agency) might decide if it must determine how a rule applies to the facts.

IRAC An acronym that stands for the components of legal analysis: issue (I), rule (R), application of the rule to the facts (A), and conclusion (C). IRAC provides a structure for legal analysis.

Legal analysis always has four components. To remember them, use the acronym **IRAC**, which stands for Issue, Rule, Application (also called Analysis), and Conclusion:

Issue: Identify the legal *issue* to be resolved in the client's case.
Rule: State the *rule* that is at the center of the issue.

Application: *Apply* the rule to the facts of the client's case. Do this from the perspective of the client and from the perspective of the client's opponent. (The latter perspective is the *counteranalysis,* which is the position of the other side on how the rule applies to the facts.)

Conclusion: State your personal *conclusion* of whether the rule applies to the facts.

These four components of IRAC constitute the structure of legal analysis. If a problem in the client's case involves more than one rule, each is "IRAC-ed" in the same manner.

IRAC can be used in memos, in essay exam answers, or in your head—in short, whenever you are doing legal analysis. If you write out your analysis in a law office, you usually do so in a **memorandum of law** (also called a legal memorandum or memo for short). It is a written explanation of how the law might apply to a set of facts. If the audience of the memo is someone in the office such as a supervisor, the memo is called an *office memorandum of law* or an *interoffice memorandum of law*. If the audience is someone outside the office, it might be called a *hearing memorandum* (submitted to an administrative law judge in an administrative agency), a *points and authorities memorandum* (submitted to a trial judge or hearing officer), or a *trial memorandum* (submitted to a trial judge).

memorandum of law A written explanation of how the law might apply to the facts of a client's case. Also called a *legal memorandum* or *memo* for short.

Often the organization of a memo consists of four parts corresponding to the four components of IRAC. Some of the essay examinations you take in school can follow the same organizational format, although your examination answer may not be as formally structured as a memo. Even less formal will be the legal analysis you will do in your head. Wherever you do legal analysis, you will use the same analytical structure outlined in Legal Analysis Guideline #2, which corresponds to IRAC:

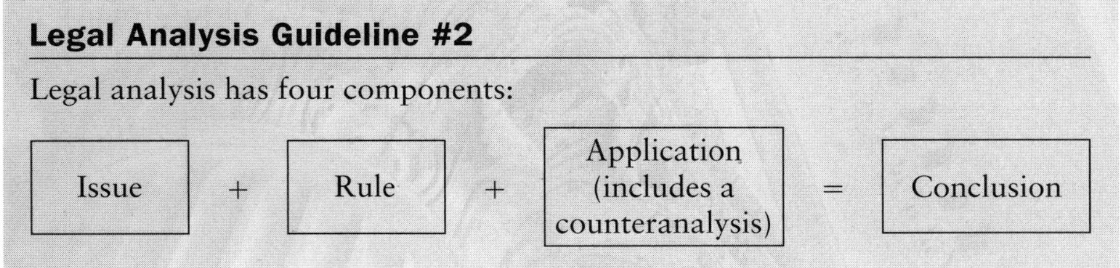

ISSUE

A **legal issue** (also called a question of law) is a question of whether a cause of action, defense, or other rule applies to the facts. During informal discussions in a law office, you will often find that attorneys and paralegals phrase legal issues very broadly, almost in shorthand. For example:

legal issue A question of whether a cause of action, defense, or other rule applies to the facts. Also called a question of law.

- Will the seller win?
- Was Tom negligent?
- What causes of action can the company use?
- Can the defendant raise the defense of necessity?

Although broad issue statements such as these can be good starting points, you need to *narrow* the issue as much as possible by limiting the issue to one cause of action, defense, or other rule and by including several of the important facts involved in the controversy. (See Legal Analysis Guideline #3.) For example, the shorthand issue, "Was Tom negligent?" might be phrased as:

- In a negligence action, did Tom breach his duty of reasonable care by failing to yield the right of way to the oncoming vehicle?

And the shorthand issue, "Can the defendant raise the defense of necessity?" might be phrased as:

- Does a boat owner have the privilege of necessity to steer the boat into a dock owned by a private person when the purpose of the entry is to prevent immediate damage to the boat from an impending storm?

Legal Analysis Guideline #3

When phrasing a legal issue, focus on one cause of action, defense, or other rule at a time and include important facts involved in the controversy.

Some issues will involve more than one rule. If so, they must be included in the statement of the issue. Most issues, however, can be limited to a single cause of action, defense, or other rule. We will have more to say about phrasing issues later in the chapter when we discuss elements of rules.

RULE

The second component of legal analysis is a statement of the rule to be applied to the facts. The rules are the primary authorities: court opinions or case law (containing the common law), statutes, constitutions, administrative regulations, administrative decisions, charters, and ordinances. See Exhibit 2–1. Although any one or more of these rules can be involved in a torts case, the rules that are most commonly raised are court opinions and statutes.

Exhibit 2–1
Legal analysis in tort law. For the definitions of these rules, see Exhibit 1–4 in Chapter 1.

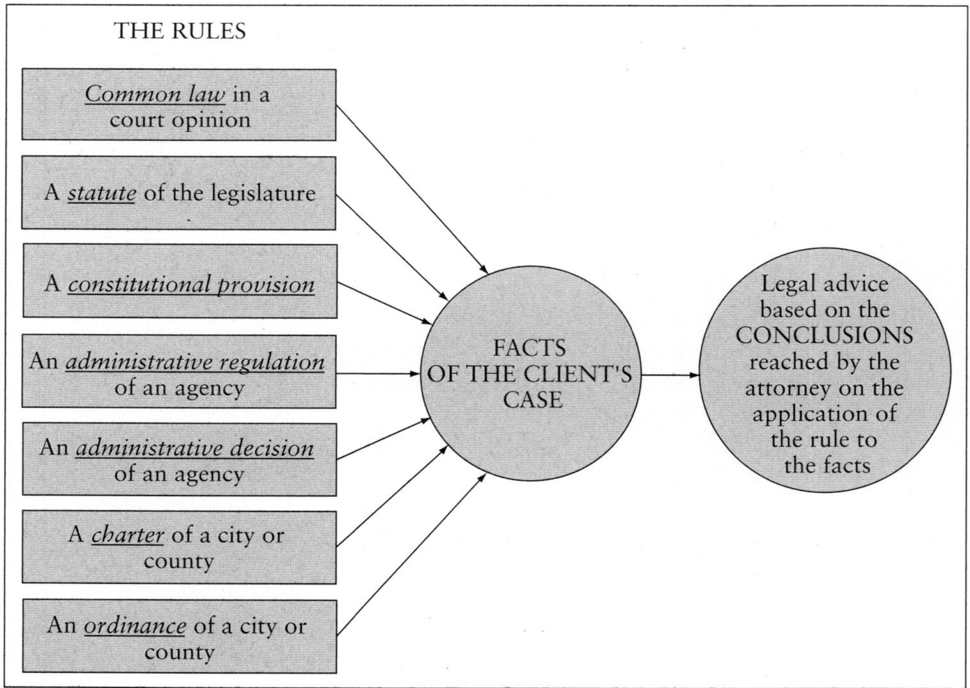

APPLICATION

We now come to the heart of legal analysis: **application**, in which you explain the extent to which the rule applies to the facts. You will be telling someone how a rule applies or does not apply to the facts. We will examine this subject through the following topics:

application An explanation of how a rule applies or does not apply to the facts. Connecting facts to the elements of a rule in order to determine whether the rule applies to the facts.

1. preliminary assessment
2. legal analysis and legal research
3. legal analysis, investigation, and interviewing
4. breaking a rule into its elements
5. definitions of the elements
6. connecting facts with elements of the rule
7. legal analysis and further research, investigation, and interviewing
8. factor analysis
9. counteranalysis

1. Preliminary Assessment

The starting point in legal analysis is always a set of facts. In the law office, these facts come from the initial client interview. (In school, the facts come from the teacher's **hypothetical**, given orally in class or in a written question. A hypothetical is a set of facts that are assumed to exist for purposes of discussion.) Your first responsibility is to make a preliminary assessment of the facts in order to determine what rules might apply to them.

hypothetical 1. A set of facts that are assumed to exist for the purposes of discussion. (The teacher asked the students to analyze the hypothetical she gave them.) 2. Assumed or based on conjecture. (The lawyer asked the witness a hypothetical question.)

The primary guide in making this assessment is the question you are asked by your supervisor or teacher. There are two kinds of such questions:

- the open-ended question
- the directed question

The open-ended question broadly asks: Who is liable for what? What torts have been committed? What defenses are available? What remedies can be used? To answer such questions, start by making a list of possible causes of action and defenses. You are not looking for *the* answer yet; you are searching for possibilities that need to be further explored. Every separate tort should be formulated into a separate issue. The same is true of every defense. If there is a reasonable possibility that the tort or defense might apply, include it in the list you make for the preliminary assessment. Obviously, this preliminary assessment cannot be done unless you know a fair amount of tort law. At a minimum, you must know the basic elements of the major tort causes of action (see Exhibit 1–3 in Chapter 1).

The directed question is more specific or narrow. (Was Dr. Davis the proximate cause of Smith's death? Did the accountant intend to deceive the broker? Did Franklin violate the "due diligence" provision of § 23.5 of the statutory code?) The directed question focuses on one of the *elements* of a rule in contention and makes that element the centerpiece of a more narrow issue. (See the discussion of elements below.)

Legal Analysis Guideline #4

Do a preliminary assessment of open-ended questions by listing the possible tort causes of action and defenses that might be involved in the fact situation. A preliminary assessment of a directed question simply involves making sure that you have identified the particular element of the tort or defense that needs to be examined.

The preliminary assessment of the open-ended or directed question (see Legal Analysis Guideline #4) has three purposes:

- to help you organize your thinking about the next stage of legal analysis
- to help you decide what legal research must be done
- to help you decide what further facts you must check through field investigation and further client interviewing

2. Legal Analysis and Legal Research

Once you have done a preliminary assessment, you have before you a list of the torts and defenses that might be applicable to the facts of the problem, or a list of elements that are most likely to be in dispute. When you are working on a client's case, the next step is to take this information to an online or a traditional brick-and-mortar law library. Legal research must be undertaken to locate the latest court opinions, statutes, rules of court, etc. You need to determine what *your state* has said about the problem you are analyzing. Your guide in undertaking this research is the list of possibilities that you compiled through a preliminary assessment of the legal analysis problem. While doing the research, the likelihood is that you will come across new options that need to be added to your list. Other tort causes of action and defense possibilities, for example, might be revealed by this research.

Following the research,

- You are in a position to evaluate the validity of your preliminary assessment. Did you initially identify the right torts and defenses? Did you initially identify the elements of the torts or defenses that will pose the most difficulty in litigation? Your preliminary assessment must be revised according to what you uncover in the law library.
- You have before you research notes containing citations to the major court opinions, statutes, regulations, etc. These are all rules that must be subjected to the IRAC legal analysis process.

3. Legal Analysis, Investigation, and Interviewing

During the initial stages of legal analysis, you will find yourself saying: "In order to provide an answer to the problem, I need to know more facts." This should happen often while you are still doing your preliminary assessment and legal research. It is rare that the initial client interview will give you every fact that you need. The same is true of a fact situation in a school exam.

Assume, for example, that you are analyzing an automobile accident case. In your preliminary assessment and initial research, you are pursuing the possibility of a negligence action. You know that it will be important to determine the foreseeability of the accident. As you start the legal analysis, you realize that foreseeability is a complex topic involving the examination of numerous factor such as:

- condition of the road
- weather
- visibility
- speed of defendant's car and other cars
- posted speed limit
- other traffic signals
- distance between the two cars
- distractions
- time of day
- parties' familiarity with the area
- when defendant first saw plaintiff
- whether anyone used a horn

As you read negligence opinions, you may come across other factors that courts considered relevant to the foreseeability of the accidents discussed in the opinions. For example, you may read an opinion in which the court emphasized the extent to which the defendant knew about prior similar accidents in the area. Also, as you think more carefully about what foreseeability means, other factors may come to you.

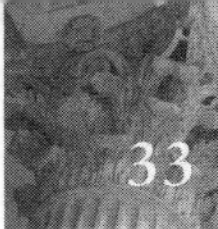

The likelihood is that your initial statement of facts is not adequate to enable you to give an intelligent answer to the question of whether the accident in question was foreseeable; you simply do not have enough facts. The deeper you go in the legal analysis and research of the problem, the wider the gap may become between the facts you have and the facts you need to discover. *Indeed, this is one of the functions of legal analysis: to help you identify facts you need to pursue through investigation and additional client interviewing.* Analysis and research regularly feed into field investigation and interviewing in this way.

Of course, if you are taking an examination in school, you do not have the opportunity to obtain more facts through investigation and interviewing. All you have is the set of facts in the exam question. What do you do when you feel that more facts are needed to answer the exam question? First, you answer the question as best you can with the facts that you have. Second, while you are analyzing the facts that you have, you also point out what further facts you need to know in order to answer the question, and why you need to know these facts. For example, you might say, "We are not told in the facts how close the defendant's car was to the plaintiff's car when they first became aware of each other. The distance could have a significant bearing on foreseeability. The closer they were, the more foreseeable the accident was or should have been." In other words, you discuss the facts that you *do not have* when they would be relevant to the analysis. You must be reasonable in discussing missing facts. There must be a logical reason why you need the fact. That reason must always be related to the rule under discussion. If the rule you are analyzing is the foreseeability of the accident, it is logical to inquire about the factors that go into a determination of foreseeability. Common sense is also a guide. If, for example, you are not told how fast the defendant was driving, logic and common sense would tell you that questions about speed must be raised because of its high relevance to foreseeability.

4. Breaking a Rule into Its Elements

One of the most important skills in legal analysis is the ability to break a rule—any rule—into its elements. An **element** is a portion of a rule that is one of the preconditions of the applicability of the entire rule. If one of the elements of the rule does not apply, the entire rule cannot apply. These rules are the categories of primary authority we discussed earlier, particularly the common law and statutory law that have given us tort causes of action and their defenses. These causes of action and defenses are rules that tell us when someone is liable for the harm they caused.

element A portion of a rule that is one of the preconditions of the applicability of the entire rule.

Element analysis is important in many areas of the law. Here are some examples:

- In drafting a tort complaint in some states, a plaintiff makes sure that the facts alleged cover every element of the tort.
- When giving instructions to a jury, judges must cover all the elements of the tort and all the elements of the defenses raised.
- When conducting a **deposition**, attorneys frequently organize questions around the elements of the torts and defenses in the case.
- The organization of a memorandum of law often follows the list of elements of the torts and defenses.
- An exam answer is often effectively organized around the list of elements of the rules being discussed.

deposition A method of discovery by which parties and their prospective witnesses are questioned outside the courtroom. Discovery is compulsory pretrial disclosure of information related to litigation by one party to another party. Discovery can also be used in postjudgment enforcement proceedings.

A major characteristic of weak legal analysis is that it fails to take the reader through the elements of a rule. Suppose that you are analyzing the following statute:

> § 100. A company that keeps or suffers to be kept upon premises owned or occupied by it within 50 yards of an inhabited building of another more than 50 pounds of nitroglycerine shall be subject to a fine of $500 per day.

The first step is to break this rule down into its elements:

1. a company
2. keeps or suffers to be kept more than 50 pounds of nitroglycerine
3. upon premises owned or occupied by the company
4. within 50 yards of an inhabited building of another

The fine of $500 will not apply until each of these four elements is established. It is the nature of an element that if one of the elements does not apply, the entire rule cannot apply. For example, if a neighbor (not engaged in a business of any kind) keeps 51 pounds of nitroglycerine within 50 yards of another's inhabited building, there is no fine, because the first element calls for a *company.*

Legal Analysis Guideline #5

The legal analysis of a rule begins when you break it into its elements. An element is a portion of a rule that is one of the preconditions to the applicability of the entire rule.

Some rules are already broken down for you into their elements. See, for example, Exhibit 1–3 in Chapter 1, which lists the elements of all the major tort causes of action. For many other rules, however, *you* must break them into their elements. This is particularly true of statutes and administrative regulations.

Use logic and common sense as your guide. In § 100, for example, notice that in the second element, we have included "nitroglycerine" with the verbs "keeps or suffers to be kept," even though "nitroglycerine" does not appear until the end of § 100. This is done because it is impractical to discuss a verb separate from its object. (Keep what?) Do not be reluctant to regroup words and phrases in a sentence so that the elements will consist of logical units. Often the more complex the rule, the more unraveling you will have to do to achieve such units.

When a rule states *alternative* conditions, the alternatives should be kept in the same element. Hence, when you see "or," "either," or like words, be alert to the existence of alternatives. The second and third elements in the nitroglycerine statute contain alternatives ("keeps or suffers to be kept") ("owned or occupied"). When the alternatives deal with the same topic, they should be kept together so that the element is a self-contained unit.

Legal Analysis Guideline #6

Keep alternative conditions covering the same topic within one element.

There are often two parts in a rule:

- the conditions of the applicability of the rule
- the consequences of the applicability of the rule

The consequence of violating the nitroglycerine statute is a $500 fine. Other kinds of consequences might be stated in the rule, such as:

- the granting of an injunction
- the waiver of an obligation
- the establishment of a particular tort
- the establishment of a particular defense to a tort

When identifying the elements of a rule, focus on the conditions (or preconditions) of the rule's applicability. The consequences follow if all the elements are met. Do not include consequences as one of the elements of the rule.

Not all rules, however, state consequences. Some rules simply make affirmations or provide definitions. For example, an administrative regulation might state that "helmets must be worn on job sites" without specifying the penalty or other consequence that will result if this rule is violated. Other administrative regulations in the same code may establish the penalty or consequence, or the code may be silent on what happens if there is a violation.

Finally, if a rule contains more than one sentence, each sentence can usually be broken into its own elements.

ASSIGNMENT 2.1

The following rules are quotations from statutes, administrative regulations, and opinions. Break them into their elements.

a. An owner of premises is prohibited from willfully or intentionally injuring a trespasser by means of force that either takes life or inflicts great bodily injury.
b. Privacy is invaded only if the information sought is of a confidential nature and the defendant's conduct was unreasonably intrusive.
c. The term *safety belt interlock* means any system designed to prevent starting or operation of a motor vehicle if one or more occupants of such vehicle are not using safety belts.
d. A public official cannot recover damages for a defamatory statement relating to his official conduct unless he proves that the statement was made with actual malice—that is, with knowledge that it was false or with reckless disregard of whether it was false or not.
e. Where an internal operation is indicated, surgeons may lawfully perform, and it is their duty to perform, such operation as good surgery demands, even when it means an extension of the operation further than was originally contemplated, and for so doing they are not to be held in damages as for an unauthorized operation.
f. When the mental or physical condition (including the blood group) of a party, or of a person in the custody or under the legal control of parties, is in controversy, the court in which the action is pending may order the party to submit to a physical or mental examination by a physician or to produce for examination the person in his custody or legal control. The order may be made only on motion for good cause shown and upon notice to the person to be examined and to all parties and shall specify the time, place, manner, conditions, and scope of the examination and the persons by whom it is to be made.

5. Definitions of the Elements

As indicated earlier, one of the most important observations you need to learn to make in legal analysis is, "In order to answer your question, I need the following additional facts because. . . ." We come now to another critical inquiry that the student of legal analysis must constantly make: *What is the definition of that word or phrase?* Legal analysis in large manner consists of the application of definitions to facts. More precisely, it consists of the application of definitions of the *elements* of the rules to facts. Hence, once you have broken a rule into its elements, the next step is to seek definitions of the major words and phrases in those elements.

Refer back to the nitroglycerine example (§ 100) discussed earlier. The definitional questions that need to be asked are:

- What is a "company"?
- What is meant by "keeps or suffers to be kept"?
- What are "premises"?
- What does "owned or occupied" mean?
- What is an "inhabited building"?
- What does "another" mean?
- What is "nitroglycerine"?

You must challenge the elements by demanding of yourself and of others that definitions be provided. The same is true if you are listening to a lecture or discussion about the law: Insist that the major terms be defined.

You will note that we did not list a number of words and phrases from the nitroglycerine statute as definitional questions, such as "or," "more than 50 pounds," "upon," and "within 50 yards." They do not appear to be unclear or in need of definitions. There may, however, be circumstances where there *will* be a need to have such words or phrases defined. It would not be unusual for a court to spend time defining a conjunction or a preposition! Trespass, for example, requires an intrusion, or an entry *on* land. Litigation has been necessary to define what is meant by "on." If you throw a rock across someone's land and the rock never touches the ground, has there been an entry *on* the land? The answer depends on the definition of "on" as well as the definition of "land." (See Chapter 23 on torts connected with land.)

Your goal is to define every *major* word and phrase in an element. The two tests to use to determine whether something is major are common sense and whether you anticipate that the word or phrase will be disputed by the parties. When in doubt about whether something is major, provide the definition.

In applying these two tests, you may decide that words such as "nitroglycerine" and "premises" do *not* need to be defined. Both parties may agree, for example, that the substance that exploded was nitroglycerine and that this occurred on premises. If so, time does not have to be wasted defining such terms. Be careful, however, in coming to such conclusions. If you must err, do so on the side of providing too many definitions.

Legal Analysis Guideline #7

Define every major word and phrase in every element of a rule, so that the definitions can be applied to the facts. When in doubt about whether a word or phrase is major, resolve the doubt in favor of providing a definition. Whenever you anticipate a dispute over a word or phrase in an element, that word or phrase is always major.

Time and again you will see and hear people analyzing the law without defining major terms. *They make the assumption that readers or listeners already know the definitions of the words or phrases being used or that the definitions are obvious from the context of the analysis.* That is a dangerous assumption to make. You are urged to avoid making this assumption in your own analysis, even though you will be surrounded by courts, legislatures, lawyers, paralegals, etc. who regularly make the assumption. Sloppy analysis does not cease to be sloppy simply because it appears that everyone is doing it!

To be sure, there is such a thing as shorthand analysis, in which people communicate through short summarizations of legal principles without providing all the definitions. Such analysis plays an important role in a busy law office. In your own career, however, it is much too early to attempt such summarizations. You must first learn how to do complete analysis before you start using shorthand analysis. Also, when people talk shorthand *to you*, do not be reluctant to slow them down so that you can better understand what is being said. This understanding comes primarily when you inquire about definitions. Take the risk that someone will think that you do not know a lot of law. At this early stage in your career, there is no shame in admitting that you don't.

Of course, even if you have a definition, you are not home free. Often you will need a definition of the definition. Suppose that you are given the following definition of hazardous substance: "Any substance that is toxic, corrosive, or an irritant." Although it is helpful to have this definition, you obviously cannot stop there. What is "toxic"? What is "corrosive"? What is an "irritant"?

Legal Analysis Guideline #8

Provide definitions for the major words or phrases contained *within* definitions.

It is important that you train your eyes and ears to recognize legal analysis that fails to provide definitions of major words or phrases. For example, suppose you read the following legal analysis in another's memo:

> The defendant acted reasonably because every safety precaution was taken before the fireworks were detonated, e.g., the area was roped off, the fireworks were inspected for defects, and extra personnel were added. Furthermore, the explosion was not the proximate cause of the injury suffered by the plaintiff. The case should be dismissed.

Such a passage should give you intellectual indigestion. There are a number of significant concepts that are not defined: "reasonably," "safety precaution," "inspected," "defects," "proximate cause," etc. The author of the passage assumes that you know what they mean. Again, this is a dangerous assumption to make in the law.

ASSIGNMENT 2.2

Examine the following passages taken from legal analysis found in memos, court opinions, appellate briefs, etc. Identify words or phrases, if any, in each passage that are not defined and that you think may have to be defined.

a. The interest in emotional and mental tranquility is not one that the law will protect from invasion in its own right.
b. Each tenant in common is equally entitled to share in the possession of the entire property and neither may exclude the other from any part of it.
c. It is not enough that the act itself is intentionally done even though the actor realizes or should realize that it contains a very grave risk of bringing about the contact or apprehension. They must realize that to a substantial certainty the contact or apprehension will result.
d. In that case, judgment for the plaintiffs was reversed where it appeared that the odors emanating from defendant's building were necessarily incident to its operation, that the business was properly operated, and that plaintiffs were not substantially injured. It appeared that disinterested witnesses had not found the odors particularly offensive. The appellate court said, "In the instant case, we have nothing more than unpleasant and disagreeable odors, and those only occasionally sickening to a few who seem to be unduly sensitive or allergic to such smells."

Having recognized the need for definitions, the next question is: Where do you obtain them? Can you go to a standard nonlegal dictionary such as *Webster's*? It is important to understand that there are many **terms of art** in the law. A term of art is a word or phrase that has a special or technical meaning. For example, in the law of trespass, battery, and many other torts, "act" means the voluntary movement of the body, and in the law of defamation, "publication" means communication to at least one person other than the plaintiff; furthermore, the communication can be printed (on paper or electronically) or it can be oral.

term of art A word or phrase that has a special or technical meaning.

To obtain the definition of a term of art, you would *not* go to *Webster's*. Unfortunately, you will not always know whether a word or phrase is a term of art or whether its ordinary "lay" definition was intended. To be safe:

- Know the "lay" definition of the word or phrase (check it in *Webster's* or another standard nontechnical dictionary).
- Assume, however, that the word or phrase is a term of art until you establish for yourself otherwise.
- Use basic research techniques to determine whether the word or phrase is a term of art, and if so, what it means.

Legal Analysis Guideline #9

Assume that all words and phrases in the law are terms of art until you satisfy yourself that a nontechnical meaning was intended. Know the nontechnical as well as the technical definition of such words and phrases.

Basic Techniques of Locating Definitions Here are some ways to try to locate definitions of a word or phrase in an element of a rule that needs a definition.

If the word or phrase is in an element of a statute, follow steps 1 through 5:

1. Check whether there is a definitions section in the statutory code. The legislature may have defined the word or phrase in another statute (often called a definitions section) that is part of the same cluster of statutes.
2. Check whether the word or phrase has been interpreted or defined in court opinions. Examine the notes of decisions that follow the text of the statute in the annotated code. The notes summarize court opinions that have interpreted the statute. A code is annotated when the code contains notes or commentary along with the text of the statutes in the code. Another way to find court opinions that have interpreted a statute is by using citators such as Shepard's and KeyCite. (A citator is a book, CD-ROM, or online service containing lists of citations that can (1) help you assess the current validity of an opinion, statute, or other item; and (2) give you leads to additional opinions, statutes, and other relevant materials.)
3. Check whether an agency has written administrative regulations that define the word or phrase.
4. Check whether an agency has written administrative decisions that define or interpret the word or phrase.
5. Check whether the legislative history of the statute gives any clues to the meaning intended by the legislature for the word or phrase.

If the word or phrase is in an element of a common-law rule such as a tort cause of action, you need to find court opinions that have interpreted or defined the word or phrase. To find such opinions, follow steps 6 through 10:

6. Check the digests, such as the *American Digest System* and the digest that covers the state court opinions of your state. Digests are volumes that contain short summaries of court opinions.

7. Check annotations in *A.L.R., A.L.R.2d, A.L.R.3d, A.L.R.4th, A.L.R.5th, A.L.R.6th, A.L.R. Fed.*, and *A.L.R. Fed. 2d.* Annotations provide extensive references to court opinions.
8. Check the legal encyclopedias such as *Corpus Juris Secundum* and *American Jurisprudence 2d.* The footnotes in them will often lead you to court opinions.
9. Check the footnotes in legal periodical literature for leads to court opinions.
10. Check the footnotes in legal treatises for leads to court opinions.

Use CALR (computer-assisted legal research), if available. Assume, for example, that you want to find definitions of "conversion" written by courts in your state. If you have access to a fee-based service such as Westlaw, you could go to the database that contains the opinions of your state courts (e.g., for New York, you would go to the ny-cs database). You could then type the following question or query for this database:

conversion /s defin!

This query tells the computer to find every opinion in which the word "conversion" and the words "define" or "defined" or "definition" are found in the same sentence (/s) anywhere in the opinion. (The "!" in the query is a wildcard that can be used to mean any character or group of characters. Here the "!" allows you to find "defin" words that end in "e," "ed," "ition," "ing," or any other characters.)

You could also try the free Internet. You would go to the web address of the state courts in your state (see Appendix A) and type words such as "conversion tort" in any available search boxes on the sites. Finally, free general search engines such as Google and Bing can be productive. A California paralegal, for example, looking for state opinions that define conversion might start with a query such as the following:

California court conversion opinion

6. Connecting Facts with Elements of the Rule

Let's recap: You have identified a series of rules, each rule has been broken down into its elements, and the definitions of the major words and phrases in the elements have been obtained. For each rule, the next step is to *connect* the facts of the problem with the elements of the rule. This connection is what is meant by "applying a rule to the facts." (See Legal Analysis Guideline #2 and the earlier discussion of IRAC.) In your mind or on paper, make a series of columns, one column per element. In each column, place those facts that are relevant to the element covered by that column. (A fact is relevant if it helps to establish that the element applies, if it helps to establish that the element does not apply, or if you have a question about how a fact may relate to an element.) To illustrate, we will briefly examine the tort of trespass to land. Although we will not cover this tort in depth until Chapter 23, you will be given enough information about the tort here so that you can follow the illustration. This legal analysis technique—connecting facts with elements—can be used when you want to apply any tort, or indeed, any rule, to a set of facts. Assume that you are analyzing the following facts:

Tom lives in a residential neighborhood. He plants a new tree along the edge of his property, two feet from Jim's land. He finishes planting at 7 A.M. on a Tuesday morning. Before Tom goes to work at 8 A.M. on this same Tuesday, he turns on his hose in front of the tree to water it. He sees that the water quickly collects around the tree and starts draining toward Jim's land. Tom decides to leave the hose on while he is at work. When he returns at 6 P.M. that day, Jim's yard is flooded by the water. Jim sues Tom for trespass to land. What result?

The elements of trespass to land are:

- an act
- intrusion on land

- in possession of another
- intent to intrude
- causation of the intrusion

Once you have obtained the definitions of the major words or phrases in these elements, the next step is to line up the facts of the problem with each of the elements. Do this on paper. After some practice, you will go though the column lineup in your head, but at least initially, write out the columns. For our trespass example, make five columns to correspond with the five elements of trespass to land. Under each column, make a note of the facts that are relevant to that column. A fact is relevant to an element if it may help to prove or disprove that element or if you need additional facts about the element. Facts that are relevant to more than one element should be repeated under each appropriate column. If you need more facts to help you analyze an element, make a note of the missing facts under the column for that element. (See Exhibit 2–2.)

Exhibit 2–2 Connecting facts to elements in a tort case: *Jim v. Tom* (trespass to land).

Act	Intrusion on Land	In Possession of Another	Intent to intrude	Causation of the Intrusion
· Tom decided to keep the hose on. · There is no indication in the facts that anyone coerced or forced Tom to turn on the hose and to leave it on when he left for work.	· The water from the hose flooded Jim's yard.	· The yard and land (where the water went) was Jim's. · We do not know if Jim was living on the land or whether anyone else was claiming the land.	· Tom saw the water start draining toward Jim's land. · We do not know whether Tom saw the water go onto Jim's land. · We do not know whether Tom wanted the water to go on Jim's land. · The tree was two feet from Jim's yard. · The water collected quickly. · We do not know whether the land was flat or inclined toward (or away from) Jim's land. · Tom decided to leave the hose on while he was at work. · Ten hours passed with the hose on.	· The yard was flooded from Tom's hose. · There is no indication in the facts that the water came from any other source.

Legal Analysis Guideline #10

Before you start writing your final analysis of a problem, make a row of columns with headings to cover each element of the rule being analyzed (e.g., a tort or a defense). Under each column heading, make a list of every fact that may be relevant to proving that the element does or does not apply. If one fact is relevant to more than one element, place the fact in the appropriate column for each of the elements involved. If there are missing facts you need to know, make a list of them in the appropriate column(s). The columns will become a checklist of what you need to discuss when you begin your written analysis.

You are now ready to write your legal analysis of the trespass problem. Your guide or checklist will be the information you collected under the columns. Assume that you are writing an answer to an examination question of whether Tom committed trespass to land in the hypothetical we have been examining. (Later we will point out some of the differences between this answer and a memorandum of law.) Notice that the discussion of each element in the model answer begins with the definition of the element. You are not expected to know these definitions; they will be covered in Chapter 23. For now, simply note the detailed connection made between the definition of an element and the facts listed under the column for that element. Note also that the organization of the analysis follows the listing of the elements. (Answers should begin with the issue—the I of IRAC—but here our focus is on lining up facts and elements. See Exhibit 2–3 for where the issue would be placed.)

Model Answer: Jim v. Tom (Trespass to Land) There are five elements to trespass to land:

(1) an act
(2) intrusion on land
(3) in possession of another
(4) intent to intrude
(5) causation of the intrusion

(1) An act is a voluntary movement of the body. There is no indication in the facts that Tom was coerced into turning on the hose. Everything that Tom did appeared voluntary, as indicated by the fact that he decided to keep the hose on. People who decide things usually act under their own willpower. Tom will concede that the first element applies.

(2) Intrusion means physically going on land or causing something physical to go on land, remaining on the land, going to a prohibited portion of the land, or failing to remove goods from the land. Water is a physical thing that went on the surface of Jim's land, since we are told that the "yard is flooded by the water." Tom will concede that the hose water is something physical that entered the land, and that the second element applies.

(3) Possession means actual occupancy of the land with the intent to have exclusive control over it, or the right to immediate occupancy when no one else is actually occupying it with intent to control it. We are told that the land is "Jim's." We do not know, however, whether Jim or anyone else was occupying the land at the time of Tom's intrusion. For example, we do not know whether Jim had a tenant living on the land at the time. Hence, we cannot tell from the facts whether Jim was in possession. I will assume, however, that Jim was in possession, since the facts indicate that Jim owned the land and there is no indication that anyone else was occupying it with the intent to control it. Hence, the third element has been established.

(4) This element poses the most difficulty. Intent to intrude is the desire to intrude or the knowledge with substantial certainty that the intrusion will result from what the defendant does or fails to do. The facts do not tell us whether Tom wanted the water from his hose to enter Jim's yard. Jim would argue, however, that there was an intent to intrude, because Tom knew with substantial certainty that the water would physically enter his land. Presumably, Tom knew that the new tree was two feet from the property line. He knew, therefore, that the water would not have far to travel. He saw the water quickly collect around the tree and start draining toward Jim's land. Tom knew, therefore, that all the water was not being absorbed into his own land. He knew that the water was headed toward Jim's land. (The facts do not tell us if the land was flat or on an incline.) Tom knew that the water was going to run from 8 A.M. until he returned from work—some ten hours later. Furthermore, since the water collected "quickly," Tom probably had it turned on high. Since Tom knew that the water was headed toward Jim's land two feet away and that it would be kept on

high for ten hours, Jim will argue that Tom knew with substantial certainty that the water would enter Jim's land. Therefore, Tom intended the entry or intrusion.

Tom disagrees. The facts do not say that he desired the water to enter. Nor do they say that he saw the water enter. He may have been negligent in causing the water to enter, but there was no intent to have it enter. There may have been carelessness in allowing the water to drain into Jim's yard, but there was no knowledge with substantial certainty that it would enter. Tom admits that it may have been careless to leave the water on, but there was no intent.

(5) There are two definitions of causation: "but for" and substantial factor. Plaintiff must establish causation by either definition. "But for" what the defendant did, the harm would not have occurred; or, the defendant was a substantial factor in producing the harm. Jim argues that "but for" Tom's leaving the hose on for ten hours, his land would not have been flooded. The facts say that the land was flooded "by the water," referring to the water from the hose. There is no indication that the water came from any other source. (Since no other causal entity is involved, Jim does not need to use the substantial factor test. But it would be easy to show that Tom was a substantial factor in producing the flooding.) Tom will concede that he caused the intrusion on Jim's land.

Conclusion I believe that Jim will win this case. The only element in contention is intent. I do not think that Tom can deny that he knew with substantial certainty that the water would enter Jim's land. He saw the water go toward the yard even before he left for a long time with the hose on. Hence, I think Jim has the stronger argument on intent.

A separate part of the answer would discuss the issue of damages for any expenses that Jim incurred as a result of the flooding. We did not discuss damages here because we limited our focus to the elements of this particular tort. Suffering harm or loss is not an element of trespass to land. The tort is committed if an intentional intrusion occurs, even if the plaintiff does not suffer specific losses as a result of the intrusion. We will see later that other torts *do* require proof of actual harm or loss in addition to the technical violation of another's rights.

The characteristics of the model answer in the trespass case of *Jim v. Tom* are outlined in Legal Analysis Guideline #11.

Legal Analysis Guideline #11

1. The analysis is organized according to the elements of the rule (here, trespass to land). The columns were used as a checklist in writing the answer.
2. Definitions of the major words and phrases in the elements are provided at the beginning of the discussion of each element.
3. The definitions are then applied to the facts. This is done by making a *specific* connection between the language of the definition and the facts. Simply restating rules without an extensive discussion of facts is weak analysis.
4. Most of the discussion centers on the elements that are most likely to be in contention (here, the element of intent).
5. The writer identifies missing facts where they are relevant to a particular element.
6. If assumptions must be made about missing facts, they are labeled as assumptions (see the discussion on possession).
7. For each element, the positions of both sides are provided, even if one of the positions amounts to a concession on an element. (Here, most of the counter-analysis centers on the element of intent.)
8. The writer's conclusion is provided at the end of the analysis.

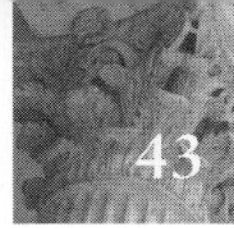

In the model answer for the case of *Jim v. Tom*, the analysis was done in the format of a school examination. A number of differences would exist in the answer if you were presenting it as a memorandum of law. First of all, there would be a heading at the top of the memo (see Exhibit 2–3). Also, the discussion portion of the memo would give citations to specific statutes, court opinions, and other authority obtained by legal research in a law library. An exam answer will also be based on such authorities, but they rarely will be cited in the answer. The core of the analysis, however, is the same in exam answers and memos:

- Issues are identified.
- Rules are broken down into their elements.
- Definitions of elements are given.
- Specific connections are made between definitions and facts (these connections are the heart of applying rules to facts).
- Conclusions are drawn about what these connections demonstrate.

Note that this sequence is based on the IRAC overview that we discussed earlier.

It is usually a good idea to begin a memorandum of law with a statement of the assignment that the supervisor has given you. This was done in Exhibit 2–3 ("You have asked me to prepare a . . ."). Note also that the legal issue is stated at the beginning of the memo just after the statement of the assignment. Finally, notice that the issue in Exhibit 2–3 contains some of the important facts involved in the controversy.

Exhibit 2–3
Heading of a legal memorandum.

MEMO TO: Supervisor's name
FROM: Your name
DATE: Today's date

RE: Jim v. Tom
Trespass to Land
OFFICE FILE NO.
09-82105

You have asked me to prepare a memo on whether Tom committed trespass to land against Jim.

Issue: Did Tom commit trespass to land when he flooded Jim's land after leaving his hose on for an extended period of time, knowing that the water was headed toward Jim's land two feet away?
Conclusion: Yes

Analysis: There are five elements to trespass to land in this state according to the recent state supreme court opinion of *Johnson v. Allen,* 487 P.2d 55 (Ct. App. 1999), which held that . . .

There is also a short conclusion stated after the issue. ("Conclusion: Yes.") If the issue is stated comprehensively (containing the rule and important facts in the controversy), the conclusion can usually be stated briefly as "yes" or "no." Of course, later in the memo, the reasons for the conclusion must be fully explained.

The major parts of the memo are often as follows:

Heading

Issue and Summary Conclusion

Facts

Discussion (also called Analysis)

Conclusion

ASSIGNMENT 2.3

Mary and Cindy are walking on the sidewalk beside Lena's house. The house is seven inches from the sidewalk. Suddenly Mary and Cindy start a violent argument. They are shouting at each other. Mary pushes Cindy. Cindy loses her balance and falls on Lena's house. Lena sues Mary and Cindy for trespass to land.

a. Analyze Lena's action against Mary.
b. Analyze Lena's action against Cindy.

Do the column exercise for each case and write your answer according to the guidelines discussed thus far in this chapter. (Do not do any legal research on the problem.)

7. Legal Analysis and Further Research, Investigation, and Interviewing

It must be emphasized that you will often find yourself rewriting the legal memorandum. New facts may be uncovered, e.g., through discovery. The ongoing research may raise factual gaps that need to be pursued through further investigation and client interviewing. You may even be asked to do research and investigation while a trial is going on, due to the facts revealed by witnesses on the stand. Analysis, legal research, and fact gathering constantly feed into each other as the client's case unfolds.

8. Factor Analysis

Thus far we have concentrated on the analysis of the *elements* of rules. Elements are preconditions to the applicability of a rule; if one of the elements does not apply, the entire rule does not apply. We now turn to a different kind of analysis: *factor* analysis.

factor One of the circumstances or considerations that will be weighed in making a decision, no one of which is usually conclusive. A factor is one of the considerations a court will examine to help it make a decision on whether a rule (or an element of a rule) applies. Unlike elements, each factor is not a precondition to the applicability of a rule.

A **factor** is simply a consideration that a court will examine to help it decide whether an element applies. A factor is not a precondition of applicability. It is simply one of a series of items a court will weigh. In negligence, for example, the court must determine the foreseeability of the accident. As we will see in Chapter 4, this determination is based on a large number of factors. The court will weigh facts and observations that center on:

- the area
- the activity
- the people
- preparation
- assumptions about human nature
- historical data
- specific sensory data
- common sense

We will also be examining other rules in this book for which a factor analysis will be required.

No one factor will usually be determinative for a court. All of the factors are examined and weighed. The question is not "Was the fire foreseeable?", but "How foreseeable or unforeseeable was the fire?" Factor analysis is most often used when the court is considering the *degree* or the *extent* of something. Hence there is a need to explore everything carefully before concluding where something falls on the scale.

You do a factor analysis by listing the factors that a court will consider and by examining one factor at a time in much the same way that you would analyze each element. State the factor, define it, list the specific facts that appear to support or not to support the applicability of the factor, integrate questions about missing facts into the discussion of each factor, etc.

Factor analysis and element analysis are not limited to the application of rules to facts. Almost every major decision you make involves elements and factors, e.g., buying a house, buying a car, or picking someone to marry. When people look for a house, they consider space, neighborhood, area schools, affordability, etc. If an item is essential, it is an element. Suppose, for example, that you will not buy a house with fewer than three bedrooms. This is a precondition to the entire purchase in the same manner as any single element of a rule is a precondition to the applicability of the entire rule. A house hunter may also want a large yard and a bus line within walking distance. But if these are not preconditions, they are simply factors to be considered, no one of which is necessarily dispositive or essential.

Legal Analysis Guideline #12

Factors are often used by courts to help decide whether a rule (or an element within a rule) applies. Examine each factor separately and then make a collective assessment of how the totality of factors helps to establish or disestablish the rule (or an element within the rule).

9. Counteranalysis

In discussing the model answer in the trespass case, we looked at the need for a counteranalysis—what the other side will say. Students of law tend to identify with clients for whom they are working, or with the side they think should win. *The more you personally believe in an argument, the greater the danger that you will have a weak counteranalysis to that argument.* This is not to say that you must invent a counterargument for the sake of having one. The safest state of mind you can have is to assume that there is a better counterargument than the one you have identified to date. Keep thinking. Often the worst kind of analysis hits the reader over the head with only one perspective. The test of whether to include a counterargument is whether a reasonable advocate would present that argument. When in doubt, include it.

Legal Analysis Guideline #13

To construct a counteranalysis, put yourself in the shoes of the opponent and ask whether he or she would warmly embrace, or would raise objections to, the conclusions you reached in applying any of the elements and factors to the facts. The objections to your arguments constitute the counteranalysis.

CONCLUSION

The fourth and final component of legal analysis (via IRAC) is the conclusion. In the model answer for the trespass case, you saw an example of a conclusion. It gives your own personal opinion as to which side has the better legal argument on a question. You will also be predicting how a particular court will rule on the question.

Another function of the conclusion is to list the next steps that should be taken to:

- initiate a lawsuit
- do further investigation on . . .
- do further research on . . .
- etc.

Generally, the conclusion should be brief and should not raise arguments that were not discussed in the analysis or counteranalysis.

Legal Analysis Guideline #14

State a brief conclusion of your personal views at the end of the analysis and counteranalysis. Tell the reader which side you think has the strongest position. Include any next steps you recommend. Do not state any new arguments in the conclusion.

Throughout this book there are many legal analysis assignments that ask you to apply rules to sets of facts in the manner in which this chapter has covered this skill. The general instructions for these assignments are as follows:

General Instructions for the Legal Analysis Assignment

1. The most important part of legal analysis is *fact* analysis. Carefully read each fact in this assignment. Give detailed attention to *every* word covering *every* fact. Hence, the first instruction is to know the facts thoroughly.
2. Review the material in this introductory chapter on legal analysis. Give particular attention to the fourteen legal analysis guidelines in the chapter (some of which are repeated and summarized here).
3. Most of the legal analysis assignments will ask you to apply an entire tort cause of action or defense, or will ask you to apply one of the elements of the tort cause of action or defense.
4. The rules you will be applying will be found on the pages immediately preceding the assignment. Do not do any legal research for the assignment unless you are specifically asked for such research.
5. Place a heavy emphasis on the application of definitions of words or phrases in the elements. All of the arguments in your analysis should relate to the definitions of these words or phrases. In effect, it is these definitions that you will be applying to the facts. In your application, draw specific, explicit connections between the definitions of the words or phrases in the element and the individual facts of the problem you are analyzing. Do the same for any factors that should be used to determine if an element applies.
6. When you need more facts to do the analysis and counteranalysis, state what facts you need, explain why you need them, and integrate these missing facts into your writing, always making clear that such facts are assumptions only.
7. Use the example of the trespass analysis in this chapter as a model.
8. Provide a counteranalysis whenever the two sides will not agree on whether an element of a tort cause of action or an element of a defense applies. When in doubt on whether they will agree, provide a counteranalysis.

ASSIGNMENT 2.4

Paul and Dave own adjoining property. Dan raises and trains dogs for hunting. Paul knew this when he bought his property. To try to prevent the dogs from going on Paul's land, Paul built a low fence around the land. Dave agrees that the hounds should not go on Paul's land. One day, as a training exercise, Dave releases a caged rabbit on Dave's property and simultaneously releases all seven of his dogs. They make a mad dash toward the fence and easily push it over in pursuit of the rabbit, which hops over the fence into Paul's yard. When Dave released the rabbit, he faced the cage away from Paul's land in the hope of steering the rabbit from Paul's land. This strategy, however, did not work. Paul sues Dave for trespass to land. Do the column exercise for this case and write your answer according to the guidelines discussed in this chapter. (Do not do any legal research on the problem.)

PROJECT

In Google, Bing, or another general search engine, run the following search: *aa* tort "court opinion." (Substitute the name of your state for *aa* in the search, e.g., Texas tort "court opinion.")

Using this search, find any tort opinion written by a court in your state.

(1) What is the name of the opinion?
(2) What court wrote it?
(3) Which of the torts listed in Exhibit 1–3 in Chapter 1 did the opinion involve?
(4) Pick one of the elements of that tort that is discussed by the court. Which element did you pick? (If the court does not discuss any of the elements of the tort, find a different opinion.)
(5) List one fact mentioned in the opinion that supports the conclusion that the element applies. List one other fact mentioned in the opinion that supports the conclusion that the element does not apply. (If you cannot find two facts in the opinion that meet these criteria, find a different opinion.)

ETHICS IN A TORTS PRACTICE

You are a paralegal working in the law office of Barton and Kiley. The firm represents Alice Garcia, who is suing her former employer, a car dealership, for slander. The dealership is represented by Walker and Walker. When Alice left the dealership, her former supervisor told Sam Powers that Alice was an "unreliable and untrustworthy worker." Alice was applying for a job with Powers, who had called the supervisor at the dealership for a reference. You are married to one of the attorneys at Walker and Walker. Any ethical problems? Would it make any difference if you and the Walker attorney were divorced?

SUMMARY

Legal analysis is the application of one or more rules to the facts of a client's case in order to answer a legal question that will help (1) keep a legal dispute from arising, (2) resolve a legal dispute that has arisen, or (3) prevent a legal dispute from becoming worse. The structure of legal analysis consists of a statement of the issue, a statement of the rule, the application of the rule to the facts (including a counteranalysis), and a conclusion on how the rule applies to the facts (IRAC). A legal issue is a question of whether a cause of action, defense, or other rule applies to the facts. Before phrasing issues, you need to break rules into their elements and identify the elements that are in contention. An issue will be based on an element in contention. (An element is a portion of a rule that is a precondition of the applicability of the entire rule.) Include in the issue important facts involved in the contention or controversy over that element. A complete statement of an issue includes both the rule (or elements of the rule in contention) and the important facts involved in the controversy. The main rules in tort litigation are (1) court opinions containing common law and (2) statutes. Other rules that can affect tort litigation include constitutions, administrative regulations, administrative decisions, charters, and ordinances.

Your preliminary analysis should make broad or general issues out of every possible tort cause of action and defense. Then try to narrow the issues by focusing on the element(s) of the rule in contention. Next, undertake legal research on the issues you have identified during the preliminary analysis. While going through these steps, you will often be identifying additional facts that you will need to try to uncover through further client interviewing and investigation. Next, break every rule under examination into its elements, noting each of the elements that have words or phrases that require definitions. Do legal research to obtain such definitions.

Then line up your facts with each of the elements of the rules under analysis, connecting the facts with the elements. Your written analysis should be organized by elements of the rules. Most of the writing should focus on the elements that will probably raise the most contention. Where needed, a factor analysis is also undertaken. A factor is one of the circumstances or considerations that will be weighed in making a decision, no one of which is usually conclusive. The perspective of the other side is presented as a counteranalysis. The conclusion in an exam answer or in a memorandum of law should state your personal opinion on which side has the better legal argument, your prediction of what a court might decide, and any next steps you recommend.

KEY TERMS

legal analysis *28*
primary authority *28*
IRAC *28*
memorandum of law *29*
legal issue *29*
application *31*
hypothetical *31*
element *33*
deposition *33*
term of art *38*
factor *44*

REVIEW QUESTIONS

1. What are the three objectives of legal analysis?
2. Explain the components of IRAC.
3. Give examples of where IRAC can be used.
4. What are the two ways to phrase a legal issue?
5. What are the different kinds of memoranda of law?
6. What kinds of rules can be the basis of tort issues?
7. What are the objectives of the application component of IRAC?
8. How is legal analysis related to legal research, investigation, and interviewing?
9. What is an element?
10. What steps do you go through to break a rule into its elements?
11. What is the distinction between the conditions of the applicability of a rule and the consequences of its applicability?
12. Where can you find definitions of the elements of rules?
13. What is a term of art?
14. Describe the method of connecting facts to elements through the use of columns.
15. How does legal analysis in exam answers differ from legal analysis in memoranda of law and other writing in a torts practice?
16. What is factor analysis and how is it similar to, and different from, element analysis?
17. What is a counteranalysis?
18. What is included in the conclusion component of IRAC?

HELPFUL WEBSITES

- **The Basics of Legal Analysis**
  www.onlineasp.org/analysis/index.htm
  www.essortment.com/all/basicsoflegal_ritg.htm
  law.hamline.edu/fundamentals_legal_analysis.html
- **IRAC**
  www.law.msu.edu/rwa/IRAC.final.pdf
  www.lawnerds.com/guide/irac.html
  law.slu.edu/academic_support/irac.html
  en.wikipedia.org/wiki/IRAC
- **Legal Analysis and the Memorandum of Law**
  www.alwd.org/publications/pdf/CM2_Appendix6.pdf
  www.alwd.org/publications/pdf/CM1_Appendix6.pdf
  sparkcharts.sparknotes.com/legal/legalwriting/section2.php
  www.ualr.edu/cmbarger (click "Format Guidelines")
  cherylstephens.com/professional/communication/Organization.pdf
  www.yourlawprof.com/21f/law34/legalmemonotes.htm

Student StudyWARE™ CD-ROM
For additional materials, please go to the student CD in this book.

CHAPTER 3

FACT GATHERING IN TORT LITIGATION

CHAPTER OUTLINE

- Overview
- Liability, Damages, and Collectibility
- Introduction to Fact Gathering
- Achieving Specificity and Comprehensiveness
- Taking a Witness Statement

CHAPTER OBJECTIVES

After completing this chapter, you should be able to:

- Identify paralegal roles in tort litigation at the agency, pretrial, trial, appeal, and enforcement stages.
- Understand the major considerations used by an office when deciding whether to take a tort case.
- Know the client background facts a law office needs to obtain in a tort case.
- Describe the guidelines a law office uses when searching for facts to establish a prima facie case.
- Organize fact gathering through versions of facts and fact particularization.
- State the major standards of proof in tort cases.
- Take a witness statement.

OVERVIEW

This chapter presents a summary of the major steps involved in tort litigation plus many of the tasks paralegals perform during those steps, particularly tasks involving fact gathering. For an overview, see the chart in Exhibit 3–1. Note that this chart includes an "Agency Stage." Most tort cases do not have this stage; they begin immediately in court. An important exception is workers' compensation, which begins by filing a claim with an administrative agency (see Chapter 28). Another

Exhibit 3–1 Overview of tort litigation with paralegal roles.

Event	Definitions	Role of Paralegal
I. Agency Stage (if applicable) **1.** Someone protests an action taken by the *administrative agency*, e.g., the state denies a tort claim alleged to have been committed by a state employee, or the state denies a workers' compensation claim for an on-the-job injury. **2.** *Agency hearing.* **3.** *Intra-agency appeal* to a commission, board of appeals, director, or secretary within the agency. (If no agency is involved, the litigation begins in court at the pretrial stage.)	**Administrative agency:** a governmental body, other than a court or legislature, that carries out (i.e., administers or executes) the statutes of the legislature, the executive orders of the chief executive, and its own regulations. **Agency hearing:** a proceeding, similar to a trial, in which the hearing examiner of the agency listens to evidence and legal arguments before deciding the case. **Intra-agency appeal:** a review within the agency of an earlier decision to determine if that decision was correct.	a. Open case file. b. Interview client. c. Conduct investigation. d. Organize and manage case file.
II. Pretrial Stage **4.** Plaintiff files a *complaint.* **5.** Clerk issues a *summons.* **6.** *Service of process* on defendant. **7.** Defendant files an *answer.* **8.** *Discovery.* **9.** Pretrial *motions.* **10.** *Settlement* efforts. **11.** *Voir dire.*	**Complaint:** a plaintiff's first pleading, stating a cause of action against the defendant (also called a petition). **Summons:** a notice directing the defendant to appear in court and answer the plaintiff's complaint or face a default judgment (also, a notice directing a witness or juror to appear in court). A *default judgment* is a judgment granted against a party who fails to appear, file an answer, or otherwise defend the action before the deadline. **Service of process:** a formal delivery of notice to a defendant that a suit has been initiated to which he or she must respond. (*Process* is the means used by the court to acquire or exercise its power or jurisdiction over a person.) **Answer:** a pleading containing the defendant's response to the plaintiff's complaint. **Discovery:** methods such as interrogatories and depositions by which one party obtains information from the other party before trial. (Discovery can also be used in postjudgment enforcement proceedings.) **Motion:** a formal request to the court, such as a motion to dismiss. **Settlement:** an agreement resolving a dispute without full litigation. **Voir dire:** a preliminary examination to assess someone's qualifications (here, to be a juror, if the case will be tried before a jury).	a.–d. Same as above if case does not begin at an agency. e. Perform legal research. f. Help draft complaint and other pleadings. g. Schedule discovery. h. Draft discovery requests and motions. i. Summarize and digest discovery data; perform other discovery tasks. j. Assemble trial notebook. k. Arrange exhibits. l. Continue investigation.

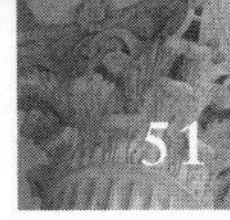

Exhibit 3–1 (Continued)

Event	Definitions	Role of Paralegal
III. Trial Stage **12.** *Opening statement* of plaintiff. **13.** *Opening statement* of defendant. **14.** Plaintiff presents its case: (a) *evidence* introduced. (b) *direct examination.* (c) *cross-examination.* **15.** *Motions* to dismiss. **16.** Defendant presents its case: (a) *evidence* introduced. (b) *direct examination.* (c) *cross-examination.* **17.** Closing arguments to jury by attorneys. **18.** *Charge* to jury. **19.** *Verdict* of jury. **20.** *Judgment* of court.	**Opening statement:** an attorney's statement to the jury, made before presenting evidence, that summarizes the case he or she intends to try to establish during the trial. **Evidence:** anything that could be offered to prove or disprove an alleged fact, e.g., testimony, documents, or fingerprints. (A separate determination must be made on whether a particular item of evidence is relevant or irrelevant, admissible or inadmissible.) **Direct examination:** the first questioning of a witness by the party who called the witness (also called examination in chief). **Cross-examination:** questioning a witness called by the other side after the other side has completed its direct examination of the witness. **Charge:** a statement of the guidelines and law given to the jury by the judge for use by the jury in deciding the issues of fact in its verdict (also called jury instructions). **Verdict:** the final conclusion of the jury. **Judgment:** the final conclusion of a court that resolves a legal dispute or that specifies what further proceedings are needed to resolve it.	a. Coordinate scheduling of witnesses. b. Help evaluate prospective jurors during voir dire. c. Take notes during trial. d. Assist attorney with documents and exhibits.
IV. Appeal Stage **21.** Filing of *notice of appeal.* **22.** Filing of *appellant's appellate brief.* **23.** Filing of *appellee's appellate brief.* **24.** Filing of appellant's reply brief. **25.** Oral argument by attorneys. **26.** Judgment of court.	**Notice of appeal:** notice given to a court (through filing) and to the opposing party (through service) of an intention to appeal. **Appellant:** the party bringing an appeal because of alleged errors made by a lower tribunal (sometimes called petitioner). **Appellee:** the party against whom the appeal is brought (sometimes called respondent) **Appellate brief:** a document filed by a party in an appellate court (and served on an opposing party) in which arguments are presented on why the appellate court should affirm (approve), reverse, or otherwise modify what a lower court has done.	a. Draft and file notice of appeal. b. Order trial transcript. c. Summarize and digest trial testimony relevant to appeal issues.
V. Enforcement Stage **27.** *Posttrial discovery.* **28.** *Execution* by sheriff.	**Posttrial discovery:** methods by which one party obtains information from another party after the trial; the usual purpose of posttrial discovery is to enable the **judgment creditor** (the party who has won a money judgment) to obtain information from the **judgment debtor** (the party ordered to pay a money judgment) that will help in the enforcement (e.g., collection) of the judgment. **Execution:** a command or writ to a court officer (e.g., sheriff) to seize and sell the property of the losing litigant in order to satisfy the judgment debt. (See the glossary for additional definitions.)	a. Investigate judgment debtor's assets. b. Schedule posttrial discovery. c. Arrange for sheriff to begin execution.

exception is a tort claim asserted against the government that is not barred by sovereign immunity (see Chapter 27). The first step is often to make the claim with a designated administrative agency of the government.

For examples of torts complaints that a paralegal might help draft, see Exhibit 3–2 in this chapter and Exhibit 19–8 in Chapter 19.

Exhibit 3–2 Example of a tort complaint.

Caption

STATE OF __________________ COUNTY OF ______________

__________________ COURT

John Smith, Plaintiff

v. Civil Action No. __________

Richard Jones, Defendant

Designation of Pleading →

COMPLAINT FOR NEGLIGENCE

Statement of Jurisdiction →

Plaintiff alleges that:

1. The jurisdiction of this court is based on section ________, title ________ of the [State] Code.

Body

2. Plaintiff is a plumber, residing at 800 Main Street in the City of ___________, ___________ County, State of _______________ .

3. Upon information and belief, defendant is a traveling salesman, residing at 210 Broadway Street in the City of Chicago, Cook County, Illinois.

4. On or about the second day of January, 2010 an automobile driven by defendant, on Highway 18 in the vicinity of East Brunswick, ________, struck an automobile being driven by the plaintiff on said highway.

5. Defendant was negligent in the operation of his automobile as to:

a. Speed,

b. Attentiveness to traffic,

c. Management and control.

6. As a result of said negligence of defendant, his automobile struck plaintiff's automobile and caused the following damage:

a. Plaintiff was subjected to great pain and suffering.

b. Plaintiff necessarily incurred medical and hospital expense.

c. Plaintiff suffered a loss of income.

d. Plaintiff's automobile was damaged.

Prayer for Relief →

Wherefore plaintiff demands judgment in the amount of two hundred thousand dollars ($200,000), together with the costs and disbursements of this action.

Subscription → (a signature, here that of the attorney drafting the complaint)

____

Plaintiff's Attorney

1 Main Street

________ , ________

Verification (a formal declaration by a party that the pleading is true to the best of his or her knowledge)

State of ______________________________

ss

County of ______________________________

John Smith, being first duly sworn on oath according to law, deposes and says that he has read the foregoing complaint and that the matters stated therein are true to the best of his knowledge, information, and belief.

____

John Smith

Subscribed and sworn to before me on this____________ day of ________, 20 ______ .

____

Notary Public

My commission expires:

Source: Adapted from MacDonald, Pick, DeWitt & Volz, *Wisconsin Practice Materials* 239 (2d ed., West Group 1959).

LIABILITY, DAMAGES, AND COLLECTIBILITY

Once a new client walks into a law office with a personal injury case, the three initial concerns of the office are liability, damages, and collectibility.

Liability

Assume the client claims that the defendant injured the client. Under our system, this does not automatically make the defendant responsible even if the client can prove that the defendant caused the injury. *We are not responsible for every harm we cause.* We are responsible:

- if the harm was wrongful because it was intentional or negligent, or
- if the harm results from a special category of conduct that leads to strict liability regardless of whether it was intentional, negligent, or innocent.

The law makes us **liable** only for harm that falls within these categories. Liability means being legally responsible for something. In the law of torts, liability occurs when a plaintiff has successfully established a cause of action, which is a legally acceptable reason for bringing a suit. To state a cause of action, the plaintiff alleges a set of facts that gives him or her a right to judicial relief.

liable Obligated in law; legally responsible.

For our purposes, the causes of action are the thirty-eight torts and related causes of action outlined in Exhibit 1–3 of Chapter 1 and examined throughout the chapters of this book. Each cause of action consists of its own elements. In order to make a preliminary assessment of whether the client "has a case," the office must decide whether enough facts can eventually be established to support the elements of any of these causes of action. If it can, liability will result, unless defenses are available that can defeat the action.

Damages

Damages are monetary payments awarded to compensate someone for a legally recognized wrong. Such payments can be one of the remedies received by a plaintiff upon establishing a cause of action against the defendant for personal injury or other harm. The amount in damages can range from $1 (which would be considered **nominal damages**) to millions of dollars. How much is awarded depends primarily on the extent of the harm proven. An attorney will probably turn away a case where liability is clear, but where the harm suffered is relatively small. For example, it may be easy to establish liability against a bottling company that left a thumbtack in a soda bottle. But if the plaintiff suffered no significant injury upon discovering the thumbtack, the case may not be worth litigating. Most personal injury attorneys are paid a **contingent fee**. They take a percentage (e.g., 33$^{1}/_{3}$ percent) of the award *if* an award is given, or a percentage of the settlement *if* the case is settled. In short, the attorney is paid contingent on the client's receiving something. But even a large percentage of a small amount is not very attractive to an attorney. Of course, the client can always offer to pay the lawyer an hourly fee rather than a contingent fee. Few clients, however, are willing to do so when the injury suffered is comparatively small. Hence, the question of damages will be a major topic of discussion with a new client.

nominal damages A trifling sum (e.g., $1) awarded to the plaintiff because there was no significant loss or injury suffered, although a technical invasion of rights did occur.

contingent fee A fee that is paid to the plaintiff's attorney only if the case is successfully resolved by litigation or settlement. (The fee is also referred to as a contingency). A *defense contingent fee* (also called a negative contingency) is a fee for the defendant's attorney that is dependent on the outcome of the case.

Collectibility

The attorney may feel that the prospects for establishing liability are very good and that the injury suffered is so substantial that the likelihood of a high damages award is also very good. A dream case for every **PI** (personal injury) attorney? Not necessarily. What good is a multimillion-dollar judgment against a bankrupt defendant with no liability insurance? During the initial contact with a new client, the

PI Personal injury. (A PI practice is a tort practice.)

deep pocket 1. An individual, business, or other organization with resources to pay a potential judgment. 2. Sufficient assets for this purpose. The opposite of *shallow pocket*.

office will start compiling information on the financial health of prospective defendants. The question is whether a defendant's pockets are deep or shallow. A **deep pocket** is a person who has resources from which a judgment can be collected. The resources can include cash, other property, insurance policies, etc. A *shallow pocket* is a person without such resources.

INTRODUCTION TO FACT GATHERING

In Chapter 20, a senior paralegal makes the following observation about paralegals in tort litigation:

> Whether you are the paralegal project manager or the newest paralegal on the team, you are the keeper of the facts.

There are two major categories of facts that a paralegal helps an office collect early in a tort case: background facts on the client and the facts needed to establish a **prima facie case**. A prima facie case is established when a party alleges enough facts to cover every element of a cause of action. A prima facie case entitles the party to win unless the other side overcomes this case with contrary evidence.

prima facie case A party's presentation of evidence that will prevail until contradicted and overcome by contrary evidence.

Background Facts

Law firms differ on the amount of background information they seek from every client. The following checklist will give you some idea of the kind of background information that can be sought.

- name of client
- birth name
- other married names
- current street address and phone (home)
- length of time lived at this address
- current street address and phone (work)
- e-mail addresses (current and past)
- web addresses (e.g., blogs, social networking sites such as MySpace and Facebook)
- prior residences
- nationality/citizenship/place of birth
- street and e-mail addresses and phone numbers where spouse (or closest relative) can be reached
- date of birth
- religion, race (may be relevant in jury selection process)
- how client was referred to this office
- whether client hired any other attorney on this case
- whether client spoke to any other attorney about this case
- if client is a minor, name of legal guardian
- marital status
- prior marriages (information on divorces or annulments)
- date of present marriage
- date(s) of divorce(s) or annulment(s)
- names of children
- ages/addresses
- name of other parent of each child
- current status of property settlement, spousal support (alimony), and child support payments
- current employer(s) of client and spouse
- job title/salary
- length of employment there
- prior employment history
- self-employment/business ventures
- tax data (filing status, gross income, availability of copies of returns, etc.)
- real property client owns in own name
- real property owned in joint names
- personal property (cash, bank accounts; approximate value of furniture, motor vehicles, etc.)
- education

- prior litigation involvement (dates, courts, attorneys, outcomes, etc.)
- present state of health
- names and addresses of doctors currently treating client
- nature of treatment
- medical problems for which no treatment has yet been sought
- medical history (for the last five years)
- prior hospital treatment (dates, addresses, doctors, care provided, outcomes)
- name of every insurance company (past/present) that has covered medical care
- list of every insurance claim client has ever filed for medical care
- names of people who could verify client's prior medical condition

Prima Facie Case

A law office uses three fact-gathering guides to determine the facts it will seek through interviewing and investigation to try to establish a prima facie case: tort law, evidence law, and common sense. (See Exhibit 3–3.) Legal interviewing is the process of gathering facts from a client (or from a prospective client if the office has not yet decided whether to take the case) in order to solve or avoid a legal problem. Legal investigation is the process of gathering additional facts and verifying presently known facts in order to solve or avoid a legal problem.

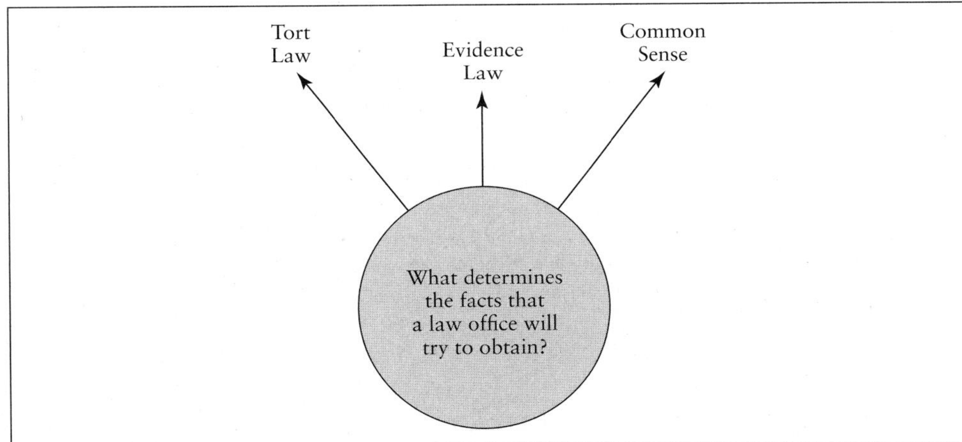

Exhibit 3–3
Guides for fact gathering in a torts practice.

Tort Law Tort law consists of the elements of the major torts and related causes of action outlined in Exhibit 1–3 of Chapter 1 plus the defenses to them. These causes of action and defenses are also outlined in the checklists called "Definitions, Relationships, Paralegal Roles, and Research References," found throughout the chapters of the book. Knowing the elements of these torts—and the elements of their defenses—will provide direction for all interviewing and investigation efforts of the office.

Evidence Law A general understanding of the law of evidence will be of assistance when asking questions during interviewing and in verifying facts through investigation. Assume, for example, that a client tells you that he or she suffered $100,000 in lost wages due to an injury. Some of the evidentiary questions related to these facts are as follows:

- Are there documents (e.g., past wage receipts) that will help document the loss?
- Are these documents **admissible** in court? (Something is admissible if a trial judge will allow a jury to consider it.)
- Are witnesses available to testify about the wage loss?

admissible Allowed into court for determination of its truth or believability.

competent Allowed (having the legal capacity) to give testimony because the person understands the obligation to tell the truth, has the ability to communicate, and has knowledge of the topic of his or her proposed testimony. The noun form is *competency*. (See glossary for another definition of competent.)

- Are these witnesses **competent** to testify and would their testimony be admissible? (A witness is competent to give testimony if he or she understands the obligation to tell the truth, has a basic ability to communicate, and has knowledge of the topic of his or her proposed testimony.)

It is not enough to be told that a $100,000 loss has been suffered. The evidence that does or does not support this amount must be considered as the interviewer interviews and the investigator investigates. They need to ask additional questions and pursue additional facts that will help build the client's case and minimize any evidentiary problems that could arise during a trial.

Common Sense Once you are working in a law practice, you will be surprised to discover the high degree to which many legal problems are solved by the use of common sense. The most effective attorneys and paralegals are those who came to the study and practice of law *already equipped* with:

- a sense of responsibility
- inquisitiveness
- common sense

Interviewers and investigators must be aggressive and imaginative in going after the facts. This reality is reflected in the following comments by an investigator who must investigate road conditions in an accident case:

> I need to find out the road conditions on the day of the accident. I can call the client—that's OK as a starter. I'm going to get a copy of the newspaper for the day of the accident to see if it has a weather report. I think copies of old newspapers are available. I'm going to check the Internet. Also, there must be some way to get a governmental weather bureau to give us something official. I think I'll give Fred a call. He once had a case like this. Maybe he can give me a lead. I wonder if the city highway department keeps a record of road conditions and road repairs. I can always ask my supervisor if she wants me to go to some of the people who live in that area to see what they might be able to tell me about the road. Sometimes you can turn up good leads just by talking to people.

Someone with this determination and common-sense instinct for thoroughness would be a prized employee in any law office.

ACHIEVING SPECIFICITY AND COMPREHENSIVENESS

Two of the major characteristics of effective fact gathering are specificity and comprehensiveness. There are a number of techniques that will help you achieve both. Checklists can be particularly helpful. There are a number of them in this book. As indicated, all of the chapters in the book that cover the major torts contain a checklist called, "Definitions, Relationships, Paralegal Roles, and Research References." In addition to checklists, there are other methods discussed in the book for achieving specificity and comprehensiveness. For example:

- The legal analysis discussion in Chapter 2 shows how to identify further facts that need to be pursued, particularly in a follow-up legal interview with a client.
- The foreseeability discussion in Chapter 4 presents guidelines for formulating numerous factual questions when foreseeability is an issue, as it is in a great many tort cases.

We turn now to two related techniques: organizing facts into versions and fact particularization.

Fact Versions

People perceive events differently. Consequently, everyone will not always have the same version of what happened. In fact, it is healthy for the interviewer and investigator to anticipate the presence of multiple versions for every important fact. This process is outlined in Exhibit 3–4.

Exhibit 3–4
Fact versions.

Starting Point:

All the facts you presently have on the case.

- Arrange the facts chronologically.
- Place a number before each fact that must be established in a legal proceeding.

State the Following Versions of Each Fact:

- Version I: The client's
- Version II: The opponent's (as revealed to you or as you assume it might be)
- Version III: A witness's
- Version IV: Another witness's
- Version V: Any other reasonable version (e.g., from your own deductions)

As to Each Version:

- State precisely (with quotations if possible) what the version is.
- State the evidence or indications that tend to support the version according to persons presenting the version.
- State the evidence or indications that tend to contradict this version.
- Determine how you will verify the evidence or indications.

Of course, all versions of facts are not of equal weight. Some versions are more believable—have more **credibility**—than others. Interviewers and investigators must be constantly evaluating the believability of all the evidence they are helping the office assemble.

credibility Believability; the extent to which something can be believed.

The **burden of proof** is the responsibility of proving a fact at trial. In general, the party asserting a cause of action has the burden of proving every fact that is essential to establishing that cause of action. And the party asserting a defense has the burden of proving every fact that is essential to establishing that defense. The **standard of proof** is the guideline that tells the trier of fact, usually the jury, how believable a party's version of a fact must be in order for it to accept that fact as true. In the vast majority of tort cases, the standard of proof is **preponderance of the evidence**. This standard is met when a party proves it is *more likely than not* that his or her version of a fact is true. (Exhibit 3–5 presents this standard along with others.)

burden of proof The responsibility of proving a fact at trial.

standard of proof How believable or convincing a version of a fact must be before the trier of fact (usually the jury) can accept it as true.

preponderance of the evidence The standard of proof that is met when the evidence establishes that it is more likely than not that the facts are as alleged. Also called fair preponderance of evidence.

EXAMPLE

Ted is suing Mary for negligence. One of Ted's arguments is that Mary failed to make a right-turn signal just before the accident. Mary swears she did make it.

Under the preponderance standard, a juror can accept whichever version of this fact is more likely true than not. To agree with Mary, a juror does not have to conclude that Ted was lying. The juror simply must be able to say, "I believe Mary more than I believe Ted." This is the meaning of preponderance of the evidence.

Although preponderance is the minimum standard that must be met, your goal in gathering facts is always to go as far beyond the minimum as possible. You keep digging for facts in the hope of finding evidence that will increase (or challenge) the believability of all the versions.

Exhibit 3–5
The spectrum of believability and the standards of proof in tort cases.

How Convincing Is the Version of the Fact?	Use of This Standard
Totally Believable: The evidence leaves no doubt whatsoever that the version of the facts is true.	This is never the standard used at trial. It may be that the trier of fact will conclude that a version of the facts offered by a party is totally believable, but it is never *required* that the evidence meet this standard to be accepted as true at trial.
Beyond a Reasonable Doubt: There may be some doubt that the version of the facts is true, but none of these doubts are reasonable. **Reasonable doubt** is doubt that would cause prudent people to hesitate before acting in matters of importance to themselves.	This is the standard used in a criminal trial. The prosecution must prove the existence of every fact needed to constitute the crime beyond a reasonable doubt. This standard is *not* used in tort cases.
Clear and Convincing: There is a high probability that the version of the facts is true.	Only rarely is this high standard of believability used in tort cases. One example of its use is the requirement in a defamation case against a media defendant that the plaintiff prove by clear and convincing evidence that the defendant knew the statement about the plaintiff was false or was reckless with regard to its truth or falsity (actual malice). The standard is also used in many contract or will cases to prove fraud or duress.
Preponderance of the Evidence: It is more likely than not that the version of the facts is true.	*This is the standard of believability that is used in the vast majority of tort cases.*
Fifty/Fifty Possibility: The evidence is evenly balanced on the facts. It is as likely that the version of the facts is true as it is that the version is false.	If the evidence establishes a fifty/fifty possibility of truth, then the fact cannot be established as true. The trier of fact would be acting on mere speculation or conjecture (guessing) if only a fifty/fifty possibility were shown.
A Possibility: The evidence establishes no more than a possibility that the version of the facts is true.	Anything is possible. Hence, to show a mere possibility is never enough to establish a version of the facts. The trier of fact would again be engaged in mere speculation or conjecture (guessing).
Highly Unbelievable: There is a high probability that the version of the facts is false.	Obviously enough to establish the falsity of a version of the facts.
Totally Unbelievable: The evidence leaves no doubt whatsoever that the version of the facts is false.	Obviously enough to establish the falsity of a version of the facts.

Fact Particularization

fact particularization A fact-gathering technique used to generate a large list of factual questions (who, what, where, how, when, and why) that will help you obtain a specific and comprehensive picture of all available facts that are relevant to a legal issue.

Perhaps the most effective technique for developing the skill of fact gathering is called **fact particularization**. It is one of the most important professional skills you can develop. Professionalism in fact gathering means to *particularize* the facts so that there is an exploration of all or almost all the details that make the facts unique. (See Exhibit 3–6.) Fact particularization involves collecting more facts in order to obtain a specific and comprehensive picture of what happened. Your main guide in accomplishing particularization is common sense.

You *particularize* a fact you already have:
1. by assuming that what you know about this fact is woefully inadequate,
2. by assuming that there is more than one version of this fact, and
3. by asking a large number of basic who, what, where, how, when, and why questions about the fact, which, if answered, will provide as specific and comprehensive a picture of that fact as is possible at this time.

Exhibit 3–6
Fact particularization.

EXAMPLE
You are working on an automobile negligence case. Two cars collide on a two-lane street. They were driven by Ed Smith and Sam Jones. Jones is a client of your law office. One of the facts in the file is that, according to Jones, Smith's car "veered into Jones's lane moments before the collision." Your job is to particularize this fact. *Design an investigation strategy consisting of questions you would like answered in order to obtain a much more detailed picture of what happened.* This is done by elaborating on the facts already collected. You ask the following common-sense questions: who, what, where, how, when, and why.

- What does Jones mean by "veered into" the other lane?
- How much veering was done? An inch? A foot? Did the entire car come into the other lane? How much of an angle was there?
- Who saw this happen? According to Jones, Smith's car veered. Did Jones see this happen himself or is he reporting what someone else said?
- Who else saw it, if anyone? Any passengers in Jones's car? Any passengers in Smith's car? Were there any bystanders? Has the neighborhood been checked for witnesses, e.g., people who live or work in the area, or people who frequently sit on public benches in the area?
- Were the police called after the accident? If so, who was the officer? Was a report made? If so, what does it say, if anything, about the car veering into the other lane? Where is this report? How can you obtain a copy?
- What time of day was it when the accident occurred?
- Why did Smith's car veer, according to Jones or anyone else who alleges that this occurred?
- How fast was Jones's car going at the time of the veering? Why was Jones going at this speed?
- Who would be able to substantiate Jones's speed? Who might have different views of how fast Jones was going?
- How fast was Smith's car going at the time of the veering? Why was Smith going at this speed?
- Who would be able to substantiate Smith's speed? Who might have different views of how fast Smith was going?
- Have there been other accidents in the area? If so, how similar have they been to this one?
- What was the condition of the road at the time Smith started to veer? At the time of the collision?
- What was the weather at the time?
- How was visibility? Describe the conditions that would affect good or poor visibility.
- What kind of a road is it? Straight? Curved at the area of the collision? Any inclines? Any hills that could affect speed and visibility?
- What kind of area is it? Residential? Commercial?
- Is there anything in the area that would distract drivers, e.g., potholes?
- Where is the nearest traffic light, stop sign, or other traffic signal? Prepare a diagram or obtain an online street map (e.g., through maps.google.com or www.mapquest.com) on which you note their location. How, if at all, did they affect traffic at the time of the accident?

- What is the speed limit in the area?
- What kind of car was Smith driving? Were there any mechanical problems with the car? Would these problems have helped cause the veering? What prior accidents has Smith had, if any?
- What kind of car was Jones driving? Were there any mechanical problems with the car? What prior accidents has Jones had, if any?

This list of questions is by no means exhaustive. Many more could be asked to try to complete the picture of what happened and to collect as many new and substantiating facts as possible on what happened. You need to develop the *habit* of generating such factual questions. Not all of the questions will turn out to be productive. Some—or perhaps many—will lead to dead ends. Be willing to take this risk.

Fact particularization can be a guide in formulating factual questions that need to be asked in different settings:

- in a client interview
- in investigations
- in interrogatories (a method of discovery consisting of written questions about a lawsuit submitted by one party to another to help the sender prepare for trial; for an example, see Exhibit 18–3 in Chapter 18)
- in a deposition (a method of discovery by which parties and their prospective witnesses are questioned outside the courtroom)
- in an administrative or court hearing in which witnesses are formally questioned

ASSIGNMENT 3.1

You work in an office that represents Mr. Floyd, who slipped on a wet floor just inside the exit door of a supermarket. He is now suing the supermarket. You are asked to interview Mr. Floyd and investigate the facts of the case. What questions would you ask in order to obtain a specific and comprehensive picture of what happened?

ASSIGNMENT 3.2

The Hazard Interview

In this assignment you will be interviewing someone about a hazard. Ask a friend, a neighbor, a relative, another student, or another employee about a hazard where they live, work, study, or play. The hazard should have the following characteristics:

- It should be a hazard about which the interviewee has personal knowledge.
- It should be a hazard about which you (the interviewer) have *no* personal knowledge.
- It should be a hazard that involves a specific thing, object, or condition—preferably relating to a building, an appliance, a motor vehicle, a sidewalk, a street area, etc. It should not deal with anything as general or vague as "the hazards of city living," "the hazards of smoking," etc.

After you conduct the interview, prepare a report on the interview. The report will be evaluated according to the following criteria:

- factual detail
- organization (no particular organization is required; select an organization that will facilitate ease of reading)
- spelling, grammar, and composition (including the structure and sequencing of sentences and paragraphs)

Type the memo—double-spaced with generous margin space. There is no minimum or maximum length for the memo. The length should be appropriate for the nature of the hazard being described.

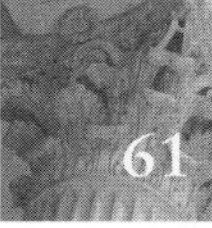

TAKING A WITNESS STATEMENT

There are four major kinds of witness statements:

1. handwritten statement
2. recorded statement in question-and-answer format (on audio or video tape)
3. responses to a questionnaire that is mailed to the witness to answer
4. statement taken in question-and-answer format before a court reporter

The most common kind of statement is the first, which we will consider here.

In a handwritten statement, the investigator writes down what the witness says, or the witness writes out the statement himself or herself. There is no formal structure to which the written statement must conform. The major requirements for the statement are clarity and accuracy.

The statement should begin by identifying (1) the witness (name, address, place of work, names of relatives, and other identifying data that may be helpful in locating the witness later); (2) the date and place of the taking of the statement; and (3) the name of the person to whom the statement is being made. See the example of the beginning of a witness statement in Exhibit 3–7.

Statement of John Wood

I am John Wood. I am 42 years old and live at 3416 34th Street, N.W., Nashua, New Hampshire 03060. I work at the Deming Chemical Plant at Region Circle, Nashua. My home phone is 603-966-3954. My work phone is 603-297-9700 x 301. I am married to Patricia Wood. We have two children, Jessica (twenty-two years old) and Gabriel (eighteen years old). I am making this statement to Rose Thompson, a paralegal at Fields, Smith and Farrell. This statement is being given on March 13, 2009 at my home, 3416 34th Street, N.W.

On February 15, 2009, I was standing on the corner of . . . .

Exhibit 3–7
Beginning of a witness statement.

Then comes the body of the statement, in which the witness provides information about the event or circumstance in question (an accident that was observed, what the witness did and saw just before a fire, where the witness was on a certain date, etc.). It is often useful to have the witness present the facts in a chronological order, particularly when many facts are involved in the statement. It is important that the witness give detailed facts that demonstrate the witness was in a good position to observe the event. This will lend credibility to the statement.

At the end of the statement, the witness should say that he or she is "making the statement of his or her own free will, without any pressure or coercion from anyone." The witness then signs the statement. The signature goes on the last page. Each of the other pages is also signed or initialed. If others have watched the witness make and sign the statement, they should also sign an **attestation clause**, which simply states that they saw the witness sign the statement.

attestation clause A clause stating that you saw (witnessed) someone sign a document or perform other tasks related to the validity of the document.

Before the witness signs, he or she should read the entire statement and make any factual corrections that need to be made. Each correction should be initialed by the witness. Each page should be numbered, with the total number of pages indicated each time. For example, if there are four pages, the page numbers would be "1 of 4," "2 of 4," "3 of 4," and "4 of 4." The investigator should not try to correct any spelling or grammatical mistakes made by the witness. The statement should exist exactly as the witness spoke or wrote it. Just before the signature of the witness at the end of the statement, the witness should say (in writing), "I have read all _____ pages of this statement, and the facts within it are accurate to the best of my knowledge."

Investigators sometimes use various tricks of the trade to achieve a desired effect. For example, if the investigator is writing out the statement as the witness speaks, the investigator may *intentionally* make an error of fact. When the witness

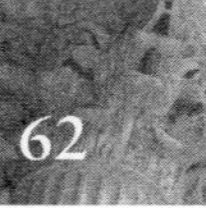

rebut To refute or oppose.

reads over the statement, the investigator makes sure that the witness catches the error and initials the correction. This becomes added evidence that the witness carefully read the statement. The witness might later try to claim that he or she did not read the statement. The initialed correction helps **rebut** this position. Try to make sure that every page of the witness statement (other than the last) ends in the middle of a sentence or somewhere before the period. This is to rebut a later allegation that someone improperly added pages to the witness statement after it was signed. The allegation is somewhat difficult to support if the bottom line of one page contains a sentence that is continued at the top of the next page.

Witness statements are generally not admitted into evidence at trial. They might be admitted to help the attorney demonstrate that the pretrial statement of the witness is inconsistent with the testimony of this witness during the trial itself. The main value of witness statements is thoroughness and accuracy in case preparation. Trials can occur years after the events that led to litigation. Witnesses may disappear or forget. Witness statements taken soon after the event can be helpful in tracking down witnesses and in helping them recall the details of the event.

ASSIGNMENT 3.3

Select any member of the class and take a witness statement from this person. The statement should concern some accident in which the witness was a participant or an observer. The witness should not, however, be a party to any litigation growing out of the accident. Write out the statement from what the witness says in response to your questions. Do not submit a statement handwritten by the witness (except for his or her signature, initials, etc.). Assume that you (the investigator–paralegal) work for the law firm of Davis and Davis, which represents someone else involved in the accident.

PROJECT

In Google, Bing, or another general search engine, enter search terms that will lead you to questionnaires that might be used or adapted in a torts practice (e.g., "personal injury questionnaire").

Draft your own comprehensive questionnaire that might be used for a client who has suffered a personal injury in an automobile accident involving two vehicles that collided at an intersection during a rain storm. For your questionnaire, adapt ideas for questions and topics discussed in this chapter and ones that you find on Internet sites through this search.

ETHICS IN A TORTS PRACTICE

You are a paralegal working in the law office of Gail Richardson, Esq., who is representing Smith in a negligence case against Jones. At the trial, Smith won a judgment of $50,000 in damages. Jones, however, has not paid the judgment. Richardson asks you to go on all the social networking sites (Facebook, MySpace, LinkedIn, etc.) to try to find out some personal information about Jones in the hope that his lifestyle will provide leads to his assets. You sign up for these sites, using a fictitious name. You trace Jones's presence on the Internet by pretending to be interested in many of the groups and subgroups that Jones is a part of. Any ethical problems?

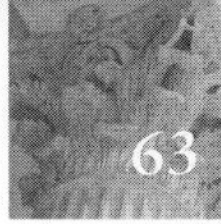

SUMMARY

Paralegals perform a large number of roles assisting attorneys during the five stages of litigation: agency (if the case begins in an administrative agency), pretrial, trial, appeal, and enforcement. Three of the initial concerns about the case of a new client are liability (has a tort been committed?), damages (what harm has resulted?), and collectability (does the wrongdoer have resources from which a judgment can be collected, i.e., is the wrongdoer a deep pocket?).

A law office needs considerable background information about a prospective client. There are three guides to the facts needed to establish a prima facie case: tort law (the elements of the tort causes of action and their defenses), evidence law (the kinds of facts that a court will consider), and common sense (making logical connections). Every important fact should be viewed from the perspectives of different versions of that fact. The believability of each version must be weighed within the context of the main standard of proof in tort cases: preponderance of the evidence. Fact particularization will help achieve specificity and comprehensiveness in fact gathering. Witness statements are important even if they are not admitted at trial. They are often needed to ensure thoroughness and accuracy. They also help everyone recall events that may have taken place a long time ago.

KEY TERMS

administrative agency *50*
agency hearing *50*
intra-agency appeal *50*
complaint *50*
summons *50*
service of process *50*
answer *50*
discovery *50*
motion *50*
settlement *50*
voir dire *50*
opening statement *51*
evidence *51*
direct examination *51*
cross-examination *51*
charge *51*
verdict *51*
judgment *51*
notice of appeal *51*
appellant *51*
appellee *51*
appellate brief *51*
posttrial discovery *51*
judgment creditor *51*
judgment debtor *51*
execution *51*
liable *53*
nominal damages *53*
contingent fee *53*
PI *53*
deep pocket *54*
prima facie case *54*
admissible *55*
competent *56*
credibility *57*
burden of proof *57*
standard of proof *57*
preponderance of the evidence *57*
reasonable doubt *58*
fact particularization *58*
attestation clause *61*
rebut *62*

REVIEW QUESTIONS

1. What are the main stages of tort litigation?
2. What are some of the major roles of paralegals at the agency, pretrial, trial, appeal, and enforcement stages of tort litigation?
3. How do liability, damages, and collectability help determine whether a law office will take a tort case?
4. What is the distinction between a judgment creditor and a judgment debtor?
5. What is a prima facie case?
6. What are some of the major categories of background facts that a law office should obtain about every new client?
7. Name three guides to fact gathering in a tort practice.
8. Distinguish between evidence that is admissible and a witness who is competent.
9. How do you organize facts into versions?
10. What is the distinction between burden of proof and standard of proof?
11. What is the distinction between preponderance of the evidence and proof beyond a reasonable doubt?
12. What is fact particularization and how does it help the office achieve specificity and comprehensiveness in fact gathering?
13. What are the main guidelines in taking a witness statement?

HELPFUL WEBSITES

- **Initial Interview**
  wiki.injuryboard.com
  (type "initial interview" in search box)
- **Obtaining Factual Information about People or Businesses**
  www.switchboard.com
  www.bigbook.com
  www.people.yahoo.com
  www.whowhere.com
  www.accurint.com
  www.iaf.net
  www.four11.com
  www.merlindata.com
  www.zabasearch.com
  www.555-1212.com
- **Finding Assets**
  www.knowx.com
  www.ussearch.com
  www.tracerservices.com
  www.members.tripod.com/proagency/ask8.html
- **More on Finding Information about Businesses**
  www.sec.gov/edgar.shtml (SEC filings; Edgar)
  www.edgar-online.com
  www.annualreports.com
  www.bloomberg.com
  www.hoovers.com
  www.onesource.com
  www.dnb.com
  www.lexisnexis.com/risk/
  www.corporateinformation.com
  www.thecorporatelibrary.com

Student StudyWARE™ CD-ROM
For additional materials, please go to the student CD in this book.

CHAPTER

4

FORESEEABILITY IN TORT LAW

CHAPTER OUTLINE

- Introduction
- Defining Foreseeability
- Foreseeability Spectrum
- Objective Standard
- Factors That Determine Foreseeability
- Review of Steps to Determine Foreseeability

CHAPTER OBJECTIVES

After completing this chapter, you should be able to:

- State the meaning of foreseeability.
- Understand the spectrum of foreseeability.
- Compare subjective standard and objective standard.
- Distinguish between intent and knowledge with substantial certainty.
- State the factors that determine foreseeability.

INTRODUCTION

Foreseeability is a critical concept in tort law. For example, in later chapters we will see that foreseeability can have a major role in three elements of negligence:

- duty
- breach of duty
- proximate cause

Foreseeability is also relevant to some of the intentional and strict-liability torts. Before studying any of these torts, we need to spend some time analyzing the concept of foreseeability. Given its critical importance, we will be referring back to this discussion throughout the remainder of the book.

The central question of this chapter is: How do we determine foreseeability? This question is explored through the following topics:

- the meaning of foreseeability
- the spectrum of foreseeability
- foreseeability as an objective standard
- phrasing the foreseeability question
- factors that determine foreseeability

The legal consequences of foreseeability will be considered in later chapters. For now, our concern is the nature of foreseeability itself.

DEFINING FORESEEABILITY

foreseeable Having the quality of being seen or known beforehand; anticipated.

In everyday language, foresee means "to see or know beforehand." **Foreseeable**, the adjective, simply describes that which one can see or know beforehand. From a legal perspective, however, the emphasis is on the *extent* to which something can be known beforehand. It is important to understand that the question, "Is it foreseeable?" is less significant than the question, "How foreseeable is it?" Or, to combine the two questions: "How foreseeable is it, if at all?" Foreseeability is primarily a question of the *extent* to which something can be anticipated.

It is also important to understand that foreseeability is determined *before the fact*. If you want to know, for example, whether a fire was foreseeable, you mentally turn the clock back to the period of time *before* the fire occurred and ask: How likely was it, if at all, that a fire would occur? This determination is not made on the basis of what happens after the fact. An event or result is not foreseeable simply because it happened.

FORESEEABILITY SPECTRUM

To assess the foreseeability of an event or result, you must pinpoint it on a scale or *spectrum of foreseeability*. Exhibit 4–1 presents this spectrum. The threshold question is whether the event or result was foreseeable in any shape, fashion, or form. If the answer is no, the inquiry is ended. If, however, the answer is yes, then the next and most important inquiry is *how* foreseeable the event or result was. Where on the spectrum did it fall before it happened?

The categories on the spectrum are not mutually exclusive. There is no scientific or measurable distinction among all the items on the spectrum. The categories are rough approximations on the higher-to-lower ranges of what could be anticipated.

intent 1. Design, plan, or purpose in performing an act. 2. The desire to cause the consequences of one's act (or failure to act), or the knowledge with substantial certainty that the consequences will follow from what you do (or fail to do).

Note the last item on the spectrum: foreseeability to a certainty. When something is that foreseeable, the law says that you *intended* the event or result to occur. The general meaning of **intent** is design, plan, or purpose in performing an act. In the law of torts, however, intent has a more specific meaning: the desire to cause the consequences of one's act (or failure to act), or the knowledge with substantial

Exhibit 4–1
Foreseeability spectrum: How foreseeable, if at all?

(Suppose, for example, you are trying to determine how forseeable it was that a child would dart in front of a car and be hit.)

- WAS IT FORSEEABLE ?
  - NO
  - YES — HOW FORSEEABLE ?
    - Highly unusual (a freakish occurrence)?
    - Unusual?
    - Slight possibility?
    - A possibility?
    - Slight probability?
    - A fair probability?
    - Highly probable?
    - Predictable almost to a certainty?
    - A certainty?

certainty that the consequences will follow from what one does (or fails to do). **Knowledge with substantial certainty** means a high degree of knowledge. This level of knowledge exists when you have no more than minimal doubt about a result that will flow from what you do or fail to do. If you pull the trigger of a gun aimed at a crowd a few feet in front of where you are standing, you cannot claim that you did not intend to shoot the person who was hit. You may have hoped and prayed that no one would be hit, but a court will probably find that you had substantially certain knowledge that someone would be hit. In the eyes of the law, you intended this result. You have committed a battery.

knowledge with substantial certainty A high degree of knowledge; having no more than minimal doubt about a result that will flow from what you do or fail to do.

OBJECTIVE STANDARD

When foreseeability is an issue in the law, we often ask two questions:

- Was the event or result foreseeable to the defendant? (You answer this question by applying a **subjective standard.**)
- Would the event or result have been foreseeable to a reasonable person? (You answer this question by applying an **objective standard.**)

subjective standard A standard by which something is measured by what a particular person actually knew, felt, or did.

objective standard A standard by which something is measured by comparing (a) what a person actually knew, felt, or did with (b) what a reasonable person would have known, felt, or done under the same circumstances.

In most cases, the second question is asked only when the answer to the first question is no.

A subjective standard simply means that everything is measured solely by what a particular person—the defendant—actually knew, felt, or did. Suppose, for example, we want to know whether it was foreseeable that Ted Vinson's dog would bite the mail carrier last Monday morning. Assume that the dog has bitten mail carriers (and others) in the past and that the dog runs loose in the front yard where the mailbox is located. Assume further that Ted is totally oblivious of the dog's biting habits and believes he owns the most gentle and friendly dog in the world. He has forgotten that the dog has bitten people before. By a subjective standard, the Monday bite was not foreseeable to Ted. He may have been silly in thinking the dog is harmless, but if he honestly (actually) believed the dog would not bite anyone, then the Monday bite was not foreseeable to him.

Suppose, however, we apply an objective standard to the dog bite case. An objective standard measures something by reference to what a **reasonable person** under the same or similar circumstances would have known, felt, or did. What do we mean by a reasonable person? We will spend a great deal of time on this topic in later chapters. For now, suffice it to say that a reasonable person is someone who uses ordinary prudence under the circumstances to avoid injury or other loss.

reasonable person Someone who uses ordinary prudence under the circumstances to avoid injury or other loss. Also called ordinary prudent person. (Called reasonable man in older cases.)

Would a reasonable person have foreseen that the dog would bite the mail carrier last Monday? An ordinary, prudent person would *not* have been oblivious of this dog's prior biting habit and would have understood that an untied dog with such a habit will probably bite again. Hence, by an objective standard, the bite was foreseeable, and probably highly foreseeable since the dog was kept near the mailbox.

If a defendant did not foresee something that a reasonable person would have foreseen, we are able to say that the defendant *should have foreseen* it. We cannot reach this conclusion, however, until we make an assessment of what a reasonable person would have foreseen—using an objective standard. This is the process that we will go through in this book when foreseeability is an issue.

FACTORS THAT DETERMINE FORESEEABILITY

Rarely do we have enough facts to determine how foreseeable something was or was not. Hence, determining foreseeability requires a probing for further facts. Questions need to be asked about the facts that you do not have, and often, about the facts that you do have. For this reason, effective interviewing and investigation are critical to reaching intelligent conclusions about foreseeability.

The foreseeability factors in Exhibit 4–2 provide a framework for asking the right questions about foreseeability. There are eight factors to consider:

area	human nature
activity	history
people	sensory data
preparation	common sense

Exhibit 4–2 Factors that determine foreseeability.

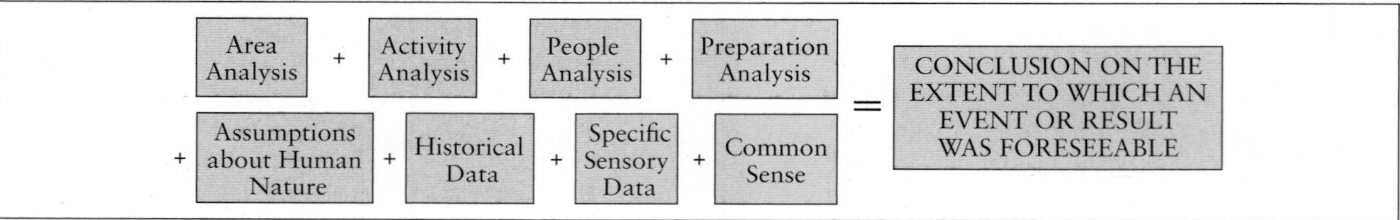

We will examine each of the eight factors separately, even though there will be overlap among them.

Area Analysis

The nature of the area can sometimes be very important. If, for example, a child is hit by a car, it is important to know whether the accident occurred in a residential area, near a school, at a playground, etc. From the nature of the area, how foreseeable is it that children will be around? If an accident occurs in a supermarket, it is equally important to assess the area. It is usually a crowded, closed area with many products stacked on shelves or on the floor. What is foreseeable given these conditions? A rotted tree branch falls and hits the plaintiff. Where did this occur? In the country? In a city? A suburb? A zoo? A park? How, if at all, would the area affect the foreseeability of what happened? An explosion occurs in a university lab. A lab is a place for experiments and the storage of chemicals. Danger is usually more foreseeable in a lab than in other areas.

Activity Analysis

Area and activity are intimately related. What specific activities were going on at the time of the accident or event whose foreseeability we are assessing? Swimming?

Driving? Walking? Running? Eating? Selling? Dynamiting? What occurs during this activity? What is frequently foreseeable? Occasionally foreseeable? Rarely foreseeable? Examine the nature of the activity or activities themselves. What do they tell you (or what should they tell you) about what might be anticipated from these activities?

People Analysis

What kind of people were involved in the activities that led to the event or result whose foreseeability is being examined? How would you characterize them, and does this characterization tell you something about what should have been foreseeable by them or by others interacting with them? Were they children? Adults? Trespassers? Doctors? Mechanics or others with special knowledge and skills? What is normally expected from such people? What precautions do they usually take or fail to take? We have expectations about certain kinds of people. What are the expectations in this case? Do these expectations help us determine what should have been foreseeable?

Preparation Analysis

What do people usually do before they engage in the activities you listed? Is any long-term preparation needed, e.g., training, testing? Short-term preparation, e.g., checking equipment, looking out for obstacles? No preparation? The data received from preparation will usually be relevant to foreseeability.

Assumptions about Human Nature

This factor is very similar to the people analysis except that it is more general. What kind of behavior is usually expected of anyone engaged in the kind of activity in question? In driving a car, for example, can you assume that other drivers will *not* always obey all traffic laws? When people are in danger, can you assume that they will act in self-defense? Can you assume that people will gravitate toward pleasurable, attractive things or events? Can you assume that many people will not read five pages of fine-print instructions? Such assumptions, when they can be made, are often relevant to what might be anticipated from people.

This is not to say that any of these assumptions are to be condoned or that they justify conduct in any way. The law that applies to conduct is a separate matter that will be considered in later chapters. Here we are limiting ourselves to a consideration of the extent of foreseeability, independent of any specific legal consequences.

Historical Data

The more something has occurred in the past, the more foreseeable is its reoccurrence. Have incidents of a similar nature occurred in the past? If so, under what circumstances? How often? How well known were they? A customer sues a restaurant for food poisoning after eating a tuna sandwich. We want to know if this sickness was foreseeable to the owner of the restaurant. Has the owner had similar complaints about this meal in the past? Has the owner heard of problems other restaurants have had? Is this the first time the owner became aware of such a problem? Historical data can be quite relevant to foreseeability.

Specific Sensory Data

What did their eyes, ears, nose, fingers, feet, etc. tell the parties just before the incident? Did any of this sensory data provide signs of what might happen? Are certain things foreseeable in certain kinds of weather? (Was this kind of weather foreseeable?) Visibility is often relevant to foreseeability. What factors affected visibility, e.g., weather, time of day, or presence of obstructions? Were there distractions that prevented people from being aware of a danger? If so, were these distractions foreseeable?

Common Sense

Common sense is a catchall factor. Include here any question that was not covered under any of the other factors. Most of the other factors should have led you to questions and observations grounded in common sense. Here we simply reinforce the central role of this factor and ask ourselves to what extent something was or was not foreseeable based on common sense.

EXAMPLE

Jones builds a swimming pool in his backyard. The use of the pool is restricted to Jones family members and guests who are present when an adult is there to supervise. One hot summer night, a neighbor's child opens an unlocked door of a fence that surrounds the Jones yard and goes into the pool. (There is no separate fence around the pool itself.) The child knows he is not supposed to be there without an adult. No one else is at the pool. The child drowns.

> **Foreseeability question:** To what extent was it foreseeable that a neighbor's child would violate a rule of the owner of the pool not to use it unless an adult was present, open a closed fence door to get to the pool, and drown in it?

From the facts, it appears that Jones built his pool in a residential area. If so, it certainly was foreseeable that children would be in the area. Jones should have anticipated that children would be drawn to the pool. The neighbor's child used the pool while no one was around. (We need to know how old the child was.) It would help to know whether people use each other's pools in this way in the neighborhood. If it is common, then it is more foreseeable to Jones that a child would use his pool without permission or supervision in spite of his rule to the contrary. Why did he impose this rule? Because of prior pool trespassing in the neighborhood? Swimming is generally considered a dangerous activity, particularly for children. It is foreseeable, however, that many children will not be able to fully protect themselves in water.

There was no separate fence around Jones's pool; there was simply an unlocked door to a fence around the yard. Was it foreseeable to Jones that this might be an inadequate precaution? Again, this may depend on the frequency with which children have made unauthorized use of pools in the area and the extent to which Jones knew about this or should have known about it. Are other pools in the area left unlocked and unguarded at night? It is true that Jones had a rule that adults must be present. But is this rule enough? Shouldn't Jones have assumed that a child would *not* obey such a rule? Has any child ever violated this rule in the past? Have there ever been children using the Jones pool without adults present? If so, then Jones was on notice that it could happen again. What steps did Jones take, if any, to make sure that neighborhood children and their parents knew about his rule?

We also need to know whether there have been any recent swimming pool accidents in the area. The drowning took place at night. (We do not know whether any of the Jones family members were at home at the time.) Common sense tells us that a child will be tempted to use an easily accessible swimming pool in the summer and that drowning is a fair probability when there is no supervision.

ASSIGNMENT 4.1

a. You have just read a series of facts and factual questions relevant to whether the swimming pool tragedy was foreseeable. Categorize each of these facts and questions under the eight categories of Exhibit 4–2. Specify what falls under area analysis, activity analysis, people analysis, preparation analysis, assumptions about human nature, historical data, specific sensory data, and common sense. Place a fact or a question under more than one category if there is overlap.
b. Under each of these eight areas, what additional questions would you want to ask to enable you to determine whether the tragedy was foreseeable?

REVIEW OF STEPS TO DETERMINE FORESEEABILITY

1. Turn the clock back to the time before the event/result in question occurred—foreseeability is determined *before* the fact.
2. Apply the foreseeability factors of Exhibit 4–2 to the situation.
3. From the range of "highly unusual" to "a certainty," draw your conclusion of where the event/result falls on the foreseeability spectrum.
4. Give a counteranalysis. If both sides are not going to agree on the extent to which the event/result was foreseeable, state the other side.

ASSIGNMENT 4.2

Assess the foreseeability of the events listed in the following situations. Go through the four steps just listed. Include a large number of factual questions you would raise, and state how these factual questions might be relevant to the foreseeability of the result or event in question.

a. The ABC Company manufactures cooking stoves. Smith buys one of the stoves. There is no heat in Smith's kitchen. Hence, Smith often turns the stove on, opens the oven door, and rests his feet on the door while sitting on a chair in front of the stove. One day, the stove collapses forward onto Smith while he is warming his feet in this way. Smith is severely injured. Was this injury foreseeable to the ABC Company?
b. A hobo hitching a ride on a railroad train falls off and injures himself. Was this injury foreseeable to the railroad?

ASSIGNMENT 4.3

Accidents happen to all of us throughout our lives. Think of an event in your life involving an accident that was somewhat of a surprise to you when it occurred. It can be a major or a minor accident. In class the teacher will select one student to be interviewed by the rest of the class (i.e., to be the interviewee) in order to determine how foreseeable the accident was to you (subjective standard) and how foreseeable it would have been to a reasonable person (objective standard).

Instructions to interviewee: If you are selected, start by telling the class what the accident was. The class will then ask you questions relevant to foreseeability. (Feel free to change any facts to preserve privacy.)

Instructions to class: Everyone in the class will conduct the interview of the interviewee. Raise your hand when you have a question. Your questions should cover the eight categories of area, activity, people, preparation, assumptions about human nature, historical data, specific sensory data, and common sense. When the teacher indicates that the interview is over, everyone should answer questions a and b below. The teacher will then lead a class discussion on the differences and similarities in the answers among the students.

a. The interviewee was asked to select an accident that was somewhat of a surprise when it occurred. Based on the interviewee's answers to the questions asked, where on the foreseeability spectrum do you think the interviewee would place the accident? Where on the foreseeability spectrum would you place it?
b. Would the accident have been foreseeable to a reasonable person? Where on the foreseeability spectrum would a reasonable person place it?

PROJECT

In Google, Bing, or another general search engine, run this single-word search: foreseeability.

(1) Quote any three sites that provide different definitions.
(2) Other than definitions, what kinds of information do you find on the Internet about foreseeability? Describe and categorize the different kinds of sites you find.

ETHICS IN A TORTS PRACTICE

You are a paralegal working in the law office of Frank Davis, Esq., who is representing a supermarket that is being sued by a customer who slipped and fell in the produce aisle. You tell your brother about this case, including the fact that the supermarket is about to be acquired by a large holding company. Unknown to you, your brother later buys shares in the stock of the holding company. It was not a good buy because the price of the stock has steadily declined since he bought it. What ethical problems, if any, might exist?

SUMMARY

Foreseeability means the extent to which we can see or know something beforehand. It is determined before the fact; something is not foreseeable simply because it happened. The spectrum of foreseeability ranges from highly unusual to a virtual certainty. (If something falls into the latter category, it was intended.) When foreseeability is an issue, we ask if the event or result was foreseeable to the defendant (answered by using a subjective standard). If not, the law sometimes requires us to ask if the event or result would have been foreseeable to a reasonable person (answered by applying an objective standard). Assessing foreseeability requires an analysis of the area involved, the activity undertaken, the people involved, the preparation involved, assumptions about human nature, historical data, specific sensory data, and common sense.

KEY TERMS

foreseeable *66*
intent *66*
knowledge with substantial certainty *67*
subjective standard *67*
objective standard *67*
reasonable person *67*

REVIEW QUESTIONS

1. In which three elements of negligence is foreseeability relevant?
2. In what other categories of torts is foreseeability relevant?
3. What is the definition of foreseeability?
4. What is the spectrum of foreseeability?
5. What is the distinction between a subjective standard and an objective standard?
6. What is a reasonable person?
7. When is something so foreseeable that it is intended?
8. What factors are considered when determining whether something is foreseeable?

HELPFUL WEBSITES

- ***Whittaker v. Saraceno***
  masscases.com/cases/sjc/418/418mass196.html
  (case discussing the foreseeability of an assault in a negligence suit against a building owner)
- **Google Books**
  Go to the Google site containing scanned books (books.google.com) and run this search: torts foreseeable foreseeability

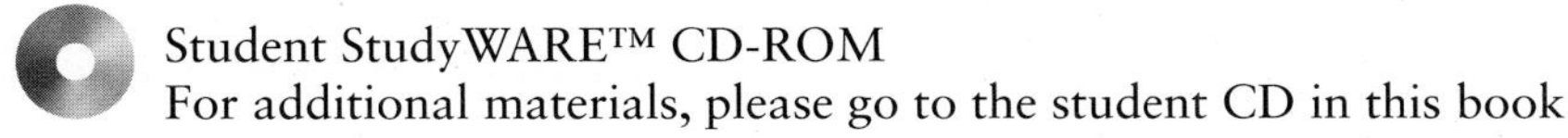

Student StudyWARE™ CD-ROM
For additional materials, please go to the student CD in this book.

CHAPTER

5

BATTERY

CHAPTER OUTLINE

- Introduction
- Act
- Material Touching
- Person
- Intent
- Harmful or Offensive Contact
- Damages
- Consent and Privilege

CHAPTER OBJECTIVES

After completing this chapter, you should be able to:

- Understand the distinction between the torts of battery and assault.
- Distinguish between civil and criminal battery.
- Identify the elements of battery.
- Identify the defenses to battery.
- State the damages that can be awarded in battery cases.
- Describe possible paralegal roles in battery litigation.
- Know the major sources (traditional and online) for researching issues in battery cases.

INTRODUCTION

battery An unpermitted and intentional physical contact with a person that is harmful or offensive.

Battery is an unpermitted and intentional physical contact with a person that is harmful or offensive. (See Exhibit 5–1 for the elements of this tort.) The easiest case is when the defendant punches the plaintiff in the nose. Many make the mistake of saying that the punch was an "assault." Although the words *battery* and *assault* are sometimes confused, we need to keep the concepts separate. As we will see in the next chapter, assault is a separate tort that does not require actual contact with the plaintiff. To commit the tort of assault all you need is the awareness (called an apprehension) of contact that is harmful or offensive. If actual contact *also* occurs, the victim may be able to sue for the tort of battery as well as for the tort of assault. The distinction between the two torts is the result—what the victim experiences. A battered victim experiences unwanted contact; an assaulted victim experiences unwanted apprehension of contact. By the time you finish studying this chapter and the next one, you should know why Sleeping Beauty, if she woke up angry, could have sued the kissing prince for battery, but not for assault.

Exhibit 5–1
Elements of the tort of battery.

Battery
1. Act
2. Intent to cause (a) an imminent contact with the plaintiff's person or (b) an apprehension of such contact
3. Contact that is harmful or offensive
4. Causation of the harmful or offensive contact

Our focus in this chapter is the tort of *civil* battery; our focus in the next chapter is the tort of *civil* assault. By civil we simply mean noncriminal. Every state also has criminal laws that cover the same or similar conduct as the torts we are examining. The terms used for these crimes differ among the states. The crimes might be called criminal battery, criminal assault, "assault and battery," etc. Exhibit 5–2 presents an overview of some of the major differences among battery and assault as torts and as crimes.

deep pocket 1. An individual, business, or other organization with resources to pay a potential judgment. 2. Sufficient assets for this purpose. The opposite of *shallow pocket*.

The tort of battery is frequently committed, but rarely litigated. A major reason for this is that most batterers are not **deep pockets**, meaning individuals who have enough resources from which a plaintiff can collect a judgment. The vast majority of people who commit intentional torts such as battery are shallow pockets—individuals without substantial assets. Furthermore, liability insurance policies generally do not cover intentional torts, whereas they do cover the most common cause of injury, automobile negligence. In typical domestic violence cases, batteries are committed among family members who often have neither the resources nor the inclination to bring civil tort actions against each other. And, as we will see in Chapter 27, the defense of *intrafamily tort immunity* may prevent such suits. Of course, criminal prosecution may be an option if the conduct falls within the definitions of criminal battery and assault.

We turn now to a closer examination of each of the elements of the tort of battery.

ACT

act A voluntary movement of the body.

There must be an **act** by the defendant that leads to contact with the plaintiff's person. An act is a voluntary movement of the body. Not all harmful or offensive contacts are the result of acts. For example, if Dan's arm hits Linda during a sleep walk, no battery exists because there is no act—no voluntary movement of Dan's body that caused the contact.

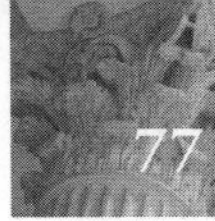

Exhibit 5–2 Battery and assault as torts and as crimes.

Category	What the Victim Experiences	What the Perpetrator Intends	Example	Comments	Court
TORT Battery (civil battery)	A physical contact that is harmful or offensive	The defendant intends that the victim receive a physical contact or an apprehension of such contact.	Dave shoves Paul when Paul cuts into a ticket line.	Dave has committed the tort of battery against Paul.	Paul can go to civil court and bring a civil cause of action (battery) against Dave. Both Paul and Dave are the parties in this civil action.
TORT Assault (civil assault)	An apprehension (awareness) of contact that is harmful or offensive	The defendant intends that the victim receive a physical contact or an apprehension of such contact. (The intent in assault is the same as the intent in battery. The difference is in the result—what the victim experiences.)	After Paul is pushed by Dave, Paul raises his cane and charges Dave, who runs away before Paul reaches him.	Paul has committed the tort of assault against Dave.	Dave can go to civil court and bring a civil cause of action (assault) against Paul. Both Paul and Dave are the parties in this civil action.
CRIME Examples of differences among the states: • *Criminal battery* requires a bodily injury or other offensive touching. • *Criminal assault* is an attempted battery. • *Criminal assault* has the same meaning as *criminal battery*. • The crime is called *assault and battery*.	States differ on what the victim of the crime suffers. It could be physical injury, offensive touching, or an apprehension (awareness) of such injury or touching.	States differ on the defendant's intent. It could be the same as for the torts of civil assault and civil battery or it could include the requirement of an intent to inflict physical injury or other offensive touching.		The same conduct can be both a tort and a crime.	The victim can go to the prosecutor (e.g., district attorney) and ask the prosecutor to bring criminal charges against the alleged wrongdoer in a criminal court. The case is brought by the state. The victim is a witness, not a party. The parties in the criminal case are the state and the alleged wrongdoer.

MATERIAL TOUCHING

In most battery cases, something concrete or material touches the body of the plaintiff, e.g., a fist, a stick, or a ball. But size is not significant. If, for example, you are given a glass of soda with poison in it, you have been battered by the poison. What about contact with smoke? Not all courts agree that smoke in the plaintiff's face can make the smoker liable for battery. In one case, a court said that there was a cause of action for battery against a smoker who intentionally blew cigar smoke in the face of the plaintiff in order to humiliate the plaintiff.[1] In general, however, when someone is subjected to secondhand smoke, most courts conclude that the contact is not "offensive" as this term is defined in the law of battery (see discussion below on harmful or offensive contact).

PERSON

person The human body, something attached to the body, or something so closely associated with the body as to be identified with it.

The definition of **person** is broad. It means one's body, anything attached to the body, or anything so closely associated with the body as to be identified with it. A kick in the shin is clearly a contact with the body. So is a yank on a tie or other item of clothing worn by the plaintiff. The following cases also illustrate the broader definition of person:

- the defendant knocks off the plaintiff's hat
- the defendant pulls a plate out of the plaintiff's hand
- the defendant stabs or shoots a horse while the plaintiff is riding it

The hat, plate, and horse are so closely associated with the body in these cases as to be practically identified with it at the time of the contact. There does not have to be contact with the physical body.

INTENT

intent (for battery) The desire (a) to bring about an imminent contact or an apprehension of such contact, or (b) the knowledge with substantial certainty that an imminent contact (or its apprehension) will result from what one does or fails to do. (See glossary for a general definition of intent.)

imminent Immediate in the sense of no significant or undue delay. Near at hand; about to occur.

For purposes of battery, **intent** is the desire to bring about an **imminent** contact or to bring about an apprehension of such contact. (As we will see in a moment, the contact must be harmful or offensive, but the victim does not have to prove that the defendant wanted or intended to do something harmful or offensive; all that is required is that the defendant intended a contact.) Imminent means immediate in the sense of no significant delay. In most cases, intent is not difficult to prove, because it is clear that the defendant wants to make contact with the plaintiff, e.g., the defendant picks up a bucket of water and pours it on the plaintiff's head. It is more difficult to prove intent when the defendant does not want contact to occur, but merely wants the plaintiff to think it will occur.

EXAMPLE
Mary throws a hammer at George. She aims it several feet above George's head, hoping to scare him. Unfortunately, it hits him in the eye.

apprehension An understanding, awareness, anticipation, belief, or knowledge of something.

Mary can accurately say that she did not intend to hit George, but this is not a defense. She wanted him to think he was about to be hit. She intended to cause an **apprehension** (i.e., an understanding or awareness) of an imminent contact. This is sufficient to establish the element of intent. Fear is not required, although fear is certainly an example of apprehension.

Suppose that there is no desire to cause a contact or even an apprehension of one.

EXAMPLE
Fred throws a stone through an open window of a crowded moving bus. His purpose is to have it pass through another open window at the other side of the bus without anyone noticing. One of the passengers, however, is hit by the stone.

knowledge with substantial certainty (for battery) A high degree of knowledge that contact (or its apprehension) will result from what one does or fails to do. (See glossary for a general definition of knowledge with substantial certainty.)

Did Fred intend to hit the passenger? In general, intent is the desire to bring about the consequences of an act or the **knowledge with substantial certainty** that the consequences will follow from the act. If Fred had substantially certain knowledge that a passenger would be imminently hit (or would have an apprehension of such a hit), then he intended that result. Note, however, that merely being **careless** or even **reckless** is not enough to establish intent. There must be substantially certain knowledge. If all you can show is carelessness or recklessness, the tort to bring is *negligence* in creating an unreasonable risk of injuring someone, not the intentional tort of battery. (There is no such thing as a negligent battery.)

careless Failing to use reasonable care; negligent.

reckless Consciously taking a risk in failing to exercise due care but without intending the consequences; wantonly disregarding a risk but neither desiring the consequences nor having substantially certain knowledge of the consequences of the risk.

CASE

Garratt v. Dailey

46 Wash. 2d 197, 279 P.2d 1091 (1955)
Supreme Court of Washington

Background: *Ruth Garratt suffered a fractured hip from a fall that occurred when five-year-old Brian Dailey removed the chair Garratt was about to use. She sued Dailey for battery. The trial court found for Dailey, holding that boy did not have the intent to commit battery. The case is now on appeal before the Supreme Court of Washington.*

Decision on Appeal: *The case is sent back (remanded) to the trial court to clarify its finding on intent. (As you read this opinion, pay careful attention to why the court said that someone can commit a battery even if that person did not have the motive of wanting to injure or embarrass anyone.)*

OPINION OF COURT

Justice HILL delivered the opinion of the court:

The liability of an infant for an alleged battery is presented to this court for the first time. Brian Dailey (age five years, nine months) was visiting with Naomi Garratt, an adult and a sister of the plaintiff, Ruth Garratt, likewise an adult, in the back yard of the plaintiff's home, on July 16, 1951. It is plaintiff's contention that she came out into the back yard to talk with Naomi and that, as she started to sit down in a wood and canvas lawn chair, Brian deliberately pulled it out from under her. . . . The trial court . . . adopted instead Brian Dailey's version of what happened, and made the following findings:

> "III. . . . that while Naomi Garratt and Brian Dailey were in the back yard the plaintiff, Ruth Garratt, came out of her house into the back yard. Some time subsequent thereto defendant, Brian Dailey, picked up a lightly built wood and canvas lawn chair which was then and there located in the back yard of the above described premises, moved it sideways a few feet and seated himself therein, at which time he discovered the plaintiff, Ruth Garratt, about to sit down at the place where the lawn chair had formerly been, at which time he hurriedly got up from the chair and attempted to move it toward Ruth Garratt to aid her in sitting down in the chair; that due to the defendant's small size and lack of dexterity he was unable to get the lawn chair under the plaintiff in time to prevent her from falling to the ground. That plaintiff fell to the ground and sustained a fracture of her hip, and other injuries. . . .
>
> "IV. That the preponderance of the evidence in this case establishes that when the defendant, Brian Dailey, moved the chair in question *he did not have any wilful or unlawful purpose in doing so; that he did not have any intent to injure the plaintiff, or any intent to bring about any unauthorized or offensive contact with her person* or any objects appurtenant thereto; that the circumstances which immediately preceded the fall of the plaintiff established that the defendant, *Brian Dailey, did not have purpose, intent or design to perform a prank or to effect an assault and battery upon the person of the plaintiff.*" (Italics ours, for a purpose hereinafter indicated.) . . .

It is urged that Brian's action in moving the chair constituted a battery. A definition (not all-inclusive but sufficient for our purpose) of a battery is the intentional infliction of a harmful bodily contact upon another. The rule that determines liability for battery is given in 1 *Restatement, Torts,* 29, § 13, as:

> "An act which, directly or indirectly, is the legal cause of a harmful contact with another's person makes the actor liable to the other, if
>
> "(a) the act is done with the intention of bringing about a harmful or offensive contact or an apprehension thereof to the other or a third person. . . .
>
> In the comment on clause (a), the *Restatement* says:
>
> "Character of actor's intention. In order that an act may be done with the intention of bringing about a harmful or offensive contact or an apprehension thereof to a particular person, . . . the act must be done for the purpose of causing the contact or apprehension or with knowledge on the part of the actor that such contact or apprehension is substantially

certain to be produced." See, also, *Prosser on Torts* 41, § 8.

We have here the conceded volitional act of Brian, i.e., the moving of a chair. Had the plaintiff proved to the satisfaction of the trial court that Brian moved the chair while she was in the act of sitting down, Brian's action would patently have been for the purpose or with the intent of causing the plaintiff's bodily contact with the ground, and she would be entitled to a judgment against him for the resulting damages. *Vosburg v. Putney,* 1891, 80 Wis. 523, 50 N.W. 403. . . .

After the trial court determined that the plaintiff had not established her theory of a battery (i.e., that Brian had pulled the chair out from under the plaintiff while she was in the act of sitting down), it then became concerned with whether a battery was established under the facts as it found them to be.

In this connection, we quote another portion of the comment on the "Character of actor's intention," relating to clause (a) of the rule from the *Restatement* heretofore set forth:

> "It is not enough that the act itself is intentionally done and this, even though the actor realizes or should realize that it contains a very grave risk of bringing about the contact or apprehension. Such realization may make the actor's conduct negligent or even reckless but unless he realizes that to a substantial certainty, the contact or apprehension will result, the actor has not that intention which is necessary to make him liable under the rule stated in this section."

A battery would be established if, in addition to plaintiff's fall, it was proved that, when Brian moved the chair, he knew with substantial certainty that the plaintiff would attempt to sit down where the chair had been. If Brian had any of the intents which the trial court found, in the italicized portions of the findings of fact quoted above, that he did not have, he would of course have had the knowledge to which we have referred. The mere absence of any intent to injure the plaintiff or to play a prank on her or to embarrass her, or to commit an assault and battery on her would not absolve him from liability if in fact he had such knowledge. *Mercer v. Corbin,* 1889, 117 Ind. 450, 20 N.E. 132. Without such knowledge, there would be nothing wrongful about Brian's act in moving the chair and, there being no wrongful act, there would be no liability.

While a finding that Brian had no such knowledge can be inferred from the findings made, we believe that before the plaintiff's action in such a case should be dismissed there should be no question but that the trial court had passed upon that issue; hence, the case should be remanded for clarification of the findings to specifically cover the question of Brian's knowledge, because intent could be inferred therefrom. If the court finds that he had such knowledge the necessary intent will be established and the plaintiff will be entitled to recover, even though there was no purpose to injure or embarrass the plaintiff. *Vosburg v. Putney,* supra. If Brian did not have such knowledge, there was no wrongful act by him and the basic premise of liability on the theory of a battery was not established.

It will be noted that the law of battery as we have discussed it is the law applicable to adults, and no significance has been attached to the fact that Brian was a child less than six years of age when the alleged battery occurred. The only circumstance where Brian's age is of any consequence is in determining what he knew, and there his experience, capacity, and understanding are of course material. . . .

The remand for clarification gives the plaintiff an opportunity to secure a judgment even though the trial court did not accept her version of the facts, if from all the evidence, the trial court can find that Brian knew with substantial certainty that the plaintiff intended to sit down where the chair had been before he moved it, and still without reference to motivation. . . .

The cause is remanded for clarification, with instructions to make definite findings on the issue of whether Brian Dailey knew with substantial certainty that the plaintiff would attempt to sit down where the chair which he moved had been, and to change the judgment if the findings warrant it. . . .

Remanded for clarification.

ASSIGNMENT 5.1

a. What was wrong with the trial court's findings of fact? Didn't the trial court find that there was no intent to cause an offensive contact?
b. Suppose that Brian Dailey was not aware of the presence of Ruth Garratt until he heard her fall just after he took the chair. Would he have had the required intent for battery under the guidelines of *Garratt v. Dailey?*
c. Two three-year-old children are standing on the edge of a bed. One says to the other, "Don't push me off." The other says, "I will so," and does so. Has there been a battery under the guidelines of *Garratt v. Dailey?*
d. Smith is an adult who suffers from severe paranoid schizophrenia that involves delusions of persecution, grandeur, and auditory hallucinations. He hits a stranger with a stick because he believed the stranger was Hitler coming to harm him. Has there been a battery under the guidelines of *Garratt v. Dailey?*

Transferred Intent

It is no defense to argue that the person hit is not the one the defendant intended to hit.

EXAMPLE
Helen fires a gun at Paul. She misses him, but strikes Rich, whom she did not see.

Helen has battered Rich. Under the **transferred-intent rule**, her intent to hit Paul is transferred to Rich. (For more on transferred intent, see Exhibit 6–2 in Chapter 6.)

transferred-intent rule The defendant may be liable for certain torts committed against the plaintiff even if the defendant intended to commit a different tort against the plaintiff (unintended tort) and even if the defendant intended to commit the tort against a different person (unintended plaintiff). (Does not apply to all torts. See Exhibit 6–2 in Chapter 6.)

Motive to Injure

To win in a battery action, the plaintiff does not have to show that the defendant's **motive** was to injure the plaintiff or that the defendant was malicious or hostile. In fact, a battery can be committed even if the defendant was trying to help the plaintiff through the contact.

motive A desire, reason, need, or emotion that induces action or inaction.

EXAMPLE
On a rainy night, John falls off the curb. When a passerby tries to help, John says, "Don't touch me." Nevertheless, the passerby lifts John to carry him out of the rain.

The passerby has battered John. The fact that the motive may have been to be of help is no defense. As long as the contact is harmful or offensive (see next section), the tort has been committed. When we study medical malpractice in Chapter 18, we will see that treatment by a doctor without the informed consent of the patient is a battery in some states. Here again, the fact that the doctor had a benevolent motive would not be a defense. Most states, however, prefer that patients use negligence as the cause of action when they are treated without their informed consent.

HARMFUL OR OFFENSIVE CONTACT

Contact is **harmful** if it brings about physical damage, impairment, pain, or illness in the body. It is **offensive** if it offends the personal dignity of a reasonable or ordinary person who is not unduly sensitive.

Any physical damage, impairment, pain, or illness—no matter how trivial or slight—is considered harmful. A slight push, for example, may cause only modest pain in one's arm, yet the pain would be classified as harmful, entitling the victim at least to **nominal damages**.

If there is no harmful contact, the plaintiff may still be able to recover if the contact is offensive. An *objective standard* is used to determine when contact is offensive. The test is whether the personal integrity or dignity of a reasonable or ordinary person—someone not unduly sensitive—would be offended by the contact. If not, there is no battery, even though the plaintiff considered the contact offensive.

harmful Involving physical damage, impairment, pain, or illness in the body.

offensive Offending the personal integrity or dignity of a reasonable or ordinary person who is not unduly sensitive.

nominal damages A trifling sum (e.g., $1) awarded to the plaintiff because there was no significant loss or injury suffered, although a technical invasion of rights did occur.

EXAMPLE
In a noisy, crowded subway, Jim approaches Cecile, a stranger. He gently taps her on the shoulder and says, "Would you please tell me the time?" Cecile is absolutely outraged by this contact, and screams.

A reasonable person would not consider this contact offensive, even though Cecile clearly does. In city life, a reasonable person expects a certain amount of contact as part of everyday living.

There is an exception to this rule when the defendant knows that the plaintiff has peculiar—even unreasonable—sensibilities about being touched. In such a case, the court will find the contact to be offensive even though someone of ordinary sensibilities would not be offended by it. The test of offensiveness is no longer objective when the defendant has such knowledge.

EXAMPLE

Same situation involving Jim and Cecile, except that she is not a stranger, and Jim knows that she would be angered by the tap.

Here the contact is offensive. Jim's knowledge of her idiosyncrasy makes it so. (Depending on the severity of the circumstances, she may even have an action for the separate tort of intentional infliction of emotional distress. See Chapter 9.)

Note, however, that some courts in battery cases refuse to extend the known-idiosyncrasy exception too far. A North Carolina court said, "it may be questioned whether any individual can be permitted, by his own fiat, to erect a glass cage around himself, and to announce that all physical contact with his person is at the expense of liability."[2]

One final point. Battery is a remedy that protects the body against intentional, unwanted contacts. The tort is committed even if one is not conscious of the contact. Patients under anesthesia, for example, can successfully bring a battery action against anyone whose contact with their bodies is harmful or offensive as we have been defining these terms.

CASE

Brzoska v. Olson

668 A.2d 1355 (1995)
Supreme Court of Delaware

Background: *The death of Delaware dentist Raymond Owens from AIDS made national news. Six hundred and thirty of his former patients took tests for HIV, which causes AIDS. None tested positive. Nevertheless, thirty-eight of the former patients sued for battery based on "offensive touching" during treatment. In the Superior Court, the plaintiffs lost; the judge ruled they had no basis to recover for "fear of AIDS" in the absence of an underlying physical injury. He granted summary judgment against them and thereby avoided a trial on the battery claim. The case is now on appeal before the Supreme Court of Delaware.*

Decision on Appeal: *Judgment is affirmed. There was no battery.*

OPINION OF COURT

Justice WALSH delivered the opinion for the majority:

In this appeal from the Superior Court, we confront the question of whether a patient may recover damages for treatment by a health care provider afflicted with Acquired Immunodeficiency Syndrome ("AIDS") absent a showing of a resultant physical injury or exposure to disease. . . . We conclude that the Superior Court correctly ruled that, under the circumstances of Dr. Owens' treatment, there can be no recovery for fear of contracting a disease in the absence of a showing that any of the plaintiffs had suffered physical harm. Specifically, plaintiffs cannot recover under battery as a matter of law because they could not show that their alleged offense was reasonable in the absence of being actually exposed to a disease-causing agent. . . .

In their Superior Court action, the plaintiffs alleged that each of them had been patients of Dr. Owens in 1990 or 1991. Each claimed to have received treatment, including teeth extraction, reconstruction and cleaning, during which their gums bled. The plaintiffs alleged that Dr. Owens was HIV-positive and that he exhibited open lesions and memory loss at the time of such treatment. The plaintiffs did not allege the contraction of any physical ailment or injury as a result of their treatment, but claimed to have suffered "mental anguish" from past and future fear of contracting AIDS. They also alleged embarrassment in going for medical testing to a State clinic which they found to be "an uncomfortable environment." Plaintiffs sought compensation and punitive damages for mental anguish. . . .

Although a battery may consist of any unauthorized touching of the person which causes offense or alarm, the test for whether a contact is "offensive" is not wholly subjective. The law does not permit recovery for the extremely sensitive who become offended at the slightest contact. Rather, for a bodily contact to be offensive, it must offend a *reasonable* sense of personal dignity. *Restatement (Second) of Torts* § 19 (1965). . . .

Plaintiffs contend that the "touching" implicit in the dental procedures performed by Dr. Owens was offensive because he was HIV-positive. We must therefore determine whether the performance of dental procedures by an HIV-infected dentist, standing alone, may constitute offensive bodily contact for purposes of battery, i.e., would such touching offend a *reasonable* sense of personal dignity? . . .

HIV is transmitted primarily through direct blood-to-blood contact or by the exchange of bodily fluids with an infected individual. In a dental setting, the most probable means of transmission is through the exchange of bodily fluids between the dentist and patient by percutaneous (through the skin) contact, by way of an open wound, non-intact skin or mucous membrane, with infected blood or blood-contaminated bodily fluids. During invasive dental procedures, such as teeth extraction, root canal and periodontal treatments, there is a risk that the dentist may suffer a percutaneous injury to the hands, such as a puncture wound caused by a sharp instrument or object during treatment, and expose the dentist and patient to an exchange of blood or other fluids. . . .

The risk of HIV transmission from a health care worker to a patient during an invasive medical procedure is very remote. In fact, even a person who is *exposed* to HIV holds a slim chance of infection. The CDC has estimated that the theoretical risk of HIV transmission from an HIV-infected health care worker to patient following actual percutaneous exposure to HIV-infected blood is, by any measure, less than one percent.

Here, plaintiffs have alleged no injuries which stem from their exposure to HIV. Instead, plaintiff's alleged "injuries" arise solely out of their *fear* that they have been exposed to HIV. In essence, they claim mental anguish damages for their "fear of AIDS.". . . As earlier noted, the offensive character of a contact in a battery case is assessed by a "reasonableness" standard. In a "fear of AIDS" case in which battery is alleged, therefore, we examine the overall reasonableness of the plaintiffs' fear in contracting the disease to determine whether the contact or touching was offensive. Since HIV causes AIDS, any assessment of the fear of contracting AIDS must, ipso facto, relate to the exposure to HIV. Moreover, because HIV is transmitted only through fluid-to-fluid contact or exposure, the reasonableness of a plaintiff's fear of AIDS should be measured by whether or not there was a channel of infection or actual exposure of the plaintiff to the virus. It is unreasonable for a person to fear infection when that person has not been exposed to a disease. . . .

In sum, we find that, without actual exposure to HIV, the risk of its transmission is so minute that any fear of contracting AIDS is *per se* unreasonable. We therefore hold, *as a matter of law,* that the incidental touching of a patient by an HIV-infected dentist while performing ordinary, consented-to dental procedures is insufficient to sustain a battery claim in the absence of a channel for HIV infection. In other words, such contact is "offensive" only if it results in actual exposure to the HIV virus. We therefore adopt an "actual exposure" test, which requires a plaintiff to show "actual exposure" to a disease-causing agent as a prerequisite to prevail on a claim based upon fear of contracting disease. Attenuated and speculative allegations of exposure to HIV do not give rise to a legally cognizable claim in Delaware. . . .

In this case, plaintiffs have not been exposed to HIV, but rather, they have been exposed only to an HIV-infected dentist. Plaintiffs merely hypothesize as to how a possible exposure to HIV could have occurred without offering any substantiating evidence to that effect. Plaintiffs have shown nothing except that their risk of HIV infection was theoretical and remote. As such, plaintiffs' claims do not rise above mere speculation. . . .

In conclusion, the tort of battery requires a harmful or offensive contact, and "offensive" conduct is tested by a reasonableness standard. We hold that the fear of contracting a disease without exposure to a disease-causing agent is *per se* unreasonable. Thus, absent actual exposure to HIV, plaintiffs cannot recover for fear of contracting AIDS. . . .

The judgment of the Superior Court [on the battery claim] is affirmed. . . .

Justice DUFFY, . . . dissenting:

The [focus of the] majority opinion . . . is on so-called "AIDS-phobia" claims which are based on fear of the virus and nothing more. But that is not this case. . . . Here there is much more than the "phobia" which the majority condemns as arising from ignorance, unreasonable suspicion, general paranoia or fragile sensibility. Indeed, there is an abundance of evidence from which a jury could conclude that the fears of plaintiffs—or some of them—that they may have contracted a fatal disease were reasonable. . . . [P]laintiffs have offered evidence to show that the contacts were offensive because the possibility of the transmission of AIDS (at the time of treatment) was greater than a statistical average because of: Dr. Owens' health, his open lesions and where they were, the stage or progression of his disease at the time of patient contact, the advice given by his own physician to stop treating patients, his casual attitude with respect to washing, and whether or not Dr. Owens complied with the advised precautions. . . .

ASSIGNMENT 5.2

a. Did the court say it did not believe the patients' statement that they felt the contact with the dentist was offensive?
b. The court says that these plaintiffs were unreasonably sensitive to find the contact with the dentist to be offensive. Would the case be different if Dr. Owens knew one of the patients was very sensitive about surface-skin contact with an infected person? Would this change the result of the court as to this patient?
c. A healthy person spits in the face of the plaintiff, a stranger. No injuries result from this act, but the plaintiff sues for battery. Was the contact offensive? If so, how does this case differ from the *Brzoska* case?
d. In January of 2009, a disease breaks out among people who live in the Southwest section of the city. Many of the infected die. No one knows what is causing the disease. Mary Smith does not live in this section. On June 4, 2009, she is on a bus in the city. John Davis is running for county supervisor. He walks up to Mary and offers to shake her hand. She does so. Later when she learns that John lives in the Southwest section of the city and has the disease, she sues him for battery. Does *Brzoska* apply? Assume that Mary does not contract the disease.
e. Tom and Linda are drug addicts. Tom knows that he has AIDS, but Linda does not know this. They have sexual relations and share each other's drug needles. Has either of them committed a battery?
f. Peterson is a professional boxer. He is in the ring with Dutton, who appears healthy. During the match, Dutton starts bleeding from a jab from Peterson. Some of the blood gets on Peterson's arm. Later Peterson learns that Dutton has AIDS and sues Dutton's estate for battery. Would the court in the *Brzoska* reach the same result on these facts?

DAMAGES

As indicated, nominal damages (e.g., $1) can be awarded if a technical battery has been committed without any significant harm suffered by the plaintiff. On the other hand, if significant harm does result, damages can be awarded for that harm even if its extent was not foreseeable by the defendant.

EXAMPLE

After a heated argument about a game, Tom throws a basketball at Bill's back while Bill is walking away. Bill has a seizure and must be hospitalized for two days. Unknown to Tom, Bill had a rare spine disease, which was activated when he was hit by the basketball, leading to the seizure.

Someone who has an unusual vulnerability to injury or illness is said to have a thin skull. Under the **thin-skull rule**, a defendant is liable for the foreseeable and unforeseeable injuries of the plaintiff that result from the defendant's negligence or intentional tort so long as the general nature or type of harm was a foreseeable consequence of the original risk created by the tort. Throwing a hard object at someone's back certainly creates a risk of injuring that person's back. It is no defense for the wrongdoer to argue that he or she never anticipated the particular kind of back injury that would result.

thin-skull rule If the general nature or type of harm was a foreseeable consequence of the original risk, the defendant will be liable for the harm even if the extent of the harm was not foreseeable. Also called eggshell-skull rule.

CONSENT AND PRIVILEGE

Consent is a complete defense. There is no liability for battery if the plaintiff voluntarily permitted the contact.

consent Voluntary agreement or permission (express or implied) that something should happen or not happen.

EXAMPLE

The plaintiff offers her arm to a doctor who is inoculating everyone in line.

The plaintiff cannot later say that the doctor battered her. She consents to the contact if certain conditions are met, e.g., she has the capacity to consent, she voluntarily does so, and she knows what she is consenting to. We will have a good deal more to say about consent when we examine *assumption of the risk* in Chapter 17 and the general nature of consent in Chapter 27.

In medical cases, consent can be an issue in three categories of cases: a doctor performs an unwanted procedure, performs a requested procedure on the wrong part of the body, or fails to provide adequate information on the risks of a particular procedure. The first two categories constitute **medical battery**. In some states, the third category of failing to obtain informed consent also constitutes battery, although most states classify it as negligence, as we saw earlier and as we will see again in Chapter 18 on medical malpractice.

medical battery An unwanted procedure performed by a health care practitioner or a requested procedure performed on the wrong part of the body.

If the defendant has a **privilege** to cause a contact with the plaintiff, the latter cannot win a suit for battery. The privileges include self-defense, the defense of others, the defense of property, discipline, and arrest. The elements of these privileges are discussed in Chapters 7 and 27.

privilege The right to act contrary to the right of another without being subject to tort or other liability. A defense that authorizes conduct that would otherwise be wrongful. (See glossary for a broader definition of privilege.)

ASSIGNMENT 5.3

a. Bill is behind the steering wheel of his parked car. He sees Helen take a baseball bat and swing it at the windshield directly in front of him. The windshield cracks but does not shatter. Has a battery been committed? Why or why not? What other torts, if any, might have been committed?

b. Ed throws a snowball at Dan's house, knowing that Dan is inside. The moment Dan hears the snowball, he is afraid that he will be hit. Battery?

c. Has a battery been committed in the following situations? If not, what other torts, if any, might have been committed?
   (1) Barbara leaves a batch of cookies with poison in them in the hall next to a telephone booth. A stranger eats one after making a call.
   (2) Sam serves a batch of cookies with bacon grease in them to George. Sam knows that George's religion forbids the eating of meat.
   (3) Fred's apartment neighbor, Jim, dislikes loud music. To annoy Jim, Fred blasts boom-box music in his apartment.

d. Diane and Bob are walking across the street. Bob is daydreaming and doesn't see a car about to hit him. Diane pushes him away from the path of the car into safety. But he falls and breaks his ankle from the push. Bob sues Diane for battery. What result?

e. Discuss whether victims of date rape can always successfully sue for battery.

BATTERY CHECKLIST

Definitions, Relationships, Paralegal Roles, and Research References

Category
Battery is an intentional tort.

Interest Protected by This Tort
The right to be free from a harmful or offensive bodily contact.

Elements
1. Act
2. Intent to cause (a) an imminent contact with the plaintiff's person or (b) an apprehension of such contact
3. Contact that is harmful or offensive
4. Causation of the harmful or offensive contact

Definitions of Major Words/Phrases in the Elements

Act: A voluntary movement of the defendant's body.

Intent:
a. The desire to bring about imminent harmful or offensive contact or an apprehension of such imminent contact, or
b. The knowledge with substantial certainty that imminent harmful or offensive contact will result from what one does or fails to do.

Harmful: Involving physical damage, impairment, pain, or illness in the body.

Offensive: Offending the personal integrity or dignity of a reasonable or ordinary person who is not unduly sensitive.

Person: The human body, something attached to the body, or something so closely associated with the body as to be identified with it.

Causation: Either
a. but for the defendant's act or omission, the consequences would not have occurred (i.e., the contact would not have occurred), or
b. the defendant's act or omission was a substantial factor in bringing about the consequences (i.e., the contact).

Major Defense and Counterargument Possibilities That Need to Be Explored
1. There was no voluntary movement of the defendant's body (no act).
2. The defendant had no desire to make contact with the plaintiff, nor any substantially certain knowledge that such contact would result from what the defendant did (no intent).
3. The contact was neither harmful nor offensive.

BATTERY CHECKLIST *(Continued)*

4. But for what the defendant did, the contact would have resulted anyway. The defendant was not a substantial factor in producing the contact. (No causation.)
5. The plaintiff consented to the defendant's contact (on the defense of consent, see Chapter 27).
6. The contact resulted while the defendant was defending him- or herself from the plaintiff (on self-defense and other self-help privileges, see Chapter 27).
7. The contact occurred while the defendant was defending someone else from the plaintiff (on the defense of others and other self-help privileges, see Chapter 27).
8. The contact occurred while the defendant was defending property or recapturing chattels from the plaintiff (on the privileges of necessity, defense of property, recapture of property, and other self-help privileges, see Chapter 27).
9. The contact occurred while the defendant was disciplining the plaintiff (on discipline and other self-help privileges, see Chapter 27).
10. The contact occurred while the defendant was arresting the plaintiff (on the privilege of arrest, see Chapter 8).
11. The plaintiff's suit against the government for a battery committed by a government employee may be barred by sovereign immunity (on sovereign immunity, see Chapter 27).
12. The plaintiff's suit against the government employee for battery may be barred by official immunity (on official immunity, see Chapter 27).
13. The plaintiff's suit against the charitable organization for a battery committed by someone working for the organization may be barred by charitable immunity (on charitable immunity, see Chapter 27).
14. The plaintiff's suit against a family member for battery may be barred by intrafamily tort immunity (on intrafamily tort immunity, see Chapter 22).
15. The plaintiff failed to take reasonable steps to mitigate the harm caused when the defendant committed battery; therefore, damages should not cover the aggravation of the harm caused by the plaintiff (on the mitigation-of-damages rule, see Chapter 16).

Damages

The plaintiff can recover compensatory damages, including pain and suffering, medical bills, and loss of wages. Damages can include unforeseeable consequences of the battery. If the defendant acts out of hatred and malice in committing the battery, punitive damages are commonly awarded as well. (On the categories of damages, see Chapter 16.)

Relationship to Criminal Law

The same act of the defendant can constitute a *civil* battery (for which the plaintiff recovers damages) and a *criminal* battery (for which the state collects a fine or imposes jail or imprisonment). The crime may be called assault, criminal battery, assault and battery, etc.

Other Torts and Related Actions

Assault: If there was no contact, but the plaintiff was placed in apprehension of an imminent contact that is harmful or offensive, the tort of assault may have been committed.

False Imprisonment: While committing the tort of false imprisonment, battery may also have been committed if contact was made with the plaintiff's person during or just before the confinement.

Negligence: (a) There may have been a harmful or offensive contact that was not intentional, hence no battery. Yet if the contact was due to carelessness or unreasonable conduct by the defendant, negligence should be explored. A negligence action requires proof of actual harm. See Chapter 16. (b) A doctor who fails to obtain informed consent from a patient may have committed negligence (although some states call it a battery). See Chapter 18 on medical malpractice.

Wrongful Death: A wrongful death action can be brought by the survivors of the deceased if death resulted from the battery.

Federal Law

a. Under the Federal Tort Claims Act, the United States government will *not* be liable for a battery committed by one of its federal employees within the scope of

BATTERY CHECKLIST *(Continued)*

employment (respondeat superior) *unless* the federal employee is an investigative or law enforcement officer. (See Exhibit 27–7 in Chapter 27.) (Most states have their own statutes that cover when tort claims can be made against the state for battery and other torts committed by state government employees. Such claims are also covered in Chapter 27.)

b. There may be liability under the Civil Rights Act if the battery was committed while the defendant was depriving the plaintiff of a federal civil right under color of state law. (See Exhibit 27–9 in Chapter 27.)

Employer–Employee (Agency) Law

A private (non-government) employee who commits a battery is personally liable for this tort. His or her employer will *also* be liable for battery if the conduct of the employee was within the scope of employment (respondeat superior). The employee must be furthering a business objective of the employer at the time. Intentional torts such as battery, however, are often outside the scope of employment. If so, only the employee is liable for the battery. (On the factors that determine the scope of employment, see Exhibit 14–9 in Chapter 14.)

Paralegal Roles in Battery Litigation

(See also Exhibit 3–1 in Chapter 3, Exhibit 20–4 in Chapter 20, and Exhibit 29–1 in Chapter 29.)

Fact finding (help the office collect facts relevant to prove the elements of battery, the elements of available defenses, and extent of injuries or other damages):

- client interviewing
- field investigation
- online research (e.g., find newspaper accounts of a public brawl)

File management (help the office control the documents involved in a battery litigation):

- open client file
- enter case data in computer database
- maintain file documents

Litigation assistance (help the trial attorney prepare for a battery trial and appeal, if needed):

- draft discovery requests
- draft answers to discovery requests
- draft pleadings
- digest and index discovery documents
- help prepare, order, and manage trial exhibits
- prepare trial notebook
- draft notice of appeal
- order trial transcript
- cite-check briefs
- perform legal research

Collection/enforcement (help the trial attorney for the judgment creditor to collect the damages award or to enforce other court orders at the conclusion of the battery case):

- draft postjudgment discovery requests
- conduct field investigation to monitor compliance with judgment
- perform online research (e.g., location of defendant's business assets)

Research References for Battery

Digests

In the digests of West Group, look for case summaries on battery under key topics such as:

Assault and Battery
Torts
Damages
Death

Corpus Juris Secundum

In this legal encyclopedia, see the discussion under topic headings such as:

Assault and Battery
Torts
Damages
Death

BATTERY CHECKLIST *(Continued)*

American Jurisprudence 2d
In this legal encyclopedia, see the discussion under topic headings such as:

Assault and Battery
Torts
Damages
Death

Legal Periodical Literature
There are two index systems to use to try to locate legal periodical literature on battery:

Index to Legal Periodicals and Books (ILP)
See literature in *ILP* under subject headings such as:
- Assault and Battery
- Damages
- Federal Tort Claims Act
- Personal Injuries
- Torts
- Wrongful Death

Current Law Index (CLI)
See literature in *CLI* under subject headings such as:
- Assault and Battery
- Torts
- Damages
- Personal Injuries

Example of a legal periodical article you will find by using *ILP* or *CLI:*

Smoker Battery: An Antidote to Second-Hand Smoke by Donald B. Ezra, 63 Southern California Law Review 1061 (1991).

A.L.R., A.L.R.2d, A.L.R.3d, A.L.R.4th, A.L.R.5th, A.L.R.6th, A.L.R. Fed., A.L.R. Fed. 2d
Use the *ALR Index* to locate annotations on battery. In this index, check subject headings such as:

Assault and Battery
Damages
Torts

Example of an annotation on battery you can locate through this index:

Civil Liability of Insane or Other Disordered Person for Assault or Battery, by C. R. McCorkle, 77 A.L.R.2d 625 (1961).

Words and Phrases
In this multivolume legal dictionary, look up *battery, harmful, offensive, apprehension,* and every other word or phrase connected with the tort discussed in this chapter. The dictionary will give you definitions of these words or phrases from court opinions.

CALR: Computer-Assisted Legal Research

Example of a query you could ask on Westlaw or on LexisNexis to try to find cases, statutes, or other legal materials on battery: **battery /p damages**

Example of search terms you could use on an Internet legal search engine such as the Public Library of Law (www.plol.org), Findlaw (www.findlaw.com), or Google Scholar (scholar.google.com) to find cases, statutes, or other legal materials on battery: **civil battery tort**

Example of search terms you could use on an Internet general search engine such Google, Bing, or AltaVista to find cases, statutes, or other legal materials on battery: **+civil +battery +tort**

More Internet sites to check for materials on battery and other torts:
www.hg.org/torts.html
www.megalaw.com/top/top.php (click "Intentional Torts," "Personal Injury Law," "Tort Law," and "Damages")
See also the online sites in Overview of Tort Law at the end of Chapter 1.

CHECK THE CITE

A teenage member of a church is suspected of being demonically possessed. She objects, however, to a "laying on of hands" by church officials to combat the demon. What difficulties will she have in suing the church for battery? Summarize the holding of *Pleasant Glade Assembly of God v. Schubert*, 264 S.W.3d 1 (Supreme Court of Texas 2008). To read the majority opinion online: (1) Go to the Texas court site (www.courts.state.tx.us). In the search box, type the names of the parties (Pleasant Glade v. Schubert). Find the opinion dated June 27, 2008. (2) Run a citation search ("264 S.W.3d 1") in the Legal Opinions and Journals database of Google Scholar (scholar.google.com).

PROJECT

In Google, Bing, or another general search engine:

(1) Run a search on smoke and the tort of battery (e.g., smoke battery tort). Write a short essay on whether tobacco smoke can be the basis of a tort action. You can consult as many websites as you wish, but you must quote from at least three separate sites.

(2) Run the following two separate searches: "Garrett v. Dailey" and "Brzoska v. Olson." For each opinion, quote commentary on the opinion from three separate sites. Do not include commentary from courts.

ETHICS IN A TORTS PRACTICE

You work in a law office that is representing John Franklin, who is suing his wealthy ex-wife, Nora Smith, for battery. After the divorce, Franklin says Smith came to his apartment and threw a glass cup at the back of his head. You are a paralegal in the office. On your own time, you do pro bono work at a women's rights office where you help draft restraining orders in domestic violence cases. While at the shelter, you see a report that says Nora Smith was a client of the office several times during her marriage with John Franklin because of beatings she received from him. What ethical problems, if any, might exist?

SUMMARY

Battery is an unpermitted and intentional physical contact with a person that is harmful or offensive. The tort of battery differs from the tort of assault; the latter does not require actual contact. The same conduct can constitute the tort of battery and the crime of battery, sometimes called assault and battery. For the tort of battery there must be a voluntary movement of the defendant's body—an act. There must be actual contact with the person or with something attached to the body or so closely associated with the body as to be identified with it. The intent must be either a desire to bring about an imminent contact or an imminent apprehension of such contact.

If the defendant intends to make contact with one person but in fact hits another, the law will transfer the intent to cover the latter. The plaintiff does not have to prove that the defendant intended to injure the plaintiff. The fact that the defendant was trying to help the plaintiff is not a defense if the conduct was harmful or offensive. Contact is harmful if it brings about physical damage, impairment, pain, or illness. It is offensive if it offends the personal integrity or dignity of a reasonable or ordinary person who is not unduly sensitive. This objective test of offensiveness is used unless the defendant has reason to know that the plaintiff has an overly sensitive reaction to the contact. The plaintiff does not have to be aware of the contact. Under the thin-skull rule, a defendant is liable for the foreseeable and unforeseeable injuries of the plaintiff that result from the defendant's battery if the general nature or type of harm was a foreseeable consequence of the original risk created by the battery. Consent and privilege are defenses to this tort.

KEY TERMS

battery *76*
deep pocket *76*
act *76*
person *78*
intent (for battery) *78*
imminent *78*
apprehension *78*
knowledge with substantial certainty (for battery) *78*
careless *79*
reckless *79*
transferred-intent rule *81*
motive *81*
harmful *81*
offensive *81*
nominal damages *81*
thin-skull rule *85*
consent *85*
medical battery *85*
privilege *85*

REVIEW QUESTIONS

1. What is a battery?
2. How does battery differ from assault?
3. How does civil battery differ from criminal battery?
4. Why is battery rarely litigated?
5. What is an act?
6. Can smoke blown in someone's face be the basis of a battery?
7. When can contact with something other than the body be the basis of a battery?
8. What intent must be proven for a battery?
9. Is apprehension the same as fear?
10. Can a reckless contact be the basis of a battery?
11. What is the transferred-intent rule?
12. When is a contact harmful? When is it offensive?
13. Does the plaintiff have to prove that the defendant wanted to harm or offend the plaintiff?
14. What is the thin-skull rule of damages?
15. What is a medical battery?
16. Name some of the privileges that constitute defenses to battery.

HELPFUL WEBSITES

- **Elements of Battery**
  In Google, Bing, or another search engine, run this search: elements battery tort
- **Battery Basics**
  injury.findlaw.com/assault-and-battery/battery-basics.html
  www.querrey.com/assets/attachments/160.pdf
  injury.findlaw.com/assault-and-battery/elements-of-a-battery.html
  battery.uslegal.com/
- **Battery Action against Nurse for Switching Medication**
  www.nursinglaw.com/nursemedication.PDF

ENDNOTES

1. *Leichtman v. WLW Jacor Communications, Inc.*, 634 N.E.2d 697 (Ohio C. App. 1994).
2. *McCracken v. Sloan*, 40 N.C. App. 214, 217, 252 S.E.2d 250, 252 (North Carolina Court of Appeals 1979) quoting W. Prosser, *Handbook of the Law of Torts* 37 (4th ed. 1971).

Student StudyWARE™ CD-ROM
For additional materials, please go to the student CD in this book.

CHAPTER 6

ASSAULT

CHAPTER OUTLINE

- Introduction
- Act
- Apprehension
- Harmful or Offensive
- Intent
- Threats of Force and a Statutory Cause of Action
- Damages

CHAPTER OBJECTIVES

After completing this chapter, you should be able to:

- Understand the distinction between the torts of assault and battery.
- Identify the elements of assault.
- Identify the defenses to assault.
- Explain how a threat of force can constitute a FACE cause of action.
- Describe paralegal roles in assault litigation.
- List the major sources (traditional and online) for researching issues in assault cases.

INTRODUCTION

assault An apprehension of an imminent harmful or offensive contact resulting from the defendant's intent to cause this apprehension or the contact itself.

Assault is an apprehension of an imminent harmful or offensive contact resulting from the defendant's intent to cause this apprehension or to cause the contact itself. The tort consists of intentionally causing an awareness of a battery. (See Exhibit 6–1 for the elements of assault.)

Exhibit 6–1
Elements of the tort of assault.

Assault
1. Act
2. Intent to cause (a) an apprehension of an imminent harmful or offensive contact or (b) the imminent harmful or offensive contact itself
3. Apprehension of an imminent harmful or offensive contact with the plaintiff's person
4. Causation of the apprehension

The average citizen thinks of assault as an unwanted, and usually violent, contact with someone. But the tort of assault does not require actual contact. If someone hits you with a stick, a battery has been committed. If you were aware of the stick coming at you, an assault has *also* been committed. The contact and the apprehension (awareness) of the contact constitute separate torts. In criminal law, assault often means a violent contact; in the law of torts, however, it is the apprehension of a harmful or offensive contact. For more on the distinction between the tort of assault and the crime of assault or battery, see exhibit 5–2 in chapter 5.

ACT

act A voluntary movement of the body.

The apprehension of a harmful or offensive contact must be caused by an **act**, which is a voluntary movement of the body.

EXAMPLE
A stranger pushes Jim, who then falls toward Ed. When Ed sees Jim coming, he quickly gets out of the way.

Ed, concerned about being hit by Jim, clearly had an apprehension of a harmful or offensive contact. But Jim did not commit an act that caused this apprehension. Because of the stranger's push, Jim involuntarily moved toward Ed. The stranger committed an act; Jim did not.

APPREHENSION

apprehension An understanding, awareness, anticipation, belief, or knowledge of something.

Apprehension is an understanding, awareness, anticipation, belief, or knowledge of something. It is not the equivalent of fear, although fear qualifies as apprehension.

EXAMPLES
- Greg (a 300-pound wrestler) swings his fist at Martha (a seventy-year-old, petite widow) because she called him a "bum" at a match. Terrified, Martha ducks just in time to avoid his punch.
- Later, Martha raises her newspaper to strike Greg in the stomach. Laughing, Greg steps back to avoid Martha's swing.

Greg and Martha have assaulted each other. Both had an awareness—an apprehension—of a harmful or offensive contact. Martha was afraid; Greg was not. But fear or intimidation is not required.

Greg laughed. Doesn't this mean the threatened contact was not harmful or offensive? It depends on the meanings of harmful and offensive. This brings us to the third element of assault.

HARMFUL OR OFFENSIVE

As we saw in Chapter 5 on battery, **harmful** means physical damage, impairment, pain, or illness in the body. A smack on the stomach with a newspaper could cause pain, no matter how slight. An *objective standard* is used to determine when an apprehension is **offensive**. The test is whether the personal integrity or dignity of a reasonable or ordinary person—someone not unduly sensitive—would be offended by the apprehension. Most people would be upset if they saw that they were about to be hit with a newspaper by someone who was angry at them. It is hardly a friendly gesture. Greg may have thought it was all a big joke. Yet note that he stepped back to avoid the newspaper. To him, the idea of a fight with an old lady may have been ludicrous, but he clearly didn't appreciate being hit. Most people wouldn't. He was not *afraid* of a harmful or offensive contact, but he surely had an *apprehension* of one, however minor it might have been.

harmful Involving physical damage, impairment, pain, or illness in the body.

offensive Offending the personal integrity or dignity of a reasonable or ordinary person who is not unduly sensitive.

Imminent

The apprehension must be of an **imminent** harmful or offensive contact. A future or **conditional threat** is not enough.

imminent Immediate in the sense of no significant or undue delay. Near at hand; about to occur.

conditional threat A communicated intent to do something dangerous or unwanted in the future if a specified event occurs.

EXAMPLE
On Monday, Ted calls Don on the phone and says, "If you don't pay your debt to me by this Friday, I'll be by Saturday to kill you." When Don hangs up the phone, he breaks out in a sweat because he knows Ted can be violent.

There is no doubt that Don apprehends a very dangerous harmful and offensive contact. Yet it is not an imminent contact. It is scheduled to happen in the future (Saturday), and is conditional (on not paying the debt by Friday). Imminent means immediate, without significant delay. Verbal threats alone are often not sufficient when they explicitly relate to future conduct. Furthermore, the defendant must have the **apparent present ability** to carry out the threat. If the defendant points a toy gun at the plaintiff and threatens to shoot, there is no imminent apprehension if the plaintiff knows that the gun is a toy that is incapable of firing anything.

apparent present ability Appearing reasonably able to do something now or very shortly.

Cyberstalking

In our digital age, **cyberstalking** has become a serious problem. It consists of the use of the Internet or other electronic means to repeatedly embarrass, humiliate, threaten, or otherwise harass someone. (If the victim is a minor, the conduct is sometimes referred to as **cyberbullying**.) When the contacts contain threats (e.g., "I will kill you"), has the tort of assault been committed? Probably not, because of the absence of an apparent *present* ability to carry out the threat. The person making the threat is sitting behind his or her own computer, often in another part of the city or state.

Yet cyberstalking can cause substantial emotional harm. Another tort to consider is intentional infliction of emotional distress (IIED). As we will see in Chapter 9, however, this is a narrow tort that does not apply to every act that causes emotional distress. Some legislatures have passed statutes that make cyberstalking a crime. Filing a complaint under such statutes with law enforcement authorities is more likely to provide relief for the victim than currently available tort remedies.

cyberstalking The use of the Internet or other electronic means to repeatedly embarrass, humiliate, threaten, or otherwise harass someone. Also called cyberharassment.

cyberbullying The use of the Internet or other electronic means to repeatedly embarrass, humiliate, threaten, or otherwise harass a minor. Also called cyberharassment.

ASSIGNMENT 6.1

a. Recall the example given in the text of the stranger pushing Jim, who then falls toward Ed. When Ed sees Jim coming toward him, he quickly gets out of the way. As we said in the text, Jim did not commit an assault on Ed. What torts, if any, did the stranger commit?

b. Several Ku Klux Klan members in white robes stand on the sidewalk five feet in front of a black person's house for about thirty minutes before walking away. The black person is terrified. Have the KKK members assaulted this person?

c. Sam puts an unloaded gun on the table in front of Mary and says, "This is for you if you don't cooperate." Mary knows the gun is unloaded but is terrified because Sam has thrown things at her in the past. Did Sam assault Mary with the gun?

d. In a secluded alley, Steve points a gun at Ed and says, "Your money or your life." Has Ed been assaulted?

e. Dan is a teenage neighbor of Harry, an eight-year-old sensitive child. Dan likes to tease Harry. One day Dan picks up Harry's toy gun and says, "I can do magic and make this gun real and I'm going to do it now so that I can shoot you." Terrified, Harry runs into the house. Has Dan assaulted Harry?

CASE

Allen v. Walker

569 So. 2d 350 (1990)
Supreme Court of Alabama

Background: *Kathryn Allen and Richard Walker both work for Gulf States Paper Company. Following an argument, she sued him for assault. The lower court granted Walker a summary judgment. The case is now on appeal before the Supreme Court of Alabama.*

Decision on Appeal: *Judgment for Kathryn Allen. There is sufficient evidence to support an action for assault.*

OPINION OF COURT

Justice ALMON delivered the opinion of the court. . . .

Kathryn and Walker were employed at Gulf States' plant in Demopolis and were members of the same union. During a conversation concerning the proper method of filing a grievance against Gulf States with the union, Walker allegedly shook his finger at Kathryn's face. Kathryn told Walker that the last man who pointed his finger at her "was sorry that he did it." Walker then allegedly stated that he would "whip [Kathryn's] ass anytime, anywhere." The conversation then ended and Kathryn returned to work. The next day she and Walker had a second confrontation, during which Walker allegedly repeated his earlier threat. Following that second incident Kathryn became "agitated and upset" and reported Walker's threats to her supervisor.

"An assault consists of '. . . an intentional, unlawful, offer to touch the person of another in a rude or angry manner under such circumstances as to create in the mind of the party alleging the assault a well-founded fear of an imminent battery, coupled with the apparent present ability to effectuate the attempt, if not prevented.' *Western Union Telegraph Co. v. Hill,* 25 Ala. App. 540, 542, 150 So. 709, 710 (1933)." *Holcombe v. Whitaker,* 294 Ala. 430, 435, 318 So.2d 289, 294 (1975). Words standing alone cannot constitute an assault. However, they may give meaning to an act, and when both are taken together they may create a well-founded fear of a battery in the mind of the person at whom they are directed, thereby constituting an assault.

Kathryn argues that Walker's alleged threats, when combined with the fact that he shook his finger in her face during their first conversation, created a question for the jury on the issue of assault. . . .

[W]e cannot say that, as a matter of law, Walker's acts and threats could not create a reasonable or well-founded apprehension of imminent physical harm. There was evidence that, after Walker's first alleged threat, [Kathryn] walked away. That evidence is not conclusive, however, as to whether she discounted the threat or whether she left to avoid the threatened harm. She also testified that, after the second alleged assault the next day, she had to leave work because she was so frightened and upset. . . .

[W]e conclude that Kathryn presented sufficient evidence that Walker's alleged threats created a well-founded fear of imminent harm and created a jury question on her claim of assault. Therefore, the summary judgment on that claim will be reversed. . . .

ASSIGNMENT 6.2

a. If someone says he can or will harm you "anytime, anywhere," isn't this a threat to do something to you in the future *if* you keep bothering him? Isn't that what Walker meant? Did the court say otherwise?
b. Kathryn told Walker that the last man who pointed his finger at her "was sorry that he did it." If she pointed her finger at Walker when she said this, would he have an assault case against her?

INTENT

The element of **intent** is the desire to bring about an imminent apprehension of a contact or the desire to bring about the contact itself. The tort can also be committed if the defendant knows with substantial certainty that an imminent apprehension will result from what the defendant does or fails to do.

intent (for assault) (a) The desire to bring about an apprehension of an imminent contact or the contact itself, or (b) the knowledge with substantial certainty that an imminent apprehension will result from what one does or fails to do. (See glossary for a general definition of intent.)

EXAMPLE
John wants to scare Barbara by running at her with the stroller he is pushing, making her think that he will ram the stroller into her knees. In fact, he intends to stop the stroller inches in front of her. John sees that Barbara has her arm around the shoulder of her younger sister, Helen, but he does not want to scare Helen.

If Barbara thinks she is going to be hit, she has been assaulted. John's intent was to scare her into thinking she would be hit (i.e., to cause Barbara to apprehend a contact). What about Helen? Has she been assaulted? The question is whether John knew with substantial certainty that Helen would apprehend being hit along with Barbara. He probably did, since he knew that they were so close together (Barbara had her arm around Helen) when he made his move. Hence, under the law, he intended Helen's apprehension as well.

Transferred Intent

Note that the intent element of assault is satisfied if the defendant's desire is to cause an apprehension *or* an actual contact. In our stroller example, let's change the facts:

EXAMPLE
John wants to hit (not just scare) Barbara by banging his stroller into her. As he moves forward, however, he trips. The stroller stops just in front of Barbara. She was not hit, but she thought she was going to be hit. (Assume that Barbara is alone when this occurs.)

John intended a contact, not an apprehension of one. Yet only an apprehension occurred. Under the **transferred-intent rule**, the element of intent is satisfied. He is liable for one tort (assault) even though he intended another tort (battery). Assault is an unintended tort for which the wrongdoer can be liable.

The transferred-intent rule is very broad. It applies to five unintended torts, not just to assault and battery. Furthermore, the rule also applies to unintended plaintiffs. Let's change the stroller example again by putting Helen back in the picture:

transferred-intent rule The defendant may be liable for certain torts committed against the plaintiff even if the defendant intended to commit a different tort against the plaintiff (unintended tort) and even if the defendant intended to commit the tort against a different person (unintended plaintiff). (Does not apply to all torts. See Exhibit 6–2.)

EXAMPLE
John wants to scare Barbara by running at her with the stroller he is pushing, making her think that he will ram the stroller into her knees. In fact, he intends to stop the stroller inches in front of her. John sees that Barbara has her arm around the shoulder of her younger sister, Helen, but he does not want to scare Helen. When John abruptly stops the carriage, Barbara is distracted so that only Helen fears being hit.

John has not assaulted Barbara because Barbara never experienced apprehension. Helen, however, clearly experienced apprehension. Has John assaulted her? The answer is "yes" under two possible theories, one of which we have already discussed. First, if John knew with substantial certainty that Helen would experience apprehension, then he intended the apprehension even though he did not want it to occur. Second, Helen is an unintended plaintiff under the transferred-intent rule. John never intended to commit a tort against Helen. Yet the tort he intended against one person (Barbara) is transferred to another person (Helen).

Exhibit 6–2 summarizes the transferred-intent rule that will make defendants liable to plaintiffs they did not intend to harm and for torts they did not intend to commit. As you can see in the exhibit, the rule applies to five intentional torts: assault, battery, false imprisonment, trespass to land, and trespass to chattels.

Exhibit 6–2 The transferred-intent rule: Unintended plaintiffs and unintended torts.

Unintended Plaintiff

a. Defendant (D) intends to commit one of the following five torts against P1:
   - Assault
   - Battery
   - False imprisonment
   - Trespass to land
   - Trespass to chattels

b. In fact, this tort is committed against P2.

c. D did not intend to commit this tort against P2.

Result: The law will transfer D's intent from P1 to P2 in order to make D liable for this tort to P2.

Examples:

- D wants to lock Mary in a room. D mistakes Fran for Mary and falsely imprisons Fran. D has committed false imprisonment against Fran.
- D throws a rock, intending to hit Paul's car. The rock misses Paul's car and hits Bill's van. D has committed trespass to chattels against Bill.

In the above two examples, it is irrelevant that D did not intend to commit any tort against Fran or Bill. They are unintended plaintiffs to whom D is liable under the transferred-intent rule.

Unintended Tort

a. Defendant (D) intends to commit acts that would constitute one of the following five torts:
   - Assault
   - Battery
   - False imprisonment
   - Trespass to land
   - Trespass to chattels

b. In fact, D commits one of the other four torts.

c. D did not intend to commit the tort that occurred.

Result: The law will transfer D's intent from the tort D intended to commit to the tort that in fact resulted in order to make D liable for the latter tort.

Example:

- D wants to lock Joe in a room. D does not succeed because the door to the room has no lock. By mistake, however, D causes Joe to be in apprehension of being hit. D has committed assault against Joe.

In the above example, it is irrelevant that D did not intend to commit assault against Joe. An unintended tort has been committed for which D is liable under the transferred-intent rule.

THREATS OF FORCE AND A STATUTORY CAUSE OF ACTION

The threat of force (e.g., "I'll kill you") can be the basis of a tort action for assault if, as we have seen, the plaintiff is reasonable in believing that the defendant will carry out the threat imminently. We will now examine the case of *Lucero v. Trosch*, in which a clergyman said that doctors who performed abortions "should be dead." At the time he made this statement, he was on a television program with a doctor who performed abortions. The doctor then sued the clergyman.

The basis of the suit was a federal statute that created a right to sue anyone who uses the "threat of force" to intimidate another when "obtaining or providing reproductive health services" (18 United States Code § 248(a)(1)). The doctor was a provider of reproductive health services. The question raised in the *Lucero* case is whether the clergyman used the threat of force to intimidate the doctor providing his services.

The doctor did not sue the clergyman for the tort of assault, although one of the questions you will be asked after you read the opinion is whether he could have done so.

The statute under which the doctor sued was the Free Access to Clinic Entrances Act—**FACE**. It is an example of a statute in which the legislature gives a citizen the right to obtain damages from someone who interferes with a basic right such as voting, protesting, or obtaining medical care. In Chapter 27 we will study more of these statutes, particularly the Civil Rights Act, the violation of which is sometimes referred to as a constitutional tort. (See Exhibit 27–9 in Chapter 27.) Anyone working in a personal injury law practice must be aware of two categories of suits for damages: (a) those based on the traditional torts and (b) those based on new causes of action created by the legislature in special statutes such as the Civil Rights Act and FACE.

FACE Free Access to Clinic Entrances Act. A federal statute that provides a remedy for victims of assault or other attack suffered while trying to obtain reproductive health services (18 United States Code § 248(a)(1) (www.usdoj.gov/crt/crim/248fin.php).

CASE

Lucero v. Trosch

904 F. Supp. 1336 (1995)
United States District Court, S.D. Alabama

Background: *Father David Trosch is an antiabortion activist. On a television talk show (Geraldo), he appeared with Dr. Bruce Lucero. On the show, Trosch said that he would kill an abortion doctor if he (Trosch) had a gun in his hand. He also said that Dr. Lucero, who performed abortions, "should be dead." Based on these statements, Lucero sued Trosch for violating the Free Access to Clinic Entrances Act (FACE). Trosch has moved to dismiss on the ground that the complaint against him does not state a cause of action. His position is that there is no need for a trial because even if he said what Lucero alleges, FACE has not been violated. Furthermore, Trosch asserts that FACE is unconstitutional. The court must now rule on Trosch's motion to dismiss.*

Decision of Court: *The motion to dismiss is denied. The case should go to trial. If Lucero can prove his allegations, FACE has been violated. Also, FACE is constitutional.*

OPINION OF COURT

Chief Judge BUTLER delivered the opinion of the court . . .:

Plaintiff Bruce Lucero, M.D. ("Lucero") is a physician who provides reproductive health services, including abortions, at the New Woman All Women Health Care Clinic in Birmingham, Alabama. On October 5, 1994, Lucero and defendant Fr. David Trosch ("Trosch") appeared as guests on the *Geraldo Show,* which was filmed in New York, New York. Transcripts of the show indicate that Trosch's responses to questions posed by the program's host included the following:

Q: Father David Trosch, would you murder an abortion doctor if you had the gun in your hand?
A: No, I would not murder him, but I would kill him, there's a difference. . . .
Q: Sitting alongside you, Dr. Bruce Lucero, a doctor who admits to performing abortions—
A: —he is a mass murder—
Q: —would you kill him?
A: He is a mass murderer and should be dead. Absolutely.
Q: He should be dead?
A: Should be dead. . . .
Q: Father Trosch, do you have the courage to say that you would kill him?
A: He deserves to be dead, [a]bsolutely. . . .

Two months previously, in August 1994, Trosch appeared on the *Shelly Stewart Show,* which was filmed in Birmingham, Alabama. The tenor of Trosch's remarks on *Shelly Stewart* was generally similar to that of his comments on *Geraldo,* as he asserted that those who provide abortions should be killed and suggested that he could possibly kill one who performed abortions.[1] Lucero was not present at the show's taping, and none of Trosch's statements on *Shelly Stewart* made specific reference to Lucero.

Lucero and the business at which he works, New Woman All Women Health Care Clinic, brought this action in the Northern District of Alabama, alleging that Trosch's conduct on the *Geraldo Show* and the *Shelly Stewart Show* violated the Free Access to Clinic Entrances Act. . . .

The Access Act creates a civil right of action against anyone who "by force or threat of force or by physical obstruction, intentionally injures, intimidates or interferes with or attempts to injure, intimidate or interfere with any person because that person is or has been, or in order to intimidate such person or any other person or any class of persons from, obtaining or providing reproductive health services." 18 U.S.C. § 248(a)(1).

---

[1]In particular, the following exchange took place on *Shelly Stewart:*

Q: If everyone listened to you, there would be people by the hundreds, by the thousands killed, wouldn't you say?
A: No, not at all. I believe if 20, 30, 40 doctors, abortionists, their staffs were killed, the rest of them would get out of the business. . . .
Q: Would you possibly yourself, pull the trigger and kill someone for performing an abortion?
A: Let me put it this way, Elijah slit the throats of 450 [prophets] of Al because of the evil they did, and they were not even murderers, so if Elijah could do it I suppose I could.
Q: You could kill?
A: In defense of innocent human beings, yes. . . .

Trosch contends that his words on the *Geraldo Show* did not rise to the level of force, threats of force, or physical obstruction sufficient to trigger the Access Act right of action, and that Lucero's claim for relief under the Act must be dismissed on that basis. In the alternative, Trosch contends that the Access Act is inapplicable because the statute excludes expressive conduct protected by the First Amendment.

Although the Access Act itself does not specifically define the term "threat of force," the Eleventh Circuit has elaborated on the term slightly, construing it as a "threat of physical force placing a person in reasonable apprehension of bodily harm." *Cheffer v. Reno,* 55 F.3d 1517, 1521 (11th Cir. 1995); see also *U.S. v. Brock,* 863 F. Supp. 851, 857 (E.D. Wis. 1994) (the Access Act is limited to "true threats", meaning those which could reasonably produce in victim a fear that threat would be carried out). . . .

Given the complaint's allegations of Trosch's words and the context in which they were spoken, the court cannot hold that a reasonable recipient could not have interpreted them as a serious expression of an intent to inflict bodily harm or death upon him. . . .

The fact that Trosch did not expressly state to Lucero that he was going to kill Lucero at some future time does not preclude a reasonable factfinder from determining that a threat was in fact made to Lucero. . . .

Trosch next contends that . . . his statements which aired on the *Geraldo Show* constituted protected speech under the First Amendment; therefore, he claims, Lucero is barred from invoking the civil remedies which would otherwise be available to him under the Access Act.

It is widely recognized that true threats of force are not cloaked in the protections afforded other types of speech by the First Amendment. . . .

If Trosch's remarks on the *Geraldo Show* were threats of force, then they cannot receive First Amendment protection. . . .

For all of the foregoing reasons, defendant's motion to dismiss the complaint for failure to state a claim upon which relief can be granted is DENIED. . . .

ASSIGNMENT 6.3

a. Would the court have reached the same result if the only comment made by Trosch was, "my conscience does not allow killing, but you, Dr. Lucero, should be stopped by any means possible"?
b. Did Father Trosch's comments constitute civil assault? Why or why not?

DAMAGES

A defendant who commits an assault is liable for the injuries of the plaintiff that result from this assault. This includes unforeseeable injuries if the general nature or type of harm was a foreseeable consequence of the original risk created by the assault. (See the discussion of the **thin-skull rule** at the end of Chapter 5.) Suppose, for example, the defendant's assault causes the plaintiff to miscarry. The plaintiff can recover damages for the miscarriage even if the miscarriage was unforeseeable to the defendant, so long as the general nature or type of harm was a foreseeable consequence of the original risk created by the assault.

thin-skull rule If the general nature or type of harm was a foreseeable consequence of the original risk, the defendant will be liable for the harm even if the extent of the harm was not foreseeable. Also called eggshell-skull rule.

ASSAULT CHECKLIST

Definitions, Relationships, Paralegal Roles, and Research References

Category
Assault is an intentional tort.

Interest Protected by This Tort
The right to be free from the apprehension of an imminent harmful or offensive contact.

Elements of This Tort

1. Act
2. Intent to cause (a) an apprehension of an imminent harmful or offensive contact or (b) the imminent harmful or offensive contact itself
3. Apprehension of an imminent harmful or offensive contact with the plaintiff's person
4. Causation of the apprehension

ASSAULT CHECKLIST *(Continued)*

Definitions of Major Words/Phrases in the Elements

Act: A voluntary movement of the defendant's body.

Intent:

a. The desire to bring about an apprehension of an imminent contact or the contact itself, or
b. The knowledge with substantial certainty that an imminent apprehension will result from what one does or fails to do.

Apprehension: An understanding, awareness, anticipation, belief, or knowledge of something (fear is not required although fear is an example of apprehension).

Imminent: Immediate in the sense of no significant or undue delay (something can be imminent without being instantaneous).

Harmful: Involving physical damage, impairment, pain, or illness in the body.

Offensive: Offending the personal integrity or dignity of a reasonable or ordinary person who is not unduly sensitive.

Causation: Either:

a. but for the defendant's act, the consequence would not have occurred (i.e., the apprehension would not have occurred), or
b. the defendant's act was a substantial factor in bringing about the consequence (i.e., the apprehension).

Major Defense and Counterargument Possibilities That Need to Be Explored

1. Defendant's conduct was involuntary (no act).
2. Defendant did not desire a contact or apprehension, or know with substantial certainty that the apprehension would result from what the defendant did or failed to do (no intent).
3. There was no apprehension.
4. The apprehension pertained to a future contact (no imminence).
5. The apprehension would have occurred even if the defendant did not do what he or she did. The defendant was not a substantial factor in producing the apprehension. (No causation.)
6. The plaintiff consented to the conduct of the defendant that led to the apprehension (on the defense of consent, see Chapter 27).
7. The apprehension resulted while the defendant was defending him- or herself from the plaintiff (on self-defense and other self-help privileges, see Chapter 27).
8. The apprehension occurred while the defendant was defending someone else from the plaintiff (on the defense of others and other self-help privileges, see Chapter 27).
9. The apprehension occurred while the defendant was defending property or recapturing chattels from the plaintiff (on the privileges of necessity, defense of property, recapture of property, and other self-help privileges, see Chapter 27).
10. The apprehension occurred while the defendant was disciplining plaintiff (on discipline and other self-help privileges, see Chapter 27).
11. The apprehension occurred while the defendant was arresting the plaintiff (on the privilege of arrest, see Chapter 7).
12. The plaintiff's suit against the government for an assault committed by a government employee may be barred by sovereign immunity (on sovereign immunity, see Chapter 27).
13. The plaintiff's suit against the government employee for assault may be barred by official immunity (on official immunity, see Chapter 27).
14. The plaintiff's suit against the charitable organization for assault committed by someone working for the organization may be barred by charitable immunity (on charitable immunity, see Chapter 27).
15. The plaintiff's suit against a family member for assault may be barred by intrafamily tort immunity (on intrafamily tort immunity, see Chapter 27).

Damages

The plaintiff can recover compensatory damages for the apprehension, including pain and suffering, medical bills, and loss of wages. Damages can include compensation for unforeseeable consequences of the assault if the general nature or type of harm was a foreseeable consequence of the original risk created by the assault. If the defendant acts out of hatred and malice in committing the assault, punitive damages are often awarded as well. (On the categories of damages, see Chapter 16.)

ASSAULT CHECKLIST *(Continued)*

Relationship to Criminal Law
The same act of the defendant can constitute a *civil* assault (for which the plaintiff recovers damages) and a *criminal* assault (for which the state collects a fine or imposes jail or imprisonment). The word "assault" in criminal law is often used interchangeably with the word "battery."

Other Torts and Related Actions

Battery: The defendant may intend to batter the plaintiff, but fail to do so. If, in the process, the plaintiff is aware of the attempted battery, the tort of assault is probably committed.

False Imprisonment: If the plaintiff is aware of the defendant's attempt to confine the plaintiff, there may be an apprehension of contact, and hence an assault as well as false imprisonment.

Intentional Infliction of Emotional Distress: This tort, unlike assault, can sometimes cover future threats if the action of the defendant is sufficiently shocking.

Negligence: If the defendant does not intentionally cause apprehension in the plaintiff, the defendant may be negligent in causing it. For the negligence action to succeed, there must be actual harm in addition to the apprehension.

Wrongful Death: A wrongful-death action can be brought by the survivors of the plaintiff if death results from the assault.

Federal Law

a. Under the Federal Tort Claims Act, the United States government will *not* be liable for an assault committed by one of its federal employees within the scope of employment (respondeat superior) *unless* the federal employee is an investigative or law enforcement officer. (See Exhibit 27–7 in Chapter 27.) (Most states have their own statutes that cover when tort claims can be made against the state for assault or other torts committed by state government employees. Such claims are also covered in Chapter 27.)
b. There may be liability under the Civil Rights Act if the assault was committed while the defendant was depriving the plaintiff of a federal civil right under color of state law. (See Exhibit 27–9 in Chapter 27.)
c. There may be liability under the federal Free Access to Clinic Entrances Act (FACE) for assaults committed against people seeking or providing "reproductive health services." See discussion of FACE and the case of *Lucero v. Trosch* in this chapter.

Employer–Employee (Agency) Law
A private (non-government) employee who commits an assault is personally liable for this tort. His or her employer will *also* be liable for assault if the conduct of the employee was within the scope of employment (respondeat superior). The employee must be furthering a business objective of the employer at the time. Intentional torts such as assault, however, are often outside the scope of employment. If so, only the employee is liable for the assault. (On the factors that determine the scope of employment, see Exhibit 14–9 in Chapter 14.)

Paralegal Roles in Assault Litigation
(See also Exhibit 3–1 in Chapter 3, Exhibit 20–4 in Chapter 20, and Exhibit 29–1 in Chapter 29.)

Fact finding (help the office collect facts relevant to prove the elements of assault, the elements of available defenses, and the extent of injuries or other damages):
- client interviewing
- field investigation
- online research

File management (help the office control the documents involved in an assault litigation):
- open client file
- enter case data in computer database
- maintain file documents

ASSAULT CHECKLIST *(Continued)*

Litigation assistance (help the trial attorney prepare for an assault trial and appeal, if needed):

- draft discovery requests
- draft answers to discovery requests
- draft pleadings
- digest and index discovery documents
- help prepare, order, and manage trial exhibits
- prepare trial notebook
- draft notice of appeal
- order trial transcript
- cite-check briefs
- perform legal research

Collection/enforcement (help the trial attorney for the judgment creditor to collect the damages award or to enforce other court orders at the conclusion of the assault case):

- draft postjudgment discovery requests
- conduct field investigation to monitor compliance with judgment
- perform online research (e.g., location of defendant's business assets)

Research References for Assault

Digests
In the digests of West Group, look for case summaries on assault under key topics such as:

Assault and Battery
Damages
Torts

Corpus Juris Secundum
In this legal encyclopedia, see the discussion under topic headings such as:

Assault and Battery
Damages
Torts

American Jurisprudence 2d
In this legal encyclopedia, see the discussion under topic headings such as:

Assault and Battery
Damages
Torts

Legal Periodical Literature
There are two index systems to use to try to locate legal periodical literature on assault:

Index to Legal Periodicals and Books (ILP)

See literature in *ILP* under subject headings such as:
Assault and Battery
Damages
Federal Tort Claims Act
Personal Injuries
Torts
Wrongful Death

Current Law Index (CLI)

See literature in *CLI* under subject headings such as:
Assault and Battery
Torts
Damages
Personal Injuries

Example of a legal periodical article you will find by using *ILP* or *CLI*:

Respondeat Superior and the Intentional Tort: A Short Discourse on How to Make Assault and Battery a Part of the Job by J. Terry Griffith, 45 University of Cincinnati Law Review 235 (1976).

A.L.R., A.L.R.2d, A.L.R.3d, A.L.R.4th, A.L.R.5th, A.L.R.6th, A.L.R. Fed., and *A.L.R. Fed.2d*
Use the *ALR Index* to locate annotations on assault. In this index, check subject headings such as:

Assault and Battery
Damages
Torts

ASSAULT CHECKLIST *(Continued)*

Example of an annotation on assault you can locate through this index:

Federal Tort Claims Act Provision Exempting from Coverage Claim Arising out of Assault, Battery, False Imprisonment, False Arrest, Malicious Prosecution, etc. by W. J. Dunn, 23 A.L.R.2d 574 (1952).

Words and Phrases
In this multivolume legal dictionary, look up *assault, apprehension, imminent, harmful, offensive, transferred intent,* and every other word or phrase connected with assault discussed in this chapter. The dictionary will give you definitions of these words or phrases from court opinions.

CALR: Computer-Assisted Legal Research
Example of a query you could ask on Westlaw or on LexisNexis to try to find cases, statutes, or other legal materials on assault: **assault /p damages**

Example of search terms you could use on an Internet legal search engine such as the Public Library of Law (www.plol.org), Findlaw (www.findlaw.com), or Google Scholar (scholar.google.com) to find cases, statutes, or other legal materials on assault: **civil AND assault AND tort**

Example of search terms you could use on an Internet general search engine such as Google, Bing, or AltaVista to find cases, statutes, or other legal materials on battery: **+civil +assault +tort**

More Internet sites to check for materials on assault and other torts:
www.hg.org/torts.html
www.megalaw.com/top/top.php (click "Intentional Torts," "Personal Injury Law," "Tort Law," and "Damages")
See also the online sites in Overview of Tort Law at the end of Chapter 1.

CHECK THE CITE

When a home-health nurse, Faye Jordan, attempted to make a home visit to a patient, she encountered resistance from Ann Wilson, a relative of the patient. During the encounter, Wilson held a .22 rifle. Read the case growing out of their dispute, *Jordan v. Wilson*, 5 So. 3d 442 (Miss. Ct. App., 2008). (a) What facts were alleged that support the conclusion that Ann Wilson committed the tort of assault against Faye Jordan? (b) What facts were alleged that there was no assault? (c) Did the court conclude that a tort cause of action for assault was properly asserted in the complaint? To read the opinion online, (1) Go to the site of the Mississippi courts (www.mssc.state.ms.us). Click Decisions Search. Select a Menu-Assisted search. In the Query Term, type the name of the parties (Jordan Wilson). (2) Run a citation search ("5 So. 3d 442") in the Legal Opinions and Journals database of Google Scholar (scholar.google.com).

PROJECT

In Google, Bing, or another general search engine, run a search on "Free Access to Clinic Entrances Act" and abortion (FACE abortion). Write a short essay on what you learn about civil actions brought under FACE. You can consult as many websites as you wish, but you must quote from at least three separate sites.

ETHICS IN A TORTS PRACTICE

You are a paralegal at a personal injury law firm. At one time you were an adjuster for an insurance company, where you still have many friends. Your boss tells you that your yearly bonus will be increased $100 for every automobile accident client you can get your insurance company contacts to refer to the law office. What ethical problems, if any, might exist?

SUMMARY

An assault is an apprehension of an imminent harmful or offensive contact resulting from the defendant's intent to cause this apprehension or intent to cause the contact itself. There is no requirement that the plaintiff fear a coming contact; he or she need only be aware of one. Harmful means physical damage, impairment, pain, or illness in the body; offensive means offending the personal integrity or dignity of a reasonable or ordinary person who is not unduly sensitive. The apprehension must pertain to an imminent (not a future or conditional) contact. The defendant must have the apparent present ability to complete the contact. This ability is usually not present in cyberstalking cases.

Intent is (a) the desire to bring about an apprehension of an imminent contact or the contact itself, or (b) the knowledge with substantial certainty that an imminent apprehension will result from what one does or fails to do. If the defendant intends to assault one person, but mistakenly assaults another, the defendant is liable for assault to the unintended plaintiff. This transferred-intent rule also covers the intentional torts of battery, false imprisonment, trespass to land, and trespass to chattels. In addition, the defendant's intent to commit one of these five torts will also make the defendant liable for one of the other four unintended torts that results from what the defendant did.

The federal Free Access to Clinic Entrances Act (FACE) provides a civil cause of action for a person who has been threatened or otherwise attacked while seeking or providing reproductive health services. Under the thin-skull rule, a defendant is liable for the foreseeable and unforeseeable injuries of the plaintiff that result from the defendant's assault if the general nature or type of harm was a foreseeable consequence of the original risk created by the apprehension.

KEY TERMS

assault *94*
act *94*
apprehension *94*
harmful *95*
offensive *95*
imminent *95*
conditional threat *95*
apparent present ability *95*
cyberstalking *95*
cyberbullying *95*
intent (for assault) *97*
transferred-intent rule *97*
FACE *99*
thin-skull rule *100*

REVIEW QUESTIONS

1. What is an assault?
2. How does an assault differ from a battery?
3. How does civil assault differ from criminal assault?
4. What is an act in an assault action?
5. What is the relationship between apprehension and fear?
6. When is contact harmful? When is it offensive?
7. When is a contact imminent?
8. Can a conditional threat constitute assault?
9. What is cyberstalking? Can it be the basis of an assault action?
10. What intent must a defendant have to be liable for assault?
11. What is the transferred-intent rule?
12. What damages can be obtained under the thin-skull rule?

HELPFUL WEBSITES

- **Assault Basics**

  injury.findlaw.com/assault-and-battery/assault-basics.html

  www.answers.com/topic/assault
  assault.uslegal.com

  www.google.com (run this search: elements assault tort)

- **FACE**

  www.prochoice.org/about_abortion/facts/face_act.html

  en.wikipedia.org/wiki/Freedom_of_Access_to_Clinic_Entrances_Act

- **Cyberstalking**

  justice.gov/criminal/cybercrime/cyberstalking.htm

  www.ncvc.org/ncvc/main.aspx?dbName=DocumentViewer&DocumentID=32458

Student StudyWARE™ CD-ROM
For additional materials, please go to the student CD in this book.

CHAPTER

7

FALSE IMPRISONMENT AND FALSE ARREST

CHAPTER OUTLINE

- Introduction
- False Imprisonment
- False Arrest

CHAPTER OBJECTIVES

After completing this chapter, you should be able to:

- Understand the nature of false imprisonment.
- Identify the elements of false imprisonment.
- Identify the defenses to false imprisonment.
- Explain the different ways a person can be confined for purposes of false imprisonment.
- State whether the plaintiff must be conscious of the confinement.
- Understand the distinction between a privilege and an immunity.
- Compare the arrest privileges of a peace officer and a citizen.
- Describe paralegal roles in false imprisonment litigation.
- List the major sources (traditional and online) for researching issues in false imprisonment cases.

INTRODUCTION

false imprisonment The intentional confinement within fixed boundaries of someone who is conscious of the confinement or is harmed by it.

The tort of **false imprisonment** is the intentional confinement within fixed boundaries of someone who is conscious of the confinement or is harmed by it. The tort covers much more than prisons and jails. It protects the right of everyone to move about freely. The most obvious example of this tort is being locked in a room of a house, business premises, or any building. But imprisonment is not limited to forcing a person to remain within an enclosed structure. It is possible to falsely imprison someone in an area where there are no walls. Recently, a celebrity brought a false imprisonment suit against *paparazzi*—photographers who stalk celebrities for candid photographs outside restaurants, in parking lots, on the sidewalk, on the freeway, etc. To understand how such conduct might constitute false imprisonment, we need to explore the broader dimension of this intentional tort. (For its elements, see Exhibit 7–1.). Following our examination of false imprisonment, we will cover false arrest, which is a major example of false imprisonment.

Exhibit 7–1
Elements of the tort of false imprisonment.

1. An act that completely confines the plaintiff within fixed boundaries set by the defendant
2. Intent to confine the plaintiff or a third party
3. Causation of the confinement
4. The plaintiff was either conscious of the confinement or suffered actual harm by it

FALSE IMPRISONMENT

Confinement

confinement The complete restraint of the plaintiff's freedom of movement within fixed boundaries.

The first element of false imprisonment is **confinement**, which is the complete restraint of the plaintiff's freedom of movement within fixed boundaries. The word "imprisonment" is misleading. To commit this tort, you do not have to place someone behind bars without authority. Such an act will constitute false imprisonment, as will an illegal delay in releasing someone from jail or prison. But false imprisonment is not limited to such extreme situations. It can also occur when there is a confinement of one's freedom of movement. The confinement or restraint can happen in five ways:

- Confinement by physical barrier
- Confinement by physical force against the plaintiff, the plaintiff's immediate family, or the plaintiff's property
- Confinement by threat of present physical force against the plaintiff, against the plaintiff's immediate family, or against the plaintiff's property
- Confinement by asserted legal authority
- Confinement by refusal to release

Confinement by Physical Barrier In this kind of confinement, tangible, physical restraints or barriers are imposed on the plaintiff.

EXAMPLES
- The defendant locks the plaintiff in a room.
- The defendant takes away the plaintiff's wheelchair.
- The defendant takes away a ladder that the plaintiff needs to climb out of a deep ditch.

Confinement by Physical Force Against the Plaintiff, the Plaintiff's Immediate Family, or the Plaintiff's Property

EXAMPLES

- If the defendant grabs or holds the plaintiff, confinement results from physical force on the plaintiff's body.
- The plaintiff can also be confined if the defendant uses physical force on the plaintiff's child or other member of his or her immediate family. Suppose that the defendant ties up the plaintiff's son. The plaintiff may be able to escape, but it is highly unlikely that he or she will do so while the child is in danger. Hence, the defendant has confined *both* the child and the plaintiff. The physical force used against the child has also resulted in the confinement of the parent.
- Finally, suppose that the defendant uses physical force against the plaintiff's valuable property, such as by seizing the plaintiff's watch. The plaintiff stays in order to try to get the watch back. The plaintiff has been confined because of the force used against the watch.

The plaintiffs in the last two examples (the parent who remains because his or her child is tied up and the plaintiff who remains to see about a watch that has been taken) have "agreed" to stay, but they have done so under such severe **duress** that the confinement is not voluntary. The confinement is imposed on the plaintiffs as effectively in these situations as when actual physical force is used on a plaintiff's body.

duress Coercion or the unlawful use of force or threats to pressure someone to do something he or she does not want to do. (See glossary for an additional definition.)

Confinement by Threat of Present Physical Force Against the Plaintiff, Against the Plaintiff's Immediate Family, or Against the Plaintiff's Property Confinement can result from a *threat* that intimidates the plaintiff into compliance with an order. A plaintiff has been confined, for example, if he or she freezes when faced with a gun and the defendant's demand, "Stop or I'll shoot!"

A threat of present physical force (restricting freedom of movement) can be (1) against the plaintiff directly, (2) against a member of the plaintiff's immediate family, or (3) against the plaintiff's property. The threat is that the force will be used if the plaintiff tries to escape or move out of an area designated by the defendant. If the plaintiff submits to the threat and remains, a confinement has occurred for purposes of establishing the first element of false imprisonment.

EXAMPLE

Jim and his brother Sam are walking down the street. Greg sees a bulging wallet in Sam's back pocket. Ignoring Jim, Greg points a gun at Sam and orders him to hand over his wallet and everything else in his pockets. Sam does so. There has been a confinement of both Sam and Jim even if Jim would have been able to flee without harm. The threat that confined Sam also confined a member of his immediate family, Jim.

Confinement by Asserted Legal Authority Here the defendant claims the legal authority or right to confine or arrest the plaintiff. Confinement occurs when the plaintiff is taken into custody. If the defendant does not have the privilege of arresting the plaintiff, as defined later in the chapter, the first element of false imprisonment has been met. No physical force or touching need be used as long as the plaintiff has reason to believe that such force will be used if the plaintiff either moves outside an area designated by the defendant or fails to follow the defendant.

Confinement by Refusal to Release Assume that the plaintiff has been validly confined, e.g., imprisoned. At the time when the plaintiff has a right to be released, he or she has been improperly confined if the defendant interferes with the release.

Confinement in any of the five ways must be complete or total, meaning that the plaintiff must know of no safe or inoffensive means of escape out of the fixed boundaries set by the defendant. There is no confinement, for example, if the defendant blocks the plaintiff's path when there is a clear and accessible way around the defendant. Nor is there confinement when the defendant locks all the doors of a house if the plaintiff is able to escape by climbing out of a window that is very close to the ground and if the inconvenience in climbing out is slight. A different result would follow, however, if the plaintiff had little or no clothing on, or would have substantial difficulty climbing out because of age or illness.

Finally, there is no set length of time that the confinement must last. Courts often say that a person can be confined for any appreciable time, however brief.

A great many false imprisonment cases result from detention in shops and department stores when a customer is suspected of stealing merchandise or services. A **shopkeeper's privilege** gives a shopkeeper the right to detain someone temporarily for the sole purpose of investigating whether theft has occurred. Reasonable force can be used to carry out this temporary investigation. The shopkeeper must be reasonable in suspecting that the person has committed the crime. If it turns out that the person is innocent and that the shopkeeper has made a mistake, the latter is still protected if the mistake was reasonable.

shopkeeper's privilege The right of a merchant to detain someone temporarily for the sole purpose of investigating whether the person has committed theft against the merchant.

Every state has a shopkeeper's privilege in one form or another. The privilege may have been created by the courts as part of the **common law** or by the legislature as part of its statutory code. One of the states with a statute is New York. Here is its statute. Note that New York extends the privilege to cover detention or confinement for the purpose of questioning someone suspected of using recording devices in a theater. Not all states would grant the privilege for this purpose.

common law Judge-made law in the absence of statutes or other controlling law.

> § 218 In any action for false arrest, false imprisonment, unlawful detention, defamation of character, assault, trespass, or invasion of civil rights, brought by any person by reason of having been detained on or in the immediate vicinity of the premises of (a) a retail mercantile establishment for the purpose of investigation or questioning as to . . . the ownership of any merchandise, or (b) a motion picture theater for the purposes of investigation or questioning as to the unauthorized operation of a recording device in a motion picture theater, it shall be a defense to such action that the person was detained in a reasonable manner and for not more than a reasonable time to permit such investigation or questioning by . . . the owner of the retail mercantile establishment or motion picture theater, his authorized employee or agent, and that such . . . owner, employee or agent had reasonable grounds to believe that the person so detained was . . . attempting to commit larceny on such premises of such merchandise or was engaged in the unauthorized operation of a recording device in a motion picture theater. As used in this section, "reasonable grounds" shall include, but not be limited to, knowledge that a person (i) has concealed possession of unpurchased merchandise of a retail mercantile establishment, or (ii) has possession of an item designed for the purpose of overcoming detection of security markings attachments placed on merchandise offered for sale at such an establishment, or (iii) has possession of a recording device in a theater in which a motion picture is being exhibited and a "reasonable time" shall mean the time necessary to permit the person detained to make a statement or to refuse to make a statement, and the time necessary to examine employees and records of the mercantile establishment relative to the ownership of the merchandise, or possession of such an item or device. . . . N.Y. General Business Law § 218 (McKinney, 1998).

The following example demonstrates the operation of the privilege.

EXAMPLE

George is a store clerk at Macy's. He sees Fred, a teenager, take a watch from the counter, put it in his pocket, and walk out the door without paying. In the parking lot, George orders Fred to the back room of the store. After about ten minutes of questioning, George concludes that Fred stole the watch. As Fred breaks down and cries, George spends about an hour lecturing Fred about the morality of stealing. He then calls the police. Later, Fred sues Macy's for false imprisonment.

The store can raise the defense of shopkeeper's privilege to cover the time when Fred was escorted to the back room and questioned about payment for the watch. The privilege, however, would *not* cover the period after George completed his investigation of Fred. There is no shopkeeper's privilege to lecture thieves about the morality of what they are doing. During the time of the lecture (about an hour), Fred was falsely imprisoned.

ASSIGNMENT 7.1

Jim is soliciting religious contributions in Leo's department store. Leo tells Jim that this is not allowed in the store. Jim nevertheless continues. Leo and four of his security guards surround Jim and tell him to come to the manager's office. Jim does so. In the manager's office, Leo shouts at Jim and tells him, "You've got thirty seconds to get out the back door." Jim leaves and sues Leo for false imprisonment. Discuss Jim's chances of winning.

CASE

The Limited Stores, Inc. v. Wilson-Robinson

317 Ark. 80, 876 S.W.2d 248 (1994)
Supreme Court of Arkansas

Background: *Perrylyn Wilson-Robinson was a customer in The Limited Stores, Inc. (referred to as Stores in the opinion). As she was walking out the front door, the sensor alarm went off. When employees asked her to come back for questioning, she agreed. After determining that there was no theft, she was told she could go. She then sued Stores for false imprisonment and won. She was awarded $6,850 in compensatory damages and $23,650 in punitive damages. The case is now on appeal before the Supreme Court of Arkansas where Wilson-Robinson is the appellee and Stores is the appellant.*

Decision on Appeal: *The judgment is reversed. There was no false imprisonment.*

OPINION OF COURT

Justice HAYS delivered the opinion of the court . . .:

Ms. Wilson-Robinson testified that she was shopping in The Limited Stores in North Little Rock. As she left the store the alarm on the sensormatic device sounded. Although she heard the alarm she continued out into the mall, thinking the alarm did not pertain to her. Two female employees from the store approached her. Ms. Wilson-Robinson testified "[t]hey asked if I would return to the store because when I left out the buzzer went off." "I said, 'Well, sure,' because I hadn't done anything."

When the two employees and Ms. Wilson-Robinson reentered the store the alarm did not go off. One of the employees then asked if she had a calculator in her bag. She said, " 'Yes, I have a calculator,' and I opened up my bag. I said, 'See, you know, here's the calculator.' " At that point one of the employees waved the calculator in front of the device but the alarm did not go off. The employee then said: "Well, okay, you know, it is fine. You can leave now." Ms. Wilson-Robinson asked to meet with the store manager and, after speaking with her, she left.

Ms. Wilson-Robinson testified there were other people leaving the store when she heard the alarm and she felt she was stopped because "I'm a heavy-set black female, and I carry a large purse." In explaining why she returned to the store, she testified: "When they stopped me on the mall, my impression was that they were accusing me of taking something, so I really didn't have a choice, so I said, 'Sure, I will go back,' because I knew I hadn't done anything. And, if I hadn't gone back, then the consequences was saying, well, maybe she is guilty. So I went back to the store because I didn't do anything." . . .

A merchant may detain, for a reasonable length of time, a person he or she has reasonable cause to believe is shoplifting. See *Arkansas Code Annotated* § 5-36-116 (Repl. 1993); 7 Speiser, Krause and Gans, *The American Law of Torts* § 27.18 (1990). However, whether Stores had grounds to detain Ms. Wilson-Robinson pursuant to the statute is not the issue. Rather, Stores contends Ms. Wilson-Robinson was not detained. Simply put, Stores contends the detention or imprisonment requirement of the tort was not met.

False imprisonment has been defined as the unlawful violation of the personal liberty of another, consisting of *detention* without sufficient legal authority. *Headrick v. Wal-Mart Stores, Inc.,* 293 Ark. 433, 738 S.W.2d 418 (1987). Any express or implied threat of force whereby one is deprived of his liberty or compelled to go where one does not wish to go is an imprisonment. *Pettijohn v. Smith* et al., 255 Ark. 780, 502 S.W.2d 618 (1973). Stores submits there was no detention, imprisonment or arrest. Ms. Wilson-Robinson contends there was a detention because *two* employees went after [her] and there was an "implied threat of arrest."

It is well established that the restraint constituting a false imprisonment may be by threats of force which intimidate the plaintiff into compliance with orders. *Restatement (Second) of Torts* § 40 (1965); Prosser and Keeton, *Prosser and Keeton on Torts* § 11 (5th ed. 1984). Although the plaintiff is not required to incur the risk of personal violence by resisting until force is actually used, it is essential that the restraint be against the plaintiff's will. 1 Harper, James and Gray, *The Law of Torts* § 3.8 (2nd ed. 1986). Submission to the mere verbal direction of another, unaccompanied by force or threats of any character, does not constitute false imprisonment. *Faniel v. Chesapeake & Potomac Telephone Co.,* 404 A.2d 147 (D.C. 1979). If one agrees of one's own free choice to surrender freedom of motion, as by accompanying another voluntarily to clear oneself of suspicion, rather than yielding to the constraint of a threat, then there is no imprisonment. . . .

[T]here is no evidence that Ms. Wilson-Robinson was threatened. She simply responded voluntarily to a request occasioned by the alarm. Nor is the testimony . . . that the employees believed Ms. Wilson-Robinson had shoplifted telling, so long as she was not forcibly detained.

Although the appellee contends there was an "implied threat of arrest," threats of future action, such as calling the police and having the person arrested, are not ordinarily sufficient in themselves to effect an unlawful imprisonment. *Morales v. Lee,* 668 S.W.2d 867 (Tex. App. 4 Dist. 1984); Prosser and Keeton, supra. Even where the confinement is attributable to the threat of *physical* force, the submission must be responsive to a threat to apply "physical force to the other's person immediately upon the other's going or attempting to go beyond the area in which the actor intends to confine him." *Restatement (Second) of Torts* § 40. Submission to the threat to apply physical force at a time appreciably later than that at which the other attempts to go beyond the given area is not confinement. *Restatement (Second) of Torts* § 40, comment b. Consequently, even if the store employees had threatened to call the police in the instant case, there would not have been a confinement.

We find the appellee failed to establish the detention element of false imprisonment. . . . [T]he appellee did not testify or allege that she had any fear of force. See Prosser and Keeton, supra. In fact, she testified repeatedly that she was *"asked"* if she would return to the store, responding, "Well, sure." When she returned to the store, she was not detained by any threat of force, she was *"asked"* if she had a calculator. There is no imprisonment when one agrees to surrender her freedom of motion. . . . In sum, there is insufficient evidence to establish a tort of false imprisonment. . . .

Reversed and dismissed.

ASSIGNMENT 7.2

a. The court said there was no confinement. Assume that the court reached the conclusion that there was a confinement because Perrylyn Wilson-Robinson did not voluntarily return to the store. Now would she have won the case?
b. Would this court reach the same result if three employees surrounded Perrylyn Wilson-Robinson and asked her to return to the store?
c. Would this court reach the same result if each of the employees wore coats with badges that said "Store Security"?
d. Is it relevant that Perrylyn Wilson-Robinson is black? Assume that the employees would not have stopped her if she was white. Would the court have found that there was false imprisonment?
e. The court said, "even if the store employees had threatened to call the police in the instant case, there would not have been a confinement." Explain why this statement is dictum.

Intent

False imprisonment is an intentional tort. To establish **intent**, one must desire to confine or know with substantial certainty that confinement will result from what one does or fails to do. If the defendant is merely negligent or reckless in causing the confinement, the intentional tort of false imprisonment has not been committed. The tort of **negligence** might be possible. A negligence suit, however, requires proof of injury or other loss, whereas for false imprisonment, no more harm than the confinement itself need be shown. (See, however, an exception in the next section on causation covering cases in which the plaintiff was unaware of the confinement.)

intent (for false imprisonment) The desire to bring about the confinement of a person or the knowledge with substantial certainty that the confinement will result from what one does or fails to do.

negligence The failure to use reasonable care that an ordinary prudent person would have used in a similar situation, resulting in injury or other loss.

EXAMPLE

The defendant locks up an old building and carelessly or even recklessly fails to check whether anyone is still inside. In fact someone is inside. These facts are not enough to establish an intent to confine, because the defendant neither desired nor knew with substantial certainty that someone would be confined. The defendant was merely careless or reckless in failing to check.

The **transferred-intent rule** applies. If the defendant intends to confine one person, but mistakenly confines a plaintiff whom the defendant never even knew existed, the requisite intent has been established. The defendant's intent to confine one person is transferred to another person who is in fact confined by the defendant's intentional conduct. (On transferred intent, see Exhibit 6–2 in Chapter 6.)

transferred-intent rule The defendant may be liable for certain torts committed against the plaintiff even if the defendant intended to commit a different tort against the plaintiff (unintended tort) and even if the defendant intended to commit the tort against a different person (unintended plaintiff). (Does not apply to all torts. See Exhibit 6-2 in Chapter 6.)

Causation

To establish the element of causation, the plaintiff must be able to show that either:

- but for the act of the defendant the plaintiff would not have been confined, or
- the defendant was a substantial factor in producing the plaintiff's confinement.

The defendant need not be the sole cause of the confinement.

EXAMPLE

A citizen makes a complaint about a person to a police officer. The latter arrests the person, who is then taken into custody. Assume that a court later determines that the arrest was improper.

In this example, the police officer made an arrest that turned out to be improper. Hence the confinement was improper. The plaintiff has an action for false imprisonment against the police officer unless the officer is protected by privilege (to be discussed at the end of the chapter). But what about the citizen? Has he or she also falsely imprisoned the plaintiff? The issue is whether the citizen caused the plaintiff's confinement. Under the second prong of our definition of causation, we need to ask whether the citizen was a substantial factor in producing the confinement through the arrest.

Courts resolve this question by distinguishing between (a) merely reporting facts to police officials who then make up their own mind on whether to arrest and (b) instigating the arrest. **Instigation** consists of insisting on, urging, goading, directing, or inciting the arrest. There must be persuasion or influencing of some kind in order for the citizen to have been a substantial factor in producing the arrest by the police officer. Without this instigation, the citizen is not a cause of the confinement.

instigation Insisting on, urging, goading, directing, or inciting.

Note that when a citizen instigates an arrest, the arrest itself is made by the government. The citizen is simply a cause of (a substantial factor in bringing about) the arrest by law enforcement personnel. We will see shortly that citizens have the right to make an arrest themselves. We will discuss this under the topic of citizen arrests.

Consciousness or Harm

The courts are split on whether plaintiffs must *know* that they are being confined. Some courts do not require consciousness of the confinement. The tort of false imprisonment can exist even if the plaintiff was ignorant of the confinement.

EXAMPLE

Sam walks into a room to sleep. After he falls asleep, someone locks the door to the room for one hour. By the time Sam wakes up, however, the door has been unlocked.

Sam was unaware that he had been confined for one hour. In some states, this is not relevant. False imprisonment has still been committed. Other states require consciousness of confinement. These states, however, make an exception if the victim suffered actual harm (e.g., an illness) during the confinement. If such harm can be shown, recovery will be allowed even though the victim was unaware of the confinement. In general, actual harm is *not* an element of false imprisonment. The confinement itself is sufficient. In cases where the plaintiff was unaware of the confinement, however, some states require a showing of actual harm.

ASSIGNMENT 7.3

In each of the following four situations, determine whether false imprisonment has been committed.

a. Luis is driving a car down the highway. His two-year-old son, Fred, is in the back seat playing. It is a three-lane highway going one way; Luis is in the middle lane. Dan's car is in the far right lane. Luis gives a right-turn signal. He wants to go to the far right lane in order to make a right turn. Dan is driving to the immediate right of Luis. Dan refuses to yield, forcing Luis to miss his turn. Luis loses fifteen minutes in taking an alternate route to where he was headed. Luis and Fred sue Dan for false imprisonment.

b. Mary calls John on the phone and threatens to kill him by 2 P.M. tomorrow unless John goes downtown to pay a debt that John owes Mary's company. John does so. He later sues Mary for false imprisonment.

c. Jane is one of the guests on the talk show called "How Nasty Can You Get?" She says she was invited on the show to receive a surprise on the air. She thought the surprise might be that she was going to receive a free trip to Germany to visit her husband who was stationed at a military base there. Instead she was told by her sister, Ann, that Jane's husband was the father of Ann's recently born baby. Jane was stunned and disgusted. She immediately stood up and tried to take her microphone off so that she could leave. Because the wire was attached through Jane's clothes, she was unable to disconnect the wire. After about five minutes, a stagehand helped her remove the microphone so that she could leave. She now brings a false imprisonment suit against the TV station for inviting her on the program under false pretenses and for the five minutes of humiliation when she could not unhook the microphone.

d. Paul Richardson is a photographer for the SinSational Daily News. He is in the parking lot of the Fillmore Maternity Clinic waiting for Sally Starr to emerge with her first-born child. Sally is an international recording artist. Suddenly he spots her coming out through a side door. He sees Sally's husband help her into a car. Paul quickly gets into his own car and races toward the exit where Sally's car is headed. Paul blocks this exit, jumps out of his car, goes over to Sally's car, and takes her picture through the car window. He then gets back into his own car and drives it out of the way of the exit. Sally's husband drives through. Paul follows behind through city streets for over three hours. Sally's husband wants to stop and confront Paul. But Sally says, "No, don't stop. I'm too sick to stop. He's got us trapped on this road." Finally Paul gives up and returns without obtaining any more pictures. Sally and her husband now sue Paul for false imprisonment.

CASE

Andrews v. Piedmont Air Lines

297 S.C. 367, 377 S.E.2d 127 (1989)
Court of Appeals of South Carolina

Background: *Clarence Andrews was not allowed to board an airplane due to the restrictions the airline imposed on customers in wheelchairs. He sued for false imprisonment. The lower court granted summary judgment for the airlines. The case is now before the Court of Appeals of South Carolina.*

Decision on Appeal: *Judgment for the airline. There was no false imprisonment.*

OPINION OF COURT

PER CURIAM.

. . . Clarence Andrews sued Piedmont Air Lines for an incident which occurred after Piedmont denied him boarding on a flight due to his physical incapacity to travel unaccompanied. . . . In 1984, Andrews, a diabetic who had previously suffered a stroke, was admitted to Greenville Memorial Hospital for circulatory problems in his right leg. As a result of the stroke, his speech was slurred, he drooled, and his left side was paralyzed. Unfortunately, the treatment for his leg was unsuccessful and it had to be amputated above the knee. During the recovery period, the hospital contacted Andrews' daughter in Florida and asked if her father could live with her. She agreed and the hospital arranged the trip.

A hospital social worker, Andrew Irwin, telephoned Piedmont and reserved a seat for Andrews. Piedmont informed Irwin that the airline had guidelines governing travel by unaccompanied physically handicapped passengers. Under the guidelines, Piedmont would accept the passenger if he (1) could use the lavatory without assistance, (2) was able to sit in a normal sitting position with the seatbelt properly fastened, and (3) required no assistance eating.

In December 1984, the hospital discharged Andrews and took him by ambulance to the Greenville/Spartanburg Airport. He was placed in an airport wheelchair and taken to the Piedmont ticket counter. He purchased a ticket and was wheeled to the gate area to wait for his flight. While waiting to embark, Andrews asked other passengers for cigarettes and asked a passenger to tie his leg to the wheelchair. The supervisor of airport security notified Milton Ward, the Piedmont station manager, of a potential problem at the departure gate.

When Ward arrived at the gate, he found Andrews slumped over in the wheelchair with saliva drooling out of the side of his mouth. Ward questioned Andrews about his ability to go to the bathroom by himself. He received a negative answer. Since Andrews did not meet Piedmont's guidelines, Ward kept him off the flight. Andrews was removed from the passenger waiting area to an area adjacent to the Piedmont office and ticket counter. Piedmont telephoned the hospital to come get Andrews.

Upon receipt of Piedmont's call, Irwin went to the airport and found Andrews in a wheelchair. He called the hospital requesting an ambulance and remained with Andrews, one and a half to two hours, until it arrived. Andrews returned to the hospital and alternate travel plans were arranged. . . .

False imprisonment is depriving the plaintiff of his liberty without lawful justification. In order to establish a cause of action, the evidence must prove: (1) that the defendant restrained the plaintiff; (2) that the restraint was intentional; and (3) that the restraint was unlawful.

The facts of the case do not support a cause of action for false imprisonment. Assuming Piedmont restrained Andrews, there is no evidence that the restraint was unlawful. Common carriers have a higher duty of care towards noticeably handicapped passengers. See *Singletary v. Atlantic Coast Line Railroad Co.,* 217 S.C. 212, 60 S.E.2d 305 (1950). Due to his physical condition, Andrews was not ambulatory. Piedmont placed Andrews in the area adjacent to the ticket counter so they could periodically check on him and find him when the ambulance arrived. There is no evidence that he protested waiting there or that he asked to be moved to another location. Further, after Irwin arrived, Andrews did not leave in Irwin's personal car, but chose to wait for the ambulance in this same area. In light of Andrews' condition, the alleged restraint was reasonable and it might well have been a breach of Piedmont's duty if they had not detained him until Irwin arrived. The trial court correctly granted the motion for summary judgment on the cause of action for false imprisonment.

ASSIGNMENT 7.4

a. Was Andrews confined by the airline? Was he confined by Greenville Memorial Hospital?
b. Assume Andrews met all the requirements for boarding the airplane. Would it have been false imprisonment for the airline to refuse to allow him to board?

false arrest An arrest for which the person taking someone into custody has no privilege.

personal liability Liability that can be satisfied out of a wrongdoer's personal assets.

official immunity Government employees are not personally liable for torts or other wrongdoing they commit within the scope of their employment.

privilege The right to act contrary to the right of another without being subject to tort or other liability. A defense that authorizes conduct that would otherwise be wrongful. (See glossary for a broader definition of privilege.)

immunity A defense that treats wrongful conduct as nonwrongful. A defense to a tort claim whether or not the defendant committed the tort. (See glossary for an additional definition.)

respondeat superior Literally, "let the master answer." An employer is responsible (liable) for the wrongs committed by an employee within the scope of employment.

sovereign immunity The sovereign (i.e., the state or government) cannot be sued in its courts without its consent. Also called governmental immunity.

peace officer A person designated by public authority to keep the peace and to arrest persons suspected of crime.

warrant A court order commanding or authorizing a specific act, e.g., the arrest of someone or the search of an area.

fair on its face Having no obvious or blatant flaws or irregularities.

FALSE ARREST

One way to commit false imprisonment is to make a **false arrest**. An arrest is false when it is not privileged. Private citizens as well as peace officers have a privilege to arrest. A summary of the protections and limitations of this privilege is presented in Exhibit 7–2.

Throughout this discussion, our concern is the **personal liability** of the individual making the arrest. When someone is personally liable for a wrong, the consequence is that an adverse judgment is satisfied (paid) out of the wrongdoer's personal assets.

When the false arrest is made by government employees (peace officers), they might still avoid personal liability if they enjoy **official immunity**. We will study this immunity in Chapter 27. Note the distinction between the defenses of **privilege** and **immunity** outlined in Exhibit 7–3.

A separate question is whether the government *employer* of the peace officer will be liable for the false arrest under the theory of **respondeat superior**. We will also discuss this question in Chapter 27 when we cover **sovereign immunity**—the right of the state not to be sued without its consent. The answer will depend on whether the government has waived its sovereign immunity and thereby given its consent to be sued for this kind of claim.

Peace Officer's Privilege to Arrest

When a **peace officer** has a **warrant** to arrest someone, the arrest is privileged as long as the warrant is **fair on its face**. Courts differ on the meaning of this phrase. Most courts will give it a broad interpretation (having no obvious or blatant flaws or irregularities) in order to protect the peace officer. A warrant is not fair on its face if it is obviously defective, e.g., the warrant does not name the party to be arrested or does not state the crime charged. An officer is not required to be an attorney who knows how to analyze the warrant in all its technicalities. The officer is required, however, to be able to recognize blatant irregularities such as these.

If the officer arrests the wrong person under the warrant, the privilege is lost in most states. In some states, however, the privilege is not lost if the officer's mistake was reasonable under the circumstances.

An officer may also make an arrest without a warrant. As Exhibit 7–2 shows, the principles of the privilege to arrest without a warrant differ depending on why the arrest is being made:

- criminal arrest for a **felony**
- criminal arrest for a **misdemeanor**
- misdemeanor that is a **breach of the peace**
- misdemeanor for which the arrest is made immediately or in **fresh pursuit**
- **civil commitment** for treatment or protection rather than as punishment for the commission of an alleged crime

Exhibit 7–2 Comparison of peace officer's and private citizen's privilege to arrest without a warrant.

Elements of Privilege to Arrest Without a Warrant

Peace Officer's Privilege

1. **Criminal Arrest: Felony**
   a. The peace officer has reasonable grounds to believe a felony has been committed.
   b. The peace officer has reasonable grounds to believe that the person arrested by the peace officer committed the felony.
   c. The peace officer uses reasonable force in making the arrest or in preventing the person from fleeing.

Notes:
- States differ on whether deadly force can be used to make the arrest or to prevent fleeing.
- Deadly force can be used if the peace officer's life becomes endangered while making the arrest or preventing fleeing (self-defense).
- A reasonable mistake on any of the three elements (a, b, and c above) will still protect the officer.

2. **Criminal Arrest: Misdemeanor**
   a. The misdemeanor must be a breach of the peace.
   b. The misdemeanor must be committed in the presence of the officer.
   c. The arrest must be made immediately or in *fresh pursuit*.
   d. Reasonable force is used to make the arrest or to prevent fleeing.

Notes:
- The peace officer's privilege to arrest for a misdemeanor is the same as that of a private citizen.
- In many states, a mistake on the first three elements (a, b, and c above) will not protect the peace officer, even if the mistake is reasonable.
- The officer can use deadly force only if the officer's life is in danger in making the arrest or in preventing fleeing (self-defense).
- Statutes may exist in a state to extend the privilege to arrest for misdemeanors not committed in the officer's presence and for misdemeanors that are not breaches of the peace.

3. **Civil Commitment**
   a. The officer must reasonably believe that an insane or mentally ill person poses a serious danger to him- or herself or to others.
   b. Reasonable force is used to bring the person to the authorities for treatment or protection.

Private Citizen's Privilege

1. **Criminal Arrest: Felony**
   a. A felony has in fact been committed.
   b. The felony committed is the one for which the citizen has made the arrest.
   c. The citizen has reasonable grounds to believe that the person arrested by the citizen committed the felony.
   d. The citizen uses reasonable force in making the arrest or in preventing the person from fleeing.

Notes:
- States differ on whether deadly force can be used to make the arrest or to prevent fleeing.
- Deadly force can be used if the citizen's life becomes endangered while making the arrest or preventing fleeing (self-defense).
- A reasonable mistake on any of the four elements (a, b, c, and d above) will not protect the citizen. Some states, however, have passed statutes that say the privilege is not lost if the citizen has reasonable grounds to believe that a felony has been committed by the person arrested—a reasonable mistake will protect the citizen in these states.

2. **Criminal Arrest: Misdemeanor**
   a. The misdemeanor must be a breach of the peace.
   b. The misdemeanor must be committed in the presence of the citizen.
   c. The arrest must be made immediately or in *fresh pursuit*.
   d. Reasonable force is used to make the arrest or to prevent fleeing.

Notes:
- The citizen's privilege to arrest for a misdemeanor is the same as that of a peace officer.
- In many states, a mistake on the first three elements (a, b, and c above) will not protect the citizen, even if the mistake was reasonable.
- The citizen can use deadly force only if the citizen's life was in danger in making the arrest or in preventing fleeing (self-defense).
- Statutes may exist in a state to extend the privilege to arrest for misdemeanors not committed in the citizen's presence and for misdemeanors that are not breaches of the peace.

3. **Civil Commitment**
   a. The citizen must reasonably believe that an insane or mentally ill person poses a serious danger to him- or herself or to others.
   b. Reasonable force is used to bring the person to the authorities for treatment or protection.

Exhibit 7–3 Privilege and immunity.

Defense	Privilege	Immunity
Definition	The right to act contrary to the right of another without being subject to tort or other liability.	The treatment of wrongful conduct as nonwrongful.
Nature of the defense	Privilege is a defense that allows the holder of the privilege to assert that his or her conduct was not wrongful and therefore no adverse legal consequences of the conduct should follow.	Immunity is a defense that allows the holder of the immunity to assert that if his or her conduct was wrongful, no adverse legal consequences of the wrongdoing should follow.
Effect of the defense	Avoids liability.	Avoids liability.

ASSIGNMENT 7.5

At a rock concert, a police officer smells marijuana coming from a section where Mary and her seven friends are sitting. The officer arrests all of them. The officer thinks that one or two are doing the smoking, but he wants to take them all in for questioning so that he can find out which ones are guilty. Mary tries to run away. The officer shoots her. An investigation reveals that none of the arrested individuals possessed or used any drugs. The police officer is sued for false arrest, false imprisonment, and battery. What result, based on the principles in Exhibit 7–2?

felony A crime punishable by death or imprisonment for a term exceeding a year; a crime more serious than a misdemeanor.

misdemeanor A crime punishable by fine or by incarceration for a term of a year or less; a crime less serious than a felony.

breach of the peace A violation or disturbance of the public tranquility and order. Disorderly conduct.

fresh pursuit Promptly, without undue delay. (See glossary for an additional definition.)

civil commitment Taking someone into custody for treatment or protection, and not as punishment for the commission of a crime.

Private Citizen's Privilege to Arrest

The privilege of a private citizen to make an arrest without a warrant must be considered under the same categories covered in Exhibit 7–2 for peace officers:

- criminal arrest for a felony
- criminal arrest for a misdemeanor
- misdemeanor that is a breach of the peace
- misdemeanor for which the arrest is made immediately or in fresh pursuit
- civil commitment for treatment or protection rather than as punishment for the commission of an alleged crime

A citizen's arrest does not mean that the citizen always takes physical custody of someone. There may be citizen-arrest forms available in the police department that the citizen fills out when he or she wishes to make a citizen's arrest. The actual arrest is then made by the police.

ASSIGNMENT 7.6

For this assignment, the facts are the same as in Assignment 7.5, except that the person who made the arrests, did the shooting, and is sued is a private citizen, rather than a peace officer. What result, based on the principles in Exhibit 7–2?

FALSE IMPRISONMENT CHECKLIST

Definitions, Relationships, Paralegal Roles, and Research References

Category
False imprisonment is an intentional tort.

Interest Protected by This Tort
The right to be free from intentional restraints on one's freedom of movement.

Elements of This Tort

1. An act that completely confines the plaintiff within fixed boundaries set by the defendant
2. Intent to confine the plaintiff or a third party
3. Causation of the confinement
4. The plaintiff was either conscious of the confinement or suffered actual harm by it

Definitions of Major Words/Phrases in These Elements

Act: A volitional movement of the defendant's body.

Confinement: The complete restraint of the plaintiff's freedom of movement within fixed boundaries:

a. by physical barriers, or
b. by physical force, or
c. by the threat of present physical force, or
d. by asserting legal authority to confine, or
e. by refusing to release the plaintiff.

Completely: Totally confined, in that the plaintiff knows of no safe or inoffensive means of escape.

Intent to Confine: The desire to bring about the confinement of a person or the knowledge with substantial certainty that the confinement will result from what one does or fails to do.

Causation: But for the defendant's act, the plaintiff would not have been confined, or the defendant was a substantial factor in producing the confinement.

Harm: Actual damage or injury in addition to the confinement itself.

Major Defense and Counterargument Possibilities That Need to Be Explored

1. There was no confinement.
2. The confinement was not total; there was a safe and inoffensive means of escape that the plaintiff did not take.
3. The threat of force related to the future.
4. The confinement was accidental. It may have been carelessly (negligently) or recklessly caused, but it was not intentional.
5. The defendant was not a substantial factor in producing the confinement.
6. The plaintiff either did not know about the confinement or was not physically harmed by it.
7. The plaintiff consented to the confinement by the defendant (on the defense of consent, see Chapter 27).
8. The confinement resulted while the defendant was defending him- or herself from the plaintiff (on self-defense and other self-help privileges, see Chapter 27).
9. The confinement occurred while the defendant was defending someone else from the plaintiff (on the defense of others and other self-help privileges, see Chapter 27).
10. The confinement occurred while the defendant was legitimately defending property or recapturing chattels from the plaintiff (on the privileges of necessity, defense of property, recapture of property, and other self-help privileges, see Chapter 27).
11. The confinement occurred while the defendant was detaining plaintiff for investigation to determine whether the plaintiff had stolen property or services (shopkeeper's privilege).
12. The confinement occurred while the defendant was disciplining the plaintiff (on discipline and other self-help privileges, see Chapter 27).
13. The confinement occurred while the defendant was properly arresting the plaintiff (privilege of arrest).

FALSE IMPRISONMENT CHECKLIST *(Continued)*

14. The plaintiff's suit against the government for false imprisonment committed by a government employee may be barred by sovereign immunity (on sovereign immunity, see Chapter 27).
15. The plaintiff's suit against the government employee for false imprisonment may be barred by official immunity (on official immunity, see Chapter 27).
16. The plaintiff's suit against the charitable organization for a false imprisonment committed by someone working for the organization may be barred by charitable immunity (on charitable immunity, see Chapter 27).
17. The plaintiff's suit against a family member for false imprisonment may be barred by intrafamily tort immunity (on intrafamily tort immunity, see Chapter 22).
18. The plaintiff failed to take reasonable steps to mitigate the harm caused when the defendant committed false imprisonment; therefore, damages should not cover the aggravation of the harm caused by the plaintiff (on the mitigation-of-damages rule, see Chapter 16).

Damages

The plaintiff does not have to prove actual harm to establish false imprisonment (unless the plaintiff was unaware of the confinement). In most cases, the confinement is harm enough. Once the elements of false imprisonment have been proven, the jury will be allowed to consider compensatory damages for humiliation, injury to plaintiff's reputation, illness or other physical discomfort, loss of earnings, damage to personal property due to the confinement, etc. Damages can include unforeseeable consequences of the false imprisonment if the general nature or type of harm that resulted was a foreseeable consequence of the original risk created by the false imprisonment. If the defendant acted out of hatred or malice, punitive damages are also possible.

Relationship to Criminal Law

In many states, false imprisonment is also a crime if the confinement is serious enough. The crime may be called false imprisonment, abduction, kidnapping, etc.

Relationship to Other Torts

Assault: An assault may also be committed if the defendant puts the plaintiff in apprehension of a harmful or offensive contact while falsely imprisoning him or her.

Battery: It is common for the defendant to touch the plaintiff while falsely imprisoning him or her. If this touching was without consent, the defendant may also be liable for a battery.

Defamation: Defamation may occur during the false imprisonment. For example, the defendant may use derogatory language while confining the plaintiff. Also, the very act of being confined may be a derogatory "communication," especially if the defendant is a police officer and the confinement is seen by others.

Intentional Infliction of Emotional Distress: This tort may also be committed if the confinement occurred by a shocking or outrageous act leading to severe emotional trauma.

Malicious Prosecution: If the defendant has instigated an unlawful arrest of the plaintiff, the defendant may be liable for false imprisonment and for malicious prosecution if the defendant acted with malice, without probable cause, and if the criminal case terminated favorably to the plaintiff.

Negligence: The defendant may have caused the confinement of the plaintiff by carelessness or recklessness rather than with the intent to confine him or her, e.g., the defendant accidentally, but carelessly or recklessly, locks the plaintiff in a room. If so, there is no false imprisonment, but there may be negligence if the plaintiff has suffered actual harm in addition to the confinement itself.

Federal Law

a. Under the Federal Tort Claims Act, the United States government will *not* be liable for a false imprisonment committed by one of its federal employees within the scope of employment (respondeat superior) *unless* the federal employee is an investigative or law enforcement officer. (See Exhibit 27–7 in Chapter 27.) (Most states have their own statutes that cover when tort claims can be made against the state for false imprisonment or other torts committed by state government employees. Such claims are also covered in Chapter 27.)

FALSE IMPRISONMENT CHECKLIST *(Continued)*

b. There may be liability under the Civil Rights Act if the false imprisonment was committed while the defendant was depriving the plaintiff of a federal civil right under color of state law. (See Exhibit 27–9 in Chapter 27.)

Employer–Employee (Agency) Law

A private (non-government) employee who commits false imprisonment is personally liable for this tort. His or her employer will *also* be liable for false imprisonment if the conduct of the employee was within the scope of employment (respondeat superior). The employee must be furthering a business objective of the employer at the time. Intentional torts such as false imprisonment, however, are often outside the scope of employment. If so, only the employee is liable for the false imprisonment. (On the factors that determine the scope of employment, see Exhibit 14–9 in Chapter 14.)

Paralegal Roles in False Imprisonment Litigation

(See Exhibit 3–1 in Chapter 3, Exhibit 20–4 in Chapter 20, and Exhibit 29–1 in Chapter 29.)

Fact finding (help the office collect facts relevant to prove the elements of false imprisonment, the elements of available defenses, and extent of injuries or other damages):

- client interviewing
- field investigation
- online research

File management (help the office control the documents involved in a false imprisonment litigation):

- open client file
- enter case data in computer database
- maintain file documents

Litigation assistance (help the trial attorney prepare for a false imprisonment trial and appeal, if needed):

- draft discovery requests
- draft answers to discovery requests
- draft pleadings
- digest and index discovery documents
- help prepare, order, and manage trial exhibits
- prepare trial notebook
- draft notice of appeal
- order trial transcript
- cite-check briefs
- perform legal research

Collection/enforcement (help the trial attorney for the judgment creditor to collect the damages award or to enforce other court orders at the conclusion of the false imprisonment case):

- draft postjudgment discovery requests
- conduct field investigation to monitor compliance with judgment
- perform online research (e.g., location of defendant's business assets)

Research References for False Imprisonment

Digests

In the digests of West Group, look for case summaries on false imprisonment under key topics such as:

False Imprisonment	Torts
Arrest	Damages

Corpus Juris Secundum

In this legal encyclopedia, look for discussions under topic headings such as:

False Imprisonment	Torts
Arrest	Damages

American Jurisprudence 2d

In this legal encyclopedia, look for discussions under topic headings such as:

False Imprisonment	Torts
Arrest	Damages

FALSE IMPRISONMENT CHECKLIST *(Continued)*

Legal Periodical Literature
There are two index systems to use to try to locate legal periodical literature on false imprisonment:

Index to Legal Periodicals and Books (ILP)
See literature in *ILP* under subject headings such as:
False Imprisonment
Arrest
Damages
Torts
Personal Injuries

Current Law Index (CLI)
See literature in *CLI* under subject headings such as:
False Imprisonment
Arrest
Torts
Damages
Duress
Personal Injuries
Privileges and Immunities

Example of a legal periodical article on this tort you will find by using *ILP* or *CLI:*

"Nowhere to Go and Chose to Stay"; Using the Tort of False Imprisonment to Redress Involuntary Confinement of the Elderly in Nursing Homes and Hospitals by Cathrael Kazin, 137 University of Pennsylvania Law Review 903 (1989).

A.L.R., A.L.R.2d, A.L.R.3d, A.L.R.4th, A.L.R.5th, A.L.R.6th, A.L.R. Fed, A.L.R. Fed 2d
Use the *ALR Index* to locate annotations on false imprisonment. In this index, check subject headings such as:

False Imprisonment
Arrest
Privileges and Immunities
Shoplifting
Torts
Damages

Example of an annotation on false imprisonment you can locate through this index:

Liability of Attorney Acting for Client for False Imprisonment or Malicious Prosecution of Third Party, 27 A.L.R.3d 1113 by J. Kraut (1969).

Words and Phrases
In this multivolume legal dictionary, look up *false imprisonment, confinement, false arrest,* and every other word or phrase connected with the tort discussed in this chapter. The dictionary will give you definitions of these words or phrases from court opinions.

CALR: Computer-Assisted Legal Research

Example of a query you could ask on Westlaw to try to find cases, statutes, or other legal materials on false imprisonment: **"false imprisonment" /p damages**

Example of a query you could ask on LexisNexis to try to find cases, statutes, or other legal materials on false imprisonment: **false imprisonment /p damages**

Example of search terms you could use on an Internet legal search engine such as the Public Library of Law (www.plol.org), Findlaw (www.findlaw.com), or Google Scholar (scholar.google.com) to find cases, statutes, or other legal materials on false imprisonment: **"false imprisonment"**

Example of search terms you could use on an Internet general search engine such as Google, Bing, or AltaVista to find cases, statutes, or other legal materials on false imprisonment: **"false imprisonment" -crime**

More Internet sites to check for materials on false imprisonment and other torts:
www.hg.org/torts.html
www.megalaw.com/top/top.php (click "Intentional Torts," "Personal Injury Law," "Tort Law," and "Damages")
See also the online sites in Overview of Tort Law at the end of Chapter 1.

CHECK THE CITE

The photo department of Wal-Mart notifies the police of nude photographs taken of a young girl. The police arrest the grandmother who left the photographs for development. She told the officials that the photographs were taken while getting her granddaughter ready for a bath. Later the charges of child exploitation were dismissed for lack of criminal intent. (1) Why was the mother of the young girl also arrested? (2) How did the court resolve the mother's tort suit against the police for false arrest and false imprisonment? See *Dull v. West Manchester Tp. Police Department,* 604 F. Supp. 2d 739 (United States District Court, Middle District Pennsylvania 2009). To read the opinion online: (1) Go to the United States District Court site (www.pamd.uscourts.gov). Click Opinions. Then click 2009 Opinions. Scroll down to the *Dull* case. (2) On the same site, click Search, type part of the names of the parties (Dull Manchester), and select the full text of the opinion that was decided on March 31, 2009. (3) Run a citation search ("604 F. Supp. 2d 729") in the Legal Opinions and Journals database of Google Scholar (scholar.google.com).

PROJECT

In Google, Bing, or another general search engine, run the following search: *aa* "false imprisonment" (substitute the name of your state for *aa* in the search). Write a short essay in which you compare false imprisonment as a tort and as a crime in your state. You can consult as many websites as you wish, but you must quote from at least three separate sites.

ETHICS IN A TORTS PRACTICE

You are a paralegal working in the law office of Thomas Riley, Esq. The office handles personal injury and other kinds of cases. Before you came to work for Riley, you were an accountant who prepared tax returns. Riley and you decide to open a tax-preparation business together in which all profits are split evenly between the two of you. You will work in the office of Riley. If one of your clients has a legal question or problem, you will refer the client to Riley. What ethical problems, if any, might exist?

SUMMARY

False imprisonment is an intentional confinement within fixed boundaries of someone who is conscious of the confinement or is harmed by it. The confinement can be by physical barriers, by physical force, by threat of present physical force, by asserted legal authority, or by a refusal to release. The confinement must be complete or total. Shopkeepers have a limited privilege to detain someone temporarily to investigate whether merchandise or services have been stolen.

The defendant must desire to confine the plaintiff or know with substantial certainty that the confinement will result from what the defendant does or fails to do. But for the act of the defendant, the confinement would not have occurred, or the defendant must be a substantial factor in producing the confinement. In most states, the plaintiff must either be aware of the confinement or suffer physical harm as a result of it.

An arrest is false when it is unprivileged. A peace officer has a privilege to arrest someone if the officer is acting on a warrant that is fair on its face. If a privilege exists, the arrest is not wrongful. If the officer has an immunity, he or she is not personally liable even if the arrest was wrongful. If no warrant exists, the peace officer has a privilege to make a felony arrest if there are reasonable grounds to believe a felony has been committed and that the plaintiff committed it. The officer is limited to reasonable force in making the arrest. The officer has a privilege to make a misdemeanor arrest if the misdemeanor is a breach of the peace or if it is committed in the officer's presence. The arrest must be made immediately or in fresh pursuit. Only reasonable force can be used. The officer can take an insane or mentally ill person into custody as a civil commitment if the officer reasonably believes the person poses a serious danger to him- or herself or to others, and if the officer uses reasonable force.

A private citizen has a privilege to make a felony arrest of a person if a felony has in fact been committed, if it is the felony the citizen arrested the person for, if the citizen has reasonable grounds to believe the person committed the felony, and if the citizen uses reasonable force. A citizen can make a misdemeanor arrest if the misdemeanor is a breach of the peace, if it is committed in the citizen's presence, if the arrest is made immediately or in fresh pursuit, and if the citizen uses reasonable force. A citizen can take an insane or mentally ill person into custody as a civil commitment if the citizen reasonably believes the person poses a serious danger to him- or herself or to others, and if the citizen uses reasonable force.

KEY TERMS

false imprisonment *108*
confinement *108*
duress *109*
shopkeeper's privilege *110*
common law *110*
intent (for false imprisonment) *113*
negligence *113*
transferred-intent rule *113*
instigation *113*
false arrest *116*
personal liability *116*
official immunity *116*
privilege *116*
immunity *116*
respondeat superior *116*
sovereign immunity *116*
peace officer *116*
warrant *116*
fair on its face *116*
felony *118*
misdemeanor *118*
breach of the peace *118*
fresh pursuit *118*
civil commitment *118*

REVIEW QUESTIONS

1. What is false imprisonment?
2. What constitutes confinement?
3. In what five ways can a plaintiff be confined?
4. How can threats constitute confinement?
5. What is the shopkeeper's privilege?
6. Under what circumstances will a merchant lose its shopkeeper's privilege?
7. What intent is needed to establish false imprisonment?
8. How does the plaintiff establish that the defendant caused the false imprisonment?
9. What is meant by the instigation of an arrest by a citizen?
10. Can someone be falsely imprisoned if he or she is not conscious of the confinement?
11. What is a false arrest?
12. What is meant by personal liability?
13. When can a peace officer avoid personal liability for a false arrest?
14. What is the distinction between a privilege and an immunity?
15. When does a warrant allow an officer to make an arrest?
16. When does a peace officer have a privilege to arrest someone without a warrant for a felony or misdemeanor, or for civil commitment?
17. When can a citizen's arrest be made for a felony or misdemeanor, or for civil commitment?

HELPFUL WEBSITES

- **False Imprisonment Overview**
  en.wikipedia.org/wiki/False_imprisonment
  www.encyclopedia.com/doc/1E1-falseimp.html
  www.mojolaw.com/info/to007
  www.law.und.edu/Class/torts/wiki/index.php/Intentional_Torts
  www.google.com (run this search: elements false imprisonment tort)
- **Shopkeeper's Privilege**
  en.wikipedia.org/wiki/Shopkeeper's_privilege
  www.civildemand.net/Articles.html
- **False Arrest Overview**
  en.wikipedia.org/wiki/False_arrest
  www.constitution.org/uslaw/defunlaw.htm
  www.google.com (run this search: elements false arrest tort)

Student StudyWARE™ CD-ROM
For additional materials, please go to the student CD in this book.

CHAPTER

8

MISUSE OF LEGAL PROCEEDINGS

CHAPTER OUTLINE

- Introduction
- Malicious Prosecution
- Wrongful Civil Proceedings
- Abuse of Process

CHAPTER OBJECTIVES

After completing this chapter, you should be able to:

- Understand why suits for torts such as malicious prosecution are disfavored in the law.
- Distinguish between malicious prosecution and wrongful civil proceedings.
- Identify the elements of malicious prosecution.
- Identify the elements of wrongful civil proceedings.
- Identify the elements of abuse of process.
- Describe paralegal roles in malicious prosecution litigation.
- List the major sources (traditional and online) for researching issues in malicious prosecution cases.

INTRODUCTION

Think of the devastating feeling you would have if:

- a police officer came to your home or your place of employment to tell you that you are under arrest for a crime (e.g., passing a forged check) that you know you did not commit; or
- a process server came to your home or place of employment to hand you a summons and complaint notifying you that you are the defendant in a civil action (e.g., negligence) that you know is frivolous.

You would not be able to close the door and refuse to cooperate with the police or refuse to accept the summons and complaint. Once the legal system is set in motion, the process must go forward to the next step. The costs to you can be substantial: damage to reputation, disruption in schedule, expense of defending yourself, emotional stress, etc. Surprisingly, it is relatively easy for a criminal or civil proceeding to be launched. Essentially, all that is needed is an allegation by someone against you.

Since you cannot walk away from legal proceedings that have been commenced, what remedy do you have once you are able to convince the system that the criminal or civil case against you was groundless or otherwise improper? You can bring a tort action. Three torts are possible: *malicious prosecution, wrongful civil proceedings,* and *abuse of process.* These torts are our concern in this chapter.

In many states, the tort of *malicious prosecution* covers two categories of misuse: the misuse of criminal proceedings and the misuse of civil proceedings. This can be confusing because the word **prosecution** is commonly used to refer to criminal cases and to the government attorney arguing a criminal case. Yet prosecution has the broader meaning of bringing and pursuing *any* legal proceedings, whether criminal or civil. Hence it is equally appropriate to refer to prosecuting a criminal case (e.g., the state prosecuted him for burglary) and a civil case (e.g., Jones prosecuted her action for negligence against Smith). In most states, the word prosecution has this broader meaning in the phrase *malicious prosecution* so that it covers the misuse of criminal or civil proceedings. Some states, however, limit the tort of malicious prosecution to the misuse of criminal proceedings. For the misuse of civil proceedings, they use the term *wrongful civil proceedings* or *malicious civil prosecution.*

prosecution 1. Bringing and pursuing criminal proceedings against someone. 2. Bringing and pursuing civil proceedings against someone. 3. The attorney representing the government in a criminal case; also called the prosecutor.

In this chapter, we will assume that malicious prosecution is limited to the misuse of criminal proceedings. We will discuss the misuse of civil proceedings separately under the heading *wrongful civil proceedings*. Keep in mind, however, that both kinds of misuse might fall under the heading of malicious prosecution in your state.

This is a delicate area of the law. As a society, we want to provide some protection against defendants who have been subjected to wrongful legal proceedings. At the same time, we do not want to discourage the public at large from filing grievances. Arguably, people will be less inclined to complain to the police or to the courts if they know that they might end up being sued themselves for the torts of malicious prosecution, wrongful civil proceedings, or abuse of process if they turn out to be wrong. One way in which the system tries to balance these concerns is to make these tort actions available, but relatively difficult to win.

malicious prosecution Instigating criminal legal proceedings without probable cause and with malice, or with an improper purpose, when the proceedings terminate in favor of the accused. (Note that some states include the initiation of civil proceedings. Here, however, we will follow those states that treat civil proceedings separately as wrongful civil proceedings.)

MALICIOUS PROSECUTION

We begin with **malicious prosecution**. This tort consists of the instigation of criminal legal proceedings without probable cause and with malice or with an improper purpose when the proceedings terminate in favor of the accused. See Exhibit 8–1 for the elements of this tort.

Malicious Prosecution

1. Instigation of criminal proceedings
2. Without probable cause
3. With malice
4. The criminal proceedings terminate in favor of the accused

Exhibit 8–1
Elements of the tort of malicious prosecution.

Instigation of Criminal Proceedings

The first element of malicious prosecution is that the accuser instigates criminal proceedings.

EXAMPLE
Dan calls the police to complain that Linda stole his car. He insists that the police arrest Linda. They do. After an investigation, she is indicted for grand larceny.

In the criminal case against Linda, Dan is the *complaining witness*. His accusation has set in motion a criminal proceeding against Linda, who becomes a defendant (the accused) in the state's criminal case of car stealing—grand larceny—against her. To **instigate** means to insist on, urge, goad, direct, or incite someone to a course of action. The instigator in the criminal case (Dan) will later become the defendant in the civil case of malicious prosecution brought by the accused (Linda) in the earlier criminal case. The two separate proceedings are as follows:

instigate To urge, goad, or incite someone to a course of action.

State v. Linda (criminal case of grand larceny)
Linda v. Dan (civil case of malicious prosecution)

Without Probable Cause

The legal proceedings must be initiated without **probable cause**. Probable cause is a reasonable belief that a specific crime has been committed and that the accused committed the crime. (Later we will see that probable cause can also mean a reasonable belief that good grounds exist to bring civil proceedings against someone.) In our example, suppose that:

probable cause 1. A reasonable belief that a specific crime has been committed and that the accused committed the crime. 2. A reasonable belief that good grounds exist to bring civil proceedings against someone.

- Dan saw Linda speeding away from his driveway in his car at night.
- Yet, Linda is eventually found not guilty of stealing Dan's car.

Linda now sues Dan for malicious prosecution. She will lose. Why? Because there was probable cause that she was guilty. She was seen speeding from Dan's driveway at night. This is probable cause that she stole the car. Probable cause does not mean conclusive proof of guilt. All that is needed for probable cause is a reasonable belief that the accused has committed a specific crime.

Now let's change the facts. Assume that Dan did not see Linda in his car speeding away from his driveway at night. The sole reason he accused Linda is that she recently broke up with him and that while they were dating she told him that she would do anything to own a car like his. This is not probable cause that Linda committed the crime. The second element of malicious prosecution, therefore, would be met in Linda's suit against Dan for this tort.

Some of the factors that a court will use to determine whether probable cause exists are outlined in Exhibit 8–2.

With Malice

Malice has many different meanings in the law. For purposes of the tort of malicious prosecution, it does *not* mean hatred or ill will. It is not necessarily

malice (for malicious prosecution) Improper purpose.

Exhibit 8–2
Probable cause in malicious prosecution suits.

Factors Considered by a Court in Determining Whether the Accuser Had Probable Cause to Instigate Criminal Proceedings Against the Accused.

1. Did the accuser honestly believe that the accused committed the crime charged?
2. Did the accuser have first-hand knowledge/observation of what the accused did?
3. If the accuser used second-hand knowledge/observation, how reliable was the source used? If, for example, an informer gave information to the accuser (which the latter used in initiating the criminal case against the accused), what was the informer's reputation for reliability? Did the accuser check into this before initiating the criminal case?
4. What was the accused's reputation in the community? Notorious? The type of person who would commit this kind of crime? Or an honest, upright citizen?
5. Did the accuser know of the accused's reputation? If not, was there time to find out?
6. Did the accuser first confront the accused before going to the authorities? If not, why not? Impractical? No time? Danger to the accuser? Fear the accused would flee?
7. Was there any time for the accuser to do any further informal or formal investigation before contacting the authorities? If there was time, was it practical to use it?
8. Did the accuser seek the advice of his or her own attorney on whether there was a reasonable basis for the accuser to initiate criminal proceedings against the accused? If so, and if the advice was that the accuser should go to the authorities, did the accuser give the attorney all the relevant facts known to the accuser so that the attorney could provide informed advice?
9. Was there any other information that was reasonably available to the accuser that should have been obtained by the accuser before he or she initiated the criminal case against the accused?

inappropriate to have such feelings against someone you think has committed a crime. To establish the element of malice in malicious prosecution, all you need to show is an improper purpose in instigating the criminal prosecution. The proper purpose to initiate criminal proceedings is to bring to justice someone you believe has committed a crime. If this was not Dan's purpose when he called the police and pursued the case against Linda, he was acting with malice. Examples of improper (and hence malicious) purposes are to exert pressure on the accused to pay a debt, to return property, or to vote a certain way in an election. Often the initiator has more than one purpose. If the primary purpose is proper, the contemporaneous presence of improper incidental purposes will not lead to the conclusion that the proceeding was instigated with malice.

Criminal Proceedings Terminate in Favor of the Accused

The criminal proceedings must be over, and the accused must have won the case. Most states require the victory to be **on the merits**, rather than be a mere technical or procedural victory. An example of a technical or procedural victory would be a dismissal of the criminal charge because it was not brought before the **statute of limitations** expired. If the accused did not win the criminal case on the merits, the strong likelihood is that the initial prosecution against the accused was made with probable cause and without malice. Examples of criminal proceedings that terminate in favor of the accused on the merits would include a verdict of not guilty, a discharge of the case because the grand jury fails to indict, and a **nolle prosequi** (i.e., a statement by the district attorney that he or she is unwilling to prosecute an individual for the commission of a crime). It must be expressly or implicitly clear that the accused was shown to be innocent of the charge.

on the merits Based on a substantive determination of who is in the right rather than on a preliminary, technical, or procedural irregularity.

statute of limitations A law that designates a time period within which a court case must be filed or it can never be brought.

nolle prosequi A statement by the prosecutor that he or she is unwilling to prosecute an individual for the commission of a crime.

The malicious prosecution case is not necessarily won, however, just because the criminal proceedings end in favor of the accused. As we have seen, the accused must also show that there was no probable cause. Winning the criminal case does not necessarily mean that there was no probable cause.

EXAMPLE

While walking in the corridor, Mary overhears Fred say on a cell phone that he is going to "bomb a federal building." They were in a federal building at the time. He was carrying a suspicious suitcase and acting erratically when Mary heard him talking. In a panic, she immediately calls the police and demands that Fred be arrested. Fred is tried but found not guilty because he convinced the jury that the statement he actually made was that "anyone who would bomb a federal building should be executed." Mary had misunderstood what he was saying. Fred now sues Mary for malicious prosecution.

The criminal proceedings certainly terminated in favor of the accused—Fred was acquitted. In the malicious prosecution case, however, he must show that Mary had no probable cause to instigate his arrest and prosecution. But Mary *did* have probable cause based on what she thought she heard, the suspicious suitcase, and the erratic behavior. She simply made a reasonable mistake in failing to hear Fred correctly. Hence, Fred loses the malicious prosecution case for failure to establish that Mary acted without probable cause. There was probable cause to believe that an innocent person committed a crime.

ASSIGNMENT 8.1

Elaine arrives home one night to find that her home has been burglarized. She calls the police. When questioned by the police, she says she does not know who did it, but that her uncle Bob recently threatened to harm her. The police conduct an investigation of Bob. He is indicted for burglary. At his trial, Elaine testifies that he once threatened her. The jury is deadlocked, and a mistrial is declared. The District Attorney (D.A.) is unsure whether to reprosecute him. By this time, Elaine is convinced Bob is guilty of the burglary. She urges the D.A. to retry Bob for the burglary. She constantly calls the D.A. Once she carries a sign outside the D.A.'s office urging prosecution. The D.A.'s decision, however, is to drop the charges. After the case is dismissed, Bob sues Elaine for malicious prosecution. What result?

Of course, the major initiators of criminal cases in our society are district attorneys and prosecutors. Rarely, however, can they be sued for malicious prosecution because of the **absolute immunity** that they enjoy. We will discuss this immunity in Chapter 27.

absolute immunity A defense that avoids personal liability when a government employee is carrying out official functions even if the employee was acting with malice.

WRONGFUL CIVIL PROCEEDINGS

The examples we have covered thus far have involved wrongful criminal litigation. Now, suppose that wrongful *civil* proceedings are initiated.

EXAMPLE

Charles files a complaint against Ted for libel. Ted is served with process, which orders Ted to file an answer within thirty days. After a trial, Ted is found not liable for libel.

Charles has initiated civil proceedings that have terminated in favor of Ted. Many states will now allow Ted to assert a tort action against Charles for bringing **wrongful civil proceedings.** The action may still be called malicious prosecution, although in this chapter we are using the terminology favored by some states that limit malicious prosecution to bringing wrongful criminal proceedings.

wrongful civil proceedings The initiation of civil proceedings without probable cause and with malice when the proceedings terminate in favor of the person against whom they were brought. (Note that some states include the initiation of civil proceedings within the tort of malicious prosecution.)

Wrongful civil proceedings is the initiation of civil proceedings without probable cause and with malice when the proceedings terminate in favor of the person against whom the civil proceedings were brought. For the elements of this tort, see Exhibit 8–3.

Exhibit 8–3
Elements of the tort of wrongful civil proceedings.

1. Initiation of civil proceedings
2. Without probable cause
3. With malice
4. The proceedings terminate in favor of the person against whom the civil proceedings were brought
5. Some states add an additional element of special injury or interference caused by the civil proceedings

In general, the same elements apply for the torts of wrongful civil proceedings and malicious prosecution. For wrongful civil proceedings, there must be an initiation of civil legal proceedings without probable cause, with malice, and the proceedings must terminate in favor of the person against whom the civil proceedings were brought. (As we will see, however, some of the definitions of the elements will differ slightly in wrongful civil proceedings.) In our libel example:

- Ted was the defendant in the libel case brought against him by Charles (Charles v. Ted for libel).
- Ted is now the plaintiff in the wrongful civil proceedings case against Charles (Ted v. Charles for wrongful civil proceedings).

For the tort of wrongful civil proceedings:

- initiation simply means filing an action in a tribunal,
- probable cause means a reasonable belief that good grounds exist for initiating the civil proceedings, and
- malice means an improper purpose in bringing the proceedings.

Ted would have to show that it was unreasonable for Charles to believe that good grounds existed to file a libel action against Ted or that Charles had an improper purpose in filing it.

Some states add an additional element to the tort of wrongful civil proceedings. In such states, Ted would have to show that he suffered some special injury or interference with person or property as a result of the wrongful civil proceedings.

CASE

Raine and Highfield v. Drasin and Fadel

621 S.W.2d 895 (1981)
Supreme Court of Kentucky

Background: *Robert Browning sued Doctors Drasin and Fadel for medical malpractice. Browning was represented by two attorneys, Raine and Highfield. The doctors won the malpractice case by a voluntary dismissal (an "agreed order of dismissal") which meant that Browning agreed to terminate his suit. Since the dismissal was with prejudice, the same claims could not be brought again on the same facts. The doctors then sued Raine and Highfield for malicious prosecution. The lower courts found that Raine, but not Highfield, was liable for malicious prosecution. The case is now on appeal before the Supreme Court of Kentucky. (In this state, the tort of malicious prosecution covers both wrongful criminal proceedings and wrongful civil proceedings.)*

Decision on Appeal: *Judgment affirmed. Raine committed malicious prosecution; Highfield did not.*

OPINION OF COURT

Justice STEPHENS delivered the opinion of the court . . .

On July 19, 1975, Robert Browning . . . suffered a massive heart attack at his home. He was taken, unconscious, to Sts. Mary and Elizabeth Hospital. Following treatment in the emergency room, he was examined by Dr. James Fitzpatrick. During his initial examination of Browning, Dr. Fitzpatrick discovered an injury to Browning's shoulder. He ordered X-rays taken which revealed that the shoulder was fractured. Dr. Fitzpatrick then called in Dr. Fadel, an orthopedic surgeon, to treat the shoulder. Dr. Drasin, a radiologist, had read the X-ray but never saw or treated Browning.

Following his release from the hospital, Browning contacted attorney Raine regarding a possible suit for the fracture of his shoulder. On September 15, 1975, Raine visited the hospital and reviewed its records which clearly showed that the fracture of the shoulder occurred before Drs. Drasin and Fadel were involved.

On November 21, 1975, a complaint was filed in the Jefferson Circuit Court against the hospital for allegedly breaking Browning's shoulder. Raine prepared the complaint, but because he represented another hospital he did not wish to sign the complaint. At his request attorney James H. Highfield, a long-time associate of Raine's, with space in his office, signed it. He did so without reading it and without investigating any of the facts. In March of 1976, the attorneys served interrogatories on the hospital, the answers to which revealed that . . . both doctors were contacted after Browning's shoulder injury was discovered. . . . On May 24, 1976, the deposition of Dr. Fitzpatrick was taken. It is clearly shown that the deponent told the attorneys that the injury occurred before he saw Browning in the emergency room and moreover that, after he discovered the injury, he then called in Drs. Fadel and Drasin. In spite of this clear and cumulative evidence, on July 15, 1976, Raine filed an amended complaint (signed by Highfield), in which the two doctors were joined as parties defendant, and were charged with malpractice in that they negligently broke Browning's shoulder. Highfield did not read the amended complaint.

[Soon thereafter, however, an order for voluntary dismissal was entered. It was an "agreed order of dismissal" that dismissed the medical malpractice case against the doctors with prejudice, meaning that the case could not be brought against them again.]

Subsequent to the dismissal, the doctors filed this suit against both attorneys, alleging malicious prosecution. . . . At the trial, no evidence was introduced by the doctors concerning any out-of-pocket expenses. They did testify as to their embarrassment, humiliation, mortification and mental anguish at having been publicly accused of malpractice. Dr. Fadel testified that he suffered an acute anxiety reaction.

Both doctors stated that the malpractice accusation (even though specious), became a permanent part of their professional and insurance records. The attorneys testified that they had no evidence to implicate the doctors. Raine had access to and was aware of this fact even when he filed the malpractice action. . . . [The trial court found that attorneys Raine and Highfield had committed malicious prosecution. On appeal, the judgment against Raine was affirmed, but reversed as to Highfield.]

On this appeal Raine argues that the order of dismissal was not a favorable determination of the action, thus eliminating a key ingredient in a malicious prosecution action . . . [and] that the testimony of an expert concerning violations of an ethical code was improperly admitted in evidence. . . . [T]he doctors argue [on appeal] that the dismissal of the . . . claim against Highfield was improper. . . .

The doctrine of malicious prosecution is an old one in our Commonwealth. Historically, it has not been favored in the law. Public policy requires that all persons be able to freely resort to the courts for redress of a wrong, and the law should and does protect them when they commence a civil or criminal action in good faith and upon reasonable grounds. It is for this reason that one must strictly comply with the prerequisites of maintaining an action for malicious prosecution.

Generally speaking, there are six basic elements necessary to the maintenance of an action for malicious prosecution, in response to both criminal prosecutions and civil action. They are: (1) the institution or continuation of original judicial proceedings, either civil or criminal, or of administrative or disciplinary proceedings, (2) by, or at the instance, of the plaintiff, (3) the termination of such proceedings in defendant's favor, (4) malice in the institution of such proceeding, (5) want or lack of probable cause for the proceeding, and (6) the suffering of damage as a result of the proceeding. With these principles in mind, we will examine the arguments.

IS AN AGREED ORDER OF DISMISSAL A FAVORABLE TERMINATION OF THE MALPRACTICE ACTION?

Shortly after the malpractice action against the doctors was filed, the order of dismissal was filed. It was, by its terms, an "agreed order of dismissal." The order provided that the amended complaint against the doctors was dismissed, with prejudice. It was signed by the plaintiff, Browning, and by his counsel, Raine and Highfield, and by counsel for the doctors. The document did not entail any compromise or settlement; it simply and effectively terminated the lawsuit as far as the defendant doctors were concerned. The dismissal declared, in effect, that there was no malpractice on the part of the defendants.

The purpose of this prerequisite to a malicious prosecution suit is to show that the action against the defendant was unsuccessful. The basis for the requirement is that courts will not tolerate inconsistent judgments on the same action between the same parties. In Kentucky, no particular form of termination in civil actions has been required. Since the order of dismissal effectively terminates the litigation, with respect to the doctors, . . . the order constituted a favorable termination so as to support this action. . . .

WAS THE TESTIMONY OF AN EXPERT CONCERNING THE ATTORNEYS' POSSIBLE VIOLATION OF ETHICAL CODE PROPERLY ADMITTED?

The deposition of Professor David Leibson, a member of the Ethics Committee of the Louisville Bar Association, was apparently read to the jury. Professor Leibson stated that, in his opinion, the actions of both Raine and Highfield did not comply with the standard of care for ordinary and prudent lawyers. Raine complains that the admission was improper. We believe that such evidence was properly introduced to show one of the key ingredients of a malicious prosecution action; viz., lack of probable cause. . . .

[WAS THE REVERSAL AGAINST HIGHFIELD PROPER?]

Attorney Highfield, it will be remembered, signed the complaint and amended complaint without reading them.

He literally knew nothing about the allegations therein, the parties therein, the factual background or the law. The evidence shows that he was a long-time friend and associate of attorney Raine and has space in Raine's office. Undoubtedly, he signed the documents as a convenience and as a favor to Raine. . . . [S]uch action does not constitute malice. At worst it was a breach of ethics, and at least, it was poor judgment on his part. . . . [Highfield] was given a plausible reason why Raine did not want to sign the complaint, and based on years of fellowship and association, he signed it. . . . [T]his is not sufficient evidence, as a matter of law, for a jury to find the necessary malice upon which to base a malicious prosecution action.

[The decision affirming the malicious prosecution claim against Raine but reversing it against Highfield is affirmed.]

ASSIGNMENT 8.2

a. The court does not like malicious prosecution cases. They have "not been favored in the law." Why?

b. Raine did not want to sign the complaint "because he represented another hospital." Why would this make any difference?

c. What did the court mean when it said, "The basis for the requirement [of favorable termination] is that courts will not tolerate inconsistent judgments on the same action between the same parties"?

d. Do you agree with the dismissal of the malicious prosecution claim against Highfield? Can you think of a reason why the court should have treated him the same as it treated Raine so that both would be liable for malicious prosecution (wrongful civil proceedings)?

ABUSE OF PROCESS

abuse of process The use of civil or criminal proceedings for an improper or ulterior motive.

process 1. The means used by a court to acquire or exercise its power or jurisdiction over a person, e.g., a writ or a summons to appear in court. 2. A court proceeding.

Abuse of process is the use of civil or criminal process for an improper or ulterior motive. (See Exhibit 8–4.) **Process** is the means by which a court acquires or exercises its power or jurisdiction over a person. Examples of process include a writ or a summons to appear in court. (Process can also mean any court proceeding.)

Unlike malicious prosecution, abuse of process involves a civil or criminal case that was *properly* initiated. Probable cause may exist, and the proceeding does not have to terminate in favor of the person now bringing the abuse-of-process action. Yet, the civil or criminal proceeding was used for an improper or ulterior motive.

EXAMPLE

Bob and Mary are married, but have been separated for over five years. They have two children. Mary believes that she is the better parent and tells Bob that if he does not agree to give her full custody, she will tell the Internal Revenue Service that he has been cheating on his business taxes for years. Bob refuses. Mary tells the IRS, which begins a criminal fraud case against Bob. He is convicted. He then sues Mary for abuse of process.

Bob would win. Mary had an ulterior motive in initiating the criminal case against Bob. She was using the courts for a purpose for which they are not designed. She may have had probable cause to accuse Bob of tax fraud, but it is improper to initiate a criminal tax proceeding against someone in order to gain agreement on a child custody matter. Note that the criminal case did not terminate in favor of Bob. This, however, is not an element of abuse of process.

Exhibit 8–4
Elements of the tort of abuse of process.

1. The use of criminal or civil process
2. For improper or ulterior motive

MALICIOUS PROSECUTION CHECKLIST

Definitions, Relationships, Paralegal Roles, and Research References

Category
Malicious prosecution is an intentional tort.

Interest Prosecuted by This Tort
The right to be free from unreasonable or unjustifiable criminal litigation brought against you. Secondarily, the tort protects your interest in not having your reputation harmed by such litigation. (This checklist covers only unjustified *criminal* proceedings. In some states, malicious prosecution also includes unjustified civil proceedings. In this chapter, however, we examined the latter as wrongful civil proceedings.)

Elements of This Tort

1. Instigation of criminal proceedings
2. Without probable cause
3. With malice
4. The criminal proceedings terminate in favor of the accused

Definitions of Major Words/Phrases in These Elements

Instigation: Insisting on, urging, goading, directing, or inciting.
Probable Cause: A reasonable belief that a specific crime has been committed and that the accused committed the crime.
Malice: (for malicious prosecution) Improper purpose.
Terminate in Favor of the Accused: The ending of the criminal proceedings expressly or by fair implication shows that the accused is innocent of the charge.

Major Defense and Counterargument Possibilities That Need to Be Explored

1. Criminal proceedings never actually began.
2. The accuser did not instigate the prosecution, but simply gave the facts to the authorities who decided to prosecute without urging from the accuser.
3. There was probable cause.
4. The primary purpose of the accuser was to bring the accused to justice (i.e., to use the court for its *proper* purpose).
5. The criminal proceedings have not yet terminated.
6. The criminal proceedings did not terminate on the merits in favor of the accused.
7. The plaintiff's suit against the government for malicious prosecution may be barred by sovereign immunity (on sovereign immunity, see Chapter 27).
8. The plaintiff's suit against the government employee for malicious prosecution may be barred by official immunity, e.g., prosecutors have an absolute immunity (on official immunity, see Chapter 27).
9. The plaintiff's suit against the charitable organization for malicious prosecution committed by someone working for the organization may be barred by charitable immunity (on charitable immunity, see Chapter 27).
10. The plaintiff's suit against a family member for malicious prosecution may be barred by intrafamily tort immunity (on intrafamily tort immunity, see Chapter 22).

Damages
In most states, malicious prosecution (unlike negligence) does not require proof of actual damages. There can be recovery for humiliation and mental suffering. Other compensatory damages include the costs of defending the underlying criminal case, medical bills, and loss of business or employment. Punitive damages are often possible when the defendant (the accuser in the criminal case) acted out of hatred for the accused. (On the categories of damages, see Chapter 16.)

Relationship to Criminal Law
One of the main purposes of the malicious prosecution tort is to provide a remedy against a person who has unjustifiably caused the criminal justice system "to go after you" because of an accusation that you have committed a crime.

MALICIOUS PROSECUTION CHECKLIST *(Continued)*

Relationship to Other Torts

Abuse of Process: Abuse of process is the improper use of legal proceedings that may have been properly initiated. If proceedings have been properly initiated, there is no malicious prosecution, but there may be abuse of process if the proceedings are used for an improper goal, e.g., to coerce the accused to pay a debt.

Battery: If the accused was touched (e.g., as part of an arrest) when criminal proceedings were initiated, the tort of battery as well as malicious prosecution may have been committed.

Defamation: Defamation (libel or slander) as well as malicious prosecution may be committed when the accuser initiates criminal proceedings against the accused. Things are probably said or written that are derogatory of the accused's character.

Disparagement: In the process of initiating criminal proceedings against the accused, the accuser may utter false statements injurious to the accused's business or property. The tort of disparagement as well as malicious prosecution may have been committed.

False Imprisonment: The accused may have been improperly restrained in his or her liberty while being maliciously prosecuted.

Intentional Infliction of Emotional Distress: It may be that the objective of the accuser was to subject the accused to severe emotional trauma by initiating criminal proceedings against the accused. A court might consider such conduct sufficiently outrageous so that the tort of intentional infliction of emotional distress is committed along with malicious prosecution.

Wrongful Civil Proceedings: Malicious prosecution covers wrongful criminal proceedings. It may also cover wrongful civil proceedings. In some states, however, wrongful civil proceedings is covered by a separate tort, sometimes called wrongful civil proceedings.

Federal Law

a. Under the Federal Tort Claims Act, the United States government will *not* be liable for malicious prosecution committed by one of its federal employees within the scope of employment (respondeat superior) *unless* the federal employee is an investigative or law enforcement officer. (See Exhibit 27–7 in Chapter 27.) (Most states have their own statutes that cover when tort claims can be made against the state for torts committed by state government employees. Such claims are also covered in Chapter 27.)
b. There may be liability under the Civil Rights Act if the malicious prosecution was committed while the defendant was depriving the plaintiff of a federal civil right under color of state law. (See Exhibit 27–9 in Chapter 27.)

Employer–Employee (Agency) Law

A private (non-government) employee who commits malicious prosecution is personally liable for this tort. His or her employer will *also* be liable for malicious prosecution if the conduct of the employee was within the scope of employment (respondeat superior). The employee must be furthering a business objective of the employer at the time. (On the factors that determine scope of employment, see Exhibit 14–9 in Chapter 14.)

Paralegal Roles in Malicious Prosecution Litigation

(See also Exhibit 3–1 in Chapter 3, Exhibit 20–4 in Chapter 20, and Exhibit 29–1 in Chapter 29.)

Fact finding (help the office collect facts relevant to prove the elements of malicious prosecution, the elements of available defenses, and the extent of injuries or other damages):

- client interviewing
- field investigation
- online research (e.g., court records)

File management (help the office control the documents involved in a malicious prosecution litigation):

- open client file
- enter case data in computer database
- maintain file documents

MALICIOUS PROSECUTION CHECKLIST *(Continued)*

Litigation assistance (help the trial attorney prepare for a malicious prosecution trial and appeal, if needed):

- draft discovery requests
- draft answers to discovery requests
- draft pleadings
- digest and index discovery documents
- help prepare, order, and manage trial exhibits
- prepare trial notebook
- draft notice of appeal
- order trial transcript
- cite-check briefs
- perform legal research

Collection/enforcement (help the trial attorney for the judgment creditor to collect the damages award or to enforce other court orders at the conclusion of the malicious prosecution case):

- draft postjudgment discovery requests
- conduct field investigation to monitor compliance with judgment
- perform online research (e.g., location of defendant's business assets)

Research References for Malicious Prosecution

Digests
In the digests of West Group, look for case summaries on this tort under key topics such as:

Malicious Prosecution
False Imprisonment
Torts
Extortion
Indictment and Information
Arrest (especially key number 63.4 on probable cause)
Damages
Compromise and Settlement
Attorney and Client (especially key number 159)

Corpus Juris Secundum
In this legal encyclopedia, see the discussion under topic headings such as:

Malicious Prosecution
Malice
False Imprisonment
Agency
Torts
Extortion
Indictment and Information
Arrest
Damages
Accord and Satisfaction
Compromise and Settlement

American Jurisprudence 2d
In this legal encyclopedia, see the discussion under topic headings such as:

Malicious Prosecution
Abuse of Process
Attachment and Garnishment (see sections 596 et seq.)
Executions (sections 750 et seq.)
Malice
False Imprisonment
Torts
Master and Servant
Damages
Arrest
Criminal Law
Extortion, Blackmail and Threats
Indictment and Information
Compromise and Settlement
Prosecuting Attorneys

Legal Periodical Literature
There are two index systems to use to locate articles on this tort:

INDEX TO LEGAL PERIODICALS AND BOOKS (ILP)
See literature in *ILP* under subject headings such as:
Malicious Prosecution
Damages
False Imprisonment
Master and Servant
Personal Injuries
Settlements
Torts

CURRENT LAW INDEX (CLI)
See literature in *CLI* under subject headings such as:
Malicious Prosecution
False Imprisonment
Torts
Damages
Personal Injuries
Employers' Liability

MALICIOUS PROSECUTION CHECKLIST *(Continued)*

Example of a legal periodical article on malicious prosecution you can locate by using these index systems:

Damages for Injury to Feelings in Malicious Prosecution and Abuse of Process by A. M. Witte, 15 Cleveland Marshall Law Review 15 (1969).

A.L.R., A.L.R.2d, A.L.R.3d, A.L.R.4th, A.L.R.5th, A.L.R.6th, A.L.R. Fed., and A.L.R. Fed. 2d
Use the *ALR Index* to find annotations relevant to malicious prosecution. In this index, check headings such as:

Malicious Prosecution
Malice
Malicious Use of Process
Torts
Damages
Libel and Slander
Master and Servant
Federal Tort Claims Act
Criminal Law

Example of an annotation on malicious prosecution you can locate by using this index:

Malicious Prosecution: Effect of Grand Jury Indictment on Issue of Probable Cause by J. D. Perovich, 28 A.L.R.3d 748 (1969).

Words and Phrases
In this multivolume legal dictionary, look up *malicious prosecution, probable cause, malice, nolle prosequi, abuse of process,* and every other word or phrase discussed in this chapter. The dictionary will give you definitions of these words or phrases from court opinions.

CALR: Computer-Assisted Legal Research

Example of a query you could ask on Westlaw to try to find cases, statutes, or other legal materials on malicious prosecution: **"malicious prosecution"/p damages**

Example of search terms you could use on an Internet legal search engine such as the Public Library of Law (www.plol.org), Findlaw (www.findlaw.com), or Google Scholar (scholar.google.com) to find cases, statutes, or other legal materials on this tort: **"malicious prosecution"**

Example of search terms you can use on an Internet general search engine such Google, Bing, or AltaVista to find cases, statutes, or other legal materials on this tort: **+"malicious prosecution" +tort**

More Internet sites to check for materials on malicious prosecution and other torts:
www.hg.org/torts.html
www.megalaw.com/top/top.php (click "Intentional Torts," "Personal Injury Law," "Tort Law," and "Damages")
See also the online sites in Overview of Tort Law at the end of Chapter 1.

CHECK THE CITE

Opponents of a shopping center development were sued by the developers. When the suit was dismissed, the opponents sued for abuse of process. One of the defendants in the abuse-of-process suit was Wal-Mart, which was scheduled to be a major tenant if the shopping center was approved. Wal-Mart argued that it should not be a defendant in the abuse-of-process suit because it was not a party to the underlying suit against the opponents. How did the court rule on this argument? The court said, "The issue we address in this case is whether a defendant can be liable for malicious abuse of process when that defendant was not a party (a non-litigant) in the underlying civil lawsuit." Explain the court's answer to this issue. Read *Valles v. Silverman*, 135 N.M. 91, 84 P.3d 1056 (C. App. N.M. 2003). To read the opinion online, (1) Use Findlaw (caselaw.lp.findlaw.com/scripts/getcase.pl?court=nm&navby=year&year=2003_12nmapp). (2) Run a citation search ("84 P.3d 1056") in the Legal Opinions and Journals database of Google Scholar (scholar.google.com).

PROJECT

Go to the *news* search pages of Google, Bing, Yahoo, or another general search engine and run the following search: "malicious prosecution." Find four news stories of four different cases in which someone sues another person for malicious prosecution. Briefly describe the facts of the case.

ETHICS IN A TORTS PRACTICE

You are a paralegal working in the law office of Myles and Myles. Your cousin was recently arrested on an accusation of theft by a neighbor of your cousin. The case was dropped when the prosecutor issued a nolle prosequi. You tell your supervisor at Myles and Myles about the case. When the supervisor learns that your cousin is furious at the neighbor because of the false accusation, your supervisor tells you that if you can convince your cousin to come in to be interviewed about a possible malicious prosecution case, you will be given a week off. What ethical problems, if any, might exist?

SUMMARY

Malicious prosecution is the instigation of criminal legal proceedings without probable cause and with malice when the proceedings terminate in favor of the accused. Probable cause is a reasonable belief that a specific crime has been committed and that the accused committed the crime. Malice means having an improper purpose, which is a purpose other than to bring someone to justice. Finally, the legal proceedings must terminate in favor of the accused on the merits.

Wrongful civil proceedings is the initiation of civil proceedings without probable cause and with malice when the proceedings terminate in favor of the person against whom they were brought. (Some states include the initiation of civil proceedings within the tort of malicious prosecution.) As an additional element, some states require the defendant to show that he or she suffered a special injury or interference with person or property as a result of the wrongful civil proceedings.

Abuse of process is the use of civil or criminal proceedings for an improper or ulterior motive. The civil or criminal proceedings were properly initiated and they do not have to terminate in favor of the party now bringing the tort of abuse of process.

KEY TERMS

prosecution *126*
malicious prosecution *126*
instigate *127*
probable cause *127*
malice (for malicious prosecution) *127*
on the merits *128*
statute of limitations *128*
nolle prosequi *128*
absolute immunity *129*
wrongful civil proceedings *129*
abuse of process *132*
process *132*

REVIEW QUESTIONS

1. What three torts cover the wrongful use of legal proceedings?
2. Why does the law disfavor these torts?
3. What are the elements of malicious prosecution?
4. What are the three meanings of prosecution?
5. How are criminal proceedings instigated?
6. What is probable cause?
7. What are the different meanings of malice, and which meaning applies to malicious prosecution?
8. What factors are considered in determining whether probable cause exists?

9. When do criminal proceedings terminate on the merits in favor of the accused?
10. What is an absolute immunity?
11. What are the elements of wrongful civil proceedings?
12. What is meant by the initiation of civil proceedings?
13. When does a party have probable cause to initiate civil proceedings?
14. What are the elements of abuse of process?
15. How does abuse of process differ from malicious prosecution?

HELPFUL WEBSITES

- **Malicious Prosecution and Wrongful Civil Proceedings**

  www.kentlaw.edu/faculty/rbrill/classes/AdvTortsSp07/Sub_Rev_misuse.html

  law.jrank.org/pages/8407/Malicious-Prosecution.html

  en.wikipedia.org/wiki/Malicious_prosecution

  www.blumberglaw.com/article-malicious-prosecution.htm

  www.justia.com/trials-litigation/docs/caci/1500/1501.html

  www.lexisnexis.com/lawschool/study/outlines/html/torts/torts20.htm

  www.google.com (run this search: elements malicious prosecution tort)

- **Abuse of Process**

  works.bepress.com/grace_giesel/5

  en.wikipedia.org/wiki/Abuse_of_process

Student StudyWARE™ CD-ROM
For additional materials, please go to the student CD in this book.

CHAPTER

9

INFLICTION OF EMOTIONAL DISTRESS

CHAPTER OUTLINE

- Introduction
- Intentional Infliction of Emotional Distress
- Tort Law and the Impeachment of the President
- Media Defendants and the Constitution
- Negligent Infliction of Emotional Distress

CHAPTER OBJECTIVES

After completing this chapter, you should be able to:

- Distinguish between intentional infliction of emotional distress (IIED) and other torts.
- Identify the elements of IIED.
- Identify the defenses to IIED.
- Understand the difficulties of bringing an IIED action for conduct on the Internet.
- Describe how courts restrict IIED when third parties try to assert the tort.
- Explain the extra rules involved when the media is the defendant in a suit alleging IIED.
- Describe the requirements for bringing an action for negligent infliction of emotional distress (NIED).
- Identify paralegal roles in litigation asserting IIED and NIED.
- List the major resources in traditional books and online when researching issues involving IIED and NIED.

INTRODUCTION

Emotional distress can be damaging to a person. Our concern in this chapter is whether the sufferer can bring a tort action against the person who caused this suffering. When someone commits a traditional tort such as battery, false imprisonment, or negligence, there is usually little difficulty recovering for the emotional distress (called **pain and suffering**) that results from this tort. In fact, damages for pain and suffering often constitute the largest portion of a successful plaintiff's judgment. Suppose, however, that the defendant causes mental distress *without* committing one of these traditional torts. For example, George is emotionally upset when Mary refuses to date him and tells him that she never wants to see him again as long as she lives. Although this statement could cause George enormous pain and suffering (in fact, an emotional breakdown), Mary has not committed a tort. The facts do not fit any of the traditional torts.

pain and suffering Physical discomfort or emotional distress; a disagreeable mental or emotional experience.

A floodgate of litigation would result if every victim of every emotional distress is allowed to sue. The filing of claims could turn into "unlimited liability for emotional distress," according to Judge Eagleson of the Supreme Court of California in the *Thing v. La Chusa* case that we will read later in the chapter. Courts are also concerned about the filing of fraudulent lawsuits because it is fairly easy to fabricate a claim of emotional distress.

One of the ways the law has dealt with these concerns is to create a new tort called **intentional infliction of emotional distress (IIED)**, also called the tort of *outrage*. It consists of intentionally causing severe emotional distress by an act of extreme or outrageous conduct. (See Exhibit 9–1 for the elements of this tort.) To prevent a flood of litigation, the tort was made relatively difficult to win, as President Bill Clinton discovered to his relief in the famous case of *Jones v. Clinton*, which we will study. After we examine the boundaries of this narrow intentional tort, we need to determine when *negligently* inflicted emotional distress can also be a basis of recovery.

intentional infliction of emotional distress (IIED) Intentionally causing severe emotional distress by an act of extreme or outrageous conduct. Also called the tort of outrage.

Exhibit 9–1
Elements of the tort of intentional infliction of emotional distress.

Intentional Infliction of Emotional Distress

1. An act of extreme or outrageous conduct
2. Intent to cause severe emotional distress
3. Severe emotional distress is suffered
4. Defendant is the cause of this distress

INTENTIONAL INFLICTION OF EMOTIONAL DISTRESS

Extreme or Outrageous Conduct

The conduct of the defendant must be so **extreme or outrageous** that it would be regarded as atrocious and totally intolerable. Of course, many (perhaps most) victims of serious wrongs would probably say that what they suffered was extreme and outrageous. Yet "merely describing conduct as outrageous does not make it so," as the court observed in *Jones v. Clinton*. Furthermore, it would be a mistake to argue that committing any intentional tort is atrocious and intolerable. It cannot be said that every battery, assault, false imprisonment, or malicious prosecution is *also* the tort of intentional infliction of emotional distress. It is possible for IIED to be committed simultaneously with other torts, but this is not necessarily the case. The act required for IIED must shock the conscience of society.

extreme or outrageous conduct Atrocious; totally intolerable; shocking the conscience of society.

EXAMPLES

- playing a practical joke on a mother by telling her that her son has just committed suicide
- putting a knife to the throat of a ten-year-old child as a threat
- surrounding a debtor and threatening to kill him and to destroy all of his business machinery if he does not pay a debt
- pushing a pregnant woman down a flight of stairs or threatening to do so

If the defendant knows that the plaintiff is vulnerable because of age, mental illness, or physical illness, it is usually easier to establish that the conduct was extreme or outrageous. Yet, vulnerability in this sense is not required. It would be extreme or outrageous, for example, for a defendant to drive a car at a high rate of speed on the sidewalk in order to scare a pedestrian directly in front of the car, whether the pedestrian is on crutches or is a healthy boxer.

As we will see elsewhere in this book, common carriers, innkeepers, and public utilities are more likely to be found liable for a tort than other categories of defendants. This is particularly true with the tort of IIED. For most defendants, the first element of this tort is not established by mere insults, threats, or obscenities directed at the plaintiff—they are not atrocious enough. Yet, such conduct might be sufficient if the defendant is a hotel or a public transit facility.

Emotional Distress on the Internet

The Internet can be an ugly arena in which people use cyberspace to embarrass, harass, and, in some instances, threaten others. New terminology has been devised to describe some of this conduct. **Cyberstalking**, for example, is the use of the Internet or other electronic means to repeatedly embarrass, humiliate, threaten, or otherwise harass someone. (If the victim is a minor, the conduct is sometimes referred to as **cyberbullying.**) Some states have passed criminal statutes that make such conduct illegal. Successful IIED cases are certainly possible, particularly if the stalker or bully knows that the victim is unusually sensitive or vulnerable.

cyberstalking The use of the Internet or other electronic means to repeatedly embarrass, humiliate, threaten, or otherwise harass someone. Also called cyberharassment.

cyberbullying The use of the Internet or other electronic means to repeatedly embarrass, humiliate, threaten, or otherwise harass a minor. Also called cyberharassment.

In several highly publicized cases, teenagers have committed suicide after reading embarrassing comments about themselves. In one case, a woman created a phony MySpace account and pretended to be a teenage boy interested in a vulnerable girl. After weeks of flirtatious communications, the "boy" changed the tone of the exchanges and sent her an e-mail telling her that "the world would be a better place" without her. Soon thereafter, she committed suicide. The girl's parents convinced the government to bring a criminal prosecution on the ground of computer fraud, but the case was thrown out because of the vagueness of the law the woman was charged with violating. If a tort case had been brought against the woman, the problem of proving that the deception caused the suicide would have been substantial.

When parties sue each other for conduct on the Internet, the victim will sometimes list IIED as one of the causes of action. If threats are made (e.g., "I'm going to kill you"), IIED has a greater chance of success than assault. The tort of assault, as we saw in Chapter 6, requires an apparent *present* ability to carry out the threat. The person behind the computer screen making the threat would be referring to future violence even if the threat referred to the present ("I'm going to kill you now"). The threat can't be carried out while at a keyboard. But threats of future violence, if sufficiently egregious, can constitute extreme and outrageous conduct for purposes of IIED.

Unfortunately, however, there is not a lot of law to provide guidance on how these cases would be resolved. In a recent case, for example, a plaintiff alleged that the defendant engaged in "Google bombing" (a slang term for manipulating the search results on Google) by hijacking a rival's website and linking it to pages with pornography. The plaintiff sued the defendant for IIED. The case, however, was either settled or dropped. Such cases rarely make it through the appellate court system. Consequently, there are very few published opinions that can guide us on what the law is. In general, the present climate is to discourage the use of the courts to police what occurs on the Internet, except for obviously criminal conduct such as identity theft. The legal system is not yet equipped with laws that cover the still-emerging modes of communication on the Internet. Furthermore, there is considerable hesitancy (and in some circles, hostility) about creating new laws that might stifle innovation and the free flow of information in cyberspace. The prevailing attitude of many is that the Internet is not a place for the timid, and if something nasty is said there about you, get over it.

ASSIGNMENT 9.1

Has extreme or outrageous conduct taken place in the following cases?

a. A creditor threatens to force the debtor into involuntary bankruptcy if a debt is not paid immediately.
b. The principal of the school suspects that a student has been smoking marijuana in the restroom. The principal threatens to use the student as an example of delinquency before the entire school assembly if the student does not confess to smoking the marijuana.
c. Defendant pretends to be a police detective and threatens to arrest the plaintiff for espionage if the plaintiff does not turn over letters received by the plaintiff from a friend in Asia.
d. A bus driver tells a seventy-five-year-old passenger that her hat is so ridiculous that she would look better bald.

Intent

intent (for intentional infliction of emotional distress) The desire to inflict severe emotional distress or the knowledge with substantial certainty that such distress will result from what one does or fails to do.

reckless Consciously taking a risk in failing to exercise due care but not intending the consequences; wantonly disregarding a risk but neither desiring the consequences of the risk nor having substantially certain knowledge of the consequences of the risk.

In most states, the defendant must have the **intent** to cause the severe emotional distress. This means that the defendant must either desire such a consequence or know with substantial certainty that it will result from what he or she does or fails to do.

In a few states, being **reckless** is enough. In such states, the second element is met if the defendant knows that his or her conduct creates the risk that the plaintiff will suffer severe emotional distress even if this result is not intended. The following is a classic example of the kind of case that meets this standard:

EXAMPLE

Bob is a good friend of Mary's. He attempts to commit suicide with a knife in Mary's kitchen. She suffers severe emotional distress upon seeing the blood and gore.

Mary sues Bob for IIED. In a state that requires intent, Mary loses because there is no indication that Bob desired Mary to suffer this distress or that Bob knew with certainty that it would result. Mary has a better chance in a state where recklessness will suffice, because a strong argument can be made that Bob knew he created a risk that Mary would suffer this distress or that Bob wantonly disregarded this risk.

The line between desiring something or knowing something with substantial certainty (intent), and knowing that you create a risk of something (recklessness) is often very difficult to draw. Yet the line may have to be drawn in a state where recklessness is not enough to establish the second element of IIED.

If the defendant is merely *negligent* in causing the severe emotional distress, there is no *intentional* infliction of emotional distress. Later in the chapter, we will consider the question of whether the plaintiff might be able to recover under the tort called *negligent* infliction of emotional distress (NIED).

Third Persons

What happens if the defendant intends to cause severe emotional distress in one person, but in fact causes such distress in another person whom the defendant had no intent to bother? What happens if two individuals suffer severe emotional distress, even though defendant's intent was directed at only one of them?

EXAMPLE

Rodney intentionally terrifies Mary and then maims her. Mary's mother suffers severe emotional distress because of this injury and the way it was brought about.

Mary has a good IIED case. What about third persons such as Mary's mother? If a state court follows § 46(2) of the *Restatement (Second) of Torts*, a third person cannot sue for IIED unless this person (a) was present at the time of the attack and (b) is a member of the immediate family of the person attacked or (if not part of the family) suffered bodily harm due to the emotional distress of witnessing the attack. Hence Mary's mother would have to show that she was present when her daughter was maimed. She is a member of her daughter's immediate family, so she meets the second condition of § 46(2). Someone who is not a member of the immediate family would have to show bodily harm from witnessing the attack.

The **transferred-intent rule** we examined earlier (see Exhibit 6–2 in Chapter 6) does not apply to IIED. Under this rule, the defendant's intent to commit a tort such as battery against one person is transferred to the person who in fact suffered the battery (the unintended plaintiff) even if the defendant had no intent to harm the latter. But the rule does not apply to IIED.

transferred-intent rule The defendant may be liable for certain torts committed against the plaintiff even if the defendant intended to commit a different tort against the plaintiff (unintended tort) and even if the defendant intended to commit the tort against a different person (unintended plaintiff).

The requirements of § 46(2) of the *Restatement* are meant to impose some limitation on liability for IIED. Think of the large number of friends and relatives, for example, who might suffer deep emotional scars upon hearing that a loved one was murdered or subjected to some other outrageous act. The requirements avoid having a potentially overwhelming number of plaintiffs suing the defendant for IIED.

Not all courts have adopted the requirements of the *Restatement*, particularly the requirement of presence. A famous example of a contrary view is the case growing out of the September 11th terrorist attacks.

9/11 and the Terrorist Attacks

It is difficult to find a clearer example of extreme and outrageous conduct than the September 11, 2001 terrorist attacks on the World Trade Center and the Pentagon. Persons who were killed could (through their estates) bring the tort of IIED against anyone who aided and abetted the hijackers who flew the airplanes into the World Trade Center and the Pentagon. What about family members of those killed? Can they also sue for IIED? Not if the court adopts the requirements of the *Restatement*. As we have seen, one of the requirements is presence at the time of the extreme or outrageous conduct. This would mean that immediate family members of those killed in the terrorist attacks could not sue for IIED because they were not present at the time of the attacks.

An important case, however, refused to adopt the presence requirement of the *Restatement* and allowed immediate family members to sue for IIED. The case is *Burnett v. Al Baraka Inv. and Development Corp.*[1] Essential to the court's conclusion was the fact that the terrorists (and those who funded and supported them) committed acts that were "sufficiently outrageous" and were intended to inflict emotional distress on family members. The court reasoned that family members were "virtually present" even though they may not have been physically present. This is what the court said:

> Given the adequacy of plaintiffs' allegations that [the defendants] aided and abetted and conspired with the September 11 hijackers, plaintiffs have also stated common law claims for . . . intentional infliction of emotional distress. . . . [T]he terrorist acts of September 11 would appear to be a perfect fit for the elements of intentional infliction of emotional distress: (i) extreme and outrageous conduct; (ii) intent to cause, or disregard of a substantial probability of causing, severe emotional distress; (iii) a causal connection between the conduct and injury; and (iv) severe emotional distress. . . . The outrageous and extreme conduct must generally be directed at the plaintiff, . . . , but a cause of action may also be stated when the conduct "causes injury to a third person, thereby intentionally or recklessly causing severe emotional distress to a member of such person's [immediate] family who is present at the time." *Maney v. Maloney,* 477 N.Y.S.2d 436, 438 (App. Div. 1984) (citing *Restatement (Second) of Torts* § 46(2)(a)). A terrorist attack on civilians is of course intended to cause emotional distress to the victims' families. . . . Family members here were not physically present at the World Trade Center, or at the Pentagon, . . . , but the whole world was virtually present, and that is enough. *See Acree v. Republic of Iraq,* 271 F. Supp. 2d 179, 215 (D.D.C. July 7, 2003) (presentation of battered POWs on television by their captors and public threats to use POWs as human shields made POWs' family members contemporaneously aware that victims were probably being tortured, thus satisfying "presence" requirement); *Jenco v. Islamic Republic of Iran,* 154 F. Supp. 2d 27, 36 (D.D.C. 2001) ("'If the defendants' conduct is sufficiently outrageous and intended to inflict severe emotional harm upon a person which is not present, no essential reason of logic or policy prevents liability'") (quoting Dan B. Dobbs, *The Law of Torts* § 307, at 834 (2000)).[2]

Severe Emotional Distress

severe emotional distress Substantial mental anguish or distress that no reasonable person should be expected to endure.

It is not enough that the defendant commit an outrageous act intended to cause **severe emotional distress** in the plaintiff. The plaintiff must in fact experience such distress. Minor inconvenience or annoyance is not enough. There must be substantial mental anguish or distress (e.g., grief, horror, fright, or humiliation) that no reasonable person should be expected to endure. The severity of these feelings is measured by their intensity and duration as well as other factors, such as the relative size and weight of the plaintiff and defendant, and how the defendant approached the plaintiff.

physical injury A wound, cut, or other detrimental change in a part of the body. An illness in the body rather than in the mind. Also called bodily harm.

Most states do not require that the plaintiff suffer **physical injury** as a result of the IIED. (See, however, the exception just discussed for third parties who are not members of the immediate family of the person attacked.) Of course, damages are increased if physical injuries do result from the IIED, but such injuries are not required in order to establish IIED in most cases. Nevertheless, the absence of physical injury may make some courts skeptical about whether severe emotional distress was in fact experienced. The judge in *Jones v. Clinton* observed that "absent physical harm, courts look for more in the way of extreme outrage as an assurance that the mental disturbance claimed is not fictitious."

Suppose the plaintiff is unusually sensitive and experiences severe emotional distress even though anyone else would not, e.g., the plaintiff goes into shock when the defendant plays a practical joke by telling the plaintiff that one of his flowers has just died. If the defendant knew of this vulnerability and still proceeded with the intent to cause severe emotional distress, the third element of the tort is established. Otherwise, the test is objective: the plaintiff will not be able to recover unless it can be said that no reasonable person should be expected to endure the distress to which the plaintiff was subjected.

ASSIGNMENT 9.2

For months Tom has been having difficulty finding work. Finally he gets a job at the XYZ gym as a judo instructor. It is the first time he has had a job in over a year and a half. A collection agency has been after Tom to pay a $500 debt. An employee of the agency calls Tom and says, "I understand that you now have a job and that you have had to go through a lot to get it. Don't do anything silly, which might cost you that job. Don't make me have to seek a wage garnishment, which would require your employer to send payments to us out of your salary. You do not want to become known as the kind of guy who doesn't pay his debts. You've got one week to pay up or else." Tom is terrified at the thought of losing his job. He has many sleepless nights worrying about the possibility that the collection agency might call his boss. Tom sues the agency for IIED. What result? (Assume that the agency has *not* violated the Fair Debt Collection Practices Act, which prohibits certain debt collection tactics (www.ftc.gov/os/statutes/fdcpajump.shtm).)

Causation

Plaintiff can use either of the following tests to establish causation:

- But for what the defendant did, the plaintiff would not have suffered severe emotional distress.
- The defendant was a substantial factor in producing the plaintiff's severe emotional distress.

The second test is used when there is more than one potential cause of the severe emotional distress. The plaintiff is not required to prove causation by the but-for test. The broader substantial factor test is sufficient.

TORT LAW AND THE IMPEACHMENT OF THE PRESIDENT

In 1999, Congress impeached and tried the president of the United States for only the second time in American history. One of the articles of impeachment against President Bill Clinton (a Democrat) was that he lied when he gave a deposition in a sexual harassment and tort case that was filed against him by Paula Corbin Jones. Her tort cause of action was IIED, called the tort of outrage in Arkansas. During the deposition the president gave in this case, he answered "none" when asked whether there were any female employees of the federal government with whom he had had sexual relations. In particular, he denied having such relations with Monica Lewinsky, a White House intern. A special prosecutor and almost all Republicans in Congress charged that his answers were intentionally false. They believed that lying in a deposition was one of the "high crimes and misdemeanors" that should lead to his removal from office. Ultimately, the Senate as a whole disagreed when it failed to convict the president by the required two-thirds vote. (The vote on this count was 55 (not guilty) and 45 (guilty). All the senators voting guilty were Republicans.) By acquitting the president, the Senate was saying either that it did not believe the president lied, or that even if he did, the lie and the other charges were not serious enough to remove him from office.

The president also won the sexual harassment and tort case when the trial court judge, Susan Webber Wright, ruled that his conduct did not constitute sexual harassment nor the tort of outrage. In a stinging rebuke, however, Judge Wright ruled that he *did* lie during his deposition and held him in civil contempt. One of the consequences of the lie was that the Jones legal team had to spend extra time preparing

its case. Hence the judge ordered the president to pay a fine of $90,000 for reasonable legal fees covering this time. The fee request included $60 an hour for the work of two paralegals on the Jones legal team.

In the meantime, Jones was set to appeal Judge Wright's ruling that the president did not commit sexual harassment nor the tort of outrage. The president did not relish the prospect of fighting the appeal, particularly since the appeal would have taken place before the impeachment proceeding in Congress was concluded. Hence the president decided that the safest legal and political strategy was to settle the case to prevent the appeal from going forward. He agreed to pay Jones $850,000 in exchange for her decision to drop her appeal of Judge Wright's ruling against her on the sexual harassment and tort claims.

For our purposes, we need to examine why the court ruled that there was no IIED (outrage). What follows is the opinion of Judge Wright on this issue.

CASE

Paula Corbin Jones v. William Jefferson Clinton and Danny Ferguson

990 F. Supp. 657 (1998)
United States District Court, Eastern District, Arkansas

Background: *Paula Corbin Jones, an Arkansas state clerical worker, alleges that when President Clinton was Governor in 1991, he made a sexual advance toward her in a Little Rock hotel, which she rejected. After Governor Clinton became President, Jones sued him and a state trooper (Danny Ferguson) in a federal trial court, the United States District Court in Arkansas. Her claims were sexual harassment and intentional infliction of emotional distress, which is called the tort of outrage in Arkansas. (Loss-of-reputation claims such as defamation were also included but later dropped.) The President argued that he should not have to defend the suit until after he left office. The United States Supreme Court disagreed (520 U.S. 681) (supreme .justia.com/us/520/681/case.html) and the case proceeded. After depositions were taken of the plaintiff, the defendants, and others, the President made a motion for summary judgment, asking that the case be dismissed without a trial. His position was that even if the plaintiff proved everything she alleged, his conduct constituted neither sexual harassment nor intentional infliction of emotional distress (outrage).*

Decision of Court: *The President's motion for summary judgment is granted. (1) There was no sexual harassment. The plaintiff's refusal to submit to unwelcome sexual advances or requests for sexual favors did not result in retaliation or other tangible job detriment and this single incident did not amount to a hostile work environment. (2) The plaintiff has not stated a claim for the tort of intentional infliction of emotional distress (outrage). The excerpts from the opinion below cover the tort claim only.*

OPINION OF COURT

Judge Susan Webber WRIGHT delivered the opinion of the court . . .:

This lawsuit is based on an incident that is said to have taken place on the afternoon of May 8, 1991, in a suite at the Excelsior Hotel in Little Rock, Arkansas. President Clinton was Governor of the State of Arkansas at the time, and plaintiff was a State employee with the Arkansas Industrial Development Commission ("AIDC"), having begun her State employment on March 11, 1991. [Danny] Ferguson was an Arkansas State Police officer assigned to the Governor's security detail.

According to the record, then-Governor Clinton was at the Excelsior Hotel on the day in question delivering a speech at an official conference being sponsored by the AIDC. Plaintiff states that she and another AIDC employee, Pamela Blackard, were working at a registration desk for the AIDC when a man approached the desk and informed her and Blackard that he was Trooper Danny Ferguson, the Governor's bodyguard. She states that Ferguson made small talk with her and Blackard. . . .

Upon leaving the registration desk, Ferguson apparently had a conversation with the Governor about the possibility of meeting with plaintiff, during which Ferguson states the Governor remarked that plaintiff had "that come-hither look," i.e. "a sort of [sexually] suggestive appearance from the look or dress." Ferguson Deposition at 50; Plaintiff's Statement of Material Facts, ¶ 3; President's Deposition at 109.[1] He states that "some time later" the Governor asked him to "get him a room, that he was expecting a call from the White House and . . . had several phone calls that he needed to make," and asked him to go to the car and get his briefcase containing the phone messages. Ferguson states that upon obtaining the room, the Governor told him that if plaintiff wanted to meet him, she could "come up."

[1]Ferguson states that plaintiff informed him that she would like to meet the Governor, remarking that she thought the Governor "was good-looking [and] had sexy hair," Ferguson Deposition at 50, while plaintiff states that Ferguson asked her if she would like to meet the Governor and that she was "excited" about the possibility, Plaintiff's Deposition at 101.

Plaintiff states that Ferguson later reappeared at the registration desk, delivered a piece of paper to her with a four-digit number written on it, and said that the Governor would like to meet with her in this suite number. She states that she, Blackard, and Ferguson talked about what the Governor could want and that Ferguson stated, among other things, "We do this all the time." Thinking that it was an honor to be asked to meet the Governor and that it might lead to an enhanced employment opportunity, plaintiff states that she agreed to the meeting and that Ferguson escorted her to the floor of the hotel upon which the Governor's suite was located.

Plaintiff states that upon arriving at the suite and announcing herself, the Governor shook her hand, invited her in, and closed the door. She states that a few minutes of small talk ensued, which included the Governor asking her about her job and him mentioning that Dave Harrington, plaintiff's ultimate superior within the AIDC and a Clinton appointee, was his "good friend." Plaintiff states that the Governor then "unexpectedly reached over to [her], took her hand, and pulled her toward him, so that their bodies were close to each other." She states she removed her hand from his and retreated several feet, but that the Governor approached her again and, while saying, "I love the way your hair flows down your back" and "I love your curves," put his hand on her leg, started sliding it toward her pelvic area, and bent down to attempt to kiss her on the neck, all without her consent. Plaintiff states that she exclaimed, "What are you doing?," told the Governor that she was "not that kind of girl," and "escaped" from the Governor's reach "by walking away from him." She states she was extremely upset and confused and, not knowing what to do, attempted to distract the Governor by chatting about his wife. Plaintiff states that she sat down at the end of the sofa nearest the door, but that the Governor approached the sofa where she had taken a seat and, as he sat down, [he lowered his trousers, fondled himself, and asked her to engage in oral sex. She states that she was horrified, jumped up from the couch, and told the Governor that she had to get back to the registration desk, to which he replied,] "Well, I don't want to make you do anything you don't want to do," and then pulled up his pants and said, "If you get in trouble for leaving work, have Dave call me immediately and I'll take care of it." She states that as she left the room (the door of which was not locked), the Governor "detained" her momentarily, "looked sternly" at her, and said, "You are smart. Let's keep this between ourselves."

Plaintiff states that the Governor's advances to her were unwelcome, that she never said or did anything to suggest to the Governor that she was willing to have sex with him, and that during the time they were together in the hotel suite, she resisted his advances although she was "stunned by them and intimidated by who he was." She states that when the Governor referred to Dave Harrington, she "understood that he was telling her that he had control over Mr. Harrington and over her job, and that he was willing to use that power." She states that from that point on, she was "very fearful" that her refusal to submit to the Governor's advances could damage her career and even jeopardize her employment.

Plaintiff states that when she left the hotel suite, she was in shock and upset but tried to maintain her composure. She states she saw Ferguson waiting outside the suite but that he did not escort her back to the registration desk and nothing was said between them. Ferguson states that five or ten minutes after plaintiff exited the suite he joined the Governor for their return to the Governor's Mansion and that the Governor, who was working on some papers that he had spread out on the desk, said, "She came up here, and nothing happened."

Plaintiff states she returned to the registration desk and told Blackard some of what had happened. Blackard states that plaintiff was shaking and embarrassed. Following the Conference, plaintiff states she went to the workplace of a friend, Debra Ballentine, and told her of the incident as well. Ballentine states that plaintiff was upset and crying. Later that same day, plaintiff states she told her sister, Charlotte Corbin Brown, what had happened and, within the next two days, also told her other sister, Lydia Corbin Cathey, of the incident. Brown's observations of plaintiff's demeanor apparently are not included in the record. Cathey, however, states that plaintiff was "bawling" and "squalling," and that she appeared scared, embarrassed, and ashamed.

Ballentine states that she encouraged plaintiff to report the incident to her boss or to the police, but that plaintiff declined, pointing out that her boss was friends with the Governor and that the police were the ones who took her to the hotel suite. Ballentine further states that plaintiff stated she did not want her fiancé to know of the incident and that she "just want[ed] this thing to go away." Plaintiff states that what the Governor and Ferguson had said and done made her "afraid" to file charges. . . .

The President moves for summary judgment on the [ground that the] claim of intentional infliction of emotional distress or outrage fails because . . . plaintiff did not as a result of the alleged conduct suffer emotional distress so severe that no reasonable person could endure it. . . . The President and Ferguson both argue that there are no genuine issues of material fact with respect to any of these issues and that they are entitled to summary judgment as a matter of law. . . .

Arkansas recognizes a claim of intentional infliction of emotional distress based on sexual harassment. *Davis v. Tri-State Mack Distribs., Inc.,* 981 F.2d 340, 342 (8th Cir. 1992) (citing *Hale v. Ladd,* 308 Ark. 567, 826 S.W.2d 244 (1992)). To establish a claim of intentional infliction of emotional distress, a plaintiff must prove that: (1) the defendant intended to inflict emotional distress or knew or should have known that emotional distress was the likely result of his conduct; (2) the conduct was extreme and outrageous and utterly intolerable in a civilized community; (3) the defendant's conduct was the cause of the plaintiff's distress; and (4) the plaintiff's emotional distress was so severe in nature that no reasonable person could be expected to endure it. *Croom v. Younts,* 323 Ark. 95, 913 S.W.2d 283, 286 (1996).

The President argues that the alleged conduct of which plaintiff complains was brief and isolated; did not result in any physical harm or objective symptoms of the requisite severe distress; did not result in distress so severe that no reasonable person could be expected to endure it; and he had no knowledge of any special condition of plaintiff that would render her particularly susceptible to distress. He argues that plaintiff has failed to identify the kind of clear cut proof that Arkansas courts require for a claim of outrage and that he is therefore entitled to summary judgment. The Court agrees.

One is subject to liability for the tort of outrage or intentional infliction of emotional distress if he or she willfully or wantonly causes severe emotional distress to another by extreme and outrageous conduct. In *M.B.M. Co. v. Counce,* 268 Ark. 269, 280, 596 S.W.2d 681, 687 (1980), the Arkansas Supreme Court stated that "[b]y extreme and outrageous conduct, we mean conduct that is so outrageous in character, and so extreme in degree, as to go beyond all possible bounds of decency, and to be regarded as atrocious, and utterly intolerable in civilized society." Whether conduct is "extreme and outrageous" is determined by looking at "the conduct at issue; the period of time over which the conduct took place; the relation between plaintiff and defendant; and defendant's knowledge that plaintiff is particularly susceptible to emotional distress by reason of some physical or mental peculiarity." *Doe v. Wright,* 82 F.3d 265, 269 (8th Cir. 1996) (citing *Hamaker,* 51 F.3d 108, 111 (8th Cir. 1995)). The tort is clearly not intended to provide legal redress for every slight insult or indignity that one must endure. *Manning v. Metropolitan Life Ins. Co.,* 127 F.3d 686, 690 (8th Cir. 1997) (citing *Hamaker,* 51 F.3d at 110). The Arkansas courts take a strict approach and give a narrow view to claims of outrage, and merely describing conduct as outrageous does not make it so.

Plaintiff seems to base her claim of outrage on her erroneous belief that the allegations she has presented are sufficient to constitute criminal sexual assault. She states that "Mr. Clinton's outrageous conduct includes offensive language, an offensive proposition, offensive touching (constituting sexual assault under both federal and state definitions), and *actual exposure of an intimate private body part,*" and that "[t]here are few more outrageous acts than a criminal sexual assault followed by unwanted exposure, coupled with a demand for oral sex by the most powerful man in the state against a very young, low-level employee." Plaintiff's Opposition to Defendant Clinton's Motion for Summary Judgment at 66 (emphasis in original).

While the Court will certainly agree that plaintiff's allegations describe offensive conduct, the Court . . . has found that the Governor's alleged conduct does not constitute sexual assault. Rather, the conduct as alleged by plaintiff describes a mere sexual proposition or encounter, albeit an odious one, that was relatively brief in duration, did not involve any coercion or threats of reprisal, and was abandoned as soon as plaintiff made clear that the advance was not welcome. The Court is not aware of any authority holding that such a sexual encounter or proposition of the type alleged in this case, without more, gives rise to a claim of outrage. Cf. *Croom,* 913 S.W.2d at 287 (use of wine and medication by a vastly older relative to foist sex on a minor cousin went "beyond a mere sexual encounter" and offended all sense of decency).

Moreover, notwithstanding the offensive nature of the Governor's alleged conduct, plaintiff admits that she never missed a day of work following the alleged incident, she continued to work at AIDC another nineteen months (leaving only because of her husband's job transfer), she continued to go on a daily basis to the Governor's Office to deliver items and never asked to be relieved of that duty, she never filed a formal complaint or told her supervisors of the incident while at AIDC, she never consulted a psychiatrist, psychologist, or incurred medical bills as a result of the alleged incident, and she acknowledges that her two subsequent contacts with the Governor involved comments made "in a light vein" and nonsexual contact that was done in a "friendly fashion." Further, despite earlier claiming that she suffered marital discord and humiliation, plaintiff stated in her deposition that she was not claiming damages to her marriage as a result of the Governor's alleged conduct and she acknowledged the request to drop her claim of injury to reputation by stating, "I didn't really care if it was dropped or not personally." Plaintiff's actions and statements in this case do not portray someone who experienced emotional distress so severe in nature that no reasonable person could be expected to endure it. Cf. *Hamaker,* 51 F.3d 108 (no claim of outrage where plaintiff, who had a speech impediment and an I.Q. of between 75 and 100, was "red-faced and angry," had an "increased heart rate and blood pressure," and had trouble sleeping four days after incident involving "rather nasty" practical joke).

Nevertheless, plaintiff submits a declaration from a purported expert with a Ph.D. in education and counseling, Patrick J. Carnes, who, after a 3.5 hour meeting with plaintiff and her husband a mere four days prior to the filing of President Clinton's motion for summary judgment, opines that her alleged encounter with Governor Clinton in 1991, "and the ensuing events," have caused plaintiff to suffer severe emotional distress and "consequent sexual aversion." The Court does not credit this declaration.

In *Angle v. Alexander,* 328 Ark. 714, 945 S.W.2d 933 (1997), the Arkansas Supreme Court noted that absent physical harm, courts look for more in the way of extreme outrage as an assurance that the mental disturbance claimed is not fictitious. In that case, the plaintiffs offered their own testimony that they had experienced emotional distress, thoughts of death, fear, anger, and worry, but little else. In concluding that there was no evidence of extreme emotional distress required to prevail on an outrage claim, the Court found it significant that none had seen a physician or mental health professional for these concerns. The Court did not allow the fact that one plaintiff "on the advice of her attorney, spoke to a psychologist," to overcome her failure of proof on this point. Id. at 937 n. 3. . . .

In sum, plaintiff's allegations fall far short of the rigorous standards for establishing a claim of outrage under Arkansas law and the Court therefore grants the President's motion for summary judgment on this claim. . . . There being no remaining issues, the Court will enter judgment dismissing this case.

ASSIGNMENT 9.3

a. The *Jones* decision on the tort of outrage was clearly incorrect. Right? Explain.
b. The *Jones* decision on the tort of outrage was clearly correct. Right? Explain.
c. Did the court dismiss the tort claim because the President's conduct was not outrageous enough, because the plaintiff did not suffer enough distress, or because the court did not think the plaintiff was telling the truth about what happened?
d. The court referred to the facts of the case of *Croom v. Younts* (use of wine and medication by a vastly older relative to foist sex on the minor went "beyond a mere sexual encounter" and offended all sense of decency). The court said that the facts of the *Croom* case were distinguishable from the facts of the *Jones* case. Do you agree?
e. Would the court have reached a different conclusion if Jones had alleged that Governor Clinton called her twice soon after the hotel incident, the first time to ask her if she would like to go to a private party with him and the second time to ask her if she wanted him to put in a good word for her with her boss? Assume that she answered "no" to both questions.

MEDIA DEFENDANTS AND THE CONSTITUTION

The First Amendment of the United States Constitution gives special protection to newspapers, magazines, broadcasters, theaters, and other media entities when they are sued because of something they publish. This includes a suit for IIED. In a famous case that reached the United States Supreme Court, Reverend Jerry Falwell asserted this tort against *Hustler Magazine* and its publisher, Larry Flynt, after the magazine printed a crude parody about him. Falwell was the host of a nationally syndicated television show and the founder and president of a political organization formerly known as the Moral Majority. Here is the Court's description of Falwell's grievance:

> Petitioner Hustler Magazine, Inc., is a magazine of nationwide circulation. Respondent Jerry Falwell, a nationally known minister who has been active as a commentator on politics and public affairs, sued petitioner and its publisher, petitioner Larry Flynt, to recover damages for . . . intentional infliction of emotional distress. . . . The inside front cover of the November 1983 issue of Hustler Magazine featured a "parody" of an advertisement for Campari Liqueur that contained the name and picture of respondent and was entitled "Jerry Falwell talks about his first time." This parody was modeled after actual Campari ads that included interviews with various celebrities about their "first times." Although it was apparent by the end of each interview that this meant the first time they sampled Campari, the ads clearly played on the sexual double entendre of the general subject of "first times." Copying the form and layout of these Campari ads, Hustler's editors chose respondent as the featured celebrity and drafted an alleged "interview" with him in which he states that his "first time" was during a drunken incestuous rendezvous with his mother in an outhouse. The Hustler parody portrays respondent and his mother as drunk and immoral, and suggests that respondent is a hypocrite who preaches only when he is drunk. In small print at the bottom of the page, the ad contains the disclaimer, "ad parody—not to be taken seriously." The magazine's table of contents also lists the ad as "Fiction; Ad and Personality Parody."[3]

The question before the Court was whether Falwell had to prove an additional element of the tort because he was suing a media defendant. The Court concluded that he did. It is not enough to show that the defendant acted outrageously. When

public official A government employee who has significant authority.

public figure A person (other than a public official) who has assumed special prominence in the affairs of society.

actual malice Knowledge that a statement of fact is false, or recklessness as to its truth or falsity. Also called constitutional malice.

a **public official** or a **public figure** such as Falwell sues the media for IIED, there must be proof that the media published a false statement of fact with **actual malice** (also called constitutional malice). This means that the media knew the statement was false or that it published the statement in reckless disregard of whether it was true or false. This standard is very difficult for most plaintiffs to meet. It would, therefore, tend to discourage an onslaught of tort claims against the media and thereby help ensure the robust exchange of ideas that the First Amendment is designed to encourage.

In the *Hustler* case, the Court ruled against Falwell because the ad parody could not reasonably be understood as describing actual facts about Falwell. Given the context of the publication, the caricature was simply not reasonably believable. Therefore, the magazine did not publish a statement of fact about Falwell, and, by definition could not have acted with actual malice. Consequently, the plaintiff cannot assert the tort of IIED.

When the media is sued for something it publishes, the more common tort asserted against it is libel. This is the area of tort law that gave birth to the Supreme Court's imposition of the actual malice standard for media defendants. When we discuss defamation in Chapter 24, we will provide a fuller treatment of actual malice, particularly when the plaintiff is a public official or a public figure.

INTENTIONAL INFLICTION OF EMOTIONAL DISTRESS CHECKLIST

Definitions, Relationships, Paralegal Roles, and Research References

Category
Intentional infliction of emotional distress (IIED) is an intentional tort. Some courts have expanded it to include recovery for reckless infliction of emotional distress.

Interest Protected by This Tort
The right to be free from emotional distress that is intentionally (or recklessly) caused by someone else.

Elements of This Tort

1. An act of extreme or outrageous conduct
2. Intent to cause severe emotional distress
3. Severe emotional distress is suffered
4. Defendant is the cause of this distress

Definitions of Major Words/Phrases in These Elements

Act: Voluntary movement of the defendant's body.
Extreme or outrageous: Atrocious; totally intolerable; shocking the conscience of society.
Intent: The desire to inflict severe emotional distress or the knowledge with substantial certainty that such distress will result from what one does or fails to do. (In some states, recklessness—wantonly disregarding risks—will be sufficient.)
Severe emotional distress: Substantial mental anguish or distress that no reasonable person should be expected to endure.
Cause: But for what the defendant did, the plaintiff would not have suffered severe emotional distress, or the defendant was a substantial factor in producing such distress.

Major Defense and Counterargument Possibilities That Need to Be Explored

1. The defendant did not act voluntarily.
2. The defendant's conduct may have been unpleasant and wrongful, but it was not extreme or outrageous.

INTENTIONAL INFLICTION OF EMOTIONAL DISTRESS CHECKLIST *(Continued)*

3. The defendant did not desire the plaintiff to suffer severe emotional distress nor know with substantial certainty that such distress would result from what the defendant did (no intent). In a state where recklessness can be a substitute for intent, the defendant did not recklessly cause such distress.
4. The plaintiff may have been embarrassed or upset, but did not suffer severe emotional distress; it was not distress that no reasonable person should be expected to endure.
5. The plaintiff suffered severe emotional distress because he or she is unusually sensitive and the defendant had no reason to know of this sensitivity.
6. But for what the defendant did, the plaintiff would still have suffered severe emotional distress; the defendant was not a substantial factor in producing plaintiff's emotional distress (no causation).
7. The defendant did not know that the statement of fact about the plaintiff was false nor was the defendant reckless as to its truth or falsity (for media defendants).
8. The plaintiff consented to the defendant's conduct that led to the severe emotional distress (on the defense of consent, see Chapter 27).
9. The plaintiff's emotional distress occurred while the defendant was defending himself or herself from the plaintiff (on self-defense and other self-help privileges, see Chapter 27).
10. The plaintiff's emotional distress occurred while the defendant was defending someone else from the plaintiff (on the defense of others and other self-help privileges, see Chapter 27).
11. The plaintiff's emotional distress occurred while the defendant was defending property or recapturing chattels from the plaintiff (on necessity, defense of property, recapture of property, and other self-help privileges, see Chapter 27).
12. The plaintiff's emotional distress occurred while the defendant was disciplining the plaintiff (on discipline and other self-help privileges, see Chapter 27).
13. The plaintiff's emotional distress occurred while the defendant was arresting the plaintiff (on the privilege of arrest, see Chapter 7).
14. The plaintiff's suit against the government for IIED committed by a government employee may be barred by sovereign immunity (on sovereign immunity, see Chapter 27).
15. The plaintiff's suit against the government employee for IIED may be barred by official immunity (on official immunity, see Chapter 27).
16. The plaintiff's suit against the charitable organization for IIED committed by someone working for the organization may be barred by charitable immunity (on charitable immunity, see Chapter 27).
17. The plaintiff's suit against a family member for IIED may be barred by intrafamily tort immunity (on intrafamily tort immunity, see Chapter 22).
18. The plaintiff failed to take reasonable steps to mitigate the harm caused when the defendant committed IIED; therefore, damages should not cover the aggravation of the harm caused by the plaintiff (on the mitigation-of-damages rule, see Chapter 16).

Damages

The plaintiff can recover compensatory damages for the mental distress suffered as well as for any physical harm or illness that may have resulted from the defendant's conduct. Punitive damages are also likely if the defendant acted out of hatred or ill will. (On the categories of damages, see Chapter 16.)

Relationship to Criminal Law

The defendant's conduct may also constitute the crime of extortion, criminal assault, breach of the peace, criminal battery, etc.

Other Torts and Related Actions

Abuse of process: While using the criminal process for an improper purpose, the defendant may have intended to cause the plaintiff severe emotional distress.

INTENTIONAL INFLICTION OF EMOTIONAL DISTRESS CHECKLIST *(Continued)*

Assault: While intending to cause severe emotional distress in the plaintiff, the defendant may have intentionally placed the plaintiff in apprehension of an imminent harmful or offensive contact. A threat of future harm rarely constitutes an assault, but future threats might constitute IIED if they are extreme or outrageous enough.
Battery: While intending to cause severe emotional distress in the plaintiff, the defendant may have intentionally made harmful or offensive contact with the plaintiff.
Conversion: Defendant may have intended to have the plaintiff suffer severe emotional distress by destroying plaintiff's personal property.
Defamation: While intentionally causing the plaintiff to suffer severe emotional distress, the defendant may have published derogatory statements that injured the reputation of the plaintiff.
False imprisonment: By intentionally locking the plaintiff up or otherwise restricting his or her movement, the defendant may have had the intent to cause the plaintiff severe emotional distress.
False light (invasion of privacy): By giving unreasonable publicity to false private facts, the defendant may have had the intent to cause the plaintiff severe emotional distress.
Intrusion (invasion of privacy): By unreasonably intruding on the plaintiff's privacy, the defendant may have had the intent to cause the plaintiff severe emotional distress.
Malicious prosecution: The defendant may have initiated legal proceedings against the plaintiff with the intent to cause the plaintiff severe emotional distress.
Negligence: If the defendant negligently caused physical harm to the plaintiff, the latter can also recover for resulting emotional distress that was not intended. Some states also allow recovery for negligent infliction of emotional distress (NIED).
Trespass to land: While trespassing on the plaintiff's land, the defendant may have had the intent to subject the plaintiff to severe emotional distress.
Wrongful death: If the plaintiff died as a result of intentional infliction of emotional distress, designated survivors may be able to bring a wrongful death action.

Federal Law

a. Under the Federal Tort Claims Act, there is no explicit exclusion that says the United States government will not be liable for IIED committed by one of its federal employees within the scope of employment (respondeat superior). (See Exhibit 27–7 in Chapter 27.) (Most states have their own statutes that cover when tort claims can be made against the state for IIED and other torts committed by state government employees. Such claims are also covered in Chapter 27.)
b. There may be liability under the Civil Rights Act if the IIED was committed while the defendant was depriving the plaintiff of a federal civil right under color of state law. (See Exhibit 27–9 in Chapter 27.)

Employer–Employee (Agency) Law

A private (non-government) employee who commits IIED is personally liable for this tort. His or her employer will *also* be liable for the tort if the conduct of the employee was within the scope of employment (respondeat superior). The employee must be furthering a business objective of the employer at the time. Intentional torts such as IIED, however, are often outside the scope of employment. If so, only the employee is liable for the tort. (On the factors that determine the scope of employment, see Exhibit 14–9 in Chapter 14.)

Paralegal Roles in Intentional Infliction of Emotional Distress Litigation

(See also Exhibit 3–1 in Chapter 3, Exhibit 20–4 in Chapter 20, and Exhibit 29–1 in Chapter 29.)

Fact finding (help the office collect facts relevant to prove the elements of IIED, the elements of available defenses, and extent of injuries or other damages):
- client interviewing
- field investigation
- online research

INTENTIONAL INFLICTION OF EMOTIONAL DISTRESS CHECKLIST *(Continued)*

File management (help the office control the documents involved in an IIED litigation):

- open client file
- enter case data in computer database
- maintain file documents

Litigation assistance (help the trial attorney prepare for an IIED trial and appeal, if needed):

- draft discovery requests
- draft answers to discovery requests
- draft pleadings
- digest and index discovery documents
- help prepare, order, and manage trial exhibits
- prepare trial notebook
- draft notice of appeal
- order trial transcript
- cite-check briefs
- perform legal research

Collection/enforcement (help the trial attorney for the judgment creditor to collect the damages award or to enforce other court orders at the conclusion of the IIED case):

- draft postjudgment discovery requests
- conduct field investigation to monitor compliance with judgment
- perform online research (e.g., location of defendant's business assets)

Research References for Intentional Infliction of Emotional Distress

Digests

In the digests of West Group, look for case summaries on this tort under key topics such as:

Torts
Threats
Death
Damages

Corpus Juris Secundum

In this legal encyclopedia, look for discussion under topic headings such as:

Torts
Threats and unlawful communications
Damages
Telegraph, telephone, radio and television
Death

American Jurisprudence 2d

In this legal encyclopedia, look for discussion under topic headings such as:

Torts
Fright, shock and mental disturbance
Damages
Death

Legal Periodical Literature

There are two index systems to use to try to locate articles on this tort:

Index to Legal Periodicals and Books (ILP)

See literature in *ILP* under subject headings such as:

Torts
Collection Agencies
Damages
Negligence
Personal Injuries
Privacy
Wrongful Death

Current Law Index (CLI)

See literature in *CLI* under subject headings such as:

Privacy, Right of Mental Distress
Negligence
Damages
Torts
Personal Injuries
Death by Wrongful Act
Collection Agencies

Example of legal periodical literature you can locate through the *ILP* or *CLI* on this tort:

Child Witnesses of Domestic Violence: Third-Party Recovery for Intentional Infliction of Emotional Distress by Mary Kate Kearney, 47 Loyola Law Review 283 (2001)

INTENTIONAL INFLICTION OF EMOTIONAL DISTRESS CHECKLIST *(Continued)*

A.L.R., A.L.R.2d, A.L.R.3d, A.L.R.4th, A.L.R.5th, A.L.R.6th, A.L.R. Fed., and A.L.R. Fed. 2d
Use the *ALR Index* to locate annotations on this tort. In this index, check subject headings such as:

Mental Anguish	Torts
Shock	Death
Emotional Disturbance	Intentional Tort
Debtors and Creditors	

Example of an annotation you can locate through this index on this tort:

Recovery by Debtor, under Tort of Intentional or Reckless Infliction of Emotional Distress, for Damages Resulting from Collection Methods by Joel E. Smith, 87 A.L.R.3d 201 (1978).

Words and Phrases
In this multivolume legal dictionary, look up *intentional infliction of emotional distress, emotional distress, outrage, outrageous, reckless, negligent infliction of emotional distress,* and every other word or phrase connected with the tort(s) discussed in this chapter. The dictionary will give you definitions of these words or phrases from court opinions.

CALR: Computer-Assisted Legal Research
Example of a query you could ask on Westlaw to try to find cases, statutes, or other legal materials on this tort: **"intentional infliction of emotional distress"/p damages**

Example of a query you could ask on LexisNexis to try to find cases, statutes, or other legal materials on this tort: **intentional infliction of emotional distress /p damages**

Example of search terms you could use on an Internet legal search engine such as the Public Library of Law (www.plol.org), Findlaw (www.findlaw.com), or Google Scholar (scholar.google.com) to find cases, statutes, and other legal materials on this tort: **"intentional infliction of emotional distress"**

Example of search terms you could use on an Internet general search engine such as Google, Bing, or AltaVista to find cases, statutes, or other legal materials on this tort: **"intentional infliction of emotional distress"**

More Internet sites to check for materials on IIED and other torts:
jurist.law.pitt.edu/sg_torts.htm
www.hg.org/torts.html
www.megalaw.com/top/top.php (click "Intentional Torts," "Personal Injury Law," "Tort Law," and "Damages")
See also the online sites in Overview of Tort Law at the end of Chapter 1.

NEGLIGENT INFLICTION OF EMOTIONAL DISTRESS

Introduction

negligent infliction of emotional distress (NIED) Carelessly causing someone to suffer emotional distress.

We now turn to a discussion of emotional distress that is not intentionally or recklessly caused but results from carelessness or negligence. Our overriding theme is whether a court will provide recovery for **negligent infliction of emotional distress (NIED)**, which is carelessly causing someone to suffer emotional distress. Not all states recognize this tort, and those that do may impose different restrictions on its availability.

Emotional Distress Following Physical Injury

The traditional rule is that you can recover for negligently caused emotional distress that results from a physical injury.

EXAMPLE
Dan negligently drives his car into Rose's car. Rose suffers a broken back and considerable emotional distress.

Rose can recover damages for the injury to her back and also for the emotional distress (pain and suffering) that grew out of or attached to the physical injury.

Emotional Distress, Zone of Danger, Physical Symptoms

A concern of the law is that it is relatively easy to fabricate emotional distress in the absence of a physical injury. Indeed, at one time such claims were simply not allowed, in large part because of this concern. Today, however, most courts allow NIED claims if the emotional distress was foreseeable to the defendant because the plaintiff was in the **zone of danger** and if the plaintiff suffered substantial physical symptoms as a result of the distress.

zone of danger The area within which injury or other loss to the plaintiff is foreseeable.

EXAMPLE

Harold negligently drives his car on the sidewalk where Jane is walking. She quickly steps aside to avoid being hit but suffers such intense emotional distress from the incident that she miscarries.

Jane was in the zone of danger; she had to step aside to avoid being hit. She suffered substantial physical symptoms (the miscarriage) from the distress. At one time, plaintiffs were denied recovery if there was no **physical impact** on their body. This is no longer the law in most states. Again, recovery for NIED is allowed in most states if the plaintiff was in the zone of danger and suffered substantial physical symptoms. Other examples of such symptoms include prolonged dizziness, nausea, headaches, vomiting, shock, or ulcers. A few courts are willing to allow NIED recovery in the absence of substantial physical symptoms, but this is a minority view.

physical impact Actual contact with the body.

There are, however, two narrow categories of cases in which almost all states allow NIED recovery even if the plaintiff was not in the zone of danger and did not suffer physical symptoms. The first involves telegraph companies (e.g., negligently delivering a false message that a child has died) and companies that deal with dead bodies (e.g., negligently misplacing or dismembering a body at a funeral home). Courts have allowed NIED recovery in such cases (primarily to relatives) without requiring a showing that the plaintiffs suffering emotional distress were in the zone of danger and had physical symptoms.

ASSIGNMENT 9.4

In the following situations, discuss whether there can be recovery for NIED.

a. Eight-year-old Johnny is on his first trip to Disneyland. While walking through the park, he is shocked to see Mickey Mouse remove his mask to get a drink of water at a fountain. Johnny is traumatized to learn that the character he idolized is not real. Johnny sues the person in the costume and Disneyland for NIED.

b. Mary is a passenger on a flight across the country. Suddenly the plane jerks. Mary looks out the window and sees that part of the wing has broken off. The pilot announces that everyone should be prepared for an emergency landing. After forty-five minutes of terror, the plane lands safely in a farm field. Mary sues the airline for NIED.

c. Harold negligently drives his car on the sidewalk where Jane is walking. She quickly steps aside to avoid being hit but suffers considerable emotional distress. After a few hours, however, she no longer thinks about the incident. In discussions with a friend who is an attorney, she realizes she may have a case for NIED against Harold. She brings the suit.

d. In a room with Leo, Fred screams that he is going to kill himself as he brandishes a knife in the air. Leo is terrified, thinking that Fred might harm him with the knife in addition to committing suicide. As Leo runs from the room while Fred's back is turned, he bumps into Fred just in front of the door, but escapes unharmed. Soon after, Leo develops ulcers and sues Fred for NIED.

Bystander Cases

bystander One who is present but is not a direct participant. (See glossary for an additional definition.)

Sometimes the emotional distress results from observing or witnessing someone else's physical injury. Observers or witnesses are referred to as **bystanders** because although they were present, they were not direct participants in the physical injury. Consider the following three variations in which a father suffers substantial physical symptoms as a result of his son's physical injury:

EXAMPLE #1

Ed, a four-year-old child, is hit by a car. At the time of the accident, George, his dad, was in the drugstore buying a newspaper. He did not see the accident. He goes into severe shock when he comes out of the store and sees Ed lying in the street.

EXAMPLE #2

Same facts as #1, but this time, George suffers severe shock when he sees Ed being hit. While in the drugstore, George looked out the window and saw the accident.

EXAMPLE #3

Same facts as #1, but this time, the accident occurs as Ed and George are walking across the street together. Although only Ed is hit by the car, George suffers severe shock upon seeing the car hit Ed.

Ed, of course, can bring a negligence action for his own physical injury and for the emotional distress it caused him. What about George? Can he, as a member of the immediate family of his son, recover for NIED? Note that only in Example #3 was George in the zone of danger himself. (Because he was walking with his son, both of them could have been hit.) In most states, George can recover for NIED in Example #3 but not in Examples #1 and #2. You must be in the zone of danger along with the person injured and be part of the latter's immediate family. Then you can recover in a NIED action for the emotional distress and resulting physical symptoms that you suffer as a result of observing another's suffering. This is the majority view. There are, however, a few states that *will* allow NIED recovery for persons who are not in the zone of danger, but only if specific conditions are met. As you read the case of *Thing v. La Chusa*, note what these conditions are.

Before we examine the *Thing* case, it should be pointed out that when recovery is denied for NIED, it is sometimes on the basis that the defendant owed no *duty* to the plaintiff (the defendant had no duty to guard against the risk of emotional distress by the plaintiff) or that the defendant was not the *proximate cause* of what the plaintiff suffered (the plaintiff's emotional distress was not foreseeable to the defendant). We will discuss duty in Chapter 13 and proximate cause in Chapter 15.

CASE

Thing v. La Chusa

48 Cal. 3d 644, 771 P.2d 814 (1989)
Supreme Court of California

Background: *Maria Thing's son, John, was injured in an automobile accident that was negligently caused by the defendant, James V. La Chusa. The son sued the defendant separately for his injuries. Maria Thing brought her own suit for negligent infliction of emotional distress (NIED) based on the distress she suffered when she came to the scene of the accident and saw the condition of her son. She did not observe the accident itself. There was no physical impact on her and she suffered no physical injury herself at the scene. The trial court dismissed her claim by granting a summary judgment for the defendant because she did not*

contemporaneously perceive the accident. On appeal, however, the Court of Appeals reversed and allowed her to recover for NIED. The case is now on further appeal before the Supreme Court of California.

Decision on Appeal: *Judgment for the defendant. The decision of the Court of Appeals is reversed. Maria Thing has failed to establish NIED since she did not witness the accident.*

OPINION OF COURT

Justice EAGLESON delivered the opinion of the court . . .

On December 8, 1980, John Thing, a minor, was injured when struck by an automobile operated by defendant James V. La Chusa. His mother, plaintiff Maria Thing, was nearby, but neither saw nor heard the accident. She became aware of the injury to her son when told by a daughter that John had been struck by a car. She rushed to the scene where she saw her bloody and unconscious child, whom she believed was dead, lying in the roadway. Maria sued defendant, alleging that she suffered great emotional disturbance, shock, and injury to her nervous system as a result of these events, and that the injury to John and emotional distress she suffered were proximately caused by defendant's negligence. . . .

The impact of personally observing the injury-producing event in most, although concededly not all, cases distinguishes the plaintiff's resultant emotional distress from the emotion felt when one learns of the injury or death of a loved one from another, or observes pain and suffering but not the traumatic cause of the injury. Greater certainty and a more reasonable limit on the exposure to liability for negligent conduct is possible by limiting the right to recover for negligently caused emotional distress to plaintiffs who personally and contemporaneously perceive the injury-producing event and its traumatic consequences.*

Similar reasoning justifies limiting recovery to persons closely related by blood or marriage since, in common experience, it is more likely that they will suffer a greater degree of emotional distress than a disinterested witness to negligently caused pain and suffering or death. Such limitations are indisputably arbitrary since it is foreseeable that in some cases unrelated persons have a relationship to the victim or are so affected by the traumatic event that they suffer equivalent emotional distress. As we have observed, however, drawing arbitrary lines is unavoidable if we are to limit liability and establish meaningful rules for application by litigants and lower courts.

No policy supports extension of the right to recover for NIED to a larger class of plaintiffs. Emotional distress is an intangible condition experienced by most persons, even absent negligence, at some time during their lives. Close relatives suffer serious, even debilitating, emotional reactions to the injury, death, serious illness, and evident suffering of loved ones. These reactions occur regardless of the cause of the loved one's illness, injury, or death. That relatives will have severe emotional distress is an unavoidable aspect of the "human condition." The emotional distress for which monetary damages may be recovered, however, ought not to be that form of acute emotional distress or the transient emotional reaction to the occasional gruesome or horrible incident to which every person may potentially be exposed in an industrial and sometimes violent society. Regardless of the depth of feeling or the resultant physical or mental illness that results from witnessing violent events, persons unrelated to those injured or killed may not now recover for such emotional upheaval even if negligently caused. Close relatives who witness the accidental injury or death of a loved one and suffer emotional trauma may not recover when the loved one's conduct was the cause of that emotional trauma. The overwhelming majority of "emotional distress" which we endure, therefore, is not compensable.

Unlike an award of damages for intentionally caused emotional distress which is punitive, the award for NIED simply reflects society's belief that a negligent actor bears some responsibility for the effect of his conduct on persons other than those who suffer physical injury. In identifying those persons and the circumstances in which the defendant will be held to redress the injury, it is appropriate to restrict recovery to those persons who will suffer an emotional impact beyond the impact that can be anticipated whenever one learns that a relative is injured, or dies, or the emotion felt by a "disinterested" witness. The class of potential plaintiffs should be limited to those who because of their relationship suffer the greatest emotional distress. When the right to recover is limited in this manner, the liability bears a reasonable relationship to the culpability of the negligent defendant. . . . Even if it is "foreseeable" that persons other than closely related percipient witnesses may suffer emotional distress, this fact does not justify the imposition of what threatens to become unlimited liability for emotional distress on a defendant whose conduct is simply negligent. . . .

We conclude, therefore, that a plaintiff may recover damages for emotional distress caused by observing the negligently inflicted injury of a third person if, but only if, said plaintiff: (1) is closely related to the injury victim;† (2) is present at the scene of the injury-producing event at the time it occurs and is then aware that it is causing

*"[A] distinction between distress caused by personal observation of the injury and by hearing of the tragedy from another is justified because compensation should be limited to abnormal life experiences which cause emotional distress. While receiving news that a loved one has been injured or has died may cause emotional distress, it is the type of experience for which in a general way one is prepared, an experience which is common. By contrast few persons are forced to witness the death or injury of a loved one or to suddenly come upon the scene without warning in situations where tortious conduct is involved. [For] example, while it is common to visit a loved one in a hospital and to be distressed by the loved one's pain and suffering, it is highly uncommon to witness the apparent neglect of the patient's immediate medical needs by medical personnel." (*Ochoa v. Superior Court* (1985) 39 Cal. 3d 159, 165, fn. 6, 703 P.2d 1.)

†In most cases no justification exists for permitting recovery for NIED by persons who are only distantly related to the injury victim. Absent exceptional circumstances, recovery should be limited to relatives residing in the same household, or parents, siblings, children, and grandparents of the victim.

injury to the victim; and (3) as a result suffers serious emotional distress—a reaction beyond that which would be anticipated in a disinterested witness and which is not an abnormal response to the circumstances. . . .

The merely negligent actor does not owe a duty the law will recognize to make monetary amends to all persons who may have suffered emotional distress on viewing or learning about the injurious consequences of his conduct. . . .

The undisputed facts establish that [Maria Thing] was not present at the scene of the accident in which her son was injured. She did not observe defendant's conduct and was not aware that her son was being injured. She could not, therefore, establish a right to recover for the emotional distress she suffered when she subsequently learned of the accident and observed its consequences. The order granting summary judgment was proper. The judgment of the Court of Appeal is reversed.

ASSIGNMENT 9.5

Jim Nester drowns while swimming in a pool operated by Fun Center, Inc. The death is solely due to the negligence of Fun Center, Inc. Jim was at the pool with his stepfather, Frank Carter. (Frank married Jim's mother a month before Jim's death. Frank had lived with the mother for about three weeks before the marriage.) Jim was accidentally pushed into the pool by a careless lifeguard. Frank did not see this, but he heard a stranger scream when Jim fell in the water. When he heard the scream, Fred looked over in the direction of Jim. Since people had gathered around, he was not certain what had happened. He walked over and saw Jim being pulled from the water. Frank gasped in horror when he saw Jim's face turn blue. As a lifeguard started carrying Jim to an ambulance, Frank panicked. He felt dizzy and almost fainted. He has been unable to sleep because of Jim's death. After the funeral, Frank sued Fun Center, Inc. for NIED. What are his chances of success? Does the *Thing* case apply?

CHECK THE CITE

Plaintiff alleged that his superiors conspired to force his coworkers to create false documentation of his poor performance, which the superiors then used to discipline the plaintiff. When the situation became intolerable and made him depressed, plaintiff sued his superiors for IIED. Why did the plaintiff lose the IIED claim? Read *Preston v. Atmel*, 560 F. Supp. 2d 1035 (D. Colo. 2008). To read the opinion online, run a citation search ("560 F. Supp. 2d 1035") or a party search (Preston Atmel) in the Legal Opinions and Journals database of Google Scholar (scholar.google.com).

PROJECT

In Google, Bing, or another general search engine, run the following searches:

1. "Catch a Predator" "intentional infliction of emotional distress". Describe the TV controversy that led to a charge of IIED.
2. *aa* "negligent infliction of emotional distress" (Substitute the name of your state for *aa* in the search.) Describe the facts and holding of a case in which a NIED action was brought in your state.

ETHICS IN A TORTS PRACTICE

You are a paralegal working in the law office that represents Fred Peterson, who is suing someone for IIED. Your assignment is to file the complaint at a courthouse across town. The cab ride takes an hour. During this hour, you use your laptop to summarize a deposition on the contracts case of another client (Ted O'Reilly). The entire trip takes three hours. When you get back to the office, you record your time as three hours on the Peterson case and one hour on the O'Reilly case. Peterson is billed your paralegal rate for the three hours and O'Reilly is billed your paralegal rate for the one hour. Any ethical problems?

SUMMARY

The tort of intentional infliction of emotional distress (IIED) is intentionally causing severe emotional distress by an act of extreme or outrageous conduct. The act must shock the conscience of society. For defendants such as common carriers and innkeepers, however, courts sometimes say that less-severe conduct will suffice. Cyberstalking and related conduct on the Internet can sometimes constitute IIED. In most states, intent for IIED is established by showing a desire to inflict severe emotional distress or the knowledge with substantial certainty that such distress will result; in some states, recklessness is enough. The transferred-intent rule does not apply to IIED.

The plaintiff must in fact suffer severe emotional distress. Physical injury is not required. The test of whether the distress was severe is an objective test unless the defendant is aware of (and takes advantage of) the plaintiff's unusual susceptibility to such distress. If a third party sues for IIED directed at another, the Restatement requires the third party to be present at the time the other is attacked and be a member of the latter's immediate family, or, if not a member, suffer bodily harm due to witnessing the attack. The plaintiff must show either that but for what the defendant did the distress would not have resulted, or that the defendant was a substantial factor in producing it.

When a media defendant is sued for intentional infliction of emotional distress and the plaintiff is a public official or public figure, the plaintiff must prove that the media published a false statement of fact and either knew the statement was false or published it in reckless disregard of whether it was true or false (actual malice).

Negligent infliction of emotional distress (NIED) consists of carelessly causing someone to suffer emotional distress. Most courts allow NIED claims if the emotional distress was foreseeable to the defendant because the plaintiff was in the zone of danger and the plaintiff suffered substantial physical symptoms as a result of the distress. If a bystander suffers emotional distress by observing or witnessing the negligently caused injury of another, most states allow the bystander to recover for NIED if he or she was in the zone of danger along with the person injured and is part of the latter's immediate family. If the bystander was not in the zone of danger, a few states will allow NIED recovery if specific conditions are met, e.g., the bystander was aware of the injury of the other at the time the injury was inflicted.

KEY TERMS

pain and suffering *140*
intentional infliction of emotional distress (IIED) *140*
extreme or outrageous conduct *140*
cyberstalking *141*
cyberbullying *141*
intent (for intentional infliction of emotional distress) *142*
reckless *142*
transferred-intent rule *143*
severe emotional distress *144*
physical injury *144*
public official *150*
public figure *150*
actual malice *150*
negligent infliction of emotional distress (NIED) *154*
zone of danger *155*
physical impact *155*
bystander *156*

REVIEW QUESTIONS

1. What is pain and suffering?
2. What are the elements of intentional infliction of emotional distress (IIED)?
3. When is conduct extreme or outrageous?
4. What is cyberstalking?
5. What difficulties is a plaintiff likely to face when bringing an action for IIED for conduct on the Internet?
6. Does the transferred-intent rule apply to IIED?
7. What requirement does the Restatement impose when someone sues for IIED that was directed at another?
8. How were families of victims of 9/11 able to sue for IIED when the families were not present at the time of the attack?
9. How was President Clinton able to win the IIED case brought against him?
10. What does a plaintiff have to prove when bringing an IIED action against the media?
11. What is negligent infliction of emotional distress (NIED)?
12. In most states, what must the plaintiff prove to bring an action for NIED?
13. How can a bystander sue for NIED?

HELPFUL WEBSITES

- **Intentional Infliction of Emotional Distress**
  www.west.net/~smith/distress.htm
  en.wikipedia.org/wiki/Intentional_infliction_of_emotional_distress
  biotech.law.lsu.edu/courses/tortsF01/IIEM.htm
  www.google.com (run this search: elements "intentional infliction of emotional distress" tort)
- **Negligent Infliction of Emotional Distress**
  en.wikipedia.org/wiki/Negligent_infliction_of_emotional_distress
  tortssymposium.law.wfu.edu/papers/keating.pdf
  tortssymposium.law.wfu.edu/papers/mathews.pdf
  www.google.com (run this search: elements "negligent infliction of emotional distress" tort)
- **Documents in the Hustler Magazine Trial**
  www.law.umkc.edu/faculty/projects/ftrials/ftrials.htm

ENDNOTES

1. 274 F. Supp. 2d 86 (D.D.C. 2003).
2. Id at 107–108.
3. *Hustler Magazine and Larry C. Flynt v. Jerry Falwell*, 485 U.S. 46, 47–8, 108 S. Ct. 876, 887–8, 99 L. Ed. 2d 41, 47 (1988).

Student StudyWARE™ CD-ROM
For additional materials, please go to the student CD in this book.

CHAPTER

10

CONVERSION AND TRESPASS TO CHATTELS

CHAPTER OUTLINE

- Introduction
- Damages
- Kind of Interference
- Mistake Defense

CHAPTER OBJECTIVES

After completing this chapter, you should be able to:

- Understand the distinction between conversion and trespass to chattels.
- Identify the elements of conversion and trespass to chattels.
- List the defenses to conversion and trespass to chattels.
- Identify paralegal roles in litigation asserting conversion or trespass to chattels.
- Identify the major resources available in traditional books and online for researching issues involving conversion or trespass to chattels.

INTRODUCTION

personal property Property other than land or other than things attached to land. Also called chattel.

chattel Personal property.

conversion An intentional interference with another's personal property, consisting of an exercise of dominion over it.

trespass to chattels An intentional interference with another's personal property, consisting of dispossession or intermeddling.

If someone accidently damages your **personal property** (also called a **chattel**) e.g., a motorist dents the right fender of your car in a collision, you may be able to sue for negligence. (Personal property and chattels are property other than land or other than things attached to land.) Suppose, however, that the interference is *intentional* rather than accidental, e.g., someone steals your fountain pen from your bag or decides to "borrow" your car for an hour without your permission. Your remedy in such cases is the tort of **conversion** or the tort of **trespass to chattels**. The major distinction between the two torts is the degree of interference that is involved. If the interference is relatively minor (dispossession or intermeddling), the tort to use is trespass to chattels. A more serious interference (exercising dominion over it) justifies an action for conversion. (See Exhibit 10–1 for the elements of these two torts that we will be examining.)

Exhibit 10–1
Elements of the torts of conversion and trespass to chattels.

Conversion
1. Personal property (chattel)
2. The plaintiff is in possession of the chattel or is entitled to immediate possession
3. Intent to exercise dominion over the chattel (a serious interference)
4. Dominion
5. Causation of the serious interference

Trespass to Chattels
1. Personal property (chattel)
2. The plaintiff is in possession of the chattel or is entitled to immediate possession
3. Intent to dispossess or intermeddle
4. Dispossession or intermeddling
5. Causation of the dispossession or intermeddling

DAMAGES

There is a dramatic difference in what can be recovered as damages in an action for conversion as opposed to an action for trespass to chattels. A successful plaintiff in a trespass-to-chattels case can recover the cost of repairing the chattel or the cost of renting a replacement while the defendant had it. In a conversion case, the recovery is the full market value of the chattel at the time it was converted. In effect, the party that seriously interfered with the chattel is forced to buy it—even if this wrongdoer later offers to return the chattel in its original condition. The victim is not required to accept the return.

KIND OF INTERFERENCE

dominion The exertion of substantial or extensive control over a chattel that is inconsistent with the right of another to control it.

dispossession 1. Taking physical control of a chattel without exercising dominion over it. 2. Depriving someone of possession or occupancy of property.

intermeddling Making physical contact with, and causing damage or harm to, a chattel without exercising dominion over it.

When is an interference serious enough to constitute conversion? There is no absolute answer to this question that will cover every case. The court will consider a number of factors, no one of which is usually conclusive. The factors are outlined in Exhibit 10–2.

Conversion requires an exercise of **dominion** over a chattel. Dominion is the exertion of substantial or extensive control over a chattel that is inconsistent with the right of another to control it. **Dispossession** consists of taking physical control or possession of a chattel but without exercising dominion over it. **Intermeddling** is making physical contact with, and causing damage or harm to, a chattel without exercising dominion over it. Dispossession and intermeddling are trespass to chattels because they are interferences that take place without consent and deprive the victim of possession or cause harm or damage to the chattel. Since, however, neither involves dominion, they do not constitute conversion.

- The extent and duration of the defendant's exercise of control over the chattel. The more substantial and lengthy the interference, the more likely it will constitute conversion.
- Whether the defendant intended to assert a right in the chattel that was inconsistent with the plaintiff's right of control. The assertion of such a right builds a stronger case for conversion.
- Whether the defendant acted in good faith or bad faith when interfering with the chattel. See the discussion below on the effect of a mistake when a plaintiff is charged with conversion or trespass to chattels.
- Whether the interference caused any damage or harm to the chattel. The more damage or harm, the greater the likelihood that the interference was a conversion.
- Whether the plaintiff suffered any inconvenience or expense as a result of the interference. The more inconvenience or expense, the greater the likelihood that the interference was a conversion.

Exhibit 10–2
Factors considered by a court to determine whether an interference with a chattel is serious enough to constitute conversion.[1]

EXAMPLES

Paul is sitting in the park, where he has brought his dog. Consider the following fact variations:

Case #1. When Paul is not looking, Dan grabs the dog and runs away to another city. At the time, the dog was wandering around some bushes near Paul's bench. Dan has committed conversion. Permanently taking someone's chattel (the dog) is clearly an exercise of dominion.

Case #2. Same facts as in #1 except that a week after taking the dog, Dan regrets what he did and returns the dog to Paul. Dan has committed conversion. Depriving someone of a chattel for an extended period is an exercise of dominion even if it is eventually returned.

Case #3. When Dan sees the dog in the park, he mistakenly thinks it belongs to his brother, who recently lost a dog of the same breed and size. Because his brother is out of town, Dan does not realize his mistake until the brother returns four days later, at which time Dan returns the dog to Paul. Dan has committed conversion. Depriving someone of a chattel for an extended period is an exercise of dominion, even if (1) it was due to an honest mistake, (2) no harm was done to the chattel, and (3) it was eventually returned.

Case #4. Same facts as in #3 except that Dan realized his mistake (that the dog did not belong to his brother) when he got to his car five minutes after picking the dog up. He immediately returns the unharmed dog to Paul. There has been a dispossession, not an exercise of dominion. Dan did not have the dog for long and did not harm it. Dan has committed trespass to chattels, not conversion. Paul would not be able to recover very much in damages for the tort of trespass to chattels because the loss suffered by Paul was minimal. Yet a dispossession, however brief, did occur.

Case #5. When Dan sees the dog in the park, it is sitting next to Paul on the bench. Dan walks over and pets the dog for about ten seconds before walking away. No tort has been committed. There was no exercise of dominion and no dispossession. Nor was there intermeddling. Dan made physical contact with the dog, but no harm or damage was done to the dog.

Case #6. Same facts as in #5 except that when Dan leans over to pet the dog, his leaking ballpoint pen falls out of his shirt pocket onto the dog. The ink from the pen stains the dog's fur. Dan has committed trespass to chattels due to intermeddling. He made contact with the dog and caused harm or damage to the dog's fur. Paul can recover any cleaning costs associated with removing the ink stain.

Spam as Trespass to Chattels

Computer networks and systems constitute personal property—chattels. Like all chattels, they can be interfered with in minimal as well as substantial ways. In one case, an Internet service provider (CompuServe) was successful in bringing a trespass-to-chattels action against a company that sent large numbers of unsolicited e-mail advertisements (spam) to users of the plaintiff's Internet service. "To the extent that defendants' multitudinous electronic mailings demand the disk space and drain the processing power of plaintiff's computer equipment, those resources are not available to serve CompuServe subscribers. Therefore, the value of that equipment to CompuServe is diminished even though it is not physically damaged by defendants' conduct . . . Many subscribers have terminated their accounts specifically because of the unwanted receipt of bulk e-mail messages. Defendants' intrusions into CompuServe's computer systems, insofar as they harm plaintiff's business reputation and goodwill with its customers, are actionable" as trespass to chattels.[2]

Conversion of Electronic Data

tangible Capable of being touched or seen. Having physical form.

intangible Without physical form, e.g., a right or an emotion.

Most conversion cases consist of an interference with personal property that is **tangible**—has a physical form. What about **intangible** property such as the right to receive a sum of money or the right to partial ownership of a corporation? The traditional rule is that intangible rights can be converted if they are represented by or merged into a physical document such as a promissory note or a stock certificate. A few cases have gone beyond this requirement and held that intangible property can be converted even if it is not embodied in a physical document. A recent New York case, for example, held that electronic data stored through an Internet connection could be converted. After an insurance company terminated its relationship with an insurance agent, the company denied the agent continued access to the company's computer system. The agent claimed that he was no longer able to access the electronic records of customer contacts and related data that the insurance company did not own. The court held that this could constitute the tort of conversion even though the records had no physical form.[3]

ASSIGNMENT 10.1

Has conversion or trespass to chattels been committed in any of the following cases?

a. After an argument, Susan places all of her boyfriend's belongings on the sidewalk in front of Susan's home. The boyfriend watches Susan do this. He sues her for converting his belongings.
b. Same facts as in *a,* except that the boyfriend does not learn about the removal of the belongings until he comes home from work on the day Susan placed them on the sidewalk.
c. George orders a very expensive meal at a restaurant where he is dining alone. He puts his silk jacket on the chair next to where he is sitting and goes to make a phone call in the hall. While away, Ralph, another patron, comes over to George's table. He tries on George's jacket in order to help decide whether he wants to buy one like it. He also pours a few drops of wine from George's glass into an empty glass Ralph brings over. Ralph wants to taste the wine in order to decide whether to order the same wine. George sues Ralph for converting his jacket and his meal.
d. Mary lies to her boyfriend, John, about her use of birth control. When she becomes pregnant, he sues her for converting his semen.

CASE

Russell-Vaughn Ford, Inc. v. E. W. Rouse

281 Ala. 567, 206 So. 2d 371 (1968)
Supreme Court of Alabama

Background: *E. W. Rouse sued Russell-Vaughn Ford for conversion when the dealer failed to return the keys to Rouse's current car, a Falcon, which he was negotiating to trade for a new car. The trial court found for Rouse and awarded him $5,000, an amount that included punitive damages. The case is now on appeal before the Supreme Court of Alabama. At the trial, the dealer was the defendant and is now the appellant, the party bringing the appeal. Rouse was the plaintiff at the trial and on appeal is the appellee, the party against whom an appeal is brought.*

Decision on Appeal: *The judgment for Rouse is affirmed. The dealer committed conversion of the Falcon.*

OPINION OF COURT

Justice SIMPSON delivered the opinion of the court . . .

On April 24, 1962, the appellee went to the place of business of Russell-Vaughn Ford, Inc., to discuss trading his Falcon automobile in on a new Ford. He talked with one of the salesmen for a while who offered to trade a new Ford for the Falcon, plus $1,900. The trade was not consummated on this basis, but Mr. Rouse went to his house and picked up his wife and children and returned to the dealer. With his wife and children there Mr. Rouse discussed further the trade but no deal was made that night.

The following night he returned with a friend where further discussions on the trade were had. At the time of this visit one of the salesmen, Virgil Harris, asked Mr. Rouse for the keys to his Falcon. The keys were given to him and Mr. Rouse, his friend, and appellant Parker [another salesman] looked at the new cars for a time and then proceeded with the negotiations with regard to the trade. The testimony indicates that in this conversation the salesman offered to trade a new Ford for the Falcon, plus $2,400. The plaintiff declined to trade on this basis.

At this stage of the negotiations, Mr. Rouse asked for the return of the keys to the Falcon. The evidence is to the effect that both salesmen to whom Rouse had talked said that they did not know where the keys were. Mr. Rouse then asked several people who appeared to be employees of Russell-Vaughn for the keys. He further asked several people in the building if they knew where his keys were. The testimony indicates that there were a number of people around who were aware of the fact that the appellee was seeking to have the keys to his car returned. Several mechanics and salesmen were, according to plaintiff's testimony, sitting around on cars looking at him and laughing at him.

After a period of time the plaintiff called the police department of the City of Birmingham. In response to his call Officer Montgomery came to the showroom of Russell-Vaughn Ford and was informed by the plaintiff that he was unable to get his keys back. Shortly after the arrival of the policeman, according to the policeman's testimony, the salesman Parker threw the keys to Mr. Rouse with the statement that he was a cry baby and that "they just wanted to see him cry a while."

The evidence is abundant to the effect that Mr. Rouse made a number of efforts to have his keys returned to him. He talked to the salesmen, to the manager, to mechanics, etc. and was met in many instances with laughter as if the entire matter was a "big joke." . . .

The appellants have . . . argued that the facts of this case do not make out a case of conversion. It is argued that the conversion if at all, [is] a conversion of the keys to the automobile, not of the automobile itself. It is further contended that there was not under the case here presented a conversion at all. We are not persuaded that the law of Alabama supports this proposition. As noted in *Long-Lewis Hardware Co. v. Abston,* 235 Ala. 599, 180 So. 261,

> "The conversion may consist, not only in an appropriation of the property to one's own use, but in its destruction, or in exercising dominion over it in exclusion or defiance of plaintiff's right. *McGill v. Hollman,* 208 Ala. 9, 93 So. 848, 31 A.L.R. 941, 948." (Emphasis added.)

It is not contended that the plaintiff here had no right to demand the return of the keys to his automobile. Rather, the appellants seem to be arguing that there was no conversion which the law will recognize under the facts of this case because the defendants did not commit sufficient acts to amount to a conversion. We cannot agree. A remarkable admission in this regard was elicited by the plaintiff in examining one of the witnesses for the defense. It seems that according to salesman for Russell-Vaughn Ford, Inc. it is a rather usual practice in the automobile business to "lose keys" to cars belonging to potential customers. We see nothing in our cases which requires in a conversion case that the plaintiff prove that the defendant appropriated the property to his own use; rather, as noted in the cases referred to above, it is enough that he show that the defendant exercised dominion over it in exclusion or defiance of the right of the plaintiff. We think that has been done here. The jury so found and we cannot concur that a case for conversion has not been made on these facts.

Further, appellants argue that there was no conversion since the plaintiff could have called his wife at home, who had another set of keys and thereby gained the ability to move his automobile. We find nothing in our cases which would require the plaintiff to exhaust all possible means of gaining possession of a chattel which is withheld from him by the defendant, after demanding its return. On the contrary, it is the refusal, without legal excuse, to deliver a chattel, which constitutes a conversion. *Compton v. Sims,* 209 Ala. 287, 96 So. 185.

We find unconvincing the appellants' contention that if there were a conversion at all, it was the conversion of the automobile keys, and not of the automobile. In *Compton v. Sims,* supra, this court sustained a finding that there had been a conversion of cotton where the defendant refused to deliver to the plaintiff "warehouse tickets" which would have enabled him to gain possession of the cotton. The court spoke of the warehouse tickets as a symbol of the cotton and found that the retention of them amounted to a conversion of the cotton. So here, we think that the withholding from the plaintiff after demand of the keys to his automobile, without which he could not move it, amounted to a conversion of the automobile.

It is next argued by appellants that the amount of the verdict is excessive. It is not denied that punitive damages are recoverable here in the discretion of the jury. In *Roan v. McCaleb,* 264 Ala. 31, 84 So.2d 358, this court held:

> "If the conversion was committed in known violation of the law and of plaintiff's rights with circumstances of insult, or contumely, or malice, punitive damages were recoverable in the discretion of the jury."

We think that the evidence justifies the jury's conclusion that these circumstances existed in this case. . . . We are clear to the conclusion that the evidence supports the verdict of the jury. . . .

Affirmed.

ASSIGNMENT 10.2

a. Would this case have reached the same result if the dealer made Rouse wait an hour in the showroom before returning the keys?

b. Sam owns a house on Main Street. He is outside his home in a wheelchair. A neighbor locks all the doors to Sam's house. Sam is not able to get into his house until the next day when he hires someone to force his way in. Has the neighbor converted Sam's house? The furnishings and other personal belongings in the house?

c. Bill and Fred have an argument over money. Bill takes Fred's wallet. In the wallet, there is a garage ticket that Fred needs to obtain his car. The garage will not return the car without the ticket or written proof that Fred owns the car. It takes Fred four days to obtain the documents needed to prove the car is his. Has Bill converted the car? Has the garage?

MISTAKE DEFENSE

mistake An unintentional act, omission, or error.

bona fide purchaser (BFP) One who has purchased property for value without notice of defects in the title of seller or of any claims against the property by others. Also called good faith purchaser, innocent purchaser.

intent (for conversion) The desire to exercise dominion over personal property that is inconsistent with another's right to control it, or the knowledge with substantial certainty that this will result from what one does or fails to do.

intent (for trespass to chattels) The desire to intermeddle with or dispossess another of personal property, or the knowledge with substantial certainty that this will result from what one does or fails to do.

It is not a defense that the defendant acted in good faith or made a reasonable **mistake**, although this is one of the overall factors that the court will take into consideration in determining whether the interference is serious enough for conversion.

EXAMPLE

Lena steals Sam's rifle. She offers to sell the rifle to Ed, who has no idea where she got it. Ed buys it for $200. Lena disappears. When Sam finds out what happened, he demands that Ed return the rifle. Ed refuses. Sam then sues Ed for conversion.

Sam will win. It is no defense that Ed is a **bona fide purchaser (BFP)** who bought the rifle mistakenly thinking that Lena had the right to sell it, i.e., thinking that Lena had title to what she sold. (A bona fide purchaser is one who purchases property for value without notice of defects in the title of the seller or of any claims against the property by others.) Lena's title to the rifle was defective—she didn't own it! Nevertheless, Ed intended to exercise total ownership and control over the gun when he tried to buy it. This was in full contradiction to Sam's rights in the rifle. If a defendant has the requisite **intent** for conversion or trespass to chattels, mistake is not a defense to an action for the resulting interference.

When we study *trespass to land* in Chapter 23, a similar conclusion will apply. If you enter the land of another without permission, you have committed trespass to land and it is not a defense that you thought you had permission to enter the land or that you did not know it was the plaintiff's land.

ASSIGNMENT 10.3

Ted grows valuable and expensive orchids in his backyard. It is the end of the growing season. He has two orchids remaining from his most expensive variety. He cuts one and places it in a basket in the yard next to the one still growing. Later that afternoon, Janice, one of Ted's houseguests, mistakenly thinks Ted is throwing away the orchid in the basket. She takes it from the basket and also cuts the one still growing. She puts them both in her suitcase. The next morning she wonders whether she made a mistake in taking the orchids without asking Ted. When Ted finds out what Janice did, he sues her for conversion. What result?

CASE

Moore v. The Regents of the University of California

51 Cal. 3d 120, 793 P.2d 479, 271 Cal. Rptr. 146 (1990)
Supreme Court of California

Background: *John Moore underwent treatment for hairy-cell leukemia at the UCLA Medical Center, which is operated by the Regents of the University of California. The doctors withdrew blood, skin, bone marrow aspirate, sperm, and his spleen. Unknown to Moore, the defendants were using his cells in research on regulating the immune system through the techniques of recombinant DNA. The research was successful. The defendants established a cell line from Moore's T-lymphocytes and applied for a patent on the cell line, which they received. Some biotechnology reports predict a potential market of over three billion dollars in this area. When Moore found out what role his cells played in this development, he sued for breach of a duty to disclose and for conversion. The trial court ruled against Moore. The case is now on appeal before the Supreme Court of California.*

Decision on Appeal: *The use of excised human cells in medical research does not amount to a conversion. Moore, however, can sue for breach of a physician's fiduciary duty to disclose information needed by a patient to make an informed consent to treatment.*

OPINION OF COURT

Justice PANELLI delivered the opinion of the court . . .

Moore . . . attempts to characterize the invasion of his rights as a conversion—a tort that protects against interference with possessory and ownership interests in personal property. He theorizes that he continued to own his cells following their removal from his body, at least for the purpose of directing their use, and that he never consented to their use in potentially lucrative medical research. Thus, to complete Moore's argument, defendants' unauthorized use of his cells constitutes a conversion. As a result of the alleged conversion, Moore claims a proprietary interest in each of the products that any of the defendants might ever create from his cells or the patented cell line. . . .

In effect, what Moore is asking us to do is to impose a tort duty on scientists to investigate the consensual pedigree of each human cell sample used in research. To impose such a duty, which would affect medical research of importance to all of society, implicates policy concerns far removed from the traditional, two-party ownership disputes in which the law of conversion arose. Invoking a tort theory originally used to determine whether the loser or the finder of a horse had the better title, Moore claims ownership of the results of socially important medical research, including the genetic code for chemicals that regulate the functions of every human being's immune system. . . .

"To establish a conversion, plaintiff must establish an actual interference with his *ownership* or *right of possession*. . . . Where plaintiff neither has title to the property alleged to have been converted, nor possession thereof, he cannot maintain an action for conversion." (*Del E. Webb Corp. v. Structural Materials Co.* (1981) 123 Cal. App. 3d 593, 610–611.)

Since Moore clearly did not expect to retain possession of his cells following their removal, to sue for their conversion he must have retained an ownership interest in them. But . . . California statutory law . . . drastically limits a patient's control over excised cells. Pursuant to Health and Safety Code section 7054.4, "[n]otwithstanding any other provision of law, recognizable anatomical parts, human tissues, anatomical human remains, or infectious waste following conclusion of scientific use shall be disposed of by interment, incineration, or any other method determined by the state department [of health services] to protect the public health and safety." Clearly the Legislature did not specifically intend this statute to resolve the question of whether a patient is entitled to compensation for the nonconsensual use of excised cells. A primary object of the statute is to ensure the safe handling of potentially hazardous biological waste materials. Yet one cannot escape the conclusion that the statute's practical effect is to limit, drastically, a patient's control over excised cells. By restricting how excised cells may be used and requiring their eventual destruction, the statute eliminates so many of the rights ordinarily attached to property that one cannot simply assume that what is left amounts to "property" or "ownership" for purposes of conversion law.

It may be that some limited right to control the use of excised cells does survive the operation of this statute. There is, for example, no need to read the statute to permit "scientific use" contrary to the patient's expressed wish. A fully informed patient may always withhold consent to treatment by a physician whose research plans the patient does not approve. That right, however . . . is protected by the fiduciary-duty and informed-consent theories.

Finally, the subject matter of the Regents' patent—the patented cell line and the products derived from it—cannot be Moore's property. This is because the patented cell line is both factually and legally distinct from the cells taken from Moore's body. Federal law permits the patenting of organisms that represent the product of "human ingenuity," but not naturally occurring organisms. . . . It is this *inventive effort* that patent law rewards, not the discovery of naturally occurring raw materials. Thus, Moore's allegations that he owns the cell line and the products derived from it are inconsistent with the patent, which constitutes an authoritative determination that the cell line is the product of invention. . . .

[A competent patient does have a right] to make autonomous medical decisions. That right . . . is grounded in well-recognized and long-standing principles of fiduciary duty and informed consent. This policy weighs in favor of providing a remedy to patients when physicians act with undisclosed motives that may affect their professional judgment. . . . [But we should] not threaten with disabling civil liability innocent parties who are engaged in socially useful activities, such as researchers who have no reason to believe that their use of a particular cell sample is, or may be, against a donor's wishes. . . .

We need not, however, make an arbitrary choice between liability and nonliability. Instead, an examination of the relevant policy considerations suggests an appropriate balance: Liability based upon existing disclosure obligations, rather than an unprecedented extension of the conversion theory, protects patients' rights of privacy and autonomy without unnecessarily hindering research.

To be sure, the threat of liability for conversion might help to enforce patients' rights indirectly. This is because physicians might be able to avoid liability by obtaining patients' consent, in the broadest possible terms, to any conceivable subsequent research use of excised cells. Unfortunately, to extend the conversion theory would utterly sacrifice the other goal of protecting innocent parties. . . . [It] would impose liability on all those into whose hands the cells come, whether or not the particular defendant participated in, or knew of, the inadequate disclosures that violated the patient's right to make an informed decision. In contrast to the conversion theory, the fiduciary-duty and informed-consent theories protect the patient directly, without punishing innocent parties or creating disincentives to the conduct of socially beneficial research. . . .

[T]he theory of liability that Moore urges us to endorse threatens to destroy the economic incentive to conduct important medical research. If the use of cells in research is a conversion, then with every cell sample a researcher purchases a ticket in a litigation lottery. . . .

If the scientific users of human cells are to be held liable for failing to investigate the consensual pedigree of their raw materials, we believe the Legislature should make that decision. Complex policy choices affecting all society are involved, and "[l]egislatures, in making such policy decisions, have the ability to gather empirical evidence, solicit the advice of experts, and hold hearings at which all interested parties present evidence and express their views. . . ." (*Foley v. Interactive Data Corp.* (1988) 47 Cal. 3d 654, 694, 765 P.2d 373.)

Finally, there is no pressing need to impose a judicially created rule of strict liability, since enforcement of physicians' disclosure obligations will protect patients against the very type of harm with which Moore was threatened. So long as a physician discloses research and economic interests that may affect his judgment, the patient is protected from conflicts of interest. Aware of any conflicts, the patient can make an informed decision to consent to treatment, or to withhold consent and look elsewhere for medical assistance. As already discussed, enforcement of physicians' disclosure obligations protects patients directly, without hindering the socially useful activities of innocent researchers.

For these reasons, we hold that the allegations of Moore's . . . complaint state a cause of action for breach of fiduciary duty or lack of informed consent, but not conversion. . . .

ASSIGNMENT 10.4

a. The doctors that treated Moore had a conflict of interest. What was the conflict?
b. In most states, you have the right to make a gift of your eyes or other organs. Is the decision in *Moore* inconsistent with this right?
c. Assume that after the UCLA Medical Center doctor extracts blood, skin, bone marrow aspirate, and sperm from Moore (plus his spleen), a doctor from another hospital breaks into the UCLA Medical Center and steals everything extracted from Moore. The doctors and researchers in this other hospital then use it in their own research, which leads to the patent. Do the UCLA doctor and the UCLA Medical Center have an action for conversion? If so, who would the plaintiff be? John Moore? UCLA?

CONVERSION AND TRESPASS TO CHATTELS CHECKLIST

Definitions, Relationships, Paralegal Roles, and Research References

Category of These Torts
They are both intentional torts.

Interest Protected by These Torts
The right to be free from intentional interference with one's ownership or possessory rights to personal property.
Conversion: The right to be free from intentional interferences with personal property that consist of an exercise of dominion or control over it.
Trespass to Chattels: The right to be free from intentional interferences with personal property that consist of dispossession or intermeddling.

Elements of These Torts
Conversion
1. Personal property (chattel)
2. The plaintiff is in possession of the chattel or is entitled to immediate possession
3. Intent to exercise dominion over the chattel (a serious interference)
4. Dominion
5. Causation of the serious interference

Trespass to Chattels
1. Personal property (chattel)
2. The plaintiff is in possession of the chattel or is entitled to immediate possession
3. Intent to dispossess or intermeddle
4. Dispossession or intermeddling
5. Causation of the dispossession or intermeddling

Definitions of Major Words/Phrases in the Elements
Chattels: Personal property; property other than land or other than things attached to land.
Intent: For conversion: The desire to exercise dominion over personal property that is inconsistent with another's right to control it, or the knowledge with substantial certainty that this will result from what one does or fails to do. For trespass to chattels: The desire to intermeddle with or dispossess another of personal property, or the knowledge with substantial certainty that this will result from what one does or fails to do.
Control: Exercising power over something.
Dominion: The exertion of substantial or extensive control over a chattel that is inconsistent with another's right to control it.
Dispossess: Take physical control of a chattel without exercising dominion over it.

CONVERSION AND TRESPASS TO CHATTELS CHECKLIST *(Continued)*

Intermeddle: Make physical contact with, and cause damage or harm to, a chattel without exercising dominion over it.
Causation: For conversion: But for what the defendant did or failed to do, dominion over the personal property would not have occurred (or the defendant was a substantial factor in producing the dominion). For trespass to chattels: But for what the defendant did or failed to do, the dispossession or intermeddling would not have occurred (or the defendant was a substantial factor in producing the dispossession or intermeddling).

Major Defense and Counterargument Possibilities That Need to Be Explored

1. The property involved was not personal property (not a chattel).
2. The plaintiff was not in possession or entitled to immediate possession.
3. There was no intent to exercise dominion (for conversion), nor to dispossess or intermeddle (for trespass to chattels).
4. The defendant did nothing that was inconsistent with the plaintiff's right to control the chattel.
5. The defendant never took possession of the chattel.
6. No harm or damage was caused by the defendant's contact with the chattel.
7. The defendant did not cause the interference with the plaintiff's chattel.
8. The plaintiff consented to what the defendant did to the chattel and the defendant did not exceed what the consent allowed (on the defense of consent, see Chapter 27).
9. The interference with the plaintiff's property occurred while the defendant was defending the defendant's own property against the plaintiff (on the privilege of defense of property and other self-help privileges, see Chapter 27).
10. The interference with the plaintiff's property occurred while the defendant was recapturing the defendant's own property from the plaintiff (on the recapture of property and other self-help privileges, see Chapter 27).
11. The interference with the plaintiff's property occurred while the defendant was protecting person or property (on necessity and other self-help privileges, see Chapter 27).
12. The interference with the plaintiff's property occurred while the defendant was abating a nuisance (on abating a nuisance and other self-help privileges, see Chapters 23 and 27).
13. The plaintiff's suit against the government for conversion or trespass to chattels committed by a government employee may be barred by sovereign immunity (on sovereign immunity, see Chapter 27).
14. The plaintiff's suit against the government employee for conversion or trespass to chattels may be barred by official immunity (on official immunity, see Chapter 27).
15. The plaintiff's suit against the charitable organization for conversion or trespass to chattels committed by someone working for the organization may be barred by charitable immunity (on charitable immunity, see Chapter 27).
16. The plaintiff failed to take reasonable steps to mitigate the harm caused when the defendant committed trespass to chattels; therefore, damages should not cover the aggravation of the harm caused by the plaintiff (on the mitigation-of-damages rule, see Chapter 16).

Damages

In conversion, the plaintiff recovers the full fair market value of the chattel at the time and place of the conversion. In trespass to chattels, the plaintiff's recovery is limited to actual damages, e.g., repair costs and cost of renting a substitute. If malice or hatred existed, punitive damages are also possible.

Relationship to Criminal Law

A number of crimes may also be involved in addition to these torts: theft or larceny, embezzlement, false pretenses, receiving stolen property, robbery, extortion, blackmail, burglary, etc.

Relationship to Other Torts

Misrepresentation: The defendant's interference with the chattel of plaintiff may have occurred through misrepresentation, so that this tort plus conversion or trespass to chattels are committed.

CONVERSION AND TRESPASS TO CHATTELS CHECKLIST *(Continued)*

Negligence: If the plaintiff cannot establish that the interference with his or her property was intentional, he or she may be able to show that the interference occurred through carelessness or negligence if there was unreasonable conduct by the defendant and actual damage to the property.

Federal Law

a. Under the Federal Tort Claims Act, the United States government will be liable for claims arising out of conversion or trespass to chattels committed by one of its federal employees within the scope of employment (respondeat superior). (See Exhibit 27–7 in Chapter 27.) (Most states have their own statutes that cover when tort claims can be made against the state for conversion, trespass to chattels, and other torts committed by state government employees. Such claims are also covered in Chapter 27.)
b. There may be liability under the Civil Rights Act if the conversion or trespass to chattels was committed while the defendant was depriving the plaintiff of a federal civil right under color of state law. (See Exhibit 27–9 in Chapter 27.)

Employer–Employee (Agency) Law

A private (non-government) employee who commits conversion or trespass to chattels is personally liable for this tort. His or her employer will *also* be liable for these torts if the conduct of the employee was within the scope of employment (respondeat superior). The employee must be furthering a business objective of the employer at the time. (On the factors that determine the scope of employment, see Exhibit 14–9 in Chapter 14.)

Paralegal Roles in Conversion or Trespass to Chattels Litigation

(See also Exhibit 3–1 in Chapter 3, Exhibit 20–4 in Chapter 20, and Exhibit 29–1 in Chapter 29.)

Fact finding (help the office collect facts relevant to prove the elements of conversion or trespass to chattels, the elements of available defenses, and extent of injuries or other damages):
- client interviewing
- field investigation
- online research (e.g., blue book value of a used car)

File management (help the office control the documents involved in a conversion or trespass to chattels litigation):
- open client file
- enter case data in computer database
- maintain file documents

Litigation assistance (help the trial attorney prepare for a conversion or trespass to chattels trial and appeal, if needed):
- draft discovery requests
- draft answers to discovery requests
- draft pleadings
- digest and index discovery documents
- help prepare, order, and manage trial exhibits
- prepare trial notebook
- draft notice of appeal
- order trial transcript
- cite-check briefs
- perform legal research

Collection/enforcement (help the trial attorney for the judgment creditor to collect the damages award or enforce other court orders at the conclusion of the conversion or trespass to chattels case):
- draft postjudgment discovery requests
- conduct field investigation to monitor compliance with judgment
- perform online research (e.g., location of defendant's business assets)

CONVERSION AND TRESPASS TO CHATTELS CHECKLIST *(Continued)*

Research References for Conversion and Trespass to Chattels

Digests
In the digests of West Group, look for case summaries on these torts under key topics such as:

Conversion
Trover and Conversion
Property
Bailments
Torts
Damages

Corpus Juris Secundum
In this legal encyclopedia, see the discussion under topic headings such as:

Conversion
Trover and Conversion
Property
Bailments
Torts
Damages

American Jurisprudence 2d
In this legal encyclopedia, see the discussion under topic headings such as:

Conversion
Property
Bailments
Abandoned, Lost and Unclaimed Property
Damages
Torts

Legal Periodical Literature
There are two index systems to use to locate legal periodical literature on these torts:

INDEX TO LEGAL PERIODICALS AND BOOKS (ILP)
See literature in *ILP* under subject headings such as:
Conversion
Personal Property
Property
Torts
Damages
Bailments

CURRENT LAW INDEX (CLI)
See literature in *CLI* under subject headings such as:
Personal Property
Torts
Property
Bailments
Intangible Property
Damages
Fraudulent Conveyances

Example of a legal periodical article you will find by using *ILP* or *CLI:*

Commercial Exploitation of DNA and the Tort of Conversion: A Physician May Not Destroy a Patient's Interest in Her Body-Matter by Aaron C. Lichtman, 34 New York Law School Law Review 531 (1989).

A.L.R., A.L.R.2d, A.L.R.3d, A.L.R.4th, A.L.R.5th, A.L.R.6th, A.L.R. Fed., A.L.R. Fed. 2d
Use the *ALR Index* to locate annotations on these torts. In this index, check subject headings such as:

Trover and Conversion
Conversion
Damages
Property Damages
Personal Property
Torts

Example of an annotation you can locate through these subject headings on these torts:

Conversion of Electronic Data, Including Domain Names by Deborah F. Buckman, 40 A.L.R.6th 295 (2008).

Words and Phrases
In this multivolume legal dictionary, look up *conversion, trespass to chattels, chattels, dispossession, intermeddling, dominion, bona fide purchaser,* and every other word or phrase connected with conversion and trespass to chattels discussed in this chapter. The dictionary will give you definitions of these words or phrases from court opinions.

CONVERSION AND TRESPASS TO CHATTELS CHECKLIST *(Continued)*

CALR: Computer-Assisted Legal Research

Example of a query you could ask on Westlaw or on LexisNexis to try to find cases, statutes, or other legal materials on conversion and trespass to chattels: **conversion /p damages**

Example of search terms you could use on an Internet legal search engine such as the Public Library of Law (www.plol.org), Findlaw (www.findlaw.com), or Google Scholar (scholar.google.com) to find cases, statutes, or other legal materials on conversion and trespass to chattels: **conversion tort damages**

Example of search terms you could use on an Internet general search engine such as Google, Bing, or AltaVista to find cases, statutes, or other legal materials on conversion and trespass to chattels: **+conversion +tort +damages**

More Internet sites to check for materials on conversion, trespass to chattels, and other torts:
www.hg.org/torts.html
www.megalaw.com/top/top.php (click "Intentional Torts," "Personal Injury Law," "Tort Law," and "Damages")
See also the online sites in Overview of Tort Law at the end of Chapter 1.

CHECK THE CITE

Ninth-grade female students e-mailed lewd photographs of themselves to other students with instructions that the photos should be deleted after viewing. When they were forwarded to others rather than deleted, the senders sued. One of the causes of action in the case was conversion of the photographs. Explain the ruling of the court on this tort claim. Read the opinion of *S.B. v. Saint James School*, 959 So. 2d 72 (Al. 2006). To read the opinion online, run a citation search ("959 So.2d 72") or a party search (SB Saint James School) in the Legal Opinions and Journals database of Google Scholar (scholar.google.com).

PROJECT

In Google, Bing, or another general search engine, run the following search: Hamadi trespass. Describe the facts of the tort action brought against Hamadi due to his e-mail activity, including the outcome in the courts.

ETHICS IN A TORTS PRACTICE

You are a paralegal working in the law office of Garvey and Garvey. The firm represents Tom Alexander, who is being sued for conversion of company records by his former employer. The company claims he took files home without authorization. While investigating the case, you become convinced that he did convert the company records and probably committed crimes in the process. What ethical problems, if any, might exist?

SUMMARY

The torts of conversion and trespass to chattels are designed to provide a remedy for intentional interferences with ownership or possessory rights in personal

property. If the interference constitutes dominion, conversion is the appropriate remedy, requiring the wrongdoer to pay the plaintiff the full market value of the chattel converted. Trespass to chattels covers less serious interferences: dispossession and intermeddling. Dispossession is the taking of physical control of a chattel without exercising dominion over it. Intermeddling is making physical contact with and causing damage or harm to a chattel without exercising dominion over it.

Most cases involve tangible personal property or intangible rights embodied in a physical document. Some courts have held that electronic data can be converted even though they have no physical form. If the act constituting interference is intentional, it is no defense that the interference was an innocent mistake, as in the case of a bona fide purchaser.

KEY TERMS

personal property *162*
chattel *162*
conversion *162*
trespass to chattels *162*
dominion *162*
dispossession *162*
intermeddling *162*
tangible *164*
intangible *164*
mistake *166*
bona fide purchaser (BFP) *166*
intent (for conversion) *166*
intent (for trespass to chattels) *166*

REVIEW QUESTIONS

1. What is a chattel?
2. What is conversion?
3. What is trespass to chattels?
4. What damages can be awarded for conversion and for trespass to chattels?
5. What factors will a court consider in deciding whether an interference is serious enough to constitute conversion?
6. What is dominion?
7. What is dispossession?
8. What is intermeddling?
9. How can spam lead to trespass to chattels?
10. What is the difference between tangible and intangible property?
11. When can intangible property be converted?
12. What is the effect of a mistake in an action for conversion or trespass to chattels?
13. What is a bona fide purchaser?
14. What is the intent element for conversion?
15. What is the intent element for trespass to chattels?

HELPFUL WEBSITES

- **Conversion and Trespass to Chattels**
  en.wikipedia.org/wiki/Conversion_(law)
  www.inc.com/articles/1999/11/15380.html
  papers.ssrn.com/sol3/papers.cfm?abstract_id=984486
  www.google.com (run this search: elements conversion tort)
- **Electronic Media**
  elr.lls.edu/issues/v23-issue2/documents/kohm.pdf
  www.internetlibrary.com/topics/conversion.cfm

ENDNOTES

1. W. Page Keeton et al., *Prosser and Keeton on the Law of Torts* (5th ed. 1984). See also *Restatement (Second) of Torts* § 222A (1965).
2. *CompuServe Inc. v. Cyber Promotions, Inc.*, 962 F. Supp. 1015, 1022 (S.D. Ohio 1997)(www.spamseminar.com/materials/compuserve.html) (cyber.law.harvard.edu/torts3y/readings/06-CvCP.html).
3. *Thyroff v. Nationwide Mut. Ins. Co.*, 8 N.Y.3d 283, 864 N.E.2d 1272, 832 N.Y.S.2d 873 (N.Y. 2007)(www.law.cornell.edu/nyctap/I07_0029.htm).

Student StudyWARE™ CD-ROM
For additional materials, please go to the student CD in this book.

CHAPTER

11

STRICT LIABILITY

CHAPTER OUTLINE

- Introduction
- Animals
- Strict Liability for Abnormally Dangerous Conditions or Activities

CHAPTER OBJECTIVES

After completing this chapter, you should be able to:

- Understand the meaning of strict liability.
- Explain liability for harm caused by an animal due to intentional conduct, negligent conduct, and strict liability.
- Know when strict liability will be imposed for harm caused by a wild animal and by a domestic animal.
- Know whether every dog is entitled to one free bite.
- Identify the elements of strict liability for abnormally dangerous conditions or activities.
- Understand the ruling of *Rylands v. Fletcher*.
- State the two components of proximate cause.
- Identify defenses to strict liability for abnormally dangerous conditions or activities.
- Identify paralegal roles in litigation asserting strict liability for abnormally dangerous conditions or activities.
- List the major resources available in traditional books and online for researching issues involving strict liability for abnormally dangerous conditions or activities.

INTRODUCTION

strict liability Responsibility for harm even if one did not intend the harm and used reasonable care to try to prevent it. Responsibility for harm whether or not the person causing the harm was at any fault or engaged in any moral impropriety. Also called absolute liability and liability without fault.

As we saw in Chapter 1, there are three main categories of torts: intentional torts, negligence, and strict liability torts. **Strict liability** (sometimes referred to as *absolute liability* or *liability without fault*) means responsibility regardless of blameworthiness or fault. Persons who engage in certain kinds of activity will be liable or responsible for the harm that results even if they did not intend the harm and used reasonable care to try to prevent it. The normal method of demonstrating blameworthiness or fault is for the plaintiff to show that the defendant's conduct fit within one of the intentional torts or was unreasonable (negligent). For some activities, however, the blameworthiness or fault of the defendant is irrelevant. As a matter of social policy, the law says that when designated activities cause harm, the defendant must pay—whether the defendant acted innocently, intentionally, or negligently. The same is true for harm that results from certain conditions that exist on the defendant's land.

In this chapter we will consider two categories of harm that lead to strict liability: harm caused by animals and harm caused by abnormally dangerous conditions or activities. In Chapter 19 on products liability, we will examine the separate tort called *strict liability in tort,* which covers harm caused by a defective product irrespective of the blameworthiness or fault of the manufacturer or distributor of the product.

One final point before we begin: there is some overlap among the three categories of torts studied in this book. For example, some of the intentional torts will lead to liability even though it may be difficult to find blameworthiness or fault in the defendant's conduct. Also, as we will see later, it is sometimes difficult to distinguish between negligence and *strict liability in tort.* Nevertheless, categorizing torts is useful as a starting point in studying tort law. Be prepared, however, to find an absence of rigid boundary lines among some of the torts.

ANIMALS

The Centers for Disease Control and Prevention estimates that each year dogs bite 4.5 million people, 885,000 of whom require medical treatment. In a recent year, more than 30,000 victims required reconstructive surgery.[1] When a dog or other animal causes harm, the major theories of liability to consider are negligence and strict liability.

EXAMPLE

Mary knows that her dog is aggressive around strangers. To prevent the dog from bothering anyone, she keeps the dog on a leash. One day in a crowded park, however, she carelessly drops the leash so that she can read a newspaper on the bench. A stranger walking by is bitten by the dog. Mary has committed negligence because her failure to use reasonable care caused harm (see Chapter 14).

What about strict liability? Can a pet owner be strictly liable for harm caused by an animal even if no negligence has been committed? The answer depends, in part, on whether the animal is wild or domestic. Exhibit 11–1 presents an overview of the law we will be discussing.

Exhibit 11–1
Elements of strict liability for harm caused by animals.

Domestic Animals

1. Keeping a domestic animal that the owner has reason to know has a dangerous propensity
2. Harm caused by the animal due to that specific propensity

Wild Animals

1. Keeping a wild animal
2. Harm caused by the animal

Wild Animals

A **wild animal** is an animal in the state of nature, e.g., lion, bear, monkey. In most states, an owner (or keeper) of a wild animal will be strictly liable for any harm it causes whether or not the owner knew of the animal's dangerous propensities, irrespective of how well trained the animal may have been, and regardless of how much care the owner took to prevent harm to others by the animal.

wild animal An animal in the state of nature.

Domestic Animals

A **domestic animal** is an animal that has been domesticated or habituated to live among humans, e.g., dog, cat, horse. (The *Restatement* defines a domestic animal as one that is "by custom devoted to the service of mankind at the time and in the place in which it is kept."[2]) An owner (or keeper) of a domestic animal will be strictly liable for the harm it causes if two elements can be established:

domestic animal An animal that has been domesticated or habituated to live among humans.

1. the owner has reason to know the animal has a specific propensity to cause harm, and
2. the harm caused by the animal was due to that specific propensity.

EXAMPLE

George knows that his dog, Fido, likes to bite joggers. Fido has never bothered anyone else. One day the dog bites Tom, a jogger. A few hours later, Fido knocks down Mary, a neighbor, while she is gardening.

In most states, George will be strictly liable to Tom since biting was a known propensity. There was no known propensity, however, for knocking people down. Therefore, there would be no strict liability to Mary. The tendency of an animal to do an act that might endanger the safety of persons or property is referred to as the animal's **dangerous propensity**. Strict liability requires a showing that the owner or possessor of the animal knew of the animal's *specific* dangerous propensity and that the harm caused by the animal was due to that propensity.

dangerous propensity A tendency to cause damage or harm as shown by prior acts or omissions that caused damage or harm.

Occasionally, you will see the phrase, "every dog is entitled to one free bite." The implication of this statement is that an owner won't know about the propensity of the dog to bite until the dog has claimed its first human victim. Yet, this is not accurate. There might be other evidence of this propensity, e.g., the dog's inclination to lunge toward everyone with its mouth wide open. Another reason the first bite may not be "free" is that an owner might be subject to negligence liability for failing to control an obviously feisty and aggressive dog even if the dog has never bitten anyone. As we will stress throughout this chapter, someone who is not liable under strict liability might still be liable under negligence. Plaintiffs prefer the former because negligence is more difficult to prove. For negligence, you must show that the defendant was careless or unreasonable, a showing that is not required under a strict liability cause of action.

A few states have passed special statutes that impose strict liability for harm caused by domestic animals with no known dangerous propensities. In effect, such statutes treat domestic animals the same as wild animals.

ASSIGNMENT 11.1

Sam knows that his dog bites other dogs. One day Sam's dog bites a stranger, the first time it has ever attacked a human. Is Sam subject to strict liability?

CASE

Nardi v. Gonzalez

165 Misc. 2d 336, 630 N.Y.S.2d 215 (1995)
City Court of Yonkers

Background: *A 110-pound German shepherd injures two small dogs. The owners of the small dogs, the Nardis, sue the owner of the German shepherd, Mrs. Gonzalez, for strict liability.*

Decision of Court: *Mrs. Gonzalez is strictly liable.*

OPINION OF COURT

Judge DICKERSON delivered the opinion of the court:

Bianca and Pepe are diminutive, curly coated Bichon Frises and are, respectively, 9 years old and 3 years old. Bianca and Pepe are owned by the plaintiffs, Dusolina and Alfred Nardi ["the Nardis"], . . . Ace is a large 5-year-old German shepherd weighing 110 pounds. Ace is owned by the defendant, Maureen Gonzalez [Mrs. Gonzalez], . . . On March 24, 1993 and again on June 16, 1994, Mrs. Gonzalez allowed Ace to run loose without a leash. On these two occasions Ace entered onto the Nardis' property and viciously attacked Bianca causing severe injuries. On both occasions, Bianca was taken to a veterinarian for treatment of the wounds inflicted by Ace. The veterinarian bills were $392 for the March 24, 1993 attack and $182 for the June 16, 1994 attack.

On June 22, 1994 the Nardis commenced a lawsuit before this Court seeking damages for the injuries sustained by Bianca and themselves. After a trial held on October 26, 1994, this Court (Smith, J.) found Ace and its owner Mrs. Gonzalez responsible ["Considering the disparate sizes of the animals and all the circumstances. . . ."] for the injuries inflicted upon Bianca ["Ace bit (Bianca) causing bite wounds and bleeding"] and awarded damages of $524.

On February 4, 1995, Pepe, the younger Bichon Frise, was with his owner, Alfred Nardi, who was in his driveway shoveling snow. Ace suddenly appeared, sniffed Pepe and then, without provocation, viciously attacked and mauled Pepe. Alfred Nardi chased Ace away and took Pepe to the veterinarian. Pepe remained hospitalized for four days undergoing surgery. The photographs introduced at trial show a 10-inch gash held together with surgical staples running from Pepe's stomach to his back. The veterinarian bills for Pepe's hospitalization, care and treatment were $819, considerably more than those incurred by Bianca just the year before.

In this action, the plaintiffs seek damages to include the costs of veterinarian services [$819], two days lost wages in caring for Pepe [$156] and all other appropriate damages. In response Mrs. Gonzalez stated that she had built a fence around her backyard to keep Ace enclosed. Unfortunately, Ace escaped from the enclosure on February 4, 1995, went to the Nardi's house and mauled Pepe. Based upon the facts of this case the Court finds that plaintiffs have stated a cognizable cause of action for strict liability for injuries caused by a vicious and dangerous dog.

Dogs can be wonderful companions and loyal guardians. On occasion, however, dogs can also be vicious animals that annoy and wound men, women and children. . . . *Coleman v. Blake,* 128 N.Y.S.2d 780, 781–782 (1954) ("Mrs. Coleman proffered the dog a bit of cheese. Man's best friend rewarded her affection by taking a bite out of her proboscis, and in so doing nipped a beautiful friendship in its origin. . .", damages of $7,500 for injuries, medical expenses and loss of earnings); *Fontecchio v. Esposito,* 108 A.D.2d 780, 485 N.Y.S.2d 113 (1985) (dog bites woman, damages of $240,000 and $70,000 reversed as excessive); *Zager v. Dimilia,* 138 Misc. 2d 448, 524 N.Y.S.2d 968 (1988) (McDuff bites Tucker, damages limited to veterinarian bills, no punitive damages without evidence of prior known bites); *Corso v. Crawford Dog and Cat Hospital, Inc.,* 97 Misc. 2d 530, 415 N.Y.S.2d 182, 183 (1979) ("a pet is not just a thing but occupies a special place somewhere in between a person and a piece of personal property", damages of $700); *Fowler v. Town of Ticonderoga,* 131 A.D.2d 919, 516 N.Y.S.2d 368 (1987) (dog shot by Dog Control Officer, no damages for owner's psychic trauma).

Some dogs can be more vicious and dangerous than others. For example, German shepherds are large, intelligent and strong and, if trained properly, can serve as trusted guard dogs and police dogs. Without proper training, however, German shepherds can be vicious, indeed [see e.g., *Ford v. Steindon,* 35 Misc. 2d 339, 232 N.Y.S.2d 473, 474 (1962) (vicious German shepherd attacks man, "the dog . . . was a German shepherd colloquially known as a police dog . . . It has been said that with respect to such dogs 'it is a matter of common knowledge that the court can almost take judicial knowledge of the fact that police dogs are, by nature, vicious, inheriting the wild and untamed characteristics of their wolf ancestors'"); *DiGrazia v. Castronova,* 48 A.D.2d 249, 368 N.Y.S.2d 898 (1975) (vicious German Shepherd [*Sam*] attacks 6-year-old boy); *Lagoda v. Dorr,* 28 A.D.2d 208, 284 N.Y.S.2d 130 (1967) (vicious German Shepherd attacks boy on bicycle knocking him to ground); *Strunk v. Zoltanski,* 62 N.Y.2d 572, 479 N.Y.S.2d 175, 468 N.E.2d 13 (1984) (dangerous German Shepherd bites infant on mouth and arms); *Application of Fugazy,* 82 Misc. 2d 135, 368 N.Y.S.2d 652 (Harrison Town Ct. West. Cty. 1974) (two dangerous German Shepherds [Kelly & Murphy] attack, bite and chase 15-year-old boy)].

New York recognizes a cause of action which imposes strict liability [no proof of negligence necessary] upon owners for injuries inflicted by their vicious dogs, the owners having knowledge thereof and viciousness being defined as prior bites and/or mischievous propensities [see e.g., *Wheaton v. Guthrie,* 89 A.D.2d 809, 453 N.Y.S.2d 480 ("strict liability 'vicious dog' cause of action . . . the proof established that (the dog) had a vicious propensity known to the defendant. A vicious propensity is the tendency of a dog to do an act which might endanger another . . ."); *Morales v. Quinones,* 72 A.D.2d 519, 420 N.Y.S.2d 899, 900 (1979) ("Liability in vicious propensity or dog bite cases is 'absolute' . . . and is not dependent upon proof of negligence in the manner of keeping the animal. . . The keeping of the animal, knowing its vicious propensities is the gravamen of the offense. . ."); *Lagoda v. Dorr,* supra, 28 A.D.2d at 209, 284 N.Y.S.2d, at 132 ("The doctrine that every dog is entitled to 'one free bite', if it ever prevailed in this State, is no longer followed. . . The gravamen of the action is the knowledge of the owner that the dog was possessed of vicious or mischievous propensities. . ."); *Coleman v. Blake,* supra, at 128 N.Y.S.2d 781 ("Knowing dog's waspish nature and a bite of record. . ."); *Fox v. Martin,* 174 A.D.2d 875, 571 N.Y.S.2d 161, 162 (1991) (cause of action requires evidence of prior bites or vicious propensities and owner's knowledge thereof)].

In this case Mrs. Gonzalez knew full well that Ace possessed vicious propensities since on two prior occasions Ace had viciously attacked Bianca causing substantial injuries for which this Court (Smith, J.) found her liable and responsible. That Mrs. Gonzalez thereafter constructed a fence to enclose Ace is of no significance [see *Lynch v. Nacewicz,* 511 N.Y.S.2d 121, 122 (1987) ("Liability is not dependent upon proof of negligence in the manner of keeping or confining the animal. . .")] since, in fact, Ace escaped on February 4, 1995 and viciously attacked and mauled Pepe. All of the elements of a strict liability cause of action–vicious dog are met herein and the Court finds Mrs. Gonzalez strictly liable for all appropriate damages.

The Court awards the following damages to the plaintiffs. First, damages will include the $819 veterinarian bills for Pepe's hospitalization, care and treatment; second, damages will include $156 lost wages incurred by Alfred Nardi in caring for Pepe; third, this Court finds defendant's misconduct to be morally culpable [see e.g., *Walker v. Sheldon,* 10 N.Y.2d 401, 223 N.Y.S.2d 488, 490, 179 N.E.2d 497 (1961)]. Ace was a dangerous instrumentality and defendant knew of the dog's vicious propensities. Punitive damages are appropriate in this case and are needed to deter other dog owners from failing to protect humans and other animals from vicious and dangerous dogs. Further, such damages will encourage defendant to take appropriate measures in the future to protect her neighbors from Ace or similar like-minded dogs. The Court awards plaintiffs punitive damages of $1,000.

Ordered accordingly.

ASSIGNMENT 11.2

a. Does the court say that all owners of German shepherds will always be strictly liable for the harm they cause?

b. Do you agree with the award of punitive damages against Mrs. Gonzalez? What could she have done to avoid punitive damages so that she would pay only the vet bills and lost wages?

c. Reread the facts of Assignment 11.1. How would *Nardi v. Gonzalez* apply to Sam? Would he be strictly liable for the harm his dog caused the stranger? Give arguments for both sides on the applicability of *Nardi.*

STRICT LIABILITY FOR ABNORMALLY DANGEROUS CONDITIONS OR ACTIVITIES

Next we examine abnormal conditions or activities causing harm that can lead to strict liability even if reasonable care was used to prevent the harm. The tort is called **strict liability for abnormally dangerous conditions or activities (SLADCA)** and sometimes, absolute liability for abnormally dangerous conditions or activities. The tort imposes liability for harm caused by abnormally dangerous conditions or activities whether the person causing the harm acted intentionally, negligently, or innocently. (See Exhibit 11–2 for the elements of SLADCA.) It is important to keep in mind that the defendant is not necessarily home free if the plaintiff fails to establish that the condition or activity of the defendant qualifies for strict liability status. The plaintiff may still be able to win by showing that the defendant committed other torts such as trespass to land, nuisance, or negligence in maintaining the condition or engaging in the activity.

strict liability for abnormally dangerous conditions or activities (SLADCA) A tort that imposes liability for harm caused by abnormally dangerous conditions or activities regardless of whether the person causing the harm acted intentionally, negligently, or innocently.

Exhibit 11–2
Elements of strict liability for abnormally dangerous conditions or activities (SLADCA).

1. Existence of an abnormally dangerous condition or activity
2. Knowledge of the condition or activity
3. Causation
4. Damages

Most of the cases on SLADCA involve the way in which the defendant uses or abuses his or her own land. It is also possible, however, to commit this tort while on someone else's land, e.g., transporting a large quantity of explosives over a neighbor's land or over a public highway.

Abnormally Dangerous Condition or Activity

abnormally dangerous condition or activity Unusual or non-natural condition or activity that creates a substantial likelihood of causing great harm.

The first element is the existence of an **abnormally dangerous condition or activity**. Some conditions or activities are so unusual or non-natural that they are abnormally dangerous in that they create a substantial likelihood of causing great harm. (A few states describe such conditions or activities as *ultrahazardous*.) The defendant will be liable for such harm even if the harm was not intended and even if the defendant used reasonable care to try to prevent it. It is not a defense for the defendant to show that he or she acted reasonably or used the greatest of care—strict liability will still be imposed.

Rylands v. Fletcher The case holding that if defendants know they are engaging in a non-natural or abnormal use of land that creates an increased danger to persons or property, they will be strictly liable for harm caused by this use. L.R. 3 H.L. 330 (1868).

A great deal of law in this area stems from a famous English case, ***Rylands v. Fletcher***.[3] The defendants built a reservoir on their land. The plaintiff owned a mine nearby. The mine was flooded when water from the defendant's reservoir broke through and reached the mine. The rule from this case, which was eventually accepted in most American states, is as follows:

> If the defendant knows he or she is engaging in:
>
> (a) a non-natural or abnormal use of land,
> (b) that creates an increased danger to persons or property,
>
> the defendant will be strictly liable for harm caused by this use. The plaintiff will not have to prove negligence.

The determination of what is abnormal or non-natural will, of course, depend on the environment. The following are examples that have been found to be abnormally dangerous:

- storing large quantities of inflammable liquids in an urban area
- blasting in a residential area
- extensive pile driving
- emitting noxious gases from a factory in a residential area

The activity or condition must be unusual for the area and present a serious threat of harm. The following are examples of cases that were *not* found to be abnormally dangerous because they did not meet both criteria:

- electric wiring in a business
- gasoline stored at a gas station underground
- a small amount of dynamite stored in a factory
- an oil well dug in a Texas field

Although damage caused by such activities may not be considered abnormally dangerous enough to qualify for strict liability status, a plaintiff may still be able to recover under other theories. If the defendant acted unreasonably, a negligence case is possible, perhaps with the help of res ipsa loquitur (see Chapter 14). Nuisance and trespass to land should also be explored (see Chapter 23).

Is airplane flying an abnormally dangerous activity? Suppose a plane crashes onto someone's land, causing substantial damage to people and property below. Strict liability? Years ago, many courts would have said yes. As aviation has become more common and accepted, however, modern courts are inclined to say no. A plaintiff, therefore, must establish negligence or some other tort in order to recover.

Statutes often play a role in this area of strict liability. A statute, for example, might require or simply authorize a common carrier to transport dangerous substances. In such cases, strict liability is usually not applied when damage results from the activity. Liability will result only if negligence can be shown. On the other hand, there may be statutes that prohibit certain activity, e.g., blasting in certain areas or selling drugs to minors. It is sometimes unclear what tort consequences, if any, the legislature intended for a violation of such statutes. Research into the legislative history of the statute must be undertaken. A court might interpret the statute as calling for strict liability, negligence liability, or no civil liability at all for its violation.

The *Restatement of Torts* lists a number of factors that a court should analyze in determining whether something is abnormally dangerous:[4]

- the degree of risk of some harm to people, land, or chattels of others
- the likelihood that the harm that results from the activity will be great
- the inability to eliminate the risk by the exercise of reasonable care
- the extent to which the activity is not a matter of common usage
- the inappropriateness of the activity to the place where the activity is carried on
- the extent to which the value of the activity to the community is outweighed by its dangerous attributes

None of these factors is usually conclusive in deciding whether an activity is abnormally dangerous. The factors are simply aids for a court to determine the extent of the abnormality and the extent of the danger posed by the defendant. (On the meaning of factors in legal analysis, see Legal Analysis Guideline #12 in Chapter 2.)

In balancing these factors, if a court tips the scale against strict liability, it does not necessarily mean that the defendant has won the case. It simply means that the plaintiff must try to fit the facts of the case under the elements of other torts: negligence, nuisance, trespass to land, etc.

ASSIGNMENT 11.3

In each of the following situations, assume that the object or activity in question has resulted in damage or harm to someone. Do you think a court will impose strict liability? Why or why not? Also discuss other tort actions that might be possible on the facts given.

a. Tom is moving his own barn. He places it on a huge truck platform and drives it on a public highway. It crashes into a bridge.
b. The XYZ Company has installed a large steam boiler in its factory. It explodes.
c. The large lake on Linda's land overflows into neighboring land after a thunderstorm.
d. From an army base in Florida, scientists send up a satellite. Unfortunately it lands on top of a barn in Newark, New Jersey.
e. Fred knows that he is HIV positive. Yet, he continues to have unprotected sex with others who are unaware of Fred's HIV status.
f. A bystander is shot when a handgun accidentally goes off during a robbery. The bystander sues the manufacturer of the handgun for engaging in an abnormally dangerous activity.

Knowledge of the Condition or Activity

A defendant will *not* be strictly liable for an abnormally dangerous condition or activity of which the defendant is unaware. The plaintiff must establish knowledge of the danger on the part of the defendant.

In the famous mink mothers case we will study in a moment (*Foster v. Preston Mill Co.*), you will see that the damages sought by the owners of the mink were limited to the period after they notified the blasting company that the blasting was harming the mink.

Causation

proximate cause A cause that is legally sufficient to impose liability for the results of one's wrongful act or omission. There are two components of proximate cause: actual cause (which answers the question of who was the cause in fact of the harm or other loss) and legal cause (which answers the question of whether the harm or other loss was the foreseeable consequence of the original risk).

The plaintiff must also establish that the defendant was the **proximate cause** of the harm. We will study proximate cause in depth in Chapter 15. As we will see, there are two components of proximate cause: actual cause and legal cause.

Actual cause: the defendant was the cause in fact of the harm or other loss of the plaintiff, as determined by one of two tests:

(1) But for the defendant's conduct, the harm or other loss would not have occurred. (This test is used when there is only one alleged cause.)
Or,
(2) The defendant was a substantial factor in producing the harm or other loss. (This test is used when there is more than one alleged cause.)

Legal cause: the harm or other loss was the foreseeable consequence of the original risk created by the defendant. To establish legal cause for the tort of SLADCA, two requirements must be met:

(1) the harm suffered by the plaintiff's person or property must be within the type of harm that was initially foreseeable, and
(2) the plaintiff's person or property must be in the group or class of people who were foreseeably at risk because of the abnormally dangerous activity or condition.

Simply stated, if an activity is abnormally dangerous because it could cause harm "A," strict liability will not be imposed if that activity causes harm "B," a totally different category of harm from "A." As you read the case of *Foster v. Preston Mill Co.*, notice how the court applies this principle.

CASE

Foster v. Preston Mill Co.

44 Wash. 2d 440, 268 P.2d 645 (1954).
Supreme Court of Washington

Background: *Blasting for road construction frightened mink mothers owned by B. W. Foster, which caused the mothers to kill their kittens. Foster brought this action against the company doing the blasting (Preston Mill) to recover damages on the theory of absolute liability (SLADCA). The trial court found for Foster in the sum of $1,953.68. The case is now on appeal before the Supreme Court of Washington where Preston Mill is the appellant and Foster is the respondent.*

Decision on Appeal: *Judgment reversed. Absolute liability does not extend this far.*

OPINION OF COURT

Justice HAMLEY delivered the opinion of the court . . . :

Respondent's mink ranch is located in a rural area one and one-half miles east of North Bend, in King County, Washington. The ranch occupies seven and one half acres on which are located seven sheds for growing mink. The cages are of welded wire, but have wood roofs covered with composition roofing. The ranch is located about two blocks from U.S. highway No. 10, which is a main east-west thoroughfare across the state. Northern Pacific Railway Company tracks are located between the ranch and the highway, and Chicago, Milwaukee, St. Paul & Pacific Railroad Company tracks are located on the other side of the highway about fifteen hundred feet from the ranch.

The period of each year during which mink kittens are born, known as the whelping season, begins about May 1st. The kittens are born during a period of about two and one-half weeks, and are left with their mothers until they are six weeks old. During this period, the mothers are very excitable. If disturbed by noises, smoke, or dogs and cats, they run back and forth in their cages and frequently destroy their young. However, mink become accustomed to disturbances of this kind, if continued over a period of time. This explains why the mink in question were apparently not bothered, even during the whelping season, by the heavy traffic on U.S. highway No. 10, and by the noise and vibration caused by passing trains. There was testimony to the effect that mink would even become accustomed to the vibration and noise of blasting, if it were carried on in a regular and continuous manner.

Appellant and several other companies have been engaged in logging in the adjacent area for more than fifty years. Early in May, 1951, appellant began the construction of a road to gain access to certain timber which it desired to cut. The road was located about two and one-quarter miles southwest of the mink ranch, and about twenty-five hundred feet above the ranch, along the side of what is known as Rattlesnake Ledge.

It was necessary to use explosives to build the road. The customary types of explosives were used, and the customary methods of blasting were followed. The most powder used in one shooting was one hundred pounds, and usually the charge was limited to fifty pounds. The procedure used was to set off blasts twice a day—at noon and at the end of the work day.

Roy A. Peterson, the manager of the ranch in 1951, testified that the blasting resulted in "a tremendous vibration, is all. Boxes would rattle on the cages." The mother mink would then run back and forth in their cages and many of them would kill their kittens. Peterson also testified that on two occasions the blasts had broken windows.

Appellant's expert, Professor Drury Augustus Pfeiffer, of the University of Washington, testified as to tests made with a pin seismometer, using blasts as large as those used by appellant. He reported that no effect on the delicate apparatus was shown at distances comparable to those involved in this case. He said that it would be impossible to break a window at two and one-fourth miles with a hundred-pound shot, but that it could cause vibration of a lightly-supported cage. It would also be audible. Charles E. Erickson, who had charge of the road construction for appellant in 1951, testified that there was no glass breakage in the portable storage and filing shed which the company kept within a thousand feet of where the blasting was done. There were windows on the roof as well as on the sides of this shed.

Before the 1951 whelping season had far progressed, the mink mothers, according to Peterson's estimate, had killed thirty-five or forty of their kittens. He then told the manager of appellant company what had happened. He did not request that the blasting be stopped. After some discussion, however, appellant's manager indicated that the shots would be made as light as possible. The amount of explosives used in a normal shot was then reduced from nineteen or twenty sticks to fourteen sticks.

Officials of appellant company testified that it would have been impractical to entirely cease road-building during the several weeks required for the mink to whelp and wean their young. Such a delay would have made it necessary to run the logging operation another season, with attendant expense. It would also have disrupted the company's log production schedule and consequently the operation of its lumber mill.

In this action, respondent sought and recovered judgment only for such damages as were claimed to have been sustained as a result of blasting operations conducted after appellant received notice that its activity was causing loss of mink kittens.

The primary question presented by appellant's assignments of error is whether, on these facts, the judgment against appellant [Preston Mill] is sustainable on the theory of absolute liability.

The modern doctrine of strict liability for dangerous substances and activities stems from Justice Blackburn's decision in *Rylands v. Fletcher,* L.R. 3 H.L. 330 (1868). *Prosser on Torts,* 449, § 59. As applied to blasting operations, the doctrine has quite uniformly been held to establish liability, irrespective of negligence, for property damage sustained as a result of casting rocks or other debris on adjoining or neighboring premises. *Patrick v. Smith,* 75 Wash. 407, 134 P. 1076. . . . However . . . strict liability should be confined to consequences which lie within the extraordinary risk whose existence calls for such responsibility. *Prosser on Torts,* 458, § 60; 3 *Restatement of Torts,* 41, § 519. . . . This restriction which has been placed upon the application of the doctrine of absolute liability is based upon considerations of policy. As Professor Prosser has said:

"It is one thing to say that a dangerous enterprise must pay its way within reasonable limits, and quite another to say that it must bear responsibility for every extreme of harm that it may cause. . . . *Prosser on Torts,* 457, § 60.

Applying this principle to the case before us, the question comes down to this: Is the risk that any unusual vibration or noise may cause wild animals, which are being raised for commercial purposes, to kill their young, one of the things which make the activity of blasting ultrahazardous?

We have found nothing in the decisional law which would support an affirmative answer to this question. The decided cases, as well as common experience, indicate that the thing which makes blasting ultrahazardous is the risk that property or persons may be damaged or injured by coming into direct contact with flying debris, or by being directly affected by vibrations of the earth or concussions of the air.

Where, as a result of blasting operations, a horse has become frightened and has trampled or otherwise injured a person, recovery of damages has been upheld on the theory of negligence. *Klein v. Phelps Lumber Co.,* 75 Wash. 500, 135 P. 226. Contra: *Uvalde Construction Co. v. Hill,* 142 Tex. 19, 175 S.W.2d 247, where a milkmaid was injured by a frightened cow. But we have found no case where recovery of damages caused by a frightened farm animal has been sustained on the ground of absolute liability.

If, however, the possibility that a violent vibration, concussion, or noise might frighten domestic animals and lead to property damages or personal injuries be considered one of the harms which makes the activity of blasting ultrahazardous, this would still not include the case we have here.

The relatively moderate vibration and noise which appellant's blasting produced at a distance of two and a quarter miles was no more than a usual incident of the ordinary life of the community. See 3 *Restatement of*

Torts, 48, § 522, comment a. The trial court specifically found that the blasting did not unreasonably interfere with the enjoyment of their property by nearby landowners, except in the case of respondent's mink ranch.

It is the exceedingly nervous disposition of mink, rather than the normal risks inherent in blasting operations, which therefore must, as a matter of sound policy, bear the responsibility for the loss here sustained. . . .

It is our conclusion that the risk of causing harm of the kind here experienced, as a result of the relatively minor vibration, concussion, and noise from distant blasting, is not the kind of risk which makes the activity of blasting ultrahazardous. The doctrine of absolute liability is therefore inapplicable under the facts of this case, and respondent is not entitled to recover damages. The judgment is reversed.

ASSIGNMENT 11.4

a. What other theories of recovery could Foster try to use against Preston Mill Co. to recover for the damages the blasting did to its mink kittens?
b. A company blasts in an area. This excites a horse, which then runs into and kills a prize cow. The owner of the cow sues the blasting company on a theory of absolute liability. What result? Does *Foster* apply?

Defenses

contributory negligence The failure of plaintiffs to take reasonable precautions for their protection, helping to cause their own injury or other loss.

Contributory negligence on the part of the plaintiff will not bar recovery for the tort of maintaining an abnormally dangerous condition or activity. This is so with all strict liability torts—the negligence of the plaintiff will not defeat liability. Suppose, for example, that Tom carelessly walks into an area where construction blasting is occurring. Tom fails to realize that blasting is going on, but if he had been exercising reasonable care for his own safety, he should have realized this. Tom is injured by the blasting. There is clear contributory negligence. This is not a defense, however, when the plaintiff is suing under the strict liability tort of maintaining an abnormally dangerous condition or activity.

assumption of the risk The knowing and voluntary acceptance of the danger or risk of being harmed by someone's negligence.

If, however, the plaintiff knows of and understands the danger posed by the defendant and voluntarily proceeds to encounter it, then the plaintiff has assumed the risk of the danger. **Assumption of the risk** *is* a defense to a strict liability tort. To avoid permitting a defendant to use this defense as an unfair weapon against a plaintiff, however, the defendant must establish that the plaintiff's assumption of the risk was unreasonable. A plaintiff has a right to the reasonable use and enjoyment of his or her property. A defendant cannot encircle the plaintiff's land with a dangerous condition or activity and then assert assumption of the risk when the plaintiff uses his or her land and is injured because of the condition or activity. The defendant must show that this use was unreasonable, and courts are reluctant to make such a finding when the defendant has prevented the plaintiff from making ordinary and reasonable use of his or her property.

STRICT LIABILITY FOR ABNORMALLY DANGEROUS CONDITIONS OR ACTIVITIES CHECKLIST

Definitions, Relationships, Paralegal Roles, and Research References

Category
Strict liability for abnormally dangerous conditions or activities (SLADCA) is a strict liability tort (neither negligence nor intent must be shown).

STRICT LIABILITY FOR ABNORMALLY DANGEROUS CONDITIONS OR ACTIVITIES CHECKLIST *(Continued)*

Interest Protected by This Tort
The right to be free from harm caused by abnormally dangerous conditions or activities.

Elements of This Tort

1. Existence of an abnormally dangerous condition or activity
2. Knowledge of the condition or activity
3. Causation
4. Damages

Definitions of Major Words/Phrases in the Elements

Abnormally dangerous condition or activity: Unusual or non-natural condition or activity that creates a substantial likelihood of causing great harm.

Causation: The defendant is the cause in fact of the plaintiff's harm and the harm was the foreseeable consequence of the original risk created by the defendant.

Major Defenses and Counterargument Possibilities That Need to Be Explored

1. The condition or activity was not abnormally dangerous. (Note: The objective of the defendant is to try to force the plaintiff to prove negligence. This is accomplished if the plaintiff fails to show that the condition or activity was abnormally dangerous. Items 2 to 5 below try to establish that the condition or activity was not abnormally dangerous.)
2. The condition or activity was usual or natural for the environment in question.
3. The likelihood of serious harm from the condition or activity was small.
4. The danger in the condition or activity could have been eliminated by the use of reasonable care. (Defendant does not admit, however, that such care was not used.)
5. The value of the condition or activity to the community outweighed any possible danger.
6. A statute required or authorized the condition or activity.
7. The defendant was not aware of the condition or activity.
8. The defendant was not the cause in fact of the harm suffered by the plaintiff.
9. The harm suffered by the plaintiff was not the foreseeable consequence of the original risk created by the defendant.
10. The plaintiff was aware of the danger, understood it, and unreasonably encountered it (assumption of the risk).
11. The plaintiff consented to what the defendant did (on the defense of consent, see Chapter 27).
12. The plaintiff's suit against the government for SLADCA committed by a government employee may be barred by sovereign immunity (on sovereign immunity, see Chapter 27).
13. The plaintiff's suit against the government employee for SLADCA may be barred by official immunity (on official immunity, see Chapter 27).
14. The plaintiff's suit against the charitable organization for SLADCA committed by someone working for the organization may be barred by charitable immunity (on charitable immunity, see Chapter 27).
15. The plaintiff failed to take reasonable steps to mitigate the harm; therefore, damages should not cover the aggravation of the harm caused by the plaintiff (on the mitigation-of-damages rule, see Chapter 16).

Damages
The plaintiff can recover compensatory damages for the harm caused by the defendant's condition or activity. Punitive damages may also be possible if the plaintiff can show that the defendant was malicious or reckless in allowing the harm to occur. (On the categories of damages, see Chapter 16.)

Relationship to Criminal Law
There may be a criminal statute that prohibits the defendant from maintaining the condition or engaging in the activity involved, e.g., a statute making it a crime to explode fireworks in public areas. The consequences of violating such a statute may include criminal penalties as well as civil liability for the strict liability tort under discussion in this chapter.

STRICT LIABILITY FOR ABNORMALLY DANGEROUS CONDITIONS OR ACTIVITIES CHECKLIST *(Continued)*

Other Torts and Related Actions

Negligence: If the condition or activity of the defendant does not qualify for strict liability status because the condition or activity is not abnormally dangerous, the plaintiff may be able to show that the defendant was negligent in connection with the condition or activity.

Nuisance: Nuisance (private or public) should be considered when the condition or activity of the defendant interferes with the use and enjoyment of the plaintiff's land. In some states, there is liability for nuisance per se on the same facts that would constitute SLADCA.

Trespass to Land: This tort can be used when there is an entry of a physical object on the land of the plaintiff due to the abnormally dangerous condition or activity of the defendant.

Wrongful Death: This action can be brought by the survivors of the plaintiff if death results from the abnormally dangerous condition or activity of the defendant.

Federal Law

Under the Federal Tort Claims Act, the United States government will *not* be liable for a claim based on SLADCA engaged in by one of its federal employees. (See Exhibit 27–7 in Chapter 27.) (Most states have their own statutes that cover when tort claims can be made against the state for SLADCA and other torts committed by state government employees. Such claims are also covered in Chapter 27.)

Employer–Employee (Agency) Law

A private (non-government) employee who commits SLADCA is personally liable for this tort. His or her employer will *also* be liable for this tort if the conduct of the employee was within the scope of employment (respondeat superior). The employee must be furthering a business objective of the employer at the time. (On the factors that determine the scope of employment, see Exhibit 14–9 in Chapter 14.)

Paralegal Roles in Litigation for Strict Liability for Abnormally Dangerous Conditions or Activities

(See also Exhibit 3–1 in Chapter 3, Exhibit 20–4 in Chapter 20, and Exhibit 29–1 in Chapter 29.)

Fact finding (help the office collect facts relevant to prove the elements of SLADCA, the elements of available defenses, and extent of injuries or other damages):
- client interviewing
- field investigation
- online research (e.g., records on weather conditions on the date of the accident)

File management (help the office control the documents involved in the litigation of a case asserting SLADCA):
- open client file
- enter case data in computer database
- maintain file documents

Litigation assistance (help the trial attorney prepare for a trial and appeal, if needed):
- draft discovery requests
- draft answers to discovery requests
- draft pleadings
- digest and index discovery documents
- help prepare, order, and manage trial exhibits
- prepare trial notebook
- draft notice of appeal
- order trial transcript
- cite-check briefs
- perform legal research

STRICT LIABILITY FOR ABNORMALLY DANGEROUS CONDITIONS OR ACTIVITIES CHECKLIST *(Continued)*

Collection/enforcement (help the trial attorney for the judgment creditor to collect the damages award or to enforce other court orders at the conclusion of the case):

- draft postjudgment discovery requests
- conduct field investigation to monitor compliance with judgment
- perform online research (e.g., location of defendant's business assets)

Research References for This Tort

Digests
In the digests of West Group, look for case summaries on this tort under key topics such as:

Explosives	Damages
Trespass	Torts
Waters and Water Courses	Death
	Nuisance

Corpus Juris Secundum
In this legal encyclopedia, see the discussion under topic headings such as:

Explosives	Damages
Trespass	Torts
Waters and Water Courses	Death
	Nuisance

American Jurisprudence 2d
In this legal encyclopedia, see the discussion under topic headings such as:

Explosions and Explosives	Damages
Waters	Torts
Premises Liability	Death
Adjoining Landowners	Nuisance

Legal Periodical Literature
There are two main index systems to use to locate legal periodical literature on this tort:

INDEX TO LEGAL PERIODICALS AND BOOKS (ILP)
See literature in *ILP* under subject headings such as:

- Water and Water Courses
- Liability Without Fault
- Animals
- Fires and Fire Prevention
- Trespass
- Real Property
- Torts
- Damages
- Adjoining Landowners

CURRENT LAW INDEX (CLI)
See literature in *CLI* under subject headings such as:

- Strict Liability
- Explosives
- Water
- Damages
- Torts
- Real Property
- Liability for Landslide Damages
- Liability for Condition and Use of Land

Example of a legal periodical article you will find by using *ILP* or *CLI:*

Strict Liability for Abnormally Dangerous Activity: The Negligence Barrier by Gerald Boston, 36 San Diego Law Review 597 (1999).

A.L.R., A.L.R.2d, A.L.R.3d, A.L.R.4th, A.L.R.5th, A.L.R.6th, A.L.R. Fed, and A.L.R. Fed 2d
Use the *ALR Index* to locate annotations on this tort. In this index, check subject headings such as:

Absolute Liability	Torts
Floods and Flooding	Damages
Explosions and Explosives	Water

STRICT LIABILITY FOR ABNORMALLY DANGEROUS CONDITIONS OR ACTIVITIES CHECKLIST *(Continued)*

Example of an annotation you can locate through this index:

Common-Law Strict Liability in Tort of Prior Landowner . . . for Contamination of Land with Hazardous Waste Resulting from . . . Abnormally Dangerous or Ultrahazardous Activity by William Johnson, 13 A.L.R.5th 600 (1993)

Words and Phrases
In this multivolume legal dictionary, look up *abnormally dangerous* and every other word or phrase connected with strict liability for abnormally dangerous conditions or activities discussed in this chapter. The dictionary will give you definitions of these words or phrases from court opinions.

CALR: Computer-Assisted Legal Research

Example of a query you could ask on Westlaw to try to find cases or other legal materials on this tort: **"strict liability for abnormally dangerous activities" /p damages**

Example of a query you could ask on LexisNexis to try to find cases or other legal materials on this tort: **strict liability for abnormally dangerous activities /p damages**

Example of search terms you could use on an Internet legal search engine such as the Public Library of Law (www.plol.org), Findlaw (www.findlaw.com), or Google Scholar (scholar.google.com) to find cases, statutes, or other legal materials on this tort: **"strict liability for abnormally dangerous activities"**

Example of search terms you could use on an Internet general search engine such as Google, Bing, or AltaVista to find cases, statutes, or other legal materials on this tort: **"strict liability for abnormally dangerous activities"**

More Internet sites to check for materials on SLADCA and other torts:
www.hg.org/torts.html
www.megalaw.com/top/top.php (click "Intentional Torts," "Personal Injury Law," "Tort Law," and "Damages")
See also the online sites in Overview of Tort Law at the end of Chapter 1.

CHECK THE CITE

James Berry was paralyzed in a ski racing accident. "In the skiercross race format, four racers simultaneously descend a course that features difficult turns and tabletop jumps. The racers compete against each other as they ski down the mountain to complete the course first. A series of elimination heats determines the race winner. On Mr. Berry's fourth trip over the course, he attempted to negotiate the course's first tabletop jump. Upon landing from the jump, Mr. Berry fell and fractured his neck, an injury that resulted in permanent paralysis." He then sued the race organizer. Why did he lose his claim for SLADCA? Read the case of *Berry v. Greater Park City Co.*, 2007 Utah 87, 171 P.3d 442 (Utah 2007). To read the opinion online, (1) Go to the site of the Utah courts (www.utcourts.gov). Click Court Publications, then Appellate Opinions. In the search box for Supreme Court opinions, type the names of the parties (Berry Greater Park City). (2) Go to www.findlaw.com (caselaw.lp.findlaw.com/data/ut/cases/supopin/berry103007.pdf). (3) Run a citation search ("171 P.3d 442") or a party search (Berry Greater Park City) in the Legal Opinions and Journals database of Google Scholar (scholar.google.com).

PROJECT

In Google, Bing, or another general search engine, run the following searches:

1. *aa* "dog bite" (substitute the name of your state for *aa* in the search). Are there any statutes or ordinances in your state on the civil or criminal liability of owners of dogs that bite someone? If so, state the terms of one.
2. *aa* "abnormally dangerous conditions or activities" (substitute the name of your state for *aa* in the search). Try the search with and without the quotation marks. Describe the facts and governing law of a court opinion in which someone was found civilly liable in your state for SLADCA.

ETHICS IN A TORTS PRACTICE

You are the only paralegal working in the law office of Alex Symms, who has just opened a practice that specializes in animal bite cases. After an extensive TV, radio, and print advertising campaign, the office is flooded with clients. Unfortunately, there is not enough staff to handle the volume of cases. Last month, the cases of two clients were lost due to the firm's failure to file their claims before the statute of limitations expired. What ethical problems, if any, might exist?

SUMMARY

Strict liability is the imposition of liability or responsibility for harm whether or not the person causing the harm intended it or failed to use reasonable care to prevent it. It is liability regardless of fault. In most states, the keeper of a wild animal will be strictly liable for harm it causes, and the keeper of a domestic animal will be strictly liable for harm it causes if the keeper had reason to know about the animal's dangerous propensity and if the harm caused by the animal was due to that specific propensity.

Strict liability for abnormally dangerous conditions or activities (SLADCA) is a tort that imposes liability for harm resulting from abnormally dangerous conditions or activities regardless of whether the harm is caused intentionally, negligently, or without fault (innocently). A condition or activity is abnormally dangerous when it is unusual or non-natural and creates a substantial likelihood of causing great harm. The *Restatement* considers a number of factors in deciding whether an activity is abnormally dangerous, such as the inappropriateness of the activity to the area and whether the value of an activity to the community outweighs its dangerous attributes. The plaintiff must establish that the defendant knew that the condition or activity was dangerous. There are two components of proximate cause. First, "but for" the defendant's conduct, the harm would not have occurred or the defendant was a substantial factor in producing the harm (cause in fact). Second, the harm was the foreseeable consequence of the original risk created by the defendant. The harm suffered by the plaintiff's person or property must be within the type of harm that was initially foreseeable, and the plaintiff's person or property must be in the group or class of people who were foreseeably at risk because of the abnormally dangerous activity or condition. Contributory negligence is not a complete defense, but unreasonable assumption of the risk is.

KEY TERMS

strict liability *176*
wild animal *177*
domestic animal *177*
dangerous propensity *177*
strict liability for abnormally dangerous conditions or activities (SLADCA) *179*
abnormally dangerous condition or activity *180*
Rylands v. Fletcher *180*
proximate cause *182*
contributory negligence *184*
assumption of the risk *184*

REVIEW QUESTIONS

1. What is strict liability?
2. What is the distinction between a wild animal and a domestic animal?
3. What is the liability for harm caused by a keeper of a wild animal?
4. When will the keeper of a domestic animal be strictly liable for the harm it causes?
5. Explain whether every dog is entitled to a free bite.
6. What is a dangerous propensity?
7. What is strict liability for abnormally dangerous conditions or activities (SLADCA)?
8. When is a condition or activity abnormally dangerous?
9. What did *Rylands v. Fletcher* hold?
10. What factors does the *Restatement* consider when deciding whether an activity is abnormally dangerous?
11. What is the knowledge requirement for the tort of SLADCA?
12. What are the two components of proximate cause?
13. How is cause in fact established?
14. To establish proximate cause, what must be foreseeable?
15. Is contributory negligence a defense to SLADCA?
16. What is assumption of the risk, and when is it a defense to SLADCA?

HELPFUL WEBSITES

- **Animals**

  Dog Bite Law

  www.dogbitelaw.com

  Animal Attacks

  attack.igorilla.com

  Animal Law

  www.animallaw.info

  www.animallaw.info/topics/spusdoglaws.htm

- **Abnormally Dangerous Conditions or Activities**

  Strict Liability

  www.lexisnexis.com/lawschool/study/outlines/html/torts/torts16.htm

  www.thelockeinstitute.org/journals/tortliability5.html

  Kent's Tort Outline

  www.docstoc.com/docs/15492/Kents-Torts-II-_Gash_

- **Element Search**

  www.google.com (run this search: elements abnormally dangerous conditions or activities tort)

ENDNOTES

1. Centers for Disease Control and Prevention, Dog Bite Prevention (www.cdc.gov/HomeandRecreationalSafety/Dog-Bites/biteprevention.html). See also Jane E. Brody, "Heeding the Warnings From Dangerous Dogs," *N.Y. Times*, May 18, 1999, at D8; Dog Bite Law (www.dogbitelaw.com/PAGES/statistics.html).
2. *Restatement (Second) of Torts* § 506 (1977).
3. L.R. 3 H.L. 330 (1868). (L.R. is the abbreviation for Law Reports; H.L. is the abbreviation for House of Lords.)
4. *Restatement (Second) of Torts* § 520 (1965).

Student StudyWARE™ CD-ROM
For additional materials, please go to the student CD in this book.

CHAPTER

12

NEGLIGENCE: A SUMMARY

CHAPTER OUTLINE

- Introduction
- Negligence and Breach of Duty
- Negligence and Insurance
- Shorthand Definition
- Gross Negligence and Ordinary Negligence
- Negligence Checklist

CHAPTER OBJECTIVES

After completing this chapter, you should be able to:

- Define negligence.
- Identify the elements of negligence.
- Understand the two different meanings of the words *negligence* and *negligent*.
- Know the shorthand definition of negligence.
- Distinguish between negligence law and insurance law.
- Distinguish between gross negligence and ordinary negligence.
- Identify paralegal roles in negligence litigation.
- List the major resources available in traditional books and online for researching issues involving the tort of negligence.

INTRODUCTION

Negligence is the largest of the three major categories of torts (the other two being the intentional torts and the various kinds of strict liability). Negligence has been called a "catchall" tort in that it encompasses a wide variety of unreasonable actions and inactions that cause injury or other loss. This chapter is an overview of negligence. Elsewhere, more specific negligence topics will be treated. (See Exhibit 12–1.)

Exhibit 12–1
Coverage of negligence topics.

Topic	Where Covered in This Book
Foreseeability	Chapter 4
Duty	Chapter 13
Breach of Duty	Chapter 14
Proximate Cause	Chapter 15
Damages	Chapter 16
Employer Liability	Chapter 14
Medical Malpractice	Chapter 18
Legal Malpractice	Chapter 18
Owners and Occupiers of Land (Premises Liability)	Chapter 23
Nuisance	Chapter 23
Manufacturers and Retailers (Products Liability)	Chapter 19
Wrongful Death	Chapter 21
Negligent Infliction of Emotional Distress	Chapter 9
Gross Negligence	Chapters 14, 17
Defenses to Negligence	Chapter 17

negligence The failure to use reasonable care that an ordinary prudent person would have used in a similar situation, resulting in harm or other loss. Injury or other loss caused by the failure to use reasonable care.

Negligence is the failure to use reasonable care that an ordinary prudent person would have used in a similar situation, resulting in harm or other loss. (See Exhibit 12–2 for its elements.) The shorthand definition of the tort is injury or other loss caused by the failure to use reasonable care.

Exhibit 12–2
Elements of the tort of negligence.

1. Duty
2. Breach of duty
3. Proximate cause
4. Damages

NEGLIGENCE AND BREACH OF DUTY

breach of duty Unreasonable conduct endangering someone to whom you owe a duty of care.

The word "negligence" is used in two different senses. It can mean the entire tort (all four elements) or only the second element (**breach of duty**). (Breach of duty is unreasonable conduct endangering someone to whom you owe a duty of care.) Hence the statement "he acted negligently" either means he acted unreasonably (the second element) or that he committed the tort itself. In this book, the words *negligence* or *negligent* mean the entire tort, although occasionally the context will make clear that the reference is to the second element only.

NEGLIGENCE AND INSURANCE

insurance A contract (called an insurance policy) under which a company agrees to compensate a person (up to a specific amount) for a loss caused by designated perils or risks.

It is commonly assumed by the public that if a driver hits a pedestrian on the street, the driver is responsible and must pay for the injury or other loss suffered by the pedestrian. This is not necessarily so. We must be careful to distinguish **insurance** law from negligence law. Insurance is a contract (called an insurance policy) under which a company agrees to compensate a person (up to a specific amount) for a loss caused by designated perils or risks. The benefits of a policy may become payable as soon as the terms of the policy have been met. For many policies, all that is needed is a covered loss, a covered person, and causation. Much more is needed to trigger the law of negligence. You are not considered negligent simply because you cause an injury or other loss. The hallmark of negligence is **fault**, which is an error or defect in someone's judgment or conduct to which blame and **culpability** attaches. Culpability refers to that which is worthy of blame (blameworthiness) because of a wrong that has been committed. In a typical negligence case, the fault or wrong involved may be simple carelessness or momentary unreasonableness. But a lapse of some kind is required. We are *not* liable for every injury that we cause. We are liable under the law of negligence for those injuries we wrongfully cause in the sense that our conduct fell below a minimum standard of conduct when we caused the injury. Some injuries are the result of **unavoidable accidents**—those that were not intended, were not foreseeable, and could not have been prevented by the exercise of reasonable care. There is no negligence liability for such injuries. Insurance might provide coverage for them, but there is no negligence liability for them. Strict liability might apply, as we saw in Chapter 11 (for abnormally dangerous conditions or activities), and as we will see in Chapter 19 when we cover strict liability for harm caused by defective products. But *negligence* law is based on a standard of fault. One of our main objectives in the following chapters is to explore what this standard is. An important first step in achieving this objective is to avoid the trap of equating negligence with causation or with insurance.

fault An error or defect in someone's judgment or conduct to which blame and culpability attach. The wrongful breach of a duty.

culpability Blameworthiness.

unavoidable accident An occurrence that led to an injury or other loss that was not intended, was not foreseeable, and could not have been prevented by reasonable care.

SHORTHAND DEFINITION

As just indicated, the shorthand definition of the tort of negligence is injury or other loss caused by the failure to use reasonable care. In the vast majority of negligence cases that are litigated, the sole questions before the court are:

- Was the defendant's conduct unreasonable?
- Did this unreasonableness cause the plaintiff's injury or other loss?

In the next seven chapters, we will examine these questions along with a large number of others. As we do so, it is important that you not lose sight of the shorthand definition of negligence as *injury or other loss caused by the failure to use reasonable care*. This definition will suffice for most negligence cases. While we must look at a maze of special rules in the law of negligence, there is a danger of thinking that the maze is the norm. It isn't.

GROSS NEGLIGENCE AND ORDINARY NEGLIGENCE

Occasionally we will need to distinguish levels or degrees of negligence. For example, a defendant might be accused of being **reckless** in causing an accident. Recklessness means consciously taking a risk in failing to exercise due care but without intending the consequences. Reckless defendants wantonly disregard a risk but have not committed an intentional tort because they neither desired the consequences of the risk nor did they have substantially certain knowledge of what the consequences would be.

reckless Consciously taking a risk in failing to exercise due care but without intending the consequences; wantonly disregarding a risk but neither desiring the consequences of the risk nor having substantially certain knowledge of the consequences.

EXAMPLES

In the rain, Ted causes an accident at an intersection when he increases the speed of his car in order to get through a light that has just turned yellow.

Same facts, except that as Ted speeds through the yellow light, he is texting a message to his girlfriend.

gross negligence The failure to use even a small amount of care to avoid foreseeable harm.

ordinary negligence Conduct that is unreasonable but not gross or reckless.

In the second case, Ted was reckless. Accelerating and texting in an intersection is high-risk behavior. Indeed, the law might call his conduct **gross negligence**, the failure to use even a small amount of care to avoid foreseeable harm. This kind of negligence is different from **ordinary negligence**, which is conduct that is unreasonable, but not gross or reckless. An example of ordinary negligence would be Ted's carelessness in speeding through a yellow light, but without other risky behavior such as dialing a cell phone, shaving, or texting.

Although most of the negligence cases we will be studying will consist of ordinary negligence, there are some issues, particularly involving defenses and damages, that will turn on whether the defendant's conduct is of a higher magnitude than ordinary negligence.

NEGLIGENCE CHECKLIST

Before we begin a detailed study of the law of negligence, briefly examine the negligence checklist containing an overview of definitions, relationships, paralegal roles, and research references for this tort. You may want to refer back to this checklist while you are studying the next seven chapters that cover specific negligence issues.

NEGLIGENCE CHECKLIST

Definitions, Relationships, Paralegal Roles, and Research References

Category
Negligence is a category unto itself. It covers harm that is neither intentional nor the basis of strict liability.

Interest Protected by This Tort
The right to be free from injury or other loss to person or property caused by the failure to use reasonable care.

Elements of This Tort
1. Duty
2. Breach of duty
3. Proximate cause
4. Damages

Definitions of Major Words/Phrases in the Elements

Duty: An obligation to conform to a standard of conduct prescribed by law. In most negligence cases, duty is the obligation to use reasonable care to avoid the foreseeable risk of causing injury or other loss to the person or property of another (see Chapter 13).

Breach of duty: Unreasonable conduct endangering someone to whom you owe a duty of care (see Chapter 14).

Proximate cause: A cause that is legally sufficient to impose liability for the results of one's wrongful act or omission. There are two components of proximate cause: actual cause (which answers the question of who was the cause in fact of the harm or other loss) and legal cause (which answers the question of whether the harm or other loss was the foreseeable consequence of the original risk) (see Chapter 15).

Damages: Actual injury or other loss (see Chapter 16). (See glossary for an additional definition.)

Major Defenses and Counterargument Possibilities That Need to Be Explored
1. The defendant owed the plaintiff no duty.
2. The injury was not foreseeable.

NEGLIGENCE CHECKLIST *(Continued)*

3. There was no breach of duty. The burden or inconvenience on the defendant to avoid the injury outweighed the risk of the injury occurring. The burden or inconvenience of avoidance was substantial, whereas the risk of injury was minimal (on breach of duty, see Exhibit 14–4 in Chapter 14).
4. The defendant was not the cause in fact of the plaintiff's injury. Under the two tests to determine actual cause: (a) it cannot be said that but for what the defendant did or failed to do, the injury to the plaintiff would not have occurred; or (b) the defendant was not a substantial factor in producing the plaintiff's injury.
5. The plaintiff's injury was not within the original risk created by the defendant (on proximate cause, see Chapter 15).
6. The plaintiff's injury was produced by a superseding cause (on proximate cause and superseding cause, see Chapter 15).
7. The plaintiff's injury was produced by an intervening cause that was highly extraordinary (on proximate cause and intervening cause, see Chapter 15).
8. The plaintiff suffered no actual injury or other loss due to the unreasonable conduct of the defendant. (There were no damages.)
9. The plaintiff was unreasonable in taking risks for his or her own safety and this helped cause the injury. (On contributory negligence, see Chapter 17).
10. The harm caused the plaintiff by his or her own negligence exceeded the minimum threshold established by the comparative negligence statute (on comparative negligence, see Chapter 17).
11. The plaintiff assumed the risk of his or her own injury (on assumption of the risk, see Chapter 17).
12. The plaintiff failed to take reasonable steps to mitigate the harm caused by the defendant's negligence; therefore, damages should not cover the aggravation of the harm caused by the plaintiff (on the mitigation-of-damages rule, see Chapter 16).
13. The plaintiff's suit against the government for negligence committed by a government employee may be barred by sovereign immunity (on sovereign immunity, see Chapter 27).
14. The plaintiff's suit against the government employee for negligence may be barred by official immunity (on official immunity, see Chapter 27).
15. The plaintiff's suit against the charitable organization for negligence committed by someone working for the organization may be barred by charitable immunity (on charitable immunity, see Chapter 27).
16. The plaintiff's suit against a family member for negligence may be barred by intrafamily tort immunity (on intrafamily tort immunity, see Chapter 22).

Damages
Negligence requires proof of actual injury or other loss. Without it, the negligence case fails and no compensatory damages can be awarded. Nominal damages are not allowed in a negligence action. In general, punitive damages are not allowed for ordinary negligence. Recklessness or malice of some kind can be the basis for an award of punitive damages. (On the categories of damages, see Chapter 16.)

Relationship to Criminal Law
There are some crimes based on negligence, e.g., negligent homicide. More than ordinary negligence, however, is usually required. Negligence in criminal law requires at least recklessness.

Relationship to Other Torts
If you are not able to prove one of the intentional torts, explore the possibility of negligence. For example, if you cannot establish the tort of battery because you cannot prove that the defendant had the intent to cause a contact that was harmful or offensive, you may be able to establish the tort of negligence if you can prove that the harmful or offensive contact was caused by the defendant's unreasonable conduct. The same may be true of other intentional torts, such as conversion and false imprisonment. Whenever you are having difficulty establishing an intentional tort, determine whether the defendant created an unreasonable risk of the same injury or other loss

NEGLIGENCE CHECKLIST *(Continued)*

occurring. If so, negligence may be an alternative cause of action. Finally, explore negligence as an alternative to strict liability torts.

Federal Law

a. Under the Federal Tort Claims Act, the United States government will be liable for negligence committed by one of its federal employees within the scope of employment (respondeat superior) as long as the employee's conduct did not involve discretion at the planning level. (See Exhibit 27–7 in Chapter 27.) (Most states have their own statutes that cover when tort claims can be made against the state for negligence or other torts committed by state government employees. Such claims are also covered in Chapter 27.)
b. There may be liability under the Civil Rights Act if the negligence was committed while the defendant was depriving the plaintiff of a federal civil right under color of state law. (See Exhibit 27–9 in Chapter 27.)
c. Under the Consumer Product Safety Act, penalties can be imposed for violations of the rules of the Consumer Product Safety Commission (CPSC) concerning dangerous products on the market (www.cpsc.gov).

Employer–Employee (Agency) Law

A private (non-government) employee who commits negligence is personally liable for this tort. His or her employer will *also* be liable for negligence: (a) vicariously, if the conduct of the employee was within the scope of employment (respondeat superior), or (b) independently, if the employer was careless in hiring or supervising an incompetent employee who posed a risk of injuring others. (On the factors that determine the scope of employment, see Exhibit 14–9 in Chapter 14.)

Paralegal Roles in Negligence Litigation

(See also Exhibit 3–1 in Chapter 3, Exhibit 20–4 in Chapter 20, and Exhibit 29–1 in Chapter 29.)

Fact finding (help the office collect facts relevant to prove the elements of negligence, the elements of available defenses, and the extent of injuries or other damages):

- client interviewing
- field investigation
- online research (e.g., records on weather conditions on the date of the accident)

File management (help the office control the documents involved in a negligence litigation):

- open client file
- enter case data in computer database
- maintain file documents

Litigation assistance (help the trial attorney prepare for a negligence trial and appeal, if needed):

- draft discovery requests
- draft answers to discovery requests
- draft pleadings
- digest and index discovery documents
- help prepare, order, and manage trial exhibits
- prepare trial notebook
- draft notice of appeal
- order trial transcript
- cite-check briefs
- perform legal research

Collection/enforcement (help the trial attorney for the judgment creditor to collect the damages award or to enforce other court orders at the conclusion of the negligence case):

- draft postjudgment discovery requests
- conduct field investigation to monitor compliance with judgment
- perform online research (e.g., location of defendant's business assets)

NEGLIGENCE CHECKLIST *(Continued)*

Research References for Negligence

Digests

In the digests of West Group, look for case summaries on negligence under key topics such as:

Negligence
Damages
Products Liability
Master and Servant
Physicians and Surgeons
Death
Animals
Drugs and Narcotics
Explosives
Torts
Automobiles
Landlord and Tenant
Health and Environment
Innkeepers
Highways
Nuisance
Contribution
Carriers
Telecommunications

Corpus Juris Secundum

In this legal encyclopedia, see the discussion on negligence under topic headings such as:

Negligence
Damages
Products Liability
Master and Servant
Physicians and Surgeons
Death
Animals
Drugs and Narcotics
Explosives
Motor Vehicles
Landlord and Tenant
Health and Environment
Inns, Hotels and Eating Places
Highways
Nuisance
Contribution
Carriers
Telegraphs, Telephones, Radio and Television

American Jurisprudence 2d

In this legal encyclopedia, see the discussion on negligence under topic headings such as:

Negligence
Products Liability
Premises Liability
Hospitals and Asylums
Damages
Contribution
Amusements and Exhibitions
Animals
Carriers
Death
Drugs, Narcotics and Poisons
Master and Servant
Automobiles and Highway Traffic
Occupations, Trades and Professions
Hotels, Motels and Restaurants
Landlord and Tenant
Highways, Streets and Bridges
Physicians and Surgeons
Health

Legal Periodical Literature

There are two index systems to use to locate legal periodical literature on negligence:

INDEX TO LEGAL PERIODICALS AND BOOKS (ILP)

See literature in *ILP* under subject headings such as:

Negligence
Accidents
Act of God
Automobile Insurance
Contributory Negligence
Damages
Highways and Streets
Inns and Innkeepers
Joint Tortfeasors

CURRENT LAW INDEX (CLI)

See literature in *CLI* under subject headings such as:

Negligence
Automobiles
Bailments
Contribution
Damages
Death by Wrongful Act
Exemplary Damages
Drugs
Employers' Liability

NEGLIGENCE CHECKLIST *(Continued)*

Landlord and Tenant
Last Clear Chance
Master and Servant
Motor Vehicles
Nuisance
Products Liability
Personal Injuries
Proximate Cause
Physicians and Surgeons
Res Ipsa Loquitur
Traffic Accidents
Vicarious Liability
Wrongful Death

Food
Hospitals
Informed Consent
Joint Tortfeasors
Landlord and Tenant
Liability for Condition and Use of Land
Malpractice
Products Liability
Respondeat Superior
Personal Injuries
Physicians
Tort Liability

Example of a legal periodical article you will find on negligence by using *ILP* or *CLI:*

What Are We Comparing in Comparative Negligence? by Paul H. Edelman, 85 Washington University Law Review 73 (2007).

A.L.R., A.L.R.2d, A.L.R.3d, A.L.R.4th, A.L.R.5th, A.L.R.6th, A.L.R. Fed., and A.L.R. 2d Fed.
Use the *ALR Index* to locate annotations on negligence. In this index, check subject headings such as:

Neglience
Aggravated Negligence
Attractive Nuisance
Comparative Negligence
Concurrent Negligence
Contributory Negligence or Assumption of Risk
Corporate Officers, Directors and Agents
Governmental Immunity or Privilege
Gross Negligence
Imputed Negligence and Liability

Landlord and Tenant
Products Liability
Rescue Doctrine
Malpractice
Hospitals
Master and Servant
Res Ipsa Loquitur
Mitigation or Aggravation of Damages
Federal Tort Claims Act
Health and Accident Insurance
Policies and Provisions

Example of an annotation on negligence you can locate through the *ALR Index:*

Liability of Clinical Laboratories for Negligence by Marjorie A. Shields, 19 A.L.R.6th 793 (2007).

Words and Phrases
In this multivolume legal dictionary, look up *negligence, duty, breach of duty, proximate cause, damages, contributory negligence, comparative negligence, assumption of the risk,* and every other word or phrase connected with negligence discussed in the next seven chapters. The dictionary will give you definitions of these words or phrases from court opinions.

CALR: Computer-Assisted Legal Research

Example of a query you could ask on Westlaw or on LexisNexis to try to find cases, statutes, or other legal materials on negligence: **negligence/p damages**

Example of search terms you could use on an Internet legal search engine such as the Public Library of Law (www.plol.org), Findlaw (www.findlaw.com), or Google Scholar (scholar.google.com) to find cases, statutes, or other legal materials on negligence: **negligence tort**

Example of search terms you could use on an Internet general search engine such as Google, Bing, or AltaVista to find cases, statutes, or other legal materials on negligence: **negligence tort**

www.hg.org/torts.html
www.megalaw.com/top/top.php (click "Intentional Torts," "Personal Injury Law," "Tort Law," and "Damages")
See also the online sites in Overview of Tort Law at the end of Chapter 1.

PROJECT

In Google, Bing, or another general search engine, run the following search: *aa* law negligence (substitute the name of your state for *aa* in the search).

(1) The search will lead to many law firms in the state that take negligence cases. Some of the sites will summarize aspects of negligence law. Identify any three firms that appear to have comprehensive summaries. Briefly compare differences and similarities among these summaries.
(2) Other than law firm sites, describe the variety of sites that cover any aspect of negligence law in the state, giving examples of sites in each category.

ETHICS IN A TORTS PRACTICE

You are a paralegal working in the law office of Williamson & Quincey. The firm has issued you a business card. In the center of the card, the name of the firm is printed along with its address and phone number. Your name is printed in the lower right hand corner. Beneath your name, your office e-mail address and phone number are printed. The card contains no other information. What ethical problems, if any, might exist?

SUMMARY

Negligence is the largest of the three major categories of torts. It covers injury or other loss caused by unreasonableness. (The other two categories are intentional torts and strict liability torts.) The broad meaning of negligence is the failure to use reasonable care that an ordinary prudent person would have used in a similar situation, resulting in harm or other loss. The shorthand definition is injury or other loss caused by the failure to use reasonable care. The four elements of negligence that we will study in detail in the next seven chapters are duty, breach of duty, proximate cause, and damages. The words *negligence* and *negligent* are sometimes used in two different senses: (1) broadly, to mean the entire tort, and (2) narrowly, to mean only the second element of the tort, breach of duty. We are not liable for every injury we cause. Negligence liability exists when someone is at fault. The injury he or she causes must be due to an error or defect in judgment or conduct to which blame and culpability attach. Some issues in the law of negligence will require a distinction between gross negligence (the failure to use even a small amount of care to avoid foreseeable harm) and ordinary negligence (conduct that is unreasonable but not gross or reckless).

KEY TERMS

negligence *192*
breach of duty *192*
insurance *192*
fault *193*
culpability *193*
unavoidable accidents *193*
reckless *193*
gross negligence *194*
ordinary negligence *194*

REVIEW QUESTIONS

1. What are the three major categories of torts?
2. What is negligence?
3. What are the elements of negligence?
4. What are the two meanings of the words *negligence* and *negligent*?
5. Are we liable for every injury that we cause?
6. What is the distinction between negligence liability and insurance?
7. What is meant by fault?
8. What is an unavoidable accident?
9. What is the shorthand definition of negligence?
10. What is reckless conduct?
11. What is the distinction between gross negligence and ordinary negligence?

HELPFUL WEBSITES

- **Negligence**
  In Google, Bing, or another search engine, run the following search: elements negligence tort.
  www.lexisnexis.com/lawschool/study/outlines/html/torts/torts03.htm
  en.wikipedia.org/wiki/Negligence
  www.expertlaw.com/library/personal_injury/negligence.html
  law.jrank.org/pages/11853/Negligence.html
  www.suite101.com/reference/negligence_law
- **State Negligence Laws**
  law.findlaw.com/state-laws/negligence

Student StudyWARE™ CD-ROM
For additional materials, please go to the student CD in this book.

CHAPTER

13

NEGLIGENCE: ELEMENT I: DUTY

CHAPTER OUTLINE

- General Rule on Duty
- Unforeseeable Plaintiff
- Nonfeasance and Special Relationships
- Gratuitous Undertaking
- Protection for the Good Samaritan
- Government Duty to Protect

CHAPTER OBJECTIVES

After completing this chapter, you should be able to:

- Understand the meaning of duty.
- State the general rule of duty in negligence cases.
- Identify the factors used by the courts to determine whether a duty exists.
- Determine whether a duty exists to an unforeseeable plaintiff.
- Distinguish between misfeasance and nonfeasance when imposing a duty of reasonable care.
- Identify the special relationships that can be the basis of a duty in nonfeasance cases.
- Determine whether a Good Samaritan has a duty of reasonable care.
- Explain when a duty attaches to a gratuitous undertaking.

GENERAL RULE ON DUTY

duty 1. An obligation to conform to a standard of conduct prescribed by law. 2. In most negligence cases, the obligation to use reasonable care to avoid the foreseeable risk of causing injury or other loss to the person or property of another.

We begin with the first element of negligence: **duty**. In the broadest sense, a duty is an obligation to conform to a standard of conduct prescribed by law. In most negligence cases, duty is the obligation to use reasonable care to avoid the foreseeable risk of causing injury or other loss to the person or property of another. Our study of duty will require us to cover the following interrelated questions:

- Who owes the duty?
- To whom is the duty owed?
- When does the duty arise?
- What is the standard of conduct to which there must be conformity? (Duty to do what?)

The general rule of duty that applies in most negligence cases is as follows:

General Rule on Duty

Whenever one's conduct creates a foreseeable risk of injury or other loss to someone's person or property, a duty of reasonable care arises to take reasonable precautions to prevent the injury or loss.

The standard embodied in the duty of reasonable care is called *due care* or *ordinary care*. In Chapter 14 we will see that this care is measured by what someone of ordinary prudence would have done under the circumstances to avoid the injury or other loss.

Throughout the law of negligence, our preoccupation will be with the presence or absence of **risk**. Note that the general rule on duty requires us to identify the foreseeable *risk* of injury or other loss. A risk is simply a danger of an unwanted (and usually unintended) result. The foreseeability of the risk gives rise to an obligation (a duty) to use reasonable care to prevent the injury or loss.

risk The chance or danger that a loss or misfortune will occur. The danger of an unwanted (and usually unintended) result.

EXAMPLE

You are driving down the road late at night. It is raining and the road is slippery.

Your driving creates the risk of someone being injured. The facts trigger the application of the general rule on duty. It is foreseeable that someone may be injured when you are driving under such conditions. Therefore, you owe a duty to take reasonable precautions to prevent such an injury—to slow down, turn on the headlights, watch extra carefully for pedestrians and other cars, keep a safe distance between your car and the car in front of you, etc. The more foreseeable the injury, the greater is the need for precautions.

Foreseeability, however, is not the sole criterion used by the courts to determine whether a duty exists. We saw in Chapter 9, for example, that the foreseeability of emotional distress does not always trigger a duty to use reasonable care to prevent the distress. When someone is negligently killed, the wrongdoer is not liable for the predictable emotional distress that a large number of relatives of the diseased will feel upon hearing the news of the death. Most courts limit claims for *negligent infliction of emotional distress* (NIED) to persons who were in the zone of danger with the injured person and who suffered substantial physical symptoms as a result of the emotional distress (see Chapter 9).

In the remainder of this chapter we will discuss other important limitations on the general rule on duty through the following topics:

- unforeseeable plaintiff
- nonfeasance
- gratuitous undertakings
- duty to protect

Elsewhere in the book we cover additional limitations and special rules governing the existence and scope of duty in the law of negligence. For example:

- duty to a guest passenger (Chapter 14)
- duty among participants in contact sports (Chapter 16)
- duty in cases of wrongful conception, birth, or life (Chapter 22)
- duty to trespassers on land (Chapter 23)

When we examine duty in these categories of cases, we will see that policy considerations are often important factors in the decisions reached by the courts. The policy considerations include the moral blameworthiness of the defendant's conduct, the prevention of similar harm in the future, the availability of insurance to cover the resulting harm, and the burden that the community would suffer if a duty were found (or were not found) to exist.

Unfortunately, this area of the law can sometimes be confusing. This is due to the close interconnection among the first three elements of negligence (duty, breach of duty, and proximate cause) and the fact that foreseeability plays a central and overlapping role in all three.

UNFORESEEABLE PLAINTIFF

Consider the sequence of events in Exhibit 13–1, based on the famous New York case of *Palsgraf v. Long Island R.R.*[1] A railroad employee carelessly pushes a passenger onto a train. (We will call this passenger Plaintiff #1.) This causes the

Exhibit 13–1 Foreseeable and unforeseeable plaintiffs.

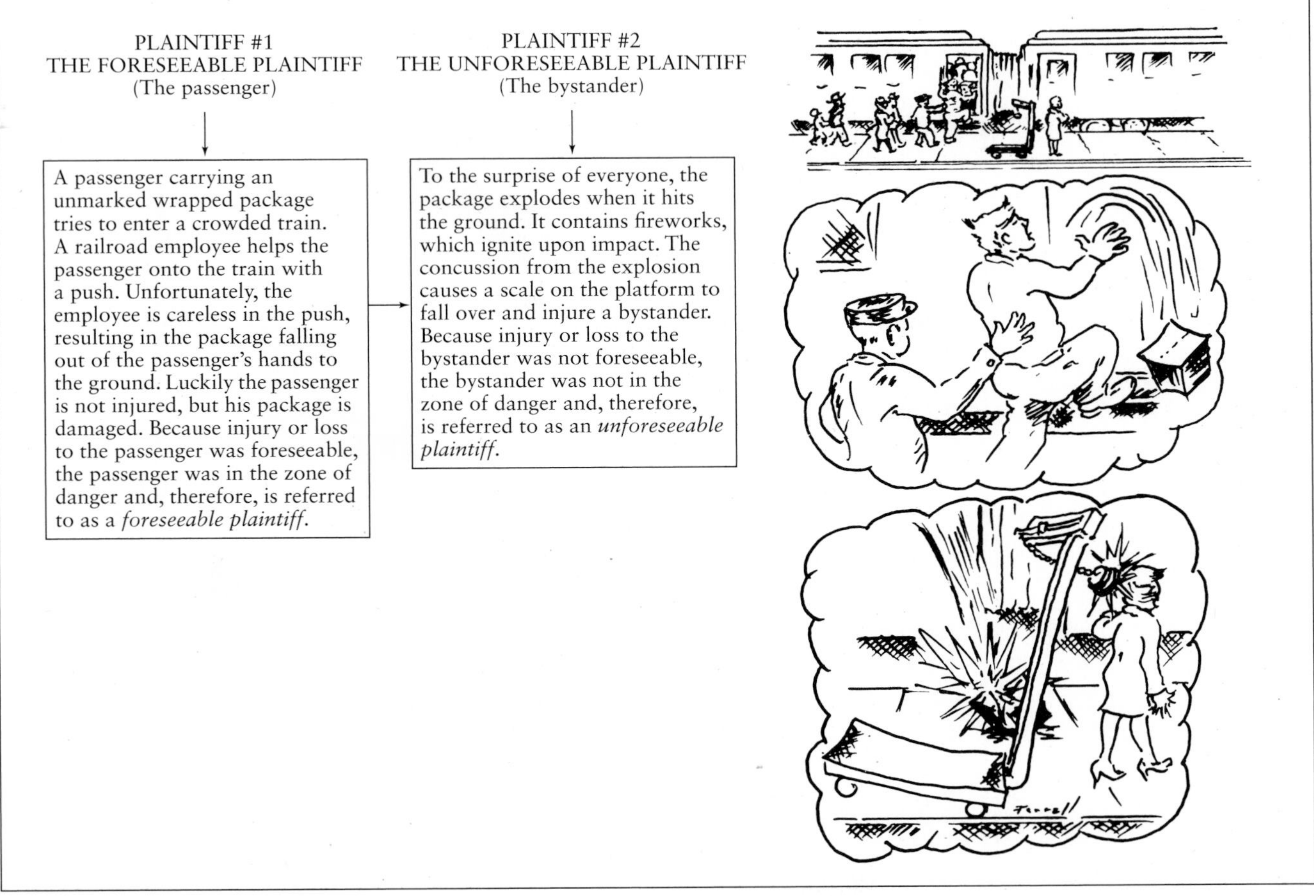

foreseeable plaintiff Someone whose presence in the zone of danger is foreseeable to the defendant.

zone of danger The area within which injury or other loss to the plaintiff is foreseeable.

unforeseeable plaintiff Someone whose presence in the zone of danger is unforeseeable to the defendant.

passenger to drop an unmarked package, which explodes. The blast causes a scale to hit a bystander. (We will call this bystander Plaintiff #2.)

Plaintiff #1 is a **foreseeable plaintiff** who will have no trouble suing the railroad for the negligence of its employee. A duty of due care is clearly owed to this passenger. Since the employee carelessly pushed the passenger, some harm was foreseeable to the passenger's property or to the person of the passenger. The passenger, therefore, was within the **zone of danger**. What about the bystander, Plaintiff #2? At the time the employee pushed the passenger onto the train, no one could foresee danger to the bystander from the falling package. Plaintiff #2 is an **unforeseeable plaintiff**. An essential question in Plaintiff #2's negligence suit against the railroad is whether a duty of due care was owed to this plaintiff. If not, then the first element of negligence cannot be established and hence the entire negligence cause of action will fall. How, then, do we determine whether a duty is owed to a person in Plaintiff #2's position? The majority and dissenting opinions in the *Palsgraf* case answered this question in very different ways. Both opinions in the case have been widely quoted, debated, and relied upon in the law of torts.

The majority opinion (written by Judge Cardozo) ruled that a duty of due care was owed only to Plaintiff #1. Unless you are foreseeably in the zone of danger, no duty is owed to you. When Plaintiff #1 was carelessly pushed by the railroad employee, harm was foreseeable to Plaintiff #1—harm to his property (the package) or harm to his person. Plaintiff #2, however, was not in the zone of danger. It was not foreseeable to the employee that harm could come to Plaintiff #2 by the careless push to Plaintiff #1. Therefore the majority opinion held that no duty was owed to Plaintiff #2. Her negligence action against the railroad failed. The dissenting opinion (written by Judge Andrews) took a broader view. A duty is owed to anyone in the world at large (in the general public) who might be injured because of the defendant's unreasonable conduct, even if the injured person was not in the zone of danger, so long as *someone* is in the zone of danger due to the defendant's unreasonable conduct. Under this principle, a duty *was* owed to Plaintiff #2 as well as to Plaintiff #1. Plaintiff #1 was in the zone of danger from the careless push by the employee. This led to an injury to Plaintiff #2 when the package exploded. To owe a duty to an injured person who is not in the zone of danger, all that is needed is for someone to be in the zone of danger.

There are limits, however, on how far the dissenting opinion would go in extending a duty to someone who was not in the zone of danger. Suppose that on the day after the railroad incident, Plaintiff #2 causes an accident that injures Plaintiff #3. Plaintiff #2 was driving her car and caused a collision with Plaintiff #3 because of the dizziness that Plaintiff #2 continued to feel after being hit by the scale on the railroad platform the day before. Would the dissenting opinion in *Palsgraf* conclude that the railroad owed a duty of due care to Plaintiff #3? Could Plaintiff #3 sue the railroad for causing Plaintiff #2 to collide with Plaintiff #3? No. The dissent would not go that far. How, then, would the dissent limit liability to persons who were not in the zone of danger when the original carelessness occurred? The answer is found in the principles of *proximate cause*. Under the dissenting opinion, a duty of due care is owed to anyone in the world who suffers an injury or other loss that is a proximate cause of the defendant's original carelessness.

Proximate cause (which we will study in detail in Chapter 15) establishes a cutoff of liability for injuries or losses that result from unreasonable conduct. As indicated, *Palsgraf* is a famous torts case. In the years since it was decided, some states have followed the majority opinion (a duty is owed only to someone in the zone of danger) and other states have followed the dissenting opinion (a duty is owed to anyone whose injury is the proximate cause of the defendant's carelessness even if the injured person was not in the zone of danger).

ASSIGNMENT 13.1

Helen and Grace are on a subway train on the way home from an office where they work together. Both are standing near one of the doors of the crowded train. Suddenly, the door opens while the train is moving and Helen falls out. Moments later, the train stops when the driver realizes what has happened. (Assume that the reason the door opened was negligent maintenance by the subway.) Grace watches in horror as Helen falls out the door. When the train stops, Grace immediately climbs down through the open door onto the tracks in order to try to help Helen. As Grace searches in the dark, she slips on a live rail and dies from electrocution. Luckily, Helen finds her way to safety with only minor injury. Helen and Grace's estate now bring separate negligence actions against the subway. Focus solely on the issue of duty.

a. Under the majority (Cardozo) opinion of *Palsgraf*, did the subway owe a duty to Helen? Explain. To Grace? Explain.
b. Under the dissenting (Andrews) opinion of *Palsgraf*, did the subway owe a duty to Helen? Explain. To Grace? Explain.

NONFEASANCE AND SPECIAL RELATIONSHIPS

Most defendants allege that their injury or other loss was due to the **affirmative conduct** (active behavior) of the defendant. Sometimes, however, the complaint is based on the defendant's *failure to act* (omission, inaction). Compare the two situations in Exhibit 13–2.

affirmative conduct Active behavior, activity; the opposite of inaction.

Exhibit 13–2
Affirmative conduct versus a failure to act.

AFFIRMATIVE CONDUCT	FAILURE TO ACT
Greg is driving his car 45 mph in a 30 mph residential zone. At an intersection, he hits the plaintiff because of excessive speed.	Tom and George are strangers in a store. Tom sees a display case about to fall on George but does nothing to prevent it even though Tom could have prevented it without hurting himself.

When Greg (in Exhibit 13–2) is sued by the plaintiff for negligence in the first situation, there will not be a problem establishing the existence of a duty. Affirmative conduct by Greg (his driving at an excessive speed) created a risk of foreseeable injury to the plaintiff. It is very easy to establish the existence of a duty when affirmative conduct (alone or in combination with inaction) creates such a risk. The vast majority of negligence cases involve at least some affirmative conduct. What about cases of inaction?

As we examine the issue of duty based on the failure to act, keep the following terminology in mind. If affirmative conduct is unreasonable, it is called **misfeasance.** The mere failure to act (whether or not the failure is unreasonable) is called **nonfeasance.** (A totally separate concept is **malfeasance**, which is wrongful conduct or inaction *by a public official.*)

misfeasance Affirmative conduct that is improper or unreasonable.

nonfeasance The failure to act; inaction; an omission. (Nonfeasance can be either wrongful or blameless.)

malfeasance Wrongful (illegal) conduct or inaction by a public official.

special relationship A relationship between persons that is the basis of a duty of reasonable care to avoid injury even in the absence of affirmative conduct.

Good Samaritan A person who comes to the aid of another without having a legal obligation to do so.

moral Pertaining to the goodness and badness of human behavior, which may or may not be embodied in the laws of our legal system.

natural law Inherent principles of conduct based on human nature rather than on formal laws imposed by society.

Now let us focus on the second hypothetical in Exhibit 13–2, involving Tom and George. Here we have *non*feasance, a failure to act. There was no affirmative conduct by Tom. He did nothing to create or increase the risk of injury to George. There is no duty in such situations to exercise care unless a **special relationship** exists between the parties.

In most cases involving strangers such as Tom and George, there is no such special relationship, and hence no duty to act with reasonable care. It is surprising to many to learn that *you have no duty to assist someone simply because it is possible for you to give assistance without harming yourself.* Nor does the mere foreseeability of injury give rise to a duty to give aid. According to the American Law Institute:

> The fact that the actor realizes or should realize that action on his part is necessary for another's aid or protection does not of itself impose upon him a duty to take such action.[2]

The classic example is the stranger who refuses to lift a finger to save the life of a drowning victim even though the stranger would be under no jeopardy in making the effort. There is no *legal* requirement to be a **Good Samaritan**. There may be a **moral** duty to help someone in distress, but many aspects of morality (e.g., kindness) are not embodied in enforceable laws. Moral duties derive from religion, customs, and principles of **natural law**. Some, but by no means all, moral duties find their way into the constitutional principles, statutes, and court holdings of our legal system.

If you become a Good Samaritan, you are volunteering your help. And you need to be careful in doing so. A Good Samaritan can be sued for negligence if he or she fails to use reasonable care in rendering assistance! Although special statutory protection for the Good Samaritan has recently been enacted, the fear of being sued continues to discourage many potential Good Samaritans from rendering assistance. (We will discuss this area of the law later in the section on Gratuitous Undertaking.)

What are the special relationships? The main ones are outlined in Exhibit 13–3.

A good deal of controversy centers on the problem of controlling the conduct of third parties who are *not* part of a special relationship.

EXAMPLE

Tom is a patient of Dr. Edward Smith, a psychotherapist. During a session, Tom tells Dr. Smith that he is going to kill his girlfriend. The latter is not a patient of Dr. Smith. The next day, Tom carries out his threat and kills his girlfriend.

The girlfriend's estate now brings a negligence action against Dr. Smith. Again, we have a nonfeasance problem. We have omissions: Dr. Smith did not warn the girlfriend of Tom's threat, he did not tell the police of the threat, he did not tell the girlfriend's family about the threat, etc. The question is whether Dr. Smith owed a *duty* to the girlfriend. He engaged in no affirmative conduct toward the girlfriend that placed her in danger or that increased the danger she was in because of Tom. Hence, we do not have misfeasance. There was no special relationship between Dr. Smith and the girlfriend. The traditional result, therefore, in such situations is that there is no duty and hence no liability for negligence. It should be noted, however, that not all states follow this traditional rule. Some states, and the *Restatement,*[3] will say that a duty of reasonable care *would* be owed by the doctor to the girlfriend in such a case.

California is one of the states that takes this position. It did so in the famous case of *Tarasoff v. Regents of University of California.*[4] This case is discussed in the *Soldano* case, which we will study on page 208.

Exhibit 13–3
Special relationships that create a duty to use reasonable care in nonfeasance cases.

Principle

In nonfeasance cases, there is no duty to use reasonable care (and hence no negligence) unless the plaintiff fits within a special relationship. If such a relationship does not exist, there is no duty to act, and hence the defendant's failure to act (nonfeasance) cannot constitute negligence. This conclusion applies only to nonfeasance cases. If the defendant has engaged in affirmative conduct, there is usually a duty to use reasonable care whether or not a special relationship exists between plaintiff and defendant.

Special Relationships

1. Common Carrier/Passenger

Duty: A passenger on a bus (Passenger #1) becomes ill or is in danger because of what another passenger (Passenger #2) is doing. A bus driver has a duty to use reasonable care to help Passenger #1 even if no affirmative conduct by the driver caused the trouble. This duty arises in nonfeasance cases because of the special relationship the law creates between a bus company (or other **common carrier**) and a passenger.

No Duty: Assume that another passenger (Passenger #3) sees that Passenger #1 is in trouble, but does nothing to assist Passenger #1. Does Passenger #1 have a negligence case against Passenger #3? No. To have a duty of reasonable care there must be affirmative conduct or a special relationship. There is no special relationship between passengers. If there was no affirmative conduct by Passenger #3 that endangered Passenger #1, then Passenger #3 had no duty to use reasonable care to help Passenger #1.

common carrier A company that holds itself out to the general public as engaged in transporting people or goods for a fee.

2. Innkeeper/Guest

Duty: A hotel guest becomes ill or is injured on the premises. The hotel has a duty to use reasonable care to help the guest even if no affirmative conduct by hotel staff caused the illness or injury. This duty arises in nonfeasance cases because of the special relationship the law creates between a hotel (or other innkeeper) and a guest.

No Duty: Assume that Guest #1 (in room 101) sees Guest #2 (a stranger in room 108) pass out in front of room 108. Guest #1 could easily use a hall phone to call for help. Instead, Guest #1 walks by and does nothing. Does Guest #2 have a negligence case against Guest #1? No. To have a duty of reasonable care there must be affirmative conduct or a special relationship. There is no special relationship between guests. If there was no affirmative conduct by Guest #1 that endangered Guest #2, then Guest #1 had no duty to use reasonable care to help Guest #2.

3. Employer/Employee

Duty: An employee is injured on the job. The employer has a duty to use reasonable care to help the employee even if no affirmative conduct by the employer caused the injury. This duty arises in nonfeasance cases because of the special relationship the law creates between employer and employee. (See also Chapter 28 on workers' compensation, which covers on-the-job injuries.)

No Duty: Assume that Employee #1 witnesses an injury suffered by Employee #2. Assume further that Employee #1 has no supervisory authority and did nothing to cause Employee #2's predicament. Employee #1 could easily call for help, but does nothing. Does Employee #2 have a negligence case against Employee #1? No. To have a duty of reasonable care there must be affirmative conduct or a special relationship. There is no special relationship between employees when one is not the supervisor of the other. If there was no affirmative conduct by Employee #1 that endangered Employee #2, then Employee #1 had no duty to use reasonable care to help Employee #2.

4. Occupier of Land/Invitee

Duty: A customer (Customer #1) in a department store becomes ill or is in danger because of what another customer (Customer #2) is doing. The store has a duty to use reasonable care to help Customer #1 even if no affirmative conduct by store employees caused the illness or danger. This duty arises in nonfeasance cases because of the

Exhibit 13–3
(Continued)

special relationship the law creates between owners or other occupiers of land (such as a department store) and **invitees** on the land (such as customers). (For more on **premises liability** and the duties owed to invitees, see Chapter 23.)

No Duty: Assume that Customer #3 witnesses the illness of Customer #1. Customer #3 could easily call for help, but does nothing. Does Customer #1 have a negligence case against Customer #3? No. To have a duty of reasonable care there must be affirmative conduct or a special relationship. There is no special relationship between customers. If there was no affirmative conduct by Customer #3 that endangered Customer #1, then Customer #3 had no duty to use reasonable care to help Customer #1.

5. Other special relationships in which a duty of reasonable care can exist in nonfeasance cases

- Parent/Child
- School/Student
- Jail or Prison/Inmate

invitee One who enters the land upon the express or implied invitation of the occupier of the land, in order to use the land for the purposes for which it is held open to the public or to pursue the business of the occupier.

premises liability The tort liability of landowners and others with possessory interests in land for injuries suffered due to conditions or activities on the land (premises). (See Chapter 23.)

ASSIGNMENT 13.2

Dr. George Donovan is treating an AIDS patient, Kevin Smith. Kevin tells Dr. Donovan that he no longer uses protection in his sexual relations with his roommate, whom Dr. Donovan has never met, and with Paul Grondon, who is also a patient of Dr. Donovan. By remaining silent about Kevin's sexual practices, could Dr. Donovan be sued for negligence by anyone who is infected with HIV by Kevin?

CASE

Soldano v. O'Daniels

141 Cal. App. 3d 443, 190 Cal. Rptr. 310 (1983)
California Court of Appeals, Fifth District

negligence claim

Background: *On August 9, 1977, Darrell Soldano was shot and killed at Happy Jack's Saloon. The defendant, O'Daniels, owns the Circle Inn, an eating establishment across the street from Happy Jack's. A patron at Happy Jack's Saloon came into the Circle Inn and informed a Circle Inn bartender that a man had been threatened at Happy Jack's. He asked the bartender either to call the police or to allow him to use the Circle Inn phone to call the police. The bartender refused even though it would have been convenient to grant either request and would have cost the defendant nothing. The victim's son sued the defendant for negligence, alleging that the Circle Inn employee (the bartender) breached a duty owed to the decedent. At the trial, the court granted the defendant a summary judgment. The plaintiff has now appealed to the California Court of Appeals for the Fifth District.*

Decision on Appeal: *The trial court judgment is reversed. The defendant had a duty to call the police or to allow the phone to be used for this purpose.*

OPINION OF COURT

Justice ANDREEN delivered the opinion of the court . . .

Does a business establishment incur liability . . . if it denies use of its telephone to a good samaritan who explains an emergency situation occurring without and wishes to call the police? . . .

There is a distinction, well rooted in the common law, between action and nonaction. It has found its way into the prestigious *Restatement Second of Torts* (hereafter cited as *"Restatement"*), which provides in section 314: "The fact that the actor realizes or should realize that action on his part is necessary for another's aid or protection does not of itself impose upon him a duty to take such action." . . .

Defendant argues that the request that its employee call the police is a request that it *do* something. He points to the established rule that one who has not created a peril ordinarily does not have a duty to take affirmative action to assist an imperiled person. It is urged that the alternative request of the patron from Happy Jack's Saloon that he be allowed to use defendant's telephone so that he personally could make the call is again a request that the defendant do something—assist another to give aid. . . .

The refusal of the law to recognize the moral obligation of one to aid another when he is in peril and when such aid may be given without danger and at little cost in effort has been roundly criticized. Prosser describes the case law sanctioning such inaction as a "refus[al] to recognize the moral obligation of common decency and common humanity" and characterizes some of these decisions as "shocking in the extreme. . . ." (Prosser, *Law of Torts* (4th ed. 1971) § 56, pp. 340–341.) . . .

As noted in *Tarasoff v. Regents of University of California* (1976) 17 Cal. 3d 425, 435, 551 P.2d 334, the courts have increased the instances in which affirmative duties are imposed not by direct rejection of the common law rule, but by expanding the list of special relationships which will justify departure from that rule. For instance, California courts have found special relationships in *Ellis v. D'Angelo* (1953) 116 Cal. App. 2d 310, 253 P.2d 675 (upholding a cause of action against parents who failed to warn a babysitter of the violent proclivities of their child), *Johnson v. State of California* (1968) 69 Cal. 2d 782, 447 P.2d 352 (upholding suit against the state for failure to warn foster parents of the dangerous tendencies of their ward), *Morgan v. County of Yuba* (1964) 230 Cal. App.2d 938, 41 Cal. Rptr. 508 (sustaining cause of action against a sheriff who had promised to warn decedent before releasing a dangerous prisoner, but failed to do so).

And in *Tarasoff,* a therapist was told by his patient that he intended to kill Tatiana Tarasoff [the patient's girlfriend]. The therapist and his supervisors predicted the patient presented a serious danger of violence. In fact he did, for he carried out his threat. The court held the patient-therapist relationship was enough to create a duty to exercise reasonable care to protect others from the foreseeable result of the patient's illness.

Section 314A of the *Restatement* lists other special relationships which create a duty to render aid, such as that of a common carrier to its passengers, an innkeeper to his guest, possessors of land who hold it open to the public, or one who has a custodial relationship to another. A duty may be created by an undertaking to give assistance. (See *Rest. 2d Torts*, § 321 et seq.)

Here there was no special relationship between the defendant and the deceased. It would be stretching the concept beyond recognition to assert there was a relationship between the defendant and the patron from Happy Jack's Saloon who wished to summon aid. But this does not end the matter. It is time to re-examine the common law rule of nonliability for nonfeasance in the special circumstances of the instant case. . . .

The [California] Supreme Court has identified certain factors to be considered in determining whether a duty is owed to third persons. These factors include: "the foreseeability of harm to the plaintiff, the degree of certainty that the plaintiff suffered injury, the closeness of the connection between the defendant's conduct and the injury suffered, the moral blame attached to the defendant's conduct, the policy of preventing future harm, the extent of the burden to the defendant and consequences to the community of imposing a duty to exercise care with resulting liability for breach, and the availability, cost, and prevalence of insurance for the risk involved." (*Rowland v. Christian* (1968) 69 Cal. 2d 108, 113, 70 Cal. Rptr. 97, 443 P. 2d 561.)

We examine those factors in reference to this case. (1) The harm to the decedent was abundantly foreseeable; it was imminent. The employee was expressly told that a man had been threatened. The employee was a bartender. As such he knew it is foreseeable that some people who drink alcohol in the milieu of a bar setting are prone to violence. (2) The certainty of decedent's injury is undisputed. (3) There is arguably a close connection between the employee's conduct and the injury: the patron wanted to use the phone to summon the police to intervene. The employee's refusal to allow the use of the phone prevented this anticipated intervention. If permitted to go to trial, the plaintiff may be able to show that the probable response time of the police would have been shorter than the time between the prohibited telephone call and the fatal shot. (4) The employee's conduct displayed a disregard for human life that can be characterized as morally wrong:* he was callously indifferent to the possibility that Darrell Soldano would die as the result of his refusal to allow a person to use the telephone. Under the circumstances before us the bartender's burden was minimal and exposed him to no risk: all he had to do was allow the use of the telephone. It would have cost him or his employer nothing. It could have saved a life. (5) Finding a duty in these circumstances would promote a policy of preventing future harm. A citizen would not be required to summon the police but would be required, in circumstances such as those before us, not to impede another who has chosen to summon aid. (6) We have no information on the question of the availability, cost, and prevalence of insurance for the risk, but note that the liability which is sought to be imposed here is that of employee negligence, which is covered by many insurance policies. (7) The extent of the burden on the defendant was minimal. . . .

As the Supreme Court has noted, the reluctance of the law to impose liability for nonfeasance, as distinguished from misfeasance, is in part due to the difficulties in setting standards and of making rules workable.

Many citizens simply "don't want to get involved." No rule should be adopted which would require a citizen to open up his or her house to a stranger so that the latter may use the telephone to call for emergency assistance. As Mrs. Alexander in Anthony Burgess' *A Clockwork Orange* learned to her horror, such an action may be fraught with danger. It does not follow, however, that use of a telephone in a public portion of a business should be refused for a legitimate emergency call. Imposing liability for such a refusal would not subject innocent citizens to possible attack by the "good samaritan," for it would be limited to an establishment open to the public during times when it is open to business, and to places within the establishment ordinarily accessible to the public. Nor would a stranger's mere assertion that an "emergency" situation is occurring create the duty to

*The moral right of plaintiff's decedent to have the defendant's bartender permit the telephone call is so apparent that legal philosophers treat such rights as given and requiring no supporting argument. (See Dworkin, *Taking Rights Seriously* (Harv. U. Press 1978) p. 99.) The concept flows from the principle that each member of a community has a right to have each other member treat him with a minimal respect due a fellow human being. (Id. at p. 98.)

utilize an accessible telephone because the duty would arise if and only if it were clearly conveyed that there exists an imminent danger of physical harm. (See *Rest. 2d Torts,* supra, § 327.)

Such a holding would not involve difficulties in proof, overburden the courts or unduly hamper self-determination or enterprise.

A business establishment such as the Circle Inn is open for profit. The owner encourages the public to enter, for his earnings depend on it. A telephone is a necessary adjunct to such a place. It is not unusual in such circumstances for patrons to use the telephone to call a taxicab or family member.

We acknowledge that defendant contracted for the use of his telephone, and its use is a species of property. But if it exists in a public place as defined above, there is no privacy or ownership interest in it such that the owner should be permitted to interfere with a good faith attempt to use it by a third person to come to the aid of another. . . .

We conclude that the bartender owed a duty to the plaintiff's decedent to permit the patron from Happy Jack's to place a call to the police or to place the call himself. It bears emphasizing that the duty in this case does not require that one must go to the aid of another. That is not the issue here. The employee was not the good samaritan intent on aiding another. The patron was.

It would not be appropriate to await legislative action in this area. The rule was fashioned in the common law tradition, as were the exceptions to the rule. To the extent this opinion expands the reach of section 327 of the *Restatement,* it represents logical and needed growth, the hallmark of the common law. . . . "Although the Legislature may of course speak to the subject, in the common law system the primary instruments of this evolution are the courts, adjudicating on a regular basis the rich variety of individual cases brought before them." (*Rodriguez v. Bethlehem Steel Corp.* (1974) 12 Cal. 3d 382, 394, 525 P.2d 669.) . . .

The creative and regenerative power of the law has been strong enough to break chains imposed by outmoded former decisions. What the courts have power to create, they also have power to modify, reject and recreate in response to the needs of a dynamic society. The exercise of this power is an imperative function of the courts and is the strength of the common law. . . .

The possible imposition of liability on the defendant in this case is not a global change in the law. It is but a slight departure from the "morally questionable" rule of nonliability for inaction absent a special relationship. . . . It is a logical extension of *Restatement* section 327 which imposes liability for negligent interference with a third person who the defendant knows is attempting to render necessary aid. However small it may be, it is a step which should be taken.

We conclude there are sufficient justiciable issues to permit the case to go to trial and therefore reverse.

ASSIGNMENT 13.3

a. Do you think the courts should provide a forum to redress every moral wrong? Should every moral duty be backed up by a legal duty? Does the *Soldano* court take this position?
b. What if the only phone at the Circle Inn were a pay phone? The Good Samaritan asks the bartender to let him borrow money for the emergency call. The bartender has the change readily available, but refuses to let him borrow the money. Does *Soldano* apply?
c. What point is the court making when it said that if "permitted to go to trial, the plaintiff may be able to show that the probable response time of the police would have been shorter than the time between the prohibited telephone call and the fatal shot"?
d. Your house is on fire. You do not have a phone. You run across the street and ask your neighbor to call 911 for help. The neighbor, who has never liked you, refuses. Later you sue the neighbor for refusing your request. Does *Soldano* apply?

GRATUITOUS UNDERTAKING

We now examine the third basis for the existence of a duty of reasonable care. The first two are affirmative conduct and special relationship. The third is a gratuitous undertaking. If you do something you do not have to do (a gratuitous undertaking), you have a duty to do it with reasonable care. To understand this area of the law, we first need to review some basic contract law.

undertaking Doing something; a task that is performed.

Doing something is referred to as an **undertaking.** There are two main kinds of undertakings: those that are gratuitous and those that are supported by consideration. A **gratuitous** undertaking is one that you are under no obligation to perform—you do it for free. For example, you like your neighbors so much that you decide to shovel their sidewalks without being asked to do so. If, however, the undertaking is supported by **consideration**, then something of value is received in exchange for the undertaking. There are four main categories of "something of value" that can be received: an act, a **forbearance**, a **promise** to perform an act, or a promise to refrain from performing an act.

gratuitous Pertaining to what is performed or given without a duty or obligation to do so; free.

consideration Something of value that is exchanged between parties. It can be an act, a forbearance (not performing an act), a promise to perform an act, or a promise to refrain from performing an act.

forbearance Refraining from exercising a right.

promise 1. A manifestation by a promisor (the person making the promise) of an intention to act or to refrain from acting in a specified way so as to justify the promisee (the person to whom the promise is made) in understanding that a commitment has been made. 2. To make a commitment.

EXAMPLES

- An act (e.g., giving someone $100)
- A forbearance (e.g., not bidding at an auction)
- A promise to perform an act (e.g., "I'll give you $100 next week")
- A promise to refrain from performing an act (e.g., "I won't bid at the auction next week)

Assume that a homeowner enters an agreement with Fred, an electrician, to rewire a house for $2,850. This is an undertaking supported by consideration. The consideration is an exchange of promises—the promise to rewire in exchange for $2,850. Because the rewiring is affirmative conduct, Fred has a duty to do the job with reasonable care. If carelessness causes a fire or some other damage, Fred is subject to negligence liability.

Now suppose that Fred *also* performs a gratuitous undertaking. While doing the rewiring, he discovers a leaking water valve in the bathroom. On his own, as a goodwill gesture, he decides to fix the valve. Because of his sloppiness and inexperience with plumbing, he causes additional damage to the water pipes. Working on the water pipes was a gratuitous undertaking. If Fred had done nothing (nonfeasance), he would not be liable for the additional damage to the water pipes. But a gratuitous undertaking can create a duty of reasonable care. Gratuitous undertakings are treated the same as affirmative conduct: both require an exercise of reasonable care. Let's look at another example.

EXAMPLE

Paula is visiting New York. She is a retired lifeguard who lives in California. While driving by a lake in New York, she sees a small, unattended child drowning close to the shore. She stops her car and decides to help. While she is carrying the child out of the water, the child's arm is broken due to Paula's carelessness in holding the child.

Paula did not have a duty to come to the aid of the child. There is no special relationship between Paula and the child. At the time she first saw the child, there was no affirmative conduct by Paula that endangered the child. But Paula did intervene (a gratuitous undertaking). Having decided to act, she now has an obligation to use reasonable care, which she arguably violated by holding the child carelessly.

A final dimension of gratuitous undertakings must be considered. In our electrician and ex-lifeguard examples, the gratuitous undertakings were carried out—Fred tried to fix the water valve and Paula tried to aid the child. Suppose, however, that the gratuitous conduct was a mere *promise* to do something.

EXAMPLE

Richard is injured on the road. A passerby sees Richard and says, "Don't do anything. Lie still. I'll get help." Soon another stranger comes by and asks Richard if he needs any help. He says, "No, someone has just gone for help." In fact, the original passerby did nothing, thinking (foolishly) that someone else would probably help Richard.

Did the original passerby owe Richard a *duty* to perform his **gratuitous promise** with reasonable care? The traditional answer has been no. More modern cases, however,

gratuitous promise A promise that one does not have a duty or obligation to make.

reliance Forming a belief, taking action, or refraining from action due in part to confidence in someone or something.

are beginning to find that a duty does exist as long as there has been **reliance** by plaintiff on the defendant's promise. Such was clearly the case with Richard, who did not seek further help because of the first passerby's promise. The promise increased the risk to Richard since it discouraged him from seeking further help.

ASSIGNMENT 13.4

a. ABC Realty Company leases space to Jones, who uses it as a grocery store. The lease agreement provides that all repairs to and maintenance of anything in the store (including the sprinkler system that is owned by ABC) are the responsibility of Jones. One day, an officer of ABC tells Jones that ABC is thinking about installing smoke detectors to replace the rusty sprinkler system. Two days later, a customer is injured in Jones's store due to a fire. The sprinkler system did not work and smoke detectors had not been installed. Did ABC owe a duty of reasonable care to the customer?

b. The B & O Railroad (RR) has a track that crosses a county street. For years, the RR stationed one of its employees at this crossing in order to warn oncoming traffic using the county street of an approaching train. There is no law that requires the RR to keep this employee at this crossing. You may assume that if the RR had never placed an employee at this crossing, a claim of negligence against the RR would not be successful. In fact, however, the RR had an employee at this crossing for years. As a train approached, the employee stepped out onto the county street and warned all traffic to stop. The employee lived in the area, and hence knew many of the automobile drivers that used the crossing. For the last three years, the RR had been experiencing declining business and never had more than two trains crossing the county street on any given day. The poor business also led to employee layoffs. On December 3rd, the employee who had worked at the county street crossing was laid off. She was not replaced. Hence, no RR employee now works at the county street crossing. In the view of the RR, the sound of an oncoming train would be warning enough to cars approaching the county street. On December 6th of the same year, Peter Blanchard was driving his truck on the county street in question. He was making a delivery from a neighboring state. He crashed into one of the RR trains at the point where the county street and the RR track meet. At all times Peter was driving carefully. It was a rainy night, and hence he did not hear the oncoming train. You may assume that Peter will be able to establish that the accident would not have happened if the RR employee (who was laid off on 12/3) had been on duty at the time of the accident. Peter Blanchard brings a negligence action against the B & O RR for its failure to have the employee present to warn traffic of oncoming trains at the crossing. Discuss the element of duty.

c. Rich is driving down the road carefully. Suddenly a storm begins. Visibility is very poor. Rich unavoidably hits a pedestrian, who suffers a broken leg. Rich gets out of the car and runs toward the pedestrian. When Rich sees the injury, he panics. He does not know what to do. Hours go by without Rich doing anything. The pedestrian dies. Did Rich owe the pedestrian a duty? Give an argument that he did. Give an argument that he did not.

PROTECTION FOR THE GOOD SAMARITAN

The Good Samaritan rules do not encourage people to come to the aid of their fellow citizens. "Try to do a good deed for someone and you end up being sued!" Some studies show that one in six potential volunteers refuse to become involved because of a fear of a lawsuit in the event that a mistake is made while trying to render aid. Even if the Good Samaritan wins the lawsuit, the embarrassment, time lost, and expense of defending oneself in court are enough to make many would-be rescuers conclude that the wiser course is to "mind my own business" rather than try to help a person in distress.

To combat this uncharitable inclination, a few states have passed laws *requiring* a citizen to become a Good Samaritan in emergency situations. Here is an example of this extreme approach:

> Minnesota Statutes Annotated § 604A.01
> Duty to assist. A person at the scene of an emergency who knows that another person is exposed to or has suffered grave physical harm shall, to the extent that the person can do so without danger or peril to self or others, give reasonable assistance to the exposed person. Reasonable assistance may include obtaining or attempting to obtain aid from law enforcement or medical personnel. A person who violates this subdivision is guilty of a petty misdemeanor.

Most states do not go this far. It is more common for a state to encourage rescue efforts by relieving Good Samaritans of civil liability for **ordinary negligence** in rendering emergency assistance. Ordinary negligence is simply unreasonable conduct that is not **recklessness** or **gross negligence.** If a mistake is made in rendering assistance, even an unreasonable mistake, there is no liability unless the mistake was reckless or grossly negligent.

ordinary negligence Conduct that is unreasonable but not gross or reckless. See also negligence.

recklessness The conscious taking of a risk by failing to exercise due care but without intending the consequences; the wanton disregard of a risk but neither desiring the consequences of the risk nor having substantially certain knowledge of the consequences.

gross negligence The failure to use even a small amount of care to avoid foreseeable harm.

In 1997, Congress passed the Volunteer Protection Act, which provides that "no volunteer of a nonprofit organization or governmental entity shall be liable for harm caused by an act or omission of the volunteer." There are exceptions, however, to this limitation of liability. For example, the volunteer can be liable for harm "caused by willful or criminal misconduct, gross negligence, reckless misconduct, or a conscious, flagrant indifference to the rights or safety of the individual harmed by the volunteer."[5] This federal act applies to every state unless the state already provides protection for the volunteer or unless the state elects not to have the act apply. If a state "opts out" of the act and does not have its own program of protection, the old rules apply—a Good Samaritan can be sued for ordinary negligence in such states. Most states, however, do have their own laws that protect Good Samaritans whose carelessness in rendering aid does not constitute more than ordinary negligence. (In Chapter 27 we will discuss the broader defense of charitable immunity. This immunity, where still applicable, protects organizations from tort liability.)

GOVERNMENT DUTY TO PROTECT

In this chapter our study of the first element of negligence (duty) has focused on whether the defendant owed a duty to the plaintiff. Most of the defendants we have examined were private parties being sued by other private parties. We shift now to the question of whether tort law can be used to enforce the government's duty to protect its citizens. Our focus here is not injury that results when a government employee injures a citizen (e.g., a police car hits a pedestrian) but rather injury that results when the government fails to protect a citizen. You will be reading the case of *Finn v. City of New York*, in which a citizen is asking the court "to proclaim a new and general duty of protection in the law of tort." New York has agreed to be sued, i.e., it has waived its **sovereign immunity** for tort claims. (As we will see in Chapter 27, sovereign immunity is the rule which provides that the state cannot be sued in its own courts without its consent.), The waiver of sovereign immunity in New York, however, does not cover all tort claims. The question in the *Finn* case is not whether the government has a duty to protect its citizens (it surely does), but rather whether a tort is committed when it fails in this duty.

sovereign immunity The sovereign (i.e., the state) cannot be sued in its courts without its consent. Also called governmental immunity.

CASE

Riss v. City of New York

22 N.Y.2d 579, 240 N.E.2d 860, 293 N.Y.S.2d 897 (1968)
Court of Appeals of New York

Background: *For more than six months, Linda Riss was terrorized by a rejected suitor, Burton Pugach. This miscreant, masquerading as a respectable attorney, repeatedly threatened to have Linda killed or maimed if she did not yield to him: "If I can't have you, no one else will have you, and when I get through with you, no one else will want you." In fear for her life, she contacted the police in February. One detective told her that she would have to be hurt before the police could do anything. In June, four months later, Linda became engaged to another man. At a party held to celebrate the event, she received a phone call warning her that it was her "last chance." Completely distraught, she called the police, begging for help, but was refused. The next day Pugach carried out his dire threats in the very manner he had foretold by having a hired thug throw lye in Linda's face. She was blinded in one eye and lost a good portion of her vision in the other. Her face was permanently scarred. After this attack, the authorities concluded that there was some basis for Linda's fears, and for the next three and one-half years, she was given around-the-clock protection. She sued the city for negligence. The trial court dismissed the complaint. The Appellate Division affirmed. The plaintiff now appeals to the Court of Appeals of New York.*

Decision on Appeal: *The judgment for the city is affirmed. The city is not liable to an assault victim for failure to supply police protection upon request.*

OPINION OF COURT

Judge BREITEL delivered the opinion of the court . . .

This appeal presents, in a very sympathetic framework, the issue of the liability of a municipality for failure to provide special protection to a member of the public who was repeatedly threatened with personal harm and eventually suffered dire personal injuries for lack of such protection. [The] . . . case involves the provision of a governmental service to protect the public generally from external hazards and particularly to control the activities of criminal wrongdoers. The amount of protection that may be provided is limited by the resources of the community and by a considered legislative-executive decision as to how those resources may be deployed. For the courts to proclaim a new and general duty of protection in the law of tort, even to those who may be the particular seekers of protection based on specific hazards, could and would inevitably determine how the limited police resources of the community should be allocated and without predictable limits. This is quite different from the predictable allocation of resources and liabilities when public hospitals, rapid transit systems, or even highways are provided.

Before such extension of responsibilities should be dictated by the indirect imposition of tort liabilities, there should be a legislative determination that that should be the scope of public responsibility. . . . When one considers the greatly increased amount of crime committed throughout the cities, but especially in certain portions of them, with a repetitive and predictable pattern, it is easy to see the consequences of fixing municipal liability upon a showing of probable need for and request for protection. To be sure these are grave problems at the present time, exciting high priority activity on the part of the national, state and local governments, to which the answers are neither simple, known, or presently within reasonable controls. To foist a presumed cure for these problems by judicial innovation of a new kind of liability in tort would be foolhardy indeed and an assumption of judicial wisdom and power not possessed by the courts. . . .

For all of these reasons, there is no warrant in judicial tradition or in the proper allocation of the powers of government for the courts, in the absence of legislation, to carve out an area of tort liability for police protection to members of the public. Quite distinguishable, of course, is the situation where the police authorities undertake responsibilities to particular members of the public and expose them, without adequate protection, to the risks which then materialize into actual losses (*Schuster v. City of New York,* 5 N.Y.2d 75, 180 N.Y.S.2d 265, 154 N.E.2d 534).

Accordingly, the order of the Appellate Division affirming the judgment of dismissal should be affirmed.

KEATING, Judge (dissenting).

No one questions the proposition that the first duty of government is to assure its citizens the opportunity to live in personal security. And no one who reads the record of Linda's ordeal can reach a conclusion other than that the City of New York, acting through its agent, completely and negligently failed to fulfill this obligation to Linda.

Linda has turned to the courts of this State for redress, asking that the city be held liable in damages for its negligent failure to protect her from harm. . . . If a private detective acts carelessly, no one would deny that a jury could find such conduct unacceptable. Why then is the city not required to live up to at least the same minimal standards of professional competence which would be demanded of a private detective?

Linda's reasoning seems so eminently sensible that surely it must come as a shock to her and to every citizen to hear the city argue and to learn that this court decides that the city has no duty to provide police protection to any given individual. What makes the city's position particularly difficult to understand is that, in conformity to the dictates of the law, Linda did not carry any weapon for self-defense. Thus, by a rather bitter irony she was required to rely for protection on the City of New York which now denies all responsibility to her. . . .

The city invokes the specter of a "crushing burden" if we should depart from the existing rule and enunciate even the limited proposition that the State and its municipalities can be held liable for the negligent acts of their police employees in executing whatever police services they do in fact provide. The fear of financial disaster is a myth. . . [I]n the past four or five years, New York City has been presented with an average of some 10,000 claims each year. The figure would sound ominous except for the fact the city has been paying out less than $8,000,000 on tort claims each year and this amount includes all those sidewalk defect and snow and ice cases about which the courts fret so often. . . . Certainly this is a slight burden in a budget of more than six billion dollars (less than two tenths of 1%) and of no importance as compared to the injustice of permitting unredressed wrongs to continue to go unrepaired. That Linda Riss should be asked to bear the loss, which should properly fall on the city if . . . her injuries resulted from the city's failure to provide sufficient police to protect Linda is contrary to the most elementary notions of justice. . . .

No one would claim that, under the facts here, the police were negligent when they did not give Linda protection after her first calls or visits to the police station in February. . . . The preliminary investigation was sufficient. If Linda had been attacked at this point, clearly there would be no liability here. When, however, as time went on and it was established that Linda was a reputable person, that other verifiable attempts to injure her or intimidate her had taken place, that other witnesses were available to support her claim that her life was being threatened, something more was required—either by way of further investigation or protection—than the statement that was made by one detective to Linda that she would have to be hurt before the police could do anything for her. . . .

If the police force of the City of New York is so understaffed that it is unable to cope with the everyday problem posed by the relatively few cases where single, known individuals threaten the lives of other persons, then indeed we have reached the danger line and the lives of all of us are in peril. If the police department is in such a deplorable state that the city, because of insufficient manpower, is truly unable to protect persons in Linda Riss' position, then liability not only should, but must be imposed. It will act as an effective inducement for public officials to provide at least a minimally adequate number of police. . . .

[I]f we were to hold the city liable here for the negligence of the police, courts would no more be interfering with the operations of the police department than they "meddle" in the affairs of the highway department when they hold the municipality liable for personal injuries resulting from defective sidewalks, or a private employer for the negligence of his employees. In other words, all the courts do in these municipal negligence cases is require officials to weigh the consequences of their decisions. If Linda Riss' injury resulted from the failure of the city to pay sufficient salaries to attract qualified and sufficient personnel, the full cost of that choice should become acknowledged in the same way as it has in other areas of municipal tort liability. Perhaps officials will find it less costly to choose the alternative of paying damages than changing their existing practices. That may be well and good, but the price for the refusal to provide for an adequate police force should not be borne by Linda Riss and all the other innocent victims of such decisions. . . .

The methods of dealing with the problem of crime are left completely to the city's discretion. All that the courts can do is make sure that the costs of the city's and its employees' mistakes are placed where they properly belong. . . . The order of the Appellate Division should be reversed and a new trial granted.

ASSIGNMENT 13.5

a. Which opinion in the *Riss* case is correct? The majority opinion of Judge Breitel or the dissenting opinion of Judge Keating? Why?
b. Is it relevant that eight months after Burton Pugach was released from a fourteen-year prison term, he married Linda Riss (en.wikipedia.org/wiki/Burt_Pugach)?
c. Is the *Riss* case consistent with the *Soldano* case? Why or why not?
d. Smith is an informant who helps the police arrest a criminal. In a news interview, the police tell a reporter that Smith was helpful in making the arrest. Two weeks later, Smith tells the police that he needs special protection because his life has been threatened. He is denied this protection. When he is murdered, his estate sues the city for negligently failing to protect him. Does *Riss* apply?

CHECK THE CITE

A father and his three children are killed by a motorist who suffered a seizure while driving. The motorist had a history of seizures. The widow and mother sued the state motor vehicle administration for negligence in failing to ensure that a driver with disabilities was capable of driving safely. Why did the court rule against the widow on this claim? Read the case of *Pulliam v. Motor Vehicle Administration*, 181 Md. App. 144, 955 A.2d 843 (Court of Special Appeals of Maryland 2008). To read the opinion online, (1) Go to the site of the Maryland courts (www.courts.state.md.us). Click Opinions. Select Court of Special Appeals for 2008. Scroll down to 181 Md. App. 144 for the *Pulliam* case. (2) Run a citation search ("955 A.2d 843") or a party search (Pulliam "Motor Vehicle" 2008) in the Legal Opinions and Journals database of Google Scholar (scholar.google.com).

PROJECT

In Google, Bing, or another general search engine, run the following search: *aa* Tarasoff (substitute the name of your state for *aa* in the search). Write a short essay in which you describe the impact of the *Tarasoff* opinion (discussed in the chapter) on the mental health profession in your state. You can consult as many websites as you wish, but you must quote from at least three separate sites.

ETHICS IN A TORTS PRACTICE

You are a paralegal working in the law office of Gavin Shirlynn, who is hired by insurance companies to represent policyholders of the insurance company in suits in which the policyholders are sued for negligence and other torts. The office limits itself to insurance defense of this kind. Shirlynn submits his hourly billings to the insurance company in compliance with the company's payment guidelines. One of the guidelines of the company is that all deposition summary work must be done by paralegals in the office. The attorney billing rate will not be paid for this task. Similarly, the office must delegate to the paralegal the task of conducting the initial interview with all policyholder clients. What ethical problems, if any, might exist?

SUMMARY

A duty is an obligation to conform to a standard of conduct prescribed by law. The general rule on duty is that whenever one's conduct creates a foreseeable risk of injury or other loss to someone else's person or property, a duty of reasonable care arises to take precautions to prevent the injury or loss. There are limitations on this general rule. For example, there are times when the foreseeability of injury will not give rise to a duty to use reasonable care to try to prevent that injury. In addition to foreseeability, other factors (e.g., the blameworthiness of the defendant's conduct) are considered by a court in deciding whether a duty of due care exists.

Under the majority opinion in the *Palsgraf* case, a duty is owed to a person who is foreseeably in the zone of danger. Under the dissenting opinion, a duty is owed to anyone in the world (in the general public) who might be injured because of defendant's unreasonable conduct even if this person is not in the zone of danger, so long as someone was in the zone of danger due to the defendant's unreasonable conduct and so long as the defendant's conduct was the proximate cause of the injury that occurred.

Nonfeasance alone does not create a duty unless there is a special relationship between the parties. Among the special relationships are common carrier and passenger, innkeeper and guest, and employer and employee. A doctor has a duty to warn (or take other reasonable steps to protect) a third party whom the doctor's patient has expressed an intent to physically harm even though there is no special relationship between the doctor and the third party.

If the defendant undertakes a task, he or she assumes a duty to perform it with reasonable care even though there was no initial duty to undertake it and even though the undertaking was gratuitous. If the defendant promises to undertake a task, he or she assumes a duty to perform the promise with reasonable care if the plaintiff relies on the promise, even though there was no initial duty to make or carry out the promise, i.e., even though the promise was gratuitous. Many states have laws that limit the liability of Good Samaritans to recklessness and gross negligence; they will not be liable for ordinary negligence. In general, a government entity is not liable in tort for failing to protect its citizens from harm by others.

KEY TERMS

duty *202*
risk *202*
foreseeable plaintiff *204*
zone of danger *204*
unforeseeable plaintiff *204*
affirmative conduct *205*
misfeasance *205*
nonfeasance *205*
malfeasance *205*
special relationship *206*
Good Samaritan *206*
moral *206*
natural law *206*
common carrier *207*
invitee *208*
premises liability *208*
undertaking *210*
gratuitous *211*
consideration *211*
forbearance *211*
promise *211*
gratuitous promise *211*
reliance *212*
ordinary negligence *213*
recklessness *213*
gross negligence *213*
sovereign immunity *213*

REVIEW QUESTIONS

1. What is a duty?
2. What is the general rule of duty in negligence cases?
3. What is a risk?
4. What is meant by a foreseeable plaintiff?
5. What is a zone of danger?
6. When does a duty arise to an unforeseeable plaintiff under the majority (Cardozo) opinion of *Palsgraf*?
7. When does a duty arise to an unforeseeable plaintiff under the dissenting (Andrews) opinion of *Palsgraf*?
8. What is affirmative conduct?
9. How does misfeasance differ from nonfeasance?
10. What is malfeasance?
11. What is a special relationship?
12. What are the major special relationships?
13. What is a common carrier?
14. What is an invitee?
15. What is premises liability?
16. When does a doctor have a duty of reasonable care to a person who is neither a patient nor someone with whom the doctor has a special relationship?
17. What is an undertaking?
18. How does a gratuitous undertaking differ from an undertaking supported by consideration?
19. What are the four categories of something of value that can constitute consideration?
20. How does a moral duty differ from a legal duty?
21. What is a Good Samaritan?
22. When does a Good Samaritan have a duty of reasonable care?
23. Can a duty arise to perform a gratuitous promise with reasonable care?
24. What is ordinary negligence?
25. What laws protect the Good Samaritan?
26. What is recklessness?
27. What is sovereign immunity?
28. Is a government body liable in tort for failing to protect its citizens?

HELPFUL WEBSITES

- **Duty in the Law of Negligence**
  law.jrank.org/pages/8788/Negligence.html
  en.wikipedia.org/wiki/Duty_of_care
- **The *Palsgraf* Case**
  www.courts.state.ny.us/history/cases/palsgraf_lirr.htm
  en.wikipedia.org/wiki/Palsgraf_v._Long_Island_Railroad_Co.
- ***Tarasoff* and the Duty to Third Parties**
  www.jaapl.org/cgi/reprint/32/3/263.pdf
  en.wikipedia.org/wiki/Tarasoff_v._Regents_of_the_University_of_California
- **In Google, Bing, or another search engine, run the following search: elements negligence duty tort.**

ENDNOTES

1. *Palsgraf v. Long Island R.R.*, 248 N.Y. 339, 162 N.E. 99, 59 A.L.R. 1253 (1928), one of the most famous tort cases in American legal history (www.courts.state.ny.us/history/cases/palsgraf_lirr.htm).
2. *Restatement (Second) of Torts* § 314 (1965).
3. *Restatement (Second) of Torts* § 315 (1965).
4. 17 Cal. 3d 425, 551 P.2d 334 (1976).
5. 42 U.S.C. § 14503 (2009) (www.law.cornell.edu/uscode/usc_sec_42_00014503----000-.html).

Student StudyWARE™ CD-ROM
For additional materials, please go to the student CD in this book.

CHAPTER

14

NEGLIGENCE: ELEMENT II: BREACH OF DUTY (UNREASONABLENESS)

CHAPTER OUTLINE

- Standard of Care: Reasonableness
- Breach-of-Duty (Unreasonableness) Equation
- Objective or Subjective Standard?
- Res Ipsa Loquitur (RIL)
- Custom and Usage
- Violation of a Statute
- Compliance with a Statute
- Gross Negligence (Unreasonableness) and Willful, Wanton, and Reckless Conduct
- Vicarious Liability

CHAPTER OBJECTIVES

After completing this chapter, you should be able to:

- State the major factors in the totality of circumstances that are assessed when determining whether a defendant acted unreasonably.
- Explain what is meant by reasonableness as a comparative standard.
- State the danger/caution hypothesis.
- State the components of the breach-of-duty equation.
- Understand the physical and mental characteristics of the reasonable person.
- Identify the elements of a res ipsa loquitur case.
- Understand how custom and usage can affect what constitutes a breach of duty.
- State the major relationships that will result in the imposition of vicarious liability.

reasonable care Ordinary prudence under the circumstances to avoid injury or other loss.

breach of duty Unreasonable conduct that endangers someone to whom you owe a duty of care. (If the duty owed is to avoid reckless conduct, then a breach of duty would be reckless conduct that endangers someone to whom you owe a duty of care.)

unreasonable The failure to use ordinary prudence under the circumstances to avoid injury or damage. A common synonym for unreasonable is *careless*.

standard of care The degree of care that the law requires in a particular case. In most cases, the standard is reasonableness—what an ordinary prudent person would do under the same or similar circumstances. In some cases, however, a lesser standard is used, such as a duty to avoid reckless conduct.

factor One of the circumstances or considerations that will be weighed in making a decision, no one of which is usually conclusive.

STANDARD OF CARE: REASONABLENESS

In Chapter 13, we studied the first element of negligence: duty. In the vast majority of cases, the duty is to use **reasonable care** to avoid injuring others, both bodily injury and property damage. Now we begin our examination of the second element of negligence: **breach of duty**. A breach of duty exists if the defendant engages in **unreasonable** conduct. When can we say that someone has acted unreasonably? One of the difficulties of tort law is defining what we mean by reasonableness as the **standard of care** by which to measure the breach of duty that leads to negligence liability. This difficulty will be our challenge in this chapter.

Totality of Circumstances

The beauty of reasonableness as a standard is that it is flexible enough to accommodate an infinite variety of situations. It is very versatile. On the other hand, the nightmare of reasonableness as a standard is that its determination requires a juggling act. All of the circumstances leading to the accident and injury must be assessed. At times, a slight change in any of the circumstances can produce a different result. Exhibit 14–1 identifies the **factors** that we must assess to determine whether someone acted reasonably. A factor is simply one of several circumstances or considerations that will be weighed in making a decision, no one of which is usually conclusive. (For more on factors, see Legal Analysis Guideline #12 in Chapter 2.) Note that the factors in Exhibit 14–1 cover a range of information such as data from the senses (e.g., what could be seen), identity and characteristics of the participants (e.g., their age and experience), earlier occurrences (e.g., prior accidents in the area), and assessment

Exhibit 14–1
Factors to be assessed in the determination of reasonableness.

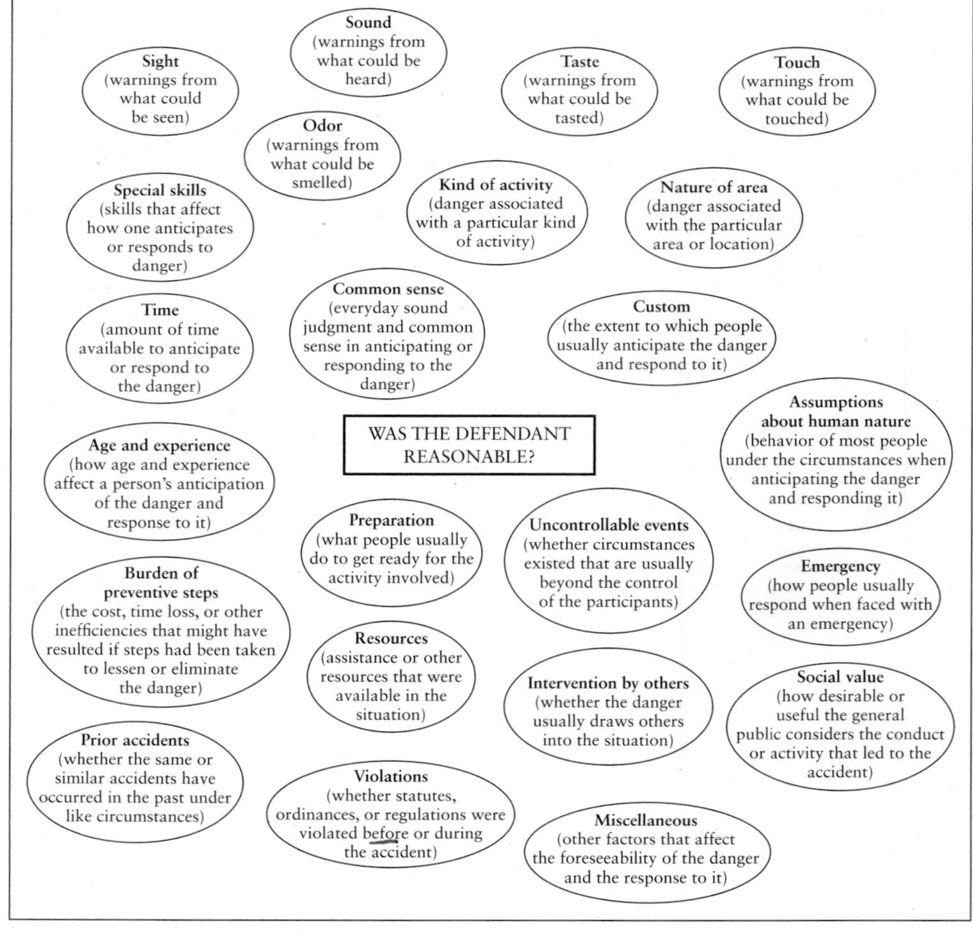

of alternatives (e.g., cost of preventive steps). It is this mix of factors that will help us answer the question of whether the defendant was reasonable.

Comparative Standard

To establish a breach of duty by showing unreasonable conduct on the part of the defendant in a negligence case, five steps are necessary:

Step 1: State the injury or other loss the plaintiff claims to have suffered because of the defendant.

Step 2: Identify the specific acts or omissions of the defendant about which the plaintiff is complaining.

Step 3: Turn back the clock in your mind to the time just before the acts and omissions identified in step 2. Ask yourself what a reasonable person would have done under the same or similar circumstances *at that time.* (You answer this question by using your common sense of what a reasonable person would have done and, most importantly, by reading what court opinions have said a reasonable person would have done in such circumstances.)

Step 4: Compare the specific acts and omissions of the defendant identified in step 2 with what you said a reasonable person would have done in step 3.

Step 5: Reach your conclusion:

a. If the comparison in step 4 tells you that the defendant did exactly what a reasonable person would have done (or that there is a substantial similarity), then you can conclude that the defendant acted reasonably, and hence there was no breach of duty.

b. If the comparison in step 4 tells you that a reasonable person would have done the opposite of what the defendant did (or would have acted substantially differently from the defendant), then you can conclude that the defendant acted unreasonably, and hence there was a breach of duty.

In flowchart form, the comparative process is outlined in Exhibit 14–2.

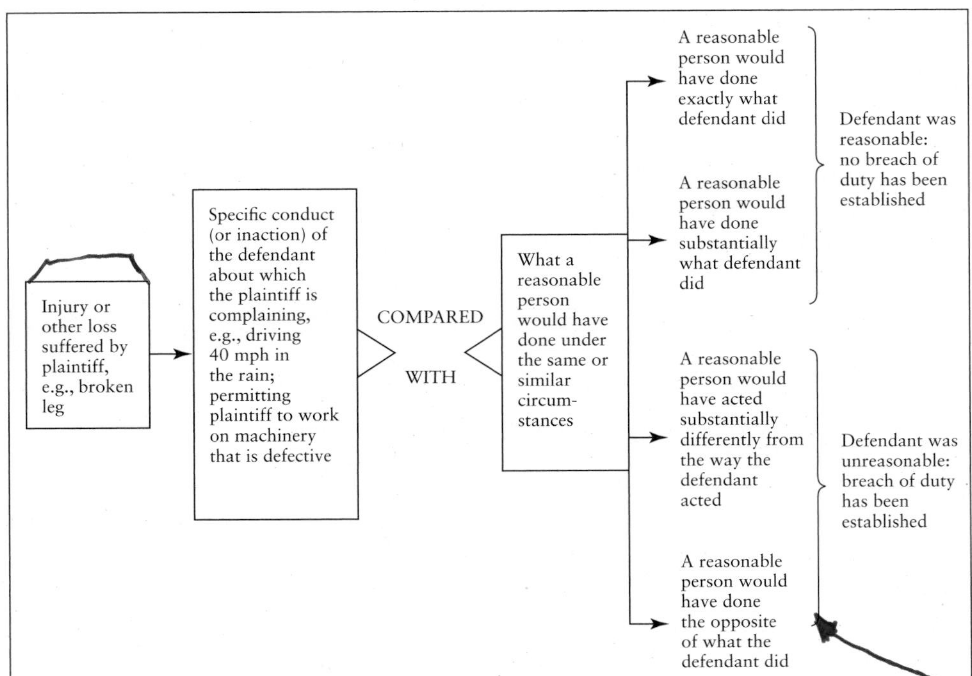

Exhibit 14–2
Reasonableness by comparison.

Examine the following excerpt from a memorandum of law that discusses the reasonableness of a truck driver who caused an accident on the road. Assume that one of the arguments against the truck driver was that he acted unreasonably when he took his eyes off the road just before the accident. Compare the following two responses to this argument:

> Response A:
>
> The truck driver took his eyes off the road to look at his instrument panel and it was at this point that the truck collided with the other car. The driver did nothing unreasonable in taking his eyes off the road for a moment.
>
> Response B:
>
> The truck driver took his eyes off the road to look at his instrument panel and it was at this point that the truck collided with the other car. It is not uncommon for truck drivers to take their eyes off the road. Reasonable drivers would not keep their eyes on the road at all times. For example, drivers glance at their gas gauge, their rear view mirror, etc. Trucks are designed with instrument panels that must be checked while the truck is moving. Drivers can't pull over every time they need to look away from the road. Hence, reasonable drivers must take their eyes off the road to look at their instrument panel, if only momentarily. It cannot be said, therefore, that the driver in this case was unreasonable simply because he took his eyes off the road momentarily.

Response A does not demonstrate an understanding of the comparative nature of reasonableness. There is no comparison between what the truck driver did and what a reasonable truck driver would have done. All we have is a *conclusory* statement that he acted reasonably. Response B, on the other hand, shows a very good grasp of the comparative nature of reasonableness. A major focus of the response is on what a reasonable truck driver would have done under the same circumstances. This is compared to what the truck driver in this case actually did. In your own legal analysis, you need to think and write like the author of Response B. Avoid the kind of conclusory analysis demonstrated in Response A.

Reasonableness versus Perfection

reasonable person Someone who uses ordinary prudence under the circumstances to avoid injury or damage; someone who is not careless. (Called the reasonable man in older cases.)

What is a **reasonable person**? Unfortunately, it is easier to define what a reasonable person is *not* than to say definitively what one is. First, let us look at the traditional definition:

> A reasonable person is someone who uses ordinary prudence under the circumstances to avoid injury or other loss. A reasonable person is someone who is not careless.

Note that the definition does not say that a reasonable person is someone who avoids injuring others. A reasonable person is not a perfect person. See Exhibit 14–3, which compares a perfect person, a reasonable person, and an unreasonable person.

BREACH-OF-DUTY (UNREASONABLENESS) EQUATION

breach-of-duty equation If the danger of a serious accident outweighs the burden or inconvenience of taking precautions to avoid the accident, the reasonable person would take those precautions. Furthermore, the more important or socially useful the activity, the more risks the reasonable person is willing to take.

To avoid injuring others, the reasonable person tries to avoid the dangers or risks of injury. How is this done? What mental process is used to decide what dangers to take precautions against? As we will see in the **breach-of-duty equation** (Exhibit 14–4), the reasonable person goes through a balancing process to decide what to do to avoid injuring someone. The foreseeability of injury is balanced against the burden of taking precautions in light of the importance or social value of what the defendant was doing before the accident. The equation is this balance; it answers the question of what is reasonable. Reasonable care is what a reasonable person would have done when balancing these factors. We know what the defendant

Perfect Person	Reasonable Person	Unreasonable Person
1. Never causes an accident.	**1.** Does cause accidents, but they are never due to carelessness.	**1.** Causes accidents due to carelessness.
2. Never makes a mistake leading to an accident.	**2.** Does make mistakes leading to accidents, but the mistakes are never careless.	**2.** Makes careless mistakes leading to accidents.
3. Reacts perfectly in an emergency in order to prevent accidents.	**3.** Reacts as cautiously as possible in an emergency, but can still make a mistake in an emergency that causes an accident. These mistakes, however, are not careless.	**3.** Reacts carelessly in an emergency, causing accidents.
4. Has the knowledge and experience needed to avoid accidents.	**4a.** Has the knowledge and experience commonly possessed, and uses them to help avoid accidents. **b.** When more expert knowledge and experience are available, the reasonable person uses them to help avoid accidents. **Note:** Even with the use of common or expert knowledge and experience, accidents can happen, but they are not due to carelessness.	**4a.** Does not have or fails to use the knowledge and experience common to everyone to help avoid accidents. **b.** When more expert knowledge and experience are available, the unreasonable person does not adequately use them to help prevent accidents.
5. Will undergo any inconvenience or burden to avoid an accident.	**5.** Will undergo only reasonable inconvenience or burden to avoid an accident.	**5.** Refuses to undergo even reasonable inconvenience or burden to avoid an accident.

Exhibit 14–3
Comparison of the conduct of a perfect person, a reasonable person, and an unreasonable person.

did or failed to do that led to the injury. Was the defendant unreasonable? Yes, if he or she did not balance the factors in substantially the same way that a reasonable person would have balanced them. No, if the defendant's balance was substantially the same as a reasonable person's balance.

Under the equation, if the danger of a serious accident outweighs the burden or inconvenience of taking precautions to avoid the accident, the reasonable person would take those precautions. The failure of the defendant to do so would mean that the defendant was unreasonable and had committed a breach of duty in the law of negligence. If, on the other hand, the danger of a serious accident is so slight that the danger would not outweigh the relatively high burden or inconvenience of the precautions that would be needed to avoid the accident, then the reasonable person would *not* take these precautions. The failure of the defendant, therefore, to take these precautions would not amount to a breach of duty. The defendant is not deemed to be unreasonable even though the precautions would have prevented the accident the defendant caused.

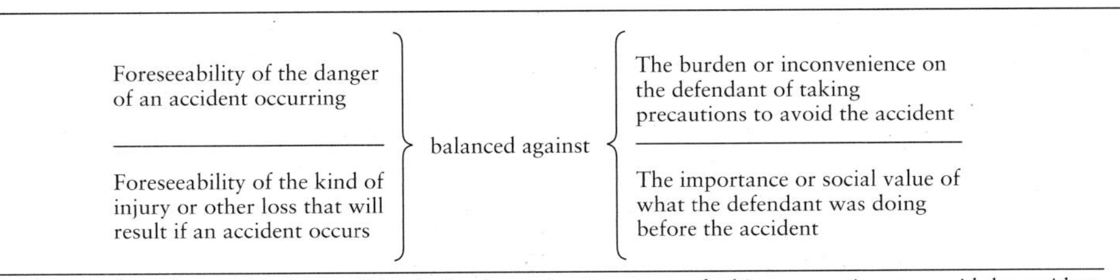

Exhibit 14–4
Breach-of-duty equation.

To better understand the breach-of-duty equation, we need to explore the following topics:

- danger/caution hypothesis
- foreseeability
- burden or inconvenience
- importance or social value

Danger/Caution Hypothesis

hypothesis An assumption or theory to be proven or disproven.

A **hypothesis** is an assumption or theory that needs to be tested. It is a statement that awaits proof or disproof. For every fact or group of facts, it is possible to state a hypothesis about the amount of danger that is present and the amount of caution that is needed to offset or eliminate the danger. The overriding principle is as follows: The greater the danger, the greater the caution needed. Here are some examples:

Facts: A sharp knife is on a table in a day care center.

Danger hypothesis: Knives are very attractive to children; knives are often easy for children to pick up; children do not appreciate the danger of knives; knives can seriously injure parts of the body with minimal force. Therefore, a sharp knife on a table in a day care center presents a *very great danger of serious injury* to one of the children.

Caution: Given the high risk of potential danger, a *great deal of caution* is needed to avoid an injury from the knife. Precautions include removing the knife from the room or locking it away so that it is not reachable by any of the children.

Facts: A sharp knife is on a table in a factory.

Danger hypothesis: Factories are places for adults; adults know how to handle sharp knives, especially if the knife is used in a factory where the workers are skilled. Therefore, a sharp knife on a table in a factory poses *almost no danger of injury* to anyone.

Caution: Given the minimal and almost nonexistent danger posed by the knife, *very little caution* is needed to avoid an injury from the knife.

ASSIGNMENT 14.1

Analyze the following fact situations. Assess the danger/caution hypothesis for each fact situation. Identify all possible dangers in each. How likely is each danger to lead to an injury? What kind of injury? In the light of your assessment of each danger, state how much caution is needed to avoid the injury. What precautions would a reasonable person take?

a. A sign on a busy three-lane street says, "USE TWO LANES GOING NORTH FROM 6 A.M. to 9:30 A.M. AND FROM 4:30 P.M. to 6:30 P.M. EXCEPT HOLIDAYS AND WEEKENDS. USE ONE LANE AT ALL OTHER TIMES."

b. Mary owns a motorcycle. Her friend, Leo, does not know how to drive it. Mary lets Leo drive the motorcycle while Mary is sitting right behind him, giving instructions as they drive in an empty lot.

c. The XYZ Chemical Company manufactures a new floor cleaner. On the label of the bottle containing the cleaner, there are very bright colors and a cartoon of a happy person cleaning the floor. The ingredients are listed on the label, plus a warning to keep the liquid away from eyes.

Of course, it can be argued that there is danger lurking in everything. It is possible to conceive of a set of acts in which any object (e.g., a tissue) could be used to injure someone in some way. This is not the kind of danger we are talking about in negligence law. It is not a breach of duty to fail to take precautions against every conceivable danger. Reasonableness does not require excessive caution.

How do we decide the amount of caution that *is* reasonable in a given set of circumstances? The answer depends on carefully weighing the elements of the breach-of-duty equation in Exhibit 14–4.

- **The FORESEEABILITY of an accident occurring.**
  The more foreseeable the accident is, the more caution a reasonable person would take to try to prevent the accident.
- **The FORESEEABILITY of the kind of injury or other loss that would result from the accident if it occurs.**
  The more serious the kind of injury or damage that is foreseeable, the more caution a reasonable person would take to prevent the accident.
- **The BURDEN or INCONVENIENCE that would be involved in taking the precautions necessary to avoid the accident.**
  The greater the burden or inconvenience, the less likely a reasonable person would take the precautions to avoid the accident.
- **The IMPORTANCE or SOCIAL VALUE of what the defendant was trying to do before the accident.**
  The more important or socially useful it is, the more likely a reasonable person would take risks in carrying it out.

Foreseeability

In Chapter 4 we took a detailed look at foreseeability and the methods by which it is determined. Review the factors that determine foreseeability in Exhibit 4–2. Our concern here is the foreseeability of the danger of an accident occurring (e.g., a customer slipping on a wet floor, a worker dropping a case of dynamite, an electric switch malfunctioning) and the danger of a particular kind of injury or damage occurring (e.g., death or crop destruction). As indicated in Exhibit 4–2, there are eight interrelated topics to be assessed:

- area analysis
- activity analysis
- people analysis
- preparation analysis
- assumptions about human nature
- historical data
- specific sensory data
- common sense

Assessing all of these topics will tell us what dangers a reasonable person would have foreseen. Once we know what a reasonable person would have foreseen, we know what the defendant *should* have foreseen.

Recall that we do not simply want to know *whether* the danger is foreseeable. The critical question is *how foreseeable* the danger is. Review the foreseeability spectrum in Exhibit 4–1 in Chapter 4. Are we talking about a danger that is only a slight possibility? A slight probability? A highly unusual danger? A certainty?

Burden or Inconvenience

Next, we examine the *burden or inconvenience* that would have to be borne in order to avoid the danger. Our focus at this point is not *who* should bear the burden or inconvenience, but *what* precisely this burden or inconvenience *is*. Suppose that the danger under discussion is a customer falling on a wet floor in a supermarket on a rainy day, and that the kind of injury posed by this danger is a broken or bruised limb. Assume that after assessing the foreseeability factors we conclude that both dangers are fairly probable. Now let us focus on the burden or inconvenience on the supermarket of eliminating the danger. Burdens or inconveniences fall into the interrelated categories of cost, time, and effectiveness:

- **Costs**
  How much money would have been needed to take steps to prevent the accident from happening? The cost of printing a sign saying "CAUTION, WET FLOOR"? The cost of an employee whose job on a rainy day is to mop the floor all day long? Every hour? The cost of a rug to absorb the water? The cost of closing the store on rainy days? Etc.
- **Time**
  How much time would have been lost in having the sign printed? How much time would have been lost in having an employee mop up all day? Every hour? Etc.
- **Effectiveness**
  As each precaution is considered, its impact on the defendant must be assessed. If a particular precaution had been taken, what impact would it have had on the overall effectiveness of what the defendant was doing before the accident? In short, how burdensome or inconvenient would it have been for the defendant to have taken the precaution? Going through the modest trouble of making and using a "WET FLOOR" sign would certainly not alter the effectiveness of the supermarket's business very much. Closing every day that it rains, however, would substantially disrupt the effectiveness of the supermarket's business. Indeed, this burden might amount to having to go out of business.

Importance or Social Value

social value The quality of something as measured by what the general public deems desirable or useful.

Finally, we examine the *importance or* **social value** of what the defendant was trying to do before the accident occurred. By social value we mean how desirable or useful the general public considers the defendant's conduct before the accident. Was the defendant driving to work? Watching a football game? Playing a practical joke? Skydiving for fun? Trying to cure cancer? Saving a child from a fire? The more beneficial or socially useful the activity, the more likely it is that a reasonable person would take risks to accomplish the goals involved. This does not mean that a reasonable person would never take any risks of injury if engaged in a mundane or frivolous task. It simply means that reasonable persons would take fewer risks of injuring someone else (or themselves) while engaged in such tasks than they would in tasks that we would all agree are more important and socially beneficial.

The reasonable person, therefore, will juggle all four components of the equation in order to decide what risks should be taken and what precautions should be taken to avoid an accident. The foreseeability of an accident, the foreseeability of the kind of injury, the burden or inconvenience of the precautions, and the importance or social value of the defendant's conduct must all be properly assessed. *Defendants will be found to have breached their duty if these factors were not assessed in the same or in substantially the same manner as a reasonable person would have assessed them.* This weighing or balancing of risks and benefits through the breach-of-duty equation is known as a **risk–benefit analysis** (also called cost-benefit analysis or risk-utility analysis).

risk–benefit analysis Deciding whether the risks outweigh the benefits. The determination of whether the benefits of proceeding without additional precautions outweigh the risk of harm that is foreseeable. Also called cost-benefit analysis and risk-utility analysis.

Cynics charge that some manufacturers distort the risk–benefit analysis when they decide whether to add a safety feature to a product. Let's look at an example of a risk–benefit analysis that a defendant should *not* make:

EXAMPLE

The XYZ Motor Company places the gas tank in the rear of its cars. Since rear-end collisions are common, this location of the tank increases the risk of fire explosion from such collisions when the tank is hit. A number of such explosions in fact occur, leading to judgments against XYZ. As the company prepares for next year's models, it must decide whether to keep the gas tank in the rear or to locate it in a place less likely to lead to such fire explosions. An XYZ engineer writes a memo that calculates how much future lawsuits might cost per vehicle if the tank is kept in the rear. To reach this figure, the cost of anticipated lawsuits is divided by the number of vehicles expected to be sold. This calculation leads to the conclusion that the litigation cost of keeping the tank in the rear would be only a few dollars per vehicle. Since this cost is less than what the company would have to spend to move the tank, the company decides to keep the tank in the rear for its new models.

Can you imagine how excited a personal-injury attorney would be to obtain a copy of such a memo? Ecstatic would be the more likely reaction. This is precisely what happened in 1999 when a California jury awarded $4.9 billion to six people who were severely burned when their General Motors car was rammed from behind by another vehicle. The verdict consisted of $107.6 million in compensatory damages and $4.8 billion in punitive damages. (The trial judge reduced the punitive damages to $1.09 billion, but allowed the compensatory award to stand. GM then announced that it would file an appeal.) The burns were caused by the explosion of the gas tank in the rear of the car in which the six plaintiffs were riding. Their attorney was able to introduce into evidence a "smoking-gun" memo written by Edward Ivey, a GM engineer. The memo estimated that the company would have to pay out $200,000 for each fatality caused by the placement of the gas tank. Based on the number of cars on the road, "Mr. Ivey came up with an estimate of the cost to GM of $2.40 per vehicle."[1] Other evidence showed that the cost of redesigning the car to prevent this kind of accident would have been $8.59 per vehicle. Although there was some controversy at the trial over what role the Ivey memo had in the design decisions of GM, there was little doubt that the memo had a major impact on the decision of the jury. GM refused to spend $8.59 to prevent the kind of tragedy that occurred. The plaintiffs' attorney told the jury that under a risk–benefit analysis, GM felt it was cheaper to pay $2.40 per car to litigate and settle the cases arising from the anticipated fatalities.

This is *not* the kind of analysis a reasonable manufacturer would make in applying the breach-of-duty equation in Exhibit 14–4. As we will see in Chapter 19 on products liability, a company should not make safety decisions solely on the basis of the cost of litigation. The question should not be how much a death or maiming is likely to cost the company through verdicts and settlements. The question should be how likely (foreseeable) is severe injury and what burdens would have to be undertaken to add a safety feature that would prevent the injury. If the burdens are relatively low and the risk of severe injury is high, a reasonable manufacturer would add the safety feature. This is very different from concluding that it would be cheaper to pay injured plaintiffs than to fix the problem by redesigning the product.

OBJECTIVE OR SUBJECTIVE STANDARD?

The reasonable person is the standard by which we judge the conduct of the defendant. Is this standard an objective standard or a subjective standard? The answer depends in part on who the defendant is and what the defendant was doing before the accident. As we will see, the reasonable person can be both an objective and a subjective standard.

A **subjective standard** means that something is assessed or measured solely by what one individual (e.g., the defendant) actually knew, felt, or did. When Bob says, "that car is attractive," he is probably using a subjective standard: attractiveness *to Bob*. An **objective standard** means that something is assessed or measured by

subjective standard A standard by which something is measured by what a person actually knew, felt, or did.

objective standard A standard by which something is measured by comparing (a) what a person actually knew, felt, or did with (b) what a reasonable person would have known, felt, or done under the same circumstances.

Exhibit 14–5
Objective and subjective standards.

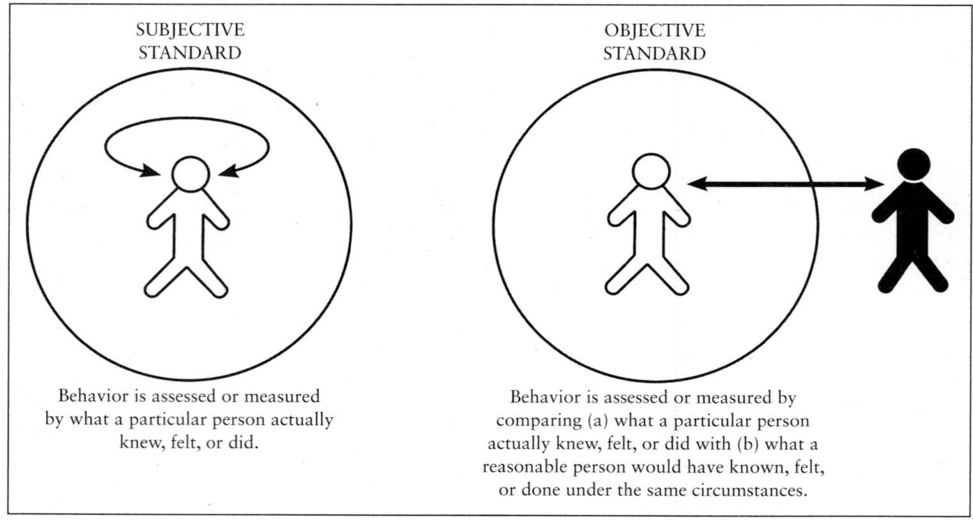

comparing what a particular person knew, felt, or did to what a reasonable person would have known, felt, or done under the same circumstances. See Exhibit 14–5.

There is, of course, no actual human being who holds the title of "reasonable person." The concept of the reasonable person was invented in order to provide juries with guidance on how to determine whether conduct that unintentionally caused injury was wrongful and hence negligent. (If the defendant *intended* the contact or injury, we are no longer talking about negligence as the cause of action. An intentional tort, e.g., battery, or a crime, e.g., aggravated assault, may have been committed.)

We now need to take a closer look at the reasonable person. We know that this person, not being perfect, can cause accidents. Such accidents, however, are never due to carelessness or imprudent behavior. (See Exhibit 14–3.) What else do we know about this person? We examine first the physical characteristics and then the mental characteristics of the reasonable person.

Physical Characteristics

If the defendant has a physical disability, the reasonableness of his or her conduct is measured by the reasonable person *with that disability.* Hence the standard is both objective (because the defendant's conduct is compared to what a reasonable person would have done) and subjective (because the reasonable person is assumed to have the physical disability of the defendant). Hence, if a blind man causes an accident and is sued, the blind man's conduct will be measured against what a reasonable *blind* person would have done under the same circumstances.

EXAMPLE
Fred is blind. While walking down the corridor, he bumps into the plaintiff, who falls and is injured. Fred was not using his cane at the time.

Assume that if Fred did not have a sight handicap, the accident would not have happened. This does not necessarily mean that Fred was negligent. The question is not how a reasonable person with no physical disabilities would have acted. The question is how a reasonable person who is blind would have acted. Phrased another way, how would a reasonable person have acted under the circumstances when one of those circumstances is his or her blindness? It may be that Fred was not acting unreasonably in walking without a cane. Suppose, for example, that he was taking a short walk in an area he was very familiar with and that he had other means of sensing objects around him. A reasonable person who is blind, therefore, might not use a cane in such a case.

Sometimes a physical handicap may require greater precautions than those expected of a person without such infirmities.

EXAMPLE

Mary has two broken legs. Yet she continues to drive. While driving one day on the freeway, she causes an accident.

If Mary is sued for negligence, the question will not be whether she was driving as best she could. This would be a totally subjective standard. Rather, the issue will be what the reasonable person with two broken legs would have done. It may be that such a person would not have driven on the freeway or would drive only cars that are specially equipped for handicapped drivers. If Mary failed to use such precautions, she acted unreasonably.

ASSIGNMENT 14.2

Fred is blind. While lighting a cigarette, he causes a fire because he did not know that he was in an area containing flammable materials. He could not see a sign that read, "Warning: Highly Flammable Vapors. No Smoking." Was Fred negligent?

Suppose that the defendant had physical capacities *beyond* that of most people, e.g., superior vision or quicker reflexes. The test of reasonableness for this defendant is what a reasonable person with these same physical strengths would have done. The reasonable person has the same physical weaknesses *and strengths* as the defendant.

Mental Characteristics (When the Defendant Is an Adult)

Here we are talking about knowledge, intelligence, and overall mental ability that comes from experience and learning. In this regard, the reasonable person is neither exceptionally bright, nor of low intelligence. The reasonable person has the basic knowledge and intelligence needed in everyday life to handle the common occurrences of living. For example, a reasonable person would know that an exposed electrical wire can be very dangerous, but is not expected to know how to repair wire cables. A reasonable person would know that a child in a large body of water can drown, but is not expected to know how to perform complicated medical procedures on a drowning victim.

Suppose that the defendant has a mental illness or deficiency that prevents him or her from knowing that electricity is dangerous or that water can drown people. Is this defendant still held to the standard of the reasonable person who has no such illness or deficiency? Yes. Such defendants are therefore held to a standard that they cannot meet. The standard as to mental characteristics is fully objective. For physical handicaps, discussed earlier, the test is what the reasonable person *with defendant's physical handicap* would have done. For mental disabilities in an adult, the test is what a reasonable person *without defendant's mental disabilities* would have done.

Suppose, however, that the defendant has mental strengths beyond that expected of everyone. For example, the defendant may be a doctor, an electrician, a police officer, etc. When this individual causes an injury, the standard of performance will be the reasonable person *with this special knowledge or skill.* Hence, the standard is subjective in the sense that we are talking about the special knowledge or skill *of the defendant,* but is objective in that we are comparing the defendant's conduct with that *of a reasonable person* with that knowledge or skill.

The special problems involving a doctor's skills (medical malpractice) and an attorney's skills (legal malpractice) will be discussed in Chapter 18.

Mental Characteristics (When the Defendant Is a Child)

An exception is made when the defendant is a child. When assessing breach of duty by a child, the standard is substantially subjective: What would a reasonable child of the age and intelligence of the defendant have done under the same or similar circumstances? There is, however, an exception to this exception. When the child is engaging in an adult activity, such as driving a car, the child will be held to the standard of a reasonable *adult.*

When we study torts associated with land in Chapter 23, we will examine the *attractive nuisance doctrine,* which is a special application of the reasonableness standard to trespassing children.

Recap on the Reasonable Person

- Reasonableness is determined by comparing the conduct of the defendant with the conduct of a reasonable person.
- Physically, a reasonable person has the same strengths and weaknesses as the defendant.
- Mentally, the reasonable person has the basic knowledge and intelligence needed in everyday life, even if the defendant does not.
- If the defendant has more than minimum knowledge and skills (e.g., has professional knowledge and skills), then the reasonable person is deemed to have the same knowledge and skills.
- If the defendant is a child, the standard is a reasonable child of the age and intelligence of the defendant, unless the defendant was engaging in an adult activity, in which case the standard is the reasonable adult.

RES IPSA LOQUITUR (RIL)

res ipsa loquitur ("the thing speaks for itself") An inference of the defendant's unreasonableness (breach of duty) that allows the plaintiff's case to go to the jury, which may then agree or disagree that the defendant was unreasonable.

Res ipsa loquitur (RIL) means "the thing speaks for itself." It is a doctrine used by a plaintiff having trouble proving the defendant's breach of duty—the defendant's unreasonableness. RIL is an evidentiary tool designed to give the plaintiff a break in certain kinds of situations.

EXAMPLE

Plaintiff sues the owner of a building for negligence after being injured in an elevator that suddenly crashed to the basement from the second floor. The *only* evidence plaintiff is able to introduce is the fact of being in the elevator when it collapsed.

Without the aid of RIL, the plaintiff would lose because of the failure to establish the second element of negligence—breach of duty. A trial judge would probably refuse to send the case to the jury. Litigants are not allowed to have the jury consider an issue unless evidence is introduced on that issue. Where is the specific evidence that the building owner was unreasonable in the maintenance of the elevator? There is none. All we know is that the accident happened. If, however, RIL applies in such a case, the jury will be allowed to draw an inference of unreasonableness. In effect, RIL simply allows the plaintiff to get his or her case to the jury. It does *not* mean that the plaintiff has won the case. Once the jury has the case, it is free to come to the conclusion that the defendant was *not* unreasonable.

What are the elements of a RIL case, in which the inference of unreasonableness can be drawn simply by reason of the fact that the accident happened? What does the plaintiff have to prove in order to get the case to the jury and require the latter to consider (but not necessarily accept) the inference of the defendant's unreasonableness? The three basic elements that must be established by the plaintiff are as follows:

Elements of Res Ipsa Loquitur

1. The event producing the harm was of a kind that ordinarily does not occur in the absence of someone's negligence. It is more likely than not due to someone's unreasonableness.
2. The event producing the harm was caused by an agency or instrumentality within the defendant's exclusive control. It is more likely than not due to the defendant's unreasonableness.
3. The event producing the harm was not due to any voluntary action or contribution on the part of the plaintiff. The plaintiff is not a responsible cause of the accident.

Let's take a closer look at each of these RIL elements.

More Likely Than Not Due to Someone's Unreasonableness

EXAMPLE

Tom is driving his car down the street. Suddenly, his front tire blows out. His car runs into plaintiff's car. Plaintiff sues Tom for negligence. The only evidence of unreasonableness introduced by the plaintiff is the fact of the tire blowout. (Assume that none of the parties have insurance and that the products liability causes of action we will consider in Chapter 19 are not involved. Here our focus is negligence.) Is this a RIL case?

No. The first element of a RIL case has not been satisfied. The most likely explanation of the tire blowout is *not* someone's unreasonableness. An equally likely explanation is that Tom unknowingly and quite innocently ran over a nail or other sharp object. To be sure, Tom's unreasonableness is a *possible* explanation. A mere possibility of unreasonableness, however, is not enough for the first element of a RIL case.

Compare the tire blowout case with the elevator case mentioned earlier. Can it be said that it is more likely than not that the explanation for an elevator falling from the second floor is someone's unreasonableness? The answer in this case is yes. One might indeed go so far as to say that it is highly likely that someone was unreasonable. Here are some of the arguments that could be made in support of this conclusion:

- It is commonly known that elevators require frequent inspections.
- If the inspections are adequate, they should reveal defects.
- A falling elevator can cause severe damage to passengers.
- Given the severity of the potential damage, one would expect very careful maintenance by those in charge of the operation and safety of the elevator; when an elevator falls, the likelihood is that this kind of care was not given.
- Elevators have been in existence for a long time; they are not mysterious machines we know very little about; hence, we cannot say that the mishap was probably due to some unknown factor.
- There is safety equipment on an elevator system; if this equipment were being maintained properly (reasonably), it is unlikely that the collapse would occur.

The plaintiff does not have to prove that the *only* explanation for the accident was someone's unreasonableness. The plaintiff does not have to prove that no other cause is possible. The test for this first element is whether unreasonableness by someone is *more likely than not* the explanation. (See Exhibit 14–6.) Hence, a defendant does not defeat a RIL case simply by showing that it is *possible* that the accident was *not* due to unreasonableness.

Exhibit 14–6
Spectrum of likelihood.

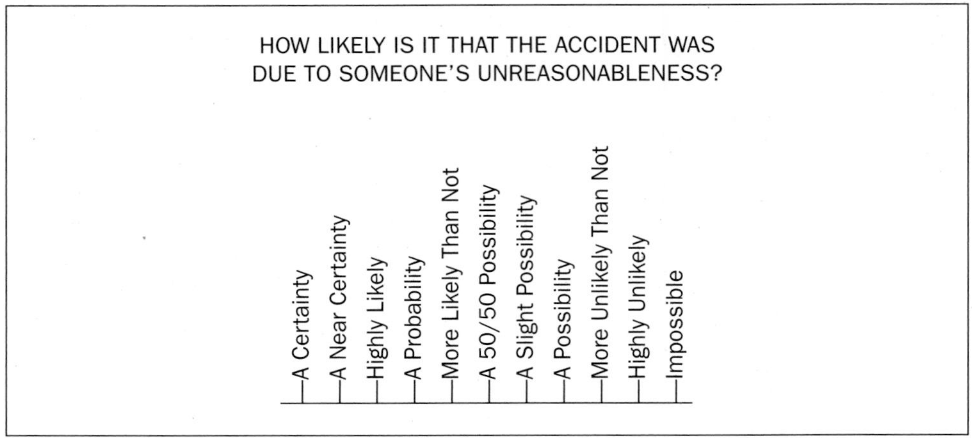

ASSIGNMENT 14.3

Examine the following list of accidents. How likely is it that each accident was due to someone's unreasonableness? Where on the "spectrum of likelihood" does each accident fall? Give reasons for your answer. If more than one answer is possible, explain all the answers. In each case you can assume that the person injured is trying to get to the jury on a RIL theory. Assume that the only evidence available is the fact of the accident.

a. A passenger is injured when an airplane explodes on the runway before takeoff.
b. Electricity leaks from a wire and injures a child.
c. A small insect is found in a can of soup, injuring a consumer.
d. A nail is found in a can of soup, injuring a consumer.
e. Two cars collide on the street, injuring a pedestrian.
f. A car collides into a parked car, damaging the latter.
g. A bottle of soda explodes, injuring a customer.
h. Cattle stray onto a road, damaging a parked car.

More Likely Than Not Due to Defendant's Unreasonableness

When the first element of RIL is established, we know that the accident was more likely than not due to *someone's* unreasonableness. In a lawsuit, of course, you do not sue a vague someone—you must sue the *defendant*. The second element of RIL requires the plaintiff to show that it is more likely than not that the accident was caused by the unreasonableness *of the defendant*. The "spectrum of likelihood" in Exhibit 14–6 for the first element applies here as well. If the unreasonableness of the defendant is a mere possibility, or if there is a 50/50 possibility that the accident was due to the unreasonableness of someone other than the defendant, then the second element of RIL has not been established.

EXAMPLE

Mary is a passenger on XYZ Airlines, which manufactures and flies its own commercial planes. While Mary's plane is flying over the ocean, it disappears. Mary's estate sues XYZ for negligence and tries to get its case to the jury on a RIL theory. The only evidence of unreasonableness offered by the estate is the fact that the plane disappeared.

Can it be said that it is more likely than not that the defendant's (XYZ's) unreasonableness caused the disappearance of the plane, e.g., due to a defectively built or maintained plane, or due to a carelessly flown plane? It is surely *possible* that other causes created the disappearance (e.g., a sudden violent storm that could not have been anticipated, a bomb concealed in luggage that could not be detected by current equipment, another passenger who went insane). It is possible that there was no unreasonableness by the defendant, XYZ Airlines. Yet, a jury could still conclude that the defendant's unreasonableness was more likely than not the cause of the accident leading to the disappearance. XYZ Airlines had exclusive control of the plane—it built and operated the plane. Airplane travel is very common in our society. Crashes are thoroughly investigated and the results usually point to some defect in the design, construction, or operation of the plane—or at least one could reasonably argue this position. Given XYZ's exclusive control, a jury could, therefore, conclude that the disappearance was more likely than not due to XYZ's unreasonableness.

Two other major issues need to be considered in connection with the second element of RIL: 1. What if the defendant was not in exclusive control of what caused the accident? 2. What if more than one person is sued and not all of them could have caused the accident?

1. What if the defendant was not in exclusive control of what caused the accident? One way to show it is more likely than not that the accident was due to the defendant's unreasonableness is to show that the event producing the harm was caused by an agency or instrumentality within the defendant's exclusive control. But such control may not exist. Assume that a soda bottle explodes in the plaintiff's hands. Before the bottle reached the plaintiff, it passed through several hands in addition to those of the manufacturer. A trucking company, for example, as well as one or more distributor/retailers may have made some contact with the bottle. It is admittedly difficult for the consumer to use RIL to show that it was the manufacturer's unreasonableness that was responsible for the explosion of the bottle. The law, however, tends to be somewhat lenient on plaintiffs in such cases, knowing the tremendous problem of proof that they have. The second element of RIL can still apply if the plaintiff submits enough evidence to enable a jury to conclude that the explosion was *probably not* due to anyone else in the chain of distribution between the manufacturer and consumer. Examples of such evidence include:

- evidence of careful handling of the bottle once it left the manufacturer, or the absence of evidence of careless handling during this time
- no evidence the bottle was dropped once it left the manufacturer
- no improper storage indicated

Such evidence, although fairly weak in itself, is usually sufficient to permit a jury to rationally eliminate other potential causes so as to conclude that it is more likely than not that the unreasonableness of the defendant (here, the manufacturer) caused the bottle to explode. If, of course, there is strong specific evidence to the contrary (e.g., evidence of vandalism or dropping after the bottle left the hands of the manufacturer), the plaintiff will have great difficulty establishing the second element of RIL.

Keep in mind that our focus here is on the tort of negligence. In Chapter 19 we will consider additional causes of action (e.g., strict liability in tort) that do not pose the kinds of proof problems that exist when one sues on a negligence cause of action.

ASSIGNMENT 14.4

In the following two cases, has the second element of RIL been established? Be sure to include a discussion of possible explanations in each case. What further evidence would you try to obtain in both cases?

a. Richard is a customer in Karen's supermarket. He slips on a ripe, yellow banana peel and is injured.
b. Bob is a customer in Karen's supermarket. He slips on a black, moldy banana peel and is injured.

2. What if more than one person is sued and not all of them could have caused the accident? The classic RIL case involving multiple defendants is *Ybarra v. Spangard*,[2] in which a patient received an injury while unconscious. The patient sued all the doctors, nurses, and other hospital employees involved. Since the plaintiff was unconscious at the time of the injury, there was no way for the plaintiff to give direct testimony about which of the defendants was or was not responsible. No other evidence was available. Hence, according to our test on the second element of RIL, the plaintiff could not show that it was more likely than not that the unreasonableness of any of the individual defendants caused the injury. Remarkably, however, the court in *Ybarra* allowed the application of RIL against all of the defendants. This had the practical effect of forcing these defendants to decide among themselves who was responsible. Failing to do this, **joint and several liability** would have resulted. This means each defendant is liable for all the damages suffered by the plaintiff, who can sue any or all of the defendants until 100 percent of the damages are recovered. (An individual defendant who is joint and severally liable cannot force the plaintiff to collect part of the damages from the other defendants. In Chapter 16 we will discuss whether defendants who have paid more than their share of the damages can obtain *contribution* from the other defendants.)

joint and several liability
Legally responsible together and individually. Each wrongdoer is individually responsible for the *entire* judgment; the plaintiff can choose to collect from one wrongdoer or from all of them until the judgment is satisfied.

Not all states follow the *Ybarra* case. Many would deny the application of RIL in such cases because of the difficulty of establishing the second element of RIL. The unusual ruling in *Ybarra* may have been due to a special duty of care that medical personnel owe patients and to the fact that when the accident occurred, there was a preexisting cooperative relationship among all the defendants.[3]

Plaintiff Is Not a Responsible Cause of the Accident

The final element of RIL the plaintiff must establish is that the plaintiff was not a responsible cause of the accident. In the vast majority of cases, this means little more than plaintiff's showing that there was no **contributory negligence** (or more accurately, showing that the plaintiff's own unreasonableness, if any, did not cause the accident). In the bottle explosion case, for example, the plaintiff must show that there is no evidence he or she mishandled or dropped the bottle while holding it.

contributory negligence The failure of plaintiffs to take reasonable precautions for their protection, helping to cause their own injury or other loss.

Recall that one of the reasons RIL was created was to help parties get to the jury when they do not have specific evidence of unreasonable conduct. Suppose, however, that a plaintiff has some evidence of unreasonableness but would also like to use RIL. Is this possible? The case of *Ward v. Forrester Day Care, Inc.* answers this question.

CASE

Ward v. Forrester Day Care, Inc.

547 So. 2d 410 (1989)
Supreme Court of Alabama

Background: *The parents of an eleven-week-old child sued a day care center for negligently causing the child's broken arm. The trial court entered summary judgment for the center. The case is now on appeal before the Supreme Court of Alabama.*

Decision on Appeal: *Reversed and remanded. Summary judgment should not have been granted. The case should have gone to the jury on a theory of RIL.*

OPINION OF COURT

Justice MADDOX delivered the opinion of the court . . .

On April 29, 1987, Radney Garrett Ward, an 11-week-old baby boy, was left at Forrester day care center in Dothan, operated by the defendant. The parents of baby Garrett, Radney Ward, Sr., and Margaret Ward, did not see their child until approximately 5:30 or 6:00 that afternoon, when he was picked up by Radney Ward, Sr. When the child was lifted out of his chair that afternoon, he screamed "a very unusual scream," according to the plaintiffs, causing them to suspect that something was wrong with him. The Wards said they examined him to determine if something was wrong with him, but they could not discover what caused him to scream. The next day, the child was brought back to Forrester day care center and was left for the day. Mr. and Mrs. Ward said that when Garrett was taken home on the afternoon of April 30, they noticed swelling on his right wrist. The next morning, they took young Garrett to his pediatrician, Dr. Barron, who instructed them to take him to Dr. Owen, a local orthopedic surgeon, and have his arm X-rayed. Dr. Owen examined the child and discovered that his arm had been broken. The parents sued Forrester Day Care, Inc.

Mr. and Mrs. Ward both testified in depositions that their child was not injured while under their care and that the only other place he had been cared for was Forrester day care center. Employees of Forrester testified that the baby was not injured while at the Forrester day care center. The same employees also testified about the operations of the center, the tendencies of their evidence being to indicate that there was no negligence.

In contrast to the testimony of the Forrester employees, Mr. and Mrs. Ward both testified in their depositions that they had witnessed conditions at the center that they contend showed the Center was improperly operated. The Wards testified in their depositions concerning several conditions that they say were potentially dangerous and could have caused the injury to their child, or to any other child under the care of the Forrester day care center. However, there is no evidence that shows the exact cause of the child's broken arm.

The plaintiffs' position is that the defendant's employees have adopted a "conspiracy of silence" and that that conspiracy should not remove their legal remedy for the injury suffered by Garrett while at the day care center. The Wards ask us to apply the doctrine of *res ipsa loquitur*. . . .

Defendant argues that "[w]here the act or instrumentality causing the injury is unknown, there is no basis for the application of the doctrine of res ipsa loquitur," citing

McClinton v. McClinton, 258 Ala. 542, 63 So. 2d 594 (1952), and *Viking Motor Lodge, Inc. v. American Tobacco Co.,* 286 Ala. 112, 237 So. 2d 632 (1970). Defendant correctly states the plaintiff's usual burden of proof, but a plaintiff is not required in every case to show a specific instrumentality that caused the injury. The drafters of comments (f) and (g) to the *Restatement (Second) of Torts* § 328D (1965) state that in making the negligence point to the defendant, this is usually done by showing that a specific instrumentality has caused the event, or that *"all reasonably probable causes were under the exclusive control of the defendant."* (Emphasis added.) The commentators note that "[i]t is not, however, necessary to the inference that the defendant have such exclusive control; and exclusive control is merely one way of proving his responsibility." *Restatement (Second) of Torts* § 328D.

In this case, the plaintiffs claim that the defendant was guilty of negligent supervision. As a general rule, a plaintiff who can prove his case by specific acts of negligence cannot avail himself of the doctrine of *res ipsa loquitur.* We do not believe that rule is applicable here.

In *Zimmer v. Celebrities, Inc.,* 44 Colo. App. 515, 519, 615 P.2d 76, 79–80 (1980), the Court addressed this question, as follows:

> "Defendant also contends that res ipsa loquitur is inapplicable in this case because plaintiffs have argued and introduced some evidence that defendant was negligent in supervision of the nursery. Defendant reasons that negligent supervision would be a specific act of negligence and therefore res ipsa is not applicable. We do not agree. *Kitto v. Gilbert,* 39 Colo. App. 374, 570 P.2d 544 (1977), is dispositive of this issue. In that case we held that:
>
> "'Res ipsa loquitur is a rule which presumes evidence which applies when it is judicially determined that a particular unexplained occurrence creates a prima facie case of negligence without proof of specific misfeasance. . . . A corollary requirement is that no direct evidence exists establishing that a specific act of negligence was *the only likely cause* for the harm. . . . *The mere introduction of evidence as to how an accident could have occurred and its possible causes* does not necessarily preclude application of res ipsa loquitur so long as that evidence does not clearly resolve the issue of culpability.'" 39 Colo. App. at 379, 570 P.2d at 548 (emphasis added except the word 'possible'.)
>
> "Even though evidence was offered concerning the probabilities of the injury being caused by a piece of equipment or by inadequate supervision on the premises, there was no direct evidence establishing a specific act of negligence which was the only likely cause of the injury, and the evidence presented did not resolve the issue of culpability." 44 Colo. App. at 519, 615 P.2d at 79–80.

We hold that the mere introduction of evidence as to how an accident could have occurred and its possible causes does not necessarily preclude the application of the doctrine of *res ipsa loquitur* so long as that evidence does not clearly resolve the issue of culpability.

Based on the foregoing, we hold that the trial court erred in entering summary judgment for the defendant.

Reversed and remanded.

ASSIGNMENT 14.5

a. Who had exclusive control of the baby during the time of the injury? The Wards took the baby home and returned him to the center the next day after hearing the "very unusual scream" at the center. Was there exclusive control by the defendant? If not, how can the Wards use RIL?

b. The Smiths are about to go on a two-week vacation. They take their pet poodle to the Dog Vacation Home. When they return, the manager of the Home says that the dog unfortunately died and had to be cremated. The manager does not know why it died. The caretaker at the Dog Vacation Home came in one morning and found it dead in its cage. Does RIL apply?

CUSTOM AND USAGE

Often in a negligence case the plaintiff alleges that the defendant failed to take specific precautionary steps and that this failure led to the plaintiff's injury. For example:

- the failure to place a safety guard on a bicycle wheel
- the failure to build a fence alongside a railroad track
- the failure to place a rubber mat in front of a store
- the failure to have two-way radios in tugboats
- the failure to perform a medical test to detect a certain disease

A common response of the defendant in these cases is that no one else in the field takes these steps. The defendant is saying: "a reasonable person in my position would not have taken these steps; it is the custom in the field to act the way I acted." Hence, the question becomes: When is it reasonable to do what everyone else is doing or to fail to do something when everyone else fails to do it as well?

As indicated in Exhibit 14–1, what is reasonable depends on a wide variety of circumstances. One of these circumstances is what others are doing. It may be unreasonable, for example, to expect a defendant to take a very expensive precaution that no other person in the defendant's position has ever taken and that is designed to avoid the small risk of very minor injury. On the other hand, it may be that an entire industry or profession is being unreasonable in failing to take a certain precautionary step. They may be acting unreasonably in spite of the fact that everyone is acting in the same way. To let them off the hook would provide little incentive to raise their standards.

Recall the breach-of-duty equation: The foreseeability of injury must be balanced against the extent of the burden or inconvenience of taking precautions against the injury occurring. (See Exhibit 14–4.) The more foreseeable the danger of serious injury, the more reasonable it is for the defendant to bear the burden or inconvenience of trying to prevent the injury. This principle helps us assess the impact of **custom and usage**.

custom and usage The general practice in a field; what is commonly done.

We need to ask *why* the business or profession acted or failed to act in a certain way. Suppose a company manufactures a product, but does not add a device that would protect the public against a particular kind of injury. Suppose further that this is the custom in the industry—no manufacturer adds the device. Why isn't the device added? Because the injury is very rare? If so, this is relevant to the foreseeability of danger in the breach-of-duty equation. Because of the cost of adding the device? Would the price to the consumer be so high that only the wealthy could afford the product with the device? Because of a loss of effectiveness? If the device were added, would the product be significantly less effective in its primary function? These questions are relevant to the burden/inconvenience component of the breach-of-duty equation.

In short, the most you can say is that custom and usage is *a* relevant factor in the law of negligence, but it almost never settles the question of what is reasonableness or unreasonableness.

VIOLATION OF A STATUTE

In a negligence case, the plaintiff will often include an allegation that the defendant violated a statute.

EXAMPLE

Ron Davis carelessly drives his truck onto Ed Packard's land and crashes into a lamppost. The impact causes a gasoline storage tank on the truck to flip over, spilling the contents on the ground. A spontaneous fire breaks out, causing extensive damage. Packard sues Davis for negligence. The complaint alleges that Davis was driving his truck carelessly (unreasonably) and also alleges that Davis violated a statute, § 200 of the state statutory code. This section prohibits the transportation of gasoline in the kind of storage container Davis was using.

What is the effect of the statute on the negligence claim? Does the violation of § 200 make it easier for Packard to establish breach of duty? How, if at all, is the violation relevant? We know that the standard of care in a negligence case is reasonableness as measured by the breach-of-duty equation of Exhibit 14–4. If the defendant violates a statute, does this violation, in effect, become the standard of care that determines the defendant's reasonableness? Can we conclude that the defendant was unreasonable *solely because* he or she violated the statute? Unfortunately, most statutes say nothing explicit about how a violation might be relevant to a negligence suit such as Packard's. The statute may impose a fine or other criminal penalties for a violation, but say nothing about whether the violation allows a victim to bring a tort action such as negligence. When the statute is silent on this point, we need a method of analyzing how a statutory violation might affect the standard of care in a negligence case.

In addition to statutes, there may also be an allegation that the defendant violated a local ordinance (e.g., a traffic ordinance) or an administrative regulation (e.g., an on-the-job safety regulation). Although the following discussion will focus on statutes, the same method of analysis can be used when the negligence case includes alleged violations of ordinances or administrative regulations.

There is an eight-part analysis to determine how to handle an alleged violation of a statute in a negligence case:

1. State what the defendant did or failed to do that the plaintiff claims was a breach of duty (unreasonableness).
2. State whether a statute might be involved. (The plaintiff's complaint may allege a violation of a statute. Your own legal research may uncover such statutes.)
3. If so, determine whether the statute was violated.
4. If so, determine whether the violation was excused.
5. If not, determine whether the violation of the statute caused the accident.
6. If so, determine whether the plaintiff was within the class of persons the statute was intended to protect.
7. If so, determine whether the statute was intended to avoid the kind of harm the plaintiff suffered.
8. If so, determine whether your state considers the violation to be negligence per se, a presumption of negligence, or simply some evidence of negligence.

negligence per se Negligence (unreasonableness) because of a violation of a statute. The jury is not asked what a reasonable person would have done; the trial judge concludes that a reasonable person would have done what the statute provides.

In most states, when an unexcused violation of a statute causes harm to a person, the violation will constitute **negligence per se** (or unreasonableness per se). This means that the trial judge won't ask the jury what a reasonable person would have done. Instead, the judge will rule that the reasonable person would have done what the statute provided. The statute, in effect, becomes the standard of care. To understand how this conclusion is reached we need to go through the eight steps. At the end of our overview of the steps you will find a flowchart (Exhibit 14–7) of all the steps.

It is important to keep in mind that a plaintiff's failure to establish the statute as the standard of care does *not* mean that the defendant wins the case. What the defendant did or failed to do may be found by a court to have been unreasonable *independent* of any statute. A given accident may involve hundreds of facts, only a small portion of which may be relevant to a particular statute. Suppose a statute requires farmers to place a fence around certain kinds of animals. No fence is erected and the plaintiff is injured by one of the farmer's animals. It may be that after we go through the eight-step analysis, we will come to the conclusion that a court would *not* adopt the statute as the standard of reasonable conduct. This would eliminate the statute from the case. It is *still* possible, however, that the court will find that the defendant acted unreasonably in failing to build the fence. If so, it will not be due to the violation of the statute; it will be due to the court's application of the breach-of-duty equation in which the absence of a fence is but one of the factors that enter into the balancing required by the equation (see Exhibit 14–4).

Now let's take a closer look at the eight steps.

Was the Statute Violated?

EXAMPLE

Tom is driving his motorcycle at thirty mph downtown when he crashes into the car of the plaintiff, who sues Tom for negligence. There is a statute in the state

(§ 100) that says, "No motor vehicle can travel more than twenty-five mph in a thickly settled district."

The first step of our analysis is to identify what the defendant did or failed to do that allegedly was unreasonable. (While driving at thirty mph downtown, Tom hit the plaintiff's car.) The second step is to identify any statutes that might apply to the case. (Section 100 provides that "No motor vehicle can travel more than twenty-five mph in a thickly settled district.") Next we ask whether this statute was violated.

Recall our discussion of legal analysis in Chapter 2 on how to determine whether a statute or other rule has been violated. We break the rule into its elements, define the major terms in the elements in contention, connect the facts to the elements, etc. (See Legal Analysis Guidelines 2 to 13 in Chapter 2.) One of the elements of § 100 is "motor vehicle." Is a motorcycle a "motor vehicle" under the statute? It depends on how broadly or narrowly we define "motor vehicle." Another element of § 100 is "thickly settled district." Tom was downtown at the time of the crash. The phrase "thickly settled district" needs to be defined in order to determine whether downtown is within such a district. These definition questions are answered by finding the **legislative intent** of § 100. What was the intent of the legislature when it enacted § 100? What was the purpose of this statute? Answering these questions through legal research (particularly by trying to find court opinions that have interpreted § 100 in the past) will help us find the definitions we need. Our conclusion might be that "motor vehicles" are those vehicles with four or more wheels and that "thickly settled district" refers to residential areas, not to downtown. If so, then Tom did not violate § 100.

legislative intent The purpose of the legislature in enacting a particular statute.

This does not mean, however, that the plaintiff loses the case for failure to convince the court that the defendant violated a particular statute. Independent of the statute, the plaintiff may be able to show that the defendant was driving unreasonably, given the totality of the circumstances. In our motorcycle case, the plaintiff will argue that going thirty mph was unreasonable in light of all of the circumstances such as the road conditions, the level of traffic, the position of the plaintiff's car, etc. The statute—§ 100—may be out of the case, but the plaintiff may still be able to show that Tom was negligent.

Was the Violation Excused?

It is not enough to show that the defendant violated a statute. If the violation was excused, it cannot be used to show that the defendant was unreasonable.

EXAMPLE

John causes an accident while driving at night. His two-week-old new car crashes into the plaintiff's cow. John's front lights suddenly went out and he could not see the plaintiff's cow in front of him. The plaintiff sues John for negligence.

Assume that there is a statute that requires headlights to be on at night. Clearly, John has violated this statute. But his violation was probably excused, particularly if he had no warning that the lights on his brand-new car might be defective. This takes the violation out of the negligence case. When we ask whether the violation of a statute constitutes proof of the defendant's unreasonableness, we are referring to unexcused violations.

Did the Violation Cause the Accident?

There was a time when all American males of a certain age were required by statute to carry a draft card on their person. Suppose such a person injures someone in a car accident while he is not carrying his draft card. The defendant has clearly violated the draft card statute. But this is not relevant to the accident. Not having a draft card certainly did not cause the car accident.

but-for test Would the event (e.g., the injury) have happened without the act or omission of the party? But for the act or omission, would the event have occurred? Also called the sine qua non test.

substantial-factor test Did the party have a significant or important role in bringing about the event (e.g., the injury)?

Use the **but-for test** or the **substantial-factor test** to determine whether the violation of the statute caused the accident. (These tests were introduced in Chapter 1 and will be covered in greater detail in Chapter 15.) If there had been no violation (i.e., "but for" the violation), would the accident still have occurred? If so, then the violation did not cause the accident. When more than one possible cause exists, the test is whether the violation was a substantial factor (along with other factors) in producing the accident. If not, then the violation did not cause the accident.

Licensing statutes often raise causation questions:

- You are in a traffic accident at a time when your driver's license has expired.
- You are a doctor whose license has been suspended and you are sued for a medical injury you caused while you were without a license.
- You are a contractor who fails to obtain the required permit to build a house; you are sued when the house collapses and injures someone.

In most license cases such as these, it cannot be said that the violation caused the harm. You may have had the same mishap if you had had the driver's license, doctor's license, or building permit. It is very weak to argue that because you did not have the license, you probably were incompetent in what you were doing. Competence is determined by a host of other factors, e.g., age, prior experience, and training. It cannot be said that simply because you did not have a license, you acted unreasonably in doing what you did. Competent doctors, for example, do not automatically become incompetent the day after their medical licenses expire.

Assume that a statute requires wall handrails on the stairs of every restaurant facility. A customer at a restaurant slips and falls on the stairs where there are no handrails. There appears to be a clear violation of the statute. But did the violation *cause* the fall? The answer appears to be yes. Of course, we need to know more facts in order to determine whether the fall would have occurred even if there were handrails, or if their absence was a substantial factor in the fall. For example, how quickly did the accident happen? How wide were the steps, and where was the plaintiff at the time of the fall? If the plaintiff fell in the center of very wide steps, it may have been impossible for him or her to have reached handrails if they were available.

ASSIGNMENT 14.6

A statute requires department stores to report all accidents occurring on elevators to a city agency. Over the years, the XYZ department store has never reported accidents on some of its elevators. Recently, a customer was injured on one of the XYZ elevators. The customer sues the XYZ store for negligence. The customer bases the entire breach-of-duty claim on the violation of the statute. Discuss causation.

Is Plaintiff Within the Class of Persons Protected by the Statute?

It is not enough that the plaintiff establishes that a violation of the statute caused the injury suffered by the plaintiff. More analysis of the statute is needed to determine whether the plaintiff is the kind of person the statute was designed to protect.

Suppose that you have a statute requiring factories to have certain safety devices on machines. A factory violates the statute by not installing these devices. One day a visitor happens to be in the factory and is injured while walking past one of the machines. Assume that there is no difficulty establishing causation. The visitor can prove that "but for" the failure to have the safety device, the accident would not have occurred. The question then becomes: Who was the statute designed to protect? Only factory employees? If so, the breach of statute cannot be the basis of the visitor's claim that the factory was unreasonable (negligent). Was it designed to protect *anyone* who is in the factory on business? If so, the visitor can use the statute.

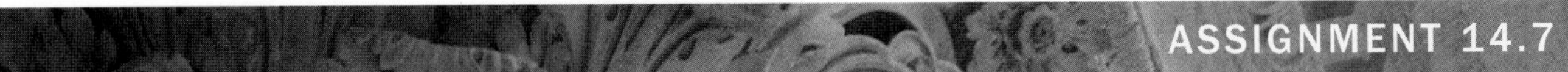

ASSIGNMENT 14.7

A statute requires all vacant lots to be fenced at all times. Tom owns a vacant lot in the city. The lot has no fence. One day a stranger cuts through Tom's lot and injures himself by falling into a hole that is very difficult to see. The stranger sues Tom for negligence. What breach-of-duty argument will the stranger make based on the statute? What will Tom's response be?

Was the Statute Intended to Avoid This Kind of Harm?

Closely related to the class-of-plaintiff problem just discussed is the question of whether the statute was meant to cover the kind of harm or injury the plaintiff suffered.

EXAMPLES

- A statute requires all traffic to drive under fifty-five mph on the highways. Defendant crashes into plaintiff while defendant is driving sixty-five mph. *Is the purpose of the statute* to:
  a. Save lives?
  b. Save gas so that the country is less dependent on foreign oil?
- A statute requires employers to have sprinkler systems in good repair at all times. One day the sprinkler system at a plant malfunctions. It is activated even though no fire exists. The entire plant is flooded. An employee, who is laid off because of the flood, sues the employer for lost wages due to the breach of the statute. *Is the purpose of the statute* to:
  a. Avoid personal injuries in case of fire?
  b. Avoid economic loss due to flooding?
- A statute requires that all commercial poison be stored in properly designated containers. A business fails to use the right containers. One day a box containing poison explodes because it was stored too close to heat. The explosion would not have occurred if the correct containers had been used. A customer is injured by the explosion. *Is the purpose of the statute* to:
  a. Prevent people (or animals) from being poisoned?
  b. Prevent explosions?

If the statute was not intended to cover the kind of harm that resulted, the plaintiff cannot use the breach of the statute as the basis of the breach-of-duty argument. Again, however, even if the statute was not intended to cover what happened, plaintiff should still try to establish unreasonableness as if the statute did not exist. In the poison example, even if the statute was not intended to cover explosions, a court could still find that the defendant was unreasonable in the method used to store the poison if, according to the breach-of-duty equation, the danger of explosion was highly foreseeable and the burden or inconvenience on the defendant of preventing this danger by proper storage was minimal.

Does the Violation of the Statute, in and of Itself, Constitute a Breach of Duty?

Finally, we assess the consequences of our analysis. Assume that you work for a law firm that represents the plaintiff in a negligence case. You have gone through all the hurdles and are able to show that:

- The defendant violated a statute.
- The violation was not excused.
- The violation caused the plaintiff's injury.
- The plaintiff is within the class of persons the statute was intended to protect.
- The injury suffered by the plaintiff was the kind of harm the statute was designed to prevent.

As indicated, most states conclude that the violation is negligence per se (unreasonableness per se). The violation, in and of itself, constitutes a breach of duty. In some states, however, the violation creates no more than a **presumption** of negligence (unreasonableness). This means that the jury must find that the defendant acted unreasonably unless the defendant offers convincing evidence that he or she acted reasonably in spite of the violation. (A presumption is an assumption of fact that can be drawn when another fact or set of facts is established. The presumption is **rebuttable** if a party is allowed to introduce evidence that the assumption is false.) Finally, a few states conclude that the violation is no more than some evidence of negligence (unreasonableness). It is neither conclusive (negligence per se) nor presumptive.

Exhibit 14–7 presents an overview of the eight-part analytical process we have been examining to determine whether a violation of a statute, in and of itself, constitutes a breach of duty.

presumption An inference or assumption of fact that can be drawn when another fact or set of facts is established. The presumption is rebuttable if a party is allowed to introduce evidence that the assumption is false. If no contrary evidence is allowed, it is called an *irrebutable presumption* or a *conclusive presumption*.

rebuttable Subject to challenge; pertaining to a conclusion that one is allowed to introduce evidence against.

CASE

Potts v. Fidelity Fruit & Produce Co., Inc.

165 Ga. App. 546, 301 S.E.2d 903 (1983)
Court of Appeals of Georgia

Background: *There are spiders on bananas of Fidelity Fruit & Produce Company in violation of the Georgia Food Act, which prohibits the packing or holding of food in a manner that is "injurious to health." An employee is bitten by one of the spiders while unloading them from a truck. He sues for negligence. The trial court enters a summary judgment in favor of the company. The employee, now the appellant, appeals to the Court of Appeals of Georgia.*

Decision on Appeal: *Judgment affirmed. Violation of the Georgia Food Act cannot be the basis of a negligence action by an employee.*

OPINION OF COURT

Judge BANKE delivered the opinion of the court. . . .

In determining whether the violation of a statute or ordinance is negligence *per se* as to a particular person, it is necessary to examine the purposes of the legislation and decide (1) whether the injured person falls within the class of persons it was intended to protect and (2) whether the harm complained of was the harm it was intended to guard against. *Rhodes v. Baker,* 116 Ga. App. 157, 160, 156 S.E.2d 545 (1967); *Huckabee v. Grace,* 48 Ga. App. 621, 636, 173 S.E. 744 (1933). Having examined the provisions of the Georgia Food Act, we agree fully with the following analysis made by the trial court: "Clearly, the Act is a consumer protection act, designed not to render the workplace a safe environment, but to prevent the sale and distribution of adulterated or misbranded foods to consumers. While safety in the workplace, and compensation for injuries arising out of work activities, are indeed matters of contemporary concern, they are the subject of other legislative enactments on both the state and federal level." Because the appellant's alleged injuries did not arise incident to his consumption of the bananas, we hold that the trial court was correct in concluding that the Act affords him no basis for recovery.

Judgment affirmed.

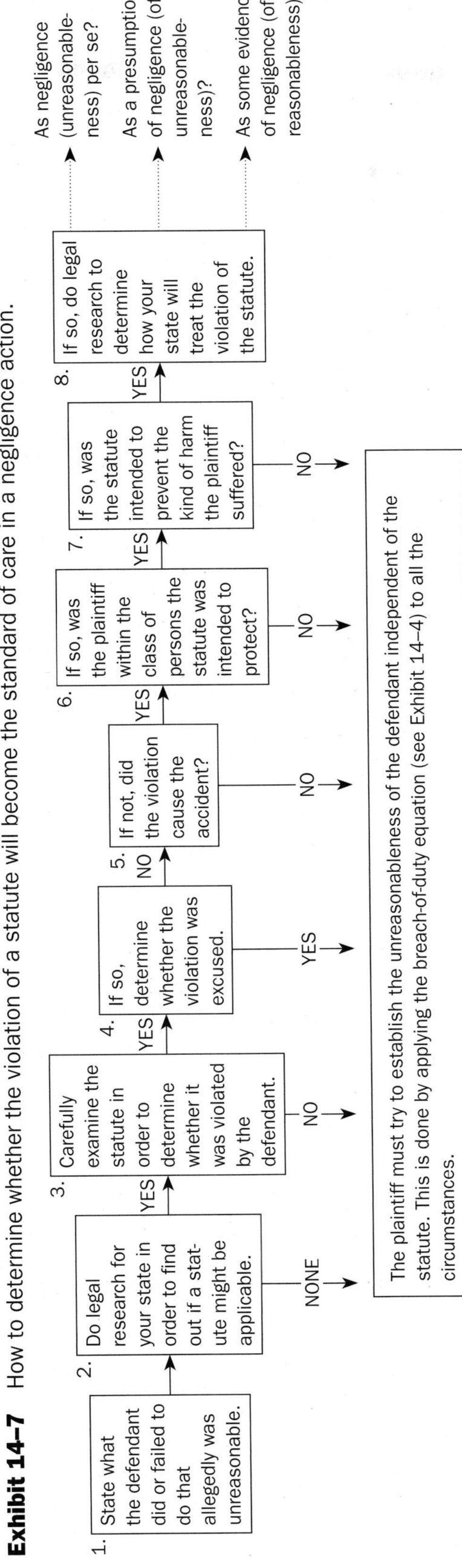

Exhibit 14–7 How to determine whether the violation of a statute will become the standard of care in a negligence action.

ASSIGNMENT 14.8

a. What if the employee ate one of the bananas while unloading them from the truck, and then was bitten by the spider? Would the *Potts* case reach the same result?
b. Assume that there was no violation of a statute in this case. Would the company be liable for negligence due to the spider bite?

COMPLIANCE WITH A STATUTE

Thus far we have seen that just because a defendant has *violated* a statute, it does not necessarily mean the defendant was unreasonable. We now look at the converse problem. If a defendant can show *compliance* with a statute, does it necessarily mean he or she acted reasonably at the time the accident occurred? *No*.

Suppose, for example, that a safety statute requires railroad companies to place flashing red lights at all points where tracks cross public highways. The fact that a railroad complies with this statute and has the lights in place does not guarantee that a court will find that the railroad acted reasonably. Suppose an accident occurs at a corner where the lights are working, but it is clear that much more is needed by the railroad to prevent injuries because of the large number of accidents in the past at this same intersection. In such a case, the statute amounts only to the *minimum* conduct expected of the railroad. Reasonableness may have called for additional precautions, e.g., a swing gate, an alarm, or an attendant on duty at the intersection during times of heavy traffic. The railroad does not get off the hook simply by showing compliance with the statute. Similarly, a motorist traveling thirty mph who causes an accident cannot claim that he or she was driving at a reasonable speed simply because he or she was well within the speed limit of forty-five mph. Compliance is evidence of reasonableness, but it is not conclusive.

To summarize, the statute merely sets the minimum standard of conduct, but reasonableness under the circumstances might call for more than what the statute requires.

GROSS NEGLIGENCE (UNREASONABLENESS) AND WILLFUL, WANTON, AND RECKLESS CONDUCT

Some states have statutes that cover special negligence cases, such as that of a *guest* injured in an automobile.

guest A passenger in a motor vehicle who is offered a ride by someone who receives no benefits from the passenger other than hospitality, goodwill, and the like. (See glossary for additional definitions.)

guest statute A statute providing that drivers of motor vehicles will not be liable for injuries caused by their ordinary negligence to nonpaying guest passengers. Also called automobile guest statute.

ordinary negligence Conduct that is unreasonable but not gross or reckless.

EXAMPLE

Mary is on her way to the post office. Her neighbor asks Mary if he could have a ride, because he also needs to go to the post office. Mary agrees. On the way, Mary negligently hits a tree. The neighbor is injured and sues Mary for negligence.

The neighbor is a **guest** in Mary's car—he did not pay for the ride and there is no indication that Mary derived any benefit from the neighbor's presence in the car other than social companionship. There are **guest statutes** in many states that make it difficult for guests to sue their automobile hosts. They are also called *automobile guest statutes*. They require guests to prove a greater degree of negligence (unreasonableness) than in non-guest/host suits. **Ordinary negligence** (unreasonableness) is not enough.

Not all states have the same guest statutes. They use different language to describe the level of unreasonableness by the driver that will allow the guest to sue. Some say that the guest must establish the driver's **gross negligence** (the failure to use even a small amount of care to avoid foreseeable harm). Other standards used in the statutes (often with overlapping definitions) include **willful** (acting with knowledge that harm will probably result), **wanton** (extremely reckless), and **reckless** (consciously taking a risk in failing to exercise due care but without intending the consequences).

In our tree case involving Mary and the neighbor, if Mary simply failed to do what a person of ordinary prudence would have done to avoid hitting the tree, the neighbor would lose his negligence case in a state that imposes standards such as those just listed. Examples of Mary's gross negligence or recklessness might include being drunk or traveling eighty mph in a twenty mph zone before hitting the tree.

As we shall see later, gross negligence (unreasonableness) or willful, wanton, and reckless conduct will often be the basis for awarding punitive damages in a negligence case.

Another example of when it is important to distinguish the degrees of negligence involves the law that governs the Good Samaritan. As we saw in Chapter 13, many states have laws that limit the liability of the Good Samaritan to recklessness; they will not be liable for ordinary negligence in such states.

gross negligence The failure to use even a small amount of care to avoid foreseeable harm.

willful 1. Acting with the knowledge that harm will probably result. 2. Voluntary and deliberate. 3. Malicious.

wanton Extremely reckless.

reckless Consciously taking a risk in failing to exercise due care but without intending the consequences; wantonly disregarding a risk but neither desiring the consequences of the risk nor having substantially certain knowledge of the consequences.

ASSIGNMENT 14.9

Matthew is driving from one city to another in your state. The distance is fifty miles. His best friend, George, asks Matthew if he could drive him to a point midway between the two cities. Matthew is delighted to do him this favor, since he enjoys his company very much. When they reach the point where George is to get off, the latter gives Matthew $5 as a contribution toward the cost of gas. As George is getting out, Matthew sneezes and steps on the accelerator by mistake, injuring George. George sues Matthew for negligence. Discuss George's chances of winning this case.

VICARIOUS LIABILITY

"Vicarious" means taking the place of another. Vicarious negligence, or more accurately, vicarious unreasonableness, means that one person will be found to be unreasonable solely because someone else is unreasonable. The unreasonableness of one person will be thrust upon or **imputed** to another person. **Imputed negligence** is a form of **vicarious liability**. As we will see, the basis of the liability is the relationship between the person whose conduct was unreasonable and the person who is vicariously liable for that conduct.

We will be looking at three categories of vicarious liability: employment, joint enterprise, and use of the family car (see Exhibit 14–8). Before we examine the three categories, two important points need to be considered: who can be sued, and how vicarious liability is distinguished from independent liability.

imputed Attributed to or imposed on someone or something.

imputed negligence Negligence liability attributed to or imposed on someone who did not act unreasonably but is liable solely because of his or her relationship with the person who did act unreasonably.

vicarious liability Liability imposed on a person because of the conduct of another, based solely on the status of the relationship between the two. The person liable is not the person whose conduct led to the liability.

Who Can Be Sued?

You will note in the three examples of Exhibit 14–8 that Sara, Joe, and Jessica were the defendants in the three negligence actions. What about the other three who, as the drivers, were more directly responsible for the accidents: Mary, Ed, and Bob? Can they also be sued for negligence? Yes. *Joint and several liability* exists. If a person is jointly and severally liable, he or she is individually responsible for 100 percent of the damages suffered by the plaintiff. The plaintiff can sue all of

Exhibit 14–8
Three categories of vicarious unreasonableness.

VICARIOUS UNREASONABLENESS

Employer/Employee (Master/Servant)	Joint Enterprise	Family Purpose Doctrine
Mary works for Sara as a truck driver. While making a delivery, Mary carelessly injures the plaintiff. The plaintiff sues Sara for negligence. Mary's unreasonableness will be imputed to Sara because of the *employer-employee relationship.*	Joe and Ed rent a car in order to buy some goods to be used in a business they are going to start together. They both contribute funds to rent the car. Ed is the driver. While driving, Ed carelessly hits the plaintiff. Joe is also riding in the car at the time. The plaintiff sues Joe for negligence. Ed's unreasonableness will be imputed to Joe because of the *joint enterprise.*	Jessica owns a car which she lets her son, Bob, drive. One day Bob is driving to the supermarket alone and carelessly hits the plaintiff. The plaintiff sues Jessica for negligence. Bob's unreasonableness will be imputed to Jessica because of the *family purpose doctrine.*

these persons together or can sue any one or more of them until 100 percent of his or her damages are recovered. An individual defendant cannot force the plaintiff to collect part of the damages from other persons. (See Chapter 16 for a discussion of *contribution* among defendants.) Since all of the individuals in Exhibit 14–8 are jointly and severally liable, here are the actions that are possible:

Plaintiff v. Sara *or*	Plaintiff v. Joe *or*	Plaintiff v. Jessica *or*
Plaintiff v. Mary *or*	Plaintiff v. Ed *or*	Plaintiff v. Bob *or*
Plaintiff v. Sara and Mary	Plaintiff v. Joe and Ed	Plaintiff v. Jessica and Bob

Hence, although the defendants in the examples in Exhibit 14–8 were Sara, Joe, and Jessica, the plaintiffs could have sued Mary, Ed, and Bob as well. It may be that the attorneys for the plaintiffs felt that Sara, Joe, and Jessica were the **deep pockets**. A deep pocket is one who has the resources (including insurance coverage) from which a negligence judgment could be satisfied.

deep pocket 1. An individual, business, or other organization with resources to pay a potential judgment. 2. Sufficient assets for this purpose. The opposite of *shallow pocket*.

Vicarious Liability and Independent Liability

In the three examples in Exhibit 14–8, there is no indication that the parties vicariously liable (Sara, Joe, and Jessica) did anything wrong, careless, or unreasonable themselves. They were not individually at fault. Suppose, however, that they were, as in the following scenarios.

Employer/Employee Case

- Sara knew that Mary was a poor driver, but let her drive anyway. This is an example of **negligent hiring**.
- Sara instructed Mary to make the delivery as fast as she could, even if it meant breaking the speed limit.
- Sara never bothered to check to determine whether her drivers were properly trained.

negligent hiring Carelessly hiring an incompetent person who poses an unreasonable risk of harm to others.

Joint Enterprise Case

- Joe knew that Ed was a poor driver, but let him drive anyway.
- The accident happened because Joe carelessly distracted Ed.
- Joe knew that the car was defective; this defect contributed to the accident.

Family Purpose Doctrine Case

- Jessica knew that Bob was a poor driver, but let him drive anyway.
- Jessica instructed Bob to get to the supermarket and back as soon as possible, even if it meant breaking the speed limit.
- Jessica knew that the car was defective; this defect contributed to the accident.

Now we have *individual* fault on the part of the parties who were not driving. Sara, Joe, and Jessica may be liable under two different theories: **independent liability** and vicarious liability.

independent liability Liability based on what an individual did him- or herself. The opposite of vicarious liability, which is liability based on what someone else has done.

In the discussion that follows, we will assume that the defendants are *not* independently liable because of any unreasonableness of their own. Our focus is on vicarious liability only. You should always keep in mind, however, the distinction between vicarious and independent liability, because in any given case a defendant may be legitimately faced with both theories of liability.

Employer/Employee Vicarious liability is based on the employer/employee relationship that is called **respondeat superior** (let the master [boss] answer). The underlying principle is that "He who does a thing through another does it himself."[4] In an **employment** relationship, the law refers to employers as *masters* and to employees as *servants*. Indeed, the employer/employee relationship is often called the master/servant relationship. Later we will see that the singular characteristic of the relationship is the degree of control that the employer has over the goals and manner of work of the employee. The employer/employee relationship is an example of a broader category of relationships called principal/agent. An **agent** is someone authorized to act for another; the agent is a *representative* of the other. A **principal** is the person who permits the agent to act on behalf of the principal.

respondeat superior "Let the master answer." An employer is responsible (liable) for the wrongs committed by an employee within the scope of employment.

employment A work relationship in which the person hiring (the employer) controls, or has the right to control, the goals and manner of work of the person hired (the employee).

agent A person authorized to act for another; a representative. (See the glossary for another meaning.)

principal One who permits another (the agent) to act on behalf of the principal. (See the glossary for additional meanings.)

Our study of the vicarious liability of an employer will center on two questions: 1. When is an employee acting within the scope of employment so that the employer is vicariously liable? and 2. When is a defendant vicariously liable for the negligence of his or her independent contractor?

1. When is an employee acting within the scope of employment? The overriding principle is that the employer is vicariously liable for the torts of his or her employee if the latter was acting within the **scope of employment** at the time. A great deal of litigation has resulted from trying to define the phrase "scope of employment." (As we shall see in Chapter 28, the comparable phrase in the law of workers' compensation is, "arising out of and in the course of employment.")

scope of employment That which is foreseeably done by an employee for the employer's business under the employer's specific or general control.

There is no absolute definition of "scope of employment." A working definition is as follows:

> Scope of employment is that which is foreseeably done by the employee for the employer's business under the employer's specific or general control.

Scope of employment is not determined by what the employer has authorized the employee to do, although authorization is one factor a court will consider. Suppose that a boss tells her hardware clerk not to allow a customer to operate the automatic paint mixer. The employee violates this instruction, resulting in an injury to a customer. This violation does not mean respondeat superior will not apply. The boss will still be vicariously liable for the negligence of her employee if the latter was acting for the boss, under the latter's control, and if what the employee did was foreseeable to the boss because of prior conduct of the employee and the nature of the work.

frolic Employee conduct that is outside the scope of employment because it is personal rather than primarily for the employer's business interests. Also called a frolic and detour.

A major concern of the courts has been the **frolic** of an employee (also called frolic and detour). There is no vicarious liability if the negligent act of the employee was committed while he or she was on a frolic of his or her own.

EXAMPLE

Bill is an employee of a delivery company. One morning while making a delivery for the company, he drives the company truck twenty-five miles out of the way to spend three hours with his girlfriend. While driving out of the girlfriend's driveway in order to return to work, Bill rams the company truck into the plaintiff's fence.

It is highly unlikely that the plaintiff can win a negligence action against the employer; the accident was not within the scope of employment because the employee was on a frolic of his own. The plaintiff will be limited to a suit against the employee (Bill). A major characteristic of a frolic is that the employee is acting for his or her personal objectives rather than acting primarily for the employer's business.

There is a large gray area where courts have had difficulty determining what is within the scope of employment. A number of factors are considered in identifying this scope. The factors are outlined in the scope-of-employment checklist in Exhibit 14–9. No single factor is determinative; a court will weigh them all. Although our emphasis has been on negligence liability (vicarious unreasonableness), the factors in the checklist would also be used by a court to determine whether the employer would be liable for any intentional torts committed by the employee, such as battery, fraud, or false imprisonment.

Exhibit 14–9
Checklist of factors used to determine scope of employment.

A "yes" answer to any of the following interrelated questions would help support a conclusion that the employee did act within the scope of employment. A "no" answer helps support the conclusion that the act was outside this scope. A single yes or no answer, however, is rarely conclusive. A court will weigh all of the factors before deciding what was within or outside of the scope of employment. The "conduct" referred to in the following eight categories of questions is what the employee did that accidentally resulted in the plaintiff's injury, which is now the basis of the plaintiff's negligence suit against the employer.

1. Authorization: Was the employee's conduct substantially within what the employer authorized the employee to do?
2. Purpose: Was the employee acting to pursue the business interests of the employer? If the employee also had personal objectives in what was done, can it nevertheless be said that the employee was acting *primarily* to pursue the business interests of the employer?
3. Normalcy: Was the employee's conduct common or usual in the job being performed?
4. Time: Was the employee's conduct undertaken substantially within the time of work for the employer?
5. Place: Was the employee's conduct undertaken substantially within the place or locale authorized by the employer for such conduct?
6. Foreseeability: Are there any additional facts (other than those listed in items 1–5 above) that would make the conduct of the employee foreseeable to the employer?
7. Special Obligation: Was the employer engaged in the kind of business on which the courts have historically placed a special obligation for the protection of its customers, e.g., common carriers, innkeepers?
8. Common Sense: As a matter of common sense, can we say that the employee's conduct was within the scope of employment?

ASSIGNMENT 14.10

Apply the scope of employment checklist of factors in Exhibit 14–9 to determine whether the employees in the following situations were acting within the scope of their employment at the time of the accident. Identify further fact investigation you may need. In each instance, the plaintiff is suing the employer on a respondeat superior theory. None of the plaintiffs work for the employer.

a. The ashes from the employee's cigarette fall onto the plaintiff's fur coat, causing substantial damage. The plaintiff sues for negligence.
b. While making a delivery in a company truck, the employee travels five miles out of the way to visit his ailing mother. He stays three hours. On his way back to the company plant to return the truck, he injures plaintiff in a traffic accident. The plaintiff sues for negligence.
c. The employee is a door-to-door salesperson. At one house, the employee gets into an argument with the plaintiff, who owns the house. The plaintiff calls the employee "stupid." The employee hits the plaintiff, who now sues for battery.

2. When is the defendant vicariously liable for the negligence of his or her independent contractor?[5] Different rules apply when the defendant hires an **independent contractor**. The distinction between an employee and an independent contractor is not always easy to draw. Some of the significant points of difference include:

- The person doing the hiring has less control over the independent contractor than over the employee.
- The independent contractor has more discretion over the way the job is done than the employee.
- The employee is on the payroll of the employer, whereas the independent contractor is hired primarily to produce a certain product or result without being on the payroll.

independent contractor One who operates his or her own business and contracts to do work for others; the latter do not control the method or administrative details of how the work is performed.

For example, compare the following two ways in which a business hires an accountant:

- Gabe's Fine Furniture, Inc. pays an accountant an annual fee of $1,500 to prepare its federal and state tax returns. The accountant comes to Gabe's business about four times a year to collect data from the company's financial books. The data is used for the tax returns.
- Ace Trucking Co. pays an accountant $1,538.46 every two weeks ($40,000.00 a year) to keep its books, pay accounts receivable, prepare the payroll, prepare tax returns, and perform other accountancy tasks in the financial office of the company.

Gabe's accountant is an independent contractor, whereas Ace's accountant is an employee. The latter is on staff and is subject to as much supervision as the company's management decides to provide. Gabe's accountant, on the other hand, probably performs his or her task with relatively little supervision from anyone at the furniture company.

The general rule is that the person who hires independent contractors is *not* liable for their torts. (See Exhibit 14–10.) If you are injured by an independent contractor, your only recourse is to sue the independent contractor. Under this general rule, respondeat superior does not apply. There are, however, two major exceptions. Vicarious liability *will* continue to apply when someone is injured while the independent contractor is performing:

- a **nondelegable duty** (e.g., a city's duty to keep its streets in repair) or
- an **inherently dangerous** task (e.g., transporting dynamite).

nondelegable duty A task considered so important or critical that you are liable for injury or other loss when the task is carelessly performed, even if you hired an independent contractor to perform it.

inherently dangerous Being susceptible to cause harm or injury due to the nature of the product, service, or activity involved.

(See other examples in Exhibit 14–10.) While performing work in either category, the independent contractor is treated as an employee for purposes of vicarious liability.

Exhibit 14–10
Liability for torts of independent contractors.

General Rule
A defendant is *not* vicariously liable for the torts of his or her independent contractor. If the independent contractor injures someone while working for the defendant, the victim is limited to suing the independent contractor.

Exceptions
There are two circumstances in which a defendant *will* be liable for the torts committed by his or her independent contractor:

1. The independent contractor is performing certain nondelegable duties of the defendant (e.g., a city's duty to keep its streets in repair, a landlord's duty to keep the leased premises safe for business visitors, a duty of a common carrier to transport passengers safely, and other special duties imposed by statute or regulation). A nondelegable duty is a task considered so important or critical that you are liable for injury or other loss when the task is carelessly performed, even if you hired an independent contractor to perform it.
2. The independent contractor is performing inherently dangerous work for the defendant (e.g., transporting dynamite, keeping vicious animals, or conducting fireworks exhibitions). Inherently dangerous means being susceptible to cause harm or injury due to the nature of the product, service, or activity involved. (See Chapter 11 on whether some of these inherently dangerous activities might also subject a party to strict liability.)

ASSIGNMENT 14.11

a. A business hires a construction company to erect a commercial building. While one of the company's executives is driving back from the job site in her car, she carelessly hits Tom's car.
b. A month later, the company is transporting a gigantic derrick along a small county road on the back of a massive trailer. An accident occurs when the derrick falls off the trailer and damages Mary's barn.

In each case, who can sue whom and on what theories? Be sure to discuss vicarious liability, if applicable.

joint enterprise An express or implied agreement to participate in a common enterprise over which the participants have a mutual right of control. Often called a *joint venture* if the purpose of the enterprise is business or profit-related.

Joint Enterprise We come now to the second example of vicarious unreasonableness listed in Exhibit 14–8, the **joint enterprise**. For parties to be engaged in a joint enterprise, the following elements must be present:

1. an express or implied agreement to participate in the enterprise together
2. a common purpose
3. a mutual right to control the enterprise

In a few states, the agreement can be to go to a picnic or to the zoo. In most states, however, the common purpose must be business or profit-related. When such a common purpose exists, the enterprise is sometimes referred to as a *joint venture*.

The third element has caused the courts the most difficulty. How, for example, do you establish that two people riding in a car for a common business purpose have the same (mutual) right to control the direction and operation of the car?

Mutuality of the right of control is not established simply because both are riding together for a business purpose. There must be more concrete indications that the passenger has the same right to control the direction and operation of the car as the driver. Such indications would include: they rented the car with their joint funds; both own the car; they share expenses on the maintenance of the car; both have driven the car in the past; on this trip, they alternate the driving; the passenger is reading the road map and giving route instructions to the driver; etc. The court must be able to find that there was a clear understanding between the parties that both had an equal say in the operation of the car, even if only one party did all the driving at the time the car had the accident injuring the plaintiff. Taking all the factors into consideration, the question is whether it would have been odd, unusual, or presumptuous for the passenger to have exercised the same authority as the driver in the operation of the car. If so, there probably was no mutual right of control.

Once a joint enterprise is established, vicarious liability comes into play. In automobile cases, the passenger is vicariously unreasonable if the driver's unreasonableness caused the accident. In a sense, the joint enterprise is treated as a partnership in which one partner becomes personally liable for the acts of all the other partners. Most joint enterprises, however, are usually more limited in their duration and less structured than the traditional partnership.

ASSIGNMENT 14.12

a. Husband and wife are in a car on their way to sign up for a motel training course in which couples are taught the motel business. The car is in both names. The wife is driving. An accident occurs. The third party sues the husband for negligence. How would you determine if there is a joint enterprise?

b. Dr. Jones and Dr. Smith practice medicine separately; they are not partners. During times of vacation, however, they cover for each other's patients. While Dr. Smith is on vacation, Dr. Jones sees one of Dr. Smith's patients. The patient suffers an injury because of negligent treatment by Dr. Jones. Assume that Dr. Jones, unlike Dr. Smith, has no liability insurance and almost no assets. Dr. Smith, therefore, is the "deep pocket." Vicarious liability? Can the patient sue Dr. Smith for the negligence of Dr. Jones? Assume that Dr. Smith had no reason to suspect that Dr. Jones would ever commit negligence.

Once a joint enterprise is established, there can *also* be **imputed contributory negligence.** Compare the following two cases:

imputed contributory negligence The defense of contributory negligence is attributed or imposed on someone who did not act unreasonably him- or herself but who is subject to this defense solely because of his or her relationship with the person who was unreasonable.

Case I (Imputed Negligence) Dan and Paul are engaged in a joint enterprise. They are in a truck on a highway. Dan is driving and Paul is a passenger. Dan carelessly crashes into Mary's car. Mary sues Paul for negligence (Mary v. Paul). Because of the joint enterprise, the negligence (unreasonableness) of Dan is imposed upon (i.e., imputed to) Paul.

Case II (Imputed Contributory Negligence) Same accident as in Case I except that this time Paul sues Mary for negligence (Paul v. Mary), claiming that her negligence caused the crash with Dan. Mary's defense is that Dan's negligence caused the accident and that this contributory negligence should be imposed upon (i.e., imputed to) Paul because of the joint enterprise between them.

The same principle of imputed contributory negligence will apply in the employer-employee relationship discussed earlier. If the employer sues a third party for damages suffered by the employer arising out of an accident in which the employee was also negligent, the contributory negligence of the employee will be imputed to the employer in the employer's negligence action against the third party. For more on contributory negligence, and its replacement by *comparative negligence*, see Chapter 17.

family purpose doctrine The owner of a car or person controlling the use of a car is liable for the negligence committed by a family member while driving the car for a family purpose. Also called family automobile rule.

Family Purpose Doctrine The final form of vicarious unreasonableness mentioned in Exhibit 14–8 is based on the **family purpose doctrine**. It makes a nondriver vicariously liable for an accident caused by a driver. Not all states have adopted the family purpose doctrine, and those that have do not all agree on its elements. In general, the elements are as follows:

- Defendant must be an owner of the car or be in control of the use of the car.
- Defendant must make the car available for family use rather than for the defendant's business. (In some states, the defendant must make it available for general family use rather than just for a particular occasion.)
- The driver must be a member of the defendant's immediate household.
- The driver must be using the car for a family purpose at the time of the accident.
- The driver must have had the defendant's express or implied consent to be using the car at the time of the accident.

The defendant does not have to be the traditional head of the household and does not have to be in the car at the time of the accident. Again, individual states, by case law or by statute, may add different elements to the doctrine or may reject it entirely.

ASSIGNMENT 14.13

Fred has just bought a used car, but it will not be ready for a week. During the week he is waiting, he rents a car. He pays a per-mile charge on the car. He tells his family that the car is to be used only to drive to work. One day while the car is at home and Fred is out of town, his child becomes sick. Fred's mother, who is staying with Fred until an opening comes up in a local nursing home, drives the child to the hospital. On the way, she has an accident, injuring the plaintiff, a pedestrian. The plaintiff sues Fred for negligence. Does the family purpose doctrine apply?

dangerous propensity A tendency to cause damage or harm as shown by prior acts or omissions that caused damage or harm.

negligent entrustment Carelessly allowing the use of a vehicle, tool, or other object by someone who poses an unreasonable risk of harm to others.

Parent and Child The traditional rule is that parents are not vicariously liable for the torts committed by their children. If a child commits negligence (or an intentional tort), the child is personally liable. The parent might be individually (not vicariously) liable for his or her own negligence in failing to use reasonable care to supervise a child with a known **dangerous propensity** or for actually participating in the unreasonable conduct of the child. Similarly, there can be individual liability for **negligent entrustment** whenever a person carelessly allows someone such as a child to use a vehicle, tool, or any other object that poses an unreasonable risk of harm to others. This kind of liability is quite separate from the parent being vicariously liable simply because he or she is the parent of a child who commits a tort.

In some states, however, there are statutes that *do* impose vicarious liability on parents for the torts of their child, but only up to a limited dollar amount, e.g., $3,000. (See also Chapter 22 on torts against and within the family.)

CHECK THE CITE

Basketball player Allen Iverson was at the Eyebar nightclub with his bodyguard. Another patron, Marlin Godfrey, was injured in a fight with the bodyguard. Godfrey sued Iverson for negligent supervision of his bodyguard. How did the court define negligent supervision? What was the main issue in the case, and why did the court find against Iverson on that issue? Read the case of *Godfrey v. Iverson*, 559 F.3d 569 (United States Court of Appeals, D.C. Cir. 2009). To read the opinion online, (1) Go to the site of the United States Court of Appeals for the District of

Columbia Circuit (www.cadc.uscourts.gov). Click Opinions, then select all opinions for March 2009. Click the pdf file for the Godfrey case. (2) Read the case on www.findlaw.com (caselaw.lp.findlaw.com/data2/circs/dc/077151p.pdf). (3) Run a citation search ("559 F.3d 569") or a party search (Godfrey Iverson) in the Legal Opinions and Journals database of Google Scholar (scholar.google.com).

PROJECT

In Google, Bing, or another general search engine, run the following search: runner scam negligence insurance. Write a short essay in which you describe cases of insurance fraud involving runners and negligence claims. You can consult as many websites as you wish, but you must quote from at least three separate sites.

ETHICS IN A TORTS PRACTICE

You are a paralegal working in the law office of Hines & Hines, which is representing Mary Ford in her automobile negligence case. The lead attorney, Paul Hines, and Mary have been good friends for years. The contingency fee agreement that Mary signed will give the firm thirty-three percent of proceeds from a favorable judgment or settlement. Paul and Mary, however, have an oral agreement that the firm will take no more than twenty-five percent because of the friendship. What ethical problems, if any, might exist?

SUMMARY

In most negligence cases, the standard of care is reasonable care, which is ordinary prudence under the circumstances to avoid injury or other loss. Reasonableness is determined by assessing the totality of circumstances, e.g., what the senses reveal, the kind of activity and area involved, and the experience of the parties. A breach of duty is unreasonable conduct endangering someone to whom you owe a duty of care. The defendant has breached this duty if his or her acts and omissions are substantially different from those of a reasonable person under the same circumstances. A reasonable person is someone who can make mistakes and cause injury, but never due to carelessness. Under the breach-of-duty equation, if the danger of a serious accident outweighs the burden or inconvenience of taking precautions to avoid the accident, the reasonable person would take those precautions. Furthermore, the more important or socially useful the activity, the more risks the reasonable person is willing to take. In assessing a burden or inconvenience, the court will consider cost, time, and the impact of the burden or inconvenience on the effectiveness of what the defendant was doing before the accident.

Physically, a reasonable person has the same strengths and weaknesses as the defendant. Mentally, the reasonable person has the basic knowledge and intelligence needed in everyday life, even if the defendant does not. If the defendant has more than minimum knowledge and skills (e.g., has professional knowledge and skills), then the reasonable person is deemed to have the same knowledge and skills. If the defendant is a child, the standard is a reasonable child of the age and intelligence of the defendant, unless the defendant was engaging in an adult activity, in which case the standard is the reasonable adult.

Res ipsa loquitur (RIL) allows a jury to infer unreasonableness simply by reason of the fact that the accident happened, even if there is no direct or specific evidence of unreasonableness. The jury is then free to agree or disagree that the defendant was unreasonable. It must be more likely than not that the accident was due to someone's unreasonableness—the defendant's—and the plaintiff must not be a responsible cause of the accident.

Custom and usage (what others in the business or industry are doing) is one of the factors a court will consider in assessing reasonableness. Following custom and usage does not necessarily make a defendant reasonable. Under the breach-of-duty equation, a defendant may be required to do more than what everyone else is doing.

If the defendant has violated a statute, the unexcused violation might be considered negligence per se, create a presumption of negligence, or simply be some evidence of negligence. We need to ask whether the statute was violated, whether the violation was excused, whether the violation caused the accident, whether the plaintiff is within the class of persons protected by the statute, and whether the plaintiff has suffered the kind of harm the statute was intended to avoid. Conversely, the defendant's compliance with a statute does not automatically establish reasonableness. Compliance may merely constitute some evidence of reasonableness. Reasonable care under the circumstances may call for more than the minimum requirements imposed by the statute.

Guest statutes often refuse to impose liability on hosts for ordinary negligence. To be liable, the host must commit gross negligence or have been willful, wanton, or reckless. Under the doctrine of respondeat superior, employers are vicariously liable for the negligence committed by their employees within the scope of employment. There is no vicarious liability for the negligence committed by independent contractors unless the latter are performing nondelegable duties or inherently dangerous work. Participants in a joint enterprise are vicariously liable for the negligence committed by each other in furtherance of the objective of the enterprise. Under the family purpose doctrine, the owner of (or one in control of) a car who makes it available for family (nonbusiness) use will be vicariously liable for the negligence of a driver in the owner's immediate household who was using the car for a family purpose at the time of the accident with the express or implied consent of the owner.

Unless modified by statute, parents are not vicariously liable for the torts of their children. A parent may be independently liable for negligence if, for example, the parent does not exercise reasonable care to supervise a child with known dangerous propensities. A parent can also be liable for negligent entrustment.

KEY TERMS

reasonable care *220*
breach of duty *220*
unreasonable *220*
standard of care *220*
factor *220*
reasonable person *222*
breach-of-duty equation *222*
hypothesis *224*
social value *226*
risk–benefit analysis *226*
subjective standard *227*
objective standard *227*
res ipsa loquitur *230*
joint and several liability *234*
contributory negligence *235*
custom and usage *237*
negligence per se *238*
legislative intent *239*
but-for test *240*
substantial-factor test *240*
presumption *242*
rebuttable *242*
guest *244*
guest statute *244*
ordinary negligence *244*
gross negligence *245*
willful *245*
wanton *245*
reckless *245*
imputed *245*
imputed negligence *245*
vicarious liability *245*
deep pocket *246*
negligent hiring *246*
independent liability *247*
respondeat superior *247*
employment *247*
agent *247*
principal *247*
scope of employment *247*
frolic *248*
independent contractor *249*
nondelegable duty *249*
inherently dangerous *249*
joint enterprise *250*
imputed contributory negligence *251*
family purpose doctrine *252*
dangerous propensity *252*
negligent entrustment *252*

REVIEW QUESTIONS

1. What is reasonable care?
2. In the law of negligence, what is a breach of duty?
3. When is someone unreasonable?
4. What is the standard of care in most negligence cases?
5. What are the factors that help determine reasonableness?
6. What do we mean when we say that reasonableness is a comparative standard?
7. How does a reasonable person differ from an unreasonable person and a perfect person?
8. What is the breach-of-duty equation?
9. What is a danger/caution hypothesis?
10. What is meant by burden or inconvenience in the breach-of-duty equation?
11. What is meant by social value in the breach-of-duty equation?
12. What is a risk–benefit analysis?
13. What are the physical characteristics of the reasonable person?
14. What are the mental characteristics of the reasonable person when the defendant is an adult?
15. What are the mental characteristics of the reasonable person when the defendant is a child?
16. What is the effect of res ipsa loquitur (RIL)?
17. What are the elements of RIL?
18. How will a court assess custom and usage in determining reasonableness?
19. What steps must be taken to determine the impact of a violation of a statute in a negligence case?
20. What is a guest statute?
21. When will a defendant not be liable for ordinary negligence?
22. What is vicarious liability?
23. When is an employer vicariously liable for the negligence of his or her employee?
24. What factors will a court use to determine whether conduct is within the scope of employment?
25. Who is liable for the negligence of an independent contractor?
26. When are participants of a joint enterprise vicariously liable for each other's negligence?
27. What is the family purpose doctrine?
28. Is a parent vicariously liable for the negligence of his or her child?
29. What is negligent entrustment?

HELPFUL WEBSITES

- **Breach of Duty**
  www.weitzlux.com/breachduty_398.html
  www.lexisnexis.com/lawschool/study/outlines/html/torts/torts04.htm
  law.findlaw.com/state-laws/negligence
  en.wikipedia.org/wiki/Negligence
  en.wikipedia.org/wiki/Reasonable_person
- **The Reasonable Person**
  www.knowledgerush.com/kr/encyclopedia/Reasonable_man
  en.wikipedia.org/wiki/Reasonable_person
- **Res Ipsa Loquitur**
  www.aana.com (type "res ipsa" in the search box)
  en.wikipedia.org/wiki/Res_ipsa_loquitur
- **Dram Shop Liability by State**
  www.wisbar.org/am/template.cfm?section=wisconsin_lawyer&template=/cm/contentdisplay.cfm&contentid=50672
- **General Search**
  In Google, Bing, or another search engine, run the following search: elements negligence "breach of duty" duty tort

ENDNOTES

1. Andrew Pollack, "Paper Trail Haunts G.M. After It Loses Injury Suit: An Old Memo Hinted at the Price of Safety," *N.Y. Times*, July 12, 1999, at A12.
2. 25 Cal. 2d 486, 154 P.2d 687 (1944).
3. W. Page Keeton et al., *Prosser and Keeton on the Law of Torts* 252 (5th ed. 1984).
4. Id at 499.
5. The distinction between an employee and an independent contractor is also important for federal purposes. Social security and withholding taxes, for example, must be deducted from payments to employees, but not to independent contractors. The Internal Revenue Service has its own tests to determine when a worker is an employee (www.irs.gov/businesses/small/article/0,,id=99921,00.html). Employers can be fined for attempting to treat employees as independent contractors.

Student StudyWARE™ CD-ROM
For additional materials, please go to the student CD in this book.

CHAPTER

15

NEGLIGENCE: ELEMENT III: PROXIMATE CAUSE

CHAPTER OUTLINE

- Introduction
- Terminology Problems
- Actual Cause
- Cutoff Test of Proximate Cause
- Overview of Steps Needed to Analyze Proximate Cause

CHAPTER OBJECTIVES

After completing this chapter, you should be able to:

- Identify the two questions that must be asked to determine if proximate cause has been established.
- State the two tests for actual cause.
- Explain how the facts of time, place, and history can be used to establish actual cause.
- Understand the cutoff test of proximate cause.
- Explain the application of the thin-skull rule and the manner-of-injury rule when an unforeseeable injury occurs.
- Explain when an intervening cause can be a superseding cause.

INTRODUCTION

Plaintiffs must show that their injury or other loss was the natural and probable result or consequence of the defendant's negligent conduct. "Natural and probable consequences are those which human foresight can anticipate because they happen so frequently they may be expected to recur."[1] This brings us to **proximate cause**, the third element of negligence. Proximate cause is defined as a cause that is legally sufficient to impose liability for the results of one's wrongful act or omission. There are two components of proximate cause: actual cause and legal cause:

proximate cause A cause that is legally sufficient to impose liability for the results of one's wrongful act or omission. There are two components of proximate cause: actual cause (which answers the question of who was the cause in fact of the harm or other loss) and legal cause (which answers the question of whether the harm or other loss was the foreseeable consequence of the original risk).

- *Actual cause*. The defendant was the cause in fact of the harm or other loss suffered by the plaintiff.
- *Legal cause*. The loss or other harm was the foreseeable consequence of the original risk created by the defendant.

In most negligence cases involving one defendant and one injury, legal cause is relatively easy to establish once actual cause is established.

EXAMPLE
Tom carelessly leaves garden tools on the front walkway of his home. One day, a neighbor injures her elbow after tripping on one of the tools.

If the tool had not been carelessly left on the walkway, the neighbor would not have been injured. The neighbor will have little difficulty establishing that this carelessness was the *actual cause* of the elbow injury. *Legal cause* is also easy to establish in this example. The risk of carelessly leaving tools on the walkway is a bodily injury by someone tripping over the tools. That's what happened. The elbow injury was a foreseeable result of the original risk that Tom took when he carelessly left the tools on the walkway. Tom, therefore, was both the actual cause and the legal cause (and hence the proximate cause) of the elbow injury.

When multiple parties and injuries are involved, however, legal cause may not be as clear.

EXAMPLE
Sam drives his car down the street at an excessive rate of speed and hits Paul's car, breaking Paul's leg. While Paul is lying in the road, another car accidentally runs over Paul's arm. When the ambulance finally arrives and takes Paul to the hospital, a doctor carelessly treats Paul, resulting in an injury to Paul's knee. After being treated, Paul discovers that someone at the hospital has stolen his wallet.

We have three injuries (leg, arm, and knee) and a property loss (the missing wallet). Our concern is whether Sam is the proximate cause of them all. Of course, Paul has other parties he can go after. He can try to sue the second car's driver who injured Paul's arm, the doctor who injured Paul's knee, the hospital where the doctor worked, and the thief (if caught) who took his wallet. He might sue them all or ignore anyone who is **judgment proof** (has insufficient assets to pay a potential judgment). There might be **joint and several liability** among Sam and others involved. For our purposes, however, we will assume that Paul is suing *only* Sam for the three injuries and the lost wallet.

judgment proof Having few or no assets from which a money judgment can be satisfied. Having shallow pockets.

joint and several liability Legally responsible together and individually. Each wrongdoer is individually responsible for the *entire* judgment; the plaintiff can choose to collect from one wrongdoer or from all of them until the judgment is satisfied.

It can be argued that Paul would not have suffered three injuries and a stolen wallet if Sam had not been speeding on the day he hit Paul. In this sense, Sam caused all four results. But was he the proximate cause of them all? That is the question we will address in this chapter. To answer it, we will focus on the two components of proximate cause: actual cause and legal cause. See Exhibit 15–1 for a summary of the tests for each that we will examine in this chapter.

1. The Actual Cause Tests
   a. But-for test (used when there is only one alleged cause): Is it more likely than not that but for the defendant's unreasonable acts or omissions, the injury would not have been suffered by the plaintiff?
   b. Substantial-factor test (used when there is more than one alleged cause): Is it more likely than not that the defendant's unreasonable acts or omissions had a significant or important role in producing the injury suffered by the plaintiff?
2. The Legal Cause Test
   Is the injury suffered by the plaintiff the *foreseeable consequence* of the *original risk* created by the defendant's unreasonable acts or omissions?

Exhibit 15–1
The tests of proximate cause.

TERMINOLOGY PROBLEMS

One final caution about terminology before we begin. Unfortunately we are stuck with the phrase *proximate cause* even though not all courts use the phrase in the same way.

- Some courts use *proximate cause* to mean its two components—actual cause and legal cause.
- Other courts use *proximate cause* to mean legal cause only; they cover actual cause (cause in fact) separately.

In this chapter, we will follow the first approach and treat proximate cause as having two components: actual cause and legal cause.

The other difficulty with the law of proximate cause is that it covers more than the topic of causation. According to one court:

> "Proximate cause"—in itself an unfortunate term—is merely the limitation which the courts have placed upon the actor's responsibility for the consequences of his conduct. In a philosophical sense, the consequences of an act go forward to eternity, and the causes of an event go back to the discovery of America and beyond. "The fatal trespass done by Eve was cause of all our woe." But any attempt to impose responsibility upon such a basis would result in infinite liability for all wrongful acts, and would "set society on edge and fill the courts with endless litigation." As a practical matter, legal responsibility must be limited to those causes which are so closely connected with the result and of such significance that the law is justified in imposing liability. Some boundary must be set to liability for the consequences of any act, upon the basis of some social idea of justice or policy.[2]

Hence the law of proximate cause will tell us when parties will not be liable for all the harms they have caused by their wrongful conduct. In this sense, proximate cause is as much about policy as it is about causation.

ACTUAL CAUSE

We begin by a close examination of **actual case** (cause in fact). There are two tests to determine whether the defendant was the actual cause of the harm or other loss suffered by the plaintiff: the **but-for test** and the **substantial-factor test**. The latter is fully adequate and often easier for a plaintiff to establish. It is important, however, that you understand both tests.

The but-for test asks the following question: Would the plaintiff have been injured but for what the defendant did or failed to do? Under this test, if the plaintiff would have been injured regardless of what the defendant did or failed to do, the defendant did not cause (was not the actual cause of) the injury.

actual cause Cause in fact. Causation established by either the but-for test or the substantial-factor test. An event (e.g., the injury) (a) would not have occurred without the act or omission of the party, or (b) the party's acts or omissions had a significant or important role in bringing about the event.

but-for test Would the event (e.g., the injury) have happened without the act or omission of the party? But for the act or omission, would the event have occurred? Also called the sine qua non test.

substantial-factor test The party had a significant or important role in bringing about the event (e.g., injury).

EXAMPLES

- Sam carelessly drives his car into Fred's barn. But for the way Sam drove, the damage to the barn would not have occurred. Sam, therefore, is the actual cause of the damage to Fred's property.
- Dwayne is an ambulance driver. One day he gets a call from the plaintiff's home for an ambulance to take the plaintiff to the hospital. Dwayne takes the call at 9:00 A.M. Because of Dwayne's careless driving, he arrives at the plaintiff's home 45 minutes later than he would have arrived if he had not been careless. When he does arrive, the plaintiff is already dead. According to the coroner's report, the plaintiff died at 9:01 A.M. Dwayne was not the actual cause of the death. Dwayne was careless and unreasonable in driving to the plaintiff, but the plaintiff would have died even if Dwayne had driven with great caution and skill. But for what Dwayne did or failed to do, the plaintiff would still have been dead when he arrived to take her to the hospital.
- Mary is a doctor whose license to practice medicine has been suspended for a year because she illegally prescribed drugs to several patients. In secret, however, Mary continues her practice. During this time, she performs a routine operation on George. George suffers serious complications following the operation and dies. His estate sues Mary for negligence. At the trial there is no evidence that Mary was careless or unreasonable in performing the operation. The estate introduces evidence that Mary performed the operation while her license was suspended. The lack of a license, however, was not the actual cause of George's death. Even if Mary had had a license, the death would still have occurred. But for Mary's not having a license, it cannot be said that George would not have died. There was no evidence that Mary did not use adequate professional skill in performing the operation. It may be that a separate criminal proceeding can be brought against Mary for practicing without a license, but the estate loses its negligence action for failure to establish actual cause.

The but-for test is sufficient for most tort cases on the issue of causation. This includes negligence cases as well as those charging intentional torts or strict liability torts. There is, however, an alternative test: the defendant will be considered the actual cause of the plaintiff's injury if the defendant was *a substantial factor* in producing the injury. Every time you establish actual cause by the but-for test, you have also established that the defendant was a substantial factor. But the converse is not necessarily true:

EXAMPLE

While hunting, Helen and Jane carelessly shoot their guns at the same time through some bushes, trying to hit an animal. Both bullets, however, hit the plaintiff, who is killed instantly. Either bullet would have killed the plaintiff. Here, the but-for test leads to a bizarre result. Helen says, correctly, that but for her bullet, the plaintiff would have died anyway. Jane says, correctly, that but for her bullet, the plaintiff would have died anyway. Hence, both Helen and Jane use the but-for test to show that she individually was not the actual cause of the plaintiff's death.

The plaintiff's estate would not be able to win a negligence action against anyone if the but-for test were the only test to determine cause in fact in such a case. Hence the need exists for an alternative test. If either Helen or Jane was *a substantial factor* in producing the death, then either one is the actual cause of the death. When two people fire a bullet at a person who is killed by the impacts, the law will say that they are both substantial factors in producing the death so long as each was independently sufficient to cause the same harm. In this case, therefore, the substantial-factor test leads to the establishment of actual cause, even though the but-for test would not.

It is usually easier for a plaintiff to establish actual cause by the substantial-factor test than by the but-for test, but in most cases, both tests will lead to the same result. In tort law, it is sufficient if the plaintiff proves actual cause by the broader substantial-factor test. *In analyzing any tort problem on the issue of actual cause, you should apply both tests, but always keep in mind that the substantial-factor test will be sufficient.*

In our hunting example, assume that it took the shots of Helen *and* Jane to kill the plaintiff—neither shot was sufficient in itself. Under these facts, both tests of actual cause would lead to the same result:

- But for Helen's bullet, the plaintiff would not have died (it took both bullets to kill the plaintiff).
- But for Jane's bullet, the plaintiff would not have died (it took both bullets to kill the plaintiff).
- Helen's bullet played a significant role (was a substantial factor) in the plaintiff's death.
- Jane's bullet played a significant role (was a substantial factor) in the plaintiff's death.

Note that the substantial-factor test requires only that the defendant be *a* substantial factor. It is not necessary that the defendant be the *sole* or *only* cause of the plaintiff's injury in order to be the actual cause of the injury. It is not even necessary to show that the defendant was the dominant factor in producing the injury. Being *a* substantial factor is enough.

ASSIGNMENT 15.1

When you phrase an actual-cause issue or question, you list relevant facts along with one of the tests for actual cause. For example, "But for the defendant's excessive speed on a slippery road at night, would the plaintiff's car have been struck by the defendant's car?" Reread the facts of the case presented at the beginning of the chapter involving Paul's injured leg, arm, and knee, and his lost wallet.

a. For each of Paul's injuries and his property loss, phrase the actual-cause question using the but-for test. (Write four separate questions.)
b. For each of Paul's injuries and his property loss, phrase the actual-cause question using the substantial-factor test. (Write four separate questions.)

You do not have to answer the questions; simply phrase them.

Evidence of Causation

What do we mean when we say that there is evidence of causation—whether we are using the but-for test or the substantial-factor test? How does one establish a connection between cause and effect? For the vast majority of cases, our most sophisticated tool in assessing causation is common sense based upon everyday experience. Our common sense depends heavily on the factors of *time, space,* and *history.* These factors present us with some fundamental hypotheses about life and human nature. (A **hypothesis** is an assumption or theory to be proven or disproven.)

hypothesis An assumption or theory to be proven or disproven.

Time: When did the injury occur? After the defendant's acts or omissions? The shorter the time between the plaintiff's injury and the acts or omissions of the defendant, the more convinced we are that those acts or omissions caused the injury. The more time that elapses between the defendant's acts or omissions and the injury of the plaintiff, the more skeptical we are that those acts or omissions caused the injury.

EXAMPLES

- Tom becomes sick seconds after drinking a beer. Common sense tells us that drinking the beer may have caused the sickness since the two events (drinking and sickness) came so close together. We would be less inclined to reach this conclusion, however, if Tom's sickness occurred two weeks later.
- Mary and Claire belong to the same social club. Mary has a pet-walking business in which all of her clients are members of the club. (Every morning, an employee of Mary's business goes to the homes of clients to get their pets for walks.) Her business drops by 80 percent within one week after Claire tells many other club members that Mary is incompetent. Common sense tells us that Claire's derogatory statement may have caused some or all of Mary's decline in business, since the decline occurred so soon after Claire made the statement. We would be less inclined to reach this conclusion if the decline occurred a year later.

In the first example, notice that we did *not* say that the beer caused the sickness because the sickness occurred seconds after drinking it. Nor did we say that the beer could not have caused the sickness if it occurred two weeks later. Rarely can such definitive conclusions be made on the basis of time evidence alone. All we can say is that our common sense suggests these conclusions, although we are willing to look at any other evidence that may suggest different conclusions. We need to be alert to the logical fallacy known as *post hoc ergo propter hoc* ("after this, therefore, because of this"). We cannot conclude that X caused Y simply because Y occurred right after X occurred. The sequence of events can, along with other facts, help us identify causation, but chronology alone is almost never conclusive.

In the second example (the one about the pet-walking business), we did *not* say that the derogatory statement caused the decline in business because the decline occurred one week after the derogatory statement was made. Nor did we say that the statement could not have caused the decline if it occurred a year later. All we can say is that time evidence is one of the relevant pieces of information that we need to consider.

Space: Did the injury occur in the same area or vicinity where the defendant acted or failed to act? The more closely we can link the defendant's acts or omissions to the area or vicinity of the plaintiff's injury, the more convinced we are that those acts or omissions caused the injury. The greater the distance between the area or vicinity of the injury and the area or vicinity of the defendant's acts or omissions, the more skeptical we are that those acts or omissions caused the injury.

EXAMPLES

- One of Bob's jobs at a printing plant is to pour a certain ink, which has a heavy odor, into the presses. Bob develops a respiratory problem. He says that the problem is due to breathing the ink fumes. Common sense tells us that the ink fumes may have caused the respiratory problem since he worked so close to the ink. We would be less inclined to reach this conclusion, however, if Bob worked 500 yards away from the presses that use the ink.
- Lena is a department store clerk where she is in charge of one of the five cosmetics counters. Occasionally she works at the other four counters. The store suspects that she is stealing cosmetics (which would constitute the crime of larceny and the tort of conversion). All of the missing cosmetics were at Lena's main counter and at those counters where she occasionally has worked. Common sense tells us that Lena may have taken the cosmetics since she was physically present at those counters where the goods were missing. We would be less inclined to reach this conclusion, however, if Lena never worked at the counters that experienced the missing cosmetics.

These observations about time and space evidence are simply hypotheses or assumptions about life and human nature. They are nothing more than points of departure in our search for causation. We must never close our minds to evidence that may point to other conclusions. Some illnesses, for example, may not appear until months or years after an accident, yet we can still be convinced that one caused the other. So, too, we can be convinced that actions taken in New York can lead to damage or injury in California. There is nothing ironclad about the hypotheses. The facts of each individual case must be carefully scrutinized. The predisposition of our common sense, however, tells us to begin this scrutiny with the hypotheses on time and space.

Assume that for years a railroad has stationed a guard at a point where the track crosses a highway. One day, the railroad removes the guard. Two days later, a train crashes into a car at the intersection. Was the absence of the guard the actual cause of the injury? Was the absence of the guard a substantial factor in producing the injury? Among the evidence to be introduced by the plaintiff's attorney are time and space evidence. The attorney will present evidence to show that the crash occurred soon after the guard was removed (time) and that the crash occurred at the very intersection where the guard was once stationed (space). Common sense tells us, according to this attorney, that the accident would not have happened if the guard had been there, or at the very least, that the absence of the guard was a substantial factor in producing the crash. Time-and-space evidence is critical on the issue of causation, but not necessarily determinative. Other evidence might show that the job function of the guard was not to try to prevent the kind of collision that occurred and that even if the guard had been present, the collision would have occurred anyway. Again, the time and space evidence is but a point of departure.

Another important source of causation evidence is *history.* Here again, a basic hypothesis is in play.

History: In the past, have the same or similar acts or omissions by the defendant or people like the defendant produced this kind of injury? The more often this kind of injury has resulted from such acts or omissions in the past, the more convinced we are that the acts or omissions of the defendant caused the injury. If this kind of injury has never or has rarely been produced by such acts or omissions, we are more skeptical that the defendant's acts or omissions caused the injury.

Of course, just because something has happened in the past does not necessarily mean that it happened in this particular case. The predisposition of our common sense, however, tells us that history does tend to repeat itself. Hence, our common sense leads us to inquire about the past. In the railroad crossing case, for example, the plaintiff's attorney may try to introduce evidence that collisions between trains and cars never occurred when the guard was on duty, as a way of proving that it is more likely than not that the absence of the guard caused the collision.

Hence, evidence of time, space, and history is critical in beginning to collect evidence of actual causation. We are drawn to search out such evidence on the basis of some basic hypotheses about time, space, and history. Such evidence will not always be conclusive—either way—on the issue of actual causation. All of the facts and circumstances of a given case must be examined. Start your examination, however, with the evidence of time, space, and history.

Weight of the Evidence

Let us shift our focus for a moment away from the tests for actual causation (but-for and substantial-factor) to the **standard of proof** needed to establish actual causation. By standard of proof we mean how convincing the evidence of

standard of proof A statement of how convincing a version of a fact must be before the trier of facts (usually the jury) can accept it as true.

To prove causation, attorneys often hire consultants to help explain why and how things went wrong. If they are engineers or scientists, they are sometimes called forensic engineers or scientists. Exponent, Inc. is a company consisting of these individuals. One of the cases for which they were hired involved the death of 113 people at the Hyatt Regency Hotel in Kansas City. An estimated 2,000 people had gathered in the lobby area to enjoy a tea dance. Suddenly, the two walkways that spanned the lobby collapsed. Forensic engineers from Exponent, Inc. sifted through the wreckage for four days. Speculation that the accident had been the result of "harmonic vibrations" caused by dancers on the walkway were disproved by mathematical models of walkways and by the sequence of events. Combined testing, materials, and stress analysis led the engineers to testify that the collapse had occurred when a bolt end on a rod that attached the walkways to the ceiling had pulled through a walkway beam.

Photo courtesy of Exponent, Inc.

something must be before a fact finder can accept it as true. (The fact finder is usually the jury; if there is no jury, it is the judge.) The overall persuasiveness of evidence is referred to as the **weight of the evidence**. The standard of proof, therefore, can be phrased as the "weight" that evidence of something must have before a fact finder can accept it as true. Here our focus is on how convincing the plaintiff's evidence must be that the defendant was the actual cause of the plaintiff's injury. There are several different "weights" that evidence can have. Evidence of something can be overwhelming, highly likely, more likely than not, fifty/fifty, possible, etc. In most tort cases, the minimum standard of proof that must be met is **preponderance of the evidence**. Under this standard, a party must prove that its version of the facts is, more likely than not, accurate as alleged. The preponderance-of-the-evidence standard ("more likely than not") is the minimum degree of believability (the minimum weight) that a plaintiff's evidence must have in order for a fact finder to be able to accept the plaintiff's version of who was the actual cause of his or her injury. Using the two tests for actual cause, the standard would be expressed as follows:

weight of the evidence The overall persuasiveness of the evidence presented; the tendency of all the evidence to support one side or another.

preponderance of the evidence The standard of proof that is met when the evidence establishes that it is more likely than not that the facts are as alleged.

> Plaintiff must produce evidence that is convincing enough for a fact finder to conclude it is *more likely than not* that the defendant was a substantial factor in producing the injury, *or*
>
> Plaintiff must produce evidence that is convincing enough for a fact finder to conclude it is *more likely than not* that but for what the defendant did, the plaintiff's injury would not have occurred.

A mere *possibility* that the defendant was a substantial factor in producing the injury is not enough. (Likewise, a mere possibility that, but for what the defendant did, the plaintiff would not have been injured is not enough.) Anything is possible. A fifty/fifty possibility is also not enough. In mathematical terms, believability must be *at least* greater than 50 percent. This is what is meant by the more-likely-than-not (preponderance of the evidence) standard.

CASE

Parra v. Tarasco, Inc. d/b/a Jiminez Restaurant

230 Ill. App. 3d 819, 595 N.E.2d 1186 (1992)
Appellate Court of Illinois, First District

Background: *Ernest Parra died when he choked on a piece of food at Jiminez Restaurant. This suit alleges that the restaurant negligently failed to post instructions in the restaurant on how to aid a choking victim and negligently failed to summon emergency medical assistance. The Illinois Choke-Saving Methods Act requires every restaurant to "have posted in a conspicuous location that is visible to patrons and employees on the premises, but which location need not be in the actual dining areas, instructions concerning at least one method of first aid assistance to choking persons." Jiminez Restaurant failed to post these instructions. The trial court dismissed the complaint for failure to state a negligence cause of action. The case is now on appeal before the Appellate Court of Illinois.*

Decision on Appeal: *Judgment affirmed. Plaintiff has not adequately alleged causation and, therefore, has not stated a negligence cause of action.*

OPINION OF COURT

Justice GORDON delivered the opinion of the court . . .

[Plaintiff has] failed to adequately allege that failure to post the sign was the proximate cause of decedent's death. The violation of a statute or ordinance designed for the protection of human life or property can be *prima facie* evidence of negligence, but the injury must have a direct and proximate connection with the violation. Plaintiff must include sufficient factual allegations that such violation was the proximate cause of his injuries. It is not sufficient to merely plead conclusions. *Horcher v. Guerin,* 94 Ill. App. 2d 244, 248–50, 236 N.E.2d 576 (complaint merely alleges conclusion that violation of building code [requiring windows in operating condition] was proximate cause of injury from fire; however, nothing indicates causal connection between inoperative windows and actual injury of plaintiff).

In order to state a cause of action, plaintiff must allege the ultimate facts which give rise to the cause of action, and liberality of pleading will not relieve plaintiff of the requirement that the complaint contain sufficient, factual averments and set out every fact essential to be proved.

In determining whether proximate cause has been sufficiently set forth, it is important to "distinguish the causal connection between what the defendant did and the plaintiff's injury from the connection between the plaintiff's injury and the class of the injuries from which the statute was intended to afford protection [choking to death]." (N.J. Singer, 2B *Sutherland Statutory Construction,* sec. 55.05, at 287–88 (5th ed. 1992) (footnotes omitted).) While clearly decedent's choking to death is precisely the class of injury for which the statute intends to afford protection; however, the necessary causal connection here runs between what defendant allegedly did—failure to post the sign, and plaintiff's injury—choking to death on his food.

The complaint here merely alleges that defendant: "5a. failed to post in a conspicuous location that was visible to patrons and employees in the premises instructions concerning first aid assistance to choking persons in violation of Illinois Revised statute; b. failed to instruct their employees in first aid assistance to choking persons; c. failed to assist the plaintiff decedent who was choking after failing to post in a conspicuous place instructions concerning first aid assistance to choking persons. 6. That as a direct and proximate result of the aforesaid negligent acts or omissions of the defendants, the plaintiff decedent . . . suffered personal injuries and died on March 18, 1989."

This broad, conclusory language fails to provide the necessary factual allegations which would establish a causal relationship between not posting the sign and decedent's death. There is no allegation, for example, that anyone tried to perform the Heimlich Maneuver but performed it incorrectly because the sign was not posted, or failed to undertake such an attempt because of a failure to post the sign.

Plaintiff additionally alleges in the complaint that defendant "failed to promptly summon emergency medical personnel." . . . [But] there is no factual allegation in the complaint which even hints at a causal connection between decedent's death, and any action or inaction by defendant. In fact, there is no allegation that anyone in the restaurant had any knowledge that decedent was choking. There is no allegation that defendant's employees had discovered decedent choking and refused to call, or delayed calling, for medical assistance. There is no allegation that, but for the failure of defendant to summon an ambulance, decedent would have lived. Cf. *Acosta v. Fuentes,* 150 Misc. 2d 1013, 571 N.Y.S. 666, 669 (1991) (if the patron choking on his food was "already doomed to die" before the restaurant's employees called an ambulance and moved him outside, then no causal connection has been shown between defendants' action or inaction and decedent's death).

We conclude that the trial court properly found that plaintiff's allegations of negligence based on defendant's failure to post a sign, or failure to secure or render first aid, did not state a cause of action. . . .

ASSIGNMENT 15.2

a. Write a complaint for Parra that *adequately* alleges causation. Make up whatever facts you need to draft this complaint. Be sure that Justice Gordon would not have the same problems with your complaint that he had with the complaint actually used in the litigation, even if your state does not require the same kind of pleading specificity that Justice Gordon required.

b. Assume that none of the employees in the Illinois restaurant spoke English, and that none of the customers in the restaurant at the time of the choking spoke English. Also assume that there are instructions clearly posted in the restaurant on what to do if someone chokes on food, but the instructions are in English. Would the result in the *Parra* case be the same? What would the complaint have to allege?

General Causation and Specific Causation

toxic tort Personal injury or property damage wrongfully caused by repeated exposure to poisons in chemicals, asbestos, radiation, waste, or other substances.

general causation In toxic tort cases, capable of bringing about or producing a particular injury or condition in the general population.

specific causation In toxic tort cases, bringing about or producing a particular injury or condition in a specific plaintiff.

There are some specific areas of tort law that have unique causation problems and terminology. An example is a **toxic tort**, which is a wrongful injury or damage caused by repeated exposure to poisons in chemicals, asbestos, radiation, waste, or other substances. When we study toxic torts later in the book, particularly in Chapter 20, we will see that some courts insist that plaintiffs establish general causation before they are allowed to establish specific causation. **General causation** addresses whether a substance is capable of causing a particular injury or condition in the general population. Example: Can cigarettes cause lung cancer? Proof of general causation is made primarily by offering scientific and medical evidence found in the literature of the field in question. **Specific causation**, on the other hand, addresses whether a substance caused the injury of a specific plaintiff. Example: Was the lung cancer caused by this plaintiff's smoking?

CUTOFF TEST OF PROXIMATE CAUSE

As indicated earlier, there are two components of proximate cause. Thus far we have been discussing the first component, *actual cause*, which answers the question of who was the cause in fact of the harm or other loss. Now we turn to the second component, *legal cause*, which answers the question of whether the harm or other loss was the foreseeable consequence of the original risk. See Exhibit 15–1.

In most negligence cases involving a single defendant and a single injury, legal cause is relatively easy to establish once actual cause is established. Cases involving multiple defendants and injuries, however, can sometimes pose difficulties. The law does not always make defendants liable for every injury they actually cause. As a matter of policy, courts impose a cutoff of liability. Defendant's liability will be limited to those injuries that were the foreseeable consequence of the original risk the defendant took by his or her carelessness or negligence.

EXAMPLE

Jim carelessly pushes Alice, who falls down and breaks her ankle. Two weeks later, while walking on crutches, Alice falls and breaks her wrist. Soon thereafter, she catches pneumonia because of her generally run-down condition due to the ankle and wrist injuries.

Let's look at Alice's ankle injury, wrist injury, and pneumonia from the perspective of both actual cause and legal cause to determine whether Jim was the proximate cause of each.

1. *Ankle injury.* But for the push by Jim, Alice would not have injured her ankle. Jim, therefore, is the actual cause of the ankle injury. Was the ankle injury a foreseeable consequence of the original risk Jim took by carelessly pushing Alice? Yes. Bodily injury is a foreseeable consequence of being pushed. Therefore, Jim is the legal cause of the ankle injury. Since he is also its actual cause, we can conclude that he is the proximate cause of the leg injury.
2. *Wrist injury.* But for the push by Jim, Alice would not have been on crutches and would not have injured her wrist. Jim, therefore, is the actual cause of the wrist injury. Was the wrist injury a foreseeable consequence of the original risk Jim took by carelessly pushing Alice? Yes. Being in a weakened condition and in need of crutches is a foreseeable consequence of a serious injury that results from being pushed. It was this weakened condition that led to the fall Alice took while on crutches. Therefore, Jim is the legal cause of the wrist injury. Since he is also its actual cause, we can conclude that he is the proximate cause of the wrist injury.
3. *Pneumonia.* But for the push by Jim, Alice would not have had pneumonia, because she would not have been in a generally run-down condition. Jim, therefore, is the actual cause of the pneumonia. Was the pneumonia a foreseeable consequence of the original risk Jim took by carelessly pushing Alice? Yes. Being in a generally run-down condition is a foreseeable consequence of a serious injury that results from being pushed. It was this generally run-down condition that resulted in Alice's catching pneumonia. Therefore, Jim is the legal cause of the pneumonia. Since he is also its actual cause, we can conclude that he is the proximate cause of the pneumonia.

Next, we'll take a closer look at the more complex example presented at the beginning of the chapter.

EXAMPLE

Sam drives his car down the street at an excessive rate of speed and hits Paul's car, breaking Paul's leg. While Paul is lying in the road, another car accidentally runs over Paul's arm. When the ambulance finally arrives and takes Paul to the hospital, a doctor carelessly treats Paul, resulting in an injury to Paul's knee. After being treated, Paul discovers that someone at the hospital has stolen his wallet.

Assume that we have been able to establish that Sam is the actual cause of the three injuries and the theft. But for Sam's speeding, none of these results would have occurred. We now want to focus on the legal-cause component of proximate cause by asking whether the injuries and theft were foreseeable consequences of the original risk that Sam took. We will limit our discussion to Sam's liability. Other parties might be sued in this example (e.g., the second driver and the doctor). As indicated earlier, joint and several liability might exist. But in order to concentrate on proximate cause in cases of multiple injuries or losses, we will limit our discussion to Sam's liability.

1. *Leg injury.* Was Paul's leg injury from Sam's car a foreseeable consequence of the original risk Sam took by driving at an excessive rate of speed? Yes. Bodily injury is certainly a foreseeable consequence of speeding. Therefore, Sam is the legal cause of the leg injury. Since he is also its actual cause, we can conclude that he is the proximate cause of the leg injury.
2. *Arm injury.* Was Paul's arm injury from the second car a foreseeable consequence of the original risk Sam took by driving at an excessive rate of speed? Yes. Car accidents are not unusual. Increased driving hazards are common at the scene of accidents due to rubbernecking and the quick decisions other drivers must make as they adjust to what has just occurred. In this tense environment, there is a danger of further accidents. That is what occurred here. The original risk Sam

took by speeding was to injure Paul in a street setting where accident victims are vulnerable to further accidents and injuries after an initial accident. Therefore, Sam is the legal cause of the arm injury. Since he is also its actual cause, we can conclude that he is the proximate cause of the arm injury.

3. *Knee injury.* Was Paul's knee injury from the careless doctor at the hospital a foreseeable consequence of the original risk Sam took by driving at an excessive rate of speed? Yes. Sam's carelessness placed Paul in the position of needing emergency medical attention. Medical errors or mistakes are not uncommon (see Chapter 18). One of the risks of speeding is that the injured party might be subjected to further injury while undergoing medical treatment. Therefore, Sam is the legal cause of the knee injury. Since he is also its actual cause, we can conclude that he is the proximate cause of the knee injury.
4. *Stolen wallet.* Was Paul's stolen wallet a foreseeable consequence of the original risk Sam took by driving at an excessive rate of speed? No. It is highly unforeseeable that a victim of careless driving will have his or her property stolen while being treated in the hospital. This is not a foreseeable consequence of speeding. Even if we can say that Sam was a substantial factor—an actual cause—in bringing about the loss of the wallet, he is not its legal cause. The law makes a policy decision to cut off liability for this loss because it is beyond the foreseeable risk that Sam took by speeding. Because Sam is not the legal cause of the loss of the wallet, he is not the proximate cause of the loss. Proximate cause requires both components to be present: actual cause and legal cause.

ASSIGNMENT 15.3

In the example involving Sam driving at an excessive rate of speed and hitting Paul, would Sam be the proximate cause of the lost wallet if it was stolen while Paul was lying on the street immediately after the accident?

ASSIGNMENT 15.4

Peter is a passenger in a bus that is carelessly speeding. The bus crashes into another car. Peter is forced forward, injuring his arm. Moments after the crash, lightning strikes a tree, which falls on the part of the bus where Peter is sitting, injuring his leg. Is the bus company the proximate cause of the arm injury and the leg injury?

Mitigation of Damages

mitigation-of-damages rule Injured parties must take reasonable steps to alleviate their injury. A wrongdoer will not be liable for any increase or aggravation of the injury caused by the injured party's failure to take such steps. Also called avoidable-consequences doctrine.

The conclusion that defendants are liable for the injuries they proximately cause is subject to the requirement that the plaintiff must take reasonable steps to mitigate the consequences of those injuries. This requirement is called the **mitigation-of-damages rule** (or the avoidable-consequences doctrine), and we will look at it in greater detail in Chapter 16. Plaintiff, for example, cannot refuse all medical attention and then hold the defendant responsible for the **aggravation** of the injury caused by the plaintiff's refusal to see a doctor.

aggravation An increase in the severity of the original injury. This may be caused by an additional injury or by a failure to take reasonable steps to prevent the increased severity of the original injury.

Foreseeability of the Extent and Manner of the Harm

Under the foreseeability test of legal cause, there is a cutoff of liability for unforeseeable consequences of the original risk. There are two important qualifications of this cutoff test that pertain to the *extent* and *manner* of the harm that results.

Foreseeability of the Extent of the Harm: Thin-Skull Rule

The *extent* of the plaintiff's injury does not have to be foreseeable if the general nature or type of harm was foreseeable. This is the effect of the **thin-skull rule** (also called the eggshell-skull rule). A thin skull is a generic phrase that means a high vulnerability to any particular kind of harm. The cutoff test of legal cause will not prevent liability in thin-skull cases.

thin-skull rule If the general nature or type of harm was a foreseeable consequence of the original risk, the defendant will be liable for the harm even if the extent of the harm was not foreseeable. Also called eggshell-skull rule.

EXAMPLE

Dave carelessly runs down the corridor and bumps into Pauline as she is turning the corner. Pauline is one month pregnant at the time. The accidental bump causes a miscarriage.

EXAMPLE

Alice is driving thirty-five mph in heavy traffic. When she carelessly takes her eyes off the road, she runs into the rear of the Jack's car. Only a slight dent is put in the car. Jack, however, dies because the collision activated a rare disease.

There is no doubt that Dave is the actual cause of Pauline's miscarriage and Alice is the actual cause of Jack's death. What about legal cause? Is there any reason to cut off liability because of the unforeseeability of the extent of the injuries that resulted? In both examples, Pauline and Jack had a very high vulnerability to injury—they have what is called thin skulls. Pauline's miscarriage and Jack's death were not foreseeable, but the *extent* of the harm need not be foreseeable if the general nature or type of harm they received was foreseeable. The general nature or type of harm that was foreseeable to Dave from the corridor bump and to Alice from the rear-end collision was bodily harm of the victims. Miscarriage and death are bodily harms. Therefore, Dave is the legal cause of Pauline's miscarriage and Alice is the legal cause of Jack's death. Since both components of proximate cause have been met, we can conclude that Dave is the proximate cause of the miscarriage and Alice is the proximate cause of the death. As courts often say, the defendant "takes the plaintiff as he finds him." There is no cutoff of liability. Defendants will be deemed to be the proximate cause of the foreseeable and unforeseeable consequences of their negligence if those consequences fit within the general nature or type of harm that was foreseeable.

A plaintiff with a thin skull may have a **preexisting condition**, consisting of a disease, injury, or other medical problem that existed before the defendant's tort against the plaintiff. The defendant, of course, will not be responsible for the original existence of the preexisting condition, but will be responsible for its aggravation—for making it worse—even if the preexisting condition was not foreseeable.

preexisting condition A medical problem that existed prior to the defendant's wrongful conduct; the defendant may have caused an aggravation of the problem but not the problem itself. (See glossary for an additional definition.)

Suppose that the plaintiff goes insane or commits suicide because of despair over the initial injuries caused by the defendant. Courts differ as to whether the defendant will be held responsible. Some courts would say that insanity or suicide is so extreme that the cutoff principle of proximate cause will prevent liability for such a drastic consequence. (See the discussion of superseding cause later in the chapter.) Other courts, however, will carry the thin-skull rule to its logical extreme and hold that the defendant is the proximate cause of the insanity or suicide if such results are within the general nature or type of harm that was foreseeable from the original risk the defendant took.

The thin-skull rule is not limited to negligence. Defendants who commit intentional torts (e.g., battery) can also be liable for foreseeable and unforeseeable injuries that result from their intentional torts.

ASSIGNMENT 15.5

Richard Williamson is an attorney who represents Leo Crowley in a breach-of-contract case involving millions of dollars. Crowley loses the case because Williamson failed to file the complaint before the statute of limitations expired. (Assume that this failure constitutes negligence and legal malpractice, which we will discuss in Chapter 18.) Crowley is so despondent at the loss of his case that he commits suicide. Is Williamson the proximate cause of the suicide?

manner-of-injury rule The manner of the plaintiff's injury does not have to be foreseeable if the general nature or type of harm was foreseeable.

Foreseeability of the Manner of the Harm: Manner-of-Injury Rule

The *manner* of the plaintiff's injury does not have to be foreseeable if the general nature or type of harm was foreseeable. This is the effect of the **manner-of-injury rule.**

EXAMPLE

Defendant is carelessly navigating a steamboat that rams into a bridge. The plaintiff was one of the workers repairing the bridge at the time. When the boat hit the bridge, the plaintiff fell onto a blowtorch he was using, resulting in blindness in both eyes.

In this case, it was foreseeable that some damage to the bridge and some kind of injury to someone on the bridge would occur from the careless navigation of a steamboat in the area of the bridge. Personal and property damage was foreseeable. But the *manner* in which the injury would result in this particular plaintiff—falling on the blowtorch—was not foreseeable to the defendant, who did not even know that the plaintiff was there working with a torch. Drowning or a severe concussion to anyone on the bridge may have been foreseeable to the defendant, but the manner in which the injury occurred in this case was not. The rule in such cases is that the manner in which an injury occurs does not have to be foreseeable in order for the defendant to be the proximate cause of the injury, as long as the general nature or type of harm was foreseeable. The general nature or type of harm that was foreseeable in the bridge case was bodily injury and property damage. This is sufficient to cover the blowtorch mishap. As one scholar commented, if "I foresee the risk in general, I need not foresee the details."[3] "The defendant is liable for the harms he negligently caused so long as a reasonable person in his position should have recognized or foreseen the general kind of harm the plaintiff suffered."[4]

The American Law Institute, in its *Restatement (Second) of Torts,* would agree that the particular manner of the occurrence of the harm need not be foreseeable in order for the defendant to be the proximate cause of the injury (or as the *Restatement* would phrase it, the "legal cause" of the injury). It is important to the *Restatement* (and to the courts that follow it) to assess whether the injury was a normal or ordinary consequence of the risk that the defendant created. Liability should be cut off, according to this view, only if we can say that the harm that resulted was unusually rare, or what it calls "highly extraordinary."[5]

ASSIGNMENT 15.6

Tom, an adult, gives a loaded gun to Bob, a young boy. Tom asks Bob to deliver the gun to Jack. Bob takes his friend Bill with him to make the delivery. Upon arrival, Bob accidentally drops the gun on Bill's toe. The toe breaks. When the gun falls, it discharges immediately, killing Jack. Bob suffers a nervous breakdown over the incident. Is Tom the proximate cause of Bill's broken toe? Of Jack's death? Of Bob's nervous breakdown?

As we examine proximate cause, it is important that this element be kept in perspective with the other elements of negligence discussed thus far—duty (Chapter 13) and breach of duty (Chapter 14). A discussion of proximate cause assumes that the plaintiff has already been able to establish that a duty of reasonable care (the first element) exists between the plaintiff and defendant, and that the defendant has breached that duty (the second element) by unreasonable conduct. Note the role that foreseeability plays in each element:

Element I: Duty
Defendant owes plaintiff a duty of reasonable care if the defendant's act or omission has created a *foreseeable* risk of injury or other loss to the plaintiff's person or property.

Element II: Breach of Duty
Defendant breaches a duty of reasonable care by failing to take precautions against injury to the plaintiff when the *foreseeability* of serious injury outweighs the burden or inconvenience of taking those precautions (see Exhibit 14–4 in Chapter 14).

Element III: Proximate Cause
Defendant is the proximate cause of an injury if the defendant is its actual cause (cause in fact) and its legal cause (the injury was a *foreseeable* consequence of the original risk the defendant took).

The foreseeability analysis that you must do to determine whether a duty exists (first element) is substantially the same foreseeability analysis that you must do to determine whether proximate cause exists (third element), or more accurately, whether the cutoff test of proximate cause will prevent the defendant from being liable for harm he or she has caused in fact. The very definition of the cutoff test requires you to refer back to the original risk created by the defendant. The relationship between the first element, duty, and the third element, proximate cause, is so close that you will sometimes see the proximate cause issue phrased in terms of duty: was the defendant under a duty to protect the plaintiff against the injury that resulted?

Intervening Causes

An **intervening cause** is a new and independent force that produces harm after the defendant's act or omission. We have already looked at intervening causes in some of the examples we have studied in this chapter. Here we examine such causes more closely.

intervening cause A new and independent force that produces harm after the defendant's act or omission.

EXAMPLE
Car #1 crashes into plaintiff's truck. While the plaintiff's truck is disabled in the middle of the road, car #2 crashes into the truck, but does not stop. Plaintiff sues car #1.

The plaintiff's truck has been damaged twice, once by the defendant (car #1) and once by the intervening cause (car #2), which has disappeared. Assume that the damage from the defendant's initial crash is $1,000 and that the damage from the crash of the intervening cause is $700. Is the defendant liable for the entire $1,700? To determine when a defendant is liable for harm from intervening causes, we must first distinguish four kinds of intervening causes:

- An *intervening force of nature* is a subsequent natural occurrence that is independent of human interference; it is an **act of God**. For example: The ABC Company carelessly builds a dam. Slight cracks become visible. A month

act of God An unpredictable and unpreventable force of nature.

after the dam is built, a severe tornado hits the area and the dam collapses. The tornado is an intervening force of nature.

- An *intervening innocent human force* is a subsequent occurrence caused by a human being who was not careless or wrongful. For example: Cynthia carelessly runs into the plaintiff as he is crossing the street. While the plaintiff is on the ground, Tom's car hits the plaintiff. Tom was driving carefully when he hit the plaintiff. Tom is an intervening innocent human force.
- An *intervening negligent human force* is a subsequent occurrence negligently caused by a human being. For example: Alex carelessly runs into the plaintiff. Plaintiff is rushed to the hospital but is given negligent medical treatment by a nurse, causing further injury. The nurse is an intervening negligent human force.
- An *intervening intentional or criminal human force* is a subsequent occurrence caused intentionally or criminally by a human being. For example: George carelessly runs into the plaintiff. While at the hospital, the plaintiff sees his archenemy, who tries to poison him. The archenemy is an intervening intentional or criminal human force.

superseding cause An intervening cause that is beyond the foreseeable risk originally created by the defendant's unreasonable acts or omissions. An intervening cause of harm that is highly extraordinary. Sometimes called supervening cause.

If any of these intervening forces can be classified as a **superseding cause** (sometimes called a supervening cause), the cutoff test of proximate cause will prevent the defendant from being responsible for the harm caused by the intervening force. If the intervening force is not a superseding cause, then the defendant will be found to be the proximate cause of the harm caused by the intervening force. Our question, therefore, becomes, When is an intervening force a superseding cause?

> An intervening force becomes a superseding cause when the harm caused by the intervening force is beyond the foreseeable risk originally created by the defendant's unreasonable acts or omissions, and/or when the harm caused by the intervening force is considered highly extraordinary.

Hence, foreseeability and the original risk created by the defendant again become critical factors. Alternatively, the "highly extraordinary" test of the *Restatement* that we saw earlier can be used as a guide.

Intervening intentional or criminal human forces are often considered superseding causes, because they are either outside the scope of the original risk (and hence do not meet the test of the legal-cause component of proximate cause) or are highly extraordinary. Examine again the example just given involving the archenemy's attempt to poison the plaintiff in the hospital. George initially hit the plaintiff in an automobile collision and is the proximate cause (i.e., the actual cause and the legal cause) of the plaintiff's injuries sustained in the collision, but he is not the proximate cause of the poisoning. The latter was highly extraordinary and far beyond the original risk that George created by his careless driving. The injuries are the natural and foreseeable consequence of bad driving. The intentional and criminal act of poisoning is not reasonably connected with George's bad driving.

Intervening intentional or criminal human forces are *not* always considered superseding causes. What the defendant does or fails to do may increase the risk of such an intervention, making the latter neither unforeseeable nor extraordinary. Suppose the defendant gives loaded guns to a group of juvenile delinquents, who intentionally shoot the plaintiff. Or suppose a motel fails to provide any security in a section of the motel where a burglary or robbery of patrons is highly likely, and such a burglary or robbery in fact occurs. In these cases, the intentional or criminal intervening force was part of the foreseeable risk created by the defendant's acts or omissions. Such intervening forces are not superseding; defendant is the proximate cause of the harm produced by them.

Intervening innocent or negligent human forces are treated the same way. If their intervention was part of the original risk, then they were foreseeable and do not become superseding causes. In those cases, for example, where the plaintiff is further injured in a hospital (whether innocently or negligently) after being brought there for treatment for the injury originally caused by the defendant, the hospital injuries are usually considered to be part of the original risk and not highly extraordinary. So, too, if the plaintiff receives a second injury by a third party (whether innocently or negligently) at the scene of the accident. In all these cases, the defendant has rendered the plaintiff highly vulnerable to further injury. It is not uncommon for individuals to receive injuries in hospitals or on the road after the first injury, although it may be highly unusual for such second injuries to be produced intentionally or criminally.

What about intervening forces of nature? Here it is important to ask whether the injury or damage is of the same kind as would have occurred if the intervening force of nature had not intervened at all. If the same kind of injury or damage results, the intervening force of nature is not a superseding cause. Suppose, for example, that the defendant carelessly leaves explosives in an area where people would be hurt by an explosion. Because of the manner of storage, assume that the explosives could detonate on their own. Hence, unreasonable storage creates a risk of serious personal and property damage to people in the area. One day, lightning strikes the explosives, leading to serious personal and property damage. The lightning may have been unforeseeable, but the damage or injury caused by the intervention of the lightning was the same kind of damage or injury that the defendant's method of storage risked. Defendant is the proximate cause of what the lightning produced. The resulting damage or injury is not highly extraordinary, even though it may have been unforeseeable that it would occur in this way.

A different result is reached in many, but not all, courts when the intervening force of nature causes a totally different kind of injury than that originally foreseeable by the defendant's act or omission. Suppose, for example, that a truck company carelessly delays the delivery of the plaintiff's food goods, and the goods are destroyed by a storm. The destruction was not within the original risk created by the defendant (spoilage due to the delay), and some courts would therefore say that the intervening force of nature was a superseding cause.

The Columbine Massacre

In 1999, two high school students in Columbine, Colorado, Dylan Klebold and Eric Harris, killed twelve students and a teacher and wounded over twenty others. In the aftermath of the massacre, the police learned that Harris and Klebold were avid consumers of violent video games and movies containing obscenity, pornography, and sexual violence. One movie the pair viewed was *The Basketball Diaries*, in which a student massacres his classmates with a shotgun.[6] Some of the Columbine survivors sued video game makers and movie producers, alleging that violent movie and video games caused the Klebold and Harris shootings. The complaint alleged that "but for the actions of the Video Game Defendants and the Movie Defendants, in conjunction with the acts of the other defendants herein, the multiple killings at Columbine High School would not have occurred."

The video and movie defendants argued that there was no proximate cause because Klebold and Harris were superseding causes. The court agreed and dismissed the complaint:

> The Video Game and Movie Defendants . . . had no reason to suppose that Harris and Klebold would decide to murder or injure their fellow classmates and teachers. Plaintiffs do not allege that these Defendants had any knowledge of Harris's and Klebold's identities, let alone their violent proclivities. Nor, for that matter, did the Video Game and Movie Defendants have any reason to believe that a shooting spree was a likely or probable consequence of exposure to their movie or video games. Plaintiffs allege that children who witness acts of violence and/or who are interactively involved with creating violence or violent

images often act more violently themselves and sometimes recreate the violence. The defendants might have speculated that their motion picture or video games had the potential to stimulate an idiosyncratic reaction in the mind of some disturbed individuals. But a speculative possibility is not enough. Foreseeability is the touchstone of proximate cause and the superseding cause doctrine. A superseding cause relieves the original actor of liability when the harm is intentionally caused by a third person and is not within the scope of the risk created by the actor's conduct. . . . I hold in this case that Harris's and Klebold's intentional violent acts were the superseding cause of [the deaths]. Moreover . . . their acts were not foreseeable. Their criminal acts, therefore, were not within the scope of any risk purportedly created by Defendants.[7]

OVERVIEW OF STEPS NEEDED TO ANALYZE PROXIMATE CAUSE

- **Actual Cause**
  Apply the two tests for actual cause. First ask if the plaintiff's injury or loss would have occurred but for the acts or omissions of the defendant. Then apply the substantial-factor test, especially when more than one cause may have produced the plaintiff's injury or loss. Was the defendant's act or omission a substantial factor in producing the plaintiff's injury or loss? Plaintiff can establish actual cause by either test.
- **Burden of Proof**
  Determine if there is enough evidence for the fact finder (e.g., a jury) to say it is more likely than not that but for the defendant's act or omission, the injury or loss would not have occurred. Or determine if there is enough evidence for the fact finder to say that it is more likely than not that the defendant's act or omission was a substantial factor in producing the plaintiff's injury or loss. If there is enough evidence to meet either test, then the most common standard of proof (preponderance of the evidence) has been met.
- **Legal Cause**
  Turn the clock back to the time of the defendant's original act or omission (e.g., speeding). What risk did the defendant take by this act or omission? Was a foreseeable consequence of this risk the kind of injury or loss that the plaintiff suffered? If so, defendant was the legal cause of the injury or loss. If the defendant was the actual and the legal cause, he or she was the proximate cause.
- **Thin-Skull Rule**
  If the plaintiff has a thin skull (i.e., a high vulnerability to any particular kind of harm) so that the *extent* of his or her injury was not foreseeable, determine whether the injury fits within the general nature or type of harm that was a foreseeable consequence of the original risk. If so, there is no cutoff of liability.
- **Manner-of-Injury Rule**
  If the *manner* in which the plaintiff's injury occurred was not foreseeable, determine whether the injury fits within the general nature or type of harm that was a foreseeable consequence of the original risk. If so, there is no cutoff of liability.
- **Intervening Human Force**
  Determine whether an intervening human force was a causal factor in producing the injury or loss. If so, determine whether this human force was innocent, negligent, intentional, or criminal. Then ask if the intervening human force was within the scope of the original risk taken by the defendant. Was it foreseeable

to the defendant? Did the human force proceed naturally out of what the defendant did or failed to do? Affirmative answers to these questions will make the defendant the proximate cause of what the intervening human force did.

- **Intervening Force of Nature**
  Determine whether an intervening force of nature was a causal factor in producing the injury or loss. If so, ask whether the injury or loss was the same kind that would have occurred if the force of nature had not intervened. If so, the defendant is still the proximate cause of the injury or loss.

- **Highly Extraordinary**
  Can it be said that the injury or loss was highly extraordinary in view of what the defendant did or failed to do? If not, then the likelihood is that a court will find that the defendant was the proximate cause of the injury or loss.

ASSIGNMENT 15.7

Examine both components of proximate cause (actual cause and legal cause) in the following situations to determine if the defendant was the proximate cause of the resulting injuries or other losses in the negligence suits indicated.

a. Tom carelessly drives his motorcycle into Dan's horse. The horse goes wild and jumps over a five-foot fence (which it has never done before) and runs into traffic. Henry tries to turn his car away from the horse and accidentally hits Pete, who is a pedestrian on the sidewalk at the time of the collision. Pete sues Tom for negligence.

b. Same facts as in (a), except that Henry just misses Pete, rather than hitting him with his car. Pete and Henry begin an argument over Henry's driving. Henry hits Pete in the jaw. Pete sues Tom for negligence.

c. Mary gives a loaded gun to a ten-year-old girl who is Mary's neighbor. The girl takes the gun home. The girl's father discovers the gun but fails to take it away from his daughter. The girl shoots Linda with the gun. Linda sues Mary for negligence.

d. Harry carelessly hits Helen, a pedestrian, with his car in a busy intersection downtown. While Helen is lying on the ground, a person in another car accidentally hits Helen, causing further injuries. This other person is a hit-and-run driver who does not stop after hitting Helen. Helen sues Harry for negligence.

e. Pat carelessly leaves her keys in her car. A thief gets in the car and starts to speed away. Moments later, the thief hits Kevin with the car one block away from where Pat parked the car. Kevin sues Pat for negligence.

f. Same facts as in (e), except that the thief hits Kevin one month after he has stolen the car, in another section of the city.

CASE

Mussivand v. David

45 Ohio St. 3d 314, 544 N.E.2d 265 (1989)
Supreme Court of Ohio

Background: *George David has a venereal disease, but does not tell the woman with whom he is having an affair. She contracts the disease from him and then gives it to her husband, Tofigh Mussivand. The latter sues David for negligence in failing to tell his wife that he had the disease. This failure allegedly caused Mussivand to contract the disease. The trial court granted David's motion to dismiss. The case is now on appeal before the Supreme Court of Ohio.*

Decision on Appeal: *The case should not have been dismissed. A husband can bring an action against his wife's paramour (lover), alleging that the paramour was* *negligent in failing to notify the wife that the paramour was at risk of passing venereal disease to the wife, who in turn could (and did) pass it to the husband.*

OPINION OF COURT

Justice RESNICK delivered the opinion of the court. . . .

The complaint basically states that [Mussivand] contracted a venereal disease due to the acts of [David]. . . . A "venereal disease" is defined as "a contagious disease, most commonly acquired in sexual intercourse or other genital contact; the venereal diseases include syphilis, gonorrhea, chancroid, granuloma inguinale, lymphogranuloma venereum, genital herpesvirus infection, and balanitis gangraenosa." *Dorland's Illustrated Medical Dictionary* (26 Ed. 1985) 394. . . .

Recently several jurisdictions have allowed tort actions for negligent, fraudulent or intentional transmission of genital herpes where the person infected with genital herpes fails to disclose to his or her sexual partner that he or she is infected with such a disease. *Maharam v. Maharam* (1986), 123 A.D.2d 165, 510 N.Y.S.2d 104; *Long v. Adams* (1985), 175 Ga. App. 538, 333 S.E.2d 852. Thus, courts have placed upon persons who have a venereal disease such as genital herpes or gonorrhea the duty to protect others who might be in danger of being infected by such a disease. In other words, people with a venereal disease have a duty to use reasonable care to avoid infecting others with whom they engage in sexual conduct. . . .

David argues that possibly Mussivand's wife, not he, was the cause of Mussivand's injuries. "Whether an intervening act breaks the causal connection between negligence and injury, thus relieving one of liability for his negligence, depends upon whether that intervening cause was a conscious and responsible agency which could or should have eliminated the hazard, and whether the intervening cause was reasonably foreseeable by the one who is guilty of the negligence. . . ." *Cascone v. Herb Kay Co.* (1983), 6 Ohio St. 3d 155, 451 N.E.2d 815.

In *Jeffers v. Olexo* (1989), 43 Ohio St. 3d 140, 144, 539 N.E.2d 614, 618, we equated foreseeability with proximate cause. This is misleading since they are not equatable. Rather, in order to establish proximate cause, foreseeability must be found. In determining whether an intervening cause "breaks the causal connection" between negligence and injury depends upon whether that intervening cause was reasonably foreseeable by one who was guilty of the negligence. If an injury is the natural and probable consequence of a negligent act and it is such as should have been foreseen in the light of all the attending circumstances, the injury is then the proximate result of the negligence. It is not necessary that the defendant should have anticipated the particular injury. It is sufficient that his act is likely to result in an injury to someone. Thus we do not equate foreseeability with proximate cause. Instead, if David knew his paramour was married, then it can be said that it was reasonably foreseeable that she would engage in sexual intercourse with her husband. In addition, if David did not inform her of the fact that he had a venereal disease, she could not be an intervening cause and, as such, David's liability to Mussivand would not be terminated. David's negligence would then be the proximate cause of Mussivand's injury.

We do not, however, mean to say that David, subsequent to his affair with Mussivand's wife, will be liable to any and all persons with whom she may have sexual contact. A spouse, however, is a foreseeable sexual partner. Furthermore, the liability of a person with a sexually transmissible disease to a third person, such as a spouse, would be extinguished as soon as the paramour spouse knew or should have known that he or she was exposed to or had contracted a venereal disease. She or he then would become a "conscious and responsible agency which could or should have eliminated the hazard." *Cascone,* supra. For example, if David told Mussivand's wife he had a venereal disease or if she noticed symptoms of the disease on herself, she then would have the duty to abstain from sexual relations or warn her sexual partner. Whether Mussivand's wife knew, or should have known, of her exposure to a venereal disease is a question of fact to be decided by the trier of fact. . . .

For the foregoing reasons we cannot say that Mussivand could not prove any set of facts entitling him to recover in negligence from David. Accordingly, the trial court erred in granting David's motion to dismiss. . . .

ASSIGNMENT 15.8

a. What test does the court use to determine when an intervening cause breaks the chain of causation and cuts off liability?
b. Why did the court say that Mrs. Mussivand may not have broken the chain of David's causation?
c. Suppose David does tell his paramour (Mrs. Mussivand) that he has VD. She tells him she doesn't care because this is the last time she will have sex with him before returning to her husband. She says, "I will never tell my husband about you or our affair." Mr. Mussivand contracts VD from her. Is David the proximate cause of Mr. Mussivand's VD?
d. Could Mr. Mussivand sue Mrs. Mussivand for negligence?

CASE

Gaines-Tabb v. ICI Explosives, USA, Inc.

160 F.3d 613 (1998)
United States Court of Appeals, Tenth Circuit

Background: *In 1995, a terrorist bomb killed 163 people when it exploded at the Alfred P. Murrah Federal Building in Oklahoma City. Timothy McVeigh and Terry Nichols were later convicted of murder for their role in the bombing. The material allegedly used to construct the bomb was ammonium nitrate (AN) that was manufactured by ICI Explosives and eventually sold as fertilizer by Mid-Kansas Co-op. It was purchased in Kansas from Mid-Kansas Co-op by either McVeigh or Nichols. This suit was brought on behalf of victims of the bombing. They sued ICI for negligence, among other theories. The trial court (district court) dismissed the negligence action. The case is now on appeal before the United States Court of Appeals for the Tenth Circuit.*

Decision on Appeal: *The judgment for ICI is affirmed. Proximate cause has not been established. The terrorist's act was a supervening cause that cut off the manufacturer's liability.*

OPINION OF COURT

Judge EBEL delivered the opinion of the court . . .:

Individuals injured by the April 19, 1995, bombing of the Alfred P. Murrah Federal Building ("Murrah Building") in Oklahoma City, Oklahoma, filed suit against the manufacturers of the ammonium nitrate allegedly used to create the bomb. . . . [The main cause of action asserted in the complaint was negligence.] The district court dismissed the complaint for failure to state a claim upon which relief may be granted, and the plaintiffs appealed. We affirm. Specifically, we hold that: plaintiffs cannot state a claim for negligence . . . because they cannot show, as a matter of law, that defendants' conduct was the proximate cause of their injuries. . . .

ICI manufactures ammonium nitrate ("AN"). Plaintiffs allege that AN can be either "explosive grade" or "fertilizer grade." According to plaintiffs, "explosive-grade" AN is of low density and high porosity so it will absorb sufficient amounts of fuel or diesel oil to allow detonation of the AN, while "fertilizer-grade" AN is of high density and low porosity and so is unable to absorb sufficient amounts of fuel or diesel oil to allow detonation.

Plaintiffs allege that ICI sold explosive-grade AN mislabeled as fertilizer-grade AN to Farmland Industries, who in turn sold it to Mid-Kansas Cooperative Association in McPherson, Kansas. Plaintiffs submit that a "Mike Havens" purchased a total of eighty 50-pound bags of the mislabeled AN from Mid-Kansas. According to plaintiffs, "Mike Havens" was an alias used either by Timothy McVeigh or Terry Nichols, the two men tried for the bombing. Plaintiffs further allege that the perpetrators of the Oklahoma City bombing used the 4000 pounds of explosive-grade AN purchased from Mid-Kansas, mixed with fuel oil or diesel oil, to demolish the Murrah Building. . . .

Plaintiffs allege that ICI was negligent in making explosive-grade AN available to the perpetrators of the Murrah Building bombing. Under Oklahoma law, the three essential elements of a claim of negligence are: "(1) a duty owed by the defendant to protect the plaintiff from injury, (2) a failure to properly perform that duty, and (3) the plaintiff's injury being proximately caused by the defendant's breach." *Lockhart v. Loosen,* 943 P.2d 1074, 1079 (Okla. 1997). . . .

"[W]hether the complained of negligence is the proximate cause of the plaintiff's injury is dependent upon the harm (for which compensation is being sought) being the result of both the natural and probable consequences of the primary negligence." *Lockhart,* 943 P.2d at 1079. . . . Under Oklahoma law, "the causal *nexus* between an act of negligence and the resulting injury will be deemed broken with the intervention of a new, independent and efficient cause which was neither anticipated nor reasonably foreseeable." *Minor v. Zidell Trust,* 618 P.2d 392, 394 (Okla. 1980). Such an intervening cause is known as a "supervening cause." Id. To be considered a supervening cause, an intervening cause must be: (1) independent of the original act; (2) adequate by itself to bring about the injury; and (3) not reasonably foreseeable. See id.; *Henry v. Merck and Co.,* 877 F.2d 1489, 1495 (10th Cir. 1989). "When the intervening act is intentionally tortious or criminal, it is more likely to be considered independent." Id.

"A third person's intentional tort is a supervening cause of the harm that results—even if the actor's negligent conduct created a situation that presented the opportunity for the tort to be committed—unless the actor realizes or should realize the likelihood that the third person might commit the tortious act." *Lockhart,* 943 P.2d at 1080. . . . If "the intervening act is a reasonably foreseeable consequence of the primary negligence, the original wrongdoer will not be relieved of liability." Id. at 1079. . . . "In determining questions relating to the foreseeability element of proximate cause, the courts have uniformly applied what might be termed a practical, common sense test, the test of common experience." 57A *Am. Jur. 2d* Negligence § 489 (1989). Oklahoma has looked to the *Restatement (Second) of Torts* § 448 for assistance in determining whether the intentional actions of a third party constitute a supervening cause of harm. See *Lay v. Dworman,* 732 P.2d 455, 458–59 (Okla. 1986). Section 448 states:

> The act of a third person in committing an intentional tort or crime is a superseding cause of harm to another resulting therefrom, although the actor's negligent conduct created a situation which afforded an opportunity to the third person to commit such a tort or crime, unless the actor at the time of his negligent conduct realized or should have realized the likelihood that such a situation might be created,

and that a third person might avail himself of the opportunity to commit such a tort or crime.

Comment b to § 448 provides further guidance in the case before us. It states:

> There are certain situations which are commonly recognized as affording temptations to which a recognizable percentage of humanity is likely to yield. So too, there are situations which create temptations to which no considerable percentage of ordinary mankind is likely to yield but which, if they are created at a place where persons of peculiarly vicious type are likely to be, should be recognized as likely to lead to the commission of fairly definite types of crime. If the situation which the actor should realize that his negligent conduct might create is of either of these two sorts, an intentionally criminal or tortious act of the third person is not a superseding cause which relieves the actor from liability.

Thus, under comment b, the criminal acts of a third party may be foreseeable if (1) the situation provides a temptation to which a "recognizable percentage" of persons would yield, or (2) the temptation is created at a place where "persons of a peculiarly vicious type are likely to be." There is no indication that a peculiarly vicious type of person is likely to frequent the Mid-Kansas Co-op, so we shall turn our attention to the first alternative.

We have found no guidance as to the meaning of the term "recognizable percentage" as used in § 448, comment b. However, we believe that the term does not require a showing that the mainstream population or the majority would yield to a particular temptation; a lesser number will do. Equally, it does not include merely the law-abiding population. In contrast, we also believe that the term is not satisfied by pointing to the existence of a small fringe group or the occasional irrational individual, even though it is foreseeable generally that such groups and individuals will exist.

We note that plaintiffs can point to very few occasions of successful terrorist actions using ammonium nitrate, in fact only two instances in the last twenty-eight years—a 1970 bombing at the University of Wisconsin-Madison and the bombing of the Murrah Building.* Due to the apparent complexity of manufacturing an ammonium nitrate bomb, including the difficulty of acquiring the correct ingredients (many of which are not widely available), mixing them properly, and triggering the resulting bomb, only a small number of persons would be able to carry out a crime such as the bombing of the Murrah Building. We simply do not believe that this is a group which rises to the level of a "recognizable percentage" of the population. Cf. *Restatement (Second) of Torts* § 302B, comment d (1965) ("Even where there is a recognizable possibility of the intentional interference, the possibility may be so slight, or there may be so slight a risk of foreseeable harm to another as a result of the interference, that a reasonable man in the position of the actor would disregard it.").

As a result, we hold that as a matter of law it was not foreseeable to defendants that the AN that they distributed to the Mid-Kansas Co-op would be put to such a use as to blow up the Murrah Building. Because the conduct of the bomber or bombers was unforeseeable, independent of the acts of defendants, and adequate by itself to bring about plaintiffs' injuries, the criminal activities of the bomber or bombers acted as the supervening cause of plaintiffs' injuries. Because of the lack of proximate cause, plaintiffs have failed to state a claim for negligence.

We AFFIRM the dismissal of plaintiffs' complaint. . . .

*In the complaint, Plaintiffs allege in a general way the detonation of AN fertilizer bombs in "Europe and especially Northern Ireland" prior to 1970 and the unsuccessful attempt in the United States to use AN to bomb certain facilities in New York.

ASSIGNMENT 15.9

a. What negligent act was alleged against ICI?

b. Would the result in *Gaines-Tabb* have been different if McVeigh or Nichols told the clerk at the Mid-Kansas Co-op that the AN was going to be used to "make the government pay for its crimes"?

c. The *Mussivand* case held that proximate cause could be established. The *Gaines-Tabb* case held the opposite. Explain the difference. Are the two cases consistent?

CHECK THE CITE

Palma was in a BP gas station making a purchase. He was injured in an altercation with someone who was apparently attempting to siphon gas from one of the pumps. Palma then sued BP for negligence. What acts of negligence did Palma allege against BP? Why did the court conclude that BP was not the proximate cause of the injuries Palma received in the altercation? Read the case of *Palma v. BP Products North America, Inc.*, 594 F. Supp. 2d 1306 (S.D., Fla. 2009). To read the opinion online ("Palma v. BP Products North America"): (1) Run a Google search for the names of the parties. (2) Run a citation search ("594 F.Supp. 2d 1306") or a party search (Palma BP Products) in the Legal Opinions and Journals database of Google Scholar (scholar.google.com).

PROJECT

In Google, Bing, or another general search engine, run one of the following searches:

1. "Oklahoma bombing" causation
2. Columbine causation

Make a list of the different causation issues and defendants involved in the disaster you selected. Briefly describe what causation issue was raised and against which defendants. You can consult as many websites as you wish, but you must quote from at least three separate sites.

ETHICS IN A TORTS PRACTICE

You are a paralegal working in the law office of O'Brien & O'Brien. When you were hired, you were never asked if you had taken an ethics course in your paralegal curriculum and none of the attorneys at the firm have ever discussed ethical rules with you. To your knowledge, there has never been an ethical violation at the firm since you have been there. Does this silence about ethics constitute a violation of ethics even if the firm is never charged with violating the ethical code?

SUMMARY

Proximate cause is a cause that is legally sufficient to impose liability for the results of one's wrongful act or omission. There are two components of proximate cause: actual cause and legal cause. Actual cause answers the question of who was the cause in fact of the harm or other loss; legal cause answers the question of whether the harm or other loss was the foreseeable consequence of the original risk. States differ in their use of terminology in this area of the law. (In some states proximate cause means only legal cause; in such states, actual cause is treated separately.) Legal cause determines when liability is cut off for injuries or other losses for which the defendant was the actual cause. There are two tests for actual cause. First, is it more likely than not that but for the defendant's unreasonable acts or omissions, the injury or loss would not have been suffered by the plaintiff? (This test is used when there is only one alleged cause.) Second, is it more likely than not that the defendant's unreasonable acts or omissions were a substantial factor in producing the injury or loss suffered by the plaintiff? (This test is often used when there is more than one alleged cause.)

In assessing actual cause, our common sense relies on time (how soon after the defendant's act or omission did the injury occur?), space (how close was the defendant's act or omission to the area where the injury occurred?), and historical data (in the past, have acts or omissions similar to the defendant's led to this kind of injury?). Time, space, and historical evidence, however, are almost never conclusive on the issue of actual cause; they are merely starting points. The standard of proof used by the fact finder to decide the actual-cause issue is preponderance of the evidence. Under the mitigation-of-damages rule, injured parties must take reasonable steps to alleviate their injury. A wrongdoer will not be liable for any increase or aggravation of injury caused by the injured party's failure to take such steps.

The legal-cause component of proximate cause is determined by asking whether the plaintiff's injury was the foreseeable consequence of the original risk the defendant took by his or her carelessness. Under the thin-skull rule, if the general nature or type of harm was a foreseeable consequence of the original risk, the defendant will be liable for the harm even if the extent of the harm was not foreseeable. Under the manner-of-injury rule, if the general nature or type of harm was a foreseeable consequence of the original risk, the defendant will be liable for the harm even if the manner in which the harm occurred was not foreseeable.

An intervening cause is a new and independent force that produces harm after the defendant's act or omission. It can be an intervening force of nature (act of God), an intervening human force, an intervening negligent human force, or an intervening intentional or criminal human force. An intervening cause is a superseding cause if it is beyond the foreseeable risk originally created by the defendant's unreasonable acts or omissions. Superseding causes are those that lead to injuries or losses that are highly extraordinary.

KEY TERMS

proximate cause *258*
judgment proof *258*
joint and several liability *258*
actual cause *259*
but-for test *259*
substantial-factor test *259*
hypothesis *261*
standard of proof *263*
weight of the evidence *264*
preponderance of the evidence *264*
toxic tort *266*
general causation *266*
specific causation *266*
mitigation-of-damages rule *268*
aggravation *268*
thin-skull rule *269*
preexisting condition *269*
manner-of-injury rule *270*
intervening cause *271*
act of God *271*
superseding cause *272*

REVIEW QUESTIONS

1. What is proximate cause?
2. What is actual cause?
3. What is legal cause?
4. What are some of the major differences in how different courts use the terminology of proximate cause?
5. When is someone judgment proof?
6. What is the but-for test of actual cause?
7. What is the substantial-factor test of actual cause, and when is it used?
8. What is the role of time evidence in the determination of actual cause?
9. What is meant by *post hoc ergo propter hoc*?
10. What is the role of space evidence in the determination of actual cause?
11. What is the role of historical evidence in the determination of actual cause?
12. How can time, space, and historical evidence be misinterpreted?
13. What is the preponderance of the evidence?
14. What is a toxic tort?
15. What is the distinction between general causation and specific causation in toxic torts cases?
16. What is the test for legal cause?
17. What is an intervening cause?
18. What is an intervening force of nature?
19. What is an act of God?
20. What is an intervening innocent human force?
21. What is an intervening negligent human force?
22. What is an intervening intentional or criminal human force?
23. When is an intervening cause a superseding cause?

HELPFUL WEBSITES

- **Proximate Cause**
  tortssymposium.law.wfu.edu/papers/zipursky.pdf
  works.bepress.com/mark_grady/6
  en.wikipedia.org/wiki/Proximate_cause
  law.jrank.org/pages/8783/Negligence-Proximate-Cause.html
  www.expertlaw.com/library/personal_injury/negligence.html
  www.txinjuryblog.com/2009/09/articles/legal-news/what-is-proximate-cause
- In Google, Bing, or another search engine, run the following search: elements negligence "proximate cause" tort

ENDNOTES

1. *State Farm Mut. Auto. Ins. Co. v. Cromwell*, 187 Kan. 573, 358 P.2d 761, 762 (Kan. 1961).
2. *Hudak v. Georgy*, 535 Pa. 152, 161, 634 A.2d 600, 605 (Pa., 1993) quoting William Prosser, *The Law of Torts*, § 41, p. 236–37 (4th ed. 1971).
3. Dan Dobs, *The Law of Torts* 467 (West 2000).
4. *Id.* at p. 466.
5. American Law Institute, *Restatement (Second) of Torts* § 435(2)(1965).
6. Columbine High School Massacre (en.wikipedia.org/wiki/Columbine_High_School_massacre).
7. *Sanders v. Acclaim Entertainment, Inc.*, 188 F. Supp. 2d 1264, 1276 (D. Colo. 2002).

Student StudyWARE™ CD-ROM
For additional materials, please go to the student CD in this book.

CHAPTER

16

NEGLIGENCE: ELEMENT IV: DAMAGES

CHAPTER OUTLINE

- Kinds of Damages
- Present Value
- Pain and Suffering
- Software
- Property Damage
- Mitigation-of-Damages Rule
- Collateral Source Rule
- Joint Tortfeasors
- Release
- Contribution
- Indemnity
- Settlement
- September 11th Victim Compensation Fund
- Taxation of Damages

CHAPTER OBJECTIVES

After completing this chapter, you should be able to:

- Understand the kinds of compensatory damages.
- Define nominal and punitive damages.
- Explain how to calculate the present value of an award that covers future damages.
- Describe how damages for pain and suffering are awarded.
- Explain the mitigation-of-damages and collateral source rules.
- Describe the liability of joint tortfeasors.
- Describe what is meant by release, contribution, and indemnity.
- Understand the tax consequences of an award of damages.

KINDS OF DAMAGES

The plaintiff in a negligence action must suffer actual harm or loss to person or property. It is not enough that the defendant has engaged in unreasonable or even reckless conduct. Without actual harm or loss, the negligence action fails. Although the focus of this chapter is on damages in a negligence action, most of the principles discussed here also apply to intentional and strict liability torts.

damages 1. Monetary payments awarded to compensate for a legally recognized wrong (noun). 2. Causes harm or other loss (verb). (The word *damage* means injury, impairment, or other loss to person or property).

Damages are monetary payments awarded for a legally recognized wrong. (The word *damage* also refers to any injury, impairment, or other loss to person or property.) Damages are a *legal* remedy, unlike an injunction, for example, which is an *equitable* remedy.[1] There are three main categories of damages: compensatory, nominal, and punitive.

Compensatory Damages

compensatory damages Monetary payments to restore an injured party to his or her position prior to the injury or other wrong.

Compensatory damages are monetary payments designed to restore an injured party to his or her position prior to suffering the injury or other loss. They seek to make the plaintiff whole. An important purpose of tort law is to return the plaintiff to the position he or she was in before the injury or loss. The payment of money, of course, cannot always accomplish this. The payment of compensatory damages is designed to come as close as possible to returning the plaintiff to the status quo before the accident.

Compensatory damages cover two kinds of losses: economic and non-economic. Economic losses can be objectively verified through specific dollar amounts that have been paid or are expected to be paid in the future to replace whatever has been lost because of the tort. Economic losses also consist of objectively verifiable lost past earnings and lost future earning capacity.

EXAMPLES

- present and future medical expenses
- burial costs
- loss of the use of property
- costs of repair
- costs of obtaining substitute domestic services
- present and future loss of wages
- loss of business or employment opportunities

Non-economic losses, on the other hand, are those losses for which no objective dollar amount can be identified.

EXAMPLES

- pain
- mental anguish
- inconvenience
- loss of companionship
- humiliation

pain and suffering Physical discomfort or emotional distress; a disagreeable mental or emotional experience.

general damages Compensatory damages that usually result from the kind of harm caused by the conduct of the defendant. Damages that usually and naturally flow from this wrong, e.g., pain and suffering. The law implies or presumes that such damages result from the wrong complained of.

Collectively, these non-economic damages are sometimes referred to as **pain and suffering** damages.

Another important classification of compensatory damages is the distinction between general and special damages. **General damages** are those compensatory damages that usually result from the kind of harm caused by the defendant's conduct. General damages naturally follow from the harm caused by such conduct. Pain and suffering, for example, naturally follow from a severe head injury. In most states, the complaint of the plaintiff does not have to allege general damages with specificity.

The law will presume that general damages result from the wrong complained of. Most plaintiffs, of course, will try to offer as much evidence on general damages as they can in order to increase the final amount of the monetary award. The point, however, is that the absence of such evidence is not fatal to the plaintiff's case; the fact finder can presume that they exist. **Special damages**, on the other hand, are economic or pecuniary losses, such as medical expenses and lost wages, that must be alleged and proven. They are compensatory damages that are not presumed to exist. They would include medical expenses, loss of earnings, destroyed property, etc. The law does not presume that they exist. They must be specifically pleaded in the complaint.

special damages Compensatory damages that consist of economic or pecuniary losses (e.g., medical expenses and lost wages) that must be alleged and proven. They are not presumed to exist. Also referred to as specials.

EXAMPLE

Sam is seeing a psychiatrist to help him overcome the anxiety he feels over the negligent conduct of the defendant who almost killed Sam with scalding water in a freak accident. His pain and suffering due to the anxiety are part of his general damages. The cost of the psychiatrist, however, is part of Sam's special damages.

Nominal Damages

Nominal damages are a small monetary payment (often $1) awarded when the defendant has committed a tort that has resulted in little or no harm, so no compensatory damages are due. Nominal damages are *not* awarded in negligence cases since one of the elements of negligence is actual damages. Nominal damages are awarded in intentional tort and strict liability tort cases when there has been a technical commission of the tort but no actual harm.

nominal damages A trifling sum (e.g., $1) awarded to the plaintiff because there was no significant loss or injury suffered, although a technical invasion of rights did occur.

Attorneys usually do not take cases that do not present the possibility of substantial damages since fees are often a percentage of the damages award. When nominal damages are likely, the plaintiff's incentive to bring the case is to vindicate a right, to make a public record of the defendant's misdeed, or to warn the defendant that future misconduct of the same kind will lead to further lawsuits. If the attorney is not taking such a case **pro bono** (for free), he or she is probably being paid an hourly or set fee rather than a percentage.

pro bono Concerning or involving legal services that are provided for the public good (*pro bono publico*) without fee or compensation. Sometimes also applied to services given at a reduced rate. Shortened to pro bono.

Punitive Damages

Punitive damages are noncompensatory damages that seek to punish the defendant and to deter similar conduct by others. Punitive damages are awarded when the defendant has acted maliciously, outrageously, recklessly, or in conscious disregard for the safety of others. **Ordinary negligence** is not enough. Nor is intentional conduct enough unless the court can conclude that the defendant acted in a morally reprehensible way.

punitive damages Damages that are added to actual or compensatory damages in order to punish malicious, outrageous, or reckless conduct and to deter similar conduct in the future. Also called exemplary damages, smart money, and vindictive damages.

ordinary negligence Conduct that is unreasonable but not gross or reckless.

In most states, the plaintiff receives all of the punitive damages that are awarded. In a few states, however, a portion of an award of punitive damages goes to the state government.

In recent years some courts have been alarmed at the size of punitive damage awards, particularly in relationship to the compensatory damages in the case. The question arises as to whether there are limits on how high punitive damages can go. For example, can punitive damages be five hundred times the compensatory damages? There is no clear answer to this question. Some states impose limits on the amount of punitive damages that can be awarded, but in many states, extraordinarily high punitive damages are allowed. Change, however, is on the horizon. The United States Supreme Court has said that to "the extent an award [of punitive damages] is grossly excessive, it furthers no legitimate purpose and constitutes an arbitrary deprivation of property."[2] To assist courts in determining whether a punitive damage award is grossly excessive and violates due process, the Court has identified three guideposts: (1) the degree of reprehensibility of the defendant's conduct, (2) the disparity between the actual or potential harm suffered by the plaintiff and the punitive damage award, and (3) the difference between the punitive damages awarded and the civil penalties authorized or imposed in comparable cases.[3] Although these guideposts do not clearly tell us when awards of punitive damages are too high, they are a signal that very high awards of punitive damages are likely to be challenged as unconstitutional.

Interrogatory Questions on Damages

interrogatories A method of discovery consisting of written questions about a lawsuit submitted by one party to another to help the sender prepare for trial.

A major tool of defendants in tort cases is the use of **interrogatories** to obtain information from the plaintiff prior to trial. In Exhibit 18–3 of Chapter 18 you will examine interrogatories on the following topics pertaining to damages:

- current injury
- treatment received to date
- anticipated future treatment
- costs of treatment
- prior injuries
- loss of wages or employment to date
- anticipated future loss of wages or employment
- collateral sources (funds received independent of the alleged tortfeasor—see discussion of collateral sources later in this chapter)
- etc.

Reading these interrogatories will provide a good overview of the kinds of evidence parties seek on the issue of damages.[4]

lump-sum payment A single amount paid at one time to cover all past and future damages.

structured settlement An agreement in which the defendant pays for damages he or she caused by making periodic payments for a designated period of time, such as during the life of the victim. The payments are often funded through an annuity.

annuity A fixed sum payable periodically (e.g., monthly or annually) for life or another specific period of time.

present value The amount of money an individual would have to be given now in order to generate a certain amount of money within a designated period of time through prudent investment, usually at compound interest. Also called present cash value and present worth.

compound interest Interest earned on money calculated on the basis of the amount of principal involved and on the interest already accrued. The latter consists of interest on interest.

simple interest Interest earned on the principal alone, not on already accrued interest.

PRESENT VALUE

By the time a trial ends, the court will want to reach one number to cover all past *and future* damages in a **lump-sum payment**. The alternative would be for the court to retain jurisdiction of the case to keep it open for the life of the plaintiff in order to take account of actual medical costs, loss of income, inflation, and other uncertainties of the economy. This would create chaos in the court system since no tort case would ever end. Hence, the court will want to have a lump-sum judgment. Normally, this judgment is paid at one time, although some states allow the amount to be paid in periodic payments over a set time. This may be required in certain kinds of tort cases such as medical malpractice.

Parties have more flexibility when negotiating a settlement. A **structured settlement**, for example, would consist of periodic payments for a designated period of time such as the life of the victim. The periodic payments are often paid through an **annuity** that the defendant funds. The settlement might call for a reduced lump sum payment now with the balance covered by future periodic payments through an annuity.

Whenever you are entitled to a payment of economic damages now to cover something that will happen in the future, the payment must be reduced to **present value**. This is the amount of money an individual would have to be given now in order to generate a certain amount of money within a designated period of time through prudent investment, usually at compound interest. **Compound interest** is interest that is calculated on the principal *and* on the interest that has accrued to date. In effect, as interest is earned, it is added to the principal. With compound interest, you are earning interest on your interest. The alternative is **simple interest**, which is interest earned on the principal alone, not on the accrued interest.

EXAMPLE

Ted negligently injures Mary in 2012. During 2012, Mary paid $15,000 in medical bills. For the next four years (2013–2016), she is expected to spend

$12,500 a year for further medical expenses. The negligence trial against Ted ends on December 31, 2012, at which time Mary's total past and future economic damages for medical expenses are calculated at $65,000.

2012:	$15,000	(past medical expenses)
2013–2016:	$50,000	(future medical expenses; $12,500 × 4)
	$65,000	(calculated at the end of the trial on December 31, 2012)

Mary has already incurred a loss of $15,000 for 2012. There is no need to reduce this amount to present value. The determination of present value pertains to future damages. Her future damages for the next four years will be $50,000. But it would be a **windfall** to give her $50,000 at the end of the trial on December 31, 2012. The reason is that she could take the $50,000 and immediately invest it. Whatever was not spent on medical expenses during the four years would be earning interest, so that by the end of four years she would have had available to her $50,000 plus the interest earned.

windfall An extra amount to which one is not entitled under the original understanding of the parties.

To prevent the windfall, $50,000 must be reduced to present value on December 31, 2012. To do this, we pick an interest rate that Mary would be assumed to earn during the four years. The higher the interest rate, the lower the amount Mary would have to be given on December 31, 2012. Assume, for example, that investing $38,000 in 2012 at 6 percent would yield $50,000 in 2016. The present value of $50,000, therefore, is $38,000. This is the amount Mary would have to be given in 2012 in order to cover her $50,000 of future expenses over the next four years. If we picked an interest rate of 10 percent, she would have to be given considerably less in 2012 because of the higher returns that 10 percent would generate over this period.

The interest rate used in calculating present value is called the **discount rate**. During negotiations, the parties may agree on what the discount rate should be. In the absence of agreement, the court will determine what the rate should be, usually based on generally accepted practice in the area. Once the discount rate is set, computer programs can quickly make the necessary calculations of compound interest over the designated period of time. For an example, see Exhibit 16–2 later in the chapter.

discount rate The interest rate used by the parties when determining the present value of money to be received in the future.

Exhibit 16–1 contains an example of jury instructions on damages. Notice that the trial judge tells the jury that it must use present value (referred to as "present cash value") for all future economic losses. Anything lost up to the date of the trial, however, is not reduced to present value.

Next we look at lost future wages more closely through the case of *O'Shea v. Riverway Towing Co.* The case provides an excellent overview of other economic factors that go into a determination of damages in a personal injury case. As you will see in the case, the downward adjustment that results from the determination of present value is not the only adjustment made in an award of damages. Make careful note of all of the factors the court uses to reach the final award. In particular, note the following questions covered by the court in reaching the result in the *O'Shea* opinion.

Guide to Reading *O'Shea v. Riverway Towing Co.*: Questions Asked by the Court in Calculating Damages for Lost Wages

- What was the injury suffered by the plaintiff? (Answer: broken leg.)
- Is the plaintiff able to continue working in her current job after the injury? (Answer: no.)
- Can the court take into consideration whether the plaintiff would have been able to find gainful employment anywhere in the economy after the accident? (Answer: yes. Wages the plaintiff could have earned in another job—discounted by the probability that she would be able to find another job—should be deducted from the future wages she would have earned in the

Exhibit 16–1
Jury instructions on damages.[5]

If you find that the plaintiff is entitled to a verdict against the defendant, you must then award the plaintiff damages in an amount that will provide reasonable and fair compensation for each of the following elements of loss proved by the evidence to have resulted from the negligence of the defendant:

(1) The reasonable value of medical, hospital, and nursing care, services, and supplies reasonably required and actually given in the treatment of the plaintiff to the present time, and the present cash value of the reasonable value of similar items reasonably certain to be required and given in the future.

(2) The reasonable value of working time lost to date. In determining this amount, you should consider evidence of plaintiff's earnings and earning capacity, how he or she ordinarily occupied him- or herself, and find what was reasonably certain to have been earned in the time lost if there had been no injury. One's ability to work may have a monetary value even though that person is not employed by another. In determining this amount, you should also consider evidence of the reasonable value of services performed by another in doing things for the plaintiff which, except for the injury, plaintiff would ordinarily have performed for him- or herself.

(3) The present cash value of earning capacity reasonably certain to be lost in the future as a result of the injury in question.

(4) In computing the damages arising from the future because of expenses and loss of earnings, you must not simply multiply the damages by the length of time you have found they will continue or by the number of years you have found that the plaintiff is likely to live. Instead, you must determine their present cash value. "Present cash value" means the sum of money needed now, which, when added to what that sum may reasonably be expected to earn in the future through prudent investment, will equal the amount of the expenses and earnings at the time in the future when the expenses must be paid and the earnings would have been received.

(5) Reasonable compensation for any pain, discomfort, fears, anxiety and other mental and emotional distress suffered by the plaintiff and of which the injury was a cause and for similar suffering reasonably certain to be experienced in the future from the same cause. No definite standard or method of calculation is prescribed by law by which to fix reasonable compensation for pain and suffering. Nor is the opinion of any witness required as to the amount of such reasonable compensation. Furthermore, the argument of counsel as to the amount of damages is not evidence of reasonable compensation. In making an award for pain and suffering, you shall exercise your authority with calm and reasonable judgment and the damages you fix shall be just and reasonable in the light of the evidence.

job she had at the time of the accident. The attorneys, however, did not ask the judge to make the calculation in this way.)

- Can the court take into consideration what the plaintiff would earn for a full year even if the plaintiff had not worked in her current job for a full year? (Answer: yes.)
- Can the court take into consideration the wages the plaintiff would have earned if she had been able to take the new job she was considering? (Answer: yes, although in this case the trial court may not have given this consideration much weight.)
- Can the court allow the plaintiff to take into account an amount by which her wages would have been increased by inflation? (Answer: yes.)
- Should a discount rate be used to reduce future lost wages to present value? (Answer: yes; at trial an accountant used an 8.5 percent discount rate.)
- Should inflation be taken into consideration in projecting lost future earnings and in the discount rate? (Answer: yes; it is illogical to build inflation into the discount rate yet ignore it in calculating the lost future wages that are to be discounted.)

- Should the court assume that the plaintiff's future wages would have increased even if there had been no inflation? (Answer: yes.)
- In calculating future lost wages to a projected age of retirement, should the amount be reduced by the probability that the plaintiff would not reach her retirement age if the accident had not occurred? (Answer: yes.)
- When determining the discount rate, should the economist take into consideration the tax bracket of the plaintiff as an indication of what safe investments she would have used? (Answer: yes, but the economist did not do so here; this is not a critical error, however, because of other offsetting errors the economist made.)
- In estimating future lost wages, should the plaintiff's entire income tax liability be deducted? (Answer: no; although the damage award is not taxable, interest earned on the award is taxable.)

CASE

O'Shea v. Riverway Towing Co.

677 F.2d 1194 (7th Cir. 1982)
United States Court of Appeals for the Seventh Circuit

Background: *Margaret O'Shea was a cook on a Mississippi towboat. After falling and breaking her leg getting off the boat, she sued her employer, Riverway, for negligently causing the fall. She won in the district court (the federal trial court), which awarded her over $86,033 in damages for lost future wages. The case is now on appeal before the United States Court of Appeals for the Seventh Circuit.*

Decision on Appeal: *The award of damages was proper.*

OPINION OF COURT

Judge POSNER delivered the opinion of the court. . . .

When the harbor boat reached shore it tied up to a seawall the top of which was several feet above the boat's deck. There was no ladder. The other passengers, who were seamen, clambered up the seawall without difficulty, but Mrs. O'Shea, a 57-year-old woman who weighs 200 pounds (she is five foot seven), balked. According to Mrs. O'Shea's testimony, which the district court believed, a deckhand instructed her to climb the stairs to a catwalk above the deck and disembark from there. But the catwalk was three feet above the top of the seawall, and again there was no ladder. The deckhand told her that she should jump and that the men who had already disembarked would help her land safely. She did as told, but fell in landing, carrying the assisting seamen down with her, and broke her leg. . . .

Mrs. O'Shea's job as a cook paid her $40 a day, and since the custom was to work 30 days consecutively and then have the next 30 days off, this comes to $7200 a year although, as we shall see, she never had earned that much in a single year. She testified that when the accident occurred she had been about to get another cook's job on a Mississippi towboat that would have paid her $60 a day ($10,800 a year). She also testified that she had been intending to work as a boat's cook until she was 70—longer if she was able. An economist who testified on Mrs. O'Shea's behalf used the foregoing testimony as the basis for estimating the wages that she lost because of the accident. He first subtracted federal income tax from yearly wage estimates based on alternative assumptions about her wage rate (that it would be either $40 or $60 a day); assumed that this wage would have grown by between six and eight percent a year; assumed that she would have worked either to age 65 or to age 70; and then discounted the resulting lost-wage estimates to present value, using a discount rate of 8.5 percent a year. These calculations, being based on alternative assumptions concerning starting wage rate, annual wage increases, and length of employment, yielded a range of values rather than a single value. The bottom of the range was $50,000. This is the present value, computed at an 8.5 percent discount rate, of Mrs. O'Shea's lost future wages on the assumption that her starting wage was $40 a day and that it would have grown by six percent a year until she retired at the age of 65. The top of the range was $114,000, which is the present value (again discounted at 8.5 percent) of her lost future wages assuming she would have worked till she was 70 at a wage that would have started at $60 a day and increased by eight percent a year. The judge awarded a figure—$86,033—near the midpoint of this range. He did not explain in his written opinion how he had arrived at this figure, but in a preceding oral opinion he stated that he was "not certain that she would work until age 70 at this type of work," although "she certainly was entitled to" do so and "could have earned something"; and that he had not "felt bound by [the economist's] figure of eight percent increase in wages" and had "not found the wages based on necessarily a 60 dollar a day job." If this can be taken to mean that he thought Mrs. O'Shea would probably have worked till she was 70, starting at $40 a day but moving up from there at six rather than eight percent a year, the economist's estimate of the present value of her lost future wages would be $75,000.

There is no doubt that the accident disabled Mrs. O'Shea from working as a cook on a boat. The break in her leg was very serious: it reduced the stability of the leg and caused her to fall frequently. It is impossible to see how she could have continued working as a cook, a job performed mostly while standing up, and especially on a boat, with its unsteady motion. But Riverway argues that Mrs. O'Shea (who has not worked at all since the accident, which occurred two years before the trial) could have gotten some sort of job and that the wages in that job should be deducted from the admittedly higher wages that she could have earned as a cook on a boat.

The question is not whether Mrs. O'Shea is totally disabled in the sense, relevant to social security disability cases but not tort cases, that there is no job in the American economy for which she is medically fit. It is whether she can by reasonable diligence find gainful employment, given the physical condition in which the accident left her. Here is a middle-aged woman, very overweight, badly scarred on one arm and one leg, unsteady on her feet, in constant and serious pain from the accident, with no education beyond high school and no work skills other than cooking, a job that happens to require standing for long periods which she is incapable of doing. It seems unlikely that someone in this condition could find gainful work at the minimum wage. True, the probability is not zero; and a better procedure, therefore, might have been to subtract from Mrs. O'Shea's lost future wages as a boat's cook the wages in some other job, discounted (i.e., multiplied) by the probability—very low—that she would in fact be able to get another job. But the district judge cannot be criticized for having failed to use a procedure not suggested by either party. The question put to him was the dichotomous one, would she or would she not get another job if she made reasonable efforts to do so? This required him to decide whether there was a more than 50 percent probability that she would. We cannot say that the negative answer he gave to that question was clearly erroneous.

Riverway argues next that it was wrong for the judge to award damages on the basis of a wage not validated, as it were, by at least a year's employment at that wage. Mrs. O'Shea had never worked full time, had never in fact earned more than $3600 in a full year, and in the year preceding the accident had earned only $900. But previous wages do not put a cap on an award of lost future wages. If a man who had never worked in his life graduated from law school, began working at a law firm at an annual salary of $35,000, and was killed the second day on the job, his lack of a past wage history would be irrelevant to computing his lost future wages. The present case is similar if less dramatic. Mrs. O'Shea did not work at all until 1974, when her husband died. She then lived on her inheritance and worked at a variety of part-time jobs till January 1979, when she started working as a cook on the towboat. According to her testimony, which the trial judge believed, she was then working full time. It is immaterial that this was her first full-time job and that the accident occurred before she had held it for a full year. Her job history was typical of women who return to the labor force after their children are grown or, as in Mrs. O'Shea's case, after their husband dies, and these women are, like any tort victims, entitled to damages based on what they would have earned in the future rather than on what they may or may not have earned in the past.

If we are correct so far, Mrs. O'Shea was entitled to have her lost wages determined on the assumption that she would have earned at least $7200 in the first year after the accident and that the accident caused her to lose that entire amount by disabling her from any gainful employment. And since Riverway neither challenges the district judge's (apparent) finding that Mrs. O'Shea would have worked till she was 70 nor contends that the lost wages for each year until then should be discounted by the probability that she would in fact have been alive and working as a boat's cook throughout the damage period, we may also assume that her wages would have been at least $7200 a year for the 12 years between the date of the accident and her seventieth birthday. But Riverway does argue that we cannot assume she might have earned $10,800 a year rather than $7200, despite her testimony that at the time of the accident she was about to take another job as a boat's cook where she would have been paid at the rate of $60 rather than $40 a day. The point is not terribly important since the trial judge gave little weight to this testimony, but we shall discuss it briefly. Mrs. O'Shea was asked on direct examination what "pay you would have worked" for in the new job. Riverway's counsel objected on the ground of hearsay, the judge overruled his objection, and she answered $60 a day. The objection was not well taken. Riverway argues that only her prospective employer knew what her wage was, and hence when she said it was $60 she was testifying to what he had told her. But an employee's wage is as much in the personal knowledge of the employee as of the employer. If Mrs. O'Shea's prospective employer had testified that he would have paid her $60, Riverway's counsel could have made the converse hearsay objection that the employer was really testifying to what Mrs. O'Shea had told him she was willing to work for. Riverway's counsel could on cross-examination have probed the basis for Mrs. O'Shea's belief that she was going to get $60 a day in a new job, but he did not do so and cannot complain now that the judge may have given her testimony some (though little) weight.

We come at last to the most important issue in the case, which is the proper treatment of inflation in calculating lost future wages. Mrs. O'Shea's economist based the six to eight percent range which he used to estimate future increases in the wages of a boat's cook on the general pattern of wage increases in service occupations over the past 25 years. During the second half of this period the rate of inflation has been substantial and has accounted for much of the increase in nominal wages in this period; and to use that increase to project future wage increases is therefore to assume that inflation will continue, and continue to push up wages. Riverway argues that it is improper as a matter of law to take inflation into account in projecting lost future wages. Yet Riverway itself wants to take inflation into account—one-sidedly, to reduce the amount of the damages computed.

For Riverway does not object to the economist's choice of an 8.5 percent discount rate for reducing Mrs. O'Shea's lost future wages to present value, although the rate includes an allowance—a very large allowance—for inflation.

To explain, the object of discounting lost future wages to present value is to give the plaintiff an amount of money which, invested safely, will grow to a sum equal to those wages. So if we thought that but for the accident Mrs. O'Shea would have earned $7200 in 1990, and we were computing in 1980 (when this case was tried) her damages based on those lost earnings, we would need to determine the sum of money that, invested safely for a period of 10 years, would grow to $7200. Suppose that in 1980 the rate of interest on ultra-safe (i.e., federal government) bonds or notes maturing in 10 years was 12 percent. Then we would consult a table of present values to see what sum of money invested at 12 percent for 10 years would at the end of that time have grown to $7200. The answer is $2318. But a moment's reflection will show that to give Mrs. O'Shea $2318 to compensate her for lost wages in 1990 would grossly undercompensate her. People demand 12 percent to lend money risklessly for 10 years because they expect their principal to have much less purchasing power when they get it back at the end of the time. In other words, when long-term interest rates are high, they are high in order to compensate lenders for the fact that they will be repaid in cheaper dollars. In periods when no inflation is anticipated, the risk-free interest rate is between one and three percent. See references in *Doca v. Marina Mercante Nicaraguense, S.A.,* 634 F.2d 30, 39 n.2 (2d Cir. 1980). Additional percentage points above that level reflect inflation anticipated over the life of the loan. But if there is inflation it will affect wages as well as prices. Therefore to give Mrs. O'Shea $2318 today because that is the present value of $7200 10 years hence, computed at a discount rate—12 percent—that consists mainly of an allowance for anticipated inflation, is in fact to give her less than she would have been earning then if she was earning $7200 on the date of the accident, even if the only wage increases she would have received would have been those necessary to keep pace with inflation.

There are (at least) two ways to deal with inflation in computing the present value of lost future wages. One is to take it out of both the wages and the discount rate—to say to Mrs. O'Shea, "we are going to calculate your probable wage in 1990 on the assumption, unrealistic as it is, that there will be zero inflation between now and then; and, to be consistent, we are going to discount the amount thus calculated by the interest rate that would be charged under the same assumption of zero inflation." Thus, if we thought Mrs. O'Shea's real (i.e., inflation-free) wage rate would not rise in the future, we would fix her lost earnings in 1990 as $7200 and, to be consistent, we would discount that to present (1980) value using an estimate of the real interest rate. At two percent, this procedure would yield a present value of $5906. Of course, she would not invest this money at a mere two percent. She would invest it at the much higher prevailing interest rate. But that would not give her a windfall; it would just enable her to replace her lost 1990 earnings with an amount equal to what she would in fact have earned in that year if inflation continues, as most people expect it to do. (If people did not expect continued inflation, long-term interest rates would be much lower; those rates impound investors' inflationary expectations.)

An alternative approach, which yields the same result, is to use a (higher) discount rate based on the current risk-free 10-year interest rate, but apply that rate to an estimate of lost future wages that includes expected inflation. Contrary to Riverway's argument, this projection would not require gazing into a crystal ball. The expected rate of inflation can, as just suggested, be read off from the current long-term interest rate. If that rate is 12 percent, and if as suggested earlier the real or inflation-free interest rate is only one to three percent, this implies that the market is anticipating 9–11 percent inflation over the next 10 years, for a long-term interest rate is simply the sum of the real interest rate and the anticipated rate of inflation during the term.

Either approach to dealing with inflation is acceptable (they are, in fact, equivalent) and we by no means rule out others; but it is illogical and indefensible to build inflation into the discount rate yet ignore it in calculating the lost future wages that are to be discounted. That results in systematic undercompensation, just as building inflation into the estimate of future lost earnings and then discounting using the real rate of interest would systematically overcompensate. The former error is committed, we respectfully suggest, by those circuits, notably the Fifth, that refuse to allow inflation to be used in projecting lost future earnings but then use a discount rate that has built into it a large allowance for inflation. See, e.g., *Culver v. Slater Boat Co.,* 644 F.2d 460, 464 (5th Cir. 1981) (using a 9.125 percent discount rate). We align ourselves instead with those circuits (a majority, see *Doca v. Marina Mercante Nicaraguense, S.A.,* supra, 634 F.2d at 35–36), notably the Second, that require that inflation be treated consistently in choosing a discount rate and in estimating the future lost wages to be discounted to present value using that rate. . . .

Applying our analysis to the present case, we cannot pronounce the approach taken by the plaintiff's economist unreasonable. He chose a discount rate—8.5 percent—well above the real rate of interest, and therefore containing an allowance for inflation. Consistency required him to inflate Mrs. O'Shea's starting wage as a boat's cook in calculating her lost future wages, and he did so at a rate of six to eight percent a year. If this rate had been intended as a forecast of purely inflationary wage changes, his approach would be open to question, especially at the upper end of his range. For if the estimated rate of inflation were eight percent, the use of a discount rate of 8.5 percent would imply that the real rate of interest was only .5 percent, which is lower than most economists believe it to be for any substantial period of time. But wages do not rise just because of inflation. Mrs. O'Shea could expect her real wages as a boat's cook to rise as she became more experienced and as average real wage rates throughout the economy rose, as they usually do over a decade or more. It would not be outlandish to assume that even if there were no inflation,

Mrs. O'Shea's wages would have risen by three percent a year. If we subtract that from the economist's six to eight percent range, the inflation allowance built into his estimated future wage increases is only three to five percent; and when we subtract these figures from 8.5 percent we see that his implicit estimate of the real rate of interest was very high (3.5–5.5 percent). This means he was conservative, because the higher the discount rate used the lower the damages calculated.

If conservative in one sense, the economist was most liberal in another. He made no allowance for the fact that Mrs. O'Shea, whose health history quite apart from the accident is not outstanding, might very well not have survived—let alone survived and been working as a boat's cook or in an equivalent job—until the age of 70. The damage award is a sum certain, but the lost future wages to which that award is equated by means of the discount rate are mere probabilities. If the probability of her being employed as a boat's cook full time in 1990 was only 75 percent, for example, then her estimated wages in that year should have been multiplied by .75 to determine the value of the expectation that she lost as a result of the accident; and so with each of the other future years. The economist did not do this, and by failing to do this he overstated the loss due to the accident.

But Riverway does not make an issue of this aspect of the economist's analysis. Nor of another: the economist selected the 8.5 percent figure for the discount rate because that was the current interest rate on Triple A 10-year state and municipal bonds, but it would not make sense in Mrs. O'Shea's federal income tax bracket to invest in tax-free bonds. If he wanted to use nominal rather than real interest rates and wage increases (as we said was proper), the economist should have used a higher discount rate and a higher expected rate of inflation. But as these adjustments would have been largely or entirely offsetting, the failure to make them was not a critical error.

Although we are not entirely satisfied with the economic analysis on which the judge, in the absence of any other evidence of the present value of Mrs. O'Shea's lost future wages, must have relied heavily, we recognize that the exactness which economic analysis rigorously pursued appears to offer is, at least in the litigation setting, somewhat delusive. Therefore, we will not reverse an award of damages for lost wages because of questionable assumptions unless it yields an unreasonable result—especially when, as in the present case, the defendant does not offer any economic evidence himself and does not object to the questionable steps in the plaintiff's economic analysis. We cannot say the result here was unreasonable. If the economist's method of estimating damages was too generous to Mrs. O'Shea in one important respect it was, as we have seen, niggardly in another. Another error against Mrs. O'Shea should be noted: the economist should not have deducted her entire income tax liability in estimating her future lost wages. While it is true that the damage award is not taxable, the interest she earns on it will be (a point the economist may have ignored because of his erroneous assumption that she would invest the award in tax-exempt bonds), so that his method involved an element of double taxation.

If we assume that Mrs. O'Shea could have expected a three percent annual increase in her real wages from a base of $7200, that the real risk-free rate of interest (and therefore the appropriate discount rate if we are considering only real wage increases) is two percent, and that she would have worked till she was 70, the present value of her lost future wages would be $91,310. This figure ignores the fact that she did not have a 100 percent probability of actually working till age 70 as a boat's cook, and fails to make the appropriate (though probably, in her bracket, very small) net income tax adjustment; but it also ignores the possibility, small but not totally negligible, that the proper base is really $10,800 rather than $7200.

So we cannot say that the figure arrived at by the judge, $86,033, was unreasonably high. But we are distressed that he made no attempt to explain how he had arrived at that figure, since it was not one contained in the economist's testimony though it must in some way have been derived from that testimony. Unlike many other damage items in a personal injury case, notably pain and suffering, the calculation of damages for lost earnings can and should be an analytical rather than an intuitive undertaking. Therefore, compliance with Rule 52(a) of the Federal Rules of Civil Procedure requires that in a bench trial the district judge set out the steps by which he arrived at his award for lost future earnings, in order to assist the appellate court in reviewing the award. The district judge failed to do that here. We do not consider this reversible error, because our own analysis convinces us that the award of damages for lost future wages was reasonable. But for the future we ask the district judges in this circuit to indicate the steps by which they arrive at damage awards for lost future earnings.

Judgment Affirmed.

ASSIGNMENT 16.1

a. What is meant by present value? What role does it play in an award of damages?
b. What tactical mistakes did the attorney representing the employer make in the trial of this case?

PAIN AND SUFFERING

Pain is often experienced when a tort is committed, at the time of medical treatment, and while recovering. During these periods, mental suffering or distress can also occur. For example:

- fright
- humiliation
- fear and anxiety
- loss of companionship
- unhappiness
- depression or other forms of mental illness

The amount recovered for pain and suffering will depend on the amount of time it was experienced and the intensity of the experience. Also considered are the age and condition of life of the plaintiff. It is, of course, very difficult to assign a dollar amount that will compensate the plaintiff for pain and suffering. The main guide available is the amount a reasonable person would estimate as fair. (See paragraph 5 in Exhibit 16–1.) A minority of states permit counsel to make a **per diem argument** to the jury whereby a certain amount is requested for every day the pain and suffering has been endured and is expected to continue. (The per diem argument is also called the unit-of-time argument.) Other states, however, do not allow such arguments on the ground that they are too arbitrary.

per diem argument A certain amount is requested as damages for every day that pain and suffering has been endured and is expected to continue. Also called the unit-of-time argument.

Damages for pain and suffering are controversial. The largest portion of an award of damages is usually the amount given for pain and suffering. Juries have been known to give amounts for pain and suffering that are fifty times the compensatory damages. It is sometimes said that pain and suffering "pays the attorney fees." Most attorneys in personal injury cases are paid a percentage of what the plaintiff receives. When the attorney walks away with a large fee, it is usually due to the pain and suffering portion of the final judgment or of the settlement if the case does not go to trial. Some states have passed reform proposals designed to set limits on damages for pain and suffering in certain categories of cases. For example, a state might pass a statute that sets limits (i.e., a **cap**) on damages for pain and suffering in medical malpractice cases at $250,000. As you might expect, trial attorneys are often vigorous opponents of such statutes.

cap A limitation or ceiling. A *damage cap* is a limitation on the amount of damages that can be awarded in tort cases.

Hedonic damages are compensatory damages that cover the victim's loss of pleasure or enjoyment for life's activities such as raising children, experiencing the morning sun, reading a good book, singing in a choir, and attending college. Some courts, however, say that an award of hedonic damages is improper because they are already provided for in the award of pain and suffering. If, however, the victim dies immediately, there may have been no pain and suffering. The concept of hedonic damages is relatively new; it is unclear how many states will allow juries to consider it.

hedonic damages Damages that cover the victim's loss of pleasure or enjoyment of life.

ASSIGNMENT 16.2

Due to medical negligence during an operation, a patient becomes permanently comatose, although she did respond to certain stimuli such as light. What damages are possible?

Before a case goes to trial, a plaintiff will usually try to settle with the insurance company of the defendant, if any. How does a claims adjuster calculate damages? Although insurance companies do not all operate in the same way, there is a rough formula that many companies use as a starting point:

> A claims adjuster begins with the medical expenses. Then the intangibles—pain and other non-economic losses—are multiplied by 1.5 to 2 times if the injuries

are relatively minor, and up to 5 times if the injuries are particularly painful, serious, or long-lasting. Finally, lost income is added to that amount. Several factors raise the damages formula toward the 5-times end:

- more painful, serious, or long-lasting injuries
- more invasive or long-lasting injuries
- clearer medical evidence of extent of injuries
- more obvious evidence of the other person's fault[6]

settlement brochure A written presentation by a party to an opponent (or its insurance company) on the merits of a cause of action (including alleged damages) in an effort to encourage settlement. The presentation is called a *settlement précis* if the case is relatively uncomplicated.

Plaintiff's attorney will often prepare a **settlement brochure** (or its shorter version, a *settlement précis*) to encourage settlement with the defendant or its insurance company. It is a written presentation on the merits of a cause of action, including documentation of alleged damages. We will examine these settlement efforts in Chapter 29.

SOFTWARE

Often a law office will use computer programs to help it calculate the damages that it will request. For example, Advocate Software, Inc. has software used in personal injury cases. It can be used to:

- convert future losses to present value
- calculate life expectancy
- calculate work life expectancy
- estimate average earnings for specific categories of work
- calculate household service values
- estimate fringe benefits a worker would have received
- prepare reports to be sent to insurers for settlement negotiations

See Exhibit 16–2, which provides damages projections for Robert T. Exemplar. When planning a case, the law office needs to calculate damages based on certain

Exhibit 16–2
Software to help calculate damages.

Source: Advocate Software, Inc., Personal Injury-Economist.

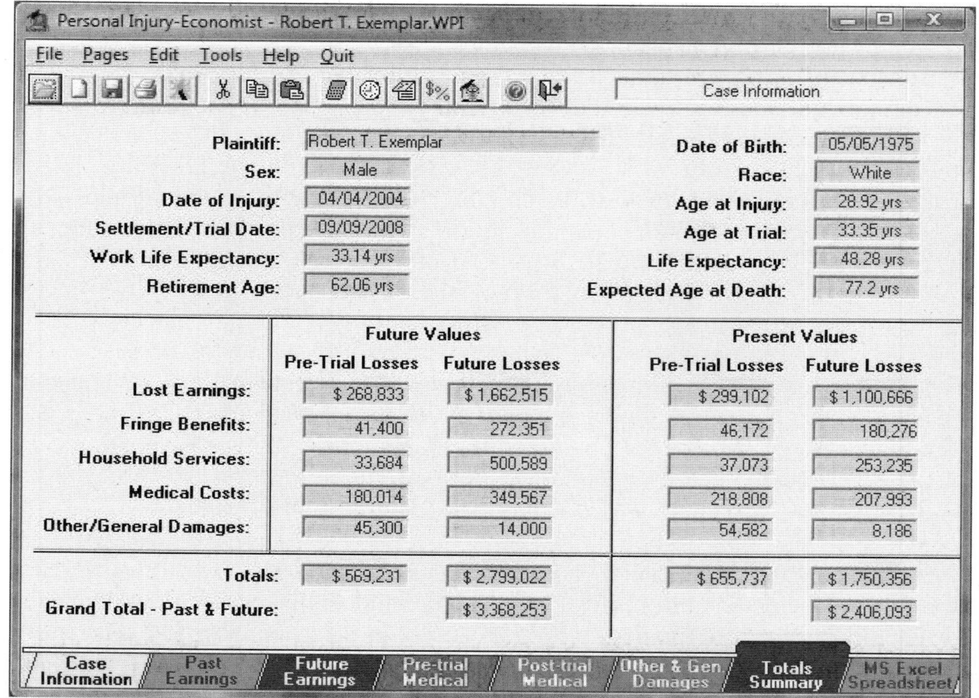

assumptions such as the discount rate and the rate of inflation. Software allows the office to change assumptions quickly and easily in order to assess alternatives.

PROPERTY DAMAGE

The defendant can inflict loss to property through the commission of a number of torts, such as negligence, trespass to chattels, and conversion. The measure of damages depends on the extent of the loss caused by the tort.

Property destroyed: The measure of damages is the **fair market value** of the property at the time of the destruction.

Property damaged but not destroyed: The measure of damages is the difference between the fair market value of the property before the damage was done and its fair market value after the damage was done.

Deprivation of the use of the property: The measure of damages is the fair market value of the use of the property during the time the plaintiff was wrongfully deprived of its use.

fair market value The price agreed upon by a willing buyer and a willing seller, neither being under any compulsion to enter the transaction and both having reasonable knowledge of the relevant facts.

Fair market value is the price agreed upon by a willing buyer and a willing seller, neither being under any compulsion to enter the transaction and both having reasonable knowledge of the relevant facts.[7] The fair market value of the use of the property might be the cost that an unpressured **lessee** would have to pay to rent the property from a willing **lessor**.

There are times when the fair market value of property is not a proper measure of damages. For example, a family portrait may have no exchange value or a dog may be trained to answer only one master. In such cases, other measures of damage might be used, e.g., replacement value, original cost, or value of the time spent producing it.[8]

lessee A person who rents or leases property from another. A tenant.

lessor A person who rents or leases property to another. A landlord.

Some plaintiffs experience considerable emotional distress when their property is destroyed or interfered with in substantial ways. In most cases, however, damages for such distress *cannot* be added to the damages for harm to the property itself even if the emotional attachment to the property (e.g., a pet) is strong. To recover for this distress, other torts would have to be tried such as intentional infliction of emotional distress (see Chapter 9).

MITIGATION-OF-DAMAGES RULE

Under the **mitigation-of-damages rule** (also called the avoidable-consequences doctrine) injured parties must take reasonable steps to alleviate their injury. A wrongdoer will not be liable for any increase or **aggravation** of the injury caused by the injured party's failure to take such steps. All recovery is not barred. The amount of the recovery is reduced to cover those damages the plaintiff brought on him- or herself by failing to use reasonable follow-up care in responding to the injury. The most obvious example is the plaintiff who fails to obtain medical help after being injured by the defendant. The plaintiff has thereby aggravated his or her own injury. The defendant will be liable for the initial injury, but not for the aggravation of that injury if the failure to seek medical assistance was unreasonable under the circumstances (e.g., such assistance was available, the plaintiff knew about it, and it had a good chance of helping the plaintiff).

The same principles apply to property loss. Suppose that the defendant negligently sets fire to a small portion of the plaintiff's barn. The plaintiff cannot sit by and watch the entire farm burn up if some reasonable steps by the plaintiff could have mitigated the loss (e.g., throwing an available bucket of water on the fire or calling the fire department).

mitigation-of-damages rule Injured parties must take reasonable steps to alleviate their injury. A wrongdoer will not be liable for any increase or aggravation of the injury caused by the injured party's failure to take such steps. Also called avoidable-consequences doctrine.

aggravation An increase in the severity of the original injury caused by an additional injury or by the failure to take reasonable steps to prevent the increase.

contributory negligence The failure of plaintiffs to take reasonable precautions for their protection, helping to cause their own injury or other loss.

The mitigation-of-damages rule differs from **contributory negligence**, which is unreasonable conduct by the plaintiff that helped cause the initial injury. Contributory negligence, where it applies, bars *all* recovery of damages by the plaintiff. The mitigation rule reduces the damages. We will cover contributory negligence in Chapter 17.

ASSIGNMENT 16.3

Mary negligently hits a pedestrian. The pedestrian is rushed to the hospital and told that a blood transfusion is necessary. The pedestrian refuses on religious grounds. The pedestrian dies. For what damages will Mary be responsible in the negligence action brought by the pedestrian's estate?

CASE

Keans v. Bottiarelli

35 Conn. App. 239, 645 A.2d 1029 (1994)
Appellate Court of Connecticut

Background: *In this action for dental malpractice, the plaintiff sued her oral surgeon for injuries resulting from a tooth extraction. The trial court found for the plaintiff, awarding her $20,000. Of this amount, $14,965.54 was for pain and suffering, and $5,034.46 was for the hospitalization the plaintiff needed because of the defendant's negligence. The trial court reduced the award by $5,034.46 after finding that the plaintiff was the cause of this hospitalization due to her failure to mitigate her damages by not following instructions after the oral surgery. Both parties appealed the award of damages. The case is now before the Appellate Court of Connecticut.*

Decision on Appeal: *The judgment affirmed. There was a failure to mitigate. The award for pain and suffering was fair.*

OPINION OF COURT

Judge SCHALLER delivered the opinion of the court . . .:

The trial court could reasonably have found the following facts. On July 19, 1990, the plaintiff consulted the defendant, an oral surgeon, to have a tooth extracted. On the initial visit to the defendant, the plaintiff informed the defendant that she suffered from myelofibrosis, a rare blood disorder that inhibits production of red blood cells and platelets, thereby affecting the blood clotting ability of afflicted individuals. The plaintiff's condition requires her to receive frequent blood and platelet transfusions and to self-administer interferon injections. The plaintiff further informed the defendant that her platelet count was 39,000. The defendant performed the extraction without first consulting the plaintiff's hematologist, concluding that the plaintiff "looked good" and would not require a platelet transfusion. The plaintiff remained in the defendant's recovery room until the area around the extraction site stopped bleeding and was sent home with a prescription for penicillin and a pamphlet detailing postoperative instructions. After returning home, the extraction site began to bleed. The plaintiff's son called the defendant, who advised him that the plaintiff should bite down on a tea bag to release tannic acid to facilitate blood clotting. The plaintiff made no further effort to contact the defendant that day, despite worsening of her condition.

The next morning, the plaintiff contacted Richard Hellman, her hematologist, who admitted her to the hospital. The plaintiff, diagnosed with neutropenia, severe thrombocytopenia, severe anemia and myelofibrosis, was hospitalized for three days and was discharged on July 23, 1990, with no permanent injuries. . . .

The plaintiff's expert testified that the conduct of the defendant deviated from prudent and standard dental practice. He testified that because the plaintiff reported a low platelet count, the defendant should have consulted her hematologist prior to attempting the extraction. One of the defendant's experts reported that on the one occasion that he himself performed an extraction on a myelofibrotic patient he consulted with a hematologist. The trial court determined that the plaintiff's expert was more credible than that of the defendant, and that a causal connection existed between the deviation from prudent and standard dental practice and the plaintiff's initial injury. We conclude that the trial court's finding that the plaintiff had established the elements necessary to prove dental malpractice by the defendant was not clearly erroneous.

The trial court applied the doctrine of mitigation of damages and reduced the award by the amount of the plaintiff's hospitalization expense. Our Supreme Court has stated that "[w]e have long adhered to the rule that one who is injured by the negligence of another must use reasonable care to promote recovery and prevent any aggravation or increase of the injuries." (Internal quotation marks omitted.) *Preston v. Keith,* 217 Conn. 12, 15, 584 A.2d 439 (1991). "When there are facts in evidence that indicate that a plaintiff may have failed to promote his recovery and do what a reasonably prudent person would be expected to do under the same circumstances, the court, when requested to do so, is obliged to charge on the duty to mitigate damages." *Jancura v. Szwed,* 176 Conn. 285, 288, 407 A.2d 961 (1978). "[A]lthough the defendant need not specially plead [a duty to mitigate damages], the defendant 'must bring forward evidence that the plaintiff could reasonably have reduced his loss or avoided injurious consequences. . . .' " *Preston v. Keith,* supra, 217 Conn. at 22, 584 A.2d 439. To prevail, the wrongdoer " 'must show that the injured party failed to take reasonable action to lessen the damages; that the damages were in fact enhanced by such failure; and that the damages could have been avoided and can be measured with reasonable certainty.' " Id., quoting 2 M. Minzer, *Damages in Tort Actions* (1989) § 16.11, p. 16–18.

The trial court concluded that the three requirements to establish a failure to mitigate damages set forth in *Preston v. Keith,* supra, 217 Conn. at 22, 584 A.2d 439 were proven. The trial court found that the plaintiff's conduct exacerbated her initial injury. The trial court found that the plaintiff failed to take reasonable action to lessen the damages by neglecting to fill the prescription for penicillin and by not following the defendant's postoperative instructions. The trial court further found that this failure on the part of the plaintiff caused the need for her hospitalization. We conclude that the trial court's reduction of the damage award for this reason was not clearly erroneous. . . .

The defendant . . . contends that the plaintiff's damage award of $14,965.54 for her pain and suffering was excessive. At the outset, we note the "question of damages in personal injury cases . . . is always a difficult one." *Prosser v. Richman,* 133 Conn. 253, 256, 50 A.2d 85 (1946). The "amount of an award is a matter peculiarly within the province of the trier of facts." *Pisel v. Stamford Hospital,* 180 Conn. 314, 342, 430 A.2d 1 (1980); *Angelica v. Fernandes,* 174 Conn. 534, 535, 391 A.2d 167 (1978). Because we find that the amount of the damage award was properly within the bounds of fair and reasonable compensation and is far from "shock[ing to our] sense of justice"; *Herb v. Kerr,* 190 Conn. 136, 139, 459 A.2d 521 (1983); we find the lower court did not abuse its discretion in assessing the damages. . . .

The judgment is affirmed.

ASSIGNMENT 16.4

a. The dentist was negligent but the only damages he was held liable for were pain and suffering. Why?
b. In the next chapter, you will learn that, in some states, if the plaintiff was also negligent in contributing to his or her own injury, the plaintiff recovers nothing no matter how negligent the defendant was. If this rule applied in Connecticut where this case was decided, would the plaintiff have recovered anything?

COLLATERAL SOURCE RULE

When a person is injured or dies, he or she often receives funds or services from a variety of sources other than the defendant:

- the plaintiff's own medical or life insurance
- company insurance
- veteran's benefits
- Social Security
- wage continuation plans
- free medical care provided by a relative

Each of these is a **collateral source**—a source to which the defendant did not contribute. When the time comes to calculate the total amount in damages owed by the defendant to the plaintiff, should this amount be reduced by what the plaintiff has received through collateral sources? Should there be an **offset**? All states do not

collateral source Someone other than (and independent of) the tortfeasor who provides direct or indirect financial assistance to the victim of the tort.

offset A deduction; that which compensates for or counters something else.

answer this question in the same way. Here are some of the approaches taken by different states:

- The damages are not reduced by collateral sources in any case even though the plaintiff, in effect, recovers twice for part or all of his or her injury. Furthermore, the defendant is not allowed to tell the jury about the collateral sources. The defendant is not given the benefit of the plaintiff's good luck or resourcefulness in obtaining benefits from collateral sources.
- The damages are not reduced by collateral sources in any case, but the defendant is allowed to tell the jury about the collateral sources in the hope that it might reduce the verdict because of them. (A reduction that is allowed but not required is called a **permissive offset**.)
- The damages are reduced by collateral sources, but only in certain kinds of cases such as medical malpractice. (A required reduction is called a **mandatory offset**.)
- The damages are reduced by collateral sources in all cases.
- The damages are reduced by some collateral sources. For example, the state may allow reduction of social security benefits, but not for life insurance proceeds or other death benefits.

When a state *refuses* to offset damages because of what is provided by collateral sources, the refusal is called the **collateral source rule**.

permissive offset An allowed (but not required) deduction that compensates for or counters something else.

mandatory offset A required deduction that compensates for or counters something else.

collateral source rule The amount of damages caused by the tortfeasor shall not be reduced by any injury-related funds received by the plaintiff from sources independent of the tortfeasor such as a health insurance policy of the plaintiff.

JOINT TORTFEASORS

Joint tortfeasors are persons who contribute to the commission of a single tort. They fall into two categories:

- persons acting in concert to produce a wrong
- persons not acting in concert whose wrongs produce a single indivisible result

joint tortfeasors Two or more persons who contribute to the commission of a single tort.

It should be noted, however, that some states disagree that the second category of persons should be classified as joint tortfeasors. According to this view, joint tortfeasors should be limited to defendants who act by mutual agreement (i.e., in concert) and should not extend to independent defendants who happen to act at the same time (i.e., **concurrently**) to produce a wrong.

The significance of being a joint tortfeasor is that each joint tortfeasor has **joint and several liability** for the entire harm suffered by the plaintiff. This means that the plaintiff can sue any individual joint tortfeasor for the entire harm or can join them all to recover for the entire harm. It does not mean that the plaintiff receives a multiple recovery. The plaintiff can receive only one **satisfaction**. Yet the plaintiff chooses whether to go after all of them or one of them. If the plaintiff sues one, but is unable to collect the full judgment, the plaintiff can sue the remaining tortfeasors until the full amount of the damages is recovered. Suppose only one joint tortfeasor pays the entire judgment. Can this person then collect anything from the other joint tortfeasors as their "share"? We will consider this separate topic later when we discuss *contribution*. It is of no concern to the plaintiff that the joint tortfeasors did not pay the judgment equally. They are left to fight this out among themselves. The plaintiff's only interest is in recovering full damages.

concurrent 1. Acting or occurring at the same time. 2. Involving or concerning the same matters.

joint and several liability Legally responsible together and individually. Each wrongdoer is individually responsible for the *entire* judgment; the plaintiff can choose to collect from one wrongdoer or from all of them until the judgment is satisfied.

satisfaction The fulfillment of an obligation, e.g., the payment of a debt based on an order to pay damages.

Persons Acting in Concert

Persons act in **concert** when they undertake an activity by mutual agreement. They are joint tortfeasors if, while acting in concert, they commit negligence or another wrong. They thereby become jointly and severally liable. If they had a business or profit purpose, their activity is often called a **joint venture**.

concert An activity undertaken by mutual agreement.

joint venture A mutually undertaken business or profit-seeking activity in which each person participates or has an equal right of participation or control.

EXAMPLES

- Mary and Jane buy a truck to make deliveries together. One day, they are late in making a delivery. Mary, the driver, starts speeding. Jane urges her to go even faster. The truck negligently hits the plaintiff. Both Mary and Jane are joint tortfeasors.
- Al and Donald agree to steal the plaintiff's goods. Al takes the goods while Donald acts as lookout. Both are joint tortfeasors.

There must be either an express agreement or a tacit understanding that each will participate in the activity that produces the wrong. No such agreement or understanding would exist, for example, with a hitchhiker in the truck of Mary and Jane at the time of the accident in the first case. The hitchhiker would not be a joint tortfeasor along with Mary and Jane. To be a joint tortfeasor, the person must cooperate in the wrong, encourage it, or otherwise be an active participant. Someone who approves or **ratifies** the wrong after it is done for his or her benefit can also be a joint tortfeasor.

ratifies 1. Adopts or confirms a prior act or transaction, making one bound by it. Formally approves.

Persons Not Acting in Concert

Assume that two individuals, acting independently of each other, cause an accident.

EXAMPLE

Two cars carelessly collide on the highway. They both run into and kill a pedestrian.

The two drivers acted concurrently, but they were not acting in concert. There was no joint venture between them. Yet, each was a substantial factor in producing a harm (the death of the pedestrian) that is **indivisible**. (A result that cannot be practically divided is considered indivisible.) In our example, we cannot separate the harm by determining which driver caused which part of the death. When two persons cause an indivisible harm, they are jointly and severally liable for the harm even though they were not acting in concert. They are treated the same as if they acted in concert.

indivisible Not separable into parts; pertaining to that which cannot be divided.

If the harm is divisible, there is no joint tortfeasorship and no joint and several liability. Suppose that two companies independently pollute a stream with different chemicals, which can be separately identified. In such a case, each company will be liable only for that portion of the damage it caused. Suppose, however, that it is difficult to **apportion** the damages, because the companies used the same chemicals or because the different chemicals cannot be separately identified. The plaintiff and the defendants are in difficult positions. The plaintiff must do more than show that "somebody caused me harm." How is the plaintiff to meet his or her burden of proving what the individual defendants caused? From the defendants' perspective, it is unfair to saddle any one of them with the harm caused by the other defendants. A few courts shift the burden to the defendants and require them to establish who caused what. Most courts do not go this far; yet, they will assist the plaintiff in such cases by accepting a rough approximation of the portion of the harm caused by each defendant.

apportion To divide into portions, e.g., to allocate or assign responsibility among parties.

ASSIGNMENT 16.5

Ten families live in an apartment complex. They are very unhappy with the maintenance service provided by the landlord. Nine of the families begin throwing their garbage in a pile in one of the alleys next to the main building. The garbage draws many rats, which infest the apartment of the tenth family. This family sues the other nine families for negligence when it is forced to move out because of the rats. Are the nine families jointly and severally liable?

RELEASE

Satisfaction is the fulfillment of an obligation, such as the payment of a debt, based on an order to pay damages. If the plaintiff receives satisfaction from one joint tortfeasor, the others can no longer be sued by the plaintiff. As indicated earlier, the plaintiff is entitled to only one satisfaction.

release The giving up or relinquishing of a right, claim, interest, or privilege.

gratuitous Pertaining to what is performed or given without a duty or obligation to do so; free.

consideration Something of value that is exchanged between parties.

Satisfaction is different from **release**. The latter is the giving up of a claim. This can be done for "free" (i.e., it is **gratuitous**) or it can be done for **consideration**.

EXAMPLE

While Tim and Fred are fishing in a lake, they negligently destroy Diane's boat, which was moored at the dock. Because they were engaged in a joint enterprise, they are jointly and severally liable to her for the damage. Diane agrees, however, to give up (i.e., release) all her claims against Tim and Fred if they stop fishing in the lake where the accident occurred. They agree. If they abide by their agreement, Diane cannot later change her mind and sue them for the damage to her boat. In this example, there was consideration for the release. Something of value was given for the release—the promise to stop fishing.

What happens if the plaintiff releases only one of the joint tortfeasors? Are the other joint tortfeasors likewise released? Yes. In most states, the release of one joint tortfeasor automatically releases the others. Statutes in some states change this result by providing that the release of one does not automatically discharge the others. The plaintiff under these statutes can still go after the other joint tortfeasors.

covenant not to sue An agreement not to bring suit against someone, e.g., an agreement not to sue one of the joint tortfeasors.

In states where the release of one discharges all the joint tortfeasors, there is a device designed to get around this result. The device works as follows: In the negotiation with one joint tortfeasor, the plaintiff does not provide a release. Rather, he or she makes a promise or **covenant not to sue** that joint tortfeasor. The covenant, unlike the release, does not act as a bar to go after the other joint tortfeasors.

CONTRIBUTION

contribution The right of one tortfeasor who has paid a judgment to be proportionately reimbursed by other tortfeasors who have not paid their share of the damages caused by all the tortfeasors.

Suppose that the plaintiff obtains satisfaction of the entire amount of damages from one of the joint tortfeasors. Can that tortfeasor now force the other joint tortfeasors to contribute their share of the amount paid? Can he or she obtain **contribution**? Contribution is the right of one tortfeasor who has paid a judgment to be proportionately reimbursed by other tortfeasors who have not paid their share of the damages caused by all the tortfeasors. States do not all agree on the availability of contribution among joint tortfeasors:

- Some states deny contribution among joint tortfeasors.
- Some states allow contribution only among joint tortfeasors against whom the plaintiff has secured a judgment. Those not sued would not be subject to contribution claims by joint tortfeasors who were sued.
- Some states allow contribution only among joint tortfeasors who were negligent. Intentional joint tortfeasors cannot obtain contribution.

pro rata Proportionately; according to a specified rate or factor.

When contribution is allowed, the allocation is usually **pro rata**, or proportionate to the number of joint tortfeasors: two would be responsible for 50 percent each, three for $33^1/_3$ each, etc. A few states, however, make the allocation according to the relative fault of the joint tortfeasors. Again, contribution is not a concern of the plaintiff who has received satisfaction. Contribution is a battle among the tortfeasors.

INDEMNITY

Indemnity is a device whereby one party who has paid the plaintiff can force another party to reimburse him or her for the full amount paid. Unlike contribution, which usually calls for a proportionate sharing of the loss, indemnity shifts the entire loss from the defendant (who has paid the judgment) onto someone else. Indemnity can arise by contract, where one person agrees to indemnify the other for any loss that results if the latter is sued. Indemnity can also arise by **operation of law** independent of any agreement between the parties.

EXAMPLES

- The ABC Company buys the tanning plant of the XYZ Company. As part of the agreement, XYZ agrees to indemnify ABC for any tort claims filed against ABC that are based on facts that arose before the sale of the plant.
- An employer who has **vicarious liability** for the tort committed by his or her employee (see Chapter 14) can seek indemnity from the employee. Seeking indemnity, of course, would be impractical if the employee is **judgment proof**.
- A supermarket found liable for **strict liability in tort** for a defective product it sold (see Chapter 19) can seek indemnity from the manufacturer that made the product.
- Someone engaged in **passive negligence** may be able to obtain indemnity from the person whose **active negligence** (or intentional tort) created the hazard.

The person seeking indemnity is liable for the tort. This person, however, is allowed to make someone else reimburse him or her for the judgment he or she has paid when it appears equitable to do so. The relationship between the party who has paid and the party against whom indemnity is sought must be such that in fairness we can say that the latter should pay.

indemnity 1. The duty of one person to pay for another's loss, damage, or liability. 2. A right to receive compensation to make one person whole from a loss that has already been sustained but which in justice ought to be sustained by the person from whom indemnity is sought.

operation of law A means by which legal consequences are imposed by law, regardless of the intent of the parties involved.

vicarious liability Liability imposed on a person because of the conduct of another, based solely on the status of the relationship between the two. The person liable is not the person whose conduct led to the liability.

judgment proof Having few or no assets from which a money judgment can be satisfied. Having shallow pockets.

strict liability in tort Liability for physical harm caused by a defective product that is unreasonably dangerous.

passive negligence The unreasonable failure to do something, e.g., carelessly allowing defects (created by others) to exist.

active negligence Unreasonable affirmative conduct, e.g., carelessly creating a defect.

SETTLEMENT

A great deal can be learned about tort damages by examining demand packages such as those found in a settlement brochure and a settlement précis. As indicated earlier, they are written by one party and sent to the other (or to the latter's insurance company) in an effort to encourage a settlement. They cover the merits of the causes of action and provide details on the damages that are alleged. We will study these documents in Chapter 29.

SEPTEMBER 11TH VICTIM COMPENSATION FUND

After the 9/11 attack against the World Trade Center towers and the Pentagon killed 2,280 people, Congress created the *September 11th Victim Compensation Fund* to compensate injured persons and relatives of those who were killed. To receive compensation from the fund, participants had to agree to waive their right to seek compensation for their injuries through tort litigation against entities involved in the attack, such as the airlines. The waiver, however, "does not apply to a civil action to recover collateral source obligations or to a civil action against any person who is a knowing participant in any conspiracy to hijack any aircraft or commit any terrorist act."[9] For those who died, the administrator of the Fund estimated the earnings they would have had if they had lived a full life. Over 98 percent of eligible families participated in the payout of over $7 billion. The average award received by relatives of those who died was approximately $2 million.

TAXATION OF DAMAGES

Compensatory damages for physical injuries are not subject to federal taxes. For example, a plaintiff does not have to pay federal taxes on an award of $100,000 in damages for pain and suffering and medical bills for a leg injury suffered in an accident due to the defendant's negligence. The same would be true if this amount is received in a settlement. Damages for nonphysical injuries and for punitive damages, however, *are* taxable. If a physically injured plaintiff receives damages of $250,000, of which $150,000 are punitive damages and $100,000 are compensatory damages for the physical injury, taxes are owed on $150,000 only. Damages for nonphysical injuries (e.g., emotional harm not connected with a physical injury) are taxable.

CHECK THE CITE

Sarah Overstreet was having supper at Shoney's Restaurant when two dinner plates fell from the tray of a waitress. A shard from one of the broken plates struck Ms. Overstreet in her left eye, blinding her in that eye. What damages issues were before the court in her action against Shoney's and how were they resolved? Read the case of *Overstreet v. Shoney's, Inc.*, 4 S.W.3d 694 (Tenn. Ct. App. 1999). To read the opinion online: (1) Go to the site of the Court of Appeals of Tennessee (www.tsc.state.tn.us/OPINIONS/TCA/Oplsttca.htm). Click the link for the opinions of 1999, Second Quarter. Locate the case in the list (www.tsc.state.tn.us/opinions/tca/PDF/992/overstre.pdf). (2) Run a citation search ("4 S.W.3d 694") or a party search (Overstreet Shoney) in the Legal Opinions and Journals database of Google Scholar (scholar.google.com).

PROJECT

Read the quote below on tort damages from plaintiff's attorney Jan Schlichtmann, played by John Travolta in the movie *A Civil Action*. In Google, Bing, or another general search engine, run the following search: "tort damages." Write a short essay in which you quote material on the Internet that supports the view of tort damages expressed in the quote by Schlichtmann. You can consult as many websites as you wish, but you must quote from at least three separate sites. Here is the Schlichtmann quote: "It's like this. A dead plaintiff is rarely worth more than a living severely maimed plaintiff. However, if it's a long, slow, agonizing death as opposed to a quick drowning or car wreck, the value can rise considerably. A dead adult in his twenties is generally worth less than one who is middle aged. A dead woman less than a dead man. A single adult less than one who's married. Black less than white. Poor less than rich. The perfect victim is a white male professional, forty years old, at the height of his earning power, struck down at his prime. And the most imperfect, well, in the calculus of personal injury law, a dead child is worth the least of all." *A Civil Action* (1998) (www.imdb.com/title/tt0120633/quotes)(www.mooviees.com/2026/quotes).

ETHICS IN A TORTS PRACTICE

You are a paralegal working in the law office of Gallagher & Gallagher, a personal injury law firm. You sometimes answer the phone when prospective clients call. Often they ask about fees. You have been instructed to tell them that there is no cost to the client unless the office wins the case through court decision or settlement. One day a caller asks what the cost would be if the client won $100,000. You answer, "One-third." What ethical problems, if any, might exist?

SUMMARY

Damages are monetary payments awarded for a legally recognized wrong. Three main categories exist: compensatory, nominal, and punitive. Compensatory damages are monetary payments to restore an injured party to his or her position prior to the injury or other wrong. The damages cover two kinds of losses: economic losses (which can be objectively verified) and non-economic losses (for which no objective dollar amount can be identified). General damages are compensatory damages that usually result from the kind of harm caused by the conduct of the defendant. Special damages are compensatory damages that consist of economic or pecuniary losses (e.g., medical expenses and lost wages) that must be alleged and proven. They are not presumed to exist. Nominal damages consist of a small monetary payment (a trifling sum) when there has been a technical violation of a right but no significant loss or injury. Punitive damages are damages that are added to actual or compensatory damages in order to punish malicious, outrageous, or reckless conduct and to deter similar conduct in the future.

Future economic losses such as lost wages and medical expenses must be reduced to present value, which is the amount of money an individual would have to be given now in order to generate a certain amount of money within a designated period of time through prudent investment, usually at compound interest.

Damages for pain and suffering are sometimes capped in certain kinds of cases. Hedonic damages are compensatory damages that cover the victim's loss of pleasure or enjoyment in life. Insurance claims adjusters sometimes use a rough formula in calculating the damages they may be willing to settle for. Software programs exist to help a law office calculate the variables involved in an assessment of damages. The measure of damages to property is often the fair market value of the property before and after the wrong. Under the mitigation-of-damages rule, a defendant will not be liable for the additional or aggravated damages that the victim's reasonable steps could have avoided. Under the collateral source rule, the amount of damages caused by the tortfeasor shall not be reduced by any injury-related funds received by the plaintiff from sources independent of the tortfeasor, such as a health insurance policy of the plaintiff. Some states, however, do allow reductions for amounts received from collateral sources.

Joint tortfeasors are two or more persons who contribute to the commission of a single tort. They are jointly and severally liable for the harm they wrongfully cause. Each wrongdoer is individually responsible for the entire judgment; the plaintiff can choose to collect from one wrongdoer or from all of them until the judgment is satisfied. Joint tortfeasors may have acted in concert or independently to produce an indivisible result. The relinquishment (release) of a claim against one joint tortfeasor usually acts to discharge the others. States differ on whether and when joint tortfeasors can seek contribution and thereby allocate the damages among themselves. Indemnity is the device whereby one party who has paid the plaintiff can force another party to reimburse him or her for the full amount paid.

Compensatory damages for physical injuries are not subject to federal taxes. Damages for nonphysical injuries and punitive damages are taxable.

KEY TERMS

damages *284*
compensatory damages *284*
pain and suffering *284*
general damages *284*
special damages *285*
nominal damages *285*
pro bono *285*
punitive damages *285*
ordinary negligence *285*
interrogatories *286*
lump-sum payment *286*
structured settlement *286*
annuity *286*
present value *286*
compound interest *286*

simple interest *286*
windfall *287*
discount rate *287*
per diem argument *293*
cap *293*
hedonic damages *293*
settlement brochure *294*
fair market value *295*
lessee *295*
lessor *295*
mitigation-of-damages rule *295*
aggravation *295*
contributory negligence *296*
collateral source *297*
offset *297*
permissive offset *298*
mandatory offset *298*
collateral source rule *298*
joint tortfeasors *298*
concurrent *298*
joint and several liability *298*
satisfaction *298*
concert *298*
joint venture *298*
ratifies *299*
indivisible *299*
apportion *299*
release *300*
gratuitous *300*
consideration *300*
covenant not to sue *300*
contribution *300*
pro rata *300*
indemnity *301*
operation of law *301*
vicarious liability *301*
judgment proof *301*
strict liability in tort *301*
passive negligence *301*
active negligence *301*

REVIEW QUESTIONS

1. What are damages?
2. What are the three main categories of damages?
3. What are compensatory damages?
4. Distinguish between economic and non-economic compensatory damages.
5. Give examples of pain and suffering.
6. How do general damages differ from special damages?
7. What are nominal damages, and when are they awarded?
8. What are punitive damages, and when are they awarded?
9. Why must future economic damages be reduced to present value?
10. What is a structured settlement?
11. Distinguish between simple and compound interest.
12. What is a discount rate?
13. How are damages for pain and suffering calculated?
14. What are hedonic damages, and why do some courts refuse to award them?
15. How are damages for property losses calculated?
16. What is the mitigation-of-damages rule?
17. What is the collateral source rule?
18. What are joint tortfeasors?
19. Define joint and several liability.
20. Distinguish satisfaction and release.
21. When can defendants who are joint tortfeasors obtain contribution?
22. Under what circumstances will indemnity be granted?
23. What is a settlement brochure? A settlement précis?
24. What right had to be waived under the law that created the September 11th Victim Compensation Fund?
25. What damages are taxable?

HELPFUL WEBSITES

- **Damages and Jury Verdicts**
  www.juryverdicts.com
  www.jvra.com
  morelaw.com
  lawyersusaonline.com (click "Verdicts & Settlements")
- **Punitive Damages**
  www.tobacco.neu.edu
  (type "punitive" as a search term)
  www.atra.org/show/7343
  en.wikipedia.org/wiki/Punitive_damages
- **Pain and Suffering**
  www.seattlepi.com/local/122105_colossus15xx.html
  en.wikipedia.org/wiki/Pain_and_suffering
- **Collateral Source Rule**
  biotech.law.lsu.edu/Books/lbb/x93.htm
  en.wikipedia.org/wiki/Collateral_source_rule
- **September 11th Victim Compensation Fund**
  www.justice.gov/archive/victimcompensation
  www.kentlaw.edu/honorsscholars/2002students/Levin.html
- **Damages in General**
  topics.law.cornell.edu/wex/Damages
  www.llrx.com
  (type "damages" as a search term)
  en.wikipedia.org/wiki/Damages
- In Google, Bing, or another search engine, run the following search: elements negligence damages tort.

ENDNOTES

1. Equity was once a court system that was separate from the common-law court system. The equity courts administered equitable remedies that were based on a somewhat flexible sense of fairness as opposed to the more rigid legal remedies available in the common-law courts. Today the two court systems have merged in most states so that equitable remedies and legal remedies are usually available in the same court.
2. *State Farm Mut. Auto. Ins. Co. v. Campbell*, 538 U.S. 408, 417, 123 S. Ct. 1513, 1520 (2003).
3. *Goff v. Elmo Greer & Sons Const. Co., Inc.*, 297 S.W.3d 175, 2009 WL 3616608 (Tenn. 2009).
4. Uniform Medical Malpractice Interrogatories, 17B Arizona Revised Statutes.
5. Adapted from David W. Robertson et al., *Torts* 349–350 (2d ed. 1998); 2 *California Jury Instructions—Civil* §§ 14.00–14.13 (7th ed. 1986) (Book of Approved Jury Instructions (BAJI) of the Committee on Standard Jury Instructions, Civil, of the Superior Court of Los Angeles County, California); Robert E. Keeton et al., *Tort and Accident Law* 449–450 (3d ed. 1998); and *Illinois Pattern Jury Instructions, Civil* §§ 30.01–30.07, 34.01, 34.02 (2d ed. 1971).
6. Joseph Matthews, *Taking the Mystery Out of Personal Injury Claims*, Nolo News 9 (Fall 1994).
7. Charles McCormick, *Handbook on the Law of Damages* 165 (1975).
8. *Restatement (Second) of Torts* § 911, comment e (1979).
9. Department of Justice, September 11th Victim Compensation Fund, www.justice.gov/archive/victimcompensation.

Student StudyWARE™ CD-ROM
For additional materials, please go to the student CD in this book.

CHAPTER

17

NEGLIGENCE: DEFENSES

CHAPTER OUTLINE

- Introduction
- Contributory Negligence
- Last Clear Chance
- Comparative Negligence
- Assumption of the Risk

CHAPTER OBJECTIVES

After completing this chapter, you should be able to:

- Understand the relationships among comparative negligence and contributory negligence, last clear chance, and assumption of the risk.
- State the different categories of the last clear chance doctrine.
- Distinguish between pure and modified comparative negligence.
- Distinguish between express and implied assumption of the risk.
- Distinguish between primary and secondary assumption of the risk.
- Explain when courts will refuse to enforce exculpatory clauses and releases.

INTRODUCTION

defense The response of a party to a claim of another party, setting forth reason(s) the claim should be denied. (See glossary for an additional definition.)

A **defense** is the response of a party to a claim of another party, setting forth the reason(s) the claim should be denied. In this chapter we consider the traditional defenses of contributory negligence, assumption of the risk, and the newest arrival, comparative negligence. Elsewhere in the book we examine other defenses to negligence such as consent, self-defense, and privileges and immunities (covered in Chapter 27).

As we will see, the defenses of contributory negligence and assumption of the risk are very harsh on the plaintiff. They nullify the effect of the defendant's negligence. The traditional rule is that if either of these defenses apply, the plaintiff recovers nothing. To avoid the seeming unfairness of this result, doctrines such as last clear chance and, in particular, comparative negligence have been created. In many states, comparative negligence has merged into and led to the partial or total abolishment of contributory negligence and assumption of the risk. We still need to cover contributory negligence and assumption of the risk, however, since not every state has adopted comparative negligence, and even in states that have, contributory negligence and assumption of the risk may still apply if the provisions of comparative negligence have not been met.

Overview

Here is an overview of the principles that apply before and after a state adopts comparative negligence. We will be examining these principles throughout the remainder of the chapter.

comparative negligence A comparison of the negligence of the defendant and the plaintiff in causing the plaintiff's injury (or other loss) in order to reduce the plaintiff's damages in proportion to the plaintiff's negligence in causing his or her own injury (or other loss).

contributory negligence The failure of plaintiffs to take reasonable precautions for their safety, helping to cause their own injury or other loss.

last clear chance Plaintiffs who have been contributorily negligent in placing themselves in peril can still recover if a negligent defendant had the last opportunity (clear chance) to avoid the accident and failed to exercise reasonable care to do so.

assumption of the risk The knowing and voluntary acceptance of the risk of being harmed by someone's negligence.

Comparative negligence: The damages between the plaintiff and the defendant are allocated according to their relative fault. There is a formula that must be met before comparative negligence can apply. When the formula has been met, the damages are allocated.

Contributory negligence: *Before comparative negligence was adopted:* If the plaintiff's unreasonable conduct contributed to his or her own injury, the defendant paid no damages. Contributory negligence was a complete defense in spite of the defendant's negligence. *If comparative negligence applies:* Contributory negligence is not a complete bar to the plaintiff's recovery. The damages are allocated between the plaintiff and the defendant according to their relative fault.

Last clear chance: *Before comparative negligence was adopted:* The last clear chance doctrine offsets the impact of contributory negligence. Contributory negligence was not a bar to the plaintiff's recovery if the defendant had the last clear chance to avoid the plaintiff's injury but failed to use this chance. *If comparative negligence applies:* There is no longer a need for the last clear chance doctrine since contributory negligence is no longer a complete bar to the plaintiff's recovery. Some states, however, kept the last clear chance doctrine after they adopted comparative negligence.

Assumption of the risk: This defense can bar recovery if the plaintiff knowingly and voluntarily accepted the danger or risk of being injured by the negligence of the defendant. The impact of contributory negligence on the assumption-of-the-risk defense is complicated. When we examine this defense later in the chapter, we will need to distinguish two kinds of assumption:

- express assumption of the risk
- implied assumption of the risk

Furthermore, we will also need to examine two kinds of implied assumption of the risk:

- primary assumption of the risk
- secondary assumption of the risk

Not all assumptions of the risk are enforceable. Consumers are often asked to accept clauses in which they assume the risk of injury. (They are called *exculpatory clauses.*) As we will see, however, for certain categories of individuals (e.g., users of public services), enforcing the clauses may be against public policy.

We turn now to a closer examination of these principles.

CONTRIBUTORY NEGLIGENCE

We begin our study of the defense of contributory negligence by examining its impact before it was changed or modified. The defense existed when the plaintiff's unreasonable conduct contributed to his or her own injury. Once established, the effect of this defense was drastic. It required the plaintiff to bear the full loss of his or her injury. The negligent defendant walked away without paying anything because the plaintiff was also negligent.

There were, however, limitations on the defense. The contributory negligence of the plaintiff prevented liability only when the defendant committed **ordinary negligence**, which is conduct that is unreasonable but not gross or reckless. If the misdeed of the defendant went beyond ordinary negligence, the plaintiff's contributory negligence was not a defense. Conduct is **reckless** when a person consciously takes a risk in failing to exercise due care but without intending the consequences. The overlapping concept of **gross negligence** is the failure to use even a small amount of care to avoid foreseeable harm. Contributory negligence was a defense to the defendant's ordinary negligence, but not to the defendant's recklessness or gross negligence. Also, contributory negligence was never a defense to any of the intentional torts the defendant might commit.

In most states, contributory negligence had to be pleaded by the defendant, who then had to prove the defense by a **preponderance of the evidence**. It is an **affirmative defense**. In a few states, however, the *plaintiff* had the burden of pleading and proving that the injury was not caused by his or her own negligence.

ordinary negligence Conduct that is unreasonable but not gross or reckless.

reckless Consciously taking a risk in failing to exercise due care but without intending the consequences; wantonly disregarding a risk but neither desiring the consequences of the risk nor having substantially certain knowledge of the consequences.

gross negligence The failure to use even a small amount of care to avoid foreseeable harm.

preponderance of the evidence The standard of proof that is met when the evidence establishes that it is more likely than not that the facts are as alleged.

affirmative defense A defense raising new facts that will defeat the plaintiff's claim even if the plaintiff's fact allegations are proven.

There are two major elements of contributory negligence:

- plaintiff's negligence (unreasonableness)
- causation

Plaintiff's Negligence (Unreasonableness)

EXAMPLE

Ben is driving forty mph in a forty mph zone in rainy weather at night. Fred runs through a red light and hits Ben's car. Ben sues Fred for negligence. In Fred's answer, he raises the defense of contributory negligence. (Assume that the parties are in a state that still allows this defense.)

In Chapter 14, we considered the standard that would apply to a defendant such as Fred who is sued for negligence: a defendant will be liable for acting unreasonably under the circumstances. This same test applies to determine whether a *plaintiff* has been contributorily negligent.

Plaintiffs must not take unreasonable risks of injuring themselves. There is a formula or equation that is used to determine whether someone has acted unreasonably. See Exhibit 17–1. This is the same equation used to determine whether the defendant was negligent or unreasonable. See Exhibit 14–4 in Chapter 14. The only difference between Exhibit 14–4 and Exhibit 17–1 is that in 17–1 our focus is on what a reasonable plaintiff would have done to prevent the injury to him- or herself,

Exhibit 17–1
Breach-of-duty equation.

Foreseeability of the danger of an accident occurring ——— Foreseeability of the kind of injury or damage that will result if an accident occurs	balanced against	The burden or inconvenience on the plaintiff of taking precautions to avoid the accident ——— The importance or social value of what the plaintiff was doing before the accident

whereas in 14–4 the focus is on what a reasonable defendant would have done to prevent the injury to the plaintiff.

When you are charged with contributory negligence, the allegation is that you acted unreasonably for your own safety. To determine whether this was so, we apply the equation by asking a series of questions. How foreseeable was it to you that your conduct would contribute to an accident? How foreseeable should it have been to you? What kind of injury was foreseeable to you? What kind of injury should have been foreseeable to you? What were you trying to do before the accident? How important or socially beneficial was it? What kind of burden or inconvenience would you have had to endure in order to take added precautions to avoid injuring yourself? These are the questions that a reasonable person would ask.

If the danger of an accident causing serious injury to yourself outweighs whatever burden or inconvenience you would have had to go through to avoid this injury, then you were unreasonable, and hence negligent, in failing to take those preventive steps. The equation also considers the importance or social value of what you were trying to do at the time. A reasonable person is more likely to take risks of injuring him- or herself when engaged in socially useful tasks than when engaged in minor or frivolous activities. "For instance, the plaintiff is not necessarily guilty of contributory negligence when she subjects herself to risks in the course of rescuing another person, because the value of saving another makes the risks reasonable."[1]

In the example involving Ben and Fred, was Ben contributorily negligent? He was driving forty mph in a forty mph zone in rainy weather at night. All of the circumstances of the accident would have to be considered in applying the equation. To determine the foreseeability of an accident, for example, we must know the condition of the road, the amount of traffic, visibility, etc. We have to *particularize* the event. (See Exhibit 3–6 in Chapter 3.) It may be that Ben's speed was not unreasonable under the circumstances. What was the burden or inconvenience on Ben of driving slower and hence taking less risk of injuring himself? All he had to do was not press down so hard on the accelerator. A minimal burden. What was the inconvenience of doing this? Arriving a few seconds or minutes later? Whether this is much of an inconvenience may depend on where he was going and whether the extra time was needed for an important or socially useful purpose.

You will recall that special allowances are made for a defendant who has a physical defect or who is a child (see Chapter 14). The same allowances are made for a plaintiff who is alleged to be contributorily negligent. The test of reasonableness is what a reasonable person with the plaintiff's physical defects would have done under the circumstances, or what a reasonable person as young as the plaintiff would have done under the circumstances. Mental deficiencies of the party, however, are not taken into consideration. The standard of reasonableness is a mentally healthy person. (As we saw in Chapter 14, however, special allowances are made for children engaged in a nonadult activities.) Finally, if the plaintiff had any special knowledge or skills that would have helped him or her to avoid the accident, the test of reasonableness is what a reasonable person with that knowledge or skill would have done under the circumstances.

In assessing the contributory negligence of a plaintiff, it is important to identify the particular risks that he or she undertook in order to determine whether these risks were in fact the risks that contributed to his or her injury. The general rule is that plaintiffs are contributorily negligent only if the risks they unreasonably created to their own safety are the *same* risks that eventually led to the injury.

EXAMPLE

Tomas goes on Jim's land knowing that there are many dangerous animals on the land. While walking, Tomas falls into a concealed hole and breaks his leg. Tomas sues Jim for negligence. Jim raises the defense of contributory negligence.

Tomas was not contributorily negligent. Tomas may have created an unreasonable risk of injury to himself when he went on the land knowing dangerous animals were present, but this is not the particular risk that produced the broken leg—Tomas was not attacked by an animal. Nor is it significant that Tomas may have been a trespasser on Jim's land. Torts can be committed against trespassers (see Chapter 23).

Suppose that the plaintiff's negligence consists of a violation of a statute, ordinance, or regulation. A court will treat a violation by the plaintiff the same way that it will treat a violation by the defendant. The same analytical process is used whether we are assessing the negligence of the defendant (see Exhibit 14–7 in Chapter 14) or the contributory negligence of the plaintiff.

ASSIGNMENT 17.1

In the following situation, will the defendant be successful in raising the defense of contributory negligence?

A trucking company uses a public alley to load and unload its trucks. The manager warns a pedestrian to keep out because of the danger. The pedestrian ignores the warning and walks through. Two of the trucks collide. The collision causes a tremor in the alley. The tremor causes a large shovel to fall off a truck and hit the pedestrian. This truck was parked and was not part of the collision. The pedestrian sues the trucking company for negligence. The company asserts contributory negligence.

Causation

Once it is determined that the plaintiff was negligent (unreasonable), the next issue is whether the plaintiff was an **actual cause** of his or her own injury, along with the defendant. Recall that actual cause covers the question of when someone was the cause in fact of an injury or other loss. Two tests can be used to determine actual cause: the but-for test and the substantial-factor test. For contributory negligence, we use the substantial-factor test: did the plaintiff's acts or omissions have a significant or important role in bringing about his or her own injury? (For more on causation, see Chapter 15.)

actual cause Causation established either by the but-for test or by the substantial-factor test. But-for test: can it be said that an event (e.g., the injury) would not have occurred without the act or omission of the party? Substantial-factor test: can it be said that the party's acts or omissions had a significant or important role in bringing about the event?

If the plaintiff acted unreasonably regarding his or her own safety, and this unreasonableness was a substantial factor in producing that injury, contributory negligence is established. It does not matter that the plaintiff was only slightly unreasonable when compared to the unreasonableness of the defendant, unless, as indicated, the defendant's unreasonableness could be categorized as reckless or gross.

Imputed Contributory Negligence

Recall the discussion in Chapter 14 on **imputed negligence**, by which the negligence of one person is attributed or transferred (imputed) to another solely because of the relationship between the parties. For example, an otherwise innocent

imputed negligence Negligence liability attributed to or imposed on someone who did not act unreasonably but is liable solely because of his or her relationship with the person who did act unreasonably.

employer is liable for the negligence of an employee committed within the scope of employment. The employee's negligence is imputed to the employer. **Imputed contributory negligence** can also exist.

imputed contributory negligence The defense of contributory negligence is attributed or imposed on someone who did not act unreasonably him- or herself but who is subject to this defense solely because of his or her relationship with the person who was unreasonable.

EXAMPLE

Ed is an employee of Greg. While on a delivery for Greg, Ed and Diane collide on the freeway. Greg sues Diane for negligence. Diane's defense is that Ed was contributorily negligent. If this defense can be proven, the contributory negligence will be imputed to Greg because of the employer-employee relationship.

Contributory Negligence and Comparative Negligence

Finally, the adoption of comparative negligence completely alters the impact of the plaintiff's contributory negligence. Under comparative negligence, damages are allocated between the plaintiff and the defendant according to their relative fault. Contributory negligence is no longer a complete defense if the state's comparative negligence law—to be examined shortly—applies.

LAST CLEAR CHANCE

Last clear chance is a pro-plaintiff doctrine that counteracts the drastic consequences of contributory negligence. A plaintiff found to be contributorily negligent can still recover if he or she can show that the defendant had the last opportunity (clear chance) to avoid the accident and failed to exercise reasonable care to do so. Unfortunately, the doctrine is surrounded by a good deal of confusion, so that it is sometimes unclear whether a court will apply it.

It is important to distinguish the different predicaments in which plaintiffs can find themselves:

helpless peril A danger (created by the plaintiff's contributory negligence) that cannot be avoided even if the plaintiff now uses reasonable care.

inattentive peril A danger (created by the plaintiff's contributory negligence) that could be avoided if the plaintiff now uses reasonable care, but the plaintiff is carelessly unaware of the danger.

Plaintiff in helpless peril: A plaintiff is in **helpless peril** when his contributory negligence has placed him in danger that he *cannot* get himself out of. Even if the plaintiff now used reasonable care, he could not avoid the danger (e.g., plaintiff's foot is carelessly caught in a machine or in a railroad track).

Plaintiff in inattentive peril: A plaintiff is in **inattentive peril** when her contributory negligence has placed her in a predicament that she *could* get herself out of by the use of reasonable care, but the plaintiff remains negligently unaware of her peril up to the time of the accident (e.g., in a noisy section of town, plaintiff carelessly fails to hear or see a bus coming right at her on the street).

Plaintiff in Helpless Peril

If the defendant discovered the plaintiff in *helpless* peril and had an opportunity to avoid the accident but did not take it, then the plaintiff's contributory negligence will not bar recovery. The reason is that the defendant had and failed to take the last clear chance to avoid the injury.

Suppose, however, that the defendant did *not* discover the helpless plaintiff. Theoretically, the defendant did not have the last clear chance to avoid the accident. How can the defendant avoid what he or she does not know? Many states say that it is impossible, and hence deny the plaintiff the use of the last clear chance doctrine. This results in the plaintiff's loss of the case because of contributory negligence. Other states, however, take a different position, but only if the defendant *could have discovered* the helpless peril if the defendant had used reasonable care in his or her observation of the situation. For example, as the defendant railroad engineer approached the scene of the accident, the engineer failed to see the helpless plaintiff because the engineer negligently failed to maintain proper attention to the track directly in front. A few states treat "should-have-discovered" in the same way as "did-discover" and permit the plaintiff to recover in spite of the latter's contributory negligence if the defendant would have had a reasonable opportunity to prevent the accident at the last moment. The defendant must have been negligent in failing to discover the plaintiff and must have had a reasonable opportunity to prevent the accident if the plaintiff had been discovered.

Plaintiff in Inattentive Peril

If the defendant discovered the plaintiff in *inattentive* peril and had a reasonable opportunity to avoid the accident but did not take it, then the plaintiff's contributory negligence will not bar his or her recovery. The reason is that the defendant had and failed to take the last clear chance to avoid the injury. Discovery of the plaintiff in inattentive peril is treated in the same way as discovery of the plaintiff in helpless peril. The defendant does not have to have definite knowledge that the plaintiff was unaware of his or her peril, but the situation must be such that the defendant did see the plaintiff and should have known that the plaintiff was unaware or inattentive.

The most troublesome case is when the defendant failed to discover the plaintiff in inattentive peril because of the defendant's negligence at the time of the accident. Very few courts would permit the plaintiff to recover here. The negligence of both plaintiff and defendant resulted in their being ignorant of each other. Neither had the last clear chance. In most courts, therefore, the plaintiff's contributory negligence would bar his or her recovery.

ASSIGNMENT 17.2

Peter is negligently driving his car, which collides with Bill's car at an intersection. Peter is not injured, but his car is thrown onto the other side of the road, upon which Dan's car is approaching from the opposite direction. Dan is driving carelessly. Dan sees Peter's car, but instead of stopping, unreasonably thinks he can cut around Peter's car. The space is too narrow and Dan collides with Peter's car, causing Peter to break his leg. Peter sues Dan for negligence. Dan raises the defense of contributory negligence. Assess Dan's chances of succeeding with this defense. What further facts would you need to know?

A state that has adopted comparative negligence does not need the doctrine of last clear chance. When comparative negligence applies, contributory negligence is not a complete bar to recovery. Hence, there is no longer a need for a defense that offsets the all-or-nothing impact of contributory negligence. As indicated earlier, however, some states kept the last clear chance doctrine even after they adopted comparative negligence principles.

COMPARATIVE NEGLIGENCE

Most states have adopted comparative negligence. The court first determines the total damages suffered by the plaintiff. Then it apportions these damages between the negligent plaintiff and the negligent defendant according to their relative fault. There are two main kinds of comparative negligence systems: pure and modified.

Pure Comparative Negligence

When the plaintiff sues the defendant for negligence and the defendant claims that the plaintiff's negligence contributed to the injury, a court will decide the percentage by which each side was negligent. Plaintiff's recovery is limited to that percentage of the award that was due to the defendant's negligence. If, for example, plaintiff suffered $100,000 in damages, and the court concludes that the defendant was 5 percent at fault and the plaintiff was 95 percent at fault in causing the injury, the plaintiff recovers $5,000 from the defendant—5 percent of $100,000. In a state with pure comparative negligence, the plaintiff always recovers something if the injury was caused by the negligence of both parties, even if the plaintiff's fault was greater than the defendant's.

Modified Comparative Negligence

Other states use different versions of comparative negligence that are not as comprehensive as the pure form. For example, some states will compare the negligence of the defendant and plaintiff in causing the plaintiff's injury and allow the plaintiff to recover only if the plaintiff's negligence was "slight" in comparison with the "gross" negligence of the defendant. Other states will compare the negligence of the defendant and that of the plaintiff in causing the plaintiff's injury and allow the plaintiff to recover only if the plaintiff's negligence is less than that of the defendant. In the latter states:

- If they are equally negligent, the plaintiff recovers nothing.
- If the plaintiff is 51 percent negligent and the defendant is 49 percent negligent, the plaintiff recovers nothing.
- If the plaintiff is 49 percent negligent and the defendant is 51 percent negligent, the plaintiff recovers 51 percent of the plaintiff's damages.

1993 World Trade Center Bombing: New York's Version of Comparative Negligence

In 1993, eight years before the World Trade Center was destroyed in a terrorist attack, another bombing occurred at the Center. In litigation growing out of the 1993 bombing, the landlord of the Center (The Port Authority of New York and New Jersey) was charged with negligence:

> On February 26, 1993, at midday, terrorists, utterly unimpeded, even by so much as a garage attendant or a gate, drove a bright yellow Ryder rental van, loaded with fertilizer-based explosive possessing the potency of 1,500 pounds of dynamite, into the subterranean public parking garage of the World Trade Center. They parked the van on the garage access ramp proximate to vital utility and communications systems and conduits, lit a ten-minute fuse and safely left the premises. The ensuing blast created a crater six stories in depth and wrought devastation over an area about half the size of a football field. Six people were killed, hundreds were injured and essential services to World Trade Center tenants were severed. . . . [The evidence] established that, years before the bombing, defendant was in receipt of reports from outside consultants and its own internal study group advising it that the World Trade Center was vulnerable to terrorist attack through its public parking garage and detailing, with exact prescience, the manner by which the identified garage vulnerability could be exploited.[2]

The jury found that the Port Authority was negligent in meeting its duty to maintain the Center's underground parking garage in a reasonably safe condition and that this negligence was a substantial factor in causing the bombing. The Port Authority was found to be 68 percent at fault and the terrorists were found to be only 32 percent at fault. Then New York's version of comparative negligence was applied. Because the Port Authority was more than 50 percent at fault, it was obligated to pay all of the damages. If it had been found to be 50 percent or less at fault, it would have been liable only for the proportionate share of noneconomic damages (e.g., pain and suffering) that it caused.[3] On the allocation of negligence, the Port Authority argued that it was "bizarre" for the court to conclude that its negligence in failing to anticipate a terrorist attack was double that of the terrorists who actually carried one out. Nevertheless, the judgment stood.

ASSUMPTION OF THE RISK

Assumption of the risk is the knowing and voluntary acceptance of the danger or risk of being injured by someone's negligence.

EXAMPLES

- Ted pays the owner of an airplane to fly him over a field where he will parachute at a designated spot. A clause in the agreement with the owner of the airplane says that Ted understands the danger of parachuting and assumes the risk of injury from the jump. During the flight, the pilot carelessly accelerates the plane, which causes Ted to injure himself in the jump.
- Bob attends many Little League baseball games as a fan. At a recent game, he volunteers to be the home plate umpire when the scheduled umpire fails to appear. Bob has never umpired before, but is very familiar with how the game is played and feels he can do the job with ease. While behind the plate, a foul ball hits Bob just above the shin padding, injuring his leg.

Both Ted and Bob assumed the risk of their injury. Ted expressly agreed to assume the risk in a signed agreement. Although Bob did not sign an agreement assuming the risk, a strong case can be made that he understood the dangers of umpiring and voluntarily accepted this risk.

Before we examine assumption of the risk in detail, we should say a word about its relationship to contributory negligence. A plaintiff's conduct may amount to both contributory negligence and assumption of the risk. In a state that still has both defenses, the defendant can choose either to avoid liability. A basic difference between the two defenses is that contributory negligence is determined by the *objective standard* of the reasonable person, whereas assumption of the risk is determined by a *subjective standard* of whether this particular plaintiff knowingly and voluntarily assumed the risk of the defendant's conduct:

Contributory negligence (objective test): The plaintiff *should have known* that he or she was creating an unreasonable risk of injuring him- or herself and *should have taken* greater precautions against this risk.

Assumption of the risk (subjective test): The plaintiff *actually knew* of the risk to his or her safety, but voluntarily chose to confront it.

Let's now take a closer look at the two main elements of the defense of assumption of the risk:

- Plaintiff understood the risks posed by the defendant's conduct to the plaintiff's safety.
- Plaintiff voluntarily chose to confront those risks.

Understanding the Risk

Suppose that Sam is injured in an electrical plant by coming into contact with large live wires that the plant negligently left on the floor. Sam never saw the wires in spite of their size. In Sam's negligence suit against the plant, can the plant use the assumption-of-the-risk defense? No. How could Sam have understood a risk in something that he did not see? If the plant says that Sam *should have seen* the wires because they were so large, the plant is confusing assumption of the risk with contributory negligence. If Sam did not see the wires but should have seen them if he had been acting reasonably as he walked, he was contributorily negligent, but it was impossible for him to have assumed the risk. Assumption of the risk, as indicated, is subjective: the risk must be known and understood by a particular plaintiff before we can say that he or she assumed that risk. If all the defendant can say is that the plaintiff was stupid in failing to understand the risk, the defendant has conceded that assumption of the risk cannot apply.

To be sure, there will be some extreme cases in which no one will believe the plaintiff's claim that he or she did not understand the danger. A plaintiff, for example, who walks into a fire negligently set by the defendant would probably not be believed if the plaintiff says he or she did not know that the fire could cause serious injury.

ASSIGNMENT 17.3

Diane is a high school freshman. She has a part-time job at a convenience store in a run-down section of the city. There have been a number of robberies at the store, several of which Diane witnessed. The store manager carelessly fails to hire a guard or to install a security system. One day, a robber confronts Diane and demands all the cash in the register. Diane complies. She is traumatized by the incident and sues the store for negligently failing to have a guard or other security system. Can the store use the defense of assumption of the risk?

Voluntarily Confronting the Risk

We need to examine two categories of assumption of the risk:

express assumption of the risk The knowing and voluntary acceptance of a danger or risk by express agreement.

- the plaintiff's **express assumption of the risk** in which the plaintiff knowingly and voluntarily accepts a risk by an explicit agreement (an example is the agreement Ted signed with the owner of the airplane containing the clause relieving the airline of liability for injuries that might result from Ted's parachute jump)

implied assumption of the risk The knowing and voluntary acceptance of a danger or risk through conduct that signifies acceptance in the absence of an express agreement.

- the plaintiff's **implied assumption of the risk** in which the plaintiff knowingly and voluntarily accepts a risk through conduct that signifies acceptance of this risk in the absence of an express agreement (an example is Bob's conduct in umpiring the Little League game)

exculpatory clause A clause in an agreement that relieves a party from liability for injury or damages he or she may wrongfully cause.

release The giving up or relinquishing of a right, claim, interest, or privilege.

Express Assumption People often enter into agreements limiting their liability to each other. (Clauses in agreements that limit liability are called **exculpatory clauses**. They constitute a **release** of the right to sue.) For example, when someone stores a car or a coat in a warehouse or other business set up for this purpose, the parties may agree that the business will not be liable for loss or damage to the car or coat. The owner of the car or coat in these situations is expressly assuming the risk of the loss or damage.

But it must be clear that the parties agreed to a limitation of liability. The plaintiff must know about the limitation. A company may try to tell the customer that it will not be liable for negligence by putting a notice to this effect on a sign buried on a wall in the rear of a room, or in very small print on the back of a receipt check.

Such communication will usually be insufficient. Customers do not agree to assume a risk of which they are unaware.

There are a number of situations in which the law will not permit or will restrict assumption-of-the-risk agreements even if the terms are clear to both parties. This occurs mainly when there is a significantly unbalanced bargaining position between the parties, particularly when the party in the weaker position is an employee, a user of a public service, or a relatively unsophisticated consumer. A court may rule that enforcing exculpatory clauses against such individuals is against **public policy**.

public policy Principles inherent in customs and societal values that are of fundamental concern to legislatures and courts.

EXAMPLES

- An employer cannot ask an employee to assume all risks of injury on the job. The employer must provide a reasonably safe workplace.
- Someone engaged in a public service (e.g., common carrier, innkeeper, public utility) cannot ask a customer to assume all risks of injury or damage while using the public service—but it may be able to limit its liability if the terms of the limitation are clearly communicated to the customer so that the latter knows what he or she is getting into.

Merchants often insist that consumers sign standard form contracts that contain important terms buried in a maze of small print and legalese. Such an agreement is called an **adhesion contract**. Adhesion contracts are standardized contracts for goods or services offered on a take-it-or-leave-it basis without any realistic opportunity for bargaining between the buyer and seller over the terms of the contract. If the adhesion contract contains an exculpatory clause or release that is not prominently brought to the attention of the consumer, a court might not enforce it, particularly if the consumer's level of sophistication is not high and the pressure on the consumer to agree borders on **coercion**.

adhesion contract A standardized contract for goods or services offered on a take-it-or-leave-it basis without any realistic opportunity for bargaining over the terms of the contract.

coercion Compelling something by force or threats. Overpowering another's free will by undue influence.

There is no single answer to the question of when a court will invalidate an exculpatory clause or release. A court will consider a number of factors to determine its validity. The most important factors are illustrated in the case of *Wagenblast v. Odessa School District No. 105-157-166J*.

CASE

Wagenblast v. Odessa School District No. 105-157-166J

110 Wash.2d 845, 758 P.2d 968 (1988)
Supreme Court of Washington

Background: *Charles Wagenblast is a public school student. To participate in high school sports, all students and their parents must sign a standardized form releasing the school district from liability for negligence. The form is an agreement containing an exculpatory clause and, as such, is an express assumption of the risk of the school's negligence. In this case, the parents and student sued the school district in Superior Court, seeking an injunction to prevent the use of the release form as a condition of participating in school sports. The Superior Court granted the injunction. The case is now on appeal before the Supreme Court of Washington.*

Decision on Appeal: *The judgment is affirmed. The release violates public policy.*

OPINION OF COURT

Justice ANDERSEN delivered the opinion of the court . . . :

Can school districts require public school students and their parents to sign written releases which release the districts from the consequences of all future school district negligence, before the students will be allowed to engage in certain recognized school related activities, here interscholastic athletics? We hold that the exculpatory releases from any future school district negligence are invalid because they violate public policy.

The courts have generally recognized that, subject to certain exceptions, parties may contract that one shall not be liable for his or her own negligence to another. As Prosser and Keeton explain: "It is quite possible for the parties expressly to agree in advance that the defendant is under no obligation of care for the benefit of the plaintiff, and shall not be liable for the consequences of conduct which would other wise be negligent. There is in the ordinary case no public policy which prevents the parties from contracting as they see fit, as to whether the plaintiff will undertake the responsibility of looking out for himself." W. Keeton, D. Dobbs, R. Keeton & D. Owen, *Prosser and Keeton on Torts* § 68, at 482 (5th ed. 1984).

In accordance with the foregoing general rule, appellate decisions in this state have upheld exculpatory agreements where the subject was a toboggan slide, a scuba diving class, mountain climbing instruction, an automobile demolition derby, and ski jumping.

As Prosser and Keeton further observe, however, there are instances where public policy reasons for preserving an obligation of care owed by one person to another outweigh our traditional regard for the freedom to contract. Courts in this century are generally agreed on several such categories of cases. Courts, for example, are usually reluctant to allow those charged with a public duty, which includes the obligation to use reasonable care, to rid themselves of that obligation by contract. Thus, where the defendant is a common carrier, an innkeeper, a professional bailee, a public utility, or the like, an agreement discharging the defendant's performance will not ordinarily be given effect. Implicit in such decisions is the notion that the service performed is one of importance to the public, and that a certain standard of performance is therefore required.

Courts generally also hold that an employer cannot require an employee to sign a contract releasing the employer from liability for job-related injuries caused by the employer's negligence. Such decisions are grounded on the recognition that the disparity of bargaining power between employer and employee forces the employee to accept such agreements.

Consistent with these general views, this court has held that a bank which rents out safety deposit boxes cannot, by contract, exempt itself from liability for its own negligence, and that if the circumstances of a particular case suggest that a gas company has a duty to inspect the pipes and fittings belonging to the owner of the building, any contractual limitation on that duty would be against public policy.

This court has also gone beyond these usually accepted categories to hold future releases invalid in other circumstances as well. It has struck down a lease provision exculpating a public housing authority from liability for injuries caused by the authority's negligence and has also struck down a landlord's exculpatory clause relating to common areas in a multi-family dwelling complex.

In reaching these decisions, this court has focused at times on disparity of bargaining power, at times on the importance of the service provided, and at other times on other factors. In reviewing these decisions, it is apparent that the court has not always been particularly clear on what rationale it used to decide what type of release was and was not violative of "public policy". Undoubtedly, it has been much easier for courts to simply declare releases violative of public policy in a given situation than to state a principled basis for so holding.

Probably the best exposition of the test to be applied in determining whether exculpatory agreements violate public policy is that stated by the California Supreme Court. In writing for a unanimous court, the late Justice Tobriner outlined the factors in *Tunkl v. Regents of Univ. of Cal.,* 60 Cal. 2d 92, 383 P.2d 441, 32 Cal. Rptr. 33, 6 A.L.R.3d 693 (1963):

> Thus the attempted but invalid exemption involves a transaction which exhibits some or all of the following characteristics. [1] It concerns a business of a type generally thought suitable for public regulation. [2] The party seeking exculpation is engaged in performing a service of great importance to the public, which is often a matter of practical necessity for some members of the public. [3] The party holds himself out as willing to perform this service for any member of the public who seeks it, or at least for any member coming within certain established standards. [4] As a result of the essential nature of the service, in the economic setting of the transaction, the party invoking exculpation possesses a decisive advantage of bargaining strength against any member of the public who seeks his services. [5] In exercising a superior bargaining power the party confronts the public with a standardized adhesion contract of exculpation, and makes no provision whereby a purchaser may pay additional reasonable fees and obtain protection against negligence. [6] Finally, as a result of the transaction, the person or property of the purchaser is placed under the control of the seller, subject to the risk of carelessness by the seller or his agents.

Tunkl, 60 Cal. 2d at 98-101. We agree.

Obviously, the more of the foregoing six characteristics that appear in a given exculpatory agreement case, the more likely the agreement is to be declared invalid on public policy grounds. In the . . . [high-school sports case] before us, *all* of the characteristics are present. . . .

1. The agreement concerns an endeavor of a type generally thought suitable for public regulation . . . . [I]nterscholastic sports in Washington are extensively regulated, and are a fit subject for such regulation.

2. The party seeking exculpation is engaged in performing a service of great importance to the public, which is often a matter of practical necessity for some members of the public. This court has held that public school students have no fundamental right to participate in interscholastic athletics. Nonetheless, the court also has observed that the justification advanced for interscholastic athletics is their educational and cultural value. As the testimony of . . . School Superintendent Robert Nelson and others amply demonstrate, interscholastic athletics is part and parcel of the overall educational scheme in Washington. The total expenditure of time, effort and money on these endeavors makes this clear. . . . Given this emphasis on sports by the public and the school system, it would be unrealistic to expect students to view athletics as an activity

entirely separate and apart from the remainder of their schooling.*. . .

3. Such party holds itself out as willing to perform this service for any member of the public who seeks it, or at least for any member coming within certain established standards. Implicit in the nature of interscholastic sports is the notion that such programs are open to all students who meet certain skill and eligibility standards. . . .

4. Because of the essential nature of the service, in the economic setting of the transaction, the party invoking exculpation possesses a decisive advantage of bargaining strength against any member of the public who seeks the services. Not only have interscholastic sports become of considerable importance to students and the general public alike, but in most instances there exists no alternative program of organized competition. . . . And, because such programs have become important to student participants, school districts possess a clear and disparate bargaining strength when they insist that students and their parents sign these releases.

5. In exercising a superior bargaining power, the party confronts the public with a standardized adhesion contract of exculpation, and makes no provision whereby a purchaser may pay additional reasonable fees and obtain protection against negligence. . . . Student athletes and their parents or guardians have no alternative but to sign the standard release forms provided to them or have the student barred from the program.

*This intimate relationship between interscholastic sports and other aspects of public education serves to distinguish this case from those involving private adult education for hazardous activities, e.g., skydiving and mountain climbing.

6. The person or property of members of the public seeking such services must be placed under the control of the furnisher of the services, subject to the risk of carelessness on the part of the furnisher, its employees or agents. A school district owes a duty to its students to employ ordinary care and to anticipate reasonably foreseeable dangers so as to take precautions for protecting the children in its custody from such dangers. This duty extends to students engaged in interscholastic sports. As a natural incident to the relationship of a student athlete and his or her coach, the student athlete is usually placed under the coach's considerable degree of control. The student is thus subject to the risk that the school district or its agent will breach this duty of care.

In sum, the attempted releases . . . before us exhibit all six of the characteristics denominated in *Tunkl v. Regents of Univ. of Cal.* Because of this, and for the aforesaid reasons, we hold that the releases . . . are invalid as against public policy. . . .

Another name for a release of the sort presented here is an express assumption of risk. If a plaintiff has released a defendant from liability for a future occurrence, the plaintiff may also be said to have assumed the risk of the occurrence. If the release is against public policy, however, it is also against public policy to say that the plaintiff has assumed that particular risk. This court has implicitly recognized that an express assumption of risk which relieves the defendant's duty to the plaintiff may violate public policy. Accordingly, to the extent that the release portions of these forms represent a consent to relieve the school districts of their duty of care, they are invalid whether they are termed releases or express assumptions of risk. . . .

The decision of the trial court in the Odessa School District case is affirmed. . . .

ASSIGNMENT 17.4

a. A fellow student asks you for a ride downtown. You do this favor on the condition that he or she signs a release of liability for any injury that may result from the ride. Assume that the student has no other way to get downtown. Is the release valid?

b. Can a public high school have a fencing class that is limited to students who, with their parents, sign a waiver of negligence liability? Why or why not? What about a furniture-making class that is similarly limited?

c. Tommy shows up for high school football. After about three weeks of practice, the coach tells Tommy that he is too thin to play football. If, however, he and his parents sign a waiver of negligence liability, he will be allowed to play. Is this waiver valid?

d. What remedy do the students have if the school district decides to cancel all school sports whether or not waivers are signed?

Implied Assumption The plaintiff can assume the risk in ways other than by express agreement. An implied assumption of the risk is the knowing and voluntary acceptance of a danger or risk through conduct that signifies acceptance in the absence of an express agreement. If, for example, the plaintiff walks very close to the spot where fireworks are exploding and fully understands the dangers involved, the plaintiff has assumed the risk of injury due to the negligent setting off of the fireworks. This is an implied assumption of the risk. Suppose that you buy a lawn mower, but before using it, you discover that it is defective. The blade has been negligently fastened to the body of the machine. You see the defect and understand the consequences of the blade's flying off while in use. If you decide to use it anyway and are injured when the blade does come off, your negligence suit against the manufacturer will be defeated because of assumption of the risk. You have impliedly assumed the risk. In effect, once you understand the risks and voluntarily proceed to confront them, you have decided to take your chances of injury caused by the negligence of the defendant.

ASSIGNMENT 17.5

Examine the following situations to determine whether the plaintiff has voluntarily assumed the risk.

a. Plaintiff runs out into the street in the path of cars that are exceeding the speed limit. One of the cars hits the plaintiff. Plaintiff sues the driver.
b. Plaintiff agrees to take a joy ride with the defendant, who will drive on the beach in very shallow water. Neither party knows that the brakes are defective. The brakes fail and the car goes out to deep water, almost drowning the plaintiff. Plaintiff sues the defendant.

There is a form of pressure that a defendant can place on the plaintiff that can negate what would otherwise be an assumption of the risk. The pressure comes in the form of negligently leaving the plaintiff no reasonable alternative in protecting the plaintiff's rights.

EXAMPLE

Defendant negligently sets fire to the plaintiff's car. The plaintiff tries to put out the fire and is burned. Plaintiff sues defendant for damage to the car and for personal injuries due to the burn. As to the personal injuries, the defendant raises the defense of assumption of the risk.

If the plaintiff acted reasonably in trying to put out the fire, he or she has not assumed the risk of being burned *even though the plaintiff fully understood the risks of being burned*. The risks were not voluntarily assumed. Defendant's negligent conduct put the plaintiff in the predicament of either watching the fire destroy the car or trying to stop the fire. The essential question is whether the plaintiff was reasonable in the course taken. This will depend on all the circumstances. How big was the fire at the time the plaintiff tried to put it out? How old was the car? What was its value? How close was a fire station, and how difficult or easy was it to contact the station? What was in the car? Nothing? Valuable papers? An infant? Would the plaintiff have been stranded in an inhospitable area if he or she were not able to use the car? Taking all of these factors into consideration, if the attempt to put out the fire was reasonable, there was no voluntary assumption of the risk. If, on the other hand, the attempt was foolhardy because of the extraordinary danger of being seriously burned to protect property of relatively little value, a court will conclude that there was an assumption of the risk. The plaintiff's protection of his or her rights or property must not be out of all proportion to the danger that the plaintiff walks or leaps into.

ASSIGNMENT 17.6

In the following cases, determine whether the defendant can successfully raise the assumption-of-the-risk defense.

a. Tony is building a new road in front of Alan's house. A ditch is dug in front of the house. Tony puts a thin piece of plywood across the ditch so that workers and Alan can cross over the ditch. A large "danger" sign is placed by Tony close to the plywood crossing. Alan sees the sign. While Alan is crossing over the plywood, it caves in, causing severe injuries. Alan sues Tony for negligence.
b. Bob's leg is injured in a hit-and-run accident. Along comes Tom in another car. Tom's car has defective brakes, and Bob knows this. Bob has no other way to get to a hospital for needed medical attention. Bob goes with Tom to the hospital. Along the way, the defective brakes cause another accident, in which Bob breaks his arm. Bob sues Tom for negligent injury to his arm.

We turn now to the effect of comparative negligence on assumption of risk.

First of all, *express* assumption of the risk remains a defense, except in those cases where the court might rule that the agreement to limit liability is against public policy. Does *implied* assumption of the risk still exist as a defense in states that have adopted comparative negligence? To answer this question, courts distinguish between two kinds of implied assumption of risk: primary and secondary.

Primary assumption of the risk: The plaintiff knowingly and voluntarily accepts a particular risk that the defendant did not have a duty to protect the plaintiff against. The plaintiff recovers nothing in such cases.

primary assumption of the risk The plaintiff's knowing and voluntary acceptance of a particular risk that the defendant did not have a duty to protect the plaintiff against.

EXAMPLE

Paul buys an expensive season ticket to a professional basketball game. He sits in the front row, a few feet from the playing court. During play, a ball bounces off a player and hits Paul in the face, breaking his glasses. He sues the stadium for negligently failing to build a net in front of spectators to protect them from stray basketballs.

Paul loses. The stadium did not have a duty to protect spectators from being hit by a ricocheted basketball during an aggressive, but normally played, basketball game. The risk of serious injury from stray balls is relatively small. The burden on the stadium of preventing such accidents outweighs the risk of the injury. It would be impossible to keep the basketball in bounds at all times without fundamentally altering the competitive nature of the game. Stray balls are inevitable. Nets all around the court would impede vision. Spectators have the option of sitting further back from the playing court. In short, the stadium simply was not negligent. Another way of phrasing this conclusion is to say that a front-row spectator assumes the risk of being hit by stray basketballs during play even if the ball was carelessly thrown by a player before it ricocheted off the court. Yet, it would be more accurate to say that there was no negligence on the part of the defendant. Unfortunately, however, assumption-of-the-risk language is still used in these cases. When the defendant had no duty to protect the plaintiff against a particular risk, many courts use the phrase *primary assumption of the risk*.

If the state has comparative negligence, does the court compare the conduct of the parties and apportion liability? No. There is nothing to compare. The defendant simply was not negligent. Plaintiff recovers nothing in cases of primary assumption of risk because the defendant was not negligent—there is no reason to invoke the comparative fault principles of comparative negligence. This is so whether the plaintiff was reasonable or unreasonable in his or her own conduct.

Secondary assumption of the risk: The plaintiff knowingly and voluntarily accepts a particular risk that the defendant had a duty to protect the plaintiff against.

secondary assumption of the risk The plaintiff's knowing and voluntary acceptance of a particular risk that the defendant had a duty to protect the plaintiff against.

EXAMPLE

At a county fair, Mary agrees to ride in a horse-drawn carriage driven by a driver who is visibly drunk. Mary sees the driver's condition as he staggers onto the carriage, but decides to take the ride with him anyway. The driver carelessly drives too close to the edge of the road. The carriage tips over, injuring Mary.

This is a case of secondary assumption of the risk. The driver had a duty to drive the carriage carefully and to protect passengers from injuries caused by unreasonable driving. Driving while intoxicated was certainly unreasonable. Mary, however, knew the driver was impaired and that this could affect the safety of the ride. She foolishly decided to ride with him. Arguably, she knowingly and voluntarily accepted the risk of injury from the ride. In cases of secondary assumption of the risk, comparative negligence applies. Recovery is not barred because of assumption of the risk. The court will compare the negligence of both parties and apportion the damages according to the comparative negligence rules in the state.

The case of *Knight v. Jewett* provides further clarification on the impact of comparative negligence on assumption of the risk as well as on contributory negligence and last clear chance.

CASE

Knight v. Jewett

3 Cal. 4th 296, 834 P.2d 696, 11 Cal. Rptr. 2d 2 (1992)
Supreme Court of California

football game

Background: *Kendra Knight had to have her finger amputated after Michael Jewett ran into her during a game of touch football. She sued him for negligence, assault, and battery. In the trial court, the defendant made a motion for summary judgment. It was sustained and the case was dismissed. The court ruled that plaintiff would not be able to win even if all the allegations made in the pleadings and during discovery were true. The Court of Appeal affirmed the dismissal. Knight has now appealed the dismissal to the California Supreme Court.*

Decision on Appeal: *The judgment is affirmed. Jewett did not owe a duty to Knight to protect her against the risk of injury she received. There was a primary assumption of the risk and therefore comparative negligence does not apply.*

OPINION OF COURT

Justice GEORGE delivered the opinion of the court . . . :

On January 25, 1987, the day of the 1987 Super Bowl football game, plaintiff Kendra Knight and defendant Michael Jewett, together with a number of other social acquaintances, attended a Super Bowl party at the home of a mutual friend. During half time of the Super Bowl, several guests decided to play an informal game of touch football on an adjoining dirt lot, using a "peewee" football. Each team had four or five players and included both women and men; plaintiff and defendant were on opposing teams. No rules were explicitly discussed before the game.

Five to ten minutes into the game, defendant ran into plaintiff during a play. According to plaintiff, at that point she told defendant "not to play so rough or I was going to have to stop playing." Her declaration stated that "[defendant] seemed to acknowledge my statement and left me with the impression that he would play less rough prospectively." In his deposition, defendant recalled that plaintiff had asked him to "be careful," but did not remember plaintiff saying that she would stop playing.

On the very next play, plaintiff sustained the injuries that gave rise to the present lawsuit. As defendant recalled the incident, his team was on defense on that play, and he jumped up in an attempt to intercept a pass. He touched the ball but did not catch it, and in coming down he collided with plaintiff, knocking her over. When he landed, he stepped backward onto plaintiff's right hand, injuring her hand and little finger.

Both plaintiff and Andrea Starr, another participant in the game who was on the same team as plaintiff, recalled the incident differently from defendant. According to their declarations, at the time plaintiff was injured, Starr already had caught the pass. Defendant was running toward Starr, when he ran into plaintiff from behind, knocked her down, and stepped on her hand. Starr also stated that, after knocking plaintiff down, defendant continued running until he tagged Starr, "which tag was hard enough to cause me to lose my balance, resulting in a twisting or spraining of my ankle."

The game ended with plaintiff's injury, and plaintiff sought treatment shortly thereafter. After three operations failed to restore the movement in her little finger or to relieve the ongoing pain of the injury, plaintiff's finger was amputated. Plaintiff then instituted the present proceeding, seeking damages from defendant on theories of negligence and assault and battery. . . .

[Defendant contended] he did not intend to step on plaintiff's hand or to injure her. Defendant also attached a copy of plaintiff's deposition in which plaintiff acknowledged that she frequently watched professional football on television and thus was generally familiar with the risks associated with the sport of football, and in which she conceded that she had no reason to believe defendant had any intention of stepping on her hand or injuring her. . . .

[P]laintiff maintained that . . . in view of the casual, social setting, the circumstance that women and men were joint participants in the game, and the rough dirt surface on which the game was played, she anticipated from the outset that it was the kind of "mock" football game in which there would be no forceful pushing or hard hitting or shoving. Plaintiff also asserted that the declarations and depositions of other players in the game, included in her opposition papers, demonstrated that the other participants, including defendant, shared her expectations and assumptions that the game was to be a "mellow" one and not a serious, competitive athletic event. Plaintiff claimed that there had been no injuries during touch football games in which she had participated on previous occasions, and that in view of the circumstances under which the game was played, "[t]he only type of injury which I reasonably anticipated would have been something in the nature of a bruise or bump.". . .

After considering the parties' submissions, the trial court granted defendant's motion for summary judgment. On appeal, the Court of Appeal . . . affirmed the judgment. . . .

As every leading tort treatise has explained, the assumption of risk doctrine long has caused confusion both in definition and application, because the phrase "assumption of risk" traditionally has been used in a number of very different factual settings involving analytically distinct legal concepts. (See, e.g., *Prosser & Keeton on Torts* (5th ed. 1984) pp. 480–481. . . .)

Prior to the adoption of comparative fault principles of liability, there often was no need to distinguish between the different categories of assumption of risk cases, because if a case fell into either category, the plaintiff's recovery was totally barred. With the adoption of comparative fault, however, it became essential to differentiate between the distinct categories of cases that traditionally had been lumped together under the rubric of assumption of risk. This court's seminal comparative fault decision in *Li v. Yellow Cab Co.* (1975) 13 Cal. 3d 804, 119 Cal. Rptr. 858, 532 P.2d 1226, explicitly recognized the need for such differentiation, and attempted to explain which category of assumption of risk cases should be merged into the comparative fault system and which category should not. . . .

In *Li,* our court undertook a basic reexamination of the common law doctrine of contributory negligence. As *Li* noted, contributory negligence generally has been defined as "'conduct on the part of the plaintiff which falls below the standard to which he should conform for his own protection, and which is a legally contributing cause cooperating with the negligence of the defendant in bringing about the plaintiff's harm.'" (*Li,* supra, 13 Cal. 3d at p. 809, quoting *Restatement (Second) Torts,* § 463.) Prior to *Li,* the common law rule was that "'[e]xcept where the defendant has the last clear chance, the plaintiff's contributory negligence *bars recovery* against a defendant whose negligent conduct would otherwise make him liable to the plaintiff for the harm sustained by him.'" (*Li,* supra, at pp. 809–810, italics added, quoting *Restatement (Second) Torts,* § 467.). . .

[The *Li* court criticized the doctrine of contributory negligence because it fails to distribute responsibility in proportion to fault. The court concluded that contributory negligence] should be replaced in this state by a system under which liability for damage will be borne by those whose negligence caused it in direct proportion to their respective fault. . . .

After determining that the "all-or-nothing" contributory negligence doctrine should be replaced by a system of comparative negligence, the *Li* court went on to undertake a rather extensive discussion of the effect that the adoption of comparative negligence would have on a number of related tort doctrines, including the doctrines of last clear chance and assumption of risk.

Under the last clear chance doctrine, a defendant was rendered totally liable for an injury, even though the plaintiff's contributory negligence had played a role in the accident, when the defendant had the "last clear chance" to avoid the accident. With regard to that doctrine, the *Li* decision observed: "Although several states which apply comparative negligence concepts retain the last clear chance doctrine, the better reasoned position seems to be that when true comparative negligence is adopted, the need for last clear chance . . . disappears and its retention results only in a windfall to the plaintiff in direct contravention of the principle of liability in proportion to fault." (*Li* at p. 824.) Accordingly, the court concluded that the doctrine should be "subsumed under the general process of assessing liability in proportion to fault." (Id. at p. 826.) . . .

[As to assumption of risk, the *Li* court said that some categories of assumption of risk are really forms of contributory negligence. When this is so, the old all-or-nothing rule of contributory negligence does not apply. Comparative negligence principles take over. The conduct of the plaintiff is called secondary assumption of risk, which does not bar recovery. There are two kinds of assumption of risk: primary and secondary. In primary assumption of risk, the defendant was under no duty of care to protect the plaintiff from a particular risk. Primary assumption of risk, therefore, bars the plaintiff from any recovery for injuries resulting from that risk. In secondary assumption of risk, however, the defendant had a duty of care to protect the plaintiff from a particular risk, but the plaintiff knowingly and unreasonably encountered that risk. Secondary assumption of risk is merged into and becomes part of comparative negligence. The fault of the plaintiff and the defendant are compared for purposes of allocating responsibility. Hence, when the defense of assumption of risk is raised, we need to ask whether the defendant had a duty to protect the plaintiff from a particular risk. If not, recovery is barred because the case falls into the category of primary assumption of risk.]

As a general rule, persons have a duty to use due care to avoid injury to others, and may be held liable if their careless conduct injures another person. (See Civ. Code, § 1714.) Thus, for example, a property owner ordinarily is required to use due care to eliminate dangerous

conditions on his or her property. (See, e.g., *Rowland v. Christian* (1968) 69 Cal. 2d 108, 70 Cal. Rptr. 97, 443 P.2d 561.) In the sports setting, however, conditions or conduct that otherwise might be viewed as dangerous often are an integral part of the sport itself. Thus, although moguls on a ski run pose a risk of harm to skiers that might not exist were these configurations removed, the challenge and risks posed by the moguls are part of the sport of skiing, and a ski resort has no duty to eliminate them. (See generally Annotation (1987) 55 *A.L.R.4th* 632.) In this respect, the nature of a sport is highly relevant in defining the duty of care owed by the particular defendant.

Although defendants generally have no legal duty to eliminate (or protect a plaintiff against) risks inherent in the sport itself, it is well established that defendants generally do have a duty to use due care not to increase the risks to a participant over and above those inherent in the sport. Thus, although a ski resort has no duty to remove moguls from a ski run, it clearly does have a duty to use due care to maintain its towropes in a safe, working condition so as not to expose skiers to an increased risk of harm. The cases establish that the latter type of risk, posed by a ski resort's negligence, clearly is not a risk (inherent in the sport) that is assumed by a participant. (See generally Annotation (1979) 95 *A.L.R.3d* 203.)

In some situations, however, the careless conduct of others is treated as an "inherent risk" of a sport, thus barring recovery by the plaintiff. For example, numerous cases recognize that in a game of baseball, a player generally cannot recover if he or she is hit and injured by a carelessly thrown ball (see, e.g., *Mann v. Nutrilite, Inc.* (1955) 136 Cal. App. 2d 729, 734-735, 289 P.2d 282), and that in a game of basketball, recovery is not permitted for an injury caused by a carelessly extended elbow (see, e.g., *Thomas v. Barlow* (1927) 5 N.J. Misc. 764, 138 A. 208). The divergent results of the foregoing cases lead naturally to the question how courts are to determine when careless conduct of another properly should be considered an "inherent risk" of the sport that (as a matter of law) is assumed by the injured participant. . . .

In the present case, defendant was a participant in the touch football game in which plaintiff was engaged at the time of her injury, and thus the question before us involves the circumstances under which a participant in such a sport may be held liable for an injury sustained by another participant.

The overwhelming majority of the cases, both within and outside California, that have addressed the issue of coparticipant liability in such a sport, have concluded that it is improper to hold a sports participant liable to a coparticipant for ordinary careless conduct committed during the sport—for example, for an injury resulting from a carelessly thrown ball or bat during a baseball game—and that liability properly may be imposed on a participant only when he or she intentionally injures another player or engages in reckless conduct that is totally outside the range of the ordinary activity involved in the sport. (See, e.g., *Gauvin v. Clark* (1989) 404 Mass. 450, 537 N.E.2d 94, 96–97 and cases cited.)

In reaching the conclusion that a coparticipant's duty of care should be limited in this fashion, the cases have explained that, in the heat of an active sporting event like baseball or football, a participant's normal energetic conduct often includes accidentally careless behavior. The courts have concluded that vigorous participation in such sporting events likely would be chilled if legal liability were to be imposed on a participant on the basis of his or her ordinary careless conduct. The cases have recognized that, in such a sport, even when a participant's conduct violates a rule of the game and may subject the violator to internal sanctions prescribed by the sport itself, imposition of *legal liability* for such conduct might well alter fundamentally the nature of the sport by deterring participants from vigorously engaging in activity that falls close to, but on the permissible side of, a prescribed rule.

A sampling of the cases that have dealt with the question of the potential tort liability of such sports participants is instructive. In *Tavernier v. Maes* (1966) 242 Cal. App. 2d 532, 51 Cal. Rptr. 575, for example, the Court of Appeal upheld a verdict denying recovery for an injury sustained by the plaintiff second baseman as an unintended consequence of the defendant baserunner's hard slide into second base during a family picnic softball game. Similarly, in *Gaspard v. Grain Dealers Mutual Insurance Company* (La. Ct. App. 1961) 131 So. 2d 831, the plaintiff baseball player was denied recovery when he was struck on the head by a bat which accidentally flew out of the hands of the defendant batter during a school game. (See also *Gauvin v. Clark* (1989) 404 Mass. 450, 537 N.E.2d 94, 96–97 [plaintiff hockey player injured when hit with hockey stick by opposing player; court held that defendant's liability should be determined by whether he acted "with reckless disregard of safety"]; . . .

In our view, the reasoning of the foregoing cases is sound. Accordingly, we conclude that a participant in an active sport breaches a legal duty of care to other participants—i.e., engages in conduct that properly may subject him or her to financial liability—only if the participant intentionally injures another player or engages in conduct that is so reckless as to be totally outside the range of the ordinary activity involved in the sport.*

As applied to the present case, the foregoing legal principle clearly supports the trial court's entry of summary judgment in favor of defendant. The declarations filed in support of and in opposition to the summary judgment motion establish that defendant was, at most,

---

*As suggested by the cases described in the text, the limited duty of care applicable to coparticipants has been applied in situations involving a wide variety of active sports, ranging from baseball to ice hockey and skating. Because the touch football game at issue in this case clearly falls within the rationale of this rule, we have no occasion to decide whether a comparable limited duty of care appropriately should be applied to other less active sports, such as archery or golf. We note that because of the special danger to others posed by the sport of hunting, past cases generally have found the ordinary duty of care to be applicable to hunting accidents. (See, e.g., *Summers v. Tice* (1948) 33 Cal. 2d 80, 83, 199 P.2d 1.)

careless or negligent in knocking over plaintiff, stepping on her hand, and injuring her finger. Although plaintiff maintains that defendant's rough play as described in her declaration and the declaration of Andrea Starr properly can be characterized as "reckless," the conduct alleged in those declarations is not even closely comparable to the kind of conduct—conduct so reckless as to be totally outside the range of the ordinary activity involved in the sport—that is a prerequisite to the imposition of legal liability upon a participant in such a sport.

Therefore, we conclude that defendant's conduct in the course of the touch football game did not breach any legal duty of care owed to plaintiff. Accordingly, this case falls within the primary assumption of risk doctrine, and thus the trial court properly granted summary judgment in favor of defendant. Because plaintiff's action is barred under the primary assumption of risk doctrine, comparative fault principles do not come into play.

The judgment of the Court of Appeal, upholding the summary judgment entered by the trial court, is affirmed.

ASSIGNMENT 17.7

a. What specific facts could Kendra have alleged about the touch football game that would have led the court to reach a different conclusion?

b. Ted and George are playing golf. Is Ted liable for negligence in any of the following situations? In your answer, include an analysis of assumption of the risk.
   (i) Ted is carelessly taking practice swings with his golf club while waiting to tee off. George says, "Watch out with that swing. You almost hit me." Laughing, Ted keeps swinging and accidently hits George in the head with the club.
   (ii) Ted and George have an argument over whether one of George's shots was over the foul line. In anger, Ted gets in the electric golf cart and drives away. Accidently, however, he drives the cart over George's foot.
   (iii) The golf course is next to a steep cliff. For fun, Ted and George decide to race the golf cart along the edge of the cliff. Ted is driving. The cart accidently goes over the cliff, injuring George.

c. The *Knight* court also ruled that Michael did not commit assault on Kendra. What facts could she have alleged to support her assault claim? (See Chapter 6 on assault.)

d. The *Knight* court also ruled that Michael did not commit battery on Kendra. What facts could she have alleged to support her battery claim? (See Chapter 5 on battery.)

CHECK THE CITE

Helene Smollett was injured in a skating rink accident. She fell when trying to avoid hitting a child on the ice. In her negligence suit against the rink, why did the court conclude that she had assumed the risk of her injury? Read the case of *Smollett v. Skayting Development Corp.*, 793 F.2d 547 (3d Cir. 1986). To read the opinion online: (1) Run a Google search for the names of the parties ("Smollett v. Skayting"). (2) Check cases.justia.com/us-court-of-appeals/F2/793/547/119290. (3) Run a citation search ("793 F.2d 547") or a party search (Smollett Skayting) in the Legal Opinions and Journals database of Google Scholar (scholar.google.com).

PROJECT

In Google, Bing, or another general search engine, run the following search: *aa* "contributory negligence" "comparative negligence" (substitute the name of your state for *aa* in the search, e.g., Texas "contributory negligence" "comparative negligence"). Does your state use contributory negligence or comparative negligence? If the latter, is it pure or modified? Describe how it operates.

ETHICS IN A TORTS PRACTICE

You are a paralegal working in the law office of Lexington & Lexington, which is representing Bill Nabors in a negligence action against someone who rear-ended Bill as Bill was slowing down at an intersection. While you are conducting a follow-up interview, Bill tells you that he had been drinking heavily an hour before the accident. Fearing that this fact could have negative consequences on damages and on defenses that might be raised against Bill, you omit this fact from your notes of the interview and decide to tell no one about it. What ethical problems, if any, might exist?

SUMMARY

Under the defense of contributory negligence, the plaintiff's unreasonableness in failing to take reasonable precautions for his or her own safety is a complete bar to recovery of damages if it was a substantial factor in causing the injury. If, however, the defendant was reckless or grossly negligent, the contributory negligence of the plaintiff does not bar recovery. Plaintiff's contributory negligence is determined by the same formula used to determine the defendant's negligence: the foreseeability of the accident and of the kind of injury or other loss that could result is weighed against the importance or social value of what plaintiff was doing at the time and the burden or inconvenience of taking precautions to avoid the accident. Under comparative negligence, damages are allocated according to the relative fault of the parties. Contributory negligence is no longer a complete defense. Just as negligence can be imputed, there can also be imputed contributory negligence.

Under the last clear chance doctrine, plaintiffs who have been contributorily negligent in placing themselves in peril can still recover if a negligent defendant had the last opportunity (clear chance) to avoid the accident and failed to exercise reasonable care to do so. If the defendant discovers the plaintiff in helpless peril and fails to take reasonable steps to avoid the accident, the plaintiff's contributory negligence is not a bar. The same is true if the defendant discovers the plaintiff in inattentive peril. A state that has adopted comparative negligence does not need the doctrine of last clear chance. Since contributory negligence is no longer a complete bar, there is no longer a need for a defense that offsets the all-or-nothing impact of contributory negligence.

Comparative negligence apportions the damages between the plaintiff and the defendant based on the extent to which each acted unreasonably. In a state that has adopted pure comparative negligence, the plaintiff's recovery is limited to the percentage of the harm that was due to the defendant's negligence. In a state that has adopted modified or restricted comparative negligence, there may be no recovery unless the plaintiff's negligence meets a designated standard, such as being "slight" as opposed to the "gross" negligence of the defendant. States apply different standards that trigger the allocation.

The plaintiff recovers nothing if he or she knowingly and voluntarily accepted (i.e., assumed) the risk of being injured by the negligence of the defendant. There must be actual knowledge of the risk (a subjective standard). Parties are free to enter exculpatory agreements that limit their liability with each other, unless such agreements are against public policy. In an express assumption of the risk, the plaintiff knowingly and voluntarily accepts a risk by express agreement. In an implied assumption of the risk, the plaintiff knowingly and voluntarily accepts a risk by reason of his or her conduct that signifies acceptance in the absence of an express agreement. Under comparative negligence, the parties can still agree to an express assumption of the risk. For implied assumption of the risk, a further distinction is made. In primary assumption of the risk, the plaintiff knowingly and voluntarily accepts a particular risk that the defendant did not have a duty to protect the plaintiff against. Plaintiff recovers nothing. In secondary assumption of the risk, the plaintiff knowingly and voluntarily accepts a particular risk that the defendant had a duty to protect the plaintiff against. Damages are allocated between the plaintiff and the defendant according to the applicable comparative-negligence rule in the state.

KEY TERMS

defense *308*
comparative negligence *308*
contributory negligence *308*
last clear chance *308*
assumption of the risk *308*
ordinary negligence *309*
reckless *309*
gross negligence *309*
preponderance of the evidence *309*
affirmative defense *309*
actual cause *311*
imputed negligence *311*
imputed contributory negligence *312*
helpless peril *312*
inattentive peril *312*
express assumption of the risk *316*
implied assumption of the risk *316*
exculpatory clause *316*
release *316*
public policy *317*
adhesion contract *317*
coercion *317*
primary assumption of the risk *321*
secondary assumption of the risk *321*

REVIEW QUESTIONS

1. What is a defense?
2. Distinguish between contributory negligence and comparative negligence.
3. What is the impact of comparative negligence on contributory negligence?
4. What is last clear chance?
5. What is the impact of comparative negligence on last clear chance?
6. What is an assumption of the risk?
7. What are the two main elements of contributory negligence?
8. Why is contributory negligence an affirmative defense?
9. How is the negligence of the plaintiff determined when the defense of contributory negligence is raised?
10. What categories of negligence by the defendant will not bar recovery even if the plaintiff was contributorily negligent?
11. When will contributory negligence be imputed?
12. When is a plaintiff in helpless peril, and what impact does it have on the contributory negligence of the plaintiff?
13. When is a plaintiff in inattentive peril, and what impact does it have on the contributory negligence of the plaintiff?
14. Distinguish between pure and modified comparative negligence.
15. Distinguish between express and implied assumption of the risk.
16. Distinguish between primary and secondary assumption of the risk.
17. What is an exculpatory clause?
18. What is an adhesion contract?
19. When is an exculpatory clause against public policy?

HELPFUL WEBSITES

- **Contributory Negligence and Comparative Negligence**

  www.mwl-law.com/PracticeAreas/Contributory-Neglegence.asp

  www.the-injury-lawyer-directory.com/negligence.html

  www.thelockeinstitute.org/journals/tortliability9.html

  lawdigest.uslegal.com/civil-laws/negligence/7124

  www.injuryboard.com/topic/tort-components-affirmative.aspx

  en.wikipedia.org/wiki/Comparative_negligence

- **Assumption of the Risk**

  www.google.com (search terms: burning man assumption of the risk)

  en.wikipedia.org/wiki/Assumption_of_risk

ENDNOTES

1. Dan Dobs, *The Law of Torts* 495 (West 2000).
2. *Nash v. The Port Authority of New York and New Jersey*, 51 A.D.3d 337, 856 N.Y.S.2d 583 (N.Y. App. Div. 2008). Anemona Hartocollis, "Port Authority Held Liable in 1993 Trade Center Bombing" *The New York Times*, April 30, 2008, at A20; en.wikipedia.org/wiki/1993_World_Trade_Center_bombing.
3. McKinney's *Civil Practice Laws and Rules* § 1601 (2009).

Student StudyWARE™ CD-ROM
For additional materials, please go to the student CD in this book.

CHAPTER

18

MEDICAL MALPRACTICE AND LEGAL MALPRACTICE

CHAPTER OUTLINE

- Introduction
- Medical Malpractice
- Legal Malpractice
- Liability of Paralegals

CHAPTER OBJECTIVES

After completing this chapter, you should be able to:

- Understand the meaning of medical malpractice.
- Distinguish between negligence and warranty.
- Distinguish between a national and a state standard of medical malpractice.
- Distinguish between the reasonable patient and the reasonable doctor standards of informed consent.
- State the major reforms proposed in the area of medical malpractice.
- Identify the major categories of questions that should be asked in discovery and other investigation when litigating a medical malpractice case.
- Understand the meaning of legal malpractice.
- Explain what is meant by a trial within a trial.
- Identify the potential tort liability of paralegals.

INTRODUCTION

In this chapter we examine the professional liability of doctors and lawyers, primarily for the tort of negligence. Other kinds of professional liability can also exist. For example, liability can be based on a breach of **fiduciary relationship**. This relationship calls for a duty of loyalty, candor, and fair treatment by doctors to their patients and by attorneys to their clients. The violation of this duty can lead to sanctions by the governing body of the profession (the medical board for doctors; the bar association and courts for attorneys). As we will see in Chapter 26, some violations of a fiduciary relationship can lead to liability for the tort of misrepresentation. Although there can be overlap in these various categories of liability, our primary focus in this chapter will be negligence—the violation of a duty of reasonable care required of doctors and attorneys. We will also cover the liability of paralegals.

fiduciary relationship The relationship that exists when one party (called the fiduciary) owes another loyalty, candor, and fair treatment. The fiduciary is required to act in the interest and for the benefit of the other. Also called a confidential relationship.

For information on the medical malpractice laws of your state, see Appendixes A and C.

MEDICAL MALPRACTICE

Malpractice is a general term that means professional misconduct or wrongdoing consisting of ethical violations, criminal conduct, and torts such as negligence and battery. More specifically, **medical malpractice** is a category of negligence consisting of the failure of a doctor to exercise the skills commonly applied by doctors in the same field under the same circumstances. A reasonable doctor is one who applies such skills.

malpractice Professional misconduct or wrongdoing consisting of ethical violations, criminal conduct, and torts such as negligence and battery.

medical malpractice The failure of a doctor to exercise the skills commonly applied by doctors in the same field under the same circumstances.

Medical malpractice is a major focus of many personal injury law practices. A crusading attorney in such an office would say that there are many medical malpractice claims because there are many victims of medical incompetence. A cynic, on the other hand, would say the main reason medical malpractice is a large part of the practice of many attorneys is simply that doctors and hospitals are deep pockets. A **deep pocket** is a defendant who has resources (i.e., personal wealth and liability insurance) with which to pay large damage awards.

deep pocket 1. An individual, business, or other organization with resources to pay a potential judgment. 2. Sufficient assets for this purpose. The opposite of *shallow pocket*.

It would be an understatement to say that many doctors do not appreciate the role of attorneys in our society. Recently, a Connecticut paralegal claimed that

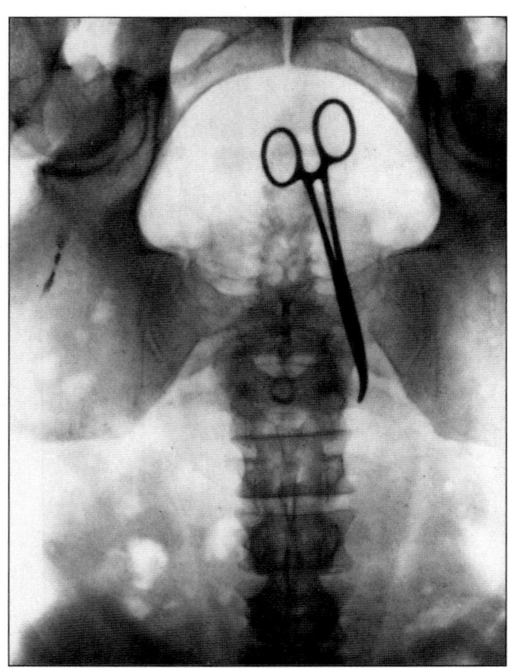

Example of a medical error.

X-ray of a retained clamp that the surgical team forgot to remove.

Source: The Turkewitz Law Firm (www.TurkewitzLaw.com).

she was denied treatment when the doctor's office found out that she worked for Koskoff, Koskoff & Bieder (www.koskoff.com), a prominent law firm that often sued doctors. She said that a "neurosurgeon told her he would have to think about treating her after she told him where she worked."[1] Several years ago a delegate of the American Medical Association proposed a resolution that would make it ethical to refuse to treat plaintiff attorneys except in emergencies! After heated debate, the proposal was soundly defeated, but the fact that the proposal was given serious discussion is telling.

The statistics on medical errors are daunting:

- A study by the Institute of Medicine concluded that preventable medical errors cause up to 98,000 deaths per year in our hospitals.[2]
- A report by the Commonwealth Fund estimated that 22.8 million people have experienced a major medical error, either personally or through at least one family member, at an annual cost of $17 billion to $29 billion.[3]
- According to the United States Agency for Healthcare Research and Quality (AHRQ), medical errors are the eighth leading cause of death in the country, more prevalent than cancer.[4]

See Exhibit 18–1 for the results of some of the litigation growing out of medical errors.

Exhibit 18–1
Medical malpractice damage award trends.

Source: Current Award Trends in Personal Injury—48th Edition, copyright 2009 by LRP Publications, P.O. Box 24668, West Palm Beach, FL 33416-4668. All rights reserved. For more information on this or other products published by LRP Publications, call 1-800-341-7874 or visit the website at www.shoplrp.com/jvr.html.

Year	Award Median	Award Range	Award Mean
2001	$712,838	$1 – $131,700,000	$2,969,737
2002	975,000	1,250 – 94,812,240	4,425,635
2003	900,000	5,000 – 118,000,000	3,537,156
2004	890,230	5,000 – 111,700,000	3,915,260
2005	1,031,300	3,620 – 212,580,000	3,446,875
2006	1,300,000	2,250 – 62,716,000	4,031,049
2007	1,000,000	2,074 – 57,632,113	4,043,416
Overall	944,879	1 – 212,580,000	3,710,561

The *median* is the middle value among awards listed in ascending order. This value provides the most accurate gauge of the norm for a specific sampling of jury award data. The statistic is also commonly referred to as the midpoint. The award *mean* is obtained by determining the sum of all the awards and dividing by the total number of awards in the sample. The median award for medical negligence in childbirth cases ($2,834,413) was the highest for all types of medical malpractice cases analyzed. The median awards for other types of malpractice were diagnosis cases, $1,250,569; medication cases, $1,250,000; patient relations cases, $971,500; nonsurgical treatment cases, $750,000; and surgical negligence cases, $582,098.

Not everyone agrees on how well our legal system responds to these statistics. An editorial in the *New York Times* cited an authoritative study of thousands of patients which "found that the vast majority who were harmed by medical errors or negligence never filed suit, whereas the vast majority of those who did file suit were not actually harmed by negligent doctors." Some studies conclude that courts do a reasonably good job of sorting out who deserves compensation, "while other research has found that juries are swayed more by the severity of a plaintiff's injuries than by evidence of negligence."[5]

liability insurance Insurance in which the insurer agrees to pay, on behalf of an insured, damages that the latter is obligated to pay to a third party because of his or her legal liability to the third person for committing a tort or other wrong.

One way to gauge the impact of litigation against doctors is the cost of **liability insurance** that doctors must pay. Most premiums are high, although there is considerable fluctuation around the country. Here are some recent figures:[6]

Annual Premiums for Medical Liability Insurance (2009)

Ob-gyns
$210,808: Miami, Florida
$194,935: Nassau County, New York
$ 20,626: Minnesota

General Surgeons
$191,422: Miami, Florida
$106,583: Nassau County, New York
$ 11,306: Minnesota

Internists
$57,859: Miami, Florida
$33,360: Nassau County, New York
$ 3,375: Minnesota

Physician-Patient Relationship

A physician-patient relationship arises when a doctor undertakes to render medical services in response to an express or implied request for services by the patient or by the patient's guardian. A doctor is not required to accept every patient. Once the physician-patient relationship exists, however, the doctor cannot withdraw at will. He or she must give reasonable notice of withdrawal so that the patient has an opportunity to find alternative treatment. On the other hand, the patient can end the relationship at any time by firing the doctor for any reason, but will remain responsible for the agreed-upon fee up to the time of termination.

Warranty

warranty A guarantee; a commitment imposed by contract or by law that a product or service will meet a specified standard.

Normally a doctor does not warrant or promise a particular cure or other result. If such a **warranty** or promise is given, the patient has a breach-of-warranty or breach-of-contract action against the doctor if the result or cure is not produced. Although doctors are understandably reluctant to give express guarantees, they sometimes use language with their patients that a court will interpret as a guarantee. Suppose, for example, that a doctor makes the following statements to a patient about an operation:

> "The operation will take care of all your troubles."
>
> "You'll be able to return to work in approximately three or four weeks at the most."

Such language could be interpreted as a promise to cure. If the patient is not cured, a breach-of-contract action may be successful against the doctor *even if the doctor was not negligent in performing the operation.*

A mere opinion by a doctor on the probable results of treatment (e.g., "there's a 50-50 chance the operation will stop the pain") is not a promise. It is sometimes very difficult, however, to distinguish between a prediction of probabilities and a promise.

strict liability Responsibility for harm even if one did not intend the harm and used reasonable care to try to prevent it. Responsibility for harm whether or not the person causing the harm was at any fault or engaged in any moral impropriety. Also called *absolute liability* and *liability without fault.*

negligence The failure to use reasonable care that an ordinary prudent person would have used in a similar situation, resulting in injury or other loss.

Negligence

Doctors are not liable for every mistake they make that causes injury. There is no **strict liability**, or liability without fault, for the services of doctors, attorneys, or other professionals. Plaintiffs must show that their injury was wrongfully caused.

The main category of wrongful conduct in this area is **negligence**, which is the failure to use reasonable care that an ordinary prudent person would have used in a similar situation, resulting in injury or other loss (see Chapters 12 and 14). Negligence by a doctor, like all negligence, is governed by state law, which can differ from state to state. Because doctors have specialized skill and knowledge, they are measured by what a reasonable doctor with that specialized skill and knowledge would have done. Simply stated, the standard is as follows:

> In diagnosing medical problems and selecting methods of treatment, a doctor must use the skill and learning commonly possessed by members of the profession in good standing.[7]

There is considerable controversy, however, as to whether this standard is to be gauged from a national or from a local perspective:

> *national*: Under this standard, a doctor is required to have and use the knowledge and skill that qualified doctors commonly have and use nationally.
>
> *same or similar community*: Under this standard, a doctor is required to have and use the knowledge and skill that qualified doctors commonly have and use in the same or in a similar community where the defendant–doctor practices. This standard is called the **locality rule**.

locality rule In a medical malpractice action, the applicable standard is that doctors must have and use the knowledge and skill that qualified doctors commonly have and use in the same or in a similar community.

custom What is commonly done. Also called *custom and usage*.

conspiracy of silence The reluctance or refusal of one member of a group to testify against another member.

In assessing reasonable care, one of the considerations of the court will be how other doctors commonly practice. What is the **custom** of sound medical practice for diagnosing and treating a particular ailment? Many states answer this question by applying the standard of what is commonly done (the custom) in the same or similar community. The trend, however, is for states to apply a national standard.

A major argument in favor of a national standard is that it will help overcome the **conspiracy of silence**, which is the reluctance or refusal of one member of a group to testify against another member. In small communities where most doctors know each other and refer business to each other, an injured patient may find it difficult, if not impossible, to find a doctor willing to testify against another doctor. A national standard, on the other hand, would allow doctors from outside the community to testify. They arguably would be more willing to do so since they would not have the close personal and professional ties that doctors in the same small community have. Another argument in favor of a national standard is the fact that medical training for all doctors has become more standardized at a high level of skill. Furthermore, doctors everywhere are close to having equal access to the most current medical science through the Internet and other online resources. All doctors may not have access to the most sophisticated equipment, but they can be expected to know (or to obtain information about) the state of the art. This should allow them to identify their limitations so that they can make appropriate referrals to other practitioners and facilities.

Regardless of which standard is used, there still may be disagreement over the treatment that should be given in a given case. Different schools of thought may exist. If there is more than one recognized method of diagnosis or treatment, and no one of them is used exclusively and uniformly by all practitioners in good standing, doctors, in the exercise of their best judgment, can select one of the approved methods. Negligence is not established simply because a method turns out to be the wrong selection or because other doctors would have used other methods. Again, the test is reasonableness. If more than one approach is reasonable, doctors will not be liable if they make a mistake as long as diligence and good judgment were otherwise used in the method selected and applied.

Informed Consent

informed consent Agreement to let something happen based on having a reasonable understanding of the benefits and risks involved.

Medical treatment requires the **informed consent** of patients. This is the agreement to let something happen based on having a reasonable understanding of the benefits and risks involved. Consent problems can arise in three categories of cases: a doctor performs an unwanted procedure, performs a requested procedure on the wrong part of the body, or fails to provide adequate information on the risks of a

medical battery An unwanted procedure performed by a health care practioner or a requested procedure performed on the wrong part of the body.

particular procedure. The first two categories constitute **medical battery**. In some states, the third category, failing to obtain informed consent, also constitutes battery, although most states classify it as negligence. See Exhibit 18–2 for the elements of informed consent. The problem of consent is serious. A study conducted by doctors reached the startling conclusion that only one of ten patient decisions are based on informed consent. Patients were simply not told enough. In effect, something was missing from the doctor-patient discussions 90 percent of the time![8]

Exhibit 18–2
Elements of informed consent.

1. Medical condition. The patient must understand his or her medical condition.
2. Treatment options. The treatment options for the condition must be explained.
3. Risks of treatment. The risks of each option must be explained, e.g., side effects or pain.
4. Risks of nontreatment. The risks of doing nothing must be explained.
5. Benefits. The benefits of each option must be explained.
6. Choice. The patient must then decide which option, if any, to pursue.

How much information on the benefits and risks of a proposed treatment must a doctor provide to a patient? To tell the patient everything might take hours of explanation and reams of printed information. States differ on what a patient must be told in order for his or her consent to be informed. Here are the two most commonly used tests:

reasonable patient standard: A doctor must disclose information on the risks and benefits of a proposed treatment that a reasonable patient with the plaintiff's condition would wish to know. In a state that adopts this standard, no expert witnesses would be needed on this issue since jurors are capable of concluding what a reasonable patient would want to know.

reasonable doctor standard: A doctor must follow the standards of the profession as to how much information on the risks and benefits of a proposed treatment would be disclosed to a patient with the plaintiff's condition. In a state that adopts this standard, expert witnesses would be needed to help the jury decide the standard practice of disclosure by doctors.

It is possible for a state that uses the reasonable patient standard to reach a different result from a state that uses the reasonable doctor standard on the same facts. Assume that a reasonable doctor decides to withhold information that a reasonable patient would have wanted to know. When this occurs, the patient would lose in a state that had adopted the reasonable doctor standard, whereas the patient would win in a state that uses the reasonable patient standard.[9]

Consent forms are often used by doctors and hospitals as a way of providing information and avoiding liability. At times, however, these forms are inadequate. Assume, for example, that a woman is in a hospital and consents to a simple appendectomy. The surgeon, however, performs a total hysterectomy as a precautionary measure, because the surgeon feels that it would be a sound medical procedure even though no emergency existed. Before the operation, the woman signed the following statement:

> "I hereby authorize the physician in charge to administer such treatment as found necessary to perform this operation which is advisable in the treatment of this patient."

A court would probably find this consent form to be invalid. It is too ambiguous. It does not designate the nature of the operation and therefore does not state what is being consented to. It is close to a blanket authorization to do whatever the doctor thinks is wise.

Suppose that the condition of the patient is such that it would be dangerous to inform him or her of all the details of a proposed treatment. Or suppose that the doctor discovers an unanticipated emergency after the patient is under anesthesia

and an incision has been made. How is consent to be handled in these situations? A court will examine all of the circumstances in order to determine whether it was reasonable for the doctor *not* to obtain consent or even to ask for it. The factors to be considered include the seriousness of the patient's condition, the patient's emotional stability, the availability of time, the extent of the emergency, and the practice in the medical community in such cases. A court might conclude that it was reasonable for the doctor to proceed without consent.

Reform

Critics of our medical malpractice laws argue that the system is in crisis. In some areas of the country, doctors have withdrawn from certain high-risk kinds of practice (e.g., delivering babies) because of the frequency of litigation and the high cost of malpractice insurance associated with those areas of practice.

Many blame the legal system for a large part of the skyrocketing cost of health care. Doctors, for example, allegedly order expensive tests solely to make them "look good" in court in the event of a later malpractice suit by a patient. This is known as the practice of **defensive medicine**—the ordering of precautionary tests and procedures intended primarily to shield doctors and other medical personnel from possible lawsuits. Studies have shown that liability premiums and defensive medical measures are a significant part of the cost of every visit to a doctor or medical facility.

defensive medicine Ordering precautionary tests and procedures intended primarily to shield doctors (or others in the medical field) from possible lawsuits rather than to benefit the patient.

Insurance companies are particularly angry about the system of compensating attorneys through the percentage fee. This kind of fee gives attorneys a percentage of any payout their clients obtain through settlement or litigation. The large amount of the percentage (e.g., 30–40 percent) arguably causes attorneys to be excessively aggressive in pursuing litigation for their clients. Attorneys, on the other hand, deny that there is a malpractice insurance crisis, arguing that if there is a problem, it is due primarily to greedy insurance companies and incompetent doctors and hospitals. Furthermore, if injured persons could not pay by percentage fee, many would not be able to use the courts for redress, because they could not afford the alternative of paying hourly fees to an attorney.

The turmoil has led to calls for reform in every state. There is a great diversity in the kinds of reforms that different states have enacted or considered. (For the status of reform in your state, see Appendix C.) Here are some examples of reform proposals:

- Limiting damage awards (**damage caps**). The state would limit the amount of damages that can be awarded in a medical malpractice lawsuit. Typically, a state might limit the amount of a plaintiff's non-economic damages, such as pain and suffering, to between $250,000 and $500,000. A similar limitation might be placed on the amount of **punitive damages** that can be awarded.
- Limiting attorney fees (**fee caps**). A state might limit the percentage of the recovery a plaintiff's attorney can receive as a fee.
- Abolishing or substantially limiting the **collateral source rule**. This rule provides that the amount of damages caused by the tortfeasor may not be reduced by any injury-related funds received by the plaintiff from sources independent of the tortfeasor (see Chapter 16). An example would be payments an injured plaintiff pedestrian receives from a medical insurance policy provided by an employer. Under the rule, a tortfeasor cannot seek the reduction of damages by amounts received from collateral sources. Juries are not even allowed to be told that collateral sources exist. There are some states, however, that have changed this rule and permit amounts received from some collateral sources to be deducted from (offset by) the total damages caused by the tortfeasor.
- Abolishing **joint and several liability**, which makes any single codefendant liable for entire judgment. Instead of joint and several liability, all defendants would have to pay damages in proportion to their degree of responsibility.

damage caps Limitations on the amount of damages that can be awarded in designated categories of cases.

punitive damages Damages that are added to actual or compensatory damages in order to punish malicious, outrageous, or reckless conduct and to deter similar conduct in the future. Also called *exemplary damages*, *smart money*, and *vindictive damages*.

fee caps Limitations on the fees that attorneys can be paid in designated categories of cases.

collateral source rule The amount of damages caused by the tortfeasor shall not be reduced by any injury-related funds received by the plaintiff from sources independent of the tortfeasor, such as a health insurance policy of the plaintiff.

joint and several liability Legally responsible together and individually. Each wrongdoer is individually responsible for the entire judgment; the plaintiff can choose to collect from one wrongdoer or from all of them until the judgment is satisfied.

statute of limitations A law that designates a time period within which a lawsuit must be filed or it can never be brought.

tolled Stopped or suspended the running of a time period within which something must be done.

alternative dispute resolution (ADR) A method or procedure for resolving a legal dispute without litigating it in a court or administrative agency.

screening panel A group of individuals who will examine a case before it can be litigated in court. The panel can often make recommendations and encourage the parties to settle.

mediation A method of alternative dispute resolution (ADR) in which the parties try to avoid litigation by submitting their dispute to a neutral third person (the mediator) who helps the parties resolve their dispute; he or she does not render a decision resolving it for them.

arbitration A method of alternative dispute resolution (ADR) in which the parties try to avoid litigation by submitting their dispute to a neutral third person (the arbitrator) who renders a decision resolving the dispute.

certificate of merit A document filed by a plaintiff with the complaint certifying that the attorney has consulted with a qualifying expert who has advised the attorney that the claim raised in the complaint has merit. Called an *affidavit of merit* if the document must be signed under oath.

National Practitioner Data Bank A collection of information such as malpractice judgments and sanctions against physicians, dentists, and other health care practitioners.

English rule The losing side in litigation must pay the winner's attorney fees and costs.

American rule The winning party cannot recover attorney fees and costs of litigation from the losing party unless (a) a statute authorizes such payment, (b) a contract between the parties provides for such payment, or (c) the court finds that the losing party acted in bad faith in the litigation.

- Requiring cooling-off periods. To encourage negotiation and settlement between the parties, some states enforce a cooling-off period (e.g., ninety days) during which litigation cannot begin. A malpractice claimant must give the doctor or hospital a formal notice of intent to file a suit. During the cooling-off period, the **statute of limitations** does not run—it is **tolled**—so that the plaintiff is not placed at a disadvantage by waiting to file. The statute of limitations is a law that designates a time period within which a lawsuit must be filed or it can never be brought.
- Requiring **alternative dispute resolution (ADR)**. A state may require the parties to attempt to resolve their dispute by using alternative dispute resolution before being allowed to litigate in court. ADR can take a number of formats. The state might have a system of screening panels. A **screening panel** tries to weed out frivolous cases before they are brought to court for trial. A panel could consist of a group of neutral attorneys and physicians who examine the evidence, consult with medical experts, and comment on whether the patient was a victim of negligence. The panel may encourage settlement or dismissal of the claim. More traditional forms of ADR include mediation and arbitration. In **mediation**, parties bring their dispute before a neutral third party—the mediator—who hears the arguments from both sides and encourages the parties to resolve the matter on their own. The mediator does not render a decision. In **arbitration**, on the other hand, the parties bring their dispute before a neutral third party—the arbitrator—who hears the arguments from both sides and renders a decision.
- Requiring a certificate of merit. A number of states require the plaintiff's attorney to file a **certificate of merit** with the complaint. The certificate states that the attorney has consulted with an expert who has concluded that the medical malpractice claim has merit.
- Providing more information about doctors. To keep track of (and to help weed out) incompetent or unprofessional physicians, dentists, and other health care practitioners, particularly those who move from one state to another, a **National Practitioner Data Bank** was created.[10] (www.npdb-hipdb.hrsa.gov). This is a federal data center that collects information on malpractice judgments, arbitration awards, disciplinary actions by medical boards, and loss of clinical privileges in hospitals. The information, however, is not available to the general public. Insurance companies and hospitals can review the information. Hospitals are required to check the information in the Data Bank whenever a doctor seeks appointment or reappointment to its medical staff.
- Adopting the **English rule.** To discourage the filing of frivolous malpractice lawsuits, some have proposed adopting the English rule under which the party who loses the trial must pay both parties' attorney fees and other legal expenses. With some exceptions, most of our courts follow the **American rule** under which each side pays its own legal expenses unless special exceptions apply.
- Adopting "sorry works" laws. Some studies indicate that if doctors apologized for medical errors, litigation would be substantially reduced. Yet many doctors are reluctant to apologize for fear that their apology would be used against them as an admission of guilt in subsequent litigation. A few states have passed "sorry works" laws that allow doctors and health care providers to apologize and offer expressions of grief without their words being used against them in court (www.sorryworks.net). For example, in Oregon, "For the purposes of any civil action against a person licensed by the Oregon Medical Board, any expression of regret or apology made by or on behalf of the person, including an expression of regret or apology that is made in writing, orally or by conduct, does not constitute an admission of liability for any purpose."[11]
- Restricting Medicare reimbursements. Medicare is a federally administered system of health insurance for persons aged 65 and over. To encourage reform, Medicare announced in 2008 that it would no longer pay hospitals for the added cost of treating patients for "reasonably preventable" conditions that

occur while the elderly are in the care of the hospital. The conditions include second operations to retrieve sponges left inside a patient's body after the first operation, incompatible blood transfusions, and urinary tract infections caused by catheters.

- Relying more on evidence-based medicine (EBM). EBM is "the conscientious, explicit and judicious use of current best evidence in making decisions about the care of the individual patient. It means integrating individual clinical expertise with the best available external clinical evidence from systematic research."[12] Currently many doctors rely on studies on the effectiveness of particular treatments, but this reliance is sometimes hit or miss. Despite the availability of Internet resources, the studies can be time-consuming to locate and assess. Instead of delving into the literature, doctors may rely on instinct and the advice of colleagues. Too often they have treatment questions that they do not take the time to answer. Unfortunately, there is no systematic collection and ranking of what does and does not work to which all doctors can refer. A system of EBM is designed to correct this problem. EBM, for example, could categorize different types of clinical evidence and rank them "according to the strength of their freedom from the various biases that beset medical research."[13] Proponents argue that EBM would create greater uniformity and standardization of best practices. Many doctors, however, fear that EBM would interfere with individualized treatment and be another weapon used by plaintiff attorneys in cataloging what the doctor failed to do. One critic referred to EBM as "microfascism."[14]
- Considering **enterprise liability**. One of the most radical proposals is called enterprise liability. It would allow injured patients to sue either the hospital where they were treated or the health plans to which doctors and other providers subscribe. Individual doctors would no longer be subject to malpractice lawsuits. One variation on this proposal would permit courts to hold health plans strictly liable for all medical injuries suffered by their beneficiaries, regardless of whether the injury was a result of negligent care. The more traditional enterprise liability proposal, however, would require a determination of negligence before a hospital's managed care organization would be held liable for a patient's injury. To date, however, enterprise liability has not been enacted into law.[15]

enterprise liability A system of spreading the costs of injuries over an entire industry or enterprise.

The turmoil—along with proposals for further change and reform—continues today.

CASE

Fein v. Permanente Medical Group

38 Cal. 3d 137, 211 Cal. Rptr. 368, 695 P.2d 665 (1985)
Supreme Court of California

Background: *A nurse practitioner and a doctor told the plaintiff that his chest pains were muscle spasms. Valium and other drugs were prescribed. In fact, the plaintiff was suffering a heart attack. In a medical malpractice action, he alleged negligence in the diagnosis. He was successful in the trial court. The case is now before the Supreme Court of California on appeal.*

Decision on Appeal: *Judgment affirmed.*

OPINION OF COURT

Justice KAUS delivered the opinion of the court . . .

On Saturday, February 21, 1976, plaintiff Lawrence Fein, a 34-year-old attorney employed by the Legislative Counsel Bureau of the California State Legislature in Sacramento, felt a brief pain in his chest as he was riding his bicycle to work. The pain lasted a minute or two. He noticed a similar brief pain the following day while he was jogging, and then, three days later, experienced another episode while walking after lunch. When the chest pain returned again while he was working at his office that evening, he became concerned for his health and, the following morning, called the office of his regular physician, Dr. Arlene Brandwein, who was employed by defendant Permanente Medical Group, an affiliate of the Kaiser Health Foundation (Kaiser).

Dr. Brandwein had no open appointment available that day, and her receptionist advised plaintiff to call Kaiser's central appointment desk for a "short appointment." He did so and was given an appointment for 4 P.M. that afternoon, Thursday, February 26. Plaintiff testified that he did not feel that the problem was so severe as to require immediate treatment at Kaiser Hospital's emergency room, and that he worked until the time for his scheduled appointment.

When he appeared for his appointment, plaintiff was examined by a nurse practitioner, Cheryl Welch, who was working under the supervision of a physician-consultant, Dr. Wintrop Frantz; plaintiff was aware that Nurse Welch was a nurse practitioner and he did not ask to see a doctor. After examining plaintiff and taking a history, Nurse Welch left the room to consult with Dr. Frantz. When she returned, she advised plaintiff that she and Dr. Frantz believed his pain was due to muscle spasm and that the doctor had given him a prescription for Valium. Plaintiff went home, took the Valium, and went to sleep.

That night, about 1 A.M., plaintiff awoke with severe chest pains. His wife drove him to the Kaiser emergency room where he was examined by Dr. Lowell Redding about 1:30 A.M. Following an examination that the doctor felt showed no signs of a heart problem, Dr. Redding ordered a chest X-ray. On the basis of his examination and the X-ray results, Dr. Redding also concluded that plaintiff was experiencing muscle spasms and gave him an injection of Demerol and a prescription for a codeine medication.

Plaintiff went home but continued to experience intermittent chest pain. About noon that same day, the pain became more severe and constant and plaintiff returned to the Kaiser emergency room where he was seen by another physician, Dr. Donald Oliver. From his initial examination of plaintiff, Dr. Oliver also believed that plaintiff's problem was of muscular origin, but, after administering some pain medication, he directed that an electrocardiogram (EKG) be performed. The EKG showed that plaintiff was suffering from a heart attack (acute myocardial infarction). Plaintiff was then transferred to the cardiac care unit.

Following a period of hospitalization and medical treatment without surgery, plaintiff returned to his job on a part-time basis in October 1976, and resumed full-time work in September 1977. By the time of trial, he had been permitted to return to virtually all of his prior recreational activities—e.g., jogging, swimming, bicycling and skiing.

In February 1977, plaintiff filed the present action, alleging that his heart condition should have been diagnosed earlier and that treatment should have been given either to prevent the heart attack or, at least, to lessen its residual effects. The case went to judgment only against Permanente.

At trial, Dr. Harold Swan, the head of cardiology at the Cedars-Sinai Medical Center in Los Angeles, was the principal witness for plaintiff. Dr. Swan testified that an important signal that a heart attack may be imminent is chest pain which can radiate to other parts of the body. Such pain is not relieved by rest or pain medication. He stated that if the condition is properly diagnosed, a patient can be given Inderal to stabilize his condition, and that continued medication or surgery may relieve the condition.

Dr. Swan further testified that in his opinion any patient who appears with chest pains should be given an EKG to rule out the worst possibility, a heart problem. He stated that the symptoms that plaintiff had described to Nurse Welch at the 4 P.M. examination on Thursday, February 26, should have indicated to her that an EKG was in order. He also stated that when plaintiff returned to Kaiser late that same night with his chest pain unrelieved by the medication he had been given, Dr. Redding should also have ordered an EKG. According to Dr. Swan, if an EKG had been ordered at those times it could have revealed plaintiff's imminent heart attack, and treatment could have been administered which might have prevented or minimized the attack.

Dr. Swan also testified to the damage caused by the attack. He stated that as a result of the attack a large portion of plaintiff's heart muscle had died, reducing plaintiff's future life expectancy by about one-half, to about 16 or 17 years. Although Dr. Swan acknowledged that some of plaintiff's other coronary arteries also suffer from disease, he felt that if plaintiff had been properly treated his future life expectancy would be decreased by only 10 to 15 percent, rather than half.

Nurse Welch and Dr. Redding testified on behalf of the defense, indicating that the symptoms that plaintiff had reported to them at the time of the examinations were not the same symptoms he had described at trial. Defendant also introduced a number of expert witnesses—not employed by Kaiser—who stated that on the basis of the symptoms reported and observed before the heart attack, the medical personnel could not reasonably have determined that a heart attack was imminent. Additional defense evidence indicated (1) that an EKG would not have shown that a heart attack was imminent, (2) that because of the severe disease in the coronary arteries which caused plaintiff's heart attack, the attack could not have been prevented even had it been known that it was about to occur, and finally (3) that, given the deterioration in plaintiff's other coronary arteries, the heart attack had not affected plaintiff's life expectancy to the degree suggested by Dr. Swan.

In the face of this sharply conflicting evidence, the jury found in favor of plaintiff on the issue of liability and, pursuant to the trial court's instructions, returned special verdicts itemizing various elements of damages. The jury awarded $24,733 for wages lost by plaintiff to the time of trial, $63,000 for future medical expenses, and $700,000 for wages lost in the future as a result of the reduction in plaintiff's life expectancy. Finally, the jury awarded $500,000 for "noneconomic damages," to compensate for pain, suffering, inconvenience, physical impairment and other intangible damages sustained by plaintiff from the time of the injury until his death. . . .

[One of the issues on appeal is whether the trial judge properly instructed the jury in the duty of care owed by a nurse practitioner. The judge] told the jury that "the standard of care required of a nurse practitioner is that of a physician and surgeon . . . when the nurse practitioner is examining a patient or making a diagnosis."*

*The relevant instruction read in full: "It is the duty of one who undertakes to perform the service of a trained or graduate nurse to have the knowledge and skill ordinarily possessed, and to exercise the care and skill ordinarily used in like cases, by trained and skilled members of the nursing profession practicing their profession in the same or similar locality and under similar circumstances. Failure to fulfill either of these duties is negligence. I instruct you that the standard of care required of a nurse practitioner is that of a physician and surgeon duly licensed to practice medicine in the state of California when the nurse practitioner is examining a patient or making a diagnosis." . . .

We agree with defendant that this instruction is inconsistent with recent legislation setting forth general guidelines for the services that may properly be performed by registered nurses in this state. Section 2725 of the Business and Professions Code . . . explicitly declares a legislative intent "to recognize the existence of overlapping functions between physicians and registered nurses and to permit additional sharing of functions within organized health care systems which provide for collaboration between physicians and registered nurses." Section 2725 also includes, among the functions that properly fall within "the practice of nursing" in California, the "[o]bservation of signs and symptoms of illness, reactions to treatment, general behavior, or general physical condition, and . . . determination of whether such signs, symptoms, reactions, behavior or general appearance exhibit abnormal characteristics. . . ." In light of these provisions, the "examination" or "diagnosis" of a patient cannot in all circumstances be said—as a matter of law—to be a function reserved to physicians, rather than registered nurses or nurse practitioners. Although plaintiff was certainly entitled to have the jury determine (1) whether defendant medical center was negligent in permitting a nurse practitioner to see a patient who exhibited the symptoms of which plaintiff complained and (2) whether Nurse Welch met the standard of care of a reasonably prudent nurse practitioner in conducting the examination and prescribing treatment in conjunction with her supervising physician, the court should not have told the jury that the nurse's conduct in this case must as a matter of law be measured by the standard of care of a physician or surgeon. (See *Fraijo v. Hartland Hospital* (1979) 99 Cal. App. 3d 331, 340–344, *White—New Approaches in Treating Nurses as Professionals* (1977) 30 Vand. Law Review 839, 871–879.)

But while the instruction was erroneous, it is not reasonably probable that the error affected the judgment in this case. As noted, several hours after Nurse Welch examined plaintiff and gave him the Valium that her supervising doctor had prescribed, plaintiff returned to the medical center with similar complaints and was examined by a physician, Dr. Redding. Although there was considerable expert testimony that the failure of the medication to provide relief and the continued chest pain rendered the diagnosis of muscle spasm more questionable, Dr. Redding—like Nurse Welch—failed to order an EKG. Given these facts, the jury could not reasonably have found Nurse Welch negligent under the physician standard of care without also finding Dr. Redding—who had more information and to whom the physician standard of care was properly applicable—similarly negligent. Defendant does not point to any evidence which suggests that the award in this case was affected by whether defendant's liability was grounded solely on the negligence of Dr. Redding, rather than on the negligence of both Dr. Redding and Nurse Welch, and, from our review of the record, we conclude that it is not reasonably probable that the instructional error affected the judgment. Accordingly, the erroneous instruction on the standard of care of a nurse practitioner does not warrant reversal. . . .

ASSIGNMENT 18.1

a. 1. What was the error committed by the trial judge on the standard of care of a nurse practitioner?
   2. Why was it an error?
   3. Why was this error harmless?

b. If an EKG had been administered the first time Lawrence Fein contacted the Permanente hospital system, could the hospital have been accused of practicing defensive medicine?

c. Nurses have a relationship to doctors that is similar to the relationship of paralegals to attorneys. What implications does the *Fein* case have for paralegals?

Interrogatories

Once litigation has commenced, pretrial discovery is used by the parties to learn about each others' cases in order to prepare for trial. One of the major discovery devices is **interrogatories**, which are a series of written questions sent by one party to another. The answers are given in writing under oath.

interrogatories A method of discovery consisting of written questions about a lawsuit submitted by one party to another to help the sender prepare for trial.

Reading interrogatories is an excellent way to understand the kind of factual detail that parties seek in medical malpractice cases. Exhibit 18–3 contains a set of sample interrogatories that a hospital defendant might send to the plaintiff.[16]

Exhibit 18–3 Sample medical malpractice interrogatories sent by a defendant hospital to plaintiff(s).

These interrogatories should be answered to provide information regarding each person claiming damages in this action and also regarding the decedent if a wrongful death action.

I. GENERAL INFORMATION AND BACKGROUND

1. A. State your full name, address, and date of birth.
   B. State any and all other names which you have ever used or by which you have been known.
2. A. Which of the following is your present marital status: single, married, separated, widowed, or divorced?
   B. State the name and last known address of your spouse and every former spouse.
   C. State the date of each such marriage.
   D. As to previous marriages, please give the date, place, and manner of each termination.
   E. State the name, age, and address of each of your children.
3. Have you ever been a party to a civil lawsuit? _____. If so, state:
   A. Were you plaintiff or defendant?
   B. What was the nature of the plaintiff's claim?
   C. When, where, and in what court was the action commenced?
   D. The names of all parties other than yourself.
4. Have you ever been convicted of a felony? _____. If so, state:
   A. What was the original charge made against you?
   B. What was the charge of which you were convicted?
   C. Did you plead guilty to the charge, or were you convicted after trial?
   D. What was the name and address of the court where the proceedings took place?
   E. Date of conviction or date plea entered.

II. EDUCATION, EMPLOYMENT, ACTIVITIES, AND IMPAIRMENT

5. State the highest grade of formal schooling completed by you and any certificate or degrees received.
6. List each job or position of employment, including self-employment, held by you on the date of and since the incident in question, stating as to each:
   A. Name and address of employer.
   B. Date of commencement and date of termination.
   C. Nature of employment and duties performed.
   D. Name and address of immediate supervisor.
   E. Rate of pay or compensation received.
   F. The reason for termination.
7. List each job or position of employment, including self-employment, held by you for the five (5) years before the incident in question, stating as to each:
   A. Name and address of employer.
   B. Date of commencement and date of termination.
   C. Place of employment.
   D. Nature of employment and duties performed.
   E. Name and address of immediate supervisor.
   F. Rate of pay or compensation received.
   G. Reason for termination.
8. Do you claim to have lost any time from gainful employment as a result of the incident in question? _____. If so, state:
   A. The specific condition which you claim caused the loss of time.
   B. The amount of time lost.
   C. The rate of pay or compensation regularly received from each such gainful employment.
   D. If you claim damage as a result of the time lost, the total amount and your method of computation.
   E. Whether or not you have in your possession or control any records or other written memoranda which show or purport to show any or all of the amount of your income for the five (5) years preceding the incident complained of to the present time, including a brief description of each such record or memorandum and the person having possession or control of the same or any copy thereof.
9. Do you claim your earning capacity will be impaired as a result of the incident complained of? _____. If so, state:
   A. The manner in which the condition will impair your ability to work.
   B. Name and address of each person who had advised you concerning the impairment.
10. Have you received any special education or training for any type of work? _____. If so, state:
    A. The names and addresses of the training or education institutions attended and the dates of attendance.
    B. The names, addresses, and inclusive dates of employment by employers from whom you received on-the-job training.
11. Do you claim that as a result of the incident complained of you have lost any opportunities for advancement or promotion in your employment? _____. If so, state:
    A. What opportunities would have been available had the incident complained of not occurred.
    B. When would each opportunity have been available.
    C. The amount of monetary damages you allege you have lost as a result of said lost opportunity.

III. INVESTIGATION

12. Have you or your attorney interviewed or spoken with any defendant, or its agents, servants, or employees, about the events in question? _____. If so, state who was present, when and where such conversation took place and the substance of any such conversations including, but not limited to, any statement or admission made by a defendant.
13. Are you aware of the existence of any oral, written, or recorded statement or admission made or claimed to have been made, by any party or witness? _____. If so, state:
    A. The name of each person making the statement or admission.
    B. The date of the statement or admission.
    C. The name, employer, occupation, and last known address of the person or persons taking or hearing the statement or admission.
    D. The name and last known address of the person now in possession of a written or recorded admission.

IV. INJURIES AND DAMAGES

14. Describe in detail all injuries, complaints, and symptoms, whether physical, mental, or emotional, each person claiming damages in this action has experienced since the alleged incident and which is claimed to have been caused, aggravated, or otherwise contributed to by the alleged incident.

15. Do you claim any of your injuries are permanent? _____. If so, state:
    A. What, if any, pains do you contend such injuries will cause in the future?
    B. What do you contend will be the course of such pains?
    C. What, if any, disabilities do you contend such injuries will cause?
    D. What do you contend will be the course of such disabilities?
    E. The name, profession, and specialty, if any, of any medical practitioner who has provided you with any of the information given in answers (A) through (D).

V. PRIOR AND SUBSEQUENT INJURIES/TREATMENT

16. Have you been hospitalized since the occurrence? _____. If so, state:
    A. The person [hospitalized].
    B. The name and location of each hospital in which each was confined.
    C. The dates of each hospitalization.
    D. The conditions treated during each hospitalization.
    E. The nature of the treatment rendered during each hospitalization.
17. Has any health care provider or any person claiming damages in this action criticized defendant's care or treatment given you? _____. If so, for each criticism, state:
    A. A description of it.
    B. The name, address, and qualifications of the person who made the criticism.
    C. The date, time, and place it was made.
18. List each injury, symptom, or complaint for which damages are claimed in this action from which you suffered at any time before the incident complained of.
19. State:
    A. The name and address of each health care provider who examined or treated you for any physical or emotional condition during the past ten years.
    B. The conditions or complaints for which the examination or treatment was performed.
    C. The date of each examination or treatment performed.
    D. Whether or not the symptoms evidencing the conditions described in your answer to paragraph (B) of this interrogatory were completely relieved and, if so, the date of relief.
20. Since the incident complained of, have you suffered any injuries, accidental or otherwise? _____. If so, state:
    A. The date and place.
    B. How the injury was sustained.
    C. A detailed description of each injury received.
    D. The name and address of each medical practitioner rendering treatment.
    E. If any permanent disability was suffered, its nature and extent.
    F. If you were compensated in any manner for any such injury, state the name and address of each person or organization against whom a claim was made or from whom payments were received.
21. Have you ever made any claim against anyone, group, organization, corporation, industrial commission, or any entity for any reason? _____. If so, state:
    A. If the claim was filed as a lawsuit, what was the style of the case?
    B. If the claim was not filed in court, with whom was it filed.
    C. Has the claim been adjudicated or settled as yet?
    D. If the answer to (C) above is in the affirmative, how much money did you receive?
22. Please identify each health care provider who has records pertaining to plaintiff(s) for the period of seven years before the incident giving rise to plaintiff(s)' claims through the present.
    A. With respect to each provider identified above, state whether plaintiff(s) will obtain and produce the records. . . .
    B. With respect to any records plaintiff(s) will not obtain and produce . . . , state the specific reason or reasons for nonproduction.

VI. MATTERS CONCERNING THE CONDUCT OF DEFENDANT(S)

23. In your Complaint you have characterized certain acts or conduct on the part of the defendant(s) as below the standard of care. As to such acts and conduct, state:
    A. Each specific act or acts, failure or failures to act by the defendant(s) which fell below the standard of care.
    B. Specifically what conduct you claim would have complied with the standard of care.
    C. Each and every fact upon which you rely when you claim:
        1. That this defendant negligently performed its professional duties to you.
        2. That this defendant's negligent performance of its professional duties to you proximately caused your injury.
24. Do you allege that any agent, servant, or employee of this defendant violated or failed to follow any rule, regulation, policy, or procedure of the hospital or some other authority? _____. If so, state:
    A. The identity of said rule, regulation, policy, or procedure.
    B. How and by whom you allege said rule, regulation, policy, or procedure was violated.
    C. How you allege said violation proximately caused injury to the plaintiff.
25. Do you contend that any agent, servant, or employee of this defendant neglected to inform, instruct, or warn you as to any matters relating to your condition, care, or treatment? _____. If so, for each matter, state:
    A. A description of what agent, servant, or employee of this defendant neglected to inform, instruct, or warn you.
    B. Whether such failure or neglect contributed to any injury of which you complain, and if so, in what way and to what extent.
26. Do you know of any person who is skilled in any particular field or science whom you may call as a witness at trial of this action and who has expressed an opinion upon any issue of this action? _____. If so, state:
    A. The name and address of each person.
    B. The field or science in which each such person is sufficiently skilled to enable him [or her] to express opinion evidence in this action.
    C. A complete list of all medical malpractice actions in which each person has rendered an opinion, whether by written report, deposition testimony, or trial testimony, including:
        1. The name of the case.
        2. The court in which filed.
        3. The docket number assigned.
        4. Whether each person rendered his [or her] opinion by written report, deposition testimony, trial testimony, or a combination thereof.
    D. Whether such person will base his [or her] opinion:
        1. In whole or in part upon facts acquired personally by him [or her] in the course of an investigation or examination of any of the issues of this case, or
        2. Solely upon information as to facts provided him [or her] by others.
    E. If your answer to Interrogatory No. 26(D) discloses that any such person has made a personal investigation or examination relating to any of the issues of this case, state the nature and dates of such investigation or examination.
    F. Each and every fact, and each and every document, item, photograph, or other tangible object supplied or made available to such person.
    G. The general subject upon which each person may express an opinion.
    H. The substance of the facts and opinions to which such person is expected to testify.

Exhibit 18–3 (Continued)

I. Whether such persons have rendered written reports. If so, state:
   1. The dates of each report.
   2. The name and address of the custodian of such reports.

VII. DAMAGES

27. State each and every expense, debt, or obligation you have incurred, amount expended, and item of special damage you will claim at trial as a result of the injuries or conditions listed in your answer to these Interrogatories other than that itemized in your answer to the foregoing Interrogatories. This Interrogatory inquires as to, but is not limited to: medical expense, ambulance expense, transportation expense, physiotherapist expense, psychologist fees, psychiatric fees, laboratory charges, hospital costs, and X-ray costs.

VIII. WITNESSES AND EXHIBITS

28. With respect to every lay witness whom you intend to or may call to testify, please state:
   A. The name, address, occupation, and employer of each such person.
   B. What information or facts such person has provided or communicated to you.
   C. What knowledge or information do you believe the witness has with respect to the matters which are at issue in this lawsuit.
   D. The subject about which such witness will or may testify, i.e., liability, damages, injuries, etc.
   E. The substance of the testimony of each witness.
29. List the names, addresses, official titles, if any, and other identification of all witnesses not previously identified who, it is contemplated, will be called upon to testify in support of your claim in this action at trial indicating the nature and substance of the testimony which is expected will be given by each such witness, and stating the relationship, if any, to the plaintiff.
30. List specifically and in detail each and every exhibit you propose to utilize at trial in this matter. This Interrogatory is directed both to exhibits you intend to use at trial and exhibits you may use.
31. At the time of trial, do you intend to use or refer to any medical textbook, periodical, or other medical publication during direct examination of your witnesses? _____. If your answer is in the affirmative, provide the citation for any text or periodical you intend to use.

IX. COLLATERAL SOURCE

32. Have you received, are you now receiving, or are you entitled to receive, collateral source benefits?_____. If so, please state:
   A. The amount of each and every payment.
   B. Schedule or frequency of such payments/benefits.
   C. If the payments have stopped, the date and reason the payments stopped.
   D. If the payments are still being received, the length of time you expect to receive these payments.
   E. If the benefits are stopped at some future time, please state when and under what circumstances the payments will terminate.
   F. The amount of payments you expect to receive in the future.

X. MISCELLANEOUS

33. Has plaintiff entered into any agreement or agreements or covenants with any other person or entity in any way compromising, settling, or in any way limiting such person's or entity's liability or potential liability for any part of the claim arising out of the occurrence alleged in plaintiff's Complaint? _____. If so, state:
   A. The name and address of each person or entity with whom such agreement or covenant was made.
   B. State the date of each such agreement or covenant.
   C. Are the agreements or covenants in writing? _____. If so, state the name and address of the individual who has custody and control of a copy of each such agreement or covenant.
   D. What are the terms of each such agreement or covenant.
   E. What was the consideration paid for each such agreement or covenant.
34. Has plaintiff asserted any claim against any person or entity, not a named party to this lawsuit, for any part of the loss or damage arising out of the occurrence alleged in plaintiff's Complaint? _____. If so, state:
   A. The name and last known address of each such person or entity.
   B. State briefly the basis upon which the claim was asserted.
35. Does any insurance company or any other person or organization have any interest in this action or any recovery herein by way of subrogation, assignment, trust receipt, or otherwise, or has any such claim been asserted? _____. If so, state the name and address of each such company, other person, or organization and the nature and amount of any such claimed interest.
36. Do you contend that any of this defendant's entries in the medical records are incorrect or inaccurate? _____. If so, state:
   A. The precise entry (entries) that you think is incorrect or inaccurate.
   B. What you contend the correct or accurate entry (entries) should have been.
   C. The name, address, and employer of each and every person who has knowledge pertaining to (A) and (B).
   D. A description, including the author and title of each and every document that you claim supports your answers to (A) and (B).
   E. The name, address, and telephone number of each and every person you intend to call as a witness in support of your contention.
37. List the names, addresses, official titles, if any, and other identification of all persons, not previously identified, who:
   A. Were present at the events in question.
   B. Claim to have information concerning the events in question.
   C. Are reported to have information concerning the events in question.
   D. Have knowledge of any pre-existing medical problems or medical treatment received by plaintiff(s) prior to the events in question.
   E. Have knowledge of medical problems or medical treatment received by plaintiff(s) from the events in question up to the present time.
   F. Participated in any investigation concerning the incident in question or of any party or witness thereto.

   Please set forth the subject and substance of the information each such person claims to have.

LEGAL MALPRACTICE

Until the 1940s, not many attorneys bought malpractice insurance because suits by clients were relatively rare. Today, the picture has changed substantially; cautious attorneys do not practice law without such insurance against their own malpractice. "Statistically, the new attorney will be subjected to three claims before finishing a legal career."[17] Therefore very few attorneys are willing to **go bare**—that is, practice without liability insurance.

go bare To engage in an occupation or profession without malpractice (liabilty) insurance.

As the practice of law becomes more complex, the likelihood of error increases. Client expectations tend to be high; hence clients are more likely to blame their attorney for an unfavorable result. And attorneys are increasingly willing to sue each other. In fact, some attorneys have developed a legal malpractice specialty in which they take clients who want to sue other attorneys. (To find attorneys with this specialty, run this search in Google or another search engine: "suing attorneys.") As malpractice awards against attorneys continue to rise, the market for malpractice insurance has dramatically increased. There are cities where the premium for insurance can be between $5,000 and $15,000 per year per attorney. This has tempted some attorneys (particularly those in solo or small firms) to go bare or to purchase very low coverage. In some states, however, attorneys without liability insurance or with coverage below a designated amount (e.g., $100,000) are ethically required to notify their clients (or prospective clients) of this fact.

Typically, claims against attorneys arise in the context of fee disputes. The sequence is often as follows: a client fails to pay agreed-upon attorney fees, the attorney sues the client for fees, and the client responds by suing the attorney for malpractice and by filing an ethics charge with the bar association alleging the same malpractice. To try to gain a strategic advantage, some attorneys wait until the statute of limitations for malpractice expires before bringing the suit against the client for nonpayment of fees.

Legal malpractice is a category of negligence consisting of the failure of an attorney to exercise the skills commonly applied by attorneys in the same area of practice under the same circumstances. A reasonable attorney is one who applies such skills. Liability for negligence will not automatically result when an attorney makes a mistake or loses the case. Unless the attorney specifically guarantees a result, the standard of care will be reasonableness, not warranty. Expressed in greater detail, the standard is as follows:

legal malpractice The failure of an attorney to exercise the skills commonly applied by attorneys in the same area of practice under the same circumstances.

> Ordinarily when an attorney engages in the practice of the law and contracts to prosecute an action in behalf of his client, he impliedly represents that (1) he possesses the requisite degree of learning, skill, and ability necessary to the practice of his profession and which others similarly situated ordinarily possess; (2) he will exert his best judgment in the prosecution of the litigation entrusted to him; and (3) he will exercise reasonable and ordinary care and diligence in the use of his skill and in the application of his knowledge to his client's cause.
>
> An attorney who acts in good faith and in an honest belief that his advice and acts are well founded and in the best interest of his client is not answerable for a mere error of judgment or for a mistake in a point of law which has not been settled by the court of last resort in his State and on which reasonable doubt may be entertained by well-informed lawyers.
>
> Conversely, he is answerable in damages for any loss to his client which proximately results from a want of that degree of knowledge and skill ordinarily possessed by others of his profession similarly situated, or from the omission to use reasonable care and diligence, or from the failure to exercise in good faith his best judgment in attending to the litigation committed to his care.[18]

If attorneys hold themselves out to the public as specialists in a particular area of the law (e.g., criminal law or patent law), the standard of competence is not the general practitioner handling such a case, but the specialist in good standing using the skill and knowledge normally possessed by such specialists. The *Restatement of Torts 2d* phrases the standard (which applies to attorneys, doctors, or anyone who claims to have special or superior skill or knowledge) this way:[19]

> An actor undertaking to render services may represent that he has superior skill or knowledge, beyond that common to his profession or trade. In that event he incurs an obligation to the person to whom he makes such a representation, to have, and to exercise, the skill and knowledge which he represents himself to have.

One way to gauge the kinds of malpractice with which attorneys have been charged is to examine the claims handled by insurance companies that sell liability insurance to attorneys. See Exhibit 18–4 for the breakdown in the categories of substantive errors, administrative errors, client relations errors, and intentional wrongs committed by attorneys.

Exhibit 18–4
Professional liability claims against law firms by error group.

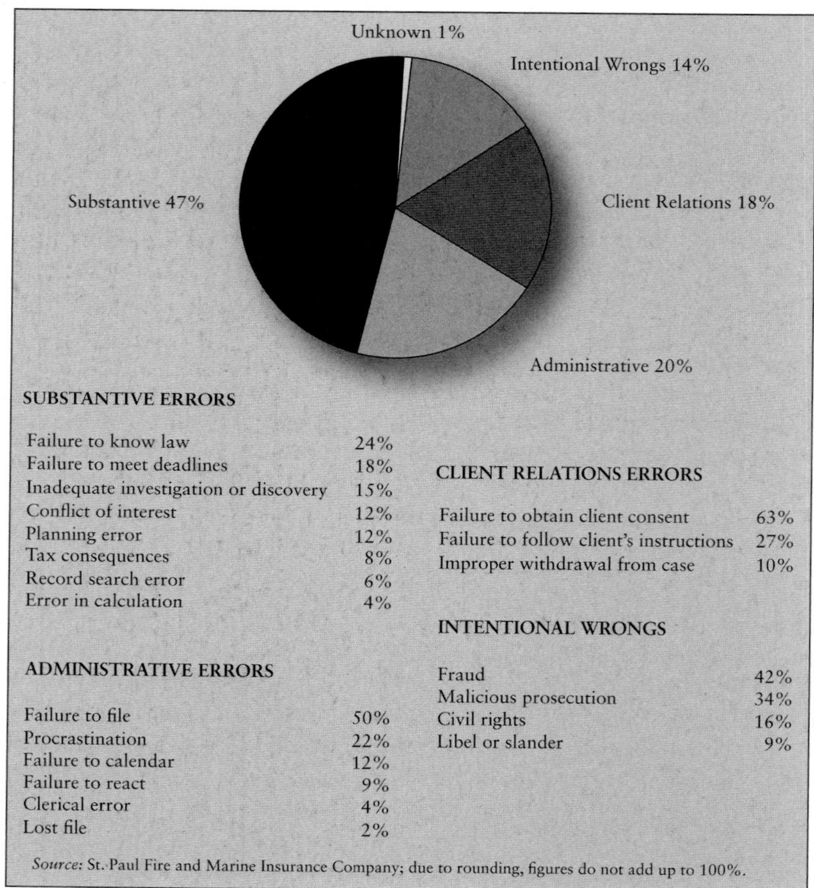

SUBSTANTIVE ERRORS

Failure to know law	24%
Failure to meet deadlines	18%
Inadequate investigation or discovery	15%
Conflict of interest	12%
Planning error	12%
Tax consequences	8%
Record search error	6%
Error in calculation	4%

ADMINISTRATIVE ERRORS

Failure to file	50%
Procrastination	22%
Failure to calendar	12%
Failure to react	9%
Clerical error	4%
Lost file	2%

CLIENT RELATIONS ERRORS

Failure to obtain client consent	63%
Failure to follow client's instructions	27%
Improper withdrawal from case	10%

INTENTIONAL WRONGS

Fraud	42%
Malicious prosecution	34%
Civil rights	16%
Libel or slander	9%

Source: St. Paul Fire and Marine Insurance Company; due to rounding, figures do not add up to 100%.

Mistakes

A distinction should be made between

- a reasonable mistake that could have been made by any attorney in good standing using the skill commonly possessed by attorneys, and
- an unreasonable mistake that would not have been made by an attorney in good standing using the skill commonly possessed by attorneys.

Only the latter kinds of mistakes will lead to liability for negligence. (See Exhibit 18–5.) The test is not whether the *average* attorney would have made the mistake. The focus is on the attorney in good standing using the skill commonly possessed by attorneys.[20]

Exhibit 18–5
Mistakes of attorneys.

Kind of Mistake	Examples	Negligence Consequences
1. Technical/mechanical mistake *not* involving the exercise of judgment and discretion.	• Attorney forgets to file the suit in court and client is thereby barred by the statute of limitations. • Attorney forgets to appear in court and client thereby has a default judgment entered against him or her.	It is relatively easy for a client to win a negligence action against an attorney based on this kind of mistake. (See, however, the discussion on causation.)
2. Tactical mistake involving the exercise of judgment and discretion in a relatively uncomplicated area of the law.	• Attorney decides not to call a certain witness who would have been able to provide valuable testimony. • Attorney does not object to the introduction of certain evidence at trial from the other side and thereby waives the right to object on appeal.	It is difficult for a client to win a negligence action against an attorney based on this kind of mistake unless what the attorney did or failed to do was blatantly contrary to what would be considered good or competent practice. (See discussion on causation.)
3. Tactical mistake involving the exercise of judgment and discretion in a complicated area of the law.	• Attorney fails to challenge the constitutionality of a guest statute. • Attorney calls an expert witness on a design defect in a products liability case and the witness unexpectedly gives very damaging testimony to the attorney's own case.	It is almost impossible for a client to win a negligence action against an attorney based on this kind of mistake. This is so not only because of the complexity of the area of the law, but also because of the difficulty of proving causation, i.e., that the mistake caused the client any harm. (See discussion on causation.)

It is important to keep in mind that the attorney is the agent of the client. While the attorney is representing the client (within the scope of the attorney's "employment"), the client is bound by what the attorney does. This includes both successes and mistakes. Hence, if the attorney makes a mistake and the client loses the case as a result, the recourse of the client is to sue the attorney and try to establish that an unreasonable mistake was made that would not have been made by an attorney in good standing using the skill commonly possessed by attorneys.[21]

There are three basic interrelated errors in the way an attorney practices law that often lead to successful negligence actions against the attorney. Errors in practicing law that can make an attorney vulnerable include:

- **Taking Too Many Cases**
  There are strong temptations to keep adding new cases to the attorney's caseload. Although one might admire "busy" attorneys, the danger exists that they have more than they can competently handle.
- **Failure to Do More Than Minimal Legal Research**
  Legal research can be difficult and time-consuming. It is much easier "to practice out of one's hip pocket." Courts, however, have warned attorneys that the failure to do needed legal research is a strong indication of incompetence.
- **Failure to Consult and/or Associate with More Experienced Attorneys**
  The tendency in legal practice is for an attorney to concentrate on certain kinds of cases—to specialize. Even many general practitioners will emphasize one or two categories of cases in their practice. What happens when the client with a new kind of case walks into the office? If the case is taken and the attorney does *not* have enough time to learn the theory and practicalities of a new area of the law, it is strong evidence of incompetence if the attorney fails to consult with attorneys who are experienced in that area of the law, and perhaps, with the client's consent, to work with such an attorney on the case.

Causation

trial within a trial A trial that takes place to establish that you would have won another trial that was lost because of the alleged negligence of your attorney. (In legal malpractice cases, plaintiffs must establish that they would have won their case if their attorney had not acted negligently.)

To win a negligence case against an attorney, it is not enough to establish that the attorney made an unreasonable mistake; causation must also be proven. For certain kinds of attorney errors, a **trial within a trial** must occur.

EXAMPLE

George hires John Taylor, Esq. to represent him in a products liability case against XYZ Motor Company. The car George bought from XYZ exploded, causing $100,000 in injuries to George. John Taylor is so tied up with other cases that he neglects to file the action within the statute-of-limitations period. Hence, George can no longer sue XYZ Motor Company; the action is barred. George now sues John Taylor for negligence (legal malpractice) in letting the statute of limitations run. Assume that the error of John Taylor was unreasonable. What can George recover from John Taylor? $100,000? Is that what he lost? Did John Taylor *cause* $100,000 in damages? The answer is yes—but only if George can establish:

1. that he would have won his case against XYZ Motor Company, and
2. that the recovery from XYZ would have been at least $100,000.

In George's negligence suit against John Taylor, George must establish that he would have won the $100,000 suit against the XYZ Motor Company if the suit had not been barred by the statute of limitations. This, then, is the suit within the suit, or the trial within a trial.

The difficulty of establishing causation can be further complicated: Suppose XYZ Motor Company is bankrupt. Even if George could have won a $100,000 judgment against XYZ, he would have been able to collect nothing or very little. Hence, it cannot be said that John Taylor's negligence in waiting too long to file the action caused George a $100,000 loss. In such circumstances, George would have to prove (in his action against John Taylor) that there would have been something to collect from XYZ Motor Company.

Indemnity

indemnity 1. The duty of one person to pay for another's loss, damage, or liability. 2. A right to receive compensation to make one person whole from a loss that has already been sustained but which in justice ought to be sustained by the person from whom indemnity is sought.

Indemnity is the right to have another person pay you the full amount you were forced to pay. In tort law, when one party is liable to a plaintiff solely because of what someone else has done (e.g., employer is liable because of what employee did), the party who is liable, and who pays as a result of the liability, can often receive indemnity from the person whose action produced the liability. Assume that an attorney is representing a *defendant* in a suit brought against the latter. Assume further that the defendant loses the suit and must pay the judgment solely because of the negligence of the attorney. In some states, the defendant can ask a court to force the attorney to *indemnify* him or her based upon the above definition of indemnity.[22]

ASSIGNMENT 18.2

(1) Karen Smith, Esq. represents Jim Noonan in the preparation of a will. It was Jim's intent that his friend Ralph Skidmore receive a bequest of $10,000. Karen Smith drafts the will. After Jim dies, it is discovered that Karen Smith made a mistake in drafting the will that resulted in Ralph receiving nothing.

a. Make an argument that Karen Smith did not *cause a* $10,000 loss to Ralph. Assume that Jim died at the age of 35, one year after the will was drafted, and that his death was a surprise to everyone—including Jim.
b. Are there any other problems that might prevent Ralph from being able to bring a negligence action against Karen Smith?

(2) Frank Jackson, Esq. represents Ted Oliver in the case of *State v. Oliver.* The state is accusing Oliver of burglary. He is convicted. Oliver is convinced that Jackson conducted the trial carelessly and now sues Jackson for negligence (legal malpractice). Assume that Oliver will be able to show that Jackson's conduct of the trial fell below the standard of how criminal lawyers commonly practice. Discuss the issue of causation in Oliver's case against Jackson.

CASE

Smith v. Lewis

13 Cal. 3d 349, 118 Cal. Rptr. 621, 530 P.2d 589 (1975)
Supreme Court of California

Background: *Rosemary Smith hired Jerome Lewis, Esq. to represent her in her divorce case. He advised her that her husband's state and federal retirement (pension) benefits were his separate property; he said they were not community property. Hence these benefits were not pleaded as items of community property, and therefore were not apportioned by the divorce court. After the divorce decree became final, Smith sued Lewis for legal malpractice in giving her negligent legal advice on the pensions. The trial court ruled for Smith (the plaintiff) against Lewis (the defendant). The case is now on appeal before the Supreme Court of California.*

Decision on Appeal: *Judgment affirmed. Lewis committed legal malpractice by failing to perform adequate research into the community property character of retirement benefits.*

OPINION OF COURT

Justice MOSK delivered the opinion of the court . . .

In determining whether defendant exhibited the requisite degree of competence in his handling of plaintiff's divorce action, the crucial inquiry is whether his advice was so legally deficient when it was given that he may be found to have failed to use "such skill, prudence, and diligence as lawyers of ordinary skill and capacity commonly possess and exercise in the performance of the tasks which they undertake." *Lucas v. Hamm* (1961) 364 P.2d 685, 689. We must, therefore examine the indicia of the law which were readily available to defendant at the time he performed the legal services in question.

The major authoritative reference works which attorneys routinely consult for a brief and reliable exposition of the law relevant to a specific problem uniformly indicated in 1967 that vested retirement benefits earned during marriage were generally subject to community [property] treatment. See, e.g., 38 *Cal. Jur. 2d*, Pensions, § 12, p. 325; 4 Witkin, *Summary of Cal. Law* (1960) pp. 2723–2724. . . .

Although it is true this court had not foreclosed all conflicts on some aspects of the issue at that time, the community character of retirement benefits had been reported in a number of appellate opinions often cited in the literature and readily accessible to defendant. *Benson v. City of Los Angeles* (1963) 384 P.2d 649; *French v. French* (1941) 112 P.2d 235. In *Benson,* decided four years before defendant was retained herein, we stated directly that "pension rights which are earned during the course of a marriage are the community property of the employee and his wife." 384 P.2d at p. 651. . . .

On the other hand, substantial uncertainty may have existed in 1967 with regard to the community character of [her husband's] *federal* pension. . . . [But] the fact that in 1967 a reasonable argument could have been offered to support the characterization of [her husband's] federal benefits as separate property does not indicate the trial court erred in submitting the issue of defendant's malpractice to the jury. The *state* benefits, the large majority of the payments at issue, were unquestionably community property according to all available authority and should have been claimed as such. As for the *federal* benefits, the record documents defendant's failure to conduct any reasonable research into their proper characterization under community property law. Instead, he dogmatically asserted his theory, which he was unable to support with authority, . . . that all noncontributory . . . retirement benefits, whether state or federal, were immune from community treatment upon divorce. The jury could well have found defendant's refusal to educate himself to the applicable principles of law constituted negligence which prevented him from exercising informed discretion with regard to his client's rights.

As the jury was correctly instructed, an attorney does not ordinarily guarantee the soundness of his opinions and, accordingly, is not liable for every mistake he may make in his practice. He is expected, however, to possess knowledge of those plain and elementary principles of law which are commonly known by well informed attorneys, and to discover those additional rules of law which, although not commonly known, may readily be found by standard research techniques. If the law on a particular subject is doubtful or debatable, an attorney will not be held responsible for failing to anticipate the manner in which the uncertainty will be resolved. But even with respect to an unsettled area of the law, we believe an attorney assumes an obligation to his client to undertake reasonable research in an effort to ascertain relevant legal principles and to make an informed decision as to a course of conduct based upon an intelligent assessment of the problem. In the instant case, ample evidence was introduced to support a jury finding that defendant failed to perform such adequate research into the question of the community character of retirement benefits and thus was unable to exercise the informed judgment to which his client was entitled.

We recognize, of course, that an attorney engaging in litigation may have occasion to choose among various alternative strategies available to his client, one of which may be to refrain from pressing a debatable point because potential benefit may not equal detriment in terms of expenditure of time and resources or because of calculated tactics to the advantage of his client. But, as the Ninth Circuit put it somewhat brutally in *Pineda v. Craven* (9th Cir. 1970) 424 F.2d 369, 372: "There is nothing strategic or tactical about ignorance. . . ." In the case before us it is difficult to conceive of tactical advantage which could have been served by neglecting to advance a claim so clearly in plaintiff's best interest, nor does defendant suggest any. The decision to forego litigation on the issue of plaintiff's community property right to a share of [her husband's] retirement benefits was apparently the product of a culpable misconception of the relevant principles of law, and the jury could have so found.

Furthermore, no lawyer would suggest the property characterization of [her husband's] retirement benefits to be so esoteric an issue that defendant could not reasonably have been expected to be aware of it or its probable resolution. *Lucas v. Hamm* (1961) 364 P.2d 685. In *Lucas* we held that the rule against perpetuities poses such complex and difficult problems for the draftsman that even careful and competent attorneys occasionally fall prey to its traps. The situation before us is not analogous. Certainly one of the central issues in any divorce proceeding is the extent and division of the community property. In this case the question reached monumental proportions, since [her husband's] retirement benefits constituted the only significant asset available to the community. In undertaking professional representation of plaintiff, defendant assumed the duty to familiarize himself with the law defining the character of retirement benefits; instead, he rendered erroneous advice contrary to the best interests of his client without the guidance through research of readily available authority. . . .

[H]ad defendant conducted minimal research into either hornbook or case law, he would have discovered with modest effort that [the husband's] state retirement benefits were likely to be treated as community property and that his federal benefits at least arguably belonged to the community as well. . . . Even as to doubtful matters, an attorney is expected to perform sufficient research to enable him to make an informed and intelligent judgment on behalf of his client. . . .

The judgment is affirmed.

ASSIGNMENT 18.3

a. Assume that Rosemary Smith's husband in *Smith v. Lewis* had a federal pension, but no state pension. Would the court still have found Lewis negligent?
b. To avoid a charge of negligence, is every attorney obligated to own a comprehensive law library?

LIABILITY OF PARALEGALS

vicarious liability Liability imposed on a person because of the conduct of another, based solely on the status of the relationship between the two. The person liable is not the person whose conduct led to the liability.

Two questions should be kept in mind. First, when are paralegal employees *personally liable* for their torts? Second, when are employers *vicariously liable* for the torts of their paralegal employees? (As we saw in Chapter 14, **vicarious liability** means liability imposed on a person because of the conduct of another, based solely on the status of the relationship between the two.) The short answer to the first question is: *always*. The short answer to the second question is: *when the wrongdoing by the paralegal was within the scope of employment.*

Several different kinds of wrongdoing are possible. The paralegal might commit:

- the tort of negligence
- an intentional tort, such as battery
- an act that is both a crime (such as embezzlement) *and* an intentional tort (such as conversion)

A client who is injured by any of these torts can sue the paralegal in the same manner that a patient in a hospital can sue a nurse. Paralegals are not relieved of liability simply because they work for, and function under the supervision of, an attorney. Every citizen has **personal liability** for the torts he or she commits.

personal liability Liability that can be satisfied out of a wrongdoer's personal assets.

Next we turn to the employers of paralegals. Are they *also* liable for the wrongdoing committed by their paralegals? There are four possible theories of employer liability for employee wrongdoing:

- Careless hiring
- Careless supervision
- Participation in the wrongdoing
- Vicarious liability

Careless hiring. Under the first theory, the employer was careless in hiring the employee; the employer should have known that the person was likely to commit wrongdoing. (This theory is sometimes called **negligent hiring.**)

negligent hiring Carelessly hiring an incompetent person who poses an unreasonable risk of harm to others.

Careless supervision. Under the second theory, the employer was careless in supervising the employee; the wrongdoing by the employee would not have occurred if the employer exercised proper oversight of the employee's work or provided proper training. (This theory is sometimes called **negligent supervision.**)

negligent supervision Carelessly monitoring or supervising an incompetent person who poses an unreasonable risk of harm to others.

Participation in the wrongdoing. Under the third theory, the employer actually participated in the wrongdoing with the employee; the two of them committed the wrongdoing together.

Vicarious liability. Under the fourth theory, the employer is liable for what the employee did solely because of the special relationship that exists between them—an employer–employee relationship. (This theory is called *vicarious liability.*[23])

Not all wrongdoing of an employee will result in vicarious liability of the employer. Under the doctrine of **respondeat superior**, an employer will be liable for the wrongdoing of his or her employee if the wrongdoing occurred within the **scope of employment.** This means the wrongdoing was foreseeably done by an employee for the employer's business under the employer's specific or general control. Slandering a client in a law office for failure to pay a law firm bill would be within the scope of employment. It's foreseeable that a paralegal would insult a client for this reason. It's not what the employer would want the paralegal to do, but it is foreseeable and it occurs within the confines and general control of the employer. However, the opposite would probably be true if the paralegal had an argument with a client over a football game and punched the client during their accidental evening meeting at a bar. In the latter example, the client could not sue the paralegal's employer under the theory of respondeat superior for the intentional tort of battery. The battery was not foreseeable by the employer, was not under the employer's control, and was unrelated to the business of the employer. Only the paralegal would be liable for the tort under such circumstances. (For more on scope of employment, see Exhibit 14–9 in Chapter 14.)

respondeat superior "Let the master answer." An employer is responsible (liable) for the wrongs committed by an employee within the scope of employment.

scope of employment That which is foreseeably done by an employee for the employer's business under the employer's specific or general control.

When a paralegal's wrongdoing is within the scope of employment (making the paralegal personally liable and the attorney employer vicariously liable under respondeat superior), the client can sue the paralegal or the attorney, or both. This does not mean that the client recovers twice; there can be only one recovery for the tort. Clients are simply given a choice on whom to collect damages from. If they are entitled to $5,000 in damages because of the tort committed by the paralegal, they can recover the entire $5,000 from the attorney, or the entire $5,000 from the paralegal, or part from each until the $5,000 is paid. In most cases, the primary target of the client will be the employer, who is the *deep pocket*—the one who has resources from which a judgment can be satisfied.

Negligence

Attorney negligence is the failure to exercise the skills commonly applied by attorneys in the same area of practice under the same circumstances. When a *traditional* paralegal (one employed by an attorney) commits negligence for which the attorney becomes liable under respondeat superior, the same standard applies. Since the work product of this paralegal blends into the work product of the supervising attorney, the attorney becomes as fully responsible for what the paralegal did as if the attorney had committed the negligence. Unreasonableness is measured by what a reasonable attorney would have done, not by what a reasonable paralegal would have done.

Independent paralegals who do not work under attorney supervision (e.g., legal document assistants) are treated differently from traditional paralegals. If the independent paralegals do not work under attorney supervision, they will be held to the standard of a reasonable independent paralegal. The standard would be the skill commonly possessed by independent paralegals in good standing. If such a paralegal is charged with negligence, he or she will not be held to the standard of a reasonable attorney, unless the paralegal led the client to believe he or she was an attorney or worked under an attorney's supervision. Independent paralegals who do not make clear that they are not attorneys may be held to the attorney standard. Furthermore, if they perform functions that only attorneys can perform (e.g., giving legal advice), they will be held to an attorney standard even if they make clear to the public that they are not attorneys.

There have not been many tort cases in which paralegals have been sued for wrongdoing in a law office. Yet as paralegals become increasingly prominent in the practice of law, more are expected to be named as defendants. The general counsel of the Mississippi Bar Association makes the unsettling point that the prominence of paralegalism means there will be more suits against them. "As paralegals become more and more professional and proficient, they . . . will become better targets for disgruntled clients looking for someone to sue."[24] The most common kinds of cases involving paralegals have occurred when the paralegal was a notary and improperly notarized signatures under pressure from the supervising attorney. For example, the paralegal may have been asked to notarize the signature of a person the paralegal did not observe signing the document.

ASSIGNMENT 18.4

Mary Smith is a paralegal at the XYZ law firm. One of her tasks is to file a document in court. She negligently fails to do so. As a result, the client loses the case through a default judgment entered against the client. What options are available to the client?

CHECK THE CITE

Sharon Black sued her doctor for negligence in failing to inform her of the availability of a drug that was a less drastic alternative to the hysterectomy that the doctor performed. What statute of limitations defense did the doctor raise? How did the court rule on this defense? Read the case of *Black v. Littlejohn*, 312 N.C. 626, 325 S.E.2d 469 (N.C. 1985). To read the opinion online, (1) Go to FindACase (www.findacase.com). Select North Carolina. Run a citation search ("325 S.E.2d 469"). (2) Run a citation search ("325 S.E.2d 469") or a party search (Black Littlejohn) in the Legal Opinions and Journals database of Google Scholar (scholar .google.com).

PROJECT

(1) Go to a site that lists a large number of diseases (e.g., www.medicinenet.com [click the Diseases & Conditions tab] or www.health.state.ny.us/diseases). Select one disease. Find two experts online that offer their services to testify about that disease. Summarize their credentials.
(2) For doctors in your state, what are the names of the main regulatory body and the governing code of medical ethics? Find the code online and quote any section in the code that covers negligence by doctors.
(3) For attorneys in your state, what are the names of the main regulatory body and the governing code of attorney ethics? Find the code online and quote any section in the code that covers negligence by attorneys.

ETHICS IN A TORTS PRACTICE

Thomas Givens, Esq. represents Helen Coderre in her negligence suit against the Daily City Hospital. David Isis is a member of the board of directors of the hospital. Givens represents David Isis in his divorce action. What ethical problems, if any, might exist?

SUMMARY

Malpractice is professional misconduct or wrongdoing consisting of ethical violations, criminal conduct, and torts such as negligence and battery. Medical malpractice is the failure of a doctor to exercise the skills commonly applied by doctors in the same field under the same circumstances. A physician-patient relationship arises when a doctor undertakes to render medical services in response to an express or implied request for services by the patient or by the patient's guardian. Doctors are not liable for breach of contract unless they guarantee a result, nor is there strict liability. They are held to the standard of negligence: A doctor must use the skill and learning commonly possessed by members of the profession in good standing. States disagree on whether this standard of care is judged from a national or a local perspective. The failure of a doctor to obtain informed consent on proposed treatment may lead to a medical battery claim, although more often the claim is negligence. The amount of disclosure a doctor must provide is determined by a reasonable patient standard or by a reasonable doctor standard. Consent forms must not be so ambiguous as to amount to a blanket authorization of whatever the doctor thinks is wise to do.

Critics say that the law of medical malpractice causes doctors to practice defensive medicine, increasing the cost and unavailability of coverage. Proposals for reform have been proposed in the areas of damage caps (particularly on noneconomic damages such as pain and suffering), fee caps (particularly on contingent fees), collateral source offsets, joint and several liability, cooling-off periods, alternative dispute resolution (particularly mediation), screening panels, certificates of merit, data banks on doctors, sorry-works laws, Medicare restrictions, evidence-based medicine, the English rule, and enterprise liability. Interrogatories are used as a pretrial discovery device for parties to learn about each other's cases and prepare for trial.

Legal malpractice is the failure of an attorney to exercise the skills commonly applied by attorneys in the same area of practice under the same circumstances. Attorneys that specialize are held to the standard of the skills commonly applied by attorneys in that specialty. Every mistake made by an attorney will not necessarily lead to negligence liability. There must be an unreasonable mistake that actually causes the client a loss. To prove causation, a trial within a trial may be necessary.

If a paralegal commits a tort, such as negligence, he or she is personally liable to the injured party. There are four theories under which employers of paralegals may be liable for the torts committed by their paralegals: careless hiring, careless supervision, participation in the wrongdoing, and vicarious liability. Under the theory of respondeat superior, a supervising attorney is vicariously liable for a wrong committed by a paralegal if it occurred within the scope of employment. When a client sues a law firm because of harm caused by paralegal negligence, the firm is held to the standard of what a reasonable attorney should have done, not what a reasonable paralegal should have done. Independent paralegals working for the public without attorney supervision who do not make clear that they are not attorneys may be held to the attorney standard. If the independent paralegals perform functions that only attorneys can perform (e.g., give legal advice), they will be held to an attorney standard even if they make clear to the public that they are not attorneys. Otherwise, independent paralegals are held to the standard of a reasonable independent paralegal.

KEY TERMS

fiduciary relationship *330*
malpractice *330*
medical malpractice *330*
deep pocket *330*
liability insurance *332*
warranty *332*
strict liability *332*
negligence *332*
locality rule *333*
custom *333*
conspiracy of silence *333*
informed consent *333*
medical battery *334*
defensive medicine *335*
damage caps *335*
punitive damages *335*
fee caps *335*
collateral source rule *335*
joint and several liability *335*
statute of limitations *336*
tolled *336*
alternative dispute resolution (ADR) *336*
screening panel *336*
mediation *336*
arbitration *336*
certificate of merit *336*
National Practitioner Data Bank *336*
English rule *336*
American rule *336*
enterprise liability *337*
interrogatories *339*
go bare *343*
legal malpractice *343*
trial within a trial *346*
indemnity *346*
vicarious liability *348*
personal liability *349*
negligent hiring *349*
negligent supervision *349*
respondeat superior *349*
scope of employment *349*

REVIEW QUESTIONS

1. What is a fiduciary relationship and what duty does it impose?
2. How many different kinds of wrongdoing can the word *malpractice* entail?
3. What is medical malpractice?
4. Why is medical malpractice a large specialty area of tort law?
5. What is the significance of the high cost of medical liability insurance?
6. How does a doctor avoid a breach-of-contract claim when treating patients?
7. What is the standard of care expected of doctors?
8. How do you distinguish between a national and the same or similar community standard of care? What is the locality rule?
9. What is the conspiracy of silence?
10. What are the elements of informed consent?
11. What causes of action are possible if a doctor provides treatment without obtaining informed consent?
12. When deciding how much information to give a patient about a procedure, what is the distinction between the reasonable person standard and the reasonable doctor standard?
13. What are damage caps and fee caps?
14. What are collateral source offsets?
15. Why do doctors dislike joint and several liability?
16. What is a cooling-off period?
17. What kinds of alternative dispute resolution (ADR) are often used?
18. What is the role of a screening panel?
19. What is a certificate of merit?
20. How do data banks on doctors work?
21. What is a sorry-works law?

22. What restriction has been imposed by Medicare on hospital reimbursements?
23. How does evidence-based medicine function in the practice of medicine?
24. How does the English rule differ from the American rule?
25. How would enterprise liability operate?
26. What happens when a professional goes bare?
27. What is legal malpractice?
28. What are some of the major errors committed by attorneys that result in liability claims?
29. What is the distinction between (and consequence of) reasonable mistakes and unreasonable mistakes made by attorneys?
30. How is causation established in a claim of legal malpractice?
31. What is indemnity?
32. When are paralegals personally liable for torts they commit?
33. When is an employer liable for negligent hiring?
34. When is an employer liable for negligent supervision?
35. What is vicarious liability?
36. How does respondeat superior make an employer liable for the torts of others?
37. When a traditional paralegal is sued for negligence, what standard of care is used?
38. What standard of care applies to independent paralegals who do not work under attorney supervision?

HELPFUL WEBSITES

- **Medical Research**
  medlineplus.gov
  www.ncbi.nlm.nih.gov/sites/entrez
  www.healthfinder.gov
- **Medical Abbreviations**
  www.medilexicon.com
- **Medical Malpractice: 50-State Summary**
  www.mcandl.com/states.html
  www.ncsl.org/print/standcomm/sclaw/tortchart04.pdf
- **Medical Malpractice**
  www.98000reasons.org
  en.wikipedia.org/wiki/Medical_malpractice
- **Expert Witnesses for Medical Malpractice Cases**
  www.tasanet.com
  www.dri.org
  expertpages.com/medical/medicalmalpractice.htm
- **Information about Doctors**
  www.npdb-hipdb.hrsa.gov
  www.fsmb.org/m_fpdc.html
  nydoctorprofile.com
  www.licensepa.state.pa.us
- **Privacy of Medical Information**
  www.hhs.gov/ocr/privacy
  www.hipaa.com
- **American Medical Association**
  www.ama-assn.com
- **Patient Safety Organization**
  www.pso.ahrq.gov
- **Legal Malpractice and Liability Insurance**
  www.abanet.org/legalservices/lpl/home.html
  www.abanet.org/legalservices/lpl/directory
  www.halt.org/reform_projects/lawyer_accountability/legal_malpractice

ENDNOTES

1. Keith Griffin, "Treatment Allegedly Denied to Paralegal," *The Legal Intelligencer* (July 19, 2004) (www.law.com/jsp/PubArticle.jsp?id=900005411630).
2. Institute of Medicine, *To Err Is Human: Building A Safer Health System* 1 (Linda T. Kohn et al., eds., 2000) (www.nap.edu/catalog.php?record_id=9728). See also *Concerning Patient Safety and Medical Errors,* Statement of Harvard Professor Lucian Leape, M.D., before the Subcommittee on Labor, Health and Human Services, and Education, U.S. Senate, January 25, 2000.
3. James H. Nichols, "Reducing Medical Errors at the Point of Care," 36 *Laboratory Medicine* 275, (May 2005). See also "Doctors Are the Third Leading Cause of Death in the U.S." (www.naturodoc.com/library/public_health/doctors_cause_death.htm) and www.commonwealthfund.org/Content/News/News-Releases/2002/Apr/New-Study-Estimates-Eight-Million-American-Families-Experienced-A-Serious-Medical-Or-Drug-Error.aspx. On costs, see www.consumersunion.org/pub/core_health_care/011324.html.

4. U.S. Department of Health and Human Services, Agency for Healthcare Research and Quality (www.ahrq.gov).
5. Editorial, "Malpractice Mythology," *N.Y. Times*, January 9, 2005, at A21.
6. Amy Lynn Sorrel, "Liability Premiums Stable, But Insurers Warn This May Not Last," *American Medical News* (November 23, 2009). (www.ama-assn.org/amendnews/2009/11/23/prl21123.htm)
7. W. Page Keeton et al., *Prosser and Keeton on the Law of Torts* 187 (5th ed. 1984).
8. Clarence H. Braddock, et al., "Informed Decision Making in Outpatient Practice," 282 *Journal of the American Medical Association* 2313 (December 22/29, 1999); "Study Shows Doctors Are Lax in Giving Information to Patients," *N.Y. Times* Nat'l Ed., December 22, 1999, at A16.
9. Kenneth S. Abraham, *The Forms and Functions of Tort Law* 77 (1997).
10. www.npdb-hipdb.hrsa.gov
11. Oregon Revised Statutes, § 677.082(1) (www.leg.state.or.us/ors/677.html).
12. Duke University, *Introduction to Evidence-Based Medicine* (2001) (www.hsl.unc.edu/services/tutorials/ebm/index.htm).
13. *Evidence-based Medicine,* en.wikipedia.org/wiki/Evidence-based_medicine.
14. Pennie Marchetti, "Does 'Evidence-Based Medicine' Diminish the Physician's Role?" *Medscape Today*, January 5, 2005.
15. Risa B. Greene, "Federal Legislative Proposals for Medical Malpractice Reform: Treating the Symptoms or Effecting a Cure?" 4 *Cornell Journal of Law and Public Policy* 563 (Spring 1995).
16. Uniform Medical Malpractice Interrogatories, 17B Arizona Revised Statutes.
17. Ronald Mallen & Jeffrey Smith, *Legal Malpractice* 2 (3d ed. 1989).
18. *Hodges v. Carter,* 239 N.C. 517, 519–20, 80 S.E.2d 144, 145–46 (1954).
19. *Restatement (Second) of Torts* § 299A, comment d (1965).
20. *Restatement (Second) of Torts* § 299A, comment e (1965).
21. Depending on the kind of mistake the attorney made, some courts might permit the client to "undo" the error by correcting it, e.g., permit a client to file a document even though the client's attorney had negligently allowed the deadline for its filing to pass. It is rare, however, that courts will be this accommodating. A client will have to live with the mistakes of his or her attorney and seek relief solely by suing the attorney for legal malpractice (negligence). See Ronald Mallen & Victor Levit, *Legal Malpractice* 45ff (1977).
22. Ronald Mallen & Victor Levit, *Legal Malpractice* 124 (1977).
23. We are talking here to vicarious *civil* liability, or more specifically, the tort liability of employers for the torts committed by their employees. Employers are not subject to vicarious *criminal* liability. If a paralegal commits a crime on the job, only the paralegal goes to jail (unless the employer actually participated in the crime).
24. Michael Martz, "Ethics, Does a Paralegal Need Insurance?" *The Assistant* 13 (Mississippi Ass'n of Legal Assistants) (Fall 1993).

Student StudyWARE™ CD-ROM
For additional materials, please go to the student CD in this book.

CHAPTER

19

PRODUCTS LIABILITY

CHAPTER OUTLINE

- Products Liability in the Media
- Categories of Defects
- Negligence
- Warranty and Strict Liability
- Express Warranty
- Sale versus Service
- Implied Warranties
- Strict Liability in Tort
- Reform
- Paralegal Roles

CHAPTER OBJECTIVES

After completing this chapter, you should be able to:

- Identify the five major causes of action that fall within the category of products liability.
- List the three kinds of product defects.
- Explain how to state a products liability case based on negligence.
- Explain how to state a products liability case based on breach of express warranty.
- Explain how to state a products liability case based on breach of implied warranty of merchantability.
- Explain how to state a products liability case based on breach of implied warranty of fitness for a particular purpose.
- Explain how to state a products liability case based on strict liability in tort.
- Identify the tests that different states use for design defects.
- Identify paralegal roles in products liability causes of action.
- Use the major resources in traditional books and online when researching issues involving a products liability causes of action.

PRODUCTS LIABILITY IN THE MEDIA

Each year 29,000 deaths are associated with consumer products (not including automobiles and trucks). In addition, an estimated 33 million people are injured. The cost of injuries treated in hospital emergency rooms alone is about $10 billion a year. (See Exhibit 19–1.) Yet the law of **products liability** is often misunderstood, particularly by the public. In part this is due to the media's fascination with the apparently frivolous case. For example:

products liability A general term that covers five causes of action for harm caused by products: negligence, breach of express warranty, breach of implied warranty of fitness for a particular purpose, breach of implied warranty of merchantability, and strict liability in tort.

- A man convinces a court that he became impotent after being shocked by a Pepsi Cola vending machine.
- A jury awards $2.8 million (later reduced to $640,000) to a woman against McDonald's because its coffee was so hot that she burned herself when she spilled some of it on her lap.

Reading about such cases in the media had many shaking their heads in disbelief. Warning labels are also ripe for comment. A sign on a baby stroller read, "Remove Child Before Folding." A Batman toy set warned that "Cape Does Not Enable User to Fly." The president of a stepladder company recently told a press conference of a case in which a man placed his ladder on frozen horse manure. He wanted to do some shingle work on his barn. As the manure melted, the ladder slipped. He fell and was injured. He then sued the ladder manufacturer and was awarded $330,000 on the theory that the manufacturer failed to provide adequate warning of the viscosity of manure! What does the need for such a warning say about the mentality of the American consumer? One commentator wonders whether we will one day see ladder warnings like the following:

- Avoid contact with electrical current. Never attempt to plug in a ladder.
- This warning sticker gets slippery when wet. That's why we put it on the side. If you're standing on this sticker, you've got the ladder pointed the wrong way.
- Never drink and climb a ladder. Always have a designated climber on hand.[1]

What's going on? Is the field of products liability law coming apart in a sea of ridicule? Not quite, but attorneys and the legal system have been taking a pounding. Talk-show hosts, late-night comics, and cartoonists are ever-available to give us the details of the latest seemingly absurd products liability case. In this environment of attack, humor, and exaggeration, it would be an understatement to say that many are confused about the law of products liability. Our goal in the following two chapters is to place this area of the law in perspective. An understanding of the basics will help separate the reality from the ridicule.

Exhibit 19–1
Annual injuries associated with selected consumer products.

Product	Injuries
Home equipment (e.g., saws, drills)	151,670
Household packaging and containers	353,989
Housewares (e.g., cookware, kitchen gadgets other than knives)	313,492
Ladders	186,732
Electric lighting equipment	20,601
Appliances (e.g., refrigerators, ranges)	61,572
Home entertainment equipment	74,424
Hair grooming equipment	20,108
Yard and garden equipment	173,008
Sports and recreation equipment	1,140,363

Source: National Safety Council, *Injury Facts, Annual* (www.nsc.org). The numbers are estimates from a representative sample of emergency room–treated cases nationwide associated with various products. Product involvement does not necessarily mean the product caused the accident or was defective. (www.census.gov/compendia/statab/tables/09s0193.xls) 2006.

CATEGORIES OF DEFECTS

The term *products liability* does not refer to a particular tort. Rather, it is a shorthand term that covers different causes of action that can be raised when a **defective** product causes injury or other harm. The major causes of action are:

defective Lacking in some particular that is essential to completeness, safety, or legal sufficiency.

- negligence
- breach of express warranty
- breach of implied warranty of merchantability
- breach of implied warranty of fitness for a particular purpose
- strict liability in tort

We will examine all five causes of action in this chapter. Some will be covered again in the next chapter when we focus on problems peculiar to what is called a **mass tort**, in which large numbers of persons are harmed by a relatively small number of defendants.

mass tort A tort cause of action asserted by a large number of persons who have been harmed by the same or similar conduct or product of a relatively small number of defendants.

The primary focus of most products liability cases is on a product that is defective. Something is wrong with the product that makes it dangerous. As a result, someone is injured, property is damaged, or both. As we shall see, however, every product that causes injury or damage is not necessarily defective. A bottle of milk that falls and breaks someone's toe has caused an injury, but it is highly unlikely that the bottle fell because it was defective. The three broad categories of defectiveness are manufacturing defects (something went wrong due to how the product was assembled), design defects (something went wrong due to how the product was planned or designed), and warning defects (something went wrong due to the inadequacy of information provided about the product). See Exhibit 19–2.

Exhibit 19–2 Categories of defects in products.

1. Manufacturing Defect The product does not conform to its design. When the product left the control of the manufacturer, it was not in the condition the manufacturer intended it to be in. Something went wrong in the manufacturing process, making the product dangerous. The defective product is different from the others. *Examples:* The screws on the wheels of the car were not tightened, a foreign substance was left in the soda bottle, a worker failed to follow instructions on the amount of a chemical to pour into the mold.
2. Design Defect The product conforms to the design, but the design is defective. When the product left the control of the manufacturer, it was in the condition the manufacturer intended it to be in, but something went wrong at the planning stage, making the product dangerous. The defective product is exactly like all the others, but something is wrong with all of them because of the very design of the product. *Examples:* The kind of metal called for by the design is not strong enough to do the work of the product, a safety shield should have been built into the product, the driver's vision through the rearview mirror was blocked because of the amount and position of the paneling in the back of the car.
3. Warning Defect There are no effective instructions on the packaging or in the literature accompanying the product covering (a) proper use of the product or (b) warnings of possible side effects of its use. When a product cannot be made safe for all foreseeable uses, there is a duty to provide effective instructions and warnings. The absence of such instructions and warnings is a defect that makes the product dangerous. The design of the product is otherwise reasonable and there are no manufacturing flaws in it, but the consumer should have been given more information about the product. *Examples:* Consumers with a certain allergy should have been told not to use the drug, or should have been told to use it only under a doctor's supervision; consumers should have been told to keep the polish out of the reach of children.

Before we begin our study of negligence and the other causes of action based on these categories of defects, it is important to note that the status of the plaintiff and of the defendant can sometimes have a dramatic effect on the outcome of a case. The various combinations are presented in Exhibit 19–3. When someone is injured by a product, one of the first tasks of a plaintiff's attorney is to identify everyone in the **chain of distribution** before the product reached the plaintiff. The attorney will be looking for parties to sue within this chain. For some causes of action, as we will see, the applicable law depends on the status of the injured party and of parties in the chain of distribution. If the status of a party changes, the applicable law will change.

chain of distribution All persons or businesses that had a role in making, selling, or leasing a product that reached the person injured by that product.

Exhibit 19–3
Status: Who is the plaintiff? Who is the defendant?

Status Possibilities of the Injured Plaintiff	Status Possibilities of the Defendant in the Chain of Distribution
• buyer of product • user of product • **lessee** (renter) of product • **bailor** of product • **bystander**	• manufacturer of entire product • manufacturer of a part of product • assembler of product • distributor of product • supplier/wholesaler of product • retail seller of product • **lessor** of product • **bailee** of product

lessee A person who rents or leases property from another. A tenant.

bailor One who delivers property to another under a contract of bailment.

bystander One who is injured by a product but who is not a seller, buyer, user, or consumer of the product. (See glossary for an additional definition.)

lessor A person who rents or leases property to another. A landlord.

bailee One to whom property is entrusted under a contract of bailment. *Bailment* is the delivery of personal property by one person (the bailor) to another (the bailee) under an express or implied contract whereby the property will be redelivered when the purpose of the contract (e.g., storage, shipment) is completed.

NEGLIGENCE

The first products liability cause of action we will examine is the traditional tort of *negligence*. For this tort, the defendant owes a duty of reasonable care to all foreseeable users of the product if it can be anticipated that substantial harm to person or property will result if the product is defective. Often this is not an easy cause of action for a plaintiff to establish because of the difficulty of proving the second element of negligence: a breach of duty (unreasonableness) by the defendant. Because of this difficulty, the law has created a new cause of action that is more plaintiff-friendly: *strict liability in tort*. We will be spending most of our time on this newer tort. Before we do, however, we need to cover some of the major issues involved in the traditional tort of negligence for injuries caused by product defects. This background will help us better understand strict liability in tort, particularly the debate on whether there is a negligence dimension to strict liability in tort.

As we saw in Chapters 12–16, there are four elements of negligence: duty, breach of duty, proximate cause, and damages.

Today, the first element, duty, is relatively easy to establish. According to the general rule on duty that we examined at the beginning of Chapter 13, whenever one's conduct creates a foreseeable risk of injury or other loss to someone's person or property, a duty of reasonable care arises to take reasonable precautions to prevent the injury or loss. In a products liability case based on negligence, the defendant's conduct that creates this duty is making, selling, or distributing a defective product.

At one time, however, the duty of a manufacturer or merchant was limited primarily to *buyers* of the product. The rule was that the defendant's duty of reasonable care covered only persons with whom the consumer was in **privity** or, more accurately, with whom there was *privity of contract*. Privity is a relationship that persons share in a transaction (e.g., a sale), in property, or in a right. The relationship between a buyer and a seller is called privity of contract. Under the old rule, an injured consumer could not bring a negligence suit against someone with whom the consumer was not in privity.

privity A relationship that persons share in a transaction, in property, or in a right. The major example of privity is *privity of contract*, which exists only between parties of a contract.

EXAMPLE

Jones goes to Wal-Mart to buy a toaster manufactured by Sunbeam. While using the toaster one day, Jones is injured when it catches fire. Jones sues Sunbeam for negligence.

Under the old rule, the case would be dismissed. There was no contract and, therefore, no privity between Jones and Sunbeam. Jones was limited to a suit against Wal-Mart, with whom he was in privity.

As we will see, the case of *MacPherson v. Buick Motor Co.* changed this privity rule. *MacPherson* is one of the most famous tort cases in American legal history. It was written by one of the giants in the field, New York State Court of Appeals Judge Benjamin Cardozo, later appointed to the United States Supreme Court. (Cardozo also wrote the majority opinion in the equally famous *Palsgraf* case we examined in Chapter 13.) The *MacPherson* case said that a duty of reasonable care is owed to all **foreseeable users** of the product (not just to those in privity) whenever it can be anticipated that harm will result if the product is defective. In our example, Jones certainly was a foreseeable user of Sunbeam's toaster. A toaster, like almost any product, can cause serious harm if it is defectively made. Under the ruling in *MacPherson,* therefore, a duty of reasonable care would be owed by Sunbeam to Jones. The existence of the duty is not based on contract. In rejecting the requirement of privity, Judge Cardozo pointed out in *MacPherson* that the source of the duty is the law "irrespective of contract," i.e., irrespective of whether the parties are in privity with each other.

foreseeable users Those persons whom a manufacturer or retailer can reasonably anticipate will use their product.

CASE

MacPherson v. Buick Motor Co.

217 N.Y. 382, 111 N.E. 1050 (1916)
Court of Appeals of New York

Background: *MacPherson was injured in his Buick because it had a defective wheel. He purchased the car from a retail dealer, not directly from the manufacturer, Buick Motor Company. Yet he sued Buick Motor Company for negligence. In the lower courts, Buick Motor Company argued that MacPherson could sue only the company with whom he was in privity—the retail dealer. Buick Motor Company also pointed out that it did not make the defective wheel itself; it purchased it from a wheel manufacturer and then assembled the wheel along with other component parts. The lower court (the Appellate Division) entered a judgment for MacPherson. The case is now on appeal before the Court of Appeals of New York.*

Decision on Appeal: *Judgment for MacPherson is affirmed. Writing for the majority, Judge Benjamin Cardozo held that a consumer can sue a manufacturer for negligence even in the absence of privity.*

OPINION OF COURT

Judge CARDOZO delivered the opinion of the court.

The defendant is a manufacturer of automobiles. It sold an automobile to a retail dealer. The retail dealer resold to the plaintiff. While the plaintiff was in the car, it suddenly collapsed. He was thrown out and injured. One of the wheels was made of defective wood, and its spokes crumbled into fragments. The wheel was not made by the defendant; it was bought from another manufacturer. There is evidence, however, that its defects could have been discovered by reasonable inspection, and that inspection was omitted. There is no claim that the defendant knew of the defect and willfully concealed it. . . . The question to be determined is whether the defendant owed a duty of care and vigilance to any one but the immediate purchaser.

The foundations of this branch of the law, at least in this state, were laid in *Thomas v. Winchester* (6 N.Y. 397). A poison was falsely labeled. The sale was made to a druggist, who in turn sold to a customer. The customer recovered damages from the seller who affixed the label. "The defendant's negligence," it was said, "put human life in imminent danger." A poison falsely labeled is likely to injure any one who gets it. Because the danger is to be foreseen, there is a duty to avoid the injury. . . . *Thomas v. Winchester* became quickly a landmark of the law. . . . [Judge Cardozo then discusses prior court opinions in order to reject the position of Buick that *Thomas v. Winchester* applies only to inherently dangerous products like poison.]

We hold, then, that the principle of *Thomas v. Winchester* is not limited to poisons, explosives, and things of like nature, to things which in their normal operation are implements of destruction. If the nature of a thing is such that it is reasonably certain to place life and limb in peril when negligently made, it is then a thing of danger. Its nature gives warning of the consequences to be expected. If to the element of danger there is added knowledge that the thing will be used by persons other than the purchaser, and used without new tests then, irrespective of contract, the manufacturer of this thing of danger is under a duty to make it carefully. That is as far as we are required to go for the decision of this case.

There must be knowledge of a danger, not merely possible, but probable. . . . There must also be knowledge that in the usual course of events the danger will be shared by others than the buyer. . . . We are dealing now with the liability of the manufacturer of the finished product, who puts it on the market to be used without inspection by his customers. If he is negligent, where danger is to be foreseen, a liability will follow. . . . We have put aside the notion that the duty to safeguard life and limb, when the consequences of negligence may be foreseen, grows out of contract and nothing else. We have put the source of the obligation where it ought to be. We have put its source in the law. . . .

Beyond all question, the nature of an automobile gives warning of probable danger if its construction is defective. This automobile was designed to go fifty miles an hour. Unless its wheels were sound and strong, injury was almost certain. It was as much a thing of danger as a defective engine for a railroad. The defendant knew the danger. It knew also that the car would be used by persons other than the buyer. This was apparent from its size; there were seats for three persons. It was apparent also from the fact that the buyer was a dealer in cars, who bought to resell. The maker of this car supplied it for the use of purchasers from the dealer. . . . The dealer was indeed the one person of whom it might be said with some approach to certainly that by him the car would not be used. Yet the defendant would have us say that he was the one person whom it was under a legal duty to protect. The law does not lead us to so inconsequent a conclusion. . . .

We think the defendant was not absolved from a duty of inspection because it bought the wheels from a reputable manufacturer. It was not merely a dealer in automobiles. It was a manufacturer of automobiles. It was responsible for the finished product. It was not at liberty to put the finished product on the market without subjecting the component parts to ordinary and simple tests. . . . The obligation to inspect must vary with the nature of the thing to be inspected. The more probable the danger, the greater the need of caution. . . .

The judgment [for MacPherson] should be affirmed.

ASSIGNMENT 19.1

a. Four people or businesses are mentioned in this opinion: Buick Motor Company, the wheel manufacturer, the retail dealer, and Mr. MacPherson. From this list, identify who was in privity with whom.
b. How are the facts in *MacPherson v. Buick Motor Co.* similar to those in *Thomas v. Winchester*? How are they different? Were the differences strong enough to lead Judge Cardozo to conclude that the *Thomas* opinion should not apply?
c. Would Judge Cardozo have ruled the same way if the person injured in the car was a backseat passenger who was in privity with no one?

The second element of negligence in a products liability case is *breach of duty*. As we saw in Chapter 14, the duty is breached when the defendant engages in unreasonable conduct under the circumstances as measured by the breach-of-duty equation (see Exhibit 14–4 in Chapter 14.) The defendant is unreasonable when the foreseeability of serious injury outweighs the burden or inconvenience of trying to avoid the accident and the defendant fails to undergo that burden or inconvenience. Also, the more important or socially useful the defendant's objective or task, the more reasonable it is to take risks of injury. A wonder drug has considerable social importance. If, however, the drug has the potential for dangerous side effects, the defendant must act reasonably to test the drug and make it as safe as reasonably possible. Some risk may still exist—even if consumer warnings are also added. Given the social importance of the drug, however, the law is less inclined to call a manufacturer negligent (unreasonable) for taking such risks by putting the drug on the market.

The same analysis is used for a product such as a lawn mower. Is it foreseeable that rocks will be thrown from the blade onto a person? If so, reasonable steps, such as the addition of a safety guard, may be needed. Lawn mowers are arguably not as socially valuable as medicine, but they are not frivolous items, and it is important to have them on the market even though they pose some risk. In all these cases, we must ask how much of a burden or inconvenience it would be for the defendant to take steps to try to eliminate the danger. The greater the potential harm, the more burden or inconvenience the defendant should undergo. It may be unreasonable for a manufacturer to fail to take extra time to do more testing and perhaps to add a safety feature (even if this will increase the cost of the product) when the foreseeability of serious harm without this feature is very high. On the other hand, it might be unreasonable to go through considerable expense to avoid a small injury that has little chance of occurring.

It is important to remember that the defendant is not an insurer. Injury caused by a manufacturing defect, a design defect, or a warning defect will *not* impose negligence liability on the defendant if the latter has taken all reasonable precautions as to safety. Under the law of negligence, the defendant does not have an obligation to produce a safe product; the obligation is to provide a *reasonably safe* product. The defendant does not have an obligation to produce a product without defects; the obligation is to take reasonable steps to avoid defects.

Later in the chapter, when we cover warranty and strict liability in tort, we will see that defendants do not always get off the hook simply by showing that they acted reasonably. It is generally much easier to establish liability under these causes of action than under negligence.

We turn now to an examination of how the status of the defendant in a negligence action affects the determination of what is reasonable.

Manufacturer

A *manufacturer* is held to the standard of an expert in the product manufactured. It must use reasonable care to discover and correct manufacturing defects. This includes the requirement of inspection and testing. Reasonable care must be used in the training of employees and in the operation of machinery on the production line. If parts are used from other manufacturers, care must be used to be sure that the parts are safe. Packaging must be reasonably safe with no misleading markings or advertising on it that could lead to a dangerous use. Once a product is made, manufacturers must inspect it for defects. This duty of inspection cannot be shifted to someone else in the chain of distribution. For example, a manufacturer of a car is not relieved of its obligation to inspect simply because it knows that a dealer will later inspect the car before final sale.

Design defects pose more of a problem. There is no absolute answer to the question of when a design is unreasonable. What, for example, is a reasonable design for a teenager's bicycle? Each year these bicycles are involved in thousands of accidental injuries. How should the bicycles be designed to avoid this danger? Theoretically, they could be designed to be extremely heavy so that they would never go very fast or designed with a very low seat so that a fall would never be more than a foot or so. But what would such bicycles cost? Would these designs render the bicycle relatively useless for recreation or sports for the vast majority of teenagers? Would they stop buying them? A reasonable design does not require a manufacturer to do that which is ridiculous—even if it could be done. In short, the breach-of-duty equation (see Exhibit 14–4 in Chapter 14) must be applied to determine whether a product design is reasonable—particularly the part of the equation calling for an assessment of the burden or inconvenience on the defendant to take design precautions that would avoid or minimize injury.

ASSIGNMENT 19.2

Is a car manufacturer unreasonable (and therefore negligent) for making a car without side air bags as standard equipment for everyone in the front and rear seats?

Warning defects also need to be considered. A manufacturer should provide reasonable instructions on the use of the product and reasonable warnings against dangers that may not be obvious. It must be emphasized, however, that a good warning is not a substitute for a reasonably safe product. Slapping a "danger" sign on an unreasonably dangerous product will not relieve the manufacturer from negligence liability. The product must be designed so that it is reasonably safe, even though it may still need a warning against dangers.

res ipsa loquitur ("The thing speaks for itself.") An inference of the defendant's unreasonableness (breach of duty) that allows the plaintiff's case to go to the jury, which may then agree or disagree that the defendant was unreasonable.

If the product defect is relatively blatant, the plaintiff may be able to use the doctrine of **res ipsa loquitur** to get the case to the jury. As we saw in Chapter 14, the elements of a res ipsa case require a showing that

1. The event producing the harm was of a kind that ordinarily does not occur in the absence of someone's negligence. It is more likely than not due to someone's unreasonableness.
2. The event producing the harm was caused by an agency or instrumentality within the defendant's exclusive control. It is more likely than not due to the defendant's unreasonableness.
3. The event producing the harm was not due to any voluntary action or contribution on the part of the plaintiff. The plaintiff is not a responsible cause of the accident.

The doctrine helps the plaintiff in cases such as the following: part of a human toe is found in a soda bottle, an aspirin contains ten times the normal ingredients, a new car explodes while someone is driving it off the dealer's lot. The special problems of applying the elements of res ipsa loquitur in a negligence case are discussed in Chapter 14.

Nonmanufacturer

merchant A person in the business of purchasing and selling goods.

A **merchant** is someone in the business of purchasing and selling goods. Merchants face negligence liability when their defective products injure a consumer. The boundary line of liability is reasonableness. The status of the defendant is relevant to the determination of what is reasonable. It may be unreasonable to ask a wholesaler or retailer to take certain safety precautions that would be quite reasonable for a manufacturer to take. A department store, for example, would not be under an obligation to safety-test every product it sells, whereas one would expect manufacturers to undertake safety tests for their products. The burden or inconvenience of this testing on a department store, a gas station, or a drugstore would be so great that it would probably mean going out of business.

Although reasonable merchants rarely need to test the products they sell, they do need to respond when injury becomes foreseeable. The following factors affect foreseeability:

Complaints If merchants have received complaints of injury from customers, they are on notice that something should be done, e.g., removing the product from the shelf. A reasonable merchant would not take a business-as-usual attitude in the face of actual knowledge that the product is being attacked by prior customers, especially if they are claiming serious injury.

Reputation of the Manufacturer A reasonable merchant who deals with a reputable manufacturer has less concern over the safety of the latter's product than when the manufacturer has had a history of problems or is relatively new on the market.

Packaging A reasonable merchant is less likely to be concerned about packaged products than about those that are sold without packaging. The package helps prevent damage. A merchant is not expected to open every package to make sure there are no dangers.

Custom in the Trade Although what other merchants do is never conclusive on the issue of reasonableness (see Chapter 14), the **custom** in the trade is relevant to determining what is reasonable. Is it the practice of similar merchants, for example, to sell the product without any inspection or warning? If so, then this may help persuade a court that a particular merchant was not unreasonable when it did not inspect or warn.

custom What is commonly done. Also called *custom and usage*.

Common Sense A reasonable merchant uses common sense. Obvious defects in the product, for example, would call for caution, especially if it is clear that the danger would not be equally apparent to every consumer, e.g., a child. Merchants may not stick their heads in the sand and play dumb in the face of obvious danger.

ASSIGNMENT 19.3

Helen is the manager of the XYZ Supermarket. While talking to a neighbor one day, Helen is told that the neighbor began feeling dizzy after using a tampon she bought from the XYZ Supermarket. Helen says, "You've got to be careful these days." Two weeks later, another customer dies while using the same product. What specific facts would you investigate to help determine whether the XYZ Supermarket was negligent in selling the tampon?

Defenses

Contributory negligence of the plaintiff is a complete defense in states where the full force of this defense is still alive. If the state has adopted **comparative negligence** (see Chapter 17), the court will compare the fault of the plaintiff and defendant and apportion responsibility according to the applicable formula in the state.

contributory negligence The failure of plaintiffs to take reasonable precautions for their protection, helping to cause their own injury or other loss.

comparative negligence A comparison of the negligence of the defendant and of the plaintiff in causing the plaintiff's injury (or other loss) in order to reduce the plaintiff's damages in proportion to the plaintiff's negligence in causing his or her own injury (or other loss).

Plaintiffs must use reasonable care to protect themselves, particularly with respect to discovering reasonably detectable defects in a product. It is contributory negligence for a plaintiff to fail to discover a defect in a product if a reasonable person in the plaintiff's position would have discovered it. Assume, for example, that the plaintiff is injured by a lawn mower, which she kept using even though she heard loud, unusual noises from the motor. These noises would have alerted any reasonable user to the probability of serious malfunction. Consumers who have paid "good money" for a product tend to be reluctant to cease using it, even when danger signs exist. The consumer keeps using the product in the hope that the machine will correct itself. After the injury, the consumer says, "I didn't know it was dangerous." If a reasonable user would have discovered the danger, the plaintiff loses the case in a contributory-negligence state (or has his or her damages reduced in a comparative-negligence state) in spite of the fact that the product was negligently designed or manufactured. Of course, consumers are not expected to conduct elaborate tests on a product in order to discover defects. They are held only to what a reasonable user would have discovered and done. (Later we will see that this negligent failure on the part of the plaintiff to discover the danger is *not* a defense when the plaintiff sues under a warranty or strict-liability-in-tort cause of action.)

Suppose that the plaintiff *does* discover the defect in the product and fully appreciates the danger. Continuing to use the product under such circumstances is an **assumption of the risk**. In many states, this is a defense to *any* cause of action in a products liability case. The plaintiff must have actual knowledge of the danger and voluntarily encounter it. There is a difference between suspecting that a problem might exist and knowing that it exists. The defense of assumption of the risk requires the latter. As pointed out in Chapter 17, however, when a state has adopted comparative negligence, an *express* assumption of the risk defeats the plaintiff's

assumption of the risk The knowing and voluntary acceptance of the danger or risk of being injured by someone's negligence.

negligence action so long as the express assumption (usually in the form of an exculpatory agreement) does not violate public policy. Not all *implied* assumptions of the risk, however, are defenses to a negligence action. There are two categories of implied assumptions: primary and secondary. In most states, plaintiffs lose if primary assumption of the risk can be established. In cases of secondary assumption of the risk, the negligence of the plaintiff and of the defendant are compared and damages are allocated according to whatever formula of comparative negligence the state uses. See the end of Chapter 17 for a discussion of these principles.

WARRANTY AND STRICT LIABILITY

warranty A guarantee; a commitment imposed by contract or by law that a product or service will meet a specified standard.

strict liability Responsibility for harm even if one did not intend the harm and used reasonable care to try to prevent it. Responsibility for harm whether or not the person causing the harm was at any fault or engaged in any moral impropriety. Also called *absolute liability* and *liability without fault*.

A **warranty** action is a form of **strict liability**, meaning that a breach of the warranty will lead to liability whether the defendant acted intentionally, negligently, or innocently. The historical development of warranty shows that it has both contract and tort dimensions. The contract dimension is that the warranty grows out of a contractual relationship. The major tort dimension is that there are consequences of violating or breaching the warranty that are imposed by law irrespective of what the parties to the contract agreed to do.

Three warranties need to be considered:

- express warranty
- implied warranty of merchantability
- implied warranty of fitness for a particular purpose

Since all three are strict liability causes of action, a plaintiff does not have to show that the defendant was negligent (or acted intentionally) in order to recover.

Do not confuse the terms *strict liability* and *strict liability in tort*. "Strict liability" is a general term that means liability without fault—the imposition of liability without the plaintiff having to show negligence or intent to injure. When we say that a cause of action imposes "strict liability," we are simply saying that there is no need to prove negligence or intent to injure. The phrase "strict liability in tort," on the other hand, has a narrower meaning. It is an actual tort cause of action. Of course, the general meaning of liability without fault also applies to this tort. But since "strict liability in tort" is an actual cause of action, it has elements, as we shall see later in this chapter. Think of "strict liability" as a phrase applying to different causes of action, one of which being "strict liability in tort."

EXPRESS WARRANTY

breach of express warranty Harm or damage caused by a false statement of fact relied on by the plaintiff and made with the intention or expectation that the statement will reach the plaintiff.

The first warranty cause of action we will examine is **breach of express warranty**, which is harm or damage caused by a false statement of fact relied on by the plaintiff and made with the intention or expectation that the statement will reach the plaintiff. See Exhibit 19–4 for its elements.

Exhibit 19–4
Elements of breach of express warranty.

1. A statement of fact that is false
2. Made with the intent or expectation that the statement will reach the plaintiff
3. Reliance on the statement by the plaintiff
4. Damage
5. Causation

Uniform Commercial Code (UCC) A state statute that governs many commercial transactions. Like all uniform laws, the UCC is proposed for adoption by state legislatures. Each state is free to accept, modify, or reject the proposal.

In most states, breach of express warranty is found within § 2-313 of the **Uniform Commercial Code (UCC)**,[2] a statute on express warranties.[3]

False Statement of Fact

The first element of a breach-of-express-warranty cause of action is that there must be a statement of **fact** that is false. A fact is a concrete statement that can be objectively established as true or false (e.g., "the mattress is nonflammable," "the wheels on the stroller cannot fall off," "the headlights on the car never have to be replaced."). An **opinion**, on the other hand, is a communication containing a relatively vague or indefinite value judgment that is not objectively verifiable (e.g., "the weather is refreshing"). The statement must be reasonably understood to be a fact.

Seller's talk or **puffing** is an expected exaggeration of quality, and as such, does not communicate facts. For example:

"The car is a great buy."

"The tool is excellent."

"It is the best buy around."

It does state a fact, however, to say that the glass in a car window is "shatter-proof," and the statement would be false if the window burst into pieces when hit with a rock. Sometimes it is difficult to classify a statement as fact or as seller's talk. Suppose that a merchant says that a chainsaw is "durable." Has a fact been stated? The answer depends on how a reasonable listener would interpret the statement. It would be unreasonable to interpret the statement to mean that it will last forever. Arguably, however, the statement communicates that the saw is safe for ordinary uses.

The creation of the express warranty does not require the use of the words "warranty" or "guarantee." Any words describing a product can be sufficient so long as the words communicate statements of fact. The warranty can also be created by showing the plaintiff a model or sample. The defendant is stating that the product conforms to the model or sample.

The plaintiff does not have to prove that the defendant knew that the statement was false; it simply must be false. Nor does the plaintiff have to show that the defendant acted negligently in communicating the false statement.

fact 1. An express or implied communication containing concrete information that can be objectively shown to be true or false. 2. A real occurrence. An event, thing, or state of mind that actually exists (or that is alleged to exist) as opposed to its legal consequences.

opinion An express or implied communication containing a relatively vague or indefinite value judgment that is not objectively verifiable. (See the glossary for another definition.)

puffing An exaggeration of quality or value that one can expect from someone, particularly a seller. Seller's talk.

ASSIGNMENT 19.4

Which of the following statements, if any, communicate statements of fact?

a. "The ladder will last a lifetime."
b. "The vaporizer is practically foolproof."
c. "These cigarettes are soothing."
d. "The detergent dissolves instantly."
e. "You can trust General Electric."
f. "If our tires save your life once, they are a bargain."

Intent or Expectation the Statement Will Reach the Plaintiff

The false statement of fact must be made to the plaintiff. If it is made to the general public, the defendant must reasonably expect that the statement will reach someone like the plaintiff. Hence, statements made in advertising would be covered. If the manufacturer makes statements in a manual that it distributes to retailers, the question will be whether the manufacturer could reasonably expect the retailer to tell consumers what is in the manual or to show the manual to them.

Reliance on Statement

reliance Forming a belief, taking action, or refraining from action in part due to confidence in someone or something. See also justifiable reliance.

material Essential or important; of influence on one's decision. (See glossary for additional meanings.)

Reliance means forming a belief, taking action, or refraining from action in part due to confidence in someone or something. The fact must be **material** to the transaction. It is material if it is essential or important in making a decision. This is so when the plaintiff either buys the product or uses it because of what the defendant said about it. Of course, plaintiffs cannot rely on a statement unless they know about it. Hence, it must be shown that the plaintiff saw or heard the statement.

Damage and Causation

The reliance on the false statement of fact must cause the plaintiff's damage or injury. The plaintiff must show that "but for" the statement, the damage or injury would not have occurred, or that the statement was a substantial factor in producing the damage or injury.

SALE VERSUS SERVICE

The final three causes of action we will examine in this chapter are:

- breach of implied warranty of merchantability
- breach of implied warranty of fitness for a particular purpose
- strict liability in tort

All three are strict liability causes of action because they do not require the plaintiff to prove that the defendant was unreasonable in causing the injury or intended the injury. A common component of all three is that they apply to sales, not to services. The distinction can be critical. If you are injured because of what the defendant *sold* you, the possible causes of action you may be able to bring include

- negligence
- breach of express warranty
- breach of implied warranty of merchantability
- breach of implied warranty of fitness for a particular purpose
- strict liability in tort

sale The transfer of title to property for a price or other consideration.

consideration Something of value that is exchanged between parties. It can be an act, a forbearance (not performing an act), a promise to perform an act, or a promise to refrain from performing an act.

personal property Property other than land or other than things attached to land. Also called chattels.

real property Land and anything attached or affixed to the land, such as buildings, fences, and trees. Also called real estate.

If, however, you are injured while the defendant is rendering a *service*, the primary causes of action you can bring are

- negligence
- breach of express warranty

It is, therefore, to the plaintiff's advantage to show that the defendant sold something. This will open more possibilities, particularly the pro-plaintiff cause of action, strict liability in tort.

The general meaning of **sale** is the transfer of title to property for a price or other **consideration**. For purposes of our three causes of action, however, the renting or leasing of property is included in the definition of a sale even though title does not pass in such transactions. Also, the sale must be by a *merchant*—someone in the business of selling. Hence the three causes of action would not apply to the sale of a car between neighbors who are not merchants.

Note that the definition of sale covers **personal property** (chattels); the definition does not cover the sale of **real property**. A few courts, however, have made

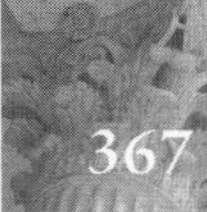

exceptions to this rule and have allowed strict liability in tort to be brought against sellers of mass-produced houses.

ASSIGNMENT 19.5

Is there a sale in the following situations?

a. Fred is at a supermarket. He takes a bottle of catsup from the shelf, puts it in his cart, and heads for the checkout counter. While he is picking up the bottle from the cart to place it on the counter, it explodes, injuring Fred.

b. Mary is test driving a car that she is considering purchasing. She is alone in the car five blocks from the dealer. On her way back to the dealer, she decides against purchasing the car. Just as she drives into the dealer's lot, the brakes malfunction, causing an accident, in which she is injured.

A **service** is an activity that is performed or a benefit that is provided as part of one's line of work, e.g., a doctor operating on a patient, an attorney conducting a trial, or a professor teaching a class. In general, if title does not pass, then what you have paid for is a service. The easiest services to recognize are the professional services of doctors, attorneys, and teachers. Such professionals are not strictly liable for the harm they cause through the three causes of action we are examining. Suits against them must establish negligence (or breach of express warranty if this cause of action can be proven).

service Activity performed or benefit provided as part of one's line of work. (See glossary for another meaning.)

A service does not become a sale simply because there is a sale dimension to what occurs. Suppose, for example, that a dentist uses a hypodermic needle in a patient's mouth. The needle is a product or a "good" for which the patient is charged. Yet this does not change the character of the event from a service to a sale. There is no implied warranty that the needle is safe. There is no implied warranty that anything the dentist does is safe or effective. If the needle breaks in the patient's mouth, a suit against the dentist must show negligence.

What about a blood transfusion at a hospital? Assume that a hemophiliac contracts AIDS by receiving infected blood during a transfusion. Is the blood a "good" (a product) that has been purchased? Most courts say no. The blood transfusion is a service. (In some states this result is mandated by statute.) Negligence, therefore, must be shown, e.g., carelessness in the screening and testing procedures for those who donate blood.

Services are not limited to the professions. Hotels provide services, as do plumbers and carpenters. The gray area is again the situation where it appears that both a sale and a service exist. A beauty parlor, for example, provides a service. Yet, it uses and charges for products in rendering this service, e.g., a permanent-wave solution. Again, the general rule is that a service does not become a sale simply because a product is used or because there is a product component to what is predominantly a service. There are courts, however, that *are* willing to chip away at this rule when nonprofessional services are involved. In the beauty parlor case, for example, there is a well-known New Jersey opinion that held there was a sale of the permanent-wave solution by a beauty parlor. When the solution caused injury, strict liability was imposed without the need to prove negligence.[4] The same result would be reached if a plaintiff at a restaurant were injured by food or drink. They are sales.

Defendants understandably want to classify what they do as services in order to avoid any form of strict liability. If they are correct that they are engaged in a service, the plaintiff must prove that the injury was negligently produced.

ASSIGNMENT 19.6

Bob is an independent paralegal in your state. He is authorized to represent clients in cases before the Social Security Administration for which he can legally charge a fee. For $25 extra, he sells clients a packet of forms that they can use to fill out themselves. Mary is one of his clients. She pays him his fee plus $25 for the forms. When opening the packet of forms at home, she cuts herself on a small razor that Bob had carelessly left in the packet. Mary wants to sue Bob. Does she have to prove negligence?

IMPLIED WARRANTIES

There are two implied warranties:

- implied warranty of merchantability
- implied warranty of fitness for a particular purpose

They are imposed by the law and not through agreement of the parties. You will find these warranties in state statutory codes. State legislatures created the warranties by modeling them on § 2-314 (merchantability) and § 2-315 (fitness) of the Uniform Commercial Code (UCC). Like the breach of an express warranty, the breach of these two implied warranties imposes strict liability, in that the plaintiff does not have to establish that the defendant intended to breach them nor that the defendant was negligent in breaching them.

Our discussion of the implied warranties will cover the following topics:

- elements of breach
- problems of privity
- defenses

breach of implied warranty of merchantability Harm or damage caused by a merchant's sale of goods that are not fit for the ordinary purposes for which they are used.

Implied Warranty of Merchantability

A **breach of implied warranty of merchantability** is harm or damage caused by a merchant's sale of goods that are not fit for the ordinary purposes for which they are used. See Exhibit 19–5 for its elements.

Exhibit 19–5
Elements of breach of implied warranty of merchantability.

1. Sale of goods
2. By a merchant of goods of that kind
3. The goods are not merchantable
4. Damage
5. Causation

Sale of Goods Sales are covered, but not services. See the earlier discussion in this chapter on the problems of distinguishing a sale (which does carry an implied warranty of merchantability) and a service (which does not).

Merchant of Goods of That Kind This warranty does not apply to the occasional seller of goods, such as a cab driver who sells a watch to a fellow cab driver or to a customer in the cab. The defendant must be a merchant in the business of selling goods of the kind in question. There is an implied warranty of merchantability in a car sold by a car dealer, but not in a rifle sold by the car dealer.

merchantable Fit for the ordinary purposes for which the goods are used.

Goods Are Not Merchantable Goods are **merchantable** when they are fit for the ordinary purposes for which the goods are used. (As we shall see in the next

section, this is a broader test than that used for *strict liability in tort*, which requires that the product be unreasonably dangerous.) The following are examples of products that are not merchantable:

- vinegar bottles that contain particles of glass
- shoes with heels that break off with normal use soon after purchase
- aspirin that causes infertility

If, however, regular shoes fall apart when the plaintiff is mountain climbing, there is no implied warranty of merchantability, because the shoes were not being used for their ordinary purpose. If the plaintiff who bought the shoes can establish the elements of an implied warranty of fitness *for a particular purpose* (see discussion below) strict liability will be imposed on that theory.

There is no requirement that plaintiffs prove they actually relied on the merchantability of the goods before purchase. This reliance is assumed. Suppose, however, that there are obvious defects in the product, which a reasonable inspection of the goods would reveal to the typical consumer. There is no implied warranty with respect to such defects so long as the consumer had full opportunity to inspect.

Damage and Causation The harm or damage to the person or property of the plaintiff must be caused by the fact that the goods were not fit for their ordinary purpose. The traditional but-for or substantial-factor tests will be applied to establish causation.

ASSIGNMENT 19.7

There is a small fire in Mary's apartment. When she tries to smother it with a blanket, she is burned by the flames that come from the blanket, which caught fire the moment she placed it on the small fire. In a suit against the manufacturer of the blanket, can she claim breach of implied warranty of merchantability?

Implied Warranty of Fitness for a Particular Purpose

Next we examine **breach of implied warranty of fitness for a particular purpose,** which is harm or damage caused by a sale of goods by a merchant who has reason to know the buyer is relying on the expertise of the merchant in selecting the goods for a particular purpose, but the goods are not fit for that purpose. See Exhibit 19–6 for its elements.

breach of implied warranty of fitness for a particular purpose Harm or damage caused by a sale of goods by a merchant who has reason to know the buyer is relying on the expertise of the merchant in selecting the goods for a particular purpose, but the goods are not fit for that purpose.

1. Sale of goods
2. By a merchant of goods of that kind
3. The merchant has reason to know the buyer's particular purpose in buying the goods
4. The merchant has reason to know that the buyer is relying on the merchant's skill or judgment in buying the goods
5. The goods are not fit for the particular purpose
6. Damage
7. Causation

Exhibit 19–6
Elements of breach of implied warranty of fitness for a particular purpose.

Particular purposes must be distinguished from the ordinary purposes of a product. Ordinary purposes are the customary uses of the product. The following are examples of particular purposes:

- shoes to be used to climb mountains
- sunglasses to be used by a professional baseball player
- a dog chain to hold a 300-pound dog

The merchant must know or have reason to know about the particular purpose, and know that the buyer is relying on the merchant's skill and judgment. The buyer must in fact rely on this skill and judgment. A buyer who makes a careful inspection of the product may have difficulty proving reliance. A good deal will depend on the extent of the inspection and on the expertise of the buyer in the use of the product. If the buyer relies on his or her own skill and judgment rather than on that of the merchant, the buyer cannot use this cause of action. Of course, if the product is also not fit for its *ordinary* purpose, the plaintiff can sue under the merchantability warranty.

Privity in Warranty Actions

Earlier, when we discussed negligence in a products liability case, we saw that all states now follow the ruling of *MacPherson v. Buick Motor Co.* that privity is not needed to bring a negligence action. Privity of contract is the relationship that two parties share because of the contract between them.

EXAMPLE

Helen buys a General Electric blender from Macy's. One day in Helen's kitchen, the blender explodes, injuring Helen, her young daughter, and a visiting neighbor. When the accident occurred, they were all gathered around the blender ready to taste a new drink the blender was mixing.

Helen is in privity with Macy's, but not with General Electric. Her daughter and neighbor are in privity with no one. Yet, under the ruling in *MacPherson,* they can all sue General Electric for *negligence*. The absence of privity will not be a bar since they are all foreseeable users of the blender, which is dangerous if defectively made.

Suppose, however, that Helen, her daughter, and her neighbor want to sue General Electric for breach of any of the warranties. Will the lack of privity be a bar? States do not answer this question in the same way:

Who Can Sue for Breach of Warranty

- A few states cling to the old rule that there must be privity, which can exist only between an immediate buyer and the immediate seller.
- Some states permit the immediate buyer and members of the buyer's family or household to bring the warranty action.
- Some states permit the immediate buyer and any person who may reasonably be expected to be affected by the goods to bring the warranty action, e.g., a bystander who is hit by a car.

Who Can Be Sued for Breach of Warranty

- A few states cling to the old rule that there must be privity, which can exist only between an immediate buyer and the immediate seller.
- Some states permit designated nonprivity plaintiffs (see "Who Can Sue" above) to bring direct warranty actions against the manufacturer when the product is designed to come into contact with the body, e.g., food, home permanent solution.
- Some states permit designated nonprivity plaintiffs (see "Who Can Sue") to bring direct warranty actions against the manufacturer for any product.

Defenses to Warranty Actions

The following defenses will be briefly discussed:

- disclaimer
- notice

- contributory negligence
- assumption of the risk

Disclaimer of Warranty Under certain conditions, parties to a sales contract can agree that some or all warranties do not exist, i.e., the warranties are disclaimed. A **disclaimer** consists of words or conduct that negate or repudiate a claim, right, or obligation. To be effective, a disclaimer must be conspicuous and unambiguous so that it is clearly communicated to the buyer. A disclaimer buried in small print on the back of a standardized contract form will probably be held to be ineffective against the ordinary consumer. A court may rule that the disclaimer is invalid because it is **unconscionable**. Something is unconscionable when it is oppressive and grossly unfair due to a highly unequal bargaining position of the parties. If the defendant is the seller or manufacturer of mass-produced goods, courts are likely to find that nonconspicuous disclaimers are unconscionable against the average consumer. Statutes may impose special requirements for disclaimers to be effective. For example, a disclaimer of the warranty of merchantability must mention the word "merchantability" in the language of the disclaimer. Furthermore, the disclaimer must be printed in a designated **point** size. Finally, if nonpurchasers are allowed to bring a warranty action (see the discussion on privity), disclaimers are generally ineffective against them.

disclaimer Words or conduct that negate or repudiate a claim, right, or obligation.

unconscionable So one-sided due to highly unequal bargaining positions as to be oppressive and grossly unfair.

point A measure of the size of printed letters of the alphabet, punctuation marks, or other characters. (One point is approximately 1/72 of an inch tall.)

Notice It is a defense to a warranty action that the injured plaintiff failed to give **notice** to the defendant of the breach of the warranty within a reasonable time after the breach was discovered or should have been discovered. Since many plaintiffs wait a good deal of time before taking action, they fall into the trap of this defense. Some courts, however, disregard the notice requirement when the breach of warranty causes personal injury or when the plaintiff is a nonpurchaser. Even if a court will not go this far, the tendency is to be lenient to plaintiffs in deciding whether they waited an unreasonable time to notify the defendant.

notice 1. Information or knowledge about something. 2. Formal notification. 3. Knowledge of facts that would naturally lead an honest and prudent person to make inquiry.

Contributory Negligence Generally, contributory negligence is not a defense to a breach-of-warranty action.

Assumption of the Risk Assumption of the risk *is* a defense to a breach-of-warranty action. The defendant must show that the plaintiff had actual knowledge and an appreciation of the danger and yet still voluntarily proceeded to use the product.

CASE

Ressallat v. Burglar & Fire Alarms, Inc.

79 Ohio App. 3d 43, 606 N.E.2d 1001 (1992)
Court of Appeals of Ohio, Third District, Crawford County

Background: *Dr. Ressallat and his wife bought a home burglary alarm from BFA (Burglar & Fire Alarms, Inc.). The contract of sale disclaimed all implied warranties. After a burglary, the Ressallats sued BFA for breach of implied warranty of merchantability seeking recovery for loss of personal property resulting from the burglary. The position of BFA was that it had disclaimed all warranties in the contract of sale. The trial court agreed with BFA, ruling that the disclaimer was sufficiently conspicuous. The Ressallats (as appellants) appealed. The case is now on appeal before the Court of Appeals of Ohio.*

Decision on Appeal: *Judgment for BFA affirmed. Although the trial court erred in ruling that the disclaimer was conspicuous, the error was harmless because there was no breach of warranty that caused harm.*

OPINION OF COURT

Judge EVANS delivered the opinion of the court. . . .

[The] Ressallats ("appellants") entered into an agreement with BFA [Burglar & Fire Alarms, Inc.] for the purchase of a burglar alarm system for their home. The system was designed to alert the Ressallats, both via warning lights and the sounding of a horn, when an unauthorized person had entered the house. The burglar alarm system was linked with the telephone system so that, simultaneous with the sounding of the alarm, a call was placed through the telephone lines to BFA's "central monitoring station." The Ressallats paid a monthly fee for these services.

On the advice of BFA's salesperson, the Ressallats arranged with the telephone company to have the phone cable, from the pole to the house, buried. However . . . the Ressallats began having problems with the telephone lines. Although General Telephone Company ("GTE") resolved the difficulties with the phone lines, the cable was not reburied. Instead, it was strung directly from the pole to the Ressallats' house, suspended just a few feet above the ground. Although Dr. Ressallat contacted GTE several times about reburying the phone cable, the company took no action until after the burglary.

[The] Ressallats' home was burglarized. The burglar apparently obtained unimpeded access to the house by cutting the exposed telephone wires so as to prevent transmission of the alarm. Inside the house, wires to the burglar alarm horn were severed at the electric service box. Jewelry and coins worth over $100,000 were stolen from the house. The Ressallats' insurance company, Physicians' Insurance Company of Ohio ("PICO"), reimbursed the Ressallats in the amount of $17,125.37, the maximum payable on their homeowners' policy. . . .

[In the Ressallats' suit against BFA for breach of warranty, the trial court ruled for BFA, concluding that all warranties had been validly disclaimed because they were conspicuous. On appeal the Ressallats argue that the disclaimer was "inconspicuous as a matter of law."]

Under R.C. [Ohio Revised Code] 1302.29, unless exclusions or disclaimers of warranty are part of the parties' "bargain in fact," a purchaser of goods in Ohio receives, in addition to any express warranty (which generally only provides for repair or replacement of defective goods), an implied warranty that the goods shall be merchantable and "fit" for their intended purpose. See R.C. 1302.27 and 1302.28. Although courts generally uphold disclaimers of implied warranties between parties who have equal bargaining power, they are reluctant to afford validity to such disclaimers when a purchaser is simply a consumer, rather than a commercial entity. As stated by the Supreme Court: ". . . [Disclaimers] of implied warranties. . . must be a part of the parties' bargain in fact. If it is contained in a printed clause which was not conspicuous or brought to the buyer's attention, the seller had no reasonable expectation that the buyer understood that his remedies were being restricted to repair and replacement." *Ins. Co. of N. Am. v. Automatic Sprinkler Corp.* (1981), 67 Ohio St. 2d 91, 96–97, 423 N.E.2d 151, 154–155.

Further, R.C. 1302.29(B) requires compliance with the following: ". . . to exclude or modify the implied warranty of merchantability or any part of it the language must mention merchantability and in case of a writing must be conspicuous, and to exclude or modify any implied warranty of fitness the exclusion must be by a writing and conspicuous. . . ."

The code itself defines "conspicuous," and provides that a determination of conspicuousness is a matter of law for the court to decide. R.C. 1301.01(J) provides:

> ". . . A term or clause is conspicuous when it is so written that a reasonable person against whom it is to operate ought to have noticed it. A printed heading in capitals (as: NONNEGOTIABLE BILL OF LADING) is conspicuous. Language in the body of a form is 'conspicuous' if it is in larger or other contrasting type or color . . . Whether a term is 'conspicuous' or not is for decision by the court."

The disclaimer of warranties at issue herein appears on the back page of the sales contract, which was signed on the front by both parties. The disclaimer is buried in the middle of a full page of small type, in a style identical to the rest of the text on the page. There are no outstanding headings alerting a purchaser to the disclaimer, and there is no mention of "merchantability" as required by R.C. 1302.29. Furthermore, Dr. Ressallat testified in his deposition that the disclaimer was not mentioned by the salesman at the time of the sale of the burglar alarm system, nor was it brought to his attention that anything was printed on the back page of the contract.

We believe the court erred in concluding that the disclaimer of warranties in these parties' contract was conspicuous. First, the disclaimer fails to mention "merchantability," a requirement of the code which must be fulfilled if a disclaimer of the implied warranty of merchantability is to be found valid. Additionally, we find that the trial court ignored the statutory language and applied an improper standard in determining that the disclaimer was conspicuous. In making that determination, the court stated: "These warranties and conditions are not hidden, but clearly spelled out in common understandable language which leaves no doubt as to what is and what is not covered, and when."

While we agree that the common, ordinary definition of "conspicuous" can be "not hidden," or "clearly spelled out," the code explicitly sets forth what the term means under the circumstances of this case. One's understanding of the terminology bears no relation to conspicuousness under the code. In the disclaimer at issue, there are no prominent headings, and there is no print of a different style or color that would draw one's attention. The disclaimer wording blends in with the surrounding "terms" and "conditions" and is in no way more noticeable. We find that the disclaimer in the contract is, as a matter of law, inconspicuous. . . .

However . . . we find that in this case the court's error was harmless, and not prejudicial to appellants. Absent evidence or testimony supporting the breach of warranty claims, the disclaimers are irrelevant, and thus provide no ground for reversal of the court's judgment. . . .

Dr. Ressallat himself testified that BFA had advised him at the time of the burglar alarm purchase to have the telephone lines buried for the sake of security. Further, after GTE had dug up the lines for repair purposes, it failed to rebury them despite several requests from appellants. Burial of the telephone cable was never a duty assumed by BFA. . . . Appellants present no evidence of failure or defect in the actual system or its components. There is simply no evidence that BFA breached any duty it could possibly have had to appellants. Appellants offer no facts evidencing how any warranty was breached, nor do the complaint, transcript, or affidavits indicate that any action of [BFA] was the proximate cause of the burglary. Furthermore, BFA's evidence that the alarm system was functioning properly immediately before and after the robbery was unrefuted.

Therefore . . . no reasonable person could find that BFA sold appellants a defective alarm system or failed in its duty to maintain and repair the system under the parties' contract, thereby becoming liable for appellants' loss of property. Indeed, sellers of goods are not required to be insurers of property, absent assumption of such a duty. . . . Having found no evidence as to BFA's . . . breach of warranties . . . we affirm the judgment of the trial court.

Judgment affirmed.

ASSIGNMENT 19.8

a. If the implied warranty on the burglar alarm was not validly disclaimed, why did the buyers of the alarm lose the case?
b. Would the result in this case have been different if the buyers had signed the contract of sale on the same page that contained the disclaimer of warranties?
c. Can the buyers sue GTE? If so, for what causes of action?

STRICT LIABILITY IN TORT

One of the most dramatic developments in the law of torts since the 1960s has been the creation of a new tort called **strict liability in tort**. As we will see, it provides considerable advantages to an injured consumer over the other products liability causes of action. For the elements of this tort, see Exhibit 19–7.

strict liability in tort Liability for physical harm caused by a defective product that is unreasonably dangerous.

Exhibit 19–7
Elements of strict liability in tort.

1. Seller
2. A defective product that is unreasonably dangerous to person or property
3. User or consumer
4. Physical harm (damages)
5. Causation

There are a number of reasons why strict liability in tort is an attractive cause of action for plaintiffs:

- The plaintiff does not have to prove that the defendant was negligent (although negligence concepts may be relevant when the plaintiff alleges that the injury was caused by a design defect).
- The plaintiff does not have to prove that the defendant knew of the defect.
- The plaintiff does not have to establish privity with the defendant.
- The defendant cannot disclaim the obligation of safety no matter how conspicuous the disclaimer.
- Before being able to sue, the plaintiff has no duty to give the defendant notice of the injury caused by the product.

The five elements of strict liability in tort are based on the highly influential **§ 402A** of the American Law Institute's *Restatement (Second) of Torts*. Many courts have adopted these five elements of § 402A. As we shall see, however, there are a number of courts that have modified some of the elements. Also, the American Law Institute has itself made significant changes in its more recent *Restatement (Third) of Torts*, particularly as to design defects. Yet, the principles that dominate this area of the law in most states continue to be those embodied in § 402A of *Restatement (Second) of Torts*.

§ 402A The main section on strict liability in tort from *Restatement (Second) of Torts*. The section provides for liability for physical harm caused by a defective product that is unreasonably dangerous.

Seller

seller Anyone in the business of selling products. (See glossary for an additional definition.)

The defendant must be a **seller**. Seller has a broad definition: any person engaged in the business of selling products for use or consumption. Not covered is the occasional seller of a product who is not engaged in selling as part of his or her business. If, for example, one student sells another student a defective car, there is no strict liability in tort, because the student is not in the business of selling products. If the student is liable at all, negligence will have to be shown. Furthermore, isolated sales that are not part of the usual course of business of the seller are not covered.

The following would be sellers under the first element:

- manufacturer of an entire product
- assembler
- wholesaler
- operator of a restaurant
- supplier of a part
- distributor
- retailer

Some states do not impose strict liability in tort on the manufacturer of a defective *component* part of a product. Its liability would have to be based on negligence. Other courts, however, treat the manufacturer of a component part like everyone else in the chain of distribution and impose strict liability in tort.

Assume that at a small neighborhood hardware store you buy a defective hammer that is manufactured by a company located a thousand miles away. Both the store (a retailer) and the manufacturer are subject to strict liability in tort. They are both in the chain of distribution to the plaintiff. The store manager cannot say, "I didn't make the hammer; go sue the manufacturer." The store is a seller engaged in the business of selling, and hence is subject to strict liability in tort. To recover, the plaintiff does not have to prove that the store manager was negligent.

For the strict liability causes of action, as we saw earlier, the sale of goods includes the leasing or renting of goods. A company that rents cars, planes, or other equipment, for example, is considered a seller, and, therefore, can be strictly liable in tort. Section 402A, however, does not apply to the sale of real property, except in the few states that are willing to extend strict liability in tort to mass-produced homes. In most states, the tort is limited to transactions involving personal property. See the earlier discussion of this theme.

Defective Product That Is Unreasonably Dangerous

The second element of strict liability in tort is that the product must be defective and unreasonably dangerous. In Exhibit 19–2, we examined the three major categories of defects:

manufacturing defects: Something never intended went wrong when the product was being put together. The product does not conform to its design.

design defects: The product conforms to what the planners intended, but something is wrong with their design.

warning defects: The instructions or warnings for the product are either missing or are inadequate.

The plaintiff does not have to prove that the defendant was negligent in creating any of these defects. A defendant who has sold a defective product can be strictly liable in tort even if the defendant used all reasonable care. The problem, however, is that it is sometimes difficult to avoid discussing negligence concepts, particularly when the product is alleged to have design defects. Part of the confusion is the use of the phrase **unreasonably dangerous** in § 402A of *Restatement (Second) of Torts*. This phrase certainly suggests the reasonableness analysis that dominates any discussion of negligence. In theory, however, we need to separate negligence from strict liability in tort. They are different causes of action:

unreasonably dangerous Dangerous to an extent beyond that which would be contemplated by the ordinary consumer who purchases it, with the ordinary knowledge common to the community as to its characteristics.

- Negligence: The primary focus of negligence is on the *conduct* of the defendant: What did the defendant do or fail to do that was reasonable or unreasonable?
- Strict liability in tort: The primary focus of strict liability in tort is the *product:* Is the product unreasonably dangerous?

When is a product unreasonably dangerous? Section 402A uses the "ordinary consumer" test:

> A product is unreasonably dangerous when it is dangerous to an extent beyond that which would be contemplated by the ordinary consumer who purchases it, with the ordinary knowledge common to the community as to its characteristics.

Note that the test is not whether the injured plaintiff thought the product was unreasonably dangerous. All injured plaintiffs undoubtedly would. The test is not *subjective* (what the plaintiff thought); the test is *objective* (what an ordinary consumer would think).

In many cases there is little difficulty establishing unreasonable danger by using the test of the ordinary consumer. Such consumers, for example, would not expect a bottle of catsup to have arsenic in it and would expect a bus to be designed with handrails that are within easy reach during a sudden stop. They are also conscious of dangers inherent in certain products, e.g., knives, matches, or bug sprays. When aware of an obvious danger, the ordinary consumer will take common-sense precautions such as lifting a knife by its handle rather than by its blade. The fact that a *particular* consumer might pick up a knife by its blade does not make the knife unreasonably dangerous.

Other products, however, are not so easy to assess. Assume, for example, that the plaintiff eats a bowl of fish chowder at a New England restaurant and suffers severe injuries when a fish bone gets caught in his or her throat. Is the product unreasonably dangerous? Probably not. An ordinary consumer would expect to find some bones in this kind of soup. There is danger from bones in the soup, but not an unreasonable danger. Note that we do not ask whether the restaurant used reasonable care to remove bones from the fish chowder. The use of reasonable care is a negligence standard. The test here is the expectation of the ordinary consumer.

Courts sometimes make the distinction between injuries caused by a foreign substance in a product (e.g., a thumbtack in a bottle of soda) and those caused by something that is intentionally present or that is natural to the product (e.g., a bone in a steak). Although it is easier to establish unreasonable danger when the substance is foreign, this is not the sole test. Injury caused by the intended or natural components of a product can sometimes make the product unreasonably dangerous (e.g., inadequate warnings of possible side effects from the ingredients of a drug).

A manufacturer or retailer is not required to sell a product that will never cause injury. Nor are they required to sell a product in the safest condition possible. A car built like a tank may be the safest vehicle on the road, but a car manufacturer is not strictly liable in tort for failing to build its cars to be as strong as tanks. Why? Because ordinary consumers do not expect cars to be built this way for their safety.

ASSIGNMENT 19.9

Are the products in the following examples unreasonably dangerous?

a. Linda goes into a bar and orders a martini. She breaks a tooth on an unpitted olive.
b. George chokes on a cherry pit in a pie he purchases from a school vending machine.

c. Sara chokes on a whole peanut found in "extra creamy" peanut butter she purchases at the supermarket.
d. Mary buys a bicycle from Cycle and Sports for her twelve-year-old son, Tom. The bike does not have a headlight on it. While carefully riding the bike at night, Tom is hit by a car. Assume that the accident would not have occurred if the bike had a headlight on it.

Many products can become dangerous to a consumer who overuses or overconsumes them, but they are not necessarily unreasonably dangerous. Good, "wholesome" whiskey is not unreasonably dangerous even though it can be deadly to alcoholics. Uncontaminated butter is not unreasonably dangerous even though it can help bring on heart attacks in people who need a low-cholesterol diet.

Nor is a product unreasonably dangerous because it fails to warn against every possible danger that could be caused by its use.

> The seller may reasonably assume that those with common allergies, as for example to eggs or strawberries, will be aware of them, and he is not required to warn against them. Where, however, the product contains an ingredient to which a substantial number of the population are allergic, and the ingredient is one whose danger is not generally known, or if known is one which the consumer would reasonably not expect to find in the product, the seller is required to give warning against it, if he has knowledge, or by the application of reasonable, developed human skills and foresight should have knowledge, of the presence of the ingredient and the danger. Likewise in the case of poisonous drugs, or those unduly dangerous for other reasons, warning as to use may be required. *Restatement (Second) of Torts* § 402A, comment j (1965).

Once a warning is clearly and conspicuously given, the seller can assume that it will be read and followed.

Stella Liebeck's Hot Coffee Case

In 1992, the Stella Liebeck case received extensive publicity in the media. Stella, a 79-year-old woman, ordered a cup of coffee from a drive-in window at a McDonald's. While sitting in a passenger seat, she placed the coffee cup between her knees and removed the lid in order to add cream and sugar. Unfortunately, the coffee spilled, causing third-degree burns that scalded her thighs, buttocks, and groin. She was in the hospital for eight days of treatment that included skin grafting. She then sued McDonald's for selling her a defective product because of the heat at which the coffee is sold. The policy of McDonald's was to sell coffee at between 180 and 190 degrees Fahrenheit. Other restaurants sold their coffee at significantly lower temperatures. Coffee made at home is usually about 135 degrees. McDonald's offered to settle the case for $800, rejecting Stella's offer to settle for $20,000. The case went to trial after further settlement efforts failed. The jury awarded Stella $2.86 million. The trial judge reduced this amount to $640,000. An appeal was avoided when the parties settled for an undisclosed but still substantial amount.

Was the coffee unreasonably dangerous? What are the expectations of the ordinary consumer when served hot coffee? Using different terminology, these questions were extensively debated by citizens throughout the country. The media had a field day with the case. There was not much sympathy for a woman who failed to avoid spilling hot coffee on herself. One organization established an annual Stella Award for the most frivolous and shocking lawsuits of the year.

Many trial lawyers, however, were quick to reject the view that the coffee case was frivolous. In the ten years before Stella brought her case, over 700 coffee burn claims were made against McDonald's. Stella's products liability case, the lawyers

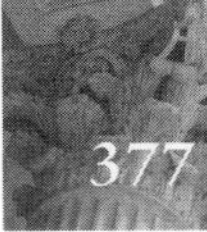

argued, was the only way to get the attention of a giant corporation in order to force it either to lower the temperature or to provide more effective warnings of the danger of spilling hot coffee.

Strict Liability in Tort for "Defective" Websites and Movies?

Most courts say that a product must have a physical form in order to give rise to strict liability in tort. Ideas or images in themselves do not have a physical form. They may be embodied in a physical form such as a DVD disk that contains a movie, or they may be accompanied by physical forms such as the electricity used to power a website. The DVD disk or the electricity can be defective and cause an injury, but the ideas and images on the DVD or website are not products for purposes of strict liability in tort. A *negligence* claim is sometimes made that violent images in the media caused a person to commit violence. Such claims usually fail for failure to prove a causal connection between the violent images and the violent conduct of an individual. But a plaintiff asserting a *strict liability in tort* claim based on ideas and images has more serious problems than proving causation. Such a claim requires a product. An idea or an image does not qualify.

Unavoidably Unsafe Products

Unavoidably unsafe products are those that are incapable of being made safe due to the current state of technology and science. A certain drug, for example, may be extremely valuable, but have a high risk of dangerous side effects. If the drug is properly prepared and marketed, and an adequate warning is given of the risk, the drug is neither defective nor unreasonably dangerous. Properly prepared means that all feasible tests were conducted on the drug before it was placed on the market. Properly marketed might mean that it is sold only by prescription through a doctor.

unavoidably unsafe product
A product that cannot be made safe by using current technology and science.

Design Defects

Design defects pose the greatest headaches for the courts. The first problem is to make the distinction between the *intended use* and the *foreseeable use* of a product:

intended use: What the manufacturer wanted the product used for; the purpose for which the product was built and placed on the market.

foreseeable use: What the manufacturer anticipates or should be able to anticipate the product will be used for; a foreseeable use may not be the intended use.

A product must not be unreasonably dangerous both for its intended use *and* for its foreseeable use.

EXAMPLES

- Chair

Intended Use:	To sit on
Foreseeable Use:	To stand on in order to store things in a closet
Unforeseeable Use:	To provide extra support for an elevated car while changing a tire

- Cleaning Fluid

Intended Use:	To clean floors
Foreseeable Use:	To be swallowed by children
Unforeseeable Use:	As a lighter fluid for a barbecue

If a plaintiff is injured when a chair on which he or she is standing collapses, the manufacturer cannot escape strict liability in tort by arguing that the plaintiff was not using the product for its intended purpose. It is foreseeable that at least a fair number of users will stand on chairs. Therefore, the product must not be unreasonably dangerous for this foreseeable purpose—the chair must be built strongly enough to accommodate this purpose, or adequate warnings against use for this purpose must be provided. An ordinary consumer would expect the product to be reasonably safe for all foreseeable purposes, including, of course, its intended purposes.

misuse Using a product in a manner that was neither intended nor foreseeable.

Defendants will sometimes claim that there was **misuse** of the product by the plaintiff. This defense will fail, however, if the plaintiff was using the product in the way it was intended or in a way that was foreseeable by the defendant. The product must be reasonably safe for such uses. A child swallowing cleaning fluid, for example, is a foreseeable use of the fluid. A reasonable consumer would expect that steps be taken to make the product reasonably safe for this use. The steps might include not having cartoon characters on the label that would be attractive to children, providing a warning on the label that the fluid is toxic, providing instructions on the label on what to do if the fluid is swallowed, and making the cap relatively difficult for a small child to turn and open.

Unforeseeable uses, however, are another matter. To make a manufacturer strictly liable in tort for injuries caused by products put to unforeseeable uses would be to make the manufacturer an insurer. Liability does not extend this far.

Of course, liability for unreasonably dangerous products put to foreseeable uses is not limited to the manufacturer that designed the defective product. The local department store is also strictly liable for such products. Anyone who is a "seller" in the chain of distribution has committed strict liability in tort.

ASSIGNMENT 19.10

For the following products, identify what you think are

- the intended uses
- possible unintended uses that are foreseeable
- possible unintended uses that are unforeseeable
  a. a screwdriver
  b. shampoo for a dog
  c. a lawn mower
  d. bug spray

ASSIGNMENT 19.11

The Smith family live in a hot climate. To keep out insects, they have placed standard removable screens on the windows of their second-floor apartment. One day their eleven-month-old, twenty-eight-pound child accidentally falls on the screen, pushing it out. The baby falls to the ground outside, sustaining severe injuries. The Smiths sue the screen manufacturer for strict liability in tort. What arguments will the Smiths make and what will be the response of the manufacturer?

crashworthiness The design of the interior of a motor vehicle so that it can avoid or minimize injury after the vehicle has been hit from outside.

Crashworthiness

An important design defect issue concerns the **crashworthiness** of automobiles—the problem of the second injury or the second collision. An automobile accident often involves two events: the impact with the other car or object and the impact of the plaintiff *inside* the car with the steering wheel, window, dashboard, or car roof. The design of the car may have nothing to do with the initial accident, yet have a great deal to do with the extent of the injury suffered by the plaintiff. The question is: how crashworthy does the car have to be? Does the manufacturer have the responsibility of designing the car so that the plaintiff is not injured through internal impact with the car's steering wheel, dashboard, gas tank, or other component? It is highly foreseeable that a plaintiff will receive serious injury following an initial crash. This risk must be weighed against the cost of designing the car to minimize the risk. A court may conclude, for example, that a dashboard made out of a hard metal is unreasonably dangerous, or that a placement of gas tank is unreasonably dangerous, because alternative designs were feasible and would have lessened the danger of the second injury.

Compliance with Statutes and Regulations

Many state and federal statutes and regulations exist on consumer products. Is a product that conforms to all of them automatically deemed to be reasonably safe even though it causes an injury? Yes, according to some courts, particularly if the statute explicitly exempts the defendant from liability when there is compliance. Many courts, however, say that a product that conforms to all of the statutes and regulations can still be unreasonably dangerous, because they may cover only what is *minimally* required for safety. Compliance is merely some evidence—or at most, raises a presumption—that the product is not defective or unreasonably dangerous.

Preemption

Considerable controversy exists when a products liability suit is brought in a *state* court against a manufacturer for a product design that complies with *federal* statutes and regulations. The question is whether the federal law takes precedence over state tort law. This is a **preemption** issue. Under the Supremacy Clause of the United States Constitution, federal laws take precedence over (preempt) state laws, including a state's tort laws, when Congress (a) expressly mandates the preemption, (b) regulates an area so pervasively that an intent to preempt the entire field may be inferred, or (c) enacts a law that directly conflicts with state law. Options (b) and (c) are called implied preemption.

preemption Under the Supremacy Clause, federal laws take precedence over (preempt) state laws when Congress (a) expressly mandates the preemption, (b) regulates an area so pervasively that an intent to preempt the entire field may be inferred, or (c) enacts a law that directly conflicts with state law.

When a drug company, for example, wants to market a new drug, it must satisfy the federal Food and Drug Administration (FDA) that the drug is safe for use. In the recent case of *Wyeth v. Levine*, a drug manufacturer of antihistamine argued that it should not be subjected to a state tort suit for failure to provide adequate warnings on the use of this drug to treat nausea. The FDA had earlier accepted the manufacturer's application on the drug's safety, including the adequacy of the warnings provided with the drug. The manufacturer said that it would be inconsistent to allow a state tort suit for a product that had already met federal standards. The United States Supreme Court ruled against the manufacturer and allowed the state products liability suit to continue.[5] The Court pointed out that there was no express preemption by Congress for prescription drugs (unlike medical devices such as catheters that *had* been given express preemption by federal statute). Nor was there implied preemption. The approval of antihistamine by the FDA was not the final word from the FDA; there were still opportunities for the manufacturer to modify its warnings and then seek FDA approval of the modifications. Because the FDA had not finalized its view of what standards were needed, a state was free to impose higher standards on warnings than those accepted by the FDA to date. In this regulatory environment, therefore, state tort law complements rather than contradicts the federal regulation of antihistamine.

Other Tests?

Thus far we have been focusing on the ordinary consumer test for unreasonable danger presented in § 402A of *Restatement (Second) of Torts*. Some states do not accept this test for determining all kinds of product defects. Everyone knows that products do not last forever. But how is an ordinary consumer supposed to identify the exact lifespan of a particular product such as a tire, engine, or drug during which it should remain reasonably safe? Ordinary consumers (with the "ordinary knowledge common to the community") often do not know enough to be able to judge the amount of danger that should have been designed out of a particular product.

In part because of this difficulty, some states do not use the ordinary consumer test when a design defect is alleged. Instead they often use language such as the following:

- The risks of the product's design outweigh its benefits.
- The risks of the product are so great that a reasonable seller, knowing the risks, would not place the product on the market.

The focus of these tests is not the expectations of the ordinary consumer. Most of the tests require the kind of **risk-benefit analysis** that courts traditionally use when determining negligence:

risk-benefit analysis Deciding whether the risks outweigh the benefits. The determination of whether the benefits of proceeding without additional precautions outweigh the risk of harm that is foreseeable. Also called risk-utility analysis.

The foreseeability of serious harm: The greater the foreseeability of serious harm, the more care, time, and expense are needed to design the product to avoid or minimize the harm.

The importance or social value of the product: How valuable or significant is the product? The more importance or social value it has, the more reasonable it is to take risks in putting the product on the market.

The burden or inconvenience on the manufacturer of redesigning the product to make it safer: What would have been the expense of adding an extra safety precaution? If it is slight, it probably should have been taken. If, however, the cost is so excessive as to make the product close to unmarketable, the precautions may not need to be taken. A warning might be sufficient. Note, however, that although warnings might be the cheapest and least burdensome precaution, they are not a substitute for reasonable design changes that would take the danger out of the product or significantly reduce it.

This kind of analysis is also referred to as *risk-utility analysis* or *risk-utility balancing*.

Frustration over defining design defects has caused some states to reject strict liability for such defects. Instead they use the standard of negligence. Strict liability continues to be available for manufacturing and warning defects in these states. For design defects, however, the plaintiff must establish negligence by the traditional breach-of-duty equation we examined in Exhibit 14–4 in Chapter 14.

CASE

Riley v. Becton Dickinson Vascular Access, Inc.

913 F. Supp. 879 (1995)

United States District Court, Eastern District of Pennsylvania

Background: *Lynda Riley contracted Human Immunodeficiency Virus (HIV) when she was stuck by a needle at the Community Hospital of Lancaster where she was a nurse. At the time of the accident, she was administering an intravenous (I.V.) conventional catheter. As she removed the needle from the catheter and was preparing to dispose of the needle, the patient's left arm unexpectedly moved. The nurse reacted to his movement by moving her hand, and the needle penetrated her left palm. She was using a conventional catheter, the*

Angiocath, manufactured by Becton Dickinson Vascular Access. She sued Becton for strict liability in tort, alleging that the catheter's design was defective, and that an alternative catheter, ProtectIV, would have prevented her accident. Becton made a motion for summary judgment, arguing that the court should rule without a trial that its product was not unreasonably dangerous. (This is a diversity of citizenship case brought in federal court because the parties are citizens of different states. The federal trial court in this diversity action applied the state tort law of Pennsylvania.)

Decision of Court: *Judgment for Becton. Motion for summary judgment is granted. The conventional catheter, Angiocath, is not unreasonably dangerous.*

OPINION OF COURT

Judge TROUTMAN delivered the opinion of the court. . . .

[W]hen presented with claims arising under § 402A of the *Restatement (Second) of Torts,* . . . Pennsylvania courts have adopted a risk/utility test which requires consideration of [seven] factors in aid of the determination whether a product is unreasonably dangerous, *Fitzpatrick v. Madonna,* 424 Pa. Super. 473, 623 A.2d 322, 324 (1993):

1. The usefulness and desirability of the product—its utility to the user and to the public as a whole. . . .

It is obvious that many medical procedures depend upon the use of sharp needles. . . . The evidence submitted by defendant demonstrates that the Angiocath is such a device and is particularly well suited for use in certain situations, such as emergencies, and with patients in whom accessing a vein is more difficult than usual, e.g., infants, small children and the elderly, since a different type of I.V. catheter is more difficult to use in those circumstances. The fact that an instrument such as the Angiocath is capable of causing injury to both the medical professional user and to the patient user does not in any way impair the usefulness of the product. Thus, we conclude that the product is both highly useful and that its availability is desirable to both the medical profession and to the public at large.

2. The safety aspects of a product—the likelihood that it will cause injury, and the probable seriousness of the injury. . . .

In analyzing this factor, we consider both the likelihood of injury from use of the product and the probable seriousness of the injury. . . . [A]lthough it is indisputable that all exposures to HIV which result in infection are terribly serious, and, because of the deadly consequences of infection, all needle stick exposures to HIV contaminated blood are serious, it does not follow that all needle stick incidents present a risk of serious injury. . . . [I]f we assume that there are 18.4 I.V. catheter needle sticks per 100,000 uses of such devices, assume an HIV contamination rate of 2%, and assume the highest likely infection rate, .47%, there could be 17 HIV infections per 1 billion I.V. catheters used . . . or between 8 and 9 infections per 500,000,000 uses of an I.V. catheter set. . . . [Using defendant's projected rate of 7.48 needle sticks per 100,000 uses of a conventional catheter set, such as the Angiocath, but assuming a 2 percent contamination rate, and a .47 percent infection rate, the likelihood of HIV infection of healthcare workers is estimated at 7 per 1 billion uses of a conventional I.V. catheter or between 3 and 4 per 500,000,000 uses thereof.] From the available evidence and projections based thereon, the Court concludes that the risk of serious injury from use of an I.V. catheter such as the Angiocath is quite low.

3. The availability of a substitute product which would meet the same need and not be as unsafe. . . .

Plaintiff does not argue that there is an acceptable substitute for an I.V. catheter. Plaintiff points out, however, that there is an available substitute for a conventional I.V. catheter which leaves the introducing needle exposed after it is withdrawn from the flexible tube. The ProtectIV, an I.V. catheter manufactured by Critikon, a competitor of defendant, permits the needle to be retracted into a plastic sheath as it is withdrawn from the tube attached to the patient's vein. . . .

A study of 1024 healthcare workers at nine hospitals in 6 states over a period of six months revealed that the incidence of needle sticks was lower with the ProtectIV, . . . Although a reduction in the total number of needle sticks would obviously lessen the likelihood of serious injury, the projected risks of HIV exposure and infection from any one such needle stick are identical to the risks associated with a needle stick from a conventional catheter, since the rate of HIV exposure and infection depend upon the patient population, not the type of I.V. catheter used. . . . [T]he projected risk of HIV infection from an I.V. catheter needle stick would be reduced from 3.5/500,000,000 uses with a conventional catheter to 2/1,000,000,000 uses or 1/500,000,000 uses with a protected catheter. Consequently, it appears that an already small risk might be somewhat reduced, but would not be eliminated, by use of a protected rather than a conventional I.V. catheter. . . .

[C]ontrary to plaintiff's argument that the ProtectIV provides "automatic" protection from an exposed needle, the record shows that the introducer needle is retracted into the protective sheath only if the person initiating the I.V. activates that mechanism by sliding the sheath front, over the needle, as the needle is withdrawn through the catheter. Failure to properly engage the mechanism by fully extending the sheath until it "clicks" allows the sharp tip of the needle to remain exposed, which can . . . result in a needle stick.*

*As defendant points out, given the undisputed circumstances of plaintiff's accident and the operation of the ProtectIV, it is not at all certain that she could have avoided the needle stick if she had been using it, since she reacted to a patient's sudden movement by an apparently reflexive movement of her own. It is not possible, therefore, to infer that plaintiff would have been able to completely engage the protective mechanism of the ProtectIV before the incident occurred. Had the needle been suddenly withdrawn from the catheter in response to the patient's movement and the tip remained exposed, a needle stick could have occurred. . . . [by a failure] to fully engage the sheath of the ProtectIV. . . .

Moreover, the available evidence also discloses that even if the incidence of needle sticks is ultimately somewhat reduced by using the ProtectIV, a healthcare worker's exposure to a patient's blood may not be significantly reduced since more blood escapes from the catheter as the needle is withdrawn than occurs with a conventional I.V. catheter. . . .

Other problems with the ProtectIV [include] . . . difficulty using the catheters on infants, small children, elderly patients and others with difficult veins. Many such problems would likely result in the need for additional I.V. initiations, thereby actually increasing the potential for a needle stick by increasing the number of times an I.V. introducer needle is used. . . .

We conclude, therefore, that although the small projected risk of a needle stick might be further reduced by substituting a protected I.V. catheter for a conventional device, assuming that the user is proficient with the new device, the danger of a needle stick cannot be eliminated. Moreover, a reduction in the incidence of needle sticks is by no means assured. . . .

Thus, although a substitute for a conventional I.V. catheter is available which may reduce the incidence of needle sticks, it is not entirely certain that such substitute is safer overall when other aspects of the alternative design are considered and it does not appear to be an alternative which can feasibly replace conventional I.V. catheters completely.

4. The manufacturer's ability to eliminate the unsafe character of the product without impairing its usefulness or making it too expensive to maintain its utility. . . .

[T]he cost of the protected catheter far exceeds that of the conventional device. At the time the Community Hospital of Lancaster first evaluated the ProtectIV in 1992, the cost was $1.40 per unit compared to $.78 for the Angiocath. Moreover, the unit cost of the catheters is not the only cost consideration. . . . [T]he evidence establishes the need for extensive training with the ProtectIV in order to gain the benefit of somewhat fewer needle sticks and to overcome the problems inherent in other aspects of the product to the greatest possible extent. . . .

[T]he unit cost of the ProtectIV . . . is very high in light of the small benefit likely to be derived from the possible reduction, but not elimination, of the risk of a needle stick. . . . Thus, we conclude that it is not possible to eliminate the unsafe feature of the Angiocath without impairing its utility since the costs of the only available alternative product are much higher; the risk associated with the allegedly unsafe design cannot be completely eliminated; and there are problems other than the risk of a needle stick associated with the use of the alternative design which require extensive training to diminish and which cannot be entirely eliminated.

5. The user's ability to avoid danger by the exercise of care in the use of the product.

Despite the suggestion by defendant that plaintiff might somehow have prevented her accident by more careful attention to proper procedures, we find nothing in the record which establishes that a lack of care on plaintiff's part contributed to her injury. Under the undisputed circumstances, it appears that anyone, using any type of sharp device, might have sustained a similar injury by reacting to a patient's unexpected movement. . . .

6. The user's anticipated awareness of the dangers inherent in the product and their avoidability, because of general public knowledge of the obvious condition of the product, or of the existence of suitable warnings or instructions. . . .

[T]here is widespread knowledge of the potential danger of a needle stick accident among healthcare workers. Indeed, plaintiff does not contend that the danger inherent in an exposed needle is hidden, generally unknown to healthcare workers, or that she was personally unaware of such danger.

7. The feasibility, on the part of the manufacturer, of spreading the loss of setting the price of the product or carrying liability insurance. . . .

[A]lthough it is unquestionably true that a manufacturer is almost always able to spread the cost of an injured plaintiff's loss over all users of a product by raising the price thereof, the feasibility of doing so depends upon balancing the . . . factors in the risk/utility analysis. . . . [W]hen consideration of the preceding six factors leads to the conclusion that the utility of product in question outweighs its risks, such determination compels the further conclusion that shifting the cost of plaintiff's loss to the manufacturer of the product is not fair, and, therefore, not feasible. . . .

SUMMARY

Having examined each factor in the risk/utility analysis, . . . we conclude that the Angiocath, although dangerous because it is capable of causing serious injury, is not unreasonably dangerous. . . . [I]n most instances the danger inherent in a needle stick is not grave, since most needle sticks do not expose the injured party to a serious illness, and even when exposed to HIV, only a small percentage of injured parties become infected. Moreover, needle sticks from I.V. catheters, specifically, are relatively rare and the likelihood of a resulting serious injury, defined herein as exposure to HIV/HIV infection, is slight in comparison to the widespread use of the product.

Although a feasible design which appears to reduce the risk of a needle stick injury is available, the potential reduction of the risk of a needle stick comes at a greatly increased cost and it is by no means certain that such design is truly "safer" overall since the available product which incorporates the alternative design is not as well-suited as the Angiocath to the primary purpose of an I.V. catheter, quick and efficient piercing of the skin and subcutaneous tissue for access to a vein. . . .

Accordingly, defendant's motion for summary judgment will be granted and judgment will be entered in favor of the defendant.

ASSIGNMENT 19.12

a. Why did the court rule that the conventional catheter was not unreasonably dangerous?
b. What was the causation problem that the nurse had in this case?
c. What does cost shifting mean? If compensation for the nurse is limited to her workers' compensation benefits, who bears the cost? If she had won this case, who would have borne the cost?
d. Assume that another hospital, Midway Hospital, must decide whether to purchase the Angiocath catheter or the ProtectIV catheter. What legal advice should Midway be given in light of the *Riley* opinion?

Risk-utility analysis has recently been adopted by the American Law Institute, the creator of the *Restatements*. As indicated earlier, the American Law Institute has made a significant change in strict liability in tort. It no longer recommends that courts use the unreasonable danger and ordinary consumer test of § 402A of the *Restatement (Second) of Torts* as the exclusive test for design defects. The new *Restatement (Third) of Torts* (1997) on products liability now recommends a different test for design defects:

> The product is defective in design when the foreseeable risks of harm posed by the product could have been reduced or avoided by the adoption of a reasonable alternative design . . . and the omission of the alternative design renders the product not reasonably safe. § 2.

Hence, the new test on design defects is the availability of a **reasonable alternative design**. It replaces the "ordinary consumer" expectations test from § 402A of *Restatement (Second) of Torts*. Of course, the availability of an alternative design was also relevant under § 402A of *Restatement (Second) of Torts*. Yet, this availability was often judged from the perspective of the ordinary consumer's expectations.

reasonable alternative design An available design that a manufacturer could have reasonably used that would have been less dangerous than the design that caused the injury.

Under the new test, how do you determine whether a reasonable alternative design was possible? By going through a risk-benefit analysis or risk-utility balancing. We just saw an example of how this is done in the *Riley* case on the competing catheter designs. The *Restatement's* new test does not mean that the expectations of the ordinary consumer are discarded. They are still considered. Under the new test, however, consumer expectations do not constitute an independent standard for judging the defectiveness of product designs.

This change has been controversial; it is unclear how many states will adopt the new test of *Restatement (Third) of Torts*. In a recent case, a court said that "the majority of jurisdictions *do not* impose upon plaintiffs an absolute requirement to prove a feasible alternative design."[6] Clearly, the law on this element of strict liability in tort is not settled. We can expect to see continued developments in the determination of what constitutes a design defect.

User or Consumer

The third element of a cause of action for strict liability in tort is that the plaintiff must be a user or consumer. The plaintiff does not have to be the purchaser of the product. A state that follows § 402A will require only that the plaintiff be a user or consumer.

EXAMPLE

Tom is driving a car that is unreasonably dangerous because of defective brakes. Jim is his passenger. There is an accident caused by the brakes. Tom and Jim are injured as well as Mary, who was a pedestrian crossing the street when the car hit her.

Tom is a user or consumer whether or not he is the purchaser of the car. So is Jim. Passengers certainly use cars. Mary, however, is not a user or consumer. She is a bystander. Under § 402A, Mary cannot sue the car manufacturer for strict liability in tort *unless* the state expands the tort to cover anyone who is foreseeably injured by the unreasonably dangerous product. There are a number of states that have done so. This would cover Mary. It is highly foreseeable that cars with defective brakes will go out of control and injure pedestrians or other bystanders.

ASSIGNMENT 19.13

In the fact situation just mentioned involving Tom, Mary, and the defective brakes, could Mary sue Tom for strict liability in tort?

Physical Harm

The tort covers actual damage to property (e.g., demolished car) or to person (e.g., broken arm, death). If no such damage has occurred, and the plaintiff has suffered economic damage only, most courts do not allow recovery under strict liability in tort. If the plaintiff is the purchaser, he or she may be able to sue under some other cause of action. The plaintiff, for example, buys a boat that is defective and unreasonably dangerous because of the design of the motor. The boat cannot be used in the plaintiff's business. No one is injured and no damage occurs to the boat itself. Only an economic loss has been suffered. The plaintiff may be able to sue for breach of contract, for breach of warranty, or perhaps for misrepresentation. Most courts, however, do not provide strict liability in tort as a remedy for purely economic loss.

Causation

The plaintiff must show that the product was defective at the time it left the hands of the defendant and that this defect caused the physical harm. Causation is established by the but-for test (but for the defect, the harm would not have resulted), or the substantial-factor test when more than one cause is involved (the defect was a substantial factor in producing the harm).

> The seller is not liable when he delivers the product in a safe condition, and subsequent mishandling or other causes make it harmful by the time it is consumed. . . . If the injury results from abnormal handling, as where a bottled beverage is knocked against a radiator to remove a cap, or from abnormal preparation for use, as where too much salt is added to food, or from abnormal consumption, as where a child eats too much candy and is made ill, the seller is not liable.[7]

Causation can sometimes be difficult to prove when the defendant is a remote manufacturer and the product has passed through many hands before it injured the plaintiff. A court will not allow causation to be established by mere speculation. This does not mean that the plaintiff must eliminate every possible cause other than the defendant. Where there is some evidence of other causes, however, the plaintiff must either negate them or show that the defendant was at least *a* substantial factor along with the other causes in producing the injury.

Causation by Market Share

In Chapter 14, we saw that the courts created the doctrine of res ipsa loquitur to help plaintiffs who would otherwise have great difficulty establishing the second element of negligence: breach of duty (unreasonableness). The doctrine allowed the jury to draw the inference of unreasonableness even though there was no direct or specific evidence of it.

We now look at a similar problem pertaining to the element of causation.

EXAMPLE

During pregnancy a woman takes DES (diethylstilbestrol), a synthetic form of estrogen, designed to prevent miscarriage. She gives birth to a daughter. When the child grows up, she develops cervical cancer, which was caused by the DES taken by her mother. Which manufacturer of DES can the daughter sue? At least 200 manufacturers used an identical formula to produce DES. But the daughter cannot determine which manufacturer made the DES pills that her mother took. The pharmacist used by her mother is no longer in business, and no records are available.

The drug was obviously defective, and unreasonably so. But *who caused the injury?* We know *what* caused the cancer, but we do not know *who* caused it. Under traditional rules, it is fundamental that the plaintiff establish which manufacturer made the defective pills taken by her mother. But she has no way of doing so on these facts.

In most states, she loses her case. A minority of states, however, are more sympathetic. In *Sindell v. Abbott Laboratories,*[8] for example, a California court held that if the plaintiff:

- established that DES caused the cancer, and
- sued a substantial share of the DES manufacturers who were selling in the market in which her mother purchased the drug,

then each defendant/manufacturer would be liable for the proportion of the plaintiff's damages represented by its share of that market unless it could prove that it could not have made the DES pill that caused plaintiff's injuries.[9] If a particular defendant/manufacturer could not prove this, then it would be liable for that part of the judgment that was proportional to its market share. This approach has been called **market share liability**.

market share liability Legal responsibility for harm caused by a product according to the proportion of the market attributable to the sales of a particular company.

Using this method of handling causation has been highly controversial. Some fear that it might open a floodgate of liability.

Although *Sindell* was dramatic in its approach, there are limitations to its use. The product made by the manufacturers must be identical, or nearly so. If the products are simply similar and are not made in the same dangerous way, this approach cannot be used. *Sindell* arguably would not apply, for example, if different manufacturers used different proportions of ingredients to make what would otherwise be considered the same product. Also, a large number of manufacturers must be sued so that it can be said that they constitute a significant or substantial share of the market. For a more extensive discussion of causation in mass tort cases, see Chapter 20.

Defenses to Strict Liability in Tort

learned-intermediary doctrine When a physician prescribes drugs or medical devices, the manufacturer's duty to the patient is limited to providing warnings and instructions to the physician; the manufacturer has no duty to provide them to the patient.

Learned-Intermediary Doctrine For some products, the duty to warn is limited by the character of the individuals involved. For example, under the **learned-intermediary doctrine**, if a physician prescribes drugs or medical devices, the manufacturer's duty to warn is limited to providing warnings and instructions *to the physician*; the manufacturer has no duty to provide them directly to the patient. If the patient sues the manufacturer for a failure to warn about the side effects or proper use of a drug or medical device, the defense of the manufacturer is that the warnings were provided to the patient's skilled agent—a learned intermediary—the doctor.

Misuse Every misuse of the product is not a defense. As indicated earlier, the simple fact that a consumer does not use a product for its intended purpose does not necessarily mean that it has been misused. A product must be reasonably safe for the foreseeable uses of the product. Furthermore, a manufacturer must plan for a certain amount of foreseeable misuse. Misuse is a defense when it is unforeseeable and when it is extreme. Such misuse occurs, for example, when the plaintiff knowingly violates the plain, unambiguous instructions on using the product or ignores the clear warnings provided.

Contributory Negligence In most states, contributory negligence is not a defense when the plaintiff's conduct consists of failing to discover the danger. Assume the defendant rents a defective car to Bob Smith. On the dashboard, there is a red light signaling trouble to the driver. Smith does not see the light and keeps driving. An accident occurs because of the defect in the car that makes it unreasonably dangerous. It is no defense that Smith failed to discover the danger—even if a reasonable person would have discovered it by checking the dashboard and seeing the red light. Smith's own negligence in failing to discover the danger to himself is not a defense.

Contributory negligence is a defense only when it constitutes the extreme, unforeseeable misuse described above, or an assumption of the risk described below.

Comparative Negligence There are some states that apply their comparative negligence rules to strict-liability-in-tort cases, even though there is no need for the plaintiff in such cases to establish the negligence of the defendant. The damages suffered by the plaintiffs are proportionately reduced by whatever percentage of the harm the plaintiffs caused themselves through carelessness.

Assumption of the Risk If the plaintiff has actual knowledge of the danger and voluntarily proceeds to use the product in spite of the danger, there has been an assumption of the risk, which *is* a defense to strict liability in tort. The plaintiff must have actually discovered the danger. For a discussion of assumption of the risk, see Chapter 17.

immunity 1. The treatment of wrongful conduct as nonwrongful. A complete defense to a tort claim whether or not the defendant committed the tort. 2. Exemption or freedom from a duty, penalty, or liability. 3. The right not to be subjected to civil or criminal prosecution.

Immunity Occasionally an industry is able to convince the legislature to grant it full or partial **immunity** from tort litigation. The immunity prevents the industry from being subjected to civil or criminal liability for injury caused by its products. After 9/11, for example, Congress passed the Support Antiterrorism by Fostering Effective Technologies Act. To encourage manufacturers to develop antiterrorism products such as gas masks and emergency radios, the Act provided that if such products fail (i.e., are defective), the liability of the manufacturer will be limited to the amount of the liability insurance the industry carries.[10] Hence the industry will not face the prospect of bankruptcy from injured plaintiffs in tort litigation that seeks large awards of punitive damages. In Chapter 23 covering public nuisance, we will examine another example of tort immunity granted to an industry—gun manufacturers.

ASSIGNMENT 19.14

Tom buys a lawn mower from a department store. A string is tied around the top of the mower attached to a tag that says "WARNING: BEFORE USING, READ INSTRUCTION BOOK CAREFULLY." Tom sees this sign but fails to read the instruction book. In the book, the consumer is told never to use the mower on a steep hill. Tom is injured while mowing on a steep hill in his yard. The mower tipped over and fell on him. Is the department store strictly liable in tort?

REFORM

Federal involvement in this area of the law has been relatively minor, including the work of the Consumer Product Safety Commission (www.cpsc.gov), whose role has primarily been that of a monitor and information collector in spite of its authority to force companies to recall their products.

Most products liability law is created and applied at the state level, which is true for most of tort law. This, of course, means that each state is free to develop its own products liability law. Critics say that this system has produced chaos, and that we need a *federal* products liability law. Although Congress has considered a number of proposals to implement such a law, none has been enacted to date. Here are selected aspects of some of the proposed reforms:

- The creation of federal standards governing the litigation of disputes arising out of injuries caused by defective products. These standards would preempt (take the place of, be controlling over) state law.
- The creation of an expedited settlement system to be available at the outset of every case.
- The imposition of a cap on non-economic damages that can be awarded.
- The creation of standards for when punitive damages can be obtained from a defendant.
- A uniform statute of limitations for bringing a case.

PARALEGAL ROLES

The checklist at the end of this chapter on strict liability in tort contains a list of paralegal roles in litigation involving this tort. Paralegals often have a great deal of responsibility in products liability cases. "Every step of the way, from investigating the accident before suit is filed to assisting at trial, paralegals are essential in product liability litigation."[11] One of their important roles is to help prepare, order, and manage trial visuals or demonstratives that are designed to help juries understand the complexities of product defects. Paralegals also assist attorneys with pleadings such as complaints and answers. (See Exhibit 19–8 for a sample complaint.) The assistance can include doing legal research in codes and legal treatises to find examples of complaints, answers, and other pleadings; summarizing or digesting the pleadings that are filed; helping to draft these pleadings; etc.

For an extensive discussion of paralegal roles when a products liability case involves mass torts, see Exhibit 20–4 in Chapter 20.

Exhibit 19–8 Sample products liability complaint.
Viagra Products Liability Litigation v. Pfizer, 2006 WL 4025693 (2006). (See also 572 F. Supp. 2d 1071 (D. Minn. 2008).)

United States District Court
District of Minnesota

In re: VIAGRA PRODUCTS LIABILITY LITIGATION — Case No. 06-md-1724 06CV4749 P4M

Ronald Richardson,
Plaintiff,
v.
PFIZER, INC., et al.,
Defendant

COMPLAINT

JURY TRIAL DEMANDED

NOW INTO COURT, through undersigned counsel, comes Plaintiff, Ronald Richardson, who respectfully represents that he has sustained personal injuries arising out of his purchase and use of the prescription drug Viagra (Sildenafil), and therefore, seeks to recover damages as a direct and proximate result of Defendant, Pfizer, Inc.'s, negligent and wrongful conduct in connection with the design, development, manufacture, testing, packaging, advertising, promoting, marketing, distribution, labeling, and/or sale of Viagra®.

I.
PARTIES

1. Plaintiff, Ronald Richardson, is a person of the full age of majority and a resident of Morgan County, City of Jacksonville, State of Illinois, which is located in the United States District Court for the District of Illinois.

2. Defendant, Pfizer, Inc., is a Delaware corporation, with its principal place of business in New York, and has committed a tort within the States of Illinois and Minnesota.

II.
JURISDICTION AND VENUE

3. This Honorable Court has subject matter jurisdiction, pursuant to 28 U.S.C. § 1332, as the amount in controversy exceeds $75,000 exclusive of interest and costs and because this action is brought by an individual who is a citizen of a state other than the Defendant.

4. Venue is proper in this district pursuant to 28 U.S.C. § 1391. At all relevant times herein, Pfizer, Inc. was in the business of designing, manufacturing, marketing, developing, testing, labeling, promoting, distributing, warranting and selling its product, Viagra. At all times relevant hereto, Pfizer, Inc., designed, developed, manufactured, promoted, marketed, distributed, tested, warranted and sold in interstate commerce, in Minnesota, the aforementioned prescription drug. Pfizer, Inc. does substantial business in the State of Minnesota, advertised in this district, received substantial compensation and profits from sales of Viagra in this district, and made material omissions and misrepresentations and breaches of warranties in this district.

III.
FACTUAL ALLEGATIONS

5. Pfizer, Inc. is in the business of designing, manufacturing, marketing, developing, testing, labeling, promoting, distributing, warranting and selling its product, Viagra. Pfizer, Inc., at all times relevant hereto, designed, developed, manufactured, promoted, marketed, distributed, tested, warranted and sold Viagra in the States of Illinois and Minnesota.

6. As a result of ingesting Viagra, Plaintiff suffered what was diagnosed as anterior ischemic optic neuropathy (NAION) in Plaintiff's right eye.

7. At all times relevant herein, Plaintiff was unaware of the serious side effects and dangerous properties of the drug as set forth herein.

8. Viagra is the trade name for the prescription drug Sildenafil, which was designed, formulated, patented, marketed, sold, tested, warranted, and ultimately distributed by Defendant as Viagra.

9. Pfizer, Inc., failed to warn consumers such as Plaintiff of the potential side effects of Viagra. One such side effect is ischemic optic neuropathy (NAION), which results from a drop in blood pressure and which restricts the flow of oxygenated blood to the optic nerve, causing irreversible vision loss and blindness.

10. Viagra was approved by the Food and Drug Administration on May 27, 1998, for the treatment of erectile dysfunction in men. By 2004, Viagra had reached $1.68 billion in sales.

11. Defendant materially breached its obligations to consumers, such as Plaintiff, through, but not limited to, its design, testing, manufacturing, warning, marketing, warranting, and sale of Viagra.

12. Defendant expressly and/or impliedly warranted to the market, including to Plaintiff, by and through statements made by Defendant or its authorized agents or sales representatives, orally and in publications, package inserts and other written materials to the health care community, that Viagra was safe, effective, fit, and proper for its intended use.

13. Defendant was aware of the substantial risks from taking Viagra but failed to fully disclose same.

14. Defendant failed to meet the applicable standards of care which were intended for the benefit of individual consumers such as Plaintiff, making Defendant liable for Plaintiff's injuries.

IV.
CAUSES OF ACTION

FIRST CAUSE OF ACTION: FRAUDULENT CONCEALMENT

15. Plaintiff adopts and re-alleges Paragraphs 1–14 above as if fully set forth herein and further alleges as follows:

16. Defendant is estopped from asserting a statute of limitations defense because it fraudulently concealed its wrongful conduct from Plaintiff.

SECOND CAUSE OF ACTION: STRICT LIABILITY—DESIGN DEFECT

17. Plaintiff adopts and re-alleges Paragraphs 1–16 above as if fully set forth herein and further alleges as follows:

18. Pfizer, Inc.'s Viagra is defectively designed because the foreseeable risks of serious side effects and injury outweigh the benefits associated with the use of the drug.

19. Viagra with design and manufacturing defects was expected to and did reach Plaintiff without substantial change or adjustment to its intended medical use.

20. Pfizer, Inc., the manufacturer or supplier of Viagra, knew or should have known of the design defect and the risk of serious bodily injury that exceeded the benefits associated with the design or formulation.

21. Furthermore, Pfizer, Inc.'s Viagra and its design and manufacturing defects presented an unreasonably dangerous risk beyond what the ordinary consumer would reasonably expect.

22. Viagra, manufactured or supplied to Plaintiff by Pfizer, Inc., was defectively designed due to inadequate warnings or instruction because the manufacturer knew or should have known through testing or otherwise that the product created a high risk of bodily injury and serious harm, yet Pfizer, Inc. failed to adequately and timely warn consumers of this risk.

23. As a direct and proximate result of Pfizer, Inc.'s failure to warn and improper conduct Plaintiff suffered and continues to suffer economic losses and other compensable injuries as alleged herein.

24. Pfizer, Inc.'s Viagra is a product inherently dangerous for its intended use due to a design defect and improper functioning. Pfizer, Inc. is therefore strictly liable to Plaintiff for damages.

THIRD CAUSE OF ACTION: STRICT LIABILITY—FAILURE TO WARN

25. Plaintiff adopts and re-alleges Paragraphs 1–24 above as if fully set forth herein and further alleges as follows:

26. Pfizer, Inc. developed, manufactured, marketed, and distributed Viagra to the general public even after learning of the design and manufacturing defect that threatened the intended use of the drug.

27. Viagra with design and manufacturing defects was expected to and did reach Plaintiff without substantial change or adjustment to its intended medical use.

Exhibit 19–8 (Continued)

28. Pfizer, Inc. knew or should have known through testing, adverse event reporting, or otherwise, that the product created a high risk of bodily injury and serious harm.

29. Pfizer, Inc. failed in providing timely and adequate warnings or instruction regarding its drug with a known design and manufacturing defect.

30. As a direct and proximate result of Pfizer, Inc.'s conduct, Plaintiff suffered bodily and mental injury, harm and other compensable injuries as alleged herein.

31. Pfizer, Inc.'s Viagra is a product inherently dangerous for its intended use due to a design and manufacturing defect and improper functioning. Pfizer, Inc. is therefore strictly liable to Plaintiff for damages.

FOURTH CAUSE OF ACTION: BREACH OF EXPRESS WARRANTY

32. Plaintiff adopts and re-alleges Paragraphs 1-31 above as if fully set forth herein and further alleges as follows:

33. Pfizer expressly warranted to the public and to Plaintiff that Viagra was effective and safe when, in fact, the product was not safe or effective for all foreseeable users. Pfizer knew or should have known of its potentially harmful side effects.

FIFTH CAUSE OF ACTION: BREACH OF IMPLIED WARRANTY

34. Plaintiff adopts and re-alleges Paragraphs 1-33 above as if fully set forth herein and further alleges as follows:

35. Defendant is the "merchant" or "seller" who sold goods to Plaintiffs.

36. The "goods," i.e., Viagra, were not merchantable or fit for their particular purposes at the time of the sale when Defendant impliedly warranted to medical professionals and Plaintiff that the product was effective and safe for its intended use.

37. The injuries and damages complained of herein were caused proximately and in fact by the defective nature of the goods.

38. Defendant has been provided notice of Plaintiff's injuries by virtue of published scientific reports and adverse events reported to the United States Food and Drug Administration.

SIXTH CAUSE OF ACTION: NEGLIGENCE

39. Plaintiff adopts and re-alleges Paragraphs 1-38 above as if fully set forth herein.

40. At all times material hereto, Defendant had a duty to Plaintiff to exercise reasonable and ordinary care in the designing, developing, manufacturing, marketing, distributing, testing, warranting, and/or selling of Viagra.

41. Independent of the foregoing, Defendant Pfizer, Inc. is liable to Plaintiff in that the damages sought by Plaintiff arose from a reasonably anticipated use of Viagra in the following nonexclusive particulars:

a. Failure to exercise reasonable care in the designing, developing, manufacturing, marketing, distributing, testing, warranting, and/or selling of Viagra;

b. Designing, developing, manufacturing, marketing, distributing, testing, warranting, and/or selling a product that it knew, or should have known, carried a risk of seriously debilitating and/or life-threatening side effects;

c. Failure to adequately test Viagra prior to placing the medication on the market;

d. Failure to use care in designing, developing, manufacturing, marketing, distributing, testing, warranting, and/or selling Viagra so as to avoid posing unnecessary health risks to users of such products;

e. Failure to conduct adequate preclinical and clinical testing and post-marketing surveillance to determine the safety of Viagra;

f. Failure to advise the consumers, such as Plaintiff, that consumption of the medication could result in severe and disabling side effects, including, but not limited to, non-arteritic anterior ischemic optic neuropathy (NAION);

g. Failure to advise the medical and scientific communities of the potential for severe and disabling side effects, including, but not limited to, non-arteritic ischemic optic neuropathy (NAION);

h. Failure to provide timely and/or adequate warnings about the potential health risks associated with the use of Viagra;

i. The unreasonably dangerous characteristics of Viagra existed at the time it left the control of the manufacturers;

j. Failure to take immediate and direct measures to ensure that consumers and users of Viagra, such as Plaintiff, were notified, or that health care providers who prescribed this medication were notified of such risks;

k. Failure to properly and adequately test Viagra to determine the potential adverse health effects; and

l. Any and all other acts of negligence with respect to Viagra which may be shown at trial.

42. The aforementioned acts and/or omissions committed by Defendant proximately caused Plaintiff to suffer non-arteritic anterior ischemic optic neuropathy (NAION) and related injuries.

SEVENTH CAUSE OF ACTION: FRAUD AND MISREPRESENTATION

43. Plaintiff adopts and re-alleges Paragraphs 1-42 above as if fully set forth herein and further alleges as follows:

44. Defendant widely advertised and promoted Viagra as a safe and effective medication.

45. Defendant had a duty to disclose material information to consumers, such as Plaintiff, about serious disabling and life-threatening side effects of using Viagra. Additionally, by virtue of Defendant's partial disclosures about the medication wherein Defendant touted its medications as safe and effective treatment, Defendant had a duty to disclose all facts about the risks of use associated with the medication, including the potential for the medication to cause non-arteritic anterior ischemic optic neuropathy (NAION). Defendant intentionally failed to disclose this information for the purpose of inducing consumers, such as Plaintiff, to purchase its dangerous product.

46. Had Plaintiff been aware of the hazards associated with use of Viagra, he would not have consumed this medication, which proximately caused his injuries.

47. In its advertisements, Defendant made material misrepresentations about Viagra to the effect that it was a safe and effective treatment, which misrepresentations Defendant knew to be false, for the purpose of fraudulently inducing consumers, such as Plaintiff, to purchase Viagra. Plaintiff relied upon these material misrepresentations in deciding to purchase and consume Viagra.

EIGHTH CAUSE OF ACTION: VIOLATION OF THE MINNESOTA DECEPTIVE TRADE PRACTICE ACT

48. Plaintiff adopts and re-alleges Paragraphs 1-47 above as if fully set forth herein and further alleges as follows:

49. Pfizer, Inc. applied advertising and marketing campaigns representing its Viagra as medically safe, while Pfizer, Inc. knew of the drugs' design and manufacturing defects.

50. Pfizer, Inc. knew or should have known of the design and manufacturing defect within Viagra, but denied public access to the information, avoiding corporate responsibility. Pfizer, Inc. knew its patients held a disadvantage in accessing information involving the safety of its drug.

51. Pfizer, Inc. concealed the design and manufacturing defects of its drug for the purposes of higher profits and increased sales.

52. Pfizer, Inc. has violated Minn. Stat. §325D.44(5) by representing Viagra as having characteristics, uses, and benefits of a safe and medically sound drug while knowing the statements were false and the drug contained inherent design and manufacturing defects.

53. Pfizer, Inc. has violated Minn. Stat. § 325D.44(7) by representing Viagra as a non-defective medical product of a particular standard, quality, or grade while knowing the statements were false and the drug contained inherent design and manufacturing defects.

54. Pfizer, Inc. has violated Minn. Stat. § 325D.44(9) by advertising, marketing, and selling Viagra as medically reliable and without a known design and manufacturing defect while knowing those claims were false and without any medical support.

Exhibit 19–8 (Continued)

55. Pfizer, Inc. has violated Minn. Stat. § 325D.44(13) by creating a likelihood of confusion about the efficacy and medical soundness of its drug, comparing its defective drug with other non-defective products.

56. The Minnesota statutes prohibiting unfair and deceptive trade practices may apply to all transactions with Pfizer, Inc. because Pfizer, Inc.'s deceptive scheme was carried out in Minnesota and affected all persons who used Viagra containing the known design and manufacturing defects.

57. Plaintiff seeks to have this practice enjoined and declared unlawful, and is entitled to recover costs, expenses, and attorneys' fees in seeking injunctive and declaratory relief. Minn. Stat. §325D.45.

NINTH CAUSE OF ACTION: VIOLATION OF THE MINNESOTA FALSE STATEMENT IN ADVERTISING ACT

58. Plaintiff adopts and re-alleges Paragraphs 1-57 above as if fully set forth herein and further alleges as follows:

59. Pfizer, Inc. produced and published advertisements and deceptive and misleading statements of the soundness and medical reliability of Viagra, after learning of its inherent design and manufacturing defect, with the intent to sell Viagra.

60. Pfizer, Inc. concealed its deceptive practices in order to increase the sale and profit from Viagra.

61. Pfizer, Inc. has violated Minn. Stat. § 325F.67 by intending to sell and create a customer demand for Viagra using deceptive or untrue statements of fact about the drug's medical soundness and reliability on Pfizer, Inc.'s website and medical brochures distributed to patients and physicians.

62. The Minnesota statutes prohibiting false statements in advertising apply to all persons with Pfizer, Inc. devices because Pfizer, Inc.'s deceptive scheme was carried out in Minnesota and affected all persons using Viagra.

63. As a result of Pfizer, Inc.'s practices, Plaintiff suffered actual damages. Plaintiff is entitled to recover those damages along with costs, expenses, and attorneys' fees. Minn. Stat. 8.31, subd. 3a.

TENTH CAUSE OF ACTION: VIOLATION OF THE MINNESOTA PREVENTION OF CONSUMER FRAUD ACT

64. Plaintiff adopts and re-alleges Paragraphs 1-63 above as if fully set forth herein and further alleges as follows:

65. Pfizer, Inc. intentionally concealed its design and manufacturing defect and failed to disclose such information for the purposes of continuing the sale and distribution of its affected drug.

66. According to Pfizer, Inc.'s 2005 Annual Report, Viagra sales generated revenues of at least one billion dollars in 2005.

67. Pfizer, Inc. represented Viagra was safe and effective and intended that patients and physicians rely on those representations when deciding if Pfizer, Inc.'s drug was optimal for meeting the patient's needs.

68. Through these misleading and deceptive statements and false promises, Pfizer, Inc. violated Minn. Stat. § 325F.69.

69. The Minnesota statutes prohibiting consumer fraud apply to all persons with Pfizer, Inc. Viagra drug because Pfizer, Inc.'s deceptive scheme was carried out in Minnesota and affected all persons using Viagra containing a design and manufacturing defect.

70. As a result of Pfizer, Inc.'s practices, Plaintiff suffered actual economic damages and is entitled to recovery of those damages along with attorneys' fees. Minn. Stat. § 8.31, subd. 3a.

ELEVENTH CAUSE OF ACTION: VIOLATION OF THE ILLINOIS CONSUMER FRAUD AND DECEPTIVE BUSINESS PRACTICES ACT

71. Plaintiff adopts and re-alleges Paragraphs 1-70 above as if fully set forth herein and further alleges as follows:

72. Pfizer, Inc. applied advertising and marketing campaigns representing its Viagra as medically safe, while Pfizer, Inc. knew of the drugs' design and manufacturing defects.

73. Pfizer, Inc. knew or should have known of the design and manufacturing defects within Viagra, but denied

public access to the information, avoiding corporate responsibility. Pfizer, Inc. knew its patients held a disadvantage in accessing information involving the safety of its drug.

74. Pfizer, Inc. concealed the design and manufacturing defects of its drug for the purposes of higher profits and increased sales.

75. Pfizer, Inc. has violated § 815 ILCS 505/2 by representing Viagra as having characteristics, uses, and benefits of a safe and medically sound drug while using unfair or deceptive acts or practices, including but not limited to the use of deception, fraud, false pretense, false promise, misrepresentation or the concealment, suppression or omission of any material fact, with intent that others rely upon the concealment, suppression or omission of such material fact.

76. The Illinois statutes prohibiting unfair and deceptive trade practices may apply to all transactions with Pfizer, Inc. because Pfizer, Inc.'s deceptive scheme was carried out in Illinois and affected all persons who used Viagra containing the known design and manufacturing defects.

77. As a result of Pfizer, Inc.'s practices, Plaintiff suffered actual economic damages and is entitled to recovery of those damages along with attorneys' fees under § 815 ILCS 505/2.

V.
DAMAGES

78. Plaintiff adopts and re-alleges Paragraphs 1-77 above as if fully set forth herein and further alleges as follows:

79. As a result of Defendant's acts, omissions and/or misconduct, Plaintiff has suffered compensatory damages, which include, but are not limited to, the following:

a. Severe and permanent physical and medical injuries and associated disabilities;

b. Severe past and future pain and suffering and mental anguish occasioned by the resulting injuries and disabilities;

c. Loss of enjoyment of life;

d. Increased risk of health problems;

e. Loss of past and future economic losses and income;

f. Past and future medical, rehabilitation, and life care expenses;

g. Past and future medical monitoring;

h. Past and future medical expenses; and

i. Any and all other damages to be shown at trial.

WHEREFORE, PREMISES CONSIDERED, Plaintiff prays for trial by jury and demands judgment of and from the Defendant, Pfizer, Inc., and that after due proceedings, Plaintiff be awarded actual and compensatory damages, together with prejudgment interest, post-judgment interest and all costs of this proceeding, as well as any other relief to which he may be entitled under the law.

JURY DEMAND

Plaintiff hereby demands a jury trial on all issues so triable.

DATED: 12/4/06 By ____________________

Michael K. Johnson (258696)
Goldenberg & Johnson, PLLC
33 South Sixth Street, Ste 4530
Minneapolis, MN 55402
Telephone: (612)335-9961

Attorney for Plaintiff

STRICT LIABILITY IN TORT CHECKLIST

Definitions, Relationships, Paralegal Roles, and Research References

Category
Strict liability in tort is a strict liability tort. There is no need to show intent or negligence. In many states, however, negligence concepts are relevant to design defects.

Interest Protected by This Tort
The right to be free from injuries due to products that are defective and unreasonably dangerous.

Elements of This Tort

1. seller
2. a defective product that is unreasonably dangerous to person or property
3. user or consumer
4. physical harm (damages)
5. causation

Definitions of Major Words/Phrases in These Elements

Seller: A person engaged in the business of selling personal property. (Note: The definition of seller includes persons in the business of leasing personal property.)

Defective: Lacking in some particular that is essential to completeness, safety, or legal sufficiency.

Unreasonably dangerous: Dangerous to an extent beyond that which would be contemplated by the ordinary consumer who purchases it, with the ordinary knowledge common to the community as to its characteristics. (Note: Some states determine unreasonable danger by a risk-benefit analysis: deciding whether the benefits of proceeding without additional precautions outweigh the risk of harm that is foreseeable.)

User or consumer: Anyone who uses or consumes the product. (Note: Some courts have extended the definition to cover bystanders.)

Physical harm: Damage to person or property.

Causation: "But for" the defect, the physical harm would not have occurred, or the defect was a substantial factor in producing the physical harm.

Major Defenses and Counterargument Possibilities That Need to Be Explored

1. The defendant is not a seller.
2. The injury came from a service, not a product.
3. The product is not defective.
4. The product is not unreasonably dangerous.
5. The plaintiff is not a user or consumer.
6. There was no physical harm to person or property of the plaintiff.
7. The defendant did not cause the physical harm.
8. There was unforeseeable, extreme misuse of the product by the plaintiff.
9. The plaintiff assumed the risk of the danger in the product.
10. The plaintiff failed to take reasonable steps to mitigate the harm caused when the defendant committed strict liability in tort; therefore, damages should not cover the aggravation of the harm caused by the plaintiff (on the mitigation-of-damages rule, see Chapter 16).

Damages
In most states, damages for strict liability in tort cover physical harm to persons or property, but not economic loss alone. Once physical harm to persons or property is established, compensatory damages can include medical bills, pain and suffering, etc. Punitive damages are also possible. (On the categories of damages, see Chapter 16.)

STRICT LIABILITY IN TORT CHECKLIST
(Continued)

Relationship to Criminal Law
A state might impose criminal penalties on a company for improperly selling designated products, e.g., drugs, explosives.

Relationship to Other Causes of Action

Breach of express warranty: Available if the product does not conform to a representation made by the seller of the product.
Breach of implied warranty of merchantability: Available if the product is not fit for its ordinary purpose.
Breach of implied warranty of fitness for a particular purpose: Available if the product is not suitable for a particular purpose when the seller knew that the buyer was relying on the seller's skill or judgment on the product's suitability for that purpose.
Misrepresentation: Available if a seller by advertising, labels, or otherwise makes a representation to the public of a material fact concerning the character or quality of a good sold by the seller and physical harm to a consumer of the good is caused by justifiable reliance on the misrepresentation.
Negligence: Available upon proof that the injury from the product was caused by the absence of reasonable care on the part of the seller.

Federal Law

a. Under the Federal Tort Claims Act, the United States government will *not* be liable for a tort based on strict liability committed by one of its federal employees within the scope of employment. Sovereign immunity is not waived as to such torts. (See Exhibit 27–7 in Chapter 27.)
b. The United States Consumer Product Safety Commission (CPSC) (www.cpsc.gov) has authority to protect the public against unreasonable risks of injury associated with designated consumer products. Penalties can be imposed for violation of CPSC mandates.
c. Other federal agencies also have jurisdiction over specific consumer products, e.g., the Food and Drug Administration (www.fda.gov), the National Highway Transportation Safety Administration (www.nhtsa.dot.gov). Such agencies write administrative regulations that impose safety and other standards governing products. These standards must be examined to assess their relevance to litigation on strict liability in tort.

Employer–Employee (Agency) Law
An employer who is a seller is strictly liable in tort for harm caused by a product sold by one of its employees within the scope of employment if the product is defective and unreasonably dangerous (respondeat superior). On the factors that determine the scope of employment, see Exhibit 14–9 in Chapter 14.

Paralegal Roles in Strict Liability in Tort Litigation
(See also Exhibit 3–1 in Chapter 3, Exhibit 20–4 in Chapter 20, and Exhibit 29–1 in Chapter 29.)

Fact finding (help the office collect facts relevant to prove the elements of strict liability in tort, the elements of available defenses, and extent of injuries or other damages):

- client interviewing
- field investigation
- online research (e.g., identity of board of directors of a manufacturer)

File management (help the office control the documents involved in a strict liability in tort litigation):

- open client file
- enter case data in computer database
- maintain file documents

STRICT LIABILITY IN TORT CHECKLIST *(Continued)*

Litigation assistance (help the trial attorney prepare for a trial and appeal, if needed, of a strict liability in tort case):

- draft discovery requests
- draft answers to discovery requests
- draft pleadings
- digest and index discovery documents
- help prepare, order, and manage trial exhibits
- help prepare trial notebook
- draft notice of appeal
- order trial transcript
- cite-check briefs
- perform legal research

Collection/enforcement (help the trial attorney for the judgment creditor to collect the damages award or to enforce other court orders at the conclusion of the strict liability in tort case):

- draft postjudgment discovery requests
- conduct field investigation to monitor compliance with judgment
- perform online research (e.g., location of defendant's business assets)

Research References for Strict Liability in Tort

Digests
In the digests of West Group, look for case summaries of court opinions on this tort under key topics such as:

Products liability
Drugs and narcotics
Food
Sales
Damages
Torts
Negligence
Death

Corpus Juris Secundum
In this legal encyclopedia, see the discussion under topic headings such as:

Products liability
Drugs and narcotics
Food
Sales
Damages
Torts
Negligence
Death

American Jurisprudence 2d
In this legal encyclopedia, see the discussion under topic headings such as:

Products liability
Drugs, narcotics and poisons
Food
Sales
Damages
Torts
Negligence
Death

Legal Periodical Literature
There are two index systems to use to locate articles on this tort:

Index to Legal Periodicals and Books (ILP)
See literature in *ILP* under subject headings such as:
Products Liability
Warranty
Strict Liability
Insurance, Products Liability
Product Recall
Manufacturers
Torts
Damages
Negligence

Current Law Index (CLI)
See literature in *CLI* under subject headings such as:
Products Liability
Insurance, Products Liability
Product Recall
Manufacturers
Torts
Damages
Negligence
Warranty

STRICT LIABILITY IN TORT CHECKLIST *(Continued)*

Example of a legal periodical article you can locate on this tort by using *ILP* or *CLI*:

Reconceptualizing Strict Liability In Tort: An Overview by Martin A. Kotler, 50 Vanderbilt Law Rev. 555 (1997).

A.L.R., A.L.R.2d, A.L.R.3d, A.L.R.4th, A.L.R.5th, A.L.R.6th, A.L.R. Fed., A.L.R. Fed 2d
Use the *ALR Index* to locate annotations on this tort. In this index, check subject headings such as:

Products liability	Negligence
Warranty	Torts
Warnings	Damages
Drugs and narcotics	Death
Absolute liability	Repairs and maintenance

Example of an annotation you can locate through this index on strict liability in tort:

Applicability of Doctrine of Strict Liability in Tort to Injury Resulting from X-Ray Radiation by Thomas E. Miller, 16 A.L.R.4th 1300 (1982).

Words and Phrases
In this multivolume legal dictionary, look up *strict liability, warranty, defect, dangerous*, and every other word or phrase connected with strict liability in tort discussed in this section of the chapter. The dictionary will give you definitions of these words or phrases from court opinions.

CALR: Computer-Assisted Legal Research

Example of a query you could ask on Westlaw to try to find cases, statutes, or other legal materials on strict liability in tort: **"strict liability in tort"/p damages**

Example of a query you could ask on LexisNexis to try to find cases, statutes, or other legal materials on strict liability in tort: **strict liability in tort /p damages**

Example of a search you can use on an Internet legal search engine such as the Public Library of Law (www.plol.org), Findlaw (www.findlaw.com), or Google Scholar (scholar.google.com): **"strict liability in tort."**

Example of a search you could use on standard search engines (www.google.com, www.bing.com, www.yahoo.com) to find material on this tort; law firms that describe the tort; and articles, cases, statutes, and other materials on the tort: **"strict liability in tort."**

More Internet sites to check for material on strict liability in tort and other torts:
www.hg.org/torts.html
www.megalaw.com/top/top.php (click "Intentional Torts," "Personal Injury Law," "Tort Law," and "Damages")
See also the online sites in Overview of Tort Law at the end of Chapter 1.

CHECK THE CITE

Gabriel Gaumer injured his arm in a farm hay baler. Gabriel's father purchased the baler used "as is." Does strict liability in tort apply to a defective product that was purchased used? Read the case of *Gaumer v. Rossville Truck and Tractor Co., Inc.*, 41 Kan. App. 2d 405, 202 P.3d 81 (Kan. 2009). To read the opinion online, (1) Go to the site of the Kansas courts (www.kscourts.org). Under Cases & Opinions, select Court of Appeals Opinions. Under G, find the Gaumer opinion. (2) Go to FindACase (www.findacase.com). Select Kansas. Run a standard search (Gaumer Rossville). (3) Run a citation search ("202 P.3d 81") or a party search (Gaumer Rossville) in the Legal Opinions and Journals database of Google Scholar (scholar.google.com).

PROJECT

In Google, Bing, or another general search engine, run the following search: *aa* "products liability" "design defect" (substitute the name of your state for *aa* in the search, e.g., Kentucky "products liability" "design defect"). What test is used in your state for a design defect in a products liability case? Cite three separate web sources for your answer, only one of which can be a law firm site that provides information on products liability in the state.

ETHICS IN A TORTS PRACTICE

Henry Costello is injured by a lawn mower manufactured by Apex, Inc. Henry calls Brenda Lyons, Esq. and asks her to represent him. She agrees to do so and asks him to come to her office in a week to discuss the case. Before the meeting, Henry is contacted by Larry Pittman, who represents Apex. Henry tells Pittman that Lyons represents him. Pittman asks Henry the name of the store where he bought the lawn mower. They hang up after Henry answers the question. Any ethical problems?

SUMMARY

Products liability is not a cause of action. It is a general term that covers different causes of action based on products that cause harm. The main causes of action are negligence, breach of express warranty, breach of implied warranty of merchantability, breach of implied warranty of fitness for a particular purpose, and strict liability in tort. There are three categories of defects in products: manufacturing defects, design defects, and warning defects.

For purposes of a negligence suit, the defendant owes a duty of reasonable care to all foreseeable users of the product if it can be anticipated that substantial harm to person or property will result if the product is defective. Privity is not necessary. Breach of duty is established when the defendant fails to take reasonable steps to prevent injury caused by the product. Contributory negligence is a defense unless the state has replaced contributory negligence with comparative negligence. Assumption of the risk is also a defense.

Breach of express warranty is harm or damage caused by a false statement of fact relied on by the plaintiff and made with the intention or expectation that the statement will reach the plaintiff.

The following causes of action apply to sales rather than to services: breach of implied warranty of merchantability, breach of implied warranty of fitness for a particular purpose, and strict liability in tort. Breach of implied warranty of merchantability is harm or damage caused by a merchant's sale of goods that were not fit for the ordinary purposes for which they are used. A breach of implied warranty of fitness for a particular purpose is harm or damage caused by a sale of goods by a merchant who has reason to know the buyer is relying on the expertise of the merchant in selecting the goods for a particular purpose, but the goods are not fit for that purpose.

To bring a warranty action, the general rule is that there must be privity, or a contractual relationship, between the defendant and the person injured. Some states, however, have abolished the privity requirement in designated kinds of cases such as when the person injured is in the immediate family of the person who bought the product. Defenses to actions for breach of warranty include valid disclaimers, failure of the plaintiff to provide notice within a reasonable time after the breach was discovered or should have been discovered, and assumption of the risk. Contributory negligence is generally not a defense.

Strict liability in tort is a cause of action imposing liability for physical harm caused by a defective product that is unreasonably dangerous. The product must be defective and unreasonably dangerous for its intended use and its foreseeable use.

States differ on the tests they use to determine when a defect is unreasonably dangerous. The predominant test is the expectations of the ordinary consumer. Some states, however, use other tests, particularly for design defects. The test might call for a risk-benefit analysis or the availability of a reasonable alternative design. The defect in the product must cause physical harm in the plaintiff, who is either a user or consumer of the product, or, in some states, anyone who is foreseeably injured, which could include a bystander. Misuse is a defense when it is unforeseeable and extreme. Assumption of the risk is also a defense. Generally, contributory negligence is not a defense. A state may compare the fault of the plaintiff and the defendant and apportion the damages according to its comparative negligence formula.

KEY TERMS

products liability *356*
defective *357*
mass tort *357*
chain of distribution *358*
lessee *358*
bailee *358*
bystander *358*
lessor *358*
bailor *358*
privity *358*
foreseeable users *359*
res ipsa loquitur *362*
merchant *362*
custom *363*
contributory negligence *363*
comparative negligence *363*
assumption of the risk *363*
warranty *364*
strict liability *364*
breach of express warranty *364*
Uniform Commercial Code (UCC) *364*
fact *365*
opinion *365*
puffing *365*
reliance *366*
material *366*
sale *366*
consideration *366*
personal property *366*
real property *366*
service *367*
breach of implied warranty of merchantability *368*
merchantable *368*
breach of implied warranty of fitness for a particular purpose *369*
disclaimer *371*
unconscionable *371*
point *371*
notice *371*
strict liability in tort *373*
§ 402A *373*
seller *374*
unreasonably dangerous *374*
unavoidably unsafe product *377*
misuse *378*
crashworthiness *378*
preemption *379*
risk-benefit analysis *380*
reasonable alternative design *383*
market share liability *385*
learned-intermediary doctrine *386*
immunity *386*

REVIEW QUESTIONS

1. How extensive are injuries caused by defective products?
2. What is meant by products liability?
3. What are the main products liability causes of action?
4. What are the three categories of product defects?
5. What are the main categories of plaintiffs who might bring a products liability cause of action?
6. What are the main categories of potential defendants in a products liability cause of action?
7. What is privity, and is it required for a products liability cause of action?
8. What is the chain of distribution?
9. In a negligence action, when is a duty owed to a foreseeable user of a product?
10. How is a breach of duty established in a negligence action for harm caused by a product?
11. What factors are considered when determining whether a manufacturer breached its duty of care in a products liability case?
12. When can res ipsa loquitur be used in a products liability case asserting negligence?
13. What factors are considered when determining whether a nonmanufacturer such as a retailer breached its duty of care in a products liability case?
14. What defenses exist to a products liability case asserting negligence?
15. What are the three warranty causes of action in a products liability case?
16. How does a plaintiff establish breach of express warranty in a products liability case?
17. Why is it important to distinguish between a sale and a service in a products liability case, and what is the distinction?
18. How does a plaintiff establish breach of warranty of merchantability in a products liability case?
19. How does a plaintiff establish breach of warranty of fitness for a particular purpose in a products liability case?

20. Who can be a plaintiff in a breach-of-warranty products liability case? Who can be a defendant?
21. What defenses exist to breach of warranty actions in products liability cases?
22. What is strict liability in tort?
23. How is *seller* defined in an action for strict liability in tort?
24. What are the different standards used by states in a case asserting strict liability in tort when determining whether there is a design defect?
25. What is preemption, and when does it apply?
26. What is market share liability?
27. What defenses can be asserted in an action for strict liability in tort?

HELPFUL WEBSITES

- **Products Liability**
  www.megalaw.com/top/products.php
  topics.law.cornell.edu/wex/Products_liability
  en.wikipedia.org/wiki/Product_liability
  www.abanet.org/litigation/committees/products
  topics.law.cornell.edu/wex/strict_liability
  topics.law.cornell.edu/wex/design_defect
  www.lexisnexis.com/lawschool/study/outlines/html/torts/torts17.htm
- **§ 402A of Restatement (Second) of Torts**
  digitalcommons.pace.edu/cgi/viewcontent.cgi?article=1149&context=lawfaculty
  biotech.law.lsu.edu/cases/products/402a-b.htm
  findarticles.com/p/articles/mi_hb6367/is_11_75/ai_n28879851
- **Reform of Products Liability Law**
  www.atra.org/show/7341
  www.vpc.org/fact_sht/gindrel.htm
  en.wikipedia.org/wiki/Tort_reform
- **Consumer Product Safety Commission**
  www.cpsc.gov

ENDNOTES

1. Andrew J. McClurg, *Rungful Suits*, 83 American Bar Association Journal 98 (June 1997).
2. § 2-313. Express Warranties by Affirmation, Promise, Description, Sample.
   (1) In this section, "immediate buyer" means a buyer that enters into a contract with the seller.
   (2) Express warranties by the seller to the immediate buyer are created as follows:
      (a) Any affirmation of fact or promise made by the seller which relates to the goods and becomes part of the basis of the bargain creates an express warranty that the goods shall conform to the affirmation or promise.
      (b) Any description of the goods which is made part of the basis of the bargain creates an express warranty that the goods shall conform to the description.
      (c) Any sample or model that is made part of the basis of the bargain creates an express warranty that the whole of the goods shall conform to the sample or model.
   (3) It is not necessary to the creation of an express warranty that the seller use formal words such as "warrant" or "guarantee" or that the seller have a specific intention to make a warranty, but an affirmation merely of the value of the goods or a statement purporting to be merely the seller's opinion or commendation of the goods does not create a warranty. . . .
3. The UCC was proposed to the states by the National Conference of Commissioners on Uniform State Laws and the American Law Institute. (www.law.cornell.edu/ucc/2/article2.htm#s2-313). See also § 402B of the *Restatement (Second) of Torts* on liability for misrepresentations of a material fact concerning the character or quality of a chattel that causes physical harm: "Section 402B. Misrepresentation by Seller of Chattels to Consumer. One engaged in the business of selling chattels who, by advertising, labels, or otherwise, makes to the public a misrepresentation of a material fact concerning the character or quality of a chattel sold by him is subject to liability for physical harm to a consumer of the chattel caused by justifiable reliance upon the misrepresentation, even though (a) it is not made fraudulently or negligently, and (b) the consumer has not bought the chattel from or entered into any contractual

relation with the seller." *Restatement (Second) of Torts* § 402B (1965).
4. *Newmark v. Gimbel's Inc.*, 102 N.J. Super. 279, 246 A.2d 11, *aff'd*, 54 N.J. 585, 258 A.2d 697 (1969).
5. *Wyeth v. Levine*, ___ U.S. ___, 129 S. Ct. 1187, 173 L. Ed. 2d 51 (2009).
6. *Potter v. Chicago Pneumatic Tool Co.*, 694 A.2d 1319, 1331 (Conn. 1997) (emphasis in original).
7. *Restatement (Second) of Torts* § 402A, Comment g (1965).
8. *Sindell v. Abbott Laboratories*, 26 Cal. 3d 588, 607 P.2d 924, 163 Cal. Rptr. 132, 2 A.L.R.4th 1061 (1980).
9. W. Page Keeton et al., *Prosser and Keeton on the Law of Torts* 271 (5th ed. 1984).
10. Safety Act, www.safetyact.gov.
11. Jan L'Hommedieu, *Products Liability: An In-House Perspective*, 23 National Paralegal Reporter 24, 25–6 (Winter 1998).

Student StudyWARE™ CD-ROM
For additional materials, please go to the student CD in this book.

CHAPTER

20

MASS TORT LITIGATION

CHAPTER OUTLINE

- Introduction
- Solicitation of Clients
- Other Ethical Violations
- Class Actions
- Junk Science and Causation
- Asbestos
- Breast Implants
- Tobacco
- Paralegal Roles in Mass Tort Litigation

CHAPTER OBJECTIVES

After completing this chapter, you should be able to:

- Understand the four categories of mass tort litigation.
- Identify the causes of action that are often asserted in mass tort litigation.
- State some of the major benefits and drawbacks of mass tort litigation.
- Understand the ethical infractions committed by personal injury attorneys seeking to solicit clients in mass tort cases.
- State the requirements for bringing a class action suit in federal court.
- Explain what is meant by junk science and how it is addressed by Federal Rule of Evidence 702 and the *Daubert* test.
- State some of the major issues that have arisen in mass tort litigation involving asbestos, breast implants, and tobacco.
- Identify paralegal roles in mass tort litigation.

INTRODUCTION

mass tort A general term for various causes of action asserted by a large number of persons who have been harmed by the same or similar conduct or product of a relatively small number of defendants. The causes of action include negligence, strict liability in tort, breach of warranty, misrepresentation, and violations of deceptive trade acts.

We live in a society in which it is relatively easy to poison the environment, contaminate the food supply, and market products that endanger the life and limb of thousands. In response, one of the most dramatic developments in tort law since the 1980s has been the increase in the litigation and settlement of **mass tort** cases. A mass tort is a general term for various causes of action asserted by a large number of persons who have been harmed by the same or similar conduct or product of a relatively small number of defendants. The causes of action include negligence, strict liability in tort, breach of warranty, misrepresentation, and violations of deceptive trade acts. According to one commentator, "If litigation is war, mass torts are the legal system's version of a nuclear exchange: Thousands of complex claims. Huge potential damages. Massive discovery and expense."[1] These will be some of the major themes in this chapter.

There are four general categories of mass tort cases, although some overlap exists among the categories: mass accident, mass-marketed product, mass exposure, and mass economic loss.[2] (See Exhibit 20–1.) As creative attorneys continue to find new ways to litigate these cases, we are likely to see additional categories emerge in the coming years.

Exhibit 20–1
Categories of mass tort litigation.

Kinds of Mass Tort Litigation	**Examples**
Mass accident: a large number of people are injured in a single catastrophic event	train wreck, plane crash, nightclub fire
Mass-marketed product: a large number of people are injured by a widely marketed product	asbestos, breast implants, tobacco, lead paint, weight loss drug, contraceptives
Mass exposure: a large number of people are injured by exposure from the same toxic source	Agent Orange, nuclear plant leakage
Mass economic loss: a large number of people suffer monetary loss from misrepresentation or consumer fraud, usually not involving bodily injury	misleading car warranty, false representations made in a stock prospectus

The focus in mass tort litigation is tortious conduct involving the same event or product that has caused harm to many people. In such cases, the major concern of the legal system is to provide a remedy for those who have been harmed without destroying the industry that caused the harm. According to federal judge Jack B. Weinstein, the need is to find the best way to "protect and compensate people exposed to toxic substances and dangerous products—particularly those with latent, after-discovered dangers—at a reasonable cost, without unnecessarily destroying industries and unduly deterring development of new products."[3]

A mass tort is not a new cause of action. In the litigation of a mass tort case, plaintiffs typically assert traditional causes of action which, as indicated, include negligence and strict liability in tort. What is new is the scope of these cases. They often involve years of litigation, thousands of plaintiffs, hundreds of millions of dollars in damages, huge attorney fees, and extensive media publicity. Although there is no such thing as a typical mass tort case, several characteristics are common to many of them.[4]

Characteristics of Many Mass Tort Cases

- numerous victims who have filed or who might file damage claims against the same defendant(s)
- injuries that are widely dispersed over time, territory, and jurisdiction
- large burdens on the court systems where cases are filed

- inconsistent judgments from different courts involving the same or similar facts
- legal issues (questions of law and fact) that are complex and expensive to litigate—frequently issues that are scientific and technological in nature
- problems in establishing causation between the plaintiff's injury and the defendant's tortious conduct—especially in **toxic tort** cases alleging toxic substance exposure where it may be difficult to identify the precise products to which there was exposure and where there is a long latency period between exposure to the toxic substance and the injury complained of
- long delays in the resolution of claims; this may lead to conflict between claimants who need prompt compensation and claimants who are willing to hold out for the largest payout possible
- huge litigation costs to plaintiffs and defendants; in some cases, attorney fees, costs of expert witnesses, and other litigation expenses far exceed the total compensation paid to victims (a common criticism of the system is that attorneys often reap millions in attorney fees while victims receive comparatively miniscule awards)
- strong pressures on defendants to settle so that litigation costs do not consume all of their business energy and resources; some defendants may face so many claims that they agree to large settlements even though their liability may be doubtful; some file for bankruptcy
- an inclination among multiple defendants to cooperate with each other even if they do not present a united defense; cooperation could include sharing experts and information
- allegations of ethical impropriety by attorneys who solicit clients, send them to friendly doctors, and claim extraordinarily high legal fees

toxic tort Personal injury or property damage wrongfully caused by repeated exposure to poisons in chemicals, asbestos, radiation, waste, or other substances.

Perhaps the most common characteristic of a mass tort case is its sheer size, as we will see when we examine paralegal roles in a toxic tort case at the end of the chapter. A mass tort case is called a "document case" because of the large volume of documents exchanged during discovery and trial. In a Minnesota tobacco case, for example, the attorney representing one of the cigarette companies (Lorillard) made the following comments in her closing argument to the jury:

> Now as you know, this case has been what we refer to as a document case. You've seen many documents. You've heard some testimony on the documents. . . . There was testimony of some 30 million pages of documents being in a depository right here in the Twin Cities area. Lorillard has produced approximately 1.8 million pages of documents in this lawsuit. If you were to take those documents and stack them, one on top of the other, they would be 666 feet high. That's the equivalent of a sixty-six-story office building. That's how many documents Lorillard has produced in this lawsuit.[5]

This comment is not an exaggeration; the quantity of documents in a mass tort case is often staggering. (The Minnesota tobacco case was eventually settled; the state of Minnesota received $6.6 billion to cover the health costs it paid to treat sick smokers. We will examine the tobacco settlement later.)

Our primary focus in this chapter will be on personal injury from a mass-marketed product, although many of the issues we will discuss apply to all of the categories listed in Exhibit 20–1. Hundreds of products have been the subject of mass tort litigation. The three we have selected for study (asbestos, breast implants, and tobacco) present vivid examples of a legal system striving to achieve justice while seeming to be on the verge of collapse. Before beginning our examination of these three products, we need to cover some preliminary topics that apply throughout this area of the law. The topics are client solicitation, class actions, and junk science in the courtroom. At the end of the chapter, we will explore paralegal roles from the perspective of a paralegal project manager who helps the office oversee the large number of tasks that must be performed in a mass tort case.

SOLICITATION OF CLIENTS

Mass tort litigation can be a lucrative area of law practice. One indication of this is the large payments law firms give search engines such as Google to have their sites appear high on the list of results of certain searches related to mass tort claims. Recently, for example, a law firm paid Google $56.24 for *each* click on a search for "mesothelioma" that led to the firm's website. Google was paid this amount whether or not the searcher hired the firm. A mere click on the link triggered the payment. The firm was willing to pay Google such a high price because someone using this search term is likely to be looking for an attorney who handles asbestos-exposure cases, which can led to unusually high attorney fees. Understandably, therefore, competition among personal injury attorneys for such cases can be fierce. One court painted the following unflattering picture of how some of these attorneys solicit clients:

> The familiar spectacle of lawyers and their agents preying on the victims of disaster has occasioned revulsion. . . . In the aftermath of the tragic release of poison gas at the Union Carbide plant in Bhopal, India, "American lawyers rushed to India in an attempt to retain clients and in their zeal brought shame and discredit to the American Bar." Eric S. Roth, *Confronting Solicitation of Mass Disaster Victims,* 2 Georgetown Journal of Legal Ethics 967, 972 (1989). The examples of abuse are chilling. Shortly after the crash of a Northwest airliner in Detroit on August 16, 1987, a man posing as a Catholic priest appeared on the scene to console the families of the victims. He "hugged crying mothers and talked with grieving fathers of God's rewards in the hereafter. He even sobbed along with dazed families. . . . Then he would pass out the business card of a Florida attorney . . . and repeatedly urge them to call the lawyer." Roth, supra, 2 Geo. J. Legal Ethics at 972. After the crash of Pan Am Flight 103 in Scotland, one victim's widow reported solicitation "by no less than 30 attorneys within 24 hours of the crash." Ibid. Other examples abound. "How much money would you like to get out of this case?" a letter asked the mother of a child who had recently suffered brain damage in an automobile accident. It was one of three letters she had received from attorneys within two weeks of her son's accident. In the same envelope was a police report with the lawyer's card stapled to it. In the view of an Oregon Bar Association commentator, "[s]uch a letter clearly offends common decency." Richard Sanders, *Lawyer Advertising and Solicitation: The Good, the Bad, the Unethical,* 50 Oregon State Bar Bulletin 5 (June 1990). An editorial cartoon in a Miami newspaper portrayed lawyers after the Delta 911 air crash disaster as " 'vultures, members of the law firm of Pickem, Pickem, Scavage & Bone . . . Don't Call Us—We'll Call You!'" Howard R. Messing, *The Latest Word on Solicitation,* Fla. Bar Journal, 17, May 1986 (quoting The Miami Herald, Aug. 16, 1985, at 20A). . . . A mother, faced with attorney solicitation shortly after her daughter's death in a car crash, reacted: "give me some time—I am still grieving." Allessandra Stanley, *Bronx Crash, Then Contest of Lawyers,* N.Y. Times, June 17, 1991, at B1.[6]

solicitation An appeal or request for clients or business. (See glossary for an additional definition.)

There are ethical rules governing the **solicitation** of prospective clients by attorneys and by those working for attorneys, such as paralegals. The policy behind these rules is that prospective clients should not be placed under undue pressure at a time when they are vulnerable and unable to make clear decisions about whom to hire, if anyone.

There are two main ways that attorneys seek to be hired by prospective clients:

real-time Occurring now; happening as you are watching; able to respond immediately.

1. *In-person, live telephone, or* ***real-time*** *electronic contact.* Examples: unannounced visits to the homes of victims or their relatives (in-person contact), cold calls to the homes of victims or their relatives (live telephone), communicating with victims in an Internet chat room (real-time electronic contact). Solicitation of clients through

such contacts is unethical if the attorney's goal is to seek fees or other financial benefit, unless the contact is with another attorney or someone with whom the attorney has a family, close personal, or prior professional relationship.

2. *Written, recorded, or standard electronic contact.* Examples: standard U.S. mail (written contact), phone messages (recorded contact), e-mail messages (electronic contact). Solicitation of clients through such contacts is ethical unless (a) the attorney knows that the prospective client does not want to be solicited; (b) the solicitation involves coercion, duress, or harassment; or (c) the solicitation is untruthful or misleading.

Although the second category of contact can be ethical, there are regulations that govern such contact. For example, a state might require that the phrase "Advertising Material" be printed prominently on the front of an envelope sent by an attorney seeking employment. In New Jersey and in many states that have adopted the *Model Rules of Professional Conduct* of the American Bar Association, Rule 7.3(b)(1) prohibits written communications through the mail if "the lawyer knows or reasonably should know that the physical, emotional or mental state of the person is such that the person could not exercise reasonable judgment in employing a lawyer."

This prohibition became an issue in an attorney solicitation letter sent to the parent of a child killed on Pan Am Flight 103 over Lockerbie, Scotland. One of the victims was Alexander Lowenstein, a student at Syracuse University and resident of Morristown, New Jersey. His remains were identified on January 3, 1989. The following day, attorney Magdy F. Anis sent the following solicitation letter to Peter Lowenstein, Alexander's father:

Dear Mr. Lowenstein:

Initially, we would like to extend our deepest sympathy for the loss of your son, Mr. Alexander Lowenstein. We know that this must be a very traumatic experience for you, and we hope that you, along with your relatives and friends, can overcome this catastrophe which has not only affected your family but has disturbed the world.

As you may already realize, you have a legal cause of action against Pan American, among others, for wrongful death due to possible negligent security maintenance. If you intend to take any legal recourse, we urge you to consider to retain our firm to prosecute your case.

Both my partner and myself are experienced practitioners in the personal injury field, and feel that we can obtain a favorable outcome for you against the airline, among other possible defendants.

We would also like to inform you that if you do decide to retain our services, you will not be charged for any attorneys fees unless we collect a settlement or verdict award for you. Before retaining any other attorney, it would be worth your while to contact us, since we will substantially reduce the customary one third fee that most other attorneys routinely charge.

Please call us to schedule an appointment at your earliest convenience. If you are unable to come to our office, please so advise us and we will have an attorney meet you at a location suitable to your needs.

Very truly yours,
(Mr.) Magdy F. Anis
MFA/seb
P.S. There is no consultation fee.

Outraged by the letter, the father immediately filed an ethics charge with the New Jersey Office of Attorney Ethics. The case was eventually resolved by the New Jersey Supreme Court, which ruled that Anis had crossed the ethical line in his mail solicitation. The attorney admitted that he did not know at the time that he mailed the letter whether Alexander's body had yet been identified. The court said, "We believe that an ordinarily prudent attorney would recognize that within the hours and days following a tragic disaster, families would be particularly weak and vulnerable." Any "reasonable lawyer would conclude that an obsequious letter of solicitation delivered the day after a death notice would reach people when they 'could not exercise reasonable judgment in employing a lawyer'" under 7.3(b)(1). The court rejected the argument of Anis that his solicitation letter was protected by his commercial speech rights under the First Amendment of the United States Constitution. Reasonable restrictions on such rights, such as those found in ethical rule 7.3(b)(1), can be imposed on attorneys.

The New Jersey court acknowledged that its ruling cast doubt on when it is permissible to send solicitation letters to potential clients. "We realize" said the court "that there may be other cases in which it will be more difficult to draw the line of ethical propriety. Would a truthful solicitation letter sent fifteen or thirty days after a tragic loss reach people when they are no longer emotionally weak or vulnerable? We cannot say with certainty, since our assumptions in such cases are largely untested. It may be that there are degrees of loss or suffering. Common sense tells us that the mildly injured survivors of an overturned-bus incident might be less vulnerable than were the Lockerbie families. Hence, we attempt no permanent bright-line rule in this opinion."[7]

Not all states follow New Jersey's reluctance to establish clear-cut (i.e., "bright-line") rules on the impropriety of solicitation. Some states, for example, prohibit attorneys from using direct mail to solicit potential personal injury or wrongful death clients within thirty days of the accident. And in 1996, Congress passed the Aviation Disaster Family Assistance Act, which restricts communications by attorneys, paralegals, or other employees of attorneys as follows: "no unsolicited communication concerning a potential action for personal injury or wrongful death may be made by an attorney (including any associate, agent, employee, or other representative of an attorney) or any potential party to the litigation to an individual injured in the accident, or to a relative of an individual involved in the accident, before the 45th day following the date of the accident."[8]

Nevertheless, the lure of mega-fees will continue to encourage some attorneys to take questionable risks in order to sign up tort victims, particularly those injured by mass torts.

OTHER ETHICAL VIOLATIONS

Paralegals need to be cautious. There are attorneys who will hire paralegals of a certain race or ethnic background for the sole purpose of soliciting mass tort victims of the same race or background. Some unscrupulous law firms have gone further. A report on a law firm that handled asbestos cases, for example, said that paralegals were encouraged to help clients manipulate facts during interviews:

> A paralegal says that in many cases, the client had no specific recollection of some products before she interviewed them. "My original caseload was a thousand, but I didn't interview that many people. It was in the hundreds. I'd say that probably in 75 percent of those cases I had people identify at least one product they couldn't recall originally." [M]anipulation of claimant memories and stories appear to have gone beyond implanting valuable facts to improve their claims. The . . . firm also conveniently helped claimants eliminate facts from their stories where that would suit their purpose. . . . According to the paralegals, their job didn't stop with implanting memories; there were also the asbestos products they had to encourage clients *not* to recall. Two lawyers told [a paralegal] to discourage identification of Johns-Manville products because

> the Manville Trust was not paying claims rendered against it at the time. . . . Thus, when a client would say he saw, for instance, a Johns-Manville pipe covering, the paralegal says, she would hand them a line. "You'd say, 'You know, we've talked to some other people, other witnesses, and they recall working with Owens-Corning Kaylo. Don't you think you saw that?' And they'd say, 'Yeah, maybe you're right.'"[9]

Clearly paralegals need to be careful to avoid letting themselves get caught up in the unethical behavior of overzealous attorneys. Most attorneys run their law firms in accordance with high professional and ethical standards. Some attorneys, however, practice law differently. This reality is by no means unique to mass tort law firms. Yet the fierce competition for clients and the lure of mega-fees require extra diligence from anyone working in this area of the law.

CLASS ACTIONS

In the vast majority of cases, a person injured by a mass tort can bring a solo or individual lawsuit, by which we mean that the injured person is usually the only party bringing the litigation (occasionally with a relative or associate) against one or more defendants. This kind of litigation, however, can be expensive. Also, obtaining attorney representation can sometimes be a challenge. Most personal injury attorneys are paid a percentage of what the plaintiff receives through settlement or litigation. Unless the accident caused a death or a major disability, damages are likely to be modest. This will discourage many attorneys from taking the case, particularly if there are difficult causation issues or other problems of proof that must be litigated.

Once an attorney does become interested, the traditional route is to launch an individual lawsuit. If there are several potential plaintiffs, they might all be joined in the lawsuit. Suppose, however, there are hundreds or thousands of injured persons due to a mass tort. Joining them all in one action may not be practical. "In the mass tort context . . . **joinder** is not feasible because it would create a 'zoo' of litigants in the courtroom, each seeking to pursue his cause of action."[10] An alternative is the **class action**, although as we will see, this kind of action has its own management problems.

A class action is a lawsuit in which one or more members of a class sue (or are sued) as representative parties on behalf of everyone in the class. A court recently defined a class action as "a nontraditional litigation procedure permitting a representative with typical claims to sue or defend on behalf of, and stand in judgment for, a class of similarly situated persons when the question is one of common or general interest to persons so numerous as to make it impracticable to bring them all before the court."[11] The representative parties act on behalf of everyone. (Here the word *representative* does not refer to an attorney; it refers to named parties who act on behalf of the class. Of course, representative parties are almost always "represented" *by* attorneys who thereby become counsel for the class.) If the parties do not intend to litigate the claims made in the complaint because they have reached a settlement before trial, the proceeding is called a **settlement class action**.

A class action can help prevent a court system from collapsing under the weight of individual lawsuits. Another benefit is that it can be attractive to injured persons who individually have not suffered greatly and hence might have difficulty attracting an attorney. As one court said:

> The policy at the very core of the class action mechanism is to overcome the problem that small recoveries do not provide the incentive for any individual to bring a solo action prosecuting his or her rights. A class action solves this problem by aggregating the relatively paltry potential recoveries into something worth someone's (usually an attorney's) labor.[12]

joinder Uniting two or more parties as plaintiffs, two or more parties as defendants, or two or more claims into a single lawsuit.

class action A lawsuit in which one or more members of a class sue (or are sued) as representative parties on behalf of everyone in the class, all of whom do not have to be joined in the lawsuit. Also called representative action.

settlement class action A class action that the parties do not intend to litigate because they have reached a settlement on the claims made.

global peace A final resolution of all claims that binds all parties, often through a class action.

opt out To choose not to participate. To bring an individual lawsuit rather than become a member of a class action.

If all victims of a mass tort are part of the class action, the benefit to the defendants is achieving **global peace**—a final resolution of all claims. In many cases, this is achieved only partially since members of the class usually have the right to **opt out** of the class (called a "request for exclusion") by deciding that they would rather bring their own individual lawsuit than be a member of the class action. In some class actions, however, claimants are not allowed to opt out.[13]

Class actions in federal court are governed by Rule 23 of the Federal Rules of Civil Procedure (FRCP). State courts follow their own rules on class actions, although many states have patterned their state class action rules on Rule 23 of the FRCP. According to the Class Action Fairness Act, some class actions, however, must be brought in federal court.[14] With some exceptions, they are class actions in which the amount in controversy exceeds $5 million and any of the defendants is a citizen of a state that is different from any member of the class of plaintiffs (**diversity of citizenship**).

diversity of citizenship The disputing parties are citizens of different states. This is one of the facts that can give jurisdiction to a United States district court.

JUNK SCIENCE AND CAUSATION

junk science Unreliable and, therefore, potentially misleading scientific evidence.

For years, critics have accused clever trial attorneys of using dubious scientific evidence to persuade juries that the defendant's product caused a particular disease or other harm. The charge is that courts are allowing juries to consider **junk science**, which simply refers to unreliable and, therefore, potentially misleading scientific evidence. Many of the cases in court are extremely complex. Scores of experts and a maze of documents can sometimes overwhelm juries. Even judges can become confused. Jurors and judges are not trained in engineering or science, yet they often must sort through and interpret a mountain of technical evidence. In this environment, critics charge that junk science has dominated many cases.

> [E]xperts peddling junk science have [led to] billions of dollars in judgments, coerced settlements, and litigation costs on the basis of speculative, unscientific theories of liability.[15]

Suppose, for example, that a plaintiff's attorney calls an expert witness to the stand to give testimony on a university study showing that 80 percent of cancer patients in the study took a particular diet supplement. Arguably, this study is junk science when it is used to prove that the diet supplement caused the cancer. *Association is not causation.* If we notice that many overweight people drink iced tea, we cannot conclude that iced tea causes obesity. In a case we will read later in the chapter, the court complains that a plaintiff's argument "is a bit like saying that if a person has a scratchy throat, runny nose, and a nasty cough, that person has a cold; if, on the other hand, that person has a scratchy throat, runny nose, nasty cough, and wears a watch, they have a watch-induced cold. Such reasoning is extremely suspect."

Frye test Expert opinion on a scientific principle or discovery is admissible if it has "gained general acceptance" as reliable in the relevant scientific community. Based on the holding of *Frye v. United States*, 293 F. 1013 (D.C. Cir. 1923).

What guidelines have trial courts used in ruling on the admissibility of scientific evidence? For years, many federal courts followed the ***Frye* test** written by a lower federal court in the case of *Frye v. United States*. Under this test, expert opinion on a scientific principle or discovery is admissible only if it has "gained general acceptance" as being reliable in the relevant scientific community. In a famous quote, the *Frye* court said:

> Just when a scientific principle or discovery crosses the line between the experimental and demonstrable stages is difficult to define. Somewhere in this twilight zone the evidential force of the principle must be recognized, and while courts will go a long way in admitting expert testimony deduced from a well-recognized scientific principle or discovery, the thing from which the deduction is made must be sufficiently established to have gained general acceptance in the particular field in which it belongs.[16]

After the *Frye* decision was written, Congress passed the Federal Rules of Evidence (FRE), which replaced the *Frye* test. Under FRE 702, technical or scientific testimony from an expert will be admitted if it is based on "sufficient facts or data," is the product of "reliable principles and methods," and will "assist the trier of fact."[17]

FRE 702, however, was criticized as being too broad and, therefore, not much of an improvement over the *Frye* test in keeping junk science out of federal trials. Further clarification was then provided by the United States Supreme Court in the *Daubert* case.[18] The Court said that FRE 702 is not an open door. Under what is now called the ***Daubert* test**, a federal trial judge must act as a "gatekeeper" to ensure that scientific evidence is relevant and reliable. The judge must carefully examine scientific evidence before allowing a jury to consider it in order to determine whether the methodology, principles, and reasoning underlying the evidence

- can be and have been empirically tested;
- have been subjected to peer review and publication;
- have a known or potential rate of error; and
- have gained general acceptance in the relevant scientific community.

Federal judges must exclude proposed scientific or other technical evidence under FRE 702 unless they are convinced that the evidence is reliable, speaks clearly and directly to an issue in dispute in the case, and will not mislead the jury. This interpretation of FRE 702 gives trial judges a very activist role in this aspect of a trial.

***Daubert* test** To assess the admissibility of scientific evidence in federal court, the judge must consider: (1) whether the theory or technique can be and has been tested; (2) whether the theory or technique has been subject to peer review and publication; (3) the known or potential rate of error; and (4) general acceptance in the relevant scientific community. Based on the United States Supreme Court's interpretation of Federal Rules of Evidence Rule 702 in *Daubert v. Merrell Dow Pharmaceuticals, Inc.*, 509 U.S. 579 (1993).

ASBESTOS

Asbestos is a fibrous material known for its resistance to acid and fire. It was used in many products such as brake linings, water pipes, blankets, rope, wall insulation, caulking, and other building materials. The fibers in asbestos are invisible. They are easily dispersed into the air when products containing asbestos are installed or removed.

There is no safe level of exposure to asbestos. It can cause mesothelioma (an untreatable terminal cancer), asbestosis (a progressive untreatable disease of the lung), and pleural disease. There is some disagreement over whether it also causes gastrointestinal tract cancers. For most victims, there is a latency period between exposure and the manifestation of disease, although the length of this latency period can widely vary. Some will have a latency period as long as forty years. Since the 1940s, the number of people estimated to have been exposed to asbestos is between 11 and 30 million. Every year tens of thousands become ill or die from asbestos-related diseases. The number of people who will develop symptoms in the future is uncertain. Some predict the death toll will reach 500,000. Asbestos has been banned or declared hazardous by the Occupational Safety and Health Administration, the National Institute for Occupational Safety and Health, the Environmental Protection Agency, and the Surgeon General. Most manufacturers stopped making asbestos in the 1970s when the lawsuits began.

Thousands of asbestos personal injury claims have been filed in almost every court in the country. In federal courts, asbestos cases constitute a substantial proportion of the docket. (See Exhibit 20–2.) The United States Supreme Court has referred to all this litigation as an "elephantine mass of asbestos cases."

Litigation delays in asbestos cases have been double that of other civil cases. Transaction costs (e.g., attorney fees, witness fees, travel, court costs) consumed 61 cents of each asbestos-litigation dollar; plaintiffs have received only 39 cents from each litigation dollar.[19] One judge painted the following picture of the large number of asbestos cases that have been filed:

> Results of jury verdicts are capricious and uncertain. Sick people and people who die a terrible death from asbestos are being turned away from the courts, while people with minimal injuries who may never suffer severe asbestos disease are being awarded hundreds of thousands of dollars, and even in excess of a

Exhibit 20–2 Asbestos cases in federal courts.

	2003	2004	2005	2006	2007
Cases total[1]	261,608	267,881	267,270	246,547	267,774
Contract actions[1]	30,789	28,413	26,712	26,671	30,631
Recovery of overpayments[2]	2,713	2,146	1,953	1,789	1,708
Real property actions	6,302	5,651	4,512	4,178	4,321
Tort actions	65,562	74,589	76,821	64,701	83,046
Personal injury	61,496	68,928	72,716	60,569	78,464
Personal injury product liability[1]	34,655	42,886	46,575	34,280	52,346
Asbestos	**5,606**	**2,528**	**1,073**	**656**	**14,525**
Other personal injury	26,841	26,042	26,141	26,289	26,118
Personal property damage	4,066	5,661	4,105	4,132	4,582
Actions under statutes[1]	158,943	159,200	157,357	150,891	149,622
Civil rights[1]	43,981	43,431	40,596	38,384	36,469
Employment	23,618	22,964	21,344	18,591	16,863
Bankruptcy suits	2,522	2,684	2,650	2,565	2,533
Commerce (ICC rates, etc.)	455	427	395	351	276
Environmental matters	2,296	2,282	1,193	1,148	1,045
Prisoner petitions	44,306	44,317	47,870	46,655	47,172
Forfeiture and penalty	1,932	2,017	2,156	2,309	2,245
Labor laws	14,621	15,131	15,725	14,014	15,111
Protected property rights[3]	8,654	8,992	10,507	10,274	9,827
Securities commodities and exchanges	5,227	5,325	5,192	4,463	4,030
Social security laws	17,526	14,853	15,420	14,202	13,214
Tax suits	1,106	1,158	1,222	1,331	1,376
Freedom of information	347	360	378	370	380

[1]Includes other types not shown separately. [2]Includes enforcement of judgments in student loan cases, and overpayments of veterans benefits. [3]Includes copyright, patent, and trademark rights.
Source: Administrative Office of the U.S. Courts, *Statistical Tables for the Federal Judiciary,* annual (www.uscourts.gov). In the statistical abstract of the United States (www.census.gov/compendia/statab) type "asbestos" in the search box.

million dollars. The asbestos litigation often resembles the casinos . . . more than a courtroom procedure.[20]

By some estimates, the total cost to asbestos defendants could eventually reach $100 billion.

In 1982, the first major bankruptcy in a mass tort case occurred when Johns-Manville Corporation, an asbestos manufacturer, filed for bankruptcy. Once bankruptcy is filed, tort victims became creditors, as do all the commercial creditors of the company. For Johns-Manville, a bankruptcy trust was established to hold and distribute funds to cover its asbestos liabilities. Within two years, however, the trust ran out of money. Over a dozen other asbestos companies have also sought bankruptcy protection due to the deluge of asbestos-related personal injury litigation.[21] The number of companies forced into bankruptcy due to asbestos liability is expected to grow to eighty-five.[22]

Many hoped that a proposed *nationwide* class action settlement would help end the chaos, at least in the federal courts. In 1997, however, the United States Supreme Court, in the case of *Amchem Products, Inc. v. Windsor,* refused to certify (i.e., approve) the proposed class.[23] This was a major event in mass tort litigation. It was a signal that class actions were being overused in the federal courts.

Judicial Panel on Multidistrict Litigation (J.P.M.L.) A special federal judicial body with the power to order that cases filed in different districts with common questions of fact be temporarily transferred to a single district for pretrial proceedings. Once the pretrial matters are completed, the cases are transferred back to the districts where they were initially filed.

The *Amchem* case began when eight federal judges who had handled asbestos cases asked the **Judicial Panel on Multidistrict Litigation (J.P.M.L.)** to transfer to one district all asbestos complaints then pending in federal courts. The panel agreed and temporarily transferred all federal cases that had been filed (but were not yet in trial) to a single district, the United States District Court for the Eastern District of Pennsylvania.

Soon after the transfer, most of the parties reached a settlement that had an estimated value of over $1 billion. They asked the United States District Court for the Eastern District of Pennsylvania to certify the class solely for purposes of settlement. (As indicated earlier, this would be called a settlement class action.) The proposed class consisted of all persons who had been exposed—occupationally or through a spouse or household member—to asbestos attributable to one of the asbestos manufacturers in the case. Potentially hundreds of thousands, perhaps millions, of individuals would fit this description. The settlement agreement:

1. detailed an administrative mechanism and a schedule of payments to compensate class members who meet defined exposure and medical criteria;
2. described four categories of compensable cancers and nonmalignant conditions, and specified the range of damages to be paid claimants for each (mesothelioma claimants, for example, were scheduled to receive between $20,000 and $200,000);
3. did not adjust payments for inflation;
4. capped the number of claims payable annually for each disease;
5. denied compensation for family members who claimed loss of consortium (see glossary and Chapter 22); and
6. proposed to settle claims not previously filed against the asbestos manufacturers in the case.

The District Court approved the settlement's plan for giving notice to the class and certified the proposed class for settlement only. Those who objected to the settlement and to the certification of the class appealed.

The United States Supreme Court in *Amchem* rejected the class certification. The Court held that the proposed class could not fairly protect the interests of those who had been exposed to asbestos but had not yet manifested injury (called exposure-only members). Their interests clashed with those of members who had already manifested injury. The Supreme Court said that the proposed class was too diverse:

> Class members were exposed to different asbestos-containing products, for different amounts of time, in different ways, and over different periods. Some class members suffer no physical injury or have only asymptomatic pleural changes, while others suffer from lung cancer, disabling asbestosis, or from mesothelioma. . . . Each has a different history of cigarette smoking, a factor that complicates the causation inquiry. The plaintiffs [who have been exposed but who manifest no injuries] share little in common, either with each other or with the presently injured class members. It is unclear whether they will contract asbestos-related disease and, if so, what disease each will suffer. They will also incur different medical expenses because their monitoring and treatment will depend on singular circumstances and individual medical histories.[24]

The Court observed that no settlement class had ever been brought to its attention "as sprawling as this one."

Notice to the exposure-only members was also flawed. Many persons in the exposure-only category may not even know of their exposure, or realize the extent of the harm they may incur. Even if they fully appreciate the significance of class notice, those without current afflictions may not have the information or foresight needed to decide, intelligently, whether to stay in or opt out. Family members of asbestos-exposed individuals may themselves fall prey to disease or may ultimately have ripe claims for loss of consortium. Yet, large numbers of people in this category—future spouses and children of asbestos victims—could not be alerted to their class membership. And current spouses and children of the occupationally exposed may know nothing of that exposure.

Consequently, the proposed settlement class action was rejected by the Supreme Court. Many argued that Congress should pass legislation to set up an administrative claims procedure similar to the one established for black lung disease. Congress, however, has not seen fit to do so. The parties in the *Amchem* case, therefore, had to return to litigate their cases or to attempt a far less ambitious settlement.

The impact of *Amchem* is being felt far beyond asbestos cases since many mass tort plaintiffs seek class action certification under the Federal Rules of Civil Procedure. Although it is still possible to have a federal class action certified, the general consensus is that certification will become much harder to obtain in the future, at least in the federal courts, particularly for those classes that have large and diverse potential membership.

Of course, asbestos cases continue to be brought in *state* courts. Some states, however, have passed "medical criteria" laws that require potential plaintiffs to present objective evidence of physical impairment in order to present a claim. Priority in these states is given to those who are sick. This has led to a substantial reduction in the number of cases filed by as-yet-unimpaired individuals.[25]

These developments in federal and state courts do not mean that asbestos litigation is going away. Quite the contrary. Asbestos filings continue to occupy a significant share of federal and state court dockets throughout the country.

BREAST IMPLANTS

Between one and two million women have breast implants. Hundreds of thousands of these women believe the implants have caused connective-tissue diseases such as rheumatoid arthritis and other immune-system disorders. For example:

- In early 1975, after the birth of her son, Mildred Valentine consulted her doctor about having a "breast lift" or maximum mastopexy. The doctor explained that the procedure would involve hospitalization, general anesthesia, and two to three incisions in each breast. He also informed Mrs. Valentine of the alternative of the silicone breast implant, performed in the office with local anesthesia. She accepted this alternative and underwent the augmentation surgery with silicone breast implants manufactured by Heyer-Schulte Corporation. Shortly thereafter, she developed complications—capsular contracture in the left breast. Her doctor performed an open capsulotomy procedure, which entailed removing the implant, dividing the scar tissue, and inserting a new implant. Contracture, however, returned to the left side. Her doctor performed a closed capsulotomy, squeezing the breast to rupture the excess scar tissue. Four years later he again performed a closed capsulotomy, once on both sides, and a month later on one side. Mrs. Valentine was diagnosed with lupus around 1976. Lupus, short for "systemic lupus erythematosus," is an autoimmune disease in which the body "turns against itself" by producing antinuclear antibodies. Characteristic manifestations of the disease include skin rashes, sensitivity to sun, hair loss, joint pain, stiffness, pleurisy, kidney involvement, nervous system involvement, lung involvement, and involvement of the gastrointestinal tract. In 1991, a pulmonary care specialist convinced her that due to the severity of her lung disease, the breast implants should be removed.
- In August 1985, as part of reconstructive surgery following a bilateral subcutaneous mastectomy, Charlotte Mahlum elected to receive silicone gel breast prostheses (breast implants). Dow Corning manufactured the two Silastic II breast implants that her surgeon implanted. The Silastic II implant is made up of several components. A clear outer shell of silicone rubber called an elastomer contains the silicone gel and is the protective barrier between the gel and the implant host. The silicone gel itself is made up of 80 to 85 percent DC 360 silicone fluid. In 1990, Mahlum's health began to deteriorate. In July 1993, one of the breast implants ruptured, requiring the surgical removal of

both implants. The surgeon was unable to remove all of the silicone gel from her body, leaving approximately 10 percent of the silicone materials embedded in muscle, tissue, and blood vessels under her arms and ribs. Her health continued to deteriorate after the explantation surgery.

- In 1978, Nancy Jennings, age 51, received silicone gel breast implants following bilateral mastectomies. (The breast implants were manufactured by Heyer-Schulte, which obtained the silicone material from Dow Corning.) Subsequently, one implant partially deflated and was replaced in 1980. The other implant partially deflated after a mammogram was performed in 1992. In 1993, Jennings had surgery to remove the implants. She now alleges that as a direct result of silicone exposure from her silicone gel breast implants, she has suffered severe and permanent injuries including silicone invasion of her tissue and cells, migration of silicone particles through her body, local and systemic inflammatory reactions, impairment of the immune system, neurological disease, and damage to her inner ear and vestibular system. These injuries have caused her physical and mental pain and suffering associated with surgical removal of her silicone gel breast implants, itching breasts, aching joints and muscles, fatigue, dry eyes and mouth, skin changes, memory loss, sleep disturbance, hearing loss, dizziness and balance problems, numbness in the extremities, increased susceptibility to disease, and emotional distress including anxiety, nervousness, irritability, and fear of future injury and/or death.
- In 1974, Erin Page Tucker had silicone gel breast implants inserted. (The responsible manufacturer was Baxter Healthcare.) About two years later, she began to experience breast hardening from her implants. To relieve the hardening, her doctor performed a closed capsulotomy (squeezing the breast by hand to rupture the scar tissue). By 1986, breast hardening reoccurred. She also suffered from other health problems such as fatigue, pain and numbness (e.g., arm pain resulted in the inability to fully use her right arm), and cognitive dysfunction. In 1988, she was diagnosed with human adjuvant disease, an incurable autoimmune disorder. In October 1989, she had her silicone gel implants replaced with saline implants. The surgery revealed that one of her silicone gel implants had ruptured. In 1990, she joined a support group for women with breast implant problems. In group discussions she was told that the Food and Drug Administration (FDA) had never reviewed manufacturer safety data on breast implants and never approved breast implants for use in humans; that breast implant manufacturers did not perform any long-term safety tests on animals or humans; that the manufacturers knew that silicone implants bled silicone oil into the body, and that silicone oil could stimulate the immune system. After learning of this misconduct, Erin Page Tucker believed that her breast implant manufacturer's wrongdoing was the cause of her autoimmune injuries.

In 1992, after several million-dollar verdicts were won by women, the FDA placed a moratorium on the sale of silicone breast implants for cosmetic or augmentation purposes because of doubts about their safety. This decision was given wide publicity. Soon manufacturers were facing thousands of products liability suits in state and federal courts throughout the country. In 1992, the federal Judicial Panel on Multidistrict Litigation (J.P.M.L.) ordered over 27,000 cases filed in federal courts to be transferred to a federal trial court (United States District Court) in Alabama where pretrial proceedings such as discovery would be coordinated. The largest manufacturer, Dow Corning, had over 30,000 claims filed against it. Dow and other manufacturers entered into extensive settlement negotiations. A proposed $4.2 billion class action settlement was abandoned because of the large number of women who sought payments under it; the amount available was simply not going to be enough. After the collapse of this settlement, the principal defendant, Dow Corning, filed for bankruptcy.

Throughout the controversy, many attorneys received considerable criticism. "Lawyers, who may take up to 40 percent of any compensation, have been advertising for clients with implants, encouraging them to believe they can get large sums of money. Some lawyers even recruit women with implants and send them to friendly physicians who will diagnose medical problems so they can participate in the lawsuits. The result has been one of the biggest legal messes in history."[26]

Perhaps the largest issue before the courts was causation. Substantial doubts were raised over whether implants caused the illnesses complained of. Thousands of women and their attorneys "have argued that exposure to silicone leaking from implants has caused serious disease like lupus. While there is little dispute that the implants can cause local inflammation and scar tissue buildup, implant manufacturers have rejected links between their products and more serious illnesses. A number of recent studies have supported that position."[27] One federal court appointed its own panel of scientific experts to study the data on causation. Their conclusions did *not* support the claim that the implants caused the illnesses. This did not stop the filing of new lawsuits. Even though manufacturers won many of these cases in court, the pressure to settle was enormous. It can cost a manufacturer up to $1 million in litigation costs alone to defend a single case that could drag on for years.

In 1995, implant makers Baxter International, Bristol-Myers Squibb, and 3M reached a settlement that resolved most of the claims against them.

In 1998, Dow Corning filed a bankruptcy reorganization plan proposing $3.1 billion to settle up to 170,000 claims from women over its silicone breast implants. If a woman wanted to bring an individual lawsuit, she could opt out of the settlement. Thousands of claims were settled through the plan, with payments ranging from $2,000 to $300,000 depending on the medical condition(s) that resulted from the implants. Dow eventually emerged from bankruptcy in 2004.

Despite the settlements and individual court judgments, many continued to dispute the conclusion that breast implants cause the diseases involved in the asserted claims. The following case of *In re Breast Implant Litigation* is a fascinating study of the controversy surrounding the causation issue. It provides an excellent overview of the challenges faced by plaintiff attorneys in this area of mass tort/product liability law.

CASE

In re Breast Implant Litigation

11 F. Supp. 2d 1217 (1998)
United States District Court, Colorado

Background: *The plaintiffs claimed that their autoimmune diseases were caused by the silicone gel breast implants made by the defendants. During the trial, the plaintiffs asked the court to allow them to introduce testimony on causation. The defendants have made a motion to exclude this testimony.*

Decision of Court: *The motion to dismiss is granted. The proposed testimony on causation is not admissible under Federal Rules of Evidence 702.*

OPINION OF COURT

Judge SPARR delivered the opinion of the court . . .:

Plaintiffs assert tort claims for negligence and strict liability, as well as claims for breach of express and implied warranty. In Colorado, "[i]n order to prevail on a tort claim, a plaintiff must prove by a preponderance of the evidence [more likely than not] that a defendant committed an act which caused an injury to that plaintiff." *Renaud v. Martin Marietta Corp.*, 749 F. Supp. 1545, 1551 (D. Colo. 1990). Plaintiffs premise many of their alleged injuries on the existence of various kinds of "atypical connective tissue disease" ("ACTD"). This "disease" allegedly manifests itself through a "constellation" of symptoms and is allegedly caused by an autoimmune response to silicone from breast implants. . . .

The Federal Rules of Evidence govern the admission of expert scientific testimony in a federal trial. *Daubert v. Merrell Dow Pharmaceuticals, Inc.*, 509 U.S. 579 (1993). Federal Rules of Evidence 702, governing expert testimony, provides:

> If scientific, technical, or other specialized knowledge will assist the trier of fact to understand the evidence or to determine a fact in issue, a witness qualified as an expert by knowledge, skill, experience, training, or education, may testify thereto in the form of an opinion or otherwise.

Under the Rules, federal trial judges "must ensure that any and all scientific testimony or evidence admitted is not only relevant, but reliable." *Daubert,* 509 U.S. at 589. The Plaintiffs have the burden of proving that the testimony of their expert witnesses is admissible pursuant to Fed. R. Evid. 702 and the standards set forth in *Daubert* governing the admissibility of scientific evidence. In applying Rule 702, the trial court has the responsibility of acting as a gatekeeper. . . .

GENERAL AND SPECIFIC CAUSATION

Causation in toxic tort cases is discussed in terms of general and specific causation. See e.g., *Raynor v. Merrell Pharmaceuticals, Inc.,* 104 F.3d 1371, 1376 (D.C. Cir. 1997). General causation is whether a substance is capable of causing a particular injury or condition in the general population, while specific causation is whether a substance caused a particular individual's injury.

In order to establish their claims, Plaintiffs "must show both general and specific causation—that is, that breast implants are capable of causing" the conditions complained of, and that "breast implants were the cause-in-fact" of the specific conditions. *Kelley v. American Heyer-Schulte Corp.,* 957 F. Supp. 873, 875 (W.D. Tex. 1997); . . . *Hall v. Baxter Healthcare Corp.,* 947 F. Supp. 1387, 1412–13 (D. Ore. 1996) (Courts "have recognized two levels of causation: general causation (i.e., can silicone gel cause disease in anyone?) and specific causation (i.e., did silicone gel breast implants cause disease in this plaintiff?)"); *Jones v. United States,* 933 F. Supp. 894, 900–01 (N.D. Cal. 1996) (plaintiff must show both "general causation," that defendant's conduct increased likelihood of injury, and "specific causation," that defendant's conduct was probable, not merely possible, cause of injury).

EPIDEMIOLOGY IS THE BEST EVIDENCE OF CAUSATION

The diseases and symptoms allegedly associated with breast implants occur in non-implanted women as well as implanted women. Many of the conditions that Plaintiffs attribute to breast implants appear in the general population. Without a controlled study, there is no way to determine if these symptoms are more common in women with silicone breast implants than women without implants. "The most important evidence relied upon by scientists to determine whether an agent (such as breast implants) cause disease is controlled epidemiologic studies. Epidemiology can be viewed as the study of the causes of diseases in humans." (Ory Affidavit, p. 7 to Defendants' Science Brief). Therefore, epidemiological studies are necessary to determine the cause and effect between breast implants and allegedly associated diseases. A valid epidemiologic study requires that study subjects, cases, and controls are chosen by an unbiased sampling method from a definable population. Epidemiology is the best evidence of causation in the mass torts context. Linda A. Bailey, et al., Reference Guide on Epidemiology, *Reference Manual on Scientific Evidence* at 126 (1994) ("In the absence of an understanding of the biological and pathological mechanisms by which disease develops, epidemiological evidence is the most valid type of scientific evidence of toxic causation"). . . .

MORE-PROBABLE-THAN-NOT BURDEN MEANS PLAINTIFFS MUST ESTABLISH A DOUBLING OF RISK

[I]f the available body of epidemiology demonstrates that breast implants do not double the risk of any known disease, then plaintiffs' causation evidence is inadmissible.

There exists in the context of breast implanted women a "background rate" of injury; that is, the injuries of which the breast implant plaintiffs complain are not unique, but occur frequently in women without breast implants. Because the injuries of which Plaintiffs complain occur commonly in women without breast implants, Plaintiffs must present expert testimony demonstrating that exposure to breast implants more than doubled the risk of their alleged injuries. *Hall v. Baxter Healthcare Corp.,* 947 F. Supp. 1387, 1403 (D. Ore. 1996). . . . If exposure to breast implants does not at least double the risk of injury, then more than half of the population suffering from the injuries allegedly caused by breast implants would be injured anyway (the background rate of injury), thereby disproving legal causation. . . .

The difference between groups is often expressed as the ratio between the incidence of the disease in the exposed group and the incidence in the unexposed group. Marcia Angell, M.D., *Science on Trial* (1996) at 164. The relative risk simply indicates how high above the background level the risk is.

> The threshold for concluding that an agent was more likely the cause of a disease than not is a relative risk greater than 2.0. . . . [A] relative risk of 1.0 means that the agent has no effect on the incidence of disease. When the relative risk reaches 2.0, the agent is responsible for an equal number of cases of disease as all other background causes. Thus, a relative risk of 2.0 implies a 50% likelihood that an exposed individual's disease was caused by the agent. *Hall,* 947 F. Supp. at 1403 (quoting *Reference Manual on Scientific Evidence* at 168).

For example, if the relative risk for a disease between women with breast implants and women without breast implants is 1.2, it means that for every 10 women without implants who develop the disease, 12 women with implants in an equal population would develop the disease. *Science on Trial* at 196.

> It is important to realize that we do not know exactly what a relative risk of 1.2 means for each of those 12 women who develop connective tissue disease. It could mean that in 2 of them, the implants were the sole cause of their disease and in the other 10 they played no role. Or it could mean that implants played a major role in 3 or 4 women and a very small one in the others. Or it could mean that implants contributed a varying amount to the disease in all 12. . . .

All we could say for sure with a relative risk of 1.2 is that on *average*, implants contributed about 17 percent (0.2/1.2) to the disease. For any one woman among the 12, then, we could not say that but for the implants, she would not have developed the disease. Further, we would have to say that some other factor or group of factors was the dominant cause. *Science on Trial* at 196–97 (emphasis in original).

THE EPIDEMIOLOGICAL EVIDENCE [IN THIS CASE] DEMONSTRATES THE ABSENCE OF A DOUBLING OF THE RISK

At least seventeen epidemiological studies of breast implants have been published in peer reviewed medical journals. (Ory Affidavit pp. 35, 36). Every controlled epidemiological study concludes that silicone breast implants do not double the risk of any known disease. None of these studies support a conclusion that breast implants cause rheumatic or connective tissue diseases, either classic or atypical, in breast implanted women. None of these studies reports a statistically significant elevation of risk of rheumatic or connective tissue disease, either classic or atypical, over 2.0. The reported results from every published controlled epidemiological study uniformly show the absence of a doubling of the risk of any known disease among breast implant recipients. . . . As a whole, these studies provide a solid body of epidemiologic evidence establishing that breast implants do not cause connective tissue disease, autoimmune disease or various symptoms. . . .

The largest study to date concluded that there is no doubling of the risk of connective tissue disease among women with breast implants. Hennekens, et al., "Self-Reported Breast Implants and Connective-Tissue Diseases in Female Health Professionals," 275 Journal of the American Medical Assoc. 616 (February 28, 1996) ("Hennekens Study"). The Hennekens Study included almost 400,000 female health professionals who completed mailed questionnaires, including more than 10,000 who reported having breast implants and almost 12,000 who reported having connective-tissue diseases between 1962 and 1991. The relative risk for all connective-tissue diseases was estimated at 1.24 (95% confidence interval, 1.08 to 1.41). As the authors themselves noted, this study suffered from bias which probably explains the slight increased relative risk. . . .

To the extent that there are case or anecdotal reports noting various symptoms or signs in breast implanted women, without controls, these suggest only a potential, untested hypothesis that breast implants may be their cause. Such case reports are not reliable scientific evidence of causation, because they simply describe reported phenomena without comparison to the rate at which the phenomena occur in the general population or in a defined control group . . . [T]hey do not isolate and exclude potentially alternative causes . . . and do not investigate or explain the mechanism of causation. An untested hypothesis cannot be a scientifically reliable basis for an opinion on causation. . . .

The reports submitted by Plaintiffs' experts fail to present a single peer-reviewed, controlled epidemiologic study that supports their causation theories. This is not to say that epidemiological studies are required in this type of tort action. Epidemiological studies are not the magical cure for legal disputes. In many instances, epidemiological data may be unavailable. A lack of epidemiology should not end the inquiry, but rather begin the inquiry into what other types of evidence a plaintiff can present to satisfy the burden of proof. There is a range of scientific methods for investigating questions of causation, for example, toxicology and animal studies, clinical research, and epidemiology, all of which have distinct advantages and disadvantages. The court's inquiry is whether reliable scientific evidence, based on sound methodology, has been presented. What is significant in this case is that the substantial body of epidemiological evidence demonstrates that silicone breast implants do not double the risk of any known disease.

DIFFERENTIAL DIAGNOSIS

Plaintiffs seek to introduce expert testimony from clinicians (i.e., treating physicians) who claim to be able to diagnose a patient with a disease caused by breast implants through the process of differential diagnosis. [A neurologist, for example, has provided a written opinion stating that he, as a treating physician of the Plaintiffs has used the medical procedure of differential diagnosis and has] determined to "a reasonable degree of medical certainty" that the illnesses and symptoms from which the Plaintiffs suffer are caused by the silicone from their silicone gel breast implants.

Such testimony is not scientifically reliable in the cases before the court because it confuses two distinct burdens. Plaintiffs must demonstrate two types of causation: general causation and specific causation. *Raynor,* 104 F.3d at 1376; *Hall,* 947 F. Supp. at 1412–1413. By using differential diagnosis, a clinician can identify possible diseases the patient may have and, through a process of elimination, rule out diseases until a disease or symptom is left as the diagnosis. Differential diagnosis is not a scientific method by which a physician can determine whether silicone breast implants can cause disease in humans. As the court explained in *Hall,*

> [d]ifferential diagnosis is a patient-specific process of elimination that medical practitioners use to identify the 'most likely' cause of a set of signs and symptoms from a list of possible causes. However, differential diagnosis does not by itself *prove* the cause, even for the particular patient. Nor can the technique speak to the issue of general causation. Indeed, differential diagnosis *assumes* that general causation has been proven for the list of possible causes it eliminates:
>
>> The process of differential diagnosis is undoubtedly important to the question of "specific causation." If other possible causes of an injury cannot be ruled out, or at least the probability of their contribution to causation minimized, then the "more likely than not" threshold for proving causation may not be met. *But, it is also important to recognize that a fundamental assumption underlying this method is that the final, suspected "cause" remaining after this process of elimination must actually be capable*

> *of causing the injury.* That is, the expert must "rule in" the suspected cause as well as "rule out" other possible causes. And, of course, expert opinion on this issue of "general causation" must be derived from a scientifically valid methodology.

947 F. Supp. at 1413 (emphasis in original) (quoting *Cavallo v. Star Enterprise,* 892 F. Supp. 756, 771 (E.D. Va. 1995)).

As a practical matter, the cause of many diseases remains unknown; therefore, a clinician who suspects that a substance causes a disease in some patients very well might conclude that the substance caused the disease in the plaintiff simply because the clinician has no other explanation. See Margaret A. Berger, "Evidentiary Framework," *Reference Manual on Scientific Evidence* at 81 (1994).

The kind of causation testimony offered by Plaintiffs' experts was summarized and rejected by Judge Prado in *Kelley:*

> [T]he witness admits that if the Plaintiff did not have breast implants but had the exact same symptoms and blood chemistry, then his diagnosis would have been non-implant-caused Sjogren's Syndrome. Essentially, this is a bit like saying that if a person has a scratchy throat, runny nose, and a nasty cough, that person has a cold; if, on the other-hand, that person has a scratchy throat, runny nose, nasty cough, and wears a watch, they have a watch-induced cold. Such reasoning is extremely suspect, which has prompted other courts to reject it as unscientific in the absence of convincing epidemiology evidence. 957 F. Supp. at 882 (citing *Brock v. Merrell Dow Pharmaceuticals, Inc.,* 874 F.2d 307, 310 n. 11 (5th Cir. 1989)).

The causation testimony offered by the Plaintiffs is precisely the kind of subjective testimony that is inadmissible pursuant to Rules 702 [of the Federal Rules of Evidence]. "Reasoning that a cause-and-effect relationship exists simply because a large number of individuals with a particular characteristic develop a particular disease is fallacious, because it totally fails to account for the fact that both characteristics and diseases are widely distributed among the general population." (Ory Affidavit p. 50). In short, "a single differential diagnosis is a scientifically invalid methodology" for the purpose of demonstrating general causation. *Hall,* 947 F. Supp. at 1414. Differential diagnosis may be utilized by a clinician to determine what recognized disease or symptom the patient has, but it is incapable of determining whether exposure to a substance caused disease in the legal sense.

TEMPORALITY

Plaintiffs' experts assert that causation may be inferred based upon the temporal sequence of implantation and the onset of illness. A temporal relationship by itself, provides no evidence of causation. Temporality at best addresses the issue of specific causation; therefore, evidence of temporality is inadmissible where no admissible evidence of general causation exists. . . . *Cavallo v. Star Enterprise,* 892 F. Supp. at 773 (a causation opinion based solely on a temporal relationship is not derived from the scientific method and is therefore insufficient to satisfy the requirements of Rule 702).

CONCLUSION

[The motion to exclude the testimony of the plaintiffs is granted].

ASSIGNMENT 20.1

a. What type of evidence of causation would this court find acceptable?
b. What is differential diagnosis and why does the court object to it?
c. What is wrong with case studies as evidence of causation?
d. What is temporality and why does the court object to it?

Breast Implants on the Market Today

In 2000 and 2006, the Federal Food and Drug Administration (FDA) reversed its moratorium and approved four breast implants for marketing:

- In 2000, Mentor and Allergan received approval for saline-filled breast implants. These implants were approved for breast augmentation in women eighteen years or older and for breast reconstruction in women of any age.
- In 2006, Allergan and Mentor received approval for their silicone gel–filled breast implants. These implants were approved for breast augmentation in women twenty-two years or older and for breast reconstruction in women of any age.

All breast implants other than these four approved devices are considered investigational devices, including the more-cohesive ("gummy bear") implants. For a woman to receive an investigational breast implant in the United States, she must enroll in a clinical study.[28] This action was taken by the FDA after the plaintiffs lost the case of *In re Breast Implant Litigation* and while thousands of women continued to receive payments under the Dow settlement plan.

TOBACCO

"Vicious!" said the plaintiff's attorney when he saw a roadside billboard display in the city where he was suing a tobacco company. The display, paid for by tobacco companies, contained a photo of an obviously wealthy and obnoxious attorney sitting by a pool with his golf clubs and Mercedes in the background. The caption on the billboard read in large letters:

"1-800-I-Sue-4-You."

In response, anti-smoking ads were available in abundance in the same city. One TV ad showed a tobacco executive at a "Demon Award" ceremony. As he accepted the award, he said, "This is for all you smokers out there." Among the executive's admirers in the audience were murderers, drug dealers, Adolf Hitler, and Joseph Stalin.[29] Such ads and counter-ads were a not-very-subtle attempt to influence juries, judges, legislators, and the general public. The tobacco wars were being waged on all fronts.

For years, smokers lost their cases in court because they were portrayed as foolish people who wanted someone else to pay for their lack of self-control. They knew smoking was hazardous to their health; since 1966 every pack of cigarettes bluntly told them so. In legal terms, they assumed the risk of health problems by continuing to smoke. Juries consistently came to this conclusion, in part, because the general public had little sympathy for the smoker. A political cartoon by Signe Wilkinson in the Philadelphia Daily News shows a distraught but sincere woman on the witness stand telling the judge and jury, "The cigarette that I was forced to smoke dropped ashes on the silicone breasts I was forced to implant and they melted over the hamburger I hadn't cooked so that's why I deserve $325 million." So prevalent was this anti-consumer attitude that a number of states even passed statutes that banned most smoker lawsuits on the ground that the dangers of tobacco use were well known. Prior to the 1990s, tobacco companies (e.g., American Tobacco Company, Brown & Williamson, Liggett & Myers, Lorillard, Philip Morris, R.J. Reynolds, and United States Tobacco Company) were not concerned by individual lawsuits brought by smokers since few of them succeeded, the awards were small, and every victorious plaintiff was overturned on appeal.

Such legal victories by the tobacco industry were remarkable in the face of a drumbeat of news that over 400,000 people per year died in the United States from smoking-related diseases such as cancer, heart disease, and emphysema. The Secretary of the United States Department of Health and Human Services estimated that smoking-related health costs exceeded $45 billion a year, particularly through Medicare and Medicaid. If you include fire damage, absenteeism, and lost productivity, the total economic cost of tobacco use was said to exceed $145 billion a year. Nevertheless, the tobacco industry kept winning in the courtroom.

Since the mid-1990s, however, the tide has turned. For years, tobacco companies denied that their product was addictive, unhealthy, or targeted at young people. Internal documents, however, have dramatically shown otherwise. For example, extensive media attention has been given to reports that the tobacco industry considered teenagers to be "replacement smokers" for the hundreds of thousands of smokers dying each year from lung cancer and other smoking-related diseases.

A 1975 memo (marked "secret") of R.J. Reynolds made the following stunning statement about children as young as fourteen:

> To ensure increased and long-term growth for Camel Filter, the brand must increase its share penetration among the 14–24 age group, which (has) a new set of more liberal values and which represent tomorrow's cigarette business.

A paralegal played a prominent role in this drama. Merrell Williams was a paralegal who once worked at Wyatt, Tarrant & Combs, the largest law firm in Kentucky. The firm represented Brown & Williamson (B&W), maker of Kool and Viceroy. While Merrell Williams worked at the firm, he secretly photocopied and distributed confidential internal memos, letters, and other documents between the law firm and its client. The documents demonstrated that the corporation knew about the danger of smoking, but tried to cover it up. The news media made extensive use of this material. Here is how a *Los Angeles Times* article described this development:

> Big tobacco is known as a formidable legal adversary, skilled and even ruthless in the courtroom. Yet the industry is being slowly undone by its former secrets. . . . Disclosure of documents [containing these secrets], many dating back 40 years, has done enormous damage, outraging citizens and forcing once-helpful politicians to climb on the anti-tobacco bandwagon. . . . The ground shifted in 1994, when an obscure paralegal, who had secretly stolen thousands of pages of documents from a [law firm representing] B&W, leaked the purloined papers to Congress and the media. The documents were an instant sensation. In one 1963 memo, for example, the [tobacco] company's former general counsel declared, "We are, then, in the business of selling nicotine, an addictive drug.". . . Now the blood was in the water, and so were the sharks. For 1994 also marked the formation of a powerful alliance of products liability lawyers and state attorneys general, who began filing immense new claims against the industry.[30]

Wyatt, Tarrant & Combs obtained an injunction against Merrell Williams to prevent him from continuing to reveal what he learned while he was a paralegal at the firm. The law firm says "Williams broke his employment contract, which requires confidentiality, and stole photocopies of documents from the law office." An ex-smoker himself, Williams has undergone quadruple bypass surgery and has sued Brown & Williamson for his own health problems.[31]

The onslaught of litigation against tobacco companies fell into several categories:

- States sued for the Medicaid costs they paid to treat smoking-related illnesses.
- Private citizens who were smokers or ex-smokers brought class action suits in state and federal courts on behalf of large numbers of sick and deceased smokers.
- Private citizens who were smokers or ex-smokers brought individual suits in state and federal courts for the illness or death brought on by smoking.
- Private citizens who were not smokers or ex-smokers brought individual or class action suits in state and federal courts for the illness or death caused by secondhand smoke.

The largest number of these cases, many of which take years to litigate, were filed during the period when the media were revealing the contents of the internal tobacco documents.

Class actions in tobacco cases have not done well in federal courts, particularly since the United States Supreme Court decided not to approve the asbestos class in *Amchem Products, Inc. v. Windsor,* as we saw earlier. For example, a federal court refused to certify a nationwide class action on behalf of "all nicotine dependent persons in the United States." The class could have involved 50 million smokers. The court concluded that the criteria for a class action in federal court had not been met.

State courts, however, have not been as reluctant as federal courts to certify a nationwide class. In 1996, one of the smaller cigarette manufacturers, Liggett Group (maker of Chesterfield and L&M), broke ranks and settled a class action that was filed in an Alabama state court on behalf of a nationwide class of smokers. The Alabama court certified this action as a settlement class and preliminarily approved the proposed settlement. A nationwide campaign of notice then took place. See Exhibit 20–3 for the "official notice" of this settlement printed in newspapers across the country. Under the settlement, Liggett admitted that smoking causes various health problems and that nicotine is addictive. Liggett also agreed to pay 7.5 percent of its pretax income to a Settlement Fund for the next twenty-five years. To the dismay of the rest of the tobacco industry, Liggett also agreed to "cooperate fully" in "lawsuits against the other cigarette manufacturers." (See paragraph 2 in the Settlement Notice of Exhibit 20–3.)

In June of 1997, the front pages of every major newspaper in the country reported that cigarette makers and forty states had reached a settlement that would provide $368.5 billion over twenty-five years to cover Medicaid money that states have paid to treat sick smokers. This settlement required legislation by Congress since it involved major policy changes such as the scope of the United States Food and Drug Administration (FDA) regulatory power. Public health groups, however, attacked the deal as too weak since companies could simply pass on their added costs to smokers. The American Lung Association called it a "bailout for the industry." In the end, Congress failed to act, and the settlement fell apart.

Several states pursued their own actions against the tobacco industry to recover their Medicaid costs. Individually, the states of Mississippi, Florida, Texas, and Minnesota reached settlements. The total involved in these four states was over $40 billion.

In the meantime, efforts to achieve a broader settlement continued. The breakthrough came in November 1998 when the other forty-six states reached a settlement that called for the payment of $206 billion over twenty-five years for smoking-related health costs. Note that the claimants in these settlements were *not* smokers who arguably assumed the known risks of smoking. The claimants were the state governments who wanted to recoup the billions of dollars they spent for smoking-related diseases. The governments had not assumed any risks. States do not inhale!

The settlements did not increase the authority of the FDA to regulate nicotine in tobacco or other aspects of the manufacture and marketing of tobacco products. The courts have ruled that the FDA would have to obtain this authority through new legislation from Congress. Nor did the settlements put an end to individual lawsuits or class actions brought by smokers. They still had the right to prove their case in court. Individual smokers were not part of the settlements that the tobacco industry made with the fifty state governments.

In 1999, a San Francisco jury awarded a smoker $51.5 million from Philip Morris Company, $50 million of which was for punitive damages. The plaintiff was a fifty-two-year-old woman who said she had inoperable lung cancer from thirty-five years of smoking. The size of the verdict frightened the tobacco companies. The punitive damages were more than three times the $15 million she asked for. She also was not expected to be a sympathetic plaintiff since she tried to stop smoking only once in thirty-five years. Yet, she walked away with a $51.5 million judgment. Although this amount was eventually cut in half on appeal, the size of the verdict has encouraged other individual smokers to bring their own cases. By the end of 2005, for example, Philip Morris said that it was defending over 450 smoking and health cases filed by individuals.

RICO (Racketeer Influenced and Corrupt Organizations Act) A federal statute imposing civil and criminal penalties for racketeering offenses such as engaging in a pattern of fraud, bribery, extortion, and other acts enumerated in the statute (18 USC § 1961). Some states have enacted similar statutes.

Looking for new strategies against the tobacco industry, the United States government sued nine tobacco companies in federal court under the Racketeer Influenced and Corrupt Organizations Act **(RICO)** to recover health care expenditures that the *federal* government paid or would pay to treat tobacco-related illnesses. (The earlier $206 billion settlement covered similar expenditures that *state* governments had to pay.) RICO is a federal statute that imposes civil and criminal penalties for racketeering offenses such as engaging in a pattern of fraud, bribery,

Exhibit 20–3 Notice printed in newspapers of tobacco class action filed against Liggett Group in Alabama State Court on behalf of smokers nationwide. (legacy.library.ucsf.edu/tid/raq64d00)

IN THE CIRCUIT COURT OF MOBILE COUNTY, ALABAMA OFFICIAL NOTICE

—ATTENTION—

ALL SMOKERS

and

ALL INDIVIDUALS OR ENTITIES WHICH MAY HAVE CLAIMS AGAINST CIGARETTE MANUFACTURERS

Your rights may be affected by a class action lawsuit pending in the Circuit Court of Mobile County, Alabama, ***Fletcher, et al. v. Brooke Group, Ltd., Liggett Group Inc., and Liggett & Myers, Inc.,*** Case No. 97-913. A settlement has been filed for this class action, and this settlement has been preliminarily approved by the Circuit Court.

If approved, the class action and settlement in ***Fletcher*** will resolve all smoking-related claims against Liggett Group, Inc. and its affiliates Brooke Group Ltd. and Liggett & Myers, Inc. (hereinafter referred to collectively as "Liggett"). Liggett is the manufacturer of Chesterfield, Eve, L & M, Lark, Pyramid, and various generic brands of cigarettes.

If you or some person or entity for whom you act as a legal representative is or was a smoker, has been exposed to cigarette smoke, or has incurred or claims to have incurred direct or indirect economic loss as a result of paying for the treatment of diseases, illnesses, or medical conditions allegedly caused by cigarettes, you may be covered by terms of the settlement as a member of the Settlement Class.

Among other things, the settlement provides for 1) compliance by Liggett with certain FDA regulations and other restrictions on Liggett's marketing and sale of cigarettes to minors and children; 2) a public statement by Liggett acknowledging that nicotine is addictive and that smoking causes various health problems; 3) placement of a prominent warning on each of Liggett's packages of cigarettes and in its advertising stating "Smoking is Addictive"; 4) cooperation with the Settlement Class and Settlement Class Counsel in pursuit of lawsuits against other cigarette manufacturers; and 5) monetary compensation—to the extent practicable given Liggett's troubled financial condition—to the Settlement Class for equitable distribution.

Liggett's assets are so limited in relation to the potential liability of Liggett for pending and potential smoking-related claims against it that even a relatively insignificant judgment could render Liggett insolvent, and members of the Settlement Class would be left unable to avail themselves of the valuable cooperation to be provided by Liggett under the settlement, and without any prospect of financial recovery from Liggett.

If the Settlement is approved and becomes effective, its main features will affect Settlement Class members as follows:

1. 7.5% of Liggett's annual pre-tax income, with a minimum yearly payment of $1 million, will be placed in a Settlement Fund for the next twenty-five (25) years. The allocation of the Settlement Fund to specific uses or among particular claimants has not been determined. Future allocation and distribution of the Settlement Fund will be administered by a Settlement Fund Board. The Settlement Fund Board shall be comprised of, among others, representatives of the public health community and by Settlement Class Counsel with the approval of the Court. The Settlement Fund Board shall be responsible for recommending and implementing guidelines and procedures for the administration of claims. The settlement agreement does not specify any particular allocation of settlement proceeds. Settlement Class members will be given notice and an opportunity to be heard and make suggestions regarding allocation before any final allocation or distribution decisions are made.

2. Liggett will cooperate fully with the Settlement Class and Settlement Class Counsel in their lawsuits against the other cigarette manufacturers. To that end, Liggett will make available to the Settlement Class and Settlement Class Counsel all relevant documents and information, including documents subject to Liggett's own attorney-client privileges and work product protections and will assist those parties in obtaining prompt court adjudication of the joint defense privilege claims of the other cigarette manufacturers. Moreover, Liggett will offer their employees, and any and all other individuals over whom they have control, to provide witness interviews of such employees and to testify, in deposition and at trial.

3. Liggett will support and not challenge Food and Drug Administration regulations concerning the sale and distribution of nicotine-containing cigarettes and smokeless tobacco products to children and adolescents. Accordingly, Liggett has agreed to comply with many of these regulations and other advertising restrictions even before they apply to the tobacco industry generally.

4. All smoking-related claims against Liggett covered by the settlement will be cut off.

5. In the event that another tobacco company merges with or acquires Liggett or Brooke Group in the future, the merging tobacco company would participate in certain aspects of the Settlement Agreement.

On March 9, 1999, a hearing will be held in the Thirteenth Judicial Circuit Court, Courtroom 8600, Mobile Government Plaza, Mobile, Alabama and will continue, if necessary, at such times as the Court orders. The purpose of this hearing is to determine whether the settlement described herein is fair, reasonable, and adequate to members of the Settlement Class and should be approved. The Court will review all aspects of the settlement and the historical events leading up to the settlement. If the Court finds the terms proposed in the settlement to be fair, reasonable and adequate, the settlement may be approved. If the Court finds any of the provisions in the proposed settlement to be unfair, it may reject the settlement.

Although you may not exclude yourself from the class, you have a right at the hearing to comment on or object to the settlement, or to any of its terms. If you desire to object or to comment on the settlement prior to the hearing, you must mail written objections or comments to Special Master John W. Sharbrough, Esq., 156 St. Anthony St., Mobile, Alabama and place on your submission the case name and the number "***Fletcher, et al. v. Brooke Group, Ltd., et al.,*** Case No. 97- 913," provided such written objections or comments are postmarked no later than March 1, 1999. If you desire to appear in person, or through counsel selected by you, at the March 9, 1999 hearing, you must mail a timely notice of intention to appear to Special Master Sharbrough on or before March 1, 1999. If you have no objections to this settlement and accept the terms of this settlement, you need not file anything with the Court. **YOU DO NEED TO MAKE ANY OBJECTIONS YOU MAY HAVE TO THE SETTLEMENT AT THIS TIME.**

You may also seek to intervene in this action as a party pursuant to either Rule 24(a) or Rule 24(b) of the Alabama Rules of Civil Procedure; however, there is no assurance that your application to intervene will be granted by the Court. A party who only objects to the settlement may not enjoy all the rights in the proceeding as a party who is permitted to intervene. For example, rights to engage in discovery may be greater for a party permitted to intervene, and there is precedent that a party who has not sought to intervene will not be permitted to appeal if dissatisfied with the outcome in the Circuit Court. If you have not intervened in this action or if you do not file a timely notice of objections or a timely intention to appear at the hearing, you will waive your right to object to the settlement.

If the Settlement Agreement is approved by the Court, and you or a person for whom you act as a legal representative fall within the definition of the Settlement Class, you will be bound by the Court's final orders and judgments. The Settlement Agreement is available for public inspection in the Court Clerk's office, 205 Government Street, Mobile, Alabama. Copies of the Settlement Agreement can be obtained from the Clerk's office by payment of the copying and mailing expense. The Settlement Agreement is also available on the World Wide Web of the Internet at stic.neu.edu/LIGGETTSETTLE.htm; www.lectlaw.com/files/cas79.htm.

extortion, and other acts enumerated in the statute.[32] RICO is not limited to these activities or to organized crime. In the tobacco case, the federal government's complaint alleged a four-decade–long conspiracy by the companies to intentionally and willfully deceive and mislead the American public about the harmful nature of tobacco products and the addictive nature of nicotine. The federal government sought injunctive relief and *disgorgement* (a forced giving up) of $280 billion dollars of ill-gotten gains for what it alleged to be companies' unlawful conspiracy to deceive the public. The court ruled that there was "overwhelming evidence" of conspiracy and ordered the companies to restrain from any further RICO violations. On appeal, however, the companies successfully argued that disgorgement of past profits was *not* a proper remedy in a RICO case.[33]

For years anti-smoking advocates tried in vain to get the United States Food and Drug Administration (FDA) to regulate tobacco products in the same way that drugs and medical devices are regulated. A major stumbling block in this goal was the case of *FDA v. Brown & Williamson Tobacco Corp.*, in which the U.S. Supreme Court held that traditional cigarettes are not subject to FDA regulation as a drug or device.[34] Some progress was made in 2009 when Congress passed the Family Smoking Prevention and Tobacco Control Act, which gave the FDA new authority to regulate "any product made or derived from tobacco that is intended for human consumption."[35] The law required more graphic label and advertising warnings. Tobacco companies had to disclose to the FDA all delivery methods of nicotine, all ingredients of their products, and any research into the health, toxicological, behavioral, or physiologic effects of tobacco products.[36] Although this new law received widespread public approval, many felt it did not go far enough. The FDA was given the authority to remove flavored cigarettes from the market, but menthol was exempted from this authority. More significantly, nicotine could not be removed from cigarettes and tobacco products could not be regulated as drugs or medical devices. Hence tobacco remains on the market despite its status as the leading cause of preventable death. With Congress unwilling to ban tobacco products, "the steady drumbeat of tobacco litigation is set to continue indefinitely."[37]

Manufacturers of other allegedly dangerous products have not been encouraged by what has happened to tobacco companies. Who is next? they wonder. Manufacturers and distributors of intoxicating liquor? Recently there has been a great deal of publicity about overweight Americans. For a while, personal injury attorneys thought that the fast-food industry could become the next source of deep-pocket defendants. Pizza Hut and Burger King, they argued, were as much a public-health menace as the maker of Camel cigarettes. Many states, however, tried to head off such litigation by passing "commonsense consumption" laws (also called "cheeseburger immunity laws") that would ban lawsuits that claimed a fast-food company made someone obese. Yet such laws will not necessarily stop the flow of litigation. Attorneys may argue that the industry violated consumer protection laws in failing to inform the public about the content of the fast food they sold. The heart of this strategy is false or misleading information rather than personal injury.

In Chapter 23 covering public nuisance, we will examine another example of an industry that obtained a measure of tort immunity—gun manufacturers.

PARALEGAL ROLES IN MASS TORT LITIGATION

Large mass tort cases present many opportunities for paralegal involvement, particularly in the area of document management. The discussion in Exhibit 20–4 of paralegal roles is by a paralegal with extensive experience in the field. Although it covers toxic torts, the discussion applies to many categories of complex tort litigation.[38]

Exhibit 20–4
Paralegal as Project/Case Manager in Toxic Tort Litigation, by Bert E. Gagnon, Director of Paralegals and Litigation Support Services, Thompson & Coburn.

INTRODUCTION

Managing complex toxic tort litigation is one of the most difficult challenges for paralegal case managers. Mountains of bewildering materials seemingly erupt in awesome magnitude during a marathon toxic tort case. The sheer volume of documents to sift and sort can appear insurmountable, so overwhelming that you want to run screaming into the morning sun. Do not take that step. A good paralegal's expert organizational skills are equal to the task at hand. With a sensible and cooperative paralegal team, you can turn this nightmare into an efficient and effective gold mine of information easily accessible to the trial litigators.

There are many types of toxic exposure, ranging from a specific incident, such as a spill, to long-term exposure of a product, such as asbestos, which takes place over a period of many years.

This author's experience in toxic tort litigation management has been for the defense in five multi-plaintiff cases involving a total of more than 300 plaintiffs, including *Kemner v. Monsanto,* the longest jury trial in the history of the United States. The systems outlined below are defense-oriented and were originally developed for a chemical spill case, but they can be applied to any type of toxic exposure litigation.

The discussion is aimed at aiding you in mapping out the elements of your case and establishing reliable document control mechanisms for each of these elements. It assumes that your firm represents a defendant involved in a complex toxic tort litigation brought by multiple plaintiffs claiming personal injury and property damage. Your goal is a meticulous support system that will provide responsive information backup to your trial counsel. The ideas outlined here are not rules carved in granite. They are merely suggestions. You should add your own creative powers to develop systems specifically tailored to the needs of your litigation.

An effective paralegal case manager is aware that what he or she becomes part of a client's bills and is a direct reflection on his or her firm. All projects should be designed to bring your case closer to settlement or to trial; it goes without saying that none should be undertaken without the consent of your supervising attorney.

I. WHERE DO I BEGIN?

Where you come into the case will determine where you start. If you are afforded the luxury of being assigned to anticipated litigation immediately after an incident has happened, rather than the day before trial, you have the opportunity to lay solid groundwork on which to build the factual information of the case. Whether you are the paralegal case manager or the newest paralegal on the team, *you are the keeper of the facts*. Factual development is the key to what every litigation paralegal does and is your team's primary responsibility.

You start at a disadvantage because the paralegals of your opponents will have already begun factual development. They may have assisted in drafting the complaint. They will have collected the factual data necessary to determine the strength of the claim and to develop their case after the complaint was filed.

If your initial contact with the lawsuit comes after it has commenced, read the complaint carefully. Know who is suing whom for what. Gain an understanding of the legal causes of action as well as the factual background. As members of the defense team, this is where most of us will enter the litigation, shortly after receipt of the complaint.

Begin with the facts of the incident. Ask to be included in initial interviews with the client and keep communication with your attorneys and their secretaries open. If you cannot be at the initial interviews, then question the attorneys who were there and read the memos they prepare. Find out as much as you can about the exposure or accident and the nature of injuries as early as possible. What parties were involved in the incident? Who was in charge? Who organized the cleanup efforts? What is the nature of the toxic agent? Who are the witnesses to the incident? What local, state, or federal agencies are involved? Find out who has taken photographs of the incident and obtain copies.

This is a good time to start files on every individual and agency you identify and to note not only pertinent contact information, but, in general terms, the nature of their involvement in the incident. Maintain an alphabetical listing of these individuals on the computer, noting names, phone numbers, street and e-mail addresses, Facebook and other social network addresses, etc. Indicate whether they are plaintiffs, defendants, eyewitnesses, government officials, or resources. Compile the same kind of information

Exhibit 20–4 (Continued)

for all other contacts you make regarding any and all aspects of the litigation. This could include plaintiffs' attorneys, secretaries and paralegals, librarians, photographers, graphic artists, police dispatchers, investigators, expert witnesses and their staff members, and many others. Keep their addresses and phone numbers and note whom you speak with at each office or agency. The next time you call, it will speed your process and assist you in getting results if you are known by the person you are calling.

Develop Checklists and Indexes

Throughout the course of any complex tort litigation you will continually be developing and updating various checklists and indexes. Although it may seem time-consuming, these working tools are essential to the management of cases of this magnitude.

Be creative in developing them and use them to monitor every project that involves a review of more than a few items—such as witnesses, depositions, or medical records. Use them to coordinate project assignments and status. Use them when you are called upon to help organize teams of attorneys. If your organizational skills are sharp (and you would not be doing this if they were not) you will be called upon to draft outlines or motions. Apply your checklists to such tasks. When preparing status reports for supervising attorneys or clients, you will know at a glance what has happened or needs to happen in each instance.

Large volumes of data require indexes (created manually or by computer). Be a compulsive indexer. You should create indexes for all aspects of a case. Develop them for expert witnesses, plaintiffs, factual witnesses, potential witnesses, witness statements, depositions, deposition exhibits, pleadings, production documents, trial transcripts, trial exhibits, scientific literature, medical literature, etc. Keep them close at hand because you will refer to them often.

At the front of every checklist or index, identify all parties who have copies of that checklist and index. When you update a checklist or index, notify all identified parties of the update. It is much easier to update your checklists and indexes as changes happen than to backtrack and try to develop them after the information is no longer fresh in your mind.

One practical checklist is a daily list of things to do. Keep one at hand at all times and note changes or updates that need to be incorporated into your other lists, new projects, comments, memos to prepare, or notes that must be placed into your tickler system. As each of these duties is taken care of, cross it off the list or click it as "done" on your computer to-do list. Seeing what you have accomplished at the end of the day will also help you in completing your daily time sheet.

Tickler System

Each of us has our own method of noting upcoming events. It does not matter whether you use a calendar system in a computer, a daily appointment book, a weekly flow chart, or a manual index card system. What matters is that you use a tickler system that prevents any important dates from "falling through the cracks." When you file interrogatories or requests for production, note the date on which a response is due. If you make a call requesting copies, put a note in your tickler system to follow up in two weeks to ensure that they were received. If a pleading or motion must be filed on a specific date, insert reminders a week before the due date, the day before the due date, and on the due date itself. Your tickler system will save you and your firm the embarrassment of missed deadlines. Check it every morning.

Coordination of Document Flow

Most attorneys and paralegals involved in the case will generate or receive correspondence, memoranda, and miscellaneous materials relating to the issues and individuals involved. Different teams will be working with various witnesses or pleadings. Establish control mechanisms for document flow within your firm to guarantee that all information regarding this litigation is filtered through the team.

Paralegals and the secretaries will usually be in position to direct documents to the proper files. Be sure all team members know who handles the pleadings, who files correspondence and memos, who codes or scans these documents into the computer database for the case, who schedules depositions, who maintains the tickler system, who receives incoming records, etc. As a case manager, you are in a pivotal position to notify team members of changes in established procedures. In an

Exhibit 20–4 (Continued)

environment where hundreds of different tasks are going on at the same time, it is not uncommon for someone to say, "I didn't know that was changed." Preventing such surprises is key.

II. DISCOVERY

Typically, in a large case, there will be more than one set of interrogatories or requests for documents. Therefore, when filing interrogatories or production requests, be sure that the individuals drafting these documents number the sets within the title or first paragraph. A number in the title (e.g., Defendant's *First Set* of Interrogatories Directed to Plaintiffs, or Defendant's *Third* Request to Produce Directed to Plaintiffs) reduces confusion as to which interrogatories are being filed or for which request for production a response is being received. If opposing parties do not use numbered sets, simply add the appropriate number to the title described in your index (e.g. Plaintiff's Request to Produce Directed to Defendant ABC Co. *Second*).

Production Requests

Plaintiffs' production requests can be extensive and sometimes burdensome. Requests can be for paper and electronic documents, films, blueprints, photographs, drawings, video and audio recordings, etc. For large cases, you may be working with e-discovery consultants that the firm has hired to help manage the volume of electronic data involved in discovery. More than likely the plaintiffs will wish to review all data regarding knowledge of the incident, product testing, manufacture, toxicity, corporate reports or minutes relating to company positions on the incident, product design, and quality control. They may also request copies of all documents previously produced in other cases.

Your firm will notify the client of the types of documentation that need to be assembled for review and possible production. Coordination of this effort is often your responsibility. If your client is a large corporation and the production request is broad and not limited by the court, your client may be required to review hundreds or even thousands of paper and computer files to comply with the request.

Find out what kinds of paper and electronic documents are available regarding day-to-day business operations. Take extensive notes, recording names and respective job titles. Know if there are diaries, handwritten notes, e-mail messages, calendars, or any special forms available, and find out how they are used. Identify any documents that may be considered confidential, privileged, or under protective order, and have stamps available for these documents. Segregate documents that are privileged or under protective order. Be sure you are not handing over such documents to the opponent! Determine which documents, if any, will need to be disclosed under special security guidelines to restrict access to the contents of the documents. Keep a separate index of such documents.

Discuss with your supervising attorney the time frame for production and the method to be used for production of documents. This could be by categories corresponding to the plaintiffs' production requests. All documents produced should be numbered sequentially with an alpha-numerical stamp. Assign a letter and a seven-digit number for all production documents no matter who is the producing party. The letter designates the producing party. If plaintiffs or co-defendants do not wish to use your numbering system, renumber their production documents upon receipt.

For documents that are turned over, obtain signed and dated receipts from opposing counsel. Each receipt should provide a brief description of the documents produced and indicate their number ranges. This can be beneficial in the future if opposing counsel claims never to have received a certain document. You will have a signed receipt indicating exactly when the document was given to the opposition.

For documents given or received, you will need to develop and maintain a master index of documents. If the documents received are not numbered, then establish and apply a numbering system to them. Record pertinent information such as the document's title and number range, the requesting party, the producing party, the date produced, and the location of the document. This tool combined with clearly numbered production requests will alleviate later confusion as to when and where certain documents became available.

If at all possible, channel all production through one individual to assure consistency. If this is not possible, ensure that all persons handling production are fully knowledgeable

Exhibit 20–4 (Continued)

about established production procedures. Not knowing exactly what has and has not been produced can lead to severe problems. Proper handling of all aspects of production can help your client avoid possible sanctions.

Building Data Summaries on Each Plaintiff

When you receive the plaintiff's interrogatory responses, you are ready to begin building your plaintiff files. Your review of these answers will be your guide for obtaining a thorough history on each plaintiff in your case. Since you are dealing with multiple plaintiffs, it is helpful to set up a data summary for each one. The data summary should include the family history, educational history, prior residences, employment history, previous medical history, health care providers consulted, instances of exposure, problems attributed to exposure, and other relevant categories of information obtainable from the interrogatory responses.

Collecting and Organizing Records on Each Plaintiff

Now it is time to start obtaining the plaintiffs' records, a process which can take days, weeks, or months, depending on the number of plaintiffs you are tracking and the number of places they have lived, worked, and obtained medical treatment. Medical records are the most obvious type of documents to obtain, but employment and military records are also important, as are school records if any of the plaintiffs are children (or adults claiming brain damage).

If most of your plaintiffs are from one area it may be beneficial to develop cross-indexes by doctor, medical institution, school, and employer prior to sending out requests for records. This way when writing to one physician, you may request records for all of the plaintiffs who claim to have received treatment from that physician. The same goes for each of the other record sources.

Moreover, do not rely on the plaintiffs to tell you all the possible sources of records. We have found that people often overlook or forget where they have received medical attention. If your plaintiffs are from a small town with relatively few sources of medical treatment, it may be fruitful to canvass all doctors and health care facilities within the nearby geographical area to determine whether they have treated any of the plaintiffs. You may also canvas physicians near plaintiffs' previous residences. A surprising number of records can be obtained in this way.

Other informative sources are within the records already obtained. A cursory review of the records received from one doctor will often yield the names of other doctors who saw the patient previously, who have referred the patient or to whom the patient was referred. These sources should not be overlooked. The same principle, of course, applies to employment, school, and military records. They are a rich source of information for further record discovery and will often tell of other employers, schools, or record sources not identified by the plaintiffs in interrogatory responses. Limiting your discovery to only the sources identified by the plaintiffs is limiting the resources available to the defense of your client.

Establishing and maintaining an ongoing log for records requested is the surest way to know the current status of your record discovery procedures. A spreadsheet or other computer chart indicating a plaintiff's name, record sources, date records were requested, and date received will provide an adequate control mechanism. Be sure to include comments on record legibility or on specific problems encountered in gathering the records.

The type of file retrieval system you establish for discovered records does not matter as long as you are able to identify the plaintiff and the source of the record. We have found that a simple index and document numbering system works best. Each plaintiff is assigned a two- or three-digit code, and each record source is given a three-digit code. Then each document is given an eight- or nine-digit number based on the plaintiff, record source, and page sequence. That way if a record is inadvertently removed from its file, it can easily be returned. For example, assume that plaintiff John Doe is plaintiff No. 5, Dr. Smith is record source No. 115, and that there are 110 pages of records received from Dr. Smith on plaintiff John Doe. The last page of these records would be numbered 05-115-110. When future records are collected from Dr. Smith regarding plaintiff John Doe, they would start at page 111 (05-115-111).

Exhibit 20–4 (Continued)

Medical Summaries

Once obtained, an initial review and summarization of medical records is essential. The medical summary should be updated as new records are received. It should also incorporate information obtained from plaintiff depositions and from expert medical examinations as these materials become available. It will be an invaluable tool for your trial attorneys.

Appendix I is a suggested medical summary format. The summarizers will need guidelines to help them identify contradictions in medical complaints and symptoms and allegations of ill health in addition to providing straightforward summaries of a plaintiff's medical, employment, and educational history. Be sure your summarizing team is using standardized medical and dental abbreviations.

APPENDIX I

Medical Summary

I. GENERAL INFORMATION AND PERSONAL DATA
(Name, address, age, employment, family history, etc.)

II. BRIEF SUMMARY OF PRE-EXPOSURE HISTORY

III. EXPOSURE
(from interrogatory answers, expert's reports, and deposition testimony)

IV. PLAINTIFF'S COMPLAINTS AND EXPERT MEDICAL FINDINGS
- A. Plaintiff's Answers to Interrogatories
- B. Complaints and Symptoms Told to Expert Medical Witnesses
- C. Complaints and Symptoms from Plaintiff's Deposition
- D. Plaintiff's Expert's Findings

V. DEFENDANT'S EXPERT'S MEDICAL FINDINGS

VI. MEDICAL RECORDS
- A. Doctor/Institution Index
- B. Detailed Chronological Summary of Doctor Visits and Hospitalizations
- C. Height, Weight, and Blood Pressure Charts
- D. Medications

VII. ADDITIONAL RECORDS
- A. School Records
  (including grades, attendance, teacher comments, athletic accomplishments, standardized test results)
- B. Employment Records
- C. Insurance or Military Records

VIII. LABORATORY CHARTS
- A. Blood Count/Blood Chemistry Charts
  (with applicable reference ranges)
- B. Urinalyses
- C. Electrodiagnostic: EKG, EMG, PNVC, EEG
- D. Audiometric
- E. Vision
- F. Other tests

As a paralegal case manager, it may be your job to recruit and interview the medical summarizers and monitor their progress. You or one of your team's paralegals may work as a liaison between them and the staff of word processors or encoders and the supervising attorneys. A simple chart indicating each plaintiff, assigned summarizer, and status of the summary will aid you in following the progress of this specialized team.

Plaintiff Depositions

Your trial counsel may decide to depose the plaintiffs prior to medical examinations by either plaintiff or defense experts. As case manager it will undoubtably fall to you to schedule and prepare notices of depositions. If you are so authorized, try to develop a friendly working relationship with the opposing attorney or paralegal who is coordinating deposition scheduling. This will make life easier for both of you.

If your lead counsel agrees, assign a member of your team to each scheduled plaintiff deposition and ensure that he or she will be available for organizing documents and

Exhibit 20–4 (Continued)

other preparatory work with the attorney taking the deposition. A paralegal can provide support at the deposition with document handling as well as taking detailed notes and keeping track of exhibits. The paralegal can guarantee that copies of the deposition and all exhibits are obtained. He or she can also prepare the deposition summary and topical index. The work already invested in the deposition preparation and execution will have provided clear insight into what medical, physical, mental, and emotional problems the plaintiff has attributed to exposure and which conditions predated exposure. The deposition information should be incorporated into the medical summaries.

The plaintiffs' depositions, together with the summaries of the depositions and the topical indexes to the depositions, can then be added to the plaintiff files. It is important to make sure you develop a standard summary format for depositions (as well as for trial testimony). When reviewing numerous deposition summaries, it increases the reviewer's speed and accuracy if all summaries are organized in the same manner. This of course applies to topical summaries as well.

Expert Medical Examinations

The plaintiffs will be examined by their team of medical experts, who will in turn issue their opinions as to the medical condition of each plaintiff. The experts' reports are, of course, discoverable and will need to be incorporated into the medical summaries previously discussed. They can be numbered and indexed into the plaintiff files in the same manner as other discovered documents. By comparing allegations of injury contained in these expert opinions with findings of the plaintiffs' treating physicians, the trial attorney will find invaluable defense ammunition. For example, an expert may attribute one condition to toxic exposure but a review of the plaintiff's records reveals that the condition predated the exposure incident.

More than likely the defendant will also wish to have the plaintiffs undergo medical examinations by its own team of medical experts. As case manager you may be asked to play an active role in these examinations by making all necessary scheduling arrangements for the examinations. Whether or not you schedule such events, it will be up to you to obtain the results and see that the defendant's medical expert reports are also numbered, incorporated into the medical summaries, and added to the plaintiff files.

Factual Review of Records

You and your team will also be called upon to conduct numerous factual reviews of the plaintiffs' records. You might chart out statistics on property damage or loss of income. You might do a comparative analysis of results of laboratory testing done by treating physicians, plaintiff experts, and defense experts. Whatever the various record reviews requested of you, it will be important for your team to have a thorough working knowledge of these records, how to read them, and what the myriad of tests stand for. Much of the factual development that you do here will ultimately be used at trial or in the preparation of trial exhibits.

Obtaining Government Reports and Other Records

Local, state, and federal government agencies are other sources of informative factual documents. The accident or exposure incident you are involved with will no doubt have been investigated or handled by various governmental agencies. You will need to locate each of the agencies involved and obtain copies of all related documentation available. You may even have to file requests under the Freedom of Information Act. It is essential to obtain everything possible. Documents from the Environmental Protection Agency, the Occupational Safety and Health Administration, state conservation organizations, local emergency teams, or the Centers for Disease Control can help to construct crucial chronologies of events as well as provide a record of government reactions and responses to the situation.

As with other production documents, number stamp any government agency documents received and add them to your master index of production.

Depositions of Expert Witnesses

Part of your team's trial preparation will be deposing the plaintiffs' expert medical witnesses to gain insight into their backgrounds, knowledge, and opinions. This will determine inconsistencies and help to develop trial strategies. Your team will function here in the same way they do for plaintiff depositions.

You will coordinate the scheduling and noticing of depositions. The paralegal team will compile and organize all relevant documentation needed for the deposition. They

Exhibit 20–4 (Continued)

may be required to review available information regarding the deponent, and draft deposition outlines for the deposing attorneys. As with plaintiff depositions, it is helpful to have the same paralegal help prepare for the deposition and do the deposition summary and topical index.

The information gathered from medical experts relating to opinions on specific plaintiffs' conditions should be added to the medical summaries, and inconsistencies should be noted. Depositions and summaries should be added to the witness files, which will be discussed later. As with all other categories of this litigation, keep an index of depositions taken.

Depositions of Non-Experts

In preparation for trial or settlement, your litigators may deem it necessary to take depositions or statements of many non-expert individuals. Eyewitness statements aid in the development of factual knowledge of the specific incident of exposure. Depositions of co-workers, health care providers, employers, and teachers provide keen insight to the moral character of a plaintiff and an excellent view of preexisting complaints or problems versus post-exposure complaints or problems. Your team's function remains the same for these as for previously discussed depositions. Paralegals can be used effectively to take some witness statements and thereby increase savings for the client. This, of course, is a choice to be made by your supervising attorneys. All statements and materials collected from record custodians will have to be numbered and produced as outlined above.

III. WITNESS FILES

By now you should be maintaining lists not only of plaintiffs and their treating physicians, schools, and employers, but also of plaintiff medical experts, plaintiff factual witnesses, defense medical experts, and other potential witnesses. These lists are the groundwork for and guide to your witness files.

Your witness files are the core of your litigation file support system. They are a compilation of the full cast of characters involved in complex tort litigation. Anything and everything you obtain on these individuals should be added to the indexes and made a part of the core files.

Witness files are not limited to people expected to testify at trial. They should include all individuals who gave statements or depositions, who were involved in any way with the accident or exposure incident, who are identified anywhere throughout the production documents, who are potential eyewitnesses, who are potential expert witnesses, who are knowledgable about some aspect of the product or incident, etc. Any individual or agency that you have information on should be included in the witness files.

The information gathered can include curriculum vitae, deposition summaries, deposition exhibits, statements given, attorney notes, relevant correspondence and memoranda, preparatory work product, related literature listings, examination outlines, relevant documents produced, chronological listings of events, proposed exhibits, testimony given in other cases, etc. Anything and everything that you gather relating to a potential witness should be kept here.

IV. PRIOR TO TRIAL

Trial Notebooks

As the trial draws closer you will start to develop trial notebooks. Whether or not your team is asked to draft them, the goal of each trial notebook at this point will be to develop the witness examination outline. Many resources discuss methodology for establishing trial notebooks. The key is that they are organized in a consistent manner allowing the user immediate access to needed information. The materials you have gathered in the witness files will undoubtably go into these notebooks, but do not surrender your only copies. The notebooks will be used and marked on. Save your witness files and use copies of necessary documents in the trial notebooks.

Review the draft examination outline and indicate in the trial notebook where each point counsel wishes to make is supported. Highlight relevant passages of deposition testimony or production documents that support these points. Be sure the trial notebooks include all production documents of which the witness has knowledge. Include depositions and previous trial testimony if applicable. If you have prepared timelines

Exhibit 20–4 (Continued)

that relate to this witness, include them as well. Be sure to discuss with the litigator what he or she will need in the trial notebook to prepare this witness for live testimony. If there are any working tools, charts, or reports needed to complete the trial notebook, develop them.

Witness Preparation Sessions

Preparatory sessions with expert witnesses on complex personal injury matters can be long and grueling. Medical experts, for example, must review hundreds of treating physicians' medical records as well as their own and other expert reports regarding each plaintiff. They may need to develop a familiarity with the toxicological literature relating to their own area of medical expertise. Your team may be assigned to work with the litigator and witness in these prep sessions.

The paralegal not only can function as a document handler during these sessions, but can take detailed notes of the expert's opinions and ensure that questions or problems that arise during preparation sessions are answered or dealt with before the next session. He or she can help monitor which records, articles, charts, or documents are to be developed for trial exhibits and can continue to supplement the trial notebooks as needed. The notebooks, now armed with outlines and materials developed during the preparatory sessions, will provide everything necessary to examine the witness at trial.

Exhibit Preparation

During witness preparation sessions and throughout the pretrial period, certain records and documents will be designated as possible exhibits. Start an index of exhibits to be used during the trial testimony of each witness. These exhibits will not be limited to discovery and production documents. Your team may be called upon to design or draft various timelines, charts, graphs, or other compilations of data to be used as trial exhibits.

If your firm does not already have business relations with photographers, computer graphic companies, commercial printers, and reproduction services, it is time to establish them. Locate and interview vendors in your area who are cost-efficient and produce quality products. Find out what their turnaround times are for the kinds of exhibits you will be using. When you are in trial and find out that you need a new exhibit in court within a few hours, you will not have time to find out who can provide that service. Do your footwork early and be prepared.

Establishing a Trial Office

The trial may be in a distant city or even in another state. If your firm is not located within close proximity of the court conducting the trial, you may be required to open a trial office close to the trial site. In-depth discussion with both the client and your litigating attorneys will be necessary to determine how much of the litigating team needs to be at the trial office, what kind of support staff and equipment will be necessary, and what files and information will need to be available at the trial office.

If the support team remains at the home office with a small satellite team at the trial office, it may be necessary to establish two complete filing systems or a secure computer network in order to transmit and share files efficiently. Whatever scenario your firm plans, try to determine it early. See that a suitable space is located and supplied appropriately to accommodate the trial team's needs. Establish a communication system between the trial office and the home office and funnel all information through the trial office paralegal. He or she should be an individual with a full grasp of the issues and facts of the litigation and a thorough working knowledge of all the systems established thus far. You will need to assure that this paralegal has the authority to manage the trial office and has the complete support of the litigation team. As you go into trial, this individual's role becomes crucial.

Final Trial Preparation

In the last weeks prior to trial there are a great number of tasks to accomplish and loose ends to tie. Your checklists will help now more than ever as your team approaches the wire. It is especially important to maintain a clear-minded, calm, unflustered approach as you apply your skills to this final organizational pretrial push. Check the status of all projects previously described and determine that they are ready for trial.

It may be your team's duty to maintain contact with and be responsible for witnesses. If necessary, arrange to serve subpoenas to guarantee witnesses' appearance at trial. Set up necessary travel and hotel accommodations. Do everything possible to put your witnesses at ease.

Exhibit 20–4 (Continued)

Become familiar with the layout of the court and instruct witnesses on the location of facilities. Know procedures for obtaining transcripts and copies of exhibits and pass this information to the trial team. Know what computer and other electronic equipment will be allowed in the courtroom and ensure that appropriate outlets or wireless connections are in place. If a trial attorney is going to use an unusually large or awkward exhibit, you may need to make prior arrangements with court personnel to accommodate the exhibit. In short, anticipate your litigator's needs.

Determine whether your trial attorneys prefer one specific paralegal to provide support at trial or a team of paralegals who rotate in and out of the position. Utilizing the same person in this role for the entire trial may maintain a small team image for the jury and provide a certain continuity. However, by rotating paralegals, you can use the individual most familiar with particular witnesses and proposed exhibits. Make sure that whoever functions as the paralegal at trial develops a checklist of basic supplies (pens, pencils, legal pads, discs, thumb drives, change for copies, etc.) to take to trial.

Meet with your team and review the extra demands that will be placed on them during the course of the trial. This will include staggering hours to provide support prior to trial in the morning, during lunch hours, and after trial each evening. During the course of the trial, unexpected projects will need to be done in rapid turnaround time. Your team must be ready at all times to provide immediate responses to the trial attorneys.

Establish a distribution list for both internal and out-of-firm recipients of exhibits, transcripts, and trial notes. Setting up a flowchart for their distributions prior to trial avoids confusion after it commences. Know who will obtain these materials and how they will be copied and disbursed.

In the last days prior to trial, it will be your team's obligation to search out whatever needs to be done to achieve trial readiness and do it. This is not the time to wait to be given assignments. If you or your team members see a problem area or have an idea for a needed project, take it to your supervising attorneys and present it assertively. Gain the authority and take the task to completion.

V. THE TRIAL

As a case manager, it is your goal to maximize efficient litigation support and to minimize obstacles to that goal. You must stay on top of every aspect of the trial and coordinate the smooth operation of all the components of the litigation team. The trial will challenge the team both at the courthouse and behind the scenes.

Be sure the paralegal at the court knows what is expected of him or her. This person will be your pipeline of information. Establish a communication routine whereby you are available to talk with the trial paralegal during court breaks to receive any comments or assignments from the in-trial team and relay it to the appropriate backup team members.

The trial paralegal will be the team's source of daily information. He or she should take detailed notes of the proceedings, noting witnesses' testimony, starting and stopping times, reasons for late starts or early dismissals, objections by all parties, bench conferences, in-chamber proceedings, juror reactions, etc. He or she will also need to keep a roster of defense and plaintiff exhibits admitted into evidence and previously marked exhibits that were used with each witness. These notes and indexes are an essential source of information and should be distributed to appropriate parties on a daily basis. Use the rosters of exhibits to build a formal log showing the history and use of each exhibit.

The trial paralegal will also be responsible for obtaining copies of all exhibits on a daily basis, obtaining transcripts as soon as they are available, maintaining and handling documents for the trial litigators, managing trial notebooks and trial boxes, providing the necessary number of copies of all proposed exhibits needed for distribution to the jury, and being available for any in-trial support needed by trial litigators and witnesses.

Behind the scenes the entire litigation support team should be available to deal with projects on a crisis basis. There will be situations where the entire staff and every available attorney and paralegal in your firm may be needed to help "put out fires."

The demands of the trial team will be numerous in this type of litigation. Throughout the course of the trial new ideas will arise and new work product and further factual development will be the result. It is important to keep indexes of all major projects, including reviews and searches that are conducted. When a new project is assigned, check to be sure that it is not something that was previously done.

Exhibit 20–4 (Continued)

You will need to have the trial transcripts summarized as fast as possible. For this purpose you can utilize either a core summarizing team or disburse the responsibility of transcript summarization throughout the entire support team.

VI. CONCLUSION

We have taken a look at the inner workings of complex tort litigation management. This discussion should inspire your own creative powers and generate ideas that you can apply to your own cases. Remember the main elements of this type of management are to define the nature of the materials you have to work with, develop standardized procedures for handling these materials, and educate all parties involved on established procedures.

Whether your title is administrative paralegal, case manager, or project coordinator, it is essential to your success that you remember your own roots. You are still a paralegal, and the skills you developed as a paralegal should not be set aside. Do not ask any of your team members to perform a task that you would not do. The other paralegals on your team today are the case managers of tomorrow. Try to maintain an even balance between being a task-oriented leader and a people-oriented leader. Your success as an administrator depends largely on the people on your litigation team. Without them you can do nothing. Shift their assignments and do not hesitate to delegate responsibilities. Mix the mundane or boring assignments with ones that really challenge their skills and help them to grow. Keep your team informed by scheduling periodic meetings to let them know what is happening with the litigation and what other team members are working on. Develop group leaders within the team and assign yourself to projects as a group member whenever time allows.

Above all, you are a proactive member of the litigation team, and it is your obligation to stay ahead of any crisis. Be accessible to both the lawyers and the other paralegals involved in the litigation. Remain open to suggestions. In accepting the position of administrator on a complex tort litigation, you have the responsibility for establishing clockwork organization and building a loyal and motivated support team. The challenge is big. The personal and professional satisfaction achieved by meeting that challenge is enormous. Good luck!

CHECK THE CITE

In Florida, smokers and their survivors brought a class action lawsuit against cigarette companies and industry organizations, seeking to recover for smoking-related injuries. The trial court awarded $12.7 million in compensatory damages and $145 billion in punitive damages. On appeal, why did the Supreme Court of Florida rule that the award of punitive damages was excessive? Read the case of *Engle v. Liggett Group, Inc.*, 945 So. 2d 1246 (Fla. 2006). To read the opinion online, (1) Go to the site of the Supreme Court of Florida (www.floridasupremecourt.org/decisions/opinions.shtml). Click 2006 and scroll down to December 21, 2006 to find the *Engle* opinion (revised opinion). (2) Go to FindACase (www.findacase.com). Select Florida. Run a standard search (Engle Liggett). (3) Run a citation search ("945 So. 2d 1246") or a party search (Engle Liggett) in the Legal Opinions and Journals database of Google Scholar (scholar.google.com).

PROJECT

In Google, Bing, or another general search engine, run one of the following issue searches:

1. asbestos litigation *aa*
2. breast implant litigation *aa*
3. tobacco litigation *aa*

Substitute the name of your state for *aa* in the search (e.g., asbestos litigation New Mexico). Write a short essay in which you describe the status of litigation in your state for the issue you selected. You can consult as many websites as you wish, but you must quote from at least three separate sites. Only one of the three sites can be that of a lawyer seeking clients who have that issue.

ETHICS IN A TORTS PRACTICE

You are a paralegal at a personal injury law firm that specializes in airline crash litigation. In your city, a plane has recently crashed. The local newspaper lists the names of the deceased. Your supervisor asks you to find the addresses of all the families of the deceased and to send each a letter that describes the specialty of the firm and invites anyone with questions about legal representation to call the firm. Unknown to you, one of the recipients of the letter is already represented by another law firm. What ethical problems, if any, might exist?

SUMMARY

There are four major categories of mass tort cases: mass accident, mass-marketed product, mass exposure, and mass economic loss. A mass tort is a general term for various causes of action asserted by a large number of persons who have been harmed by the same or similar conduct or product of a relatively small number of defendants. In a mass tort case, the plaintiffs assert traditional causes of action such as negligence and strict liability in tort; mass tort is not a new tort cause of action.

Most in-person, live telephone, and real-time electronic solicitation is unethical unless the attorney is not seeking fees or other financial gain or already has a professional or family relationship with the prospective client. Most other solicitation (e.g., by mail) is ethical unless the lawyer knows or reasonably should know that the physical, emotional, or mental state of the person is such that the person could not exercise reasonable judgment in making a decision on employing a lawyer.

A person injured by a mass tort may seek relief through an individual lawsuit. An alternative is a class action, in which one or more members of a class sue (or are sued) as representative parties on behalf of everyone in the class. If the parties do not intend to litigate because they have settled, the action is called a settlement class action. Under the Class Action Fairness Act some class actions must be brought in federal court.

Junk science is unreliable and, therefore, potentially misleading scientific evidence. Under Federal Rule of Evidence 702, technical or scientific testimony from an expert will be admitted if it is based on sufficient facts or data, is the product of reliable principles and methods, and will assist the trier of fact.

Asbestos is a fibrous material used in products such as wall insulation and other building materials. Asbestos causes diseases such as mesothelioma and asbestosis. Millions of people have been exposed to asbestos and hundreds of thousands of personal injury claims have been filed throughout the country. Many asbestos manufacturers have filed for bankruptcy. An attempt at a nationwide class action settlement failed when the United States Supreme Court refused to certify the class because the members of the class were too diverse. In particular, the class could not fairly protect the interests of those of persons who have been exposed to asbestos but had not yet manifested injury. Their needs clashed with those of persons who have already manifested injury. Also, there were flaws in the plan to give notice to everyone in the class, particularly those who had not yet manifested injury.

Hundreds of thousands of women have sued breast implant manufacturers for diseases the implants have allegedly caused. So many claims were filed that manufacturers like Dow Corning sought bankruptcy protection. Causation was a big issue since many studies did not support the conclusion that the implants caused serious diseases. Nevertheless, litigation costs pressured some manufacturers to settle.

For years, tobacco companies were very successful in court, particularly with the argument that smokers were assuming a known risk. The tide, however, has turned, in large part because of leaked tobacco company documents that showed that the companies knew about the danger of smoking and targeted young people. States sued for Medicaid costs; the federal government brought a RICO suit; and private citizens brought class actions and individual lawsuits for the illnesses caused by direct and secondhand smoke.

Paralegals play many roles in mass tort cases. They assist in drafting complaints, prepare extensive checklists and document indexes, maintain a tickler system, coordinate document flow and discovery, summarize medical records, keep witness files, develop trial notebooks, help prepare witnesses, coordinate trial exhibits, and respond to ongoing and emergency needs prior to and during the trial.

KEY TERMS

mass tort *404*
toxic tort *405*
solicitation *406*
real-time *406*
joinder *409*
class action *409*
settlement class action *409*
global peace *410*
opt out *410*
diversity of citizenship *410*
junk science *410*
Frye test *410*
Daubert test *411*
Judicial Panel on Multidistrict Litigation (J.P.M.L.) *412*
RICO *422*

REVIEW QUESTIONS

1. What is a mass tort?
2. What are the four main categories of mass torts?
3. What are the main causes of action raised in mass tort cases?
4. What are some of the characteristics of mass tort litigation?
5. State some examples of ethical improprieties in mass tort litigation.
6. What is a class action?
7. Why are class actions allowed?
8. What is junk science?
9. How does the *Frye* test compare with the *Daubert* test?
10. What does FRE 702 require?
11. What is asbestos?
12. Why did the Court in *Amchem* reject the proposed class certification?
13. What are medical criteria laws?
14. What is the function of the J.P.M.L.?
15. What causation problems exist in breast implant litigation?
16. What kinds of litigation have been brought against tobacco companies?
17. To what extent can the FDA regulate tobacco products?
18. What are some of the main roles of paralegals in mass tort litigation?

HELPFUL WEBSITES

- **Mass Torts**

  www.ncsconline.org/WC/Publications/MassTorts/MassTortIndex.htm

  www.ncsconline.org/WC/Publications/MassTorts/MaTortPPA_Final.pdf

  lawprofessors.typepad.com/mass_tort_litigation

  www.abanet.org/litigation/committees/masstorts

  www.masstortdefense.com

  www.facebook.com/pages/Mass-Tort-Litigation/116869087803?ref=nf

- **Class Actions**

  classactiondefense.jmbm.com

  www.consumerclassactionsmasstorts.com

- **Asbestos Litigation**

  www.claimsres.com

www.citizen.org (enter "asbestos" in the search box)

- **Breast Implant Litigation**
  www.sfdct.com/_sfdct/index.cfm
  mason.gmu.edu/~dbernste/BreastImplants.html

www.manhattan-institute.org/html/research_memorandum_5.htm

- **Tobacco Litigation**
  www.tobacco.neu.edu
  www.tobacco.neu.edu/box

ENDNOTES

1. Michael Higgins, *Mass Tort Makeover?* 84 American Bar Association Journal 52 (November 1998).
2. Anne E. Cohen, *Mass Tort Litigation After Amchem,* 57 ALI-ABA Course of Study Materials 269 (February 25, 1998).
3. Jack B. Weinstein, *Notes for a Discussion of Mass Tort Cases and Class Actions,* 63 Brooklyn Law Review 581 (Summer 1997).
4. American Law Institute, *Enterprise Responsibility for Personal Injury* 389 (Reporters' Study, 1991); Mark A. Peterson and Molly Selvin, *Resolution of Mass Torts* 31 (Rand, 1988).
5. *State of Minnesota and Blue Cross and Blue Shield of Minnesota v. Philip Morris, Inc.*, Trial Transcript, Closing Statements, May 7, 1998, P.M. Session (1998 WL 242426).
6. *In the Matter of Magdy F. Anis*, 126 N.J. 448, 451, 599 A.2d 1265, 1266 (1992).
7. *In the Matter of Magdy F. Anis*, 126 N.J. at 460, 599 A.2d at 1271.
8. 49 U.S.C. § 1136(g)(2) (uscode.house.gov/search/criteria.shtml)
9. *S4247 Fairness in Asbestos Injury Resolution Act of 2004—Motion to Proceed*, 150 Cong. Rec. S4247-02, S4247, Proceedings and Debates of the 108th Congress, Second Session Thursday, April 22, 2004; www.dallasobserver.com/1998-08-13/news/toxic-justice/1.
10. Kevin H. Hudson, *Catch-23(b)(1)(B): The Dilemma of Using the Mandatory Class Action to Resolve the Problem of the Mass Tort Case*, 40 Emory Law Journal 665, 677 (1991).
11. *Bourgeois v. A.P. Green Industries, Inc.*, 939 So.2d 478, 486 (La. App. 5 Cir., 2006).
12. *Mace v. Van Ru Credit Corp.*, 109 F.3d 338, 344 (7th Cir. 1997).
13. A class action in which a member of the class can opt out is a *permissive class action*. A class action in which a member of the class cannot opt out is a *mandatory class action*. The latter is often attempted if the defendant(s) have limited resources (constituting a so-called "limited fund") out of which to pay a judgment. Allowing individual lawsuits might quickly deplete the assets of the defendant(s), leaving little or nothing for others similarly injured. This is particularly true if the plaintiff in an individual lawsuit is allowed to collect punitive damages.
14. fl1.findlaw.com/news.findlaw.com/hdocs/docs/clssactns/cafa05.pdf.
15. Daniel J. Popeo, *Truth for Sale*, New York Times, September 21, 1998, at A23.
16. *Frye v. United States*, 293 F. 1013, 1014 (D.C. Cir. 1923).
17. www.law.cornell.edu/rules/fre/rules.htm#Rule702.
18. *Daubert v. Merrell Dow Pharmaceuticals, Inc.*, 509 U.S. 579, 113 S. Ct. 2786, 125 L. Ed. 2d 469 (1993).
19. Rand Corporation, *Annual Report*, April 1, 1990–March 31, 1991.
20. Rand Corporation, *Asbestos in the Court* 42 (1985).
21. Anne E. Cohen, *Mass Tort Litigation After Amchem*, 57 ALI-ABA 269, 277–78 (1998).
22. Martha Neil, *Backing Away from the Abyss*, 92 American Bar Association Journal 26 (September 2006).
23. *Amchem Products, Inc. v. Windsor*, 521 U.S. 591, 117 S. Ct. 2231, 138 L. Ed. 2d 689 (1997).
24. *Amchem*, 117 S. Ct. at 2250 (citing the lower court opinion in the case).
25. Mark Behrens, *What's New in Asbestos Litigation?*, 28 Review of Litigation 501 (2009).
26. Joan Beck, Hidden Agenda on Breast Implants, San Diego Union-Tribune, March 2, 1996, at B6.
27. Barry Meier, "Judges Set Up Panel for Lawsuits on Implants," *New York Times*, April 4, 1996, at A12.
28. www.fda.gov/SiteIndex/ucm148497.htm (click "Breast Implants").
29. *Blowing Smoke: Cigarette Maker Taunts Lawyers in Ad Campaign*, Wall Street Journal, October 20, 1998, at B1.
30. Myron Levin, *Years of Immunity and Arrogance Up in Smoke*, Los Angeles Times, May 10, 1998, at D1, D17.
31. Mark Curriden, *DOJ (Department of Justice) Probes Law Firms: Paralegal Who Copied Documents Subpoenaed*, 80 American Bar Association Journal 14 (June 1994); *It Started with a Paralegal*, 13 Legal Assistant Today 18 (May/June 1996).

32. 18 USC § 1961.
33. *U.S. v. Philip Morris USA, Inc.*, 449 F. Supp. 2d 1 (D.D.C. 2006); *U.S. v. Philip Morris USA, Inc.*, 396 F.3d 1190 (DC Cir. 2005).
34. 529 U.S. 120, 120 S.Ct. 1291, 146 L. Ed. 2d 121 (2000).
35. 21 U.S.C. § 321(rr)(1). Pub.L. 111-31, 123 Stat. 1776 (2009); frwebgate.access.gpo.gov/cgi-bin/getdoc.cgi?dbname=111_cong_bills&docid=f:h1256enr.txt.pdf.
36. Barak Orbach, "The New Regulatory Era–An Introduction," 51 *Arizona Law Review* 559, 563 (Fall 2009); U.S. Food and Drug Administration, *Tobacco Products*, www.fda.gov/TobaccoProducts/default.htm.
37. Micah Berman, *Smoking Out the Impact of Tobacco-Related Decisions on Public Health Law*, 75 Brooklyn Law Review 1 (2009).
38. Reprinted with permission from Toxic Law Reporter, vol. 4, no. 21, pp. 628–37, October 25, 1989 (as "The Administrative Legal Assistant: A Nuts-and-Bolts View of Complex Toxic Tort Litigation Management"). Copyright 1989 by the Bureau of National Affairs, Inc. (800-372-1033).

Student StudyWARE™ CD-ROM
For additional materials, please go to the student CD in this book.

CHAPTER

21

SURVIVAL AND WRONGFUL DEATH

CHAPTER OUTLINE

- Introduction
- Survival of Torts Unrelated to Death
- Wrongful Death
- Avoiding Double Recovery

CHAPTER OBJECTIVES

After completing this chapter, you should be able to:

- Understand the distinction between survival actions and wrongful death actions.
- Know which actions survived at common law and which survive by statute.
- State the characteristics of a survival action.
- Explain when a wrongful death action is allowed.
- Explain how states resolve the problem of double recovery when survival and wrongful death actions are possible.

INTRODUCTION

Distinguish between the following situations:

Case I. Dan steals Paul's watch. Paul then sues Dan for the tort of conversion. Within two weeks of filing the suit, Paul dies in a car accident and Dan dies in an earthquake.

Case II. Barbara negligently drives her car into Sam's car. Sam dies from the injuries resulting from the crash. Six months later, Barbara dies of cancer.

wrongful death A death caused by a tort or other wrong.

tortious Pertaining to conduct that can lead to tort liability.

tortfeasor A person who has committed a tort.

In Case I, the plaintiff (Paul) died from a cause unrelated to Dan's tort of conversion; the tort did not cause Paul's death. The same is true of the defendant (Dan)—his death had nothing to do with the tort. Case II presents a very different situation. Barbara's negligence caused the death of Sam. It was a **wrongful death** because it was caused by a tort. (It, therefore, is also referred to as a **tortious** death.) We need to determine whether the tort action survives the death of either the victim or the **tortfeasor** in Cases I and II. (A tortfeasor is a wrongdoer who has committed a tort.) As we will see, not all tort actions survive.

SURVIVAL OF TORTS UNRELATED TO DEATH

First, we examine the survival of a tort cause of action when a death has occurred that had nothing to do with the tort (Case I in the preceding example). The survival of the tort depends in part on the kind of injury or harm that the tort inflicts. Two main categories of torts need to be discussed: personal torts and property torts. The latter is further divided into real property torts and personal property torts. Here are the definitions of these terms and examples involving Tom and Pete:

personal tort A tort that injures a person's body, reputation, or feelings.

property tort A tort that damages a person's real property or personal property.

- **Personal torts** injure a person's body, reputation, or feelings.

Examples of personal torts:
Tom batters Pete, defames him, or invades his privacy.

- **Property torts** damage a person's real property or personal property.

Real property (also called real estate and realty) is land and anything permanently attached or affixed to the land such as buildings, fences, and trees.

Examples of real property torts:
Tom trespasses on Pete's land or negligently sets fire to Pete's house.

Personal property (also called chattels) is anything that can be owned, other than real property.

Examples of personal property torts:
Tom steals (i.e., converts) Pete's car or negligently poisons Pete's dog.

estate All of the assets and liabilities of a decedent after he or she dies. See glossary for additional definitions.

personal representative A person appointed to administer the estate and legal affairs of someone who has died or who is incapacitated.

In all of these examples, assume that Tom or Pete dies from a cause *unrelated* to the tort. What survives? Logically, you would think that the death of the victim or of the tortfeasor from an unrelated cause would not affect the litigation of the tort action. If the tortfeasor dies, the victim's **estate** should be able to bring the tort claim against the tortfeasor. (An estate consists of all the assets and debts left by a decedent. The estate can sue and be sued; it acts through a **personal representative** appointed by the decedent's will or by the court.) If, on the other hand, it is the tortfeasor who dies, the victim should be able to bring the tort action against the tortfeasor's estate. Logic, however, has not always ruled this area of the law.

common law Judge-made law in the absence of statutes or other controlling law.

Common Law and Statutory Law

First, we will examine survival of torts (personal, personal property, and real property) at **common law**. (Common law is judge-made law in the absence of statutes or other controlling law; the phrase **at common law** refers to the time in history when the controlling law on an issue was the common law rather than statutory law.) Then, more importantly, we will examine what survives under statutory law that has changed the common law. Such statutes are often called *survival statutes*.

at common law During the time in history when the controlling law on an issue was the common law rather than statutory law. (See glossary for additional definitions.)

Personal Torts

Common law: At common law, torts against the person of the victim did not survive the death of either the victim or the tortfeasor. If the victim died, the action could not be brought by the victim's estate. If the tortfeasor died, the action could not be brought against the estate of the tortfeasor.

Statutory law: All states have passed survival statutes that have changed the common law, but not completely. In most states, the personal torts that are invasions of **tangible** interests survive, but the personal torts that are invasions of **intangible** interests do not. Something is tangible if it has physical form and we can make contact with it through our senses of touch or sight. For example, a human body is tangible. Since battery is a tort against the body, it is a tort that protects a tangible interest and, therefore, would survive. Something is intangible, however, if it is without physical form. For example, a person's reputation or privacy is intangible. Hence, personal torts that protect these interests such as defamation and invasion of privacy would not survive.

tangible Capable of being touched or seen. Having physical form.

intangible Without physical form, e.g., an emotion, a right.

Personal Property Torts

Common law: At common law, torts against the personal property of the victim survived the death of the victim but did not survive the death of the tortfeasor.

Statutory law: Survival statutes have changed the common law. In all states, torts against personal property survive both the victim and the tortfeasor.

Real Property Torts

Common law: At common law, torts against the real property of the victim did not survive the death of the victim or the tortfeasor.

Statutory law: Survival statutes have changed the common law. In all states, torts against real property survive the death of either the victim or the tortfeasor.

Hence, if a tort action survives today, it is because the action is one of the few that survived at common law, or because a survival statute has established that it survives.

Characteristics of Actions That Survive

Let us focus on a tort action that survives the death of the victim, again keeping in mind that we are not yet talking about a death that is caused by the tort. Before the victim brings any action against the tortfeasor, the victim dies from a cause unrelated to the tort. The action is brought after this death. Note the following characteristics of this action:

- The action is brought by the estate of the victim through the personal representative of the estate.
- The action is not a new or independent action. It is the same action that the victim would have had if he or she had lived.
- The plaintiff in the action is not an heir or relative of the victim unless the heir or relative happens to be the personal representative of the victim's estate.
- Heirs or relatives do not directly receive any benefit from a damage award in the tort action that survives. If they benefit from the award, they do so through the estate as beneficiaries of a will or via **intestacy** (the distribution of a decedent's estate when no valid will exists).
- In general, the damages recoverable (including pain and suffering) are the same damages that the victim would have recovered if he or she had not died. (Some exceptions exist. For example, a state might not allow the personal

intestacy Dying without leaving a valid will. The deceased is called the intestate.

representative to recover any punitive damages the victim would have been able to recover.)
- There is no recovery for the death of the victim, because we are examining a case in which the tort did not cause the death of the victim; the decedent was the victim of a tort that did not cause death.
- Any defenses the tortfeasor would have had against the victim, had the latter lived (e.g., contributory negligence, assumption of the risk, self-defense), are available to the tortfeasor in the action that survives.

survival action An action brought on behalf of a decedent against a defendant (who did not cause the death of the decedent) to recover what the decedent would have recovered if he or she had not died.

A suit with these characteristics is called a **survival action.**

WRONGFUL DEATH

Common Law

Now we move to the situation in Case II presented at the beginning of this chapter: what happens when the victim of a tort dies *because* of the tort? Here we are talking about a tortious or wrongful death. At common law, a tort action for this death could not be brought against the wrongdoer. If, however, the act that caused the death of the victim constituted a crime, the wrongdoer might be prosecuted in a criminal court, but no civil tort action could be brought. If the wrongdoer committed a nondeadly tort against the victim or a tort against the property of a victim who was still alive, there *could* be recovery against the wrongdoer, but not if the latter had killed the victim. It was cheaper, therefore, to kill the victim!

Needless to say, statutes were passed to change this absurdity. Every state now has a remedy for wrongful death. The remedy is not the same in each state. Although your primary concern will be the law of your state, you will need to be aware of the major remedies available in other states; it is not uncommon for an office to work on a case involving the death of someone in another state.

Elsewhere in this book, we discuss the law of workers' compensation (Chapter 28). If an employee dies from an injury that arises out of and in the course of employment, compensation to heirs or relatives is received through the workers' compensation statute, whether or not the employer wrongfully caused the death. In most states, workers' compensation replaces any other civil remedy. Hence, the following discussion does not apply to death due to an employment accident or employment-related illness.

Recovery for Wrongful Death

States differ on how they allow recovery for wrongful death. Two common methods are

- enlarging the survival statute to include wrongful death, and
- enacting a wrongful death statute (Lord Campbell's Act).

Enlarging the Survival Statute to Include Wrongful Death We saw earlier that survival statutes have been passed to permit most kinds of tort actions to survive the death of the victim of the tort. In some states, the death of the victim caused by the tort is handled as follows:

- The tort action of the victim survives his or her death and covers damages that accrued up to the moment of death.
- Damages resulting from the death can be recovered in the same survival action.

No new cause of action is created because of the death. The victim's cause of action is continued by the personal representative of his or her estate. In this action, any

defense is available that could have been brought had the victim lived. The damages that are recoverable in this action usually include

- pain and suffering of the victim from the time of the injury to the time of death
- medical, hospital, and funeral expenses
- lost net earnings and savings the victim would have accumulated if he or she had lived to his or her life expectancy

Enacting a Wrongful Death Statute (Lord Campbell's Act) Most states create a *new* cause of action for designated relatives of the deceased victim, e.g., spouse and children. The action is called a **wrongful death action**. The statute creating this wrongful death cause of action is usually modeled after **Lord Campbell's Act** in England and is sometimes referred to as a "pure" death action, as distinguished from the enlarged survival action, which continues the victim's claim. The new cause of action is brought by a representative for the benefit of the relatives or beneficiaries or, in some states, by the beneficiaries themselves. The damages that are recoverable in this action are usually limited to **pecuniary** (i.e., money) losses. They cover the loss of the economic value of the support, services, and contributions that the beneficiaries would have received if the victim had lived to his or her life expectancy.

wrongful death action An action by a decedent's next of kin for their damages resulting from a wrongful injury that killed the decedent.

Lord Campbell's Act An early English statute giving certain relatives of a decedent a wrongful death claim for a tort that caused the death of the decedent.

pecuniary Pertaining to money.

Damages are *not* recoverable in this action for

- Pain and suffering of the victim, medical bills, lost wages, or any other loss that the victim would have had against the tortfeasor (damages for such items are recoverable in a separate survival action, which is often brought along with the beneficiaries' action—see the following discussion on Avoiding Double Recovery)
- Mental suffering and grief experienced by the survivor-beneficiaries because of the death of the victim, particularly due to the loss of companionship with the deceased (we will discuss companionship and consortium in greater detail in Chapter 22). Some states, however, have changed the rule and will allow recovery for such **nonpecuniary losses**

nonpecuniary losses Mental suffering, grief, and other noneconomic losses that cannot be measured in money.

Under most wrongful death statutes, the defendant can raise any defense he or she would have had against the victim if death had not occurred. For example, the defendant may assert that the death was not wrongful. The defendant may have caused the death—but not tortiously. There must be an underlying intentional, negligence, or strict liability tort before the beneficiaries can recover anything in the wrongful death action. Also, defenses of contributory negligence (if available in the state), assumption of the risk, or any of the privileges will usually defeat the wrongful death action. In most states, the statute of limitations runs from the time of death and not from the date of the injury.

AVOIDING DOUBLE RECOVERY

Some states have both a survival statute (covering the victim's pain and suffering, loss of earnings, medical expenses up to death, etc.) *and* a wrongful death statute (covering the beneficiaries' pecuniary loss of the support, services, and contributions that the victim would have provided them if he or she had not died). The survival action and the wrongful death action can usually be brought concurrently. When both actions are possible, there is a fear of double recovery, especially with respect to the lost earnings of the victim. The following describes the basic conflict and how it may be handled:

> An injured person's own cause of action in tort, which at common law would have ended abruptly at death, is now preserved and vested in his personal representative by means of a survival statute, one of which obtains in every

jurisdiction. The existence of such a measure side by side with a wrongful death provision has proved to be a source of concern arising from fear that a duplication of damages could result. Indeed such a fear is not without foundation: Whenever an injured victim while still alive can demonstrate that the impairment of his bodily condition is sufficiently serious to shorten his life expectancy he will become entitled to damages sufficient to replace the lost earnings that otherwise would have been in prospect for him. It is not to be expected that this right would be expunged in the event that death does indeed foreshorten his life before the award has been made. In theory, this element of loss should persist and remain available to his personal representative under a survival statute. If, however, to this survived claim for lost future earnings there were superadded a separate award for his dependents' loss of support under a [wrongful] death statute, the prospect of a duplication of damages would face the defendant. This dilemma has been dealt with in a bewildering variety of ways. In a few states a binding election must be made between a survival claim and an action for wrongful death (e.g., Ky. and Wyo.). Occasionally the survival suit is arbitrarily restricted to those claims of the deceased that were unrelated to his death (e.g., W. Va.). In other states the lawmakers have deliberately omitted a separate death statute, and lost future earnings in full are provided under the survival measure (e.g., Conn.). There are numerous other varieties in approach. The one that is most satisfactory and which has been most widely adopted is that of affording recognition of both the survival claim and the wrongful death claims but with damages for loss of earnings under the survival suit limited exclusively to those earnings that were lost between the time of accident and the moment of death. All pecuniary loss accruing thereafter must be recovered solely under the [wrongful] death statute. It is noteworthy, however, that funeral expenses, which do not accrue, of course, during the lifetime of the deceased, are frequently made recoverable by express provision in the survival statute.[1]

CASE

Cassano v. Durham

180 N.J. Super. 620, 436 A.2d 118 (1981)
Superior Court of New Jersey, Law Division, Passaic County

Background: *The plaintiff had a "live-in" relationship with decedent; they never married. He died intestate—without leaving a valid will. Following his death, she claimed benefits as the equivalent of a "surviving spouse" under the New Jersey intestacy statute and Wrongful Death Act. In the trial court, a motion for summary judgment has been made that would strike plaintiff's claim.*

Decision of Court: *The motion is granted. Only spouses can claim benefits under the Wrongful Death Act.*

OPINION OF COURT

Judge SCHWARTZ delivered the opinion of the court . . .

In this case the [plaintiff] had lived with decedent for seven years and they intended to get married. The court is asked to permit her to recover for her pecuniary loss as if she qualified as a "surviving spouse" under N.J.S.A. 3A:2A-34 of the intestacy statute. . . .

In *Wood v. State Farm Mutual Automobile Ins. Co.,* 178 N.J. Super. 607, 429 A.2d 1082 (App. Div. 1981) the court held that an economically independent companion who lived in the same home as the insured for three and one-half years before he suffered a vehicular accident and who married her almost two years later, had not been a member of her "family" residing in her household and therefore was not entitled to coverage under the personal injury protection provision of the insurance policy.

But even when a claimant relies upon the companion for support, the issue of dependency is irrelevant since the right of the spouse to partake of the benefits of the Wrongful Death Act is not conditioned on dependency. In this respect, it differs from the Worker's Compensation Act in which our Supreme Court in *Parkinson v. J. & S. Tool Co.,* 64 N.J. 159, 313 A.2d 609 (1974) recognized as a proper petitioner a live-in partner who had previously been married to and divorced from the decedent and who became entitled to the benefits of that statute having proved dependency upon the decedent who suffered death during and arising out of employment. . . .

Is it arbitrary to provide a remedy for a surviving spouse and to deny a like remedy for a live-in companion who may equally suffer as the result of the tort? There is no constitutional impediment to the legislative determination to designate one, who has entered into the bonds of matrimony with decedent, as a beneficiary under the Wrongful Death Act among those who will inherit under the intestacy statute. That is solely a legislative function and the court cannot enlarge the reach of the statute.

Changed attitudes toward marriage are temporal, reflecting the temper of the times as they may still relate to the permissiveness of the 1960s and the early '70s. But the reaction to freedom of thought as it extends to consensual sexual conduct outside of the family tradition has not found ready acceptance by the Legislature in areas where the stability and responsibility of family life may be affected.

It was in 1939 that the Legislature determined (now N.J.S.A. 37:1–10) that no marriage subsequently contracted shall be valid unless the contracting parties obtained a marriage license and the marriage was legally solemnized. This was an expression of public policy which precluded common law marital relationships acquired through cohabitation and matrimonial repute, and the statute has not been amended. . . .

The family has been the genesis of our society since the birth of civilization, and the laws of inheritance were intended to buttress the stability and continuance of the family unit. The preservation of familial law is so essential that where questions of inheritance, property, legitimacy of offspring and the like are involved, an adherence to conventional doctrine is demanded.

Since the live-in plaintiff cannot be classified as a "surviving spouse" under the legislative designation in the intestacy laws, and the Wrongful Death Act was intended to apply for the exclusive benefit of persons eligible to inherit under the succession provisions of the statute, the motion for summary judgment striking the claim of plaintiff shall be granted.

ASSIGNMENT 21.1

Would this case be decided in the same way if the decedent died the moment before he was scheduled to say "I do" to the plaintiff at the altar?

CHECK THE CITE

Donna Green, a high school student, was killed in an automobile accident for which the defendant was found negligent in a separate trial. Later, Donna's parents brought a wrongful death action against the defendant. In this action, the jury awarded no damages. The trial judge concluded that "it would be reasonable for this jury to come to (the) conclusion that the value of [Donna's] services to babysit or to dry dishes was far exceeded by the cost to the family of feeding, clothing and educating her." Why was this result rejected on appeal by the Supreme Court of New Jersey? What measure of damages did the Supreme Court say should govern actions for the wrongful death of a child? Read the case of *Green v. Bittner*, 85 N.J. 1, 424 A.2d 210 (N.J. 1980). To read the opinion online, (1) Go to FindACase (www.findacase.com). Select New Jersey. Run a citation search (424 for the Volume, A.2d for the reporter, and 210 for the page). (2) Run a citation search ("424 A.2d 210") or a party search (Green Bittner) in the Legal Opinions and Journals database of Google Scholar (scholar.google.com).

PROJECT

In Google, Bing, or another general search engine, run the following two searches:

(1) wrongful death action *aa*
(2) survival action *aa*

Substitute the name of your state for *aa* in the search (e.g., survival action Texas). Summarize the law in your state for wrongful death and survival actions. Who can bring them and what damages can be recovered in them?

ETHICS IN A TORTS PRACTICE

You are a paralegal at the law office of Robert Fitzgerald, Esq. The office represents Dan and Paula Gomez in their wrongful death action against Ace Trucking Company. One of its truck drivers killed John Gomez (Dan and Paula's son) in a collision. While interviewing Dan Gomez, he tells you that John played the lottery every day and hoped that he would win big one day so that he would never have to work. You receive a call from a newspaper reporter writing a story on the accident. The reporter asks you if John Gomez was a regular lottery player. You answer yes. What ethical problems (in addition to breach of confidentiality) might exist?

SUMMARY

A survival action is an action brought on behalf of a decedent against a defendant (who did not cause the death of the decedent) to recover what the decedent would have recovered if he or she had not died. Under survival statutes of most states, (1) personal torts that are invasions of tangible interests (e.g., bodily integrity) survive; (2) personal torts that are invasions of intangible interests (e.g., reputation or privacy) do not survive; (3) personal property torts and real property torts survive. The tort action that survives is the same action that the victim would have brought if he or she had lived.

When the tort causes the death of the victim, a state might enlarge its survival statute to allow the personal representative of the deceased's estate to recover damages for wrongful death in the survival action. Alternatively, the state might create a separate cause of action for wrongful death for designated relatives of the deceased. A wrongful death action is an action by a decedent's next of kin for their damages resulting from a wrongful injury that killed the decedent. Special provisions are often necessary to avoid double recovery for lost earnings (in the survival action) and loss of support (in the wrongful death action).

KEY TERMS

wrongful death *440*
tortious *440*
tortfeasor *440*
personal tort *440*
property tort *440*
estate *440*
personal representative *440*
common law *440*
at common law *441*
tangible *441*
intangible *441*
intestacy *441*
survival action *442*
wrongful death action *443*
Lord Campbell's Act *443*
pecuniary *443*
nonpecuniary losses *443*

REVIEW QUESTIONS

1. What is a wrongful death?
2. When is an act tortious?
3. What is the distinction between a personal tort and a property tort?
4. What is an estate?
5. Who is a personal representative?
6. What is meant by the phrases *common law* and *at common law*?
7. What is the distinction between a tangible and intangible interest?
8. At common law, what personal torts survived?
9. By statute in most states, what personal torts survived?
10. At common law, what real property torts survived?
11. By statute in most states, what real personal torts survived?
12. Describe the characteristics of survival actions for torts that survive.
13. What is intestacy?
14. What is a wrongful death action?
15. What are the two methods that states use to provide recovery for wrongful death?

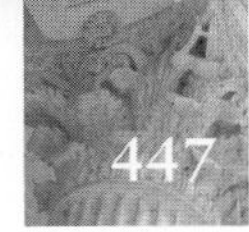

16. What is Lord Campbell's Act?
17. What damages are recoverable in a wrongful death action? What damages are not recoverable in such an action?
18. What is the danger of double recovery in survival and wrongful death actions, and what are some of the ways that states have solved this problem?

HELPFUL WEBSITES

- **Survival Actions**

  www.fsmlaw.org/kosrae/code/title06/t06p03c27.htm

  www.gencourt.state.nh.us/RSA/html/LVI/556/556-9.htm

- **Wrongful Death Actions**

  www.ehlinelaw.com/pages/3093/Wrongful-Death-Survival-Action-Differences.htm

  en.wikipedia.org/wiki/Wrongful_death_claim

ENDNOTE

1. W. Malone, *Injuries to Family, Social and Trade Relations* 44–45 (1979).

Student StudyWARE™ CD-ROM
For additional materials, please go to the student CD in this book.

CHAPTER

22

TORTS AGAINST AND WITHIN THE FAMILY

CHAPTER OUTLINE

- Torts Derived from Other Torts
- Torts Not Derived from Other Torts
- Prenatal Torts
- Wrongful Life, Birth, Pregnancy
- Wrongful Adoption
- Intrafamily Tort Immunity
- Other Family-Related Torts

CHAPTER OBJECTIVES

After completing this chapter, you should be able to:

- State the elements of an action for loss of consortium.
- Explain when an action for loss of services can be brought.
- Identify the major actions based on a broken heart or loss of love.
- Explain what a heart-balm statute is.
- State the kinds of damages sought in actions for wrongful life, birth, pregnancy, and adoption.
- Explain what is meant by intrafamily torts.
- State which torts are subject to the defense of intrafamily tort immunity.

TORTS DERIVED FROM OTHER TORTS

Loss of Consortium

consortium 1. The benefits that one spouse is entitled to receive from the other, e.g., companionship, services, affection, and sexual relations. 2. The companionship and affection a parent is entitled to receive from a child and that a child is entitled to receive from a parent.

loss of consortium Interference with the companionship, services, affection, and sexual relations one spouse receives from another.

Consortium is the companionship, love, affection, sexual relationship, and services (e.g., cooking, making repairs around the house) that a spouse is entitled to receive from his or her spouse. There can be a recovery for a tortious injury to consortium. At one time, only the husband could recover for **loss of consortium**. In every state, this view has been changed by statute or has been ruled unconstitutional as a denial of the equal protection of the law. Either spouse can now recover for loss of consortium.

EXAMPLE

- Rich and Ann are married.
- Paul, a stranger, injures Ann by negligently hitting her with his car.
- Ann sues Paul for negligence. She receives damages to cover her medical bills, lost wages, and pain and suffering.
- Rich then brings a *separate* action against Paul for loss of his wife's consortium. He receives damages to compensate him for whatever loss or impairment he can prove to the relationship he had with Ann before the accident—to the love, affection, sexual intercourse, and services that she gave him as his wife before the accident.

In Rich's action against Paul, Rich cannot recover for injuries sustained by Ann. Ann must recover for such injuries in her own action against Paul. (A spouse's action for loss of consortium is usually brought in the same suit brought by the other spouse for the latter's own damages.) Paul's liability to Rich is limited to the specific injuries sustained by Rich—the loss or impairment of his wife's consortium. If Ann loses her suit against Paul, e.g., because she was contributorily negligent, Rich will not be able to bring his consortium suit. To recover for loss of consortium, there must be an underlying successfully litigated tort.

Most states deny recovery for loss of consortium to individuals who are not married.

EXAMPLES

- Jim and Rachel are engaged to be married. The defendant negligently incapacitates Rachel the day before the wedding. Rachel sues the defendant to recover for her injuries.
- Mary and John have lived together for forty years. They have never married and do not live in a state that recognizes common law marriage. The defendant negligently incapacitates John, who sues the defendant to recover for his injuries.
- George and Bob are homosexuals who have lived together as a couple for ten years but have never married nor entered into a **domestic partnership** or **civil union**. The defendant negligently incapacitates Bob, who sues the defendant to recover for his injuries.

domestic partnership Two persons in a same-sex (or unmarried opposite-sex) relationship who are emotionally and financially interdependent and who register with the government to receive marriage-like benefits.

civil union A same-sex relationship with the same *state* benefits and responsibilities the state grants spouses in a marriage.

Clearly, Jim, Mary, and George have experienced a loss of consortium. They arguably have suffered in the same manner as Rich, whose wife, Ann, was negligently hit by Paul. The difference, however, is that Jim, Mary, and George (unlike Rich) were not married at the time their consortium was damaged. Most states deny an unmarried person the right to sue for loss of consortium. This may seem unfair, particularly to a couple who is hours away from being married. The law, however, must draw a line somewhere. A court would have a difficult time distinguishing between Jim and Rachel (a day away from their wedding) and an engaged couple whose wedding is one or two years away. What about someone six months or six weeks away? The practical problem of drawing the line plus the bias of the law in favor of marriage has led courts to limit the action for loss of consortium to married individuals.

If, however, two individuals have entered a valid domestic partnership or civil union, they *would* be granted most, if not all, the state rights accorded a married couple, including the right to sue for the loss of consortium.

The word *consortium* sometimes also refers to the normal companionship and affection that exists between a parent and a child. The right of a child to the companionship and affection of a parent is referred to as **parental consortium.** The right of a parent to the companionship and affection of a child is referred to as **filial consortium**.

parental consortium The right of a child to the normal companionship and affection of a parent.

filial consortium The right of a parent to the normal companionship and affection of a child.

EXAMPLES

- Bill is the father of Sam.
- Case 1: The defendant negligently incapacitates Bill, who sues the defendant to recover for Bill's injuries.
- Case 2: The defendant negligently incapacitates Sam, who sues the defendant to recover for Sam's injuries.

In the first case, Sam has also suffered a loss—a loss of parental consortium. Yet, most states do *not* allow suits for damage to this kind of consortium. Suppose, however, that the parent (Bill) dies from the defendant's negligence. There are some states whose wrongful death statutes give children the right to damages for the loss of companionship and affection they had with their parent (in addition to the financial losses caused by the death). But most states would *not* allow a suit for loss of parental consortium when the injured parent is still alive. (On wrongful death, see Chapter 21.)

In the second case, Bill has also suffered a loss—a loss of filial consortium. As we will see in a moment, parents can sue someone who interferes with their right to receive the services of their children, such as doing household chores. States differ, however, on the parent's right to recover for interference with the companionship and affection the parent has with a child—filial consortium. Many states deny such recovery. There are, however, a fair number of states that take a different position and allow recovery for interference with filial consortium.

Loss of Services and Earnings

A parent has the right to the services of his or her **unemancipated** child. This would include tasks such as cutting the grass and running errands for the household. (Unemancipated means legally dependent on one's parent or legal guardian. A child is **emancipated** if he or she becomes legally independent, such as by marrying.)

unemancipated Still under the legal control of a parent or other legal guardian.

emancipated Married or otherwise living independently with the express or implied consent of a parent or former legal guardian.

EXAMPLE

Mary is the twelve-year-old child of Victor and Helen. The defendant negligently injures Mary in a car accident. In a negligence action against the defendant, Mary can recover damages for her injuries.

Victor and Helen can also recover damages from the defendant for causing a **loss of services** by Mary to them. As a twelve-year-old who is dependent on her parents, Mary is unemancipated. She probably helps around the house. The parents can recover for any interference with such services that is wrongfully caused.

loss of services An action by a parent for interference with an unemancipated child's ability to perform household chores and other tasks for the parent.

Parents are also entitled to the earnings of their unemancipated children, such as from part-time jobs. If the defendant's negligence against the child interferes with the earning capacity of the child, the parents can recover for this loss.

TORTS NOT DERIVED FROM OTHER TORTS

At common law, there were a number of tort actions that could be brought by one family member because of what the defendant did with or to another family member:

- alienation of affections
- criminal conversation
- enticement of a spouse
- abduction or enticement of a child
- seduction

heart-balm statute A law abolishing heart-balm actions, which are actions based on a broken heart or loss of love (e.g., breach of promise to marry, alienation of affections, and criminal conversation).

To establish one of these causes of action, there is no need to prove an underlying tort; they are torts in their own right. Many states, however, have passed statutes (sometimes called **heart-balm statutes**) that have abolished some or all of these tort actions.

alienation of affections The tort of causing a diminishment of the marital relationship or interference with consortium rights between the plaintiff and his or her spouse.

Alienation of Affections

Elements

1. The defendant intended to diminish the marital relationship (love, companionship, and comfort) between the plaintiff and the latter's spouse.
2. Affirmative conduct by the defendant.
3. Affections between the plaintiff and spouse were in fact alienated.
4. The defendant caused the alienation (but for the defendant, the alienation would not have occurred, or the defendant was a substantial factor in producing the alienation).

criminal conversation The tort that occurs when the defendant has sexual relations with the plaintiff's spouse.

Criminal Conversation

Element

The defendant had sexual relations with the plaintiff's spouse (adultery).

enticement of a spouse A tort in which the defendant encourages the plaintiff's spouse to leave or to stay away from the plaintiff.

Enticement of a Spouse

Elements

1. The defendant intended to diminish the marital relationship between the plaintiff and the latter's spouse.
2. The defendant engaged in affirmative conduct either:
   a. to entice or encourage the spouse to leave the plaintiff's home, or
   b. to harbor the spouse and encourage the latter to stay away from the plaintiff's home.
3. The plaintiff's spouse left home.
4. The defendant caused the plaintiff to leave home or to stay away (but for what defendant did, the plaintiff would not have left home or stayed away; or, the defendant was a substantial factor in the spouse's leaving or staying away).

abduction or enticement of a child A tort involving serious interference with a parent's custody over his or her child.

Abduction or Enticement of a Child

Elements

1. The defendant intended to interfere with the parent's custody of the child.
2. Affirmative conduct by the defendant:
   a. to abduct or force the child from the parent's custody,
   b. to entice or encourage the child to leave the parent, or
   c. to harbor the child and encourage the latter to stay away from the parent's custody.

3. The child left the custody of the parent.
4. The defendant caused the child to leave or to stay away (but for what the defendant did, the child would not have left or stayed away; or, the defendant was a substantial factor in the child's leaving or staying away).

ASSIGNMENT 22.1

Olivia is the mother of Irene, who is married to George. Olivia had begged Irene not to marry George—to no avail. After the marriage and the birth of a son, Olivia warns Irene that George has a violent disposition. Irene and George separate. Irene takes their son to live with Olivia. Has Olivia committed any torts?

Seduction

seduction The tort of engaging in sexual relations with the plaintiff's minor daughter by force or with the consent of the daughter. (See glossary for an additional meaning.)

Element

The defendant had sex with the plaintiff's minor daughter by force or with the consent of the daughter.

CASE

Franklin v. Hill

264 Ga. 302, 444 S.E.2d 778 (1994)
Supreme Court of Georgia

Background: *Nancy Franklin sued her daughter's high school teacher, Andrew Hill, when he seduced her daughter. His defense was that the tort of seduction is unconstitutional because it applied to men only. The trial court agreed and dismissed the case. The mother appealed to the Supreme Court of Georgia.*

Decision on Appeal: *The tort is unconstitutional. Judgment of dismissal is affirmed.*

OPINION OF COURT

Justice FLETCHER delivered the opinion of the court:

This case involves the constitutionality of the state statute that gives parents a cause of action for the seduction of their unmarried daughter. We hold that OCGA [the Official Code of Georgia] § 51-1-16 is a gender-based classification that violates the equal protection clause of the Georgia Constitution because only men may be civilly liable for seduction under the statute.

Nancy Franklin sued her daughter's former high school teacher, Andrew Hill, seeking damages for Hill's alleged seduction of the daughter under OCGA § 51-1-16.[1] . . . Hill moved for summary judgment, challenging the constitutionality of the statute on equal protection grounds. The trial court declared the statute violated the equal protection clauses of the United States and Georgia constitutions and granted summary judgment. We affirm.

The protection of the equal protection clause in the State Constitution is similar to the protection provided in the Federal Constitution.[2] To withstand constitutional challenge, a gender-based classification "'must serve important governmental objectives and must be substantially related to achievement of those objectives.' " *Lamar v. State,* 243 Ga. 401, 254 S.E.2d 353 (1979) (quoting *Orr v. Orr,* 440 U.S. 268, 99 S. Ct. 1102, 59 L. Ed. 2d 306 (1979)). Applying this standard, this court has held unconstitutional several state laws that created a gender classification in violation of the federal equal protection clause. We have relied on the state's equal protection guarantee to invalidate a state statute that treated children differently based on the sex of their deceased parents. See *Tolbert v. Murrell,* 253 Ga. 566, 571, 322 S.E.2d 487 (1984) (finding wrongful death act violated equal protection by denying to children of deceased fathers rights granted to children of deceased mothers).

---

[1]The challenged statute provides: The seduction of a daughter, unmarried and living with her parent, whether followed by pregnancy or not, shall give a right of action to the father or to the mother if the father is dead, or absent permanently, or refuses to bring an action. No loss of services need be alleged or proved. . . . OCGA § 51-1-16.

[2]The equal protection clause in the Georgia Constitution provides: "Protection to person and property is the paramount duty of government and shall be impartial and complete. No person shall be denied the equal protection of the laws." Ga. Const. Art. I, Sec. I, Para. II (1983).

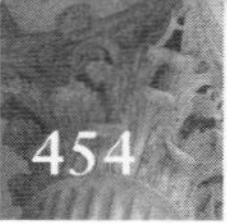

Hill argues that the seduction statute establishes a gender classification in three ways. First, only unmarried daughters, not sons, are protected from seduction; second, mothers are permitted to bring a seduction action only if the father is unable or unwilling to sue; and third, only men are liable for seduction. Because Hill limits his challenge to the third classification where his rights as a male are implicated, we do not address the constitutionality of the first two classifications. . . .

Seduction is defined as the "[a]ct of man enticing woman to have unlawful intercourse with him by means of persuasion, solicitation, promises, bribes, or other means without employment of force." *Black's Law Dictionary* p. 1218 (5th ed. 1979). This court has defined "seduction" as a term substantially similar to "debauchery." *Mosley v. Lynn,* 172 Ga. 193, 201, 157 S.E. 450 (1930). "'Seduction, as a civil injury, may generally be defined as the act of a man in inducing a virtuous woman to commit unlawful sexual intercourse with him.'" Id. at 201, 203, 157 S.E. 450 (quoting *Dwire v. Stearns,* 44 N.D. 199, 172 N.W. 69). Therefore, by definition the statute makes a gender classification in that only men may be liable for the seduction of unwed daughters. . . .

A gender-based classification violates equal protection only if it fails to serve important government interests that are substantially related to those interests. The mother argues that the seduction statute advances the important state interests of "protect[ing] females from the emotional and physical consequences of non-marital sexual intercourse," including unwanted pregnancies and the physical and emotional scars of seduction.

Although preventing unwanted pregnancies, particularly of minors, is a legitimate government interest, the seduction statute is not substantially related to that goal. First, the statute has no age limitation, such as restricting the claim to parents of minor children. Second, the statute does not give the cause of action to the girl or woman who has the unwanted pregnancy and endured the "scars," but instead gives the right only to the parent. Third, the statute does not restrict the claim to parents whose daughters become pregnant, but extends the claim to seduction "whether followed by pregnancy or not." . . . [T]he statute is aimed at compensating a father or mother for personal injuries suffered by the daughter's seduction.[3]

Rather than seeking to prevent the pregnancy of unwed daughters, the statute was passed to hold men civilly liable for corrupting the morals and compromising the chastity of unmarried women. Passed in 1863 at a time when women and children were the legal property of their husbands or fathers, the statute vindicates the outraged feelings of the father whose daughter's virtue has been ruined. See *Mosley,* 172 Ga. at 199, 157 S.E. 450. As Justice Lumpkin explained:

> Never, so help me God, while I have the honor to occupy a seat upon this bench, will I consent to control the Jury, in the amount of compensation which they may see fit to render a father for the dishonor and disgrace thus cast upon his family; for this atrocious invasion of his household peace. There is nothing like it, since the entrance of Sin and Death into this lower world.

Kendrick v. McCrary, 11 Ga. 603, 606 (1852) (quoted with approval in *Mosley,* 172 Ga. at 200, 157 S.E. 450). Based on the language, history, and judicial interpretation of the seduction statute, we conclude it does not bear a substantial relationship to any important government objective.

We hold that the statute, which by definition applies only to men, violates the equal protection of laws and must be struck down as unconstitutional. . . .

Judgment affirmed.

[3][As to the argument that the statute is] . . . related to the deterrence of unwanted pregnancies, . . . [note that] it does not cover the seduction of married women or any woman living in a household away from her parents, but does include single, divorced, and widowed women who are past child-bearing age.

ASSIGNMENT 22.2

a. Rewrite the Georgia statute (§ 51-1-16 found in footnote 1 of the case) so that it will not be subject to any constitutional objection mentioned by the court.
b. Are there any other tort actions against the teacher that should be considered?

PRENATAL TORTS

It is possible to commit a tort against an unborn child.

EXAMPLE

Mary is pregnant. While on the freeway one day, Tom negligently drives his car into Mary's car. The impact causes a head injury to the unborn child Mary is carrying.

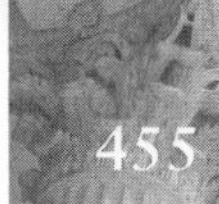

Mary, of course, can sue for her own injuries and for damage to her car caused by the defendant's negligence. Also, if the child is later born alive, an action can be brought on its behalf to cover the head injury. Suppose, however, the prenatal injury results in the death of the child. In such cases, many states will allow a wrongful death action to be brought (see Chapter 21), but only if the child was **viable** at the time of death. (*Viable* means able to live indefinitely outside the womb by natural or artificial support systems.)

viable Capable of surviving indefinitely outside the womb of the mother by natural or artificial support systems.

WRONGFUL LIFE, BIRTH, PREGNANCY

Doctors and pharmaceutical companies have been sued for negligence that results in the birth of an unwanted child. When the child is born deformed or otherwise impaired, two categories of suits have been attempted:

> **Wrongful life:** An action by or on behalf an unwanted child who is impaired; the child seeks its own damages in this action.
>
> **Wrongful birth**: An action by the parents of an unwanted child who is impaired; the parents seek their own damages in this action.

wrongful life An action by or on behalf of an unwanted impaired child for negligence that precluded an informed parental decision to avoid the child's conception or birth. The child seeks its own damages.

wrongful birth An action by parents of an unwanted impaired child for negligence in failing to warn them of the risks that the child would be born with birth defects. The parents seek their own damages.

Suppose, for example, a woman contracts German measles early in her pregnancy. Her doctor negligently advises her that the disease will not affect the health of the child. In fact, the child is born with severe defects caused by the disease. If the woman had known the risks, she would have had an abortion.

In such cases, a small number of states allow suits for wrongful life to cover the child's damages. The vast majority of states, however, do not. Courts are very reluctant to recognize a right *not* to be born. Several reasons account for this result. One is the enormous difficulty of calculating damages. According to the New Jersey court in a case we will examine in a moment, it is literally impossible to measure the difference in value between life in an impaired condition and the "utter void of nonexistence." Some courts also feel that allowing the suit might encourage unwanted children to sue for being born to a poverty-stricken family or to parents with criminal records. Finally, anti-abortion activists have argued that no one should be allowed to sue for missing the opportunity to have been aborted.

Wrongful birth cases, on the other hand, have been more successful. Here the parents sue for their own damages to cover their emotional distress and the cost of prenatal care and delivery. Courts disagree on whether other categories of damages (e.g., extra caretaking expenses due to the impairment) can be obtained in a wrongful-birth action.

Finally, we examine negligence that leads to the birth of an unwanted *healthy* child:

> **Wrongful pregnancy**: An action by the parents of an unwanted child who is healthy; the parents seek their own damages in this action.

wrongful pregnancy An action by parents of an unwanted healthy child for a wrong related to pregnancy such as negligent performance of a sterilization procedure. Also called wrongful conception.

Cases of wrongful pregnancy (also called wrongful conception) are allowed in most states. The most common example is a suit against a doctor for negligently performing a vasectomy or against a pharmaceutical company for producing defective birth control pills. Damages are limited to the expenses of prenatal care and delivery; they rarely extend to the costs of raising a healthy child. Furthermore, the unwanted healthy child is usually not allowed to bring the same kind of action in his or her own right.

CASE

Berman v. Allen

80 N.J. 421, 404 A.2d 8 (1979)
Supreme Court of New Jersey

Background: *Sharon Berman was born with Down's syndrome, a genetic defect formerly referred to as mongolism. The mother would have had an abortion if she had known this before birth. Doctors Allen and Attardi, specialists in gynecology and obstetrics, failed to tell her about the availability of amniocentesis as a technique to discover the presence of Down's syndrome. In this medical malpractice action, the parents sue for wrongful life on behalf of Sharon and for wrongful birth on their own behalf. The trial court granted the doctors a summary judgment because the plaintiffs failed to state a cause of action. The case is now on appeal before the Supreme Court of New Jersey.*

Decision on Appeal: *The child cannot sue for wrongful life, but the parents can sue for wrongful birth.*

OPINION OF COURT

Justice PASHMAN delivered the opinion of the court . . .

Plaintiffs allege that defendants deviated from accepted medical standards by failing to inform Mrs. Berman during her pregnancy of the existence of a procedure known as amniocentesis. This procedure involves the insertion of a long needle into a mother's uterus and the removal therefrom of a sample of amniotic fluid containing living fetal cells. Through "karyotype analysis," a procedure in which the number and structure of the cells' chromosomes are examined, the sex of the fetus as well as the presence of gross chromosomal defects can be detected. Prenatal diagnosis of genetic abnormalities is potentially available for approximately 60 to 90 metabolic defects, including Tay-Sachs disease and Down's syndrome. Recent studies indicate that amniocentesis is highly accurate in predicting the presence of chromosomal defects, and that the risk of even minor damage to mother or fetus deriving from the procedure is less than 1 percent.

Due to Mrs. Berman's age at the time of her conception [38], plaintiffs contend that the risk that her child, if born, would be afflicted with Down's syndrome was sufficiently great that sound medical practice at the time of pregnancy required defendants to inform her both of this risk and the availability of amniocentesis as a method of determining whether in her particular case that risk would come to fruition. Had defendants so informed Mrs. Berman, the complaint continues, she would have submitted to the amniocentesis procedure, discovered that the child, if born, would suffer from Down's syndrome, and had the fetus aborted.

As a result of defendants' alleged negligence, the infant Sharon, through her guardian *ad litem,* seeks compensation for the physical and emotional pain and suffering which she will endure throughout life because of her mongoloid condition. Mr. and Mrs. Berman, the child's parents, request damages in their own right both for the emotional anguish which they have experienced and will continue to experience on account of Sharon's birth defect, and the medical and other costs which they will incur in order to properly raise, educate and supervise the child. . . .

The claim for damages asserted on behalf of the infant Sharon has aptly been labeled a cause of action grounded upon "wrongful life." Sharon does not contend that absent defendants' negligence she would have come into the world in a normal and healthy state. There is no suggestion in either the pleadings below or the medical literature which we have scrutinized that any therapy could have been prescribed which would have decreased the risk that, upon birth, Sharon would suffer from Down's syndrome. Rather, the gist of the infant's complaint is that had defendants informed her mother of the availability of amniocentesis, Sharon would never have come into existence.

As such, this case presents issues different from those involved in malpractice actions where a plaintiff asserts that a defendant's deviation from sound medical practices *increased* the probability that an infant would be born with defects. Nor are we here confronted with a situation in which an individual's negligence while a child was in gestation caused what otherwise would have been a normal and healthy child to come into the world in an impaired condition. Here, defendants' alleged negligence neither caused the mongoloid condition nor increased the risk that such a condition would occur. . . . In essence, Sharon claims that her very life is "wrongful. . . ."

The primary purpose of tort law is that of compensating plaintiffs for the injuries they have suffered wrongfully at the hands of others. As such, damages are ordinarily computed by "comparing the condition plaintiff would have been in, had the defendants not been negligent, with plaintiff's impaired condition as a result of the negligence." *Gleitman v. Cosgrove,* 49 N.J. 22, 28, 227 A.2d 689, 692. In the case of a claim predicated upon wrongful life, such a computation would require the trier of fact to measure the difference in value between life in an impaired condition and the "utter void of nonexistence." *Gleitman,* supra. Such an endeavor, however, is literally impossible. As Chief Justice Weintraub noted, man, "who knows nothing of death or nothingness," simply cannot affix a price tag to non-life. *Gleitman* at 63.

Nevertheless, although relevant to our determination, we would be extremely reluctant today to deny the validity of Sharon's complaint solely because damages are difficult to ascertain. The courts of this and other jurisdictions have long held that where a wrong itself is of such a nature as to preclude the computation of damages with precise exactitude, it would be a "perversion of fundamental principles of justice to deny all relief to the injured [party], and thereby relieve the wrongdoer from making any amend for his acts." *Story Parchment Co. v. Paterson Parchment Paper Co.,* 282 U.S. 555, 563 (1931). To be sure, damages may not be determined by mere speculation or guess and, as defendants emphasize, placing a value upon non-life is not simply difficult—it is humanly impossible. Nonetheless, were the measure of damages our sole concern, it is possible that some judicial remedy could be fashioned which would redress plaintiff, if only in part, for injuries suffered.

Difficulty in the *measure* of damages is not, however, our sole or even primary concern. Although we conclude, as did the . . . majority [in *Gleitman v. Cosgrove*] that Sharon has failed to state an actionable claim for relief, we base our result upon a different premise [:] that Sharon has not suffered any damage cognizable at law by being brought into existence.

One of the most deeply held beliefs of our society is that life whether experienced with or without a major physical handicap is more precious than non-life. See *In re Quinlan,* 70 N.J. 10, 19 & n. 1, 355 A.2d 647 (1976). Concrete manifestations of this belief are not difficult to discover. The documents which set forth the principles upon which our society is founded are replete with references to the sanctity of life. The federal constitution characterizes life as one of three fundamental rights of which no man can be deprived without due process of law. U.S. Const., Amends. V and XIV. Our own state constitution proclaims that the "enjoying and defending (of) life" is a natural right. N.J. Const. (1947), Art. I, § 1. The Declaration of Independence states that the primacy of man's "unalienable" right to life is a "self-evident truth." Nowhere in these documents is there to be found an indication that the lives of persons suffering from physical handicaps are to be less cherished than those of non-handicapped human beings.

State legislatures and thus the people as a whole have universally reserved the most severe criminal penalties for individuals who have unjustifiably deprived others of life. Indeed, so valued is this commodity that even one who has committed first degree murder cannot be sentenced to death unless he is accorded special procedural protections in addition to those given all criminal defendants. Moreover, it appears that execution is constitutionally impermissible unless the crime which a defendant has perpetrated was one which involved the taking of another's life. Again, these procedural protections and penalties do not vary according to the presence or absence of physical deformities in the victim or defendant. It is life itself that is jealously safeguarded, not life in a perfect state. . . .

We recognize that as a mongoloid child, Sharon's abilities will be more circumscribed than those of normal, healthy children and that she, unlike them, will experience a great deal of physical and emotional pain and anguish. We sympathize with her plight. We cannot, however, say that she would have been better off had she never been brought into the world. Notwithstanding her affliction with Down's syndrome, Sharon, by virtue of her birth, will be able to love and be loved and to experience happiness and pleasure[,] emotions which are truly the essence of life and which are far more valuable than the suffering she may endure. To rule otherwise would require us to disavow the basic assumption upon which our society is based. This we cannot do.

Accordingly, we hold that Sharon has failed to state a valid cause of action founded upon "wrongful life."

The validity of the parents' [own] claim for relief calls into play considerations different from those involved in the infant's complaint. As in the case of the infant, Mr. and Mrs. Berman do not assert that defendants increased the risk that Sharon, if born, would be afflicted with Down's syndrome. Rather, at bottom, they allege that they were tortiously injured because Mrs. Berman was deprived of the option of making a meaningful decision as to whether to abort the fetus, a decision which, at least during the first trimester of pregnancy, is not subject to state interference. See *Roe v. Wade,* 410 U.S. 113, 93 S. Ct. 705, 35 L. Ed. 2d 147 (1973). They thus claim that Sharon's "birth" as opposed to her "life" was wrongful.

Two items of damage are requested in order to redress this allegedly tortious injury: (1) the medical and other costs that will be incurred in order to properly raise, supervise and educate the child; and (2) compensation for the emotional anguish that has been and will continue to be experienced on account of Sharon's condition.

The . . . majority [in *Gleitman v. Cosgrove*] refused to recognize as valid a cause of action grounded upon wrongful birth. Two reasons underlay its determination. The first related to measure of damages should such a claim be allowed. In its view,

> In order to determine [the parents'] compensatory damages a court would have to evaluate the denial to them of the intangible, unmeasurable, and complex human benefits of motherhood and fatherhood and weigh these against the alleged emotional and money injuries. Such a proposed weighing is . . . impossible to perform. . . . [*Gleitman,* 49 N.J. at 29, 227 A.2d at 693]

Second, even though the Court's opinion was premised upon the assumption that Mrs. Gleitman could have legally secured an abortion, the majority concluded that "substantial [public] policy reasons" precluded the judicial allowance of tort damages "for the denial of the opportunity to take an embryonic life." 49 N.J. at 30, 227 A.2d at 693.

In light of changes in the law which have occurred in the 12 years since *Gleitman* was decided, the second ground relied upon by the *Gleitman* majority can no longer stand in the way of judicial recognition of a cause of action founded upon wrongful birth. The Supreme Court's ruling in *Roe v. Wade* clearly establishes that a woman possesses a constitutional right to decide whether her fetus should be aborted, at least during the first trimester of pregnancy. Public policy now supports, rather than militates against, the proposition that she not be impermissibly denied a meaningful opportunity to make that decision.

As in all other cases of tortious injury, a physician whose negligence has deprived a mother of this opportunity should be required to make amends for the damage which he has proximately caused. Any other ruling would in effect immunize from liability those in the medical field providing inadequate guidance to persons who would choose to exercise their constitutional right to abort fetuses which, if born, would suffer from genetic defects. Accordingly, we hold that a cause of action founded upon wrongful birth is a legally cognizable claim.

Troublesome, however, is the measure of damages. As noted earlier, the first item sought to be recompensed is the medical and other expenses that will be incurred in order to properly raise, educate and supervise the child. Although these costs were "caused" by defendants' negligence in the sense that but for the failure to inform, the child would not have come into existence, we conclude that this item of damage should not be recoverable. In essence, Mr. and Mrs. Berman desire to retain all the benefits inhering in the birth of the child, i.e., the love and joy they will experience as parents while saddling defendants with the enormous expenses attendant upon her rearing. Under the facts and circumstances here alleged, we find that such an award would be wholly disproportionate to the culpability involved, and that allowance of such a recovery would both constitute a windfall to the parents and place too unreasonable a financial burden upon physicians.

The parents' claim for emotional damages stands upon a different footing. In failing to inform Mrs. Berman of the availability of amniocentesis, defendants directly deprived her and, derivatively, her husband of the option to accept or reject a parental relationship with the child and thus caused them to experience mental and emotional anguish upon their realization that they had given birth to a child afflicted with Down's syndrome. We feel that the monetary equivalent of this distress is an appropriate measure of the harm suffered by the parents deriving from Mrs. Berman's loss of her right to abort the fetus. . . .

[W]e do not feel that placing a monetary value upon the emotional suffering that Mr. and Mrs. Berman have and will continue to experience is an impossible task for the trier of fact. . . . [C]ourts have come to recognize that mental and emotional distress is just as "real" as physical pain, and that its valuation is no more difficult. Consequently, damages for such distress have been ruled allowable in an increasing number of contexts. Moreover . . . to deny Mr. and Mrs. Berman redress for their injuries merely because damages cannot be measured with precise exactitude would constitute a perversion of fundamental principles of justice.

Consequently, we hold that Mr. and Mrs. Berman have stated actionable claims for relief. Should their allegations be proven at trial, they are entitled to be recompensed for the mental and emotional anguish they have suffered and will continue to suffer on account of Sharon's condition. Accordingly, the judgment of the trial court is affirmed in part and reversed in part, and this case remanded for a plenary trial.

ASSIGNMENT 22.3

a. Did the two doctors owe a duty of care to Sharon Berman? Why or why not?
b. Assume that the doctors owed Sharon a duty and that it was breached by a failure to render competent medical advice and services in connection with the pregnancy. What harm did the doctors cause Sharon? They clearly did not cause the Down's syndrome. What was Sharon's loss?

WRONGFUL ADOPTION

Suppose that an adoption agency misrepresents the physical or mental health of a child or misrepresents the medical history of the child's birth family.

EXAMPLE

Alice and Stan Patterson want to adopt a child. They go to the Riverside Adoption Agency (RAA), which introduces them to Irene, an infant available for adoption. The Pattersons adopt Irene. Before the adoption, RAA told the Pattersons that Irene did not have any genetic disorders. This turned out to be false. Also, RAA knew that Irene had phenylketonuria (PKU) (a disorder that affects how the body processes protein), but they did not inform the Pattersons of this. After Irene has been living with the Pattersons for a while, they discover that she has severe medical and psychological problems.

Can the Pattersons sue RAA for damages covering the increased cost of child rearing? The period for challenging the adoption itself may have passed. Furthermore, the adoptive parents may have bonded with the child and do not want to "send" the child back even if it were possible to annul or abrogate the adoption. In such cases, some states have allowed the adoptive parents to sue, particularly when they made clear to the agency that they did not want to adopt a problem child. Their argument is that they would not have adopted the child if they had been presented with all the facts. They cannot expect a guarantee that the child will be perfect. But they are entitled to available information that might indicate a significant likelihood of future medical or psychological problems. The failure to provide such information may constitute the tort of **wrongful adoption.** In an action for this tort, the adoptive parents sue the adoption agency for wrongfully stating or failing to disclose available facts on the health or other condition of the child (the adoptee) that would have been relevant to their decision of whether to adopt.

wrongful adoption Wrongfully stating or failing to disclose to prospective adoptive parents any available facts on the health or other condition of a child that would be relevant to their decision to adopt the child.

intrafamily tort A tort committed by one family member against another.

immunity The treatment of wrongful conduct as nonwrongful. A complete defense to a tort claim whether or not the defendant committed the tort. (See glossary for additional definitions.)

INTRAFAMILY TORT IMMUNITY

Finally, we consider **intrafamily torts**, which are torts committed by one family member against another. Historically, an intrafamily **immunity** existed for most of these torts. (An immunity is a defense that prevents someone from being sued for what would otherwise be wrongful conduct.) Courts have always been reluctant to permit tort actions among any combination of wife, husband, and unemancipated child. When the law prevents family members from suing each other for certain torts, the prohibition is called the **intrafamily tort immunity.** It covers suits between spouses, although the prohibition on spouses has its own name—**interspousal immunity** or husband–wife immunity.

The reluctance to allow family members to sue each other is based on the theory that family harmony will be threatened if members know they can sue each other in tort. If the family carries **liability insurance**, there is also a fear that family members will fraudulently try to collect under the policy by fabricating tort actions against each other. A more technical and brutal reason was given at common law for why husbands and wives could not sue each other—the husband and wife were considered to be one person, and that one person was the husband! Hence, to allow a suit between spouses would theoretically amount to one person suing himself. With the passage of the **Married Women's Property Acts** and the enforcement of the laws against sex discrimination, a wife now retains her separate identity so that she can sue and be sued like anyone else.

Reform in the law, however, has not meant that intrafamily tort immunity no longer exists. A distinction must be made between a **personal tort** (one that injures a person's body, reputation, or feelings, e.g., battery) and a **property tort** (one that damages a person's real property or personal property, e.g., conversion). For torts against property, most states allow suits between spouses and between parent and child. Many states, however, retain the immunity in some form when the suit involves a tort against the person. The state of the law is outlined in Exhibit 22–1.

intrafamily tort immunity Family members cannot sue each other for designated categories of torts.

interspousal immunity Spouses cannot sue each other for personal torts, e.g., battery. Also called husband–wife immunity.

liability insurance Insurance in which the insurer agrees to pay, on behalf of an insured, damages the latter is obligated to pay to a third party because of his or her legal liability to the third person for committing a tort or other wrong.

Married Women's Property Acts Statutes removing legal disabilities on married women, e.g., the right to sue and the right to convey property in their own right.

personal tort A tort that injures a person's body, reputation, or feelings.

property tort A tort that damages a person's real property or personal property.

Exhibit 22–1
Intrafamily torts.

Spouse against Spouse

1. *Property torts.* In most states, spouses can sue each other for intentional or negligent damage to their property, e.g., negligence, trespass, conversion. (Negligence, of course, can be committed against the person or against property.)
2. *Personal torts.* In some states, spouses cannot sue each other for intentional or negligent injury to their person, e.g., negligence, assault, battery.
3. *Personal torts.* Some states will permit personal tort actions if the man and woman are divorced or if the tort is covered by liability insurance. (Note that some insurance policies have a "family exclusion clause" that denies liability coverage among family members living in the same household.)
4. *Personal torts.* Some states will permit intentional tort actions against the person to be brought by spouses against each other, but continue to forbid negligence actions for injury to the person.

Exhibit 22–1
(Continued)

Child against Parent(s)

1. *Property torts.* In all states, a child can sue the parent for intentional or negligent damage caused by the parent to the child's property, e.g., negligence, trespass, conversion.
2. *Personal torts.* In many states, a child cannot sue a parent for intentional or negligent injury caused by the parent to the child's person, e.g., negligence, assault, battery, particularly in cases where the parent was disciplining the child. Parents have a privilege to discipline their children.
3. *Personal torts.* If the child is emancipated (e.g., married, member of the armed forces, self-supporting), the child in all states can sue the parent for intentional or negligent injury caused by the parent to the child's person, e.g., negligence, assault, battery.
4. *Personal torts.* Some states will permit any child (emancipated or not) to sue the parent for intentional torts causing injury to the person, but continue to forbid actions for negligence causing injury to the person.
5. *Personal torts.* A few states allow the child to sue the parent for all intentional torts causing injury to the person, except where a tort arises out of the parent's exercise of discipline over the child.

Other Related Persons

Brothers and sisters, aunts and uncles, grandparents and grandchildren, and other relatives can sue each other in tort. The restrictions imposed on spouse suits and child suits do not apply to tort actions involving other relatives.

ASSIGNMENT 22.4

Dave knows that he has contagious genital herpes, but does not tell Alice, who contracts the disease from Dave. Can Alice sue Dave for battery? For intentional infliction of emotional distress? For misrepresentation? Does it make any difference whether the disease was communicated before or after Dave and Alice were married? Does it make any difference that they are now divorced?

OTHER FAMILY-RELATED TORTS

vicarious liability Liability imposed on a person because of the conduct of another, based solely on the status of the relationship between the two. The person liable is not the person whose conduct led to the liability.

negligent entrustment Carelessly allowing the use of a vehicle, tool, or other object by someone who poses an unreasonable risk of harm to others.

At the end of Chapter 14, we discussed the extent to which parents are liable for the torts of their children. Unless modified by statute, parents are not **vicariously liable** for the torts of their children. A parent may be independently liable for negligence if, for example, the parent does not exercise reasonable care to supervise a child with known dangerous propensities. A parent can also be liable for **negligent entrustment**—carelessly allowing the use of a vehicle, tool, or other object by a child or other person who poses an unreasonable risk of harm to others.

CHECK THE CITE

The following quote is from the opening paragraph of an opinion of the Supreme Court of California:

> This case presents the question of whether a child born with an hereditary affliction may maintain a tort action against a medical care provider who—before the child's conception—negligently failed to advise the child's parents of the possibility of the hereditary condition, depriving them of the opportunity to choose not to conceive the child.

How did the court answer this question, and how does its answer differ from the answer given by the Supreme Court of New Jersey in the *Berman* case you read in this chapter? To find out, read *Turpin v. Sortini*, 31 Cal.3d 220, 643 P.2d 954, 182 Cal. Rptr. 337 (Cal. 1982). To read the opinion online, (1) Go to the site of the Supreme Court of California (www.courtinfo.ca.gov/courts/supreme). Click Opinions. Then click Searchable Opinions 1850–Present. Follow the instructions on cookies and click Continue. Click View Opinions after deciding whether to accept the terms of proceeding. In the citation box, enter 31 for Cal.3d and enter 220 for the page. (2) Go to FindACase (www.findacase.com). Select California. Run a standard search (Turpin Sortini) after following the instructions for proceeding. (3) Run a citation search ("643 P.2d 954") or a party search (Turpin Sortini) in the Legal Opinions and Journals database of Google Scholar (scholar.google.com).

PROJECT

In Google, Bing, or another general search engine, run the following search: *aa* "loss of consortium" (substitute the name of your state for *aa* in the search, e.g., Georgia "loss of consortium"). Write a short essay in which you describe the circumstances under which someone can claim consortium damages in your state. You can consult as many websites as you wish, but you must quote from at least three separate sites, only one of which can be a law firm site.

ETHICS IN A TORTS PRACTICE

You are a paralegal working in the law office of Emerson & Emerson, which represents Barbara Kirkland in a wrongful pregnancy case. Barbara is very pleased with your performance in the case. On your birthday, she gives you her time-share apartment by the lake. She asks one of the attorneys at Emerson & Emerson to draft the needed documents to finalize this gift to you. What ethical problems, if any, might exist?

SUMMARY

Loss of consortium is an interference with the companionship, services, affection, and sexual relations one spouse receives from another. When a parent is injured, most states do not recognize an action for loss of parental consortium in which a child sues for tortious interference with the normal companionship and affection children have with their parents. When a child is injured, states differ on whether parents can sue for tortious interference with filial consortium, the normal companionship and affection parents have with their children. An action for loss of services can be brought by a parent against a defendant who has tortiously injured an unemancipated child to the extent that the child cannot render services that rightfully are due the parent. Parents can also recover for wrongful interference with their right to the earning capacity of their unemancipated children.

Other torts against the family include alienation of affections, criminal conversation, enticement of a spouse, abduction or enticement of a child, and seduction. Many states, however, have abolished these torts via heart-balm statutes.

Unborn children can sue for prenatal injuries. If the child dies from the injuries, many states allow a wrongful death action if the child was viable at the time of death. Courts are reluctant to allow an unwanted impaired child to bring an action for wrongful life for his or her own damages in being negligently born. Wrongful birth actions in which parents seek damages for negligence in the birth of an unwanted impaired child are usually permitted, as are wrongful pregnancy actions, in which parents seek damages for negligence in the birth of an unwanted healthy child. The failure of an adoption agency to give prospective adoptive parents available information about the health or other condition of the prospective adoptee may constitute the tort of wrongful adoption.

Intrafamily property torts are often treated differently from intrafamily personal torts. Generally, spouses can sue each other for negligent or intentional damage to property. The same is true for wrongful damage caused by the parent to a child's property. There is no immunity for property torts. For torts against the person, in some states, one spouse cannot sue another, and an unemancipated child cannot sue a parent; immunity does apply to torts against the person in such states. There are some exceptions. For example, many states grant this immunity only for negligent injury to the person; thus, any family member can sue another for intentional injury to the person in such states. Other family members such as siblings and other relatives do not have intrafamily tort immunity. Unless modified by statute, parents are not vicariously liable for the torts of their children. A parent may be independently liable for a child's torts if there has been negligent supervision or negligent entrustment.

KEY TERMS

consortium *450*
loss of consortium *450*
domestic partnership *450*
civil union *450*
parental consortium *451*
filial consortium *451*
unemancipated *451*
emancipated *451*
loss of services *451*
heart-balm statute *452*
alienation of affections *452*
criminal conversation *452*
enticement of a spouse *452*
abduction or enticement of a child *452*
seduction *453*
viable *455*
wrongful life *455*
wrongful birth *455*
wrongful pregnancy *455*
wrongful adoption *459*
intrafamily tort *459*
immunity *459*
intrafamily tort immunity *459*
interspousal immunity *459*
liability insurance *459*
Married Women's Property Acts *459*
personal tort *459*
property tort *459*
vicarious liability *460*
negligent entrustment *460*

REVIEW QUESTIONS

1. What is consortium?
2. When can an action for loss of consortium be brought?
3. What is a domestic partnership? A civil union?
4. What are parental consortium and filial consortium, and when can suits be brought for interference with them?
5. What is an emancipated child?
6. Who is entitled to the services and earnings of a child?
7. What are the elements of an action for alienation of affections?
8. What are the elements of an action for criminal conversation?
9. What are the elements of an action for enticement of a spouse?
10. What are the elements of an action for abduction or enticement of a child?
11. What are the elements of an action for seduction?
12. What is a heart-balm statute?
13. How can a tort be committed against an unborn child?
14. What is an action for wrongful life?
15. Why are most courts against allowing an action for wrongful life?
16. What is an action for wrongful birth?
17. What is an action for wrongful pregnancy?
18. What is an action for wrongful adoption?
19. What is an intrafamily tort?
20. What is an immunity?
21. What is intrafamily tort immunity?
22. What is liability insurance?
23. What is a Married Women's Property Act?
24. What is the distinction between a personal tort and a property tort?
25. What torts can one spouse commit against another?
26. What torts can a parent commit against his or her child?
27. What torts can other relatives commit against each other?
28. Is a parent vicariously liable for the torts of his or her child?
29. When is a parent independently liable for the torts of his or her child?

HELPFUL WEBSITES

- **Loss of Consortium**
  en.wikipedia.org/wiki/Loss_of_consortium
  www.newyorkinjurycasesblog.com (type consortium in the search box)
  www.txinjuryblog.com (type consortium in the search box)
- **Heart-Balm Statutes**
  www.divorcesource.com/NC/ARTICLES/gilpin11.html
  en.wikipedia.org/wiki/Alienation_of_affections
- **Intrafamily Tort Immunity**
  www.querrey.com/assets/attachments/271.pdf
  www.jud.ct.gov/LawLib/Notebooks/Pathfinders/SpousalImmunity/spousal.htm

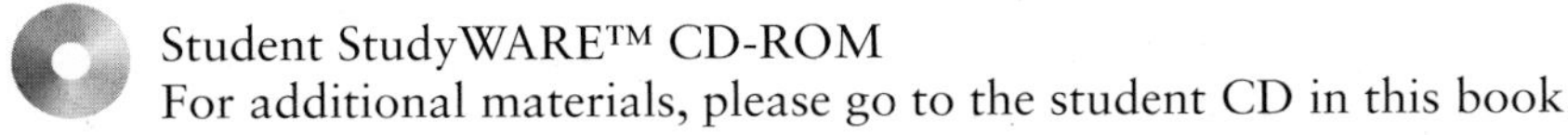

Student StudyWARE™ CD-ROM
For additional materials, please go to the student CD in this book.

CHAPTER

23

TORTS CONNECTED WITH LAND

CHAPTER OUTLINE

- Introduction
- Nuisance
- Traditional Negligence Liability

CHAPTER OBJECTIVES

After completing this chapter, you should be able to:

- Identify the variety of plaintiffs and defendants who are often parties in premises liability litigation.
- State the elements of an action for trespass to land.
- Distinguish between a private and a public nuisance.
- Describe the nature of a private nuisance, the main ways in which it can be created, who can sue, and the defenses that are available.
- Explain the components of reasonableness in determining whether an interference is unreasonable.
- Describe the nature of a public nuisance, the main ways in which it can be created, who can sue, and the defenses that are available.
- State the duty owed by occupiers to persons outside the land.
- State the duty owed by occupiers to trespassers, licensees, and invitees.
- Explain the components and legal consequences of the attractive nuisance doctrine.
- State the duty owed by a vendor to third persons injured on land sold to a vendee.
- State the duty owed by a landlord to third persons injured on leased land.

INTRODUCTION

interest A right, claim, title, or legal share in something; a right to have the advantage accruing from something. (See glossary for additional definitions.)

occupier Anyone in possession of land who has a right to possess it.

lessor A person who rents or leases property to another. A landlord.

lessee A person who rents or leases property from another. A tenant.

adverse possession A method of acquiring title to land without buying it or receiving it as a gift through a will or other traditional means. A trespasser can obtain title to land by occupying it in a hostile and visible manner for a designated number of continuous years.

possessory interest 1. A present or future right to possess land. 2. The right to exert control over specific property to the exclusion of others, whether or not the right is based on title.

premises liability The tort liability of landowners and others with possessory interests in land for injuries suffered due to conditions or activities on the land (premises).

trespass to land An intentional entry or intrusion on land in possession of another.

There are a variety of **interests** you can have in land based on your relationship to the land. (An interest is a right, claim, title, or legal share in something.) You can be:

- an **occupier**
- an owner who is occupying the land
- a nonoccupying owner who is the landlord (i.e., **lessor**) of a tenant (i.e., **lessee**) who is occupying the land
- a nonoccupying owner of vacant land
- a tenant (lessee) of the land
- a subtenant (sublessee) who is renting the land from the tenant
- a trespasser who now claims to own the land through **adverse possession**

This chapter is primarily about the torts that can be committed by and against individuals with these relationships to—these interests in—land. Most of these individuals have interests that are called **possessory interests.** Collectively, torts committed by or against persons with possessory interests are referred to as **premises liability.** The main torts we will consider are

- trespass to land
- nuisance due to trespass, negligence, or strict liability
- negligence

In Chapter 11, we examined a separate tort called strict liability of abnormally dangerous conditions or activities, which is often committed by occupiers of land.

We begin with an overview of **trespass to land**. (See Exhibit 23–1 for the elements of this tort.)

Plaintiffs in a Trespass Action

You do not have to own land to bring a suit against someone who is trespassing on the land. Plaintiffs in trespass cases can include tenants and anyone else who has an immediate right to possess the land (referred to as someone with a possessory interest). A major reason to bring a trespass action is to prevent someone from taking it away by *adverse possession*. This is a method of acquiring title to land without buying it or receiving it as a gift through a will or other traditional means. The law allows a trespasser to obtain title to land by occupying it in a hostile and visible manner for a designated number of continuous years. This method of acquiring title is designed to prevent speculators from buying land and leaving it vacant for long periods of time until its price increases. If these speculators want to avoid losing their land, they must bring trespass actions against anyone claiming it by adverse possession.

Act

The act required for trespass to land is any volitional movement of the body that leads to an intrusion on land. If someone trips on the sidewalk and falls onto the plaintiff's land, there is no trespass to land because there was no intrusion by a volitional movement of the body.

Exhibit 23–1
Elements of the tort of trespass to land.

1. An act
2. Intrusion on land
3. In possession of another
4. Intent to intrude
5. Causation of the intrusion

Intrusion on Land

Intrusion means physically going on the land, remaining on the land, going to a prohibited part of the land, or failing to remove goods from the land. If there are nonphysical entries (e.g., noise, odor, vibration, and light), courts are more likely to treat the entry under the category of nuisance, which we will consider shortly. (Alternatively, strict liability might apply to nonphysical entries. See Chapter 11 for a discussion of strict liability for abnormally dangerous conditions or activities.)

Intrusion Physically going on the land, remaining on the land, going to a prohibited part of the land, or failing to remove goods from the land. (See glossary for an additional definition.)

Land does not consist solely of ground surface. It also includes that portion of the air space above the surface and the land below the surface for which the plaintiff can claim a **reasonable beneficial use.** If a defendant throws a brick over the plaintiff's land, a trespass has occurred even if the brick never touches the plaintiff's home or ground. Assume that it finally lands beyond the plaintiff's property line. The plaintiff has the use of the air space immediately above the ground. Hence, there has been a trespass to land. The case is different, however, for the space one mile above the ground that is used by airplanes. The latter do not commit trespass. Similar reasoning applies to the space below the surface. There is no trespass to land if someone enters subterranean space of which the plaintiff can make no reasonable use.

reasonable beneficial use Space above and ground below the surface of land of which reasonable use can be made.

Possession of Another

As indicated, the plaintiff does not have to be the owner of the land. The tort protects anyone with a possessory interest, which could include a tenant. Most plaintiffs are in actual occupancy of the land with the intent to have exclusive control over the land. If, however, the land is unoccupied, the plaintiff must have the right to immediate occupancy.

Intent to Intrude

The **intent** required is the intent to enter. The defendant does not have to show that the plaintiff intended to violate defendant's rights. Hence, it is no defense for the plaintiff to be able to show that he or she was reasonable in thinking there was a right to enter. For example, the defendant has committed trespass to land even though the defendant reasonably, but mistakenly, believed that he or she owned the land. "The defendant is liable for an intentional entry although he acted in good faith, under the mistaken belief, however reasonable, that he was committing no wrong."[1]

intent (for trespass to land) The desire to intrude on the land of another or the knowledge with substantial certainty that this will result from what one does or fails to do.

Suppose that the defendant does not intend to enter the land but does so negligently or recklessly (e.g., the defendant does not see clearly visible "no trespassing" signs on the driveway where he steers his car). In the absence of an intent to intrude there is no trespass to land. The plaintiff may be able to bring a *negligence* cause of action, but negligence requires proof of actual harm or damage. When the entry is intentional, there is no need to prove actual harm; the entry itself is sufficient to establish trespass to land. If nothing more has occurred, the plaintiff can at least recover **nominal damages** and prevent someone else from acquiring title by adverse possession. But in a negligence action, actual harm or damage is required, as we saw in Chapter 16.

nominal damages A trifling sum (e.g., $1) awarded to the plaintiff because there was no significant loss or injury suffered, although a technical invasion of rights did occur.

Finally, see Exhibit 6–2 in Chapter 6 on the **transferred-intent rule.** Trespass to land is one of the five torts that can be committed when the defendant intended a different tort against someone other than the plaintiff.

transferred-intent rule The defendant may be liable for certain torts committed against the plaintiff even if the defendant intended to commit a different tort against the plaintiff (unintended tort) and even if the defendant intended to commit the tort against a different person (unintended plaintiff). (Does not apply to all torts. See Exhibit 6–2 in Chapter 6.)

Causation of the Intrusion

The plaintiff must show that but for what the defendant did, the intrusion would not have occurred, or that the defendant was a substantial factor in bringing about the intrusion.

ASSIGNMENT 23.1

Has a trespass to land been committed in the following cases?

a. Bill's truck collides with the trees on Tim's land.
b. Snow accumulating on the roof of Mary's house occasionally slides off the house and strikes the roof of an adjacent house, causing damage.

TRESPASS TO LAND CHECKLIST

Definitions, Relationships, Paralegal Roles, and Research References

Category
Trespass to land is an intentional tort.

Interest Protected by This Tort
The interest in the exclusive possession of land.

Elements of This Tort

1. An act
2. Intrusion on land
3. In possession of another
4. Intent to intrude
5. Causation of the intrusion

Definitions of Major Words/Phrases in These Elements

Act: A voluntary movement of the body that leads to the intrusion.

Intrusion:

a. Physically going on the land,
b. Remaining on the land,
c. Going to a prohibited portion of the land, or
d. Failing to remove goods from the land.

Possession:

a. Actual occupancy with intent to have exclusive control over the land, or
b. The right to immediate occupancy when no one else is actually occupying it with intent to control it.

Intent to Intrude: The desire to intrude on the land or the knowledge with substantial certainty that an intrusion will result from what you do or fail to do.

Causation: But for what the defendant did, the intrusion would not have occurred, or the defendant was a substantial factor in producing the intrusion.

Major Defenses and Counterargument Possibilities That Need to Be Explored

1. The defendant did not voluntarily go on the land, remain on the land, go to a prohibited portion of the land, or fail to remove goods from the land.
2. The plaintiff did not have possession of the land or the right to immediate possession.
3. The plaintiff had no reasonably beneficial use of the land that the defendant entered (e.g., the air space over the land).
4. There was no intent to intrude: the defendant did not desire to intrude or know with substantial certainty that an intrusion would result from what the defendant did.
5. The defendant did not cause the intrusion (but for what the defendant did or failed to do, the intrusion would have occurred anyway; the defendant was not a substantial factor in bringing about the intrusion).
6. The plaintiff consented to the defendant's intrusion (on the defense of consent, see Chapter 27).
7. The intrusion occurred while the defendant was defending property (on necessity and other self-help privileges, see Chapter 27).

TRESPASS TO LAND CHECKLIST *(Continued)*

8. The intrusion occurred while the defendant was abating a nuisance (see discussion of this self-help privilege later in this chapter).
9. The plaintiff's suit against the government for trespass committed by a government employee may be barred by sovereign immunity (on sovereign immunity, see Chapter 27).
10. The plaintiff's suit against the government employee for trespass may be barred by official immunity (on official immunity, see Chapter 27).
11. The plaintiff's suit against the charitable organization for trespass committed by someone working for the organization may be barred by charitable immunity (on charitable immunity, see Chapter 27).

Damages
Actual harm or damage to the land does not have to be shown for a plaintiff to maintain an action for trespass to land. If actual harm or damage *was* done to the land, the plaintiff can recover compensatory damages, e.g., cost or repair. If no harm or damage was done (a technical violation only), nominal damages can be recovered. If the defendant acted out of hatred and malice, punitive damages are possible. (On the categories of damages, see Chapter 16.)

Relationship to Criminal Law
It may be a crime in certain states to enter designated land, e.g., government property.

Relationship to Other Torts
Negligence: If the defendant does not intentionally enter the plaintiff's land, the defendant may have entered negligently. The tort of negligence is committed if actual harm or damage results from the negligent entry.
Nuisance: The defendant may commit a private or public nuisance while entering the plaintiff's land.
Strict Liability for Abnormally Dangerous Activities: The defendant may enter the land while engaged in abnormally dangerous activities, which could be the basis of strict liability.

Federal Law

a. Under the Federal Tort Claims Act, the United States government *will* be liable for trespass to land committed by one of its federal employees within the scope of employment (respondeat superior). (See Exhibit 27–7 in Chapter 27.) (Most states have their own statutes that cover when tort claims can be made against the state for trespass to land and other torts committed by state government employees. Such claims are also covered in Chapter 27.)
b. There may be liability under the Civil Rights Act if the trespass to land was committed while the defendant was depriving the plaintiff of a federal right under color of state law. (See Exhibit 27–9 in Chapter 27.)

Employer–Employee (Agency) Law
A private (non-government) employee who commits a trespass to land is personally liable for this tort. His or her employer will *also* be liable for trespass to land if the conduct of the employee was within the scope of employment (respondeat superior). The employee must be furthering a business objective of the employer at the time. Intentional torts such as trespass to land, however, are often outside the scope of employment. If so, only the employee is liable for the trespass to land. (On the factors that determine the scope of employment, see Exhibit 14–9 in Chapter 14.)

Paralegal Roles in Trespass to Land Litigation
(See also Exhibit 3–1 in Chapter 3, Exhibit 20–4 in Chapter 20, and Exhibit 29–1 in Chapter 29.)

Fact finding (help the office collect facts relevant to prove the elements of trespass to land, the elements of available defenses, and extent of injuries or other damages):
- client interviewing
- field investigation
- online research (e.g., identity of owners of land)

TRESPASS TO LAND CHECKLIST *(Continued)*

File management (help the office control the documents involved in a trespass to land litigation):
- open client file
- enter case data in computer database
- maintain file documents

Litigation assistance (help the trial attorney prepare for a trespass to land trial and appeal, if needed):
- draft discovery requests
- draft answers to discovery requests
- draft pleadings
- digest and index discovery documents
- help prepare, order, and manage trial exhibits
- prepare trial notebook
- draft notice of appeal
- order trial transcript
- cite-check briefs
- perform legal research

Collection/enforcement (help the trial attorney for judgment creditor to collect the damages award or to enforce other court orders at the conclusion of the trespass to land case):
- draft postjudgment discovery requests
- conduct field investigation to monitor compliance with judgment
- perform online research (e.g., location of defendant's business assets)

Research References for Trespass to Land

Digests
In the digests of West Group, look for case summaries on trespass to land under key topics such as:

Trespass
Forcible Entry and Detainer
Ejectment
Landlord and Tenant
Torts
Damages
Adverse Possession
Animals

Corpus Juris Secundum
In this legal encyclopedia, see the discussion under topic headings such as:

Trespass
Forcible Entry and Detainer
Ejectment
Landlord and Tenant
Torts
Damages
Adverse Possession

American Jurisprudence 2d
In this legal encyclopedia, see the discussion under topic headings such as:

Trespass
Property
Damages
Forcible Entry and Detainer
Ejectment
Landlord and Tenant
Torts
Adverse Possession
Animals

Legal Periodical Literature
There are two index systems to use to locate legal periodical literature on trespass to land:

Index to Legal Periodicals and Books (ILP)
See Literature in *ILP* under subject headings such as:
Trespass
Forcible Entry and Detainer
Real Property
Air Law
Torts
Damages
Adjoining Landowners

Current Law Index (CLI)
See literature in *CLI* under subject headings such as:
Trespass
Torts
Riparian Rights
Real Property
Damages

TRESPASS TO LAND CHECKLIST *(Continued)*

Example of a legal periodical article you will find using *ILP* or *CLI:*

Tort Law—Trespass: Michigan Does Not Recognize a Cause of Action in Trespass for Airborne Particles, Noise, or Vibrations by Demrie Wilkinson, 78 University of Detroit Mercy Law Review 129 (2000).

A.L.R., A.L.R.2d, A.L.R.3d, A.L.R.4th, A.L.R.5th, A.L.R.6th, A.L.R. Fed., A.L.R. Fed. 2d
Use the *Index to Annotations* to locate annotations on trespass to land. In this index, check subject headings such as:

Trespass	Adverse Possession
Forcible Entry and Detainer	Torts
Real Property	Damages
	Air Space

Example of an annotation on trespass to land you can locate through this index:

Liability for Personal Injury or Death Caused by Trespassing or Intruding Livestock by James L. Rigelhaupt, 49 A.L.R.4th 710 (1987).

Words and Phrases
In this multivolume legal dictionary, look up *trespass to land, intrusion, land, real property, ejectment, detainer,* and every other word or phrase connected with trespass to land discussed in this section of the chapter. The dictionary will give you definitions of these words or phrases from court opinions.

CALR: Computer-Assisted Legal Research
Example of a query you could ask on Westlaw or on LexisNexis to try to find cases, statutes, or other legal materials on trespass to land: **trespass /s damages**

Example of search terms you can use on an Internet legal search engine such as the Public Library of Law (www.plol.org), Findlaw (www.findlaw.com), or Google Scholar (scholar.google.com): **"trespass to land"**

Example of a search you could use on standard search engines (www.google.com, www.bing.com, www.yahoo.com) to find material on this tort; law firms that describe the tort; and articles, cases, statutes, and other materials on the tort: **"trespass to land"**

More Internet sites to check for material on trespass to land and other torts:
www.hg.org/torts.html
www.megalaw.com/top/top.php (click "Intentional Torts," "Personal Injury Law," "Tort Law," and "Damages")
See also the online sites in Overview of Tort Law at the end of Chapter 1.

NUISANCE

The first obstacle to understanding this topic is to realize that the word **nuisance** has been very loosely used throughout the law. There is *no* separate tort of nuisance, although the language of many opinions would appear to indicate otherwise. Nuisance is a word that describes two different kinds of harm that are produced by some other tortious or wrongful conduct. The two kinds of harm are private nuisance and public nuisance. A **private nuisance** is an unreasonable interference with the use and enjoyment of private land. A **public nuisance** is an unreasonable interference with a right that is common to the general public.

There are a variety of ways that these interferences can be brought about:

- The interferences may be due to negligence.
- The interferences may be due to abnormally dangerous conditions or activities that impose strict liability.
- The interferences may be intentional.
- The interferences may be due to a violation of a statute.

nuisance The separate harms of private nuisance (an unreasonable interference with the use and enjoyment of private land) and public nuisance (an unreasonable interference with a right that is common to the general public).

private nuisance An unreasonable interference with the use and enjoyment of private land.

public nuisance An unreasonable interference with a right that is common to the general public.

Although nuisance is often thought to apply to land, only private nuisance is primarily concerned with land. In the main, public nuisance is a separate category of a wrong that often has nothing to do with land. As we shall see, however, there are some public nuisances that can also constitute private nuisances.

Private Nuisance

A private nuisance (see Exhibit 23–2 for its elements) is different from a trespass to land in that the latter protects one's interest in the exclusive possession of land, whereas the former protects one's right to the reasonable use and enjoyment of land. Of course, the same conduct of the defendant can constitute a private nuisance and a trespass to land, e.g., building a fence on the plaintiff's land without permission. In such cases, the plaintiff can sue either for trespass to land or for a private nuisance.

Exhibit 23–2
Elements of private nuisance.

Private Nuisance
1. An act
2. Unreasonable interference with the use and enjoyment
3. Of private land
4. Based on negligence, intent, or strict liability
5. Causation

We approach the subject of private nuisance through five basic questions:

1. What is the nature of a private nuisance? What type of harm does it cover?
2. How is it created?
3. Who can sue?
4. What remedies are available?
5. What defenses are available?

See Exhibit 23–3 for an overview of the law governing these questions.

1. What Is the Nature of a Private Nuisance and What Type of Harm Does It Cover?

There are a number of forms that the interference can take:

- loud noises
- vibrations from blasting
- odors or gases
- pollution of air, land, or water
- flooding
- damage to crops or to structures on the land
- keeping a house of prostitution next door
- bringing insects into the area
- constant knocking on the door, constant telephone calls

Any of these examples can interfere with the use and enjoyment of one's land. It is not necessary that the physical condition of the land be altered or damaged, although this will certainly qualify. Interference with use and enjoyment of land also occurs when the plaintiff's peace of mind is disturbed while on the land because of what the defendant has done or failed to do.

Of course, every interference with the use and enjoyment of land is not a private nuisance. It is not a private nuisance for one's relative to move into the state, no matter how upsetting this might be! The interference must be unreasonable. The determination of when this is so has caused the greatest difficulty in this area of the law. The difficulty arises when *both* plaintiff and defendant are claiming the

Exhibit 23–3
Private nuisance: An overview.

1. What type of harm does private nuisance cover?	1. Unreasonable interference with the use and enjoyment of private land.
2. What are the ways in which a private nuisance can be created?	2. a. Negligently causing unreasonable interference with the use and enjoyment of land. b. Intentionally causing unreasonable interference with the use and enjoyment of land. c. Strict liability in maintaining an abnormally dangerous condition or activity, which causes an unreasonable interference with the use and enjoyment of land. d. Violation of a statute, ordinance, or regulation.
3. Who can sue for the private nuisance?	3. Anyone who has a right to the use and enjoyment of the land, e.g., owner, tenant.
4. What remedies can be obtained when a private nuisance has been committed?	4. a. Damages (money). b. Injunction—if the unreasonable interference is threatened or is continuous. c. The plaintiff may be able to exercise the privilege to abate the nuisance (self-help).
5. What defenses are available?	5. a. Contributory negligence. This may be a defense if the defendant negligently created the unreasonable interference with the use and enjoyment of the land. Contributory negligence is not a defense if the defendant recklessly or intentionally created this interference. (Note: comparative negligence applies if the state no longer uses contributory negligence.) b. Assumption of the risk. This is a defense no matter how the defendant caused the unreasonable interference. c. Failure to mitigate damages. A plaintiff must mitigate damages no matter how the defendant produced the unreasonable interference. d. Official authorization. The government authorized or required the defendant's activity that caused the interference.

reasonable use and enjoyment of their own land. A delicate balancing process must be used to determine unreasonableness. There are a number of factors that a court will consider.

Factors to Consider When Determining Unreasonableness

- the gravity and character of the harm
- the social value of the use that the plaintiff is making of the land
- the character of the locality
- the extent of the burden on the plaintiff of avoiding or minimizing the interference
- the motive of the defendant
- the social value of the defendant's conduct that led to the interference
- the extent of the burden on the defendant of avoiding or minimizing the interference

The gravity and character of the harm The interference must be substantial. There is a certain level of annoyance that we are all required to endure in society.

A restaurant next door that occasionally makes noises or a neighbor whose garden sprinkler occasionally throws drops of water on someone else's land does not constitute substantial interference with the use and enjoyment of land.

It is important to know the extent of the harm in order to assess its gravity. Has there been serious physical damage done to the land? Even if the physical condition of the land has not been altered, is the plaintiff experiencing significant mental discomfort as a result of what the defendant has done? Can such discomfort be passed off as the whining of a grouchy neighbor, or would people generally agree that plaintiff's adverse reaction is understandable? The duration of the harm is also important to measure. Is the interference momentary or is it continuous?

The spectrum of the gravity and character of harm can be viewed in Exhibit 23–4. Of course, something less than total interruption can qualify as a private nuisance. How much less? This question can never be answered in isolation. All of the other factors would also have to be examined and weighed.

Exhibit 23–4
Spectrum of interference.

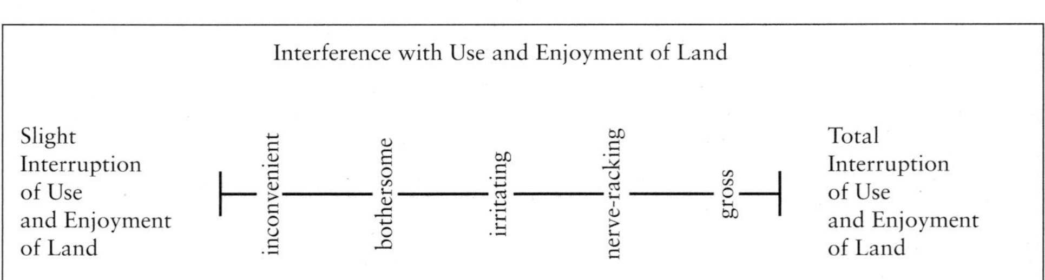

When the physical condition of the land has been damaged, a court will usually have little trouble measuring the gravity of the interference. When, however, the interference involves personal discomfort or annoyance alone, the difficulties of assessment are sometimes acute. A rough objective standard is used in such cases. The test is: How would a normal person in that locality view the interference? Would a person who is not unduly sensitive be substantially annoyed or disturbed? Suppose that a halfway house is opened next door to the plaintiff. The halfway house will provide rehabilitation services for men just released from prison as a transition to parole. The plaintiff fears that his children may be molested and that property values in the area will go down as a result of the halfway house. Has there been a substantial interference with the use and enjoyment of the plaintiff's land? This question is answered by determining how a normal person, who is not hypersensitive, would react to the halfway house. If the fears of the plaintiff are based on sheer speculation on what *might* happen, then a normal person would not consider the interference to be a serious one. If, however, the fears are based on substantive data, e.g., the fact that the men in the house will receive very little supervision from trained staff, or the fact that many of the ex-inmates have a history of child molestation, or the fact that property assessments have actually gone down due to the halfway house, then a normal person might agree that the interference is a substantial one.

The social value of the use that the plaintiff is making of the land For what purpose is the plaintiff using his or her land? How valuable is that use to society? What is the **social value** of the use? (Social value means quality as measured by what the general public deems desirable or useful.) The following uses have considerable social value: use as a residence, use for business purposes, and use for recreational purposes. This is not to say that vacant or unoccupied land has no social value. In balancing all of the factors, however, a court is less likely to conclude that an interference with such land is unreasonable than an interference with land actively used for residential, commercial, or recreational purposes.

social value The quality of something as measured by what the general public deems desirable or useful. Also called social utility.

The character of the locality This factor is one of the most important in determining the reasonableness or unreasonableness of the interference. How suitable to the environment is the use the plaintiff is making of his or her land? Zoning ordinances are one measure of suitability. Even if no such ordinances exist, however, a court will still ask whether an area is used primarily or exclusively for residences, for heavy industry, for small businesses, for agriculture, etc. Having made this determination, a court will then use the following rough equation:

> If the plaintiff's use of his or her land is suitable to the locality, a court will be more likely to conclude that an interference with this use by the defendant is unreasonable than if the use is not suitable or compatible.

If, for example, the plaintiff is using land as a home in an area that is predominantly residential, a court will be more inclined to find that noise, odor, or other pollution from a nearby business is unreasonable than if the area is predominantly commercial. Of course, the equation becomes more difficult to apply when an area consists of a significant mixture of residential, commercial, and recreational structures, such as in many of our cities where use patterns change over the years. When there is such a mixture, it simply means that a plaintiff cannot be as sensitive to interferences as a plaintiff living in a purer or more homogeneous area.

The character of the locality can also be looked at from the perspective of the defendant's conduct. How compatible is the conduct with the predominant nature of the environment? The more incompatible it is, the more likely that a court would find that the interference with the plaintiff's use and enjoyment of land is unreasonable.

The extent of the burden on the plaintiff of avoiding or minimizing the interference A court will probably be unwilling to find an interference by the defendant to be unreasonable if the burden on the plaintiff of avoiding or minimizing the interference is modest. The plaintiff, in effect, has an obligation to avoid the consequences of the defendant's tort when it is practical to do so. Suppose, for example, that all the plaintiff had to do to prevent occasional factory odors from coming into the house was to close some of the windows a few times during the week. The minor nature of this burden would weigh against calling the interference unreasonable. On the other hand, if the only way for the plaintiff to minimize or avoid the interference were to rebuild the house or business or to move away, then the substantial nature of the burden might help to tip the scale toward concluding that the interference is unreasonable.

The motive of the defendant Why has the defendant interfered with the use and enjoyment of the plaintiff's land? If it can be shown that the defendant acted out of spite to harm the plaintiff, then it is highly likely that a court will conclude that any significant interference is unreasonable. On the other hand, if the interference is simply the product of the defendant's pursuit of his or her own self-interest, unreasonableness may be more difficult to establish.

The social value of the defendant's conduct that led to the interference Just as we needed to ask about the social value of the plaintiff's use of his or her land, so too we must ask about the social value of the defendant's conduct that produced the interference. Conduct can have social value even if the defendant is acting for his or her own private interests, e.g., using a backyard for a barbecue or running a machine in a farm or other business. The question is rarely: does the defendant's conduct have social value? Rather, the question is: how much social value does it have? How much is the general public good advanced by the conduct? Operating a hospital or school has high social value. Operating a farm or living in a home also has social value. The court must assess where on the scale the activity falls. The greater the social value, the less likely that a court will conclude that the conduct or condition causing the interference is unreasonable. This does not mean, however, that a cancer-curing hospital cannot commit a private nuisance. Again, all of the factors must be considered. The ultimate test is whether the social value of the defendant's conduct outweighs the hardship of the interference the plaintiff is suffering.

The extent of the burden on the defendant of avoiding or minimizing the interference What would the defendant have to do to stop or minimize the interference? Install an inexpensive shield? Radically change the nature of the business? Close down? The more minimal the burden, the more likely the court will find the continued interference to be unreasonable. This does not mean, however, that the defendant is home free simply by showing that the burden of avoiding or minimizing the interference would be great. The extent of the burden is but one factor that must be weighed.

ASSIGNMENT 23.2

Examine the following situations. What questions would you want answered in order to determine whether there has been an unreasonable interference with the use and enjoyment of land for purposes of establishing a private nuisance?

a. The plaintiff lives next door to a small nursing home. The home has a large air-conditioner motor in the backyard. The plaintiff is very upset about the noise given off by this motor.
b. The defendant is an excellent mechanic. She works on cars as a hobby after her regular job hours. She frequently works on her car and the cars of her friends until late at night. The plaintiff, a neighbor, is bothered by the bright lights the defendant uses while working on the cars and by the constant coming and going of her friends, who visit to talk about cars.
c. The local church runs a bingo game every Thursday night. This is extremely upsetting to the plaintiff, who lives next door to the church.
d. A factory employing five hundred people has a chimney that sends black smoke into the air. Particles in the smoke sometimes fall on the plaintiff's house. The plaintiff is worried that the particles will damage her property.
e. Tom lives two floors above Mary's apartment in a four-story apartment building. Mary is a cigarette smoker and her boyfriend smokes cigars. Whenever either of them smokes, the secondhand smoke travels up through the walls into Tom's apartment. It also goes into several of Tom's windows when they are open.

2. What Are the Ways in Which a Private Nuisance Can Be Committed?

There are four main ways in which a private nuisance can be created:

Negligence: There is no intent to interfere. The defendant creates an unreasonable risk of interfering. Suppose, for example, that the defendants dump what they think is harmless waste into a stream that flows through the plaintiff's land before going out to sea. In fact, the waste is not harmless. As a result, the plaintiff's land becomes totally useless. If the defendants had taken reasonable precautions, they would have discovered the harmful nature of the waste. The defendants have negligently created an unreasonable interference with the plaintiff's use and enjoyment of land.

Intent: Intent here means that the defendant knows the interference will occur or has knowledge with substantial certainty that the interference will result from what the defendant does or fails to do. If the defendant, for example,

knows that foul pollutants are going from its factory to the plaintiff's land, the defendant, in the eyes of the law, has intended this interference.

Strict liability. The unreasonable interference can be created through conduct that would impose strict liability—an abnormally dangerous condition or activity, such as blasting.

Violation of a statute, ordinance, or regulation: The defendant violates a statute, ordinance, or regulation—for example, opens a house of prostitution.

3. Who Can Sue for a Private Nuisance?

Since private nuisance protects the use and enjoyment of private land, an owner, a tenant, or anyone else who has rights to the use and enjoyment of the land can sue for a private nuisance. This includes individuals in possession of the land who are claiming an interest in the land as well as their families. Landlords who do not live on or use the land themselves can bring the suit when the damages caused by the defendant are permanent.

4. What Remedies Can Be Obtained When a Private Nuisance Has Been Committed?

Damages can be awarded for the harm caused by the private nuisance. The measure of damages is usually the difference between the value of the land before the harm and its value after the harm. Some courts will permit a plaintiff to choose as the measure of damages the **cost of restoration**. Additional compensatory damages include the loss in the rental value of the land, the loss of the plaintiff's own personal use of the land, and an amount to compensate the plaintiff for any discomfort or annoyance that has been experienced.

damages Monetary payments awarded to compensate for a legally recognized wrong. (See glossary for an additional definition.)

cost of restoration The amount of money damages that will restore property to its condition before the defendant's tort.

There are times when an award of damages is not adequate, particularly when the interference is threatened or is continuous. The issue will be whether the plaintiff can obtain an **injunction** against the defendants to prevent or stop the interference. (An award of damages is a legal remedy; an injunction is an **equitable remedy**. A court will not consider equitable remedies unless it determines that there are no adequate legal remedies, referred to as "no adequate remedy at law.") Most courts are reluctant to grant the equitable relief of an injunction because of its drastic nature. The court must first be satisfied that an award of damages will not be adequate to remedy the problem. If the interference is threatened, the court will want to be convinced that there is a high likelihood that the interference will in fact occur. The effect of an injunction could be to close down a defendant's business. This may lead to the loss of many jobs. Hence, before a court will grant an injunction, it will weigh (a) the economic hardship that will be suffered by the defendant due to an injunction, and (b) the nature of the interference the plaintiff is suffering. The court will also consider the hardship that the entire community might suffer if the injunction is granted. In short, the court will go through a similar kind of analysis on the injunction issue that it went through to determine whether the interference was unreasonable. A court may decide that the interference is unreasonable, but that injunctive relief against it is unwarranted because it is too drastic. If so, the court will permit the defendant to proceed, but require damages to be paid to the plaintiff. This is an unsatisfactory result, because the practical effect of refusing to grant the injunction is a kind of court "permission" to continue with an unreasonable interference with the plaintiff's land.

injunction A court order requiring a person or organization to do or to refrain from doing something.

equitable remedy A form of relief (e.g., injunction or specific performance) that is available when remedies at law (e.g., damages) are not adequate.

Another remedy that might be available is **self-help**, in which the victim of a tort takes corrective steps on his or her own without resort to the courts. This would include the common law privilege to **abate a nuisance**. This is the privilege to take reasonable steps to correct a nuisance that is interfering with the use and enjoyment of land.

self-help Acting on one's own to prevent or correct the effects of a tort or other wrong without using the courts or other public authority.

abate a nuisance To take steps to eliminate a nuisance that is interfering with the use and enjoyment of land.

EXAMPLE

Tom and Mary live next to each other. When Tom returns late one evening from a two-month business trip, he is surprised to find Mary's car parked in his driveway, preventing him from getting into his garage. Tom goes over to Mary's house to complain, but no one is home. He then gets in Mary's car, releases the emergency brake, and rolls it to the side of the street away from his driveway entrance.

Tom has properly exercised his privilege to abate a nuisance. Aggrieved parties, such as Tom, must act within a reasonable amount of time after they discover interference with the use and enjoyment of their land. If practical, they must give notice to the wrongdoers to determine whether they will remove the interference on their own. Only reasonable force can be used to abate the nuisance. One cannot blow up a polluting factory in order to stop the flow of offending smoke.

5. What Defenses Are Available to a Defendant?

contributory negligence The failure of plaintiffs to take reasonable precautions for their protection, helping to cause their own injury or other loss.

comparative negligence A comparison of the negligence of the defendant and plaintiff in causing the plaintiff's injury (or other loss) in order to reduce the plaintiff's damages in proportion to the plaintiff's negligence in causing his or her own injury (or other loss).

assumption of the risk The knowing and voluntary acceptance of the danger or risk of being harmed by someone's negligence.

Contributory negligence The **contributory negligence** of the plaintiff in helping to cause his or her own injury or interference is a defense if the defendant produced the private nuisance negligently. It normally would not be a defense, however, if the defendant acted recklessly or intentionally in causing the nuisance. If the state has adopted **comparative negligence**, the damages would be apportioned according to the extent of the defendant's negligence and the plaintiff's negligence as determined by the comparative negligence formula followed in the state. (On comparative negligence, see Chapter 17.)

Assumption of the risk **Assumption of the risk** is a defense if the plaintiff voluntarily accepted a risk from the nuisance, a risk that the plaintiff fully understands. The defense applies no matter how the defendant caused the unreasonable interference. It is not often, however, that a defendant can establish that the plaintiff assumed the risk of a private nuisance. The defense is more frequently raised in cases of a public nuisance, to be discussed shortly.

Suppose that the plaintiff has "come to the nuisance," e.g., the plaintiff moves to an industrial town knowing that a lot of noise and pollution exists in that town. Hasn't the plaintiff assumed the risk of the private nuisance? Not necessarily. A plaintiff is not barred from complaining about a nuisance simply because the nuisance was there before the plaintiff arrived. To say that someone has "moved to the nuisance" may beg the question of whether there is in fact a private nuisance. All of the factors discussed previously must be analyzed to determine whether there is an unreasonable interference, e.g., the suitability of the activity to the locale. If the plaintiff clearly knew about and understood a nuisance before moving to the area, a court will take this into consideration in determining the extent of the burden that the nuisance has placed on the plaintiff, but "coming to the nuisance" in and of itself is not an absolute defense to the action.

An interference may be unreasonable in an exclusively residential area, but quite reasonable in an industrial area. On the separate question of whether a court will grant an injunction against what it has found to be a nuisance, the fact that the plaintiff has "come to the nuisance" will be a factor to be weighed *against* the granting of the injunction. This is different, however, from the problem of whether a private nuisance in fact exists.

mitigation-of-damages rule Injured parties must take reasonable steps to alleviate their injury. A wrongdoer will not be liable for any increase or aggravation of the injury caused by the injured party's failure to take such steps. Also called avoidable-consequences doctrine.

Mitigation of damages Under the **mitigation-of-damages rule**, the plaintiff must take reasonable steps to avoid the damages or other harmful consequences of the defendant's wrongful conduct. If, for example, the plaintiff knows that the defendant's private nuisance has resulted in the poisoning of the plaintiff's drinking water, the plaintiff cannot proceed to drink the water anyway or continue to let his or her animals drink it. The defendant will be responsible for the poisoning of the water, but not for the consequences of the poisoning that the plaintiff could have eliminated. The plaintiff has failed to take reasonable steps to mitigate the consequences of the defendant's wrong.

Official authorization Special statutes, ordinances, or regulations may exist that either authorize or require the defendant to engage in the activity that is later being challenged as a nuisance. For example, zoning ordinances authorize certain kinds of activities and structures, and statutes may require public utilities to transport dangerous substances. Such official sanction, however, is never an authorization to carry on the activity carelessly or negligently. Damages and injunctive relief will be granted only to the extent that harm is caused or threatened by carrying on the activity in an unreasonable manner. The entire operation will rarely be enjoined, because that would have the effect of rescinding the official authorization.

Even if the defendant is not conducting the activity unreasonably, a plaintiff may have an argument that the official sanction of the activity has, in effect, resulted in a **taking** of property for which the government is responsible and therefore liable for just compensation.

taking The forced acquisition of private property by the government for a public purpose, for which the government must pay just compensation. (A requirement of the Fifth Amendment.) The acquisition can consist of a forced purchase, a substantial interference with the enjoyment of the property, or the deprivation of substantially all productive use of the property.

Public Nuisance

We saw earlier that a public nuisance is an unreasonable interference with a right that is common to the general public. (See Exhibit 23–5 for the elements of public nuisance.)

Exhibit 23–5
Elements of public nuisance.

1. An act
2. Unreasonable interference with the use and enjoyment
3. Of a right common to the general public
4. Based on negligence, intent, strict liability, or violation of a statute
5. Causation

We will examine public nuisance by asking the same five basic questions we used to discuss a private nuisance:

1. What is the nature of a public nuisance? What type of harm does it cover?
2. How is it created?
3. Who can sue?
4. What remedies are available?
5. What defenses are available?

For some of the questions, the answers are very similar to those given for private nuisance. The answers to the first and third questions, however, are substantially different.

1. What Is the Nature of a Public Nuisance and What Type of Harm Does It Cover?

A public nuisance often has nothing to do with the use and enjoyment of private land. It is an unreasonable interference with a right that is common to the public.

EXAMPLES

- keeping diseased animals that will be sold for food
- operating a house of prostitution
- operating an illegal gambling parlor
- obstructing a public highway
- polluting a public river
- wiretapping conversations in a judge's chambers or in a jury room
- maintaining unsafe apartment buildings used by many people
- using public profanity

Very often, the conduct of the defendant constitutes a crime.

To be a public nuisance, there must be some public right involved. Every member of the public does not have to be actually affected by it. If only a small number of people are affected, however, there is usually no public nuisance. To obstruct a public highway, e.g., by leaving a truck on it or by causing boulders to be placed on it, is a public nuisance, because there is a public right to use the highway, and this right is taken away from everyone who tries to use it.

The interference with the public right must be unreasonable. If the defendant has violated a specific statute, ordinance, or regulation, there is usually little difficulty establishing unreasonableness. Otherwise, many of the same factors described earlier to determine the reasonableness of an alleged private nuisance must also be used to determine the reasonableness of an alleged public nuisance, e.g., the gravity of the interference and the burden of removal or mitigation.

Craigslist

Craigslist.com is a popular free Internet classified service. It creates search categories into which users can post their ads. The site is viewed over nine billion times each month around the world. Among the choices on the site is a section in which adults seeking sexual contacts can exchange photographs and messages that can lead to in-person meetings. At one time the section was called "erotic services," later changed to services for "adults" and "personals." In a suit against Craigslist, the sheriff of Cook County, Illinois alleged that the service facilitated prostitution and constituted a public nuisance. Despite a warning on the site that prohibits illegal conduct, code words (e.g., "roses" for dollars) were routinely used as a way of communicating what payment was expected for specified sexual acts. The sheriff asserted that "Craigslist is now the single largest source for prostitution, including child exploitation, in the country."

In its defense, Craigslist cited a federal statute, which provides that "No provider . . . of an interactive computer service shall be treated as the publisher or speaker of any information provided by another information content provider."[2] In response the sheriff said that Craigslist knowingly "arranges" meetings for the purpose of prostitution and "directs" people to places of prostitution. It was foreseeable that prostitution would be a likely result of a section named "erotic services" with twenty-one categories based on sexual preference.

The court disagreed:

> The phrase "adult," even in conjunction with "services," is not unlawful in itself nor does it necessarily call for unlawful content. The same is true of the subcategories. Plaintiff is simply wrong when he insists that these terms are all synonyms for illegal sexual services. A woman advertising erotic dancing for male clients ("w4m") is offering an "adult service," yet this is not prostitution. It may even be entitled to some limited protection under the First Amendment. Plaintiff's argument that Craigslist causes or induces illegal content is further undercut by the fact that Craigslist repeatedly warns users not to post such content. While we accept as true for the purposes of this motion plaintiff's allegation that users routinely flout Craigslist's guidelines, it is not because Craigslist has caused them to do so. . . . The fact that Craigslist also provides a word-search function does not change the analysis. The word-search function is a "neutral tool" that permits users to search for terms that they select in ads created by other users. It does not cause or induce anyone to create, post, or search for illegal content. . . . [The sheriff] can use Craiglist's website to identify and pursue individuals who post allegedly unlawful content. But he cannot sue Craigslist for their conduct."[3]

Hence there was no violation of prostitution laws by Craigslist and no public nuisance.

Guns

Firearms are the second leading cause of death in the United States. There are over 109,000 licensed firearms dealers in the United States. Suits have been brought by or on behalf of gunshot victims on the theory that the firearms industry has created a public nuisance by negligently flooding the firearms market. Such suits have met with mixed results.

Some early New York cases, for example, dismissed the suits on the ground that the law of public nuisance did not cover the manufacture and sale of a lawful product. It was the job of the legislature, these courts concluded, to decide whether additional firearm regulation and control was needed.[4] Other cases, however, have reached a different result. In a major recent case, the Supreme Court of Ohio held that a public nuisance theory can be used against the firearm industry. The city of Cincinnati alleged that handgun manufacturers and distributors manufactured, marketed, distributed, and sold firearms in ways that unreasonably interfered with public health, welfare, and safety in the city; that city residents had a common right to be free from such conduct; that defendants knew or reasonably should have known that their conduct would cause handguns to be used and possessed illegally; and that such conduct produced an ongoing nuisance that had a detrimental effect upon the public health, safety, and welfare of city residents. The court held that these allegations stated a valid cause of action.[5]

To counter such suits, the firearms industry has had some success in lobbying legislatures to pass laws that grant them immunity from the suits. In Pennsylvania, for example, a court held that the state's Uniform Firearms Act (UFA) prevented manufacturers from being held liable for public nuisance for the distribution practices of their legal, nondefective products.[6] Over thirty states have passed similar laws protecting the firearms industry.[7]

In 2005, Congress passed the Protection of Lawful Commerce in Arms Act. It included the finding that "[t]he possibility of imposing liability on an entire industry for harm that is solely caused by others is an abuse of the legal system." The purpose of the act was to "prohibit causes of action against manufacturers, distributors, dealers, and importers of firearms . . . for the harm solely caused by the criminal or unlawful misuse of firearm products or ammunition products by others when the product functioned as designed and intended."[8] This Act, however, did not mean the end of public nuisance suits against the firearm industry. Under an exception in the Act, civil liability actions are allowed against firearms sellers who violate a state or federal statute applicable to the sale or marketing of firearms. There is a tremendous volume of such statutes on the books. Hence plaintiffs will always include a laundry list of statutes that the industry has allegedly violated to try to convince the court that a public nuisance suit comes within the exception of the Act and hence is not barred.

ASSIGNMENT 23.3

What do you think are the social problems that pose the most severe risk to the health or morals of Americans? Obesity? Pollution? Alcoholism? Gambling? Pornography? What kinds of public nuisance suits against industries (not just an individual company) do you think might be possible to combat these social problems? What obstacles would such suits face?

2. What Are the Ways in Which a Public Nuisance Can Be Created?

Negligence: The defendant can negligently create the public nuisance, e.g., carelessly allowing logs to fall off a truck and obstruct a public highway.

Intent: Here the defendant knows that the interference with a public right will occur or is substantially certain that it will occur based on what the defendant does or fails to do, e.g., the defendant knows that the pollutants being poured into a lake will make the lake unusable by the public for fishing.

Strict liability: The defendant, for example, conducts blasting in an area, which causes substantial damage to all surrounding buildings through vibrations—an abnormally dangerous condition or activity.

Violation of a statute, ordinance, or regulation: The defendant, for example, opens a house of prostitution.

3. Who Can Sue for the Public Nuisance?

Because public rights are involved, a public official can always bring a civil action or a criminal prosecution against the defendant.

standing 1. A person's right to seek relief from a court. 2. The right to bring a court action because of the sufficiency of one's personal interest in the outcome of the proposed court action or because of a special statute that grants this right.

When can a *private* citizen bring a suit for a public nuisance? A private person has **standing** only when he or she suffered in a way that is different from every other member of the public affected by the public nuisance. (Standing is a person's right to seek relief from a court.) Every person who has suffered a wrong does not necessarily have standing. To bring an action for a public nuisance, the plaintiff must have suffered special or particular damage. The harm must be different in kind. If the plaintiff has "only" suffered more of the same harm everyone else has suffered (a difference in degree only), very few courts will allow the plaintiff to bring an independent action for the public nuisance. If the defendant obstructs a public highway resulting in the need for a substantial detour, the citizens who must suffer this inconvenience have *not* suffered an inconvenience that is different in kind from everyone else. Hence, a private suit cannot be brought. All that a citizen can do is ask the public authorities to take the defendant to court. Suppose, however, that one citizen crashes into the obstruction. This individual has suffered personal or property damage that is different in kind from having to make a detour. Such an individual, therefore, *can* bring a private action for the public nuisance. Also, if the plaintiff can show special financial damage that other members of the public do not suffer, the plaintiff will often be able to bring the public nuisance action.

Some public nuisances are also private nuisances when the conduct of the defendant interferes with a public right *and* interferes with the use and enjoyment of a particular plaintiff's land. For example, the defendant builds a dam that prevents the public from using the water that would otherwise flow into a lake used for recreational purposes, and the dam also floods the plaintiff's land; or the defendant opens a gambling hall next door to the plaintiff, whose peace of mind is substantially disrupted as a result.

The violation of some environmental statutes may constitute a public nuisance. It is important to check whether such statutes allow a private citizen to sue whomever caused the violation. If so, the private citizen has standing. He or she may be able to act on behalf of a class or group of similarly situated citizens. (On class actions, see Chapter 20.)

4. What Remedies Can Be Obtained When a Public Nuisance Has Been Committed?

When a public official brings the public nuisance action, the remedies often include a fine or imprisonment. The government may also be able to collect damages for harm that may have been done to public property.

As with a private nuisance, it is sometimes difficult to obtain an injunction against a public nuisance, particularly when a crime has been committed or is threatened. If criminal conduct is being alleged, elaborate criminal trial procedures must be followed. They cannot be bypassed simply because someone is seeking an injunction rather than punishment for a crime. If criminal conduct is not involved in the action to seek an injunction against a public nuisance, a court will go through a balancing analysis similar to the one it uses to decide whether to issue an injunction against a private nuisance.

Self-help—the privilege to abate a nuisance—is also a possible remedy. Only reasonable force can be used, and the steps taken by the plaintiff to stop the nuisance must occur very soon after the nuisance is discovered and after notice is given to the defendant, unless such notice is impractical under the circumstances.

Statutes in some states allow officials to remove vehicles and other objects that constitute a public nuisance. In Michigan, for example, a man's car was forfeited as a public nuisance after he engaged in sexual activity in the car with a prostitute. The man's wife, who was a co-owner of the car, argued unsuccessfully that her half ownership in the car should not have been forfeited since she never knew her wayward husband used the car for this purpose.[9]

5. What Defenses Are Available to a Defendant in a Public Nuisance Case?

The four main categories of defenses discussed under private nuisance apply equally to public nuisances:

- contributory negligence (or comparative negligence)
- assumption of the risk
- mitigation of damages
- official authorization

Nuisance Per Se

Finally, we need to distinguish nuisance in fact from nuisance per se. Many of the examples of public and private nuisances we have examined in the chapter are *nuisances in fact*, which simply means that we determined whether they were nuisances by examining all of the circumstances involved. A **nuisance per se**, on the other hand, is a nuisance in all circumstances. For example, nuisances that are clear violations of statutes or ordinances are usually nuisances per se. In many instances the legislature has explicitly labeled the act or condition a nuisance per se. A major consequence of a finding that an act or condition is a nuisance per se is that it is much easier to obtain a court injunction against its continuance.

nuisance per se An act, occupation, or structure that is a nuisance at all times and under any circumstances, regardless of location or surroundings. Also called nuisance at law.

CASE

Armory Park Neighborhood Assn v. Episcopal Community Services

148 Ariz. 1, 712 P.2d 914 (1985)
Supreme Court of Arizona

Background: *St. Martin's Center is run by Episcopal Community Services (ECS). The Center operates a free food distribution program for indigent persons in Tucson. The Armory Park Neighborhood Association sought an injunction against the center as a public nuisance. Although it did not violate any zoning or health codes, the trial court granted a preliminary injunction against the Center on the ground that its activities constituted a public and a private nuisance. The case is now on appeal before the Supreme Court of Arizona.*

Decision on Appeal: *The injunction against the Center's free meal program is appropriate.*

OPINION OF COURT

Justice FELDMAN delivered the opinion of the court . . .

Before [St. Martin's] Center opened, the area had been primarily residential with a few small businesses. When the Center began operating in December 1982, many transients crossed the area daily on their way to and from the Center. Although the Center was only open from 5:00 to 6:00 P.M., patrons lined up well before this hour and often lingered in the neighborhood long after finishing their meal. The Center rented an adjacent fenced lot for a waiting area and organized neighborhood cleaning projects, but the trial judge apparently felt these efforts were inadequate to control the activity stemming from the Center. Transients frequently trespassed onto residents' yards, sometimes urinating, defecating, drinking and littering on the residents' property. A few broke into storage areas and unoccupied homes, and some asked residents for handouts. The number of arrests in the area increased dramatically. Many residents were frightened or annoyed by the transients and altered their lifestyles to avoid them. . . .

We have previously distinguished public and private nuisances. In *City of Phoenix v. Johnson*, 51 Ariz. 115, 75 P.2d 30 (1938), we noted that a nuisance is public when it affects rights of "citizens as a part of the public, while a private nuisance is one which affects a single individual or a definite number of persons on the enjoyment of some private right which is not common to the public." Id. at 123, 75 P.2d 34. A public nuisance must also affect a considerable number of people. . . .

Defendant claims that its business should not be held responsible for acts committed by its patrons off the premises of the Center. It argues that since it has no control over the patrons when they are not on the Center's premises, it cannot be enjoined because of their acts. We do not believe this position is supported either by precedent or theory.

In *Shamhart v. Morrison Cafeteria Co.*, 159 Fla. 629, 32 So. 2d 727 (1947), the defendant operated a well-frequented cafeteria. Each day customers waiting to enter the business would line up on the sidewalk, blocking the entrances to the neighboring establishments. The dissenting justices argued that the defendant had not actually caused the lines to form and that the duty to prevent the harm to the plaintiffs should be left to the police through regulation of the public streets. The majority of the court rejected this argument, and remanded the case for a determination of the damages. See, also, *Reid v. Brodsky*, 397 Pa. 463, 156 A.2d 334 (1959) (operation of a bar enjoined because its patrons were often noisy and intoxicated; they frequently used the neighboring properties for toilet purposes and sexual misconduct); *Barrett v. Lopez*, 57 N.M. 697, 262 P.2d 981, 983 (1953) (operation of a dance hall enjoined, the court finding that "mere possibility of relief from another source [e.g., the police] does not relieve the courts of their responsibilities"); *Wade v. Fuller*, 12 Utah 2d 299, 365 P.2d 802 (1961) (operation of drive-in cafe enjoined where patrons created disturbances to nearby residents); *McQuade v. Tucson Tiller Apartments*, 25 Ariz. App. 312, 543 P.2d 150 (1975) (music concerts at mall designed to attract customers enjoined because of increased crowds and noise in residential area). . . .

Since the rules of a civilized society require us to tolerate our neighbors, the law requires our neighbors to keep their activities within the limits of what is tolerable by a reasonable person. However, what is reasonably tolerable must be tolerated; not all interferences with public rights are public nuisances. As Dean Prosser explains, "[t]he law does not concern itself with trifles, or seek to remedy all of the petty annoyances and disturbances of everyday life in a civilized community even from conduct committed with knowledge that annoyance and inconvenience will result." Prosser, W. and W. P. Keeton, *Handbook on the Law of Torts*, § 88, at 626 (5th ed. 1984). Thus, to constitute a nuisance, the complained-of interference must be substantial, intentional and unreasonable under the circumstances. *Restatement (Second) of Torts*, § 826 comment c and § 821F. Our courts have generally used a balancing test in deciding the reasonableness of an interference. The trial court should look at the utility and reasonableness of the conduct and balance these factors against the extent of harm inflicted and the nature of the affected neighborhood. We noted in the early case of *MacDonald v. Perry*:

> What might amount to a serious nuisance in one locality by reason of the density of the population, or character of the neighborhood affected, may in another place and under different surroundings be deemed proper and unobjectionable. What amount of annoyance or inconvenience caused by others in the lawful use of their property will constitute a nuisance depends upon varying circumstances and cannot be precisely defined. 32 Ariz. 39, 50, 255 P. 494 (1927).

The trial judge did not ignore the balancing test and was well aware of the social utility of defendant's operation. His words are illuminating:

> It is distressing . . . [that this activity] should be restrained. Providing for the poor and the homeless is certainly a worthwhile, praisworthy [sic] activity. It is particularly distressing to this Court because it [defendant] has no control over those who are attracted to the kitchen while they are either coming or leaving the premises. However, the right to the comfortable enjoyment of one's property is something that another's activities should not affect, the harm being suffered by the Armory Park Neighborhood and the residents therein is irreparable and substantial, for which they have no adequate legal remedy. . . .

We believe that a determination made by weighing and balancing conflicting interests or principles is truly one which lies within the discretion of the trial judge. We defer to that discretion here. The evidence of the multiple trespasses upon and defacement of the residents' property supports the trial court's conclusion that the interference caused by defendant's operation was unreasonable despite its charitable cause.

The common law has long recognized that the usefulness of a particular activity may outweigh the inconveniences, discomforts and changes it causes some persons to suffer. We, too, acknowledge the social value of the Center. Its charitable purpose, that of feeding the hungry, is entitled to greater deference than pursuits of lesser intrinsic value. It appears from the record that ECS' purposes in operating the Center were entirely admirable. However, even admirable ventures may cause unreasonable interferences. See, e.g., *Assembly of God Church of Tahoka v. Bradley*, 196 S.W.2d 696 (Tex. Civ. App. 1946). We do not believe that the law allows the costs of a charitable enterprise to be visited in their entirety upon the residents of a single neighborhood. The problems of dealing with the unemployed, the homeless and the mentally ill are also matters of community or governmental responsibility.

ECS argues that its compliance with City of Tucson zoning regulations is a conclusive determination of reasonableness. We agree that compliance with zoning provisions has some bearing in nuisance cases. . . . We decline, however, to find that ECS' compliance with the applicable zoning provisions precludes a court from enjoining its activities. The equitable power of the judiciary exists independent of statute. Although zoning and criminal provisions are binding with respect to the type of activity, they do not limit the power of a court acting in equity to enjoin an unreasonable, albeit permitted, activity as a public nuisance. . . .

The trial court's order granting the preliminary injunction is affirmed. By affirming the trial court's preliminary orders, we do not require that [the trial judge] close the Center permanently. It is, of course, within the equitable discretion of the trial court to fashion a less severe remedy, if possible. . . .

ASSIGNMENT 23.4

a. Suppose that a church operated the same kind of free meal program in New York City. Would the result be the same?
b. What is the logical consequence of this opinion? That programs such as those operated by St. Martin's Center will always be kept in the inner city and never be allowed in the suburbs?

TRADITIONAL NEGLIGENCE LIABILITY

In this section, we consider negligence liability to persons who are injured on someone's premises or in the immediate environment. In Chapters 12 through 16, we studied the elements of negligence:

- duty
- breach of duty
- proximate cause
- damages

A major issue in the area of premises liability is the first element: duty. In Chapter 13 the general rule on duty is stated as follows:

> Whenever one's conduct creates a foreseeable risk of injury or other loss to someone else's person or property, a duty of reasonable care arises to take precautions to prevent that injury or loss.

When discussing the negligence liability of occupiers of land, this general rule on duty is unfortunately riddled with exceptions depending on the status of the parties.

Categories of Plaintiffs in Premises Liability Cases:

- Someone not on the defendant's land when injured
- An adult trespasser injured on the land (defendant had no reason to know the trespasser was there)
- An adult trespasser injured on the land (defendant knew the trespasser was there)
- An adult trespasser injured on the land (the trespasser was foreseeable because of repeated prior trespasses on limited parts of the land)
- A child trespasser injured on the land
- A licensee injured on the land
- An invitee injured on the land

Categories of Defendants in Premises Liability Cases:

- An occupier of the land
- An owner of unoccupied land
- A seller of the land
- A landlord of the land

Every time the status of the plaintiff or defendant changes, we must ask whether the court will apply a different standard of duty (other than the general duty of reasonable care) for purposes of negligence liability.

A few courts have recently discarded all these special rules and exceptions, and have declared that the duty is reasonable care for all categories of plaintiffs and defendants. In these courts, the status of the plaintiff or defendant is simply one of the factors to be taken into consideration in deciding whether there has been a breach of this duty. The status of the plaintiff as trespasser, licensee, or invitee, for example, would be relevant solely in determining the extent to which their presence on the land was foreseeable to the defendant. A separate duty would not exist for each category of plaintiff under this minority view. Because most courts, however, do not take this position, we must examine each status separately.

reasonable care Ordinary prudence under the circumstances to avoid injury or other loss.

Throughout the discussion, we will be asking whether a duty of **reasonable care** is owed by the defendant, and if not, what *lesser standard of care* is owed. In some situations, it may be that *no duty* of care is owed, so that the defendant will not be liable for the injury suffered by the plaintiff on or just outside the premises.

The following themes will guide our discussion:

1. the duty of occupiers of land to persons outside the land
2. the duty of occupiers of land to trespassers, licensees, and invitees on the land
3. the special problems of the seller and buyer of land (vendor and vendee)
4. the special problems of the landlord and tenant (lessor and lessee)

By occupier we mean anyone in possession of the land who has a right to possess it, e.g., tenant, owner-occupant of land, or adverse possessor. If land is unoccupied, our discussion of the duty and liability of an occupier will generally apply to the owner of the unoccupied land.

Causes of Injury

When a plaintiff is injured on land, the cause will fall into one of the following three categories:

- *Natural Conditions on the Land.* Examples include someone who drowned in a natural lake or was bit by an insect on the land.
- *Artificial or Non-natural Conditions on the Land.* Examples include someone who drowned in a man-made lake or who was hit by glass falling from the broken window of a building on the land.
- *Activities Occurring on the Land.* Examples include someone who was blinded by fireworks or who was hit by a high-speed train on the land.

Exhibit 23–6 presents an overview of the law that we will be examining in the remainder of the chapter.

1. Persons Outside the Land

First we examine injuries to persons who were not on the occupier's land at the time they were injured. Examples include injuries to someone traveling in front of the defendant's land or someone living adjacent to the defendant. The injury can come from an *artificial condition* on the defendant's land (e.g., a building collapses on a car parked on a street in front of the defendant's land); from a *natural condition* on the defendant's land (e.g., a limb from a native tree falls on the plaintiff who is walking on a sidewalk), or from business or personal *activity* taking place on the defendant's land (e.g., a bucket falls from a plank used by painters, and the bucket hits a pedestrian).

As indicated in Exhibit 23–6, reasonable care is owed to persons outside the land to protect them from danger in artificial conditions on the land. Reasonable care is also owed to protect them from danger resulting from activities conducted by the occupier on the land. No duty is owed persons outside the land from natural conditions on the land unless the occupier has done something affirmative to increase the danger from the natural condition. (In some states, however, a duty of reasonable care is owed for trees in urban, but not rural, areas.)

The rules in Exhibit 23–6 apply if the injury results from what the employees of the occupier do or fail to do within the scope of their employment. Suppose, however,

Exhibit 23–6 Negligence liability of occupiers of land.
(Abbreviations. ND: no duty. RC: reasonable care)

Status of Injured Plaintiff	Injuries Due to Artificial Conditions on the Land	Injuries Due to Natural Conditions on the Land	Injuries Due to Activities on the Land
Anyone outside the land	*How injured:* by an artificial condition on the land, e.g., derrick *Duty of occupier*: RC	*How injured:* by a natural condition on the land, e.g., natural lake *Duty of occupier:* ND *Exception:* In some states, RC is owed for trees in urban (but not rural) areas	*How injured:* by an activity on the land, e.g., steam cleaning a wall *Duty of occupier:* RC
Adult trespasser on the land who is unknown and unforeseeable to the occupier	*How injured:* by an artificial condition on the land, e.g., derrick *Duty of occupier:* ND	*How injured:* by a natural condition on the land, e.g., natural lake *Duty of occupier:* ND	*How injured:* by an activity on the land, e.g., excavating a tunnel *Duty of occupier:* ND
Adult trespasser known or discovered by the occupier to be on the land	*How injured:* by an artificial condition on the land, e.g., high-voltage electric wire *Duty of occupier:* Use RC to provide a warning if the danger is not obvious and is likely to cause serious bodily injury	*How injured:* by a natural condition on the land, e.g., natural lake *Duty of occupier:* ND	*How injured:* by an activity on the land, e.g., excavating a tunnel *Duty of occupier:* RC
Adult foreseeable trespasser on limited portions of the land	*How injured:* by an artificial condition on the land, e.g., high-voltage electric wire *Duty of occupier:* Use RC to provide a warning if the danger is not obvious and is likely to cause serious bodily injury	*How injured:* by a natural condition on the land, e.g., natural lake *Duty of occupier:* ND	*How injured:* by an activity on the land, e.g., excavating a tunnel *Duty of occupier:* RC
Foreseeable child trespasser on the land	*How injured:* by an artificial condition on the land, e.g., high-voltage electric wire *Duty of occupier:* Use RC if the danger of serious bodily injury is unreasonable and the child is unlikely to appreciate it	*How injured:* by a natural condition on the land, e.g., natural lake *Duty of occupier:* ND	*How injured:* by an activity on the land, e.g., excavating a tunnel *Duty of occupier:* RC
Licensee	*How injured:* by an artificial condition on the land, e.g., high-voltage electric wire *Duty of occupier:* RC to warn of dangers that are known to the occupier but are latent (not obvious) to the licensee. More than a warning may be required for extreme dangers.	*How injured:* by a natural condition on the land, e.g., natural lake *Duty of occupier:* RC to warn of dangers that are known to the occupier but are latent (not obvious) to the licensee. More than a warning may be required for extreme dangers.	*How injured:* by an activity on the land, e.g., excavating a tunnel *Duty of occupier:* RC if the danger is nonobvious
Invitee	*How injured:* by an artificial condition on the land, e.g., high-voltage electric wire *Duty of occupier:* RC, which may include a duty to inspect and discover dangers	*How injured:* by a natural condition on the land, e.g., natural lake *Duty of occupier:* RC which may include a duty to inspect and discover dangers	*How injured:* by an activity on the land, e.g., excavating a tunnel *Duty of occupier:* RC, which may include a duty to inspect and discover dangers

independent contractor One who operates his or her own business and contracts to do work for others; the latter do not control the method or administrative details of how the work is performed.

the occupier hires an **independent contractor** over whom the occupier usually has little control concerning the method or administrative details of how the work is done. If injury occurs to plaintiffs not on the land due to the activity of independent contractors on the land, the independent contractors and not the occupier will be liable for the negligence. An exception exists when the occupier hires the independent contractor to do inherently dangerous work. The occupier will be liable for injuries resulting from such activities. When, however, the injury results from the manner or method of work of the independent contractor not involved in inherently dangerous work, the defendant-occupier of the land is not liable.

2. Trespassers, Licensees, and Invitees on the Land

Everyone who comes *on* the land will fall into one of the three categories of trespasser, licensee, or invitee. The highest standard of care is owed the invitee.

Trespassers

trespasser One who enters or remains on land without the consent of the occupier and without any privilege to do so. One who commits a trespass to land.

Trespassers have neither consent nor privilege to be on the land or on designated portions of the land. The privileges include necessity, recapture of chattels, and abatement of a nuisance. (The first two self-help privileges will be discussed in Chapter 27; the last was covered earlier in this chapter.)

Four categories of trespassers need to be considered:

- adult trespassers on the land who are unknown by and unforeseeable to the occupier
- adult trespassers discovered by the occupier to be on the land (known or discovered adult trespassers)
- adult trespassers whose presence on the land is not known but who are foreseeably present on a limited portion of the land because there have been frequent trespassers there in the past (foreseeable adult trespassers)
- child trespassers who are foreseeably present anywhere on the land

Our focus is on the negligence liability that occupiers do or do not have to these categories of trespassers.

One rule that applies to all trespassers is that an occupier cannot do any *intentional* harm to a trespasser unless the occupier has a privilege (e.g., self-defense or defense of others) to use such force. A spring gun, for example, cannot be used to catch an unsuspecting trespasser. (See *Katko v. Briney* in Chapter 27 on the use of such guns.)

Adult trespassers on the land who are unknown and unforeseeable to the occupier No duty is owed to an adult trespasser who has not been discovered on the land by the occupier and whom the occupier has no reason to expect is on the land. There is no duty to warn such a trespasser of hidden dangers on the land nor to make the land safe from dangerous artificial conditions, natural conditions, or activities the occupier is conducting on the land.

Adult trespassers discovered by the occupier to be on the land (known or discovered adult trespassers) Assume that the occupier has actual knowledge of an adult trespasser on the land. For highly dangerous artificial conditions on the land (likely to cause death or serious bodily injury) that are not obvious, the occupier owes the known trespasser a duty to use reasonable care to provide a warning of the danger. No duty is owed the known trespasser for dangers in natural conditions on the land. For activities on the land, the occupier has a duty to use reasonable care for the safety of the known trespasser.

Adult trespassers who are foreseeably present on a limited portion of the land where there have been frequent trespassers in the past The occupier may not know about the presence of a particular trespasser, but may know that frequent trespassers have been present on a limited portion of the land. Hence it is foreseeable that trespassers will continue to be on that portion of the land. For example, a railroad may know (or should know) that large numbers of people regularly walk across the track at a designated spot. The area must be limited and the trespassing in that area must be constant or frequent. For highly dangerous artificial conditions on the land (likely to cause death or serious bodily injury) that are not obvious, the occupier owes the foreseeable adult trespasser a duty to use reasonable care to provide a warning of the danger. No duty is owed the foreseeable trespasser for dangers in natural conditions on the land. For activities on the land, the occupier has a duty to use reasonable care for the safety of the foreseeable trespasser.

Child trespassers foreseeably present anywhere on the land Children are given special protection in the law of premises liability. A **child** is usually defined as someone who is too young to appreciate the dangers that could be involved in a given situation. There is no age limit that sets the boundary line for the level of immaturity that is required, but in the vast majority of cases that have provided this special protection, the plaintiff has been under fifteen.

child Someone too young to appreciate the dangers that could be involved in a given situation. (See glossary for an additional definition.)

The special protection is embodied in the **attractive nuisance doctrine**, which says a duty of reasonable care is owed to prevent injury:

1. to a foreseeable trespassing child
2. too young to appreciate the danger
3. of an unreasonable risk of death or serious bodily injury
4. due to an artificial condition on the land

attractive nuisance doctrine When an artificial condition on land creates an unreasonable risk of death or serious bodily injury to a foreseeable trespassing child too young to appreciate the danger, a duty of reasonable care exists to protect the child. Also called *turntable doctrine*, because the doctrine originated in cases involving railroad turntables.

The word "nuisance" in the name of the doctrine is used in the generic sense of danger; it does not refer to the rules of public and public nuisance we discussed earlier in the chapter. Also, the word "attractive" does not mean that the artificial condition on the land must be particularly alluring or inviting to the child, although such a condition would qualify. The attractiveness of the condition bears mainly on the issue of the foreseeability of the child's presence.[10] The question is whether it was foreseeable that a trespassing child would be present, not whether the particular condition lured the child to it.

Artificial conditions include railroad tracks, vehicles, rope, fences, barns, and factories—any condition that has the potential of causing death or serious bodily injury. *Natural* conditions on the land are not covered by the doctrine. The occupier is not under a duty to childproof the land from all of the dangers that a child could encounter with natural lakes, animals, trees, and rock formations on the land unless the defendant has significantly altered these conditions through strip-mining or other processes.

The artificial condition must be one whose danger the child is not expected to understand. If the danger in the condition is obvious, the attractive nuisance doctrine does not apply. In one case, the court refused to apply the doctrine to a trespassing ten-year-old boy who drowned in a swimming pool. The child was intelligent, had completed the fourth grade, and had been told that the water was deep. The court said that "there are many dangers, such as those of fire and water or falling from a height, which under ordinary conditions may be reasonably expected to be fully understood and appreciated by any child old enough to be allowed at large."[11] It should be noted, however, that other courts may be more inclined to give the benefit of the doubt to a child and conclude that he or she did not understand the danger.

Furthermore, only *unreasonable* dangers from artificial conditions are covered. A danger is unreasonable if the burden or inconvenience of preventing injury is outweighed by the foreseeability of serious injury. The more likely that a child may suffer serious injury, the greater the responsibility of the occupier to take reasonable measures to try to prevent it. This is the same equation that is used when reasonableness must be assessed in any negligence case. (See Exhibit 14–4 in Chapter 14 where we introduced the equation.) Assume, for example, that an occupier has exposed electrical wires on the land. It's foreseeable that a child could be seriously injured by the wires. Reasonable precautions, therefore, must be taken to prevent such injuries. A "danger" sign may not be enough. More appropriate may be building a difficult-to-climb fence around the wires. On the other hand, it may be too extreme to require the occupier to station around-the-clock guards throughout the land where the wires exist. The occupier is not required to prevent the injury; the duty owed to the trespassing child is limited to taking reasonable steps to try to prevent it.

When an occupier engages in *activities* on the land (e.g., dynamiting), he or she owes a duty of reasonable care to persons who could be injured by the activity. This includes trespassers so long as they are foreseeable. For example, an occupier cannot continue blasting operations without taking reasonable precautions to protect known or foreseeable trespassers in the area. This, of course, includes a child trespasser. The duty to the child is based on the foreseeability of harm from a dangerous activity (blasting); it is not based on the attractive nuisance doctrine, which applies only to artificial conditions on the land.

ASSIGNMENT 23.5

What questions would you investigate to decide whether the defendant in the following cases owed and breached a duty of reasonable care to the plaintiff?

a. A ten-year-old boy is trespassing on the defendant's land. He leans against a fence on the land and badly injures his back on a protruding nail.
b. A nine-year-old girl is trespassing on the defendant's land. She watches workers climb a pole on the land. After the workers leave, the girl puts on a pair of spiked or cleated shoes that she owns and tries to climb the pole. She falls and severely injures herself.

Licensees

licensee One who enters the land for his or her own purposes, but with the express or implied consent of the occupier.

Licensees are on the land with the express or implied permission of the occupier. The licensees, however, are present for their own purposes.

EXAMPLES

- someone taking a shortcut through the land
- someone soliciting money for charity
- a loiterer or other trespasser who has been allowed to remain
- a person who comes to borrow a tool
- a social guest, even if invited

social guest One who receives a social invitation, and who comes on the premises for a social (not a business) purpose to enjoy hospitality as a guest of the occupier. An example of a licensee.

business guest Someone who has been expressly or impliedly invited to be present, primarily for a business purpose. Also called a business invitee.

latent Not readily visible; hidden.

The last example has caused some difficulty. Because **social guests** are invited, one would normally tend to classify them as invitees. Only a few courts, however, take this position. A social guest is someone who has received a social invitation and is on the premises to enjoy hospitality as a guest of the occupier. In most states, a social guest is a mere licensee, no matter how much urging the occupier may have used to get the guest to come and even though the guest may perform some incidental chores or tasks for the occupier while there. A **business guest**, however, who has been invited primarily for the purpose of doing business with the occupier, *is* an invitee.

What standard of care is owed by the occupier to the licensee?

1. First, the occupier owes the licensee at least the same duty of care that he or she owes the adult trespasser, as discussed previously.
2. The occupier must warn the licensee of dangerous artificial *or* natural conditions (a) if the owner knows about these conditions or has reason to know about them, and (b) if they are **latent** or nonobvious so that the occupier should expect that the licensee would not discover them. (Note: the occupier

does not have a duty to inspect his or her premises to discover such danger. This duty to inspect *will* exist for the protection of an invitee.)

3. Third, if a warning is unlikely to be adequate for extremely dangerous conditions, the occupier must take additional reasonable precautions to protect the licensee.
4. Fourth, for any activities being conducted on the land that pose nonobvious dangers to the licensee, the occupier owes a duty of reasonable care to avoid injuring the licensee, which may call for a warning or for safety precautions that are more active.

Suppose that there is a fence on the land in a state of disrepair. The occupier does not know or have reason to know about this problem with the fence. A licensee is injured by a protruding nail on the fence. The occupier is not liable to the licensee for this injury. An occupier has no duty to inspect for dangerous conditions. If the occupier has actual knowledge (or reason to know) of the dangerous condition (artificial or natural), then the occupier must either warn the licensee of it or take additional reasonable precautions, depending on the nature of the danger. Activities, however, such as operating machinery on the land, call for reasonable care if the danger in the activity would not be obvious to the licensee.

If the occupier knows that third persons are on the land who are likely to injure the licensee, the occupier has a duty to at least warn the licensee of the presence of such third persons, e.g., known criminals or individuals who have told the occupier that they want to harm the licensee.

An analogous situation involves automobiles. The same rules apply to a social guest/licensee in an automobile: the driver has a duty to use reasonable care in driving the car (an activity), but has no duty to inspect the condition of the car to make sure that it is safe. When the driver knows of defective conditions in the car, a warning to the guest is usually sufficient. As indicated in Chapter 14, there are *automobile guest statutes* in some states that change this rule, often making the driver liable only for wanton or reckless conduct in driving the car. A **passenger**, however, is often treated differently than a mere social guest. In many states, a duty of full reasonable care is owed passengers. To be a passenger, the plaintiff's presence must confer some benefit on the driver other than the benefit of his or her company or the mere sharing of expenses. The sharing of expenses can help show that the plaintiff is a passenger if other benefit to the driver is also shown. If the plaintiff is paying for the ride, or if the driver is trying to solicit business from the plaintiff, the latter is a passenger to whom a duty of reasonable care is owed.

passenger Someone riding in a car who confers a benefit on the driver, other than the benefit of social company.

ASSIGNMENT 23.6

A door-to-door salesperson slips and falls on a child's skate upon approaching the front door of a residence. What standard of care would the occupier owe this person?

Invitees

The highest degree of care by the occupier of land is owed an **invitee**. An invitee is someone present on the land with the express or implied invitation of the occupier to use the land for a purpose for which it is open to the public or to use the land to pursue the business of the occupier.

invitee One who enters the land upon the express or implied invitation of the occupier of the land, in order to use the land for the purposes for which it is held open to the public or to pursue the business of the occupier.

EXAMPLES

- a customer in a department store
- someone browsing in a department store, even if nothing is purchased

- a user of a laundromat to wash clothes (a person who is present in the laundromat to wait for a bus or to get out of the rain, however, is probably a licensee only)
- someone attending a free public lecture on religion
- a user of a library (a person who is there to meet a friend, however, is probably only a licensee)
- a patron at a restaurant, theater, amusement park, or similar establishment
- someone who goes to a garage to find out if it sells a certain part for a car

There must be an element of invitation that is much stronger than mere permission or consent that the person be on the land. The invitation is an implied or direct statement of a desire by the occupier that the person be present. A greater standard of care is owed to an invitee than to a trespasser or a licensee because the invitation justifies the invitee's belief that the premises are safe.

Public employees injured on the premises often pose a problem. They include police officers, fire fighters, sanitation workers, postal workers, and meter readers. What is their status? If they are not present in their official capacity within working hours, their status is determined like that of any other citizen. Indeed, they could have the status of trespasser. When present in an *official* role, are they invitees or licensees?

In most states, police officers and firefighters are licensees only, to whom a duty of reasonable care is owed for activities conducted on the premises, but to whom no duty is owed concerning dangerous conditions unknown to the occupier. The theory behind this position is that these public employees are likely to go to parts of the premises that the occupier has no reason to expect, especially in emergency situations. As to such areas, the occupier has made no implied or direct representation that they are safe. Other public official entrants, however, are given the status of invitees on the somewhat strained theory they are present for a business purpose of the occupier. A few states disregard this distinction and classify all public entrants as invitees.

firefighter's rule Firefighters (and police officers) cannot recover against an occupier for injuries related to the risks they are expected to assume as part of their job.

ordinary negligence Conduct that is unreasonable but not gross or reckless.

Finally, many states apply the **firefighter's rule** to emergency public employees. Under this rule, firefighters and police officers cannot recover for injuries that result from risks that are inherent in their jobs. In effect such personnel cannot recover for injuries related to risks they are expected to assume as part of their job. This limitation, however, applies only when their injuries were due to the **ordinary negligence** of the occupier. The firefighter's rule would not apply if the emergency worker was injured by the occupier's recklessness.

ASSIGNMENT 23.7

Are the following individuals invitees, licensees, or trespassers?

a. Tom enters a restaurant solely to use its bathroom. He slips on the bathroom floor.

b. Mary wants to visit a friend who is staying at a hotel. She goes to the room of the friend. While there, she is assaulted by another guest.

c. Fred goes to a railroad station to meet a passenger. While there, he falls over a hose on the ramp.

d. Linda goes to a soccer game to pass out religious literature. She falls down a flight of steps.

e. Jim is in a restaurant eating. He notices that there are cries of distress coming from the kitchen. He passes through the kitchen door on which a sign is posted reading, "Authorized Personnel Only." He discovers that nothing is wrong, but slips on the kitchen floor.

What is the duty of care owed by an occupier to an invitee?

1. First, the occupier owes the invitee at least the same standard of care owed the adult trespasser, as discussed previously.
2. Second, the occupier owes the invitee at least the same standard of care owed the licensee, as discussed previously.
3. Third, if a warning is unlikely to be adequate for extremely dangerous conditions, the occupier must take additional reasonable precautions to protect the invitee.
4. Fourth, the occupier must usually take reasonable steps to *inspect and discover* dangerous artificial conditions, dangerous natural conditions, and dangerous activities on the land. In the main, this inspect-and-discover rule does not apply to trespassers and licensees.

Again, no more than reasonable care is required to discover the danger and protect the invitee from it. The occupier is not the insurer of the invitee.

CASE

Donnell v. California Western School of Law

200 Cal. App. 3d 715, 246 Cal. Rptr. 199 (1988)
California Court of Appeal, Fourth District, Division 1

Background: *William Donnell is a law student at California Western School of Law in San Diego. While going home from school late one night, he was attacked on a dark city-owned sidewalk adjoining the school. He sued the law school for negligence. The trial court denied the claim. Donnell has now appealed to the Court of Appeals.*

Decision on Appeal: *The judgment is affirmed. The law school did not have a duty to place lights on the exterior of its building nor to install security monitors in the area.*

OPINION OF COURT

Justice KREMER delivered the opinion of the court . . .:

Donnell's complaint alleged: Cal Western runs a law school at 350 Cedar Street in a San Diego building it owns, possesses and controls. Cal Western provides no parking for its students at or near its law school. On January 30, 1984, Cal Western's library and school grounds were open for student use until midnight. About 10 P.M., Cal Western law student William Donnell left Cal Western's building after studying in its library and headed toward his parked car. While walking along the west side of Cal Western's building, William was attacked, stabbed and injured by an unknown assailant. William called for help, but no security personnel came to his assistance. Cal Western's building had no exterior lights on its west side. No security guards patrolled the building's west side.

Donnell further alleged: Defendants knew criminal activity had occurred in the immediate area but negligently failed to provide adequate lighting and security around the law school building. Students, including William, going to and from the law school were forced to traverse the dangerous area because Cal Western did not provide parking for its students. Despite knowing about prior criminal activity perpetrated on persons and property around its law school premises, defendants did not warn William of the dangerous conditions, provide adequate security forces or otherwise safeguard law school students from criminal acts. . . .

We decline . . . to impose on Cal Western a duty to insure its adult students' safety once they have left Cal Western's premises. Mature students are generally considered business invitees. . . . [N]othing in the record suggests Cal Western voluntarily assumed a duty to protect its students from criminal acts outside its premises.

A right to protection from the dangerous conduct of another may arise from the special relationship between a landholder and its invitees. (*Peterson v. San Francisco Community College Dist.,* (1984) 36 Cal. 3d 799, 806, 685 P.2d 1193.) Thus, the issue here is the extent of Cal Western's premises liability to its invitee William.

"A defendant cannot be held liable for the defective or dangerous condition of property which it [does] not own, possess, or control. Where the absence of ownership, possession, or control has been unequivocally established, summary judgment is proper." (*Isaacs v. Huntington Memorial Hospital* (1985) 38 Cal. 3d 112, 134, 695 P.2d 653.)

Donnell contends Cal Western had a duty to take reasonable steps to protect its invitees from foreseeable criminal assaults on sidewalks giving immediate access to its building. Donnell seeks to hold Cal Western liable for a dangerous condition of a City-owned sidewalk adjoining Cal Western's property, asserting Cal Western had the power to "control" the sidewalk by placing lights on its own building to shine on the sidewalk. Donnell also asserts Cal Western should perhaps have mounted exterior monitors on its building walls to permit its students to view the dangerous area before traversing it. However, Donnell attempts to expand the principle of "control" of property to include situations where an adjoining landowner merely has the ability to influence or affect such property. Donnell in effect attempts to hold Cal Western responsible for the dangerous condition of "something with which [its] only connection is the fact of [its] ownership or use of the abutting land." (*Kopfinger v. Grand Central Pub. Market* (1964) 60 Cal. 2d 852, 858, 389 P.2d 529.) The law of premises liability does not extend so far as to hold Cal Western liable merely because its property exists next to adjoining dangerous property and it took no action to influence or affect the condition of such adjoining property.

In *Kopfinger,* as a result of the defendant merchant's business operation, meat fell to the sidewalk in the course of defendant's activities rendering the walkway dangerous to pedestrians. . . . [T]he court held the defendant could be held liable because its business activities *affirmatively* created a dangerous physical condition on the adjacent public sidewalk which was not timely remedied by the defendant. The court specifically distinguished the "numerous cases to the effect that in the absence of statute there is no common-law duty on the occupant of land abutting a sidewalk to repair or maintain the sidewalk." (Id. at p. 858.) Unlike the plaintiff in *Kopfinger,* Donnell has presented no evidence Cal Western's business activities affirmatively created a dangerous physical condition on the City-owned sidewalk. . . .

[Nor has he offered evidence that] Cal Western had any right to control the City-owned sidewalk where Donnell was assertedly injured. At most Cal Western merely had the ability to influence or affect the condition of the City's property. Further, Donnell presented no evidence Cal Western assumed any responsibility for or exercised control over the means of lighting the City-owned sidewalk where Donnell was injured. Indeed, Donnell asserts Cal Western should be liable precisely because it did not assume responsibility over the City-owned sidewalk.

Donnell's heavy reliance on *Schwartz v. Helms Bakery Limited* (1967) 67 Cal. 2d 232, 235, 430 P.2d 68, is misplaced. In *Schwartz* the court . . . [held] that by undertaking to direct a child to an assigned rendezvous with a doughnut truck the defendants assumed a duty to exercise due care for the child's safety. In discussing earlier cases involving premises liability, the court stated: "The physical area encompassed by the term 'the premises' does not, however, coincide with the area to which the invitor possesses a title or a lease." (Id. at p. 239.) However, this language in *Schwartz* did not expand the law of premises liability beyond those premises owned, possessed or controlled by the defendant. . . . The court in *Schwartz* stated the "premises" may be greater than the invitor's property: "The premises may include such means of ingress and egress as a customer may reasonably be expected to use. The crucial element is *control.*" (Id. at p. 239, italics added.). . . "An invitor bears a duty to warn an invitee of a dangerous condition existing on a public street or sidewalk adjoining his business which, because of the invitor's special benefit, convenience, or use of the public way, creates a danger." (Id. pp. 239–240.)

The court in *Schwartz* also emphasized it was applying established premises liability law to the unique facts before it involving the mobile doughnut truck:

> "It may be argued that defendants, as business invitors, cannot incur a duty to protect invitees from injury on a public street. We have pointed out, however, that the jury could have found that the dangerous circumstances which caused the injury were *created* by defendants. Moreover, . . . the concept of 'business premises' may no longer be mechanically defined by the geographical area in which the invitor holds a property interest. An invitor may be liable for an injury, whether it occurs on his property or on a common passageway or on an adjacent sidewalk or street being used for his special benefit, if, and only if, the injury is caused by a dangerous condition, or unreasonable risk of harm, within the invitor's *control.* [Citation.] Defendants' business consisted of selling bakery goods from a truck. In coming to the truck for the convenience of defendants, patrons used the public streets and sidewalks as means of access for the special benefit of defendants' business. Defendants may therefore be held liable for an injury occurring to their customer in the immediate vicinity of the truck if the circumstances causing the injury are within the range of defendants' *reasonable supervision and control.* Obviously, defendants are not insurers for all accidents occurring in areas through which their truck passes. They may not be held liable, for example, for a fall caused by an unobserved defect in a sidewalk next to which their truck stops. They may be responsible, however, for harm occurring in the immediate vicinity of the truck, wherever it may be stopped at a given time, if the harm is of the kind that defendants could have prevented by exercising reasonable care for the safety of their customers." (*Schwartz,* supra, 67 Cal. 2d at p. 243, fn. 10, italics added.)

Donnell also relies on *O'Hara v. Western Seven Trees Corp.* (1977) 75 Cal. App. 3d 798, 142 Cal. Rptr. 487. However, [this case does] not help Donnell. *O'Hara* involved a landlord-tenant relationship not involved here. Alleging she was raped in her apartment, plaintiff tenant sued her landlord for not providing adequate security and not warning her of the danger of rape. The court held the plaintiff had stated a cause of action. The court noted "the landlord-tenant relationship, at least in the urban, residential context, has given rise to liability under circumstances where landlords have failed to take reasonable steps to protect tenants from criminal activity. . . . It has been held that since *only the landlord is in the position to secure common areas,* he has a duty to protect against types of crimes of which he has notice and which are likely to recur if the common areas are not secure." (Id. at pp. 802–803, italics added.) Cal Western's position was unlike the landlord's in *O'Hara.* Here the City could remedy any dangerous condition of its sidewalk.

Donnell's asserted premises liability case against Cal Western fails under the analysis of *Steinmetz v. Stockton City Chamber of Commerce* (1985) 169 Cal. App. 3d 1142, 214 Cal. Rptr. 405. In a case involving "a landowner's liability for a criminal assault by a third person upon an invitee which occurs off the landowner's premises," the court in *Steinmetz* affirmed summary judgment favoring defendant tenant. (Id. at p. 1144.) The court found "the record establishes without question the decedent was murdered off the premises leased by [defendant tenant] on property not within the possession or control of [defendant tenant], but rather on the premises of another tenant in the industrial park. . . . Plaintiffs have not cited nor are we aware of any case where a *landowner* was held responsible for injuries to an invitee from criminal activity occurring off the landowner's premises." (Id. at p. 1146, italics in original.) Discussing *Schwartz v. Helms Bakery Limited,* supra, 67 Cal. 2d 232, the court stated *Schwartz's* "elastic concept of business premises is uniquely appropriate to the vendor whose commercial activities are conducted from a mobile vehicle at shifting locations on the public streets. However, we know of no decision which has applied this standard to one whose business is conducted on private property in a fixed location. Indeed, it is difficult to perceive how such a rule could be fashioned." (*Steinmetz,* supra, at p. 1146.) . . .

[P]remises liability is based on ownership, possession or control. The mere possibility of influencing or affecting the condition of property owned or possessed by others does not constitute "control" of such property. . . .

The judgment is affirmed.

ASSIGNMENT 23.8

a. Assume that Cal Western holds a forum at the law school on prison reform. The speakers include ex-felons discussing their experiences. Would the *Donnell* case have reached the same result if a law student was assaulted by one of the ex-felons (i) in a restroom at the law school during the forum, or (ii) on a city-owned sidewalk adjacent to the law school after the forum?
b. Assume that two days after the attack on William Donnell, another student is assaulted on the adjacent sidewalk by an unknown stranger. Would the *Donnell* case reach the same result when this other student sues the law school?
c. Assume that two days after the attack on William Donnell, another student is assaulted on the adjacent sidewalk by a fellow law student. Would the *Donnell* case reach the same result when this student sues the law school?
d. In the *Armory Park* case we read earlier in the chapter, the landowner (Episcopal Community Services) said that it should not be held responsible for the criminal acts committed by its patrons off the premises of the food distribution center. The landowner lost this argument. Is *Armory Park* consistent with the *Donnell* case, which held that the landowner (Cal Western) was not responsible for the criminal act that was committed off the school premises?

3. The Special Problems of the Seller and Buyer of Land (Vendor and Vendee)

When land is sold, the general rule is that the seller (**vendor**) has no further tort liability for injuries that occur on the land, either to the buyer (**vendee**) or to a third person. The buyer, under the theory of **caveat emptor** (buyer beware), takes the land as he or she finds it. The buyer is expected to make an inspection of the premises before purchasing. The seller will not be liable if the buyer is injured by a condition on the land, even if the condition was present when the land was sold. Third parties injured by such conditions must look to the new owner for liability.

A number of exceptions exist to this rule. If there is a hidden or latent condition on the land that is dangerous and if the seller knows about the condition (or has reason to know about it), the seller has a duty either to warn the buyer of the condition or to repair it before turning the land over to the buyer. Examples of latent conditions include deep holes in the yard covered by thin plywood, and ceilings infested with termites not visible on the surface. A seller does not have a duty to inspect the premises to discover defects that are latent. There is a duty to warn or repair only when the seller knows about such defects or has reason to believe they exist. If this duty is breached, injuries sustained by the buyer can lead to negligence liability against the seller. The buyer may also be able to assert the tort of fraud or misrepresentation.

vendor Seller.

vendee Buyer.

caveat emptor ("buyer beware") A seller of real property will not be liable for injuries caused by a defect in the property if (1) the defect was discoverable upon reasonable inspection by the buyer, (2) the buyer had an unimpeded opportunity to inspect the premises, and (3) the seller did not commit fraud.

Another exception concerns conditions on the land that are dangerous to persons *outside the land* at the time of the sale. These conditions sometimes amount to a public or private nuisance, although the seller's liability for injury caused to a plaintiff outside the land is not dependent on the existence of a nuisance. The seller's liability exists only for a reasonable time to enable the buyer to discover such conditions and therefore assume responsibility for them.

4. The Special Problems of the Landlord and Tenant (Lessor and Lessee)

reversionary interest The right of a grantor of land (who has transferred less than his or her full interest in the land) to the future possession and enjoyment of land presently occupied by another. The right in land that is retained by one who transfers property (the grantor).

Normally, a landlord (lessor) is not entitled to possession of the land, but has a **reversionary interest** in the land, which comes into effect after the tenancy is over. (A reversionary interest is a right to the future possession and enjoyment of land that is presently occupied by another.) The general rule is that the tenant (lessee) assumes all liability for injuries caused by conditions or activities on the land. There are a number of exceptions to this general rule.

Statutes may exist in a state requiring the landlord to maintain the premises, particularly apartment houses, in a safe condition. The violation of such statutes may impose negligence (and in severe cases, criminal) liability on the landlord.

The landlord will be liable to the tenant and to third parties for injuries caused by latent dangerous conditions on the land at the time of the lease if the landlord had actual knowledge of the dangerous conditions or had reason to believe they existed. In most states, the landlord has no duty to inspect and discover such conditions, but must know of them or have reason to believe that they are present. The conditions must be latent or concealed—not obvious to the tenant.

common area An area used by more than one tenant that is controlled by (and under the responsibility of) the landlord.

Often the landlord does not lease the entire building or land to the tenant(s). The landlord may retain control over certain **common areas**, such as hallways, stairways, elevators, boiler rooms. The landlord has a duty of reasonable care to inspect these common areas and make sure that they are safe for those who are entitled to use them, e.g., the tenants and people using the land as invitees.

Another exception occurs when the landlord leases the premises for a purpose that involves the admission of the public, e.g., theater, pier, hotel, or department store. In such cases, the landlord has a duty to inspect the premises and to repair any dangerous conditions that exist at the time of the lease, *before* the tenant takes over. Reasonable care must be used to make sure that the land is not turned over to the tenant in a dangerous condition. If a member of the public is injured by such a condition that was unreasonably not discovered and repaired by the landlord before the tenant took over, the landlord will be liable, even if the lease agreement provides that the tenant shall assume all responsibility for repairs. The landlord cannot shift the responsibility to the tenant in this way. The duty is **nondelegable**.

nondelegable Pertaining to a duty for which one remains responsible even if another is asked to (or agrees to) carry it out.

Suppose that the dangerous condition arises *after* the land is leased. The general rule is that injured third parties must look to the tenant for liability rather than to the landlord. If, however, the landlord is obligated to make repairs by the terms of the lease, failure to do so will lead to negligence liability in most states. In such cases, the tenant can argue that the tenant did not make the repairs because of reasonable reliance on the landlord's contract obligation to do so. There are some states, however, that do not impose tort liability on the landlord for a failure to make agreed-upon repairs. In such states, only the tenant is liable in tort to injured third parties. The tenant's recourse in such states is a breach-of-contract action against the landlord.

CHECK THE CITE

Homeowners living near an outdoor music venue complained about the noise from the facility. How did the court resolve their claims of public nuisance and private nuisance? Read the case of *Whaley v. Park City Mun. Corp.*, 190 P.3d 1

(Ct. App. Utah 2008). To read the opinion online, (1) Go to the site of the Utah courts (www.utcourts.gov). Click Court Publications, then Appellate Opinions. In the search box for Court of Appeals Opinions, type the names of the parties (Whaley Park City). Find the June 19, 2008 opinion. (2) Go to www.findlaw.com (caselaw.lp.findlaw.com/data/ut/cases/appopin/whaley061908.pdf). (3) Run a citation search ("190 P.3d 1") or a party search (Whaley Park City) in the Legal Opinions and Journals database of Google Scholar (scholar.google.com).

PROJECT

In Google, Bing, or another general search engine, run the following search: "attractive nuisance" liability *aa* (substitute the name of your state for *aa* in the search (e.g., "attractive nuisance" liability Georgia). Summarize the law in your state on attractive nuisance liability for injuries to children. You can consult as many websites as you wish, but you must quote from at least three separate sites, only one of which can be a law firm site.

ETHICS IN A TORTS PRACTICE

You are a paralegal working in the law office of Taylor & Taylor, which represents Metro Ltd., the owner of the East End apartment complex in the city. Metro is being sued for maintaining a private nuisance and a public nuisance at the East End complex. Four months ago you were evicted from the West End apartment complex, also owned by Metro. The reason for the eviction was nonpayment of rent. You stopped paying rent because you felt that the building services were poor. What ethical problems, if any, might exist?

SUMMARY

Trespass to land is an intentional entry or intrusion on land in possession of another. The intent to enter does not require proof of an intent to enter wrongfully. Land includes the space above (and the ground below) of which the plaintiff has reasonable beneficial use. Actual harm to the land does not have to be shown. The action can be brought by someone with a possessory interest in the land. The plaintiff does not have to be the owner.

A private nuisance is an unreasonable interference with the reasonable use and enjoyment of private land. This occurs when one's peace of mind is disturbed while on the land. In determining whether the interference is unreasonable, the court will consider a number of factors: the gravity and character of the harm, the social value of the use the plaintiff is making of the land, the character of the locality, the extent of the burden on the plaintiff of avoiding or minimizing the interference, the motive of the defendant, the social value of the defendant's conduct, and the extent of the burden on the defendant of avoiding or minimizing the interference. A private nuisance can be created negligently; intentionally; through an abnormally dangerous condition or activity; or by a violation of a statute, ordinance, or regulation. Any person who has the right to the use and enjoyment of the land can bring the action. The remedies might include money (damages), injunction, and self-help via the privilege to abate the nuisance. Possible defenses include contributory negligence (or comparative negligence), assumption of the risk, the failure to mitigate damages, and official authorization.

A public nuisance is an unreasonable interference with a right common to the general public. It can be created negligently; intentionally; through an abnormally dangerous condition or activity; or by violating a statute, ordinance, or regulation. A public official can sue the wrongdoer. A private citizen can also sue if he or she has suffered in

a way that is different in kind from that of every other member of the public affected by the public nuisance. The remedies are similar to those for a private nuisance. The government may also be able to impose a fine or imprisonment. The defenses to a public nuisance are similar to those available in private nuisance cases.

Traditional negligence liability may depend on the status of the parties. To persons outside the land, occupiers owe (1) a duty of reasonable care as to artificial or non-natural conditions on the land; (2) no duty as to natural conditions on the land, except for trees in urban areas; and (3) a duty of reasonable care as to activities taking place on the land. For adult trespassers whom the occupier does not know are present, no duty of care is owed for natural conditions, artificial conditions, or activities on the land. To discovered trespassers (and to foreseeable trespassers on limited portions of the land), occupiers owe (1) a duty of reasonable care as to artificial conditions to provide a warning if the danger is not obvious and is likely to cause serious bodily injury, (2) no duty as to natural conditions, and (3) a duty of reasonable care as to activities on the land. To foreseeable child trespassers on the land, occupiers owe (1) a duty of reasonable care as to artificial conditions if the danger of serious bodily injury is unreasonable and the child is unlikely to appreciate it, (2) no duty as to natural conditions on the land, and (3) a duty of reasonable care as to activities taking place on the land. To licensees, occupiers owe (1) a duty of reasonable care as to artificial conditions to warn of dangers that are known to the occupier but are latent (not obvious) to the licensee; (2) a duty of reasonable care as to natural conditions to warn of dangers that are known to the occupier but are latent (not obvious) to the licensee; and (3) a duty of reasonable care as to activities on the land if the danger is nonobvious. To invitees, an occupier owes (1) a duty of reasonable care as to artificial conditions which may include a duty to inspect and discover dangers, (2) a duty of reasonable care as to natural conditions which may include a duty to inspect and discover dangers, and (3) a duty of reasonable care as to activities, which may include a duty to inspect and discover dangers.

The seller of land can be liable for known latent defects that injure the buyer or a third person on the land. A landlord can be liable to tenants and others injured by latent dangerous conditions on the land that the landlord knows about or should know about. The landlord must use reasonable care to make common areas safe.

KEY TERMS

interest *466*
occupier *466*
lessor *466*
lessee *466*
adverse possession *466*
possessory interest *466*
premises liability *466*
trespass to land *466*
intrusion *467*
reasonable beneficial use *467*
intent (for trespass to land) *467*
nominal damages *467*
transferred-intent rule *467*
nuisance *471*
private nuisance *471*
public nuisance *471*
social value *474*
damages *477*
cost of restoration *477*
injunction *477*
equitable remedy *477*
self-help *477*
abate a nuisance *477*
contributory negligence *478*
comparative negligence *478*
assumption of the risk *478*
mitigation-of-damages rule *478*
taking *479*
standing *482*
nuisance per se *483*
reasonable care *486*
independent contractor *488*
trespasser *488*
child *489*
attractive nuisance doctrine *489*
licensee *490*
social guest *490*
business guest *490*
latent *490*
passenger *491*
invitee *491*
firefighter's rule *492*
ordinary negligence *492*
vendor *495*
vendee *495*
caveat emptor *495*
reversionary interest *496*
common area *496*
nondelegable *496*

REVIEW QUESTIONS

1. What is an interest in land?
2. What is an occupier?
3. How does a lessor differ from a lessee?
4. How is land acquired by adverse possession?
5. What is meant by premises liability?
6. What is trespass to land?
7. Who can bring an action for trespass to land?
8. What are the ways land can be intruded upon?
9. What intent must be established for trespass to land?
10. What is a reasonable beneficial use?
11. How does trespass to land differ from negligence?
12. How is private nuisance different from public nuisance?
13. What is the nature of a private nuisance?
14. In what ways can a private nuisance be created?
15. Who can sue for private nuisance?
16. What remedies can be obtained for a private nuisance?
17. What defenses can be raised against a claim of private nuisance?
18. What is the nature of a public nuisance?
19. In what ways can a public nuisance be created?
20. Who can sue for public nuisance?
21. What remedies can be obtained for a public nuisance?
22. What defenses can be raised against a claim of public nuisance?
23. What is nuisance per se?
24. What duty does an occupier owe to persons outside the land injured by artificial conditions, natural conditions, or activities on the land?
25. What duty does an occupier owe to an unknown adult trespasser injured by artificial conditions, natural conditions, or activities on the land?
26. What duty does an occupier owe to a known adult trespasser injured by artificial conditions, natural conditions, or activities on the land?
27. What duty does an occupier owe to a foreseeable trespasser on a limited portion of the land injured by artificial conditions, natural conditions, or activities on the land?
28. What duty does an occupier owe to a foreseeable child trespasser injured by artificial conditions, natural conditions, or activities on the land?
29. What duty does an occupier owe to a licensee injured by artificial conditions, natural conditions, or activities on the land?
30. What duty does an occupier owe to an invitee injured by artificial conditions, natural conditions, or activities on the land?
31. What duty does a seller (vendor) owe to a buyer (vendee) or to third parties injured on the land that is sold?
32. What duty does a landlord owe to a tenant or to third parties injured on the land that is leased?

HELPFUL WEBSITES

- **Premises Liability**
  www.justia.com/injury/premises-liability
  www.expertlaw.com (enter "premises liability" in the search box)
- **Trespass to Land**
  en.wikipedia.org/wiki/Trespass_to_land
  law.jrank.org/pages/10898/Trespass-Trespass-Land.html
- **Element Search**
  www.google.com (run this search: elements "trespass to land" tort)
- **Private and Public Nuisance**
  en.wikipedia.org/wiki/Nuisance
  www.lexisnexis.com/lawschool/study/outlines/html/prop/prop29.htm
  www.nuisancelaw.com
- **Element Search**
  www.google.com (run this search: elements nuisance tort)
- **Negligence Liability to Trespassers, Licensees, and Invitees**
  en.wikipedia.org/wiki/Licensee
  www.expertlaw.com/library/premises_liability/premises_liability.html

ENDNOTES

1. W. Page Keeton et al., Prosser and Keeton on the Law of Torts 74 (5th ed. 1984).
2. 47 U.S.C §230(c)(1); (www.law.cornell.edu/uscode/47/230.html).
3. *Dart v. Craigslist*, 665 F. Supp. 2d 961 (N.D. Ill. 2009).
4. Matthew Kliegman and Mary Yelenick, *Public Nuisance Claims Have Mixed Success,* www.internationallawoffice.com/Newsletters/Detail.aspx?r=8478#firearms (2004).
5. *Cincinnati v. Beretta U.S.A. Corp.*, 95 Ohio St.3d 416, 768 N.E.2d 1136 (Ohio 2002).
6. *City of Philadelphia v. Beretta U.S.A.,* 126 F. Supp. 2d 882, 895 (E. D. Pa. 2000).
7. John Tierney, *A New Push to Grant Gun Immunity from Suits*, New York Times, April 4, 2003, at A10.
8. 15 U.S.C. § 7901 (2010).
9. *Michigan ex rel. Wayne County Prosecutor v. Bennis*, 447 Mich. 719, 527 N.W.2d 483 (1994); *Bennis v. Michigan*, 516 U.S. 442, 116 S. Ct. 994, 134 L. Ed. 2d 68 (1996).
10. *Restatement (Second) of Torts* § 339 (1965).
11. *Gordon v. C.H.C. Corporation*, 236 So.2d 733, 735 (Supreme Court of Mississippi, 1970).

Student StudyWARE™ CD-ROM
For additional materials, please go to the student CD in this book.

CHAPTER

24

DEFAMATION

CHAPTER OUTLINE

- Introduction
- Defamatory Statement
- Extrinsic Facts
- Falsity of the Statement
- Of and Concerning the Plaintiff
- Publication
- Republication
- Cyberspace Defamation
- Damages
- Privilege
- SLAPP Suits
- "Veggie Libel"

CHAPTER OBJECTIVES

After completing this chapter, you should be able to:

- Understand the harm a defamation action is designed to remedy.
- Distinguish between libel and slander.
- Know when a statement is defamatory.
- Distinguish fact from opinion.
- Explain the effect of having to prove extrinsic facts in a libel or slander action.
- State the major differences in bringing a defamation action against a media defendant and against a nonmedia defendant.
- Know when actual malice must be established in a defamation action.
- Know when a defamatory statement is of and concerning a plaintiff.
- State the meanings of publication and republication.
- Describe the protection given to interactive computer services.
- Distinguish between libel per se and libel per quod.
- Distinguish between slander per se and slander per quod.
- Identify the major defenses to defamation actions.
- Know the impact of an anti-SLAPP motion.
- Identify paralegal roles in defamation actions.
- List the major resources in traditional books and online to use when researching issues involving the defamation torts.

INTRODUCTION

In Shakespeare's *Othello,* Iago says to Othello:

Good name in man and woman, dear my lord,
Is the immediate jewel of their souls:
Who steals my purse steals trash; 'tis something, nothing;
'Twas mine, 'tis his, and has been slave to thousands;
But he that filches from me my good name
Robs me of that which not enriches him,
And makes me poor indeed. Act III, scene 3.

defamation The publication of a written or gestured defamatory statement (libel) or an oral one (slander) that is of and concerning the plaintiff and that harms the plaintiff's reputation.

libel Defamation that is written or embodied in a physical form.

slander Defamation that is oral or gestured.

defamacast Defamation communicated via radio or television.

Iago, however, is not without a remedy. He can bring a suit for **defamation**, which covers injuries to a person's good name and reputation. There are two defamation torts: libel and slander. **Libel** consists of defamation that is written (e.g., in a book) or embodied in a physical form (e.g., a photograph, a film, an effigy). **Slander** consists of defamation that is spoken (e.g., a conversation) or gestured as a substitute for speech (e.g., a nod of the head, a wave of the hand). Defamation in an e-mail message or on a website is libel. Defamation on a television program would be considered libel (even if the defendant is not talking from a prepared script) since it has relative permanence in the physical form of film or video. A few states refer to defamation on radio or television as **defamacast.**

It's not easy to state the elements of libel and slander because the elements may differ depending on the status of the plaintiff, the status of the defendant, and the subject matter of the defamatory statement. Exhibit 24–1 contains our starting point on identifying elements. Throughout the chapter, we will be examining modifications of these elements.

Exhibit 24–1
Elements of the torts of libel and slander.

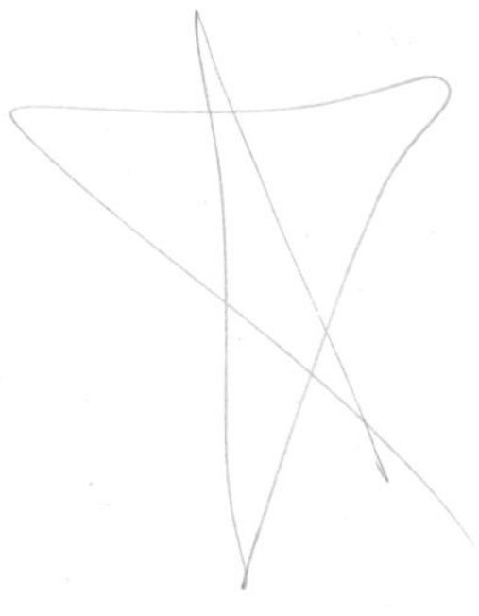

Elements of Libel	Elements of Slander
1. Written defamatory statement by the defendant 2. Of and concerning the plaintiff 3. Publication of the statement 4. Damages: a. In some states, special damages never have to be proven in a libel case b. In other states, libel per se does not require special damages, but libel per quod does 5. Causation Note: In media cases, the plaintiff must also prove that the statement was false and that the defendant exhibited some degree of fault in determining the truth or falsity of the statement. The amount of fault depends on the status of the plaintiff and the content of the libel.	1. Oral defamatory statement by the defendant 2. Of and concerning the plaintiff 3. Publication of the statement 4. Damages: a. Special damages are not required for slander per se b. Special damages are required for slander per quod 5. Causation Note: In media cases, the plaintiff must also prove that the statement was false and that the defendant exhibited some degree of fault in determining the truth or falsity of the statement. The amount of fault depends on the status of the plaintiff and the content of the slander.

Since 1964, the United States Supreme Court has made major changes in the common law of defamation, particularly when the defendant is the press, the media, or book publishers and when the defamation concerns a matter of public concern. (For convenience, we will refer to press, media, and book defendants collectively as media defendants.)

- Under the common law, when a plaintiff alleged defamation, the defendant's statement was assumed to be false. Truth was an **affirmative defense** that the defendant had to prove. This has now been reversed for media defendants. The plaintiff must prove the falsity of the statement.
- Under the common law, the court did not require the plaintiff to prove that the defendant knew the statement was false, was reckless as to its truth or falsity, or was negligent in determining its truth or falsity before publishing the statement. This too has been changed for media defendants. Some degree of **fault** must now be proven as to how the defendant reached its conclusion on the truth or falsity of the statement. The amount of fault depends on the status of the plaintiff and the content of the libel or slander.

affirmative defense A defense raising new facts that will defeat the plaintiff's claim even if the plaintiff's fact allegations are proven.

fault An error or defect in someone's judgment or conduct to which blame and culpability attaches. The wrongful breach of a duty.

The Supreme Court has made these changes in order in order to balance the plaintiff's need to redress injury to reputation and good name with the First Amendment's protection of free speech and press. The changes have been so dramatic that they are referred to as the constitutionalization of defamation law, meaning that principles in the United States Constitution now control a good deal of defamation law.

Do these changes also apply to nonmedia defendants such as a grocery store manager who commits one of the defamation torts by accusing a customer of using a stolen credit card? The answer to this question is not clear. The Supreme Court has not yet defined the full reach of the First Amendment in this area of the law. Some states have applied the law governing media defendants to nonmedia defendants even though the Supreme Court has not yet required them to do so. In short, defamation is a mix of common law and constitutional law that is still in the process of evolving.

DEFAMATORY STATEMENT

Introduction

The first element of both libel and slander is that the defendant has made a **defamatory statement**. This is a statement of fact that would tend to harm the reputation of the plaintiff in the eyes of at least a substantial and respectable minority of people by lowering the plaintiff in the estimation of those people or by deterring them from associating with the plaintiff. More specifically, it is a statement of fact that tends to disgrace a person by holding him or her up to hatred or ridicule, or by causing others to avoid him or her. The people who express this hatred or ridicule must not be extreme or antisocial in their reaction. For example, although it is possible to find people who hate members of a particular race, it is not defamatory for someone to say that you like or support the rights of members of that race, even if a large number of bigots hold you in contempt for this position and refuse to associate with you because of it.

defamatory statement A statement of fact that would tend to harm the reputation of the plaintiff in the eyes of at least a substantial and respectable minority of people by lowering the plaintiff in the estimation of those people or by deterring them from associating with the plaintiff.

actionable Furnishing a legal basis for a cause of action.

Facts and Opinions

Defamatory opinions are rarely **actionable**. An **opinion** is defined as a relatively vague or indefinite value judgment that is not objectively verifiable. ("The speaker was boring.") Opinions are often the basis of endless debate. A **fact**, on the other hand, is a concrete statement that can be objectively established as true or false. ("He does not have a college degree.") There is a difference between saying "Helen's behavior is disgraceful" and saying "Helen stole $100." Only the latter is a statement of fact. In general, you cannot sue someone for expressing a defamatory opinion unless the opinion implies the existence of undisclosed defamatory facts as the basis for the opinion. The statement, "The food at the City Deli is inedible" is an

opinion An express or implied communication containing a relatively vague or indefinite value judgment that is not objectively verifiable. (See the glossary for an additional meaning.)

fact An express or implied communication containing concrete information that can be objectively shown to be true or false. (See the glossary for an additional meaning.)

opinion, but it is arguably based on the unstated defamatory fact that the speaker has eaten spoiled food at this restaurant. According to one court:

> [E]xpressions of "opinion" may often imply an assertion of objective fact. If a speaker says, "In my opinion John Jones is a liar," he implies a knowledge of facts which lead to the conclusion that Jones told an untruth. Even if the speaker states the facts upon which he bases his opinion, if those facts are either incorrect or incomplete, or if his assessment of them is erroneous, the statement may still imply a false assertion of fact. Simply couching such statements in terms of opinion does not dispel these implications. . . .[1]

Suppose that someone says, "Marx and Lenin have had major negative effects on world history." The truth or falsity of such a statement would be the subject of endless debate. It is not a fact that can be objectively proven true or false. What about this statement: "Professor Smith abysmally misinterprets the teachings of Marx and Lenin." It would be impossible to prove that someone misinterprets a particular political or social philosophy. By implication the statement *does* communicate the fact that Professor Bob Smith has tried to interpret Marx and Lenin. Such fact, however, would not be defamatory unless perhaps it is made in the context of a prior assertion by Professor Smith that he has never discussed or tried to interpret Marx and Lenin. (Later in the chapter we will see how context can demonstrate the defamatory meaning of statements.)

No one doubts that opinions can be derogatory and hurtful. Yet it is very difficult to win suits that grow out of derogatory opinions. Everyone has a privilege to express opinions on matters of public concern. For example, Mary says of a fellow worker who refuses to join the union, "He is a traitor to God, country, family, and class." The subject of union membership is certainly a matter of public concern in our society. The privilege to express such opinions is known as **fair comment**. It prevents liability for defamation, no matter how unreasonable the comment, so long as it (1) concerns a matter of public interest, (2) is the actual opinion of the critic, (3) was not made solely to harm the subject of the comment, and (4) does not contain undisclosed facts that are defamatory.

fair comment An honest observation or opinion on a matter of public concern.

When the media is the defendant, the First Amendment to the United States Constitution gives wide latitude in the expression of ideas and opinions. In a famous line in *Gertz v. Welch,* the United States Supreme Court said,

> Under the First Amendment, there is no such thing as a false idea. However pernicious an opinion may seem, we depend for its correction not on the conscience of judges and juries but on the competition of other ideas.[2]

This does not mean that the media has a constitutional right to express any opinion. Again, opinions based on undisclosed defamatory facts can lead to liability for defamation. Yet, winning a defamation suit based on such an opinion is extremely difficult for reasons we will examine shortly.

ASSIGNMENT 24.1

Are any of the following statements defamatory? Assume that each of the statements is made in front of third persons.

a. A disgruntled former client says of his attorney, "He will say or do just about anything to win, typically at the expense of the truth."
b. Author Mary McCarthy says of author Lillian Hellman, "Every word she writes is a lie, including 'and' and 'the'."
c. Alice says of Bill, "He doesn't have the manners of a chimp." When asked for a retraction, Alice says, "He does have the manners of a chimp."
d. Vince calls Nick a "closet Republican." Nick is a registered Democrat.

e. Tom calls Juanita a "Socialist."
f. Ed calls Bill a "tree-hugger."
g. Rich is a member of a union who returns to work during a strike. Hank, another union member, calls Rich a traitor.
h. Mary is the ex-wife of John, now married to Linda. Mary says she had a dream last night and knows it is going to come true. In the dream, Linda wanted to "murder me."
i. Don Adams is a sports talk show host. Sam says, "Adams is the only sportscaster in town who is enrolled in a course for remedial speaking."

CASE

Van Duyn v. Smith

173 Ill. App. 3d 523, 527 N.E.2d 1005 (1988)
Appellate Court of Illinois, Third District

Background: *Margaret Van Duyn directs an abortion clinic. Smith is a pro-life activist who distributed a "Wanted" poster and a "Face the American Holocaust" poster to Van Duyn's friends, neighbors and acquaintances living in the three-block area surrounding Van Duyn's residence. She sued Smith for defamation and other causes of action. Her complaint was dismissed by the trial court for failure to state a cause of action. The case is now before the Appellate Court of Illinois.*

Decision on Appeal: *Defamation was not committed because there was no statement of fact; the posters contained opinions.*

OPINION OF COURT

Justice SCOTT delivered the opinion of the court . . .

Plaintiff claims that the "Wanted" poster . . . resembling those used by the Federal Bureau of Investigation and seen on bulletin boards in public places, states: that plaintiff is a wanted person "for prenatal killing in violation of the Hippocratic oath and Geneva Code"; that plaintiff uses the alias "Margaret the Malignant"; that plaintiff has participated in killing for profit and has presided over more than 50,000 killings; and the plaintiff's modus operandi is a small round tube attached to a powerful suction machine that tears the developing child limb from limb. The poster further contains a statement at the bottom which indicates in part, that "(n)othing in this poster should be considered unethical. Once abortion was a crime but it is not now considered a crime."

The "Face the American Holocaust" poster . . . contains pictures of fetuses between 22 and 29 weeks gestational age that have been aborted. Under each picture the "cause of death" of the fetus is listed; referring to the method used to perform the abortion. Among the techniques listed are dismemberment, salt poisoning, and massive hemorrhaging. The poster also contains four paragraphs of information regarding the discovery of some 17,000 fetuses stored in a 3½ ton container in California, the number of abortions performed per day in "America's abortion mills", and how "America's Holocaust is the responsibility of us all." The poster additionally gives the name and address of Pro-Life Action League and lists the defendant's name and telephone number for those who choose to call locally. . . . [Plaintiff alleges] that as a result of defendant's actions, her good name, character and reputation were impaired and brought into disrepute before her friends and acquaintances. . . .

Generally, defamation, which consists of the identically treated branches of libel and slander, is the publication of anything injurious to the good name or reputation of another, or which tends to bring him into disrepute. Illinois courts have held that a statement is defamatory if it impeaches a person's integrity, virtue, human decency, respect for others, or reputation and thereby lowers that person in the estimation of the community or deters third parties from dealing with that person. Each defamation case must be decided on its own facts. . . .

Plaintiff maintains that the "Wanted" poster, when read alone, or in conjunction with the "Face the American Holocaust" poster, contains false statements of fact that are libelous. . . . In particular, plaintiff argues that defendant's use of the word "killing" would cause the average reader to believe that plaintiff has committed a criminal offense. . . .

We acknowledge, however, that the Supreme Court has recognized a constitutional privilege for expressions of opinion. (*Gertz v. Welch,* 418 U.S. 323.) Whether a statement is one of opinion or fact is a matter of law. Moreover, the alleged defamatory language must be considered in context to determine whether or not it is an expression of opinion. . . .

In *Ollman v. Evans,* the court drew upon theories used in prior cases to devise the totality of the circumstances analysis for determining whether a publication is a statement of fact or an expression of opinion. The four-part analysis is explained as follows: "First, we will analyze the common usage or meaning of the specific language of the challenged statement itself. Our analysis of the specific language under scrutiny will be aimed at determining whether the statement has a precise core of meaning for which a consensus of understanding exists or, conversely, whether the statement is indefinite and ambiguous. Readers are, in our judgment, considerably less likely to infer facts from an indefinite or ambiguous statement than one with a commonly understood meaning. Second, we will consider the statement's verifiability—is the statement capable of being objectively characterized as true or false? Insofar as a statement lacks a plausible method of verification, a reasonable reader will not believe that the statement has specific factual content. And, in the setting of litigation, the trier of fact obliged in a defamation action to assess the truth of an unverifiable statement will have considerable difficulty returning a verdict based upon anything but speculation. Third, moving from the challenged language itself, we will consider the full context of the statement—the entire article or column, for example —inasmuch as other, unchallenged language surrounding the allegedly defamatory statement will influence the average reader's readiness to infer that a particular statement has factual content. Finally, we will consider the broader context or setting in which the statement appears. Different types of writing have . . . widely varying social conventions which signal to the reader the likelihood of a statement's being either fact or opinion. . . ." *Ollman v. Evans,* 750 F.2d 970, 979 (D.C. Cir. 1984).

We believe defendant's statement that plaintiff is involved in "killing" can be commonly understood as meaning that plaintiff has terminated a life of something or someone that was previously living. In itself the accusation that plaintiff is involved with "killing the unwanted and unprotected" is a potentially damaging fact. Our difficulty, however, is that the type of killing being referred to in this instance is not, in our opinion, objectively capable of being proven or disproven. This is especially true when the allegedly defamatory statements are read in the context in which the statements occur. It becomes apparent when looking at the "Wanted" poster in its entirety that defendant's use of the word "killing" is his description of what takes place during an abortion procedure. We are not prepared to find that the word "killing" in this context is verifiable and, thus, a defamatory statement of fact. Additionally, when the statements are considered within the social context, it becomes quite clear that defendant's use of the word "killing" merely describes his opinion of the results of an abortion procedure. Since the Supreme Court decision of *Roe v. Wade* (1973), 410 U.S. 113, wherein a woman's right to have an abortion was determined to be constitutionally protected, one of the primary issues has been, and still is, whether or not there is an actual killing of a human life as the result of an abortion. Pro-life activists certainly maintain that abortion is a killing; however, pro-choice activists believe the contrary, especially before the fetus has reached viability. Regardless of which position may ultimately be considered correct, at the present we find that the average reasonable reader of the "Wanted" poster would not believe as an actual fact that plaintiff has been involved in killing, as that word is commonly understood by our society. In fact, we believe that the average reader would quickly realize that the central theme of the "Wanted" poster is that abortion is a killing, to which plaintiff plays a part, and should be a crime in the opinion of those siding with the pro-life movement.

Although we consider the "Wanted" poster repulsive, explicit, unnecessary and in bad taste, we adhere to the belief that "(u)nder the First Amendment there is no such thing as a false idea. However pernicious an opinion may seem, we depend for its correction not on the conscience of judges and juries but on the competition of other ideas." (*Gertz v. Welch,* 418 U.S. at 339–40.) As elaboration, we cite *Sloan v. Hatton,* wherein the court stated: "Free speech is not restricted to compliments. Were this not so there could be no verbal give and take, no meaningful exchange of ideas, and we would be forced to confine ourselves to platitudes and compliments. But members of a free society must be able to express candid opinions and make personal judgments. And those opinions and judgments may be harsh or critical— even abusive—yet still not subject the speaker or writer to civil liability." (*Sloan v. Hatton* (1978), 383 N.E.2d 259, 260.)

We consider the above rationale applicable to all the other allegedly defamatory statements with the exception of the allegedly false statement that plaintiff performs abortions on 29-week-(gestationally) old fetuses. This alleged statement requires reading the two posters in conjunction. In this regard we perceive plaintiff's reasoning to be that the two posters were distributed at the same time, therefore, the average reader would look at the pictures of apparently aborted fetuses on the "Face the American Holocaust" poster and infer that plaintiff was involved with abortions involving fetuses as old as 29 weeks gestationally. Without more information, we note that an abortion at 29 weeks may be a crime. (Ill. Rev. Stat. 1987, ch. 38, ¶ 81–21 et seq. . . .) [Yet defendant did not state] that plaintiff performs abortions on 29-week-(gestationally) old fetuses. . . . First, there is absolutely no cross-referencing between the two posters which would lead the average reader to infer that the two posters should be read and considered together. Second, the "Face the American Holocaust" poster tells the story of how 17,000 fetuses were found in a 3½ ton container in Los Angeles, California. Nowhere does it state that plaintiff was responsible for any of the fetuses found in the container. . . .

The average reasonable reader would realize that the "Wanted" poster is referring to the practice of abortion and that the basis for defendant's opinion that plaintiff is "killing for profit the unwanted and unprotected" is that plaintiff is somehow involved in the abortion process. Moreover, the average reader of the "Wanted" poster would recognize that it is merely another restatement of the pro-life movement's opinion regarding abortion; an opinion that has been publicized since at least the *Roe v. Wade* decision in 1973. The "Wanted" poster does not imply that plaintiff has been involved in any "killing for profit" outside of her involvement with abortions. The "Face the American Holocaust" poster simply does not refer to plaintiff and cannot be read in conjunction with the "Wanted" poster for reasons previously stated. Accordingly, we affirm the trial court's dismissal. . . .

ASSIGNMENT 24.2

Has defamation been committed in the following circumstances?

a. Sam is the mayor. Because he refuses to say in advance that he will never raise taxes, Alice calls him a "coward and a fraud." "It's highway robbery what you're doing," she says to him in a corridor in front of many people.

b. George Harrison is a doctor who performs abortions. Ed carries a poster in front of Harrison's office that reads, "Dr. Harrison is a murderer who pressures young women to kill their babies."

EXTRINSIC FACTS

As we have seen, some statements are not defamatory on their face because you cannot understand the defamatory meaning simply by examining the words or images used. For example, to say that "Mary gave birth to a child today" is not defamatory **on its face** because you need to know the **extrinsic fact** that Mary has been married only a month. When extrinsic facts are needed, they are alleged in the part of the complaint called the **inducement**. The explanation of the defamatory meaning of words alleged by inducement is called the **innuendo**. The innuendo in the birth statement is that Mary engaged in sexual intercourse when she was not married—conduct that a substantial number of people consider to be immoral.

on its face Without reference to extrinsic facts. What is readily observable.

extrinsic fact A fact, not evident on the face of a statement, that is needed to establish the defamatory meaning of the statement.

inducement The part of a defamation complaint that alleges extrinsic facts to show a defamatory meaning.

innuendo The explanation of the defamatory meaning of words alleged by inducement in the complaint. The portion of a complaint that explains a statement's defamatory meaning when this is not clear on its face.

FALSITY OF THE STATEMENT

The issue of falsity is a major area in which the United States Supreme Court has changed the common law of defamation for media defendants. Two separate questions need to be asked. First, does the plaintiff have to prove that the defendant's statement is false? Second, does the plaintiff have to prove the defendant's fault on the truth or falsity of the statement? At common law, the answer to both questions was *no*. Truth was a defense that the defendant had to prove, and the plaintiff did not have to prove fault concerning the defendant's conclusion on whether the statement was true or false. Today, however, the answer to both questions is *yes* for media defendants. The plaintiff must prove both falsity and fault.

Let's focus on the question of fault. Three categories of fault are possible: knowing, reckless, and negligent.

- *Knowing falsehood:* The defendant knew the statement was false when publishing it.
- *Reckless falsehood:* The defendant was **reckless** in determining the truth or falsity of the statement before publishing it.
- *Negligent falsehood:* The defendant was careless or **negligent** in determining the truth or falsity of the statement before publishing it.

reckless Consciously taking a risk in failing to exercise due care but without intending the consequences; wantonly disregarding a risk but not having substantially certain knowledge of the consequences of the risk.

negligent Failing to use reasonable care; careless.

A fourth category of falsehood involves no fault at all.

- *Innocent falsehood:* The defendant's statement about the plaintiff was false, but there was no knowing, reckless, or negligent falsehood; the defendant made an honest mistake.

The first two categories (knowing falsehood and reckless falsehood) are called **actual malice**. The word *malice* in this context does not mean ill will or animosity. It simply means a knowing or reckless falsehood.

actual malice Knowledge that a statement of fact is false, or recklessness as to its truth or falsity. Also called constitutional malice and *New York Times* malice because the definition is based on the case of *New York Times v. Sullivan*, 276 U.S. 254 (1964).

EXAMPLE

A local newspaper publishes a story that Jim Franklin recently sold a stolen Picasso painting. Unfortunately, this statement turns out to be false. Examine the following four possibilities:

A. The editor knew that the painting was not stolen.

B. The editor did not know the story was false. An anonymous source told the editor that the painting was stolen. This is the basis of the story. The editor was also told that three other sources would cast serious doubt on whether the painting was stolen. The editor, however, decides not to check these sources or any other evidence.

C. The editor did not know the story was false. An anonymous source told the editor that the painting was stolen. This is the basis of the story. The editor does no more checking to find out if there are any other sources that will confirm or deny the claim that the painting was stolen.

D. The editor did not know the story was false. An anonymous source told the editor that the painting was stolen. Another source casts doubt on whether the painting was stolen. The editor carefully checks both of these sources as well as others.

In all four examples, a falsehood was published by the newspaper. In what category was each falsehood?

- Case A: knowing falsehood. The editor knew the story was false.
- Case B: reckless falsehood. The editor printed the story in reckless disregard for the truth or falsity of the story. Not checking three known sources seems to be extraordinarily poor judgment. Recklessness consists of an egregious or blatant disregard of what should appear to be an obvious step to take to determine the accuracy of a story. To rely on one anonymous source and to disregard known contrary sources is reckless.
- Case C: negligent falsehood. There was no checking by the editor to determine if the anonymous source was reliable and if there were other sources. Negligence consists of sloppiness or carelessness in disregarding reasonable steps to determine the accuracy of a story.
- Case D: innocent mistake. The editor was innocently wrong. There was no fault involved. All sources were carefully checked.

Which of the three standards of fault must the plaintiff prove in a defamation action against a media defendant? Knowing falsehood, reckless falsehood, or negligent falsehood? The answer depends on the *status* of the plaintiff (public official, public figure, or private person) and on whether the statement is about a matter of *public concern* or *private concern*. Exhibit 24–2 summarizes the law that we will be examining.

public official A government employee who has significant authority.

public figure A person (other than a public official) who has assumed special prominence in the affairs of society.

all-purpose public figure A person of general power, influence, or notoriety.

limited-purpose public figure A person who has voluntarily become involved in a controversy of interest to the general public.

private person Someone who is not a public official or a public figure.

Status There are three categories of plaintiffs in media cases: public officials, public figures, and private persons. A **public official** is a government employee who has significant authority, e.g., mayor, police officer. A **public figure** is a nongovernment employee who has assumed special prominence in the affairs of society. There are two categories of public figures. An **all-purpose public figure** is a person of general power, influence, or notoriety (e.g., a prominent actor). A **limited-purpose public figure** is a person who has voluntarily become involved in a controversy of interest to the general public (e.g., a death-penalty activist). A **private person** is everyone else. Private persons are those who are neither public officials nor public figures. An example might be your retired Uncle Ed or the local supermarket clerk.

Public concern/private concern Defamatory statements about a plaintiff fall into two main categories: those that involve public issues or matters of public concern and those that involve matters of private concern. The general public has a

Exhibit 24–2 Falsity: Standards of proof in defamation cases against media defendants.

STATUS OF THE PARTIES TO THE DEFAMATION SUIT	WAS THE DEFAMATORY STATEMENT A MATTER OF PUBLIC CONCERN OR PRIVATE CONCERN?	ACTUAL MALICE: KNOWING OR RECKLESS FALSEHOOD (Defendant knew the statement was false or was reckless as to truth or falsity)	NEGLIGENCE (Defendant was careless about the truth or falsity of the statement)	INNOCENCE (There was neither actual malice nor negligence in determining the truth or falsity of the statement)
Public official or public figure sues a media defendant	Public concern (A public concern is a matter in which the general public has a legitimate interest.)	Plaintiff must prove actual malice	No liability if all the plaintiff can prove is negligence	No liability if the falsehood was published innocently
Public official or public figure sues a media defendant	Private concern (A private concern is a matter in which the general public does not have a legitimate interest.)	Plaintiff can win by proving actual malice	Plaintiff can win by proving negligence	No liability if the falsehood was published innocently
Private person sues a media defendant	Public concern or private concern	Plaintiff can win by proving actual malice	Plaintiff can win by proving negligence	No liability if the falsehood was published innocently

legitimate interest in matters of public concern; it has no such interest in matters of private concern.

EXAMPLES

- The Detroit *Daily News* prints a story that says Sam Smith tried to pour poison into the drinking reservoir of the city.
- A TV show called *Revelations* says that Sam Smith once took a male impotency pill.

Assume that both statements are false and defamatory. For the moment, we will not concern ourselves with whether Smith is a public official, public figure, or private person. Let us simply classify the category of defamatory statement in each example. The statement about the poison clearly involves a matter of public concern. The public has an interest in the safety of its drinking water. The statement about impotency medication, however, is little more than barnyard gossip. The kind of medication someone may have taken for a sexual problem is a private concern, not a public one.

Once we identify the status of the plaintiff and the public or private nature of the statement, we can then turn to the law that applies to the media defendant. Three main categories of cases need to be considered:

Category #1: *The plaintiff is a public official or a public figure who is suing the media for a defamatory statement about the plaintiff that pertains to a matter of public concern.*

In all states,

- A public official/public figure must prove that the defendant (1) knew a statement on a matter of public concern was false (knowing falsehood) *or* (2) was reckless in determining the truth or falsity of the statement (reckless falsehood). Either of these fault standards is called actual malice.
- There can be no liability if the media was merely careless or negligent in determining the truth or falsity of a statement on a matter of public concern about a public official/public figure. Knowledge or recklessness must be shown.

- Similarly, there can be no liability if the media innocently publishes a defamatory falsehood about a public official/public figure concerning a public matter. Knowledge or recklessness must be shown.

Negligence is *not* one of the fault standards that can be used when a public official/public figure alleges defamation on a matter of public concern. The public official/public figure loses if all that can be shown is that the defendant was careless or negligent in determining the truth or falsity of the statement before publishing it. And, of course, the plaintiff loses if the defendant made an innocent mistake in thinking that the statement was true. All of this means that it is very difficult for a public official/public figure to win a category #1 case against a media defendant. The Supreme Court has set the bar high in order to avoid undue First Amendment restrictions on the media.[3]

Category #2: *The plaintiff is a public official or a public figure who is suing the media for a defamatory statement about the plaintiff that pertains to a matter of private concern.*

When the public official/public figure sues the media about a statement on a private concern, the states have more leeway. They can allow the public official/public figure to win by proving actual malice *or* by proving the lower standard of negligence.

- If a state has an *actual malice* standard, the public official/public figure can win the case by proving that the media (1) knew the defamatory statement on a matter of private concern was false (knowing falsehood) *or* (2) was reckless in determining the truth or falsity of the statement (reckless falsehood).
- If a state has a *negligence* standard, the public official/public figure can win the case by proving that the media was careless in determining the truth or falsity of the statement on a matter of private concern.
- There can be no liability if the media innocently published a defamatory falsehood about a public official/public figure on a matter of private concern. Actual malice or negligence must be shown.

Category #3: *The plaintiff is a private person who is suing the media for a defamatory statement about the plaintiff that pertains to a matter of public concern or a matter of private concern.*

Category #3 cases involve defamation of a private person on a matter of public or private concern. Such cases are treated the same as category #2 cases. States can require private persons to prove actual malice or the lower standard of negligence.

- If a state has an *actual malice* standard, the private person can win the case by proving that the media (1) knew the defamatory statement on a matter of public or private concern was false (knowing falsehood) *or* (2) was reckless in determining the truth or falsity of the statement (reckless falsehood).
- If a state has a *negligence* standard, the private person can win the case by proving that the media was careless in determining the truth or falsity of a statement on a matter of public or private concern.
- There can be no liability if the media innocently published a defamatory falsehood about a private person on a matter of public or private concern. Actual malice or negligence must be shown.

Most states allow the private person to win by proving either of the fault standards: actual malice or negligence.

ASSIGNMENT 24.3

Explain why the following statement is true: The media has a constitutional right to negligently publish defamatory statements about public officials or public figures on matters of public concern.

ASSIGNMENT 24.4

In the following cases, what is the standard of fault that the plaintiff must prove in order to win the defamation case against the defendant?

a. A national television news report says that the president of the United States is a "philanderer."
b. Dr. Adams is a twenty-five-year-old biologist who teaches at the local community college. He applies for and is given a $1,500 government grant to study whether fleas can understand Italian. A columnist in a local newspaper awards him the "Golden Fleece Award of the Month" for the absurd use of public funds.

ASSIGNMENT 24.5

The front page of a newspaper contains a story that the mayor illegally grants city contracts to his "cronies and friends." The mayor sues for defamation. You are a paralegal who works for the law firm that represents the mayor. What facts would you try to investigate in order to determine whether the newspaper published the story with actual malice?

Next we turn to the other elements of libel and slander (defamation) outlined in Exhibit 24–1 at the beginning of the chapter. Except where indicated, these elements apply to both media defendants (e.g., a newspaper that defames someone) and to nonmedia defendants (e.g., one neighbor who defames another or a department store that defames a customer).

OF AND CONCERNING THE PLAINTIFF

The defamatory statement must be **of and concerning the plaintiff.** This requires proof by the plaintiff that a recipient of the statement reasonably understood that it referred to the plaintiff. Occasionally, extrinsic facts are needed to make this determination. Suppose the defendant says that "the head guard at Fulton Prison has stolen state funds." On the face of this statement, we cannot identify who was defamed. We need to know who was the head guard at the time the statement was made. The plaintiff can introduce the extrinsic fact that he or she was the head guard at the time, and that, therefore, the statement was reasonably understood to refer to the plaintiff. The part of the complaint in which the plaintiff alleges that the defamatory statement was of and concerning the plaintiff is called the **colloquium.**

of and concerning the plaintiff Reasonably understood by the recipient to refer to the plaintiff.

colloquium Extrinsic facts showing that a defamatory statement was of and concerning the plaintiff. A part of the complaint alleging such facts.

Suppose that the defendant defames a group, e.g., "all Russians are thieves" or "Boston doctors are quacks." The groups defamed here are too large; no individual Russian or Boston doctor can say that the statement can be reasonably understood to refer to him or her as an individual. The larger the group, the less reasonable such an understanding would be.

ASSIGNMENT 24.6

Can defamation actions be brought because of the following statements? If so, by whom?

a. "The jury that acquitted John Gotti was bribed."
b. "Cab drivers always cheat."
c. "The Titon University football players take steroids."
d. "The money was stolen by Tom or Fred."

PUBLICATION

publication Communication of a statement to someone other than the plaintiff.

There must be a **publication** of the defamatory statement by the defendant. Publication is not limited to widespread dissemination, although such dissemination certainly qualifies as publication. A statement is published if it is communicated by anyone to at least one person other than the plaintiff.

EXAMPLE

Ted telephones Paulette in order to accuse her of being a thief.

There is no publication if Paulette is the only person who heard the statement.

Publication is a fault element for all defendants. The plaintiff must prove that the defendant intentionally or negligently allowed someone to see or hear the statement.

EXAMPLES

Ted telephones Paulette in order to accuse her of being a thief. He knows that she has her speakerphone on.

Ted sends Paulette a postcard in which he accuses her of being a thief.

In both of these cases, Paulette will try to prove that Ted knew or should have known that someone other than Paulette would hear or see the statement, e.g., evidence that Ted knew that Paulette had roommates who would probably listen to all phone messages, or that others picked up her mail for her and could easily read a postcard. If such evidence does not exist, the publication of the defamatory statement was unintentional or innocent and therefore not actionable.

EXAMPLE

Alice sends Dan a letter in which she says he is a child molester. On the cover of the envelope, Alice prints the words, "PERSONAL AND CONFIDENTIAL." Unknown to Alice, however, Dan has asked his mother to open and sort all his mail. Or, Dan's neighbor steals the letter and reads it.

In both instances, Alice was not at fault in communicating the statement to a third person. She did not intend someone else to read it and there is no indication that she was careless or negligent in allowing this to occur. She sealed the letter in an envelope, using language alerting everyone that the letter was for Dan's eyes only. Hence, the element of publication has not been established.

ASSIGNMENT 24.7

Nina writes a note on a piece of paper in which she says that George's divinity degree is a fake. She intends to hand the note to George in person. She places the note in her purse and boards a bus. Carelessly, however, she leaves her purse on the bus. A bus driver finds the purse and reads everything in it, including the note to George. Has Nina published the note?

REPUBLICATION

Someone who repeats another's defamatory statement has *republished* it and can sometimes be subject to the same tort liability as the person who originated the statement.

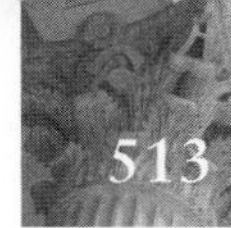

EXAMPLE

Ted works for the Ajax Company in the town of Salem. At a staff meeting, he hears Thomas Sanford, another employee, say that "Senator Bill Crowley is a crook." The next morning, Ted says to a friend, "Thomas Sanford said that Senator Bill Crowley is a crook."

If Sanford made this statement, he published a defamatory statement at the meeting. But Ted *also* published (or republished) the defamatory statement the next morning when he repeated the statement to a friend. Ted's **republication** is treated as a publication. Crowley can sue Sanford and Ted for slander.

republication Repetition of a defamatory statement originally made by someone else.

The media can also be a republisher.

EXAMPLE

The *Salem News* prints a news article on a staff meeting held at the Ajax Company in Salem. The article reports that Thomas Sanford told several employees that "Senator Bill Crowley is a crook."

The newspaper has republished the defamatory statement. Winning a defamation case against the media, however, can be difficult. As we have seen, a public official like Senator Crowley must establish that a defamatory falsehood on a matter of public concern was published with actual malice. Also, many states give the media a **fair-report privilege**. This privilege allows the media to publish fair and accurate stories on government reports and proceedings, even if the stories contain defamatory statements made in the government reports or proceedings. This privilege would not apply to the *Salem News* case in our example since the news story was not about a government report or proceeding. However, Senator Crowley would still have a difficult time suing *Salem News* because he would have to prove actual malice.

fair-report privilege A newspaper or other media entity is not liable for defamation when it publishes fair and accurate stories on government reports and proceedings even if the stories contain defamatory statements made in the government reports or proceedings.

Other individuals and businesses are also engaged in republication. Examples include bookstores, news carriers, libraries, message deliverers, and printers. Are they liable for the defamatory statements contained in the products that they deliver or transmit? Since it would be too burdensome for them to check the content of everything they distribute, they are *not* liable for defamation unless they have reason to know that the book, article, message, or other communication contains defamatory material. The same is true of telephone and telegraph companies.

CYBERSPACE DEFAMATION

The prevalence of the Internet has raised the issue of defamation in e-mails, instant messages, chat rooms, blogs, bulletin boards, social networks, and other sites on the World Wide Web. Most computer users get access to the Internet by subscribing to Internet service providers (ISPs), e.g., AT&T and Comcast. What happens when one subscriber defames someone in an e-mail message or on a social network such as Facebook or Twitter? What happens when someone posts a scathing critique of a person or a business on rating or so-called "gripe" sites?

EXAMPLE

Mary and George are AT&T Internet subscribers. On an e-mail **listserv**, Mary sends a message to George that says, "Jim Thompson beats his wife." Thousands of other members of the listserv read this.

listserv A program that manages computer mailing lists automatically, receiving and distributing messages from and to members of the list.

Mary has published a defamatory statement to George. Clearly, Thompson can sue her for defamation. What about AT&T? Hasn't it *also* published the defamatory statement?

Congress has definitively answered *no* to this question. In 1996, it passed a law that prohibited tort actions that seek to treat an entity such as AT&T or Facebook as the "publisher or speaker" of messages transmitted over its service by third parties:

> "No provider . . . of an interactive computer service shall be treated as the publisher or speaker of any information provided by another information content provider. . . . No cause of action may be brought and no liability may be imposed under any State or local law that is inconsistent with this section."[4]

In our example, AT&T is a "provider" of an "interactive computer service." Mary is an "information content provider;" she provided the "information" that "Thompson beats his wife." Under the protection granted by Congress, the victim of defamation delivered in this manner cannot sue the interactive computer service. The victim must go after the originator of the defamatory speech. (If the originator's posting was anonymous, the owner of the website may be forced to reveal the identity of the originator during litigation.) Online service providers will not be treated as newspapers, magazines, and television and radio stations that have more control over the content of their products. In effect, Congress granted tort **immunity** to Internet intermediaries that are providers of interactive computer services. This was done to encourage further robust development of the Internet:

immunity The treatment of wrongful conduct as nonwrongful. A complete defense to a tort claim whether or not the defendant committed the tort. (See glossary for additional definitions.)

> The purpose of this statutory immunity is not difficult to discern. Congress recognized the threat that tort-based lawsuits pose to freedom of speech in the new and burgeoning Internet medium. The imposition of tort liability on service providers for the communications of others represented, for Congress, simply another form of intrusive government regulation of speech. [The immunity] was enacted, in part, to maintain the robust nature of Internet communication and, accordingly, to keep government interference in the medium to a minimum.[5]

The immunity is also a recognition of the near impossibility of requiring providers of online services to edit the vast quantity of information passed among the millions of connected computers all over the world.

ASSIGNMENT 24.8

Ted writes a blog on environmental issues. There is space on his blog for readers to post comments on his content. On a recent blog, someone leaves a comment that says, "The mayor accepts kickbacks from the major polluters in the state." The comment is signed "Concerned Citizen." Has defamation been committed? If so, by whom?

DAMAGES

At common law, once the plaintiff proved that the defendant published a defamatory statement, the jury was allowed to presume that the plaintiff suffered humiliation or harm to reputation. There was no need for the plaintiff to offer specific evidence of these consequences. Such damages were called **presumed damages**. If, in addition, the plaintiff suffered actual dollar losses such as medical expenses or lost income, they could be recovered as **special damages**. These are actual economic or pecuniary losses. Today, there can be no presumed damages against media defendants charged with making defamatory statements on matters of public concern *unless* the plaintiff can prove actual malice—the defendant knew the statement was false or was reckless as to its truth or falsity. A private person, however, can obtain presumed damages if the defamatory statement did not involve an issue of public concern.

presumed damages Damages that a jury is allowed to assume were suffered by the plaintiff, who does not have to introduce specific evidence that these damages were in fact suffered.

special damages Economic or pecuniary losses, such as medical expenses and lost wages, that result from a particular tort. Also referred to as specials.

The following discussion of damages in libel and slander is limited to suits against nonmedia defendants.

Libel

States differ on how they treat the element of damages against nonmedia defendants:

- Most states say that all libel is **libel per se**, meaning that all written defamatory statements are actionable without proof that the plaintiff suffered special damages. Presumed damages are allowed. This conclusion does not depend on whether extrinsic facts are needed for one to understand the defamatory meaning of the statement.
- A few states use a different definition of libel per se. It means any written statement that does not require extrinsic facts to demonstrate the defamatory nature of the statement. For such libel, there is no need for the plaintiff to prove special damages. Presumed damages are allowed. **Libel per quod**, however, does require proof of special damages. Libel per quod is any written statement that requires one to use extrinsic facts to prove the defamatory nature of the statement.

libel per se 1. A written defamatory statement that is actionable without proof that the plaintiff suffered special damages; presumed damages are allowed. 2. A written statement that does not require the use of extrinsic facts to demonstrate the defamatory nature of the statement.

libel per quod A written statement that requires one to use extrinsic facts to understand its defamatory meaning.

Slander

Slander per se does not require proof of special damages, but slander per quod does.

Slander per se is an oral statement that is defamatory in one of the following four ways:

- It accuses the plaintiff of committing a crime of **moral turpitude** (e.g., "Ed stole a car").
- It accuses the plaintiff of having a loathsome communicable disease (e.g., "Ed has venereal disease").
- It accuses the plaintiff of serious sexual misconduct (e.g., "Ed is an adulterer").
- It accuses the plaintiff of being inept at or unfit for his or her trade or profession (e.g., "Ed forged his license to sell liquor").

Most states have all of these categories, although some states have made modifications. A slanderous statement that does *not* fall into one of these four categories (e.g., "Ed is illegitimate") is called **slander per quod**. In a few states, this phrase has the additional meaning of an oral statement that requires extrinsic facts to understand its defamatory meaning.

The *Becker* case raises the question of whether an attorney committed slander per se against three independent paralegals that the attorney hired to work on specific cases. The paralegals are the Becker brothers—Steven, Thomas, and Jeffrey Becker. (See Exhibit 24–3.) They were not salaried employees of the attorney; they

slander per se An oral statement that is defamatory because it accuses a person of (1) committing a crime of moral turpitude, (2) having a loathsome communicable disease, (3) committing serious sexual misconduct, or (4) being inept at or unfit for his or her trade or profession.

moral turpitude Conduct that is dishonest, contrary to moral rules, or reprehensible.

slander per quod 1. An oral defamatory statement that does not fit into one of the four categories that constitute slander per se. 2. An oral defamatory statement that requires one to use extrinsic facts to understand its defamatory meaning.

Exhibit 24–3
From left to right: Steven Becker, Thomas Becker, and Jeffrey Becker. Independent paralegals in Illinois who sued an attorney for slander per se in the case of *Becker v. Zellner*.

were independent paralegals, sometimes called freelance paralegals. Such individuals often work for more than one attorney on a short-term basis. Their work for Kathleen Zellner, Esq. in the Chicago area did not go well, as you will see in the case of *Becker v. Zellner.*

CASE

Jeffrey Becker, Steven Becker, and Thomas Becker
v.
Kathleen Zellner and Associates
292 Ill. App. 3d 116, 684 N.E.2d 1378
Appellate Court of Illinois, Second District (1997)

Background: *Jeffrey, Steven, and Thomas Becker (the plaintiffs) are independent paralegals in Illinois. Among the attorneys for whom they worked were Kathleen Zellner and Associates (the defendants). The Beckers brought a defamation complaint against the defendants for saying*

- *the plaintiffs submitted "a $45,000 bill for five pages of worthless memorandum,"*
- *a client should not contact the plaintiffs, and*
- *the plaintiffs were "devious" in how they conducted their independent paralegal business, and would "try to get into the back door" when charging for their paralegal services.*

The trial court dismissed the complaint. The case is now on appeal before the Appellate Court of Illinois, Second District where the paralegal brothers are representing themselves (pro se).

Decision on Appeal: *The judgment dismissing the complaint is reversed. The attorney's statements about the paralegals were defamatory per se and the case should proceed to trial.*

OPINION OF COURT

Justice BOWMAN delivered the opinion of the court. . . .:

On May 6, 1996, plaintiffs filed a . . . [defamation] complaint against defendants in which they alleged that, as paralegals, they assisted defendants in their representation of Frank Lyons during the fall of 1994. On May 9, 1995, Sharon Wendt, a friend of Lyons, called defendants in order to obtain plaintiffs' telephone number for Lyons. Lyons apparently wanted plaintiffs to work with his new attorney. In the presence of an associate of her firm, defendant Zellner accepted Wendt's call and placed it on a speakerphone. Zellner then allegedly told Wendt (1) that during plaintiffs' employment with her, they had submitted "a $45,000 bill for five pages of worthless memorandum"; (2) that Lyons should not contact plaintiffs; and (3) that plaintiffs were "devious" and that they would try to "get into the back door" when charging Lyons for their services. Plaintiffs' complaint further alleged that later on May 9, 1995, Lyons "left a message on their answering machine stating that he wanted to know whether plaintiffs were going to stick him with a $45,000.00 bill." Lyons did not hire plaintiffs to assist him in the preparation of his case, and their "business relationship and reputation" with Lyons were "never the same" after Zellner's telephone conversation with Wendt. . . . [The] defendants filed a motion to dismiss . . . [the paralegals' defamation complaint, which] the trial court granted. . . .

Defendants' motion to dismiss . . . sought the dismissal of plaintiffs' complaint for "failure to make a claim for which relief may be granted." Accordingly, the question on review is "whether sufficient facts are contained in the pleadings which, if established, could entitle [plaintiffs] to relief." *Illinois Graphics v. Nickum,* 159 Ill. 2d 469, 488, 639 N.E.2d 1282 (1994). A cause of action should be dismissed when it is apparent that no set of facts can be proved that would entitle the nonmovant to relief.

In . . . their complaint, plaintiffs alleged that Zellner had committed slander *per se* during her conversation with Wendt. Specifically, plaintiffs pointed to Zellner's alleged statements that they had submitted "a $45,000 bill for five pages of worthless memorandum," that Lyons should not contact them, and that they were "devious" and "would try to get into the back door." According to plaintiffs, these alleged statements constituted slander *per se* because they pertained to plaintiffs' "profession and employment." The trial court found the statements "susceptible of an innocent construction as a matter of law" and dismissed the *per se* [cause of action].

The four categories of statements which are considered actionable *per se* [in Illinois] include ". . . words that prejudice a party, or impute lack of ability, in his or her trade, profession or business." *Bryson v. News America Publications, Inc.,* 174 Ill. 2d 77, 88, 672 N.E.2d 1207 (1996).

Even if words fall into a *per se* category, the claim will not be actionable if the words are capable of an innocent construction. *Bryson,* 174 Ill. 2d at 90. Under the innocent construction rule, courts consider the statement "in context, giving the words, and their implications, their natural and obvious meaning." *Bryson,* 174 Ill. 2d at 90. Importantly, only a *reasonable* innocent construction will negate the *per se* effect of an allegedly defamatory statement. Courts decide, as a matter of law, whether an allegedly defamatory statement is reasonably capable of being innocently construed.

Plaintiffs argue that Zellner's alleged statements fall into the . . . *per se* category, as words that impute their lack of abilities as paralegals. We agree. In context, Zellner's allegedly defamatory statements were obviously intended to describe and denigrate plaintiffs' abilities as paralegals. She allegedly called plaintiffs' work product "worthless," labeled them as "devious," and, in an apparent attempt to further impugn their character, told Wendt that they would try to "get into the back door" during their billing process. The natural and obvious meaning of these words prejudices plaintiffs and imputes a lack of ability in their profession as paralegals.

Despite counsel's . . . creative attempt at oral argument to the contrary, the natural and obvious meanings of "worthless" and "devious" are negative. Webster's Dictionary defines "devious" as "hard to pin down or bring to agreement" and lists as synonyms "shifty, tricky, unscrupulous, [and] unfair." *Webster's Third New International Dictionary* 619 (1986). Moreover, Webster's defines "worthless" as "lacking value or material worth" and lists "useless" as a synonym. *Webster's Third New International Dictionary* 2637 (1986). Counsel's alternative definitions of these words at oral argument were accurate, but the mere existence of other dictionary definitions does not automatically indicate an innocent construction. Rather, under the innocent construction rule, we are neither required to "strain to find an unnatural but possibly innocent meaning for words where the defamatory meaning is far more reasonable," nor are we required to "espouse a naïveté unwarranted under the circumstances." *Bryson,* 174 Ill. 2d at 94. Thus, we reject defendants' contention that Zellner's alleged statements can be innocently construed. . . .

For the foregoing reasons, the judgment [dismissing the slander *per se* complaint] is . . . reversed . . . and the cause is remanded for proceedings consistent with this opinion.

ASSIGNMENT 24.9

a. The attorney tried to argue that the words "worthless" and "devious" are not necessarily negative. What meanings do you think the attorney tried to offer?
b. Chris Eagan is a paralegal who works for David Vinson, Esq. Both live in the same neighborhood. One day, Vinson tells a neighbor that Chris "is barely making it" at the office. Is this slander per se under the *Becker* case?
c. Same facts as (c), only this time Vinson makes this comment to his law partner.

PRIVILEGE

There are a number of situations in which a defendant has, in effect, a **privilege** to defame. A privilege is the right to act contrary to another individual's right without being subject to tort or other liability. The existence of a privilege is a defense to the tort action. Two kinds of privileges exist: absolute and qualified.

privilege 1. The right to act contrary to the right of another without being subject to tort or other liability. A defense that authorizes conduct that would otherwise be wrongful. 2. A special legal benefit, right, immunity, or protection.

Absolute Privilege

An **absolute privilege** is a privilege that cannot be lost because of the bad motives of the party asserting the privilege. The holder of such a privilege is not subject to defamation liability even though he or she knows the statement is false and has personal ill will toward or intends to harm the subject of the defamation. In short, the privilege is absolute.

absolute privilege A privilege that cannot be lost because of the bad motives of the party asserting the privilege.

EXAMPLE

Judge Smith says to attorney Jones during a trial, "your incompetence knows no equal among the practicing bar in the state."

Judge Smith has an absolute privilege to utter this defamatory statement even if the judge knows it is false and utters it solely out of hatred of Jones.

There are very few categories of individuals who can assert this absolute privilege:

1. Judges, attorneys, parties, witnesses, and jurors while performing their functions during judicial proceedings.
2. Members of Congress, the state legislature, and city councils or other local legislative bodies while the members are performing their functions during

legislative proceedings. Witnesses testifying before these bodies also have an absolute privilege to defame.
3. High executive or administrative officers of the government while performing their official duties.

Qualified Privilege

qualified privilege A privilege that can be lost if it is not exercised in a reasonable manner for a proper purpose. Also called *conditional privilege*.

A **qualified privilege** (also called a *conditional privilege*) is a privilege that can be lost if it is not exercised in a reasonable manner for a proper purpose.[6] Some states are more specific on how this privilege can be lost in defamation cases. For example, some states say it is lost if the defamer did not believe the statement was true or did not have reasonable grounds to believe the statement was true. Other states say that the privilege is lost only if the defamer was reckless in determining its truth or falsity.

Who can assert qualified privileges? As we saw earlier, everyone has a right to make a *fair comment* on a matter of public concern. This is a qualified privilege that can be lost if it is abused. We also saw that many states have a *fair-report privilege* that allows the media to publish stories on government reports and proceedings, even if the stories contain defamatory statements made in the government reports or proceedings. This privilege can be lost if the media's story is not fair and accurate.

The most common qualified privilege is the privilege to protect your own legitimate interests.

EXAMPLE
Tony calls Diane a "liar" after Diane says Tony stole her money.

Tony has defamed Diane. If she sues him for defamation, his defense is the qualified privilege of protecting his interest in his own integrity. The privilege would be lost, however, if Tony goes beyond the scope of protecting his interest such as by calling Diane a prostitute or by responding solely out of revenge to hurt Diane.

Under limited circumstances, a person also has a qualified privilege to defame in order to protect *others*. The defamer must be under a legal or moral obligation to protect the other and must act reasonably in believing the protection is necessary.

EXAMPLE
Lena tells her daughter that it would be disastrous for her to marry "a bum and a gigolo like Paul."

Finally, people who share a *common interest* have a qualified privilege to communicate about matters that will protect or advance that interest.

EXAMPLE
One employee of a company says to another, "Don't buy anything from the Eagle Supplier Corp. since all of its goods are stolen."

ASSIGNMENT 24.10

In the following cases, what defenses, if any, can the defendant raise in the defamation action?

a. Alex calls ABC Insurance Company and says that Jackson, his neighbor, has filed fraudulent automobile-accident claims against the company. The neighbor sues Alex for defamation.
b. Same facts as in (a). ABC Insurance Company tells a different insurance company that Jackson has been charged with filing fraudulent claims. Jackson sues ABC Insurance Company for defamation.

SLAPP SUITS

It is relatively easy to sue someone. All you need is an allegation and court filing fees. Many defendants, however, are quite upset when they find out they are being sued, particularly after a process server formally hands them the official documents that signal the beginning of litigation. In this environment of tension, some individuals use defamation suits to intimidate those who have complained about something.

EXAMPLE

Mary Adams tries to organize fellow trailer-home owners against the fees imposed by the park where the trailers are located. She writes a blog in which she says that the park owner, Ron Ullson, should be reported to the government for imposing "greedy" fees. Ullson then sues Adams for defamation.

Arguably, the defamation suit is meritless and Ron Ullson is simply trying to use the suit to intimidate Mary Adams—to scare her off. Even if he loses the defamation suit, he may cause her so much agony that she will drop her efforts to organize the trailer-home owners. Emotional and financial costs of defending the defamation action can be overwhelming.

If this is Ullson's motive, his suit is known as an intimidation suit. It is also called a **SLAPP suit**, which stands for "strategic lawsuit against public participation." It is a meritless suit brought primarily for the purpose of chilling the defendant's exercise of the right to free speech and to petition the government for a redress of grievances. The cause of action in these suits is usually defamation, but other causes of action are also common such as the tort of interference with economic advantage, which we will consider in Chapter 26.

SLAPP (Strategic Lawsuit Against Public Participation) suit A meritless suit brought primarily for the purpose of chilling the defendant's exercise of the right to free speech and to petition the government for a redress of grievances.

What can a defendant do in such cases, particularly the defendant who does not have the economic resources of the party who "slapped" the defendant with the intimidation suit? As we discussed in Chapter 8, the defendant can sue the plaintiff for the tort of malicious prosecution, but this can be a cumbersome and expensive remedy. The defendant can also file an ethics charge against the attorney who helped the plaintiff bring the SLAPP suit. It is unethical for an attorney to assert a frivolous claim for a client. The ethics charge, however, does not stop the SLAPP suit.

A more direct method of relief is to use the anti-SLAPP statute that about eight states have passed to help curb the use of intimidation suits to muzzle citizens. In California, for example, victims of SLAPP suits can assert a special motion to strike the defamation or other suit. The motion will be granted unless there is a probability that the plaintiff will prevail on the claim. If the motion is granted, it can end a meritless suit well before the full ordeal of a trial is played out. Furthermore, the defendant may be able to recover his or her attorney fees and costs of defending the SLAPP suit.

In a widely publicized case, a photographer asserted an anti-SLAPP motion against the entertainer Barbra Streisand, who objected to the online posting of an aerial photograph of her Malibu house.[7] The case involved a privacy claim, but would be equally applicable to defamation claims. Streisand sued the photographer and others (e.g., pictopia.com) for invasion of her privacy. The photo was included among 12,000 online photos that were taken to document coastal erosion for the non-profit California Coastal Records Project. The photographer moved to strike Streisand's privacy complaint under California's anti-SLAPP law. He won. The court concluded that the aerial photographs were an exercise of the photographer's First Amendment free speech right to participate in an issue of public concern, namely coastal erosion. Furthermore the court held that it was highly unlikely that Streisand could win her privacy claim. The photo of her home was one of thousands taken from a distance of about 2,000 feet in the air. In **dictum**, the court said that a different conclusion might be reached if the photographer was in a low-hovering

dictum An observation made by a judge in an opinion that is not essential to resolve the issues before the court; comments that go beyond the facts before the court. Also called obiter dictum.

helicopter waiting to photograph activity of people on the grounds of the Streisand home. Because Streisand's privacy claim was so thin, she was anti-slapped in order to prevent her litigation from curtailing a constitutionally protected activity.[8]

"VEGGIE LIBEL"

Occasionally, people will make unflattering comments about certain consumer products, e.g., "there are dangerous pesticides in Idaho potatoes." Can you defame a potato? Several states have enacted statutes that allow suits for maligning or disparaging certain products. The media has labeled such suits "veggie libel cases." We will consider them in Chapter 26.

DEFAMATION CHECKLIST

Definitions, Relationships, Paralegal Roles, and Research References

Category
At common law, defamation was a strict-liability tort except for the element of publication. For media defendants, this has been changed by constitutional law. For such defendants, defamation is now a tort that requires a showing of fault.

Interest Protected
The right to one's good name and reputation.

Elements
Defamation consists of two torts: libel and slander.

Elements of Libel

1. Written defamatory statement by the defendant
2. Of and concerning the plaintiff
3. Publication of the statement
4. Damages:
   a. In some states, special damages never have to be proven in a libel case
   b. In other states, libel per se does not require special damages, but libel per quod does
5. Causation

Elements of Slander

1. Oral defamatory statement by the defendant
2. Of and concerning the plaintiff
3. Publication of the statement
4. Damages:
   a. Special damages are not required for slander per se
   b. Special damages are required for slander per quod
5. Causation

Note: In libel and slander cases against the media, the plaintiff must also prove that the statement was false and that the defendant exhibited some degree of fault in determining the truth or falsity of the statement. The amount of fault depends on the status of the plaintiff and the content of the libel or slander.

Definitions of Major Words/Phrases in These Elements

Defamatory Statement: A statement of fact that would tend to harm the reputation of the plaintiff in the eyes of at least a substantial and respectable minority of people by lowering the plaintiff in the estimation of those people or by deterring them from associating with the plaintiff.

Of and Concerning the Plaintiff: Reasonably understood by the recipient to refer to the plaintiff.

Publication: A communication of the statement to someone other than the plaintiff.

DEFAMATION CHECKLIST *(Continued)*

Special Damages: Compensatory damages that consist of economic or pecuniary losses (e.g., medical expenses and lost wages) that must be alleged and proven. They are not presumed to exist.

Causation: But for the defendant's statement, the plaintiff would not have suffered harm to reputation; or, the defendant's statement was a substantial factor in bringing about the harm to the plaintiff's reputation.

Major Defenses and Counterargument Possibilities That Need to Be Explored
(Constitutional law has changed a good deal of the common law of defamation as it applies to the media. In the following list, if the item has been applied only to media defendants, it will so indicate.)

1. The defendant's statement was true.
2. The statement did not tend to harm the reputation of the plaintiff in the eyes of at least a respectable and substantial minority of the community.
3. Only the plaintiff thought that the statement harmed his or her reputation, or that it had a tendency to do so.
4. The defendant's statement cannot reasonably be understood in a defamatory sense.
5. The defendant's statement was not in fact understood in a defamatory sense.
6. The defendant merely stated an opinion, which did not expressly or impliedly communicate any statements of fact.
7. The defendant's statement could not reasonably be understood to refer to the plaintiff.
8. The group the defendant defamed was too large for the plaintiff (who was part of the group) to be able to reasonably say that the statement was of and concerning the plaintiff.
9. The defendant's statement was not communicated to someone other than the plaintiff.
10. The defendant neither intended to communicate the statement to someone other than the plaintiff nor was negligent in this regard.
11. The defendant's oral defamatory statement is not slander per se and the plaintiff has failed to prove special damages.
12. The defendant's statement is libel per quod and the plaintiff has failed to prove special damages.
13. The harm suffered by the plaintiff was not caused by the defendant's defamatory statement.
14. The defamatory statement pertained to a matter of public concern about a public official or a public figure and the plaintiff has not shown actual malice (for media defendants only).
15. The defamatory statement pertained to a matter of private concern about a public official or a public figure and the plaintiff has not shown the defendant's actual malice or negligence (depending on the fault standard that applies in the state) as to truth or falsity (for media defendants only).
16. The defamatory statement pertained to a matter of public or private concern about a private person and the plaintiff has not shown the defendant's actual malice or negligence (depending on the fault standard that applies in the state) as to truth or falsity (for media defendants only).
17. The defendant had an absolute privilege to utter the defamatory statement.
18. The defendant had a qualified or conditional privilege to utter the defamatory statement and the privilege was not lost by abusing it.
19. The defendant consented to the publication of the defamatory statement (on the defense of consent, see Chapter 27).
20. The plaintiff's defamation suit is a SLAPP suit that should be dismissed.
21. The plaintiff's suit against the government for defamation committed by a government employee may be barred by sovereign immunity (on sovereign immunity, see Chapter 27).
22. The plaintiff's suit against the government employee for defamation may be barred by official immunity (on official immunity, see Chapter 27).
23. The plaintiff's suit against the charitable organization for a defamation committed by someone working for the organization may be barred by charitable immunity (on charitable immunity, see Chapter 27).

DEFAMATION CHECKLIST *(Continued)*

24. The plaintiff's suit against a family member for defamation may be barred by intrafamily tort immunity (on intrafamily immunity, see Chapter 22).
25. The plaintiff failed to take reasonable steps to mitigate the harm caused when the defendant committed defamation; therefore, damages should not cover the aggravation of the harm caused by the plaintiff (on the mitigation-of-damages rule, see Chapter 16).

Damages
At common law, defamation plaintiffs could receive presumed damages; special damages did not have to be proven. In many states, special damages must be proven if the defamation is slander per quod. In most states, libel never requires special damages. In others, this is so only for libel per se. There can be no presumed damages against media defendants charged with making defamatory statements on matters of public concern unless the plaintiff can prove actual malice.

Relationship to Criminal Law
Certain forms of defamation are crimes in some states if the defamatory statement is intentionally published.

Relationship to Other Torts

Abuse of Process: While abusing legal process, the defendant may also defame the plaintiff.

Alienation of Affections: While alienating the affections of a spouse, the defendant may also defame the plaintiff.

Disparagement: Defamation protects the personal reputation of the plaintiff. Disparagement is an attack against the goods or property of the plaintiff beyond ordinary commercial competition. While committing disparagement, the defendant may also defame the plaintiff if the attack against the plaintiff's goods or property is also an express or implied personal attack on the reputation of the plaintiff.

False Imprisonment: While falsely imprisoning the plaintiff, the defendant may also defame the plaintiff.

Intentional Infliction of Emotional Distress: The defendant's defamatory statement may not be actionable because it is true or because it is not communicated to a third person. Yet, the statement might be so outrageous as to constitute the tort of intentional infliction of emotional distress.

Invasion of Privacy: The facts that give rise to false light invasion of privacy often also give rise to an action for defamation.

Malicious Prosecution: While committing malicious prosecution, the defendant may also defame the plaintiff.

Federal Law

a. Under the Federal Tort Claims Act, the United States government will *not* be liable for libel or slander committed by one of its federal employees within the scope of employment (respondeat superior). (See Exhibit 27–7 in Chapter 27.)
b. There may be liability under the Civil Rights Act if the libel or slander was committed while the defendant was depriving the plaintiff of a federal right under color of state law. (See Exhibit 27–9 in Chapter 27.) (Most states have their own statutes that cover when tort claims can be made against the state for libel and slander and other torts committed by state government employees. Such claims are also covered in Chapter 27.)

Employer–Employee (Agency) Law
A private (non-government) employee who commits libel or slander is personally liable for this tort. His or her employer will *also* be liable for libel or slander if the conduct of the employee was within the scope of employment (respondeat superior). The employee must be furthering a business objective of the employer while defaming the plaintiff. (On the factors that determine scope of employment, see Exhibit 14–9 in Chapter 14.)

Paralegal Roles in Defamation Litigation
(See also Exhibit 3–1 in Chapter 3, Exhibit 20–4 in Chapter 20, and Exhibit 29–1 in Chapter 29.)

DEFAMATION CHECKLIST *(Continued)*

Fact finding (help the office collect facts relevant to prove the elements of libel or slander, the elements of available defenses, and extent of injuries or other damages):

- client interviewing
- field investigation
- online research (e.g., locating news stories about the defendant)

File management (help the office control the documents involved in a libel or slander litigation):

- open client file
- enter case data in computer database
- maintain file documents

Litigation assistance (help the trial attorney prepare for a libel or slander trial and appeal, if needed):

- draft discovery requests
- draft answers to discovery requests
- draft pleadings
- digest and index discovery documents
- help prepare, order, and manage trial exhibits
- help prepare trial notebook
- draft notice of appeal
- order trial transcript
- cite-check briefs
- perform legal research

Collection/enforcement (help the trial attorney for the judgment creditor to collect the damages award or to enforce other court orders at the conclusion of the libel or slander case):

- draft postjudgment discovery requests
- conduct field investigation to monitor compliance with judgment
- perform online research (e.g., location of defendant's business assets)

Research References for Defamation

Digests
In the digests of West Group, look for case summaries on defamation under key topics such as:

Libel and Slander
Constitutional Law (90)
Damages
Torts

Corpus Juris Secundum
In this legal encyclopedia, see the discussions under topic headings such as:

Libel and Slander
Constitutional Law (585)
Damages
Torts

American Jurisprudence 2d
In this legal encyclopedia, see the discussions under topic headings such as:

Libel and Slander
Damages
Constitutional Law
Torts

Legal Periodical Literature
There are two index systems to use to try to locate articles on defamation:

Index to Legal Periodicals and Books (ILP)

See literature in *ILP* under subject headings such as:

Libel and Slander
Constitutional Law
Freedom of the Press
Liability without Fault
Radio and Television
Torts
Damages

Current Law Index (CLI)

See literature in *CLI* under subject headings such as:

Libel and Slander
Liberty of the Press
Constitutional Law
Strict Liability
Torts
Damages

DEFAMATION CHECKLIST *(Continued)*

Examples of legal periodical articles on defamation you will find by using *ILP* or *CLI*:

Defamation on the Internet—A New Approach to Libel in Cyberspace by Yuval Karniel, 2 Journal of International Media and Entertainment Law 215 (2009).

A Libel Law Analysis of Media Abuses in Reporting on the Duke Lacrosse Fabricated Rape Charges by David Elder, 11 Vanderbilt Journal of Entertainment and Technology Law 99 (2008).

A.L.R., A.L.R.2d, A.L.R.3d, A.L.R.4th, A.L.R.5th, A.L.R.6th, A.L.R. Fed., A.L.R. Fed. 2d
Use the *ALR Index* to find annotations on defamation. In this index, check subject headings such as:

- Libel and Slander
- Freedom of Speech and Press
- Privileges and Immunities
- Newspapers
- Radio and Television
- Damages
- Torts
- New York Times Rule

Example of an annotation on defamation you will find by using this index:

Defamation by Television—Actual Malice by Ann K. Wooster, 42 A.L.R.6th 353 (2009).

Words and Phrases
In this multivolume legal dictionary, look up *slander per se, libel per quod, defamatory statement, publication, special damages*, and every other word or phrase connected with defamation discussed in this chapter. The dictionary will give you definitions of these words or phrases from court opinions.

CALR: Computer-Assisted Legal Research

Example of a query you could ask on Westlaw to try to find cases, statutes, or other legal materials on defamation: **"defamatory statement" /p slander**

Example of a query you could ask on LexisNexis to try to find cases, statutes, or other legal materials on defamation: **defamatory statement /p slander**

Example of search terms you can use on an Internet legal search engine such as the Public Library of Law (www.plol.org), Findlaw (www.findlaw.com), or Google Scholar (scholar.google.com): **libel slander defamation tort**

Example of a search you could use on standard search engines (www.google.com, www.bing.com, www.yahoo.com) to find material on this tort; law firms that describe the tort; and articles, cases, statutes, and other materials on the tort: **libel slander defamation tort**

More Internet sites to check for material on strict liability in tort and other torts:
www.hg.org/torts.html
www.megalaw.com/top/top.php (click "Intentional Torts," "Personal Injury Law," "Tort Law," and "Damages")
See also the online sites in Overview of Tort Law at the end of Chapter 1.

CHECK THE CITE

Gus Chafoulias sued ABC and an attorney for defamation, alleging that ABC published a defamatory statement made by the attorney pertaining to sexual harassment. What standard of fault was Chafoulias required to meet, and how did the court rule on his claim? Read the case of *Chafoulias v. Peterson*, 668 N.W.2d 642 (Minn. 2003). To read the opinion online, (1) Go to the site of the Minnesota courts (www.courts.state.mn.us). Click Find Court Records, then Supreme Court and Court of Appeals Opinion Archive. For the Supreme Court Opinions & Orders, click Index by case name, then letter *C*. Scroll down to the *C* opinions until you find the Chafoulias case. (2) Go to FindACase (www.findacase.com). Select Minnesota. Run a citation search (for volume enter 668, for reporter, select N.W.2d, for page enter 642). (3) Run a citation search ("668 N.W.2d 642") or a party search (Chafoulias Peterson) in the Legal Opinions and Journals database of Google Scholar (scholar.google.com).

PROJECT

In Google, Bing, or another general search engine, run the following search: "public official" defamation *aa* (substitute the name of your state for *aa* in the search, (e.g., "public official" defamation California). Find a case in which a court ruled on a defamation action brought by a public official in your state. Summarize the facts and decision of the court.

ETHICS IN A TORTS PRACTICE

You are a paralegal working in the law office of Francis Robertson, who has a large personal injury practice. When settlement checks or paid judgment awards arrive at the office, your instructions are to deposit the funds in the account Robertson keeps at a local bank. It is also the account the office uses to pay the law firm's rent and other office expenses. What ethical problems, if any, might exist?

SUMMARY

Defamation is the publication of a written or gestured defamatory statement (libel) or an oral one (slander) that is of and concerning the plaintiff and that harms the plaintiff's reputation. A statement of fact is defamatory if it would tend to harm the reputation of the plaintiff in the eyes of at least a substantial and respectable minority of people by lowering the plaintiff in the estimation of those people or by deterring them from associating with the plaintiff. In general, defamatory opinions are not actionable unless they imply the existence of defamatory facts that can be objectively established as true or false.

When extrinsic facts had to be alleged for the explanation of the defamatory statement (the innuendo), the facts were pleaded in the inducement. At common law, the falsity of the statement was assumed; truth was an affirmative defense. For media defendants, the U.S. Constitution requires plaintiffs to prove that the statement was false and that the defendant exhibited some degree of fault in deciding whether the statement was true or false before publishing it. The fault must be actual malice (knowing falsehood or reckless falsehood) if the plaintiff is a public official/public figure and the statement is on a matter of public concern. The fault must be actual malice *or* negligence if the plaintiff is a public official/public figure and the statement is on a matter of private concern. The fault must be actual malice *or* negligence if the plaintiff is a private person and the statement is on a matter of public or private concern.

The defamatory statement must be of and concerning the plaintiff. Extrinsic facts may need to be pleaded in the colloquium of the complaint to establish that the defamatory statement was of and concerning the plaintiff. Publication of the statement occurs when it is intentionally or negligently communicated to someone other than the plaintiff. The repetition or republication of a defamatory statement by someone else is treated as a publication of the statement, although some protection is available to defendants under the fair-report privilege. Entities such as bookstores and telephone companies that merely deliver or transmit the defamatory statement are not liable for defamation unless they have reason to know that they are transmitting defamatory material. Providers of interactive computer services on the Internet have an immunity from tort liability based on defamatory statements made by others using the online services of the providers.

In nonmedia cases, most libel on its face does not require special damages. Libel per quod does in some states. Slander per se does not require special damages; slander per quod does. There can be no presumed damages against media defendants charged with making defamatory statements on matters of public concern unless the plaintiff can prove actual malice—that the defendant knew the statement was false or was reckless as to its truth or falsity.

Judges, attorneys, parties, witnesses, and jurors have an absolute privilege to make defamatory statements while performing their duties in judicial proceedings. The same is true of legislators, legislative witnesses, and high executive officers. An absolute privilege cannot be lost by bad motives. Under certain circumstances, defendants have a qualified privilege to defame in order to protect their own legitimate interests, the interests of others, or common interests. Everyone has the qualified privilege of fair comment on a matter of public interest or concern, and in many states, the media has the qualified fair-report privilege. A qualified privilege can be lost if it is not exercised in a reasonable manner for a proper purpose.

Plaintiffs sometimes SLAPP defendants with meritless defamation suits solely to intimidate them. Several states give SLAPP victims the right to assert special motions designed to end such suits quickly.

KEY TERMS

defamation *502*
libel *502*
slander *502*
defamacast *502*
affirmative defense *503*
fault *503*
defamatory statement *503*
actionable *503*
opinion *503*
fact *503*
fair comment *504*
on its face *507*
extrinsic fact *507*
inducement *507*
innuendo *507*
reckless *507*
negligent *507*
actual malice *507*
public official *508*
public figure *508*
all-purpose public figure *508*
limited-purpose public figure *508*
private person *508*
of and concerning the plaintiff *511*
colloquium *511*
publication *512*
republication *513*
fair-report privilege *513*
listserv *513*
immunity *514*
presumed damages *514*
special damages *514*
libel per se *515*
libel per quod *515*
slander per se *515*
moral turpitude *515*
slander per quod *515*
privilege *517*
absolute privilege *517*
qualified privilege *518*
SLAPP suit *519*
dictum *519*

REVIEW QUESTIONS

1. What is defamation?
2. How does libel differ from slander?
3. What is a defamacast?
4. On the issue of who had to prove the truth or falsity of the statement, how has the U.S. Constitution changed the common law?
5. On the issue of fault on the truth or falsity of the statement, how has the U.S. Constitution changed the common law?
6. How does a fact differ from an opinion?
7. When can an opinion be defamatory?
8. What is fair comment?
9. When is an inducement needed?
10. What is innuendo?
11. How does knowing falsehood differ from reckless falsehood?
12. How does actual malice differ from negligent falsehood?
13. How does a matter of public concern differ from a matter of private concern?
14. How does a public official differ from a public figure?
15. How does an all-purpose public figure differ from a limited-purpose public figure?
16. What degree of fault must a public official/public figure prove when suing the media on a matter of public concern?

17. What degree of fault must a public official/public figure prove when suing the media on a matter of private concern?
18. What degree of fault must a private person prove when suing the media on a matter of public or private concern?
19. When is a statement of and concerning the plaintiff?
20. What is the colloquium?
21. What is a publication?
22. In what respect is the element of publication a fault element?
23. When is republication actionable?
24. What is the fair-report privilege?
25. Can an Internet service provider be liable for defamation based on what a third party posts on its service?
26. How does libel per se differ from libel per quod?
27. Are special damages required for libel per se?
28. Are special damages required for libel per quod?
29. How does slander per se differ from slander per quod?
30. Are special damages required for slander per se?
31. Are special damages required for slander per quod?
32. Are presumed damages allowed in defamation actions against the media?
33. How does an absolute privilege differ from a qualified privilege?
34. Who is entitled to an absolute privilege?
35. Who is entitled to a qualified privilege?
36. What is a SLAPP suit?

HELPFUL WEBSITES

- **Defamation**
  www.megalaw.com/top/defamation.php
  cyber.law.harvard.edu/ (type defamation in the search box)
  www.abbottlaw.com/defamation.html
  en.wikipedia.org/wiki/Defamation
  www.expertlaw.com/library/personal_injury/defamation.html
  www.freedomforum.org (type defamation in the search box)
  members.mobar.org/civics/DefamePubOff.htm
- **Internet Defamation**
  www.uiowa.edu/~cyberlaw/cls01/small3.html
  writ.news.findlaw.com/hilden/20080723.html
  www.eff.org/issues/bloggers/legal/liability/defamation
  www.cyberlibel.com
  www.digitaldefamation.com
  reputationdefender.com
- **Element Search**
  In Google (www.google.com) run the following searches:
  elements libel tort
  elements slander tort
  elements defamation tort
  elements Internet tort

ENDNOTES

1. *Milkovich v. Lorain Journal Co.*, 497 U.S. 1, 19, 110 S. Ct. 2695, 2706, 111 L. Ed. 2d 1 (1990).
2. 418 U.S. 323, 339, 94 S. Ct. 2997, 3007, 41 L. Ed. 2d 789, 805 (1974).
3. *New York Times v. Sullivan*, 376 U.S. 254, 84 S. Ct. 710, 11 L. Ed. 2d 686 (1964).
4. 47 U.S.C. §230(c)(1)&(e)(3) (www.law.cornell.edu/uscode/47/230.html).
5. *Zeran v. America Online, Inc.*, 129 F.3d 327, 330 (4th Cir. 1997).
6. W. Page Keeton et al., *Prosser and Keeton on the Law of Torts* 832 (5th ed. 1984).
7. www.californiacoastline.org/streisand/lawsuit.html.
8. *Streisand v. Adelman*, Case No. SC 077 257 (Cal. Super. Ct. Dec. 31 2003) (www.californiacoastline.org/streisand/slapp-ruling.pdf).

Student StudyWARE™ CD-ROM
For additional materials, please go to the student CD in this book.

CHAPTER

25

INVASION OF PRIVACY

CHAPTER OUTLINE

- Four Torts
- Intrusion
- Appropriation
- Public Disclosure of Private Fact
- False Light
- Media Defendants

CHAPTER OBJECTIVES

After completing this chapter, you should be able to:

- List the names of the four torts that constitute invasion of privacy.
- State the elements of the four invasion-of-privacy torts.
- Identify the factors that a court will consider when determining whether an activity is private for purposes of the torts of intrusion and public disclosure of private fact.
- Explain some of the main differences between suing media and nonmedia defendants in invasion-of-privacy suits.
- Identify paralegal roles in invasion-of-privacy litigation.
- List the major resources in traditional books and online to use when researching issues involving invasion-of-privacy torts.

FOUR TORTS

invasion of privacy 1. Four torts (intrusion, appropriation, public disclosure of private fact, and false light). 2. An unwarranted interference into someone's private life or misappropriation of someone's name, likeness, or personality.

In general, something is private if it pertains to facts about an individual's personal life that have no reasonable or logical connection to what the person does in public, and that the person does not consent to reveal. When this privacy is invaded, tort law may provide a remedy in the form of four separate **invasion-of-privacy** torts: intrusion, appropriation, public disclosure of private fact, and false light. They are designed to protect an individual's interest (1) in being left alone and (2) in not having someone use the individual's name, likeness, or personality for personal gain.

intrusion 1. Prying, peering, or probing. 2. A highly offensive invasion into another's personal seclusion or private life. It is one of the four invasion-of-privacy torts. (See glossary for an additional definition.)

INTRUSION

Intrusion is a highly offensive invasion into another's personal seclusion or private life. It is one of the four invasion-of-privacy torts. (See Exhibit 25–1 for its elements.)

Exhibit 25–1
Elements of the tort of intrusion.

1. An act of intrusion into someone's private affairs or concerns
2. Highly offensive to a reasonable person

private affairs Information that cannot reasonably be considered of legitimate public concern. Non-newsworthy facts.

Intrusion consists of prying, peering, or probing of some kind, e.g., wiretapping, opening mail, filing subpoenas that require disclosure of records, making persistent phone calls. Such methods of intrusion must be directed at something that is considered one's **private affairs.** It is usually not an intrusion to follow the plaintiff in a department store or to photograph him or her in a park. In these settings, the plaintiff is engaging in public activity. There are a number of factors a court will consider in determining whether something is private, none of which is usually conclusive alone. These factors are outlined in Exhibit 25–2.

Exhibit 25–2
Factors a court will consider when deciding whether plaintiff was engaged in a private activity.

A. "Yes" answers to the following questions will help persuade a court that the activity was *not* private:

- Was the plaintiff in a public place at the time?
- Was the activity of the plaintiff observable by normal methods of observation?
- Was the activity of the plaintiff already a matter of public record before the defendant became involved?
- Was the plaintiff drawing attention to him- or herself?

B. "Yes" answers to the following questions will help persuade a court that the activity *was* private:

- Was the plaintiff caught off guard through no fault of his or her own?
- Did the defendant take advantage of a vulnerable position that the plaintiff was in?
- Was the activity of the plaintiff something that society would consider none of anyone else's business?

highly offensive Extremely distasteful or unpleasant to a reasonable person.

Not every intrusion into private matters is tortious. The intrusion must be **highly offensive** to a reasonable person. The test is objective—what the reasonable person considers extremely distasteful or unpleasant. The plaintiff may be greatly offended by a call from an ex-boyfriend at the plaintiff's workplace. But a reasonable person would probably not be highly offended by such a call. The case may be different, however, if calls are made every fifteen minutes starting at midnight while the plaintiff is trying to sleep at home.

ASSIGNMENT 25.1

Has the tort of intrusion been committed in any of the following situations?

a. Fred has purchased the latest smartphone. Henry passes Fred on the street. Henry has his cell phone on. Without Henry knowing it, Fred's smartphone is able to download personal information from Henry's cell phone (e.g., his name and phone number). Fred uses this information to do a background check on Henry and finds out that Henry has a criminal record.

b. Tim photographs Karla at an amusement park in the fun house at the moment an air vent on the floor blows up her dress.

c. At a bus terminal, a wall television camera is clearly visible in the men's room.

d. General Motors hires a prostitute to solicit consumer advocate (and presidential candidate) Ralph Nader to engage in sexual activities. Ralph refuses.

CASE

Hamberger v. Eastman

106 N.H. 107, 206 A.2d 239, 11 A.L.R.3d 1288 (1964)

Supreme Court of New Hampshire

Background: *The Hambergers are husband and wife. They are weekly tenants of Eastman. When they discovered that he had installed a concealed listening and recording device in their bedroom, they sued him for invasion of privacy. The defendant moved to dismiss on the ground that the plaintiffs had not stated a cause of action. The trial court transferred the case to the Supreme Court without making a ruling, probably because the invasion-of-privacy cause of action had not yet been recognized in the state. The case is now before the Supreme Court of New Hampshire.*

Decision on Appeal: *Motion to dismiss should be denied. The plaintiffs have stated an invasion-of-privacy cause of action for intrusion. The case is sent back (remanded) to the trial court for the trial.*

OPINION OF COURT

Justice KENISON delivered the opinion of the court:

The question presented is whether the right of privacy is recognized in this state. There is no controlling statute and no previous decision in this jurisdiction which decides the question. . . . In capsule summary the invasion of the right of privacy developed as an independent and distinct tort from the classic and famous article by Warren and Brandeis, *The Right to Privacy,* 4 Harvard Law Review 193 (1890). . . . It is not one tort, but a complex of four. The law of privacy comprises four distinct kinds of invasion of four different interests of the plaintiff which are tied together by the common name, but otherwise have almost nothing in common except that each presents an interference with the right of the plaintiff "to be let alone." Prosser, *Torts,* § 112, p. 832 (3d ed. 1964).

The four kinds of invasion comprising the law of privacy include: (1) intrusion upon the plaintiff's physical and mental solitude or seclusion; (2) public disclosure of private facts; (3) publicity which places the plaintiff in a false light in the public eye; (4) appropriation, for the defendant's benefit or advantage, of the plaintiff's name or likeness. In the present case, we are concerned only with the tort of intrusion upon the plaintiffs' solitude or seclusion. . . .

The tort of intrusion upon the plaintiff's solitude or seclusion is not limited to a physical invasion of his home or his room or his quarters. As Prosser points out, the principle has been carried beyond such physical intrusion "and extended to eavesdropping upon private conversations by means of wire tapping and microphones." Prosser, supra, p. 833. . . . The right of privacy has been upheld in situations where microphones have been planted to overhear private conversations. *Roach v. Harper,* 143 W. Va. 869, 105 S.E.2d 564.

We have not searched for cases where the bedroom of husband and wife has been "bugged" but it should not be necessary—by way of understatement—to observe that this is the type of intrusion that would be offensive to any person of ordinary sensibilities. What married "people do in the privacy of their bedroom is their own business so long as they are not hurting anyone else." Ernst and Loth, *For Better or Worse,* 79 (1952). The *Restatement, Torts* § 867 provides that "a person who unreasonably and seriously interferes with another's interest in not having his affairs known to others . . . is liable to the other." As is pointed out in comment d "liability exists only if the defendant's conduct was such that he should have realized that it would be offensive to persons of ordinary sensibilities. It is only where the intrusion has gone beyond the limits of decency that liability accrues. These limits are exceeded where intimate details of the life of one who has never manifested a desire to have publicity are exposed to the public. . .".

The defendant contends that the right of privacy should not be recognized on the facts of the present case as they appear in the pleadings because there are no allegations that anyone listened or overheard any sounds or voices originating from the plaintiffs' bedroom. The tort of intrusion on the plaintiffs' solitude or seclusion does not require publicity and communication to third persons although this would affect the amount of damages, as Prosser makes clear. Prosser, supra, 843. The defendant also contends that the right of privacy is not violated unless something has been published, written or printed and that oral publicity is not sufficient. Recent cases make it clear that this is not a requirement. *Carr v. Watkins,* 227 Md. 578, 177 A.2d 841.

If the peeping Tom, the big ear and the electronic eavesdropper (whether ingenious or ingenuous) have a place in the hierarchy of social values, it ought not to be at the expense of a married couple minding their own business in the seclusion of their bedroom who have never asked for or by their conduct deserved a potential projection of their private conversations and actions to their landlord or to others. Whether actual or potential such "publicity with respect to private matters of purely personal concern is an injury to personality. It impairs the mental peace and comfort of the individual and may produce suffering more acute than that produced by a mere bodily injury." III Pound, *Jurisprudence* 58 (1959). The use of parabolic microphones and sonic wave devices designed to pick up conversations in a room without entering it and at a considerable distance away makes the problem far from fanciful. . . . [T]he invasion of the plaintiffs' solitude or seclusion, as alleged in the pleadings, was a violation of their right of privacy and constituted a tort for which the plaintiffs may recover damages to the extent that they can prove them. . . .

The motion to dismiss should be denied. Remanded.

ASSIGNMENT 25.2

a. Would the *Hamberger* court have reached a different result if the landlord installed the listening devices because of his suspicion that the married couple was planning to set fire to his building?
b. How would the *Hamberger* court have decided the bus terminal case in Assignment 25.1(c)?

CASE

Smyth v. The Pillsbury Co.

914 F. Supp. 97 (1996)
United States District Court, Eastern District, Pennsylvania

Background: *Michael Smyth was an at-will employee of The Pillsbury Company. (At-will employees can be terminated at any time for any reason that does not violate public policy.) Smyth was fired after sending an e-mail that contained threats to "kill the backstabbing bastards" and that referred to a planned holiday party as the "Jim Jones Kool-Aid affair." (Jim Jones was a cult leader who persuaded hundreds of his followers to commit mass suicide by drinking poison-laced Kool-Aid.) Smyth sued the company in District Court for wrongful termination. He argued that the reading of his e-mail messages constituted the tort of intrusion and that a firing that resulted from this invasion of privacy was wrongful. At the trial, the defendant moved to dismiss on the ground that the plaintiff has failed to state a claim on which relief can be granted. In effect, the company denied that there was an invasion of privacy. The portions of the opinion excerpted below pertain to this tort claim.*

Decision of Court: *The District Court granted the motion to dismiss. The firing for transmitting inappropriate and unprofessional comments over Pillsbury's e-mail system was not wrongful since there was no invasion of privacy.*

OPINION OF COURT

Judge WEINER delivered the opinion of the court. . . .

[P]laintiff, an at-will employee, claims he was wrongfully discharged from his position as a regional operations manager by the defendant [Pillsbury]. Defendant maintained an electronic mail communication system ("e-mail") in order to promote internal corporate communications between its employees. Defendant repeatedly assured its employees, including plaintiff, that all e-mail communications would remain confidential and privileged. Defendant further assured its employees, including plaintiff, that e-mail communications could not be intercepted and used by defendant against its employees as grounds for termination or reprimand.

In October 1994, plaintiff received certain e-mail communications from his supervisor over defendant's e-mail system on his computer at home. In reliance on defendant's assurances regarding defendant's e-mail system, plaintiff responded and exchanged e-mails with his supervisor. At some later date, contrary to the assurances of confidentiality made by defendant, defendant, acting through its agents, servants and employees, intercepted plaintiff's private e-mail messages made in October 1994. On January 17, 1995, defendant notified plaintiff that it was terminating his employment effective February 1, 1995, for transmitting what it deemed to be inappropriate and unprofessional comments over defendant's e-mail system in October, 1994. . . . [The e-mails concerned sales management and contained threats to "kill the backstabbing bastards" and referred to the planned holiday party as the "Jim Jones Kool-Aid affair."]

Plaintiff claims that his termination was [improper because it was based on an invasion of privacy.] . . . [O]ne of the torts which Pennsylvania recognizes as encompassing an action for invasion of privacy is the tort of "intrusion upon seclusion." . . . [T]he *Restatement (Second) of Torts* defines the tort as follows: One who intentionally intrudes, physically or otherwise, upon the solitude or seclusion of another or his private affairs or concerns, is subject to liability to the other for invasion of his privacy, if the intrusion would be highly offensive to a reasonable person. *Restatement (Second) of Torts* 652B. Liability only attaches when the [intrusion is substantial]. . . .

Applying the *Restatement* definition of the tort of intrusion upon seclusion to the facts, . . . we find that plaintiff has failed to state a claim upon which relief can be granted. In the first instance, . . . we do not find a reasonable expectation of privacy in e-mail communications voluntarily made by an employee to his supervisor over the company e-mail system notwithstanding any assurances that such communications would not be intercepted by management. Once plaintiff communicated the alleged unprofessional comments to a second person (his supervisor) over an e-mail system which was apparently utilized by the entire company, any reasonable expectation of privacy was lost. . . . We find no privacy interests in such communications.

In the second instance, even if we found that an employee had a reasonable expectation of privacy in the contents of his e-mail communications over the company e-mail system, we do not find that a reasonable person would consider the defendant's interception of these communications to be a substantial and highly offensive invasion of his privacy. [We] note that by intercepting such communications, the company is not . . . requiring the employee to disclose any personal information about himself or invading the employee's person or personal effects. Moreover, the company's interest in preventing inappropriate and unprofessional comments or even illegal activity over its e-mail system outweighs any privacy interest the employee may have in those comments.

In sum, we find that the defendant's actions did not tortiously invade the plaintiff's privacy. . . . As a result, the motion to dismiss is granted.

ASSIGNMENT 25.3

a. What legitimate business reasons might exist that could make it reasonable for a company to monitor and read all e-mail correspondence on its system?
b. Is the court's conclusion in the *Hamberger* case consistent with the conclusion reached in the *Smyth* case? Why or why not?
c. Suppose that in the *Smyth* case the director of the personnel department at Pillsbury sends all employees the following e-mail message: "As you know, the Red Cross will be here next week to collect blood. We want 100 percent participation." Michael Smyth sends an e-mail back that says he cannot contribute blood because of a rare disease he has. The director sends a copy of this response to Smyth's supervisor and to a co-worker, neither of whom knew about this health problem. Would the *Smyth* court say it was an invasion of privacy for the personnel director to have allowed these individuals to read the e-mail?

Several states have passed statutes that are designed to curb some of the most blatant kinds of intrusion, particularly by *paparazzi*, photographers who stalk celebrities for photographs. For example, the Hollywood community cheered the enactment of the following California law, which they argued was long overdue:

California Civil Code § 1708.8 (1998)

(a) A person is liable for physical invasion of privacy when the defendant knowingly enters onto the land of another without permission or otherwise committed a trespass in order to physically invade the privacy of the plaintiff with the intent to capture any type of visual image, sound recording, or other physical impression of the plaintiff engaging in a personal or familial activity and the physical invasion occurs in a manner that is offensive to a reasonable person. . . .

(i) It is not a defense to a violation of this section that no image, recording, or physical impression was captured or sold. . . .

(k) For the purposes of this section, "personal and familial activity" includes, but is not limited to, intimate details of the plaintiff's personal life, interactions with the plaintiff's family or significant others, or other aspects of plaintiff's private affairs or concerns. . . .

APPROPRIATION

appropriation The unauthorized use of a person's name, likeness, or personality for the user's benefit.

Appropriation is the unauthorized use of a person's name, likeness, or personality for the benefit of someone other than that person. It is one of the four invasion-of-privacy torts. (See Exhibit 25–3 for its elements.)

Exhibit 25–3
Elements of the tort of appropriation.

1. The use of the plaintiff's name, likeness, or personality
2. For the benefit of the defendant

The first element is met if the defendant uses the name, likeness, or personality of the plaintiff. The plaintiff must be identifiable in this use. To make a statue or mannequin of the plaintiff is not sufficient unless the plaintiff is clearly recognizable.

pecuniary Pertaining to money.

The defendant must derive benefit from the use. In some states, the benefit must be commercial or **pecuniary**, e.g., impersonating the plaintiff to obtain credit, or using the plaintiff's name or picture in a business ad to give the appearance of an endorsement. But in most states the benefit does not have to be financial. The second element would be met, for example, if the defendant pretended to be a well-known photographer as part of his effort to seduce women.

ASSIGNMENT 25.4

The plaintiff is a "human cannonball" who shoots himself out of a cannon at county fairs. Do either of the following situations constitute appropriation?

a. The defendant tapes a video of the stunt and shows it at home to friends and relatives.
b. The defendant is a television station. One of its employees videotapes the stunt and shows it both on the evening news and on its "Incredible People" variety show. (See the last section of this chapter, on media defendants.)

PUBLIC DISCLOSURE OF PRIVATE FACT

public disclosure of private fact Unreasonable publicity concerning private facts about an individual's life that are not matters of legitimate public concern.

Public disclosure of private fact is unreasonable publicity concerning private facts about an individual's life that are not matters of legitimate public concern. It is one of the four invasion-of-privacy torts. (See Exhibit 25–4 for its elements.)

Exhibit 25–4
Elements of the tort of public disclosure of private fact.

1. Publicity
2. Concerning the private life of the plaintiff
3. Highly offensive to a reasonable person

For purposes of this tort, "publicity" has a different meaning from "publication" in the law of defamation. **Publication** is the communication of the defamatory statement to at least one person other than the plaintiff. **Publicity**, however, means communication to the public at large. More than a few people must hear or read the statement.

publication Communication of a statement to someone other than the plaintiff.

publicity Communication to the public at large, i.e., to more than a few people.

Review the factors mentioned in the section on intrusion that are used to determine whether something is private (see Exhibit 25–2). Most of these factors are also relevant to determine whether there has been a public disclosure of a private fact.

In most instances, there has not been a disclosure of a private fact when publicity is given to something that is already a matter of public record (e.g., a document recently filed in court, the names of contributors to a political candidate). Some subject matter, however, is clearly private, either by law or by custom. Data provided on income tax returns and census forms, for example, are protected from disclosure by law. Also legally protected are confidential communications between attorney and client, doctor and patient, and minister and penitent. One's sexual inclinations are also private, because in our society such matters are considered no one's business. Of course, if a plaintiff flaunts such information, he or she may be considered to have consented to the disclosure.

If there has been a disclosure of a private fact, it is no defense that the fact is true. Falsity is not one of the elements of this tort.

It is not enough that the plaintiff considers the publicity discomforting or embarrassing. It must be highly offensive to a reasonable person. A reasonable person, for example, would not be highly offended by a story about an individual's having his deceased dog cremated, but would probably be offended by a story about the individual's three unsuccessful (or successful) operations to cure incontinence. Here are some other disclosures that might be highly offensive to a reasonable person:

- a sign placed in the defendant's window stating that the plaintiff does not pay his or her debts
- an interoffice memo sent to thirty employees stating that a fellow employee is a homosexual
- a video shown in a tavern of a woman nursing her baby on her backyard porch

ASSIGNMENT 25.5

a. Tom is an ex-convict who served time for murder twenty-five years ago. He is now a reformed citizen living an outstanding life in a new community. Bill finds out about Tom's past and lets everyone know at a town meeting. Does Tom have a cause of action against Bill?

b. George recently had plastic surgery. Helen, his neighbor, tells every member of her garden club, of which Helen is the president.

FALSE LIGHT

False light is untrue and unreasonably offensive publicity about a person. It is one of the four invasion-of-privacy torts. (See Exhibit 25–5 for the elements of false light.)

false light Untrue and unreasonably offensive publicity about a person.

Exhibit 25–5
Elements of the tort of false light.

1. Publicity
2. Placing the plaintiff in a false light
3. Highly offensive to a reasonable person

The first element of false light is publicity. It has the same meaning as publicity in the tort of public disclosure of private fact: communication to the public at large—not just to a few people.

False light is similar to defamation in that the statement about the plaintiff must be false. Unlike defamation, however, false light can be established without the statement harming the plaintiff's reputation, although most usually do. When is a person placed in a false light? Broadly speaking, whenever an impression or conclusion is given about a person that is not accurate.

EXAMPLES

- falsely stating in a report that a doctor has given AIDS to one of his patients during an operation
- falsely claiming that the plaintiff has written a pornographic novel
- signing the name of a pro-choice plaintiff on a pro-life petition without permission

newsworthy Pertaining to information the general public would like to have; of legitimate public interest.

public official A government employee who has significant authority.

These cases of false light would be considered highly offensive by a reasonable person. Not all false light, however, falls into this category. Misspelling the plaintiff's name on a notice places him or her in a false light, but this would hardly be deemed highly offensive, even if the plaintiff was very embarrassed by the incident. A reasonable person would not take such offense.

ASSIGNMENT 25.6

a. At a banquet honoring the retirement of Linda, her boss rises to make a speech. The boss gives some details of Linda's life, including the fact that she was married on June 26, 1968 and gave birth to her first child on July 1, 1968. In fact, the child was born on June 30, 1969. Linda sues her boss for false light. What result?
b. George Jones is a practicing attorney. He decides to hire two attorneys as associates (not partners). The name of the firm is "Jones & Associates." Jones decides to take out a Yellow Pages listing under this name. When the Yellow Pages come out, his firm is listed as "Jones & Ass". Have any torts been committed?

public figure A person (other than a public official) who has assumed special prominence in the affairs of society. An *all-purpose public figure* is a person of general power, influence, or notoriety. A *limited-purpose public figure* is a person who has voluntarily become involved in a controversy of interest to the general public.

actual malice Knowledge that a statement of fact is false, or recklessness as to its truth or falsity. Also called constitutional malice and *New York Times* malice.

MEDIA DEFENDANTS

Special protections exist for the press, media, and book publishers (referred to collectively in this book as media defendants). The media has a constitutional right under the First Amendment to publicize **newsworthy** people and events. This covers a broad range of matters of legitimate public interest. Media defendants are often charged with false light invasion of privacy, particularly by a **public official** or a **public figure.** In such a case, there must be proof that the media defendant either knew that the publication placed the plaintiff in a false light or acted in reckless disregard of whether it did so. (This is known as **actual malice.**) These rules also apply to defamation cases against the media. See Chapter 24 where the rules are more fully discussed.

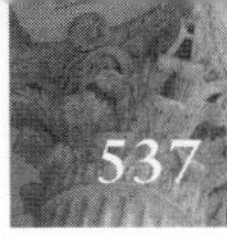

CASE

Peoples Bank and Trust Co. of Mountain Home, Conservator of the Estate of Nellie Mitchell, an Aged Person v. Globe International Publishing, Inc. doing business as "Sun"

978 F.2d 1065 (1992)
United States Court of Appeals for the Eighth Circuit

Background: *The Sun, a supermarket tabloid owned by Globe International, published photographs of Nellie Mitchell to illustrate a story about a 101-year-old pregnant woman. Mitchell sued for false light invasion of privacy and won a jury verdict in federal district court. Globe now appeals to the United States Court of Appeals for the Eighth Circuit.*

Decision on Appeal: *Globe committed false light invasion of privacy. A judgment against Globe does not violate the First Amendment.*

OPINION OF COURT

Judge HEANEY delivered the opinion of the court . . .

Plaintiff Mitchell is a ninety-seven-year-old woman from the city of Mountain Home, in Baxter County, Arkansas. After having operated a newsstand and delivered newspapers in Mountain Home for almost fifty years, Mitchell has become a well-recognized figure in her community and something of a local legend. She was recognized for her long service in 1980 when major newspapers ran human interest stories about her and she appeared for interviews on television talk shows.

Defendant Globe publishes several supermarket tabloids, including the *National Examiner* and the *Sun*. Globe published a fairly accurate account of Mitchell in the November 25, 1980, issue of the *National Examiner*. A photograph of Mitchell, purchased from the Baxter County News, accompanied that story.

The same photograph appeared again on the cover page of the October 2, 1990, edition of the *Sun* with the headline "Pregnancy forces granny to quit work at age 101." Customers at supermarket checkout lines in Baxter County who scanned the cover page of the *Sun* saw only that Nellie Mitchell was featured next to a headline about a "granny" forced to quit work because of pregnancy. Purchasers of the tabloid who turned to the story on page eleven also would have seen a second photograph of Mitchell next to a fictitious story about a woman named "Audrey Wiles," living in Australia, who quit her paper route at the age of 101 because an extramarital affair with a millionaire client on her route had left her pregnant.

Word spread quickly in Mountain Home that Nellie Mitchell, "the paper lady," was featured in the offending edition of the *Sun*. This edition of the *Sun* was a "sell-out" in the northern region of Arkansas where Mitchell lives. . . .

The district court gave the following instruction regarding "false light" invasion of privacy:

> to prevail on this claim, the plaintiff has the burden of proving by clear and convincing evidence the following: one, that the false light in which she was placed by the publicity would be highly offensive to a reasonable person; and two, that the defendant acted with actual malice in publishing the statements at issue in this case. Actual malice means that Globe International intended, or recklessly failed to anticipate, that readers would construe the publicized matter as conveying actual facts or events concerning Mrs. Mitchell. A finding of actual malice requires a showing of more than mere negligence.

Globe does not dispute that the published story was false; indeed, its principal defense is that the story was "pure fiction." Nor does Globe dispute that the story would be highly offensive to a reasonable person, or that it was in fact highly offensive to Mitchell. The central issue on appeal is the existence of actual malice: whether Globe intended, or recklessly failed to anticipate, that readers would construe the story as conveying actual facts or events concerning Mitchell. Globe contends that, as a matter of law, no reader reasonably could construe the story as conveying actual facts about Mitchell, and that no evidence supports a finding that Globe intended that result.

Globe . . . asserts it is biologically impossible for a woman of either 101 or 95 years of age to become pregnant, and therefore, as a matter of law, no reasonable reader could have believed the story represented true facts about Mitchell. . . .

Every other aspect of the charged story, however—such as the implication of sexual impropriety and that Mitchell was quitting her life-long profession—is subject to reasonable belief. Even the report of the pregnancy—a physical condition, not an opinion, metaphor, fantasy, or surrealism—could be proved either true or false. In the context of this case, therefore, we cannot say as a matter of law that readers could not reasonably have believed that the charged story portrayed actual facts or events concerning Mitchell. . . .

The circumstances of the instant case suggest the story in the *Sun* may well be believed by readers as conveying actual facts about Mitchell despite the apparent absurdity of a pregnant centenarian. Indeed, there is more than sufficient evidence to conclude that Globe intends its readers to believe the *Sun* generally. Although there is less evidence to conclude that Globe intended its readers to believe facts specifically about Mitchell, we conclude there is sufficient evidence to find that it recklessly failed to anticipate that result. . . .

The format and style of the *Sun* suggest it is a factual newspaper. Globe advertises the *Sun* as publishing "the weird, the strange, and the outlandish *news* from around the globe," and nowhere in the publication does it suggest its stories are false or exaggerated. The *Sun* also mingles factual, fictional, and hybrid stories without overtly identifying one from the other. At trial, even its own writers could not tell which stories were true and which were completely fabricated.

In the October 2, 1990, issue submitted as evidence, the *Sun* consistently alerted its readers to advertisements with small-print caveats above the text of those advertisements. The *Sun* even published a disclaimer above certain personal advertisements warning its readers that those notices had not been investigated—implying that other advertisements and the news stories *had* been investigated. These disclaimers and caveats on advertisements, and the absence of any warning or explanation on the admittedly fictional "news" stories, bolster our conclusion that Globe intends for its 366,000 readers to believe the *Sun* prints factual material. It is the kind of *calculated* falsehood against which the First Amendment can tolerate sanctions without significant impairment of its function. See *Time, Inc. v. Hill,* 385 U.S. 374 (1967).

Globe was on notice that the photographs of Mitchell it published in its October 2, 1990, issue of the *Sun* were purchased from Baxter County, Arkansas—an area where Globe circulated the *Sun.* Counsel at oral argument conceded that the photographs were identified on the back as having been purchased from the *Baxter County Bulletin*. The editor who chose the photograph testified that he knew the individual pictured in the photograph was a real person, but that he assumed she was dead. This was the same editor who, ten years before, had worked for the *Examiner* when it published the essentially truthful story about Mitchell.

Although Globe's failure to investigate and confirm its assumption of Mitchell's death will not alone support a finding of actual malice, the purposeful avoidance of the truth is in a different category. Globe contends it made a simple mistake, and that it was not on notice that Mitchell was alive. The jury, however, had sufficient evidence to determine that Globe purposefully avoided the truth about Mitchell.

[Judgment affirmed. The case is remanded, however, to reconsider the issue of damages.]

ASSIGNMENT 25.7

a. Was Nellie Mitchell a public figure? If so, would it be relevant to her invasion-of-privacy claim?
b. Was the case correctly decided? Some may think that tabloids deserve to be sued, but is it accurate to say that readers could interpret the photos and story as conveying actual facts or events concerning Mrs. Mitchell?
c. What other torts do you think Globe may have committed against Nellie Mitchell?

INVASION-OF-PRIVACY CHECKLIST

Definitions, Relationships, Paralegal Roles, and Research References

Interests Protected by the Four Invasion-of-Privacy Torts

Intrusion: The right to be free from unreasonable intrusions into a person's private affairs or concerns.

Appropriation: The right to prevent the unauthorized use of a person's name, likeness, or personality for the user's benefit.

Public Disclosure of Private Fact: The right to be free from unreasonable disclosures of private facts about a person's life that are not matters of legitimate public concern.

False Light: The right to be free from false statements that unreasonably place a person in a false light in the public eye.

Elements of These Torts

- Intrusion:
  1. an act of intrusion into someone's private affairs or concerns
  2. highly offensive to a reasonable person
- Appropriation:
  1. the use of the plaintiff's name, likeness, or personality
  2. for the benefit of the defendant

INVASION-OF-PRIVACY CHECKLIST *(Continued)*

- Public disclosure of private fact:
  1. publicity
  2. concerning the private life of the plaintiff
  3. highly offensive to a reasonable person
- False light:
  1. publicity
  2. placing the plaintiff in a false light
  3. highly offensive to a reasonable person

Definitions of Major Words/Phrases in These Elements

Intrusion: Prying, peering, or probing.

Private: Pertaining to facts about an individual's personal life that have no reasonable or logical connection to what the person does in public and that the person does not consent to reveal.

Reasonable Person: An ordinary person who is not unduly sensitive.

Benefit: Deriving some advantage.

Publicity: Communication to the public at large or to a large group of people.

Major Defense and Counterargument Possibilities That Need to Be Explored

1. There was no prying, peering, or probing (for intrusion).
2. What the defendant did related to the public activities of the defendant (for intrusion, public disclosure of private fact, and false light).
3. The defendant did not use plaintiff's name, likeness, or personality (for appropriation).
4. The defendant did not derive benefit from the use of the plaintiff's name, likeness, or personality—or derived only incidental benefit from such use (for appropriation).
5. The statement about the plaintiff was not communicated to the public at large nor to a large group of people (for public disclosure of private fact and false light).
6. No inaccurate impression or statement was made about the plaintiff (for false light).
7. The plaintiff consented to what the defendant did (for all four torts) (on the defense of consent, see Chapter 27).
8. The defendant's conduct occurred while the defendant was arresting the plaintiff, protecting the defendant's own property, or giving testimony in a public proceeding (for intrusion, public disclosure of private fact, and false light) (on the privilege of arrest, see Chapter 7; on defense of property and other self-help privileges, see Chapter 27).
9. The plaintiff's suit against the government for invasion of privacy committed by a government employee may be barred by sovereign immunity (on sovereign immunity, see Chapter 27).
10. The plaintiff's suit against the government employee for invasion of privacy may be barred by official immunity (for all four torts) (on official immunity, see Chapter 27).
11. The plaintiff's suit against the charitable organization for invasion of privacy committed by someone working for the organization may be barred by charitable immunity (for all four torts) (on charitable immunity, see Chapter 27).
12. The plaintiff's suit against a family member for invasion of privacy may be barred by intrafamily tort immunity (for all four torts) (on intrafamily tort immunity, see Chapter 27).
13. The plaintiff failed to take reasonable steps to mitigate the harm caused by the defendant's invasion of privacy; therefore, damages should not cover the aggravation of the harm caused by the plaintiff (for all four torts) (on the mitigation-of-damages rule, see Chapter 16).

Damages

The plaintiff can recover compensatory damages for humiliation or embarrassment caused by the defendant. If the plaintiff suffered mental or physical illness due to the tort committed by the defendant, recovery can also include damages for the illness.

INVASION-OF-PRIVACY CHECKLIST *(Continued)*

If the defendant acted with a malicious motive to harm or injure the plaintiff, punitive damages are possible. Against media defendants, however, there can be no punitive damages in the absence of actual malice. (On the categories of damages, see Chapter 16.)

Relationship to Criminal Law
If the defendant committed intrusion by wiretapping or other electronic devices, the conduct may also violate the criminal law.

Relationship to Other Torts

Defamation: Libel or slander may be committed along with false light if the statement is also derogatory (harms the plaintiff's reputation).
Intentional Infliction of Emotional Distress: This tort is committed along with any of the four invasion-of-privacy torts if the defendant committed an outrageous act with the intent to cause severe emotional distress.
Malicious Prosecution: One example of intrusion is prying into the plaintiff's private affairs through procedural devices such as subpoenas. In such cases, malicious prosecution may also be committed.
Misrepresentation: Misrepresentation may be committed along with false light when the following elements can be established: a false statement of fact, intent to deceive, justifiable reliance, and actual damages.
Prima Facie Torts: If the plaintiff cannot establish the elements of any of the four invasion-of-privacy torts, the plaintiff should check prima facie tort in those states that recognize it.

Federal Law

a. Under the Federal Tort Claims Act, the United States government can be liable for invasion of privacy committed by one of its federal employees within the scope of employment (respondeat superior) (see Exhibit 27–7 in Chapter 27). (Most states have their own statutes that cover when tort claims can be made against the state for invasion of privacy and other torts committed by state government employees. Such claims are also covered in Chapter 27.)
b. There may be liability under the Civil Rights Act if the invasion of privacy was committed while the defendant was depriving the plaintiff of a federal right under color of state law (see Exhibit 27–9 in Chapter 27).

Employer–Employee (Agency) Law
A private (non-government) employee who commits an invasion of privacy is personally liable for this tort. His or her employer will also be liable for invasion of privacy if the conduct of the employee was within the scope of employment (respondeat superior). The employee must be furthering a business objective of the employer at the time. (On the factors that determine scope of employment, see Exhibit 14–9 in Chapter 14.)

Paralegal Roles in Invasion-of-Privacy Litigation
(See also Exhibit 3–1 in Chapter 3, Exhibit 20–4 in Chapter 20, and Exhibit 29–1 in Chapter 29.)

Fact finding (help the office collect facts relevant to prove the elements of the four invasion-of-privacy torts, the elements of available defenses, and the extent of injuries or other damages):

- client interviewing
- field investigation
- online research (e.g., obtaining public records)

File management (help the office control the volume of paperwork in an invasion-of-privacy litigation):

- open client file
- enter case data in computer database
- maintain file documents

INVASION-OF-PRIVACY CHECKLIST *(Continued)*

Litigation assistance (help the trial attorney prepare for an invasion-of-privacy trial and appeal, if needed):

- draft discovery requests
- draft answers to discovery requests
- draft pleadings
- digest and index discovery documents
- prepare trial notebook
- draft notice of appeal
- order trial transcript
- cite-check briefs
- perform legal research

Collection/enforcement (help the trial attorney for the judgment creditor to collect the damages award or to enforce an injunction or other court order at the conclusion of the invasion-of-privacy case):

- draft postjudgment discovery requests
- conduct field investigation to monitor compliance with judgment
- perform online research (e.g., location of defendant's business assets)

Research References for Invasion-of-Privacy Torts

Digests

In the digests of West Group, look for case summaries on these torts under key topics such as:

Torts
Damages
Constitutional Law (274)

Corpus Juris Secundum

In this legal encyclopedia, see the discussions under topic headings such as:

Constitutional Law (582)
Right of Privacy
Torts
Damages

American Jurisprudence 2d

In this legal encyclopedia, see the discussions under topic headings such as:

Privacy
Constitutional Law (503)
Torts
Damages
Fright, Shock, and Mental Disturbance

Legal Periodical Literature

There are two index systems to use to locate articles and other legal periodical literature on these torts:

Index to Legal Periodicals (ILP)

See literature in *ILP* under subject headings such as:

Right of Privacy
Eavesdropping
Torts
Freedom of the Press
Damages

Current Law Index (CLI)

See literature in *CLI* under subject headings such as:

Privacy, Right of Liberty of the Press
Torts
Damages

Example of a legal periodical article you can find by using *ILP* or *CLI*:

Looking out for Your Employees: Employers' Surreptitious Physical Surveillance of Employees and the Tort of Invasion of Privacy by Daniel O'Gorman, 85 Negligence Law Review 212 (2006).

A.L.R., A.L.R.2d, A.L.R.3d, A.L.R.4th, A.L.R.5th, A.L.R.6th, A.L.R. Fed., A.L.R. Fed. 2d

Use the *ALR Index* to locate annotations on these torts. In this index, check subject headings such as:

Privacy
Harassment
Eavesdropping
Newspapers
Torts
Damages

INVASION-OF-PRIVACY CHECKLIST *(Continued)*

Example of an annotation you can locate through this index on these torts:

Intrusion by News-Gathering Entity as Invasion of Right of Privacy by Edward L. Raymond, 69 A.L.R.4th 1059 (1989).

Words and Phrases
In this multivolume legal dictionary, look up *invasion of privacy, intrusion, appropriation, false light*, and every other word or phrase connected with the four invasion-of-privacy torts discussed in this chapter. The dictionary will give you definitions of these words or phrases from court opinions.

CALR: Computer-Assisted Legal Research

Example of a query you could ask on Westlaw to try to find cases, statutes, or other legal materials on these four torts: **"invasion of privacy"/p damages**

Example of a query you could ask on LexisNexis to try to find cases, statutes, or other legal materials on these four torts: **invasion of privacy /p damages**

Example of search terms you can use on an Internet legal search engine such as the Public Library of Law (www.plol.org), Findlaw (www.findlaw.com), or Google Scholar (scholar.google.com): **"invasion of privacy"**

Example of a search you could use on standard search engines (www.google.com, www.bing.com, www.yahoo.com) to find law firms that describe the torts; and articles, cases, statutes, and other materials on these torts: **"invasion of privacy"**

More Internet sites to check for material on invasion-of-privacy and other torts:
www.hg.org/torts.html
www.megalaw.com/top/top.php (click "Intentional Torts," "Personal Injury Law," "Tort Law," and "Damages")
See also the online sites in Overview of Tort Law at the end of Chapter 1.

CHECK THE CITE

A Yale professor, Elena Grigorenko, sued her fellow teachers for false light. What was the basis of her claim? How did the court rule on the claim? What other torts did she allege, and how did the court rule on them? Read the case of *Grigorenko v. Pauls*, 297 F. Supp. 2d 446 (D. Conn. 2003). To read the opinion online, run a citation search ("297 F. Supp. 2d 446") or a party search (Grigorenko Pauls) in the Legal Opinions and Journals database of Google Scholar (scholar.google.com).

PROJECT

In Google, Bing, or another general search engine, run the following search: *aa* "invasion of privacy" tort (substitute the name of your state for *aa* in the search, e.g., Arizona "invasion of privacy" tort). Write a short essay in which you describe the four invasion-of-privacy torts in your state. You can consult as many websites as you wish, but you must quote from at least three separate sites, only one of which can be a law firm site.

ETHICS IN A TORTS PRACTICE

You are a paralegal working in the law office of Charles Benson, a solo practitioner who handles real estate, probate, and personal injury cases. You are the only paralegal in the office. Often you perform secretarial and administrative tasks in addition

to your paralegal duties. Charles has been depressed lately due to his own divorce. He has started drinking, leaving the office in the early afternoon and not returning. You have become frantic with phone calls from clients trying to reach him and from opposing attorneys attempting to schedule settlement negotiations. Last week, a case was almost dismissed because of the statute of limitations. When you have tried to talk with him about the chaos in the office, he is indignant at the suggestion that the office is not being run properly. What ethical problems, if any, might exist?

SUMMARY

There are four invasion-of-privacy torts: intrusion, appropriation, public disclosure of private fact, and false light. They are designed to protect an individual's interest (1) in being left alone and (2) in not having someone use the individual's name, likeness, or personality for personal gain.

Intrusion is prying, peering, or probing into the plaintiff's private affairs or concerns when it is considered highly offensive to a reasonable person. Appropriation is the unauthorized use of the plaintiff's name, likeness, or personality for the benefit of the user. In most states, this benefit does not have to be pecuniary. Public disclosure of private fact is unreasonable publicity concerning private facts about an individual's life that are not matters of legitimate public concern. False light is untrue and unreasonably offensive publicity about a person.

The media has a First Amendment right to publicize newsworthy people and events that are matters of legitimate public interest. When media defendants are charged with false-light invasion of privacy by a public official or a public figure, there must be proof of actual malice—that the defendant either knew that the publication placed the plaintiff in a false light or acted in reckless disregard of whether it did so.

KEY TERMS

invasion of privacy *530*
intrusion *530*
private affairs *530*
highly offensive *530*
appropriation *534*
pecuniary *534*
public disclosure of private fact *534*
publication *535*
publicity *535*
false light *535*
newsworthy *536*
public official *536*
public figure *536*
actual malice *536*

REVIEW QUESTIONS

1. What is meant by private?
2. What are the invasion-of-privacy torts?
3. What interests do they protect?
4. How is intrusion committed?
5. What are the factors a court will consider in deciding whether someone in engaged in a private activity?
6. How is appropriation committed?
7. How is public disclosure of private fact committed?
8. What is the distinction between publication and publicity?
9. How is false light committed?
10. What special protections are enjoyed by the media when sued for public disclosure of private fact by a public official or public figure?

HELPFUL WEBSITES

- **Privacy and Tort Law**
  cyber.law.harvard.edu/privacy/Privacy_R2d_Torts_Sections.htm
  www.privacyjournal.net
  www.cas.okstate.edu/jb/faculty/senat/jb3163/privacytorts.html

www.personal-injury-info.net/invasion-of-privacy.htm

www.rcfp.org/photoguide/intro.html

en.wikipedia.org/wiki/Privacy_law

www.encyclopedia.com/doc/1G1-19532960.html

www.rbs2.com/privacy.htm

www.netatty.com/privacy/privacy.html

www.scribd.com/doc/4076365/Complaint-for-Defamation-and-False-Light-Invasion-of-Privacy

- **Element Search**

  In Google (www.google.com) run the following searches:

  elements "invasion of privacy" tort

  elements "invasion of privacy" intrusion tort

  elements "invasion of privacy" appropriation tort

  elements "invasion of privacy" "public disclosure of private fact" tort

  elements "invasion of privacy" "false light" tort

Student StudyWARE™ CD-ROM
For additional materials, please go to the student CD in this book.

CHAPTER

26

MISREPRESENTATION, TORTIOUS INTERFERENCE, AND OTHER TORTS

CHAPTER OUTLINE

- Misrepresentation
- Interference with Contract Relations
- Interference with Prospective Advantage
- Wrongful Discharge
- Disparagement
- Injurious Falsehood
- Prima Facie Tort
- Bad Faith Liability
- Dram Shop Liability

CHAPTER OBJECTIVES

After completing this chapter, you should be able to:

- State the elements of misrepresentation.
- Distinguish fact from opinion.
- Explain when silence can constitute misrepresentation.
- Identify paralegal roles in actions for misrepresentation.
- Use the major resources in traditional books and online when researching issues involving the tort of misrepresentation.
- Explain when a suit can be brought for interference with contract relations.
- Explain when a suit can be brought for interference with prospective advantage.
- Explain when a suit can be brought for wrongful discharge.
- Distinguish among disparagement, defamation, and "veggie libel."
- Explain when a suit can be brought for injurious falsehood and prima facie tort.
- Explain when a party can be subject to bad faith liability and dram shop liability.

MISREPRESENTATION

Misrepresentation is an intentionally false statement of fact that is material, made to induce reliance by the plaintiff, and results in harm because of the reliance. (See Exhibit 26–1 for the elements of this tort.) The tort covers **pecuniary** (money) losses caused by false statements to the **representee.** (See also Exhibit 19–8 in Chapter 19 for a complaint that alleges misrepresentation as one of its causes of action or counts.)

Exhibit 26–1
Elements of the tort of misrepresentation.

1. Statement of fact
2. Statement is false
3. Scienter (intent to deceive)
4. Justifiable reliance
5. Actual damages

misrepresentation 1. An intentionally false statement of fact that is material, made to induce reliance by the plaintiff, and results in harm because of the reliance. Also called intentional misrepresentation, fraudulent misrepresentation, deceit, or fraud. 2. An incorrect, false, or misleading statement, which can be communicated intentionally, negligently, or innocently.

pecuniary Pertaining to money.

representee The person to whom a representation is made.

EXAMPLE

When George sells Brenda a used computer for $500, he tells her that it has an internal modem. He knows that this is not true.

George lied about the features of the computer. Contrary to his statement, it does not have a modem. He probably has committed the tort of misrepresentation, although we must examine all of the elements of this tort to be sure. Brenda has suffered a pecuniary loss. She received a computer that is worth less than the one George described.

There has been no property damage or bodily injury as a result of what George did. If such damage or injury does result from a false statement (e.g., Sam becomes ill after drinking what Mary told him was a healthy fruit drink when she knew there was poison in it), many courts will allow recovery for the property damage or bodily injury in the misrepresentation suit. It would be more common, however, for this kind of recovery to be sought under other torts such as battery, conversion, or negligence.

The word misrepresentation can also mean any incorrect, false, or misleading statement, even one that is not intended to deceive anyone. In this chapter, however, we will use the word to mean the tort with the elements outlined in Exhibit 26–1. Occasionally you will see other terms used for the tort, such as deceit, fraud, fraudulent misrepresentation, and intentional misrepresentation.

Sometimes a defendant will make a false statement *negligently*, without the intent to mislead the plaintiff. We will examine negligent misrepresentation as a separate basis of liability after covering intentional misrepresentation.

Statement of Fact That Is False

fact An express or implied communication containing concrete information that can be objectively shown to be true or false. (See glossary for an additional definition.)

opinion An express or implied communication containing a relatively vague or indefinite value judgment that is not objectively verifiable. (See the glossary for another definition.)

puffing An exaggeration of quality or value that one can expect from someone, particularly a seller. Seller's talk.

The first element of misrepresentation is that the defendant has made a statement of **fact.** The second element is that the fact is false. (Sometimes the first element is expressed as a statement of material fact. In this chapter, however, we will cover materiality under a different element of the tort—the element of justifiable reliance.) A fact is an express or implied communication containing concrete information that can be objectively established as true or false. When I tell you that a particular pen has red ink in it, I have communicated a fact. There is an objective way to find out if my statement is true: we simply write with the pen to check the color of its ink. An **opinion**, on the other hand, is an express or implied communication containing a relatively vague or indefinite value judgment that is not objectively verifiable. When I tell you that a particular product is "wonderful," I have communicated an opinion. Whether something is "wonderful" could be the subject of endless debate. There is no way to prove—objectively—that the statement is true or false.

Controversy often arises in sales transactions, where **puffing** is common. Puffing is an expected exaggeration of quality. An example would be a seller telling a buyer

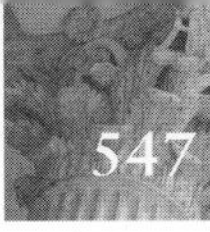

that the XYZ brand of shampoo is "fabulous." Such comments are mere puffing, not statements of fact. Furthermore, there cannot be justifiable reliance (an element we will consider later) on puffing.

Some opinions contain implied statements of fact.

EXAMPLE

Vince is trying to sell Linda an automobile online. He tells her that the car is in "excellent condition." Once Linda buys the car, and goes to pick it up, she discovers that it has no engine.

Vince's comment about the car is an opinion, but it implied the fact that the car had at least the basic equipment in it—such as an engine!

If you state an opinion that you do not believe, you have lied about your state of mind. When you communicate your state of mind, you are communicating a fact. While an opinion itself is not a fact, a communication about your state of mind is a fact.

EXAMPLE

Ted, a stockbroker says, "This stock is a dream come true." Ted, however, knows that the stock is worthless and highly unlikely to appreciate in value or to earn income.

The statement that the stock is a "dream come true" is an opinion. It is a vague value judgment that cannot be objectively proven or disproved. But whether Ted believed the statement at the time he made it is a fact that can be proven or disproved—although not always easily. He either thought highly of the stock or he didn't. A false representation of a state of mind is a false representation of a fact.

Words are not always necessary to communicate a fact. Someone who turns back the odometer without saying a word, for example, is making a factual statement about the number of miles a vehicle has traveled to date. Occasionally, the active concealment of a fact can lead to liability for misrepresentation. An example is a defendant who paints over cracks in an engine in order to conceal its defects from a potential buyer.

Silence can also communicate facts, e.g., not telling someone that a house has termites could constitute a communication that the house is termite-free. Communicating facts through silence, however, is not sufficient to impose liability for misrepresentation unless there is an obligation to disclose the facts. Two strangers usually do not have this obligation to each other. Suppose, however, that two people have a **fiduciary relationship**, sometimes called a confidential relationship. A fiducuary relationship exists when one of the parties owes the other loyalty, candor, and fair treatment. Examples would be business partners, doctor and patient, attorney and client, bank and depositor, and husband and wife. When this relationship exists, silence can be the basis for the tort of misrepresentation when the fact should have been communicated because of the fiduciary relationship.

fiduciary relationship The relationship that exists when one party (called the fiduciary) owes another loyalty, candor, and fair treatment. The fiduciary is required to act in the interest and for the benefit of the other. Also called a confidential relationship.

CASE

Dushkin and Others v. Desai

18 F. Supp. 2d 117 (1998)

United States District Court, D. Massachusetts

Background: *This is a misrepresentation action brought against a yoga guru, Amrit Desai, by some of his former followers. The complaint in the United States District Court in Massachusetts alleges that Desai "misrepresented his celibacy, honesty, and status as an authentic guru." Desai has made a motion to dismiss on the grounds that he made no statements of fact to the plaintiffs. To rule on this motion, the court must assume that the allegations in the complaint are true and decide whether the allegations contain facts* *that constitute a cause of action—here, the tort of misrepresentation.*

Decision of Court: *Motion to dismiss is denied. Desai did make statements of fact. The complaint alleges sufficient facts that, if proved, entitle the plaintiffs to succeed in their misrepresentation action.*

OPINION OF COURT

Judge PONSOR delivered the opinion of the court . . . :

Fourteen former "disciples" of self-proclaimed yoga guru Amrit Desai have brought this suit against their former leader for losses suffered when Desai was (according to their allegations) revealed to be a charlatan. Plaintiffs resided and labored for many years at the Kripalu Ashram, a yoga retreat center in Lenox, Massachusetts, where Desai, plaintiffs' revered spiritual leader, presented himself as a "true and authentic guru." [The quotes are from the complaint of the plaintiffs.] Plaintiffs devoted themselves to emulating Desai, who promoted a celibate and ascetic lifestyle to which he himself outwardly proclaimed to adhere. . . .

After coming to the United States in the 1960s to study at the Philadelphia College of Art, defendant Amrit Desai formed the Kripalu Yoga Ashram, a small intentional living community, sometime in 1974. Desai appointed himself as the Kripalu Ashram's "guru," or spiritual leader. The ashram included approximately twenty resident members and operated a small public center for the purpose of teaching yoga. In the late 1970s, Desai's ashram became a Pennsylvania nonprofit charitable corporation called the Kripalu Yoga Fellowship ("KYF").

In 1983, KYF moved to a 350-acre site in Lenox, Massachusetts. KYF began to operate a large-scale retreat center for holistic health and education at the Lenox site, which contained several large facilities that housed up to 500 people. Over 15,000 paying guests per year visited KYF "to relax, take yoga classes, meditate, have massages, and otherwise take a break from the routine of their daily lives." Approximately 250 resident members of the ashram (including the plaintiffs) operated the facility, working for room and board and a small monthly stipend in exchange for the opportunity to live at the Kripalu Ashram as Desai's "disciples."

Plaintiffs allege that the resident members, paying guests, and KYF donors were attracted to the facility precisely because of Desai's presence. Desai's picture hung throughout the facilities, his videos ran continuously in the public areas, and his books, tapes, and other items were offered for sale by KYF. Publicly, Desai claimed to be an authentic guru—a "teacher and object of veneration" who attains his status in part through several forms of abstinence, including refraining from sexual activity and material pursuits. Desai outwardly professed to live the proper life of an authentic guru, which he identified as demanding "honesty, selfless devotion to the well-being of his followers," and "absolute personal trust" between guru and followers, in addition to celibacy and commitment to a non-material, physically and financially simple lifestyle. As resident guru at KYF, he conducted a combination of life counseling, spiritual leadership, and health and educational services.

Plaintiffs characterize Desai as cultivating in his followers an intense emotional dependence. The plaintiffs, as "disciples," were told to identify themselves and their well-being with Desai's personality and integrity, and to regard Desai as the most important person in their lives. Desai deemed himself the plaintiffs' "personal life counselor," and frequently offered guidance with respect to the most intimate aspects of the plaintiffs' personal lives. Plaintiffs state that over many years, each of them developed a "close and deeply personal relationship" with Desai.

Plaintiffs claim that during their years at the ashram they strove to emulate Desai's professed lifestyle, in that they endeavored to be celibate or chaste, honest, selfless, and devoted to the well-being of others, within the framework of a simple, non-material way of life. In addition, on numerous occasions, Desai allegedly urged the plaintiffs to donate literally all of their possessions to KYF. One plaintiff claims to have donated more than $30,000, and another more than $100,000 in earnings to KYF upon Desai's instruction.

Behind his carefully cultivated image, plaintiffs charge, Desai was in fact a fraud. Plaintiffs' complaint alleges that, from the 1970s until 1994, KYF entered into a series of lucrative contractual relationships with Desai, the purpose of which was "to induce Desai to remain physically present at KYF, teaching yoga courses, meeting with guests and visitors, serving as advisor, mentor and exemplar to the residents," and performing the role of guru at KYF. In exchange, Desai, as an independent contractor, received an annual fee, free housing, free transportation (both domestic and international), a percentage of the proceeds from literature, video, and audiotape sales, and free sponsorship of Desai's seminars throughout the world, all revenue from which he retained. Plaintiffs aver that Desai secretly received payments and benefits from KYF totaling many hundreds of thousands of dollars.

Moreover, between 1974 and 1994, Desai engaged in a series of secret sexual relationships with several female "disciples" in the KYF community (none of whom is a party to this litigation). Plaintiffs assert that these relationships, like his material self-enrichment, were deliberately concealed by Desai in order to preserve his reputation as a true and authentic guru. In 1985, a woman apparently revealed to KYF officers and directors that Desai had had abusive sexual relations with her. Desai accused the woman of deceit and mental illness, and "prevailed on KYF and its residents and members, including each of the plaintiffs, to ostracize, expel, or otherwise usher her out of the KYF community." In 1994, another woman brought similar accusations against Desai, at which time he publicly admitted to some past sexual activities. In an audiotaped statement, Desai apologized for his behavior and acknowledged that it had caused his disciples much emotional pain and suffering. KYF ended its contractual relationship with Desai, who moved to Florida. The Kripalu Ashram still operates in Lenox, Massachusetts, but without any connection to Desai.

[The complaint of the plaintiffs asserts fraud and misrepresentation in that] Desai knowingly misrepresented his celibacy, honesty, and status as an authentic guru, and that plaintiffs reasonably relied on these misrepresentations to their detriment. In essence, plaintiffs contend that they were induced by defendant's misrepresentations to devote years of their lives—and in some cases, large sums in personal savings—to Desai and the overall interests of KYF. . . .

Defendant argues that his alleged misrepresentations did not concern matters of fact—that they were merely promissory in nature, or simple expressions of opinion—and therefore could not form the basis of an action for fraud. If the allegations of the complaint are accepted, as they must be at this stage of the litigation, this contention is manifestly untrue. Desai's representations regarding his manner of living—especially his celibacy and lack of interest in material things—concerned verifiable facts regarding his life habits.

Furthermore, his representations regarding these habits and attitudes were . . . the kinds of representations to which potential disciples such as the plaintiffs would attach importance in distinguishing a "true and authentic guru" from an ordinary layperson, or even an ordinary teacher of yoga. . . . [T]he complaint . . . depicts that Desai and KYF depended on the virtually free labor provided by the plaintiffs and other resident members of the Kripalu Ashram in order to keep the center operating for outside paying visitors. The court may readily infer that it was in Desai's interest to perpetuate his image as an authentic guru in order to retain the plaintiffs' devotion and free labor, continue to attract a steady stream of outside customers, and thereby maintain the benefits that flowed to him from his status.

In short, plaintiffs have offered sufficient allegations from which the court reasonably may infer that Desai made false representations with respect to his status . . . and that plaintiffs in fact relied on defendant's representations, as evidenced by their significant donations of time, labor, and money to the facility. . . .

For the foregoing reasons, defendant's motion [to dismiss the misrepresentation claim is] DENIED. . . .

ASSIGNMENT 26.1

a. Is it relevant that none of the women with whom Desai was sexually intimate were plaintiffs in this case?
b. Make specific arguments that communications about a person's manner of living, selflessness, devotion to the well-being of others, and lack of interest in material things:
   (i) are matters of opinion,
   (ii) are not matters of opinion.

Scienter

Scienter is the intent to mislead. This means that the defendant knows a statement is false, or does not believe in its truth, or acts in **reckless** disregard for its truth or falsity. Scienter also includes an intent that the audience of the statement believe it and act in reliance on its truth. The audience consists of those individuals the defendant intends to reach with the statement. Some states go further and extend liability to those individuals the defendant has reason to expect will learn about and act on the statement, even though the defendant never actually intended to reach them.

scienter 1. Intent to deceive or mislead. 2. Knowingly done.

reckless Consciously failing to exercise due care but without intending the consequences; wantonly disregarding a risk but not having substantially certain knowledge of the consequences of the risk.

Negligent Misrepresentation

Suppose the defendant's misrepresentation does not encompass scienter because there was no knowledge of the statement's falsity, no lack of belief in its truth, or no reckless disregard for truth or falsity. The defendant may simply have been careless in making the false statement, such as by not taking reasonable steps to check the accuracy of the statement before making it. If this leads to physical harm (e.g., plaintiff is injured because the car brakes failed after defendant carelessly told the plaintiff that the brakes were safe), a traditional negligence suit can be brought. If, however, only pecuniary harm results (e.g., the plaintiff loses $10,000 because of

negligent misrepresentation A careless communication of a false statement of fact received and relied upon by someone the statement was intended to reach.

a careless statement by the defendant on the value of a painting), many states will allow the plaintiff to sue for **negligent misrepresentation** as long as he or she was one of the individuals the defendant intended to reach by the careless statement. In many states, individuals within a relatively small group can also sue if the defendant knows that at least someone in a group will learn about the statement and rely on it, even if the defendant does not know which specific individual will do so.

Justifiable Reliance

justifiable reliance Being reasonable in taking action (or in refraining from taking action) because of the circumstances, such as what someone has said or done. Dependence or trust that is legally or morally excusable or defensible.

material Essential or important; of influence on one's decision. (See glossary for additional meanings.)

To recover, the plaintiff must rely on the statement of the defendant, and it must be a **justifiable reliance**. If the plaintiff is foolish in believing and acting on the defendant's statement, recovery for misrepresentation may be denied unless the defendant knew about and took advantage of the plaintiff's intellectual vulnerabilities. The fact on which the plaintiff relies must be **material**, meaning that it was essential or important to the transaction. In selling the plaintiff a car, for example, it is not material that the defendant falsely tells the plaintiff that the defendant likes bananas, if all the statements about the car itself are accurate. If, however, the defendant knows that the plaintiff attaches significance to a peculiar fact and intentionally misleads him or her as to that fact, recovery may be allowed.

ASSIGNMENT 26.2

Diane has just been hired as a telemarketer for a museum. She calls Harry, a stranger, to solicit a contribution. She tells Harry that the museum has important works of art in it and therefore deserves the support of the community. In fact, none of the works of art is valued over $500. During the conversation, Diane learns that Harry is a Catholic. She tells Harry that she too is a Catholic. In fact, she has always been a practicing Lutheran. She is married to a Catholic and attends Catholic church services once or twice a year. Harry tells his wife about the museum. His wife decides to donate $10,000. When she finds out that the museum has a very weak collection and that Diane is not a Catholic, she sues Diane for misrepresentation. What result?

CASE

Vokes v. Arthur Murray, Inc.
212 So. 2d 906 (1968)
District Court of Appeal of Florida, Second District

Background: *After spending over $31,000 for 2,302 hours of dancing lessons in the 1960s, which today would be the equivalent of over $225,000, Audry Vokes sued the dancing school for misrepresentation. The trial dismissed the complaint for failure to state a cause of action. The case is now before the Florida District Court of Appeal.*

Decision on Appeal: *The dismissal is reversed. Audry Vokes has alleged enough to state a cause of action.*

OPINION OF COURT

Judge PIERCE delivered the opinion of the court . . .

Defendant Arthur Murray, Inc., a corporation, authorizes the operation throughout the nation of dancing schools under the name of "Arthur Murray School of Dancing" through local franchised operators, one of whom was defendant J. P. Davenport, whose dancing establishment was in Clearwater.

Plaintiff Mrs. Audry E. Vokes, a widow of 51 years and without family, had a yen to be "an accomplished dancer" with the hopes of finding "new interest in life". So, on February 10, 1961, a dubious fate, with the assist of a motivated acquaintance, procured her to attend a "dance party" at Davenport's "School of Dancing" where she whiled away the pleasant hours, sometimes in a private room, absorbing his accomplished sales technique, during which her grace and poise were elaborated upon and her rosy future as "an excellent dancer" was

painted for her in vivid and glowing colors. As an incident to this interlude, he sold her eight ½-hour dance lessons to be utilized within one calendar month therefrom, for the sum of $14.50 cash in hand paid, obviously a baited "come-on".

Thus she embarked upon an almost endless pursuit of the terpsichorean art during which, over a period of less than sixteen months, she was sold fourteen "dance courses" totalling in the aggregate 2,302 hours of dancing lessons for a total cash outlay of $31,090.45, all at Davenport's dance emporium. All of these fourteen courses were evidenced by execution of a written "Enrollment Agreement—Arthur Murray's School of Dancing" with the addendum in heavy black print, "No one will be informed that you are taking dancing lessons. Your relations with us are held in strict confidence", setting forth the number of "dancing lessons" and the "lessons in rhythm sessions" currently sold to her from time to time, and always of course accompanied by payment of cash of the realm.

These dance lesson contracts and the monetary consideration therefor of over $31,000 were procured from her by means and methods of Davenport and his associates which went beyond the unsavory, yet legally permissible, perimeter of "sales puffing" and intruded well into the forbidden area of undue influence, the suggestion of falsehood, the suppression of truth, and the free exercise of rational judgment, if what plaintiff alleged in her complaint was true. From the time of her first contact with the dancing school in February, 1961, she was influenced unwittingly by a constant and continuous barrage of flattery, false praise, excessive compliments, and panegyric encomiums, to such extent that it would be not only inequitable, but unconscionable, for a Court exercising inherent chancery power to allow such contracts to stand.

She was incessantly subjected to overreaching blandishment and cajolery. She was assured she had "grace and poise"; that she was "rapidly improving and developing in her dancing skill"; that the additional lessons would "make her a beautiful dancer, capable of dancing with the most accomplished dancers"; that she was "rapidly progressing in the development of her dancing skill and gracefulness", etc., etc. She was given "dance aptitude tests" for the ostensible purpose of "determining" the number of remaining hours [of] instructions needed by her from time to time.

At one point she was sold 545 additional hours of dancing lessons to be entitled to award of the "Bronze Medal" signifying that she had reached "the Bronze Standard", a supposed designation of dance achievement by students of Arthur Murray, Inc. Later she was sold an additional 926 hours in order to gain the "Silver Medal", indicating she had reached "the Silver Standard", at a cost of $12,501.35. At one point, while she still had to her credit about 900 unused hours of instructions, she was induced to purchase an additional 24 hours of lessons to participate in a trip to Miami at her own expense, where she would be "given the opportunity to dance with members of the Miami Studio". She was induced at another point to purchase an additional 123 hours of lessons in order to be not only eligible for the Miami trip but also to become "a life member of the Arthur Murray Studio", carrying with it certain dubious emoluments, at a further cost of $1,752.30. At another point, while she still had over 1,000 unused hours of instruction she was induced to buy 151 additional hours at a cost of $2,049.00 to be eligible for a "Student Trip to Trinidad", at her own expense as she later learned. Also, when she still had 1,100 unused hours to her credit, she was prevailed upon to purchase an additional 347 hours at a cost of $4,235.74, to qualify her to receive a "Gold Medal" for achievement, indicating she had advanced to "the Gold Standard". On another occasion, while she still had over 1,200 unused hours, she was induced to buy an additional 175 hours of instruction at a cost of $2,472.75 to be eligible "to take a trip to Mexico". Finally, sandwiched in between other lesser sales promotions, she was influenced to buy an additional 481 hours of instruction at a cost of $6,523.81 in order to "be classified as a Gold Bar member, the ultimate achievement of the dancing studio".

All the foregoing sales promotions, illustrative of the entire fourteen separate contracts, were procured by defendant Davenport and Arthur Murray, Inc., by false representations to her that she was improving in her dancing ability, that she had excellent potential, that they were developing her into a beautiful dancer, whereas in truth and in fact she did not develop in her dancing ability, she had no "dance aptitude", and in fact had difficulty in "hearing that musical beat". The complaint alleged that such representations to her "were in fact false and known by the defendant to be false and contrary to the plaintiff's true ability, the truth of plaintiff's ability being fully known to the defendants, but withheld from the plaintiff for the sole and specific intent to deceive and defraud the plaintiff and to induce her in the purchasing of additional hours of dance lessons". It was averred that the lessons were sold to her "in total disregard to the true physical, rhythm, and mental ability of the plaintiff". In other words, while she first exulted that she was entering the "spring of her life", she finally was awakened to the fact there was "spring" neither in her life nor in her feet.

The complaint prayed that the Court decree the dance contracts to be null and void and to be cancelled, that an accounting be had, and judgment entered against, the defendants "for that portion of the $31,090.45 not charged against specific hours of instruction given to the plaintiff". The Court held the complaint not to state a cause of action and dismissed it with prejudice. We disagree and reverse.

The material allegations of the complaint must, of course, be accepted as true for the purpose of testing its legal sufficiency. Defendants contend that contracts can only be rescinded for fraud or misrepresentation when the alleged misrepresentation is as to a material fact, rather than an opinion, prediction or expectation, and that the statements and representations set forth at length in the complaint were in the category of "trade puffing", within its legal orbit.

It is true that "generally a misrepresentation, to be actionable, must be one of fact rather than of opinion". *Tonkovich v. South Florida Citrus Industries, Inc.*, Fla. App. 1966, 185 So. 2d 710. But this rule has significant qualifications, applicable here. It does not apply where there is a fiduciary relationship between the parties, or where there has been some artifice or trick employed by the representor, or where the parties do not in general deal at "arm's length" as we understand the phrase, or where the representee does not have equal opportunity to become apprised of the truth or falsity of the fact represented. As stated by Judge Allen of this Court in *Ramel v. Chasebrook Construction Company,* Fla. App. 1961, 135 So. 2d 876: "A statement of a party having . . . superior knowledge may be regarded as a statement of fact although it would be considered as opinion if the parties were dealing on equal terms."

It could be reasonably supposed here that defendants had "superior knowledge" as to whether plaintiff had "dance potential" and as to whether she was noticeably improving in the art of terpsichore. And it would be a reasonable inference from the undenied averments of the complaint that the flowery eulogiums heaped upon her by defendants as a prelude to her contracting for 1,944 additional hours of instruction in order to attain the rank of the Bronze Standard, thence to the bracket of the Silver Standard, thence to the class of the Gold Bar Standard, and finally to the crowning plateau of a Life Member of the Studio, proceeded as much or more from the urge to "ring the cash register" as from any honest or realistic appraisal of her dancing prowess or a factual representation of her progress.

Even in contractual situations where a party to a transaction owes no duty to disclose facts within his knowledge or to answer inquiries respecting such facts, the law is if he undertakes to do so he must disclose the *whole truth.* From the face of the complaint, it should have been reasonably apparent to defendants that her vast outlay of cash for the many hundreds of additional hours of instruction was not justified by her slow and awkward progress, which she would have been made well aware of if they had spoken the "whole truth".

In *Hirschman v. Hodges, etc.,* 1910, 59 Fla. 517, 51 So. 550, it was said that—"what is plainly injurious to good faith ought to be considered as a fraud sufficient to impeach a contract", and that an improvident agreement may be avoided—"because of surprise, or mistake, *want of freedom, undue influence, the suggestion of falsehood, or the suppression of truth*". (Emphasis supplied.)

We repeat that where parties are dealing on a contractual basis at arm's length with no inequities or inherently unfair practices employed, the Courts will in general "leave the parties where they find themselves". But in the case sub judice, from the allegations of the unanswered complaint, we cannot say that enough of the accompanying ingredients, as mentioned in the foregoing authorities, were not present which otherwise would have barred the equitable arm of the Court to her. In our view from the showing made in her complaint, plaintiff is entitled to her day in Court.

It accordingly follows that the order dismissing plaintiff's . . . complaint . . . is reversed.

ASSIGNMENT 26.3

a. If you owned a small struggling business, how would you feel about *Vokes v. Arthur Murray, Inc.?* Consumers love it. What do you think the business community feels about this opinion?

b. What could the defendants have done to avoid losing their dance sales agreements because of misrepresentation? Should they have told Audry Vokes that she has two left feet? (Wouldn't she then be able to sue for slander?) Should they have refused to take her money for more lessons? (Wouldn't she then charge them with some form of discrimination or violation of her consumer right to spend her money as she pleased?) Assume that she is determined to become a good dancer no matter how much it costs. Where is she supposed to turn? Is it true that Arthur Murray, Inc. can continue to take her money forever as long as it explicitly insults her by telling her that she is wasting her time and money?

c. Ted Smith has a problem losing weight. He attends the Avis Weight Reduction Center. The literature of the Center says, "We guarantee nothing, but eventually, we will help you lose it all." The Center costs $1,000 a week. Ted has been attending every week for the past six years. Center personnel work regularly with Ted. They encourage him to keep a good attitude and never give up. Is the Center liable under the reasoning of *Vokes v. Arthur Murray, Inc.?*

MISREPRESENTATION CHECKLIST

Definitions, Relationships, Paralegal Roles, and Research References

Category
Misrepresentation is an intentional tort. (In many states, however, negligence is also a basis for liability—negligent misrepresentation.)

Interest Protected by This Tort
The right to be free from pecuniary loss resulting from false statements.

Elements of This Tort
1. Statement of fact
2. Statement is false
3. Scienter (intent to mislead)
4. Justifiable reliance
5. Actual damages

Definitions of Major Words/Phrases in These Elements

Fact: An express or implied communication containing concrete information that can be objectively established as true or false. (An opinion is an express or implied communication containing a relatively vague or indefinite value judgment that is not objectively verifiable.)

Intent to Mislead (Scienter): Intent to deceive or mislead. Making a statement knowing it is false, or without a belief in its truth, or in reckless disregard of its truth or falsity—with the desire that the statement be believed and relied upon.

Justifiable Reliance: Being reasonable in taking action (or in refraining from taking action) because of the circumstances such as what someone has said or done.

Major Defense and Counterargument Possibilities That Need to Be Explored
1. The defendant made no statement of past or present fact.
2. The defendant concealed no past or present fact.
3. The defendant had no duty to disclose the fact; there was no fiduciary or other relationship of trust and confidence between the parties.
4. The statement was not false, incomplete, ambiguous, or misleading.
5. The defendant did not have a state of mind that differed from what he or she expressed.
6. The defendant did not know or believe the statement was false or inaccurate.
7. The defendant did not act in reckless disregard of the truth or falsity of his or her statement.
8. The defendant did not intend the plaintiff to rely on the defendant's statement, and had no reason to expect that the plaintiff would rely on it.
9. The plaintiff did not in fact rely on the defendant's statement.
10. The defendant's statement was not a substantial factor in the plaintiff's action or inaction.
11. The plaintiff's reliance was not justifiable.
12. The defendant did not take advantage of idiosyncrasies of the plaintiff.
13. A cursory investigation by the plaintiff would have revealed the truth or falsity of the defendant's statement.
14. The plaintiff suffered no actual damages.
15. The plaintiff's suit against the government for misrepresentation committed by a government employee may be barred by sovereign immunity (on sovereign immunity, see Chapter 27).
16. The plaintiff's suit against the government employee for misrepresentation may be barred by official immunity (on official immunity, see Chapter 27).
17. The plaintiff's suit against the charitable organization for misrepresentation committed by someone working for the organization may be barred by charitable immunity (on charitable immunity, see Chapter 27).

MISREPRESENTATION CHECKLIST *(Continued)*

18. The plaintiff failed to take reasonable steps to mitigate the harm caused when the defendant committed misrepresentation; therefore, damages should not cover the aggravation of the harm caused by the plaintiff (on the mitigation-of-damages rule, see Chapter 16).

Damages

Actual damages must be proved. Some courts use the out-of-pocket measure of damages, whereas other courts allow a benefit-of-the-bargain measure of damages. Traditionally, misrepresentation covered only pecuniary or economic damages. Many courts now also allow recovery for injury to person or property caused by the false statement. Punitive damages are also possible. (On the categories of damages, see Chapter 16.)

Relationship to Criminal Law

In all states, embezzlement is a crime. In many states there is a crime called false pretenses. False statements of fact are often made by the defendant in the commission of both crimes.

Other Torts and Related Actions

Battery: One way to commit battery is to induce the plaintiff to give consent to a touching by falsely stating facts (e.g., defendant falsely claims to be a doctor and examines the plaintiff).

Breach of Express Warranty: Under the Uniform Commercial Code (UCC), a cause of action for breach of an express warranty is possible if the defendant makes a false statement of fact with the intent or expectation that the plaintiff rely on the statement, which in fact occurs, to the detriment of the plaintiff.

Conversion: One way to commit this tort is to take possession of the plaintiff's property for an extended period by falsely stating the authority to do so.

Defamation: Defendant can defame the character of the plaintiff by making false statements about the plaintiff.

False Imprisonment: One way to commit this tort is to confine the plaintiff by falsely stating the authority to do so.

Intentional Infliction of Emotional Distress: One way to commit this tort is to tell a particularly vicious lie to an unsuspecting and vulnerable plaintiff.

Negligence: The tort of negligence can be committed when the defendant causes injury to plaintiff's person or property by carelessly stating facts (e.g., carelessly telling the plaintiff that milk is safe to drink when in fact it is not).

Trespass to Land: One way to commit this tort is to get someone to go onto the plaintiff's land by making false statements about who owns the land.

Federal Law

a. Under the Federal Tort Claims Act, the United States government will *not* be liable for misrepresentation committed by one of its federal employees within the scope of employment. (See Exhibit 27–7 in Chapter 27.) (Most states have their own statutes that cover when tort claims can be made against the state for misrepresentation and other torts committed by state government employees. Such claims are also covered in Chapter 27.)
b. There may be liability under the Civil Rights Act if the misrepresentation was committed while the defendant was depriving the plaintiff of a federal right under color of state law. (See Exhibit 27–9 in Chapter 27.)

Employer–Employee (Agency) Law

A private (non-government) employee who commits a misrepresentation is personally liable for this tort. His or her employer will *also* be liable for misrepresentation if the conduct of the employee was within the scope of employment (respondeat superior). The employee must be furthering a business objective of the employer at the time. Many times, intentional torts such as misrepresentation, however, are outside the

MISREPRESENTATION CHECKLIST *(Continued)*

scope of employment. If so, only the employee is liable for the misrepresentation. (On the factors that determine scope of employment, see Exhibit 14–9 in Chapter 14.)

Paralegal Roles in Misrepresentation Litigation
(See also Exhibit 3–1 in Chapter 3, Exhibit 20–4 in Chapter 20, and Exhibit 29–1 in Chapter 29.)

Fact finding (help the office collect facts relevant to prove the elements of misrepresentation, the elements of available defenses, and the extent of injuries or other damages):

- client interviewing
- field investigation
- online research (e.g., identification of financial data relevant to the defendant's alleged misrepresentation)

File management (help the office control the documents involved in the litigation of a misrepresentation case):

- open client file
- enter case data in computer database
- maintain file documents

Litigation assistance (help the trial attorney prepare for a trial and appeal, if needed, of a misrepresentation case):

- draft discovery requests
- draft answers to discovery requests
- draft pleadings
- digest and index discovery documents
- help prepare, order, and manage trial exhibits
- prepare trial notebook
- draft notice of appeal
- order trial transcript
- cite-check briefs
- perform legal research

Collection/enforcement (help the trial attorney for the judgment creditor to collect the damages award or to enforce other court orders at the conclusion of the misrepresentation case):

- draft postjudgment discovery requests
- conduct field investigation to monitor compliance with judgment
- perform online research (e.g., location of defendant's business assets)

Research References for Misrepresentation

Digests
In the digests of West Group, look for case summaries on this tort under the following key topics:

Fraud
Vendor and Purchaser
Negligence
Torts
Damages

Corpus Juris Secundum
In this legal encyclopedia, see the discussion under topic headings such as:

Fraud
Vendor and Purchaser
Negligence
Torts
Damages

American Jurisprudence 2d
In this legal encyclopedia, see the discussion under topic headings such as:

Fraud and Deceit
Fraudulent Conveyances
Vendor and Purchaser
Negligence
Sales
Damages
Torts

MISREPRESENTATION CHECKLIST *(Continued)*

Legal Periodical Literature
There are two index systems to use to locate legal periodical articles on this tort:

INDEX TO LEGAL PERIODICALS AND BOOKS (ILP)	***CURRENT LAW INDEX (CLI)***
See Literature in *ILP* under subject headings such as: Fraud Damages Fraudulent Conveyance Negligence Torts Debtor and Creditor	See literature in *CLI* under subject headings such as: Fraud Fraudulent Conveyance Debtor and Creditor Negligence Torts Damages

Example of a legal periodical article you can find by using *ILP* or *CLI:*

> *Negligent Misrepresentation: High School Guidance Counselors Can Be Held Liable When Their Erroneous Advice Prevents a Student-Athlete from Obtaining an Athletic Scholarship* by Timothy Bennett, 12 Seton Hall Journal of Sport Law 311 (2002).

A.L.R., A.L.R.2d, A.L.R.3d, A.L.R.4th, A.L.R.5th, A.L.R.6th, A.L.R. Fed., A.L.R. Fed. 2d.
Use the *ALR Index* to locate annotations on this tort. In this index, check subject headings such as:

Fraud and Deceit	Negligence
Fraudulent Conveyance	Torts
Vendor and Purchaser	Damages
Debtors and Creditors	

Example of an annotation you can find through this index:

> *When Statute of Limitations Begins to Run on Action Against Attorney for Malpractice Based Upon Negligence . . . Application of Rule to Negligent Misrepresentation . . .* by George Blum, 16 A.L.R.6th 653 (2006).

Words and Phrases
In this multivolume legal dictionary, look up *misrepresentation, deceit, fraud, scienter, fact, opinion, justifiable reliance,* and every other word or phrase connected with misrepresentation discussed in this chapter. The dictionary will give you definitions of these words or phrases from court opinions.

CALR: Computer-Assisted Legal Research

Example of a query you could ask on Westlaw or on LexisNexis to try to find cases, statutes, or other legal materials on misrepresentation: **misrepresentation /p damages**

Example of search terms you can use on an Internet legal search engine such as the Public Library of Law (www.plol.org), Findlaw (www.findlaw.com), or Google Scholar (scholar.google.com): **misrepresentation deceit tort**

Example of search terms you could use on standard search engines (www.google.com, www.bing.com, www.yahoo.com) to find material on this tort; law firms that describe the tort; and articles, cases, statutes, and other materials on the tort: **misrepresentation deceit tort**

More Internet sites to check for material on misrepresentation and other torts:
www.hg.org/torts.html
www.megalaw.com/top/top.php (click "Intentional Torts," "Personal Injury Law," "Tort Law," and "Damages")
See also the online sites in Overview of Tort Law at the end of Chapter 1.

INTERFERENCE WITH CONTRACT RELATIONS

Suppose that Fred has a contract to build a bridge for Sam. If Fred fails to build the bridge, Sam can sue Fred in an action for breach of contract. Now suppose that a third party, Dan, persuades Fred not to build Sam's bridge so that Fred can build one for Dan. At this point two legal actions are possible:

- a *contract* action (Sam v. Fred) for breaching the contract to build a bridge for Sam
- a *tort* action (Sam v. Dan) for inducing a breach of the contract Sam had with Fred

The tort is **interference with contract relations** (also called **tortious** interference with contractual relations). See Exhibit 26–2 for the elements of this tort.

interference with contract relations Intentionally encouraging or provoking a breach of contract between two other persons. Also called tortious interference with contractual relations.

1. An existing contract
2. Interference with the contract by the defendant
3. Intent to interfere
4. Damages
5. Causation

Exhibit 26–2
Elements of the tort of interference with contract relations.

Existing Contract

There must be a contract with which the defendant interferes. The enforcement of the contract must not violate **public policy**. For example, it is not a tort to induce the breach of a prostitution contract or an illegal gambling contract. Such contracts are against public policy. Similarly, inducing a breach of a contract to marry would not lead to liability for this tort. Jane's promise to marry Dan is unenforceable; the law will not force someone to enter a marriage he or she no longer wants, despite an earlier promise to the contrary. Hence it would not be a tort for Fred to induce Jane to break her contract to marry Jim and call off the wedding.

public policy Principles inherent in customs and societal values that are of fundamental concern to legislatures and courts.

Suppose that the contract is **voidable**, i.e., cancelable at the option of one of the parties. A voidable contract remains in effect if the option to terminate is not exercised. A contract might be voidable because it is not in writing or because one of the parties is a minor. Is it a tort to interfere with such a contract? Yes, as long as the contract is in existence and is not contrary to public policy as just discussed. There is always the possibility that the party to the contract will *not* exercise his or her option to get out of it; hence, it is a wrong (a tort) for a third party (the defendant) to induce its breach.

voidable Valid, but subject to being cancelled or annulled at someone's option.

Many contracts are **terminable at will**, meaning that either party can get out at any time for any reason. (They are sometimes called contracts at will.) The most common example of such contracts is an *employment at will*, which is an employment relationship that either the employee or the employer can terminate at any time for any reason without liability so long as the termination does not violate public policy. Some courts conclude that it is *not* a tort to induce the termination of a contract at will since the parties to the contract are always free to terminate it without committing a breach of contract to each other. Most courts, however, disagree. It is a tort in most states to interfere with a contract at will. The injured party to the contract had a valuable expectation that the other party would not terminate—until the defendant came along. It is a tort to upset the contract relationship that existed.

terminable at will Something (e.g., a contract) that can be ended at any time for any reason without liability.

Interference

The interference with the contract can take a number of forms:

- inducing one party to the contract to breach it
- making it impossible for one party to perform the contract
- making it substantially more difficult for one party to perform the contract

Intent

The plaintiff must show that the defendant intended to interfere with the contract relation by inducing the breach, or by rendering performance impossible or more burdensome. The defendant must desire this interference or know with substantial certainty that the interference will result from what the defendant does or fails to do. Negligence is not enough. Suppose that the XYZ Company has a contract to supply lake water to a city, and the defendant (a third party) negligently pollutes this water before delivery. The defendant has surely interfered with XYZ's contract with the city, but no intentional tort has been committed by the defendant because there was no intent to interfere with the contract. The XYZ Company or the city may be able to sue the defendant for negligence in polluting the water, but there can be no suit for interference with contract. The defendant must know about the contract and intend to interfere with it.

Damages

The damages for this tort cover the loss of the contract or the diminished value of its performance. Most courts require a showing of actual damages, even though they may be minimal. In addition, damages for mental suffering are usually allowed, and if malice is shown, punitive damages can be awarded. As indicated in the bridge example at the beginning of this section involving Fred, Sam, and Dan, the plaintiff may have a breach of contract action against the other party to the contract *and* a tort action against the third party for inducing the breach or for diminishing the value of performance. To avoid double recovery, however, the amount recovered in the tort action is reduced by whatever the plaintiff recovers in the contract action. When the defendant has threatened an interference with the contract, or when the interference is continuing, many courts will grant an **injunction** against the defendant because of the inadequacy of damages as a remedy.

injunction A court order requiring a person or organization to do or to refrain from doing something.

Causation

The plaintiff must show that either:

- but for the action or inaction of the defendant, the plaintiff would not have suffered the damages that are provable, or
- the defendant was a substantial factor in producing these damages

Privilege to Interfere

One of the major defenses to this tort is the privilege to interfere in order to protect one's own interest. Assume, for example, that Len has a contract to furnish goods to Ted. Len will obtain these goods from Mary with whom Len has a separate contract. If Mary feels that Len is violating his contract with her, she can take steps to protect her own interest. This might include stopping delivery of the goods to Len. This, of course, would have the effect of interfering with Ted's contract with Len. Mary has not committed a tort, however, as long as she is acting reasonably to protect her own interest.

There may also be a privilege to interfere in order to protect the interest of someone else if there is a legal or moral duty to protect this other person (e.g., a doctor caring for a patient, an attorney advising a client). The interference could take the form of a recommendation that the person remove him- or herself from certain contract obligations that are reasonably thought to be detrimental to the welfare of that person. For example, the doctor might tell the patient that continuing to work at a particular plant could lead to a further deterioration of the patient's health.

This privilege is lost if the interference was **malicious.** In this context, malice means not acting reasonably—acting for a purpose other than to protect a legitimate interest, e.g., interfering with someone's contract in order to seek revenge.

malicious Acting with malice, e.g., with an improper purpose. (See glossary for additional meanings.)

ASSIGNMENT 26.4

Helen works for Linda. One day, Helen borrows $500 from Linda to repair a fence at Helen's home. Linda has difficulty collecting this money from Helen. Linda tells her father, Ed, about the loan. He advises Linda to fire Helen if she does not repay the loan. Linda tells Helen that she will lose her job if she does not repay the loan within a week. Helen is fired when she does not make the payment within the time designated. Does Helen have a cause of action against Ed?

CASE

Texaco, Inc. v. Pennzoil Co.

729 S.W.2d 768 (1987)

Court of Appeals of Texas, Houston (1st District)

Background: *This case involves a multibillion-dollar verdict for committing the tort of interference with contract relations. In 1984 Getty Oil was for sale. It agreed "in principle" to be purchased by Pennzoil in a leveraged buyout for $110 per share (plus a $5 "stub," payable later). Although there was no formal contract between Getty and Pennzoil, both issued a "news release" that announced an "agreement in principle" based on a Memorandum of Agreement. The day after this announcement, Texaco offered to buy Getty for $125 per share. Getty withdrew from its relationship with Pennzoil and agreed to merge with Texaco. Pennzoil then sued Texaco for the tort of interfering with its contract with Getty. A Houston jury found that (1) at the end of a board meeting on January 3, 1984, the Getty entities intended to bind themselves to an agreement providing for the purchase of Getty Oil stock by Pennzoil; (2) Texaco knowingly interfered with the agreement between Pennzoil and the Getty entities; (3) as a result of Texaco's interference, Pennzoil suffered damages of $7.53 billion; (4) Texaco's actions were intentional, willful, and in wanton disregard of Pennzoil's rights; and (5) Pennzoil was entitled to punitive damages of $3 billion. The case is now on appeal before the Court of Appeals of Texas.*

Decision on Appeal: *The Court of Appeals affirmed the trial court and held that Texaco did commit the tort. Following this opinion, the parties negotiated to try to settle the case. After further court proceedings (including a Chapter 11 bankruptcy by Texaco) Pennzoil and Texaco agreed to a settlement of $3 billion dollars to be paid by Texaco.*

OPINION OF COURT

Justice WARREN delivered the opinion of the court. . . .

Texaco argues first that there was no evidence [Getty intended to bind itself] to an agreement with Pennzoil. . . . Second, Texaco asserts that the evidence is legally and factually insufficient to support the . . . [finding that] it had actual knowledge of a legally enforceable contract, or that Texaco actively induced a breach of the alleged contract. . . . Pennzoil contends that the evidence showed that the parties intended to be bound to the terms in the Memorandum of Agreement plus price terms of $110 plus a $5 stub, even though the parties may have contemplated a later, more formal document to memorialize the agreement already reached. . . .

[If] parties do not intend to be bound to an agreement until it is reduced to writing and signed by both parties, then there is no contract until that event occurs. If there is no understanding that a signed writing is necessary before the parties will be bound, and the parties have agreed upon all substantial terms, then an informal agreement can be binding, even though the parties contemplate evidencing their agreement in a formal document later. . . .

Texaco states that the use of the term "agreement in principle" in the press release was a conscious and deliberate choice of words to convey that there was not yet any binding agreement. . . . There was sufficient evidence at trial on the common business usage of the expression "agreement in principle" and on its meaning in this case for the jury reasonably to decide that its use in the press release did not necessarily establish that the parties did not intend to be bound before signing a formal document. . . . There was sufficient evidence for the jury to conclude that the parties had reached agreement on all essential terms of the transaction with only the mechanics and details left to be supplied by the parties' attorneys. Although there may have been many specific items relating to the transaction agreement draft that had yet to be put in final form, there is sufficient evidence to support a conclusion by the jury that the parties did not consider any of Texaco's asserted "open items" significant obstacles precluding an intent to be bound. . . .

Texaco asserts that Pennzoil failed to prove that Texaco had actual knowledge that a contract existed. [There must be] knowledge by a defendant of the existence of contractual rights as an element of the tort of inducing a breach of that contract. However, the defendant need not have full knowledge of all the detailed terms of the contract. . . . Since there was no direct evidence of Texaco's knowledge of a contract in this case, the question is whether there was legally and factually sufficient circumstantial evidence from which the trier of fact reasonably could have inferred knowledge. . . .

Pennzoil responds that there was legally and factually sufficient evidence to support the jury's finding of knowledge, because the jury could reasonably infer that Texaco knew about the Pennzoil deal from the evidence of (1) how Texaco carefully mapped its strategy to defeat Pennzoil's deal by acting to "stop the train" or "stop the signing"; (2) the notice of a contract given by a January 5 *Wall Street Journal* article reporting on the Pennzoil agreement—an article that Texaco denied anyone at Texaco had seen; [and] (3) the knowledge of an agreement that would arise from comparing the Memorandum of Agreement with the Getty press release. . . . Pennzoil contends that these circumstances indicated Texaco's knowledge of Pennzoil's deal too strongly to be overcome by Texaco's "self-serving verbal protestations at trial" that Texaco was told and believed that there was no agreement. . . .

We find that an inference could arise that Texaco had some knowledge of Pennzoil's agreement with the Getty entities, given the evidence of Texaco's detailed studies of the Pennzoil plan, its knowledge that some members of the Getty board were not happy with Pennzoil's price, and its subsequent formulation of strategy to "stop the [Pennzoil] train." . . .

The second major issue Texaco raises . . . is that the evidence was legally and factually insufficient to show that Texaco actively induced breach of the alleged Pennzoil/Getty contract. A necessary element of the plaintiff's cause of action is a showing that the defendant took an active part in persuading a party to a contract to breach it. Merely entering into a contract with a party with the knowledge of that party's contractual obligations to someone else is not the same as inducing a breach. It is necessary that there be some act of interference or of persuading a party to breach, for example by offering better terms or other incentives, for tort liability to arise. . . .

The evidence . . . on Texaco's calculated formulation and implementation of its ideal strategy to acquire Getty is . . . inconsistent with its contention that it was merely the passive target of Getty's aggressive solicitation campaign and did nothing more than to accept terms that Getty Oil . . . proposed. The evidence showed that Texaco knew it had to act quickly, and that it had "24 hours" to "stop the train." . . .

[The judgment of the trial court is affirmed.]

ASSIGNMENT 26.5

You and Bob are applying for the job of president of a major corporation. The contract will be for three years. Both of you are equally qualified. After the chairman of the board of the corporation meets with Bob, the chairman tells the press that the board is very impressed with Bob and that "no one should be surprised if the formality of an announcement is made soon that Bob will be joining us very soon." This announcement troubles you. You decide to speak to a friend who was once on the board of directors of the corporation. You tell this friend that Bob is not serious about joining the corporation. "He is really using the job discussions with the corporation as leverage to negotiate better employment terms with a rival company where he really wants to work." Your friend tells the chairman of the board, who investigates and finds out that in fact Bob is actively pursuing a position at the rival company. The corporation decides to give you the job. Have you committed the tort of interference with contract relations? Has your friend? Does the *Texaco* case apply?

INTERFERENCE WITH PROSPECTIVE ADVANTAGE

interference with prospective advantage Intentionally interfering with another's reasonable expectation of an economic advantage. Also called tortious interference with prospective advantage.

Next, we consider the tort called **interference with prospective advantage,** (also called **tortious** interference with prospective advantage). In this tort, the plaintiff intentionally interferes with another's reasonable expectation of an economic advantage. (See Exhibit 26–3 for the elements of this tort.)

1. Reasonable expectation of an economic advantage
2. Interference with this expectation
3. Intent to interfere
4. Damages
5. Causation

Exhibit 26–3
Elements of the tort of interference with prospective advantage.

In this tort, the plaintiff does not have to prove that the defendant has interfered with an existing contract. All that is needed is a reasonable expectation of some economic advantage.

In the business world, most of the cases that have arisen under the tort of interference with prospective advantage have involved what is loosely called **unfair competition**, which is a dishonest or fraudulent practice directed at a commercial rival.

unfair competition Dishonest or fraudulent rivalry in trade or commerce.

EXAMPLES

- The plaintiff is trying to lure ducks at a public pond, which he or she will then kill and try to sell. The defendant intentionally fires a gun into the air in order to scare the ducks out of the plaintiff's range. The defendant is a competitor of the plaintiff in the sale of ducks.
- The defendant threatens a third party not to go to work for the plaintiff (no employment contract yet exists). The goal of the defendant is to get the third party to go to work for the defendant.
- The defendant pours some foul-smelling chemicals on his or her own property, which is next door to the plaintiff's, in order to scare the latter's potential customers away. The defendant wants the plaintiff to leave the area so that the defendant can rent the premises now occupied by the plaintiff.

The defendant has a privilege to protect his or her own business interests by engaging in fair competitive practices. Deceptive advertising and monopolistic steps, of course, constitute unfair (and illegal) competition. When such devices are not used, the defendant is free to use tactics such as high-pressure advertising, price cutting, and rebates in order to lure prospective customers away from other merchants.

Courts are often reluctant to allow the tort of interference with prospective advantage when business or commercial interests are not involved, e.g., a defendant pressures a person to remove the plaintiff as the beneficiary of a will. There are a few courts, however, that will allow recovery in such situations, when there is a reasonable degree of certainty that the plaintiff would have received the expected benefit if there had been no interference by the defendant.

In most cases of interference with prospective advantage, causation is a problem. It can be very difficult to prove that the benefit would have been obtained but for what the defendant did, or that the defendant was a substantial factor in the loss of the benefit. This is because the plaintiff had no contractual right to the benefit at the time of the interference. Yet, if causation can be shown by a preponderance of the evidence, recovery is allowed.

ASSIGNMENT 26.6

Tom Peterson is a paralegal at Smith & Smith (S&S). He receives a job offer from Jones & Jones (J&J), which he seriously considers accepting. When S&S hears about this, it notifies J&J that S&S will file a conflict of interest challenge to J&J if J&J hires Tom. In the last month, Tom did some filing work on a case in which S&S and J&J were opposing counsel. The case is still pending. J&J then withdraws its offer to hire Tom. Tom quits his job at S&S. Can Tom now sue S&S for interference with contract relations or interference with prospective advantage?

WRONGFUL DISCHARGE

cause A justifiable reason. Sometimes phrased as good cause or just cause. (See glossary for an additional definition.)

employment at will An employment relationship that either the employee or the employer can terminate at any time for any reason without liability so long as the termination does not violate public policy. The employee (called an at-will employee) has no union or special contract protection.

To terminate workers covered by a union contract, the employer must usually establish **cause.** This is a justifiable reason spelled out in the union contract. Some government workers also have this protection. The vast majority of workers, however, are employees at will who are not entitled to a showing of cause before being terminated. An **employment at will** is an employment relationship that either the employee or the employer can terminate at any time for any reason without liability so long as the termination does not violate public policy. The employee has no union or special government protection.

Here are some examples of terminations of at-will employees that violate public policy:

An employer fires an employee after the employee

- exercises a right (e.g., files a workers' compensation claim),
- refuses to engage in illegal conduct (e.g., tells the boss that he or she will not falsely notarize a document), or
- blows the whistle on the employer's illegal conduct (e.g., alerts the fire department of a fire hazard on the job).

retaliatory discharge Dismissing someone from a job for a reason that violates public policy, e.g., for reporting a fire hazard at work.

A termination for such reasons is called a **retaliatory discharge**. Such discharges violate public policy because they can discourage the exercise of rights, encourage illegal conduct, or prevent the state from enforcing safety laws.

wrongful discharge 1. A termination that violates public policy because the employee was terminated for exercising a right, refusing to engage in illegal conduct, or blowing the whistle on the employer's illegal conduct. 2. Terminating an employee for any invalid reason.

What is the remedy for such retaliation? It is difficult to categorize the remedy within the traditional causes of action. A breach of contract action is somewhat strained, because there is no express contract that was violated. Some courts say that in the employment relationship there is an implied condition that forbids the employer from terminating the relationship for a reason that violates public policy. Most courts take a different approach by concluding that a tort has been committed—**wrongful discharge**. This phrase sometimes has the broad meaning of termination for any improper reason. But the tort of wrongful discharge is more narrowly connected to retaliatory conduct by the employer. See Exhibit 26–4 for the elements of the tort.

Exhibit 26–4
Elements of the tort of wrongful discharge.

1. Termination of an employee by an employer
2. Retaliation
3. Violation of public policy

disparagement The intentional and false discrediting of a plaintiff's business, products, or title to property, resulting in specific monetary loss.

DISPARAGEMENT

The tort of **disparagement** covers the wrongful discrediting of the plaintiff's business, products, or title to property. (See Exhibit 26–5 for the elements of this tort.)

Exhibit 26–5
Elements of the tort of disparagement.

1. False statement of fact
2. Disparaging the plaintiff's business, products, or title to property
3. Publication
4. Intent
5. Special damages
6. Causation

slander of title The wrongful denigration or discrediting of the plaintiff's title to property.

trade libel The wrongful denigration or discrediting of the plaintiff's products.

The attack might cast doubt on the plaintiff's title to property (called **slander of title**) or attribute a quality to goods that make them undesirable for sale or other commercial use (called **trade libel**). The effect of the disparaging statement is to cause others not to deal with the plaintiff or to cause some other similar disadvantage.

EXAMPLES

- Sam falsely states that he holds a mortgage on Paul's farm, which Paul just listed for sale.
- Tom falsely says that he owns the land that Jim is trying to sell.
- Sarah falsely states that the tires being sold by XYZ as radials are not radials.

Some statements constitute the tort of disparagement *and* the tort of defamation. Disparagement discredits the quality of or title to *goods or property.* Defamation consists of a derogatory statement about the *person* of the plaintiff (see Chapter 24). Compare the following statements:

"Prostitutes regularly use the XYZ Hotel for their clients."
"Fred, the manager of the XYZ Hotel, takes a cut of the fee charged by prostitutes in exchange for the use of the hotel for their clients."

The first statement disparages the hotel—the business. The second statement disparages the hotel *and* personally defames the manager.

The plaintiff must plead and prove **special damages**, which are specific economic or pecuniary losses. It is usually not enough for the plaintiff to prove that there was a *general* loss of business following the disparaging statements of the defendant. The plaintiff must show specifically identified contracts or customers that were lost. Or, the plaintiff must show he or she had to sell goods at a lower price to specific customers as a result of the disparagement.

special damages Compensatory damages that consist of economic or pecuniary losses (e.g., medical expenses and lost wages) that must be alleged and proven. They are not presumed to exist. Also referred to as specials.

Defendants have a privilege to protect their own interest. For example, a defendant can state that he or she owns property the plaintiff is trying to sell. This disparages the property of the plaintiff, but it is privileged as long as the defendant is acting in the honest belief that he or she is protecting his or her own interest. Malice, however, defeats the privilege.

There is also a general privilege to compete in the business world by exaggerating the qualities of your own products compared to the products of others. There is a privilege, for example, to say that "no car is more economical" than the car being offered for sale. As indicated earlier, such statements are viewed as nonfactual statements (hence not qualifying as the first element of disparagement), as *puffing*, or as **fair competition**.

fair competition Open, honest, nonfraudulent rivalry in commerce.

Deceptive Trade Practices

Many states have statutes that outlaw deceptive trade practices. Violations of these statutes are often added as causes of action when businesses bring tort actions against other businesses. For an example of a products liability complaint that asserts such causes of action, see Exhibit 19–8 in Chapter 19. Here is an example of a statute on deceptive trade practices:

Subdivision 1. A person engages in a deceptive trade practice when, in the course of business, vocation, or occupation, the person:

(1) passes off goods or services as those of another;
(2) causes likelihood of confusion or of misunderstanding as to the source, sponsorship, approval, or certification of goods or services; . . .
(4) uses deceptive representations or designations of geographic origin in connection with goods or services;
(5) represents that goods or services have sponsorship, approval, characteristics, ingredients, uses, benefits, or quantities that they do not have or that a person has a sponsorship, approval, status, affiliation, or connection that the person does not have; . . .
(7) represents that goods or services are of a particular standard, quality, or grade, or that goods are of a particular style or model, if they are of another;

(8) disparages the goods, services, or business of another by false or misleading representation of fact;
(9) advertises goods or services with intent not to sell them as advertised; . . .
(13) engages in any other conduct which similarly creates a likelihood of confusion or of misunderstanding.

Subdivision 2. Proof. In order to prevail . . . , a complainant need not prove competition between the parties or actual confusion or misunderstanding.

Subdivision 3. Other law. This section does not affect unfair, deceptive, or misleading trade practices otherwise actionable at common law or under other statutes of this state.

Minnesota Statutes Annotated, Uniform Deceptive Trade Practices, §325D.44.

Special Statutes: "Veggie Libel"

Some statements about consumer products can have a major impact on their sale. Suppose, for example, that a guest, a reporter, or a host on a national talk show or newsmagazine says, "The pesticides used on all broccoli cause cancer in children." This could devastate the broccoli market.

Several states have passed special statutes that give producers of perishable food products a cause of action when they lose business because of false statements that disparage the safety of their products. The media has called such actions "**veggie libel**."

"veggie libel" A cause of action created by statute that allows producers of perishable food products to sue when they lose business because of false statements that disparage the safety of their products. Also called *agricultural product disparagement*.

EXAMPLES

- Ranchers sued television talk-show host Oprah Winfrey and a guest who said American beef was largely infected with bovine spongiform encephalopathy, or "mad cow disease." (WINFREY: "You said this disease could make AIDS look like the common cold?" GUEST: "Absolutely." WINFREY: "Now doesn't that concern you-all a little bit right here, hearing that? It has just stopped me cold from eating another burger. I'm stopped.")
- Washington State apple growers sued the CBS television show *60 Minutes* for alleging in a segment called, "*A* is for Apple" that Alar, a chemical growth regulator, dramatically increased cancer risks.
- Emu ranchers sued Honda Motor Company for a Honda advertisement that said the emu was the "pork of the future."

Almost all cases of this kind are lost by the plaintiffs who bring them. It can be very difficult to prove that the statements are false. This is particularly true in those states where the plaintiff must prove that the defendant knew the statement was false. (In the Oprah Winfrey case, for example, the court held that she did not knowingly make false statements about the beef industry.) Also, some courts are not receptive to an allegation of group disparagement that is not directed at a particular grower or food producer. Furthermore, there is reason to believe that the United States Supreme Court will eventually impose severe constitutional limitations on disparagement suits of this kind against the media, as it has in the area of defamation. The inclination of the Court is to interpret the First Amendment as encouraging robust speech. "Veggie libel" laws arguably do the opposite.

ASSIGNMENT 26.7

Did President George Bush commit a tort when he told the media, "I hate broccoli and we don't serve it here at the White House"?

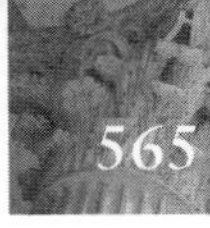

INJURIOUS FALSEHOOD

The phrase **injurious falsehood** is sometimes used interchangeably with the word "disparagement," but injurious falsehood is a broader concept. Disparagement is an example of an injurious falsehood. An injurious falsehood can consist of a false statement of fact that injures someone economically in a way other than disparaging a business, a product, or title to property.

injurious falsehood The publication of a false statement that causes special damages.

EXAMPLES

- a false statement to the immigration officials that results in the deportation of the plaintiff
- a false statement by an employer of the income paid to an employee, resulting in tax evasion charges against the employee

The same elements for disparagement are required for injurious falsehood, except for the second element. Instead of showing that the statement disparages the business, product, or title to property of the plaintiff, the broader tort of injurious falsehood requires only that the statement be harmful to the pecuniary interests of the plaintiff. The other elements are the same: false statement of fact, publication, intent, special damages, and causation. (See Exhibit 26–6.)

1. False statement of fact
2. Harmful to the pecuniary interest of the plaintiff
3. Publication
4. Intent
5. Special damages
6. Causation

Exhibit 26–6
Elements of the tort of injurious falsehood.

ASSIGNMENT 26.8

Tom dies intestate, i.e., without a valid will. There are only two survivors: Mary, a daughter, and George, a nephew. Under the intestate law of the state, all property goes to legitimate children. If no legitimate children survive, the property goes to other relatives. George claims that Mary is illegitimate. Mary hires an attorney who helps establish that she is legitimate. What tort or torts, if any, has George committed?

PRIMA FACIE TORT

Negligence is a catchall tort that encompasses a very wide variety of wrongful conduct that is considered unreasonable. There is no comparable catchall tort for conduct that is intentional. We cannot say that all intentional conduct causing harm is tortious. If the defendant's actions or inactions do not fall within the elements of negligence, the plaintiff must try to fit the facts within one of the other traditional torts such as battery, slander, or malicious prosecution. If these torts do not fit, then the plaintiff must suffer the loss, unless no-fault systems such as workers' compensation (see Chapter 28) provide some form of relief.

Some consider it unfortunate that the law does not provide a clear tort remedy for a defendant's intentional conduct that harms someone even though the facts do not come within the traditional torts. In a sense, the torts of injurious falsehood and interference with prospective advantage try to fill some of the holes left by the traditional torts.

prima facie tort The intentional infliction of harm without justification, resulting in special damages.

In a few states (including New York), small efforts toward the creation of a generic intentional tort have been made in the form of what is called a **prima facie tort**. Although this tort is not limited to the business world, most of the cases applying it have involved commercial matters. The elements of the prima facie tort are stated in Exhibit 26–7.

Exhibit 26–7
Elements of the prima facie tort.

1. Infliction of harm
2. Intent to do harm (malice)
3. Special damages
4. Causation

It is sometimes said that this tort does not exist unless the defendant acted "maliciously and without justification." It is not always clear whether malice means a desire to harm someone or simply an intentional act or omission.

In theory, the prima facie tort is available when the facts of the case do not fit the pigeonholes of any of the traditional torts. It does not follow, however, that the prima facie tort will apply every time the other torts do not. The requirement of special damages, for example, tends to limit the applicability of the prima facie tort, due to the difficulty of proving specific economic or pecuniary loss (i.e., special damages).

The vast majority of states do *not* recognize the prima facie tort. Too many problems exist in defining it and in defining the defenses to it. Rather than create a new tort, most states would prefer to try to stretch the boundaries of the existing torts so that plaintiffs will not be without a remedy when defendants have intentionally caused injury.

BAD FAITH LIABILITY

bad faith liability Civil liability for an unreasonable denial or delay by an insurance company in response to an insurance claim.

A relatively recent basis of liability against insurance companies is called **bad faith liability**. It consists of an unreasonable denial or delay in paying an insurance claim within policy limits.

EXAMPLE
Jackson has a $100,000 liability policy with an insurance company. He has an accident and is sued for $250,000 by Pamela. The latter offers to settle for $80,000. Jackson's attorney notifies the insurance company of the offer, but the company takes an unreasonable amount of time to respond. Pamela proceeds with litigation and obtains a $200,000 judgment against Jackson. The insurance company pays $100,000 of this judgment, the maximum under the policy.

Jackson can now sue the company for the tort of bad faith in handling the insurance claim. His argument is that the company's unreasonable delay in processing his claim led to a judgment far in excess of policy limits.

DRAM SHOP LIABILITY

dram shop liability Civil liability imposed on the seller of intoxicating liquor to a buyer who then injures a third person. Sometimes also applied to a social host who serves liquor to intoxicated guests.

A number of states have what is called a Civil Damage Act or Dram Shop Act that imposes liability on those who give liquor to someone who is visibly intoxicated when the intoxication causes an injury to a third person. (A dram shop is a tavern or other establishment that sells liquor, usually in small amounts called drams.) The basis of **dram shop liability** can differ from state to state. Negligence may have to be shown, i.e., that the person giving the liquor created an unreasonable risk that the person receiving the liquor might injure others. Some states impose **strict liability,** especially if the person receiving the liquor is a minor. In such states there is no need for the injured third party to show that the person giving the liquor was negligent.

Many states impose dram shop liability only when the liquor is *sold* and only when the buyer is already visibly intoxicated. In a few states, however, liability is not dependent on a sale. A social host can also be held to dram shop liability when a *gift* of intoxicating liquor causes an injury.

strict liability Responsibility for harm even if one did not intend the harm and used reasonable care to try to prevent it. Responsibility for harm whether or not the person causing the harm was at any fault or engaged in any moral impropriety. Also called *absolute liability* and *liability without fault.*

EXAMPLE

Bob holds a high school graduation party in his home for his daughter and her friends. He serves liquor at the party. One of the guests is Kelly, who is intoxicated. While driving home from the party, Kelly hits a pedestrian. Kelly became intoxicated at the party and the intoxication was a substantial factor in causing the pedestrian's injury. The latter can now seek dram shop liability against Bob if she lives in a state that has extended such liability to social hosts.

ASSIGNMENT 26.9

The XYZ Supermarket has a liquor section. Davidson, an adult, buys a six-pack of beer at XYZ. At the time of the purchase, his speech was slightly slurred from drinking earlier in the day. He goes to his car in the parking lot of XYZ and drinks all the beer he just bought. Would dram shop liability apply in the following cases?

a. After Davidson drives out of the XYZ Supermarket parking lot, he goes to a nearby parking lot. He has a fist fight with another driver in an argument over a parking space. Davidson knocks the other driver unconscious. This driver now wants to sue the XYZ Supermarket for selling Davidson the beer.
b. After Davidson drives out of the XYZ Supermarket parking lot, he hits a tree and is killed. His family now wants to sue the XYZ Supermarket for selling Davidson the beer.

CHECK THE CITE

A well-drilling company mistakenly drilled a water well on a landowner's land. What was the basis of the landowner's slander of title action against the company? What other tort did the landowner assert? What did the court decide? Read the case of *Wharton v. Tri-State Drilling & Boring*, 175 Vt. 494, 824 A.2d 531 (Vermont 2003). To read the opinion online, (1) Go to the site of the Supreme Court of Vermont (libraries.vermont.gov/law/supct). Select 175 VT Reports (unofficial). Find the *Wharton* case in the list. (2) Go to FindACase (www.findacase.com). Select Vermont. Select Vermont Appellate Courts. Run a standard search (Wharton Tri-State). (3) Run a citation search ("824 A.2d 531") or a party search (Wharton Tri-State) in the Legal Opinions and Journals database of Google Scholar (scholar.google.com).

PROJECT

In Google, Bing, or another general search engine, run the following search: *aa* "negligent misrepresentation" tort (substitute the name of your state for *aa* in the search, e.g., Michigan "negligent misrepresentation" tort). Write a short essay in which you describe the law in your state on the tort of negligent misrepresentation.

Explain whether the state recognizes the tort and, if so, what its elements are. You can consult as many websites as you wish, but you must quote from at least three separate sites, only one of which can be a law firm site.

ETHICS IN A TORTS PRACTICE

You are a paralegal working in the corporate law department of Eaton Chemical Company. The company manufactures many consumer products. Scores of contract and tort actions are filed against the company every month throughout the country. Most of the actions involve small sums of money. You work for two attorneys who handle slip-and-fall cases and charges of misrepresentation against the company and its subsidiaries. Even when the liability of the company is clear, the policy of the office is to force the plaintiffs to respond to lengthy and expensive discovery demands of Eaton. The more drawn out the process, the more likely it is that plaintiffs will drop their actions or settle for small amounts. If a case does go to trial, Eaton attorneys call numerous witnesses and present duplicative evidence whenever possible. What ethical problems, if any, might exist?

SUMMARY

Misrepresentation is an intentionally false statement of fact that is material, made to induce reliance by the plaintiff, and results in harm because of the reliance by the representee. It covers pecuniary loss caused by the active concealment of a fact, by the nondisclosure of a fact that someone had a duty to disclose, or by the statement of an opinion containing false implied facts. There must be scienter, the intent to mislead, which is established by showing that the defendant made a statement knowing it was false, without a belief in its truth, or in reckless disregard of its truth or falsity, with the desire that the statement be believed and relied upon. An action for negligent misrepresentation can be brought in many states for the careless communication of a false statement of fact to someone whom the statement was intended to reach. There must be justifiable reliance, which means that the plaintiff was reasonable in taking action because of the defendant's statement. The exception is when the defendant knows the plaintiff is particularly vulnerable to whatever the defendant says.

It is a tort to interfere with contract relations by intentionally inducing a breach of a contract between two other persons or to make it impossible or more difficult for them to perform their contract. There must be an existing contract with which the defendant intends to interfere. The plaintiff's damages include compensation to cover the loss of the contract or the diminished value of its performance. One of the defenses to this tort is the privilege to protect one's own interest or the interest of another. If the plaintiff does not have a contract, but the defendant interferes with the plaintiff's reasonable expectation of an economic advantage, the defendant may have committed the tort of interference with prospective advantage. An employment at will is an employment relationship that either the employee or the employer can terminate at any time for any reason without liability so long as the termination does not violate public policy. A retaliatory discharge can be a wrongful discharge. The latter is a termination of employment that violates public policy because the employee was terminated for exercising a right, refusing to engage in illegal conduct, or blowing the whistle on the employer's illegal conduct.

Disparagement is the intentional and false discrediting of a plaintiff's business, products, or title to property, resulting in specific monetary loss. The defendant must publish a false statement of fact that casts doubt on the plaintiff's title to property (slander of title) or attributes a quality to the plaintiff's goods that makes them undesirable for commercial use (trade libel). A defendant has the privilege to protect his or her own interest and to engage in fair competition in the business world. Another basis of liability in many states is the violation of deceptive trade practice statutes. Some states have passed "veggie libel" statutes that give producers of perishable food products a cause of action when they lose business because of false statements that disparage the safety of their products. These cases are difficult to prove and may be subject to constitutional challenge.

Injurious falsehood is the publication of a false statement that causes special damages. This tort is broader than the tort of disparagement. In a few states, if the defendant causes special damages by intentionally inflicting harm, the plaintiff may be able to bring an action for prima facie tort when the conduct does not fit within any of the traditional torts.

Insurance companies that unreasonably deny or delay acting on insurance claims within policy limits may be subject to bad faith liability when the litigated claim results in a judgment against the plaintiff that is over the limits of the policy. Businesses that sell liquor to intoxicated persons who then injure others can be subject to dram shop liability. Some states also impose this liability on hosts who serve liquor to intoxicated guests at social gatherings.

KEY TERMS

misrepresentation *546*
pecuniary *546*
representee *546*
fact *546*
opinion *546*
puffing *546*
fiduciary relationship *547*
scienter *549*
reckless *549*
negligent misrepresentation *550*
justifiable reliance *550*
material *550*
interference with contract relations *557*
public policy *557*
voidable *557*
terminable at will *557*
injunction *558*
malicious *559*
interference with prospective advantage *560*
unfair competition *561*
cause *562*
employment at will *562*
retaliatory discharge *562*
wrongful discharge *562*
disparagement *562*
slander of title *562*
trade libel *562*
special damages *563*
fair competition *563*
"veggie libel" *564*
injurious falsehood *565*
prima facie tort *566*
bad faith liability *566*
dram shop liability *566*
strict liability *567*

REVIEW QUESTIONS

1. What is misrepresentation?
2. What kinds of damages can be recovered in an action for misrepresentation?
3. How is a fact distinguished from an opinion?
4. Can an opinion be the basis of misrepresentation?
5. What is puffing?
6. When can silence be the basis of misrepresentation?
7. What is scienter?
8. Can negligence be the basis of misrepresentation?
9. When is reliance by a representee justifiable?
10. When is a representation material?
11. What are the elements of interference with contract relations?
12. Can interference with a voidable contract be tortious?
13. What privileges does one have to interfere with another's contract?
14. What are the elements of interference with prospective advantage?
15. What is a retaliatory discharge?
16. What is an employment at will?
17. What are the elements of wrongful discharge?
18. What are the elements of disparagement?
19. How does slander of title differ from trade libel?
20. What are deceptive trade practices?
21. What is "veggie libel?"
22. What are the elements of injurious falsehood?
23. What are the elements of prima facie tort?
24. What are the elements of bad faith liability?
25. What are the elements of dram shop liability?

HELPFUL WEBSITES

- **Misrepresentation**
  www.west.net/~smith/deceit.htm
  www.answers.com/topic/misrepresentation
  en.wikipedia.org/wiki/Misrepresentation
  www.insurancejournal.com/magazines/southcentral/2000/04/10/legalbeat/21184.htm
- **Business Torts**
  www.lexisnexis.com/lawschool/study/outlines/html/torts/torts19.htm
  www.gastonandgaston.com/business-attorney-california/business-torts.shtml
- **Bad Faith Liability**
  www.hg.org/article.asp?id=7485
  library.findlaw.com/insurance/bad-faith-and-unfair-practices/liability-insurance/
  en.wikipedia.org/wiki/Insurance_bad_faith
  www.docstoc.com/docs/21944601/BAD-FAITH-AND-PUNITIVE-DAMAGES-IN-LIABILITY-INSURANCE-Asim
- **Dram Shop Liability**
  www.marininstitute.org/alcohol_policy/dramshop.htm
  www.cfif.org/htdocs/freedomline/current/guest_commentary/dram_shop_liability.htm
  en.wikipedia.org/wiki/Dram_shop
  www.wisbar.org/am/template.cfm?section=wisconsin_lawyer&template=/cm/contentdisplay.cfm&contentid=50672
- **Element Search**
  In Google (www.google.com), run the following searches:
  elements misrepresentation tort
  elements deceit tort
  elements interference with contract relations tort
  elements interference with prospective advantage tort
  elements disparagement tort
  elements injurious falsehood tort
  elements "prima facie tort"
  elements "bad faith liability" tort
  elements "dram shop liability" tort

Student StudyWARE™ CD-ROM
For additional materials, please go to the student CD in this book.

CHAPTER

27

ADDITIONAL TORT DEFENSES

CHAPTER OUTLINE

- Introduction
- Consent in Tort Law
- Self-Help Privileges
- The Defense of Sovereign Immunity
- The Defense of Official Immunity: The Personal Liability of Government Employees
- The Defense of Charitable Immunity
- The Defense of Intrafamily Tort Immunity

CHAPTER OBJECTIVES

After completing this chapter, you should be able to:

- Understand the distinction between privilege and immunity.
- List the elements of consent.
- Explain what is meant by self-help.
- Understand when self-defense is a valid defense to a tort.
- Understand when defense of others is a valid defense to a tort.
- Explain the distinction between private and public necessity.
- Understand when defense of property is a valid defense to a tort.
- Distinguish between sovereign immunity and official immunity.
- Know when the federal government has waived sovereign immunity under the Federal Tort Claims Act.
- Know when state governments waive sovereign immunity.
- Explain the distinction between governmental functions and proprietary functions in determining when local governments have waived sovereign immunity.
- Know when government employees are personally liable for common-law and constitutional torts they commit.
- Distinguish between absolute and qualified official immunity.
- Explain what are meant by charitable immunity and intrafamily tort immunity.

INTRODUCTION

defense The response of a party to a claim of another party, setting forth the reason(s) the claim should be denied. (See glossary for an additional definition.)

privilege 1. The right to act contrary to the right of another without being subject to tort or other liability. A defense that authorizes conduct that would otherwise be wrongful. 2. A special legal benefit, right, immunity, or protection.

immunity The treatment of wrongful conduct as nonwrongful. A complete defense to a tort claim, whether or not the defendant committed the tort. (See glossary for additional definitions).

A **defense** is the response of a party to a claim of another party, setting forth the reason(s) the claim should not be granted. Sometimes the defense is a simple denial ("I didn't do it"). More often the response is more specific (e.g., "the law allowed me to do what I did because. . . ."). Throughout this text, we have studied defenses to specific torts, e.g., Chapter 17 (defenses to negligence) and Chapter 24 (defenses to defamation). In this chapter, almost all the defenses we will study apply to more than one tort.

Many defenses are privileges or immunities. A **privilege** is a justification for what would otherwise be wrongful or tortious conduct. A privilege is the right of an individual to act contrary to the right of another individual without being subject to tort or other liability. Self-defense is an example. Using physical force against another usually constitutes a battery. If, however, you used this force to protect yourself against attack, you may have a defense when you are sued for battery—the privilege of self-defense. Technically, a tort cannot exist if the defendant had a privilege to do what the plaintiff is now complaining about. An **immunity**, on the other hand, is a special protection given to someone who *has* committed a tort. Sovereign immunity is an example. Suppose, for example, that a government employee defames you. As we will see later, the defense of sovereign immunity may prevent you from suing the government for this tort, and the defense of official immunity may prevent you from suing the employee for this tort. The practical effect of privileges and immunities is the same: they both are defenses that prevent liability for damage or injury. Because of this similarity of effect, you will sometimes see the words "privilege" and "immunity" used interchangeably. Indeed, immunity is sometimes defined as protection from tort liability whether or not the defendant has committed a tort.

Privileges that are defenses to tort actions are different from *evidentiary* privileges that operate to prevent a jury from considering otherwise admissible evidence. Examples of evidentiary privileges are attorney-client privilege, doctor-patient privilege, and privilege against self-incrimination. In this chapter, we are concerned with the privileges that prevent tort liability.

CONSENT IN TORT LAW

volenti non fit injuria "To a willing person it is not wrong." There is no cause of action for injury or harm endured by consent that is knowingly and voluntarily given.

consent Voluntary agreement or permission (express or implied) that something should happen or not happen.

A central principle of the law is **volenti non fit injuria**: no wrong is done to one who consents. If the plaintiff consented to the defendant's conduct, the defendant should not be liable for the resulting harm. When the defendant is charged with negligence or strict liability in tort, the consent defense is the closely related concept of assumption of the risk, which we examined in Chapters 17 and 19. Here, our focus is consent as a defense to intentional torts such as assault, battery, and trespass.

Consent is a voluntary agreement or permission (express or implied) that something should happen or not happen. The basic elements of consent are presented in Exhibit 27–1.

Exhibit 27–1
Elements of consent.

1. Plaintiff (P) must have the capacity to consent to the conduct of Defendant (D).
2. There is an express or implied manifestation from P of a willingness to let the conduct of D occur.
3. P's willingness is voluntary.
4. D reasonably believes that P is willing to let D's conduct occur.
5. P has knowledge of the nature and consequences of D's conduct.
6. D's conduct is substantially the same as the conduct P agreed to.

Capacity to Consent

The person giving consent must have the capacity to consent. A young girl, for example, may agree to sexual intercourse with an older male, but the latter can still be guilty of statutory rape. If the girl later sues the male for battery in a civil case, the male cannot raise the defense of consent, just as he could not raise it in the criminal case of rape. The young girl does not have the capacity to consent if she is below the age designated by law. So too, there are statutes intended to protect children from working in dangerous conditions. If a child is injured in working conditions that violate the statute, the employer will not be able to say that the child consented to work there and took the risk of being injured—even if the child understood those risks and willingly proceeded. The statutes will be interpreted as taking away the child's capacity to consent.

A person can also lack the capacity to consent by being too young or ill to understand the conduct involved. Unless an authorized parent or guardian gives consent for this person, the consent is invalid.

Suppose that the conduct to which consent is given is criminal conduct. Paul and Dan agree to a duel or boxing match that is a crime in the state. Both are prosecuted under criminal law. Paul then sues Dan for damages in a civil battery case. Dan's defense is that Paul consented to being hit. Courts differ on how they handle this problem. Some hold that the consent is a defense, barring the civil action. Other courts, however, do not recognize the consent as valid on the theory that no one has the power or capacity to consent to a crime. Since the consent is invalid, the civil battery action can be brought. As a consequence, a plaintiff can receive damages growing out of a criminal act in which the plaintiff willingly participated. Of course, if both Paul and Dan were injured in their illegal fight with each other, each of them could sue the other for civil battery in a state where the consent will not be recognized.

ASSIGNMENT 27.1

Henry and Fred are having an argument. Henry is about to hit Fred with a baseball bat. In response, Fred punches Henry with his fist and breaks Henry's jaw. While Henry is unconscious on the ground, Fred stabs him in the leg. Henry later sues Fred for injury to his leg in a civil battery case. Fred raises the defense of consent. What result and why?

Manifestation of Willingness

A person can demonstrate or manifest willingness in a variety of ways. There can be an express manifestation such as telling someone he or she can enter the land or use a car. Written or verbal manifestation is not always needed. The wave of a hand can indicate consent to come on one's land. Consent by silence is also common if the person would normally be expected to speak if he or she objected to conduct about to occur. If a trespasser enters your yard and you fail to object or fail to take steps to remove the individual, your silence or nonaction is strong evidence that you do not object. This is an **implied consent**. If you voluntarily agree to play football, you are implying consent to the kind of rugged contact that is usually associated with this sport. If you walk downtown into a crowded store, you are implying consent to the kind of everyday contact that is normal in crowds.

implied consent An inference that consent has been given based on the surrounding circumstances, including signs, affirmative conduct, inaction, or silence.

ASSIGNMENT 27.2

At a college dance, Jessica asks Dan, a stranger, to dance. After the dance, Jessica kisses Dan on the cheek and walks away. Dan sues Jessica for battery. Does she have a defense?

Voluntariness

coercion Compelling something by force or threats; overpowering another's free will by undue influence.

If the plaintiff has been coerced into agreeing to the defendant's conduct, the consent is invalid. **Coercion** is compelling something by force or threats and thereby overcoming free will by undue influence. Coercion renders consent involuntary, invalidating the defense. When, for example, you hand over your wallet at the point of a gun, you have not consented to the conversion of your wallet. Suppose that a foreign passenger about to enter port does not want to be vaccinated, but nevertheless rolls up her sleeve to the doctor injecting the vaccine. Her conduct led the doctor to believe that she consented. She may have been under pressure to be vaccinated in order to avoid the hassle of being detained at port, yet the consent was still the product of a free will. The consent was voluntary.

Extreme or drastic pressure, however, can be enough to invalidate consent, e.g., a threat of force against the plaintiff or a member of the plaintiff's family, or a threat against the valuable property of the plaintiff. The plaintiff's agreement as a result of such pressure would probably not be voluntary.

ASSIGNMENT 27.3

Tom calls Linda on the phone and tells her that he has her very valuable painting, which he will destroy if she does not come to his apartment and engage in sexual intercourse. Linda is frantic about the painting. She goes to his apartment and has sex with him. He then gives her the painting. Later, she brings a civil battery action against him. Does he have a defense? Would it make any difference if his threat was to harm Linda's neighbor?

Reasonable Belief

The defendant must be reasonable in believing that the plaintiff has consented to the conduct in question. Problems often arise when the defendant claims to have relied on the plaintiff's implied consent. Suppose that the defendant has always played practical jokes on the plaintiff, to the latter's great amusement, e.g., squirting the plaintiff with a water pistol or pretending to steal the plaintiff's hat. It would be reasonable for the defendant to believe that the plaintiff would continue to agree to such jokes as long as they were of the same kind as practiced in the past. If the plaintiff has decided that enough is enough and does not want to be subjected to such jokes anymore, he or she must communicate this to the defendant. Otherwise, the defendant is justified in believing that plaintiff continues to consent. The test of consent is not what the plaintiff subjectively thinks, but what someone reasonably interprets the plaintiff to be communicating based upon the latter's words, actions, silence, and any relevant cultural customs in the area on how people normally interpret each other's behavior.

ASSIGNMENT 27.4

Mary is riding in her car when she spots Alex injured on the side of the road. Mary pulls over to try to help. She sees that his arm is broken and puts it in a sling. Later, Alex sues Mary for battery. Does she have a defense? Does it make any difference that Mary is a doctor? Why or why not?

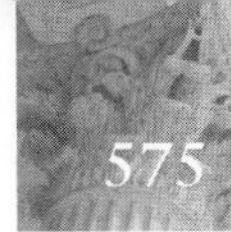

Knowledge

The plaintiff must know what conduct is being consented to and its probable consequences in order for the consent to be an effective bar to a later tort action against the defendant. If a doctor obtains the consent of a patient to undergo an operation, but fails to tell the patient of the very serious probable side effects of the operation, the patient has not consented to the operation. The defendant has not provided the patient with the basic knowledge to enable the patient to give an **informed consent**. As we saw in Chapter 18, if an emergency exists, the doctor can proceed with treatment to save the patient's life or to avoid serious further injuries if it is not possible or practical to obtain the patient's consent and the doctor does not have an express prior direction to the contrary from the patient.

informed consent Agreement to let something happen based on having a reasonable understanding of the benefits and risks involved.

Consent obtained by trickery or misrepresentation is not effective. The classic case is the plaintiff who buys candy that turns out to be poisoned. The implied representation of the seller is that the candy is wholesome. The plaintiff consented to eat candy, not poison. So too if the defendant entices the plaintiff to play a game of ice hockey in order to get the plaintiff into a position where the defendant can intentionally cut the plaintiff with skates, the defendant cannot later claim that the plaintiff consented to such contact. The plaintiff's consent was obtained by misrepresentation.

When the plaintiff has made a mistake about what he or she is consenting to, it is important to know whether the defendant caused the plaintiff's mistake and whether the defendant knew about it. If the mistake was not caused by and was not known to the defendant, the consent is still valid as long as the defendant was reasonable in believing that the plaintiff consented.

EXAMPLE

Mary tells her assistant to let Ted know that he cannot drive over the portion of Mary's land where she is building a golf course. By mistake, however, the assistant tells Ted that he can drive there. When he does so, Mary sues him for trespass. Ted's defense of consent will defeat the action so long as he did not know that a mistake was made, did not procure or cause the mistake by Mary's assistant, and was reasonable in believing that the permission (consent) was valid.

Substantially the Same Conduct

If the defendant's conduct deviates in a minor way from the conduct the plaintiff consented to, the consent is still effective. The deviation must be substantial for the consent to be invalid. If, for example, the plaintiff agrees to let the defendant throw a bucket of water on him or her, the consent is still effective if the same approximate amount of water is poured on the plaintiff by using a garden hose. The defendant's conduct is substantially different, however, if the bucket of water contains rocks, unknown to the plaintiff.

Sexual fidelity can sometimes raise consent issues.

EXAMPLE

Thomas and Mary Neal are married. They engage in sexual relations during a time when Thomas is having an affair. When Mary finds out about the affair, she brings a battery action against Thomas for those times they had sexual relations while the affair was going on. Tom's defense is that Mary consented to these relations. (Assume that the intrafamily tort immunity discussed in Chapter 22 does not apply.)

If Mary had known of Thomas's sexual involvement with another woman, she says she would not have consented to continue having sex with him since sexual relations

ASSIGNMENT 27.5

In the example of Thomas and Mary Neal, assume that several weeks after Mary found out about Thomas's affair, she resumed sexual relations with her husband. Later, however, she still sues him for battery to cover the time they had sexual relations when she was unaware of the affair. Does Thomas now have a better argument that her consent was valid during this time?

under those circumstances would have been offensive to her. Therefore, his failure to disclose the fact of the affair rendered her consent ineffective.[1]

The defendant must substantially comply with any restrictions or conditions imposed on the consent by the plaintiff that are communicated to the defendant. If, for example, the plaintiff tells the defendant that he or she can cut one truckload of timber from the plaintiff's land on January 3 or 4, the defendant will be liable for trespass to land if he or she cuts three truckloads on those dates, or if any timber is cut on January 10.

ASSIGNMENT 27.6

Ted and Maureen agree to have sexual intercourse. Maureen gets a venereal disease from Ted and sues him for battery. How, if at all, would the following factors affect Ted's defense of consent?

a. Ted was a prostitute and Maureen knew it.
b. Ted led Maureen to believe that he was a virgin.
c. Ted and Maureen confided to each other that both had had many lovers before.
d. Ted lied to Maureen about wanting to marry her.
e. Maureen lied to Ted about wanting to marry him.
f. This was the first time Ted and Maureen met.
g. Ted and Maureen are married to each other.

CASE

Peterson v. Sorlien

299 N.W.2d 123 (1980)

Supreme Court of Minnesota

Background: *Susan Jungclaus Peterson joined a religion called The Way Ministry. Her father, Norman Jungclaus, enlisted the support of Susan's former minister, Paul Sorlien, and of deprogrammers to try to separate her from what the father believed was a cult. Later Susan sued for false imprisonment. The lower courts dismissed the suit. The case is now on appeal in the Supreme Court of Minnesota.*

Decision on Appeal: *Judgment affirmed. There was no false imprisonment.*

OPINION OF COURT

Chief Justice SHERAN delivered the opinion of the court. . . .

This action by plaintiff Susan Jungclaus Peterson for false imprisonment . . . arises from an effort by her parents . . . to prompt her disaffiliation from an organization known as The Way Ministry. . . . [T]his case marks the emergence of a new cultural phenomenon: youth-oriented religious or pseudoreligious groups which utilize the techniques of what has been termed "coercive persuasion" or "mind control" to cultivate an uncritical and devoted following. Commentators have used the term "coercive persuasion," originally coined to identify the experience of American prisoners of war during the Korean conflict to describe the cult-induction process. The word "cult" is not used pejoratively but in its dictionary sense to describe an unorthodox system of belief characterized by "[g]reat or excessive devotion or dedication to some person, idea, or thing." Webster's *New International Dictionary of the English Language Unabridged* 552 (1976). Coercive persuasion is fostered through the creation of a controlled environment that heightens the susceptibility of a subject to suggestion and manipulation through sensory deprivation,

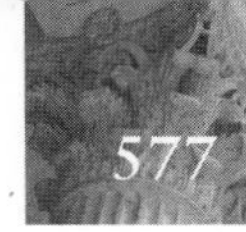

physiological depletion, cognitive dissonance, peer pressure, and a clear assertion of authority and dominion. The aftermath of indoctrination is a severe impairment of autonomy and the ability to think independently, which induces a subject's unyielding compliance and the rupture of past connections, affiliations and associations. See generally Delgado, *Religious Totalism: Gentle and Ungentle Persuasion under the First Amendment,* 51 Southern California Law Review 1 (1977). One psychologist characterized the process of cult indoctrination as "psychological kidnapping." Id. at 23.

At the time of the events in question, Susan Jungclaus Peterson was 21 years old. For most of her life, she lived with her family on a farm near Bird Island, Minnesota. In 1973, she graduated with honors from high school, ranking second in her class. She matriculated that fall at Moorhead State College. A dean's list student during her first year, her academic performance declined and her interests narrowed after she joined the local chapter of a group organized internationally and identified locally as The Way of Minnesota, Inc.

The operation of The Way is predicated on the fund-raising activities of its members. The Way's fund-raising strategy centers upon the sale of pre-recorded learning programs. Members are instructed to elicit the interest of a group of ten or twelve people and then play for them, at a charge of $85 per participant, a taped introductory course produced by The Way International. Advanced tape courses are then offered to the participants at additional cost, and training sessions are conducted to more fully acquaint recruits with the orientation of the group and the obligations of membership. Recruits must contribute a minimum of 10 percent of their earnings to the organization; to meet the tithe, student members are expected to obtain part-time employment. Members are also required to purchase books and other materials published by the ministry, and are encouraged to make larger financial contributions and to engage in more sustained efforts at solicitation.

By the end of her freshman year, Susan was devoting many hours to The Way, listening to instructional tapes, soliciting new members and assisting in training sessions. As her sophomore year began, Susan committed herself significantly, selling the car her father had given her and working part-time as a waitress to finance her contributions to The Way. Susan spent the following summer in South Dakota, living in conditions described as appalling and overcrowded, while recruiting, raising money and conducting training sessions for The Way.

As her junior year in college drew to a close, the Jungclauses grew increasingly alarmed by the personality changes they witnessed in their daughter; overly tired, unusually pale, distraught, and irritable, she exhibited an increasing alienation from family, diminished interest in education and decline in academic performance. The Jungclauses, versed in the literature of youth cults and based on conversations with former members of The Way, concluded that through a calculated process of manipulation and exploitation Susan had been reduced to a condition of psychological bondage.

On May 24, 1976, defendant Norman Jungclaus, father of plaintiff, arrived at Moorhead to pick up Susan following the end of the third college quarter. Instead of returning to their family home, defendant drove with Susan to Minneapolis to the home of Veronica Morgel. Entering the home of Mrs. Morgel, Susan was greeted by Kathy Mills and several young people who wished to discuss Susan's involvement in the ministry. Each of those present had been in some way touched by the cult phenomenon. Kathy Mills, the leader of the group, had treated a number of former cult members, including Veronica Morgel's son. It was Kathy Mills, a self-styled professional deprogrammer, to whom the Jungclauses turned, and intermittently for the next sixteen days, it was in the home of Veronica Morgel that Susan stayed.

The avowed purpose of deprogramming is to break the hold of the cult over the individual through reason and confrontation. Initially, Susan was unwilling to discuss her involvement; she lay curled in a fetal position in the downstairs bedroom where she first stayed, plugging her ears and crying while her father pleaded with her to listen to what was being said. This behavior persisted for two days during which she intermittently engaged in conversation, at one point screaming hysterically and flailing at her father. But by Wednesday Susan's demeanor had changed completely; she was friendly and vivacious and that night slept in an upstairs bedroom. Susan spent all day Thursday reading and conversing with her father and on Saturday night went roller-skating. On Sunday she played softball at a nearby park, afterwards enjoying a picnic lunch. The next week Susan spent in Columbus, Ohio, flying there with a former cult member who had shared with her the experiences of the previous week. While in Columbus, she spoke every day by telephone to her fiancé who, playing tapes and songs from the ministry's headquarters in Minneapolis, begged that she return to the fold. Susan expressed the desire to extricate her fiancé from the dominion of the cult.

Susan returned to Minneapolis on June 9. Unable to arrange a controlled meeting so that Susan could see her fiancé outside the presence of other members of the ministry, her parents asked that she sign an agreement releasing them from liability for their past weeks' actions. Refusing to do so, Susan stepped outside the Morgel residence with the puppy she had purchased in Ohio, motioned to a passing police car and shortly thereafter was reunited with her fiancé in the Minneapolis headquarters of The Way. Following her return to the ministry, she was directed to counsel and initiated the present action.

Plaintiff [alleges] that defendants unlawfully interfered with her personal liberty by words or acts which induced a reasonable apprehension that force would be used against her if she did not otherwise comply. The jury, instructed that an informed and reasoned consent is a defense to an allegation of false imprisonment and that a nonconsensual detention could be deemed consensual if one's behavior so indicated, exonerated defendants with respect to the false imprisonment claim.

The period in question began on Monday, May 24, 1976, and ceased on Wednesday, June 9, 1976, a period of 16 days. The record clearly demonstrates that Susan willingly remained in the company of defendants for at least 13 of those days. During that time she took many excursions into the public sphere, playing softball and picnicking in a city park, roller-skating at a public rink, flying aboard public aircraft and shopping and swimming while relaxing in Ohio. Had Susan desired, manifold opportunities existed for her to alert the authorities of her allegedly unlawful detention; in Minneapolis, two police officers observed at close range the softball game in which she engaged; en route to Ohio, she passed through the security areas of the Twin Cities and Columbus airports in the presence of security guards and uniformed police; in Columbus she transacted business at a bank, went for walks in solitude and was interviewed by an F.B.I. agent who sought assurances of her safety. At no time during the 13- day period did she complain of her treatment or suggest that defendants were holding her against her will. If one is aware of a reasonable means of escape that does not present a danger of bodily or material harm, a restriction is not total and complete and does not constitute unlawful imprisonment. Damages may not be assessed for any period of detention to which one freely consents.

In his summation to the jury, the trial judge instructed that to deem consent a defense to the charge of false imprisonment for the entire period or for any part therein, a preponderance of the evidence must demonstrate that such plaintiff voluntarily consented. The central issue for the jury, then, was whether Susan voluntarily participated in the activities of the first three days. The jury concluded that her behavior constituted a waiver.

We believe the determination to have been consistent with the evidence. See *Faniel v. Chesapeake & Potomac Telephone Co.,* 404 A.2d 147 (D.C. 1979); *Schneckloth v. Bustamonte,* 412 U.S. 218, 93 S. Ct 2041, 36 L. Ed. 2d 854 (1973); F. Harper & F. James, *The Law of Torts* § 3.10, at 235 (1956). Were the relationship other than that of parent and child, the consent would have less significance.

To determine whether the findings of the jury can be supported upon review, the behavior Susan manifested during the initial three days at issue must be considered in light of her actions in the remainder of the period. Because, it is argued, the cult conditioning process induces dramatic and non-consensual change giving rise to a new temporary identity on the part of the individuals whose consent is under examination, Susan's volitional capacity prior to treatment may well have been impaired. Following her readjustment, the evidence suggests that Susan was a different person, "like her old self." As such, the question of Susan's consent becomes a function of time. We therefore deem Susan's subsequent affirmation of defendants' actions dispositive.

In *Weiss v. Patrick,* 453 F. Supp. 717 (D. R.I.), aff'd, 588 F.2d 818 (1st Cir. 1978), the federal district court in Rhode Island confronted a situation similar to that which faces us. Plaintiff, a devotee of the Unification Church, brought an action for false imprisonment against individuals hired by her parents to prompt her disassociation from the church. Because plaintiff's mother was dying of cancer, the church authorities permitted her to join her family for the Thanksgiving holiday. Met at the airport by her mother, she testified that she was restrained against her will in the home of one of the defendants and subjected to vituperative attacks against the church until she seized an opportunity to flee. Despite the evidently traumatic experience sustained by plaintiff, the district court found that she failed to demonstrate a meaningful deprivation of personal liberty, reasoning that "any limitation upon personal mobility was not her primary concern." Id. at 722. In so reasoning, the court underscored a parental right to advocate freely a point of view to one's child, "be she minor or adult." To assure freedom, the court observed, "the right of every person 'to be left alone' must be placed in the scales with the right of others to communicate." Id. (quoting *Rowan v. United States Post Office Department,* 397 U.S. 728, 736, 90 S. Ct. 1484, 1490, 25 L. Ed. 2d 736 (1970)).

In light of our examination of the record and rules of construction providing that upon review the evidence must be viewed in a manner most favorable to the prevailing party, we find that a reasonable basis existed for the verdict exonerating defendants of the charge of false imprisonment. Although carried out under colorably religious auspices, the method of cult indoctrination, viewed in a light most favorable to the prevailing party, is predicated on a strategy of coercive persuasion that undermines the capacity for informed consent. While we acknowledge that other social institutions may utilize a degree of coercion in promoting their objectives, none do so to the same extent or intend the same consequences. Society, therefore, has a compelling interest favoring intervention. The facts in this case support the conclusion that plaintiff only regained her volitional capacity to consent after engaging in the first three days of the deprogramming process. As such, we hold that when parents, or their agents, acting under the conviction that the judgmental capacity of their adult child is impaired, seek to extricate that child from what they reasonably believe to be a religious or pseudo-religious cult, and the child at some juncture assents to the actions in question, limitations upon the child's mobility do not constitute meaningful deprivations of personal liberty sufficient to support a judgment for false imprisonment. But owing to the threat that deprogramming poses to public order, we do not endorse self-help as a preferred alternative. In fashioning a remedy, the First Amendment requires resort to the least restrictive alternative so as to not impinge upon religious belief. *Cantwell v. Connecticut,* 310 U.S. 296, 60 S. Ct. 900, 84 L. Ed. 2d 1213 (1940). . . .*

Affirmed.

Justice WAHL (dissenting in part).

I must respectfully dissent. In every generation, parents have viewed their children's religious and political beliefs with alarm and dismay if those beliefs were different from their own. Under the First Amendment, however,

*While we decline at this time to suggest a particular alternative, we observe that some courts have permitted the creation of temporary guardianships to allow the removal of cult members to therapeutic settings. If the individuals desire, at the end of the conservatorship they may return to the cult. Actions have also been initiated against cult leaders on the basis of criminal liability. See generally Delgado, supra, at 73–97.

adults in our society enjoy freedoms of association and belief. In my view, it is unwise to tamper with those freedoms and with longstanding principles of tort law out of sympathy for parents seeking to help their "misguided" offspring, however well-intentioned and loving their acts may be. . . .

Any imprisonment "which is not legally justifiable" is false imprisonment, *Kleidon v. Glascock,* 215 Minn. 417, 10 N.W.2d 394 (1943); therefore, the fact that the tortfeasor acted in good faith is no defense to a charge of false imprisonment. . . .

The majority opinion finds, in plaintiff's behavior during the remainder of the 16-day period of "deprogramming," a reasonable basis for acquitting [her father] of the false imprisonment charge for the initial three days, during which time he admittedly held plaintiff against her will. Under this theory, plaintiff's "acquiescence" in the later stages of deprogramming operates as consent which "relates back" to the events of the earlier three days, and constitutes a "waiver" of her claim for those days. . . . Certainly, parents who disapprove of or disagree with the religious beliefs of their adult offspring are free to exercise their own First Amendment rights in an attempt, by speech and persuasion without physical restraints, to change their adult children's minds. But parents who engage in tortious conduct in their "deprogramming" attempts do so at the risk that the deprogramming will be unsuccessful and the adult children will pursue tort remedies against their parents. To allow parents' "conviction that the judgmental capacity of their [adult] child is impaired [by her religious indoctrination]" to excuse their tortious conduct sets a dangerous precedent.

Here, the evidence clearly supported a verdict against Norman Jungclaus on the false imprisonment claim. . . .

ASSIGNMENT 27.7

a. Explain why the court said Susan consented to the confinement during the first three days. Is the court saying that she did not have the capacity to consent during these three days? Or is the court saying that there really was no confinement during these three days?
b. Susan's parents asked her to sign an agreement releasing them from liability for their past weeks' actions. Suppose she had signed. Would the agreement have had legal effect?
c. Can you falsely imprison someone who is mentally retarded?
d. Does this opinion set good social policy? Why or why not?

SELF-HELP PRIVILEGES

When serious conflict arises, our society encourages people to use the legal system—the police and the courts—to resolve the conflict. In effect, we say, "Don't take the law into your own hands; tell it to a judge!" There are situations, however, where it simply is not practical to ask the courts to intervene. A person may need to act immediately to protect an interest or a right. Such immediate, protective action is called **self-help.** It consists of acting on one's own to prevent or correct the effects of a tort or other wrong without using the courts or other public authority. Self-help is a form of **extrajudicial** enforcement. It is justified when there is a privilege to act without first obtaining the permission or involvement of the legal system.

self-help Acting on one's own to prevent or correct the effects of a tort or other wrong without using the courts or other public authority. Also called *extrajudicial enforcement.*

extrajudicial Outside of court and litigation. Pertaining to what is done or given outside the course of regular judicial proceedings.

We shall consider nine self-help privileges:

1. self-defense
2. defense of others
3. necessity
4. abating a nuisance
5. defense of property
6. recapture of chattels
7. retaking possession of land forcibly
8. discipline
9. arrest

The question often arises whether a defendant loses the protection of a privilege because the defendant has made a *mistake.* As we shall see, some reasonable mistakes do not destroy the privilege, whereas other mistakes—even if reasonably made—do destroy it.

Self-Defense

self-defense The use of reasonable force to prevent an immediate harmful or offensive contact to one's person. (Self-defense sometimes has a broader meaning of repelling threatened danger to one's person *or property*.)

The privilege of **self-defense** is the use of reasonable force to prevent an immediate harmful or offensive contact against you by someone who is making an apparent threat of this contact. In short, it is the right to protect yourself from immediate physical harm. (Occasionally self-defense has a broader meaning—protecting one's property as well as one's person. Later we will consider the former separately as defense of property.) If you are in your residence, you do not have to retreat before inflicting deadly force or serious bodily harm in self-defense if this response is otherwise reasonable. If you are *not* in your residence, states differ on whether you must retreat before inflicting death or serious bodily harm in self-defense. The threat must be immediate (today, you cannot hit someone who has threatened to hurt you tomorrow) and the force used to prevent the threat must be reasonable (you cannot shoot someone who has threatened to blow smoke in your face). Aside from the rule on residences, you cannot inflict death or great bodily harm unless you are threatened with death or serious bodily harm yourself.

What happens if you make a mistake in trying to protect yourself?

EXAMPLE

Nathan sees Diana running toward him with a raised baseball bat. Thinking that she is going to hit him, Nathan throws a brick at Diana, breaking her leg. In fact, unknown to Nathan, Diana was simply expressing jubilation after just coming from a softball game that her team won.

Nathan acted in self-defense, but he made a mistake. There was no actual threat to him from Diana. In most states, the defense is not lost if this mistake was reasonable as to the amount of force needed for self-protection or, indeed, as to whether *any* protection was needed.

Exhibit 27–2 presents an overview of the elements of the privilege of self-defense, the effect of a mistake, examples of the kinds of torts to which this privilege can be used as a defense, examples of paralegal interviewing and investigation tasks to uncover facts that are relevant to proving that the privilege applies (including the reasonableness of mistakes), and a list of facts that could make it impossible to use the privilege.

ASSIGNMENT 27.8

In the following situations, assess whether the defendant can successfully use the privilege of self-defense.

a. Richard raises his cane over his head and shouts at Gary, saying, "If my daughter wasn't here with me, I'd smash you in the head." Gary is afraid. He grabs Richard's cane and knocks him down. Richard then sues Gary for battery.
b. Jane asks Clayton to leave Jane's store because she does not like the style of Clayton's hair. Clayton refuses to leave. Jane comes at Clayton with a broom. Jane is over twenty-five feet away and walks with a cane. As Jane approaches, Clayton shoots her. Jane sues Clayton for battery.
c. Lou is in Robin's home. Lou starts yelling obscenities at Robin in front of Robin's family. Lou spits in Robin's face and throws Robin's coat out the window. Just as Lou is about to spit in Robin's face again, Robin stabs Lou. Lou sues Robin for battery.

Exhibit 27–2 An overview of the privilege of self-defense.

Elements of the Privilege of Self-Defense	Effect of Mistake on the Privilege	The Torts Involved (Examples)	Paralegal Tasks: What to Find Out Through Interviewing and Investigation	Facts That Destroy the Privilege
a. Reasonable belief by D that P will immediately inflict harmful or offensive contact on D. b. Reasonable force used by D to prevent P from carrying out the apparent threat of an immediate harmful or offensive contact on D. (See entry below on the use of deadly force in a residence.) c. In most states, D cannot use deadly force in self-defense unless D is threatened with death or serious bodily harm by P, the attacker. d. If D is in his or her residence, D does not have to retreat before inflicting deadly force or serious bodily harm in self-defense if this response is otherwise reasonable. e. If D is *not* in his or her residence, states differ on whether D must retreat before inflicting death or serious bodily harm in self-defense.	• If D makes a mistake about whether P is about to inflict an immediate harmful or offensive contact on D, the privilege of self-defense is still valid if the mistake was reasonable under the circumstances. • If D makes a mistake about the amount of force needed to prevent the immediate threat, the privilege of self-defense is still valid if the mistake was reasonable under the circumstances. • In most states, the law is different if D's mistake is made when defending a third person. Even a reasonable mistake will not protect D in these states. See Exhibit 27–3 on "defense of others."	• *Battery* P is about to hit D. To prevent this, D knocks P down. P sues D for battery. D can raise the defense of self-defense. • *Assault* P is about to hit D. To prevent this, D threatens to hit P. P sues D for assault. D can raise the defense of self-defense. • *False Imprisonment* P is about to hit D. To prevent this, D locks P in a room. P sues D for false imprisonment. D can raise the defense of self-defense.	• Has P threatened D in the past? • Has P hit D in the past? • Does P have a reputation for aggressiveness? • What age and strength differences appear to exist between P and D? • How close was P to D at the time of the threat? • What did P threaten D with? • Did the threat occur in D's residence? • What did P say that would indicate how serious the threat was? • How much time did D have before P would carry out P's threat? • Was P's threat to inflict future or present harm on D? • Did D know or believe that P was only bluffing? • Did D have time to warn P that D would inflict force on P? • In the past, has D ever consented to the kind of contact that P threatened?	• D's response to the threat of P was disproportionate to the danger posed by P. (D cannot kill P to prevent a shove by P when the shove does not threaten D's life or limb with serious bodily harm.) • P's threat was to inflict future harm on D. • P was merely insulting D and not threatening D with bodily harm or offensive contact. • D was acting solely to protect D's honor and not to prevent a harmful or offensive contact by P. • D was acting out of revenge and not to prevent immediate harm to D. • D was not threatened at D's residence and could have retreated without responding with deadly force or force calculated to impose serious bodily harm on P. • D knew or believed that P was only bluffing.

Defense of Others

We are also allowed to defend others. The privilege of the **defense of others** is the use of reasonable force to prevent an immediate harmful or offensive contact against a third person by someone who is making an apparent threat of this contact. This privilege is similar to self-defense in that the threat must be immediate and the use of force must be proportionate to the threat. A major distinction between the two privileges concerns the effect of a mistake. As we just saw, the privilege of self-defense is not lost if you make a reasonable mistake in what you thought was needed to protect yourself. Suppose, however, you make a mistake when trying to protect a third person.

defense of others The use of reasonable force to prevent an immediate harmful or offensive contact against a third person.

EXAMPLE

Dan sees that Paul is about to knock Bill down. To prevent this, Dan runs over and pushes Paul away. Paul sues Dan for battery. Dan raises the defense of the defense of others—Dan was trying to prevent Paul from harming Bill. Unknown to Dan, however, Bill had just pulled a knife on Paul. Paul was acting in self-defense when he was about to knock Bill down. Hence, Paul had a privilege to harm Bill.

In this case, the third person—Bill—was the aggressor against Paul. Dan didn't know this. He made a mistake. Does this mistake mean that Dan loses the defense of defense of others? Yes, in most states. Even a reasonable mistake will not save Dan. When you intervene to protect a third person, you take the risk that this third person has no right to be protected. In a minority of states, however, a reasonable mistake *will* preserve the defense. In our example, if Dan was reasonable in thinking that Bill needed protection, Dan can use the defense of defense of others to defeat Paul's battery action against him. But this is so only in a minority of states.

Exhibit 27–3 presents an overview of the elements of this privilege, the effect of mistake on the privilege, examples of the kinds of torts to which this privilege

Exhibit 27–3 An overview of the privilege of defense of others.

Elements of the Privilege of Defense of Others	Effect of Mistake on the Privilege	The Torts Involved (Examples)	Paralegal Tasks: What to Find Out Through Interviewing and Investigation	Facts That Destroy the Privilege
a. Belief by D that P will immediately inflict harmful or offensive contact on a third person. (The third person does *not* have to be a member of D's family.) **b.** Reasonable force used by D with the intent to prevent P from carrying out the apparent threat of an immediate harmful or offensive contact on the third person. **c.** On the amount of force that D can use, D stands in the shoes of the third person. D can use the amount of force that the third person could have reasonably used to protect him- or herself. This could include deadly force only if the third person was in danger of death or serious bodily harm from P.	• In most states, if D makes a mistake on whether P is about to inflict an immediate harmful or offensive contact on the third person, the defense is lost even if the mistake was reasonable under the circumstances. • In a minority of states, D's mistake on whether P is about to inflict an immediate harmful or offensive contact on the third person does not invalidate the defense so long as the mistake was reasonable under the circumstances.	• *Battery* P is about to hit a third person. D sees this and hits P to prevent P's attack on the third person. P sues D for battery. D can raise the defense of the defense of others. • *Assault* P is about to hit a third person. D sees this and threatens to hit P if P does not stop. P sues D for assault. D can raise the defense of defense of others. • *False Imprisonment and Battery* P is about to hit a third person. D sees this and locks P in a "bear hug" until the third person can escape. P sues D for false imprisonment and for battery. D can raise the defense of the defense of others.	• Has P threatened the third person in the past? • Has P hit the third person in the past? • Does P have a reputation for aggressiveness? • What age and strength differences appear to exist between P and the third person? Between P and D? • How close was P to the third person at the time of P's threat? • What gestures or words were used by P to the third person that D could observe or hear? • How much time appeared to exist before P would carry out P's threat against the third person? • Was P's threat against the third person immediate or for the future? • Did P appear to be bluffing? • Did D have time to warn P that D would use force against P if the latter did not stop trying to harm the third person? • Did the third person appear to be consenting to contact from P, e.g., in a football game?	• D's response was disproportionate to the harm P was threatening the third person with. • P's threat was to impose future harm on the third person. • P was merely insulting the third person and not threatening the latter with immediate harm. • D knew P was bluffing. • D was acting out of revenge and not to prevent immediate harm to the third person. • In most states, D loses the privilege if D made a mistake and the third person turns out to have been the aggressor against P. This is so even if the mistake was reasonable. In a minority of states, however, the privilege is not lost if D's mistake was reasonable.

can be used as a defense, examples of paralegal interviewing and investigation tasks to uncover facts that are relevant to proving that the privilege applies, and a list of facts that could make it impossible to use the privilege.

Necessity

Necessity is the privilege to make a reasonable use of the property of others to avoid immediate harm or damage to persons or property. The property can be personal property or real property.

necessity The privilege to make reasonable use of someone's property to avoid immediate harm or damage to persons or property.

EXAMPLES

Without permission, you use a stranger's car to drive a member of your family to the emergency room of a hospital.

Without permission, you bulldoze a wide path over the crops of a neighbor in order to stop the spread of a fire that is headed toward the town on the other side of the neighbor's field containing the crops.

When you use someone's property in this way, do you have to compensate them for any damage that you do? The answer depends on the kind of necessity that existed. You must provide compensation if a **private necessity** existed. This is the privilege to make a reasonable use of someone's property to avoid immediate private harm or damage. The use of the car in the first example demonstrates a private necessity. You were trying to protect a member of your family. A **public necessity**, on the other hand, is the privilege to make a reasonable use of someone's property to avoid immediate public harm or damage. This was the case in the second example. There was a danger of the town going up in flames—clearly a public danger. There is no requirement to provide compensation to someone whose property is used to prevent public harm or danger. In many states, however, special statutes exist that provide compensation in these cases, particularly when the damage is done by public employees such as the police or fire department.

private necessity A privilege to make reasonable use of another's property to avoid an immediate private harm or damage.

public necessity A privilege to make reasonable use of another's property to avoid an immediate public harm or damage.

Exhibit 27–4 presents an overview of the elements of the privilege of necessity, examples of the kinds of torts to which the privilege can be used as a defense, examples of paralegal interviewing and investigation tasks to uncover facts that are relevant to proving that the privilege applies, and a list of facts that could make it impossible to use the privilege.

ASSIGNMENT 27.9

Tom has a highly contagious disease. He has no money to buy medicine and no hospitals are in the area. Tom breaks into a doctor's office at night and steals what he thinks is medicine that will help. In fact, he takes the wrong medicine. The doctor sues Tom for conversion. Does Tom have a defense? If Tom has a defense, does he still have to pay the doctor for losses sustained due to the break-in?

Abating a Nuisance

There are times when a defendant has a privilege to enter someone's land in order to **abate a nuisance**. This is the privilege to take reasonable steps to correct a nuisance that is interfering with the use and enjoyment of your land. The privilege is a defense to the tort of trespass to land. For a discussion of this privilege, see Chapter 23.

abate a nuisance To take self-help steps to eliminate a nuisance that is interfering with the use and enjoyment of land.

Exhibit 27–4 An overview of the privilege of necessity.

Elements of the Privilege of Necessity	The Torts Involved (Examples)	Paralegal Tasks: What to Find Out Through Interviewing and Investigation	Facts That Destroy the Privilege
a. Reasonable belief by D that persons or property will be immediately harmed or damaged. b. Reasonable use by D of the personal or real property of another to avoid the immediate harm or damage to the persons or property.	· *Conversion* D destroys P's liquor to prevent it from getting into the hands of an invading army. P sues D for conversion. D can raise the defense of public necessity and avoid paying P for the loss D caused. · *Conversion* D is injured in a car accident and uses P's scarf as a tourniquet. The scarf is ruined. P sues D for conversion. D can raise the defense of private necessity, but must compensate P for any damage done to P's scarf. · *Trespass to Land* D runs onto P's land to escape a bear. P sues D for trespass to land. D can raise the defense of private necessity but must compensate P for any damage D does to P's land, e.g., to a fence.	· What alternatives, if any, were available to D and how realistic were they? · How much time did D have to act? · How much damage did D do? · What were the indications that the public was in danger (for public necessity)? · Did D seek advice on what to do—if any time was available?	· D's belief in the existence of the danger was unreasonable. · D's use of P's personal or real property was disproportionate to the danger. (For example, D cannot blow up P's house to prevent the spread of a fire when the fire is minor and water is easily available to put it out.)

Defense of Property

defense of property The right to use reasonable force to prevent a present threat of interference with the possession of your personal or real property or to end an interference with such property that just started.

The privilege of the **defense of property** is the right to use reasonable force to prevent a present interference with the possession of your personal or real property or to end an interference with such property that just started. You cannot use deadly force, however, to protect your property. This kind of force was one of the main issues in the *Katko* case we will examine shortly.

There are two major kinds of mistakes that can occur when trying to use this privilege:

- mistake about the amount of force needed to protect your possession, and
- mistake about whether you had the right to possess the property you protected.

A reasonable mistake about the amount of force needed will not defeat the privilege. Any mistake, however, about your right to possession *will* defeat the privilege, regardless of how reasonable your mistake might have been.

EXAMPLE

Dan buys a painting from Kevin, a reputable art dealer, not knowing that Kevin stole the painting from Peter. When Peter sees the painting on Dan's wall, Peter starts to take the painting off the wall. To prevent this, Dan pushes Peter away. Peter sues Dan for battery.

In the battery action, Dan cannot use the defense of defense of property. He made a reasonable mistake in believing that he had a right to possess the painting since he bought it from a reputable dealer without knowing the dealer was a thief. Mistakes about the right to possession, however, destroy the privilege to defend

property—even reasonable mistakes. The only exception would be if the person with the superior right to possession caused the other person to make the mistake.

Exhibit 27–5 presents an overview of the elements of this privilege, the effect of mistake on the privilege, examples of the kinds of torts to which this privilege can be used as a defense, examples of paralegal interviewing and investigation tasks to uncover facts that are relevant to proving that the privilege applies, and a list of facts that could make it impossible to use the privilege.

Exhibit 27–5 Overview of the privilege of defense of property.*

Elements of the Privilege of Defense of Property	Effect of Mistake on the Privilege	The Torts Involved (Examples)	Paralegal Tasks: What to Find Out Through Interviewing and Investigation	Facts That Destroy the Privilege
a. D has possession of personal or real property. **b.** D's right to possession is superior to P's claim of possession, if any. **c.** D has a reasonable belief that immediate force is needed to prevent P's present threat of interference with D's possession or to end an interference that P just started. **d.** D requests that P cease the interference with D's possession, unless the request would be unsafe or impractical for D. **e.** D uses reasonable force against P to prevent the interference by P of D's possession. **f.** In most states, D cannot use deadly force or force calculated to cause serious bodily harm (e.g., shoot P), even if D adequately warns P that such force will be used. D has a privilege to use great force only if P's interference with property also threatens life or limb.	• If D makes a mistake about whether P has a right to possession of the personal or real property, the defense-of-property privilege is lost even if the mistake was reasonable, unless P caused D to make this mistake. • If D makes a mistake about the amount of force that is needed to stop the interference, the defense-of-property privilege is not lost if the mistake was reasonable under the circumstances.	• *Battery* P enters D's land and refuses to leave when D asks him to do so immediately after P entered. D takes P by the collar and pushes him out. P sues D for battery. D can raise the defense of defense of property. • *Assault* P reaches for D's purse on the table. D raises her fist at P and shouts at him to keep away from her purse. P sues D for assault. D can raise the defense of defense of property.	• Did D have possession of the personal or real property? • What indications were there that P was going to interfere immediately or was going to continue the interference shortly after it began? • What did P say or do? • What alternatives to force, if any, were available to D? • What age and strength differences existed between P and D? • What harm was P subjected to by D's use of force to prevent P's interference? • Did D ask P to stop the interference? Would such a request have been realistic? • Did P's interference with D's property in any way threaten D's personal safety or that of others?	• P had a privilege to be on the real property or to have the personal property. • P's right to possession was superior to D's. • P's threat to interfere was in the future—it was not an immediate threat. • D's use of force was disproportionate to the threat posed by P to D's possession. • D was motivated solely by hatred and revenge. D was not trying to prevent interference by P. • D knew that P was bluffing when P threatened interference. • D did not ask P to cease the threatened interference by P. Such a request would have been reasonable or practical. • D used deadly force or force calculated to cause serious bodily harm even though neither D nor anyone else was threatened with death or serious bodily harm by P.

**Recapture* of property is covered separately in Exhibit 27–6.

CASE

Katko v. Briney

183 N.W.2d 657 (1971)
Supreme Court of Iowa

***Background:** The Brineys own an unoccupied farm house that had been broken into several times. Boarding up the windows and posting no-trespassing signs did not deter the break-ins. On June 11, 1967 Mr. Briney set "a shotgun trap" in the north bedroom. He secured the gun to an iron bed with the barrel pointed at the bedroom door. It was rigged with wire from the doorknob to the gun's trigger so it would fire when the door was opened. He first pointed the gun so an intruder would be hit in the stomach. At Mrs. Briney's suggestion, however, it was lowered to hit the legs. He admitted he did so "because I was mad and tired of being tormented" but "he did not intend to injure anyone." Tin was nailed over the bedroom window. The spring gun could not be seen from the outside and no warning of its presence was posted. When Katko and a companion tried to break in, Katko was seriously injured when he triggered the gun. Much of his leg, including part of the tibia, was blown away. In a criminal proceeding, Katko pled guilty to larceny, was fined $50, and was paroled during good behavior from a sixty-day jail sentence. He then brought a civil suit against the Brineys for damages. At the trial, the jury returned a verdict for Katko for $20,000 actual and $10,000 punitive damages. The case is now on appeal before the Supreme Court of Iowa.*

***Decision on Appeal:** Judgment affirmed. Deadly force cannot be used to protect uninhabited property.*

OPINION OF COURT

Chief Justice MOORE delivered the opinion of the court.

The primary issue presented here is whether an owner may protect personal property in an unoccupied boardedup farm house against trespassers and thieves by a spring gun capable of inflicting death or serious injury. We are not here concerned with a man's right to protect his home and members of his family. Defendants' home was several miles from the scene of the incident. . . .

In the statement of issues the trial court stated plaintiff and his companion committed a felony when they broke and entered defendants' house. In instruction 2 the court referred to the early case history of the use of spring guns and stated under the law their use was prohibited except to prevent the commission of felonies of violence and where human life is in danger. The instruction included a statement [that] breaking and entering is not a felony of violence.

Instruction 5 stated: "You are hereby instructed that one may use reasonable force in the protection of his property, but such right is subject to the qualification that one may not use such means of force as will take human life or inflict great bodily injury. Such is the rule even though the injured party is a trespasser and is in violation of the law himself."

Instruction 6 stated: "An owner of premises is prohibited from willfully or intentionally injuring a trespasser by means of force that either takes life or inflicts great bodily injury; and therefore a person owning a premise is prohibited from setting out 'spring guns' and like dangerous devices which will likely take life or inflict great bodily injury, for the purpose of harming trespassers. The fact that the trespasser may be acting in violation of the law does not change the rule. The only time when such conduct of setting a 'spring gun' or a like dangerous device is justified would be when the trespasser was committing a felony of violence or a felony punishable by death, or where the trespasser was endangering human life by his act." . . .

The overwhelming weight of authority, both textbook and case law, supports the trial court's statement of the applicable principles of law.

Prosser on Torts, Third Edition, pages 116–118, states: "the law has always placed a higher value upon human safety than upon mere rights in property. [It] is the accepted rule that there is no privilege to use any force calculated to cause death or serious bodily injury to repel the threat to land or chattels, unless there is also such a threat to the defendant's personal safety as to justify a self-defense. . . . [S]pring guns and other mankilling devices are not justifiable against a mere trespasser, or even a petty thief. They are privileged only against those upon whom the landowner, if he were present in person, would be free to inflict injury of the same kind." . . .

Affirmed.

ASSIGNMENT 27.10

a. Do you agree with the result in this case? Why or why not?
b. Would the case have been decided differently if the Brineys had posted a large sign on the farm property saying, "WARNING: Property Protected by Spring Guns"? Would assumption of the risk bar recovery?
c. Smith owns a liquor store that has been burglarized often. He buys a pit bull dog to stay in the store after he closes. A midnight burglar is mauled by the dog. Does *Katko* apply?

Mr. and Mrs. Briney in front of the vacant farmhouse they tried to protect with a spring gun, leading to the famous case of *Katko v. Briney*.

chattel Personal property; property other than land or things attached to land.

ASSIGNMENT 27.11

In the following situations, examine what defenses, if any, can be raised in the suits brought.

a. George is invited to Henry's house for dinner. They have an argument and Henry asks George to leave. George refuses. Henry pushes George through a glass window. George sues Henry for battery.
b. Tom is terrified by dogs. Leo's little dog starts barking at Tom in the street. Tom picks up a stick and is about to hit the dog. Leo sees this and clubs Tom with a baseball bat. Tom sues Leo for battery.
c. Helen is in her boat when a storm suddenly begins. Helen takes the boat to Kevin's private dock in order to prevent the destruction of her boat. When Kevin sees Helen's boat at his dock, he tells her to leave immediately or he will punch her in the nose. Helen leaves even though the storm is still raging. Helen sues Kevin for assault.

Recapture of Chattels

The defense-of-property privilege is used when you have possession of property with which someone is interfering. Suppose, however, you no longer have possession. Someone has *wrongfully* dispossessed you of a **chattel** (personal property) and you want to recapture it. The privilege you need to try to use in this situation is called **recapture of chattels**. It is the right to use reasonable force to obtain the return of personal property promptly after someone obtains it wrongfully. The attempt to regain possession must occur promptly after the **dispossession**. This is sometimes referred to as **fresh pursuit**, which means promptly, without undue delay. (Fresh pursuit also refers to the right to retake the property if done promptly.) If a long period of time elapses after the dispossession, the preference of the law is that the victim use the courts (rather than self-help) to resolve any dispute over the right of possession.

Merchants often use the recapture-of-chattels privilege when they suspect a person of stealing merchandise in their store. As we saw in Chapter 7, their right is referred to as the **shopkeeper's privilege**.

Before force is used to recapture a chattel, a request for its return must be made unless such a request would be impractical or unsafe. Like the defense of property, you cannot use deadly force to recapture the chattels. Also, the privilege of recapture does not apply unless the chattel was taken from you wrongfully.

recapture of chattels The right to use reasonable force to obtain the return of personal property (chattels) shortly after someone obtained them wrongfully.

dispossession Depriving someone of possession or occupancy of property. (See glossary for another definition.)

fresh pursuit 1. Promptly, without undue delay. 2. The right of a victim whose property has been dispossessed to use reasonable force to take the property back just after it is taken. Also called hot pursuit.

shopkeeper's privilege The right of a merchant to detain someone temporarily for the sole purpose of investigating whether the person has committed any theft against the merchant.

EXAMPLE

David lets his friend, Paul, use David's bike for a brief ride in the playground. When Paul is on the bike for a few moments, he decides not to return it and tells David this. David immediately pushes Paul off the bike and retrieves it. Paul sues David for battery.

Paul wins. David cannot use the defense of recapture of chattels because Paul initially obtained possession of the bike rightfully—David agreed to let him use it. The privilege does not apply unless it is being used to obtain it back from someone who obtained it wrongfully. Paul rightfully obtained possession, but he has wrongfully kept it. To get the bike back in such a case, David must resort to the courts. The case would be different if Paul took the bike without permission. Then David would have the privilege to recapture.

You must be sure that you have the right to possess the chattel you want to recapture. If you make a mistake—even a reasonable one—the privilege is destroyed and you can be liable for any torts resulting from your use of force. To demonstrate this, let's look at another bike example:

EXAMPLE

David sees Pete, a total stranger, take a bike out of the playground. David immediately pushes Pete off the bike and retrieves it. In fact, Pete was riding his own bike, which looks exactly the same as David's bike. Pete sues David for battery.

Pete wins. David made a mistake about his right to possess the bike. Even though the mistake may have been reasonable since the bikes looked alike, the mistake is fatal. If you use force to recapture a chattel, you must have the right to possess that chattel. The only exception would be if the person with the superior right to possession caused the other person to make the mistake.

Exhibit 27–6 presents an overview of the elements of this privilege, the effect of mistake on the privilege, examples of the kinds of torts to which this privilege can be used as a defense, examples of paralegal interviewing and investigation tasks to uncover facts that are relevant to proving that the privilege applies, and a list of facts that could make it impossible to use the privilege.

ASSIGNMENT 27.12

In the following situations, determine whether the defendant can claim the defense of recapture of chattels.

a. Tom is playing football. He asks Fred to hold his watch. While Tom is on the field, Fred suddenly must leave. Fred asks Joe to hold the watch for Tom. Fred does not know that Joe is Tom's archenemy. When Tom finds out that Joe has the watch, he asks for it back. Joe refuses. Tom hits Joe over the head with a football helmet and takes the watch back. Joe sues Tom for battery.
b. Sam steals John's ring and sells it for $1 in a dark alley to Fred, who knows neither John nor Sam. Two weeks after John finds out that Fred has the ring, John breaks into Fred's house and takes the ring from Fred's jewelry box. Fred sues John for trespass to land.

Retaking Possession of Land Forcibly

squatter One who settles on land without legal title or authority.

Assume that someone is on land wrongfully, e.g., a **squatter** moves into a vacant building or a tenant remains in an apartment long after ceasing to pay rent. Can

Exhibit 27–6 Overview of the privilege of recapture of chattels (personal property).

Elements of the Privilege of Recapture of Chattels	Effect of Mistake on the Privilege	The Torts Involved (Examples)	Paralegal Tasks: What to Find Out Through Interviewing and Investigation	Facts That Destroy the Privilege
a. P acquired possession of the chattel wrongfully, e.g., by fraud or force. **b.** D has the right to immediate possession. **c.** D requests that P return the chattel. This request is made before D uses force to recapture it unless the request would be unrealistic or unsafe for D. **d.** D's use of force to recapture the chattel occurs promptly after P took possession of the chattel (fresh pursuit). **e.** D uses reasonable force (not force calculated to cause death or serious bodily injury) with the intent to recapture the chattel from P.	• If D makes a mistake about whether P has a right to possession of the chattel, the recapture-of-chattel privilege is lost even if the mistake was reasonable, unless P caused D to make this mistake.	• *Battery* P has just stolen D's television, and refuses to return it. D pushes P aside in order to take the television back. P sues D for battery. D can raise the defense of recapture of chattels. • *Assault* Same facts as above, except that instead of pushing P, D raises his fist and threatens to hit P if P does not return the television. P sues D for assault. D can raise the defense of recapture of chattels. • *Trespass to Land* Same facts as above on the television. P has the television in his garage. When D finds out, D immediately goes into the garage to recapture the television. P sues D for trespass to land. D can raise the defense of recapture of chattels.	• How did P get possession of the chattel? • Did P claim P had a right to possession? If so, on what basis? • What is D's basis for the claim that D had a right to possess the chattel? • Did either P or D claim that they owned the chattel, that they had properly rented it, or that they were properly holding it for someone else? • Did P originally get possession with the consent of D? • Did D request P to return the chattel? Was such a request realistic and safe? • When did D discover that P had possession, and how long after discovery did D try to recapture it? • Could D have discovered that P had possession sooner? Why or why not? • Could D have acted sooner to recapture the chattel? Why or why not? • How much force was necessary to take the chattel back from P? Could less force have been used? Why or why not? • What did P and D say to each other just prior to D's use of force?	• P did not have actual possession nor did P control possession. • P in fact got possession rightfully (even though P's *continued* possession may now be wrongful, in which case D does not have the privilege of recapture—D must use the courts to get the chattel back). • D has no right to possession. • D failed to request a return when such a request was practical and safe. • D took too long to discover that P had possession. • D took too long to recapture after D knew that P had possession. • D used a disproportionate amount of force to recapture the chattel. • D was acting solely from the motive of hatred and revenge and did not limit the force to what was necessary to recapture the chattel.

the owner use force to regain possession by ousting the wrongdoer? In general, the answer is no. The law requires the owner to use the courts (rather than self-help) to regain possession of land through eviction proceedings and actions for **unlawful detainer** or **ejectment**. If, however, the rightful owner is in possession, which a wrongdoer attempts to seize, the rightful owner can use reasonable force (self-help) to prevent the dispossession. But the courts must be used to oust a wrongdoer who has already settled into his or her wrongful possession of the land.

unlawful detainer Remaining in possession of real property unlawfully by one whose original possession was lawful.

ejectment An action for the recovery of the possession of land and for damages for the wrongful dispossession.

Discipline

Parents have the privilege of disciplining their children. This can include physically hitting and confining the children, as long as such force is reasonable. (Teachers and others who stand in the place of parents—***in loco parentis***—also have this privilege unless it has been restricted by special statute.) Suits within the family are discussed elsewhere. See Exhibit 22–1 in Chapter 22.

in loco parentis "In the place of the parent." Acting in place of or assuming some or all of the duties of a parent without adopting the child.

Arrest

When a public officer or a private citizen tries to arrest someone, the latter might respond with a suit for battery, assault, or false imprisonment. The privilege of **arrest** can be raised as a defense to such suits. The elements of this privilege and its special circumstances are considered in Chapter 7 on false imprisonment and false arrest. The arrest of an individual can also raise issues of defamation, invasion of privacy, malicious prosecution, and abuse of process. Finally, the arrested person might claim a violation of his or her civil rights.

arrest Take another into custody to bring him or her before the proper authorities.

THE DEFENSE OF SOVEREIGN IMMUNITY

When is a government liable for the torts committed on its behalf? The old answer was: never. The king cannot be sued because the king can do no wrong. This was the essence of the doctrine of **sovereign immunity**. Over the years, however, the government (i.e., the sovereign) has agreed to be sued for torts in limited situations. In this section, we will discuss the boundaries of what is now a limited sovereign immunity. Government, of course, acts only through its agents or employees. Hence, when the government is liable, it will be on a theory of **respondeat superior**: let the master answer for the wrongful acts of its servants committed within the scope of employment. The servant is the government employee. We also need to explore when this employee is *personally* liable for the torts he or she commits while carrying out governmental functions. In summary, the issues are:

1. When has the *federal* government agreed to be liable for the torts of its employees?
2. When have the *state* governments in the country agreed to be liable for the torts of their employees?
3. When have *local* governments agreed (on their own or on order from the state government) to be liable for the torts of their employees?
4. When is a federal, state, or local government employee independently and personally liable for the torts he or she commits on the job? As we will see later, when **official immunity** applies, government employees are exempt from personal liability for torts they commit within the scope of their employment. Official immunity is separate from sovereign immunity.

If you are the victim of a tort committed by a government employee (e.g., slander, conversion), you will have no one to sue if both sovereign immunity and official immunity apply.

Before we examine these immunities, two closely related issues need to be mentioned. First, legislatures sometimes pass special legislation that allows a private individual to sue the government when the individual's suit would otherwise be barred by sovereign or official immunity. This individualized or private waiver from immunity is more narrow than the general waiver for designated classes of torts or other claims that are our concern here. Second, if the government forces you to give up your land for a public purpose (e.g., to build a road through it), you must receive **just compensation**. This is because the constitution forbids government **taking** of property from a private individual without just compensation. To the extent that the government is forced by the constitution to provide compensation for a "taking," the government is waiving its sovereign immunity.

sovereign immunity The sovereign (i.e., the state or the government) cannot be sued in its courts without its consent. Also called governmental immunity.

respondeat superior "Let the master answer." An employer is responsible (liable) for the wrongs committed by an employee within the scope of employment. (On the factors that determine the scope of employment, see Exhibit 14–9 in Chapter 14.)

official immunity Government employees are not personally liable for torts or other wrongdoing they commit within the scope of their employment.

just compensation Compensation from the government that is fair to the owner and the public, paid when the owner's property is taken by the government for a public purpose.

taking The forced acquisition of private property by the government for a public purpose for which the government must pay just compensation. (A requirement of the Fifth Amendment.) The acquisition can consist of a forced purchase, a substantial interference with the enjoyment of the property, or the deprivation of substantially all productive use of the property.

Federal Government

The basic law containing the federal government's consent to be sued is the **Federal Tort Claims Act (FTCA)**.[2] The FTCA does not abolish sovereign immunity for the federal government. The general rule established by the FTCA is as follows: The United States (this phrase refers to the federal government) will be liable for its torts in the same manner as a private individual would be liable according to the local law in the place where the tort occurs, *unless* the United States is specifically exempted for that tort in the FTCA.

Federal Tort Claims Act (FTCA) The federal statute that specifies the torts for which the federal government can be sued because it waives sovereign immunity for those torts (28 U.S.C. §§ 2671 et seq., 1346).

Assume that a federal employee in Delaware commits a tort such as negligence against you. According to the general rule, if the negligence law of the state of Delaware would make a private person liable for negligence for doing what the federal employee did, then the federal government will be liable for the tort—unless there is a specific exemption for that tort in the FTCA. Hence, we need to know what the FTCA specifically excludes and covers. Exhibit 27–7 tells us.

Before a citizen tries to bring a claim under the Federal Tort Claims Act, the administrative agency involved must be given the chance to settle the case on its own within certain dollar limits. If the citizen is still dissatisfied, he or she can sue under the Act in a federal court.

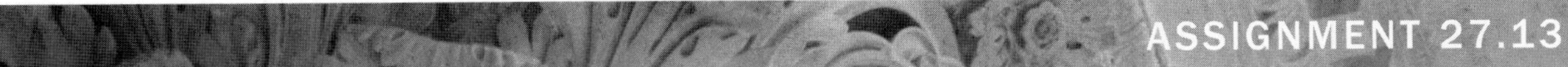

ASSIGNMENT 27.13

When delivering a letter, a mail carrier carelessly left a package on the porch. The owner of the house trips over the package and sues the U.S. Postal Service for negligence. Is sovereign immunity a defense in this suit? How does the Federal Tort Claims Act apply?

Federal employees themselves are generally excluded as claimants under the Federal Tort Claims Act. Injuries that they receive on the job are covered by other statutory schemes, such as the Federal Employees' Compensation Act.

State Government

A state government consists of the governor's office, state agencies such as the state police, state hospitals, and state commissions and boards. To what extent has a state government waived its own sovereign immunity so that citizens can sue the state for the torts of state employees? States differ in their answers to this question. Some states have come close to abolishing sovereign immunity. Other states have schemes modeled in whole or in part on the Federal Tort Claims Act. Finally, other states have retained most of the traditional immunity.

Special protection is always given to agencies and offices when they are carrying out policy deliberations involving considerable judgment and discretion. It is sometimes said that it is not a tort for a government to govern! Rarely, for example, will any government waive immunity for tortious injury caused a citizen by a judge, legislator, or high administrative officer. Negligence by a lower-level employee in the judicial, legislative, or executive branches, however, may constitute a wrong for which the state will waive immunity, e.g., when a court clerk negligently loses a pleading that was properly filed. Acts that do not involve much discretion and that do not involve the formulation of policy will often subject the state to tort liability because the state has waived immunity for such acts.

Keep in mind that we are *not* talking about individual or personal liability of the government employee at this point. Personal liability will be discussed later. Our focus is on the government's liability via respondeat superior for the torts its employees commit within the scope of their employment.

Exhibit 27–7
Federal Tort Claims Act (FTCA).

THE SCOPE OF THE FEDERAL GOVERNMENT'S TORT IMMUNITY UNDER THE FTCA
(The FTCA states a broad waiver of sovereign immunity, but then provides *numerous* exceptions to the waiver.)

■ **Broad Waiver:** The federal government is treated like a private person. If a private person would be liable for harm resulting from an act or omission (in the state where the act or omission occurred), then the federal government will be liable when a federal employee's act or omission within the scope of employment causes the harm.

■ **Exception: Discretionary Action or Inaction.** The federal government will not be liable (sovereign immunity is not waived) for harm that results while a government employee performs or fails to perform a *discretionary* act, whether or not the discretion is abused. Examples: the decision of a federal agency to deny a waste permit to a business or to parole a prisoner. Discretionary decisions are policy judgments—those that result from an analysis of social, economic, or political policy concerns. A federal park ranger's decision on how fast to drive a truck would be an *operational* decision rather than a policy decision. Sovereign immunity would not prevent a suit against the federal government for an injury caused by negligent driving by such a driver.

■ **Exception: Enforcing a Statute or Regulation.** The federal government will not be liable (sovereign immunity is not waived) for harm that results while a government employee is using due care in carrying out a statute or regulation, even if the statute or regulation is ruled to be invalid.

■ **Exception: Some Intentional Torts.** The federal government's immunity for intentional torts depends on which intentional torts we are talking about and which federal employee committed them. Here are the rules:

- The federal government will be liable (sovereign immunity is waived) if a federal investigative or law enforcement officer commits one of the following six torts:

  - assault
  - battery
  - false imprisonment
  - false arrest
  - abuse of process
  - malicious prosecution

  Example: a police brutality claim.
- The federal government will not be liable (sovereign immunity is not waived) if a federal investigative or law enforcement officer commits one of the following four torts:

  - libel
  - slander
  - misrepresentation (deceit)
  - interference with contract rights

  Example: a claim that a police officer called a pedestrian a thief.
- For federal employees other than investigative or law enforcement officers, the federal government will not be liable (sovereign immunity is not waived) for the following ten torts:

  - assault
  - battery
  - false imprisonment
  - false arrest
  - malicious prosecution
  - abuse of process
  - libel
  - slander
  - misrepresentation (deceit)
  - interference with contract rights

■ **Exception: Strict Liability.** The federal government will not be liable (sovereign immunity is not waived) for harm based on strict liability. Example: a claim based on harm caused by leakage of ultrahazardous materials being transported by the federal government on a highway.

■ **Exception: Combatant Activity.** The federal government will not be liable (sovereign immunity is not waived) for claims arising out of combatant activities during a time of war.

■ **Exception: Mail and Taxes.** The federal government will not be liable (sovereign immunity is not waived) for claims based on the negligent transmission of mail or for the assessment or collection of taxes.

Local Government

Local government units have a variety of names: cities, municipalities, municipal corporations, counties, towns, villages, etc. Also part of local government are public schools, transportation agencies, some hospitals, recreational agencies, and some utilities. Whether any of these local units of government can be sued in tort is again a problem of sovereign immunity. A number of possibilities exist:

- Sovereign immunity has been completely or almost completely waived.
- The sovereign immunity of the units of local government is the same as that enjoyed by the state government.
- The sovereign immunity of the units of local government is different from that of the state government.
- Different units of local government have different sovereign immunity rules.

In short, extensive legal research must be done every time you want to sue a unit of local government. You must determine its category or status. What is it called? Who created it? Why was it created? What are its powers? Is it part of the state government? Is it separate from the state government? Is it a hybrid combination of both state and local government? Many cities and counties receive substantial state aid. Does such aid entitle them to the same sovereign immunity protection as the state? You may find that for some purposes, the unit of government is considered part of the state, whereas for other purposes it is considered entirely separate and local. Over the years, a great deal of litigation has dealt with the problem of determining the nature of the unit of government in order to decide what sovereign immunity principles apply.

Units of local government perform many different kinds of functions. These functions are often grouped into two classifications: governmental and proprietary. The sovereign immunity rules may differ depending on what category of function the employee was carrying out when the tort was committed. The general rule is that sovereign immunity is *not* waived when the tort grows out of a *governmental* function, whereas it *is* waived when it grows out of a *proprietary* function. (An important exception is when the city, county, town, or other unit has created a public or a private nuisance. Even if this nuisance grows out of a governmental function, sovereign immunity will usually not prevent the suit.) Of course, there is always the possibility that a government will waive its sovereign immunity for torts arising out of both governmental and proprietary functions. The waiver, however, is usually limited to proprietary functions.

Unfortunately, there are few clear rules on the distinction between a governmental and a proprietary function.

Governmental Functions A **governmental function** is one that can be performed adequately only by the government. The operation of local courts and local legislatures (e.g., a city council) is considered governmental. The same is true of the chief administrative offices of the local government (e.g., office of the mayor, office of the county commissioner) where basic policy is made. Police and fire departments also fall into the category of governmental functions where sovereign immunity will prevent suits for the torts that grow out of these functions.[3]

governmental function A function that can be performed adequately only by the government.

Proprietary Functions A **proprietary function** is one that (1) traditionally or principally has been performed by private enterprise, or (2) is conducted primarily to produce a profit or benefit for the government rather than for the public at large. Examples include government-run airports, docks, garages, and utilities such as water and gas. For some of these functions, the local government often collects special fees or revenue. The test for a proprietary function, however, is not whether a "profit" is made. This is simply one factor that tends to indicate a proprietary function. Some functions are very difficult to classify, such as the operation of a city hospital. You will find courts going both ways for these and similar functions.

proprietary function A function of government that (1) traditionally or principally has been performed by private enterprise, or (2) is conducted primarily to produce a profit or benefit for the government rather than for the public at large.

There are courts that do not rely totally on the distinction between governmental and proprietary functions to decide whether sovereign immunity prevents the suit against the local government. Some courts make the same distinction we saw earlier under the Federal Tort Claims Act between a claim arising out of discretionary or policy decisions made by the government (for which sovereign immunity will not be waived) and claims arising out of nondiscretionary or operational decisions (for which sovereign immunity will be waived). For example, a city may be immune from liability for damages resulting from its negligent decision on where to construct sewers, but would be liable for damages resulting from the negligent construction or repair of a particular sewer.

Finally, some governments have tied the waiver of sovereign immunity to the purchase of liability insurance: the waiver extends only to the maximum coverage provided by the insurance.

ASSIGNMENT 27.14

Select any three agencies: one that is part of the federal government, one that is part of your state government, and one that is part of your local government. For each agency, assume that one of its employees has committed a tort against you for which sovereign immunity has been waived. For example, while in a government car, the employee negligently hit your car. What steps are required to file a tort claim against each agency? Check guidelines available online, including relevant statutes and ordinances on tort claims against the government.

THE DEFENSE OF OFFICIAL IMMUNITY: THE PERSONAL LIABILITY OF GOVERNMENT EMPLOYEES

personal liability Liability that can be satisfied out of a wrongdoer's personal assets.

vicarious liability Liability imposed on a person because of the conduct of another, based solely on the status of the relationship between the two. The person liable is not the person whose conduct led to the liability.

What about a suit against the *individual* government employee as opposed to one against the sovereign, or the government itself? If the employee is sued *personally*, any judgment is paid out of the employee's own pocket. Although there are circumstances in which **personal liability** is imposed on government employees, it should be pointed out that the law is reluctant to impose such liability. Public employees must be "free to exercise their duties unembarrassed by the fear of damage suits in respect of acts done in the course of those duties—suits which would consume time and energies which would otherwise be devoted to governmental service and the threat of which might appreciably inhibit the fearless, vigorous, and effective administration of policies of government."[4] On the other hand, critics argue that public employees should not be treated differently from employees in the private sector. When an employee of a business commits a tort, the employer is **vicariously liable** if the tort was committed within the scope of employment, but the employee is also *personally liable*. The critics say that the same rule should apply to government employees. For the most part, however, it does not.

When government employees are *not* liable, it is because of *official immunity*. If this defense applies, government employees will not be personally liable for the torts they commit within the scope of employment. Three questions need to be asked in this area of the law:

- Was a tort committed by the government employee?
- If so, was the tort within the scope of employment?
- If so, can the employee avoid personal liability by using the defense of official immunity?

The first question to ask is whether a tort has been committed by the government employee. It may be that the government employee had a privilege to act so that there was no tort. For example, a police officer has the privilege to arrest someone. (See Exhibit 7–2 in Chapter 7.) The privilege prevents liability for torts such as battery and false imprisonment. If, however, a tort was committed, the second question is whether it was committed within the scope of employment. (See Exhibit 14–9 in Chapter 14 on the factors that determine scope of employment.) Judges may have official immunity for defamation they commit from the bench against attorneys or defendants, but not for defamation they commit against their neighbor in an argument over a football game. The latter is clearly outside the judge's scope of employment. A government employee is as liable for torts outside the scope of employment as any citizen would be. If a tort was committed by the government employee and if it was within the scope of employment, we then ask a third question: Can the employee avoid personal liability under the doctrine of official immunity?

A citizen who has been the victim of a government tort may face one of several scenarios in looking for a defendant to sue:

- Sovereign immunity may prevent a suit against the government, and official immunity may prevent a suit against the employee; the citizen is without remedy.
- Sovereign immunity may have been waived so that the government can be sued, but official immunity may prevent a suit against the employee; the citizen can sue only the government.
- Sovereign immunity may have been waived so that the government can be sued, and official immunity may not apply so that the employee can also be sued; the citizen can sue either or both.

If the citizen can sue both the government and the employee, and successfully does so, the citizen does not receive double damages for the same injury. There is one recovery only. The plaintiff can usually collect from either defendant until there has been a satisfaction of the judgment.

Official immunity must be examined under two main categories: the employee's personal liability for a traditional common-law tort (e.g., negligence, battery, defamation), and the employee's personal liability for a **civil rights** violation. First, let us examine civil rights violations.

Section 1983 of the **Civil Rights Act of 1871** provides as follows:

> "Every person who, under color of any statute, ordinance, regulation, custom, or usage, of any State . . . subjects . . . any citizen . . . to the deprivation of any rights, privileges, or immunities secured by the Constitution and laws, shall be liable to the party injured in an action at law, . . ." 42 U.S.C. § 1983.

Under this statute, a person who acts or pretends to act as a state official in a governmental capacity is said to be acting under **color of law**, or, to be specific, under color of *state* law. If that person deprives someone of a federal civil right, a special cause of action arises.

civil rights Basic individual rights guaranteed by the U.S. Constitution and by special federal statutes. Included are the right to vote, to choose one's vocation, to marry, to be accorded due process, and to equal protection under law.

Civil Rights Act of 1871 A federal statute that gives a person a right to sue a government employee who deprives the person of a federal right under color of state law (42 U.S.C. § 1983).

color of law Acting or pretending to act in an official, governmental capacity. Usually refers to state official or state governmental capacity.

EXAMPLE

Fred Jamison is a state police officer. He sees Loretta Walker driving down the street. Jamison decides to give Walker a speeding ticket solely because she is black. Jamison knows that she was not speeding at the time.

Such racial discrimination is forbidden by the Equal Protection Clause of the United States Constitution. Since Jamison was charging Walker with violating the speeding law (a state law), the police officer was acting under color of law when he deprived Walker of the constitutional right not to be subjected to racial discrimination. Walker can sue Jamison under § 1983 of the Civil Rights Act. A civil rights suit seeking damages under this Act is called a **1983 action**, which asserts a federal cause of action called a **1983 tort**. The phrase **constitutional tort** refers to a special cause of action that arises when someone is deprived of federal civil rights. The generic name for this constitutional law tort cause of action is *civil rights violation*. For its elements, see Exhibit 27–8.

Exhibit 27-8
Elements of a civil rights violation.

1. A person acting under color of law
2. Deprives someone of a federal right

1983 action A suit based on § 1983 of the Civil Rights Act of 1871 against a government employee who deprives someone of a federal civil right under color of state law. The deprivation is called a *1983 tort*.

1983 tort A deprivation of a federal civil right under color of state law.

constitutional tort A special cause of action that arises when someone is deprived of a federal civil right under color of state law. Also called a *1983 tort*.

Liability for a traditional common-law tort such as battery is separate from liability for a constitutional tort. It is possible for a government employee to commit a constitutional tort that is not, in addition, a common-law tort. An example is the Jamison/Walker case just discussed. There is no indication that the police officer committed a common-law tort when he wrote the ticket, but he did commit a constitutional tort for which he might be liable in a 1983 action. Sometimes, however, the wrong committed by the employee is both a common-law tort and a constitutional tort:

EXAMPLES

- A police officer punches a citizen (battery) to prevent him or her from voting.
- A government tax auditor destroys the flag of a citizen (conversion) in order to stop him or her from participating in a lawful demonstration.

A plaintiff can assert the common-law tort and the constitutional tort in the same lawsuit. A major benefit of winning a constitutional tort is that attorney fees can be awarded, whereas for common-law torts, the parties pay their own attorneys.

Finally we come to the third question posed earlier. Can a government official who has committed a tort within the scope of employment avoid liability through the defense of official immunity? It may be clear that a government official has committed a common-law tort, a constitutional tort, or both within the scope of employment. Yet the official will not be personally liable if he or she is covered by official immunity.

absolute immunity A defense that avoids personal liability when a government employee is carrying out official functions, even if the employee was acting with malice.

qualified immunity A defense that avoids personal liability when a government employee is carrying out official functions, unless the employee was acting with malice.

Two kinds of official immunity exist: absolute and qualified. **Absolute immunity** avoids personal liability when a government employee is carrying out official functions, and the immunity cannot be lost if the employee was acting with malice. **Qualified immunity** avoids personal liability when a government employee is carrying out official functions, but the immunity can be lost if the employee was acting with malice. Here is an overview of who can claim these immunities:

- Judges and legislators. These employees have absolute immunity for common-law torts and for constitutional torts.
- High administrative officials. In most states, these officials have absolute immunity for common-law torts and qualified immunity for constitutional torts.
- Lower-level administrative officials who exercise considerable discretion in their job. These officials have qualified immunity for common-law torts and qualified immunity for constitutional torts.
- Lower-level administrative officials who function at the **ministerial** level with little or no discretion. In many states, these employees have no immunity for common-law torts (unless a special statute provides otherwise) and qualified immunity for constitutional torts.

ministerial Involving a duty that is to be performed in a prescribed manner with little or no judgment or discretion involved.

See also Exhibit 27–9 for an outline of who can claim the immunities and how they can be lost.

Exhibit 27–9 Official immunity of government employees for common-law torts and for violations of the Civil Rights Act.

The Government Employees	Official Immunity for Common-Law Torts	How the Official Immunity for Common-Law Torts Can Be Lost	Official Immunity for Violations of the Civil Rights Act (Constitutional Torts)
Judges and legislators	Absolute immunity for torts committed in the scope of their employment even if they acted maliciously.	a. They did not commit the tort while performing their judicial or legislative role. b. They acted totally outside their authority or jurisdiction. **Note:** The immunity is not lost if they acted merely in excess of their authority.	Absolute immunity for violations of the Act committed under color of law even if they acted maliciously. (The immunity is lost, however, for the same two reasons listed in the third column.)
High administrative officials	Same as for judges and legislators.	Same as for judges and legislators. In some states, however, they have a qualified immunity that is defeated by malice.	Qualified immunity, which is lost if a reasonable official would believe that the conduct violated a "clearly established" constitutional or statutory right.
Lower-level administrative officials (e.g., prosecutors) who exercise considerable discretion in their job	Qualified immunity for torts committed within the scope of their employment.	a. They did not commit the tort within the scope of their employment. b. They acted totally outside their authority. c. They acted maliciously or not in good faith.	Qualified immunity. Same as for high administrative officials.
Lower-level administrative officials who function at the ministerial level with little or no discretion	No immunity in many states. They are personally liable for their torts, whether or not they acted in good faith or without malice. Statutes may have been passed, however, that provide absolute or qualified immunity for such employees.		Qualified immunity. Same as for high administrative officials.

Note: The words "immunity" and "privilege" are sometimes used interchangeably in this area of the law. Absolute immunity, for example, is often referred to as absolute privilege, and qualified immunity as qualified privilege. The practical effect of either word, however, is the same with respect to the ultimate question of whether the government official will be personally liable. (For more on the distinction between immunity and privilege, see Exhibit 7–3 in Chapter 7.)

Unfortunately, the distinction between discretionary functions and ministerial functions is often unclear. In general, ministerial functions are duties performed in a prescribed manner with little or no judgment or discretion involved. Ministerial functions occur at the operational level of government. Discretionary functions, on the other hand, involve the choice of options, usually at the policy level.

In Exhibit 27–9, note that when high administrative officials are charged with a violation of the Civil Rights Act (see the fourth column), they have a qualified immunity that is lost if a reasonable official would have believed that his or her conduct violated a "clearly established" constitutional or statutory right. In the case of *Conn and Najera v. Gabbert* on the practice of law, we will examine an allegation by an attorney that such a right was violated.

CASE

Conn and Najera v. Gabbert

119 S. Ct. 1292, 143 L. Ed. 2d 399 (1999)
United States Supreme Court

Background: *Paul Gabbert was an attorney for Traci Baker, a witness appearing before the grand jury in a nationally-publicized state criminal trial involving two brothers accused of murdering their wealthy parents in Beverly Hills. While Baker was being questioned, the prosecutors obtained a search warrant and searched Gabbert for evidence Baker may have given him earlier. Gabbert then brought a § 1983 action against the prosecutors for damages, claiming that their search interfered with his "clearly established" constitutional right to practice law. The Fourteenth Amendment says that no state shall "deprive any person of life, liberty, or property without due process of law." Part of the "liberty" protected by this clause is the right to practice one's employment. If the state unreasonably interferes with this liberty right, the victim can sue for damages under § 1983. Government officials such as prosecutors have a qualified immunity against such suits as long as they have not violated a "clearly established" right. Gabbert argued that his right to practice law without unreasonable interference was "clearly established" at the time the prosecutors violated it. The trial court (a U.S. Federal District Court) disagreed and dismissed the § 1983 action. Gabbert appealed to the Court of Appeals. During oral argument at the Court of Appeals, one of the judges expressed shock at what had occurred: "If you described what happened in this case to a stranger and didn't [say] what country it had happened in, America is not the first place that would come to mind." The Court of Appeals reversed the District Court and held that the prosecutors had violated Gabbert's right to practice law, thus reinstating his § 1983 action. The prosecutors then petitioned to the United States Supreme Court to reverse the Court of Appeals. They are the petitioners; Gabbert, the respondent, is responding to their petition.*

Decision on Appeal: *Judgment reversed. Gabbert's Fourteenth Amendment right to practice his calling was not violated by the search ordered by the prosecutors. His client had no right to have him present during the grand jury proceeding. An attorney has a Fourteenth Amendment right to practice his profession, but this right can be restricted by reasonable government regulation. Since Gabbert was subjected to no more than reasonable regulation when he was forced to submit to a search warrant, his right to practice law was not violated. This defeats the basis of the § 1983 action. There is no need, therefore, to decide whether the prosecutors lost their qualified immunity by violating a "clearly established" right.*

OPINION OF COURT

Chief Justice REHNQUIST delivered the opinion of the court . . .:

This case arises out of the high-profile California trials of the "Menendez Brothers," Lyle and Erik Menendez, for the murder of their parents. Petitioners David Conn and Carol Najera are Los Angeles County Deputy District Attorneys, and respondent Paul Gabbert is a criminal defense attorney. In early 1994, after the first Menendez trial ended in a hung jury, the Los Angeles County District Attorney's Office assigned Conn and Najera to prosecute the case on retrial. Conn and Najera learned that Lyle Menendez had written a letter to Traci Baker, his former girlfriend, in which he may have instructed her to testify falsely at trial. Gabbert represented Baker, who had testified as a defense witness in the first trial. Conn obtained and served Baker with a subpoena directing her to testify before the Los Angeles County grand jury and also directing her to produce at that time any correspondence that she had received from Lyle Menendez. After Gabbert unsuccessfully sought to quash the portion of the subpoena directing Baker to produce the Menendez correspondence, Conn and Najera obtained a warrant to search Baker's apartment for any such correspondence. When police tried to execute the warrant, Baker told the police that she had given all her letters from Menendez to Gabbert.

Three days later, on March 21, 1994, Baker appeared as directed before the grand jury, accompanied by Gabbert. Believing that Gabbert might have the letter on his person, Conn directed a police detective to secure a warrant to search Gabbert. . . . California law provides that a warrant to search an attorney must be executed by a court-appointed special master. When the Special Master arrived, Gabbert requested that the search take place in a private room. He did not request that his client's grand jury testimony be postponed. The Special Master searched Gabbert in the private room, and Gabbert produced two pages of a three-page letter from Lyle Menendez to Baker.

At approximately the same time that the search of Gabbert was taking place, Najera called Baker before the grand jury and began to question her. After being sworn, Najera asked Baker whether she was acquainted with Lyle Menendez. Baker replied that she had been unable to speak with her attorney because he was "still with the special master." A short recess was taken during which time Baker was unable to speak with Gabbert. He was aware that Baker sought to speak with him, but apparently stated that the prosecutors would simply have to delay the questioning until they finished searching him. Baker returned to the grand jury room and declined to answer the question "upon the advice of my counsel" on the basis of her Fifth Amendment privilege against self-incrimination. Najera asked a follow-up question, and Baker again asked for a short recess to confer with Gabbert. Baker was again unable to locate Gabbert, and she again returned to the grand jury room and asserted her Fifth Amendment privilege. At this point, the grand jury recessed.

Believing that the actions of the prosecutors were illegal, Gabbert brought suit against them and other officials in Federal District Court under 42 U.S.C. § 1983. Relevant to this appeal by Conn and Najera, he contended that his Fourteenth Amendment right to practice his profession without unreasonable government interference was violated when the prosecutors executed a search warrant at the same time his client was testifying before the grand jury. [The District Court ruled for the prosecutors on the basis that their actions were protected by qualified immunity.]

The Court of Appeals reversed in part, holding that Conn and Najera were not entitled to qualified immunity on Gabbert's Fourteenth Amendment claim. 131 F.3d 793 (C.A.9 1997). Relying on *Board of Regents of State Colleges v. Roth,* 408 U.S. 564 (1972), and earlier cases of this Court recognizing a right to choose one's vocation, the Court of Appeals concluded that Gabbert had a right to practice his profession without undue and unreasonable government interference. The Court of Appeals also held that . . . the right allegedly violated in this case was clearly established, and as a result, Conn and Najera were not entitled to qualified immunity: "The plain and intended result [of the prosecutors' actions] was to prevent Gabbert from consulting with Baker during her grand jury appearance. These actions were not objectively reasonable, and thus the prosecutors are not protected by qualified immunity from answering Gabbert's Fourteenth Amendment claim." Id., at 802–803. We granted certiorari and now reverse.

Section 1983 provides a federal cause of action against any person who, acting under color of state law, deprives another of his federal rights. 42 U.S.C. § 1983. In order to prevail in a § 1983 action for civil damages from a government official performing discretionary functions, the defense of qualified immunity that our cases have recognized requires that the official be shown to have violated "clearly established statutory or constitutional rights of which a reasonable person would have known." *Harlow v. Fitzgerald,* 457 U.S. 800 (1982). Thus a court must first determine whether the plaintiff has alleged the deprivation of an actual constitutional right at all, and if so, proceed to determine whether that right was clearly established at the time of the alleged violation. See *Siegert v. Gilley,* 500 U.S. 226, 232–233 (1991).

We find no support in our cases for the conclusion of the Court of Appeals that Gabbert had a Fourteenth Amendment right which was violated in this case. The Court of Appeals relied primarily on *Board of Regents v. Roth.* In *Roth,* this Court repeated the pronouncement in *Meyer v. Nebraska,* 262 U.S. 390, 399 (1923) that the liberty guaranteed by the Fourteenth Amendment "'denotes not merely freedom from bodily restraint but also the right of the individual to contract, to engage in any of the common occupations of life, to acquire useful knowledge, to marry, establish a home and bring up children, to worship God according to the dictates of his own conscience, and generally to enjoy those privileges long recognized . . . as essential to the orderly pursuit of happiness by free men.'" *Roth,* supra, at 572 (quoting *Meyer,* supra, at 399). But neither *Roth* nor *Meyer* even came close to identifying the asserted "right" violated by the prosecutors in this case. *Meyer* held that [a state could not pass a law] that prohibited teaching in any language other than English. And *Roth* . . . held that an at-will college professor had no "property" interest in his job within the meaning of the Fourteenth Amendment so as to require the university to hold a hearing before terminating him. . . . Neither case supports the conclusion that the actions of the prosecutors in this case deprived Gabbert of a liberty interest in practicing law.

Similarly, none of the other cases relied upon by the Court of Appeals or suggested by Gabbert provide any more than scant metaphysical support for the idea that the use of a search warrant by government actors violates an attorney's right to practice his profession. In a line of earlier cases, this Court has indicated that the liberty component of the Fourteenth Amendment's Due Process Clause includes some generalized due process right to choose one's field of private employment, but a right which is nevertheless subject to reasonable government regulation. See, e.g., *Dent v. West Virginia,* 129 U.S. 114 (1889) (upholding a requirement of licensing before a person can practice medicine); *Truax v. Raich,* 239 U.S. 33 (1915) (invalidating on equal protection grounds a state law requiring companies to employ 80% United States citizens). These cases all deal with a complete prohibition of the right to engage in a calling, and not the sort of brief interruption which occurred here.

Gabbert also relies on *Schware v. Board of Bar Examiners of N.M.,* 353 U.S. 232, 238–239, 77 S. Ct. 752, 1 L. Ed. 2d 796 (1957), for the proposition that a State cannot exclude a person from the practice of law for reasons that contravene the Due Process Clause. *Schware* held that former membership in the Communist Party and an arrest record relating to union activities could not be the basis for completely excluding a person from the practice of law. Like *Dent,* supra, and *Truax,* supra, it does not deal with a brief interruption as a result of legal process. No case of this Court has held that such an intrusion can rise to the level of a violation of the Fourteenth Amendment's liberty right to choose and follow one's calling. That right is simply not infringed by the inevitable interruptions of our daily routine as a result of legal process which all of us may experience from time to time. . . .

We hold that the Fourteenth Amendment right to practice one's calling is not violated by the execution of a search warrant, whether calculated to annoy or even to prevent consultation with a grand jury witness. In so holding, [there is no need to address] the question of whether such a right was "clearly established" as of a given day. The judgment of the Court of Appeals holding to the contrary is therefore reversed.

It is so ordered.

ASSIGNMENT 27.15

a. Why didn't the Court have to decide whether the prosecutors had lost their qualified immunity?
b. Would the Court have reached a different result and ruled in favor of Gabbert if the state had revoked his license to practice law because he had the letter?

THE DEFENSE OF CHARITABLE IMMUNITY

charitable immunity A charitable organization is not liable for the torts that its workers commit.

There was a time when a charitable, educational, religious, or other benevolent organization enjoyed an immunity for the torts it committed in the course of its work. The law was reluctant to allow the resources of such organizations to be depleted in a suit brought against the organization because of a tort committed by one of its employees or volunteers. **Charitable immunity**, however, was never complete. An organization, for example, was liable for its negligence in selecting personnel and in raising money. Most states, however, have abolished the immunity altogether, and other states have severely restricted its applicability, particularly in light of the availability of liability insurance that charitable organizations can purchase to cover tort actions against them.

At the end of the twentieth century, numerous lawsuits were brought against priests and the Catholic Church for the sexual abuse of children by priests and the resulting cover-up of this abuse by church officials. If a state still had the defense of charitable immunity, it was often raised in the suits. In some of these states, the defendants were successful with the defense. In others, the defense was interpreted narrowly. For example, a court might rule that the defense protected the church but not individual perpetrators. Some courts ruled that the defense was available for negligent conduct that led to the abuse or the church's response to it, but did not prevent liability for the extensive intentional conduct that most of the abuse entailed.

THE DEFENSE OF INTRAFAMILY TORT IMMUNITY

intrafamily tort immunity Family members cannot sue each other for designated categories of torts.

Suppose that one family member wrongfully injures another. Can they sue each other in tort? If they are not allowed to do so, it is because of the **intrafamily tort immunity**. This topic is covered in Exhibit 22–1 at the end of Chapter 22 on Torts Against and Within the Family.

CHECK THE CITE

Plaintiffs alleged that defendants induced the plaintiffs to enter a residential group psychiatric treatment program by false representations as to the therapeutic value and limited term of the program. In fact, the plaintiffs claimed that the defendants used the program as a pretext to employ psychological coercion, humiliation, and physical violence to subjugate the plaintiffs, to coerce them to remain in the residential program, to give the defendants donations, to recruit new patients, and to believe that their well-being depended upon remaining in the program and loyally serving defendants to the exclusion of the outside world. How did the court resolve the defense of the defendants that the plaintiffs consented to the treatment program? Read the case of *Rains v. Superior Court*, 150 Cal. App. 3d 933, 198 Cal. Rptr. 249 (Ct. App. 1984). To read the case online, (1) Go to Findlaw (caselaw .lp.findlaw.com/ca/calapp3d/150.html). You will need to sign up for a free account.

(2) Go to FindACase (www.findacase.com). Select California. Run a citation search. Select 198 for the volume, Cal. Rptr. for the reporter, and 249 for the page. (3) Run a citation search ("198 Cal. Rptr. 249") or a party search (Rains Superior Court) in the Legal Opinions and Journals database of Google Scholar (scholar.google.com).

PROJECT

In Google, Bing, or another general search engine, run the following search: *aa* "sovereign immunity" tort (substitute the name of your state for *aa* in the search, e.g., Louisiana "sovereign immunity" tort). Write a short essay in which you describe the law in your state on when the state can be sued for torts committed by a state employee. Explain the extent to which sovereign immunity prevents suits for such torts in your state. You can consult as many websites as you wish, but you must quote from at least three separate sites, only one of which can be a law firm site.

ETHICS IN A TORTS PRACTICE

You are a paralegal working in the law office of Harold Dunton, Esq. You are also a notary. Dunton wants you to notarize a document for one of the clients in the office. The notarized document must be filed in court by tomorrow noon. Dunton gives you the document and asks you to notarize it. The client already signed it yesterday before going out of town for two weeks. You make a long-distance call to the client to confirm that the client signed the document. You then notarize it as instructed. What ethical problems, if any, might exist?

SUMMARY

A defense is the response of a party to a claim of another party, setting forth the reason(s) the claim should not be granted. The defense of privilege is the right to act contrary to the right of another without being subject to tort or other liability. It authorizes conduct that would otherwise be wrongful. The defense of immunity treats wrongful conduct as nonwrongful. It is a complete defense to a tort claim, whether or not the defendant committed the tort.

Consent is a defense to most torts. The plaintiff must have the capacity to consent and must voluntarily manifest the consent. The test is the reasonableness of the defendant's belief that the plaintiff consented, not the plaintiff's subjective state of mind. For the consent to be valid, the plaintiff must know the nature and consequences of what the defendant wants to do; gaining consent by misrepresentation renders the consent invalid.

There are several self-help privileges. The defendant can use reasonable force to protect him- or herself in the reasonable belief that the plaintiff will immediately inflict harmful or offensive contact on the defendant (self-defense). The defendant can use reasonable force to prevent the plaintiff from immediately inflicting on a third person harmful or offensive contact, which the plaintiff does not have the privilege to inflict (defense of others). If the defendant reasonably believes that persons or property will be immediately injured or damaged, he or she can make reasonable use of the plaintiff's personal property or land to prevent the injury or damage (necessity). If the defendant possesses land or chattels and this right of possession is superior to the plaintiff's claim of possession, the defendant can use reasonable force to prevent the plaintiff's immediately threatened interference with the defendant's possession or to end an interference with such property that just started (defense of property). If the plaintiff wrongfully acquires possession of a chattel and the defendant has the right to immediate possession, the defendant can use reasonable force to recapture it shortly after the plaintiff takes possession (recapture of chattels).

Under the Federal Tort Claims Act, the federal government has waived sovereign immunity for designated torts. Examples include negligence at the operational (non-policy-making) level, trespass to land committed by any federal employee, and battery or false arrest committed by a federal law enforcement officer. Further exceptions apply for which sovereign immunity is not waived, such as claims based on the negligent transmission of the mail.

State governments differ on the extent to which sovereign immunity is waived. The state often retains its immunity to cover the conduct of its judges, legislators, and high administrative officers. The less discretion and policy involvement a state employee has, the more likely the state will waive its sovereign immunity for harm caused by that employee. Local governments often waive their sovereign immunity for the proprietary functions they perform, but not for their governmental functions.

Government employees with official immunity cannot be personally liable for the common-law or constitutional torts they commit within the scope of their employment. (A constitutional tort is a special cause of action, such as a 1983 action, that arises when someone is deprived of a federal civil right under color of state law.) Generally, judges, legislators, and high administrative officials have an absolute immunity; lower-level officials who exercise considerable discretion in their jobs have a qualified immunity; and lower-level officials who exercise little or no discretion in their jobs have no official immunity unless changed by statute.

Most states have eliminated or substantially restricted the charitable immunity that once relieved charities and similar organizations of liability for their torts.

KEY TERMS

defense *572*
privilege *572*
immunity *572*
volenti non fit injuria *572*
consent *572*
implied consent *573*
coercion *574*
informed consent *575*
self-help *579*
extrajudicial *579*
self-defense *580*
defense of others *581*
necessity *583*
private necessity *583*
public necessity *583*
abate a nuisance *583*
defense of property *584*
chattel *587*
recapture of chattels *587*
dispossession *587*
fresh pursuit *587*
shopkeeper's privilege *587*
squatter *588*
unlawful detainer *589*
ejectment *589*
in loco parentis *590*
arrest *590*
sovereign immunity *590*
respondeat superior *590*
official immunity *590*
just compensation *590*
taking *590*
Federal Tort Claims Act (FTCA) *591*
governmental function *593*
proprietary function *593*
personal liability *594*
vicarious liability *594*
civil rights *595*
Civil Rights Act of 1871 *595*
color of law *595*
1983 action *596*
1983 tort *596*
constitutional tort *596*
absolute immunity *596*
qualified immunity *596*
ministerial *596*
charitable immunity *600*
intrafamily tort immunity *600*

REVIEW QUESTIONS

1. What is a defense?
2. How does a privilege differ from an immunity?
3. What is the meaning of *volenti non fit injuria*?
4. What are the elements of consent?
5. Can someone consent to criminal conduct?
6. What is implied consent?
7. How does someone decide if his or her conduct is consented to?
8. What is informed consent?
9. What is a self-help privilege?
10. What are the major self-help privileges?
11. What are the elements of the defense of self-defense?
12. What is the effect of mistake in using this privilege?
13. Can deadly force be used?

14. What are the elements of the defense of defense of others?
15. What is the effect of mistake in using this privilege?
16. Can deadly force be used?
17. What are the elements of the defense of necessity?
18. How does private necessity differ from public necessity?
19. What are the elements of the defense of defense of property?
20. What is the effect of mistake in using this privilege?
21. Can deadly force be used?
22. What is the defense of abating a nuisance?
23. What are the elements of the defense of recapture of chattels?
24. What is the shopkeeper's privilege?
25. What actions are the preferred methods of retaking possession of land?
26. What is the defense of discipline?
27. What is sovereign immunity?
28. When has the federal government waived sovereign immunity?
29. When has a state government waived sovereign immunity?
30. When has a local government waived sovereign immunity?
31. How does sovereign immunity differ from official immunity?
32. What is a constitutional tort?
33. How does absolute immunity differ from qualified immunity?
34. Who is entitled to absolute immunity?
35. Who is entitled to qualified immunity?
36. What is charitable immunity?
37. What is intrafamily tort immunity?

HELPFUL WEBSITES

- **Defenses to Intentional Torts**
  sparkcharts.sparknotes.com/legal/torts/section3.php
  www.myazbar.org/seccomm/committees/ciji/ciji-pdf/intentionaltorts.pdf
- **Consent in Tort law**
  www.lexisnexis.com/lawschool/study/outlines/html/torts/torts02.htm
  en.wikipedia.org/wiki/Consent
  www.answers.com/topic/consent
- **Sovereign Immunity**
  topics.law.cornell.edu/wex/sovereign_immunity
  www.justicelives.com
  en.wikipedia.org/wiki/Sovereign_immunity
  www.copyright.gov/docs/regstat72700.html
- **Charitable Immunity**
  www.ohioafp.org/pdfs/members/CharityImmunityLaws.pdf
  www.premack.com/links/cil-stat.htm
  www.lexisnexis.com/lawschool/study/outlines/html/torts/torts02.htm

ENDNOTES

1. See *Neal v. Neal*, 125 Idaho 617, 873 P.2d 871 (1994).
2. 28 U.S.C. §§ 2671 et seq., 1346.
3. W. Page Keeton et al., *Prosser and Keeton on the Law of Torts* 1053 (5th ed. 1984). See also *Restatement (Second) of Torts* § 895C (1965).
4. *Barr v. Matteo*, 360 U.S. 564, 571, 79 S. Ct. 1335, 3 L. Ed. 2d 1434 (1959).

Student StudyWARE™ CD-ROM
For additional materials, please go to the student CD in this book.

CHAPTER

28

WORKERS' COMPENSATION

CHAPTER OUTLINE

- Introduction
- On-the-Job Injuries at Common Law
- Workers' Compensation Statutes
- Injuries and Diseases Covered
- Filing a Claim
- Benefits Available
- Tort Claims Against Third Parties
- Reform

CHAPTER OBJECTIVES

After completing this chapter, you should be able to:

- Understand how worker injuries were handled at common law.
- State the three major defenses that often defeated tort litigation for employee injuries at common law.
- Describe the system of workers' compensation as an alternative to tort litigation.
- Determine whether an injury is within the course of employment.
- Explain how to determine whether an injury arises out of employment.
- Explain how a workers' compensation claim is filed.
- State how tort litigation can be brought against third parties in cases of employee injuries.
- Describe some of the major reform proposals for the workers' compensation system.

INTRODUCTION

Every year, about $170 billion is spent by businesses on costs associated with on-the-job injuries and illnesses. Just under $1 billion is paid every week to injured or ill workers and their doctors or other medical providers.[1] According to the U.S. Bureau of Labor Statistics, in 2007 there were

- 5,657 fatal occupational injuries
- 4,002,700 nonfatal occupational injuries and illnesses[2]

Under the common law, the major remedy of the worker was to sue the employer for negligence. This was not a satisfactory option. Not only was negligence difficult to prove, but also, as we will see, the employer could use some powerful defenses that effectively defeated the vast majority of such negligence suits. After 1910, however, a separate system was created under which the cost of worker injuries was spread over an entire industry or enterprise regardless of who was negligent or at fault. This **no-fault** system of enterprise responsibility is called **workers' compensation**. Before examining its scope, we need to take a closer look at the common-law fault system that workers' compensation was designed to replace for most workers.

no fault Pertaining to legal consequences (e.g., paying insurance benefits or granting a divorce) that will occur regardless of who was at fault or to blame.

workers' compensation A no-fault system of paying for medical care and providing limited wage benefits to a worker for an employment-related injury or illness regardless of who was at fault in causing the injury or illness.

contributory negligence The failure of plaintiffs to take reasonable precautions for their protection, helping to cause their own injury or other loss.

willful 1. Acting with the knowledge that harm will probably result. 2. Voluntary and deliberate. 3. Malicious.

wanton Extremely reckless.

last clear chance Plaintiffs who have been contributorily negligent in placing themselves in peril can still recover if a negligent defendant had the last opportunity (clear chance) to avoid the accident and failed to exercise reasonable care to do so.

assumption of the risk The knowing and voluntary acceptance of the danger or risk of being harmed by someone's negligence.

fellow-servant rule An employer will not be liable for injuries to an employee caused by the negligence of another employee—a fellow servant—unless the negligent employee was a superior or someone with responsibility for safety on the job (referred to as a vice principal).

strict liability Responsibility for harm even if one did not intend the harm and used reasonable care to try to prevent it. Responsibility for harm whether or not the person causing the harm was at any fault or engaged in any moral impropriety. Also called absolute liability and liability without fault.

ON-THE-JOB INJURIES AT COMMON LAW

Before workers' compensation was created, an employee with a work-related injury or illness had to bring a negligence action that tried to prove that the employer unreasonably failed to provide a safe work environment. It was relatively easy for the employer to win such cases because of the ready availability of the following three defenses:

Contributory negligence: The employee acted unreasonably, which contributed to his or her own injury or illness along with the negligence of the employer. The contributory negligence of the employee prevented recovery against the employer (unless the latter's negligence was **willful** or **wanton**, or unless the employer failed to take the **last clear chance** (see Chapter 17) to avoid the injury).

Assumption of the risk: The employee knew about the hazards of the job and voluntarily took the job or voluntarily remained on the job, even though the employee understood the dangers involved. Assumption of the risk defeated the employee's recovery for the employer's negligence.

Fellow-servant rule: The employer was not liable for an employee injury or illness that was caused by the negligence of a fellow employee. An exception existed when the fellow employee was a vice principal, i.e., an employee with supervisory authority over other employees or an employee of any rank who has been given some responsibility for the safety of the work environment. The employer *will* be liable if the employee suffers an injury or illness because of the negligence of a fellow employee who is a vice principal.

WORKERS' COMPENSATION STATUTES

Throughout the country, workers' compensation statutes have been passed by the legislatures as an alternative to the common-law negligence system. Under these statutes, an employee will receive compensation for a work-related injury or illness without having to prove that the employer was negligent. Hence, the liability of the employer under such a statute is a form of **strict liability**. This means there is no need to prove that the employer caused the injury negligently. It is a no-fault system. The defenses of contributory negligence, assumption of the risk, and the

fellow-servant rule are abolished. See Exhibit 28–1 for an overview of the advantages and disadvantages of workers' compensation.

Exhibit 28–1
Benefits/disadvantages of workers' compensation (WC).

ADVANTAGES	
To Employee	**To Employer**
• In a WC case, there is no need to prove the employer was negligent. • Contributory negligence, assumption of risk, and the fellow-servant rule cannot defeat a WC case—they are not defenses in a WC case. • The WC administrative procedure is quicker and less costly than a suit for negligence in court. • Recovery of benefits in a WC case is usually quicker than filing an action for negligence in court.	• Limited liability: the cash benefits awarded an employee under WC are limited to set amounts specified by statute, whereas a negligence judgment in court against the employer could be much higher. • The WC administrative procedure is quicker and less costly than a negligence suit in court.
DISADVANTAGES	
To Employee	**To Employer**
• Recovery of cash benefits in a WC case is usually smaller than damages awarded in a successful negligence case in court. • Critics charge that employers (1) pressure injured workers not to file for WC benefits and (2) cause undue delays by disputing claims that are filed.	• Critics charge that the WC system is riddled with fraud. The temptation to fabricate a WC claim is large. Consequently, WC insurance premiums paid by employers are very high.

Not all employers and employees are covered under workers' compensation. When employees are not covered, they are left with a traditional negligence action in which they must face the "unholy trinity" of defenses: contributory negligence,[3] assumption of risk, and the fellow-servant rule.

The primary way in which the workers' compensation system is financed is through insurance. An employer must either purchase insurance or prove that it is financially able to cover any risks on its own. The latter is called **self-insurance.** When insurance is purchased, it comes either from a state-operated insurance fund or from a private insurer or carrier.

self-insurance The ability to pay government-mandated benefits (e.g., workers' compensation) out of one's own funds rather than through a government fund or an insurance policy.

Every state has an agency or commission that administers the workers' compensation law for employees in the private sector. (See Appendix A for the agency or commission in your state.) It may be an independent entity or be part of the state's department of labor. Government employees have a separate workers' compensation system to cover their employment. Workers' compensation for nonmilitary employees of the federal government, for example, is administered by the Office of Workers' Compensation Programs within the U.S. Department of Labor.[4] In this chapter, our focus is workers' compensation for employees in the private sector.

The statutory code of your state will list the categories of employers and employees covered by workers' compensation in the private sector. It is important to note the definitions of employer, employee, employment, and any other word that will tell you who is and who is not covered. Some codes may say that everyone is covered except those specifically excluded, such as domestic workers, farm workers, casual workers, independent contractors, or people who work for employers with fewer than a certain number of employees.

ASSIGNMENT 28.1

List the name, address, phone number, e-mail address, and World Wide Web address of the central office of the agency in your state that administers the workers' compensation law for employees in the private sector? This information should be available online. (See also Appendix A for this and related sites for your state.)

INJURIES AND DISEASES COVERED

Not every on-the-job misfortune is covered under workers' compensation. A few states, for example, do not cover certain diseases that occur as a result of long-term exposure to conditions or hazards at a job. In most states, however, diseases as well as accidents are covered.

arise out of To be a causal link or connection; to cause; to stem from.

in the course of Pertaining to the time, place, and circumstances of the injury or illness in connection with the employment. Occurring while at work or in the service of the employer.

The basic requirement is that the employee's injury must **arise out of** and occur **in the course of** employment. "Arising out of" refers to the causal connection between the injury and the employment; "in the course of" refers to the time, place, and circumstances of the injury in connection with the employment. We will explore both issues through the following themes:

In the Course of Employment
1. while clearly at work
2. while going to or coming from work
3. during trips
4. during horseplay and misconduct
5. while engaged in personal comfort

Arising Out of Employment
1. causal-connection tests
2. acts of nature
3. street risks
4. assault and battery
5. personal risks

In the Course of Employment

1. While Clearly at Work The vast majority of injuries occur while the worker is clearly at work, e.g., a hand is injured while operating a printing press, or death results from an explosion while the worker is in a mine. In most cases of this kind, there is little doubt that the worker will receive workers' compensation benefits.

going-and-coming rule Workers' compensation is denied if the employee is injured "off the premises" while going to or coming back from work or lunch. (See glossary for an additional meaning.)

incident to employment Sufficiently connected or related to an employee's job duties.

2. While Going to or Coming from Work A **going-and-coming rule** exists in most states: workers' compensation is denied if the employee is injured "off the premises" while going to or coming back from work or while going to or coming back from lunch. The company parking lot is usually considered part of the employer's premises, so that there *is* coverage if the employee is injured while on the lot. A number of exceptions have been created to the going-and-coming rule. For example, if the route to work exposes the worker to special dangers or risks (e.g., passing through a "rough" neighborhood to get to the plant), the injury will be considered within the "course of employment" even though it technically occurred beyond the premises owned or leased by the employer. Such risks are said to be **incident to employment**. The court will conclude that there is a close association between the access route and the premises of the employer.[5] Some courts also make an exception if the injury occurs when the employee is on a public sidewalk or street that is close to the premises of the employer.

3. During Trips Of course, any trip made by the employee that is part of a job responsibility is within the course of employment, and an injury that occurs on such a trip will be covered by workers' compensation, e.g., injury while making a sales trip or a delivery. Even if the employee is going to or from work, the trip will be considered part of the employment if the trip is a special assignment or service for the employer, e.g., an employee is injured when asked to return to the shop after work hours to check on an alarm or to let someone in. It is not always necessary to show that the employee is paid extra compensation for such a trip, but when such compensation is paid, the argument is strengthened that the trip is within the course of employment.

Suppose, however, that the trip serves a *personal* purpose of the employee as well as a business purpose of the employer. This is a **dual-purpose trip**.

dual-purpose trip An employee trip that has both a business and a personal purpose. Also called a mixed-purpose trip.

EXAMPLE

Helen is asked by her boss to rent a car so that she can deliver a package to a certain city. She takes along two of her friends so that the three of them can attend a party after Helen makes the delivery. While on her way to the city, Helen is injured in a traffic accident.

Helen had a business purpose for the trip (make the delivery) and a personal purpose (go to a party with her friends). Under the law of workers' compensation, a dual-purpose trip will be considered a business trip (and hence covered by workers' compensation) if the trip would have been made even if the personal objective did not exist. The business nature of the trip is established once it can be said that the trip must be made at some time by someone whether or not the person making the trip will also attend to personal matters.

Suppose that an employee is on a purely business trip. While on the trip, however, the employee decides to take a detour for personal reasons, e.g., to visit a relative or to inquire into another job. The general rule is that the employee is not covered by workers' compensation if injured while on a personal detour (sometimes called a **frolic**). Once the personal detour has been completed and the employee is once more attending to the business purpose of the trip, coverage under the compensation statute resumes.

frolic Employee conduct outside the scope of employment because it is personal rather than primarily for the employer's business. Also called a frolic and detour.

4. During Horseplay and Misconduct It is not uncommon for workers on the job to be playful with each other or to engage in horseplay. What happens if an employee is injured during such horseplay? If the employee is the innocent victim of the horseplay, he or she will be covered by workers' compensation, e.g., the employee is hit on the head by a hard aluminum-foil ball that other employees were using to "play catch," in which the injured employee was not participating.

Suppose, however, that one of the employees participating in or instigating the horseplay is injured. Such injuries are often not covered by workers' compensation unless it can be shown that the horseplay was a very minor departure from normal work responsibilities, or that the horseplay had been occurring over a long period of time and had, in effect, become customary.

The employee's injury may be caused by his or her own misconduct on the job. Recall what was said earlier about the defense of contributory negligence: the employee's own negligence is not a defense to recovery under workers' compensation. Some workers' compensation statutes, however, provide that if the employee is injured while engaged in willful misconduct, such as the willful failure to use a safety device, workers' compensation benefits *will* be denied or reduced.

It is important to distinguish between the following:

- what the employee has been asked to do—the goal or *objective* of the job, and
- the *method* that the employee uses to carry out the objective

The general rule is that employee misconduct related to the objective of a job leads to no coverage under workers' compensation, but misconduct related to method is still covered.

> **Objective:** A bus ticket clerk who works in a ticket booth violates specific instructions never to drive a bus, and is injured. The injury is not covered under workers' compensation.
>
> **Method:** A bus driver is injured because of careless operation of the bus. The injury is covered by workers' compensation.

Other examples of injuries that grow out of the method of doing the job and hence are covered under workers' compensation include reaching into a machine before stopping it, climbing over a fence rather than walking around it, repairing a machine while it is still operating, and using a machine with its safety guard removed.[6] Even if these methods of doing the job were specifically prohibited by the employer, workers' compensation will still be allowed unless the statute has an exception for certain willful violations, as already mentioned.

5. While Engaged in Personal Comfort Simply because an employee is injured while taking care of a personal need on the job does not mean that coverage is denied under workers' compensation. When an injury occurs while a worker is taking a lunch break, going to the restroom, or stepping out for a moment of fresh air, workers' compensation is usually provided.[7] Factors that will be considered in reaching this result include whether the accident occurred on the premises and within an authorized area for the activity, whether it occurred within working hours, whether the hazard that led to the accident is considered normal for that work environment, and whether the employer prohibited the activity that led to the accident. (On factor analysis, see Legal Analysis Guideline #12 in Chapter 2.)

Suppose that the employee is injured while engaged in a sports contest at a picnic or other social event involving coworkers. Workers' compensation is applicable if the activity is sponsored by the employer or if the workers are otherwise encouraged to participate by the employer. The more benefit the employer is likely to derive from the activity, the more inclined an agency or a court will be to conclude that the activity was within the course of employment and hence covered by workers' compensation.

ASSIGNMENT 28.2

Examine the following situations to determine whether the injury was within the "course of employment."

a. An employee is killed while crossing a public street immediately in front of her office. She is on her way home when hit by the car of another employee on the way to work.
b. The street in front of the company building is over fifty feet wide and is heavily traveled. An employee, walking to a restaurant during a lunch break, is hit by a car on this street. Another route to the restaurant is available through the rear of the company building. If the employee had used this other route, the trip would have taken an extra twelve minutes.
c. An employee is injured in a public parking lot 800 feet from his place of work. The company parking lot has spaces for only 200 of its 500 employees. The public parking lot is the closest alternative parking lot available.
d. During the work day, the employee is given an old company computer and allowed to take it home on company time. While putting the computer in her car in the company parking lot, she drops the computer and injures her foot.

e. An employee is a company salesperson who travels extensively throughout the city. At 6:00 P.M., the employee makes the last call and is on the way home. The employee is killed in an automobile collision one mile from home.
f. A teacher attends an evening PTA meeting and is on the way home. The teacher stops for a few minutes at a tavern and has half a glass of beer. After leaving the tavern, the teacher is injured in an automobile collision one mile from home.
g. An employee is a lawyer who works for a title insurance company. She usually takes a bus to work. On Tuesday, her employer asks her to come to work as soon as possible. The lawyer takes her car and has a collision on the way to work.
h. A real estate appraiser leaves home to inspect property listed by his employer. On the way, he stops at a jewelry store to buy a present for his wife. He slips in the store and injures his back.
i. An employee is a salesperson. While on a sales trip, she stops at a store to buy some groceries for that evening. The stop takes her ten miles out of the way. While in the store buying her groceries, she meets a prospective customer. After a brief discussion about a possible sale, she injures herself in a fall just outside the store.
j. An employee injures his back while putting out a cigarette in the lunchroom during his lunch break. The employee was leaning down to extinguish the cigarette in a bucket that had sand in it.
k. An employee has a heart attack while dancing at a Christmas party in the company hall.
l. An employee is injured while playing handball in the rear of the plant during a break. Employees have been playing handball there for months in spite of a company sign forbidding play in that area.
m. The elevator door in a company building is broken. All employees are forbidden to use it until it is repaired. Two employees use this elevator and are both injured during a friendly wrestling match while the elevator is in motion.

CASE

Colvin v. Industrial Indemnity

83 Or. App. 73, 730 P.2d 585
Court of Appeals of Oregon (1986)

Background: *Leslie Colvin was a paralegal at a fifty-attorney law firm. While at a law firm picnic, she suffered low back and neck injuries after a fall. No one saw the incident, but she told Ms. Kreft, the firm's senior paralegal, about her injury shortly after it happened. She also told Mr. Lilly, an associate attorney of the firm for whom she frequently worked. Although Leslie missed two days of work following the fall, she did not file a workers' compensation claim because she thought the pain would go away. Two years after the party, however, she filed for workers' compensation because of recurring symptoms during this period. The Workers' Compensation Board denied her claim because she failed to inform her employer about the injury and to file her claim in a timely manner. It also ruled that the injury was not work-related. She appealed to the Court of Appeals, which affirmed the Board's decision. She further appealed to the Supreme Court of Oregon, which reversed and sent the case back (remanded it) to the Court of Appeals. The case is now before the Court of Appeals of Oregon for the second time.*

Decision on Appeal: *Reversed and remanded. The paralegal did give timely notice of her claim to the employer and the injury was in the course of employment.*

OPINION OF COURT

Judge WARDEN delivered the opinion of the court . . . :

We first address the issue of whether the persons claimant told of her injury had supervisory authority over her. [Under the workers' compensation statute in Oregon, a claim is barred if the claimant fails to give a formal notice of injury to the employer unless someone with supervisory authority over the claimant already "had knowledge of the injury." Oregon Revised Statutes 656.265(4)(a).] Claimant was a paralegal in a large law firm. Her injury occurred at a firm picnic. She told Kreft, the firm's senior paralegal, about her injury shortly after it occurred. The next week she mentioned to Lilly, an associate attorney of the firm, that she had fallen and injured her back at the picnic. After reviewing the record, we find that both Kreft and Lilly had supervisory authority over claimant. Both testified that the firm's organization was loosely structured at the time of claimant's injury. Kreft's uncontroverted testimony was that she was the senior paralegal, that she had interviewed claimant before the firm had hired her and that she always represented the paralegals when speaking with the firm's partners concerning issues such as salaries and the need for more secretaries. Lilly . . . said that he worked at least weekly, and often daily, with claimant on cases assigned to him. Both Kreft and Lilly therefore exercised a degree of supervisory authority over claimant. Claimant's failure to give [formal notice of the injury] does not bar her claim, because her employer had knowledge of the injury.

Employer's knowledge, however, is not determinative, by itself, of the issue of compensability. To be compensable, the injury must be one "arising out of and in the course of employment." Oregon Revised Statutes (ORS) 656.005(8)(a). Some discussion of the facts is required for an analysis of whether the picnic at which the injury occurred was sufficiently work-related to make the injury compensable. The facts are undisputed. The picnic was an annual affair, sponsored and paid for entirely by the firm. The organizing committee planned it on company time. It started at noon on a regular workday and lasted until late in the evening. Only the firm's legal and paralegal staff and their spouses were allowed to participate. No clients were present. The paralegals perceived the picnic as one of their job benefits. Attendance was not compulsory, but people were encouraged to attend. If those eligible to attend did not, they were expected to be at work that afternoon. Business was discussed only on an informal and casual basis. Some humorous or "fun" awards were made by the firm to those who participated in athletic events in the afternoon. Claimant was injured at the picnic between 6:30 and 7:00 P.M.

We address the issue of whether "the relationship between the injury and the employment [is] sufficient that the injury should be compensable." *Rogers v. SAIF*, 289 Or. 633, 642, 616 P.2d 485 (1980). [We accept the tests proposed by the commentator, Larson]:

> "Recreational or social activities are within the course of employment when
>
> "(1) They occur on the premises during a lunch or recreation period as a regular incident of the employment; or
>
> "(2) The employer, by expressly or impliedly requiring participation, or by making the activity part of the services of an employee, brings the activity within the orbit of the employment; or
>
> "(3) The employer derives substantial direct benefit from the activity beyond the intangible value of improvement in employee health and morale that is common to all kinds of recreation and social life." 1A. Larson, *Workmen's Compensation Law*, 5-52, § 22.00 (1985).

The three tests are stated in the disjunctive. If claimant's attendance at the picnic satisfies any one of them, it would be within the course of her employment. She concedes that Larson's first test is not met, because the picnic occurred off the firm's premises.

The second test involves the extent to which an employer requires participation or makes the activity part of the services of an employee. We find Larson's analysis helpful: "When the degree of employer involvement descends from compulsion to mere sponsorship or encouragement, the questions become closer, and it becomes necessary to consult a series of tests bearing on work-connection. The most prolific illustrations of this problem are company picnics and office parties. Among the questions to be asked are: Did the employer in fact sponsor the event? To what extent was attendance really voluntary? Was there some degree of encouragement to attend in such factors as taking a record of attendance, paying for the time spent, requiring the employee to work if he did not attend, or maintaining a known custom of attending? Did the employer finance the occasion to a substantial extent? Did the employees regard it as an employment benefit to which they were entitled as a right? Did the employer benefit from the event, not merely in a vague way through better morale and good will, but through such tangible advantages as having an opportunity to make speeches and awards?" 1A. Larson, supra, 5-110, § 22.23 (1985).

The law firm sponsored the picnic and allowed it to be organized on company time. Although attendance was voluntary, the firm did provide encouragement to attend by requiring staff members to work if they did not attend and by paying those who did attend. The firm financed the picnic in its entirety, including box lunches, barbecue dinners and cocktails. The paralegal staff regarded the picnic as one of their employment benefits. Although the firm presumably derived intangible benefits from the picnic through better morale among its employees, we cannot say that it received any more tangible benefits. [We note that under Larson's third test, the picnic does not fall within the course of employment, because the firm gained no benefit from the picnic other than boosting employee morale.] Nevertheless, consideration of all of the factors that Larson lists leads us to conclude that the picnic was an "activity within the orbit of employment."

Employer's insurer argues that, because the injury occurred between 6:30 and 7:00 P.M. and because the normal workday at the firm ended at 5:00 P.M., the injury occurred after any work-connection had terminated. We reject that argument. We hold that claimant's injury arose out of and was within her course of employment. . . . Reversed and remanded to the Workers' Compensation Board with instructions to accept the claim and for determination of compensation.

ASSIGNMENT 28.3

a. How, if at all, do you think the following facts would have affected the outcome of the *Colvin* case, assuming all the other facts remain the same?
   i. The picnic where the claimant fell was held at the home of the senior partner at the firm.
   ii. The picnic where the claimant fell was held at the home of the paralegal claimant.
b. Assume that the only person the claimant told about the fall was a fellow paralegal, Ed Davis, who had just applied for the job of senior paralegal. He was told a week before the picnic that he would get the promotion effective the day after the picnic. Would this change the result in *Colvin?*
c. Assume that the claimant fell at a Tuesday afternoon meeting of the local paralegal association. The dues for membership are paid by the employer. The only person from the paralegal's firm present at the meeting was the paralegal who fell. Does *Colvin* apply?

Arising Out of Employment

1. Causal-Connection Tests "Arising out of employment" refers to the workers' compensation requirement that the injury must be caused by the employment. Various tests have been used by the courts to determine whether the requisite causal connection exists between the conditions under which the employee works and the injury sustained.[8]

Increased-risk test: The risk of injury to the employee is quantitatively greater than the risk of injury to nonemployees. The employment must increase the risk of an injury, even if others are also exposed to the risk of the injury.

Peculiar-risk test: The source of the harm is peculiar to the employment. The danger must be incidental to the character of the business and dependent on the existence of an employer-employee relationship. The risk must not be one that the employee shares with every citizen, e.g., injury due to cold weather. The risk must differ in quality.

Positional-risk test: The injury of the employee would not have occurred but for the fact that the job placed the employee in a position where the employee could be injured.

Proximate-cause test: The injury is foreseeable, and no intervening factor breaks the chain of causation between the conditions of employment and the injury.

Actual-risk test: The injury is a risk of this particular employment. Whether or not the employment increases the risk, there is causation if the injury comes from a risk that is actually present in this employment.

Most states use the increased-risk test to determine whether the injury arises out of the employment. You must be aware of the other tests, however, because they are used by some states as sole tests, and they are sometimes used along with the increased-risk test.

2. Acts of Nature There is usually no problem showing that an injury arose out of (was caused by) the employment when it was due to an **act of God** such as a storm or freezing weather that occurred during work. The increased-risk test is most often applied to reach this result. An injury received by an employee by lightning, for example, arises out of the employment if the job places the employee on an

act of God An unpredictable and unpreventable force of nature.

elevation, near metal, or in any place where there is an increased risk of this injury's occurring.

Suppose, however, that the act of nature delivers the same harm to everyone, e.g., a tornado levels an entire town. In such a case, it cannot be said that the employee was subjected to any increased risk by being on the job as opposed to being at home. Workers' compensation will be denied, because the injury did not arise out of the employment. Many courts make an exception to this rule if there is contact with the premises: if the act of God produces a force that makes actual contact with the employment premises, e.g., the hurricane blows down a company pole that hits the employee.

Exposure to the elements may bring on diseases such as Rocky Mountain spotted fever, which many people in an area may contract. If the employment increases the employee's chances of getting the disease, causation is established.

3. Street Risks Traveling salespersons and employees making deliveries or soliciting sales are sometimes injured by falls or traffic accidents. Even though everyone is exposed to the risk of such injuries, most states will say that if the job increases the risk of their occurring, compensation will be allowed. Other courts will go even further and say that workers' compensation will be awarded simply by the plaintiff's showing that the job requires that public streets be used.

4. Assault and Battery What happens if the employee is injured because of an assault or a battery? If the employee is the aggressor and the quarrel is personal, having nothing to do with the job, the injury does not arise out of the employment and workers' compensation is denied. It does not take much, however, for the assault or battery to be connected with the employment. The following are examples of injuries due to assault or battery that are sufficiently connected with the employment so that it can be said that the injury arises out of the employment:

- A police officer is hit by someone under arrest.
- A cashier is killed in a robbery attempt.
- A lawyer is raped in an office located in a dangerous area.
- A supervisor is struck by a subordinate being disciplined.
- A worker is struck by a coworker in an argument over who is supposed to perform a certain task.
- A union member and a nonunion member have a fight over whether the latter should join the union.

Fights on the job pose some difficulty. It is not always easy to determine whether a fight is due solely to personal animosity or vengeance (not compensable under workers' compensation) or whether the fight has its origin in the employment, so that it can be said that the employment is a contributing factor to the fight (compensable under workers' compensation). In most states, the fact that the injured employee is the aggressor in the fight does not mean that compensation will be denied to him or her, as long as the employment itself contributed to the fight.

5. Personal Risks Some employees are more susceptible to injury or illness than others, e.g., employees with a heart condition or epilepsy. An on-the-job injury or illness suffered by such an employee will be said to arise out of the employment only if it can be shown that the employment increased the risk of the injury or illness occurring, or if the employment **aggravated** the extent of the harm resulting from the injury or illness. Workers' compensation, of course, cannot be awarded for any **preexisting condition**—a physical or mental health problem that existed prior to the claimed starting date of workers' compensation. By definition, injuries or illnesses that the employee brings to the job are not caused by the job. Workers' compensation will be granted, however, when the job contributes to the risk or aggravates the resulting injury or illness. For example, if an employee falls on a machine after

aggravation An increase in the severity of the original injury.

preexisting condition A physical or mental health problem that existed prior to the starting date of an insurance policy or other benefit.

blacking out due to a preexisting condition, the dangerous consequences of a blackout have been increased by the employer because the employee was stationed next to such a machine. Since the employer increased the risk of serious injury, workers' compensation will be awarded. Most courts, however, would reach a different result if the injury resulted from a fall onto the floor (without hitting any objects) while the employee was standing on a level surface. The injury following the blackout was not increased by the employment; it is the same injury that would have occurred if the employee had blacked out at home.

An employer cannot insist that all employees be fully healthy or normal at the time of employment. The employer takes employees as he or she finds them. If the employment produces stress, exertion, or strain that activates or aggravates a preexisting condition, the resulting injury or illness is said to arise out of the employment. Workers' compensation will be awarded.

ASSIGNMENT 28.4

Examine the following situations to determine whether the injury "arises out of the employment."

a. A caddie is struck by lightning while under a tree on a golf course during a sudden storm.
b. While digging a ditch, an employee is stung by a wasp, resulting in a severe fever.
c. A professor contracts infectious hepatitis due to exposure to an infected student.
d. An employee is killed in an airplane explosion on the way to a business meeting. The plane exploded because of a bomb planted by another passenger.
e. An employee had an ulcer before taking her job. She becomes worried about being laid off. The employee is hospitalized for further treatment of the ulcer during a period of depression about the possible loss of the job.
f. An employee is a door-to-door salesperson. While at a home trying to make a sale, he asks the prospective customer if she would go out with him to a dance that evening. Insulted, she breaks his arm.
g. Two employees have an intense argument on the job over which employee is entitled to go to lunch first. Thirty minutes after the argument, one of the employees walks up behind the other and hits him over the head.
h. An employee has a weak leg due to an injury sustained before she began her present employment. As part of her job, she is required to use a ladder to store supplies on shelves. While on the second rung of the ladder, she falls due to the weak condition of her bad leg.

CASE

Seitz v. L&R Industries, Inc.

437 A.2d 1345 (1981)
Supreme Court of Rhode Island

Background: *Beulah Seitz (referred to in the opinion as "the employee") sought worker's compensation for mental distress allegedly caused by her job. Under § 28-33-1 of the Rhode Island statutory code, benefits can be awarded if there has been a "personal injury arising out of and in the course of employment." The Rhode Island Worker's Compensation Commission awarded her compensation. The case is now before the Supreme Court of Rhode Island on appeal.*

Decision on Appeal: *Her mental injury was the result of the ordinary stresses of her job, not a physical or unexpected emotional trauma. Worker's compensation, therefore, is denied.*

OPINION OF COURT

Justice WEISBERGER delivered the opinion of the court. . . .

The employee had worked as secretary to the vice president and general manager of the Worcester Pressed Aluminum Corporation (Worcester) for approximately six years. The place of employment during this period was Worcester, Massachusetts. In 1975 portions of the Worcester enterprise were placed on the market for sale. One of the divisions known as Palco Products Division was sold to L&R Industries, Inc. (employer). At some time during the month of September 1975, the employer ordered the Palco operations to be moved from Worcester, Massachusetts, to Smithfield, Rhode Island. This change necessitated physical movement of office equipment, furniture, inventory, records, invoices, and machinery. The moving operation began on a Friday afternoon and was completed in a thirty-six-hour period. The employee and a former vice president of Palco Products Division, one Francis Maguire, were active in supervising and implementing the moving activities.

When Palco Products, under the new ownership, began operation on the following Monday, conditions in the new location were confusing and abnormal to a marked degree. Records were unavailable, the telephone service was inadequate, the previous tenants had not vacated the premises, and personnel were untrained. The employee sought to perform duties as office manager and secretary to Mr. Maguire but was also required to do janitorial and cleaning work and to protect office equipment from potential damage due to a leaking roof. She encountered difficulties in interpersonal relations with other employees in the new location. Her authority as office manager was not recognized, and office protocol was not satisfactory to her. She attempted to arrange a meeting with Mr. Maguire and other key personnel in order to work out these difficulties and to improve the organization of the employer's business at the new location. The meeting was scheduled for October 3, 1975, but because of the intervention of another employee, the meeting did not take place. As a result, the employee became so upset that she terminated her employment on the afternoon of October 3, 1975, and has not returned to work since that time.

Dr. Elliot R. Reiner, a psychiatrist who practices in the city of Worcester, had earlier begun treatment of the employee on June 10, 1967, for a condition he described as a depressive neurosis. After three office visits, the employee was discharged. The employee next visited the doctor on October 9, 1975, and described the emotional disruption she had experienced in association with occupational problems and conflicts during the period she had worked with the employer in Smithfield. The doctor diagnosed the employee's condition as an "obsessive compulsive personality disorder." The doctor stated, and the [workers' compensation] commission found, that the employee's rigid personality characteristic had been of long standing but had been aggravated by her employment from September 15, 1975 to October 3, 1975. The doctor testified that the employee had sustained an emotional trauma but had not experienced any physical trauma as the result of her employment.

The commission found that this aggravation qualified within the terms of G.L. 1956 (1979 Reenactment) § 28-33-1 as a "personal injury arising out of and in the course of [her] employment." Although the commission determined the aggravation to be entirely psychic, it found as a matter of fact and held as a matter of law that the conditions under which the employee had been required to work resulted in a malfunction of the body which gave rise to an incapacity to perform her customary work. Therefore, the appellate commission, with one dissenting member, sustained the decree of the trial commissioner and ordered that compensation for total disability be paid to the employee. We reverse.

Professor Larson in this treatise . . . has set forth an analysis of three broad types of psychic injury. 1B Larson, *The Law of Workmen's Compensation* §§ 42.21–.23 (1980). The first type is a physical injury caused by mental stimulus. An analysis of case law on this subject leads Professor Larson to conclude that the "decisions uniformly find compensability." . . . The second broad type of psychic injury is that caused by physical trauma. The courts, including this court, have almost universally awarded compensation for this type of physically produced psychic injury upon an appropriate showing of causal connection. *Greenville Finishing Co. v. Pezza,* 81 R.I. 20, 98 A.2d 825 (1953) (neurosis produced by traumatic loss of eye). . . .

The third type of psychiatric injury mentioned by Professor Larson is a mental injury produced by mental stimulus in which there are neither physical causes nor physical results. Professor Larson finds "a distinct majority position supporting compensability in these cases" but concedes that "[t]he contra view, denying compensation in the 'mental-mental' category continues, however, to command a substantial following." 1B Larson, *The Law of Workmen's Compensation* §§ 42.23 at 7-628 (1980). In this field, of course, it is difficult to compare holdings in various jurisdictions because of the variation among the statutory provisions. Some statutes require accidental injuries. Other statutes, such as that of Rhode Island, require "personal injury" without the necessity of an accident. . . .

The Supreme Court of Wisconsin has succinctly encapsulated the distinction in *School District No. 1 v. Department of Industry, Labor & Human Relations,* 62 Wis. 2d 370, 215 N.W.2d 373 (1974), in which it stated: "Thus it is the opinion of this court that mental injury nontraumatically caused must have resulted from a situation of greater dimensions than the day-to-day emotional strain and tension which all employees must experience. Only if the 'fortuitous event unexpected and unforeseen' can be said to be so out of the ordinary from the countless emotional strains and differences that employees encounter daily without serious mental injury will liability . . . be found." Id. at 377–78, 215 N.W.2d at 377.

In *School District No. 1 v. Department of Industry, Labor & Human Relations,* compensation was denied to a school guidance teacher who suffered psychic injury in the form of an acute anxiety reaction upon seeing a recommendation from a group of students that she be dismissed from her position as a member of the guidance counseling staff of the school. . . .

The courts are reluctant to deny compensation for genuine disability arising out of psychic injury. However, since screening of such claims is a difficult process, the courts recognize the burden that may be placed upon commerce and industry by allowing compensation for neurotic reaction to the ordinary everyday stresses that are found in most areas of employment. Indeed, it is a rare situation in which some adverse interpersonal relations among employees are not encountered from time to time. Employers and managers must admonish their subordinates and correct perceived shortcomings. The stress of competitive enterprise is ever present and attendant upon all types of commercial and industrial activity.

Great care must be taken in order to avoid the creation of voluntary "retirement" programs that may be seized upon by an employee at an early age if he or she is willing or, indeed, even eager to give up active employment and assert a neurotic inability to continue.

It is all very well to say that the adversary system will expose the difference between the genuine neurotic and the malingerer. We have great fears that neither the science of psychiatry nor the adversary judicial process is equal to this task on the type of claim here presented. An examination of the evidence in the instant case discloses that the employee's psychiatrist largely accepted her statement that she was unable to return to work. The patient, who had exhibited neurotic tendencies, arising out of family relationships as early as 1967, apparently suffered an aggravation during her sixteen-day period of employment with the employer. An analysis of the testimony in the case would clearly indicate that this stressful period contained conditions that, though scarcely tranquil, did not exceed the intensity of stimuli encountered by thousands of other employees and management personnel every day. If psychic injury is to be compensable, a more dramatically stressful stimulus must be established. . . .

[The decision of the Worker's Compensation Commission is reversed.]

KELLEHER, Justice, with whom BEVILACQUA, Chief Justice, joins, dissenting. . . .

An overriding objective of worker's compensation legislation is to impose upon the employer the burden of caring for the casualties occurring in its employment by preventing an employee who has suffered a job-related loss of earning capacity from becoming a public charge. . . . An employer takes its workers as it finds them, and when the employee aggravates an existing condition and the result is an incapacity for work, the employee is entitled to compensation for such incapacity. Here, the commission, in awarding Beulah compensation, believed her psychiatrist when he testified that the office chaos that ensued following her employer's weekend move from Massachusetts to Rhode Island aggravated a preexisting psychiatric condition. Credibility and fact-finding are part of the commission's job. However, this award goes for naught because of the . . . imposition by my brother of a standard calling for a "more dramatically stressful stimulus." With all due deference to my learned associate, this standard represents judicial legislation. . . .

ASSIGNMENT 28.5

Can workers' compensation be granted in the following situations?

a. Smith and Jones are working on a scaffold when one end gives way. Jones falls to his death as Smith watches. Smith had the sensation that he might fall himself, but he didn't. After this experience, Smith is unable to continue in this employment as a structural steelworker. He blanks out and freezes, experiencing complete paralysis, when attempting work in a high place.
b. Edward works as an assistant manager at a food processing plant. The last year has been very stressful. For three months he was temporarily laid off because of a small fire that seriously damaged the plant's electrical system. He was accused of stealing and of sexually harassing another worker. (After an investigation, the owners of the plant concluded that he was innocent of both charges.) Due to declining profits, the plant seriously considered filing for bankruptcy. All of these events led to Edward's having a mental breakdown requiring hospitalization.

FILING A CLAIM

States differ on the steps involved in making a workers' compensation claim. (See Exhibit 28–2 for an example.) The basic procedure is often as follows:

1. The worker reports the injury or illness to the supervisor and/or to the insurance carrier.
2. The worker receives medical attention.
3. The doctor, worker, and employer fill out forms provided by the workers' compensation agency and/or insurance carrier.
4. The worker receives disability benefits after a designated waiting period.

Each state has a statute of limitations within which the worker must make a claim, e.g., one year from the date of the injury.

uncontested Unopposed; without opposition.

Most claims for workers' compensation are **uncontested**. No questions of liability for compensation arise. The employer or insurance carrier and the employee

Exhibit 28–2
Filing a claim.

WORKERS'
COMPENSATION NOTICE
And Instructions to
Employers & Employees

All employees of this establishment, entitled to benefits under the provisions of the Arkansas Workers' Compensation Law, are hereby notified that their Employer has secured the payment of such compensation as may at any time be due a disabled employee or his dependents.

IN CASE OF JOB-RELATED INJURIES OR OCCUPATIONAL DISEASES
The Employer Shall:

1. Provide all necessary medical, surgical and hospital treatment, as required by the Law, following the disability and for such additional time as ordered by the Commission.
2. Keep a record of all injuries received by his employees, and make a prompt report thereof in writing to the Arkansas Workers' Compensation Commission on blanks procured for this purpose.
3. Determine the average weekly wage of the employee and provide compensation in accordance with the provisions of the Act. The first installment of compensation becomes due on the 15th day after the employer has notice of the injury or death, except in those cases where liability has been denied by the employer. Additional compensation shall be paid every two weeks, except where the Commission directs that installment payments be made at other periods.

The Employee Should:

1. Immediately give or cause to be given to the employer notice in writing of disability or upon the first distinct manifestation of an occupational disease and request medical services. Failure to give notice within sixty (60) days after an accident or injury or ninety (90) days after the first distinct manifestation of an occupational disease, or to accept the medical services provided, may deprive the employee of the right to compensation.
2. Give promptly to the employer and to the Workers' Compensation Commission, on forms approved by the latter, notice of any claim for compensation for the period of disability. In case of fatal injuries, notice must be given by one or more dependents of the deceased or by a person in their behalf. (Act, Sec. 17.)

ARKANSAS WORKERS' COMPENSATION COMMISSION
Justice Building
State Capitol Grounds
Little Rock, Ark. 72201

All employers, who come within the operation of the Arkansas Workers' Compensation Law, and have complied with its provisions, MUST POST THIS NOTICE IN A CONSPICUOUS PLACE in or about his place or places of business, in addition to the prescribed notice as required by the Commission for insured employers.

ALLYN C. TATUM, Chairman
JOHN E. COWNE, JR., Commissioner
JIMMIE D. CLARK, Commissioner
OGDEN BERRY, Executive Director

INSURED EMPLOYERS make all reports to the insurance carrier in all cases where the employee loses time or is sent to the doctor. The insurance carrier then makes the necessary reports to the Commission. SELF-INSURED employers, State agencies, counties and cities under the State Plan, and public schools shall report directly to the Workers' Compensation Commission.

sign an agreement on the benefits to be received consistent with any state laws on the extent of such benefits. The state workers' compensation agency will usually approve such agreements as a matter of course. Some states do not use this agreement system. In such states, the employer or insurance carrier simply begins to make direct payments to the employee or to the dependents of the employee.

If there is a dispute, it will be resolved by the agency responsible for the workers' compensation program, often a board or commission. The procedure is frequently as follows:

- A hearing is held before a hearing officer, arbitrator, or referee of the agency. The proceeding is usually informal, unlike a court trial. Paralegals are sometimes allowed to represent claimants at these hearings.
- A decision is made by the hearing officer, arbitrator, or referee. A party disagreeing with the decision can appeal it to the agency's commission or board.
- The commission or board makes the final decision of the agency. This decision can then be appealed to a court.

BENEFITS AVAILABLE

Most statutes are very specific on the number of weeks of disability benefits that are available to an employee who establishes a workers' compensation claim. For an example, see Exhibit 28–3.

Exhibit 28–3 Example of a schedule of weeks of benefits.

Injury	Weeks of Compensation Benefits	Injury	Weeks of Compensation Benefits
Loss of thumb	60	Loss of first finger	35
Loss of second finger	30	Loss of third finger	25
Loss of fourth finger	20	Loss of hand	190
Loss of arm	250	Loss of great toe	40
Loss of any other toe	15	Loss of foot	150
Loss of leg	220	Loss of eye	140
Loss of hearing in one ear	50	Loss of hearing in both ears	175
Permanent disfigurement, face or head	150		

Note: The schedule of weeks is based on a 100 percent loss of the body member indicated. If the disability rating is less than 100 percent, the percentage rated should be multiplied by the number of weeks shown. For example, a 20 percent loss of function of a thumb would be computed as 20 percent of sixty weeks, or twelve weeks of compensation benefits.

The weekly disability benefit is usually based on a percentage of the employee's weekly pay over a designated period of time. The percentage is often 66⅔ percent. This benefit is in addition to the cost of medical services. Different benefit periods, percentages, and amounts are provided depending on which of the following the employee has suffered:

- permanent total disability
- temporary total disability
- permanent partial disability
- temporary partial disability
- disfigurement
- death

TORT CLAIMS AGAINST THIRD PARTIES

As we have seen, a covered injured worker cannot sue his or her employer for negligence when the benefits of workers' compensation are available. Tort litigation between employer and employee is barred in such cases, but tort law may still play a role in the incidents involved in the employee's injury. There is no bar of tort actions against *third parties* involved in the worker's injury. For example:

- A worker is injured on defective machinery. Although a suit against the employer is not possible, a products liability suit (see Chapter 19) against the machinery's manufacturer is possible.
- An injured worker files a workers' compensation claim. The workers' compensation insurance carrier fails to process the worker's claim in a reasonable and timely manner. A bad faith action (see Chapter 26) against the carrier is possible.

Attorney fees in workers' compensation are often not large enough to entice attorneys to take workers' compensation cases. However, an attorney may become very interested in handling a workers' compensation case if the attorney sees the possibility of suing a deep-pocket third party in a related tort case that is not barred by the workers' compensation statute.

REFORM

Every state has expressed concern about the high cost of workers' compensation insurance. Companies may leave a state that has a reputation for excessive costs. Employers may feel that a particular state is too generous in the amount of workers' compensation benefits available and too lax in preventing fraud in the filing of workers' compensation claims. Some states have responded by enacting a variety of reforms,[9] such as

- no longer awarding benefits for mental or psychological disorders unless they are the result of an injury
- eliminating cost-of-living adjustments
- denying benefits to a worker who cannot identify the day and time of injury
- establishing a special fund to pay for teams that go after fraudulently filed applications

Although many of these reforms are the result of deep frustration, no one is thinking about eliminating workers' compensation. A return to the tort system as the sole vehicle to obtain compensation for injured workers is out of the question.

CHECK THE CITE

Khamtamh Keovorabouth was injured in an automobile accident while traveling to her attorney's office to prepare for a deposition. Why was her claim for workers' compensation denied? Read the case of *Keovorabouth v. Industrial Com'm*, 222 Ariz. 378, 214 P.3d 1019 (Ct. App. 2009). To read the opinion online, (1) Go to the site of the Arizona Court of Appeals, Division One (www.cofad1.state.az.us). Click "Search Opinions Div 1." Type Keovorabouth in the search box. (2) Go to FindACase (www.findacase.com). Select Arizona. Select "Arizona Appellate courts." Run a standard search (Keovorabouth). (3) Run a citation search ("214 P.3d 1019") or a party search (Keovorabouth) in the Legal Opinions and Journals database of Google Scholar (scholar.google.com).

PROJECT

In Google, Bing, or another general search engine, run the following search: *aa* "workers' compensation" representation (substitute the name of your state for *aa* in the search, e.g., New York "workers' compensation" representation). Determine whether a paralegal or other nonattorney is allowed to represent clients before the administrative agency, board, or commission that handles workers' compensation claims. If they can, cite and summarize the law that allows this representation. If they cannot, cite and summarize the law that so provides.

ETHICS IN A TORTS PRACTICE

You are an independent paralegal working in a state that allows nonattorneys to represent clients before the workers' compensation board. One of your clients is David Howard. After he loses the workers' compensation case at the agency, you tell him that he can appeal in court but that you cannot represent him in court. Howard decides to represent himself. He asks you to draft the complaint that he will file in court. You do so. What ethical problems, if any, might exist?

SUMMARY

Traditional common-law negligence actions brought by employees for on-the-job injuries/illnesses were often won by employers who used the defenses of contributory negligence, assumption of the risk, or the fellow-servant rule. An alternative remedy is workers' compensation, which is a form of strict liability, because recovery is not dependent on establishing the negligence or fault of the employer. For workers' compensation to apply, the worker must be a covered employee and the injury or illness must arise out of and occur in the course of employment.

Generally, injuries off the premises while going to or coming back from work or lunch are not within the course of employment and hence are not covered. Injuries that occur while on a mixed-purpose trip are covered if the trip is primarily business, because the trip would have been made even if the employee did not also have a personal purpose in making the trip. But an injury that occurs during a personal detour while on a business trip is not covered.

An employee who is the innocent victim of horseplay is covered, but not the employee who participated in or instigated the horseplay, unless the horseplay was a very minor departure from normal work responsibility or had become customary. The employee's own misconduct is usually not a bar to recovery unless it amounted to a willful failure to use a safety device. An injury that results from misconduct in the method of doing a job is covered, whereas one that results from misconduct in what the employee has been asked to do, or the objective of the job, is not. Whether there is coverage for an injury that occurs while an employee is engaged in personal comfort on the job, e.g., during a break, depends on factors such as whether the injury occurred on the premises, within an authorized area for the activity, and within working hours.

Courts use different tests to determine whether an injury/illness arose out of, and hence was caused by, the employment. The most common is the increased-risk test, whereby the risk of injury/illness to the employee is quantitatively greater than the risk of that injury/illness to nonemployees. An injury/illness that results from an act of God is covered if the job increased the risk of that injury/illness occurring. The same is true of an injury/illness incurred from street risks. An employee who is injured from an assault and battery or a fight is covered if the event was sufficiently connected with the employment. Workers' compensation does not cover a preexisting injury/illness, but does cover its aggravation due to the job.

Claims are made to the employer, to the insurance carrier, or both. If the claim is disputed, the workers' compensation agency will attempt to resolve it. If this is unsuccessful, the denial can be appealed in court.

When workers' compensation applies, tort actions between employer and employee are barred. There may, however, be tort actions that can still be brought against third parties, such as a products liability suit against the manufacturer of a machine that caused the worker's on-the-job injury. Many of the efforts to reform workers' compensation center on reducing the number of fraudulent claims filed by workers.

KEY TERMS

REVIEW QUESTIONS

1. What is workers' compensation?
2. How does an action for negligence at common law differ from a workers' compensation claim?
3. What three defenses often defeated a worker's negligence claim for a work-related injury/illness?
4. What is self-insurance?
5. What is meant by an injury/illness being in the course of employment?
6. What is the going-and-coming rule?
7. When is a risk incident to employment?
8. What is a frolic?
9. What horseplay by a worker can disqualify him or her from eligibility?
10. What misconduct by a worker can disqualify him or her from eligibility?
11. How is workers' compensation eligibility determined when an injury occurs on a dual-purpose trip?
12. What is meant by an injury/illness arising out of employment?
13. What is the main causal connection test?
14. When is an injury caused by an act of God covered?
15. When are street risks covered?
16. Can a worker involved in an assault and battery be covered?
17. What personal risks are covered?
18. How does a worker file a claim?
19. What benefits are available?
20. What third-party tort actions are sometimes possible in workers' compensation cases?

HELPFUL WEBSITES

- **Workers' Compensation**
  www.workerscompensation.com
  www.law.cornell.edu/topics/workers_compensation.html
  www.bls.gov/iif
  www.workerscompensationinsurance.com
  en.wikipedia.org/wiki/Workers'_compensation
  www.spamlaws.com/workers-compensation.html
  www.lawguru.com/answers/search/category/02

ENDNOTES

1. *Injuries, Illnesses, and Fatalities*, Bureau of Labor Statistics (2007) (www.bls.gov/iif).
2. *The Effects of the Economy on Workplace Safety* by Frank Pennachio, EHS Today (May 1, 2009) (ehstoday.com/columns/effects-economy-workplace-0309)
3. Or comparative negligence if the state has abolished contributory negligence. See Chapter 17.
4. Federal Employees' Compensation Act, 5 U.S.C. §§ 8101 et seq.
5. Arthur Larson, *Workmen's Compensation Law* § 15.13, pp. 4–22 (1978).
6. Id. at § 31.22, pp. 6–20 (1978).
7. *Crilly v. Ballou*, 353 Mich. 303, 326, 91 N.W.2d 493, 505 (1958). See also Malone, Plant, & Little, *Workers' Compensation and Employment Rights* 126 (2d. ed. 1980).
8. Arthur Larson, *Workmen's Compensation Law* § 6, pp. 3–1 (1978).
9. Michael Quint, *Crackdown on Job-Injury Costs*, N.Y. Times, March 16, 1995, at C1.

Student StudyWARE™ CD-ROM
For additional materials, please go to the student CD in this book.

CHAPTER

29

SETTLEMENT

CHAPTER OUTLINE

- Introduction
- Paralegal Roles During Settlement
- Settlement Précis
- Settlement Brochure

CHAPTER OBJECTIVES

After completing this chapter, you should be able to:

- Understand why parties agree to settle cases.
- Explain the function of a settlement précis.
- Distinguish between a settlement précis and a settlement brochure.
- State paralegal roles in the settlement process.
- Explain the main components and functions of a settlement précis.
- Explain the main components and functions of a settlement brochure.

INTRODUCTION

settlement An agreement resolving a dispute without full litigation.

settlement précis A relatively brief written presentation by a party to an opponent (or its insurance company) on the merits of a cause of action (including alleged damages) in an effort to encourage settlement. A more elaborate version for more complex cases is called a *settlement brochure*.

settlement brochure A detailed written presentation by a party to an opponent (or its insurance company) on the merits of a cause of action (including alleged damages) in an effort to encourage settlement. The presentation is called a *settlement précis* if the case is relatively uncomplicated.

The vast majority of legal disputes are settled in one form or another without the need for a complete trial. In fact, the moment a case is initiated, the opposing attorneys are usually thinking about the possibilities of **settlement**. There are substantial incentives for the parties to settle, such as the enormity of the cost of a trial and of the amount of time needed to complete the litigation through the appeal process.

This chapter presents two documents used by attorneys to encourage settlement—the settlement précis and the settlement brochure. They are documents presented by one attorney to the other side and to the insurance company in an effort to settle the case. A **settlement précis** is a relatively brief document used by a party to advocate a settlement. It states an amount the party is willing to settle the case for. To support this request, the précis summarizes facts, theories of recovery, medical expenses, lost wages or profits, and other components of damages. If the document is more elaborate, it is often called a **settlement brochure**.

PARALEGAL ROLES DURING SETTLEMENT

There are a number of important roles that a paralegal can play to assist the attorney during settlement efforts. For an overview, see Exhibit 29–1.

Exhibit 29–1
Paralegal roles during settlement.[1]

- Make sure you have the name, address, phone number, fax number, and e-mail address of the insurance adjuster assigned to your case.
- Make sure the insurance adjuster has the name, address, social security number, and phone number of the client.
- Maintain the office tickler system containing reminder calendar dates such as the date the statute of limitations is scheduled to run, deposition appointments, and medical appointments of the client.
- Obtain waiver of confidentiality letters or forms from client that will authorize you to obtain medical files and other personal records of the client.
- Continue collecting medical records from client's past medical history and for the current case.
- Collect records relevant to the client's loss of income, e.g., current wage stubs, salary and fringe benefits history, past tax returns.
- Arrange for witness statements to be taken.
- Arrange for photographs to be taken of client's injury, accident scene, and property damage.
- Every few weeks send a brief letter to the insurance adjuster explaining the status of the case, particularly the client's medical condition and care received. (Attach copies of bills.)
- Contact the client regularly to ensure that he or she is following the prescribed medical treatment.
- Authenticate all medical records and bills.
- Research jury verdict awards to assess settlement range for this kind of case. Check the Internet for jury research sites (e.g., www.juryverdictresearch.com).
- Help prepare or design *life activity charts* that provide a graphic presentation of the kinds of activities the client enjoyed before the injury as opposed to now.
- Help draft the *demand package* based on the settlement précis or settlement brochure. (The package seeks—demands—a settlement of the case.)
- Draft the cover letter for the settlement précis or settlement brochure.
- Contact insurance adjuster to confirm his or her receipt of documents sent such as medical reports, settlement précis, or settlement brochure.
- Contact the insurance adjuster to request a status report on the insurer's response to the settlement demand.

SETTLEMENT PRÉCIS

Lawyers are constantly reminded that theirs is "a profession, not a business."[2] Unfortunately, this plea for competence and high ethical standards has been interpreted by some to mean that lawyers should give little thought to the economic realities of their profession. Obviously, a case with a potential settlement value of less than ten thousand dollars cannot be handled in the same fashion as one with a settlement value of ten or twenty times that much. The client is concerned with the net amount of the settlement. A lawyer who diverts a substantial percentage of that settlement for photographs, plats, etc., when the potential of the case does not deserve it, is guilty of dissipating his or her time and the money of his or her client. Neither client nor lawyer can afford to swat flies with sledgehammers.

But the smaller case has the same need of effective presentation as the larger one. Some format should be adopted that will have the advantages of a persuasive disclosure without the expense of time and money in its preparation.

The use of a *settlement précis* seeks to meet that need. Its primary purpose is to present the claim in as persuasive a fashion as possible. It is divided into six main sections:

- identity of the plaintiff
- facts of the case
- theories of recovery
- medical (reports)
- expenses
- analysis of evaluation

The preparation of such a précis has two secondary advantages: it will discipline lawyers to analyze their liability, marshal their evidence, and appraise the case; and it will provide a dress rehearsal for trial in the event that efforts at settlement are fruitless.

Settlement Précis—Illustration

Identity of the Plaintiff

Social History Sharon Williams was born July 10, 2003, the fourth of four children born to John and Virginia Williams. The family lives at 2305 Grand Vista, Columbus, Missouri. Mr. Williams is employed as a machinist at Eagle Air Craft Co., a position he has held for six years.

Sharon is a student in the second grade of Middleton Grade School. She is a member of Girl Scout Troop 378 and is a member of the YMCA girls' swimming team.

Medical History Sharon had a normal prenatal history and a normal birth. She has been attended by Dr. Grant Fry, a pediatrician, from birth. She has suffered from the childhood diseases of chicken pox and measles. She has never suffered any disability to her lower limbs and has never sustained any injuries to her legs, back, or spine. Dr. Fry's medical report is attached.

Facts of the Case On April 5, 2010, Sharon was en route from her home to school. The attached police report confirms that the day was clear and warm and the streets were dry. Sharon was by herself and crossing Grand Avenue at its intersection with Washington Street moving westwardly from the southeast to the southwest corner approximately six feet south of the south curb line and within the designated crosswalk. Grand Avenue is forty feet wide with two lanes of traffic moving in each direction. It is straight and level and surfaced with asphalt.

There were no cars parked within sixty feet of the intersection. A sign located one hundred feet south of the intersection on Grand has a legend "Caution Children." A police report confirming the description of the scene of the accident is attached.

Sharon was struck by the northbound automobile of defendant at a point five feet from the center line. The attached photographs show the following:

Photo 1: skid marks ten feet long, blood on street.

Photo 2: damage to left headlight.

Sharon states that when she left the southeast corner of the intersection the light was in her favor. She never looked at the light again. She walked at a normal pace until she was hit. She was looking forward and never saw or heard the defendant's automobile. The accident occurred at 8:35 A.M. The school is two blocks away and convenes at 8:45 A.M.

A statement taken from the defendant, a copy of which is attached, acknowledges that he didn't see the plaintiff until she was fifteen feet from him and that his automobile came to a stop twenty feet after impact.

Theories of Recovery The plaintiff has three theories of recovery:

1. that defendant violated a red light
2. that defendant failed to keep a lookout
3. that defendant failed to exercise the highest degree of care to bring his automobile to a stop or slacken after plaintiff came into a position of immediate danger

The proof of the first theory is supported by plaintiff's testimony that when she left the curb the light was green for westbound traffic. By reason of the plaintiff's age, the court might decide not to permit her to testify. In that event, the defendant's failure to keep a lookout could be submitted as an alternate theory of recovery. Defendant has acknowledged that he didn't see plaintiff until he was fifteen feet away from her and she was already in his path. This would place Sharon at least twelve feet from the curb. The court will judicially notice that the pace of walk is approximately two or three miles an hour or 2.9 to 4.4 feet per second. *Wofford v. St. Louis Public Service Co., Mo.*, 252 S.W.2d 529. Sharon was in the street and visible to defendant for almost three seconds before the accident. At defendant's acknowledged speed of twenty-five miles per hour, he was traveling at approximately thirty-six feet per second or was approximately one hundred feet away when he should have seen Sharon. He was further alerted by the warning sign as he approached the intersection.

By reason of her age, it is questionable whether Sharon would be held responsible for her own actions. *Mallot v. Harvey*, 199 Mo. App. 615, 204 S.W. 940; *Quirk v. Metropolitan St. Ry. Co.*, 200 Mo. App. 585, 210 S.W. 103.

In the event Sharon could be held accountable for not maintaining a proper lookout, a third theory of recovery is available: defendant's failure to stop or slacken after plaintiff came into a position of immediate danger. By defendant's admission, he came to a stop twenty feet after the impact and he did not attempt evasive action until he was fifteen feet from Sharon; therefore, his overall stopping distance was thirty-five feet. A jury could find that by reason of Sharon's obliviousness that she was in immediate danger as she approached the path of the vehicle and when defendant's automobile was more than the thirty-five feet that was available to bring his vehicle to a stop.

The skid marks indicate that no slackening took place until the defendant's vehicle was within ten feet of the impact. The damage to the automobile indicates it was the left front headlight which struck Sharon. Sharon was within two feet of safety beyond the path of the car when she was struck. Moving at 4.4 feet per second, in one-half second she would have escaped injury. From this the jury could assume that a failure to slacken at an earlier time was the proximate cause of the injury.

Medical Records The police report states that Sharon was "bleeding about the face and mouth" complaining of "pain in the right hip." She was taken by police cruiser to Welfare Hospital where it was discovered that she had suffered the loss of a front upper left tooth which was permanent, a laceration of the lip necessitating six stitches, and a bruise of the right hip. Portions of the hospital record are attached. She was examined by her pediatrician, Dr. Fry, who referred her to Dr. William Jones, a dentist, for examination. He confirms the loss of the permanent tooth and outlines the dental prostheses which will be needed throughout her growth stage and into adulthood. His report is attached. The stitches were removed after six days by Dr. Fry, leaving a hairline scar one-fourth inch long near the upper lip.

Expenses

Emergency room Welfare Hospital	$12,250
Dr. Grant Fry	$ 1,750
Dr. William Jones	$ 500
Anticipated treatment	$10,000

Analysis of Evaluation

The loss of the tooth is permanent and will necessitate special prophylactic care to maintain the prosthetic devices which must be employed. The scar above the lip is discernible and will be permanent.

It is anticipated that a jury verdict could fall within the $100,000 to $125,000 range. If the case could be settled without further legal procedure, I would recommend a settlement of $80,000.

SETTLEMENT BROCHURE

Larger cases often require more than a settlement précis. If the case is of sufficient potential to warrant the necessary time and expense, a settlement brochure should be utilized in pretrial settlement negotiations. It will attempt to serve the same functions as outlined for the settlement précis, but on a larger scale.

A settlement brochure presents the plaintiff's case in a relatively extensive documentary form consisting of statements, reports, and exhibits. Generally, there is little oratorical flourish or emotional argument. The claims agent or representative of the insurance company receives the information "in cold blood" and can appraise the case rationally.

A well-ordered, carefully planned settlement brochure carries with it an aura of importance. The bulk alone suggests value. Plaintiff files might not be sold by the pound, but there seems to be some correlation between the bigness of the file and the bigness of the case. The preparation of a brochure demonstrates that the plaintiff has sufficient confidence in the magnitude of the case to warrant a detailed presentation. It immediately creates an impression of importance.

Settlement Brochure—Illustration

DEMAND FOR SETTLEMENT

TO: ALL-RISK INSURANCE COMPANY

IN THE MATTER OF THE CLAIM OF

SARAH ANDERSON

CLAIMANT AND POTENTIAL PLAINTIFF

VERSUS

DONALD M. SWANSON

AND

JACK G. SWANSON D/B/A
SWANSON LOGGING

PRESENTED BY:
REX PALMER
ATTORNEYS, INC., P.C.
126 E. BROADWAY
MISSOULA, MT 59802
(406) 728-4514
ATTORNEY FOR CLAIMANT

TABLE OF CONTENTS

DISCLAIMER

The matters set forth herein are stated solely for purposes of expediting possible settlement at this stage of this claim, and as such, are not to be used or referred to in any way should these matters proceed to trial, except as set forth in the paragraph immediately below. All photographs, attachments, and other exhibits set forth herein shall remain the property of Claimant and Claimant's attorney, the originals of which are to be returned promptly upon oral or written request. All figures utilized herein are subject to change without notice, as discovery and investigation are continuing, medical attention continues to be required, and all figures will accordingly require supplementation and updating at or prior to trial, and are not to be construed as final figures should these matters proceed to trial.

Potential plaintiff, Sarah Anderson, and her legal counsel, reserve the right to present a copy of this Settlement Brochure as evidence in a secondary action directly against All-Risk Insurance Company to recover compensatory and punitive damages if the Claimant and her legal counsel, in their sole discretion, deem that All-Risk has violated the provisions of the Montana Fair Claims Practices Act, Sec. 33-18-201(6), MCA (Montana Code Annotated), or the Montana common law obligation of good faith and fair dealing in insurance claims settlement practices. A review of applicable statutory and case law on settlement practices is set forth in Appendix I to this brochure.

SUMMARY

This is a personal injury claim resulting from an automobile collision in Yellowstone County, Montana. On August 20, 2009, Sarah Anderson was making a left turn off a secondary highway into her driveway. Donald Swanson, who was delivering a check for his father's logging company, Swanson

2

Logging, tried to pass Sarah Anderson's vehicle in a no-passing zone as she was completing her turn. Swanson's pickup hit Anderson's Datsun station wagon in the left rear corner, knocking it sideways and off the roadway into a power pole. In the wreck, Sarah Anderson was injured. For the direct medical costs resulting from these injuries, for the pain and suffering, for her continued impairment and future losses, she demands compensation in the amount of Two Hundred Eighty-five Thousand and no/100 Dollars ($285,000.00).

Liability, jointly and severally, of the prospective defendants is clearly demonstrated by the facts set forth in this brochure. All-Risk, the insurer for the potential defendants, is therefore under a legal obligation to effectuate a settlement at or near the figure set forth above, or the policy limits of their insurance policies, whichever is less, within a reasonable period of time.

If All-Risk disagrees with the evaluation of this claim as set forth herein, it should respond within a reasonable period of time by providing Sarah Anderson's counsel with a written statement of its analysis and evaluation of this claim, together with its payment of the sum supported by its own evaluation.

For the purposes of this brochure, we consider thirty (30) days a reasonable period of time. This period will end on the 20th day of April, 2011. Thereafter, no further settlement negotiations will be initiated by Claimant, and Claimant will initiate legal action against the insurance carrier and its insured under the provisions of Montana statutory and case law, in an action for compensatory, general, and punitive damages in courts of appropriate jurisdiction.

STATEMENT OF FACTS

Family Background

Sarah Anderson was born March 10, 1965. At the time of this collision, Sarah was 44 years old. She resides with her husband, Ross and her family approximately one mile east of Laurel, Montana, on Devlin Road. Sarah and Ross have two (2) daughters, namely: Marsha, age 17, who still resides in the family home, and Teresa, age 20, who is currently residing in the family home but has lived outside the home on occasion. Sarah has two (2) other children from a prior marriage which ended in divorce: Jerry Landquer, who has been on his own for the past ten (10) years, and Roxanne Aist, who is married and resides in Red Lodge, Montana. Sarah has a close relationship with Roxanne and generally sees her once each week. Sarah also enjoys her relationship with her grandchild, Roxanne's daughter.

Prior Medical History

Sarah has had a complex medical history including surgeries on her pituitary gland, bladder, and colon. As well, she has had bilateral carpel tunnel repairs and a complete hysterectomy. In spite of this checkered medical history, she has always been able to return to her normal activities without restriction after a reasonable healing period.

The Collision

On August 20, 2009, Sarah Anderson drove her house guests, Lisa Weston and Lisa's children, Samuel and Laura, to visit a friend. After this visit, Sarah and her guests drove to the grocery store. After purchasing groceries, Sarah and her guests returned to the car and drove away from Laurel east on Devlin Road toward home, which is a little over one mile from Superior. (See Appendix III, Witnesses and Testimony.)

Devlin Road is a paved two-lane secondary highway. Sarah's home is immediately north of Devlin Road so that she must cross over the center line to turn into her driveway whenever she is returning home from town. When traveling east from town, Devlin Road dips down to cross a bridge, then immediately develops an uphill grade throughout the approach to Sarah Anderson's driveway and beyond. These physical characteristics of the road make passing very unsafe. The Highway Department has marked the entire area with solid double yellow lines, indicating that this is a no-passing zone.

3

On the day of this collision, it was daylight, approximately 5:00 P.M. Though the sky was somewhat overcast with patchy clouds, the road was dry. (See Highway Patrol's Accident Report in Exhibit D.)

At the time of the collision, Sarah was driving a 1980 Datsun 710 station wagon. She had driven this vehicle for some time and was completely familiar with its operation.

She is a cautious driver, and as a matter of practice she turns on her left turn indicator several hundred feet before turning into her driveway from Devlin Road. She is so regular in this practice that, a few days before this collision, Laura Weston asked Sarah why she began signaling her turn so early, referring to the fact that Sarah turns on her blinker before crossing the bridge.

On the day of this collision, Sarah followed her normal routine and triggered her left-turn indicator before crossing the bridge and before beginning the uphill grade to her driveway. Sarah slowed from approximately 45 m.p.h. at the bridge to approximately 3–4 m.p.h. at the immediate approach to her driveway. Immediately before initiating her turn, she checked her rear-view mirrors for approaching vehicles and saw none. (See Appendix III, Witnesses and Testimony.)

After she had completely crossed the center line with the front tires of her compact vehicle completely off the paved roadway, Donald Swanson smashed into the left rear corner of Sarah's car with the left front corner of his 1985 four-wheel-drive Chevrolet pickup. (See photos 1–5 in Exhibit C.)

Donald Swanson was traveling at an excessive rate of speed (passing speed) with his vehicle traveling east in the passing lane when he collided with Sarah Anderson's vehicle. At the time of the collision, he was on an errand, delivering a check for his father Jack G. Swanson, d/b/a Swanson Logging.

If Donald Swanson had remained in his own lane of traffic, there would have been no collision even at his excessive rate of speed.

Donald Swanson left skid marks of over 60 feet prior to the point of impact. After impact, his vehicle continued to skid, leaving skid marks with a total length of approximately 119 feet. The impact of the collision threw Sarah Anderson's vehicle into a violent spin, off the roadway, and into a telephone pole approximately 65 feet from the point of impact. The force of the impact and the sudden stop against the telephone pole was so great that it broke the front passenger's seat belt and threw Lisa Weston completely out of the vehicle. Fortunately for Sarah Anderson, her seat belt did not break. Nevertheless, she was seriously injured when the car smashed into the telephone pole at precisely the point where her shoulder and left side were inside the car.

The Anderson vehicle was a total loss. (See photos 1–4 in Exhibit C.)

The Injuries

The hospital records and medical reports now in your possession, as well as the medical reports that have been furnished to you herewith, are self-explanatory as to the injuries received. Basically, Sarah sustained musculoskeletal strain and chronic myofascitis of the left shoulder and neck region. As well, her dentures were broken, and she suffered an injury to her left side temporomandibular joint. The above were apparently the direct result of the rear-end collision and her subsequent left side contact with the telephone pole. She also required the surgical repair of a rectocele. Sarah had suffered a previous rectocele which had required surgical repair, and this recurrence was apparently due to the pressure exerted on her abdomen by her seat belt.

Immediately following the accident, Sarah was admitted to Billings Community Hospital on August 20, 2009, and was discharged five (5) days later on August 25. She was subsequently admitted to Deaconess Hospital on October 2, 2009 for repair of her rectocele. She was discharged five (5) days later on October 7. Over the eighteen (18) months since the accident, she has undergone an extensive regimen of physical therapy in an attempt to control her pain and return to her normal activities. Her primary treating physician, Sid Silker, M.D., was not satisfied with Sarah's progress and referred her to the Pain Center at Billings Community Rehabilitation Center for evaluation. (See Dr. Silker's Sept. 23, 2010 letter, Exhibit A.)

Sarah appeared for evaluation at the Billings Community Hospital Diagnostic Pain Clinic on December 9, 2010. She was evaluated by a team of six (6) professionals: Physiatric evaluation by Sandy T. Bickett, M.D.; Psychological evaluation by Keith Makie, Ph.D.; Neurologic evaluation by

4

Edward B. Runk, M.D.; Orthopedic evaluation by W. J. McConnell, M.D.; Physical Therapy evaluation by Todd Rockler, R.P.T.; and Social Service Intake Interview by Rick Wysil, B.S.W. The results of this diagnostic evaluation are attached hereto in full as Appendix II. In addition to the diagnostic team's results, the Pain Clinic Director, Keith Makie, Ph.D., provided a letter dated January 21, 2011, summarizing the process and costs of the Pain Clinic program. (See attached letter, Exhibit B.)

The Pain Clinic team unanimously recommends that Sarah seek out a highly structured, interdisciplinary chronic pain treatment program such as that offered by the Billings Community Hospital Pain Clinic.

Prior to the accident, Sarah and her family routinely engaged in such activities as camping, gold mining, digging crystals, hiking, and searching for arrowheads. Through all these activities, whether summer or winter, Sarah would bring her easel and create portrait paintings. (See photos of her paintings in Exhibit E.) She particularly excelled in painting miniatures. Until the accident, Sarah usually entered the Yellowstone County Art Fair. One year she even painted small figures on people's fingernails at the art and craft show in Laurel. (See Exhibit F.) Often she sold and bartered her art work.

The pain, stiffness, and muscle spasms resulting from Sarah's injuries preclude her participation in the family's outdoor activities described above. The injuries also interfere with her indoor activities.

Now, Sarah is almost entirely unable to engage in her art work. The muscle spasms and stiffness in her shoulder and neck interfere with the delicate work generally required in her paintings. Aside from these physical restrictions, her ongoing pain substantially precludes the intricate detail and concentration required by her art work. As well, these restrictions and pain make it impossible to enjoy her art work even when she is physically able to do it.

Before the accident, Sarah was constantly sewing. She sewed for her family as well as for others. Sarah not only enjoyed sewing as an activity, her sewing saved her family clothing expense and provided her income from the sale of some of her work. This in turn gave her satisfaction and fulfillment from contributing to her family's welfare. Now, Sarah cannot even bend over the sewing machine and concentrate on her sewing work in any meaningful fashion.

The same is true of her cake decorating activities. Before the accident, she was able to engage in such activities to augment her family's income and to fulfill her creative desires. Now, her pain and physical limitations simply preclude any substantial participation in such activities.

Sarah has calculated that her income from cake decorating, paintings, jewelry, and sewing of shirts and coats for sale and barter has grown from between $700–$800 in 2006 to approximately $2,000 in 2009. From this we have calculated that her injuries have diminished her income by approximately $2,000 to date. These losses will continue into the future unless the Pain Clinic program is as successful as expected by Dr. Makie.

To date, Sarah has been primarily a housewife. Through her services she has nurtured and cared for her children and husband. Now that her children have reached adulthood, she could easily begin to pursue her sewing, cake decorating, and art as full-time occupations, or even work outside the home if she chose. But this is not possible because of the pain and restrictions she suffers from the accident.

Sarah's current diagnosis remains: musculoskeletal strain and chronic myofascitis of the left shoulder and neck region, and chronic pain syndrome. We understand that the proposed treatment at the Pain Clinic will not relieve her of ongoing pain. The muscle problem and pain are probably a fact of life for her. However, with the treatment recommended by the pain evaluation team, the pain should no longer dominate her life. She should be able to substantially return to her previous active lifestyle by learning to manage her pain.

The next Pain Clinic starts April 27, 2011. As is evident from Dr. Keith Makie's January 21st letter, it is urgent that she receive the funds to participate in this or a similar program.

All indications are that Sarah's pain and physical limitations are a direct result of the accident, which either caused the particular condition or significantly aggravated a preexisting condition such as with the aggravation of her prior depression and the recurrence of her rectocele.

5

Medical Expenses (through 2011)

As a result of the injuries sustained by Sarah Anderson, the following medical expenses were incurred:

Billings Community Hospital	$ 3,786.75
Yellowstone Co. Hospital	3,921.14
Laurel Vol. Fire Dept.	177.30
Jason Pharmacy	135.95
Doug Bard (dentures 1 TMJ)	850.00
Billings Radiology	125.70
Matterson Surgical Supply	40.00
Dr. B. J. Halst (glasses)	288.00
John Raysmer (dentist)	35.00
R. K. Hersh, M.D., P.C. (Radiologist)	16.00
Billings Medical Clinic	273.00
Deaconess Hosp. (Rectocele)	3,841.75
Family Practice Clinic	906.90
Vern Chase, M.D., (Anesthesiologist)	330.00
Neurological Associates	180.00
Medical reports	45.00
Billings Clinic Pharmacy	163.60
Edward B. Runk, M.D.	148.00**
Community Hosp., Diag. Pain Clinic	845.00**
Yellowstone Co. Hospital	253.50**
Yellowstone Co. Hospital	122.50**
Yellowstone Co. Hospital	45.00**
Billings Medical Clinic	20.00**
TOTAL:	$16,550.09

The sums indicated "**" have not yet been paid. In addition, as stated in Dr. Makie's letter of January 21st (see Exhibit B), Sarah is in urgent need of enrollment in the Pain Clinic program at a cost of between $25,000.00–$27,000.00 for a seven (7)-week treatment program.

EVALUATION OF THE CASE

Legal Issues

From our investigation and our understanding of the facts, we feel that we will obtain a directed verdict in this case in favor of the Plaintiff, leaving only the issue of damages for the jury. We base this upon our research and briefing of the law.

Under Sec. 61-8-326 MCA (Montana Code Annotated), your insured should not have been driving on the left side of the roadway within the no-passing zone as indicated by the double yellow striping on the pavement. Furthermore, your insured was very familiar with this particular area; he knew that it was a low-visibility area with a no-passing zone throughout, and that several homes adjoined the roadway, requiring residents to enter and leave the highway to reach their homes. In this instance, the Andersons' driveway was clearly marked by their mailbox, which would call for additional caution on the part of a would-be passing vehicle. (See photos 6–9 in Exhibit C.)

6

It has been held repeatedly that the primary duty of avoiding a collision rests upon the following driver (*Custer Broadcasting Corp. v. Brewer,* 163 Mont. 519, 518 P.2d 257 (1974)). In a case directly on point with the present claim, a jury entered a verdict for the defendant where the defendant rear-ended the plaintiff while the plaintiff was turning into his driveway. *Garza v. Peppard,* 51 St. Rptr. 1922 (Mont.). In *Garza,* as with this claim, both vehicles were proceeding in the same direction, and both vehicles had passed over the double yellow lines on the pavement. The District Court entered judgment for the plaintiff notwithstanding the verdict. On appeal the Supreme Court affirmed the District Court and found that the defendant, who had been driving the following vehicle, was guilty of negligence as a matter of law for failing to keep a proper lookout. The Court stated:

> Under Montana law, a motorist has a duty to look not only straight ahead but laterally ahead as well and to see that which is in plain sight. Furthermore, a motorist is presumed to see that which he could see by looking, and he will not be permitted to escape the penalty of his negligence by saying that he did not see that which is in plain view. *Nissen v. Johnson,* 135 Mont. 329, 333, 339 P.2d 651, 653 (1959); *Sorrells v. Ryan,* 129 Mont. 29, 289 P.2d 1028 (1955); *Koppang v. Sevier,* 106 Mont. 79, 75 P.2d 790 (1938).
>
> Clearly, a person is negligent in either not looking or looking but not seeing if he claims not to have seen an object which is so clearly visible that all reasonable minds would agree the person must see the object if he were to look with reasonable diligence. *Payne v. Sorenson,* 183 Mont. 323, 326-327, 599 P.2d 362, 364 (1979).

Having these cases and other cases in mind, we strongly feel that this is a case in which the only issue will be the amount of damages to be awarded the plaintiff.

Damages

As to the question of damages, we have taken into consideration the initial hospitalization as well as the subsequent hospitalization for surgical repair of the rectocele, the extreme pain at the outset and during the initial recovery period, the continuing pain in therapy as well as the permanent pain, which Sarah hopes to manage with the assistance of the Pain Clinic program. We have also considered Sarah's lost income and changed course of life.

Sarah still receives treatment in connection with this injury, and even if the Pain Clinic program is successful in managing the pain, it is expected that she will continue to require intermittent physical therapy indefinitely. She will continue to suffer the effects of this injury, and we have considered her life expectancy, which at the present age of 46 is 34.5 years.

We have considered the substantial medical testimony indicating the relationship between Sarah's injuries and the automobile accident. We have considered the magnitude of medical expenses already incurred and those immediately required. We have adjusted our calculations downward to recognize the preexisting nature of her rectocele problem and intermittent depression.

We feel that in our evaluation of this matter, a probable jury verdict in this case would be the sum of Three Hundred Thousand Dollars ($300,000.00). This figure includes the following:

Pain and suffering: PAST:	
10 days or 240 hours for the 2 hospital stays of 5 days each:	
Physical pain at $25.00/hour (muscular and skeletal strain and sprain, temporomandibular joint injury, headaches, surgical rectocele repair):	$ 6,000.00
Mental anguish at $25.00/hour (restricted to hospital and trauma of surgery):	$ 6,000.00

7

Lost pleasure at $5.00/hour (inability to perform any activities):	$ 3,000.00
Remaining 18 months since the accident, approx. 12,960 hours:	
Physical pain at $2.00/hour (therapy, rehabilitation, pain related to muscle and skeletal strain and sprain, TMJ and surgery, etc.):	$25,920.00
Mental anguish at $3.00/hour (depression from pain and inability to pursue normal activities, 16 waking hours/day = 8,640 hours):	$17,280.00
Lost pleasure at $2.00/hour (limitations 8 hours/day = 4,320 hours, on sports, physical activities with friends, and self-fulfillment in pursuing established course of life, etc.):	$ 8,640.00
TOTAL PAST PAIN AND SUFFERING:	$66,840.00

Pain and suffering: FUTURE:

Sarah Anderson is 46 years old and has a life expectancy of 34.5 years pursuant to the life expectancy tables prepared by the U.S. Department of Health & Human Services. 34.5 years is 12,592 days or 302,220 hours:

Physical pain at $.10/hour (muscular and skeletal strain and sprain, myofascitis syndrome and chronic pain syndrome, future arthritis, etc.):	$30,222.00
Mental anguish at $.10/hour (includes concerns for diminished active physical relationship with immediate family and grandchildren, etc., for 16 waking hours/day = 199,465 hours):	$19,946.00
Lost pleasure at $.10/hour (this recognizes partial limitations in active sports and intricate detail work, and the need to be careful due to the injury, for 16 waking hours each day):	$19,946.00
TOTAL FUTURE PAIN AND SUFFERING:	$70,114.00
MEDICAL SPECIALS:	
Past:	$10,550.00
Future—Pain Clinic:	$27,000.00
—Occasional physical therapy etc., @ $500.00/year:	$17,250.00
TOTAL MEDICAL SPECIALS:	$54,800.00

8

INCOME AND PRODUCTIVITY LOSSES:

Past—outside earnings and barter:	$ 2,000.00
—household activities:	$ 6,000.00
TOTAL INCOME AND PRODUCTIVITY LOSSES:	$ 8,000.00

The calculations of pain, suffering, medical expenses, income, and productivity losses anticipate successful pain management by the Pain Clinic program as is expected by Dr. Makie in his January 21, 2011 letter.

Conclusion

As we have stated, our investigation discloses that the liability of your insured is certain in our opinion, and the injuries and actual damages sustained by our client are in excess of the amount of Two Hundred Eighty-Five Thousand Dollars ($285,000.00) for which we now offer to settle. In the event that you do not notify us to the contrary, we will proceed on the assumption that the offer of settlement made in this case is within the coverage of your insurance contract with your insured.

This offer and material is submitted in good faith and we expect you to carefully examine the material contained and honestly evaluate the same, responding to it in the same good faith with which it is submitted to you. Thank you for your cooperation.

Sincerely yours,

Rex Palmer

Rex Palmer
ATTORNEYS, INC., P.C.

Encs.

9

APPENDIX I: GOOD FAITH AND FAIR CLAIMS PRACTICES IN MONTANA

Public policy in the State of Montana encourages timely settlement of insurance claims without litigation. Montana statutory and case law history support this conclusion. Sec. 33-18-201(6), MCA, states:

> Unfair claims settlement practices prohibited. No person may, with such frequency as to indicate a general business practice, do any of the following: . . . (6) neglect to attempt in good faith to effectuate prompt, fair, and equitable settlements of claims in which liability has become reasonably clear. . . .

The above statute creates a duty that runs from the insurer to the insured as well as to third-party claimants. The duty includes an obligation to negotiate in good faith and promptly settle claims when liability has become "reasonably clear." An action based upon a breach of this obligation by the insurer may be prosecuted by a third-party claimant after an action against the insured to determine liability.

The case generally cited for the above proposition is *Klaudt v. Flink,* 658 P.2d 1065 (Mont. 1983). Justice Daley for the majority wrote:

> We therefore hold that Sec. 33-18-201(6), MCA, does create an obligation running from the insurer to the claimant. When such an obligation is breached, the claimant has a basis for a civil action.
>
> The obligation to negotiate in good faith and to promptly settle claims does not mean that liability has been determined. Sec. 33-18-201(6) states that the insurer's obligation arises when liability has become "reasonably clear". . . . 658 P.2d 1065, 1067.

The *Klaudt* result was to be expected. In Montana, the State District Courts and Supreme Court have accepted the principle of third-party liability and the duty to deal in good faith in *Fowler v. State Farm Mutual Automobile Ins. Co.,* 153 Mont. 74, 454 P.2d 76 (1969), and *Thompson v. State Farm Mutual Automobile Ins. Co.,* 161 Mont. 207, 505 P.2d 423 (1973). *Klaudt* was immediately followed by *St. Paul Fire & Marine Ins. Co. v. Kumiskey,* 665 P.2d 223 (Mont. 1983); *Reno v. Erickstein,* 679 P.2d 1204 (Mont. 1984); and *Gibson v. Western Fire Ins. Co.,* 682 P.2d 725 (Mont. 1984).

In this rapidly expanding area of tort law, the relatively old federal case of *Jensen v. O'Daniel,* 210 F. Supp. 317 (D. Mont. 1962), hereinafter *Jensen,* establishes six (6) "elements of bad faith." In that case by an insured against his carrier, the carrier refused a pretrial settlement offer below policy limits.

The six (6) elements examined in *Jensen* and cited with approval by the court in *Gibson v. Western Fire Insurance Co., supra,* are as follows:

1. the likelihood of a verdict in excess of policy limits,
2. whether a defendant's verdict is doubtful,
3. the company's trial counsel's own recommendations,
4. whether insured has been informed of all settlement offers,
5. whether there has been a demand for settlement within policy limits, and
6. whether any offer of contribution has been made by the insured.

The *Gibson* court easily discarded the *Jensen* factors that were inapplicable, and relied upon as many of them as are clearly applicable.

> As the court said in *Jensen,* no one factor is decisive, and all of the circumstances must be considered as to whether the insurance company acted in good faith . . . [T]he failure of *Western* through its agents to follow established standards of investigation, evaluation, negotiation, and communication with its insured are the deciding factors upon which we base this conclusion . . . (682 P.2d 725, 737).

10

Among the "standards of evaluation" mentioned in the *Gibson* decision is the fact that the insured's attorney evaluated the claim as being reasonably worth the amount demanded by the claimant in the insured's malpractice case.

The second issue is raised by the statute, namely, the requirement that bad faith be shown to be "general business practice" of that particular company.

> [I]t is possible that multiple violations occurring in the same claim could be sufficient to show a frequent business practice, as would violations by the same company in different cases. (*Klaudt v. Flink,* 658 P.2d 1065, 1068).

The court concedes that its ruling in *Klaudt* could be viewed by many as "harsh," but offers the following rationale:

> [T]he legislature has reacted to what it perceives to be an important problem. Insurance companies have, and are able to exert, leverage against individual claimants because of the disparity in resource base. Justice delayed is often justice denied. Public policy calls for a meaningful solution. The legislature has spoken and we, by this decision, breathe life into the legislative product. (*Ibid.*)

APPENDIX II: DIAGNOSTIC PAIN CLINIC REPORTS

Billings Community Hospital
Rehabilitation Center

Gregory M. Wies, EXECUTIVE DIRECTOR

January 9, 2011

Sid R. Silker, M.D.
Post Office Box 1045
Laurel, Montana 59248

Dear Dr. Silker:

Sarah Anderson was evaluated at Billings Community Rehabilitation Center's Outpatient Diagnostic Pain Clinic on December 9, 2010, by the following clinic team members: Keith Makie, Ph.D., Psychologist; Sandy Bickett, M.D., Physiatrist; Todd Rockler, R.P.T., Physical Therapist; Rick Wysil, B.S.W., Social Worker; and the following consultants: Edward B. Runk, M.D., Neurologist, and W. J. McConnell, M.D., Orthopedist.

Enclosed for your review are their reports, together with the Summary and Recommendations. If you wish to follow through with the recommendations, please contact the Pain Program Secretary at 248-2400 extension 3634 or by letter.

Thank you for referring your patient to the Billings Community Rehabilitation Center's Outpatient Diagnostic Pain Clinic.

Sincerely,

Keith Makie

Keith Makie, Ph.D.
Pain Program Director

KCM:pdr
enclosures
xc: Rex Palmer, Attorney

REPORTS

Billings Community Rehabilitation Center
OUTPATIENT DIAGNOSTIC PAIN CLINIC

December 9, 2010

SUMMARY AND RECOMMENDATIONS . . . . Keith Makie, Ph.D.
Albert Fremont, M.D.

PHYSIATRIC EVALUATION . . . . Sandy Bickett, M.D.

PSYCHOLOGICAL EVALUATION . . . . Keith Makie, Ph.D.

NEUROLOGIC EVALUATION . . . . Edward Runk, M.D.

ORTHOPEDIC EVALUATION . . . . W. J. McConnell, M.D.

PHYSICAL THERAPY EVALUATION . . . . Todd Rockler, R.P.T.

SOCIAL SERVICE INTAKE INTERVIEW . . . . Rick Wysil, B.S.W.

SUMMARY AND RECOMMENDATIONS
(DIAGNOSTIC PAIN CLINIC)

Billings Community
Rehabilitation Center

PATIENT: Sarah Anderson
MEDICAL RECORD NUMBER: 0113075
DATE OF EVALUATION: 12-9-10
PROGRAM: Diagnostic Pain Clinic

On December 9, 2010 Sarah Anderson and her husband, Ross, participated in a comprehensive pain evaluation. Sarah was seen by an orthopedic surgeon, a psychiatrist, a psychologist, a physical therapist, and a neurologist; Ross was seen by a social worker. The reports from these various people are included; this will serve as a summary of their findings and the recommendations of the Diagnostic Pain Clinic Team.

It was the consensus of the individuals who examined Sarah from a physical standpoint that she was suffering from a rather long-standing problem with chronic shoulder, neck, and headache pain. Those who examined her agreed that the pain was of a musculoskeletal chronic myofascitis origin and there was a consensus that Sarah was in the midst of what they would term chronic pain syndrome. Upon examination there was evidence of rather marked limitation of range of motion in her neck due to pain. There was a good deal of evidence of muscle tightness and some tenderness. There was no evidence of radiculopathy or other neurologic involvement upon examination and in general those who examined her from a physical standpoint saw her problem as mainly musculoskeletal with resultant problems in muscle tightness, deconditioning, and general inactivity. There were comments upon the large number of treatments that had been tried with Sarah to no avail and suggestions that an interdisciplinary, highly structured, intensive treatment program would be necessary to turn around the problem.

The Psychological Evaluation indicates that Sarah is a woman who, at the present time, is in a great deal of obvious psychological distress. She reports being extremely agitated and nervous. She clearly

13

states that the stresses in her life that are enumerable at this time tend to directly contribute to her pain. She has many, many family and relationship problems with her husband, from her standpoint. She gave the impression during the psychological evaluation of being distressed to the point of being desperate and not being in control of her life and this very high level of general psychological distress was definitely reflected on the MMPI. She appeared to be very motivated to do something about her problem because, as she said in the evaluation, she was coming to the "end of her rope," and very much wanted something to change.

In the social worker's interview with Ross, there was a marked discrepancy between Ross's report of the problem situation with Sarah's chronic pain and Sarah's own report. Ross appeared to be a rather poor historian and to be relatively uninvolved in Sarah's chronic pain problem. He continued to have past expectations of her even though she reports to be in great pain and is unable to do many things physically. The social worker commented that their relationship is quite traditional with Ross's expectations being that Sarah carry her load as a traditional wife. The social worker noted that Ross was quite ambivalent about supporting an intensive treatment program that could remove her from home, even if Sarah decided that was the best thing for her. The social worker questioned Ross's involvement and motivation to work with Sarah on solving this problem.

It was the overwhelming consensus of the Diagnostic Pain Clinic Team that Sarah seek out an inpatient, interdisciplinary, behaviorally oriented chronic pain treatment program. The team felt it was imperative that such a program be implemented very soon. They were concerned not only with Sarah's obvious decline physically and lack of ability to engage in most activities in her daily life, but also about the extreme degree of psychological distress reflected in the evaluation. The Team agreed that unless such an interdisciplinary, highly structured pain treatment program were implemented, Sarah's situation would continue to deteriorate to the point where she became more and more distressed psychologically and already-serious family concerns would become even more serious. The Team felt that given Sarah's level of motivation to do something about her problem, she would be a good candidate for chronic pain treatment.

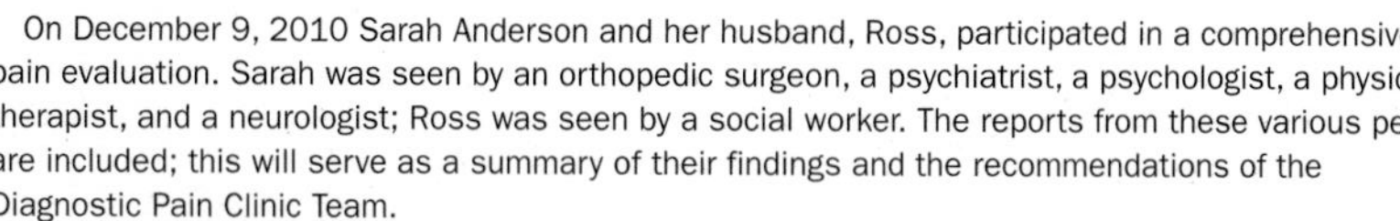

Keith Makie, Ph.D.
Pain Program Director

Albert Fremont, M.D.
Medical Director
Community Rehabilitation Center

KCM/brm
dic 1/8/11
tran 1/8/11

14

PHYSIATRIC EVALUATION
(SANDY BICKETT, M.D.)

Billings Community Hospital

DIAGNOSTIC PAIN CLINIC

NAME: Sarah Anderson
MEDICAL RECORD NUMBER: 0113075
EVALUATION: Physiatrist Evaluation
EVALUATOR: Sandy Bickett, M.D.
DATE OF EVALUATION: December 9, 2010

Sarah is a 45-year-old woman who was involved in a motor vehicle accident in August of 2009. She reports that at that time she was pulling into her driveway when a four-wheel-drive pickup truck was passing in a no-passing zone and struck the rear of her car going approximately 80 to 90 miles an hour. The impact was sufficient to break the seat belt that the passenger was wearing and the passenger was thrown from the car. Sarah stayed in the car; she did have her seat belt on. The car was spun around and wrapped around the telephone pole on the driver's side and Sarah was wedged in the car and found herself wrapped around the telephone pole as well. She reports that she lost consciousness briefly and when she came to, the daughter of the woman who had been thrown from the car was calling out for her mother. Sarah reports being able to get out of the car though she felt like she was in slow motion and walked over to her friend who was injured and there passed out. They were taken initially to the Emergency Room in Laurel and from there to the Emergency Room in Billings. She remembers having no feeling in her left leg or foot at the time of the accident and for the rest of that night. She was initially seen by Dr. Coots who evaluated her and managed her during that stay, which he reports as a few days. She reports that from the moment she began to be fully conscious she had numbness in her left leg, but an aching feeling as well; she had an aching, burning pain in her left arm and shoulder and neck. She reports having been bruised over that entire shoulder and upper-arm region. She was sent home from the hospital and the pain was still there. She reports that the pain has continued to be present continuously ever since. It may wax and wane in intensity, but is always present in her shoulder and neck. Her leg and low back pain has subsided and only recurs once in a while. She notices pain in her lower back and leg when she has to do any bending or stooping. She attempted to pick some strawberries this summer and had the recurrence of her back and leg pain. She was unable to have a garden as she usually does.

When Sarah describes her shoulder and neck pain, which is her chief complaint, she reports that the pain is always present. It has a nagging, burning quality as well as a deep itching. It is not an itch which can be scratched on the surface, but is an itch or a tingle deep within. When she moves or stretches, she has a pulling, burning pain throughout that area that is being stretched. She has currently been instructed in some exercises for stretching her neck and shoulder and when she does those it brings on the pulling, burning pain, which does not subside during that hour. She also reports having headaches since the time of the accident, at least one a day. She reports she cannot remember a day since the accident when she did not have a headache. There are days when it is worse than others and some days where she is unable to function because of the headache and neck pain, but in general, the intensity waxes and wanes.

Sarah reports that things that increase the intensity of her pain include activity and stress. Activities that she describes that are particularly painful or pain-producing include doing paperwork, when she leans forward and concentrates. Vacuuming is particularly painful. She reports having been an avid seamstress prior to her accident and would finish two or three garments per day. Now, if she sews a half a garment she will hurt for the entire week. She does not do heavy housekeeping including mopping or vacuuming, but does do dishes, cooking, baking, and washing. Her husband is

15

self-employed, so she does some of his bookwork on a daily basis. Sarah reports having tried multiple medications at the recommendation of her physicians and this includes Valium, which she reports "put her in outer space," but helped the pain. She discontinued that because although it reduced the pain she was unable to function. Xanax she will take on occasion when the pain is particularly severe and she is unable to relax and go to sleep at night. The Xanax causes her bad dreams and so she takes it only rarely, but will take it when the pain is severe. She reports having tried Naprosyn, which was not helpful, and is now taking Clinoril, which she finds somewhat better than Tylenol. In addition to the medications which she has tried, she has also tried physical therapy. The ultrasound helped and made her feel better and lasted approximately one-half an hour. She has tried hot baths and hot showers and finds that if she can lie down in the tub and relax and get the water as hot as possible, this will help for a short period of time. She had a cortisone injection into her left shoulder by Dr. Todd on two occasions, both of which helped; however, she is fearful of having too much cortisone and Dr. Todd warned against having too many injections. She was seen by Dr. Dowell, who placed her on exercises for stretching, which she is supposed to do on an hourly basis. However, the exercise consistently makes her worse and so she is reluctant to do it hourly and does it somewhat less than that.

Sarah Anderson reports that her sleeping has been poor since the time of the accident. She reports she cannot remember sleeping through a whole night and is up three or four times a night because of the pain waking her, and she cannot get back to sleep. At these times, she will get up, read a little or walk around, or have a glass of warm milk in an attempt to go back to bed and go to sleep. She is finding that she will fall asleep during the day if she is sitting, because of her fitful night sleep. She reports occasionally staying in bed the whole day and sleeping essentially all day. This has only begun to occur in the last two months and she feels that this is an indication of her becoming worn out by the pain. She reports a bad appetite, comments that this seems unreasonable given her overweight condition, but reports not really having a good appetite or enjoying food, but that she considers herself a nervous eater and that when she is in pain, in order to make herself feel better she begins to eat and eat and not even taste what she is eating. She reports that after the injury, her weight got down to 155 pounds for a period of time; however, her usual weight is between 172 and 184 and has remained there for the last several years, and she is in that range at the present time. Sarah also reports that her social life and recreational life have taken a real reduction since her accident. She went to a Bible study both Tuesday and Wednesday nights and to church on Sunday regularly before her accident and now occasionally gets to Sunday services, which is a dramatic reduction for her. She used to visit people regularly; however, now she reports being anxious and hating to be around people. She finds they make her nervous and she thinks she rattles on. She also does not like to talk about her pain and yet people will comment on how bad she looks and this makes her feel worse. She also reports that she dislikes being around people because she has lost touch with the activities that she used to do and to do with them, and feels like she has nothing to talk about anymore. Prior to her accident, she liked to do a variety of activities, including camping, some gold mining, searching for arrowheads, and hiking. She reports that she usually does a lot of activities with her family in the summer. However, last summer after the accident, she was left at home alone frequently while they went off to do their usual activities. She has done oil painting in the past, doing both miniatures and canvas. Since the time of the accident, she is unable to do miniatures because she cannot lean forward and concentrate or do the fine work. She has been unable to do her canvas oil painting because of the pain and the nervousness. Sewing was one of Sarah Anderson's other areas of release and enjoyment, as well as substantially contributing to the family's well-being. She finds she cannot do that anymore. She not only made her own clothing and that of her children, but she also made jeans for her husband and did the winter coats for her adult daughters, as well as undergarments. The cost of doing it herself was so much less than the cost of purchasing that she and her family are experiencing a substantial burden by her inability to continue to do this activity and she is feeling a particular loss because this was an area of outlet for her.

16

Physical examination reveals a very short, stout woman in no apparent distress.

HEENT: The pupils are equal and react to light and accommodate. Extraocular muscles are intact. Sensation over the face is intact as are facial movements.
BACK: Back was examined and though there is no back deformity, the left shoulder is carried approximately an inch lower than the right without causing a spinal curve. Hips and pelvis are equal and level. Palpation of the back, neck, and shoulders reveals multiple areas of tautness of muscle and trigger point tenderness as demonstrated on the attached diagram.
NECK: Neck range of motion is limited in flexion to chin one inch from the chest. Extension is essentially normal. Rotation is approximately 60 degrees in both directions.
UPPER EXTREMITIES: Upper extremity strength is Grade V minus on the right and IV on the left including grip. These are all reduced because of the pain that they reportedly produce in the left shoulder. Range of motion of the left upper extremity is also limited by pain produced in the left shoulder area and limited to 120 degrees of flexion, 100 degrees of abduction, external rotation lacks 45 degrees.
NEUROLOGIC: Deep tendon reflexes and coordination are intact in both upper and lower extremities, as is sensation to pin prick and light touch.

IMPRESSION:
1. Musculoskeletal strain and chronic myofascitis of the left shoulder and neck region.
2. Chronic pain syndrome.

RECOMMENDATIONS: Sarah Anderson has had good episodic physical therapy, which produced short-term relief. All of the previous persons who have examined her have recommended physical therapy and stretching which have produced some positive results, but have not fully resolved this problem. For this reason, it is recommended that she become involved in an inpatient program that combines treatment for her myofascitis, tenseness, and tightness as well as her chronic pain syndrome in order to achieve maximal results.

Sandy Bickett

Sandy Bickett, M.D.

STB: ajf

PSYCHOLOGICAL EVALUATION
(KEITH MAKIE, PH.D.)

Billings Community
Rehabilitation Center

PATIENT: Sarah Anderson
DATE OF EVALUATION: 12/9/10
EVALUATION PROCEDURES: Review of records and questionnaires, interview, Minnesota Multiphasic Personality Inventory (MMPI)
STATUS: outpatient
AGE: 45
PROGRAM: Diagnostic Pain Clinic
EVALUATOR: Keith Makie, Ph.D.

17

Background Information

Sarah is a 45-year-old married woman who lives with her husband and family in Laurel, Montana. She was referred for this Psychological Evaluation, which is part of a larger interdisciplinary pain evaluation, because of her long-standing debilitating problem with chronic shoulder, neck, and headache pain. It was obvious from the onset of the interview part of this evaluation that Sarah was extremely agitated and distressed. She came into the interview reporting that she was very nervous, that her pain is getting worse, that she had numerous family and personal problems, and was even having a hard time concentrating on the evaluation. She talked at a rapid rate, much of her thinking was confused, her speech was forced at times, she became quite emotional in several parts of the interview, and in general she presents herself as someone who is operating under a great deal of pressure and that pressure was steadily mounting to the point where she was feeling out of control.

She presented a history of her injury which happened in August of 2009 as a result of a motor vehicle accident. She indicated that since that time she has had rather excruciating and constant pain in her shoulder and neck and has had headaches. She says that this pain increases with any kind of activity, but definitely increases when she has problems with anxieties and worries at home. She said that nothing really helps the pain, other than taking medication and getting rest and quiet, which she never gets in her rather crisis-filled, tumultuous life. At the present time she takes Xanax, Tylenol Extra-Strength, and Clinoril. She says that these medications tend to help her somewhat, although the pain is usually there. She says that the pain does disturb her sleep but is not sure whether the disturbance is due to the pain, per se, or the many other worries and rapid thoughts she has going through her mind most of the time.

I did not have to ask her how the chronic pain had affected her life because she quickly launched into a long description of how out of control she feels and how awful her life has become since the accident. She indicated that before the accident she still had a number of concerns and problems, but was able to "roll with the punches" and handle the situations as they arose. She said that since the accident, her physical limitations, and the constant pain, she is just unable to handle the pressures in her life and finds herself wishing things like going to sleep and never waking up and then her family just all going away, which are very disturbing to her. She describes herself as a very responsible, caring, caretaking kind of person who watches out for the needs of everybody else before she takes care of her own needs. She again said that it was fine for her to operate that way before the chronic pain situation, but now she is finding she is "at her wit's end," she is losing control of her emotions, she feels that her life is a mass of confusion and she doesn't know which way to turn. All of this was presented in a rather distressed, agitated manner with Sarah shifting around in her chair, talking rapidly, and in general appearing as if she was having a difficult time. At several points during the interview she commented on the fact that she didn't know why she was telling me all these details because usually she presents a rather calm, stoic front when underneath she is seething with distress and agitation.

One of the things that came out clearly in the interview is that Sarah is a woman who takes responsibility for almost everybody she comes in contact with. She described her relationship with her husband as extremely problematic. She said that she does the work around the house, even though she has days where she cannot get out of bed; her husband still pretty much demands that she keep up the pace. She says at times she feels like a slave in her own home, and then again feels very badly for even having those unacceptable thoughts. She says there has been some recent trouble in her home because of a 21-year-old who has been living with them because he has nowhere else to go; this individual has gotten in trouble with the law and caused a great deal of stress and conflict in her life. She described her home as a motel for anybody who wants to stay there.

She doesn't feel like she has control over who impinges on her life. She said that she constantly works hard and doesn't seem to get anywhere and is feeling quite desperate. In general, it appeared that she was unable to draw any limits on what people in her life could expect from her and she did

18

not know how she was going to get out of a situation that she definitely saw herself as getting into because of her wanting to help other people and meet their needs. There was a definite tone in the whole interview of her being trapped in a situation that she does not know how to get out of.

We talked about alternative treatments to chronic pain, including structured chronic pain treatment. She said she had heard about such a program and thought that would be exactly what she needed. She thought she needed to be removed from the very stressful environment she now lives in. She thought her family needed to learn more about her pain and the effects of stress on her pain and she seemed very interested in anything that could relieve what she describes as a desperate, intolerable situation.

TEST RESULTS: The Welsh Code for Sarah's MMPI is as follows: 83**1*76"429'0/5# F'K/L:

The first thing about this Welsh Code is the significantly elevated 'F' Scale, suggesting that Sarah is in a good deal of general psychological distress, which she is openly admitting. There are a number of extremely elevated clinical scales, suggesting a number of themes for this profile. The two high points suggest an individual who appears to be in a great deal of psychological turmoil. These individuals report feeling anxious, tense, nervous, fearful, and worried. They tend to be very dependent in interpersonal relationships and seek attention and affection; they tend to be depressed with feelings of hopelessness. They tend to present a large number of physical complaints of a vague nature. There tends to be a disturbance in their thinking and they often report memory lapses, poor concentration, and intrusive thoughts. A second theme is that of someone who is overly involved in her physical complaints and bodily functions; these complaints tend to increase in times of stress. There is also a suggestion of an individual who tends to convert psychological problems into physical symptoms. Other suggestions from the profile are someone who is quite distrustful and suspicious of the motives of others. There is a suggestion from this profile of an individual who is quite dependent in interpersonal relationships and tends to defer in decision-making matters, especially to males. This MMPI Profile fits in very well with my interview observations of Sarah, that of an extremely distressed, obviously upset, rather desperate woman who sees herself as trapped in a situation that she cannot solve with her own resources.

SUMMARY AND RECOMMENDATIONS: This evaluation indicates that Sarah has a rather long-standing, complicated chronic pain problem that is made even more complicated by an obviously stressful family and social situation. She comes across as quite desperate, confused, and psychologically distressed. This distress definitely worsens her chronic pain, which then, in a circular fashion, increases her distress. My main recommendation at this point is that she seek out an inpatient, interdisciplinary, behaviorally oriented chronic pain treatment program. Only in such a program could the multiplicity of factors contributing to her chronic pain problem be reasonably addressed. I would think without such an intervention she will continue to deteriorate and eventually the family situation will most likely collapse.

Keith Makie

Keith Makie, Ph.D.
Licensed psychologist

KCM/brm
dic 12/12/10
tran 12/16/10

19

NEUROLOGIC EVALUATION
(EDWARD RUNK, M.D.)

Billings Community
Rehabilitation Center

HX: This 45 YOWF is referred via the Pain Clinic for evaluation. Apparently she was injured in a MVA in 8/09. She was a driver wearing a belt, but apparently it was not tight. She was struck from behind by another vehicle that caused her vehicle to go into a spin and strike a tree. Apparently the tree was struck on the driver's door. The patient feels that her head struck a telephone pole through the open window and her shoulder was pinched between the seat and the door. The patient thinks she may have been unconscious for one minute, and was subsequently hospitalized for four days. She had a CAT scan that was reportedly negative. The patient had residual neck, shoulder, and trapezius pain on the left, with continued symptoms until this time. This consists of a burning in the left arm, with some numbness in the hand. This is called a constant nagging pain. This is worse with bending, vacuuming, and other activity and better with rest. Heat seems to help, such as in the bath.

The patient has had an ultrasound, heat, massage, etc. via PT, without any continued benefit. Shoulder injection seems to help temporarily. Various checks in the past have shown spasm but no clear neurologic changes. The patient had nightmares on Xanax and amitriptyline. Imipramine apparently helped some, but it was DC'd for reasons that are unclear to the patient. Of the anti-inflammatories, she has had the best response on Clinoril but currently is only taking it intermittently, about three times per week. The patient is not currently in PT, and has never had a TENS unit.

PMH: The patient has had a transphenoidal hypophysectomy for a micropituitary tumor. She has had a prior hysterectomy, bil. carpal tunnel repairs, Marshall-Marketti procedure, and T and A. She has been treated in the past for depression. Current meds include the Clinoril, HCTZ, Premarin, K^+, and occasional Xanax or Tylenol. The patient has no allergies. The patient had a grade-eight education, but later received a GED. She is right-handed.
PH: Neg.
SH: The patient did sewing and painting for work in the past, is having difficulty pursuing these at the current time due to her problems. The patient's husband is out of work and currently is trying to get SSI for lowback pain and reported emotional problems. The patient denies use of tobacco and drinks alcohol rarely.

EXAM: Weight is 183 pounds. Height is 4'11". BP is 120-78. General: pleasant, obese 45 YOWF who appears quite comfortable at rest. Head: normocephalic, atraumatic without bruits. ENT: unremarkable. Neck: reasonably supple with full active ROM. Carotids 2+ without bruits. Lhermitte's sign was negative. Chest: clear. Cor: S1, S2 without murmur. Abdomen: soft. The patient had bil. CTS scars. The patient was very tight and tender throughout the left trapezius area.
Mental Status: The patient was alert and oriented ×3. She knew the recent presidents, was minimally right-left confused, but had normal praxis and naming skills. She read a grade-six passage well with good recall. Serial 3s were well done. The patient remembered two of three objects after five minutes and confabulated on the third. With a hint she came up with it. The patient's speech was normal. The patient had a lot of nervous laughter. Cranial nerves: 1. intact. 2. fields and OKNs were normal. Fundi: benign. PERRL. The patient had full EOMs but seemed to have a minimal right exotropia at rest. Remaining cranial nerves are unremarkable. On motor exam, the patient has pain around the left shoulder girdle, leading to difficulty testing the biceps and deltoids. There was no winging of the scapula or other clear weakness. Sensation was intact to fine touch, sharp/dull, vibration, position, and graphesthesia testing throughout. A Romberg test was neg.

On coordination testing, the patient performed finger-to-nose, heel-to-shin, and rapid alternating movement tests well. Gait including toe and tandem was normal. Reflexes were 2–3+ and symmetrical with down going toes.

20

A: 45 YOWF seems to have a myofascial pain syndrome. I see no evidence of specific radiculopathy or other neurologic involvement at this time. The patient might respond to another round of PT, especially including such modalities as a TENS Unit. She might benefit additionally from imipramine as it has been used in the past. More frequent use of Clinoril might be of value as well. I will discuss the situation further with other members of the Pain Clinic team.

Edward Runk

Edward Runk, MD/jh
trans: 12/12/10

ORTHOPEDIC EVALUATION
(W. J. McCONNELL, M.D.)

Billings Community
Rehabilitation Center

OUTPATIENT DIAGNOSTIC PAIN CLINIC

NAME: Sarah Anderson
MEDICAL RECORD NUMBER: 0113075
AGE: 45
PROGRAM: Outpatient Diagnostic Pain Clinic
EVALUATION: Orthopedic Evaluation
EVALUATOR: W. J. McConnell, M.D., Orthopedic Surgeon
EVALUATION: December 9, 2010

Sarah Anderson, a 45-year-old, Caucasian female, was evaluated on December 9, 2010 for purpose of the Pain Clinic Evaluation Unit.

She reported that on August 20, 2009, she was the driver of a Datsun pickup which was rear-ended by a 4 × 4 Chevy while she was turning into her driveway near Laurel, Montana. She reported injuring her left shoulder, neck and head as well as her left leg. According to her, she went to the Laurel Hospital where Dr. Gosten saw her and then was transferred to Billings Community Hospital. She further reported that Dr. Coots saw her upon her entrance to the Community X-Ray Department. She further stated that since that time she has been bothered by a lot of headaches, left neck, and shoulder pain extending down into the posterior aspect of the left arm to above the elbow; also to the front of her chest, indicating the anterior pectoral region.

In addition to being seen by Dr. Coots, she has also had neurosurgical consultation by Dr. Dowell, orthopedic consultation by Dr. Todd, and has also been seen by Dr. Sid Silker of Laurel. Dr. Silker is her doctor of record, according to her.

Past medical history is quite complex surgically as she reported that she has had a brain tumor removed by Dr. Grost in Seattle. She has had bilateral carpal tunnel since three to four years ago, a number of D & C's, followed by a complete hysterectomy.

PRESENT CONDITION: According to her, she continues having frequent headaches, which she localizes by placing the palm of her hand to the occipital region, which she indicated progressed upwards and forwards, indicating the parietal-temporal regions, continuing into the frontal area. She characterized the pain as dull, deep, aching pain that she can partially alleviate, when severe, by taking Xanax or Tylenol. She also reported other medical intake, including blood pressure medications and Premarin.

21

In regards to her headaches she denied any oral or auditory auras and denied any memory loss, type of seizures, dizziness, or syncope. She also indicated that the left shoulder bothered her and here, again, placing the palm of her hand onto the trapezii areas, extending up into the cervical region to the occiput on the left. She also reported that this pain extended into the posterior arm area, by her description and stopping at a level just above the elbow. She further related that the pain also extended forward, indicating the pectoralis area on the left. She also indicated that her upper back, and here indicated the infrascapular region, mainly on the left paraspinal musculature, bothers her at times when she is tense or with extended arm use.

She also indicated to this evaluator that actually her back is doing pretty well now and that she is not having any particular leg problem currently, at the time she was being seen here.

According to her, her last medical attention was provided by Dr. Silker who saw her approximately one month prior to her being seen here. Examination revealed a rather short, moderately obese female of stated age who did not appear in acute or chronic distress. She appeared awake, alert, and oriented and proved to be a good historian. She was noted to move about without a visible gait disturbance and offered no complaints during the interview, with her sitting on the examining table throughout.

She was able to stand in the mode of attention upon request and the spine appeared to be in good alignment when viewed posteriorly and laterally. The scapular angles were noted to be level and scapular motion was full in all planes, as was range of motion of the upper extremities and the cervical spine. She produced forward flexion to approximately 60°, extension to 15°, right and left lateral flexion and rotation to 25° each. Motor power of the upper extremities, including grip, was considered to be within normal limits throughout. Digit dexterity was opinioned to be intact. There was no atrophy, in opinion noted, with special reference to the hand intrinsics.

She was able to stand and walk on toes and heels and tandem walk without apparent difficulty or complaint. Sitting straight-leg raise was negative, bilaterally, to beyond 90°. Passive ankle dorsiflexion was performed readily. Motor power of the lower extremities was considered to be within normal limits throughout, with special reference to the great toe extensors and feet evertors.

Deep tendon reflexes of the upper and lower extremities were considered to be bilaterally equal and active and produced without clonus. There were no sensory changes elicited to pin involving the upper extremities, with special reference to the left upper extremity.

It should be noted that while passive range of motion of the left shoulder was able to be performed fully, she was unable, according to her, to lift her arm in lateral elevation to above 90° and was able to forward elevate to approximately 120° with complaints of pain and pulling. At this point in time, palpation of this shoulder was accomplished and she indicated that the greatest amount of tenderness lay in the specific region of the bicipital groove on this side.

The question of left bicipital tendonitis is unanswered at this point and it may prove beneficial to form appropriate injection(s). Other than this suggestion, no other opinions to any further treatment, medically or surgically, are able to be projected by this evaluator.

Following further X-ray reviews and file review, will discuss at the appropriate scheduled conference.

W. J. McConnell

W. J. McConnell, M.D.
Orthopedic Surgeon

WJM/brm
dic 12/16/10
tran 12/22/10

22

PHYSICAL THERAPY EVALUATION
(TODD ROCKLER, R.P.T.)

Billings Community
Rehabilitation Center

PHYSICAL THERAPY EVALUATION
NAME: Sarah Anderson
MEDICAL RECORD NUMBER: 0113075
AGE: 45
DIAGNOSIS: Chronic left arm and cervical pain.
PHYSICIAN ORDERS: Evaluation
PHYSICIAN: Dr. Sandy Bickett
FREQUENCY/DURATION: one time only
DATE OF EVAL: 12/9/10
STATUS: Outpatient Diagnostic Pain Clinic

HISTORY: This is a 45-year-old woman who was involved in a motor vehicle accident in August of 2009 in which she was hit from behind and spun around and struck a telephone pole. The patient stated she had immediate onset of shoulder and neck pain, and left upper extremity pain. She describes this pain as a nagging, dull, constant pain. She is worse with forward bending and doing desk work, lifting over 5 pounds. Patient said she is better with heat and ultrasound temporarily side bending to the right. She stated her upper extremity pain comes and goes, and that she has a problem sleeping and is up walking around, three to four times a night. She has been treated with stretching exercises, hot packs, ultrasound, and massage. Isometric exercises made her worse. She has been treated by an osteopath who gave her acupressure which temporarily helped relieve her pain. She has had two cortisone shots in the cervical area which she stated helped her pain for approximately one month. She currently has hypertension and is on medication for this. She feels that her pain is staying about the same over the last several months.

SUBJECTIVE: Patient's chief complaint is of dull, nagging, constant pain in her cervical area and left shoulder with intermittent radiations down her left upper extremity.

OBJECTIVE: Evaluation of patient showed her to have good posture with a slightly forward head. Range of motion of her cervical spine was approximately 75 percent in backward bending, approximately 90 percent in forward bending, within normal limits in left rotation and left side bending, approximately 75 percent of right rotation and right side bending. Palpation of patient's upper cervical and thoracic area showed her to be sore over her left sterno-clavicular joint and over the left clavicle, the subacrominal triangle, the sterno-cleidomastoids, and the scalenes on the left were all tender to palpation. The facet joints, bilaterally were tender to palpation and patient had a difficult time swallowing. Passive mobility of her cervical spine was difficult due to muscle guarding, but did show some significant tightness in the muscles on the left cervical and thoracic area. Temporomandibular test showed patient to have a late opening click on the left with a late closing click. She also had a late opening click on the right with an early closing click on the right. The patient has dentures and has had dentures since she was fifteen years old. Soft tissue testing showed her to be extremely tight on the left upper thoracic area and cervical area. Upper extremity range of motion was decreased on the left, both actively and passively, and internal and external rotation and abduction. Her strength was decreased to good-minus and sensation seemed to be increased on the left. Evaluation of her cervical spine was difficult due to her obesity.

PROBLEMS: Soft tissue tightness on the left in her upper thoracic and cervical area. Decreased strength. Decreased range of motion and increased sensation in the left upper extremity. Possible TMJ problems and slightly poor posture with a forward head.

GOALS: Not applicable.

23

TREATMENT RECOMMENDATIONS: Patient would probably do well with an intensive physical therapy program for stretching, strengthening, and mobilization of her left upper extremity. It is recommended that patient would do well with inpatient behavioral modification pain program with extensive physical therapy.

Todd Rockler

Todd Rockler, RPT
12/10/10

TR/brm
dic 12/10/10
tran 12/12/10

SOCIAL SERVICE INTAKE INTERVIEW
(RICK WYSIL, B.S.W.)

Billings Community
Rehabilitation Center

OUTPATIENT DIAGNOSTIC PAIN CLINIC EVALUATION

NAME: Sarah Anderson
MEDICAL RECORD NUMBER: 0113075
PROGRAM: Chronic Pain Program
DATE OF INTAKE: 12/9/10

EVALUATION: Social Services
EVALUATOR: Rick Wysil, BSW
SIGNIFICANT OTHER: Ross Anderson, husband

DESCRIPTIVE STATEMENT: The following information was obtained from a personal interview with Sarah's husband, Ross Anderson. He was a poor historian; he had particular trouble providing details or estimation of dates. Ross shared he is hard of hearing. He also stated he is "absent-minded" and if he is required to "think fast" he gets confused. Sarah Anderson, a 45-year-old married female, was injured in a two-vehicle accident during the summer of 2009. According to Ross, the other driver was at fault. Ross stated that Sarah was hospitalized for a number of days following this accident. He said she suffered injury to her left shoulder, neck, and upper back. As a result of the accident, Ross said she has had numerous surgeries and suffers from headaches.

Ross said Sarah has had a complicated medical history for the past twenty years, which has included surgeries on her bladder, intestines, and pituitary gland (he said she has had many other surgeries, but he couldn't remember them all).

FAMILY COMPOSITION AND SUPPORT NETWORK: Sarah and her 49-year-old husband, Ross, have been married between 20 and 25 years; this is the second marriage for both people. Ross indicated their attraction for each other was the cause of dissolvement of both their first marriages. He indicated this was a traumatic period for all parties involved; in fact, Sarah's husband somehow convinced her to go to Warm Springs State Mental Hospital for a month or so. Sarah has two adult children from her first union: Jerry Landquer, and Roxanne Aist, who is married and resides in Red Lodge (Ross adopted her). Ross and Sarah see Roxanne at least once a week. Roxanne has one daughter. Ross stated Sarah is very close to her daughter and grandchild and enjoys spending time with them. Sarah's son by her first marriage, Jerry Landquer, is in the service and has been out of the family home for the past ten years. Ross had two children from his first marriage: his son died in an accident shortly after

24

the divorce; his daughter Jolene lives in Florida. He has little contact with his daughter. Ross and Sarah have two daughters, Theresa, age 20, who occasionally still resides in the family home and Marsha, age 17, who is still in the family home. Ross reports Sarah has close relationships with both daughters. He added they are having typical trouble with Marsha that one would expect from a teenager; he indicated he and Sarah both believe in physical punishment when they cannot manage Marsha in any other manner. Ross described Sarah as a good mother and stated she has very close family ties.

Ross stated his relationship with Sarah has had the "usual ups and downs," but "nothing terrible." He added they have always been able to overcome their problems. As far as communication between the two, Ross admitted Sarah probably feels he does not talk to her enough. He shared he tends not to discuss his feelings, but instead tends to keep things to himself. Ross said he and Sarah believe in traditional male/female values in their marriage, i.e., her place is in the home caring for the children and he is responsible for providing for their financial security. Ross added, "I'm in charge, I don't believe in a woman leading a family."

Sarah's father is deceased; her mother, Lisa Scoon, lives in Laurel. Ross stated Sarah sees her mother weekly, but does not believe they are terribly close; he stated Sarah's relationship with her mother has improved over the years. Ross said he believes Sarah's childhood was difficult. He said because her parents were divorced, the children (he did not know how many siblings she has) were "shoved around in the family." He believes Sarah's mother was physically and mentally abusive to her. He stated Sarah came from an extremely poor family. Sarah was born and raised in Wyoming. Ross said Sarah married at age 15 or 16; he suspects she married at such a young age as a means of getting out of her family situation.

Ross's father is deceased; his mother, Donna Anderson, resides in Laurel except during the summer when she lives with her daughter in Oregon. Ross believes his mother provides Sarah with much emotional support, but does not interfere.

Sarah apparently receives good emotional support from her sister, Lena Morgal, who lives in Laurel. Ross stated that she sees her at least weekly and they talk on the phone frequently.

According to Ross, Sarah has many friends, but none of them are particularly close. He has noticed her friends seem to come over less often; Sarah also does less with friends because of her pain.

Ross stated he has no one that he confides in; probably for emotional support he depends on Sarah.

CURRENT LIVING ARRANGEMENTS: Sarah and her family reside approximately one mile east of Laurel, Montana, on Devlin Road. They have lived in this home for the past ten years. Ross stated it is a two-bedroom, single-story home with a basement. They use the basement for storage, particularly of their canned goods; Sarah is able to go up and down the basement stairs without problems. They are buying their home.

Prior to her injury, Sarah was responsible for all homemaking tasks, including housework, laundry, meal preparation, and grocery shopping. Ross stated, as far as her homemaking duties, he always felt she enjoyed this work but now she asks the girls to share more in the chores. Ross stated the children do assist with cooking, dishes, and are responsible for their own rooms. He has noticed they are doing more of the home chores than they did before Sarah's accident. Ross stated, "I have never done housework, and never changed a baby's diapers."

Ross stated Sarah typically gets up around 7 A.M., at which time she may cook breakfast for Marsha (Teresa often does her own). After Marsha goes to school, Sarah may go back to bed. She then gets up around 8:30 and prepares Ross's breakfast. After that she does housework and may work on sewing projects for the children. Ross has noticed her housework is not at the level it used to be and he added, "she is not the greatest housekeeper." At noon Sarah prepares lunch for Ross. After lunch he is uncertain what she does with her time; he suspects she may lie down if the pain is severe. The evening meal is prepared by either Sarah or one of the daughters. Sarah tends to spend

25

her evening time reading, watching television, or working on a craft project. She usually retires by 10:30 P.M.

Ross has noticed since her accident Sarah is less "energetic." He explained she still does the day-to-day tasks, but not all the extras she used to do. He has noticed she has given more responsibility to their daughters. When the daughters prepare a meal she usually sits in the kitchen with them and provides instructions.

EFFECT OF CHRONIC PAIN: Ross said Sarah's pain is constant; however, he has noticed the degree does vary. He is uncertain what makes her pain worse, but has noticed that when she uses her left arm during housework, her pain seems to increase. Ross believes Sarah's pain has progressively worsened. Ross said it is hard to know what her pain level is because she is not a complainer. He stated, "she doesn't tell me that much, and I haven't tried to find out." He believes Sarah continues to do her homemaking tasks even when she is in a lot of pain. He stated that Sarah has "an iron constitution." He added, "I don't try to keep her from doing her tasks, because I think she needs to as things would fall apart if she didn't." Ross stated her pain is primarily in her shoulders and neck area and that she is also bothered with extreme headaches. He was uncertain how often she gets the headaches, but they are frequent. Unless Sarah has had an extremely bad day as far as her pain goes, she does not talk about it. Ross believes she has a very high pain tolerance.

Ross stated he can tell when Sarah's pain is worse because she becomes short-tempered with him and the girls, she grimaces, or she may hold the back of her neck or put her hand on her forehead.

Ross believes Sarah attempts to manage her pain by lying down with a pillow under her neck and a cold washcloth on her forehead, and with the use of medication. Ross was uncertain what type of medication Sarah is on, but he believes it is a muscle relaxant. He stated she is not taking any pain medication, as she does not wish to be "zonked out."

Ross stated there is little he does to assist Sarah when she is in pain. He said he seldom waits on her. Occasionally he will ask if there is something she needs. However, for the most part, he will ask the children to assist her. Ross shared it is emotionally difficult for him to provide the comfort she may wish.

Sarah is suffering from sleep disturbance due to her chronic pain. Ross said she changes position often during the night and she is up and down frequently. When she is up she may sit and have a cup of tea. Ross said she has been bothered with sleep disturbance for many years, but since the accident it has gotten worse. She is unable to sleep on her left side, due to the shoulder pain.

Ross was uncertain if Sarah's injury has affected her appetite. He stated he does not know what she weighs, but she may be losing some weight. He stated she has always had a weight problem and diets frequently. He believes she is 4'11" tall.

Ross believes the only way Sarah's chronic pain has changed her relationship with their daughters is that she is shorter-tempered with them. He stated the girls often complain to him about this, but he reminds them of what Sarah is going through. He said when Sarah is particularly upset with Marsha, she may slap her or hit her with a belt. Ross stated Sarah does not overuse physical punishment, nor does he believe this has increased since her injury. He stated when Sarah physically punishes Marsha, he believes Marsha "has it coming." He stated, "I sit in the background to see if it is justified." Ross believes Sarah has difficulty with Marsha because Marsha is "headstrong and talks back."

Ross believes he is able to understand Sarah's chronic pain because of the pain he has suffered in his back since he injured it skiing when he was in his twenties. Apparently because of his back injury, Ross has been self-employed for the past ten years so he is able to work at his own pace and for the number of hours he feels physically capable. Ross said when his back pain becomes severe he may be down for two or three days; however, this does not happen very often. He stated, "I have learned to live with it and know when to take it easy." He added he is uncertain whether Sarah has learned her physical limitations. Ross also senses because of his back pain he, too, is shorter-tempered. He

26

stated, "If people leave me alone I get over it fast." When he is upset he tends to yell, swear, and throw objects. He stated he does not physically abuse Sarah when he is upset. He explained they used to fight a lot and in the early days occasionally hit each other; he added that this was many years ago.

When this worker asked Ross what he would do if their situation does not change, he indicated he can continue to cope and he does not plan to leave Sarah. He added he tends to look at the situation a day at a time, and does not plan ahead.

COMMUNITY AGENCIES AND TRANSPORTATION: Ross stated their family is receiving assistance through County Social Services and Human Resources.

Sarah is capable of driving; however, she often has one of the daughters run errands for her. Ross has noticed she does not want to go out of the house as much as she used to; he stated he is unsure why.

INCOME, FINANCIAL RESOURCES, AND MEDICAL COVERAGE:
- Ross stated his income varies from month to month, but probably averages around $500 a month.
- The family receives $100+ a month in food stamps.
- They are receiving energy assistance for their utility costs through Human Resources.
- Sarah's medical costs that relate to the accident are covered by the other driver's insurance, All-Risk.
- Ross thinks Sarah is considering applying for Social Security.
- Ross said their finances are extremely tight, and it is a stress area for the couple—he said that it tends to create friction between them.
- Sarah manages the family's finances; however, Ross oversees their money and makes the decisions as to how it will be spent.

EDUCATION AND MILITARY SERVICE:
- Sarah did not complete high school. Ross believes she was an average student; she quit school to get married.
- Sarah has her GED.
- Ross completed the ninth grade.
- Ross served in the Air Force for three years and received an honorable discharge.
- Sarah has no military experience.

EMPLOYMENT:
- Sarah has primarily been a homemaker throughout their marriage. Ross stated she has on several occasions worked as a waitress. This lasted for a short period of time as he was opposed to her working outside the home. Ross believes Sarah enjoyed working as a waitress, but stated, "a woman's place is in the home raising children."
- Ross has been self-employed as a "handyman" for the past ten years. He works four to five hours a day doing such things as plumbing, carpentry, welding, and furniture construction.
- Until ten years ago he worked as a welder. He held this position until he could no longer tolerate the pain. Prior to working as a welder he worked in the sawmills.

LEISURE ACTIVITIES AND ORGANIZATIONS:
Sarah enjoys the following:
- cards (pinochle)
- board games with the children
- sewing
- reading (romance novels)
- television
- knitting and crocheting
- listening to music (classical and country-western)
- working crossword puzzles

27

Prior to her injury she also enjoyed spending her time camping, going on short car trips, rock hunting, painting (oil and acrylics), and making jewelry. Ross has attempted to encourage her to do her art work, but stated, "mentally she can't get into it." Ross shared that they do little as a couple. He said he tends to watch television a lot.

Sarah is a member of the Jehovah's Witnesses; she attends meetings at least once a week. Prior to her accident she attended Jehovah's Witnesses meetings five times a week.

PATIENT AND FAMILY COPING HISTORY:
Ross described Sarah in the following terms:
- friendly and easy to get along with
- even-tempered
- optimistic
- poorly organized in housework and generally; this has been a friction area for the couple
- has always "bounded back" from surgeries; seems to endure "a lot"
- a humanitarian

Ross has noticed the following changes in Sarah since her accident:
- mentally seems less able to tolerate the pain; Ross believes it may be too much after all of the medical problems she has had to deal with
- cries much more easily
- more irritable
- moody
- seems withdrawn

Ross believes Sarah copes with her situation through the support she receives from her family and her strong religious faith. Ross indicated he has always relied strongly on Sarah's optimistic attitude to help him get through difficult times. Ross shared that he often feels anxious due to the amount of stress in his life caused by his inability to work, their limited financial resources, and during peak work times, the number of jobs he has to do. Ross stated he had a mild heart attack some time after Sarah's accident; he believes it was brought on by stress.

HISTORY OF DRUG AND ALCOHOL USE:
Ross stated Sarah does not have a problem with drugs or alcohol. He said at times he has been concerned that she may "get hooked on prescription drugs." However, he does not believe this has, as yet, been a problem. Ross shared that in the past he has been a heavy drinker; he believes in the past year or so he has decreased his amount of consumption. He stated that he at times uses alcohol to relax. When he drinks it is beer or whiskey.

Sarah drinks approximately three to four cups of coffee a day, and also often drinks black tea; she is not a smoker.

Ross indicated both his father and Sarah's mother were problem drinkers.

ASSESSMENT OF CURRENT SOCIAL SITUATION AND PROBLEMS:
From this report, Ross adamantly believes in traditional male and female roles within the marriage. He very clearly views himself as the head of the family and the individual who makes the major decisions. According to Ross it is out of the question that Sarah will work outside of the home because he does not approve of it. Apparently when Sarah has worked in the past she has acquiesced to his wishes for her to quit. Ross believes they have a strong relationship, although the communication is limited. He indicated there are some problems regarding their 17-year-old daughter; however, he minimized these problems by indicating they are typical teenage concerns. Ross and Sarah both subscribe to physical punishment when they feel their youngest daughter is out of line. This family does appear to be experiencing financial stress. Nonetheless, Ross does not consider it appropriate for Sarah to work to help ease the financial burden.

Sarah has apparently dealt with many medical problems over the last twenty years. Ross described her as highly resilient through all of her medical concerns. However, at this point he does not feel she is dealing with her injuries from the accident with the same mental strength and attitude she has

28

demonstrated in the past. Ross is concerned she may "give up." Ross has noticed the following changes in Sarah since her accident: increased irritability, moodiness, more withdrawn behavior, and a change in her mental attitude (less optimistic). These changes, particularly the mental attitude, are probably very frightening to Ross as he indicated he has always depended on her to help him manage his own stress. By Ross's admission, his use of alcohol in the past has been heavy; it's possible he may revert back to that if he feels overwhelmed with the situation.

GOALS OF CLIENT AND FAMILY:
Ross stated his primary goal for Sarah is for her to be more comfortable and for her to again pursue past projects such as her painting. Ross strongly indicated he does not plan for her to go to work (even though she has indicated a desire to). As far as her working goes, he said, "I just wouldn't let her; what I say is what happens."

Ross said they hope to receive a settlement from the other driver's insurance company.

SOCIAL SERVICE PLAN:
This worker provided Ross with information on a residential chronic pain program. Ross was particularly troubled by the thought of Sarah being out of their home for six to seven weeks. He said it would be extremely hard on both of them. He was unwilling to commit himself to supporting such a program, even if Sarah would choose to participate. Unless Sarah is highly motivated to work in such a program (if one is deemed appropriate) and is able to solicit Ross's support, I suspect her chances of succeeding are slim. If Ross's perception is accurate of his being the final decision-maker, his support is crucial. If Ross's concern about Sarah's mental attitude and thus her inability to provide him with the kind of support he found uplifting is strong enough, this may be an issue that would push him to seek change. In general, I believe Ross would find the separation and the program highly threatening.

If Sarah takes part in the pain program, weekly sessions with Ross and occasional sessions with their daughters would be necessary to

1. Assist them to understand Sarah's chronic pain and behavior.
2. Assist them to understand their roles in Sarah's chronic pain.
3. Help them to understand the program's goals and expectations.
4. Help promote generalization of progress Sarah would make in a pain program to their home environment.

Rick Wysil

Rick Wysil, BSW
Medical Social Services
12/18/10

RW/brm
dic 12/18/10
tran 12/29/10

29

APPENDIX III: WITNESSES AND TESTIMONY

Transcript of Telephone Interview Between All-Risk Insurance Agent and Sarah Anderson

This is Tim Taner recording a telephone interview with Sarah Anderson, who is speaking from her attorney's office in Missoula, Montana. The date of this conversation is September 4, 2009. The time is 9:50 A.M. and we're going to be talking about an accident that Mrs. Anderson was involved in on or about August 20, 2009.

Q. Mrs. Anderson, would you give me your full name and spell your last name?
A. Sarah Anderson. A-n-d-e-r-s-o-n.

Q. And Mrs. Anderson, you're aware that I'm recording this conversation?
A. Yes.

Q. It's being done with your consent?
A. Yes.

Q. Your age?
A. 45.

Q. You're married. Your husband's first name?
A. Ross.

Q. And what is your home address and phone number?
A. It's Box 336, Laurel, Montana, 59044. And my phone number's 248-6733.

Q. Are you employed other than as a housewife?
A. No.

Q. And were you operator of a car involved in this accident?
A. Yes, I was.

Q. What kind of a car is it and who is the owner of it?
A. It's a 1980 Datsun 710, and my husband and I own it.

Q. What was the purpose of your trip that day? Where had you been? Where were you going?
A. Okay, we were, we went to a friend's house. Then we went to the store to get groceries and came home. And we were on the way home when this happened.

Q. What was the date and time of this accident as near as you can recollect?
A. It was on a Tuesday, August 20th.

Q. This year?
A. 2009.

Q. And the time?
A. About 5:00.

Q. And where did this accident occur?
A. Just right near my driveway on Devlin Road as we were, as I was almost turned in to go into the drive.

Q. All right. Where is this accident location relative to Laurel, Montana?
A. It's a mile-and-three-tenths from the Town Pump station.

Q. It's not in the city limits then?
A. No.

Q. It's in the county?
A. Um huh.

Q. And the county is?
A. Yellowstone.

30

Q. Devlin Road at this point, what direction does it run?
A. East and west.

Q. Is this a two-lane, two-way road or is it wider than that?
A. It's a two-lane road.

Q. Paved?
A. Yes.

Q. Were there any traffic controls in the immediate vicinity that regulated the flow of traffic, like stop signs?
A. There was no stop signs. There was a double yellow line.

Q. The double yellow line which indicated no passing?
A. Right.

Q. Is there a speed limit in the area?
A. Yes, it's 50.

Q. At the time this accident occurred, what other traffic was in the vicinity?
A. Coming to the town of Laurel, there was none. But going out, there was myself and there was a semi behind us, way behind us. And that's all I could see.

Q. All right. The terrain where this happened, is it level or is there a hill crest or curve involved?
A. Well there's a hill crest, but it's, uh, oh, how many—about 2,200 feet to the crest of the hill. Oh it's more than that, but you can see. You can see the crest of the hill from my drive real easy.

Q. The road isn't level then. Are you going uphill or downhill?
A. It's going uphill as you turn into my drive.

Q. All right.
A. Just starting to go uphill.

Q. Would you classify this as a business, residential, or rural area?
A. A rural area.

Q. Were there any obstructions to your view either in your vehicle or outside it which would cause you or the other driver to fail to see each other?
A. No. My mirror was, I even looked in my rear-view mirror, and there was a truck coming just over the crest of the hill, but it was a semi.

Q. This was an oncoming vehicle or one that . . .
A. It was an oncoming one behind me. And my side mirror, there was nothing coming from it when I turned either.

Q. I see. This was a vehicle behind you, not coming at you?
A. Right.

Q. All right.
A. And it's not the vehicle that hit us.

Q. Yes. We've established that you were the driver of the car you were in. Would you indicate your passengers and their position in the vehicle?
A. Okay. Mrs. Weston was in the front seat with a seat belt on. And I had my seat belt on. And her son, Samuel, was behind her and her daughter, Laura, was behind me.

Q. So you had a total of three people besides yourself?
A. Right.

Q. Who was the operator of the other vehicle involved in this accident?
A. Donald Swanson.

Q. Was he alone in his vehicle?
A. Yes.

31

Q. And what kind of a vehicle was he operating?
A. It was a pickup truck, and I have no idea what kind. It's a four-wheel-drive, but what the make was I don't know.

Q. What was the weather like that day?
A. Clear.

Q. Pavement's dry?
A. Um huh.

Q. And at that time of day, it's still daylight?
A. Oh yeah.

Q. What was your direction of travel and speed?
A. Okay, I was going east. At the time of the accident, I wasn't going, oh maybe, three or four miles an hour because I had to turn in.

Q. Okay. You were making a turn, what direction?
A. To the left.

Q. Were you signaling for that turn?
A. Yes, I was.

Q. For what interval of time did you give your signal?
A. It started at the, the other side of the bridge, and, how far was the bridge from there?. . .

Q. That would be adequate for me. The other side of the bridge?
A. Um huh.

Q. All right. That's as you approach the bridge and before you crossed it you started . . .
A. I started signaling.

Q. And what was your speed at the time you started signaling and then again as you were in your turn?
A. Well, I started, well I started slowing it down right at the bridge to about, oh 45 maybe. And then I slowed continually down till I came to where we turn in. And then I looked and nobody's coming up. And then as I turned in I don't think I was going more than two or three miles an hour.

Q. Did you at any time reduce your speed suddenly?
A. No. It was just all gradual.

Q. When were you first aware of Swanson's vehicle?
A. I never was.

Q. You didn't see it before the impact?
A. No, I didn't. And I had looked behind me and I looked in my rear-view mirror, too, and I didn't see him at all. I, in the side mirror I looked.

Q. How far into your turn or, well, you indicated that your intention was to turn. Had you started that turn?
A. Yes, I'd started the turn and I was almost down into my driveway. I was across the double yellow line.

Q. All right, so your car would be, would you say entirely in the left-hand lane or westbound lane when it was hit?
A. Well, I think part of my wheels were on my own driveway.

Q. So you had completed more than half of your turn?
A. Oh yeah.

Q. When were you first aware, you said you weren't aware of the other vehicle. Were you aware of it at impact?
A. Well, yes (inaudible).

32

Q. You didn't lose consciousness?
A. I did. I heard a crash and glass breaking. And um, I saw my friend going past me through my window. And then I must have hit the telephone pole because I blacked out completely.

Q. The Swanson vehicle as far as you're able to deduce at this time was traveling what direction?
A. East towards Billings.

Q. Overtaking you then, apparently?
A. Um huh.

Q. To your knowledge, was it apparent that Swanson had done anything to try and avoid this impact?
A. Well, no. As a matter of fact, I felt that he was going so fast, he'd have to have been going so fast that there's no way he could have avoided it except staying in his own lane. Staying in the right lane instead of turning into my passing lane.

Q. On what basis do you come to the conclusion that he was traveling too fast or that he was traveling fast?
A. Because I hadn't seen him as I turned. And he'd have to have been coming at a tremendous amount of speed in order for him to get up on us so close and so fast.

Q. Was there anything going on inside of the car that might have been a momentary distraction to you?
A. No, cause I don't play the radio or the, I don't even have a tape deck in the car, so I don't play that when I'm driving cause I don't like. . .

Q. Any conversation going on at the time?
A. No, nothing heavy. Just, in fact I can't even remember anything with it going on as far as conversations go that would even begin to cause a distraction.

Q. What was the point of impact on your car?
A. Okay. It was on the driver's side in the rear.

Q. Did you observe the other vehicle, the Swanson pickup, after the accident?
A. Yes, I've been down to see it.

Q. Where was the impact on it?
A. Okay, the right front fender on his.

Q. Following . . .
A. (Is that right?)

Q. Following this impact, where did your vehicle end up?
A. Well, just a minute. It's the left front fender.

Q. On the Swanson truck?
A. Yes.

Q. All right.
A. And where did my vehicle end up?

Q. Um huh.
A. Against the telephone pole.

Q. It actually came in contact with the pole?
A. Yes, and it dented the car. And the pole pushed it in quite a bit.

Q. Are you completely off the road?
A. Yes.

Q. And headed what direction?
A. Okay, headed north, nope, just a minute. I think south.

Q. All right, if you're not sure.
A. Okay.

33

Q. Yet, this would be on the right or left side of the road?
A. On the left side.

Q. Are you beyond your driveway?
A. Yes, well, a few feet off of the driveway if that. Yeah, a few feet off the driveway.

Q. Where was the Swanson pickup when it came to rest?
A. I have no idea because I didn't see it.

Q. Did you have any conversation with Mr. Swanson after the accident?
A. I didn't, no.

Q. To your knowledge, was it, had Mr. Swanson had anything intoxicating to drink?
A. No.

Q. Had you or your passengers?
A. No.

Q. Do you know of any witnesses to this accident other than the people involved?
A. My daughter seen a car get hit, but it was down in our yard. And she, she just knew there was an accident because our yard sits down a ways from where the highway was.

Q. You mentioned a semi.
A. Um huh.

Q. Is there, has that party been identified?
A. I don't think so. It was a chip truck from, uh, . . .

Q. I see. Would it have been in a position to have seen the accident?
A. I think so, yes.

Q. Mrs. Anderson, I still have a few questions. I'm coming to the end of this side of the tape. I'll have to stop the recorder and turn over to the other side. Before I do, you are aware that I've recorded the entire conversation thus far? And it's been done with your consent?
A. Yes.

Mr. Taner: If you will hold, I'll change over the tape.

(End Tape, Side 1)

This is Tim Taner recording an in-person interview with Sarah Anderson on September 4, 2009. It concerns her accident on August 20, '09.

Q. All right, Mrs. Anderson, you're still with me?
A. Yes.

Q. And you're aware I'm once again recording?
A. Right.

Q. Was either car driveable following this accident?
A. I don't know if his was, but I know mine is completely totaled out.

Q. All right. Were, what injuries were sustained in your car to you and your passengers? Now that, anything that you're actually aware of by personal knowledge. Doesn't have to be anything too great.
A. Okay, I had a concussion, um, all my left side is bruised internally, all the soft tissue is bruised, um, my shoulder and my neck. Okay, and then I'm going to go in today and I think there's been damage to my bladder and to my colon. And then, um, Mrs. Weston, she had three broken ribs. Her leg was broke in two places. She has a broken clavicle, a concussion, and problems with her neck, too, I think. I'm not, I'm not sure. Then to Laura Weston, she had a whiplash and Samuel did also. And Laura had bruises, a concussion too.

Q. Following the accident, where did you receive your first medical attention?
A. At Yellowstone County Hospital.

34

Q. Your doctor there?
A. Dr. Gosten.
Q. And how did you get to the hospital?
A. Ambulance.
Q. You had subsequent medical attention, you personally. Where did you receive that?
A. They put an I.V. in me in the emergency room and got Mrs. Weston ready, and they took some X-rays of me there. And then they took us both into Billings.
Q. Did the, the police were at the scene?
A. I think they were, yes.
Q. You don't recall them specifically?
A. Yeah, I do. I recall Alice, um, Pracel there.
Q. The vehicles to your knowledge had not been moved by the time the police arrived?
A. Oh no, nothing had been.
Q. What relation is Mrs. Weston to you?
A. She's just a good friend.
Q. I see. Does she live in this area?
A. No, she lives in Spokane, Washington.
Q. She had come to visit you?
A. Right.
Q. A social-type visit?
A. Yes. She just came for a vacation.
Q. Had your passengers registered any kind of complaint about your driving prior to this accident?
A. No.
Q. Mrs. Anderson, I think that completes my interview, but is there anything further you would comment on? Something we haven't discussed to this point?
A. No, there isn't.
Q. You are aware that I've recorded this entire conversation using one side of a tape and part of another?
A. Yes, I have.
Q. It was done with your full knowledge and consent?
A. Right.
Q. Everything you've told me in the course of this interview is true?
A. Yes.
Q. Then that completes the recording and I'll turn off the machine.

EXHIBIT A: SID SILKER, M.D., LETTER OF SEPTEMBER 23, 2010

September 23, 2010

Attorneys, Inc. P. C.
126 E Broadway, Suite 25
P. O. Box 7742
Missoula, MT 59807

RE: Sarah Anderson

To Whom It May Concern:

35

I have referred Sarah Anderson to the Pain Center at Billings Community Rehabilitation Center for evaluation of her shoulder pain and neck pain. This pain she initially began experiencing as the result of a rear-end automobile collision in the summer of 2009.

Despite multiple modalities of treatment locally, we have not succeeded in reducing her pain to an acceptable degree, either for her or for us. It is my belief that the pain that she is currently experiencing is the result of the motor vehicle accident that occurred last year.

If you have any other questions please feel free to contact me.

Sincerely,

Sid Silker

Sid Silker, M.D.
P. O. Box 1045
Laurel, MT 59248

SRS/bd
C: File

EXHIBIT B: KEITH MAKIE, PH.D. PAIN CLINIC DIRECTOR, LETTER OF JANUARY 21, 2011

January 21, 2011

Mr. Rex Palmer
Attorneys, Inc.
126 East Broadway
Missoula, Montana
59802

RE: Sarah Anderson

Dear Mr. Palmer:

The purpose of this letter is to answer your questions about the program we have recommended for your client, Sarah Anderson, and the cost of that program. Sarah, as you know, was evaluated in our Diagnostic Pain Clinic on 12/9/10; it was the unanimous recommendation of the Evaluation Team that she seek out a highly structured, interdisciplinary chronic pain treatment program. The evaluation suggested that not only does Sarah have an extremely complicated physical pain problem, but this physical pain problem is exacerbated by a great deal of general emotional distress and innumerable family problems.

Your specific question about our program was what exactly would we be recommending for Sarah and what would the cost be, and what outcomes might be expected. Our program is truly interdisciplinary and residential. We have the best of both worlds in that we have a highly trained interdisciplinary team affiliated with Billings Community Rehabilitation Center to do the treatment while we have the people stay in a home-like residential facility with twenty-four-hour nursing care. Our program is aimed specifically at increasing activity level, returning people to as much of their function, prior to the injury, as possible, given the physical effects of the injury. Our goal is to get people active, to strengthen and stretch their muscles, to get them back into activities of daily living, and to eventually, in most cases, return them to work. Our program is seven weeks in length, involves a large vocational component, and addresses not only physical factors, but also psychological and family factors. The cost of the program at the present time is between $25,000 and $27,000 for the seven-week program. By the end of the program the Evaluation Team felt that Sarah would very likely be able to return to her former, fairly active lifestyle, and even work outside the home, if she chose to. The

36

Evaluation Team predicted that by the end of the program the chronic pain and its attendant problems would cease to dominate Sarah's life. Much of the psychological upheaval we found in the evaluation would be reduced and we would also be able to improve her family situation. There was no doubt in the minds of the Evaluation Team that Sarah would not only find some relief from her seemingly unrelenting pain, but she would also be able to resume the activities of her life very close to what they had been before the accident.

The Evaluation Team was also unanimous in their prediction that unless Sarah took advantage of such an interdisciplinary, highly structured, intensive pain treatment program, she would continue to deteriorate. The Team felt this deterioration not only would manifest itself in decreased activity level, increased deconditioning, lack of mobility, but also that the great deal of psychological distress she reports at the present time would worsen; her family situation would worsen to the point where the prediction was that the family would break down.

I hope this general description provides you with the information you need. If you need any more specific information I would be more than happy to provide it to you. You can either write to me or call me at 248-2400, extension 3634.

Sincerely,

Keith C. Makie

Keith C. Makie, Ph.D.
Pain Clinic Director

KCM/brm

EXHIBIT C: PHOTOGRAPHS RELEVANT TO THE ACCIDENT

Photo 1: Sarah Anderson's Vehicle

37

Photos 2–5: Sarah Anderson's Vehicle; Donald Swanson's Vehicle

Photo 2

Photo 3

Photo 4

38

Photo 5

Photos 6–9: Devlin Road

Photo 6

39

Photo 7

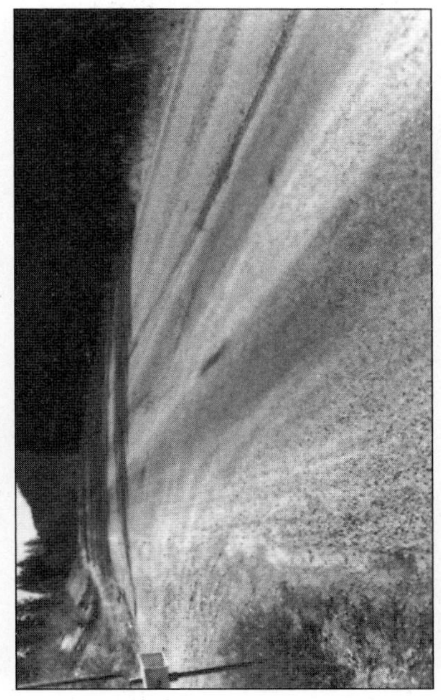
Photo 8

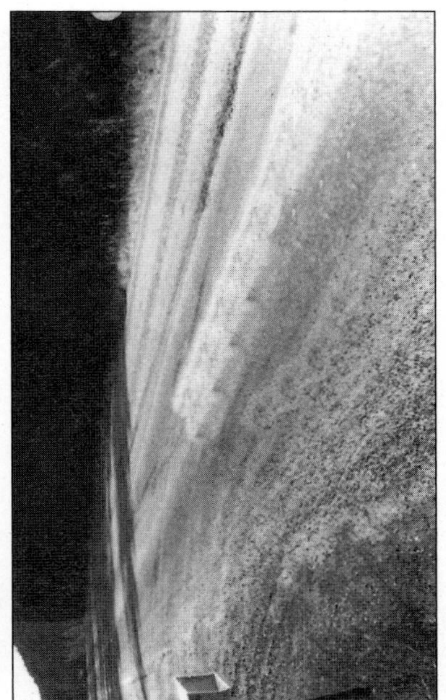
Photo 9

40

EXHIBIT D: ACCIDENT REPORT, MONTANA HIGHWAY PATROL

Exhibit D: Accident Report, of Montana Highway Patrol

STATE OF MONTANA — ACCIDENT INVESTIGATOR'S REPORT

ACCIDENT NUMBER: 09 (YEAR) 00 (AGENCY) 155 (BADGE) 08 (MONTH) 02 (SEQ NO) — DATE OF ACCIDENT: 082009 — TIME: 1655 — CITY: YELLOWSTONE — COUNTY: 54

OCCURRED ON: DEVLIN ROAD — AT INTERSECTION OF: PVT ROAD — MILES: - - 7 — N S E W — OF: LAUREL

IF NOT AT INTERSECTION: FEET / MILES N S E W OF — FUNCTIONAL CLASS — HIGHWAY: 52570 — MILEPOST: 01 + 0450

Diagram labels: Pvt. Road; power pole; 2; 2 1; 2; DEVLIN Rd.; INDICATE NORTH WITH ARROW; 131

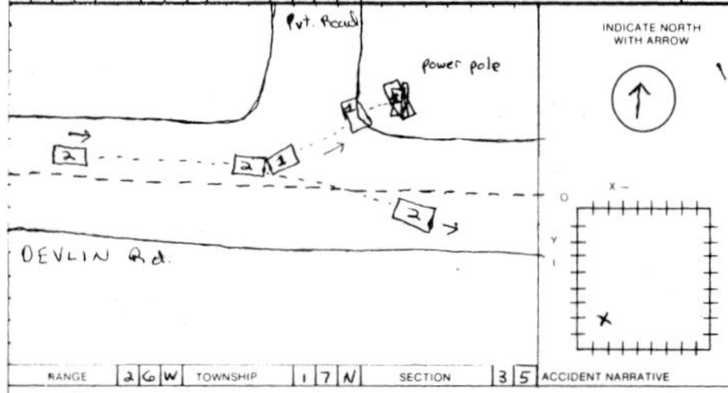

FIRST HARMFUL EVENT	C 4
FIRST OBJECT HIT OFF RDWY	0 7
INJURY SEVERITY	2
DAMAGE SEVERITY	1
CLASS OF TRAFFICWAY	4
BIKEWAY	0
GRADE & HORIZ ALIGN	3
ROADWAY RELATED LOC	1
RELATIONSHIP TO JUNCTION	0
NUMBER OF VEHICLES	C 2
NUMBER OF PEDESTRIANS	0 0
NUMBER OF FATALITIES	0 0
NUMBER OF INJURIES	0 5
WEATHER CONDITION	5
ROAD CONDITION	1
LIGHT CONDITION	1
TRAFFIC CONTROLS	1 4
DAMAGE TO OTHER PROPERTY — TYPE	0 0
SEVERITY	0
OWNERSHIP	0
POSTED SPEED	5 0
ENGINEERING STUDY REQUEST	0
ACCIDENT ANALYSIS I	0 2
ACCIDENT ANALYSIS II	0 0
TYPE OF COLLISION	3

RANGE: 26W — TOWNSHIP: 17N — SECTION: 35

ACCIDENT NARRATIVE:
VEH. #1 WAS MAKING LEFT TURN AND VEH #2 WAS ATTEMPTING TO PASS #1 IN A NO PASSING ZONE. #2 IN PASSING LANE STEPPED ON BRAKES AND TURNED TO RIGHT. VEH #2 HIT #1 IN THE LEFT REAR CORNER, KNOCKING #1 SIDEWAYS AND OFF RDWY. & INTO POWER POLE. #2 WENT STRAIGHT AHEAD AND STOPPED IN MIDDLE OF ROAD

OFFICER'S SIGNATURE: Alice Procel — BADGE NO: 155 — DEPT: MHP — DATE: 8/22/09 — DATE NOTIFIED: 082009 — TIME: 1709 — DATE ARRIVED: 082009 — TIME: 1755

DRIVER (1) — NAME (LAST): ANDERSON — FIRST: SARAH — MIDDLE: T. — ADDRESS: Box 336, LAUREL, MT
DRIVER LICENSE NUMBER: 519468505 — STATE: MONTANA — OPER/CHAUF/OTHER: X — DRIVER LICENSE STATUS: 1 — RESTRICTION COMPLIANCE: 1 — DATE OF BIRTH: 031065
CONTRIBUTING FACTORS: 000000 — DRIVER: 0 44 F 1 0 2

SEAT POSITION	NAME	ADDRESS	A/C	AGE	SEX	BELT	LOC	INJ
FRONT CENTER								
FRONT RIGHT	LISA WESTON		0	37	F	[illegible]	2	2
REAR LEFT	LAURA WESTON		0	16	F	0	0	2
REAR CENTER								
REAR RIGHT	SAMUEL WESTON		0	17	M	0	2	3

INSURANCE CARRIER: STATE FARM — POLICY NO: 5062-3-13-43
THIS DRIVER WAS HEADED N S E W ON DEVLIN RD. — VEHICLE NO: 01 — INTENDED TO: 04 — WRECKER CO: GREGORY'S
VEHICLE MAKE: DATSUN — BODY: 23 — TRLR: 0 — VEH YEAR: 80 — VEHICLE DAMAGE (X) IF OVER $400: X
VEHICLE ID NUMBER: JHL760845886 — LICENSE PLATE NO: 591-3981 — STATE: MONTANA — LIC YEAR: 09
OWNER OF VEHICLE: ROSS ANDERSON — ADDRESS: Box 336 LAUREL MT — DAMAGE SEVERITY: 1

DRIVER (2) — NAME (LAST): SWANSON — FIRST: DONALD — MIDDLE: M. — ADDRESS: 212 CREEK LOOP RD, LAUREL MT
DRIVER LICENSE NUMBER: 5670703 — STATE: MONTANA — DRIVER LICENSE STATUS: 1 — RESTRICTION COMPLIANCE: 1 — DATE OF BIRTH: 070791
VIOLATION CODE: 52600 2 — SUMMONS NO: 510 MO 1 2025
CONTRIBUTING FACTORS: 000050 — DRIVER: 0 18 M 2 0 4

SEAT POSITION	NAME	ADDRESS
FRONT CENTER		
FRONT RIGHT		
REAR LEFT		
REAR CENTER		
REAR RIGHT		

INSURANCE CARRIER: ALL-RISK — POLICY NO: 020626048
THIS DRIVER WAS HEADED N S E W ON DEVLIN RD. — VEHICLE NO: 02 — INTENDED TO: 02 — WRECKER CO: GREGORY'S
VEHICLE MAKE: CHEVROLET — BODY: 18 — TRLR: 0 — VEH YEAR: 85 — VEHICLE DAMAGE: X
VEHICLE ID NUMBER: CKL1HA7783577 — LICENSE PLATE NO: 0061E — STATE: MONTANA — LIC YEAR: 91
DAMAGE SEVERITY: 1

HQ-1599 60

41

EXHIBIT E: OIL PAINTINGS BY SARAH ANDERSON

Four (4) Original Oil Paintings by Sarah Anderson

EXHIBIT F: NEWSPAPER CLIPPING SHOWING SARAH ANDERSON PAINTING MINIATURE FIGURES ON FINGERNAILS

PAGE TWELVE–THURSDAY, NOVEMBER 10, 2007

Jacki Sander took home a miniature souvenir from the Art and Craft show over the weekend. Sarah Anderson paints a very small figure on her fingernail. A continuous slide show, toys, stained glass work and other beautiful examples of county crafts were on display.

42

CHECK THE CITE

Brian Neiman was found to have engaged in the unlicensed practice of law (UPL). What conduct pertaining to settlement did Neiman engage in that constituted UPL? Read the case of *The Florida Bar v. Neiman*, 816 So. 2d 587 (Supreme Court of Florida, 2002). To read the opinion online, (1) Go to the site of the Supreme Court of Florida (www.floridasupremecourt.org). Select "Court Decisions and Rules" and then "Unofficial Archives of Opinions." Select the docket range "94501–94750." Then select docket number SC94738. (2) Go to FindACase (www.findacase.com). Select Florida. Run a citation search. For the volume, type 816. For the reporter, select So. 2d. For the page, enter 587. (3) Run a citation search ("816 So. 2d 587") or a party search (Florida Bar Neiman) in the Legal Opinions and Journals database of Google Scholar (scholar.google.com).

PROJECT

In Google, Bing, or another general search engine, run the following search: *aa* settlement tort (substitute the name of your state for *aa* in the search, e.g., Minnesota settlement tort. Find and summarize a court opinion in your state in which one of the issues in the case pertained to the settlement of a tort case, e.g., the fairness of the settlement, the attorney's misconduct in communicating the settlement.

ETHICS IN A TORTS PRACTICE

You are a paralegal working in the law office of Upton and Upton, which represents a client in a negligence case against Wal-Mart. The client has authorized the Upton attorney to negotiate a minimum settlement of $50,000. During the negotiation, Wal-Mart offers $60,000, but payable as follows: the first payment of $10,000 to be made in four years and the remaining payments to be made in $10,000 installments for the next five years. When this offer is made, the Upton attorney immediately rejects it. What ethical problems, if any, might exist?

SUMMARY

A settlement is a resolution of a legal dispute without the need for a complete trial. To achieve this goal, a party may use a settlement précis. This is an advocacy document that tries to persuade the opponent (or the insurance company of the opponent) to settle the case in a certain way—or more accurately, for a certain amount. The précis presents the facts of the case, the theories of liability, the nature of past and anticipated expenses, and other matters that pertain to damages. If the case is more complex or elaborate, the advocacy document is often called a settlement brochure.

KEY TERMS

settlement *626*

settlement précis *626*

settlement brochure *626*

REVIEW QUESTIONS

1. How are most legal disputes resolved?
2. What is a settlement?
3. What are the advantages of a settlement?
4. What is a settlement précis?
5. How does a settlement précis differ from a settlement brochure?
6. What are some major paralegal roles in the settlement stage of litigation?
7. What are the main components of a settlement précis and settlement brochure?

HELPFUL WEBSITES

- **Settlement**
  www.nolo.com/legal-encyclopedia/article-29858.html
  www.settlementcentral.com/page0262.htm
  www.settlementconsultants.com
  insurance.freeadvice.com/information/auto/article/63
  personal-injury.lawyers.com/Personal-Injury-Settlement-FAQ.html
  ezinearticles.com/?Personal-Injury-Settlement-Calculators&id=268676

ENDNOTES

1. Adapted from Melynda Hill-Teter, *Building the Perfect PI Settlement Demand Package*, 15 Legal Assistant Today 70 (July/August 1998) and Lori R. Hoesing, *The Settlement Brochure*, 10 In Brief 5 (Nebraska Association of Legal Assistants, May 1990).
2. The discussion and illustration of a settlement précis is taken in large part from J. Jeans, *Trial Advocacy* 549–53 (2d ed. 1993). Reprinted with permission from West, a Thomson Reuters business.

Student StudyWARE™ CD-ROM
For additional materials, please go to the student CD in this book.

APPENDIX

A

RESOURCES FOR A TORTS PRACTICE

A. INTRODUCTION

In this appendix you will find links to some of the major sites that are relevant to a personal injury/torts law practice. Note the sites for the state where you will be employed as a paralegal. Because a good deal of tort litigation involves multiple jurisdictions, sites for other states are provided as well.

B. STATE RESOURCES

The state resources fall into the following categories:

State Court System: Links to the courts that handle tort cases in the state.

Accident/Driver Records; Public Safety: Links to information on how to obtain accident reports, particularly for highway accidents. (Some of the links may be to fee-based sites.)

Statute of Limitations in State Tort Cases: Links to the time periods within which tort cases must be brought.

Medical Malpractice in the State: Links to medical malpractice laws of the state, including law reform efforts. (See also Appendix C on medical malpractice.)

State Workers' Compensation & Occupational Safety: Links to sites relevant to on-the-job injuries and illnesses.

Researching State Tort Law: Links to substantive and procedural law governing torts as well as other legal issues governed by state law.

Definitions of State Tort Principles in Jury Instructions: Links to jury instructions, which often contain succinct definitions of tort causes of action and defenses in the state.

Summaries of State Tort Laws: Links to selected law firms in the state that provide summaries of aspects of tort law in the state (often useful as a starting point in learning about general principles of tort law).

Jury Verdicts in State Tort Cases: Links to (mostly fee-based) sites that provide data on tort verdicts in the state.

Trial Attorney Bar in the State: Links to the association of trial attorneys, whose members often represent plaintiffs in personal injury litigation, and to the state bar.

Defense Bar in the State: Link to trial attorneys that defend individuals, companies, and organizations in tort cases.

Google Searches on State Tort Law: Search queries to run in Google (and other general search engines) to find material on tort law and law firms in the state.

Miscellaneous Sites on State Tort Law: Links to blogs and sites on state tort law, tort reform, and other sites of interest to someone working in a personal injury practice.

Alabama

- **Alabama State Court System**
  www.judicial.state.al.us
- **Accident/Driver Records; Public Safety**
  www.dps.state.al.us
  www.dps.state.al.us/DriverLicense/Forms.aspx
  www.hooveral.org/Default.asp?ID=188
  search.dmv.org/dmv/alabama/accident-report
  publicrecords.onlinesearches.com/Alabama.htm

- **Statute of Limitations in Alabama Tort Cases**
  www.statutes-of-limitations.com
- **Medical Malpractice in Alabama**
  www.mcandl.com/alabama.html
  www.atra.org/show/7338
- **Alabama Workers' Compensation & Occupational Safety**
  dir.alabama.gov/wc
  alabamasafestate.ua.edu/safe_state_osha.htm
- **Researching Alabama Tort Law**
  www.judicial.state.al.us/links.cfm
  www.library.law.ua.edu/links/bama.htm
  www.megalaw.com/al/alweb.php
- **Definitions of Alabama Tort Principles in Jury Instructions**
  west.thomson.com/productdetail/2069/13997606/productdetail.aspx
- **Summaries of Alabama Tort Law (from selected attorney sites)**
  www.alabamatortlaw.com
  guides.gottrouble.com/Tort_law_Alabama-r1179156-Alabama.html
- **Jury Verdicts in Alabama Tort Cases**
  www.juryverdicts.com/alabama.html
  www.ll.georgetown.edu/guides/jury.cfm
- **Alabama Trial Lawyers Association & State Bar**
  www.alabamajustice.org/AL
  www.alabar.org
- **Defense Bar in Alabama**
  www.adla.org
  www.dri.org/open/SLDO.aspx
- **Google Searches on Alabama Tort Law**
  "Alabama tort"
  "Alabama tort reform"
  "Alabama negligence"
  Alabama "intentional tort"
  Alabama "medical malpractice"
- **Miscellaneous Sites on Alabama Tort Law**
  www.legalreforminthenews.com/Tort%20Profiles/AL_Tort_Laws.htm
  www.alabamainjurylawyerblog.com
  www.alabamaproductinjurylawyer.com
  alabamavotersagainstlawsuitabuse.com

Alaska

- **Alaska State Court System**
  www.courts.alaska.gov
- **Accident/Driver Records and Public Safety**
  www.dot.state.ak.us/stwdplng/accreptapp/index.shtml
  doa.alaska.gov/dmv/akol/recordfx.htm
  www.state.ak.us/dmv

www.dps.state.ak.us
publicrecords.onlinesearches.com/Alaska.htm

- **Statute of Limitations in Alaska Tort Cases**
  www.statutes-of-limitations.com
- **Medical Malpractice in Alaska**
  www.mcandl.com/alaska.html
  www.atra.org/show/7338
- **Alaska Workers' Compensation & Occupational Safety**
  labor.state.ak.us/wc
  labor.state.ak.us/lss/oshhome.htm
- **Researching Alaska Tort Law**
  www.state.ak.us/courts/aklegal.htm
  www.romingerlegal.com/state/alaska.html
  www.megalaw.com/ak/ak.php
- **Definitions of Alaska Tort Principles in Jury Instructions**
  www.state.ak.us/courts/juryins.htm
- **Summaries of Alaska Tort Laws (from selected attorney sites)**
  www.alaskainjurylawgroup.com
  www.aktriallaw.com
- **Jury Verdicts in Alaska Tort Cases**
  www.juryverdicts.com/alaska.html
  www.ll.georgetown.edu/guides/jury.cfm
- **Alaska Trial Lawyers Association & State Bar**
  www.alaskatriallawyers.org/AK
  www.alaskabar.org
- **Defense Bar in Alaska**
  www.dri.org/open/SLDO.aspx
- **Google Searches on Alaska Tort Law**
  "Alaska tort"
  "Alaska tort reform"
  "Alaska negligence"
  Alaska "intentional tort"
  Alaska "medical malpractice"
- **Miscellaneous Sites on Alaska Tort Law**
  www.alaskainjurylawblog.com/sitemap.html
  Tort Liability of Volunteers
  www.iciclesoftware.com/vlh7/VLH9Torts.html
  Tort Reform in Alaska
  www.law.duke.edu/shell/cite.pl?16+Alaska+L.+Rev.+61

Arizona

- **Arizona State Court System**
  www.supreme.state.az.us
- **Accident/Driver Records; Public Safety**
  www.azdps.gov/Services/Records/Department_Records

www.azdot.gov/mvd/index.asp
www.dmv.org/az-arizona/driving-records.php
publicrecords.onlinesearches.com/Arizona.htm
www.azdps.gov

- **Statute of Limitations in Arizona Tort Cases**
  www.statutes-of-limitations.com
- **Medical Malpractice in Arizona**
  www.mcandl.com/arizona.html
  www.atra.org/show/7338
- **Arizona Workers' Compensation; Occupational Safety**
  www.ica.state.az.us
  www.workerscompensationinsurance.com/workers_compensation/arizona.htm
- **Researching Arizona Tort Law**
  www.supreme.state.az.us/nav2/legalref.htm
  www.lexisone.com/legalresearch/legalguide/states/arizona.htm#l1
- **Definitions of Arizona Tort Principles in Jury Instructions**
  www.myazbar.org/SecComm/Committees/CIJI/CIJI-PDF/FrontMatter.pdf
  www.myazbar.org/SecComm/Committees/CIJI/raji4.cfm
- **Summaries of Arizona Tort Laws (from selected attorney sites)**
  www.breyerlaw.com
  www.riggslaw.com
- **Jury Verdicts in Arizona Tort Cases**
  www.morelaw.com/arizona/cases
  www.ll.georgetown.edu/guides/jury.cfm
- **Arizona Trial Lawyers Association & State Bar**
  www.aztla.org/AZ
  www.azbar.org
- **Defense Bar in Arizona**
  www.azadc.org
  www.dri.org/open/SLDO.aspx
- **Google Searches on Arizona Tort Law**
  "Arizona tort"
  "Arizona tort reform"
  "Arizona negligence"
  Arizona "intentional tort"
  Arizona "medical malpractice"
- **Miscellaneous Sites on Arizona Tort Law**
  www.arizonaaccidentlawyerblog.com
  www.justia.com/us-states/arizona/law-blog-posts.html

Arkansas

- **Arkansas State Court System**
  courts.state.ar.us
- **Accident/Driver Records & Public Safety**
  https://www.ark.org/grs/app/asp

www.arkansas.gov/dfa/driver_services/ds_index.html
www.state.ar.us/dfa/driver_services/ds_faqs.html
publicrecords.onlinesearches.com/Arkansas.htm

- **Statute of Limitations in Arkansas Tort Cases**
  www.statutes-of-limitations.com
- **Medical Malpractice in Arkansas**
  www.mcandl.com/arkansas.html
  www.atra.org/show/7338
- **Arkansas Workers' Compensation & Occupational Safety**
  www.awcc.state.ar.us
  www.state.ar.us/labor/divisions/aosh_p1.html
- **Researching Arkansas Tort Law**
  www.romingerlegal.com/state/arkansas.html
  www.lexisone.com/legalresearch/legalguide/states/arkansas.htm
- **Definitions of Arkansas Tort Principles in Jury Instructions**
  west.thomson.com/productdetail/148909/22065781/productdetail.aspx
  courts.state.ar.us/boards_committees/model_jury_civil.cfm
- **Summaries of Arkansas Tort Laws (from selected attorney sites)**
  www.ggreen.com
  www.pfeiferlawfirm.net
  www.owingslawfirm.com
- **Jury Verdicts in Arkansas Tort Cases**
  www.ll.georgetown.edu/guides/jury.cfm
- **Arkansas Trial Lawyers Association & State Bar**
  www.arktla.org/AR
  www.arkbar.com
- **Defense Bar in Arkansas**
  www.arkansasdefensecounsel.com
  www.dri.org/open/sldoview.aspx?state=Arkansas
  www.dri.org/open/SLDO.aspx
- **Google Searches on Arkansas Tort Law**
  "Arkansas tort"
  "Arkansas tort reform"
  "Arkansas negligence"
  Arkansas "intentional tort"
  Arkansas "medical malpractice"
- **Miscellaneous Sites on Arkansas Tort Law**
  www.legalreforminthenews.com/Tort%20Profiles/Arkansas.htm
  www.childproductsafety.com
  guides.gottrouble.com/Tort_law_Arkansas-r1179156-Arkansas.html

California

- **California State Court System**
  www.courtinfo.ca.gov
  www.courtinfo.ca.gov/courts
  www.courtinfo.ca.gov/courts/about.htm

- **Accident/Driver Records; Public Safety**
  www.chp.ca.gov/programs/aiuswitrs.html
  www.dmv.ca.gov
  www.mrtraffic.com/dmv.htm
  publicrecords.onlinesearches.com/California.htm
- **Statute of Limitations in California Tort Cases**
  www.statutes-of-limitations.com
- **Medical Malpractice in California**
  www.mcandl.com/california.html
  www.atra.org/show/7338
- **California Workers' Compensation & Occupational Safety**
  www.dir.ca.gov/DWC/dwc_home_page.htm
  www.workerscompensation.com/california.php
  www.cwci.org
- **Researching California Tort Law**
  www.megalaw.com/ca/ca.php
  www.lexisone.com/legalresearch/legalguide/states/california.htm
  california.lp.findlaw.com/index.html
- **Definitions of California Tort Principles in Jury Instructions**
  www.courtinfo.ca.gov/jury/civiljuryinstructions
  www.californiajuryinstructions.net
  www.saclaw.lib.ca.us/pages/jury-instructions.aspx
- **Summaries of California Tort Law (from selected attorney sites)**
  www.kinseylaw.com (click Legal Library, then Injury and Tort Law)
  www.scarlettlawgroup.com (under Practice Areas, click Professional Negligence)
  www.toxictorts.com
- **Jury Verdicts in California Tort Cases**
  www.ll.georgetown.edu/guides/jury.cfm
  www.morelaw.com/california/cases
  www.verdictsearch.com/index.jsp
- **California Trial Lawyers Association & State Bar**
  www.caoc.com/CA (now called Consumer Attorneys of California)
  www.calbar.ca.gov
- **Defense Bar in California**
  www.ascdc.org
  www.dri.org/open/SLDO.aspx
- **Google Searches on California Tort Law**
  "California tort"
  "California tort reform"
  "California negligence"
  California "intentional tort"
  California "medical malpractice"
- **Miscellaneous Sites on California Tort Law**
  www.tortlawcases.com/california-tort-claims-act
  www.hg.org/article.asp?id=18154

www.californiatortlaw.com
www.lexisnexis.com/store/catalog/booktemplate/productdetail.jsp?pageName=relatedProducts&prodId=10295

Colorado

- **Colorado State Court System**
  www.courts.state.co.us
  www.courts.state.co.us/Courts/Index.cfm
  www.courts.state.co.us/Forms/Index.cfm
- **Accident/Driver Records; Public Safety**
  crash.state.co.us
  www.colorado.gov/revenue
  publicrecords.onlinesearches.com/Colorado.htm
- **Statute of Limitations in Colorado Tort Cases**
  www.statutes-of-limitations.com
- **Medical Malpractice in Colorado**
  www.mcandl.com/colorado.html
  www.atra.org/show/7338
- **Colorado Workers' Compensation & Occupational Safety**
  www.colorado.gov/cs/Satellite/CDLE-WorkComp/CDLE/1240336932511
  www.workerscompensation.com/colorado.php
  www.coworkerscomp.com
- **Researching Colorado Tort Law**
  www.cobar.org/index.cfm/ID/3149/DPLPM/Legal-Research-Links
  www.loc.gov/law/help/guide/states.php
  www.lexisone.com/legalresearch/legalguide/states/colorado.htm
- **Definitions of Colorado Tort Principles in Jury Instructions**
  openlibrary.org/b/OL391017M/Colorado_jury_instructions_4th--civil
  www.llrx.com/columns/reference19.htm
- **Summaries of Colorado Tort Law (from selected attorney sites)**
  www.statutes-of-limitations.com/state/colorado
  www.mcandl.com/colorado.html
  www.hg.org/law-firms/Torts/USA-Colorado.html
- **Jury Verdicts in Colorado Tort Cases**
  www.jvrc.com
  www.ll.georgetown.edu/guides/jury.cfm
  www.verdictsearch.com/index.jsp
- **Colorado Trial Lawyers Association & State Bar**
  www.ctlanet.org/CO
  www.cobar.org
- **Defense Bar in Colorado**
  codla.org
  www.dri.org/open/SLDO.aspx
- **Google Searches on Colorado Tort Law**
  "Colorado tort"
  "Colorado tort reform"

"Colorado negligence"
Colorado "intentional tort"
Colorado "medical malpractice"

- **Miscellaneous Sites on Colorado Tort Law**
  www.tortlawcases.com/colorado-tort-law
  research.lawyers.com/Colorado/Personal-Injury-in-Colorado.html
  www.lexblog.com/network/midsize-firms/colorado-toxic-torts-law-blog-davis-graham-stubbs-law-firm.html

Connecticut

- **Connecticut State Court System**
  www.jud.ct.gov
  www.courtreference.com/Connecticut-Courts.htm
- **Accident/Driver Records; Public Safety**
  www.ct.gov/dot/cwp/view.asp?a=1383&q=259794
  www.ct.gov/dmv/site
  publicrecords.onlinesearches.com/Connecticut.htm
- **Statute of Limitations in Connecticut Tort Cases**
  www.statutes-of-limitations.com
- **Medical Malpractice in Connecticut**
  www.mcandl.com/connecticut.html
  www.atra.org/show/7338
- **Connecticut Workers' Compensation & Occupational Safety**
  wcc.state.ct.us
  www.workerscompensation.com/connecticut.php
  www.expertlaw.com/library/comp_by_state/Connecticut.html
- **Researching Connecticut Tort Law**
  www.jud.ct.gov/lawlib/state.htm
  www.cslib.org/law.htm
  www.romingerlegal.com/state/connecticut.html
  www.loc.gov/law/help/guide/states.php
- **Definitions of Connecticut Tort Principles in Jury Instructions**
  www.jud.ct.gov/JI/Civil
  www.jud.ct.gov/JI/civil/part3
  www.llrx.com/columns/reference19.htm
- **Summaries of Connecticut Tort Law (from selected attorney sites)**
  www.stangerlaw.com
  www.morelaw.com/connecticut/law/negligence.asp
  www.jacobslaw.com/PracticeAreas/Medmal.asp
- **Jury Verdicts in Connecticut Tort Cases**
  www.ll.georgetown.edu/guides/jury.cfm
  www.verdictsearch.com/index.jsp
- **Connecticut Trial Lawyers Association & State Bar**
  www.cttriallawyers.org
  www.ctbar.org

- **Defense Bar in Connecticut**
  www.ctdefenselawyers.org
  www.dri.org/open/SLDO.aspx
- **Google Searches on Connecticut Tort Law**
  "Connecticut tort"
  "Connecticut tort reform"
  "Connecticut negligence"
  Connecticut "intentional tort"
  Connecticut "medical malpractice"
- **Miscellaneous Sites on Connecticut Tort Law**
  www.jud.state.ct.us/lawlib/Law/domestic_torts.htm
  www.jud.ct.gov/lawlib/Notebooks/Pathfinders/TortsofMinors.htm
  law.findlaw.com/state-laws/negligence/connecticut

Delaware

- **Delaware State Court System**
  courts.delaware.gov
  courts.delaware.gov/courts/Superior%20Court
  www.findlaw.com/11stategov/de/courts.html
- **Accident/Driver Records; Public Safety**
  www.dmv.de.gov
  dsp.delaware.gov
  publicrecords.onlinesearches.com/Delaware.htm
- **Statute of Limitations in Delaware Tort Cases**
  www.statutes-of-limitations.com
- **Medical Malpractice in Delaware**
  www.mcandl.com/Delaware.html
  www.atra.org/show/7338
  www.expertlaw.com/library/malpractice_by_state/Delaware.html
  www.atra.org/states/DE
- **Delaware Workers' Compensation & Occupational Safety**
  www.delawareworks.com/industrialaffairs/services/WorkersComp.shtml
  www.workerscompensation.com/delaware.php
- **Researching Delaware Tort Law**
  www2.lib.udel.edu/subj/stdc/resguide/dellegal.htm
  www.lexisone.com/legalresearch/legalguide/states/delaware.htm
  www.romingerlegal.com/state/delaware.html
  www.loc.gov/law/help/guide/states.php
- **Definitions of Delaware Tort Principles in Jury Instructions**
  courts.delaware.gov/jury%20services
  www.llrx.com/columns/reference19.htm
- **Summaries of Delaware Tort Law (from selected attorney sites)**
  www.rawle.com/Reports_Articles_Details.asp?fileID=70
  www.delawarebusinesslitigation.com/articles/case-summaries/toxic-torts

- **Jury Verdicts in Delaware Tort Cases**
  www.ll.georgetown.edu/guides/jury.cfm
  www.verdictsearch.com/index.jsp
- **Delaware Trial Lawyers Association & State Bar**
  www.dtla.org/DE
  www.dsba.org
- **Defense Bar in Delaware**
  www.dri.org/open/SLDO.aspx
- **Google Searches on Delaware Tort Law**
  "Delaware tort"
  "Delaware tort reform"
  "Delaware negligence"
  Delaware "intentional tort"
  Delaware "medical malpractice"
- **Miscellaneous Sites on Delaware Tort Law**
  law.findlaw.com/state-laws/negligence/delaware
  www.ehow.com/list_5974247_delaware-medical-malpractice-laws.html

District of Columbia

- **District of Columbia Court System**
  www.dccourts.gov/dccourts/index.jsp
  www.dccourts.gov/dccourts/about/prose.jsp
- **Accident/Driver Records; Public Safety**
  search.dmv.org/dmv/washington-dc/accident-report-form
  publicrecords.onlinesearches.com/DistrictofColumbia.htm
- **Statute of Limitations in District of Columbia Tort Cases**
  www.statutes-of-limitations.com
- **Medical Malpractice in District of Columbia**
  www.mcandl.com/DC.html
  www.atra.org/show/7338
- **District of Columbia Workers' Compensation & Occupational Safety**
  www.does.dc.gov/does/cwp/view.asp?a=1232&Q=537428
- **Researching District of Columbia Tort Law**
  www.ll.georgetown.edu/research/browse_jurisdictions.cfm
  www.law.gwu.edu/Library/Research/Documents/Guides/DC_09.pdf
  www.loc.gov/law/help/guide/states.php
- **Definitions of District of Columbia Tort Principles in Jury Instructions**
  www.ll.georgetown.edu/states/dc-in-depth.cfm
  www.llrx.com/columns/reference19.htm
- **Summaries of District of Columbia Tort Law** (from selected attorney sites)
  www.ashcraftandgerel.com
  www.chaikinandsherman.com

- **District of Columbia Trial Lawyers Association & Local Bar**
  www.tla-dc.org/DC
  www.dcbar.org
  www.badc.org
- **Jury Verdicts in District of Columbia Tort Cases**
  www.ll.georgetown.edu/guides/jury.cfm
  www.verdictsearch.com/index.jsp
- **Defense Bar in District of Columbia**
  www.dri.org/open/SLDO.aspx
- **Google Searches on District of Columbia Tort Law**
  "DC tort"
  "DC tort reform"
  "DC negligence"
  DC "intentional tort"
  DC "medical malpractice"

Florida

- **Florida State Court System**
  www.flcourts.org
  www.floridasupremecourt.org
- **Accident/Driver Records; Public Safety**
  www.stateofflorida.com/Portal/DesktopDefault.aspx?tabid=23
  publicrecords.onlinesearches.com/Florida.htm
- **Statute of Limitations in Florida Tort Cases**
  www.statutes-of-limitations.com
- **Medical Malpractice in Florida**
  www.mcandl.com/Florida.html
  www.atra.org/show/7338
- **Florida Workers' Compensation & Occupational Safety**
  www.myfloridacfo.com/wc
  www.myfloridacfo.com/wc/pdf/WC-System-Guide-v2.pdf
- **Researching Florida Tort Law**
  floridalegalblog.blogspot.com
  www.floridasupremecourt.org/library/index.shtml
  www.loc.gov/law/help/guide/states.php
- **Definitions of Florida Tort Principles in Jury Instructions**
  www.flcourts18.org/PDF/civil.pdf
  www.flcourts.org/gen_public/jury/jury_management.shtml
  www.llrx.com/columns/reference19.htm
- **Summaries of Florida Tort Law (from selected attorney sites)**
  www.southfloridapersonalinjurylawyers.com
  www.johnbales.com
  www.chaliklaw.com
  www.dnslaw.com

- **Jury Verdicts in Florida Tort Cases**
  www.ll.georgetown.edu/guides/jury.cfm
  www.verdictsearch.com/index.jsp
- **Florida Trial Lawyers Association & State Bar**
  www.floridajusticeassociation.org
  www.floridabar.org
- **Defense Bar in Florida**
  www.fdla.org
  www.dri.org/open/SLDO.aspx
- **Google Searches on Florida Tort Law**
  "Florida tort"
  "Florida tort reform"
  "Florida negligence"
  Florida "intentional tort"
  Florida "medical malpractice"
- **Miscellaneous Sites on Florida Tort Law**
  www.megalaw.com/fl/top/fltorts.php
  www.floridapersonalinjurylawyerblog.com
  www.legalreforminthenews.com/Tort%20Profiles/FL_Tort_Laws.html

Georgia

- **Georgia State Court System**
  www.georgiacourts.org
- **Accident/Driver Records; Public Safety**
  www.georgia.gov/00/channel_title/0,2094,5635600_40829891,00.html
  publicrecords.onlinesearches.com/Georgia.htm
- **Statute of Limitations in Georgia Tort Cases**
  www.statutes-of-limitations.com
- **Medical Malpractice in Georgia**
  www.mcandl.com/Georgia.html
  www.atra.org/show/7338
- **Georgia Workers' Compensation & Occupational Safety**
  sbwc.georgia.gov/portal/site/SBWC
  www.workerscompensation.com/georgia.php
- **Researching Georgia Tort Law**
  www.megalaw.com/ga/ga.php
  www.romingerlegal.com/state/georgia.html
  www.loc.gov/law/help/guide/states.php
- **Definitions of Georgia Tort Principles in Jury Instructions**
  www.law.mercer.edu/library/GeorgiaResources/GeorgiaResources.cfm#verdicts
  www.llrx.com/columns/reference19.htm
- **Summaries of Georgia Tort Law (from selected attorney sites)**
  www.garymartinhays.com
  www.millarandmixon.com
  www.christophersimon.com

- **Jury Verdicts in Georgia Tort Cases**
  www.ll.georgetown.edu/guides/jury.cfm
  www.verdictsearch.com/index.jsp
- **Georgia Trial Lawyers Association & State Bar**
  www.gtla.org/GA
  www.gabar.org
- **Defense Bar in Georgia**
  www.gdla.org
  www.dri.org/open/SLDO.aspx
- **Google Searches on Georgia Tort Law**
  "Georgia tort"
  "Georgia tort reform"
  "Georgia negligence"
  Georgia "intentional tort"
  Georgia "medical malpractice"
- **Miscellaneous Sites on Georgia Tort Law**
  www.atlantainjurylawblog.com
  www.legalreforminthenews.com/Tort%20Profiles/GA_Tort_Laws.html

Hawaii

- **Hawaii State Court System**
  www.courts.state.hi.us
- **Accident/Driver Records; Public Safety**
  www.hawaii.gov/dot/highways
  publicrecords.onlinesearches.com/Hawaii.htm
- **Statute of Limitations in Hawaii Tort Cases**
  www.statutes-of-limitations.com
- **Medical Malpractice in Hawaii**
  www.mcandl.com/Hawaii.html
  www.atra.org/show/7338
- **Hawaii Workers' Compensation & Occupational Safety**
  hawaii.gov/labor/dcd/aboutwc.shtml
  hawaii.gov/labor/hiosh/index.shtml
- **Researching Hawaii Tort Law**
  www.state.hi.us/jud/library/index.htm
  www.courts.state.hi.us/legal_references/resources/internet_resources.html
  www.loc.gov/law/help/guide/states.php
- **Definitions of Hawaii Tort Principles in Jury Instructions**
  www.courts.state.hi.us/legal_references/circuit_court_standard_jury_instructions.html
  www.llrx.com/columns/reference19.htm
- **Summaries of Hawaii Tort Law (from selected attorney sites)**
  www.turbin.net
  www.janweinberg.com

www.croninfried.com
accidentlawyerhawaii.com

- **Jury Verdicts in Hawaii Tort Cases**
  www.ll.georgetown.edu/guides/jury.cfm
  www.verdictsearch.com/index.jsp
- **Hawaii Trial Lawyers Association & State Bar**
  www.hsba.org
  www.theatla.com/top-100-lawyers-hawaii.html
- **Google Searches on Hawaii Tort Law**
  "Hawaii tort"
  "Hawaii tort reform"
  "Hawaii negligence"
  Hawaii "intentional tort"
  Hawaii "medical malpractice"
- **Miscellaneous Sites on Hawaii Tort Law**
  pibureau.com/cases/torts.htm
  theinvestigatorsllc.com/Torts_Hawaii_Investigation.html

Idaho

- **Idaho State Court System**
  www.isc.idaho.gov
- **Accident/Driver Records; Public Safety**
  idahofallspdid.policereports.us
  www.isp.idaho.gov
  publicrecords.onlinesearches.com/Idaho.htm
- **Statute of Limitations in Idaho Tort Cases**
  www.statutes-of-limitations.com
- **Medical Malpractice in Idaho**
  www.mcandl.com/Idaho.html
  www.atra.org/show/7338
- **Idaho Workers' Compensation & Occupational Safety**
  www.iic.idaho.gov
  www.boisestate.edu/oshcon
- **Researching Idaho Tort Law**
  www.isu.edu/library/law/legalresearch.htm
  www.lexisone.com/legalresearch/legalguide/states/idaho.htm
  www.loc.gov/law/help/guide/states.php
- **Definitions of Idaho Tort Principles in Jury Instructions**
  www.isc.idaho.gov/juryinst_cov.htm
  www.isc.idaho.gov/rules/CV_JURYINST.pdf
  www.llrx.com/columns/reference19.htm
- **Summaries of Idaho Tort Law (from selected attorney sites)**
  www.hepworthlaw.com
  idaho.gregoryswapp.com

- **Jury Verdicts in Idaho Tort Cases**
  www.ll.georgetown.edu/guides/jury.cfm
  www.verdictsearch.com/index.jsp
- **Idaho Trial Lawyers Association & State Bar**
  www.itla.org/ID
  isb.idaho.gov
- **Defense Bar in Idaho**
  www.idahodefense.org
  www.dri.org/open/SLDO.aspx
- **Google Searches on Idaho Tort Law**
  "Idaho tort"
  "Idaho tort reform"
  "Idaho negligence"
  Idaho "intentional tort"
  Idaho "medical malpractice"

Illinois

- **Illinois State Court System**
  www.state.il.us/court
- **Accident/Driver Records; Public Safety**
  www.isp.state.il.us/traffic/crashreports.cfm
  publicrecords.onlinesearches.com/Illinois.htm
- **Statute of Limitations in Illinois Tort Cases**
  www.statutes-of-limitations.com
- **Medical Malpractice in Idaho**
  www.mcandl.com/Illinois.html
  www.atra.org/show/7338
  medicalmalpractice.levinperconti.com/970tort_reform
- **Illinois Workers' Compensation & Occupational Safety**
  www.state.il.us/agency/IIC
  www.illinois.gov/working/workplace_safety.cfm
- **Researching Illinois Tort Law**
  www.lawsource.com/also/usa.cgi?il
  www.romingerlegal.com/state/illinois.html
  www.loc.gov/law/help/guide/states.php
- **Definitions of Illinois Tort Principles in Jury Instructions**
  www.state.il.us/court/circuitcourt/juryinstructions/default.asp
  www.llrx.com/columns/reference19.htm
- **Summaries of Illinois Tort Law (from selected attorney sites)**
  www.chicagotriallaw.com
  www.vlaw.com
  www.seidmanlaw.net
- **Jury Verdicts in Illinois Tort Cases**
  www.ll.georgetown.edu/guides/jury.cfm
  www.verdictsearch.com/index.jsp

- **Illinois Trial Lawyers Association & State Bar**
  www.iltla.com
  www.isba.org
- **Defense Bar in Illinois**
  www.iadtc.org
  www.dri.org/open/SLDO.aspx
- **Google Searches on Illinois Tort Law**
  "Illinois tort"
  "Illinois tort reform"
  "Illinois negligence"
  Illinois "intentional tort"
  Illinois "medical malpractice"
- **Miscellaneous Sites on Illinois Tort Law**
  www.illinoispersonalinjurylawyerblog.com
  www.legalreforminthenews.com/Tort%20Profiles/IL_Tort_Laws.html

Indiana

- **Indiana State Court System**
  www.in.gov/judiciary
- **Accident/Driver Records; Public Safety**
  www.in.gov/bmv
  bloomington.in.gov/documents/viewDocument.php?document_id=670
  publicrecords.onlinesearches.com/Indiana.htm
- **Statute of Limitations in Indiana Tort Cases**
  www.statutes-of-limitations.com
- **Medical Malpractice in Indiana**
  www.mcandl.com/Indiana.html
  www.atra.org/show/7338
- **Indiana Workers' Compensation & Occupational Safety**
  www.in.gov/wcb
  www.in.gov/dol/iosha.htm
- **Researching Indiana Tort Law**
  www.in.gov/judiciary/library/about.html
  www.lawsource.com/also/usa.cgi?in
  www.loc.gov/law/help/guide/states.php
- **Definitions of Indiana Tort Principles in Jury Instructions**
  www.llrx.com/columns/reference19.htm
- **Summaries of Indiana Tort Law (from selected attorney sites)**
  www.tortslaw.com
  www.sevenishlaw.com
- **Jury Verdicts in Indiana Tort Cases**
  www.ll.georgetown.edu/guides/jury.cfm
  www.verdictsearch.com/index.jsp
- **Indiana Trial Lawyers Association & State Bar**
  www.indianatriallawyers.org/IN
  www.inbar.org

- **Defense Bar in Indiana**
  www.dtci.org
  www.dri.org/open/SLDO.aspx
- **Google Searches on Indiana Tort Law**
  "Indiana tort"
  "Indiana tort reform"
  "Indiana negligence"
  Indiana "intentional tort"
  Indiana "medical malpractice"
- **Miscellaneous Sites on Indiana Tort Law**
  www.earlham.edu/~peters/courses/ct/ctlinks.htm
  law.findlaw.com/state-laws/negligence/indiana

Iowa

- **Iowa State Court System**
  www.iowacourts.gov
  www.iowacourts.gov/Representing_Yourself
- **Accident/Driver Records; Public Safety**
  accidentreports.iowa.gov
  publicrecords.onlinesearches.com/Iowa.htm
- **Statute of Limitations in Iowa Tort Cases**
  www.statutes-of-limitations.com
- **Medical Malpractice in Iowa**
  www.mcandl.com/Iowa.html
  www.atra.org/show/7338
- **Iowa Workers' Compensation & Occupational Safety**
  www.iowaworkforce.org/wc
  www.iowaworkforce.org/labor/iosh
- **Researching Iowa Tort Law**
  www.law.drake.edu/library/?pageID=iowaResearch
  www.lexisone.com/legalresearch/legalguide/states/iowa.htm
  www.loc.gov/law/help/guide/states.php
- **Definitions of Iowa Tort Principles in Jury Instructions**
  www.law.drake.edu/library/?pageID=juryInstructions
  www.llrx.com/columns/reference19.htm
- **Summaries of Iowa Tort Law (from selected attorney sites)**
  www.walklaw.com
  www.hixsonlaw.com
  www.roxanneconlinlaw.com
- **Jury Verdicts in Iowa Tort Cases**
  www.ll.georgetown.edu/guides/jury.cfm
  www.verdictsearch.com/index.jsp
- **Iowa Trial Lawyers Association & State Bar**
  www.iowajustice.org/IA
  www.iowabar.org

- **Defense Bar in Iowa**
  www.iowadefensecounsel.org
  www.dri.org/open/SLDO.aspx
- **Google Searches on Iowa Tort Law**
  "Iowa tort"
  "Iowa tort reform"
  "Iowa negligence"
  Iowa "intentional tort"
  Iowa "medical malpractice"
- **Miscellaneous Sites on Iowa Tort Law**
  www.law.uiowa.edu/alumni/cle/books/books-iowatortguide.php
  www.legis.state.ia.us/lsadocs/Legal_Update/2009/LULSL004.PDF

Kansas

- **Kansas State Court System**
  www.kscourts.org
- **Accident/Driver Records; Public Safety**
  https://www.accesskansas.org/ssrv-khp-crashlogs/index.do
  publicrecords.onlinesearches.com/Kansas.htm
- **Statute of Limitations in Kansas Tort Cases**
  www.statutes-of-limitations.com
- **Medical Malpractice in Kansas**
  www.mcandl.com/Kansas.html
  www.atra.org/show/7338
- **Kansas Workers' Compensation & Occupational Safety**
  www.dol.ks.gov/WC/html/wc_ALL.html
  www.dol.ks.gov/safety/html/workplacesafety.html
- **Researching Kansas Tort Law**
  www.findlaw.com/11stategov/ks/index.html
  www.kscourts.org/kansas-courts/law-library/default.asp
  www.loc.gov/law/help/guide/states.php
- **Definitions of Kansas Tort Principles in Jury Instructions**
  www.llrx.com/columns/reference19.htm
  west.thomson.com/productdetail/159891/40705472/productdetail.aspx
- **Summaries of Kansas Tort Law (from selected attorney sites)**
  www.warnerlawoffices.com
  www.pistotniklaw.com
- **Jury Verdicts in Kansas Tort Cases**
  www.ll.georgetown.edu/guides/jury.cfm
  www.verdictsearch.com/index.jsp
- **Kansas Trial Lawyers Association & State Bar**
  www.ksaj.org/KS
  www.ksbar.org
- **Defense Bar in Kansas**
  www.kadc.org
  www.dri.org/open/SLDO.aspx

- **Google Searches on Kansas Tort Law**
  "Kansas tort"
  "Kansas tort reform"
  "Kansas negligence"
  Kansas "intentional tort"
  Kansas "medical malpractice"
- **Miscellaneous Sites on Kansas Tort Law**
  www.caakansas.org/files/ktca.pdf
  washburnlaw.edu/wlj/39-1/articles/smith-kevin.pdf
  www.kscoplaw.com/outlines/civ&crim.html

Kentucky

- **Kentucky State Court System**
  courts.ky.gov
- **Accident/Driver Records; Public Safety**
  www.kentuckystatepolice.org
  www.kytc.state.ky.us
  publicrecords.onlinesearches.com/Kentucky.htm
- **Statute of Limitations in Kentucky Tort Cases**
  www.statutes-of-limitations.com
- **Medical Malpractice in Kentucky**
  www.mcandl.com/Kentucky.html
  www.atra.org/show/7338
- **Kentucky Workers' Compensation & Occupational Safety**
  www.labor.ky.gov/workersclaims
  www.labor.ky.gov/ows/osh
- **Researching Kentucky Tort Law**
  www.kybar.org/117
  courts.ky.gov/research
  www.loc.gov/law/help/guide/states.php
- **Definitions of Kentucky Tort Principles in Jury Instructions**
  www.law.uky.edu/files/docs/library/guides/jury%20instructions.pdf
  www.llrx.com/columns/reference19.htm
- **Summaries of Kentucky Tort Law (from selected attorney sites)**
  www.poppelawfirm.com
  www.bluegrassinjury.com
  www.franklingrayandwhite.com
- **Jury Verdicts in Kentucky Tort Cases**
  www.ll.georgetown.edu/guides/jury.cfm
  www.law.uky.edu/files/docs/library/guides/jury%20instructions.pdf
  www.verdictsearch.com/index.jsp
- **Kentucky Trial Lawyers Association & State Bar**
  www.kentuckyjusticeassociation.org/KY
  www.kybar.org

- **Defense Bar in Kentucky**
  www.kentuckydefensecounsel.com
  www.dri.org/open/SLDO.aspx
- **Google Searches on Kentucky Tort Law**
  "Kentucky tort"
  "Kentucky tort reform"
  "Kentucky negligence"
  Kentucky "intentional tort"
  Kentucky "medical malpractice"
- **Miscellaneous Sites on Kentucky Tort Law**
  kytortlaw.blogspot.com
  www.legalreforminthenews.com/Tort%20Profiles/Kentucky.htm
  www.hg.org/law-firms/Personal-Injury/USA-Kentucky.html

Louisiana

- **Louisiana State Court System**
  www.louisiana.gov/Government/Judicial_Branch
- **Accident/Driver Records; Public Safety**
  lhsc.lsu.edu
  www.dps.state.la.us
  publicrecords.onlinesearches.com/Louisiana.htm
- **Statute of Limitations in Louisiana Tort Cases**
  www.statutes-of-limitations.com
- **Medical Malpractice in Louisiana**
  www.mcandl.com/Louisiana.html
  www.atra.org/show/7338
- **Louisiana Workers' Compensation & Occupational Safety**
  www.laworks.net/WorkersComp/OWC_MainMenu.asp
  appl003.lsu.edu/pubsafety/oes.nsf/index
- **Researching Louisiana Tort Law**
  www.lasc.org/law_library/library_information.asp
  www.megalaw.com/la/la.php
  www.loc.gov/law/help/guide/states.php
  www.lexisone.com/legalresearch/legalguide/states/louisiana.htm
- **Definitions of Louisiana Tort Principles in Jury Instructions**
  west.thomson.com/productdetail/1054/22112364/productdetail.aspx
  www.judgeconque.com/Jury%20Charges/juryciv.html
  www.llrx.com/columns/reference19.htm
- **Summaries of Louisiana Tort Law (from selected attorney sites)**
  www.cuerialawfirm.com
  www.dueprice.com/lawyer-attorney-1503213.html
- **Jury Verdicts in Louisiana Tort Cases**
  www.ll.georgetown.edu/guides/jury.cfm
  www.verdictsearch.com/index.jsp

- **Louisiana Trial Lawyers Association & State Bar**
  www.lafj.org/LA
  www.lsba.org
- **Defense Bar in Louisiana**
  ladc.org
  www.dri.org/open/SLDO.aspx
- **Google Searches on Louisiana Tort Law**
  "Louisiana tort"
  "Louisiana tort reform"
  "Louisiana negligence"
  Louisiana "intentional tort"
  Louisiana "medical malpractice"
- **Miscellaneous Sites on Louisiana Tort Law**
  www.legalreforminthenews.com/Tort%20Profiles/LA_Tort_Laws.html
  www.gallagherlawfirm.com/blog
  www.richardvlaw.com/blog/index.asp

Maine

- **Maine State Court System**
  www.courts.state.me.us
  www.courts.state.me.us/citizen_info/representing_yourself.html
- **Accident/Driver Records; Public Safety**
  www.informe.org/mcrs
  publicrecords.onlinesearches.com/Maine.htm
- **Statute of Limitations in Maine Tort Cases**
  www.statutes-of-limitations.com
- **Medical Malpractice in Maine**
  www.mcandl.com/Maine.html
  www.atra.org/show/7338
- **Maine Workers' Compensation & Occupational Safety**
  www.maine.gov/wcb
  www.maine.gov/labor/workplace_safety/datagroup/index.shtml
- **Researching Maine Tort Law**
  www.courts.state.me.us/citizen_info/links.html
  www.romingerlegal.com/state/maine.html
  www.loc.gov/law/help/guide/states.php
- **Definitions of Maine Tort Principles in Jury Instructions**
  www.llrx.com/columns/reference19.htm
- **Summaries of Maine Tort Law** (from selected attorney sites)
  www.peter-thompson-associates.com
  www.maineinjurylawyerblog.com
- **Jury Verdicts in Maine Tort Cases**
  www.ll.georgetown.edu/guides/jury.cfm
  www.verdictsearch.com/index.jsp

- **Maine Trial Lawyers Association & State Bar**
  www.mtla.org/ME
  www.mainebar.org
- **Defense Bar in Maine**
  www.tristatedefenselawyers.org
  www.dri.org/open/SLDO.aspx
- **Google Searches on Maine Tort Law**
  "Maine tort"
  "Maine tort reform"
  "Maine negligence"
  Maine "intentional tort"
  Maine "medical malpractice"
- **Miscellaneous Sites on Maine Tort Law**
  www.marcheseassociates.net/resources.html
  www.dmv.org/me-maine/personal-injury.php
  www.lexblog.com/network/small-solo-firms/maine-personal-injury-law-blog-joe-bornstein.html

Maryland

- **Maryland State Court System**
  www.courts.state.md.us
- **Accident/Driver Records; Public Safety**
  www.mdsp.org/services/services_intro.asp
  search.dmv.org/dmv/maryland/accident-report
  publicrecords.onlinesearches.com/Maryland.htm
- **Statute of Limitations in Maryland Tort Cases**
  www.statutes-of-limitations.com
- **Medical Malpractice in Maryland**
  www.mcandl.com/Maryland.html
  www.atra.org/show/7338
- **Maryland Workers' Compensation & Occupational Safety**
  www.wcc.state.md.us
  www.dllr.state.md.us/labor/mosh
- **Researching Maryland Tort Law**
  www.lawlib.state.md.us
  www.lexisone.com/legalresearch/legalguide/states/maryland.htm
  www.loc.gov/law/help/guide/states.php
- **Definitions of Maryland Tort Principles in Jury Instructions**
  www.millerandzois.com/jury_instructions.html
  www.llrx.com/columns/reference19.htm
- **Summaries of Maryland Tort Law (from selected attorney sites)**
  www.millerandzois.com
  www.marylandinjuryattorney.net
  www.youhavealawyer.com

- **Jury Verdicts in Maryland Tort Cases**
  www.ll.georgetown.edu/guides/jury.cfm
  www.verdictsearch.com/index.jsp
- **Maryland Trial Lawyers Association & State Bar**
  www.marylandassociationforjustice.com/MD
  www.msba.org
- **Defense Bar in Maryland**
  www.mddefensecounsel.org
  www.dri.org/open/SLDO.aspx
- **Google Searches on Maryland Tort Law**
  "Maryland tort"
  "Maryland tort reform"
  "Maryland negligence"
  Maryland "intentional tort"
  Maryland "medical malpractice"
- **Miscellaneous Sites on Maryland Tort Law**
  www.peoples-law.org/misc/personal_injury/MD_personal_injury.htm
  www.mdinjurydisabilitylaw.com
  www.marylandaccidentlawblog.com

Massachusetts

- **Massachusetts State Court System**
  www.mass.gov/courts/index.html
  www.mass.gov/courts/selfhelp/index.html
- **Accident/Driver Records; Public Safety**
  www.mhd.state.ma.us/default.asp?pgid=content/traffic/crashrateeval&sid=about
  publicrecords.onlinesearches.com/Massachusetts.htm
- **Statute of Limitations in Massachusetts Tort Cases**
  www.statutes-of-limitations.com
- **Medical Malpractice in Massachusetts**
  www.mcandl.com/Massachusetts.html
  www.atra.org/show/7338
- **Massachusetts Workers' Compensation & Occupational Safety**
  www.mass.gov (type Workers Compensation in the search box)
  www.mass.gov (type Occupational Safety in the search box)
- **Researching Massachusetts Tort Law**
  www.bu.edu/lawlibrary/research/mass/index.html
  www.romingerlegal.com/state/massachusetts.html
  www.lawlib.state.ma.us
  www.loc.gov/law/help/guide/states.php
- **Definitions of Massachusetts Tort Principles in Jury Instructions**
  www.llrx.com/columns/reference19.htm
- **Summaries of Massachusetts Tort Law (from selected attorney sites)**
  www.giacoppelaw.com

www.margolinlaw.com
www.frobertallison.com

- **Jury Verdicts in Massachusetts Tort Cases**
  www.ll.georgetown.edu/guides/jury.cfm
  www.verdictsearch.com/index.jsp
- **Massachusetts Trial Lawyers Association & State Bar**
  www.massacademy.com/MA
  www.massbar.org
- **Defense Bar in Massachusetts**
  www.massdla.org/mdla
  www.dri.org/open/SLDO.aspx
- **Google Searches on Massachusetts Tort Law**
  "Massachusetts tort"
  "Massachusetts tort reform"
  "Massachusetts negligence"
  Massachusetts "intentional tort"
  Massachusetts "medical malpractice"
- **Miscellaneous Sites on Massachusetts Tort Law**
  www.massbar.org (type "tort" in the search box)
  www.christopherfearley.typepad.com
  www.mass.gov/legis/laws/mgl/90-34m.htm

Michigan

- **Michigan State Court System**
  courts.michigan.gov
  courts.michigan.gov/scao/selfhelp/selfhelphome.htm
- **Accident/Driver Records; Public Safety**
  www.michigan.gov/msp
  publicrecords.onlinesearches.com/Michigan.htm
- **Statute of Limitations in Michigan Tort Cases**
  www.statutes-of-limitations.com
- **Medical Malpractice in Michigan**
  www.mcandl.com/Michigan.html
  www.atra.org/show/7338
- **Michigan Workers' Compensation & Occupational Safety**
  www.michigan.gov/wca
  www.oseh.umich.edu
- **Researching Michigan Tort Law**
  www.ll.georgetown.edu/states/michigan.cfm
  www.romingerlegal.com/state/michigan.html
  www.loc.gov/law/help/guide/states.php
- **Definitions of Michigan Tort Principles in Jury Instructions**
  courts.mi.gov/mcji-index.htm
  www.llrx.com/columns/reference19.htm

- **Summaries of Michigan Tort Law (from selected attorney sites)**
  www.cochranfoley.com
  www.bredell.com
  www.2keller.com
- **Jury Verdicts in Michigan Tort Cases**
  www.ll.georgetown.edu/guides/jury.cfm
  www.verdictsearch.com/index.jsp
- **Michigan Trial Lawyers Association & State Bar**
  www.michiganjustice.org/MI
  www.michbar.org
- **Defense Bar in Michigan**
  www.mdtc.org
  www.adtc.org
  www.dri.org/open/SLDO.aspx
- **Google Searches on Michigan Tort Law**
  "Michigan tort"
  "Michigan tort reform"
  "Michigan negligence"
  Michigan "intentional tort"
  Michigan "medical malpractice"
- **Miscellaneous Sites on Michigan Tort Law**
  www.michbar.org/generalinfo/libraries/tort_june99.cfm
  www.alexanderandangelas.com/michigan_tort_law_summary.htm
  www.a2lawyer.com/articles/injury/personal.html
  www.legalreforminthenews.com/Tort%20Profiles/MI_Tort_Laws.html

Minnesota

- **Minnesota State Court System**
  www.courts.state.mn.us
  www.courts.state.mn.us/selfhelp
- **Accident/Driver Records; Public Safety**
  www.ci.minneapolis.mn.us/police/records/accident_report_request.asp
  publicrecords.onlinesearches.com/Minnesota.htm
- **Statute of Limitations in Minnesota Tort Cases**
  www.statutes-of-limitations.com
- **Medical Malpractice in Minnesota**
  www.mcandl.com/Minnesota.html
  www.atra.org/show/7338
- **Minnesota Workers' Compensation & Occupational Safety**
  www.dli.mn.gov/WorkComp.asp
  www.dli.mn.gov/mnosha.asp
- **Researching Minnesota Tort Law**
  www.lawlibrary.state.mn.us
  www.lawmoose.com

www.courts.state.mn.us/?page=318
www.loc.gov/law/help/guide/states.php

- **Definitions of Minnesota Tort Principles in Jury Instructions**
  west.thomson.com/productdetail/138948/15674006/productdetail.aspx
  www.llrx.com/columns/reference19.htm
- **Summaries of Minnesota Tort Law (from selected attorney sites)**
  lawyerbob.com
  www.schwebel.com
  www.minnesotapersonalinjury.com
- **Jury Verdicts in Minnesota Tort Cases**
  www.ll.georgetown.edu/guides/jury.cfm
  www.verdictsearch.com/index.jsp
- **Minnesota Trial Lawyers Association & State Bar**
  www.mnaj.org
  www.mnbar.org
- **Defense Bar in Minnesota**
  www.mdla.org
  www.dri.org/open/SLDO.aspx
- **Google Searches on Minnesota Tort Law**
  "Minnesota tort"
  "Minnesota tort reform"
  "Minnesota negligence"
  Minnesota "intentional tort"
  Minnesota "medical malpractice"
- **Miscellaneous Sites on Minnesota Tort Law**
  www.lawmoose.com/internetlawlib/110.htm
  www.minncle.org/materials/publications/57709-CA.htm
  www.hg.org/law-firms/Torts/USA-Minnesota.html

Mississippi

- **Mississippi State Court System**
  www.mississippi.gov/ms_sub_sub_template.jsp?Category_ID=13
  www.mssc.state.ms.us
  www.courtreference.com/Mississippi-Courts.htm
- **Accident/Driver Records; Public Safety**
  www.dps.state.ms.us/dps/dps.nsf/main?OpenForm
  publicrecords.onlinesearches.com/Mississippi.htm
  motorvehicles.org/mississippi/driving-records
- **Statute of Limitations in Mississippi Tort Cases**
  www.statutes-of-limitations.com
- **Medical Malpractice in Mississippi**
  www.mcandl.com/Mississippi.html
  www.atra.org/show/7338
- **Mississippi Workers' Compensation & Occupational Safety**
  www.mwcc.state.ms.us

- **Researching Mississippi Tort Law**
  www.romingerlegal.com/state/mississippi.html
  www.lexisone.com/legalresearch/legalguide/states/mississippi.htm
  www.loc.gov/law/help/guide/states.php
- **Definitions of Mississippi Tort Principles in Jury Instructions**
  west.thomson.com/productdetail/3308/22081545/productdetail.aspx
  www.llrx.com/columns/reference19.htm
- **Summaries of Mississippi Tort Law (from selected attorney sites)**
  www.ingramlawyers.com
  www.baileyandwomble.com
  www.jayfosterlaw.com
- **Jury Verdicts in Mississippi Tort Cases**
  www.ll.georgetown.edu/guides/jury.cfm
  www.verdictsearch.com/index.jsp
- **Mississippi Trial Lawyers Association & State Bar**
  www.msaj.org/MS
  www.msbar.org
- **Defense Bar in Mississippi**
  www.msdefenselaw.org
  www.dri.org/open/SLDO.aspx
- **Google Searches on Mississippi Tort Law**
  "Mississippi tort"
  "Mississippi tort reform"
  "Mississippi negligence"
  Mississippi "intentional tort"
  Mississippi "medical malpractice"
- **Miscellaneous Sites on Mississippi Tort Law**
  www.dfa.state.ms.us/Offices/Tort/Tort.htm
  www.mslitigationreview.com
  www.kingsoftort.com

Missouri

- **Missouri State Court System**
  www.courts.mo.gov
  www.selfrepresent.mo.gov/page.jsp?id=5240
- **Accident/Driver Records; Public Safety**
  www.mshp.dps.mo.gov/HP68/search.jsp
  publicrecords.onlinesearches.com/Missouri.htm
- **Statute of Limitations in Missouri Tort Cases**
  www.statutes-of-limitations.com
- **Medical Malpractice in Missouri**
  www.mcandl.com/Missouri.html
  www.atra.org/show/7338
  www.missouriinjuryattorneysblog.com/medical-malpractice

- **Missouri Workers' Compensation & Occupational Safety**
  www.labor.mo.gov
  www.workerscompensation.com/missouri.php
- **Researching Missouri Tort Law**
  www.megalaw.com/mo/mo.php
  www.courts.mo.gov/page.jsp?id=587
  www.findlaw.com/11stategov/mo/index.html
  www.loc.gov/law/help/guide/states.php
- **Definitions of Missouri Tort Principles in Jury Instructions**
  www.courts.mo.gov/page.jsp?id=589
  www.llrx.com/columns/reference19.htm
- **Summaries of Missouri Tort Law (from selected attorney sites)**
  www.sansonelaw.com
  www.brownandcrouppen.com
  www.petersonlawfirm.com
- **Jury Verdicts in Missouri Tort Cases**
  www.ll.georgetown.edu/guides/jury.cfm
  www.verdictsearch.com/index.jsp
- **Missouri Trial Lawyers Association & State Bar**
  www.matanet.org/MO
  www.mobar.org
- **Defense Bar in Missouri**
  www.modllaw.com
  www.dri.org/open/SLDO.aspx
- **Google Searches on Missouri Tort Law**
  "Missouri tort"
  "Missouri tort reform"
  "Missouri negligence"
  Missouri "intentional tort"
  Missouri "medical malpractice"
- **Miscellaneous Sites on Missouri Tort Law**
  www.missouripersonalinjurylawyerblog.com
  www.missouriinjurylawblog.com

Montana

- **Montana State Court System**
  courts.mt.gov/default.mcpx
- **Accident/Driver Records; Public Safety**
  www.doj.mt.gov/driving/default.asp
  www.madison.mt.gov/departments/sheriffs_office/mv.asp
  publicrecords.onlinesearches.com/Montana.htm
- **Statute of Limitations in Montana Tort Cases**
  www.statutes-of-limitations.com

- **Medical Malpractice in Montana**
  www.mcandl.com/Montana.html
  www.atra.org/show/7338
- **Montana Workers' Compensation & Occupational Safety**
  erd.dli.mt.gov/wcregs/wcrhome.asp
  erd.dli.mt.gov/safetyhealth/sbhome.asp
- **Researching Montana Tort Law**
  courts.mt.gov/library/default.mcpx
  www.lexisone.com/legalresearch/legalguide/states/montana.htm
  www.loc.gov/law/help/guide/states.php
- **Definitions of Montana Tort Principles in Jury Instructions**
  www.llrx.com/columns/reference19.htm
- **Summaries of Montana Tort Law (from selected attorney sites)**
  www.montana-injury-lawyer.com
  montanaattorney4personalinjury.com
  www.skaggslaw.com
- **Jury Verdicts in Montana Tort Cases**
  www.ll.georgetown.edu/guides/jury.cfm
  www.verdictsearch.com/index.jsp
- **Montana Trial Lawyers Association & State Bar**
  www.monttla.com/MT
  www.montanabar.org
- **Defense Bar in Montana**
  www.mdtl.net
  www.dri.org/open/SLDO.aspx
- **Google Searches on Montana Tort Law**
  "Montana tort"
  "Montana tort reform"
  "Montana negligence"
  Montana "intentional tort"
  Montana "medical malpractice"
- **Miscellaneous Sites on Montana Tort Law**
  rmtd.mt.gov
  www.dhmlaw.com/CM/FSDP/PracticeCenter/Personal-Injury/Personal-Injury-General.asp

Nebraska

- **Nebraska State Court System**
  www.supremecourt.ne.gov
  www.courtreference.com/Nebraska-Courts.htm
  www.supremecourt.ne.gov/self-help
- **Accident/Driver Records; Public Safety**
  www.dor.state.ne.us/highway-safety
  publicrecords.onlinesearches.com/Nebraska.htm
- **Statute of Limitations in Nebraska Tort Cases**
  www.statutes-of-limitations.com

- **Medical Malpractice in Nebraska**
  www.mcandl.com/Nebraska.html
  www.atra.org/show/7338
- **Nebraska Workers' Compensation & Occupational Safety**
  www.wcc.ne.gov
  www.nesafetycouncil.org
- **Researching Nebraska Tort Law**
  www.lawsource.com/also/usa.cgi?ne
  www.megalaw.com/ne/ne.php
  www.loc.gov/law/help/guide/states.php
- **Definitions of Nebraska Tort Principles in Jury Instructions**
  www.llrx.com/columns/reference19.htm
- **Summaries of Nebraska Tort Law (from selected attorney sites)**
  www.friedmanlaw.com
  www.harriskuhn.com/practiceareas.html
- **Jury Verdicts in Nebraska Tort Cases**
  www.ll.georgetown.edu/guides/jury.cfm
  www.verdictsearch.com/index.jsp
- **Nebraska Trial Lawyers Association & State Bar**
  www.nebraskatrial.com/NE
  www.nebar.com
- **Defense Bar in Nebraska**
  www.nebraskadefense.org
  www.dri.org/open/SLDO.aspx
- **Google Searches on Nebraska Tort Law**
  "Nebraska tort"
  "Nebraska tort reform"
  "Nebraska negligence"
  Nebraska "intentional tort"
  Nebraska "medical malpractice"
- **Miscellaneous Sites on Nebraska Tort Law**
  www.das.state.ne.us/risk/types%20of%20claims.htm
  dockets.justia.com/browse/state-nebraska/court-nedce/noscat-3

Nevada

- **Nevada State Court System**
  www.nevadajudiciary.us
- **Accident/Driver Records; Public Safety**
  www.dmvstat.com/drivers/history.htm
  publicrecords.onlinesearches.com/Nebraska.htm
- **Statute of Limitations in Nevada Tort Cases**
  www.statutes-of-limitations.com
- **Medical Malpractice in Nevada**
  www.mcandl.com/Nevada.html
  www.atra.org/show/7338

- **Nevada Workers' Compensation & Occupational Safety**
  dirweb.state.nv.us
  dirweb.state.nv.us/OSHA/osha.htm
- **Researching Nevada Tort Law**
  lawlibrary.nevadajudiciary.us
  www.lawsource.com/also/usa.cgi?nv
  www.loc.gov/law/help/guide/states.php
- **Definitions of Nevada Tort Principles in Jury Instructions**
  www.llrx.com/columns/reference19.htm
- **Summaries of Nevada Tort Law (from selected attorney sites)**
  www.sprenzlaw.com
  www.personalinjuryofnevada.com
- **Jury Verdicts in Nevada Tort Cases**
  www.ll.georgetown.edu/guides/jury.cfm
  www.verdictsearch.com/index.jsp
- **Nevada Trial Lawyers Association & State Bar**
  www.nevadajustice.org/NV
  www.nvbar.org
- **Defense Bar in Nevada**
  www.adcnc.org
  www.dri.org/open/SLDO.aspx
- **Google Searches on Nevada Tort Law**
  "Nevada tort"
  "Nevada tort reform"
  "Nevada negligence"
  Nevada "intentional tort"
  Nevada "medical malpractice"
- **Miscellaneous Sites on Nevada Tort Law**
  www.nevada-corp.net/tort_reform_in_Nevada.htm
  leg.state.nv.us/nac/NAC-041.html

New Hampshire

- **New Hampshire State Court System**
  www.courts.state.nh.us
- **Accident/Driver Records; Public Safety**
  www.nh.gov/safety/dmv
  publicrecords.onlinesearches.com/NewHampshire.htm
- **Statute of Limitations in New Hampshire Tort Cases**
  www.statutes-of-limitations.com
- **Medical Malpractice in New Hampshire**
  www.mcandl.com/NewHampshire.html
  www.atra.org/show/7338
- **New Hampshire Workers' Compensation & Occupational Safety**
  www.labor.state.nh.us/workers_compensation.asp
  www.nhcosh.org

- **Researching New Hampshire Tort Law**
  www.lawsource.com/also/usa.cgi?nh
  www.courts.state.nh.us/lawlibrary/index.htm
  www.loc.gov/law/help/guide/states.php
- **Definitions of New Hampshire Tort Principles in Jury Instructions**
  www.llrx.com/columns/reference19.htm
- **Summaries of New Hampshire Tort Law (from selected attorney sites)**
  www.arbd.com
  www.shaheengordon.com
- **Jury Verdicts in New Hampshire Tort Cases**
  www.ll.georgetown.edu/guides/jury.cfm
  www.verdictsearch.com/index.jsp
- **New Hampshire Trial Lawyers Association & State Bar**
  www.nhaj.org/NH
  www.nhbar.org
- **Defense Bar in New Hampshire**
  www.tristatedefenselawyers.org
  www.dri.org/open/SLDO.aspx
- **Google Searches on New Hampshire Tort Law**
  "New Hampshire tort"
  "New Hampshire tort reform"
  "New Hampshire negligence"
  New Hampshire "intentional tort"
  New Hampshire "medical malpractice"
- **Miscellaneous Sites on New Hampshire Tort Law**
  www.donahuelawfirm.com/blog
  lawyers.findlaw.com/lawyer/practicestate/Personal-Injury----Plaintiff/New-Hampshire

New Jersey

- **New Jersey State Court System**
  www.judiciary.state.nj.us
  www.judiciary.state.nj.us/prose/index.htm
- **Accident/Driver Records; Public Safety**
  www.njsp.org
  www.state.nj.us/mvc
  publicrecords.onlinesearches.com/NewJersey.htm
- **Statute of Limitations in New Jersey Tort Cases**
  www.statutes-of-limitations.com
- **Medical Malpractice in New Jersey**
  www.mcandl.com/NewJersey.html
  www.atra.org/show/7338
- **New Jersey Workers' Compensation & Occupational Safety**
  lwd.dol.state.nj.us/labor/wc/wc_index.html
  www.nj.gov/health/ohs

- **Researching New Jersey Tort Law**
  law-library.rutgers.edu/ilg/njlaw.php
  www.njstatelib.org/Research_Guides/Law/index.php
  www.loc.gov/law/help/guide/states.php
- **Definitions of New Jersey Tort Principles in Jury Instructions**
  www.llrx.com/columns/reference19.htm
- **Summaries of New Jersey Tort Law (from selected attorney sites)**
  www.njatty.com
  injury.stark-stark.com
  www.keefebartels.com
- **Jury Verdicts in New Jersey Tort Cases**
  www.ll.georgetown.edu/guides/jury.cfm
  www.verdictsearch.com/index.jsp
- **New Jersey Trial Lawyers Association & State Bar**
  www.nj-justice.org/NJ
  www.njsba.com
- **Defense Bar in New Jersey**
  www.njdefenseassoc.com
  www.dri.org/open/SLDO.aspx
- **Google Searches on New Jersey Tort Law**
  "New Jersey tort"
  "New Jersey tort reform"
  "New Jersey negligence"
  New Jersey "intentional tort"
  New Jersey "medical malpractice"
- **Miscellaneous Sites on New Jersey Tort Law**
  www.judiciary.state.nj.us/mass-tort/index.htm
  www.njcaraccidentlawblog.com
  www.njlra.org

New Mexico

- **New Mexico State Court System**
  www.nmcourts.gov
  www.nmcourts.gov/othercourts.html
- **Accident/Driver Records; Public Safety**
  www.nmshtd.state.nm.us/main.asp?secid=14478
  publicrecords.onlinesearches.com/NewMexico.htm
- **Statute of Limitations in New Mexico Tort Cases**
  www.statutes-of-limitations.com
- **Medical Malpractice in New Mexico**
  www.mcandl.com/NewMexico.html
  www.atra.org/show/7338
- **New Mexico Workers' Compensation & Occupational Safety**
  www.workerscomp.state.nm.us
  www.nmenv.state.nm.us/Ohsb_Website/index.htm

- **Researching New Mexico Tort Law**
  www.nmbar.org/legalresearch/lrproviders.html
  www.lawsource.com/also/usa.cgi?nm
  www.loc.gov/law/help/guide/states.php
- **Definitions of New Mexico Tort Principles in Jury Instructions**
  www.llrx.com/columns/reference19.htm
- **Summaries of New Mexico Tort Law (from selected attorney sites)**
  www.carusolaw.com
  www.thefinelawfirm.com/lawyer-attorney-1053056.html
  www.maherlawfirm.com
- **Jury Verdicts in New Mexico Tort Cases**
  www.ll.georgetown.edu/guides/jury.cfm
  www.verdictsearch.com/index.jsp
- **New Mexico Trial Lawyers Association & State Bar**
  www.nmtla.org/NM
  www.nmbar.org
- **Defense Bar in New Mexico**
  www.nmdla.org
  www.dri.org/open/SLDO.aspx
- **Google Searches on New Mexico Tort Law**
  "New Mexico tort"
  "New Mexico tort reform"
  "New Mexico negligence"
  New Mexico "intentional tort"
  New Mexico "medical malpractice"
- **Miscellaneous Sites on New Mexico Tort Law**
  www.legalreforminthenews.com/Tort%20Profiles/NM_Tort_Laws.html
  www.newmexicoinjury.com/new_mexico_laws
  www.hg.org/law-firms/Personal-Injury/USA-New-Mexico.html

New York

- **New York State Court System**
  www.courts.state.ny.us
- **Accident/Driver Records; Public Safety**
  www.nydmv.state.ny.us/abstract.htm
  publicrecords.onlinesearches.com/NewYork.htm
- **Statute of Limitations in New York Tort Cases**
  www.statutes-of-limitations.com
- **Medical Malpractice in New York**
  www.mcandl.com/NewYork.html
  www.atra.org/show/7338
- **New York Workers' Compensation & Occupational Safety**
  www.wcb.state.ny.us
  www.nycosh.org

- **Researching New York Tort Law**
  www.aallnet.org/chapter/llagny/ny.html
  law-library.rutgers.edu/resources/nyresearch.php
  www.lawsource.com/also/usa.cgi?ny
  www.loc.gov/law/help/guide/states.php
- **Definitions of New York Tort Principles in Jury Instructions**
  west.thomson.com/productdetail/159981/13509494/productdetail.aspx
  www.llrx.com/columns/reference19.htm
- **Summaries of New York Tort Law (from selected attorney sites)**
  www.nbrlawfirm.com
  www.zifflaw.com
  www.perecman.com
- **Jury Verdicts in New York Tort Cases**
  www.ll.georgetown.edu/guides/jury.cfm
  www.verdictsearch.com/index.jsp
- **New York Trial Lawyers Association & State Bar**
  www.nystla.org
  www.nysba.org
- **Defense Bar in New York**
  www.defenseassociationofnewyork.org
  www.dri.org/open/SLDO.aspx
- **Google Searches on New York Tort Law**
  "New York tort"
  "New York tort reform"
  "New York negligence"
  New York "intentional tort"
  New York "medical malpractice"
- **Miscellaneous Sites on New York Tort Law**
  www.newyorkpersonalinjuryattorneyblog.com
  www.nytortreformnow.org
  www.nylawsuitreform.org

North Carolina

- **North Carolina State Court System**
  www.nccourts.org
- **Accident/Driver Records; Public Safety**
  www.ncdot.org/DMV/other_services/recordsstatistics/copyCrashReport.html
  publicrecords.onlinesearches.com/NorthCarolina.htm
- **Statute of Limitations in North Carolina Tort Cases**
  www.statutes-of-limitations.com
- **Medical Malpractice in North Carolina**
  www.mcandl.com/NorthCarolina.html
  www.atra.org/show/7338
- **North Carolina Workers' Compensation & Occupational Safety**
  www.ic.nc.gov
  www.nclabor.com/osha/osh.htm

- **Researching North Carolina Tort Law**
  www.romingerlegal.com/state/northcarolina.html
  www.lawsource.com/also/usa.cgi?nc
  www.law.duke.edu/lib/researchguides/ncprac
  www.loc.gov/law/help/guide/states.php
- **Definitions of North Carolina Tort Principles in Jury Instructions**
  www.law.duke.edu/lib/researchguides/ncprac
  www.llrx.com/columns/reference19.htm
- **Summaries of North Carolina Tort Law (from selected attorney sites)**
  www.demayolaw.com
  www.pgoodson.com
  www.rflaw.net
- **Jury Verdicts in North Carolina Tort Cases**
  www.ll.georgetown.edu/guides/jury.cfm
  www.verdictsearch.com/index.jsp
- **North Carolina Trial Lawyers Association & State Bar**
  www.ncaj.com
  www.ncbar.gov
- **Defense Bar in North Carolina**
  www.ncada.org
  www.dri.org/open/SLDO.aspx
- **Google Searches on North Carolina Tort Law**
  "North Carolina tort"
  "North Carolina tort reform"
  "North Carolina negligence"
  North Carolina "intentional tort"
  North Carolina "medical malpractice"
- **Miscellaneous Sites on North Carolina Tort Law**
  www.ic.nc.gov/ncic/pages/tortrule.htm
  www.ncsu.edu/legal_affairs/legal_topics/tort.php
  www.cap-press.com/isbn/9780890898475

North Dakota

- **North Dakota State Court System**
  www.ndcourts.gov/court/Courts.htm
- **Accident/Driver Records; Public Safety**
  www.dot.nd.gov
  www.dmv.org/nd-north-dakota/if-you-have-an-accident.php
  publicrecords.onlinesearches.com/NorthDakota.htm
- **Statute of Limitations in North Dakota Tort Cases**
  www.statutes-of-limitations.com
- **Medical Malpractice in North Dakota**
  www.mcandl.com/NorthDakota.html
  www.atra.org/show/7338

- **North Dakota Workers' Compensation & Occupational Safety**
  www.nd.gov/risk/workers-compensation
  www.workforcesafety.com
- **Researching North Dakota Tort Law**
  www.court.state.nd.us/Research
  www.ndcourts.gov/Research
  www.loc.gov/law/help/guide/states.php
- **Definitions of North Dakota Tort Principles in Jury Instructions**
  www.sband.org/pattern_jury_instructions
  www.llrx.com/columns/reference19.htm
- **Jury Verdicts in North Dakota Tort Cases**
  www.ll.georgetown.edu/guides/jury.cfm
  www.verdictsearch.com/index.jsp
- **North Dakota Trial Lawyers Association & State Bar**
  www.ndaj.org/ND
  www.sband.org
- **Defense Bar in North Dakota**
  www.defenseassociationofnewyork.org
  www.dri.org/open/SLDO.aspx
- **Google Searches on North Dakota Tort Law**
  "North Dakota tort"
  "North Dakota tort reform"
  "North Dakota negligence"
  North Dakota "intentional tort"
  North Dakota "medical malpractice"
- **Miscellaneous Site on North Dakota Torts**
  www.hg.org/law-firms/Personal-Injury/USA-North-Dakota.html

Ohio

- **Ohio State Court System**
  www.supremecourt.ohio.gov
- **Accident/Driver Records; Public Safety**
  www.statepatrol.ohio.gov/crash.stm
  publicrecords.onlinesearches.com/Ohio.htm
- **Statute of Limitations in Ohio Tort Cases**
  www.statutes-of-limitations.com
- **Medical Malpractice in Ohio**
  www.mcandl.com/Ohio.html
  www.atra.org/show/7338
- **Ohio Workers' Compensation & Occupational Safety**
  www.ohiobwc.com
  www.ohiobwc.com/employer/services/safetyhygiene.asp
- **Researching Ohio Tort Law**
  www.law.csuohio.edu/lawlibrary/resources/lawpubs/ohio/index.html
  www.romingerlegal.com/state/ohio.html

www.supremecourt.ohio.gov/LegalResources/LawLibrary/default.asp
www.loc.gov/law/help/guide/states.php

- **Definitions of Ohio Tort Principles in Jury Instructions**
  www.law.csuohio.edu/lawlibrary/resources/lawpubs/juryinstructions.html
  www.llrx.com/columns/reference19.htm
- **Summaries of Ohio Tort Law (from selected attorney sites)**
  www.castellilaw.com
  www.rothchildlaw.com
  www.clarkperdue.com
- **Jury Verdicts in Ohio Tort Cases**
  www.ll.georgetown.edu/guides/jury.cfm
  www.verdictsearch.com/index.jsp
- **Ohio Trial Lawyers Association & State Bar**
  www.oajustice.org/OH
  www.ohiobar.org
- **Defense Bar in Ohio**
  www.oacta.org
  www.cacta.org
  www.dri.org/open/SLDO.aspx
- **Google Searches on Ohio Tort Law**
  "Ohio tort"
  "Ohio tort reform"
  "Ohio negligence"
  Ohio "intentional tort"
  Ohio "medical malpractice"
- **Miscellaneous Sites on Ohio Tort Law**
  ohiolegalblog.blogspot.com
  www.legalreforminthenews.com/Tort%20Profiles/OH_Tort_Laws.html
  www.moshea.com/TORT.html

Oklahoma

- **Oklahoma State Court System**
  www.oscn.net/applications/oscn/start.asp
  www.courtreference.com/Oklahoma-Courts.htm
- **Accident/Driver Records; Public Safety**
  www.oktrooper.com/ohp-info.html
  publicrecords.onlinesearches.com/Oklahoma.htm
- **Statute of Limitations in Oklahoma Tort Cases**
  www.statutes-of-limitations.com
- **Medical Malpractice in Oklahoma**
  www.mcandl.com/Oklahoma.html
  www.atra.org/show/7338
- **Oklahoma Workers' Compensation & Occupational Safety**
  www.owcc.state.ok.us
  www.ok.gov/odol/Public_Employee_Occupational_Safety_and_Health/index.html

- **Researching Oklahoma Tort Law**
  www.oscn.net/applications/oscn/start.asp?viewType=LIBRARY
  www.lawresearch.com/v2/state/csokj.htm
  www.loc.gov/law/help/guide/states.php
- **Definitions of Oklahoma Tort Principles in Jury Instructions**
  www.oscn.net/applications/oscn/index.asp?ftdb=STOKJU&level=1
  www.llrx.com/columns/reference19.htm
- **Summaries of Oklahoma Tort Law (from selected attorney sites)**
  www.garrettlawoffice.com
  www.oklalawyer.com
  www.cherrylawfirm.com
- **Jury Verdicts in Oklahoma Tort Cases**
  www.ll.georgetown.edu/guides/jury.cfm
  www.verdictsearch.com/index.jsp
- **Oklahoma Trial Lawyers Association & State Bar**
  www.okforjustice.org/OK
  my.okbar.org
- **Defense Bar in Oklahoma**
  www.oadc.org
  www.dri.org/open/SLDO.aspx
- **Google Searches on Oklahoma Tort Law**
  "Oklahoma tort"
  "Oklahoma tort reform"
  "Oklahoma negligence"
  Oklahoma "intentional tort"
  Oklahoma "medical malpractice"
- **Miscellaneous Sites on Oklahoma Tort Law**
  www.legalreforminthenews.com/Tort%20Profiles/OK_Tort_Laws.html
  www.okphysiciansalliance.org
  law.justia.com/oklahoma/codes/os76.html

Oregon

- **Oregon State Court System**
  www.oregon.gov/OJD/courts/index.page
  www.oregon.gov/OJD/selfhelp/index.page?
- **Accident/Driver Records; Public Safety**
  www.oregon.gov/ODOT/DMV/records/generalpublic.shtml
  publicrecords.onlinesearches.com/Oregon.htm
- **Statute of Limitations in Oregon Tort Cases**
  www.statutes-of-limitations.com
- **Medical Malpractice in Oregon**
  www.mcandl.com/Oregon.html
  www.atra.org/show/7338

- **Oregon Workers' Compensation & Occupational Safety**
  www.cbs.state.or.us/wcd
  www.orosha.org
- **Researching Oregon Tort Law**
  www.oregon.gov/SOLL
  lawlib.lclark.edu/research/oregonlaw.php
  www.loc.gov/law/help/guide/states.php
- **Definitions of Oregon Tort Principles in Jury Instructions**
  www.osbar.org/store/pub/pubcat.asp?action=view&cat=Trial+Practice+%26+Litigation
  www.llrx.com/columns/reference19.htm
- **Summaries of Oregon Tort Law (from selected attorney sites)**
  www.mdkaplanlaw.com
  www.vangelisti.com
  www.oregonautoaccidentattorney.com
- **Jury Verdicts in Oregon Tort Cases**
  www.ll.georgetown.edu/guides/jury.cfm
  www.verdictsearch.com/index.jsp
- **Oregon Trial Lawyers Association & State Bar**
  www.oregontriallawyers.org
  www.osbar.org
- **Defense Bar in Oregon**
  www.oadc.com
  www.dri.org/open/SLDO.aspx
- **Google Searches on Oregon Tort Law**
  "Oregon tort"
  "Oregon tort reform"
  "Oregon negligence"
  Oregon "intentional tort"
  Oregon "medical malpractice"
- **Miscellaneous Sites on Oregon Tort Law**
  oregonlegalresearch.blogspot.com
  www.oregonpersonalinjury.com
  www.oregoninjurylawyerblog.com
  www.legalreforminthenews.com/Tort%20Profiles/Oregon.htm

Pennsylvania

- **Pennsylvania State Court System**
  www.aopc.org/default.htm
- **Accident/Driver Records; Public Safety**
  www.dmv.state.pa.us
  publicrecords.onlinesearches.com/Pennsylvania.htm
- **Statute of Limitations in Pennsylvania Tort Cases**
  www.statutes-of-limitations.com

- **Medical Malpractice in Pennsylvania**
  www.mcandl.com/Pennsylvania.html
  www.atra.org/show/7338
- **Pennsylvania Workers' Compensation & Occupational Safety**
  www.dli.state.pa.us
  www.pasafetyconference.com/zencart
- **Researching Pennsylvania Tort Law**
  www.pennsylvanialegalresearch.com
  www.law.pitt.edu/library/PA
  www.jenkinslaw.org
  www.loc.gov/law/help/guide/states.php
- **Definitions of Pennsylvania Tort Principles in Jury Instructions**
  www.jenkinslaw.org/cgi-bin/search/search.pl?Terms=jury+instructions
  www.llrx.com/columns/reference19.htm
- **Summaries of Pennsylvania Tort Law (from selected attorney sites)**
  www.rosenbaumandassociates.com
  www.dallashartman.com
  www.ppl-law.com
- **Jury Verdicts in Pennsylvania Tort Cases**
  www.ll.georgetown.edu/guides/jury.cfm
  www.verdictsearch.com/index.jsp
- **Pennsylvania Trial Lawyers Association & State Bar**
  www.pajustice.org/PA
  www.pabar.org
- **Defense Bar in Pennsylvania**
  www.padefense.org
  www.dri.org/open/SLDO.aspx
- **Google Searches on Pennsylvania Tort Law**
  "Pennsylvania tort"
  "Pennsylvania tort reform"
  "Pennsylvania negligence"
  Pennsylvania "intentional tort"
  Pennsylvania "medical malpractice"
- **Miscellaneous Sites on Pennsylvania Tort Law**
  www.pennsylvaniapersonalinjuryblog.com
  www.legalreforminthenews.com/Tort%20Profiles/PA_Tort_Laws.html
  www.hg.org/article.asp?id=6727

Rhode Island

- **Rhode Island State Court System**
  www.courts.ri.gov
- **Accident/Driver Records; Public Safety**
  www.dmv.state.ri.us/accidents
  publicrecords.onlinesearches.com/RhodeIsland.htm

- **Statute of Limitations in Rhode Island Tort Cases**
  www.statutes-of-limitations.com
- **Medical Malpractice in Rhode Island**
  www.mcandl.com/RhodeIsland.html
  www.atra.org/show/7338
- **Rhode Island Workers' Compensation & Occupational Safety**
  www.dlt.state.ri.us/wc
  www.courts.ri.gov/workers/defaultnew-workers.htm
  www.dlt.ri.gov/occusafe
- **Researching Rhode Island Tort Law**
  www.findlaw.com/11stategov/ri/index.html
  www.lexisone.com/legalresearch/legalguide/states/rhode_island.htm
  www.loc.gov/law/help/guide/states.php
- **Definitions of Rhode Island Tort Principles in Jury Instructions**
  www.llrx.com/columns/reference19.htm
- **Summaries of Rhode Island Tort Law (from selected attorney sites)**
  www.slepkowlaw.com
  www.karnslaw.com
- **Jury Verdicts in Rhode Island Tort Cases**
  www.ll.georgetown.edu/guides/jury.cfm
  www.verdictsearch.com/index.jsp
- **Rhode Island Trial Lawyers Association & State Bar**
  www.rijustice.org/RI
  www.ribar.com
- **Google Searches on Rhode Island Tort Law**
  "Rhode Island tort"
  "Rhode Island tort reform"
  "Rhode Island negligence"
  Rhode Island "intentional tort"
  Rhode Island "medical malpractice"
- **Miscellaneous Sites on Rhode Island Tort Law**
  www.hg.org/law-firms/Personal-Injury/USA-Rhode-Island.html
  www.resminiweb.com/tortpractice.htm
  www.freedomworks.org/publications/rhode-island-needs-tort-reform

South Carolina

- **South Carolina State Court System**
  www.judicial.state.sc.us
- **Accident/Driver Records; Public Safety**
  www.scdmvonline.com/DMVNew/default.aspx?n=accident_reports
  publicrecords.onlinesearches.com/SouthCarolina.htm
- **Statute of Limitations in South Carolina Tort Cases**
  www.statutes-of-limitations.com

- **Medical Malpractice in South Carolina**
  www.mcandl.com/SouthCarolina.html
  www.atra.org/show/7338
- **South Carolina Workers' Compensation & Occupational Safety**
  www.wcc.sc.gov
  www.scosha.llronline.com
- **Researching South Carolina Tort Law**
  www.ll.georgetown.edu/states/southcarolina.cfm
  www.lexisnexis.com/infopro/zimmerman/disp.aspx?z=1942
  www.loc.gov/law/help/guide/states.php
- **Definitions of South Carolina Tort Principles in Jury Instructions**
  www.charlestonbar.org/CM/Custom/Jury-Charges.asp
  www.llrx.com/columns/reference19.htm
- **Summaries of South Carolina Tort Law (from selected attorney sites)**
  www.mcwhirterlaw.com
  www.grimesandteich.com
  www.tanenbaumlaw.com
- **Jury Verdicts in South Carolina Tort Cases**
  www.ll.georgetown.edu/guides/jury.cfm
  www.verdictsearch.com/index.jsp
- **South Carolina Trial Lawyers Association & State Bar**
  www.scaj.com/SC
  www.scbar.org
- **Defense Bar in South Carolina**
  www.scdtaa.com
  www.dri.org/open/SLDO.aspx
- **Google Searches on South Carolina Tort Law**
  "South Carolina tort"
  "South Carolina tort reform"
  "South Carolina negligence"
  South Carolina "intentional tort"
  South Carolina "medical malpractice"
- **Miscellaneous Sites on South Carolina Tort Law**
  www.scpilaw.com
  legalreforminthenews.com/Tort%20Profiles/SC_Tort_Laws.html
  www.scinjurylawjournal.com

South Dakota

- **South Dakota State Court System**
  www.sdjudicial.com
- **Accident/Driver Records; Public Safety**
  dps.sd.gov
  publicrecords.onlinesearches.com/SouthDakota.htm
- **Statute of Limitations in South Dakota Tort Cases**
  www.statutes-of-limitations.com

- **Medical Malpractice in South Dakota**
  www.mcandl.com/SouthDakota.html
  www.atra.org/show/7338
- **South Dakota Workers' Compensation & Occupational Safety**
  dol.sd.gov/workerscomp/default.aspx
  www.southdakotasafetycouncil.org/courses/workplace.htm
- **Researching South Dakota Tort Law**
  www.ll.georgetown.edu/states/southdakota.cfm
  www.lexisone.com/legalresearch/legalguide/states/south_dakota.htm
  www.loc.gov/law/help/guide/states.php
- **Definitions of South Dakota Tort Principles in Jury Instructions**
  www.llrx.com/columns/reference19.htm
  www.law.uiowa.edu/library/south_dakota.php
- **Jury Verdicts in South Dakota Tort Cases**
  www.ll.georgetown.edu/guides/jury.cfm
  www.verdictsearch.com/index.jsp
- **South Dakota Trial Lawyers Association & State Bar**
  www.sdtla.com
  www.sdbar.org
- **Defense Bar in South Dakota**
  www.sddla.com
  www.dri.org/open/SLDO.aspx
- **Google Searches on South Dakota Tort Law**
  "South Dakota tort"
  "South Dakota tort reform"
  "South Dakota negligence"
  South Dakota "intentional tort"
  South Dakota "medical malpractice"

Tennessee

- **Tennessee State Court System**
  www.tsc.state.tn.us
  www.tncourts.gov/geninfo/help/selfhelp.htm
- **Accident/Driver Records; Public Safety**
  www.tennessee.gov/safety
  search.dmv.org/dmv/tennessee/accident-report
  publicrecords.onlinesearches.com/Tennessee.htm
- **Statute of Limitations in Tennessee Tort Cases**
  www.statutes-of-limitations.com
- **Medical Malpractice in Tennessee**
  www.mcandl.com/Tennessee.html
  www.atra.org/show/7338
- **Tennessee Workers' Compensation & Occupational Safety**
  www.state.tn.us/labor-wfd/wcomp.html
  www.workerscompensation.com/tennessee.php

- **Researching Tennessee Tort Law**
  www.romingerlegal.com/state/tennessee.html
  www.tncourts.gov/geninfo/clinks1.htm
  www.loc.gov/law/help/guide/states.php
- **Definitions of Tennessee Tort Principles in Jury Instructions**
  www.kevinsnider.com/images/Jury%20Instructions-5thedition.pdf
  west.thomson.com/productdetail/159497/14043723/productdetail.aspx
  www.llrx.com/columns/reference19.htm
- **Summaries of Tennessee Tort Law (from selected attorney sites)**
  www.hillboren.com
  www.summersandwyatt.com
  www.sidgilreath.com
- **Jury Verdicts in Tennessee Tort Cases**
  www.ll.georgetown.edu/guides/jury.cfm
  www.verdictsearch.com/index.jsp
- **Tennessee Trial Lawyers Association & State Bar**
  www.tnaj.org/TN
  www.tba.org/index.php
- **Defense Bar in Tennessee**
  www.tdla.net
  www.dri.org/open/SLDO.aspx
- **Google Searches on Tennessee Tort Law**
  "Tennessee tort"
  "Tennessee tort reform"
  "Tennessee negligence"
  Tennessee "intentional tort"
  Tennessee "medical malpractice"
- **Miscellaneous Sites on Tennessee Tort Law**
  www.dayontorts.com/cat-forms-for-tennessee-tort-practice.html
  www.triallawreport.com

Texas

- **Texas State Court System**
  www.courts.state.tx.us
- **Accident/Driver Records; Public Safety**
  www.dot.state.tx.us/drivers_vehicles/crash_records/reports.htm
  search.dmv.org/dmv/texas/accident-report
  publicrecords.onlinesearches.com/Texas.htm
- **Statute of Limitations in Texas Tort Cases**
  www.statutes-of-limitations.com
- **Medical Malpractice in Texas**
  www.mcandl.com/Texas.html
  www.atra.org/show/7338

- **Texas Workers' Compensation & Occupational Safety**
  www.tdi.state.tx.us/wc/indexwc.html
  www.workerscompensation.com/texas.php
- **Researching Texas Tort Law**
  tarlton.law.utexas.edu/vlibrary/online/internet
  www.stcl.edu/library/lrtexas.html
  www.sll.state.tx.us/collection/databases.html
  www.loc.gov/law/help/guide/states.php
- **Definitions of Texas Tort Principles in Jury Instructions**
  west.thomson.com/productdetail/124489/22023065/productdetail.aspx
  texasbarbooks.net/texas-pattern-jury-charges
  www.llrx.com/columns/reference19.htm
- **Summaries of Texas Tort Law (from selected attorney sites)**
  www.thetexaspersonalinjurylawyer.com
  www.injuryrelief.com
  www.jimadler.com
- **Jury Verdicts in Texas Tort Cases**
  www.ll.georgetown.edu/guides/jury.cfm
  www.verdictsearch.com/index.jsp
- **Texas Trial Lawyers Association & State Bar**
  www.ttla.com/TX
  www.texasbar.com
- **Defense Bar in Texas**
  www.tadc.org
  www.dri.org/open/SLDO.aspx
- **Google Searches on Texas Tort Law**
  "Texas tort"
  "Texas tort reform"
  "Texas negligence"
  Texas "intentional tort"
  Texas "medical malpractice"
- **Miscellaneous Sites on Texas Tort Law**
  www.sll.state.tx.us/collection/databases.html (enter Tort in the subject search box)
  research.lawyers.com/Texas/Personal-Injury-In-Texas.html
  www.legalreforminthenews.com/Tort%20Profiles/TX_Tort_Laws.html

Utah

- **Utah State Court System**
  www.utcourts.gov
  www.utcourts.gov/selfhelp
- **Accident/Driver Records; Public Safety**
  publicsafety.utah.gov/dld/documents/DI8-RequestforAccidentReport Records12-08.pdf
  search.dmv.org/dmv/utah/accident-report
  publicrecords.onlinesearches.com/Utah.htm

- **Statute of Limitations in Utah Tort Cases**
  www.statutes-of-limitations.com
- **Medical Malpractice in Utah**
  www.mcandl.com/Utah.html
  www.atra.org/show/7338
- **Utah Workers' Compensation & Occupational Safety**
  www.laborcommission.utah.gov/IndustrialAccidents
  www.workerscompensationinsurance.com/workers_compensation/utah.htm
- **Researching Utah Tort Law**
  www.utcourts.gov/lawlibrary/research
  www.utcourts.gov/lawlibrary/research/utah.asp
  www.utahbar.org/public/useful_information.html
  www.loc.gov/law/help/guide/states.php
- **Definitions of Utah Tort Principles in Jury Instructions**
  www.utcourts.gov/resources/muji
  www.llrx.com/columns/reference19.htm
- **Summaries of Utah Tort Law (from selected attorney sites)**
  www.robertdebry.com
  www.siegfriedandjensen.com
  www.eisenbergandgilchrist.com
- **Jury Verdicts in Utah Tort Cases**
  www.ll.georgetown.edu/guides/jury.cfm
  www.verdictsearch.com/index.jsp
- **Utah Trial Lawyers Association & State Bar**
  www.utahassociationforjustice.org/UT
  www.utahbar.org
- **Defense Bar in Utah**
  www.udla.org
  www.dri.org/open/SLDO.aspx
- **Google Searches on Utah Tort Law**
  "Utah tort"
  "Utah tort reform"
  "Utah negligence"
  Utah "intentional tort"
  Utah "medical malpractice"
- **Miscellaneous Sites on Utah Tort Law**
  utahinjuredworker.com
  dockets.justia.com/browse/state-utah/court-utdce/noscat-3

Vermont

- **Vermont State Court System**
  www.vermontjudiciary.org/default.aspx
  www.vermontjudiciary.org/GTC/default.aspx

- **Accident/Driver Records; Public Safety**
  www.dps.state.vt.us/vtsp/records.htm
  dmv.vermont.gov
  publicrecords.onlinesearches.com/Vermont.htm
- **Statute of Limitations in Vermont Tort Cases**
  www.statutes-of-limitations.com
  www.whatistortreform.com/vermont-statutes-of-limitation.html
- **Medical Malpractice in Vermont**
  www.mcandl.com/Vermont.html
  www.atra.org/show/7338
- **Vermont Workers' Compensation & Occupational Safety**
  www.labor.vermont.gov
  www.labor.vermont.gov/Business/WorkersCompensation/tabid/114/ Default.aspx
- **Researching Vermont Tort Law**
  www.findlaw.com/11stategov/vt/index.html
  www.lexisone.com/legalresearch/legalguide/states/vermont.htm
  www.megalaw.com/vt/vt.php
  www.loc.gov/law/help/guide/states.php
- **Definitions of Vermont Tort Principles in Jury Instructions**
  openlibrary.org/b/OL1418710M/Vermont_jury_instructions_civil_and_criminal
  www.llrx.com/columns/reference19.htm
- **Summaries of Vermont Tort Law (from selected attorney sites)**
  www.sylvestermaley.com
  www.okglawyers.com
  www.greenmountainlaw.com
- **Jury Verdicts in Vermont Tort Cases**
  www.ll.georgetown.edu/guides/jury.cfm
  www.verdictsearch.com/index.jsp
- **Vermont Trial Lawyers Association & State Bar**
  www.vermontjustice.org/VT
  www.vtbar.org/index.asp
- **Defense Bar in Vermont**
  www.tristatedefenselawyers.org
  www.dri.org/open/SLDO.aspx
- **Google Searches on Vermont Tort Law**
  "Vermont tort"
  "Vermont tort reform"
  "Vermont negligence"
  Vermont "intentional tort"
  Vermont "medical malpractice"
- **Miscellaneous Sites on Vermont Tort Law**
  law.findlaw.com/state-laws/negligence/vermont
  www.dayontorts.com/wrongful-death-vermont-supreme-court-allows-wrongful-death-recovery-for-death-of-a-sibling.html

Virginia

- **Virginia State Court System**
  www.courts.state.va.us
  www.courts.state.va.us/courts/home.html
- **Accident/Driver Records; Public Safety**
  www.vsp.state.va.us/AccidentReport.shtm
  www.dmv.state.va.us
  publicrecords.onlinesearches.com/Virginia.htm
- **Statute of Limitations in Virginia Tort Cases**
  www.statutes-of-limitations.com
- **Medical Malpractice in Virginia**
  www.mcandl.com/Virginia.html
  www.atra.org/show/7338
- **Virginia Workers' Compensation & Occupational Safety**
  www.vwc.state.va.us
  www.dhrm.virginia.gov/workerscomp.html
- **Researching Virginia Tort Law**
  www.lexisone.com/legalresearch/legalguide/states/west_virginia.htm
  www.megalaw.com/va/va.php
  www.aallnet.org/chapter/vall/varesrch.htm
  www.loc.gov/law/help/guide/states.php
- **Definitions of Virginia Tort Principles in Jury Instructions**
  openlibrary.org/b/OL398373M/Virginia_model_jury_instructions
  www.lexisnexis.com/store/catalog/booktemplate/productdetail.jsp?pageName=relatedProducts&prodId=7357
  www.llrx.com/columns/reference19.htm
- **Summaries of Virginia Tort Law (from selected attorney sites)**
  www.marksandharrison.com
  www.allenandallen.com
  www.hallandsickels.com
- **Jury Verdicts in Virginia Tort Cases**
  www.ll.georgetown.edu/guides/jury.cfm
  www.verdictsearch.com/index.jsp
- **Virginia Trial Lawyers Association & State Bar**
  www.vtla.com/VA
  www.vsb.org
- **Defense Bar in Virginia**
  www.vada.org
  www.dri.org/open/SLDO.aspx
- **Google Searches on Virginia Tort Law**
  "Virginia tort"
  "Virginia tort reform"
  "Virginia negligence"
  Virginia "intentional tort"
  Virginia "medical malpractice"

- **Miscellaneous Sites on Virginia Tort Law**
  www.legalreforminthenews.com/Tort%20Profiles/VA_Tort_Laws.html
  dockets.justia.com/browse/state-virginia/noscat-3
  www.northernvirginiapersonalinjuryattorney.com

Washington

- **Washington State Court System**
  www.courts.wa.gov/index.cfm
  www.courts.wa.gov/newsinfo/resources/?fa=newsinfo_jury.brochure_guide&altMenu=Citi
- **Accident/Driver Records; Public Safety**
  www.kingcounty.gov/safety/sheriff/Services/Accident.aspx
  www.dol.wa.gov/driverslicense/collision.html
  publicrecords.onlinesearches.com/Washington.htm
- **Statute of Limitations in Washington Tort Cases**
  www.statutes-of-limitations.com
- **Medical Malpractice in Washington**
  www.mcandl.com/Washington.html
  www.atra.org/show/7338
- **Washington Workers' Compensation & Occupational Safety**
  www.lni.wa.gov
  www.lni.wa.gov/ClaimsIns/claims
- **Researching Washington Tort Law**
  www.courts.wa.gov/library/?fa=library.display&fileID=netsrch
  www.legalwa.org
  www.loc.gov/law/help/guide/states.php
- **Definitions of Washington Tort Principles in Jury Instructions**
  www.courts.wa.gov/index.cfm?fa=home.contentDisplay&location=PatternJuryInstructions
  www.llrx.com/columns/reference19.htm
- **Summaries of Washington Tort Law (from selected attorney sites)**
  www.washingtoninjury.com
  www.personalinjurywashington.com
  www.kornfeldlaw.com
- **Jury Verdicts in Washington Tort Cases**
  www.ll.georgetown.edu/guides/jury.cfm
  www.verdictsearch.com/index.jsp
- **Washington Trial Lawyers Association & State Bar**
  www.washingtonjustice.org/WA
  www.wsba.org
- **Defense Bar in Washington**
  www.dri.org/open/SLDO.aspx
  www.wdtl.org
- **Google Searches on Washington Tort Law**
  "Washington State tort"

"Washington State tort reform"
"Washington State negligence"
Washington State "intentional tort"
Washington State "medical malpractice"

- **Miscellaneous Sites on Washington Tort Law**
  www.legalreforminthenews.com/Tort%20Profiles/WA_Tort_Laws.htm
  www.ofm.wa.gov/rmd/tort
  omwtortlaw.com
  research.lawyers.com/Washington/Personal-Injury-in-the-State-of-Washington.html

West Virginia

- **West Virginia State Court System**
  www.state.wv.us/wvsca/wvsystem.htm
  www.courtreference.com/West-Virginia-Courts.htm
- **Accident/Driver Records; Public Safety**
  www.wvstatepolice.com/traffic/mvi.htm
  search.dmv.org/dmv/west-virginia/accident-report-form
  publicrecords.onlinesearches.com/WestVirginia.htm
- **Statute of Limitations in West Virginia Tort Cases**
  www.statutes-of-limitations.com
- **Medical Malpractice in West Virginia**
  www.mcandl.com/WestVirginia.html
  www.atra.org/show/7338
- **West Virginia Workers' Compensation & Occupational Safety**
  www.wvinsurance.gov/Default.aspx?tabid=73
  www.workerscompensation.com/west_virginia.php
  www.workerscompensationinsurance.com/workers_compensation/west_virginia.htm
- **Researching West Virginia Tort Law**
  www.megalaw.com/wv/wv.php
  www.loc.gov/law/help/guide/states.php
- **Definitions of West Virginia Tort Principles in Jury Instructions**
  www.llrx.com/columns/reference19.htm
- **Summaries of West Virginia Tort Law (from selected attorney sites)**
  www.law-wv.com
  www.belllaw.com
  www.wfbmlaw.com
- **Jury Verdicts in West Virginia Tort Cases**
  www.ll.georgetown.edu/guides/jury.cfm
  www.verdictsearch.com/index.jsp
- **West Virginia Trial Lawyers Association & State Bar**
  www.wvaj.org/WV
  www.wvbar.org
- **Defense Bar in West Virginia**
  www.dri.org/open/SLDO.aspx
  www.dtcwv.org

- **Google Searches on West Virginia Tort Law**
  "West Virginia tort"
  "West Virginia tort reform"
  "West Virginia negligence"
  West Virginia "intentional tort"
  West Virginia "medical malpractice"
- **Miscellaneous Sites on West Virginia Tort Law**
  www.legalreforminthenews.com/Tort%20Profiles/WV_Tort_Laws.html
  www.civtrial.com

Wisconsin

- **Wisconsin State Court System**
  www.wicourts.gov
- **Accident/Driver Records and Public Safety**
  www.dot.wisconsin.gov/drivers/index.htm
  www.dot.wisconsin.gov/drivers/drivers/traffic/accident.htm
  publicrecords.onlinesearches.com/Wisconsin.htm
- **Statute of Limitations in Wisconsin Tort Cases**
  www.statutes-of-limitations.com
- **Medical Malpractice in Wisconsin**
  www.mcandl.com/wisconsin.html
  www.atra.org/show/7338
  www.expertlaw.com/library/malpractice_by_state/Wisconsin.html
- **Wisconsin Workers' Compensation and Occupational Safety**
  www.dwd.state.wi.us/wc
  www.wiscosh.org
- **Researching Wisconsin Tort Law**
  wilawlibrary.gov
  law.marquette.edu/cgi-bin/site.pl?2130&pageID=101
  www.loc.gov/law/help/guide/states.php
- **Definitions of Wisconsin Tort Principles in Jury Instructions**
  wilawlibrary.gov/topics/justice/jury.php
  www.law.wisc.edu/clew/publications/jury_instructions_civil.htm
- **Summaries of Wisconsin Tort Laws (from selected attorney sites)**
  www.frankpasternak.com
  www.brabazonlawoffice.com
- **Jury Verdicts in Wisconsin Tort Cases**
  www.ll.georgetown.edu/guides/jury.cfm
  www.verdictsearch.com/index.jsp
- **Wisconsin Trial Lawyers Association & State Bar**
  www.wisjustice.org/WI
  www.wisbar.org
- **Defense Bar in Wisconsin**
  www.wdc-online.org

www.dri.org/open/sldoview.aspx?state=Wisconsin
www.dri.org/open/SLDO.aspx

- **Google Searches on Wisconsin Tort Law**
  "Wisconsin tort"
  "Wisconsin tort reform"
  "Wisconsin negligence"
  Wisconsin "intentional tort"
  Wisconsin "medical malpractice"
- **Miscellaneous Sites on Wisconsin Tort Law**
  wilawlibrary.gov/topics/justice/civil/torts.php
  wisconsinpersonalinjurylawyers.blogspot.com
  dhs.wisconsin.gov/health/injuryprevention
  www.dot.wisconsin.gov/safety/motorist/crashfacts
  www.law.wisc.edu/blogs/wisblawg

Wyoming

- **Wyoming State Court System**
  www.courts.state.wy.us
- **Accident/Driver Records; Public Safety**
  www.dot.state.wy.us/wydot/driver_license_records/accident_ procedures/accident_reports
  www.dot.state.wy.us/wydot
  www.dot.state.wy.us/wydot/safety
  publicrecords.onlinesearches.com/Wyoming.htm
- **Wyoming Workers' Compensation and Occupational Safety**
  wydoe.state.wy.us/doe.asp?ID=9
  wydoe.state.wy.us/doe.asp?ID=7
- **Statute of Limitations in Wyoming Tort Cases**
  www.statutes-of-limitations.com
- **Medical Malpractice in Wyoming**
  www.mcandl.com/wyoming.html
  www.atra.org/show/7338
- **Researching Wyoming Tort Law**
  www.courts.state.wy.us/LawLibrary
  www.lawsource.com/also/usa.cgi?wy
  www.loc.gov/law/help/guide/states.php
- **Definitions of Wyoming Tort Principles in Jury Instructions**
  wyomingbar.org/bookstore/index.html?id=3&-session=wybar_user:42F94421164ad2AA15SWo1679466
- **Summaries of Wyoming Tort Laws (from selected attorney sites)**
  www.bklawfirm.com (click "Newsletters")
  www.vanmeverenlaw.com
  cheyenne.injuryboard.com

- **Jury Verdicts in Wyoming Tort Cases**
  www.ll.georgetown.edu/guides/jury.cfm
  www.verdictsearch.com/index.jsp
- **Wyoming Trial Lawyers Association & State Bar**
  www.wytla.org
  wyomingbar.org
- **Defense Bar in Wyoming**
  www.dri.org/open/SLDO.aspx
- **Google Searches on Wyoming Tort Law**
  "Wyoming tort"
  "Wyoming tort reform"
  "Wyoming negligence"
  Wyoming "intentional tort"
  Wyoming "medical malpractice"
- **Miscellaneous Sites on Wyoming Tort Law**
  www.insurancejournal.com/magazines/west/2004/03/08/features/39861.htm
  www.justia.com/us-states/wyoming/law-blog-posts.html

C. FEDERAL RESOURCES

Here you will find the major federal agencies and boards that are relevant to a torts or personal injury practice.

- **Bureau of Alcohol, Tobacco, Firearms, and Explosives**
  www.atf.gov
- **Chemical Safety and Hazard Investigation Board**
  www.csb.gov
- **Consumer Product Safety Commission**
  www.cpsc.gov
- **Federal Aviation Administration**
  www.faa.gov
- **Federal Highway Administration**
  safety.fhwa.dot.gov
- **Federal Motor Carrier Safety Administration**
  www.fmcsa.dot.gov
- **Federal Railroad Administration**
  www.fra.dot.gov
- **Food and Drug Administration**
  www.fda.gov
- **Food and Drug Administration MedWatch**
  www.fda.gov/Safety/MedWatch/SafetyInformation/default.htm
- **Mine Safety and Health Administration**
  www.msha.gov

- **National Highway Traffic Safety Administration**
  www.nhtsa.dot.gov
- **National Interagency Fire Center**
  www.nifc.gov/safety.html
- **National Transportation Safety Board**
  www.ntsb.gov
- **National Weather Service**
  www.weather.gov/safety.php
- **Occupational Safety and Health Administration**
  osha.gov
- **Pipeline and Hazardous Materials Safety Administration**
  www.phmsa.dot.gov
- **Transportation Safety Institute** (U.S. Department of Transportation)
  www.tsi.dot.gov/Default.aspx?AspxAutoDetectCookieSupport=1
- **U.S. Department of Agriculture** (Food Safety)
  www.fsis.usda.gov/news_&_events/Food_Safety_at_Home_Podcasts/index.asp
- **U.S. Department of Health & Human Services** (Food Safety)
  www.foodsafety.gov
- **U.S. Department of Transportation** (Safety)
  www.dot.gov/safety.html
- **U.S. National Library of Medicine**
  www.nlm.nih.gov

APPENDIX B

AUTOMOBILE INSURANCE

Different categories of insurance cover motor vehicles:

- *Liability insurance* protects others who are injured by your vehicle. It is insurance in which the insurer agrees to pay, on behalf of an insured, damages the latter is obligated to pay to a third party because of his or her legal liability to the third person for committing a tort or other wrong.
- *Collision insurance* covers damage to your vehicle from a roll-over or collision with an object. It does not cover bodily injury or property damage to another's property, such as someone else's vehicle.
- *Comprehensive insurance* covers multiple risks to your vehicle, such as theft, vandalism, and fire.
- *Medical-payments insurance* (also called MedPay insurance) covers medical costs for each person injured while riding in your vehicle. It can also cover vehicle-related injuries such as those incurred when you or a member of your family is hit by a vehicle while walking.
- *Uninsured/underinsured motorist insurance* protects you and the occupants of your car for bodily injury and property damage caused by someone who is uninsured or by a hit-and-run driver. Underinsured motorist coverage is used when an at-fault driver has insufficient insurance to pay for the insured's total loss.[1]

Every state requires motorists to demonstrate "financial responsibility" by carrying a minimum level of liability insurance. For example, the minimum level might be $25,000/$50,000/$15,000. This means:

- $25,000 coverage for a single bodily injury in one accident
- $50,000 coverage for multiple bodily injuries in one accident
- $15,000 coverage for property damage in one accident

Motorists must apply for liability insurance on their own. The cost depends on factors such as the applicant's driving record, where the applicant lives, the age of the applicant, and anticipated use of the vehicle. If no insurance company agrees on its own to sell liability insurance to a particular motorist in the voluntary market (e.g., because of the applicant's bad driving record), he or she becomes an *assigned risk* in the involuntary market. Insurance companies are required to write liability insurance for assigned risks (at higher rates than they charge in the voluntary market) in proportion to the amount of business they do in the state.

Under our tort system, an injured party sues a defendant in court in order to prove that the defendant was at fault in causing the accident. Most liability insurance, on the other hand, is not based on fault. Each person's own insurance company pays for covered injury or damage up to policy limits, regardless of who was at fault in causing the accident.

Liability insurance is *third-party insurance* in the sense that the insurance company pays a third party—someone other than the insured—who has been wrongfully injured by the insured. Fire insurance and collision insurance are examples of *first-party insurance* because the insurance company pays the insured for a covered loss; third parties are not directly involved.

> The term "no-fault" auto insurance is often used loosely to denote any auto insurance program that allows policyholders to recover financial losses from their own insurance company, regardless of fault. But in its strictest form, no-fault applies only to state laws that both provide for the payment of no-fault first-party benefits and restrict the right to sue, the so-called "limited tort" option. The first-party (policyholder) benefit coverage is known as personal injury protection (PIP).[2]

Liability insurance has not replaced the tort system. No state has a no-fault scheme that eliminates for all automobile injury cases the option of bringing a tort suit in court. Some states have what is called *add-on no-fault*. Here, liability insurance is simply added onto, but does not replace, the tort system. The injured party can recover

No-Fault: State auto insurance laws governing liability coverage

	First-party benefits (PIP) (1)		Restrictions on lawsuits		Thresholds for lawsuits	
"True" no-fault	**Compulsory**	**Optional**	**Yes**	**No**	**Monetary**	**Verbal**
Florida	X		X			X
Hawaii	X		X		X	
Kansas	X		X		X	
Kentucky	X		X	X (2)	X (2)	
Massachusetts	X		X		X	
Michigan	X		X			X
Minnesota	X		X		X	
New Jersey	X		X	X (2)		X (2), (3)
New York	X		X			X
North Dakota	X		X		X	
Pennsylvania	X		X	X (2)		X (2)
Puerto Rico	X		X		X	
Utah	X		X		X	
Add-on						
Arkansas	X			X		
Delaware	X			X		
D.C.		X	X (4)	X (4)		
Maryland	X			X		
New Hampshire		X		X		
Oregon	X			X		
South Dakota		X		X		
Texas		X		X		
Virginia		X		X		
Washington		X		X		
Wisconsin		X		X		

(1) Personal injury protection.

(2) "Choice" no-fault state. Policyholder can choose a policy based on the no-fault system or traditional tort liability.

(3) Verbal threshold for the Basic Liability Policy, the Special Policy, and the Standard Policy where the policyholder chooses no-fault. The Basic and Special Policies contain lower amounts of coverage.

(4) The District of Columbia is neither a true no-fault nor add-on state. Drivers are offered the option of no-fault or fault-based coverage, but in the event of an accident a driver who originally chose no-fault benefits has 60 days to decide whether to receive those benefits or file a claim against the other party.

Source: Property Casualty Insurers Association of America (www.iii.org/media/hottopics/insurance/nofault).

under his or her liability insurance policy *and* can bring a tort suit in court against the person who caused the accident. If, however, the plaintiff wins anything in court, his or her insurance company is reimbursed for whatever benefits it paid the plaintiff. Other states have a *modified no-fault*. States have different versions of modified no-fault. In general, the right of a victim to collect certain kinds of tort damages in court depends on whether a threshold has been met. There are two kinds of thresholds:

- A *dollar threshold* covers medical costs.
- A *verbal threshold* or descriptive threshold covers the kind of injury involved, such as death, serious disfigurement, or dismemberment.

Some laws also include minimum requirements for the days of disability incurred as a result of the accident.[3] Meeting a threshold means that the medical expenses of the victim exceed a designated amount (in a dollar-threshold state) or that the victim's injury was of a designated severity (in a verbal-threshold state). If the threshold has been met, the injured party can sue the other party in court for a tort. If, however, the threshold has not been met, the courts cannot be used; the parties are limited to the insurance coverage.[4]

ENDNOTES

1. Insurance Information Institute, www2.iii.org/individuals/AutoInsurance.
2. Id. at www.iii.org/media/hottopics/insurance/nofault.
3. Ibid.
4. 1998 The Council of State Governments, *The Book of States*; State Farm Insurance Companies, *No-Fault Press Reference Manual*.

APPENDIX

C

MEDICAL LIABILITY/MALPRACTICE LAWS

Here is an overview of some of the major medical liability/malpractice laws in the country.[1] Unless otherwise indicated, the section numbers refer to the statutory codes of the state.

Alabama

• *Damage Award Limits or Caps:*
No limitations. Limits on noneconomic damages (§ 6-5-547) declared unconstitutional by state supreme court (see *Mobile Infirmary Medical Center v. Hodgen*, 884 So.2d (Ala. 2003)).

• *Limits on Attorney Fees:*
No limitations

Alaska

• *Damage Award Limits or Caps:*
§ 09.55.549. Noneconomic damages limited to $250,000; limited to $400,000 for wrongful death or injury over 70 percent disabling; limits not applicable to intentional or reckless acts or omissions.

§ 9.17.020. Punitive damages limited to the greater of three times the amount of compensatory damages or $500,000. Except as provided, if the conduct was motivated by financial gain and the adverse consequences of the conduct were actually known by the defendant or the person responsible for making policy decisions on behalf of the defendant, it may award an amount of punitive damages not to exceed the greatest of (1) four times the amount of compensatory damages awarded to the plaintiff in the action; (2) four times the aggregate amount of financial gain that the defendant received as a result of the defendant's misconduct; or (3) the sum of $7,000,000.

• *Limits on Attorney Fees:*
§ 09.60.080. If an attorney contracts for or collects a contingency fee in connection with an action for personal injury, death, or property damage and the damages awarded by a court or jury include an award of punitive damages, the contingent fee due the attorney shall be calculated before that portion of punitive damages due the state under AS 09.17.020(j) has been deducted from the total award of damages.

Arizona

• *Damage Award Limits or Caps:*
No limitations. **Arizona Constitution Article 2, § 31:** No law shall be enacted in this state limiting the amount of damages to be recovered for causing the death or injury of any person.

• *Limits on Attorney Fees:*
§ 12-568. The court shall, at the request of any party in any action under this chapter, determine the reasonableness of each party's attorneys' fees.

Arkansas

• *Damage Award Limits or Caps:*
§§ 16-55-205 to 16-55-209. Punitive damages award for each plaintiff shall not be more than the greater of the following: (1) $250,000; or (2) Three times the amount of compensatory damages awarded in the action, not to exceed $1 million. Limits adjusted for inflation at three-year intervals. Limits shall not apply when the finder of fact: (1) Determines by clear and convincing evidence that, at the time of the injury, the defendant intentionally pursued a course of conduct for the purpose of causing injury or damage; and (2) Determines that the defendant's conduct did, in fact, harm the plaintiff.

• *Limits on Attorney Fees:*
No limitations.

California

• *Damage Award Limits or Caps:*
Civil Code § 3333.2. $250,000 limit for noneconomic damages.

• *Limits on Attorney Fees:*
Business and Professions § 6146. Sliding scale, not to exceed 40 percent of first $50,000, 33-1/3 percent of next $50,000, 25 percent of next $500,000, and 15 percent of damages exceeding $600,000.

Colorado

• *Damage Award Limits or Caps:*
§ 13-64-302. $1 million total limit on all damages; $300,000 noneconomic limitation.

• *Limits on Attorney Fees:*
No limitations.

Connecticut

• *Damage Award Limits or Caps:*
§ 52-228c. If the jury renders a verdict specifying noneconomic damages in an amount exceeding $1 million, the court shall review the evidence presented to the jury to determine if the amount of noneconomic damages specified in the verdict is excessive as a matter of law in that it so shocks the sense of justice as to compel the conclusion that the jury was influenced by partiality, prejudice, mistake or corruption. If the court so concludes, it shall order a remittitur and, upon failure of the party so ordered to remit the amount ordered by the court, it shall set aside the verdict and order a new trial.

• *Limits on Attorney Fees:*
§ 52-251c. Sliding scale, not to exceed an amount equal to a percentage of 33-1/3 percent of first $300,000; 25 percent of next $300,000; 20 percent of next $300,000; 15 percent of next $300,000; and 10 percent of damages exceeding $1.2 million. A claimant may waive the percentage limitations of said subsection if the claim or civil action is so substantially complex, unique or different from other wrongful death, personal injury or property damage claims or civil actions as to warrant a deviation from such percentage limitations.

Delaware

• *Damage Award Limits or Caps:*
18 § 6855. Punitive damages may be awarded only on finding of malicious intent to injure or willful or wanton misconduct. No specified limit.

• *Limits on Attorney Fees:*
18 § 6865. Sliding scale, not to exceed 35 percent of first $100,000; 25 percent of next $100,000; and 10 percent of all damages exceeding $200,000. A claimant has the right to elect to pay for the attorney's services on a mutually satisfactory per diem basis.

District of Columbia

• *Damage Award Limits or Caps:*
No applicable statute.

• *Limits on Attorney Fees:*
No limitations.

Florida

• *Damage Award Limits or Caps:*
§ 766.118. Noneconomic damages limited to $500,000 per claimant. Noneconomic damages shall not exceed $1 million for cases involving death or permanent vegetative state, or 1) a manifest injustice would occur unless increased noneconomic damages are awarded, based on a finding that because of the special circumstances of the case, the noneconomic harm sustained by the injured patient was particularly severe; and 2) The trier of fact determines that the defendant's negligence caused a

catastrophic injury to the patient. Noneconomic damages limited to $150,000 per claimant for cases arising from medical negligence of practitioners providing emergency services and care, the total noneconomic damages recoverable by all claimants from all such practitioners shall not exceed $300,000.

§ 768.73. Punitive damages limited to the greater of three times amount of compensatory damages or $500,000. Where the wrongful conduct was motivated solely by unreasonable financial gain and the unreasonably dangerous nature of the conduct, together with the high likelihood of injury resulting from the conduct, was actually known by the managing agent, director, officer, or other person responsible for making policy decisions on behalf of the defendant, the amount of punitive damages shall not to exceed the greater of four times the amount of compensatory damages or $2 million. Where the defendant had a specific intent to harm, and the defendant's conduct did in fact harm the claimant, there shall be no cap on punitive damages.

- *Limits on Attorney Fees:*

Fla. Atty. Conduct Reg. § 4-1.5. Attorneys' fees in excess of the following amounts are presumed unreasonable: (1) In cases that settle before filing an answer or appointing an arbitrator: 33-1/3 percent of any recovery up to $1 million; plus 30 percent of any recovery between $1 million and $2 million; plus 20 percent of any portion exceeding $2 million. (2) In cases after filing an answer, demanding an arbitrator through the entry of judgment: 40 percent of any recovery up to $1 million; plus 30 percent of any recovery between $1 million and $2 million; plus 20 percent of any portion exceeding $2 million. (3) If all defendants admit liability and request a trial only on damages: 33-1/3 percent of any recovery up to $1 million; plus 20 percent of any recovery between $1 million and $2 million; plus 15 percent of any portion exceeding $2 million. An additional five percent of any recovery after institution of any appellate proceeding is filed or post-judgment relief or action is required for recovery on the judgment.

Georgia

- *Damage Award Limits or Caps:*

§ 51-13-1. Noneconomic damages in medical malpractice actions limited to $350,000 against providers, regardless of number of defendants. Noneconomic damages limited to $350,000 against a single medical facility; $700,000 against multiple facilities. Aggregate amount of noneconomic damages limited to $1.05 million.

- *Limits on Attorney Fees:*

No limitations.

Guam

- *Damage Award Limits or Caps:*

7 § 12116. Any exemplary damages awarded to a client in a tort suit based on health care or professional services shall be placed in a special fund that may be expended at the discretion of the administrator, Guam Memorial Hospital, for the improvement of medical services within the territory of Guam.

- *Limits on Attorney Fees:*

7 § 26601. Sliding scale, not to exceed (1) 50 percent on the first $1,000 recovered; (2) 40 percent on the next $2,000 recovered; (3) 33-1/3 percent on the next $47,000 recovered; (4) 20 percent on the next $50,000 recovered; (5) 10 percent on any amount recovered over $100,000; and (6) Where the amount recovered is for the benefit of an infant or incompetent and the action is settled without trial the foregoing limits shall apply, except that the fee on any amount recovered up to $50,000 shall not exceed 25 percent.

Hawaii

• *Damage Award Limits or Caps:*
§ 663-8.7. Noneconomic damages recoverable for pain and suffering shall be limited to a maximum award of $375,000.

• *Limits on Attorney Fees:*
§ 607-15.5. Attorneys' fees for both the plaintiff and the defendant shall be limited to a reasonable amount as approved by the court.

Idaho

• *Damage Award Limits or Caps:*
§ 6-1603. $250,000 limit on noneconomic damages, adjusted annually according to state's average annual wage.

§ 6-1604. Punitive damages limited to the greater of $250,000 or amount three times of compensatory damages.

• *Limits on Attorney Fees:*
No limitations.

Illinois

• *Damage Award Limits or Caps:*
735 § 5/2-1115. Punitive damages not recoverable in medical malpractice cases. Noneconomic damages: There are no limitations on noneconomic damages.

• *Limits on Attorney Fees:*
735 § 5/2-1114. Sliding scale, not to exceed 33-1/3 percent of first $150,000; 25 percent of next $850,000; 20 percent of any amount recovered over $1 million of the sum recovered.

Indiana

• *Damage Award Limits or Caps:*
§ 34-18-14-3. The total amount recoverable may not exceed $500,000. A health care provider is not liable for an amount in excess of $250,000 for an occurrence of malpractice.

• *Limits on Attorney Fees:*
§ 34-18-18-1. When a plaintiff is represented by an attorney in the prosecution of the plaintiff's claim, the plaintiff's attorney's fees from any award made from the patient's compensation fund may not exceed 15 percent of any recovery from the fund.

Iowa

• *Damage Award Limits or Caps:*
§ 147.136. In an action for damages the damages awarded shall not include actual economic losses incurred or to be incurred in the future by the claimant by reason of the personal injury, including but not limited to, the cost of reasonable and necessary medical care, rehabilitation services, and custodial care, and the loss of services and loss of earned income, to the extent that those losses are replaced or are indemnified by insurance, or by governmental, employment, or service benefit programs or from any other source except the assets of the claimant or of the members of the claimant's immediate family.

• *Limits on Attorney Fees:*
§ 147.138. The court shall determine the reasonableness of any contingent fee arrangement between the plaintiff and the plaintiff's attorney.

Kansas

• *Damage Award Limits or Caps:*
§ **60-19a02.** $250,000 limit on noneconomic damages for personal injury recoverable by each party from all defendants.

§ **16-1903.** Wrongful death damages, other than pecuniary loss sustained by an heir at law, cannot exceed in the aggregate the sum of $250,000 and costs.

§ **60-3702.** No award of exemplary or punitive shall exceed the lesser of: (1) The annual gross income earned by the defendant, as determined by the court based upon the defendant's highest gross annual income earned for any one of the five years immediately before the act for which such damages are awarded, unless the court determines such amount is clearly inadequate to penalize the defendant, then the court may award up to 50 percent of the net worth of the defendant, as determined by the court; or (2) $5 million. If the court finds that the profitability of the defendant's misconduct exceeds or is expected to exceed the limitation above, the limitation on the amount of exemplary or punitive damages which the court may award shall be an amount equal to 1 1/2 times the amount of profit which the defendant gained or is expected to gain as a result of the defendant's misconduct.

• *Limits on Attorney Fees:*
§ **7-121b.** Compensation for reasonable attorney fees to be paid by each litigant in the action shall be approved by the judge after an evidentiary hearing and prior to final disposition of the case by the district court. Compensation for reasonable attorney fees for services performed in an appeal of a judgment in any such action to the court of appeals shall be approved after an evidentiary hearing by the chief judge or by the presiding judge of the panel hearing the case. Compensation for reasonable attorney fees for services performed in an appeal of a judgment in any such action to the supreme court shall be approved after an evidentiary hearing by the departmental justice for the department in which the appeal originated.

Kentucky

• *Damage Award Limits or Caps:*
No limitations. **Kentucky Constitution** § **54:** The General Assembly shall have no power to limit the amount to be recovered for injuries resulting in death, or for injuries to person or property.

• *Limits on Attorney Fees:*
No limitations.

Louisiana

• *Damage Award Limits or Caps:*
RS § **40:1299.42.** $500,000 limit for total recovery. Health care provider liability limited to $100,000. Any award in excess of all liable providers paid from Patient's Compensation Fund.

• *Limits on Attorney Fees:*
No limitations.

Maine

• *Damage Award Limits or Caps:*
No applicable statute.

• *Limits on Attorney Fees:*
24 § **2961.** Sliding scale, not to exceed 33-1/3 percent of first $100,000; 25 percent of next $100,000; and 20 percent of damages exceeding $200,000. For purposes of determining any lump-sum contingent fee, any future damages recoverable by the plaintiff in periodic installments shall be reduced to lump-sum value. If the plaintiff prevails in the action for professional negligence, the plaintiff's attorney may petition the court to review the reasonableness of the fees permitted above.

Maryland

• *Damage Award Limits or Caps:*

Courts & Judicial Proceedings Code § 3-2A-09(A). Noneconomic damages for a cause of action arising between January 1, 2005, and December 31, 2008, inclusive, may not exceed $650,000. The limitation on noneconomic damages shall increase by $15,000 on January 1 of each year beginning January 1, 2009. The increased amount shall apply to causes of action arising between January 1 and December 31 of that year, inclusive. In a wrongful death action, where there are two or more claimants or beneficiaries, the noneconomic damages for all actions may not exceed 125 percent of the above limitation.

• *Limits on Attorney Fees:*

Courts & Judicial Proceedings § 3-2A-07. If a legal fee is in dispute, an attorney may not charge or collect compensation for services rendered in connection with an arbitration claim unless it is approved by the arbitration panel, or by the court in the event an action to nullify a panel determination has been filed therein.

Massachusetts

• *Damage Award Limits or Caps:*

Ch. 231 § 60H. $500,000 limit for pain and suffering, loss of companionship, embarrassment and other items of general damages unless there is a determination that there is a substantial or permanent loss or impairment of a bodily function or substantial disfigurement, or other special circumstances. Except as provided, if two or more plaintiffs have received verdicts or findings of such damages in a total amount, for all plaintiffs claiming damages from a single occurrence, transaction, act of malpractice, or injury which exceeds $500,000, the amount of such damages recoverable by each plaintiff will be reduced to a percentage of $500,000 proportionate to that plaintiff's share of the total amount of such damages for all plaintiffs.

• *Limits on Attorney Fees:*

Ch. 231 § 60I. No contingent fee agreement, shall be enforced, and no attorney shall recover a fee thereunder, as a result of services rendered in an action against a provider of health care for malpractice, negligence, error, omission, mistake, or the unauthorized rendering of professional services if, at the time of judgment, the court determines that the amount of the recovery paid or to be paid to the plaintiff, after deduction of the attorney's reasonable expenses and disbursements for which the plaintiff is liable and the amount of the attorney's fee, is less than the total amount of the plaintiff's unpaid past and future medical expenses included in the recovery, unless the contingent attorney's fee: (a) is 20 percent or less of the plaintiff's recovery; (b) is reduced to 20 percent or less of the plaintiff's recovery; or (c) is reduced to a level which permits the plaintiff to be paid his unpaid past and future medical expenses included in the recovery. Sliding scale, not to exceed 40 percent of first $150,000; 33-1/3 percent of next $150,000; 30 percent of next $200,000 and 25 percent of award over $500,000.

Michigan

• *Damage Award Limits or Caps:*

§ 600.1483. $280,000 limit on noneconomic damages; $500,000 limit on noneconomic damages if (a) The plaintiff is hemiplegic, paraplegic, or quadriplegic resulting in a total permanent functional loss of one or more limbs caused by one or more of the following: (i) Injury to the brain. (ii) Injury to the spinal cord. (b) The plaintiff has permanently impaired cognitive capacity rendering him or her incapable of making independent, responsible life decisions and permanently incapable of independently performing the activities of normal, daily living. (c) There has been permanent loss of or damage to a reproductive organ resulting in the inability to procreate. The limitation is adjusted annually by state treasurer according to consumer price index.

- *Limits on Attorney Fees:*

§ **600.919** The measure of the compensation of members of the bar is left to the express or implied agreement of the parties subject to the regulation of the supreme court.

Minnesota

- *Damage Award Limits or Caps:*

§ **549.20.** Punitive damages shall be allowed in civil actions only upon clear and convincing evidence that the acts of the defendant show deliberate disregard for the rights or safety of others. The court shall specifically review the punitive damages award and shall make specific findings. The appellate court, if any, also shall review the award. Nothing in this section may be construed to restrict either court's authority to limit punitive damages.

- *Limits on Attorney Fees:*

§ **548.251.** If the fees for legal services provided to the plaintiff are based on a percentage of the amount of money awarded to the plaintiff, the percentage must be based on the amount of the award as adjusted under the collateral source rule.

Mississippi

- *Damage Award Limits or Caps:*

§ **11-1-60.** $500,000 limit on noneconomic damages.

§ **11-1-65.** In any civil action where an entitlement to punitive damages shall have been established under applicable laws, no award of punitive damages shall exceed the following: (i) $20 million for a defendant with a net worth of more than $1 billion; (ii) $15 million for a defendant with a net worth of more than $750 million but not more than $1 billion; (iii) $5 million for a defendant with a net worth of more than $500 million but not more than $750 million; (iv) $3,750,000 for a defendant with a net worth of more than $100 million but not more than $500 million; (v) $2,500,000 for a defendant with a net worth of more than $50 million but not more than $100 million; or (vi) Two percent of the defendant's net worth for a defendant with a net worth of $50 million or less.

- *Limits on Attorney Fees:*

No limitations.

Missouri

- *Damage Award Limits or Caps:*

§ **538.210.** Noneconomic damages limited to $350,000 regardless of number of defendants.

§ **510.265.** No award of punitive damages against any defendant shall exceed the greater of: (1) $500,000; or (2) Five times the net amount of the judgment awarded to the plaintiff against the defendant.

- *Limits on Attorney Fees:*

No limitations.

Montana

- *Damage Award Limits or Caps:*

§ **25-9-411.** $250,000 limit on past and future damages for noneconomic loss.

§ **27-1-220.** A judge or jury may award, in addition to compensatory damages, punitive damages for the sake of example and for the purpose of punishing a defendant. An award for punitive damages may not exceed $10 million or three percent of a defendant's net worth, whichever is less.

- *Limits on Attorney Fees:*

No limitations.

Nebraska

- *Damage Award Limits or Caps:*

§ 44-2825. Total damages limited to $1,750,000. Health care provider liability limited to $500,000. Any excess of total liability of all health care providers paid from Excess Liability Fund.

- *Limits on Attorney Fees:*

§ 44-2834. In all cases against a health care provider for malpractice or professional negligence, upon motion of either party the court shall review the attorney's fees incurred by that party and allow such compensation as the court shall deem reasonable.

Nevada

- *Damage Award Limits or Caps:*

§ 41A.035. $350,000 limit on noneconomic damages.

§ 42.005. Exemplary or punitive damages made pursuant to this section may not exceed: (a) Three times the amount of compensatory damages awarded to the plaintiff if the amount of compensatory damages is $100,000 or more; or (b) $300,000 if the amount of compensatory damages awarded to the plaintiff is less than $100,000.

- *Limits on Attorney Fees:*

§ 7.095. Sliding scale for attorney fees, not to exceed 40 percent of first $50,000; 33-1/3 percent of next $50,000; 25 percent of next $500,000; 15 percent of any amount over $600,000.

New Hampshire

- *Damage Award Limits or Caps:*

No limitations. Limits on noneconomic damages (§ 507-C:7) declared unconstitutional by state supreme court (see *Carson v. Maurer*, 120 N.H. 925, 424 A.2d 825 (1980) and *Brannigan v. Usitalso*, 134 N.H. 50, 587 A.2d 1232 (1991)).

- *Limits on Attorney Fees:*

§ 508:4-e. Contingent fee agreements between attorney and client shall be governed by Rules of Professional Conduct, Rule 1.5 as it may be amended by the [New Hampshire] supreme court from time to time and by any other rules regarding fees which are adopted or amended by the court. All fees and costs for actions, resulting in settlement or judgment of $200,000 or more, shall be subject to approval by the court.

New Jersey

- *Damage Award Limits or Caps:*

§ 2A:15-5.14. No defendant shall be liable for punitive damages in any action in an amount in excess of five times the liability of that defendant for compensatory damages or $350,000, whichever is greater.

- *Limits on Attorney Fees:*

Court Rules § 1:21-7. Sliding scale, not to exceed 33-1/3 percent of first $500,000; 30 percent of next $500,000; 25 percent of third $500,000; 20 percent of fourth $500,000; on all amounts recovered in excess of the above by application for reasonable fee in accordance with the provisions of paragraph (f) hereof; and where the amount recovered is for the benefit of a client who was a minor or mentally incapacitated when the contingent fee arrangement was made, the foregoing limits shall apply, except that the fee on any amount recovered by settlement without trial shall not exceed 25 percent.

New Mexico

- *Damage Award Limits or Caps:*

§ 41-5-6. $600,000 total limit on all damages. The value of accrued medical care and related benefits shall not be subject to the $600,000 limitation. Monetary damages shall not be awarded for future medical expenses in malpractice claims. A health care provider's personal liability is limited to $200,000 for monetary damages and medical care and related benefits as provided in § 41-5-7 NMSA 1978. Any amount due from a judgment or settlement in excess of $200,000 shall be paid from the patient's compensation fund.

§ 41-5-7. Awards of future medical care and related benefits shall not be subject to the $600,000 limitation imposed in § 41-5-6.

- *Limits on Attorney Fees:*

No limitations.

New York

- *Damage Award Limits or Caps:*

No applicable statute.

- *Limits on Attorney Fees:*

Jud. 30 § 474-a. Sliding scale, not to exceed 30 percent of first $250,000; 25 percent of second $250,000; 20 percent of next $500,000; 15 percent of next $250,000; 10 percent over $1.25 million. In the event the attorney believes in good faith that the fee schedule, because of extraordinary circumstances, will not give adequate compensation, application for greater compensation may be made upon affidavit with written notice and an opportunity to be heard to the claimant or plaintiff and other persons holding liens or assignments on the recovery.

North Carolina

- *Damage Award Limits or Caps:*

§ 1D-25. Punitive damages shall not exceed three times the amount of compensatory damages or $250,000, whichever is greater.

- *Limits on Attorney Fees:*

No limitations.

North Dakota

- *Damage Award Limits or Caps:*

§ 32-42-02. $500,000 limit on noneconomic damages.

§ 32-03.2-08. Economic damage awards in excess of $250,000 subject to court review.

- *Limits on Attorney Fees:*

§ 28-26-01. The amount of fees of attorneys in civil actions must be left to the agreement, express or implied, of the parties.

Ohio

- *Damage Award Limits or Caps:*

§ 2315.21. Punitive and exemplary damages limited to twice the amount of compensatory damages. If the defendant is a small employer or individual, the court shall not enter judgment for punitive or exemplary damages in excess of the lesser of two times the amount of the compensatory damages awarded to the plaintiff from the defendant or 10 percent of the employer's or individual's net worth when the tort was committed up to a maximum of $350,000.

§ 2323.43. No limitation on compensatory damages that represent the economic loss of the person who is awarded the damages in the civil action. Noneconomic damages shall not exceed the greater of $250,000 or an amount that is equal to three times the plaintiff's economic loss, as determined by the trier of fact, to a maximum of $350,000 for each plaintiff or a maximum of $500,000 for each occurrence. Noneconomic damages may exceed the amount described above but shall not exceed $500,000 for each plaintiff or $1 million for each occurrence if the noneconomic losses of the plaintiff are for either of the following: (a) Permanent and substantial physical deformity, loss of use of a limb, or loss of a bodily organ system; (b) Permanent physical functional injury that permanently prevents the injured person from being able to independently care for self and perform life sustaining activities.

- *Limits on Attorney Fees:*

§ 2323.43 (F). If the amount of the attorney's fees exceed the applicable amount of the limits on compensatory damages for noneconomic loss, the attorney shall apply to the court and the attorney's fees shall be subject to the approval of the probate court of the county in which the civil action was commenced or in which the settlement was entered.

Oklahoma

- *Damage Award Limits or Caps:*

23 § 9.1. Where the jury finds by clear and convincing evidence that: The defendant has been guilty of reckless disregard for the rights of others; the jury . . . may award punitive damages in an amount not to exceed the greater of: a. $100,000, or b. the amount of the actual damages awarded. Where the jury finds by clear and convincing evidence that: The defendant has acted intentionally and with malice towards others; the jury may award punitive damages in an amount not to exceed the greatest of: a. $500,000, b. twice the amount of actual damages awarded, or c. the increased financial benefit derived by the defendant as a direct result of the conduct causing the injury to the plaintiff and other persons or entities. Where the jury finds by clear and convincing evidence that: The defendant has acted intentionally and with malice towards others; and the court finds that there is evidence beyond a reasonable doubt that the defendant acted intentionally and with malice and engaged in conduct life-threatening to humans, the jury . . . may award punitive damages in any amount the jury deems appropriate, without regard to the limitations set forth above.

23 § 61.2. No limitation on the amount of noneconomic damages in a civil action arising from a claimed bodily injury resulting from professional negligence against a physician if the judge and jury finds, by clear and convincing evidence, that: 1. The plaintiff or injured person has suffered permanent and substantial physical abnormality or disfigurement, loss of use of a limb, or loss of, or substantial impairment to, a major body organ or system; or 2. The plaintiff or injured person has suffered permanent physical functional injury which prevents them from being able to independently care for themselves and perform life sustaining activities; or 3. The defendant's acts or failures to act were: a. in reckless disregard for the rights of others, b. grossly negligent, c. fraudulent, or d. intentional or with malice.

63 § 1-1708.1F-1. Except as provided, noneconomic damages awarded shall not exceed the hard cap amount of $300,000, provided: 1. The defendant has made an offer of judgment pursuant to § 1101.1 of Title 12 of the Oklahoma Statutes; and 2. The amount of the verdict awarded to the plaintiff is less than 1 1/2 times the amount of the final offer of judgment. The $300,000 cap shall be adjusted annually based upon any positive increase in the Consumer Price Index. If nine or more members of the jury find by clear and convincing evidence that the defendant committed negligence or if nine or more members of the jury find by a preponderance of the evidence that the conduct of the defendant was willful or wanton, the limits on noneconomic damages provided above shall not apply.

63 § 1-1708.1F. In a medical liability action in which the health care services at issue were provided for: 1. Pregnancy or labor and delivery, including the immediate post-partum period; or 2. Emergency care in the emergency room of a hospital or as follow-up to the emergency care services provided in the emergency room; the amount of noneconomic damages awarded shall not exceed $300,000. Where the judge finds by clear and convincing evidence that the defendant committed negligence in one of these types of cases, the court shall articulate its findings into the record out of the presence of the jury and shall lift the noneconomic damage cap.

- *Limits on Attorney Fees:*

5 § 7. Fee may not exceed 50 percent of net judgment.

Oregon

- *Damage Award Limits or Caps:*

No limitations. Limits on noneconomic damages (§ 31.710) declared unconstitutional by state supreme court (see *Lakin v. Senco Products, Inc.*, 329 Or. 62, 987 P.2d 463 (Or. 1999)).

§ 31.740. Punitive damages may not be awarded against a health practitioner, as defined, if the health practitioner was engaged in conduct regulated by the license, registration or certificate issued by the appropriate governing body and was acting within the scope of practice for which the license, registration or certificate was issued and without malice.

- *Limits on Attorney Fees:*

§ 31.735. In no event may more than 20 percent of the amount awarded as punitive damages be paid to the attorney for the prevailing party.

Pennsylvania

- *Damage Award Limits or Caps:*

No limitations. **Pennsylvania Constitution Article 3, § 18:** The General Assembly may enact laws requiring the payment by employers, or employers and employees jointly, of reasonable compensation for injuries to employees arising in the course of their employment, and for occupational diseases of employees, whether or not such injuries or diseases result in death, and regardless of fault of employer or employee, and fixing the basis of ascertainment of such compensation and the maximum and minimum limits thereof, and providing special or general remedies for the collection thereof; but in no other cases shall the General Assembly limit the amount to be recovered for injuries resulting in death, or for injuries to persons or property, and in case of death from such injuries, the right of action shall survive, and the General Assembly shall prescribe for whose benefit such actions shall be prosecuted.

40 § 1303.505. Except in cases alleging intentional misconduct, punitive damages against an individual physician shall not exceed 200 percent of the compensatory damages awarded. Punitive damages, when awarded, shall not be less than $100,000 unless a lower verdict amount is returned by the trier of fact. Upon the entry of a verdict including an award of punitive damages, the punitive damages portion of the award shall be allocated as follows: (1) 75 percent shall be paid to the prevailing party; and (2) 25 percent shall be paid to the Medical Care Availability and Reduction of Error Fund.

40 § 1303.509. The trier of fact may incorporate into any future medical expense award adjustments to account for reasonably anticipated inflation and medical care improvements as presented by competent evidence.

- *Limits on Attorney Fees:*

Limits declared unconstitutional by state supreme court (see *Heller v. Frankston*, 475 A.2d 1291 (Pa. 1984)).

Puerto Rico

- *Damage Award Limits or Caps:*

32 § 3077. Actions for damages for alleged acts of malpractice to the health professionals who work in the areas of obstetrics, orthopedics, general surgery or trauma exclusively at public health institutions of the Commonwealth of Puerto Rico, its

dependencies, instrumentalities and/or municipalities, regardless of whether said institutions are being administered or operated by a private entity limited to up to the sum of $75,000. Damages shall not exceed $150,000 when, because of said act or omission, damages are caused to more than one person or when there are several causes of action to which a single prejudiced party is entitled. If according to the conclusions of the court it should arise that the sum of the damages caused to each of the persons exceeds $150,000, the court shall proceed to distribute said sum prorated among the plaintiffs, taking as [basis] the damages suffered by each one.

- *Limits on Attorney Fees:*

4 § 742. No attorney shall charge fees of a contingent nature in actions to recover damages in an amount that exceeds, for any reason, 25 percent of the final proceeds of the judgment, compromise or agreement if the client is a minor or mentally disabled, or 33 percent of the final proceeds of the judgment, compromise or agreement if it is any other client. Notwithstanding the foregoing, where clients are minors or mentally disabled, the court may authorize the charge of contingent fees up to 33 percent of the final proceeds of the judgment, compromise or agreement if the attorney so requests, and presents good cause therefor.

Rhode Island

- *Damage Award Limits or Caps:*

No applicable statute.

- *Limits on Attorney Fees:*

No limitations.

South Carolina

- *Damage Award Limits or Caps:*

§ 15-32-220. Noneconomic damages limited to $350,000 against single health care provider or facility. In actions against more than one facility, provider or combination, the limit of civil liability for noneconomic damages for each health care institution and each health care provider is limited to an amount not to exceed $350,000 for each claimant, and the limit of civil liability for noneconomic damages for all health care institutions and health care providers is limited to an amount not to exceed $1,050,000 for each claimant. Limits increased or decreased annually based on Consumer Price Index. No limits on noneconomic or punitive damages if defendant is grossly negligent, wilful, wanton, or reckless, and such conduct was the proximate cause of the claimant's noneconomic damages, or if the defendant has engaged in fraud or misrepresentation related to the claim, or if the defendant altered or destroyed medical records with the purpose of avoiding a claim or liability to the claimant.

- *Limits on Attorney Fees:*

No limitations.

South Dakota

- *Damage Award Limits or Caps:*

§ 21-3-11. The total general damages which may be awarded may not exceed the sum of $500,000. No limitation on the amount of special damages which may be awarded.

§ 21-3-2. Punitive damages in discretion of jury.

- *Limits on Attorney Fees:*

No limitations.

Tennessee

- *Damage Award Limits or Caps:*

No applicable statute.

- *Limits on Attorney Fees:*

§ 29.26.120. Contingent fees shall be awarded in an amount to be determined by the court on the basis of time and effort devoted to the litigation by the claimant's attorney, complexity of the claim and other pertinent matters in connection therewith, not to exceed 33-1/3 percent of all damages awarded to the claimant.

Texas

- *Damage Award Limits or Caps:*

Civil Practice & Remedies § 74.301. $250,000 limit per claimant for noneconomic damages against physician or provider. $250,000 limit per claimant against single institution. For claims against multiple institutions, the limit of civil liability for noneconomic damages for each health care institution, inclusive of all persons and entities for which vicarious liability theories may apply, shall be limited to an amount not to exceed $250,000 for each claimant and the limit of civil liability for noneconomic damages for all health care institutions, inclusive of all persons and entities for which vicarious liability theories may apply, shall be limited to an amount not to exceed $500,000 for each claimant.

Civil Practice & Remedies § 74.303. In wrongful death claims against physician, the limit of civil liability for all damages, including exemplary damages, shall be limited to an amount not to exceed $500,000 for each claimant. The limitation will be adjusted by the Consumer Price Index.

- *Limits on Attorney Fees:*

No limitations.

Utah

- *Damage Award Limits or Caps:*

§ 78B-3-410. $400,000 limit on noneconomic damages. Adjusted annually for inflation by state treasurer.

- *Limits on Attorney Fees:*

§ 78B-3-411. An attorney may not collect a contingent fee for representing a client seeking damages in connection with or arising out of personal injury or wrongful death caused by the negligence of another which exceeds 33-1/3 percent of the amount recovered.

Vermont

- *Damage Award Limits or Caps:*

No applicable statute.

- *Limits on Attorney Fees:*

No limitations.

Virginia

- *Damage Award Limits or Caps:*

§ 8.01-581.15. $1.5 million limit on recovery damages. Increased by $50,000 each year from 2001 to 2006. Increased by $75,000 each year in 2007 and 2008. The July 1, 2008, increase shall be the final annual increase.

- *Limits on Attorney Fees:*

No limitations.

Virgin Islands

- *Damage Award Limits or Caps:*

27 § 166b. The total amount recoverable for any injury of a patient may not exceed $250,000 per occurrence. Only economic damages and noneconomic damages may be awarded. The total amount awarded for noneconomic damages for any injury to a patient as a result of a single occurrence may not exceed $75,000. No punitive damages may be awarded.

- *Limits on Attorney Fees:*

5 § **541.** The measure and mode of compensation of attorneys shall be left to the agreement, express or implied, of the parties.

Washington

- *Damage Award Limits or Caps:*

No limitations. Limits on noneconomic damages (§ 4.56.250) declared unconstitutional by state supreme court (see *Sofie v. Fireboard Corp.*, 112 Wash. 2d 636, 771 P.2d 711 (1989)).

- *Limits on Attorney Fees:*

§ **7.70.070.** Court to determine reasonableness of each party's attorney fees.

West Virginia

- *Damage Award Limits or Caps:*

§ **55-7B-8.** $250,000 limit for noneconomic damages per occurrence. Plaintiff may recover compensatory damages for noneconomic loss in excess of the limitation above, but not in excess of $500,000 for each occurrence, where the damages for noneconomic losses suffered by the plaintiff were for: (1) Wrongful death; (2) permanent and substantial physical deformity, loss of use of a limb or loss of a bodily organ system; or (3) permanent physical or mental functional injury that permanently prevents the injured person from being able to independently care for himself or herself and perform life sustaining activities. Limits are adjusted annually for inflation by the Consumer Price Index.

- *Limits on Attorney Fees:*

No limitations.

Wisconsin

- *Damage Award Limits or Caps:*

No limitations. Limits on noneconomic damages (§ 893.55) declared unconstitutional by state supreme court (see *Ferdon ex rel. Petrucelli v. Wisconsin Patients Compensation Fund*, 701 N.W.2d 440 (2005)).

- *Limits on Attorney Fees:*

§ **655.013.** Sliding scale, not to exceed (a) Except as provided in par. (b), 33-1/3 percent of the first $1 million recovered. (b) 25 percent of the first $1 million recovered if liability is stipulated within 180 days after the date of filing of the original complaint and not later than 60 days before the first day of trial. (c) 20 percent of any amount in excess of $1 million recovered.

Wyoming

- *Damage Award Limits or Caps:*

No limitations. **Wyoming Constitution Article 10, § 4:** (a) No law shall be enacted limiting the amount of damages to be recovered for causing the injury or death of any person. (b) Any section of this constitution to the contrary notwithstanding, for any civil action where a person alleges that a health care provider's act or omission in the provision of health care resulted in death or injury, the legislature may by general law: (i) Mandate alternative dispute resolution or review by a medical review panel before the filing of a civil action against the health care provider.

- *Limits on Attorney Fees:*

Ct. Rules, R. 1 *et seq*. Contingent fees which do not exceed the following schedule will be presumed to be reasonable and not excessive where the total recovery does not exceed $1 million: (1) 33-1/3 percent of the recovery if the claim is settled prior to or within 60 days after suit is filed; (2) 40 percent of the recovery if the claim is settled more than 60 days after filing suit or if a judgment is entered upon a verdict. For those amounts of a recovery in excess of $1 million a contingent fee of 30 percent of such excess sum over $1 million shall be presumed reasonable and not excessive.

ENDNOTE

1. National Conference of State Legislatures, Medical Liability/Malpractice Laws (2009) (www.ncsl.org/default.aspx?tabid=18516).

GLOSSARY

A

abate a nuisance. Take steps to eliminate a nuisance that is interfering with the use and enjoyment of land.

abduction or enticement of a child. A tort involving serious interference with a parent's custody over his or her child.

abnormally dangerous condition or activity. Unusual or non-natural condition or activity that creates a substantial likelihood of causing great harm.

absolute immunity. A defense that avoids personal liability when a government employee is carrying out official functions, even if the employee was acting with malice.

absolute liability. See strict liability.

absolute privilege. A privilege that cannot be lost because of the bad motives of the party asserting the privilege. See also privilege.

abuse of process. The use of civil or criminal proceedings for an improper or ulterior motive.

act. A voluntary movement of the body.

actionable. Furnishing a legal basis for a cause of action.

active negligence. Unreasonable affirmative conduct, e. g., carelessly creating a defect.

act of God. An unpredictable and unpreventable force of nature.

actual cause. Cause in fact. Causation established by either the but-for test or the substantial-factor test. But-for test: can it be said that an event (e.g., the injury) would not have occurred without the act or omission of the party? Substantial-factor test: can it be said that the party's acts or omissions had a significant or important role in bringing about the event? See also proximate cause.

actual malice. Knowledge that a statement of fact is false, or recklessness as to its truth or falsity. Also called constitutional malice and *New York Times* malice because the definition is based on the case of *New York Times v. Sullivan*, 276 U.S. 254 (1964).

adhesion contract. A standardized contract for goods or services offered on a take-it-or-leave-it basis without any realistic opportunity for bargaining over the terms of the contract.

administrative agency. A governmental body, other than a court or legislature, that carries out (i.e., administers or executes) the statutes of the legislature, the executive orders of the chief executive, and its own regulations.

administrative code. A collection of administrative regulations organized by subject matter rather than chronologically by date enacted.

administrative decision. An administrative agency's resolution of a controversy (often following a hearing) on the application of the regulations, statutes, or executive orders that govern the agency. Sometimes called an administrative *ruling*.

administrative regulation. A law written by an administrative agency designed to explain or carry out the statutes, executive orders, or other regulations that govern the agency. Also called *administrative rule*.

admissible. Allowed into court for determination of its truth or believability.

ADR. See alternative dispute resolution.

adverse possession. A method of acquiring title to land without buying it or receiving it as a gift through a will or other traditional means. A trespasser can obtain title to land by occupying it in a hostile and visible manner for a designated number of continuous years.

affidavit of merit. See certificate of merit.

affirmative conduct. Active behavior, activity; the opposite of inaction.

affirmative defense. A defense raising new facts that will defeat the plaintiff's claim even if the plaintiff's fact allegations are proven.

agency hearing. A proceeding, similar to a trial, in which the hearing examiner of an administrative agency listens to evidence and legal arguments before deciding the case. See also administrative agency.

agent. 1. A person authorized to act for another; a representative. See also principal. 2. A power or force that produces an effect.

aggravation. An increase in the severity of the original injury. This may be caused by an additional injury or by a failure to take reasonable steps to prevent the increased severity of the original injury.

alienation of affections. The tort of causing a diminishment of the marital relationship or interference with consortium rights between the plaintiff and his or her spouse.

all-purpose public figure. See public figure.

alternative dispute resolution (ADR). A method or procedure for resolving a legal dispute without litigating it before a court or administrative agency. Examples include arbitration and mediation.

American rule. The winning party cannot recover attorney fees and costs of litigation from the losing party unless (1) a statute authorizes such payment, (2) a contract between the parties provides for such payment, or (3) the court finds that the losing party acted in bad faith in the litigation. See also English rule.

Andrews test. A duty is owed to anyone in the world at large (in the general public) who might be injured because of the defendant's unreasonable conduct even if this person is not in the zone of danger so long as someone is in the zone of danger due to the defendant's unreasonable conduct (from the *Palsgraf* case).

annuity. A fixed sum payable periodically (e.g., monthly or annually) for life or another specific period of time.

answer. A pleading containing the defendant's response to the plaintiff's complaint.

apparent present ability. Appearing reasonably able to do something now or very shortly.

appellant. The party bringing an appeal because of alleged errors made by a lower tribunal. Sometimes called petitioner.

appellate brief. A document filed by a party in an appellate court (and served on an opposing party) in which arguments are presented on why the appellate court should affirm (approve), reverse, or otherwise modify what a lower court has done.

appellee. The party against whom an appeal is brought. Also called the respondent.

application. An explanation of how a rule applies or does not apply to the facts. Connecting facts to the elements of a rule in order to determine whether the rule applies to the facts.

apportion. To divide into portions, e.g., to allocate or assign responsibility among parties.

apprehension. An understanding, awareness, anticipation, belief, or knowledge of something.

appropriation. The unauthorized use of a person's name, likeness, or personality for the user's benefit.

arbitration. A method of alternative dispute resolution (ADR) in which the parties try to avoid litigation by submitting their dispute to a neutral third person (the arbitrator) who renders a decision resolving the dispute.

arise out of. To be a causal link or connection; to cause; to stem from. See also workers' compensation.

arrest. Take another into custody to bring him or her before the proper authorities.

assault. An apprehension of an imminent harmful or offensive contact resulting from the defendant's intent to cause this apprehension or the contact itself.

assumption of the risk. The knowing and voluntary acceptance of the danger or risk of being harmed by someone's negligence. There are two main categories: express and implied assumption of risk. *Express assumption of the risk:* the knowing and voluntary acceptance of a danger or risk by an explicit agreement. *Implied assumption of the risk:* the knowing and voluntary acceptance of a danger or risk through conduct that signifies acceptance in the absence of an express agreement. There are two main categories of implied assumption: primary and secondary. *Primary assumption of the risk:* the knowing and voluntary acceptance of a particular risk that the defendant did not have a duty to protect the plaintiff against. *Secondary assumption of the risk:* the knowing and voluntary acceptance of a particular risk that the defendant had a duty to protect the plaintiff against.

at common law. 1. The case law and statutory law that existed during the Colonial period of American history. 2. During the time in history when the controlling law on an issue was the common law rather than statutory law. 3. The common law that existed before it was changed by statute. See also common law.

attestation clause. A clause stating that you saw (witnessed) someone sign a document or perform other tasks related to the validity of the document.

attractive nuisance doctrine. When an artificial condition on land creates an unreasonable risk of death or serious bodily injury to a foreseeable trespassing child too young to appreciate the danger, a duty of reasonable care exists to protect the child. Also called *turntable doctrine*, because the doctrine originated in cases involving railroad turntables.

at-will employee. See employment at will.

authority. Any written material a court could rely on to reach its decision. Primary authority is any law and secondary authority is any nonlaw that a court could rely on to reach its decision. See also legal authority.

automobile guest statute. See guest statute.

avoidable-consequences doctrine. See mitigation-of-damages rule.

B

bad faith liability. Civil liability for an unreasonable denial or delay by an insurance company in response to an insurance claim.

bailee. The person to whom property is entrusted under a contract of bailment. See also bailment.

bailment. The delivery of personal property by one person (the bailor) to another (the bailee) under an express or implied contract whereby the property will be redelivered when the purpose of the contract (e.g., storage, shipment) is completed.

bailor. The person who delivers property to another under a contract of bailment. See also bailment.

battery. An unpermitted and intentional physical contact with a person that is harmful or offensive.

beyond a reasonable doubt. See reasonable doubt.

BFP. See bona fide purchaser.

bodily harm. See physical injury.

bona fide purchaser (BFP). One who has purchased property for value without notice of defects in the title of the seller or of any claims against the property by others. Also called good faith purchaser and innocent purchaser.

breach of duty. Unreasonable conduct that endangers someone to whom you owe a duty of care. (If the duty owed is to avoid reckless conduct, then a breach of duty would be reckless conduct that endangers someone to whom you owe a duty of care.)

breach-of-duty equation. If the danger of a serious accident outweighs the burden or inconvenience of taking precautions to avoid the accident, the reasonable person would take those precautions. Furthermore, the more important or socially useful the activity, the more risks the reasonable person is willing to take.

breach of express warranty. Harm or damage caused by a false statement of fact relied on by the plaintiff and made with the intention or expectation that the statement will reach the plaintiff.

breach of implied warranty of fitness for a particular purpose. Harm or damage caused by a sale of goods by a merchant who has reason to know the buyer is relying on the expertise of the merchant in selecting the goods for a particular purpose, but the goods are not fit for that purpose.

breach of implied warranty of merchantability. Harm or damage caused by a merchant's sale of goods that were not fit for the ordinary purposes for which they are used.

breach of the peace. A violation or disturbance of the public tranquility and order. Disorderly conduct.

brief. A summary of a court opinion. See also appellate brief.

burden of proof. The responsibility for proving a fact at trial.

business guest. Someone who has been expressly or impliedly invited to be present, primarily for a business purpose. Also called a business invitee.

but-for test. Would the event (e.g., the injury) have happened without the act or omission of the party? But for the act or omission, would the event have occurred? Also called the sine qua non test.

bystander. 1. One who is injured by a product but who is not a seller, buyer, user, or consumer of the product. 2. One who is present but is not a direct participant.

C

cap. A limitation or ceiling. A damage cap is a limitation on the amount of damages that can be awarded in tort cases.

***Cardozo* test.** A duty is owed to anyone who is foreseeably in the zone of danger (from the *Palsgraf* case).

careless. Failing to use reasonable care, negligent.

case. 1. A court opinion. See also opinion. 2. A client matter.

cause. 1. Bring something about; causation. 2. A justifiable reason. Sometimes phrased as good cause or just cause.

cause in fact. Causation established either by the but-for test or by the substantial-factor test. An event (e.g., the injury) (a) would not have occurred without the act or omission of the party, or (b) the party's acts or omissions had a significant or important role in bringing about the event.

cause of action. 1. A legally acceptable reason for bringing a suit. A rule that constitutes a legal theory for bringing a suit. 2. The facts that give a person a right to judicial relief. When you state a cause of action, you list the facts that give you a right to judicial relief against the wrongdoer. When you state a tort cause of action, you list the facts that give you a right to judicial relief against the tortfeasor.

caveat emptor. "Buyer beware." A seller of real property will not be liable for injuries caused by a defect in the property if (1) the defect was discoverable upon reasonable inspection by the buyer, (2) the buyer had an unimpeded opportunity to inspect the premises, and (3) the seller did not commit fraud.

certificate of merit. A document filed by a plaintiff with the complaint certifying that the attorney has consulted with a qualifying expert who has advised the attorney that the claim raised in the complaint has merit. Called an *affidavit of merit* if the document must be signed under oath.

certify the class. The court's permission to allow a member of a class to represent every other member of the class in a class action.

chain of distribution. All persons or businesses that had a role in making, selling, or leasing a product that reached the person injured by that product.

charge. A statement of the guidelines and law given to the jury by the judge for use by the jury in deciding the issues of fact in its verdict. Also called jury instructions.

charitable immunity. A charitable organization is not liable for the torts that its workers commit.

charter. The fundamental law of a municipality or other local unit of government authorizing it to perform designated governmental functions.

chattels. Personal property; property other than land or things attached to land.

child. 1. Someone too young to appreciate the dangers that could be involved in a given situation. 2. Someone under the age of majority.

civil commitment. Taking someone into custody for treatment or protection, and not as punishment for the commission of a crime.

civil law. 1. The law that governs rights and duties between private persons or between private persons and the government concerning matters other than the commission of a crime. 2. Any law other than criminal law. 3. The statutory or code law applicable in Louisiana and in many Western European countries other than England.

civil rights. Basic individual rights guaranteed by the U.S. Constitution and by special federal statutes. Included are the right to vote, to choose one's vocation, to marry, to be accorded due process, and to equal protection under law.

Civil Rights Act of 1871. A federal statute that gives a person a right to sue a government employee who deprives the person of a federal right under color of state law (42 U.S.C. § 1983).

civil union. A same-sex relationship with the same *state* benefits and responsibilities the state grants spouses in a marriage.

class action. A lawsuit in which one or more members of a class sue (or are sued) as representative parties on behalf of everyone in the class, all of whom do not have to be joined in the lawsuit. If a prospective class member can decide not to join the class (i.e., can opt out), it is a *permissive class action*; if he or she cannot opt out, it is a *mandatory class action*.

***Code Napoléon*.** The law that is the basis of civil law systems such as that of France.

code of regulations. The text containing administrative regulations.

coercion. Compelling something by force or threats. Overpowering another's free will by undue influence.

collateral source. Someone other than (and independent of) the tortfeasor who provides direct or indirect financial assistance to the victim of the tort.

collateral-source rule. The amount of damages caused by the tortfeasor shall not be reduced by any injury-related funds received by the plaintiff from sources independent of the tortfeasor such as a health insurance policy of the plaintiff.

colloquium. Extrinsic facts showing that a defamatory statement was of and concerning the plaintiff. A part of the complaint alleging such facts.

color of law. Acting or pretending to act in an official, governmental capacity. Usually refers to state official or state governmental capacity.

commercial speech. Communications made in the pursuit of business, e.g., product advertising.

common area. An area used by more than one tenant that is controlled by (and under the responsibility of) the landlord.

common carrier. A company that holds itself out to the general public as engaged in transporting people or goods for a fee.

common law. Judge-made law in the absence of statutes or other controlling law. See also *at common law*.

comparative negligence. A comparison of the negligence of the defendant and of the plaintiff in causing the plaintiff's injury (or other loss) in order to reduce the plaintiff's damages in proportion to the plaintiff's negligence in causing his or her own injury (or other loss).

compensatory damages. Money paid to restore an injured party to his or her position prior to the injury or other loss.

competent. 1. Using the knowledge and skill that are reasonably necessary to represent a particular client. 2. Allowed (having the legal capacity) to give testimony because the person understands the obligation to tell the truth, has the ability to communicate, and has knowledge of the topic of his or her proposed testimony. The noun form is *competency*.

complaint. 1. A plaintiff's first pleading, stating a cause of action against the defendant. Also called petition. 2. A formal criminal charge.

complete. Total; confinement is complete if the victim knows of no safe or inoffensive means of escape from the boundaries set by the defendant.

component part. A part of a consumer product that is often manufactured by a company other than the assembler of the final product.

compound interest. Interest earned on money, calculated on the basis of the amount of principal involved and on the interest already accrued. The latter consists of interest on interest. See also simple interest.

concert. An activity undertaken by mutual agreement.

conclusive presumption. See presumption.

concurrent. 1. Acting or occurring at the same time. 2. Involving or concerning the same matters.

conditional privilege. See privilege.

conditional threat. A communicated intent to do something dangerous or unwanted in the future if a specified event occurs.

confidential relationship. See fiduciary relationship.

confinement. The complete restraint of the plaintiff's freedom of movement within fixed boundaries.

consent. Voluntary agreement or permission (express or implied) that something should happen or not happen. See also implied consent.

consideration. Something of value that is exchanged between parties. It can be an act, a forbearance (not performing an act), a promise to perform an act, or a promise to refrain from performing an act.

consortium. 1. The benefits that one spouse is entitled to receive from the other, e.g., companionship, cooperation, services, affection, and sexual relations. 2. The companionship and affection a parent is entitled to receive from a child and that a child is entitled to receive from a parent.

conspiracy of silence. The reluctance or refusal of one member of a group to testify against another member.

constitution. The fundamental law that creates the branches of government, allocates power among them, and defines some basic rights of individuals.

constitutional malice. See actual malice.

constitutional tort. A special cause of action that arises when someone is deprived of a federal civil right under color of state law. Also called a 1983 tort.

contingent fee. A fee that a paid to the plaintiff's attorney only if the case is successfully resolved by litigation or settlement. (The fee is also referred to as a contingency.) A *defense contingent fee* (also called a negative contingency) is a fee for the defendant's attorney that is dependent on the outcome of the case.

contract. A legally enforceable agreement. An agreement supported by consideration, which can be an act, a forbearance (not performing an act), a promise to perform an act, or a promise to refrain from performing an act.

contribution. The right of one tortfeasor who has paid a judgment to be proportionately reimbursed by other tortfeasors who have not paid their share of the damages caused by all the tortfeasors.

contributory negligence. The failure of plaintiffs to take reasonable precautions for their protection, helping to cause their own injury or other loss.

conversion. An intentional interference with another's personal property, consisting of an exercise of dominion over it.

cost of restoration. The amount of money damages that will restore property to its condition before the defendant's tort.

court rules. See rules of court.

covenant not to sue. An agreement not to bring suit against someone, e.g., an agreement not to sue one of the joint tortfeasors.

crashworthiness. The design of the interior of a motor vehicle so that it can avoid or minimize injury after the vehicle has been hit from outside.

credibility. Believability; the extent to which something can be believed.

criminal conversation. The tort that occurs when the defendant has sexual relations with the plaintiff's spouse.

criminal law. The law that governs crimes alleged by the government. Criminal law defines crimes, punishments, and procedures for investigation and prosecution. Also called penal law.

cross-examination. Questioning a witness called by the other side after the other side has completed its direct examination of the witness.

cut-off test. A policy test to determine whether a person should be liable for what he or she has caused in fact. See also proximate cause.

culpability. Blameworthiness.

culpable. At fault; blameworthy.

custom. What is commonly done. Also called *custom and usage*.

custom and usage. The general practice in a field; what is commonly done.

cyberbullying. The use of the Internet or other electronic means to repeatedly embarrass, humiliate, threaten, or otherwise harass a minor. Also called cyberharassment.

cyberharassment. See cyberbullying, cyberstalking.

cyberstalking. The use of the Internet or other electronic means to repeatedly embarrass, humiliate, threaten, or otherwise harass someone. Also called cyberharassment.

D

damage caps. Limitations on the amount of damages that can be awarded in designated categories of cases.

damages. 1. Monetary payments awarded to compensate someone for a legally recognized wrong (noun). 2. Causes harm or other loss (verb). (The word *damage* means injury, impairment, or other loss to person or property.)

dangerous propensity. A tendency to cause damage or harm because of prior acts or omissions that caused damage or harm.

Daubert. The United States Supreme Court opinion in *Daubert v. Merrell Dow Pharmaceuticals, Inc.*, which defined the gatekeeper role of federal trial judges on the admissibility of scientific evidence under Federal Rules of Evidence 702 (designed to limit admissibility of junk science).

deceit. See misrepresentation.

deep pocket. 1. An individual, business, or other organization with resources to pay a potential judgment. 2. Sufficient assets for this purpose. The opposite of *shallow pocket*.

defamacast. Defamation communicated via radio or television.

defamation. The publication of a written or gestured defamatory statement (libel) or an oral one (slander) that is of and concerning the plaintiff and that harms the plaintiff's reputation. See also defamatory statement, disparagement.

defamatory statement. A statement of fact that would tend to harm the reputation of the plaintiff in the eyes of at least a substantial and respectable minority of people by lowering the plaintiff in the estimation of those people or by deterring them from associating with the plaintiff.

default judgment. A judgment granted against a party who fails to appear, file an answer, or otherwise defend the action before the deadline.

defective. Lacking in some particular that is essential to completeness, safety, or legal sufficiency.

defense. 1. The response of a party to a claim of another party, setting forth reason(s) the claim should be denied. 2. The defendant and his or her attorney.

defense contingent fee. See contingent fee.

defense of others. The right to use reasonable force to prevent an immediate harmful or offensive contact against a third person.

defense of property. The right to use reasonable force to prevent a present threat of interference with the possession of your personal or real property or to end an interference with such property that just started.

defensive medicine. Ordering precautionary tests and procedures intended primarily to shield doctors (or others in the medical field) from possible lawsuits rather than to benefit the patient.

deposition. A method of discovery by which parties and their prospective witnesses are questioned outside the courtroom. Discovery is compulsory pretrial disclosure of information related to litigation by one party to another party. Discovery can also be used in postjudgment enforcement proceedings.

derivative action. A plaintiff's action against a defendant to recover for a loss that is dependent on an underlying tort committed by that defendant against another plaintiff.

derogation. A partial repeal or abolition of a law. For example, a statute in derogation of common law changes the common law.

dictum. An observation made by a judge in an opinion that is not essential to resolve the issues before the court; comments that go beyond the facts before the court. Also called obiter dictum.

differential diagnosis. A method by which a clinician can identify possible diseases the patient may have and, through a process of elimination, rule out diseases until a disease or symptom is left as the diagnosis.

digest. 1. A set of volumes of small-paragraph summaries of court opinions. 2. To summarize a document according to a given organizational principle.

direct examination. The first questioning of a witness by the party who called the witness. Also called examination in chief.

disclaimer. Words or conduct that negate or repudiate a claim, right, or obligation.

discount rate. The interest rate used by the parties when determining the present value of money to be received in the future.

discovery. 1. Methods such as interrogatories and depositions by which one party obtains information from the other party before trial. 2. Methods by which one party obtains postjudgment information from the other party to assist in enforcing the judgment.

disparagement. The intentional and false discrediting of a plaintiff's business, products, or title to property, resulting in specific monetary loss. See also slander of title and trade libel.

dispossession. 1. Taking physical control of a chattel but without exercising dominion over it. 2. Depriving someone of possession or occupancy of property.

diversity of citizenship. The disputing parties are citizens of different states. This fact gives jurisdiction (called diversity jurisdiction) to a United States district court when the amount in controversy exceeds $75,000.

domestic animal. An animal that has been domesticated or habituated to live among humans.

domestic partnership. Two persons in a same-sex (or unmarried opposite-sex) relationship who are emotionally and financially interdependent and who register with the government to receive marriage-like benefits.

dominion. The exertion of substantial or extensive control over a chattel that is inconsistent with another's right to control it.

dram shop liability. Civil liability imposed on the seller of intoxicating liquor to a buyer who then injures a third person. Sometimes also applied to a social host who serves liquor to intoxicated guests.

dual-purpose trip. An employee trip that has both a business and a personal purpose. Also called a mixed-purpose trip.

due care. The standard embodied in the duty of reasonable care is called *due care* or *ordinary care*. This care is measured by what someone of ordinary prudence would have done under the circumstances to avoid the injury or other loss.

duress. 1. Coercion or the unlawful use of force or threats to pressure someone to do something he or she does not want to do. 2. Wrongful confinement or imprisonment.

duty. 1. An obligation to conform to a standard of conduct prescribed by law. 2. In most negligence cases, the obligation to use reasonable care to avoid the foreseeable risk of causing injury or other loss to the person or property of another.

E

economic loss. An objectively verifiable monetary loss such as medical expense, burial expense, loss of earnings, and cost of repair. See also non-economic loss.

eggshell skull. See thin-skull rule.

ejectment. An action for the recovery of the possession of land and for damages for the wrongful dispossession.

element. A portion of a rule that is one of the preconditions of the applicability of the entire rule. A cause of action is also a rule. Hence, a cause of action has elements. See also factor.

emancipated. Married or otherwise living independently with the express or implied consent of a parent or former legal guardian.

emotional distress. Mental anguish such as fright, worry, and humiliation.

employment. A work relationship in which the person hiring (the employer) controls, or has the right to control, the goals and manner of work of the person hired (the employee).

employment at will. An employment relationship that either the employee or the employer can terminate at any time for any reason without liability so long as the termination does not violate public policy. The employee (called an at-will employee) has no union or special contract protection.

English rule. The party who loses the trial must pay the other side's attorney fees and other legal expenses. See also American rule.

enterprise liability. A system of spreading the costs of injuries over an entire industry or enterprise.

enticement of a child. See abduction or enticement of a child.

enticement of a spouse. A tort in which the defendant encourages the plaintiff's spouse to leave or to stay away from the plaintiff.

entrustment. The transfer of possession to someone's care. See also negligent entrustment.

epidemiology. The study of the causes of diseases in humans.

equitable remedy. A form of relief (e.g., injunction or specific performance) that is available when remedies at law (e.g., damages) are not adequate.

equity. 1. The system of justice administered in courts of equity. 2. Fairness.

estate. 1. An interest in real or personal property. 2. The extent and nature of one's interest in real or personal property. 3. All of the assets and liabilities of a decedent after he or she dies. 4. All of the property of whatever kind owned by a person. 5. Land.

evidence. Anything that could be offered to prove or disprove an alleged fact, e.g., testimony, documents, fingerprints (a separate determination must be made on whether a particular item of evidence is relevant or irrelevant, admissible or inadmissible).

examination in chief. See direct examination.

exculpation. Exoneration; release from liability.

exculpatory clause. A clause in an agreement that relieves a party from liability for injury or damages he or she may wrongfully cause.

execution. 1. Signing and doing whatever else is needed to finalize a document and make it legal. 2. Carrying out or performing some act to its completion, e.g., the process of carrying into effect the decisions in a judgment. 3. A command or writ to a court officer (e.g., sheriff) to seize and sell the property of the losing litigant in order to satisfy the judgment debt. Also called general execution and writ of execution. 4. Implementing a death sentence.

executive order. A law issued by the chief executive (e.g., president, governor, mayor) pursuant to specific statutory authority or to the executive's inherent authority (e.g., to direct the operation of governmental agencies).

exemplary damages. See punitive damages.

exhibit. An item of physical or tangible evidence offered to the court for inspection.

express assumption of the risk. See assumption of the risk.

express warranty. See breach of express warranty.

extrajudicial. Outside of court and litigation. Pertaining to what is done or given outside the course of regular judicial proceedings.

extreme or outrageous. Atrocious; totally intolerable; shocking the conscience of society.

extrinsic fact. A fact, not evident on the face of a statement, that is needed to establish the defamatory meaning of the statement.

F

FACE. Free Access to Clinic Entrances Act. A federal statute that provides a remedy for victims of assault or other attack suffered while trying to obtain (or provide) reproductive health services (18 United States Code § 248(a)(1); (www.usdoj.gov/crt/crim/248fin.php).

fact. 1. An express or implied communication containing concrete information that can be objectively shown to be true or false. 2. A real occurrence. An event, thing, or state of mind that actually exists (or that is alleged to exist) as opposed to its legal consequences.

factor. One of the circumstances or considerations that will be weighed in making a decision, no one of which is usually conclusive. A factor is one of the considerations a court will examine to help it make a decision on whether a rule (or an element of a rule) applies. Unlike elements, each factor is not a precondition to the applicability of a rule.

fact particularization. A fact-gathering technique used to generate a large list of factual questions (who, what, where, how, when, and why) that will help you obtain a specific and comprehensive picture of all available facts that are relevant to a legal issue.

factual issue. A question of fact; a question of what happened.

fair comment. An honest observation or opinion on a matter of public interest. Fair comment is a qualified privilege to a defamation action.

fair competition. Open, honest, nonfraudulent rivalry in commerce.

fair market value. The price agreed upon by a willing buyer and a willing seller, neither being under any compulsion to enter the transaction and both having reasonable knowledge of the relevant facts.

fair on its face. Having no obvious or blatant flaws or irregularities.

fair preponderance of evidence. See preponderance of the evidence.

fair-report privilege. A newspaper or other media entity is not liable for defamation when it publishes fair and accurate stories on government reports and proceedings even if the stories contain defamatory statements made in the government reports or proceedings.

false arrest. An arrest for which the person taking someone into custody has no privilege.

false imprisonment. The intentional confinement within fixed boundaries of someone who is conscious of the confinement or is harmed by it.

false light. Untrue and unreasonably offensive publicity about a person.

family purpose doctrine. An owner of a car (or a person controlling the use of a car) is liable for the negligence committed by a family member using the car for a family purpose. Also called family automobile rule.

fault. An error or defect in someone's judgment or conduct to which blame and culpability attach. The wrongful breach of a duty.

Federal Tort Claims Act (FTCA). The federal statute that specifies the torts for which the federal government can be sued because it waives sovereign immunity for those torts (28 USC §§ 2671 et seq., 1346).

fee caps. Limitations on the fees that attorneys can be paid in designated categories of cases.

fellow-servant rule. An employer will not be liable for injuries to an employee caused by the negligence of another employee—a fellow servant—unless the negligent employee was a superior or someone with responsibility for safety on the job (referred to as a vice principal).

felony. A crime punishable by death or imprisonment for a term exceeding a year; a crime more serious than a misdemeanor.

fiduciary relationship. The relationship that exists when one party (called the fiduciary) owes another loyalty, candor, and fair treatment. The fiduciary is required to act in the interest of and for the benefit of the other. Also called a confidential relationship.

filial consortium. The right of a parent to the normal companionship and affection of a child.

firefighter's rule. Firefighters (and police officers) cannot recover against an occupier for injuries related to the risks they are expected to assume as part of their job.

fitness for a particular purpose. See breach of implied warranty of fitness for a particular purpose.

forbearance. Refraining from exercising a right.

foreseeable. Having the quality of being seen or known beforehand; anticipated.

foreseeable plaintiff. Someone whose presence in the zone of danger is foreseeable to the defendant.

foreseeable users. Those persons whom a manufacturer or retailer can reasonably anticipate will use their product.

§ 402A. The main section on strict liability in tort from *Restatement (Second) of Torts*. The section provides for liability for physical harm caused by a defective product that is unreasonably dangerous.

fraud. See misrepresentation.

fresh pursuit. 1. Pursuit undertaken promptly, without undue delay. 2. The right of a victim whose property has been dispossessed to use reasonable force to take the property back just after it is taken. Also called hot pursuit.

frolic. Employee conduct outside the scope of employment because it is personal rather than primarily for the employer's business interests. Also called a frolic and detour.

***Frye* test.** Expert opinion on a scientific principle or discovery is admissible if it has "gained general acceptance" as reliable in the relevant scientific community. Based on the holding of *Frye v. United States*, 293 F. 1013 (D.C. Cir. 1923), which has been replaced by Federal Rules of Evidence Rule 702 and by *Daubert v. Merrell Dow Pharmaceuticals, Inc.*, 509 U.S. 579 (1993).

G

general causation. In toxic tort cases, capable of bringing about or producing a particular injury or condition in the general population. See also specific causation.

general damages. Compensatory damages that usually result from the kind of harm caused by the conduct of the defendant. Damages that usually and naturally flow from this wrong, e.g., pain and suffering. The law implies or presumes that such damages result from the wrong complained of. General damages differ from special damages, which are awarded for actual economic loss, such as medical costs and loss of income.

general rule on duty. Whenever one's conduct creates a foreseeable risk of injury or other loss to someone else's person or property, a duty of reasonable care arises to take reasonable precautions to prevent the injury or loss.

global peace. A final resolution of all claims that binds all parties, often through a class action.

go bare. To engage in an occupation or profession without malpractice (liabilty) insurance.

going-and-coming rule. 1. Workers' compensation is denied if the employee is injured "off the premises" while going to or coming back from work or lunch. 2. Commuting to and from work is outside the scope of employment. Torts committed by an employee during this period are not covered by respondeat superior; the employer is not liable for them.

good cause. See cause.

Good Samaritan. A person who comes to the aid of another without a legal obligation to do so.

governmental function. A function that can be performed adequately only by the government.

governmental immunity. See sovereign immunity.

gratuitous. Pertaining to what is performed or given without a duty or obligation to do so; free.

gratuitous promise. A promise that one does not have a duty or obligation to make.

gross negligence. The failure to use even a small amount of care to avoid foreseeable harm.

guest. 1. A passenger in a motor vehicle who is offered a ride by someone who receives no benefits from the passenger other than hospitality, goodwill, and the like. 2. One who pays for the services of a restaurant or place of lodging. 3. A recipient of one's hospitality, especially at home.

guest statute. A statute providing that drivers of motor vehicles will not be liable for injuries caused by their ordinary negligence to nonpaying guest passengers. Also called automobile guest statute.

H

harmful. Involving physical damage, impairment, pain, or illness in the body.

harmless. Not affecting substantial rights.

hearing. A proceeding in court or in an administrative agency.

hearing memorandum of law. See memorandum of law.

heart-balm statute. A law abolishing heart-balm actions, which are actions based on a broken heart or loss of love (e.g., breach of promise to marry, alienation of affections, and criminal conversation).

hedonic damages. Damages that cover the victim's loss of pleasure or enjoyment of life.

helpless peril. A danger (created by the plaintiff's contributory negligence) that cannot be avoided even if the plaintiff now uses reasonable care.

highly offensive. Extremely distasteful or unpleasant to a reasonable person.

hypothesis. An assumption or theory to be proven or disproven.

hypothetical. 1. A set of facts that are assumed to exist for purpose of discussion. (The teacher asked the students to analyze the hypothetical she gave them.) 2. Assumed or based on conjecture. (The lawyer asked the witness a hypothetical question.)

I

imminent. Immediate in the sense of no significant or undue delay. Near at hand; about to occur.

immunity. 1. The treatment of wrongful conduct as non-wrongful. A complete defense to a tort claim, whether or not the defendant committed the tort. 2. Exemption or freedom from a duty, penalty, or liability. 3. The right not to be subjected to civil or criminal prosecution.

impeach. Discredit or attack.

implied assumption of the risk. See assumption of the risk.

implied consent. An inference that consent has been given based on the surrounding circumstances, including signs, affirmative conduct, inaction, or silence. See also consent.

implied warranty. See breach of implied warranty of fitness for a particular purpose, breach of implied warranty of merchantability.

imputed. Attributed to or imposed on someone or something.

imputed contributory negligence. The defense of contributory negligence is attributed or imposed on someone who did not act unreasonably him- or herself but who is subject to this defense solely because of his or her relationship with the person who was unreasonable.

imputed negligence. Negligence liability attributed to or imposed on someone who did not act unreasonably but is liable solely because of his or her relationship with the person who did act unreasonably.

inattentive peril. A danger (created by the plaintiff's contributory negligence) that could be avoided if the plaintiff now uses reasonable care, but the plaintiff is carelessly unaware of the danger.

incident to employment. Sufficiently connected or related to an employee's job duties.

increased-risk test. The risk of injury to the employee is quantitatively greater than the risk of injury to nonemployees (a causal connection test for workers' compensation).

indemnity. 1. The duty of one person to pay for another's loss, damage, or liability. 2. A right to receive compensation to make one person whole from a loss that has already been sustained but which in justice ought to be sustained by the person from whom indemnity is sought.

independent contractor. One who operates his or her own business and contracts to do work for others; the latter do not control the method or administrative details of how the work is performed.

independent liability. Liability based on what an individual did him- or herself. The opposite of vicarious liability, which is liability based on what someone else has done.

indivisible. Not separable into parts; pertaining to that which cannot be divided.

inducement. The part of a defamation complaint that alleges extrinsic facts to show a defamatory meaning.

inference. A logical conclusion drawn from facts. A conclusion deduced from other facts.

informed consent. Agreement to let something happen based on having a reasonable understanding of the benefits and risks involved.

inherently dangerous. Being susceptible to cause harm or injury due to the nature of the product, service, or activity involved.

initiate. To instigate, urge on, or incite.

injunction. A court order requiring a person or organization to do or to refrain from doing something.

injurious falsehood. The publication of a false statement that causes special damages.

injury. See physical injury.

in loco parentis. "In the place of the parent." Acting in place of or assuming some or all the duties of a parent without adopting the child.

innocently. Done without negligence, intent, recklessness, malice, or other wrongful state of mind.

innuendo. The explanation of the defamatory meaning of words alleged by inducement in the complaint. The portion of a complaint that explains a statement's defamatory meaning when this is not clear on its face.

in-person solicitation. Seeking employment on the phone or in a face-to-face setting such as at home or in the office.

instigate. To insist on, urge, goad, direct, or incite someone to a course of action.

insurance. A contract (called an insurance policy) under which a company agrees to compensate a person (up to a specific amount) for a loss caused by designated perils or risks. See also liability insurance.

insured. The person designated as being protected against specified loss under an insurance policy.

intangible. Without physical form, e.g., a right or an emotion. See also tangible.

intent. 1. Design, plan, or purpose in performing an act. 2. The desire to cause the consequences of one's act (or failure to act), or the knowledge with substantial certainty that the consequences will follow from what one does (or fails to do).

intent (for assault). (a) The desire to bring about an apprehension of an imminent contact or the contact itself, or (b) the knowledge with substantial certainty that an imminent apprehension will result from what one does or fails to do.

intent (for battery). (a) The desire to bring about an imminent contact or an apprehension of such contact, or (b) the knowledge with substantial certainty that an imminent contact (or its apprehension) will result from what one does or fails to do.

intent (for conversion). (a) The desire to exercise dominion over personal property that is inconsistent with another's right to control it, or (b) the knowledge with substantial certainty that this will result from what one does or fails to do.

intent (for false imprisonment). (a) The desire to bring about the confinement of a person, or (b) the knowledge with substantial certainty that the confinement will result from what one does or fails to do.

intent (for intentional infliction of emotional distress). (a) The desire to inflict severe emotional distress, or (b) the knowledge with substantial certainty that such distress will result from what one does or fails to do.

intent (for trespass to chattels). (a) The desire to intermeddle with or dispossess another of personal property, or (b) the knowledge with substantial certainty that this will result from what one does or fails to do.

intent (for trespass to land). (a) The desire to intrude on the land of another, or (b) the knowledge with substantial certainty that this will result from what one does or fails to do.

intentional infliction of emotional distress (IIED). Intentionally causing severe emotional distress by an act of extreme or outrageous conduct. This tort is also called the tort of *outrage*.

intentional tort. A tort in which a person either desired to bring about the result or knew with substantial certainty that the result would follow from what the person did or failed to do.

interest. 1. A right, claim, title, or legal share in something; a right to have the advantage accruing from something. 2. A charge that is paid to borrow money or for a delay in its return when due. 3. The object of any human desire.

interference with contract relations. Intentionally encouraging or provoking a breach of contract between two other persons. Also called tortious interference with contractual relations.

interference with prospective advantage. Intentionally interfering with another's reasonable expectation of an economic advantage. Also called tortious interference with prospective advantage.

intermeddling. Making physical contact with, and causing damage or harm to, a chattel without exercising dominion over it.

interoffice memorandum of law. See memorandum of law.

interrogatories. A method of discovery consisting of written questions about a lawsuit submitted by one party to another to help the sender prepare for trial.

interspousal immunity. Spouses cannot sue each other for designated categories of torts. Also called husband–wife immunity.

intervening cause. A new and independent force that produces harm after the defendant's act or omission.

intestacy. Dying without leaving a valid will. The deceased is called the intestate.

in the course of. Pertaining to the time, place, and circumstances of the injury or illness in connection with the employment. Occurring while at work or in the service of the employer. See also workers' compensation.

intra-agency appeal. A review within the agency of an earlier decision to determine if that decision was correct. See also agency hearing.

intrafamily tort. A tort committed by one family member against another.

intrafamily tort immunity. Family members cannot sue each other for designated categories of torts.

intrusion. 1. Prying, peering, or probing. 2. A highly offensive invasion into another's personal seclusion or private life. It is one of the four invasion-of-privacy torts. 3. Physically going on land, remaining on land, going to a prohibited part of the land, or failing to remove goods from the land. (An element of trespass to land.)

invasion of privacy. 1. Four torts (intrusion, appropriation, public disclosure of private fact, and false light). 2. An unwarranted interference into someone's private life or misappropriation of someone's name, likeness, or personality.

invitee. One who enters the land upon the express or implied invitation of the occupier of the land, in order to use the land for the purposes for which it is held open to the public or to pursue the business of the occupier.

IRAC. An acronym that stands for the components of legal analysis: issue (I), rule (R), application of the rule to the facts (A), and conclusion (C). IRAC provides a structure for legal analysis.

irrebuttable presumption. See presumption.

issue. See factual issue, legal issue.

J

joinder. Uniting two or more parties as plaintiffs, two or more parties as defendants, or two or more claims in a single lawsuit.

joint and several liability. Legally responsible together and individually. Each wrongdoer is individually responsible for the entire judgment; the plaintiff can choose to collect from one wrongdoer or from all of them until the judgment is satisfied.

joint enterprise. An express or implied agreement to participate in a common enterprise over which the participants have a mutual right of control. Often called a *joint venture* if the purpose of the enterprise is business or profit related.

joint tortfeasors. Two or more persons who contribute to the commission of a single tort.

joint venture. A mutually undertaken business or profit-seeking activity over which each person participates or has an equal right of participation or control.

judgment. The final conclusion of a court that resolves a legal dispute or that specifies what further proceedings are needed to resolve it.

judgment creditor. The person to whom a court-awarded money judgment (damages) is owed.

judgment debtor. The person ordered by a court to pay a money judgment (damages).

judgment proof. Having few or no assets from which a money judgment can be satisfied. Having shallow pockets.

Judicial Panel on Multidistrict Litigation (J.P.M.L.). A special federal judicial body with the power to order that cases filed in different districts with common questions of fact be temporarily transferred to a single district for pretrial proceedings. Once the pretrial matters are completed, the cases are transferred back to the districts where they were initially filed.

junk science. Unreliable and, therefore, potentially misleading scientific evidence. See also *Daubert*.

jurisdiction. 1. The authority or power of a court to resolve a dispute. Its *personal jurisdiction* is its power to order a particular defendant to do or to refrain from doing something. Its *subject matter jurisdiction* is its power to hear certain kinds of cases. 2. The geographic area over which a particular court has authority.

just cause. See cause.

just compensation. Compensation from the government that is fair to the owner and the public, paid when the owner's property is *taken* by the government for a public purpose.

justifiable reliance. Being reasonable in taking action (or in refraining from taking action) because of the circumstances, such as what someone has said or done. Dependence or trust that is legally or morally excusable or defensible.

K

knowledge with substantial certainty. A high degree of knowledge; having no more than very minimal doubt about a result that will flow from what you do or fail to do.

L

last clear chance doctrine. Plaintiffs who have been contributorily negligent in placing themselves in peril can still recover if a negligent defendant had the last opportunity (clear chance) to avoid the accident and failed to exercise reasonable care to do so.

latent. Not readily visible; hidden.

law journals. See law reviews.

law reviews. Legal periodicals published by law schools. Also called law journals.

learned-intermediary doctrine. When a physician prescribes drugs or medical devices, the manufacturer's duty to the patient is limited to providing warnings and instructions to the physician; the manufacturer has no duty to provide them to the patient.

legal analysis. The application of one or more rules to the facts of a client's case in order to answer a legal question that will help (1) prevent a legal dispute from arising, (2) resolve a legal dispute that has arisen, or (3) prevent a legal dispute from becoming worse.

legal authority. 1. The power of the government; the right to do something. 2. Any law (primary authority) or nonlaw (secondary authority) on which a tribunal can rely to help it resolve a legal dispute before it.

legal cause. The loss or other harm was the foreseeable consequence of the original risk created by the defendant. See also proximate cause.

legal encyclopedia. A multivolume set of books that summarizes almost every important legal topic.

legal issue. A question of whether a cause of action, defense, or other rule applies to the facts. Also called a question of law.

legal malpractice. The failure of an attorney to exercise the skills commonly applied by attorneys in the same area of practice under the same circumstances. See also malpractice.

legal memorandum. See memorandum of law.

legal reasoning. See legal analysis.

legal remedy. A method of enforcing a legal right or redressing the violation of a legal right. See also remedy at law; remedy.

legal treatise. A book written by a private individual (or by a public official writing as a private citizen) that provides an overview, summary, or commentary on a legal topic.

legislative intent. The purpose of the legislature in enacting a particular statute.

legitimate public interest. Information the general public would like to have.

lessee. A person who rents or leases property from another. A tenant.

lessor. A person who rents or leases property to another. A landlord.

liability insurance. Insurance in which the insurer agrees to pay, on behalf of an insured, damages that the latter is obligated to pay to a third party because of his or her legal liability to the third person for committing a tort or other wrong. See also insurance.

liability without fault. See strict liability.

liable. Obligated in law; legally responsible.

libel. Defamation that is written or embodied in a physical form. See also defamation.

libel per quod. A written statement that requires one to use extrinsic facts to understand its defamatory meaning.

libel per se. 1. A written defamatory statement that is actionable without proof that the plaintiff suffered special damages; presumed damages are allowed. 2. A written statement that does not require the use of extrinsic facts to demonstrate the defamatory nature of the statement.

licensee. One who enters the land for his or her own purposes, but with the express or implied consent of the occupier.

limited-purpose public figure. A person who has voluntarily become involved in a controversy of interest to the general public. See also public figure.

listserv. A program that manages computer mailing lists automatically, receiving and distributing messages from and to members of the list.

locality rule. In a medical malpractice action, the applicable standard is that doctors must have and use the knowledge and skill that qualified doctors commonly have and use in the same or in a similar community.

Lord Campbell's Act. An early English statute giving certain relatives of a decedent a wrongful death claim for a tort that caused the death of the decedent.

loss of consortium. Interference with the companionship, services, affection, and sexual relations one spouse receives from another.

loss of services. An action by a parent for interference with an unemancipated child's ability to perform household chores and other tasks for the parent. See also derivative action.

lump sum payment. A single amount paid at one time to cover all past and future damages.

M

made whole. Restored to the condition that existed before the wrong was committed against the victim insofar as this is possible. To be compensated for a loss.

malfeasance. Wrongful (illegal) conduct or inaction by a public official.

malice. 1. Ill will, hatred, or a desire to harm. 2. Recklessness. 3. Knowledge of consequences. 4. Improper purpose. See also actual malice.

malicious. Acting with malice, e.g., an improper purpose. See also malice.

malicious civil prosecution. See wrongful civil proceedings.

malicious prosecution. Initiating criminal legal proceedings without probable cause and with malice, or with an improper purpose, when the proceedings terminate in favor of the accused. (Note that some states include the initiation of civil proceedings. Here, however, we follow those states that treat civil proceedings separately as *wrongful civil proceedings*. See this phrase.)

malpractice. Professional misconduct or wrongdoing consisting of ethical violations, criminal conduct, and torts such as negligence and battery. See also legal malpractice, medical malpractice.

mandatory class action. See class action.

mandatory offset. A required deduction that compensates for or counters something else. See also permissive offset.

manner. A method or way of performing a task.

manner-of-injury rule. If the general nature or type of harm was a foreseeable consequence of the original risk, the defendant will be liable for the harm even if the manner in which the harm occurred was not foreseeable.

manufacturer. A business that makes a product.

manufacturing defect. The product is dangerous because of the way in which it was assembled; the product does not conform to its design.

market share liability. Legal responsibility for harm caused by a product according to the proportion of the market attributable to the sales of a particular company.

Married Women's Property Acts. Statutes removing legal disabilities on married women, e. g., the right to sue and the right to convey property in their own right.

mass tort. A general term for various causes of action asserted by a large number of persons who have been harmed by the same or similar conduct or product of a relatively small number of defendants. The causes of action include negligence, strict liability in tort, breach of warranty, misrepresentation, and violations of deceptive trade acts.

master/servant relationship. An employer/employee relationship. See employment.

material. 1. Essential or important; of influence on one's decision. 2. Relevant; logically connected. 3. Pertaining to matter; physical.

mediation. A method of alternative dispute resolution (ADR) in which the parties try to avoid litigation by submitting their dispute to a neutral third person (the mediator) who helps the parties resolve their dispute; he or she does not render a decision resolving it for them.

medical battery. An unwanted procedure performed by a health care practitioner or a requested procedure performed on the wrong part of the body.

medical malpractice. The failure of a doctor to exercise the skills commonly applied by doctors in the same field under the same circumstances.

memo. Shorthand for memorandum.

memorandum of law. A written explanation of how the law might apply to the facts of a client's case. Also called a legal memorandum or *memo* for short. If the audience of the memo is someone in the office such as a supervisor, the memo is called an *office memorandum of law* or an *interoffice memorandum of law*. If the audience of the memo is someone outside the office, it might be called a *hearing memorandum* (submitted to an administrative law judge in an administrative agency), a *points and authorities memorandum* (submitted to a trial judge or hearing officer), or a *trial memorandum* (submitted to a trial judge).

merchant. A person in the business of purchasing and selling goods.

merchantable. Fit for the ordinary purposes for which the goods are used. See also breach of implied warranty of merchantability.

merits. See on the merits.

method. The means used to accomplish something; the manner of performing a task.

ministerial. Involving a duty that is to be performed in a prescribed manner with little or no judgment or discretion involved.

misdemeanor. A crime punishable by fine or by incarceration for a term of a year or less; a crime less serious than a felony.

misfeasance. Affirmative conduct that is improper or unreasonable.

misrepresentation. 1. An intentionally false statement of fact that is material, made to induce reliance by the plaintiff, and results in harm because of the reliance. Also called intentional misrepresentation, fraudulent misrepresentation, deceit, or fraud. 2. An incorrect, false, or misleading statement, which can be communicated intentionally, negligently, or innocently.

mistake. An unintentional act, omission, or error.

misuse. Using a product in a manner that was neither intended nor foreseeable.

mitigation-of-damages rule. Injured parties must take reasonable steps to alleviate their injury. A wrongdoer will not be liable for any increase or aggravation of the injury caused by the injured party's failure to take such steps. Also called avoidable-consequences doctrine.

mixed-purpose trip. See dual-purpose trip.

moral. Pertaining to the goodness and badness of human behavior, which may or may not be embodied in the laws of our legal system.

moral turpitude. Conduct that is dishonest, contrary to moral rules, or reprehensible.

motion. A formal request to a court.

motive. A desire, reason, need, or emotion that induces action or inaction.

N

National Practitioner Data Bank. A collection of information such as malpractice judgments and sanctions against physicians, dentists, and other health care practitioners.

national standard. 1. A doctor is required to have and use the equipment, knowledge, and experience that doctors have and use nationally. 2. Evaluation based on what is acceptable nationally rather than locally.

natural law. Inherent principles of conduct based on human nature rather than on formal laws imposed by society.

necessity. The privilege to make reasonable use of someone's property to avoid an immediate threat of harm or damage to persons or property. If the threat is to private interests, the privileged use is a private necessity. If the threat is to the public, the privileged use is a public necessity.

negligence. The failure to use reasonable care that an ordinary prudent person would have used in a similar situation, resulting in injury or other loss. *Ordinary negligence* consists of conduct that is unreasonable but that is not gross or reckless. *Willful, wanton, or reckless negligence* consists of unreasonable conduct that creates a very great risk that harm will result; acting with the knowledge that the harm will probably result. See also gross negligence.

negligence per se. Negligence (unreasonableness) found because of a violation of a statute. The jury is not asked what a reasonable person would have done; the trial judge court concludes that a reasonable person would have done what the statute provides.

negligent. Failing to use reasonable care; careless.

negligent entrustment. Carelessly allowing the use of a vehicle, tool, or other object by someone who poses an unreasonable risk of harm to others.

negligent hiring. Carelessly hiring an incompetent person who poses an unreasonable risk of harm to others.

negligent infliction of emotional distress (NIED). Carelessly causing someone to suffer emotional distress.

negligent misrepresentation. A careless communication of a false statement of fact received and relied upon by someone the statement was intended to reach.

negligent supervision. Carelessly monitoring or supervising an incompetent person who poses an unreasonable risk of harm to others.

neighborhood justice center (NJC). A government or private center where disputes can be resolved by mediation or other method of alternative dispute resolution (ADR).

newsworthy. Pertaining to information the general public would like to have; pertaining to matters of legitimate public interest.

***New York Times* malice.** See actual malice.

NIED. See negligent infliction of emotional distress.

1983 action. A suit based on § 1983 of the Civil Rights Act of 1871 against a government employee who deprives someone of a federal right under color of state law. The deprivation is called a 1983 tort.

1983 tort. A deprivation of a federal civil right under color of state law. See 1983 action.

no fault. Pertaining to legal consequences (e.g., paying insurance benefits or granting a divorce) that will occur regardless of who was at fault or to blame.

nolle prosequi. A statement by the prosecutor that he or she is unwilling to prosecute an individual for the commission of a crime.

nominal damages. A trifling sum (e.g., $1) awarded to the plaintiff because there was no significant loss or injury suffered, although a technical invasion of rights did occur.

nondelegable. Pertaining to a duty for which one remains responsible even if another is asked to (or agrees to) carry it out.

nondelegable duty. A task considered so important or critical that you are liable for injury or other loss when the task is carelessly performed, even if you hired an independent contractor to perform it.

non-economic loss. A non-monetary harm such as emotional pain, suffering, inconvenience, mental anguish, loss of enjoyment of life, loss of companionship, damage to reputation, and humiliation. A nonpecuniary loss.

nonfeasance. The failure to act; inaction; an omission. (Nonfeasance can be either wrongful or blameless.)

nonpecuniary losses. Mental suffering, grief, and other noneconomic losses that cannot be measured in money.

notice. 1. Information or knowledge about something. 2. Formal notification. 3. Knowledge of facts that would naturally lead an honest and prudent person to make inquiry.

notice of appeal. Notice given to a court (through filing) and to the opposing party (through service) of an intention to appeal.

nuisance. An unreasonable interference with the use and enjoyment of private land (*private nuisance*); or an unreasonable interference with a right that is common to the general public (*public nuisance*).

nuisance per se. An act, occupation, or structure that is a nuisance at all times and under any circumstances, regardless of location or surroundings. Also called nuisance at law.

O

objective. Goal or purpose. See also objective standard.

objective standard. A standard by which something is measured by comparing (1) what a person actually knew, felt, or did with (2) what a reasonable person would have known, felt, or done under the same circumstances.

occupier. Anyone in possession of land who has a right to possess it.

of and concerning the plaintiff. Reasonably understood by the recipient to refer to the plaintiff.

offensive. Offending the personal integrity or dignity of a reasonable or ordinary person who is not unduly sensitive.

office memorandum of law. See memorandum of law.

official immunity. Government employees are not personally liable for torts or other wrongdoing they commit within the scope of their employment. See also absolute immunity and qualified immunity.

offset. A deduction; that which compensates for or counters something else.

on its face. Without reference to extrinsic facts. What is readily observable. See also extrinsic fact.

online. 1. Connected to another computer or computer network, often through the Internet. 2. Residing on a computer and available for use; activated and ready for use on a computer.

on the merits. Based on a substantive determination of who is in the right rather than on a preliminary, technical, or procedural irregularity.

opening statement. An attorney's statement to the jury made before presenting evidence that summarizes the case he or she intends to try to establish during the trial.

operation of law. A means by which legal consequences are imposed by law, regardless of the intent of the parties involved.

opinion. 1. An express or implied communication containing a relatively vague or indefinite value judgment that is not objectively verifiable. 2. A court's written explanation of how it applied the law to the facts before it to resolve a legal dispute. Also called a case.

opt out. To choose not to participate. To bring an individual lawsuit rather than become a member of a class action. See also class action.

ordinance. A law passed by the local legislative branch of government (e.g., city council or county commission) that declares, commands, or prohibits something. (An ordinance operates like a statute, but at the local level.)

ordinary care. The standard embodied in the duty of reasonable care is called *due care* or *ordinary care*. This care is measured by what someone of ordinary prudence would have done under the circumstances to avoid the injury or other loss.

ordinary negligence. Conduct that is unreasonable but not gross or reckless. See also negligence.

out-of-pocket. Pertaining to amounts actually paid or to be paid to cover losses.

outrage. See intentional infliction of emotional distress.

outrageous. See extreme or outrageous.

P

pain and suffering. Physical discomfort or emotional distress; a disagreeable mental or emotional experience.

palimony. Support payments ordered after the end of a nonmarital relationship if the party seeking support was induced to initiate or maintain the relationship by an express or implied promise of support or if support is otherwise equitable.

parental consortium. The right of a child to the normal companionship and affection of a parent.

passenger. Someone riding in a car who confers a benefit on the driver, other than the benefit of social company.

passive negligence. The unreasonable failure to do something, e.g., carelessly allowing defects (created by others) to exist.

peace officer. A person designated by public authority to keep the peace and to arrest persons suspected of crime.

peace of mind. The lack of anguish due to serious interference.

peculiar-risk test. The source of the harm is peculiar to the employment (a causal connection test for workers' compensation).

pecuniary. Pertaining to money.

pecuniary loss. A money loss. Examples include cost of repair and the amount needed to replace the loss of support and services that would have been received.

penal law. See criminal law.

percentage fee. Payment in the form of a percentage of the amount involved in the award, settlement, or transaction.

per-diem argument. A certain amount is requested as damages for every day that pain and suffering has been endured and is expected to continue. Also called the unit-of-time argument.

permissive class action. See class action.

permissive offset. An allowed (but not required) deduction that compensates for or counters something else. See also mandatory offset.

person. The human body, something attached to the body, or something so closely associated with the body as to be identified with it.

personal liability. Liability that can be satisfied out of a wrongdoer's personal assets.

personal property. Property other than land or other than things attached to land. Also called chattels. See also property.

personal property tort. See tort.

personal representative. A person appointed to administer the estate and legal affairs of someone who has died or who is incapacitated.

personal tort. A tort that injures a person's body, reputation, or feelings. See also tort.

persuasive authority. Any authority a court could rely on in reaching its decision even though it is not required to rely on it. (The opposite of persuasive authority is *mandatory authority*, which is any authority a court must rely on in reaching its decision.)

petitioner. See appellant.

physical impact. Actual contact with the body.

physical injury. A wound, cut, or other detrimental change in a part of the body. An illness in the body rather than in the mind. Also called bodily harm.

physician-patient relationship. The relationship that arises when a doctor undertakes to render medical services in response to an express or implied request for services by the patient or by the patient's guardian.

PI. Personal injury. (A PI practice is a tort practice.)

point. A measure of the size of printed letters of the alphabet, punctuation marks, or other characters. (One point is approximately 1/72 of an inch tall.)

points and authorities memorandum. See memorandum of law.

positional-risk test. The injury of the employee would not have occurred but for the fact that the job placed the employee in a position where the employee could be injured (a causal connection test for workers' compensation).

possessory interest. 1. A present or future right to possess land. 2. The right to exert control over specific property to the exclusion of others, whether or not the right is based on title.

posttrial discovery. Methods by which one party obtains information from another party after the trial; the usual purpose of posttrial discovery is to enable the *judgment creditor* (the party who has won a money judgment) to obtain information from the *judgment debtor* (the party ordered to pay a money judgment) that will help in the enforcement (e.g., collection) of the judgment.

preemption. 1. Under the Supremacy Clause, federal laws take precedence over (preempt) state laws when Congress (a) expressly mandates the preemption, (b) regulates an area so pervasively that an intent to preempt the entire field may be inferred, or (c) enacts a law that directly conflicts with state law. 2. The right of first purchase.

preexisting condition. 1. A medical problem that existed prior to the starting date of an insurance policy or other benefit. 2. A medical problem that existed prior to the defendant's wrongful conduct; the defendant may have caused an aggravation of the problem but not the problem itself.

premises liability. The tort liability of landowners and others with possessory interests in land for injuries suffered due to conditions or activities on the land (premises).

preponderance of the evidence. The standard of proof that is met when the evidence establishes that it is more likely than not that the facts are as alleged. Also called fair preponderance of evidence.

present cash value. See present value.

present value. The amount of money an individual would have to be given now in order to generate a certain amount of money within a designated period of time through prudent investment, usually at compound interest. Also called present cash value and present worth.

presumed damages. Damages that a jury is allowed to assume were suffered by the plaintiff, who does not have to introduce specific evidence that these damages were in fact suffered.

presumption. An inference or assumption of fact that can be drawn when another fact or set of facts is established. The presumption is rebuttable if a party is allowed to introduce evidence that the assumption is false. If no contrary evidence is allowed, it is called an *irrebuttable presumption* or a *conclusive presumption*.

prima facie. Sufficient to establish a fact or a presumption of a fact unless refuted by other evidence.

prima facie case. A party's presentation of evidence that will prevail unless the other side offers more convincing counterevidence.

prima facie tort. The intentional infliction of harm without justification, resulting in special damages.

primary assumption of risk. See assumption of the risk.

primary authority. Any law (e.g., case or statute) that a court could rely on in reaching a decision. See also authority.

principal. 1. One who permits another (the agent) to act behalf of the principal. 2. A perpetrator of a crime. 3. One with prime responsibility for an obligation.

private affairs. Information that cannot reasonably be considered of legitimate public concern. Non-newsworthy facts.

private necessity. A privilege to make reasonable use of another's property to avoid an immediate private harm or damage.

private nuisance. An unreasonable interference with the use and enjoyment of private land.

private person. Someone who is not a public official or a public figure.

privilege. 1. The right to act contrary to the right of another without being subject to tort or other liability. A defense that authorizes conduct that would otherwise be wrongful. 2. A special legal benefit, right, exemption, or protection.

privity. A relationship that persons share in a transaction, in property, or in a right. The major example of privity is *privity of contract*, which exists only between parties to a contract.

privity of contract. The relationship that exists between persons who enter a contract with each other.

probable cause. 1. A reasonable belief that a specific crime has been committed and that the accused committed the crime. 2. A reasonable belief that good grounds exist to bring civil proceedings against someone.

pro bono. Concerning or involving legal services that are provided for the public good (*pro bono publico*) without fee or compensation. Sometimes also applied to services given at a reduced rate. Shortened to pro bono.

process. 1. The means used by a court to acquire or exercise its power or jurisdiction over a person, e.g., a writ or a summons to appear in court. 2. A court proceeding. See also service of process.

products liability. A general term that covers five causes of action for harm caused by products: negligence, breach of express warranty, breach of implied warranty of fitness for a particular purpose, breach of implied warranty of merchantability, and strict liability in tort.

promise. 1. A manifestation by a promisor (the person making the promise) of an intention to act or to refrain from acting in a specified way so as to justify the promisee (the person to whom the promise is made) in understanding that a commitment has been made. 2. To make a commitment.

property. Real property is land and anything attached to the land. Personal property (also called chattels) is every other kind of property. See also tangible.

property tort. A tort that damages a person's real property or personal property.

proprietary function. A function of government that (1) traditionally or principally has been performed by private enterprise, or (2) is conducted primarily to produce a profit or benefit for the government rather than for the public at large.

pro rata. Proportionately; according to a specified rate or factor.

prosecution. 1. Bringing and processing criminal proceedings against someone. 2. Bringing and processing civil proceedings against someone. 3. The attorney representing the government in a criminal case, also called the prosecutor.

proximate cause. A cause that is legally sufficient to impose liability for the results of one's wrongful act or omission. There are two components of proximate cause: actual cause (which answers the question of who was the cause in fact of the harm or other loss) and legal cause (which answers the question of whether the harm or other loss was the foreseeable consequence of the original risk).

proximate-cause test. The injury is foreseeable and no intervening factor breaks the chain of causation between the conditions of employment and the injury (a causal connection test for workers' compensation).

publication. Communication of a statement to someone other than the plaintiff.

public disclosure of private fact. Unreasonable publicity concerning private facts about an individual's life that are not matters of legitimate public concern.

public figure. A person (other than a public official) who has assumed special prominence in the affairs of society. An all-purpose public figure is a person of general power, influence, or notoriety. A limited-purpose public figure is a person who has voluntarily become involved in a controversy of interest to the general public.

publicity. Communication to the public at large, i.e., to more than a few people.

public necessity. The privilege to make reasonable use of another's property to avoid an immediate public harm or damage.

public nuisance. An unreasonable interference with a right that is common to the general public.

public official. A government employee who has significant authority.

public policy. Principles inherent in customs and societal values that are of fundamental concern to legislatures and courts.

puffing. An exaggeration of quality or value that one can expect from someone, particularly a seller. Seller's talk.

punitive damages. Damages that are added to actual or compensatory damages in order to punish malicious, outrageous, or reckless conduct and to deter similar conduct in the future. Also called exemplary damages, smart money, and vindictive damages.

Q

qualified immunity. A defense that avoids personal liability when a government employee is carrying out official functions, unless the employee was acting with malice.

qualified privilege. A privilege that can be lost if it is not exercised in a reasonable manner for a proper purpose. Also called conditional privilege.

question of law. See legal issue.

R

Racketeer Influenced and Corrupt Organizations Act (RICO). A federal statute imposing civil and criminal penalties for racketeering offenses such as engaging in a pattern of fraud, bribery, extortion, and other acts enumerated in the statute (18 USC § 1961). Some states have enacted similar statutes.

ratifies. 1. Adopts or confirms a prior act or transaction, making one bound by it. 2. Formally approves.

real property. Land and anything attached or affixed to the land, such as buildings, fences, and trees. Also called real estate. See also property.

real property tort. See tort.

real-time. Occurring now; happening as you are watching; able to respond immediately.

reasonable alternative design. An available design that a manufacturer could have reasonably used that would have been less dangerous than the design that caused the injury.

reasonable beneficial use. Space above and ground below the surface of land of which reasonable use can be made.

reasonable care. Ordinary prudence under the circumstances to avoid injury or other loss.

reasonable doubt. Doubt that would cause prudent people to hesitate before acting in matters of importance to themselves. The standard of proof needed to convict someone of a crime is proof beyond a reasonable doubt.

reasonable person. Someone who uses ordinary prudence under the circumstances to avoid injury or other loss; someone who is not careless. Also called ordinary prudent person. (Called reasonable man in older cases.)

rebut. To refute or oppose.

rebuttable. Subject to challenge; pertaining to a conclusion that one is allowed to introduce evidence against. On irrebuttable presumptions, see presumption.

recapture of chattels. The right to use reasonable force to obtain the return of personal property (chattels) shortly after someone obtained them wrongfully.

reckless. Consciously taking a risk in failing to exercise due care but without intending the consequences; wantonly disregarding a risk but neither desiring the consequences of the risk nor having substantially certain knowledge of the consequences.

release. The giving up or relinquishing of a right, claim, interest, or privilege.

reliance. Forming a belief, taking action, or refraining from action due in part to confidence in someone or something. See also justifiable reliance.

remedy. 1. The means by which a right is enforced or the violation of a right is prevented, compensated for, or otherwise redressed. 2. To correct.

remedy at law. A remedy available in a court of law (e.g., damages) as opposed to one available in a court of equity (e.g., injunction).

reporter. 1. A volume (or set of volumes) of court opinions. Also called case reports. 2. The person who takes down and transcribes proceedings.

representative action. See class action.

representee. The person to whom a representation is made.

republication. Repetition of a defamatory statement originally made by someone else. See also publication.

res ipsa loquitur. ("The thing speaks for itself.") An inference of the defendant's unreasonableness (breach of duty) that allows the plaintiff's case to go to the jury, which may then agree or disagree that the defendant was unreasonable.

respondeat superior. "Let the master answer." An employer is responsible (liable) for the wrongs committed by an employee within the scope of employment.

respondent. The party against whom an appeal is brought. Also called the appellee.

retainer. An agreement to hire someone.

retaliatory discharge. Dismissing someone from a job for a reason that violates public policy, e.g., for reporting a fire hazard at work.

reversionary interest. The right of a grantor of land (who has transferred less than his or her full interest in the land) to the future possession and enjoyment of land presently occupied by another. The right in land that is retained by one who transfers property (the grantor).

RICO. See Racketeer Influenced and Corrupt Organizations Act.

risk. The chance or danger that a loss or misfortune will occur. The danger of an unwanted (and usually unintended) result.

risk–benefit analysis. Deciding whether the risks outweigh the benefits. The determination of whether the benefits of proceeding without additional precautions outweigh the risk of harm that is foreseeable. Also called cost–benefit analysis and risk–utility analysis.

rule. A law or other governing principle.

rules of court. The procedural laws that govern the mechanics of litigation (practice and procedure) before a particular court. Also called court rules.

Rylands v. Fletcher. The case holding that if defendants know they are engaging in a non-natural or abnormal use of land that creates an increased danger to persons or property, they will be strictly liable for harm caused by this use. L.R. 3 H.L. 330 (1868).

S

sale. The transfer of title to property for a price or other consideration.

satisfaction. The discharge or performance of an obligation; full payment of a debt.

scienter. 1. Intent to deceive or mislead. 2. Knowingly done.

scope of employment. That which is foreseeably done by an employee for the employer's business under the employer's specific or general control.

screening panel. A group of individuals who examine a case before it can be litigated in court. The panel can often make recommendations and encourage the parties to settle.

secondary assumption of risk. See assumption of the risk.

secondary authority. Any nonlaw that a court could rely on to reach its decision. See also legal authority.

§ 402A. The main section on strict liability in tort from *Restatement (Second) of Torts*. The section provides for liability for physical harm caused by a defective product that is unreasonably dangerous.

seduction. 1. The tort of engaging in sexual relations with the plaintiff's minor daughter by force or with the consent of the daughter. 2. Wrongfully inducing another, without the use of force, to engage in sexual relations.

self-defense. The use of reasonable force to prevent an immediate harmful or offensive contact to one's person. (Self-defense sometimes has a broader meaning of repelling threatened danger to one's person *or property*.)

self-help. Acting on one's own to prevent or correct the effects of a tort or other wrong without using the courts or other public authority.

self-insurance. The ability to pay government-mandated benefits (e.g., workers' compensation) out of one's own funds rather than through a government fund or an insurance policy.

seller. 1. Anyone in the business of selling products. See also merchant. 2. One who sells or enters a contract to sell. See also sale.

service. 1. Activity performed or benefit provided as part of one's line of work. 2. Household chore or other task an unemancipated child owes his or her parent. See also loss of services.

service of process. A formal delivery of notice to a defendant that a suit has been initiated to which he or she must respond. *Process* is the means used by the court to acquire or exercise its power or jurisdiction over a person.

settlement. An agreement resolving a dispute without full litigation.

settlement brochure. A detailed written presentation by a party to an opponent (or its insurance company) on the merits of a cause of action (including alleged damages) in an effort to encourage settlement. The presentation is called a *settlement précis* if the case is relatively uncomplicated.

settlement class action. A class action that the parties do not intend to litigate because they have reached a settlement on the claims made.

settlement précis. A relatively brief written presentation by a party to an opponent (or its insurance company) on the merits of a cause of action (including alleged damages) in an effort to encourage settlement. A more elaborate version for more complex cases is called a *settlement brochure*.

severe emotional distress. Substantial mental anguish or distress that no reasonable person should be expected to endure.

shallow pockets. 1. An individual, business, or other organization without resources to pay a potential judgment. 2. Insufficient assets for this purpose. The opposite of *deep pockets*.

shopkeeper's privilege. The right of a merchant to detain someone temporarily for the sole purpose of investigating whether the person has committed theft against the merchant.

simple interest. Interest earned on the principal alone, not on already accrued interest. See also compound interest.

sine qua non test. See but-for test.

slander. Defamation that is spoken or gestured. See also defamation.

slander of title. The denigration or discrediting of the plaintiff's title to property. See also disparagement.

slander per quod. 1. An oral defamatory statement that does not fit into one of the four categories that constitute slander per se. 2. An oral defamatory statement that requires one to use extrinsic facts to understand its defamatory meaning.

slander per se. An oral statement that is defamatory because it accuses a person of (1) committing a crime of moral turpitude, (2) having a loathsome communicable disease, (3) committing serious sexual misconduct, or (4) being inept at or unfit for his or her trade or profession.

SLAPP (Strategic Lawsuit Against Public Participation) suit. A meritless suit brought primarily for the purpose of chilling the defendant's exercise of the right to free speech and to petition the government for a redress of grievances.

social guest. One who receives a social invitation, and who comes on the premises for a social (not a business) purpose to enjoy hospitality as a guest of the occupier. An example of a licensee.

social value. The quality of something as measured by what the general public deems desirable or useful. Also called social utility.

solicitation. 1. An appeal or request for clients or business. 2. An attempt to obtain something by persuasion or application.

sovereign immunity. The sovereign (i.e., the state or the government) cannot be sued in its courts without its consent. Also called governmental immunity.

special damages. Compensatory damages that consist of economic or pecuniary losses (e.g., medical expenses and lost wages) that must be alleged and proven. They are not presumed to exist. Also referred to as specials.

special relationship. A relationship between persons that is the basis of a duty of reasonable care to avoid injury even in the absence of affirmative conduct.

specific causation. In toxic tort cases, bringing about or producing a particular injury or condition in a specific plaintiff. See also general causation.

squatter. One who settles on land without legal title or authority.

standard of care. The degree of care that the law requires in a particular case. In most negligence cases, the standard is reasonableness—what an ordinary prudent person would do under the same or similar circumstances. In some cases, however, a lesser standard is used, such as to avoid reckless conduct. See also locality rule, national standard.

standard of proof. How believable or convincing a version of a fact must be before the trier of facts (usually a jury) can accept it as true.

standing. 1. A person's right to seek relief from a court. 2. The right to bring a court action because of the sufficiency of one's personal interest in the outcome of the proposed court action or because of a special statute that grants this right.

state a cause of action. See cause of action.

statute. A law passed by the state or federal legislature that declares, commands, or prohibits something. Also called *act* and *legislation*. (Statute, act, and legislation are sometimes used in a broader sense to include laws passed by any legislature, which would include ordinances passed by a city council.)

statute of limitations. A law that designates a time period within which a court case must be filed or it can never be brought.

statutory code. A collection of statutes organized by subject matter rather than chronologically by date enacted.

strict liability. Responsibility for harm even if one did not intend the harm and used reasonable care to try to prevent it. Responsibility for harm whether or not the person causing the harm was at any fault or engaged in any moral impropriety. Also called absolute liability and liability without fault.

strict liability for abnormally dangerous conditions or activities (SLADCA). A tort that imposes liability for harm resulting from abnormally dangerous conditions or activities regardless of whether the person causing the harm acted intentionally, negligently, or innocently.

strict liability in tort. Liability for physical harm caused by a defective product that is unreasonably dangerous.

structured settlement. An agreement in which the defendant pays for damages he or she caused by making periodic payments for a designated period of time, such as during the life of the victim. The payments are often funded through an annuity.

subjective standard. A standard by which something is measured by what a particular person actually knew, felt, or did.

sub judice. Before the court; under judicial consideration.

subrogation. The process by which one insurance company seeks reimbursement from another company or person for a claim it has already paid.

substantial factor. A significant role.

substantial-factor test. Did the party's acts or omissions have a significant or important role in bringing about the event (e.g., the injury)?

substantially certain knowledge. See knowledge with substantial certainty.

summary judgment. A decision based on the pleadings, facts revealed through discovery, and other facts placed in the record, without going through a trial, because there is no genuine dispute on any material facts.

summary jury trial. A method of alternative dispute resolution (ADR) in which the parties present their evidence and arguments to an advisory jury, which renders a nonbinding verdict. Also called mock trial or minitrial.

summons. 1. A notice directing the defendant to appear in court and answer the plaintiff's complaint or face a default judgment. (A default judgment is a judgment granted against a party who fails to appear, file an answer, or otherwise defend the action before the deadline.) 2. A notice directing a witness or juror to appear in court.

superseding cause. An intervening cause that is beyond the foreseeable risk originally created by the defendant's unreasonable acts or omissions. An intervening cause of harm that is highly extraordinary.

survival action. An action brought on behalf of a decedent against a defendant (who did not cause the death of the decedent) to recover what the decedent would have recovered if he or she had not died.

T

taking. The forced acquisition of private property by the government for a public purpose, for which the government must pay just compensation. (A requirement of the Fifth Amendment.) The acquisition can consist of a forced purchase, a substantial interference with the enjoyment of the property, or the deprivation of substantially all productive use of the property.

tangible. Capable of being touched or seen. Having physical form.

terminable at will. Something (e.g., a contract) that can be ended at any time for any reason without liability, so long as the reason does not violate public policy.

term of art. A word or phrase that has a special or technical meaning.

testate. Die leaving a valid will.

thin skull. A high vulnerability to a particular kind of harm.

thin-skull rule. If the general nature or type of harm was a foreseeable consequence of the original risk, the defendant will be liable for the harm even if the extent of the harm was not foreseeable. Also called eggshell-skull rule.

tolled. Stopped or suspended the running of a time period within which something must be done.

tort. A civil wrong (other than a breach of contract) that causes injury or other loss for which our legal system deems it just to provide a remedy such as damages. Injury or loss can be to the person (a personal tort), to movable property (a personal property tort), or to land and anything attached to the land (a real property tort).

tortfeasor. A person who has committed a tort.

tortious. Pertaining to conduct that can lead to tort liability.

tortious interference with employment. A wrongful discharge.

tortious interference with contractual relations. See interference with contractual relations.

tortious interference with prospective advantage. See interference with prospective advantage.

toxic tort. Personal injury or property damage wrongfully caused by repeated exposure to poisons in chemicals, asbestos, radiation, waste, or other substances.

trade libel. The wrongful denigration or discrediting of the plaintiff's products. See also disparagement.

transferred-intent rule. The defendant may be liable for certain torts committed against the plaintiff even if the defendant intended to commit a different tort against the plaintiff (unintended tort) and even if the defendant intended to commit the tort against a different person (unintended plaintiff). (Does not apply to all torts. See Exhibit 6–2 in Chapter 6.)

treatise. See legal treatise.

trespasser. One who enters or remains on land without the consent of the occupier and without any privilege to do so. One who commits a trespass to land.

trespass to chattels. An intentional interference with personal property, consisting of dispossession or intermeddling.

trespass to land. An intentional entry or intrusion on land in possession of another.

trial memorandum. See memorandum of law.

trial within a trial. A trial that takes place to establish that you would have won another trial that was lost because of the alleged negligence of your attorney. (In legal malpractice cases, plaintiffs must establish that they would have won their case if their attorney had not acted negligently.)

U

unavoidable accident. An occurrence that led to an injury or other loss that was not intended, was not foreseeable, and could not have been prevented by reasonable care.

unavoidably unsafe product. A product that cannot be made safe by using current technology and science.

unconscionable. So one-sided due to highly unequal bargaining positions as to be oppressive and grossly unfair.

uncontested. Unopposed; without opposition.

undertaking. Doing something; a task that is performed.

unemancipated. Still under the legal control of a parent or other legal guardian.

unfair competition. A dishonest or fraudulent practice directed at a commercial rival.

unforeseeable plaintiff. Someone whose presence in the zone of danger is unforeseeable to the defendant.

Uniform Commercial Code (UCC). A state statute that governs many commercial transactions. Like all uniform laws, the UCC is proposed for adoption by state legislatures. Each state is free to accept, modify, or reject the proposal.

United States. Any entity of the federal government.

unlawful detainer. The remaining in possession of real property unlawfully by one whose original possession was lawful.

unreasonable. The failure to use ordinary prudence under the circumstances to avoid injury or other loss. A common synonym for unreasonable is *careless*.

unreasonably dangerous. Dangerous to an extent beyond that which would be contemplated by the ordinary consumer who purchases it, with the ordinary knowledge common to the community as to its characteristics.

V

"veggie libel." A cause of action created by statute that allows producers of perishable food products to sue when they lose business because of false statements that disparage the safety of their products. Also called agricultural product disparagement.

vendee. Buyer.

vendor. Seller.

verdict. The final conclusion of the jury.

viable. Capable of surviving indefinitely outside the womb of the mother by natural or artificial support systems.

vicarious liability. Liability imposed on a person because of the conduct of another, based solely on the status of the relationship between the two. The person liable is not the person whose conduct led to the liability.

vice principal. An employee with supervisory authority over other employees.

voidable. Valid, but subject to being cancelled or annulled at someone's option.

voir dire. "To speak the truth." A preliminary examination to assess someone's qualifications to be a juror or witness.

volenti non fit injuria. "To a willing person it is not wrong." There is no cause of action for injury or harm endured by consent that is knowingly and voluntarily given.

W

waiver. The loss of a right or privilege because of an explicit rejection of it or because of a failure to claim it at the appropriate time.

wanton. Extremely reckless.

warning defect. The product is dangerous because its instructions or warnings are ineffective.

warrant. A court order commanding or authorizing a specific act, e.g., the arrest of someone or the search of an area.

warranty. A guarantee; a commitment imposed by contract or by law that a product or service will meet a specified standard.

warranty, breach of. See breach of express warranty, breach of implied warranty of fitness for a particular purpose, and breach of implied warranty of merchantability

weight of the evidence. The overall persuasiveness of the evidence presented; the tendency of all the evidence to support one side or another.

whole. See made whole.

wild animal. An animal in the state of nature.

willful. 1. Acting with the knowledge that harm will probably result. 2. Voluntary and deliberate. 3. Malicious.

windfall. An extra amount to which one is not entitled under the original understanding of the parties.

workers' compensation. A no-fault system of paying for medical care and providing limited wage benefits to a worker for an employment-related injury or illness regardless of who was at fault in causing the injury or illness.

world at large. The Andrews test of duty. See Andrews test.

wrongful adoption. Wrongfully stating or failing to disclose to prospective adoptive parents any available facts on the health or other condition of a child that would be relevant to their decision to adopt the child.

wrongful birth. An action by parents of an unwanted impaired child for negligence in failing to warn them of the risks that the child would be born with birth defects. The parents seek their own damages.

wrongful civil proceedings. The initiation of civil proceedings without probable cause and with malice when the proceedings terminate in favor of the person against whom they were brought. (Note that some states include the initiation of civil proceedings within the tort of malicious prosecution.)

wrongful death. A death caused by a tort or other wrong.

wrongful death action. An action by a decedent's next of kin for their damages resulting from a wrongful injury that killed the decedent. See also Lord Campbell's Act.

wrongful discharge. Terminating employment for a reason that violates public policy. Tortious interference with employment.

wrongful life. An action by or on behalf of an unwanted impaired child for negligence that precluded an informed parental decision to avoid the child's conception or birth. The child seeks its own damages.

wrongful pregnancy. An action by parents of an unwanted healthy child for a wrong related to pregnancy such as negligent performance of a sterilization procedure. Also called wrongful conception.

Z

zone of danger. The area within which injury or other loss to the plaintiff is foreseeable.

INDEX

A

B

C

D

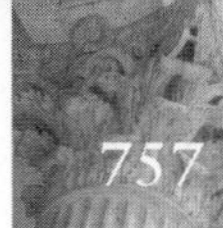

J

K

Q

R

S

T

U

V

W

XYZ

Exam*View*® Submission Form (Revised 4/09)

Version and Type of Project:

☒	**ExamView 6**	☒	**Full license**
☐	**Include Content Update feature**	☐	**Upgrade only**
		☐	**Reprint**
		☐	**Reprint – Using Update feature**
		☐	**Content Update**
		☐	**State Standard Update**
		☐	**Both**

Question information will be supplied in the following format:

☒ **Exam***View* Question Banks ☐ Word .rtf files ☐ Quark/.pdf

The following must be supplied to your Account Manager prior to beginning project:

Cover Art (.tif, .jpg, or .bmp format) ______________________

Textbook Table of Contents ______________________

Graphics Will question banks include graphics? ☐ Yes ☒ No

Will graphic work within the banks be done by el*? ☐ Yes ☒ No

* If yes, provide hard copy along with the art in Windows black & white or 256-color bitmap (.bmp) format at 140 dpi (dots per inch). B&W (1-bit) images require much less disk space and print faster.

Submission Date:		**Exact Title of Text:**	Torts: Personal Injury Litigation, Fifth Edition
Contact:	Jim Zayicek		
Address:	Delmar Cengage Learning	**Teacher Ed ISBN:**	
	5 Maxwell Drive	**Textbook ISBN:**	1-4018-7962-4
	Clifton Park, NY 12065	**Invoicing ISBN:**	1-4018-7963-2
Phone:	(800) 998-7498 ext 2501	**Author(s):**	William P. Statsky
Fax:		**Copyright Year:**	2011
Email:	Jim.zayicek@cengage.com	**Publisher Imprint:**	Delmar Cengage Learning
Shipping Acct:		**Discipline:**	Paralegal

Grade Level: ☐ K-6 ☐ 6-12 ☒ Postsecondary ☐ Adult Education ☐ Trade and Industry

# of Files or Banks: 29 **# of English Questions:** 270 **# of Canned Tests:** ______

Gold Master Delivery Date: ______________________

☐ RUSH Delivery Requested: Two week or less turnaround needed. ($500.00 charge)

☒ Standard Delivery Requested: More than two week turnaround needed.

Question Bank Folder Name: ______________ *(31 characters max. including Publisher ID)*

Alternate Language: ☐ Yes ☒ No **If yes**, please indicate language: ______________

Dynamic Content: ☐ Yes ☒ No ☐ Algorithmic Technical Review Requested

GM Delivery Media: ☐ Post to ftp site ☐ CD-ROM ☐ Content Update Server

Exam *View*® Submission Form (Revised 4/09)

Platform Required: ☒ Hybrid ☐ Windows only ☐ Macintosh only

Question Types

☒ True/False ☐ Yes/No ☐ Case
☐ Modified True/False ☐ Matching ☐ Other
☒ Multiple Choice/Bi Modal ☐ Completion ☐ Problem
☐ Multiple Response ☐ Numeric Response ☐ Short Answer
☐ Essay

Question Information used (provide sample in space provided)

☒ Difficulty DIF: PTS: 1
☐ Reference REF: ______
☐ Learning Objective OBJ: ______
☐ Topic TOP: ______
☐ Notes NOT: ______
☐ Rationale RAT: ______
☐ Keywords KEY: ______
☐ Miscellaneous MSC: ______
☐ Feedback ______

Standards and Descriptions**

**Please contact eI for the spreadsheet to complete if including National, State, or Local Standards and/or Standard Descriptions. *Only Excel spreadsheets supplied by eInstruction will be accepted.*

☐ National Standard ☐ Local Standard ☐ State Standards (specify below)

___ AL	___ AK	___ AZ	___ AR	___ CA	___ CO	___ CT	___ DE	___ FL	___ GA	___ HI	___ ID
___ IL	___ IN	___ IA	___ KS	___ KY	___ LA	___ ME	___ MD	___ MA	___ MI	___ MN	___ MS
___ MO	___ MT	___ NE	___ NV	___ NH	___ NJ	___ NM	___ NY	___ NC	___ ND	___ OH	
___ OK	___ OR	___ PA	___ RI	___ SC	___ SD	___ TN	___ TX	___ UT	___ VT	___ VA	
___ WA	___ WV	___ WI	___ WY								

☐ State Standard Descriptions

Notes/Comments to Project Manager: ______

MindPoint™ Quiz Show will accompany this project: ☐ Yes ☒ No

Shipping Instructions: Please provide the name and address of those who should receive shipment of final product.

______

Other quality products brought to you by the developers of Exam *View*:

MindPoint Quiz Show – Helps students prepare for formal assessment by competing in a game show quiz format.

Exam *View* QuickTake – Allows instructors to incorporate interactive quizzing with PowerPoint presentations.

Lesson *View* – A state-of-the-art electronic lesson planner and resource library that allows educators to quickly and easily create lessons plans.

Puzzle *View* – Allows teachers to create Crossword, Word Search, Jumble, and Cryptogram puzzles from publisher vocabulary terms.

Contact your Account Manager to learn more!